THE CAMBRIDGE HISTORY OF THE
BYZANTINE EMPIRE *c.* 500–1492

Byzantium lasted a thousand years, ruled to the end by self-styled 'emperors of the Romans'. It underwent kaleidoscopic territorial and structural changes, yet recovered repeatedly from disaster: even after the near-impregnable Constantinople fell in 1204, variant forms of the empire reconstituted themselves. *The Cambridge History of the Byzantine Empire* tells the story, tracing political and military events, religious controversies and economic change. It offers clear, authoritative chapters on the main events and periods, with more detailed chapters on outlying regions and neighbouring societies and powers of Byzantium. With aids such as maps, a glossary, an alternative place-name table and references to English translations of sources, it will be valuable as an introduction. However, it also offers stimulating new approaches and important findings, making it essential reading for postgraduates and for specialists.

JONATHAN SHEPARD was for many years a Lecturer in History at the University of Cambridge, and was a Fellow of Selwyn College and of Peterhouse. He is the co-editor (with Simon Franklin) of *Byzantine Diplomacy* (1992), co-author (also with Simon Franklin) of *The Emergence of Rus, 750–1200* (1996), author of *Nespokoini s'sedi: b'lgaro-vizantiiska konfrontatsiia, obmen i s'zhitelstvo prez srednite vekove* [*Uneasy Neighbours: Bulgaro-Byzantine Confrontation, Exchange and Co-existence in the Middle Ages*] (2007) and editor of *The Expansion of Orthodox Europe: Byzantium, the Balkans and Russia* (2007). Shepard is Doctor Honoris Causa of St Kliment Ohrid University in Sofia.

THE CAMBRIDGE
HISTORY OF THE
BYZANTINE EMPIRE

c. 500–1492

Edited by

JONATHAN SHEPARD

CAMBRIDGE
UNIVERSITY PRESS

CAMBRIDGE UNIVERSITY PRESS
Cambridge, New York, Melbourne, Madrid, Cape Town, Singapore, São Paulo, Delhi

Cambridge University Press
The Edinburgh Building, Cambridge CB2 8RU, UK

Published in the United States of America by Cambridge University Press, New York

www.cambridge.org
Information on this title: www.cambridge.org/9780521832311

First published 2008

Printed in the United Kingdom at the University Press, Cambridge

A catalogue record for this publication is available from the British Library

Library of Congress Cataloguing in Publication data
The Cambridge history of the Byzantine Empire c. 500–1492 / edited by
Jonathan Shepard.
p.   cm.
Includes bibliographical references and index.
ISBN 978-0-521-83231-1
1. Byzantine Empire – History – 527–1081.   2. Byzantine Empire – History – 1081–1453.
I. Shepard, Jonathan.   II. Title.
DF571.C34   2008
949.5′02 – dc22   2008038886

ISBN 978-0-521-83231-1 hardback

CONTENTS

v

PART III: THE BYZANTINE LANDS IN THE LATER MIDDLE AGES 1204–1492

MAPS

ILLUSTRATIONS

TABLES

To Nicola

PREFACE

This is a short preface for quite a lengthy book, but it is a means of paying tribute to those principally involved in the development, shaping and production of *The Cambridge history of the Byzantine empire* (or *CHBE*). Like the empire itself, the process of formation has been protracted, without a clear-cut starting-point, and such sense of direction as has been attained owes more to collaborative effort than it does to untrammelled autocracy.

Given the sizable number of persons contributing in one way or another, the preface's brevity entails a mere sketch of those without whose help and advice *CHBE* would have been a far more onerous and lengthy task. It was Bill Davies who originally encouraged me to take on remodelling materials already available, and several anonymous readers helped structure the volume. Michael Sharp took over from Bill at Cambridge University Press and he has been an extremely patient and supportive editor, ably assisted at various times by Liz Davey, Sinead Moloney, Liz Noden and Annette Youngman. Particular thanks should go to the following key players: Bernard Dod, our indefatigable and eagle-eyed copy-editor, whose attention to detail and wise counsel averted many a mishap; to Barbara Hird, our expert indexer, whose care and clarity have created a valuable additional pathway to Byzantium; to Patricia Jeskins, our assiduous proofreader; and to David Cox, our cartographer, whose splendid maps are closely integrated with the text of our chapters.

For bibliographic help I have to thank the following colleagues, who have supplied references and answered tiresome queries with speed and good grace: Jean-Claude Cheynet, Florin Curta, Peter Frankopan, Judith Gilliland, Michael Grünbart, Paul Herrup, James Howard-Johnston, Elizabeth Jeffreys, Lester Little, Margaret Mullett, Angel Nikolov, Paolo Odorico, Maureen Perrie, Günter Prinzing, Charlotte Rouché, Maciej Salamon, Alexios Savvides, Teresa Shawcross, John Smedley, Tsvetelin Stepanov, Alice-Mary Talbot, George Tcheishvili, Ida Toth, Vladimir Vavřínek and Mark Whittow. I should also like to thank the staff at the Bodleian, Taylorian Slavonic, Sackler, Oriental Institute and the other Oxford libraries, as well as the staff of the University Library in Cambridge.

Colleagues who clarified various points along the thousand-year trek, or who freely provided access to unpublished materials of value for this work include Jane Baun, Jeffrey Featherstone, Paul Fouracre, John Haldon, Rosemary Morris, Pananos Sophoulis and Monica White. Particular thanks are due to Catherine Holmes, Mike Maas and Andrew Roach, who read the introduction and some of the chapters that follow, and who warned of culs-de-sac and quicksands to be charted or – hopefully – avoided.

On the technical side, help with translation and transliteration was given by Lawrence Conrad, Jeffrey Featherstone, Tim Greenwood, Mona Hamami and Marina Kujić. Jenny Perry saved me on several occasions when Macs failed to talk to PCs, and vice versa, while Nigel James of the Bodleian initiated me into the mysteries of digital map-making. Locating and sourcing illustrations was made easier through the assistance of Nancy Alderson, Michel Balard, Theodore van Lint, Cyril Mango, Nicholas Mayhew, Dorothy McCarthy, Denys Pringle, Michael Stone and Robert Thomson. Particular thanks go to our neighbours, Vanessa and Peter Winchester, to whom I am indebted for several pictures of Constantinople. These thanks should be accompanied by apologies for a certain lack of sociability in recent years – and extended to all remaining friends.

It is a commonplace to thank one's immediate family for their help and endurance in these endeavours. However, I must single out my wife, Nicola, who took on the role of editorial assistant on the project without, I think, appreciating the sheer scale of activity involved. As I have often pointed out to her, this could be seen as due penance for failing to attend my lectures on Byzantium and its neighbours all those years ago in Cambridge! Without Nicola, the volume would probably not have been published this decade, and I am profoundly grateful for her patience, counsel and support.

However, those most indispensable are the volume's contributors. The chapters whose first incarnation was in *The Cambridge ancient history* or *The new Cambridge medieval history* have been joined by important new contributions expanding and elaborating on relevant themes. But it goes without saying that, notwithstanding all the help and advice received along the way, I take responsibility for such mistakes or errors as may have crept into the finished work.

NOTES ON USING THIS VOLUME

Our approach to transliteration may induce unease among some colleagues – and invite charges of inconsistency – but we have tried to make proper names and technical terms accessible to the English-speaking world wherever possible. Greek has been transliterated and bars have been used to distinguish *ēta* from *epsilon* and *ōmega* from *omicron* in the case of individual words and technical terms, but abandoned for proper names. Greek forms of proper names have generally been adopted in Parts II and III – Komnenos instead of the Latinised Comnenus, for example – in contrast to Part I, set in late antiquity, when Latinised names seem appropriate. In general, we have adopted a 'b' and not 'v' when transliterating the Greek letter *bēta*. However, where a name is more or less domiciled in English usage, we have let it be, e.g. Monemvasia and not Monembasia. Where the names of places are probably so familiar to most readers in their Latinised forms that the use of a Greek form might distract, the Latinised form has been retained in Parts II and III – Nicaea instead of Nikaia, for example. Familiar English forms have been preferred out of the same consideration – Athens not Athenai, for example – and in Part III, when the empire's possessions were being taken over by speakers of other tongues, the place names now prevalent have generally been preferred – Ankara instead of Ankyra, for example.

Arabic diacritics have been discarded in proper names, with only the ayn (') and hamza (') retained in the form shown, on the assumption that the diacritics will not help non-Arabic readers and may actually distract from name recognition and recall; however, full diacritics have been retained for individual words and technical terms. We have tried to be consistent yet accessible in transliterating other key scripts, such as Armenian and Cyrillic, using for the latter a modified version of the Library of Congress system.

Detailed notes on how to use the bibliography can be found below at pp. 936–8. Chronological sectioning for the secondary bibliography is – like the periodisation of history itself into mutually exclusive compartments – rather arbitrary. **The bibliography of secondary works should therefore be treated as a whole and the reader failing to find a work in one section should try the others**.

The Glossary and Tables are not intended to be comprehensive guides. The Glossary offers a selection of the technical terms, foreign words and names of peoples and institutions appearing in *CHBE*. But wherever possible, these are explained in the context of a chapter and only the more problematic proper names have a Glossary entry (see also Maps 3 and 52). Likewise, the lists of rulers and genealogies have been kept to a minimum, since they are available in more specialised works. The list of alternative place names is intended to help the reader locate some towns and regions which were known under radically different names by diverse occupants or neighbours, and to offer modern equivalents where known.

The maps are designed to reconcile accessibility for anglophone readers with a sense of the form prevalent during the chronological section of *CHBE* in question, not wholly compatible goals. The maps are intended to be viewed as an ensemble, and readers unable to spot a place in a map positioned in one chapter should look to adjoining chapters, or (aided by the list of alternative place names and the index) shop around.

GENERAL INTRODUCTION

APPROACHING BYZANTIUM

JONATHAN SHEPARD

Many roads lead to Byzantium, 'the New Rome', and guidance comes from dozens of disciplines, including art history and archaeology, theology and expertise in stone inscriptions, coins or handwriting. Indeed, those general historians who act as guides have themselves often majored in other fields, such as ancient Greece and Rome, the medieval west, the Slav or Mediterranean worlds, and even the Italian renaissance. The surest fact about the elusive 'New Rome' is that it lasted over a thousand years, albeit with a fifty-seven-year dislocation from 1204. Across this millennium, the questions of how, why and where the empire survived, receded and (most importantly) revived as a more or less functioning organism – and as an idea – underlie this book.

We take a narrower road than the one chosen by this volume's predecessor, *The Cambridge medieval history* IV,[1] whose first part recounted political, military and ecclesiastical history in detail from 717 until the end of the empire, and devoted several authoritative chapters to neighbouring peoples and powers; its second part contained thematic chapters, on for example law, government, the church, music, the visual arts and literature. No such comprehensive treatment of Byzantium's culture will be attempted here. Our chapters follow the fortunes of the empire, as shifting politico-military organisation and as abiding ideal and state of mind, but do not attempt portrayal of Byzantium and its civilisation from every angle; however, some important alternative approaches to its history are sketched in the third section of this introduction (see below, pp. 53–75).

Our narrative picks out those occurrences salient to the political organism, with an eye for the many problems, external and internal, facing the upholders of imperial order from their capital in the New Rome. Unfashionable weight is given to individual emperors' characters, and to the statecraft of such giants as Justinian (527–65), Leo III (717–41), Basil I (867–86) and Basil II (976–1025), Alexios I Komnenos (1081–1118) and Manuel I Komnenos (1143–80). Their diverse, often successful, solutions to problems

---

[1] Hussey (ed.) (1966–7).

of governance are outlined, and a recurring theme is the pragmatism of Byzantium's rulers in coping with plague, financial straits and the inroads of 'barbarians', and also with unexpected problems of success. The dynamics of these improvisations, abrupt overhauls and longer-term shifts are traced through the course of events rather than through detailed analysis of institutions as such, a justifiable approach given that the precise workings of so many of Byzantium's institutions – from the army to provincial administration – are so hard to determine and highly controversial.

Topics of relevance to Byzantine political culture are brought into the narrative, from religious devotions to patronage of the visual arts, and the broader, provincial society revolving around that of the metropolis is outlined. Thematic chapters look at the economy and Christian missions, and there is treatment of several societies, elites and powers that had long-term dealings with Byzantium. Here, too, coverage is less than comprehensive: for example, no chapter is dedicated to ties between the empire and the lands of the Rus. But enough is provided to demonstrate the impact of Byzantium on various cultures of world significance: the world of Islam, the Eurasian and the Slav worlds, and the Christian west. The aim is to outline and analyse interaction rather than to recount every known detail of relations with a particular state. The importance of Byzantium to neighbouring or newly forming societies and powers emerges more clearly when their individual situations and needs are taken into account. This is particularly true of the tortuous interrelationship with the Christian west across the centuries, and the vitality of the exchanges, cultural as well as ecclesiastical and political, between 'Latins' and 'Greeks' is brought out in full here.

The chronological range of our chapters spans from just after the formal termination of the western half of the Roman empire (476) to the fifteenth century, when the Christian west was viewed by some Byzantines as a potential saviour from the Turks. This broad yet careful sweep takes in the numerous communities and towns of Greek-speakers who came under new rulers after the empire's collapse in 1204, sometimes Venetians or French-speakers, sometimes Bulgarian or Serbs. The ebb and flow of the imperial dominions in the thirteenth and fourteenth centuries is presented in more detail than is usual with this kind of survey, and it shows up qualities of the Byzantine body politic too easily overlooked: its 'variable geometry', a capacity to function quite effectively even without the use of apparently vital members; and resilience, its constituent parts realigning themselves with imperial dominion more or less of their own accord, without much prompting from the top.

The conspectus offered here, at once authoritative and unusually wide-ranging, should yield some fresh insights to specialists in, and postgraduate students of, the Byzantine world. But it also has something to offer new-comers to the enigma variations of Byzantium. No prior knowledge of the subject, or indeed of pre-modern history, is presupposed, and every effort has been made to provide guidelines for readers whose mother tongue or first foreign language is English. Translations of primary texts are cited in the footnotes where available, and a guide to sources in English trans-lation is offered in the fourth section of this introduction (see below, pp. 76–90).

Our introduction is divided into four sections, The first – this one – looks at Byzantine notions of empire, their tenacity in the face of adversity and the significance of religious rites for believers at grass-roots, consti-tuting Byzantium's special blend of faith and power. It concludes with a discussion of the nature of the interrelationships between outsiders and insiders, and of their bearing on the broader question of the Byzantine identity.

The second section addresses the book's time-frame and considers pos-sible alternatives. It is followed by a survey of the book's three main parts, which run from *c.* 500 to *c.* 700, *c.* 700 to 1204 and 1204 to 1492. Themes running through chapters that may, at first sight, seem rather disparate are picked out, part by part. The chapters are not surveyed in strict order of their sequence in the book: thus the topic- or region-specific chapters of Part II are considered *en bloc*, after the chapters forming the main narrative spine. Part III's contents, lacking a single fixed point, and encompassing a wide variety of populations and polities, receive fairly lengthy treatment without close adherence to the order of the chapters.

The third section outlines other possible approaches to those taken in this book, which mostly follow the course of recorded events of political, ecclesiastical or military significance for the empire. The outline draws attention to some more or less recent introductions to art, institutions and the human condition among the Byzantines. It is nonetheless slanted towards topics germane to the idea or substance of empire, whether political imagery, size of armies, or castration.

The fourth and final section of the introduction addresses some of the problems of approaching Byzantium without benefit of Greek and offers short-cuts that may help towards the study – and teaching – of the empire's story: historical atlases covering Byzantium and neighbouring peoples, chronologies, art-historical lexicons and whole dictionaries devoted to the subject. Far more works penned by the Byzantines or about the Byzantines by contemporary outsiders are available in English translation than is gen-erally realised and further translations are underway. These make aspects of Byzantium readily accessible to newcomers from the English-speaking world, and this section of the introduction points to some of the online guides to English-language translations now available.

NOTIONS OF EMPIRE, RESILIENCE AND RELIGION

The phenomenon of Byzantium has multiple connotations and even the name which its rulers used of their polity, 'Roman', was controversial.[2] 'Greeks' was the name by which they and their subjects were known to many of their neighbours. This was a reflection of the language in everyday use in Constantinople and provincial towns and in which most imperial business was done from the sixth century onwards. To Goths fanning Italians' prejudices, 'Greeks' carried intimations of frippery and rapaciousness (see below, pp. 214–15). Yet a certain readiness to accept the empire's claim to be 'Roman' surfaces spasmodically among Frankish courtiers, for all their fulminations to the contrary (see below, p. 397). And while some Arabic writers in the Abbasid era stressed the Byzantines' cultural inferiority to the ancient Greeks or Romans,[3] Rum ('Romans') was the name by which Muslims called the Byzantines, and the Turkish potentates who made themselves masters of south-central Anatolia from the late eleventh century became known as sultans of Rum.[4]

The very terms Rome and Roman had overtones of unimpeachably legitimate sovereign authority, evoking the greatest empire the world had yet seen. Fantastic as popular notions might be concerning the imagery of classical monuments in Constantinople,[5] Byzantine rulers still acted out triumphal parades through its streets and enlisted the citizens' support in staging them, manifesting the classical Roman concept of 'eternal victory'.[6] Less flamboyantly, the City's water-supply kept flowing through an intricate network of pipes and cisterns established in the sixth century, to standards set by Roman engineers. The workings of this system, ensuring the pure water vital to Constantinople's survival, were seldom if ever set down in writing,[7] and in fact the importance of this state secret features in a late thirteenth-century treatise on Byzantine political thought.[8]

In contrast to mundane matters of pipelines, the supernatural protection enjoyed by the 'God-protected City' of Constantinople was a leitmotif of imperial pronouncements from the seventh century onwards,[9]

---

[2] The term 'Byzantium' only came into use in the sixteenth century, when it was introduced to distinguish the medieval eastern Mediterranean state from the 'Roman' empire of antiquity. Byzantium is a Latinised form of the name of the city chosen by Constantine the Great (306–37) to be his residence, Byzantion, renamed Constantinople after him.

[3] El-Cheikh (2004a), pp. 103–11.

[4] See below, p. 708; *EI*, VIII, s.v. Saldjuks, pp. 948–50 (C. E. Bosworth).

[5] *Parastaseis syntomoi chronikai*, ed. Preger; tr. Cameron and Herrin; Dagron (1984b).

[6] McCormick (1990), pp. 3, 21–31, 205–8; Morris (2003).

[7] Greek fire's workings are likewise ill-documented: see below, pp. 233–4; Haldon and Byrne (1977); Haldon (2006a); Pryor and Jeffreys (2006), pp. 607–31.

[8] Crow *et al.* (2001); Crow and Bayliss (2005); Angelov, D. G. (2004), p. 520; below, pp. 114, 471, 485.

[9] Fenster (1968), pp. 97–8, 104 and n. 2.

becoming engrained in the consciousness of Christians in the eastern Mediterranean world. The dedication of the new City by Constantine the Great in AD 330 symbolised his conversion to Christianity and was commemorated each year on 11 May.[10] Constantine's espousal of Christianity marked a new beginning not just for the emperor but for all mankind, whose spiritual salvation now became his avowed concern. Bishop Eusebius of Caesarea, Constantine's counsellor and biographer, interpreted the turning-point thus, laying the foundations for an ideology that would treat the history of the church as being coterminous with the bounds of the Roman empire.[11]

The emperor thus became a pivotal figure in God's grand design for believers and unbelievers alike, and the conception gained monumental expression in stone from Justinian's building of St Sophia in Constantinople (see below, pp. 111–12, 114). Justinian's building-works were undertaken when, for all the pressures from external enemies on several fronts, military feats could still bring confirmation that the Christian God conferred victory, and churchmen ranged far and wide on missions to bring remaining groups of pagans within the emperor's fold (see below, pp. 307–12).

The association of the empire of the Christians with the future of mankind remained vital even when the tide abruptly turned and, following a Persian occupation, the empire's eastern provinces were overrun by bands of Arab warriors in the mid-seventh century. Formerly deemed poor, divided and readily manipulable by the Romans, these Arabs now acted in concert, united in responding to their own revealed truth, as conveyed by God to the prophet Muhammad (see below, pp. 173–95, 365–9). Little more than a generation later, Pseudo-Methodius[12] explained 'the Ishmaelites'' extraordinary victories as God's punishment on the Christians for their sins. He prophesied that 'the Ishmaelites' would carry all before them until the emperor awoke 'like a man from sleep after drinking much wine', arose and put them to flight; the emperor would subsequently make for Jerusalem, and his arrival there would lead to the appearance of the anti-Christ and Christ's second coming.[13] The text was soon translated from Syriac into Greek and the surviving version contains an interpolation alluding to actual Arab expeditions against Constantinople of the late seventh or early eighth century.

[10] *DC*, I.79 (70), ed. Reiske, I, pp. 340–9; ed. and French tr. Vogt, II, pp. 143–50; Dagron (2000), pp. 60–71.

[11] Eusebius of Caesarea, *Life of Constantine*, II.3–5, II.44–61, IV.74–5, ed. Winkelmann, pp. 48–50, 66–72, 150–1; tr. Cameron and Hall, pp. 95–7, 110–15, 182; Dvornik (1966), II, pp. 614–22; Brock (1994), p. 70.

[12] A seventh-century Syriac author, who wrote in the name of the fourth-century bishop of Patara.

[13] Pseudo-Methodius, *Apocalypse*, [13], 11, ed. Aerts and Kortekaas, I, p. 174; below, p. 247. See also Psalms 78: 65.

It also represents the Ishmaelites as momentarily entering the City before the emperor's resurgence.[14]

The Arabs never did penetrate the walls of Constantinople and so these events were not, strictly speaking, relevant to Pseudo-Methodius' prophecy. But the interpolation reflects widely held Byzantine beliefs: that they were acting out events foretold in sacred writings, and empire and capital were closely bound up with the fate of mankind.[15] Sudden strikes against the City by barbarians such as the Rus in 860 were interpreted as divine punishment for its sins,[16] and after Constantinople's fall to the Crusaders in 1204, many believed this was God's warning that the Byzantines should mend their ways before He showed His displeasure terminally (see below, p. 735).

Faith and empire could no longer be held to be indissoluble to the same extent after 1204, yet eastern orthodox emperors remained at large and upon seizing control of Constantinople in 1261, Michael VIII Palaiologos (1258–82) presented himself as a new Constantine: his success in occupying the City was in itself a mark of God's favour towards him and of God's mercy for His people. Apocalyptic writings and sayings, some deriving from Pseudo-Methodius, circulated widely among orthodox Greek- and Slavonic-speakers alike. The Byzantine emperors' predicament in the face of Ottoman Turk advances from the mid-fourteenth century onwards, the collapse of other orthodox polities and then, in 1453, the City's fall to these Ishmaelites, appeared to bear out the prophecies.

These developments could be aligned with other computations that earthly time would cease upon expiry of the seventh millennium from the creation, a date corresponding with the year 1492.[17] Such computations were commonplace in the higher echelons of the church, and Patriarch Gennadios II Scholarios (1454–6, 1463, 1464–5) foretold doomsday on 1 September 1492. He thus assumed the City's occupation by infidels could only be provisional, now that the empire was no more. Meanwhile, at grass-roots, orthodox Christian faith was integral to Roman identity; even today, a villager in north-eastern Turkey can explain that 'this was Roman country; they spoke Christian here' (see below, pp. 852, 853).

Thus Byzantium is best viewed as an amalgam of communities of religious ritual and faith in the power of God, and of administrative institutions and defence works, some kept to a high degree of efficiency.[18] True

---

[14] Pseudo-Methodius, *Apocalypse*, [13], 9–10, ed. Aerts and Kortekaas, I, p. 172 (text); II, p. 49 (commentary). Already in 654, a large Arab fleet may have advanced far towards Constantinople before being destroyed by a storm: O'Sullivan (2004). See also below, p. 372, n. 17; Magdalino (2005), p. 42.

[15] Alexander (1962), pp. 341–55.

[16] Photios, *Homilies*, ed. Laourdas, pp. 29–52; tr. Mango, pp. 82–110.

[17] Nicol (1979); Magdalino (1993b), pp. 27–8; Polyviannyi (2000), pp. 207–8, 218–23.

[18] On 'political orthodoxy' among the Byzantines as well as orthodoxy's doctrinal and ritual mould, see Beck (1978), pp. 87–108.

believers, however far removed from the material protection of the imperial authorities, could hope for spiritual salvation and perhaps physical protection through prayer, regular celebration of the eucharist and access to the holy. As with the bread and wine bringing the body and blood of Christ to mankind, other rites of worship and also the decor and layout of the structure within which they were celebrated symbolised higher things, the medley standing for an infinitely superior, harmonious whole. Willingness to see providential design in the domed interior of a Byzantine church was articulated by Maximus the Confessor, and it was further elaborated upon by Patriarch Germanos I (715–30) in his influential treatise on the liturgy. Theological meaning was assigned to even the humblest example of ecclesiastical architecture and its interior furnishings: proceedings inside the church building mirrored those in heaven.[19]

The 'corporate consciousness' generated by rites revolving round the liturgy could hold communities of Christians together, so long as priests could be mustered to perform the church services. In a sense, therefore, imperial governmental apparatus was superfluous, and orthodox communities could carry on even under barbarian occupation. This was the case in the thirteenth and fourteenth centuries, when the populations under Frankish or Italian rule were still, in their hearts, 'turned towards Greek matters'. Such 'Greek matters', which did not distinguish very sharply between this world and the next, gave Marino Sanudo, a fourteenth-century Venetian observer, grounds for unease (see below, p. 778). In similar spirit the eminent holy man, Neophytos, ignored the Latins' occupation of his island of Cyprus, and as Catia Galatariotou has remarked, judging by his writings alone, one 'would be forgiven for believing that Cyprus never ceased to be a province of Byzantium'.[20]

Byzantine writings about the apocalypse offer little coverage of rebounds of imperial power before the final awakening from drunken sleep, but individual emperors showed resilience, sometimes recovering territories after generations of barbarian occupation. An emperor's expectations of acceptance and collaboration from the orthodox under outsiders' rule could be misplaced, as in the case of Manuel I Komnenos (see below, pp. 716–17). But after the Latin occupation of Constantinople and the emergence of rival orthodox emperors, widely scattered populations still proved receptive to the idea of belonging to the original Christian Roman empire. Not even the well-organised, culturally accommodating regime of the Villehardouin lords of the Peloponnese could counteract this magnetism, and Marino

---

[19] Germanos I, *Historia ecclesiastica*, ed. and tr. Meyendorff; Taft (1984), p. 111–26; see below, pp. 111–12, 244. On the (sometimes varying) interpretations of Maximus and Germanos, see Mathews (1971), pp. 113–15, 121–2, 140–4, 150, 159–60. See also Déroche (2002), pp. 177–80 and, for later developments, Ševčenko, N. P. (2006).

[20] Galatariotou (1991), p. 218.

Sanudo's apprehensions were voiced at a time when the Palaiologoi were gaining ground on the peninsula (see below, pp. 803–33, 860). Only out-siders with overwhelming military might, bonded together by distinctive religious beliefs and able to count on numerous like-minded enthusiasts, had fair prospects of implanting themselves lastingly in the 'God-protected City'. This conjuncture did not come about swiftly or inevitably: the subtle, tentative quality of Mehmet II's (1444–6, 1451–81) measures even after his capture of Constantinople in 1453, suggests as much (see below, pp. 858, 865–72).

This is not to claim that the amalgam of faith-zone, imperial idea and state apparatus which the Byzantine empire represented was an unqualified asset, or that it was sustainable indefinitely. The bonds were coming apart as Athonite monks and some senior churchmen and officeholders denounced the overtures to the Roman papacy which beleaguered emperors, pressured by *raisons d'état*, were constrained to make. The implacable opponents of ecclesiastical subordination to the Latins accused John VIII Palaiologos (1425–48) of betraying orthodoxy when he accepted a form of union with Rome at the Council of Florence in 1439 (see below, pp. 862–3). Perhaps other, un-imperial socio-political structures could better have served the earthly needs of Greek-speaking orthodox in the thirteenth and fourteenth centuries, allowing for the development of their burgeoning urban centres, trading enterprises and *littérateurs*.[21] But the plasticity, even virulence, of the orthodox Roman order during its protracted decomposition goes some way to answering the question of why the empire lasted so long.

INSIDE OUT: EMPERORS, OUTSIDERS AND ROMAN ORTHODOX IDENTITY

The relations of Byzantium with the Christian west loom large through the chapters that follow, tracing political, military and ecclesiastical encounters and exchanges. This does not necessarily mark over-simplification of the issues for the sake of narrative formatting. To recount Byzantium's rela-tionship with all the peoples and areas around it in equal measure would not be feasible, given the kaleidoscopic movement of the peoples and, in many cases, the dearth of source-materials for their relations with the empire. The only institution whose dealings with Byzantium can be tracked continuously across a thousand years is the papacy, offering an alternative universalist scheme of things. The minutiae of this relationship are not analysed or recounted here, but Byzantino-papal relations form a baseline

---

[21] See below, pp. 43–4, 45, 49–50, 824–5, 830–3. The flurry of late Byzantine writings on political economy signals interest in alternative constitutions, as well as reinforcement of the imperial order: Angelov, D. G. (2007); Gaul (forthcoming); see below, p. 862.

for Byzantium's relations with the Christian west, a story offering extensive windows on, if not a key to, the empire's longevity. Time and again, they also show how 'Old Rome' and its adherents impinged on the empire's domestic affairs.

There was an epic turning of the tables in the balance of power and wealth between Byzantium and the west from the sixth century, when Justinian's armies restored most of Italy to his dominion, through to the eleventh century, when emperors could still harness western martial and commercial resources on their own terms, and up to the thirteenth and fourteenth century, when westerners often, but not invariably, had the upper hand. By the late Byzantine era, the empire was in many ways an economic colony of the west, the Genoese and Venetians controlling the islands and other strategically important vantage-points in the Aegean, backed up by formidable naval resources and exchanging manufactured goods for primary produce. The renown of western arms was such that Manuel II Palaiologos (1391–1425) spent years touring the west in hopes of military aid.[22] Yet by this time much of the Peloponnese had been restored to imperial dominion after decades of Frankish rule in the thirteenth century, and – against the Turkish odds – 'hot-spots' such as Thessaloniki still aligned themselves with the emperor in Constantinople under the encouragement of their church leaders (see below, pp. 857–9).

In tracing these shifts in power one glimpses the silhouette, if little more, of that 'silent majority' of orthodox Greek-speaking country-dwellers whose customs and beliefs stood in the way of occupiers' maximal exaction of resources and consolidation of their regimes. In its way, the imperviousness of 'Greek matters' to land-based Latin warlords and churchmen offers as strong a clue as any to the reasons for the resilience of the Byzantine empire (see above and below, pp. 777–8). Yet it also stood in the way of Palaiologan emperors seeking some form of union with Rome (see below, pp. 829, 863–4).

This work pays pronounced attention to emperors' dealings with non-members of their empire, those considered not quite 'Romans' for one reason or another, laying it open to the charge of undue attention to 'Byzantium's foreign relations with little regard for its internal history'.[23] This plaint cited the then-published volumes of the *New Cambridge medieval history* and is pertinent, seeing that over half our chapters derive from contributions made to that series; the series' framing of the middle ages is maintained in this work.[24] Moreover our chapters, in line with the *New Cambridge medieval history*, aim to present the interplay between

---

[22] See below, p. 829; Barker (1969), pp. 171–99; Nicol (1974); Mergiali-Sahas (2001b), pp. 56–7.
[23] Treadgold (2003), pp. 1002–3.
[24] Chapters 1, 3 and 4 were published in substantially similar form in *NCMH*, I; chapters 10 and 11 in *NCMH*, II; chapters 13, 14 and 15 in *NCMH*, III; chapters 16 and 17 in *NCMH*, IV; chapters 20a,

socio-economic developments, the turn of events and vicissitudes of successive political regimes – the stuff of narrative. There are, as emphasised above, many roads to Byzantium, but the trails left by contacts with outsiders are numerous and quite well documented. They bear closely on Byzantium's one undeniable characteristic, its durability, and on our opening questions: how on earth did the empire last so long, as political entity and as idea? The empire was continuously confronting armed outsiders, and constructing a balanced account of this requires frequent recourse to non-Byzantine sources. So attention to alternative polities seems not merely excusable, but advisable, particularly since those which veered between merging with and separating from Byzantium often provide invaluable information about the empire's internal affairs. Four considerations may support this proposition.

Firstly, a geopolitical fact no less important for being obvious: Constantinople lay at the hub of many routes by land and sea. Constantine the Great chose Byzantium because major military highways converged there and because its accessibility by sea would facilitate provisioning of the increased population he envisaged for his new residence. For almost 300 years corn supplies were regularly shipped from Egypt, free of charge. But the assumption that overwhelming advantage would lie with the emperor against all comers already needed qualification in Justinian's era. Once Byzantium became a kind of *empire sans frontières*, the very accessibility of Constantinople and its environs exposed citizens to abrupt arrivals of aliens. Even lulls were apt to be rudely interrupted by the onset of 'barbarians', as for example the appearance off the City walls of 800 Rus or Scandinavians who refused to disarm and whose ships had to be dealt with around 1025.[25] And the speed with which Suleiman ibn Qutlumush (1081–6) and his Turkomans advanced north-westwards along the military road towards the Bosporus in 1075 shows the mixed blessings of the highways inherited from ancient Rome.[26] The state of emergency generated by the Arabs' onset eased after the seventh and eighth centuries, but the challenge posed by potentially formidable foes on two or more fronts at a time never wholly lifted.[27] Goings-on among outsiders were therefore of keenest concern to imperial statesmen. Through maintaining a stance of eternal vigilance against barbarians, they could hope for loyalty and order among the City's inhabitants.

The capital was, in effect, permanently in a frontline position and this raises a second aspect of the empire's involvement with outsiders: every generation or so Constantinople's citizens faced a major 'barbarian' incursion

20b and 21 in *NCHM*, V; chapters 22 and 23 in *NCMH*, VI; chapter 24 in *NCMH*, VII; and chapters 2a, 2b and 2c in *CAH*, XIV.
[25] Skyl., ed. Thurn, pp. 367–8; French tr. Flusin and Cheynet, p. 305.
[26] See below, p. 707.   [27] Haldon (1999a), pp. 37–8.

Map 1 Physical geography of the Byzantine world

0   250   500   750   1000 km

0   250   500 miles

Fertile crescent

Passes

Land over 1000 metres

EURASIAN STEPPES

Dnieper

Don

Volga

BLACK SEA STEPPES

Sea of Azov

CASPIAN SEA

BLACK SEA

CAUCASUS MTS

Caspian Gates

TRANSCAUCASUS

Lake Sevan

PONTIC ALPS

ANATOLIAN PLATEAU

Lake Van

Lake Urmia

Bitlis Pass

ANTI-TAURUS MTS

Cilician Gates

IRANIAN PLATEAU

ELBURZ MTS

GREAT KAVIR SALT DESERT

TAURUS MTS

Euphrates

Tigris

ZAGROS MOUNTAINS

CYPRUS

SYRIAN DESERT

Baghdad

Ctesiphon

PERSIAN GULF

Nile

RED SEA

or at least an alert.[28] The more fertile tracts of territory in the provinces were mostly either at risk of raids from Muslims or juxtaposed to Slavonic-speaking populations. Those few which were not, such as the inner sanctum around the Sea of Marmara or the north-eastern Peloponnese (see below, p. 501), were of considerable economic and fiscal value to the empire, enabling it to carry on. In fact the very fragmentation of Byzantium's territories from the seventh century onwards made it the harder for marauders to hit all the prize areas simultaneously. With a modicum of naval capability, the imperial government could tap these fertile areas' resources and maintain an administrative infrastructure and armed forces of a sort. Revenues reliant on agrarian produce, porous borders and painstaking (and therefore slow) methods of assessing and collecting taxes in consultation with locals were not wholly incompatible with one another (see below, p. 63). But in such circumstances the government could seldom afford very large, full-time armed forces, and the more convincing estimates favour a generally modest scale.[29]

This brings us to a third aspect of the emperors' ready recourse to external regimes and keen interest in direct dealings with them: the value of military manpower from other societies, whether as individuals in the imperial forces, companies serving alongside them, or self-sustaining hosts attacking Byzantium's enemies on home ground. Sizable field armies recruited from 'Romans' and geared to combat were not only costly to equip and maintain. They also posed a standing temptation for ambitious generals. Military coups, apprehended and actual, formed part of the empire's heritage from ancient Rome and the double-edged qualities of glorious victories won by generals, however trustworthy, underlie Justinian's differing treatment of Narses, who as a eunuch was debarred from the throne, and Belisarius (see below, pp. 206, 208). During the Byzantine emperors' centuries-long confrontation with their Muslim counterparts they were ever watchful of their *stratēgoi* (see below, pp. 259, 266, 380–1, 394). These provincial governors had sweeping powers, but neither the revenues nor high-calibre manpower sufficient to make a bid for the throne easy.

Themselves disposing of finite military resources, emperors had good reason to concern themselves with elites and power structures other than their own. It was not merely a matter of cost-effectiveness, substituting battle-hardened 'barbarian' brawn for that of Christian Romans, nor even that outsiders were generally less likely to show enthusiasm for attempts on the throne. Diplomacy amounted to negotiating arrangements with external or subordinate powers and with other elements not quite – or not

---

[28] Beck (1965), p. 13; see below, pp. 260, 299.
[29] Haldon (1999a), pp. 99–106; see below, pp. 60–1.

at all – Roman. This was an activity that an emperor could direct from his palace, relying on court counsellors and hand-picked agents, notably the *basilikoi* who often acted as his emissaries to another potentate or notable. In this way the emperor could swiftly mobilise armed units, even whole armies. They served his ends but with minimal employment of his administrative apparatus, and payment was at least partly conditional upon results. Thus the 'flat-management' style discernible in central governmental bureaus of middle Byzantium suited the emperor's dealings with outsiders particularly well.

And in this special relationship of the emperor with barbarians lies a fourth reason for our paying particular attention to un-Roman peoples beyond the City walls. It is in the field of diplomacy that Byzantine statecraft can claim responsibility for a text without any known precursor from the ancient Roman epoch. The title of *De administrando imperio* ('Concerning the governance of the empire') given by a seventeenth-century scholar to Constantine VII's handbook addressed to his son Romanos II (959–63) has been criticised as a misnomer, since internal affairs feature only briefly, far more coverage being devoted to 'the nations' (*ethnē*), outsiders beyond his direct dominion. But the highly personal nature of the text does not make it unrepresentative: Constantine's order of priorities registers where palace-bound emperors saw their strengths lying. Constantine's rhetoric in his preface demonstrates the way in which workaday considerations of cost-effectiveness could be dignified into positive affirmations of the emperor's ascendancy, couched in biblical tones: God has raised up Romanos 'as a golden statue on a high place', 'that the nations may bring to thee their gifts' and bow down before him (Psalms 17.34, 71.10, 32.14).[30] Through the incessant reception of embassies from other potentates, the emperor could demonstrate his authority in majestic form and signal his hegemony to subjects as well as to outsiders. In addition, and with less ceremony, he dealt directly with individual foreign notables.

The logothete of the Drome was the first official to have an audience with the emperor in the Chrysotriklinos each morning, and he had a further session every evening. External affairs and matters arising from them were the logothete's principal brief, and one reason for his close attendance on the emperor was probably the steady flow of outsiders through this hall. The *Book of ceremonies* treats the reception there of 'several foreigners' as routine.[31] These were not necessarily ambassadors, representing another potentate, but individuals. Such face-to-face encounters enabled the emperor to forge personal ties with a wide range of notables, encounters

[30] *DAI*, preface; Shepard (1997), pp. 90–4.
[31] *DC*, II.1, ed. Reiske, pp. 520–2. A high-ranking official (*ho epi tōn barbarōn*) was responsible for barbarians in the empire, especially Constantinople itself: Seibt and Wassiliou, *Byzantinischen Bleisiegel*, II, pp. 50–1.

which might involve bestowal of a court-title but had no necessary institutional framework. Through his 'diplomacy of hospitality' the emperor
could make the acquaintance of individuals who might return to a position
of prominence in their home society – or might return to acquire as much.
Besides, there was always the possibility that a visiting *ethnikos* would opt
to remain at Constantinople, becoming the emperor's *doulos*, even ultimately a Roman. Young barbarians from across the steppes or from the
other end of Europe were apt to spend stints at court.[32] The princely and
noble families among the Armenians offered particularly rich pickings for
talent-spotters at Constantinople, and lower-born individuals could rise
through merit, usually initially military, in the emperor's service. The families of the Kourkouases and the Lekapenoi are examples of such recruitment.
Instances of Armenian princes and, still more strikingly, of middle-ranking
notables holding court-titles while resident in their homeland will feature
in chapters below.[33]

The Armenian lands and their multifarious links with Byzantium were
to an extent a special case, but similar processes were underway on most
approaches to Byzantium other than central and south-eastern Anatolia
in the era of the jihad. They underline the way in which governance
shaded into dealings with separate societies and cultures. During the earlier
middle ages military governors supplemented central officials in treating
with Slavonic-speaking and other non-Roman notables on the outskirts
of Thessaloniki, Dyrrachium and other fortresses and strongholds on the
Balkan and Peloponnesian coast, while headmen of Slav groupings such as
the Belegezitai were termed *archontes* and given responsibilities as well as
titles. In this way, and complemented by ecclesiastical organisation, imperial enclaves very gradually extended their reach to the point where taxes
were imposed or services exacted.[34] In the western portions of the Byzantine
'archipelago' what might be termed 'internal diplomacy' was continually
in play, operating by devices not dissimilar to the higher-profile encounters of the emperor with potentates and notables in the Chrysotriklinos or
Magnaura at Constantinople.

Thus encounters and negotiations of many kinds between the emperor
and his senior officials and outsiders – whether informal meetings, ties
solemnised by a court-title, or actual administrative posts – were the sinews
of Byzantine governance. This networking process was necessarily unend-
ing, occurring at many different points and social levels across the imperial
dominions, not merely the capital. This is one reason why the question
of Roman identities is so complex. A senior army commander, Philaretos

---

[32] Shepard (2006d).
[33] See below, pp. 340–2, 345, 347, 357–8, 509, 709; *ODB*, II, pp. 1203–4 (A. Kazhdan); Savvides
(1990); Brousselle (1996).
[34] Turlej (2001), pp. 105–24; Seibt (2003a), p. 462; below, p. 258.

Brachamios, could carve out a power structure having markedly Armenian characteristics to the point where he was dubbed first of the Armenian rulers of Cilicia by a later Armenian chronicler.[35] And a century earlier the sons of an Armenian *komēs* in the imperial armed forces had transmuted into leaders of a Bulgarian insurrection against Byzantine occupation, the Kometopouloi (see below, p. 522). Collation of Byzantine with western sources shows several persons prominent in the imperial service, intellectual life and even the Byzantine patriarchate in the eleventh and twelfth centuries to have had close Italian connections, if not actually to have been of Italian origin.[36]

It is by considering some of the other elites with which the imperial court had so much to do that one may hope to understand the workings of the Byzantine empire. If this attention to 'foreign relations' appears excessive, such is the price of prying into the human, and not very institutionalised, organs of that empire. Byzantium's workings involved compromise and accommodation on the part of both outsiders and imperial authorities. The latter were in practice willing to make concessions. For example, the Rus trading in Constantinople in the tenth century were allowed to have their disputes with Byzantines resolved partly in accordance with Rus custom,[37] while the Armenian princes allocated territories in eastern Anatolia had commands over sizable communities of fellow Armenians, maintaining their own culture and church organisation.[38] At any stage in the course of these encounters, individual outsiders could opt for Roman ways and religious orthodoxy in their entirety. Hence the need to keep orthodoxy clear and pure, and to be on guard against deviance. It is no accident that lists of 'the errors of the Latins' (i.e. western Christians) began to be circulated at the very time when westerners were becoming a familiar sight in the larger Byzantine towns and on highways, and when social intercourse with them was on the rise.[39]

It was, in fact, their ongoing accommodation of exogenous groups and individuals within the empire in varying degrees of assimilation and their flexibility in dealings with them and with externally based traders, elites and potentates that made Byzantine rulers so adamant concerning certain prerogatives. So long as key marks of uniquely legitimate hegemony were reserved, all manner of concessions – jurisdictional, territorial, honorific – might be vouchsafed according to circumstances. Foremost among these 'brandmarks' was the name of 'Roman,' with all its connotations of cultural and moral superiority, antiquity, rightful sovereignty and, from Constantine the Great's time on, manifest Christian destiny (see above, p. 6). It is

---

[35] Dédéyan (2003), I, pp. 6–7, 69. See also Yarnley (1972); below, pp. 707, 709.
[36] Magdalino (2003); Magdalino (2007a).
[37] Stein-Wilkeshuis (1991).   [38] Dédéyan (1975); see below, pp. 360, 692, 701.
[39] Kolbaba (2000); Kolbaba (2001); Kolbaba (2006); see below, pp. 73–4.

no accident that the Byzantines reacted promptly to those external rulers and their emissaries (usually western) who impugned their monopoly of Romanness, whether by terming the *basileus* 'Greek' or by purporting to brand their own regime Roman (see below, pp. 417, 432, 540, 545). From the same considerations, efforts were made to maintain consistent protocols, terminology and, even (for centuries at a time), media in formal communications of the *basileus* with other rulers. As Anthony Bryer observes, John VIII was still styling himself 'emperor and autocrat of the Romans' and signing in purple ink at the council of Florence in 1439.[40]

Court ceremonial and indeed the whole ambiance of the emperor's 'sacred palace' in Constantinople, its orders of precedence, titles, vestments and other trappings, were likewise presented as quintessentially 'Roman'. As the chapters below suggest, the style of the court could alter as new emperors sought to distance themselves from immediate predecessors, and certain authority symbols changed appearance over time. Yet even emperors invoking 'renewal' to legitimise their regime tended to present themselves as 'new Constantines', harking back to the very first Constantine.[41] Conscious efforts were made to use *de luxe* baths, antique dining styles, buildings and other monuments, together with chariot-racing and spectacles patently associated with ancient traditions for the grander state occasions.[42] Such observances seem mostly to have continued until the twelfth century. Some involved sizable numbers of Constantinople's citizens as well as the elite,[43] and the games and races occasionally yet regularly held in the Hippodrome symbolised the emperor's 'marriage' to his City as well as his other attributes, such as eternal victory (see below, p. 521). Even banquets in the palace drew hundreds of invited guests, and the purpose of official orders of precedence was to maintain 'good form' and order (*taxis*) against the ever-present risk of confusion and loss of imperial composure.[44] But there was also a sense that the imperial court was the repository, breeding-ground and citadel of true Romanness, the place where those 'born in the purple' would first see light of day.[45]

The conviction that being raised in the palace conferred moral qualities as well as legitimacy was volubly expressed by a prime (and far from disinterested) beneficiary, Constantine VII Porphyrogenitus. Decrying his former

---

[40] See below, p. 853 and fig. 62. For continuities and changes in diplomatic forms, see Dölger (1938–9); Dölger and Karayannopulos (1968), pp. 89–107; Kresten (1992–3); Kresten (1998); Kresten and Müller (eds.), 'Die Auslandsschreiben der byzantinischen Kaiser'; Schreiner (2005).

[41] Magdalino (ed.) (1994).   [42] Mango (1981a), p. 352; Dagron (2000); Featherstone (2006).

[43] Morris (2003), pp. 241–2, 253.

[44] Philotheos, *Kletorologion*, ed. and French tr. Oikonomides, pp. 82–3; McCormick (1985), p. 5; Kazhdan and McCormick (1997), pp. 175–6; Oikonomides (1997a).

[45] Attempts to concretise 'the purple' as birth in the Porphyra chamber in the palace were, however, subsequent to the notion that special qualities were inherent in those born to reigning emperors: Dagron (1994).

co-emperor, Romanos I Lekapenos (920–44) as 'common and illiterate', he opined that only 'those raised up in the palace' were imbued with 'Roman customs from the very beginning', as if the court were a kind of crucible of Romanness.[46] Classical, Attic Greek was also prized by Constantine, aware as he was of his own deficiencies in writing it.[47] Attic was the dialect in which orations and other formal statements were composed for delivery at court occasions, and in which official accounts of emperors' deeds were composed. Thus the Byzantine court, with its regard for 'good form' and preoccupation with continuity, religious orthodoxy and linguistic correctness might seem to epitomise a 'mandarin' political culture. Literary works from this quarter are among the readiest sources for the general history of the empire (see below, p. 58).

Such priorities and shibboleths are, however, best viewed against a background of barbarians frequenting the imperial court, *ad hoc* arrangements continually being made with useful potentates, and titles bestowed on outsiders with barely a smattering of spoken Greek. The proportion of families in the ruling elite comprising first-, second- or third-generation immigrants probably made up around a quarter of the total.[48] The number of persons of external stock who made it, or almost made it, to the imperial throne is striking. Romanos Lekapenos' uncouthness made an easy target for Constantine VII's jibes since he was of quite recent Armenian origins. But the Porphyrogenitus was himself the grandson of a low-born opportunist, conceivably of Slavonic stock; the tendentious ancestry claimed for Basil 'the Macedonian' in the *Life of Basil* composed under Constantine's auspices even represents him as of Armenian kingly descent.[49] Once sole occupant of the throne, Basil I had displayed his orthodox piety and staged triumphs to parade his supposed qualities of victorious generalship.[50] He also undertook spectacular works to restore churches in and around Constantinople and to refurbish the Great Palace, the setting for imperial ceremonies.[51] Basil's measures were designed to legitimise a palace coup, but they demonstrate how certain 'core values' such as doctrinal orthodoxy and regard for palace ceremonial lent themselves to assimilation by highly ambitious, capable outsiders. Basil's adaptation and manipulation of establishment forms and conventions was extraordinarily skilful, enabling him to work, charm and perhaps sleep his way to the very top. But his career pattern was played out less spectacularly – and through more straightforward merits such as military talent – by many individuals intent on merely attaining the higher reaches of the imperial establishment, or gaining a footing there for their offspring. Many were members, if not from the dominant family, of elites

---

[46] *DAI*, ch. 13, pp. 72–3; see below, pp. 508–9.   [47] Ševčenko, I. (1992a), pp. 178–80.
[48] Kazhdan and Ronchey (1999), pp. 346–7.
[49] *Life of Basil*, pp. 212–13, 215–16; see below, p. 294.   [50] McCormick (1990), pp. 154–7, 212–23.
[51] Ousterhout (1998), pp. 115–19, 129.

beyond Byzantium's borders, external or internal.[52] Thus one of Basil's early
patrons, the widow Danelis, appears to have belonged to the ruling family
of a *Sklavinia* in the Peloponnese. Basil's way of thanking her upon seizing
power was to confer a court-title on her son and to stage a reception in the
Magnaura, befitting 'someone of substance and distinction who is at the
head of an *ethnos*'.[53]

The concern with 'form' and general inclination to stand on ceremony
of imperial Byzantines were, unquestionably, obstacles to casual infiltration by outsiders belonging to different cultures. Their presence in sizable
numbers in the imperial milieu was predicated by the 'diplomacy of hospitality'. An abiding apprehension was that this might lead to dilution of the
'Roman customs' which were integral to Byzantium's credentials for hegemony. Such apprehensions are seldom vented in as many words in extant
written sources. But they go far to explaining the limitations of the historical sources emanating from the Byzantine establishment, their preference
for a classicising prose style and tendency to present events in terms of
antique or scriptural precedents. The insistence on *taxis* in the more functional works composed in palace circles is, in fact, an index of the pressures
making for the reverse. Prominent among those pressures' drivers was the
steady stream into Constantinople – and, often, out again – of outsiders,
whether from the 'outer territories' beyond the City walls[54] or out-and-out
ethnikoi. The maelstrom of constant interaction between the imperial leadership and significant outsiders and alternative power structures underlies
the glassy surface that establishment-derived literature tends to present to
us. This interaction, the opportunities as well as the problems it posed for
Byzantium's rulers, is a theme running through the chapters of this book
and it has a bearing on the empire's longevity.

---

[52] Brousselle (1996), pp. 47–50, 53–4; Garsoïan (1998), pp. 59–61, 66, 88.
[53] *Life of Basil*, pp. 217–18; Ševčenko, I. (1992a), p. 192 and n. 68.
[54] Magdalino (2000b); pp. 149–52. For Skylitzes' sense of virtual 'home counties' of the 'Romans'
in the vicinity of Constantinople itself, see Bonarek (2003).

INTRODUCTION – PART ii

PERIODISATION AND THE CONTENTS OF THIS BOOK

JONATHAN SHEPARD

WHEN DID BYZANTIUM END – OR BEGIN?

Byzantium is an elusive phenomenon because so many of its constituent parts altered in place and over time. The overarching façade of the imperial order remained, with certain fixed points: religious doctrine, use of the Greek language, and the City of Constantinople itself. But many other elements were mutable – from court fashions, administrative methods and commercial undertakings, to forms of warfare or territorial possessions. Byzantium's distinctive qualities lie in this interplay between the fixed and the changeable, the expendable and the non-negotiable, ensuring its endurance across a millennium or so, longevity which only the Chinese and Japanese empires can unequivocally be said to have surpassed.

However, even the chronological limits of the Byzantine empire are contentious. In a material sense, the Constantinopolitan-based emperor could be regarded as powerless, politically dead by the time Sultan Mehmed II's technicians closed the Bosporus and trained their guns on the City in 1453. Yet alternative or affiliated imperial regimes were still functioning, and to all appearances the empire of Trebizond and the despotate of the Morea could have carried on indefinitely, even flourished, had the Ottomans not determined to put paid to them, too, while reducing other robust polities in the Balkans to tributary status (see below, pp. 831–2, 860–1). And the idea of the central place of the empire and the City in God's scheme of things persisted among the orthodox well after 1453. From that point of view, 1492 – when the world had been predicted to end following upon the empire's fall (see above, p. 7) – seems as good a date as any to conclude. And it is not wholly coincidental that 1492 saw the discovery of the New World: Christopher Columbus, himself of Genoese stock, was sailing a refined version of the type of cog which plied directly between Genoese Chios, England and Flanders until the Turks began putting pressure on their trading activities in the Levant (see below, pp. 847–8).

Our story might accordingly begin with the new covenant between God and mankind which Constantine the Great (306–37) made upon accepting the Christian religion and basing himself in the city of Byzantion. That is when the emperor became a figure of universal value to influential Christian churchmen such as Eusebius (see above, p. 6). Triumphalist notions about the Christian empire's destiny and hopes of individual spiritual rebirth started to filter through the lettered and propertied classes of the Roman Mediterranean and other strata of society, providing a sense of purpose and consolation through military setbacks and periodic devastation. In other words, something of the amalgam of Christian faith and eschatological hopes that characterised medieval Byzantium was already being mixed in the fourth century, when the Roman empire encompassed much of continental Europe, was a formidable presence in Africa and western Asia and still harboured notions of conquering Persia. To begin the story with Constantine among his bishops has all the more to recommend it, in that the Christian empire's longevity and perseverance through a variety of changes of fortune and circumstances is the connecting theme of this book. Besides, Constantine's conversion is roughly the point where several other authoritative surveys of Byzantium begin, whether focused on the ups and downs of the Byzantine state and its ruling classes;[1] on the thought-world of the faithful and the dissenters of Byzantium;[2] or dealing with culture and society as well as matters of state.[3]

However, both practical and theoretical considerations have discouraged us from beginning with the fourth century. Constantine accepted Christianity in 312 but the processes by which Christian observance became irreversible, an indispensable attribute of Romanness, were intricate and protracted. At the time of Constantine's death in 337 and for many decades to come, the majority of the population were non-Christian. The diffusion of Christianity can partly, but only partly, be charted through the injunctions of senior churchmen, the edicts of emperors and the feats of holy men. The decisions of individuals, families or communities to adopt the Christian faith and forms of worship could be made for many different reasons, not least peer-group pressure. These processes are seldom set out in reliable detail in our surviving sources, and such records as there are come from highly partisan writers.[4]

The fifth century saw the construction of important platforms and spectacular pinnacles of Christian empire that would be admired and utilised by

---

[1] Ostrogorsky (1968).   [2] Mango (1980).
[3] Cavallo (ed.) (1997); Treadgold (1997); Angold (2001); Treadgold (2001); Mango (ed.) (2002); Harris (ed.) (2005); Gregory (2005); Haldon (2005b); Cameron, Averil (2006b).
[4] See Brown, P. (1998); contributions to Lenski (ed.) (2006); Casiday and Norris (eds.) (2007).

much later regimes in the Christian west as well as the east. The 'rhetoric of empire', already well worked upon by Eusebius, Themistius, John Chrysostom and others in the fourth century, was further elaborated.[5] A vibrant court culture and ceremonial accrued around the figure of the emperor ensconced in his 'sacred palace', the majesty and dignitaries of his court evoking the heavenly court above.[6] The monuments of this architecture of empire took both material and institutional form, from the walls of Constantinople, built for Theodosius II (402–50) (fig. 2), to the almost as massive law-code, the *Codex Theodosianus*, that he promulgated. This law-code marks a milestone in emperors' attempts to codify law and governance across the spectrum of society, providing for church property and the jurisdiction of bishops and the religious observances and way of life of ordinary subjects. An entire book of the *Codex* is devoted to religious issues, heretics, Jews and pagans among them.[7]

These new materials of empire-building did not, however, make unreservedly for the consolidation of imperial power. The leadership of the church was prone to bitter disagreements over elements of doctrine such as the interrelationship of the divine and human qualities of Christ. These controversies periodically reached boiling-point and assemblies of patriarchs and bishops were convened under the supervision of emperors to try and reach an agreement. Of these 'universal' – ecumenical – councils, the council of Chalcedon (451) stands out as of particular importance. Its outcome was a formula concerning Christ: that He was 'recognised in two natures' while also 'in one person and hypostasis'. This was acceptable to the papacy, being very close to the terms which it had formulated, and Emperor Marcian's commissioners pressed the council to accept it. Serious fault-lines, however, remained both among eastern churchmen and between easterners and the papacy.[8] The divisions would reopen and become still more acrimonious in the following century.

A case could be made for bringing these achievements and controversies within the compass of this book, treating 'the Byzantine empire' as already in place in the fifth century. However, such identification of the empire's development and well-being with the formal elaboration of Christian doctrine by councils and the spread of Christian observance in everyday life raises three major difficulties. Firstly, as already stated, Christianity spread along multifarious channels and its effects – or otherwise – on social attitudes and behaviour patterns in town and country varied greatly between

---

[5] Cameron, Averil (1991b).   [6] Cameron, Averil (2002b); McCormick (2000), pp. 156–63.
[7] Theodosius, *Codex Theodosianus*, XVI, tr. Pharr *et al.*, pp. 440–76. On the making of the *Codex*, see contributions in Harries and Wood (eds.) (1993). For the impact of Christianisation on the family, see Giardina (2000).
[8] Gray (1979); Allen (2000), pp. 814–16; Gray (2005), pp. 221–5.

communities and regions. The onset of the new religion in its various guises has been much discussed in recent English-speaking scholarship and might seem to provide grounds for studying the Christianising empire of the fifth and sixth centuries *en bloc*. But scholarly voices have also sounded in favour of closer attention to the nuts and bolts of empire, institutions of governance such as the law and its enforcement, the state apparatus for revenue raising and expenditure, and coinage.[9] These institutions remained in working order across much of the eastern empire throughout the fifth century, and the continuing *pax romana* rested on impressive reserves of military manpower, coordinated to awesome effect. So long as the empire presented obvious and overwhelming advantages of martial strength, prosperity and public welfare, these material benefits spoke for themselves. Christian preachers and holy men might inveigh against alternative cults, indifference, materialism and – in matters of discipline and doctrine – against one another, and their written outpourings have survived in bulk, as has the Christian framing which orators and senior churchmen now provided for imperial power. But while that power still appeared to underwrite general well-being out of its own vast resources, in the heterogeneous and multi-cult towns and settlements of the eastern Mediterranean region,[10] Christian worship and observance had a wide range of alternative connotations for their inhabitants – whether as an optional extra supplementing other devotions; an imposition; a familial or communal tradition of cult practices and obligations; or an avenue for individual spiritual development. Christian court culture and splendiferous trappings supplemented, embellished and enhanced imperial power, rather than virtually substituting for it. Faith and worship were a valued asset in bringing the emperor victories and the empire dominance, but they were not yet generally seen as vital to the empire's survival: the empire did not yet, in the fifth century, amount to a faith-zone.[11]

Secondly, many shades of Christian belief, practices and organisation were developing under their own momentum, on a geographical scale extending far beyond the empire's frontiers. The ferment of Christianity in the fertile crescent and other parts of the orient posed obstacles for the Roman emperor as well as openings. When Armenia's King Tiridates IV adopted Christianity early in the fourth century, the Armenian church organisation and distinctive Armenian script provided building-blocks for the development of a separate political identity. Yet occasionally

---

[9] Millar (2000), pp. 754, 757–9; Giardina (1999); Marcone (2004), pp. 30–6. For a response (focusing on problems of periodisation) see Bowersock (2004), with a rejoinder by Giardina (2004). See also Harries (1999); Cameron, Averil (2002b); pp. 180, 190; Fowden (2002), pp. 683–4.

[10] On widespread well-being in the eastern provinces, see Whittow (1990); below, pp. 467–9.

[11] See Brown, P. (1998), p. 653.

prospects opened up of bringing Armenia – ever a region of keen strategic interest – under Roman hegemony, if only Armenian churchmen would subscribe to imperially approved church doctrine (see below, pp. 169–70, 337–8). Persia is another example of how Christianity was something of a double-edged sword for the Roman empire. The Sasanians offered safe haven for dissidents, vociferously at odds with the established church and (often) with the imperial authorities; by the sixth century the Nestorians made up a substantial portion of the Persian population and Persian-occupied Nisibis was a school for dissenters from the imperial line. Yet there flickered the prospect of further Christian converts in Sasanian ruling circles and it was not inconceivable that key individuals might opt for Chalcedonian orthodoxy (see below, pp. 136, 142–4, 311).

Meanwhile, and less spectacularly, ruling families and local communities adopted Christianity in the Arabian peninsula, Abyssinia and the Sudan for a variety of reasons, sometimes thanks to proselytisation by sects which operated in rivalry with missionaries sponsored by the emperor (see below, pp. 180, 188–9, 308–11). These movements and cross-currents among other societies and powers posed anomalies and challenges to an empire purporting to embody Christianity on earth. It has therefore seemed appropriate to include chapters which look back in detail to the more important developments on the empire's eastern approaches around the time of Constantine's conversion.[12] They put in perspective the church councils of Ephesus (431) and Chalcedon and those of the sixth century,[13] and also the tug of culturo-religious forces working on imperial decision-making from east and west.

However, a balanced presentation of the fifth century for its own sake would require full coverage of the western half of the empire, too, and this constitutes a third reason why overall treatment of the fifth-century empire is not attempted here. Law and order ceased to be the sole preserve of the imperial authorities in the west long before the abdication of the last legitimate emperor, Romulus Augustulus, in 476. In the west, the adoption of Christianity as the official religion of the empire appeared to usher in political turbulence and disorder, rather than consolidating military effectiveness, state-maintained infrastructure and prosperity, as it did in the east. Furthermore issues such as the diffusion of power; the levels of law and order sustained and of everyday violence; and the calibre of urban living and economic activity in the Mediterranean world and the Roman provinces further north are highly contentious.[14] The contrasts and cross-currents between the eastern Mediterranean world and the Christian

---

[12] See below, chs. 2a, 2b, 2c, 7.   [13] See below, ch. 1.

[14] See, for example, Liebeschuetz (2001); Cameron, Averil (2002b); Brown, P. (2003); Ward-Perkins (2005); Heather (2005); Wickham (2005). The question of whether conditions in the Germanic kingdoms were more violent than in the empire preceding them, together with comparison with the eastern empire, feature in contributions to Drake *et al.* (eds.) (2006).

west are a key theme of this work, but the dissolution of empire in the west has distinctive, often quite local, explanations. The broader implications for the eastern empire of the formation of more or less 'barbarian' regimes in the central and western Mediterranean regions will be discussed below (see ch. 3). That their existence was unprecedented, posing new problems yet also diplomatic and strategic openings for the rulers of Constantinople, is hard to deny, and this goes some way towards justifying the starting-point of this book around AD 500.[15]

We have therefore begun our story around the time when Byzantium first stood alone as a working Christian empire, surrounded by potentially formidable predators. Those seeking balanced treatment of the economic, social and politico-administrative history of the earliest centuries of the Christianising Roman empire have only to turn to the three final volumes of the *Cambridge ancient history*, which have advanced the bounds of classical antiquity up to around AD 600.[16] They will also find the progress of the Christian faith and its practices traced from its beginnings, across the length and breadth of the Roman empire and beyond, in the *Cambridge history of Christianity*. The first volume includes accounts of Constantine's reign and the first council of Nicaea.[17] Also of use are discussions by individual scholars or teams of conference speakers on the problems of the sense in which late antiquity may be said to have ended and the Byzantine empire begun, of how far the sixth century marks an end or a beginning.[18]

PART I: THE EARLIER EMPIRE *c.* 500–*c.* 700

The age of Justinian: flexibility and fixed points in time of uncertainty (Chapters 1–4)

In the sixth century, imperial armies were still large, the infantry tactics and military units of Rome's heyday were still in use, and they functioned on the strength of an urban economy whose structure was older still (see below, pp. 99–100). Expeditionary forces reconquered the coastline of north Africa and southern Spain and took back Sicily and Italy; their spoils bolstered Justinian's (527–65) triumphalist claim to have restored the Roman empire to former worldwide glories (see below, pp. 201–3, 207, 208–10). Yet these were protestations in the face of uncertainties arising from plague, natural disasters, incursions of armed outsiders and internal religious dissent.

---

[15] On periodisation, see Cameron, Averil (2002b); Fowden (2002).
[16] *CAH*, XII; *CAH*, XIII; *CAH*, XIV.
[17] Cameron, Averil (2006a); Edwards (2006). See also contributions in Casiday and Norris (eds.) (2007).
[18] Allen and Jeffreys (eds.) (1996); Cameron, Averil (2002b), pp. 165, 190–1; Mango (2002b), pp. 2–5. The effective starting-point of Whittow (1996) is *c.* 600.

Characteristics of Byzantium following the seventh-century 'transformation of a culture'[19] can already be discerned in the era of Justinian – notably
the fusion of faith and *imperium*; penny-pinching and a cast of defensive-
ness behind imperial bluster; and the assumption that a correct approach
to the divine held the key to earthly imperial as well as spiritual salvation.

The uncertainties of the sixth century made divine sense, if one accepted
the numerous predictions of the end of the world then in circulation.[20]
While individual responses ranged from the traditional to the Christian,
involving amulets, relics and incantations,[21] church-going congregations
and monasteries looked to the scriptures, priest-directed worship and holy
men. In enumerating the fortified towns and refuges furnished by Justinian for rural populations in the Balkans, Procopius acknowledged the
inevitability of barbarian incursions: yet he also stressed that the emperor
was manifestly doing everything within his powers to protect, offering his
subjects both a literal and spiritual safe haven (see below, p. 111).[22] Thus the
imperial order joined forces with faith and public acts of worship to offer
a modicum of security: it is likely that by the later sixth century, images
of the Mother of God and of the saints were being venerated with mounting intensity and orchestration.[23] The emperor also offered underpinnings
for social peace and order in the form of clear, accessible codification and
distillation of Roman law (see below, pp. 107–9).

A peculiar blend of military triumphalism, strenuous intercession for
divine support and careful husbanding of assets helped the Byzantines
survive as a collective the drastic turn of events in the seventh century
and beyond. The medieval empire's components were scattered and disparate, from the *basileus* in his God-protected City down to the inhabitants of fortified towns and self-sufficient, semi-pastoral hill-country kin-
groups in Anatolia or the Balkans. Their material circumstances and degrees
of security varied considerably. But a substantial proportion even of the
country-dwellers were within reach of refuges of some kind, and also of
churches. Since the blend began to be brewed in Justinian's era – when
elaborate earthly measures of protection for the civilian population were
instituted, first put constantly to the test and found only partly wanting –
so do our opening chapters. They also take full account of the empire's
eastern neighbours and rivals, current and to come. Persia's rulers, the
Sasanians, made much of their victories over the Romans, defining their

---

[19] Haldon (1997a).   [20] See below, pp. 121, 122; Meier (2003), pp. 73–100, 373–87, 405–26, 459–70.
[21] Krueger (2005), pp. 302–10.
[22] Pr *B*, IV, tr. Dewing and Downey, pp. 218–315; Gregory (1992 [1993]), pp. 246–50; Sarantis, 'The
Balkans during the reign of Justinian' (DPhil thesis, 2005). On Anastasius' building programme and
appreciation of the need for a network of fortifications, see Haarer (2006), pp. 65–70, 109–14, 230–45.
See also Dunn (1994).
[23] Cameron, Averil (1978); Cameron, Averil (1992c), pp. 18–20; Cameron, Averil (2000), pp. 12–13;
Belting (1994), pp. 109–14, 134.

own power in terms of these. Yet their institutional base may not have been quite as firm as this implies, while substantial minority groups within their realm worshipped the Christian God (see below, pp. 144, 153–5). The coexistence and cultural interaction of these two great powers prefigures that of Byzantium and the Abbasid caliphate, whose court in Baghdad drew on Persian customs, political thought and high culture.[24] The Arabs in the age of the Prophet Muhammad lacked the Persians' sophistication, yet their capacity for literacy, diplomacy and organised warfare was more advanced than hostile Romans, or their own later writers, allowed. To that extent their adroitness in exploiting the aftermath of 'the last great war of antiquity' between Byzantium and Persia is perhaps unsurprising (see below, pp. 174, 193–5).

By the seventh century, the Armenians had long been Christian. The inventor of their distinctive script, Mashtots', based it on the Greek alphabetical model. He had received a Greek education, and Christian Armenia's literary culture drew heavily on the fourth-century Greek fathers as well as Syriac writings (see below, p. 161). But the Armenians had their own church hierarchy, headed by a catholicos, and the princely and noble families in mountain strongholds debarred Romans and Sasanians alike from outright control over their respective sectors in Caucasia. For Justinian and his successors, the Armenian church posed a conundrum as intractable as was the papacy to their west: Christian, notionally beneath their umbrella, and yet highly articulate and prepared to defy the emperor and his senior churchmen on matters of doctrine (see below, pp. 171–2). The Armenians stood in the way of the idea of a Christian church coterminous with the empire even as, individually and collectively, they made an extraordinary contribution to its workings.[25]

Justinian's legacy was, then, a singular concoction in unpredictable circumstances. Its supreme and understated asset was flexibility, the capability to withstand military setbacks through a blend of material safeguards, *ad hoc* diplomacy, spiritual purity, ideological vision – and bluff. The 'beacon' was not only St Sophia but Constantinople itself, where law and order were upheld and where the unceasing rites of empire and worship were performed, shielded by imperial orthodoxy (see below, pp. 111–12, 114). The emperor as beacon-keeper could still convincingly take charge of these essentials, although in reality he was unable to direct the course of events in all his provinces. Justinian's reign can therefore be seen as prologue and scene-setter for all that was to come, until the City of Constantinople actually did fall to barbarians, albeit fellow Christians, in 1204. In many ways the sixth century was the starting-point of the cycles of rebuffs and recoveries that characterised the middle Byzantine period.

---

[24] Kennedy (2004a).   [25] Charanis (1961); Garsoïan (1998).

An alternative starting-point for our story might indeed have been the sensational events of the mid-seventh century. The chapters below subscribe to the widely held view that the eastern empire underwent massive shocks in the seventh century: thereafter things were never quite the same again, for all the restoration of order in many provinces and the semblance of Roman continuity maintained in the capital.

The Arabs' overrunning of the Levant and Egypt halted inflows to Constantinople of taxes and resources from what had been by far the richest provinces of the empire, dislocated distribution networks and military funding, and in the words of a mid-seventh-century text left the empire 'humiliated'.[26] Few, if any, men of letters could see the point of celebrating imperial deeds in the guise of classical heroics. Grand historical narratives in the mould of Thucydides, such as Procopius' or Theophylact Simocatta's, and rhetorical poems such as George of Pisidia's in praise of Heraclius' campaigns against the Persians in the 620s, could scarcely be cast from collapsing frontiers and incessant improvisation. As Averil Cameron has pointed out, much was still written, but with regard to the world of the spirit and the transcendent meaning of things, sermons, theological tracts and disputations.[27] The lights go out, so far as straightforward narrative is concerned, and our main surviving Byzantine accounts of events from around 640 onwards were not composed before the early ninth century.

Yet this change in source-materials does not necessarily imply a corresponding rupture in every single aspect of governance or of spiritual priorities for all the inhabitants of the empire at that time. The differences in civil administration and military organisation which are clear from our sources for the ninth century cannot be dated precisely, and few scholars now subscribe to George Ostrogorsky's thesis that systematic military reforms and creation of a theme system were carried out by Heraclius in immediate response to the Arab invasions (see below, pp. 239–40, 266). The shifts of overall responsibilities to military commanders (*stratēgoi*) and their staffs in the provinces may well have been provisional and fluctuating, with independent civilian authorities still functioning through the eighth century. The sixth and seventh centuries show sufficiently similar administrative arrangements still in place and important processes of change continuously underway to be viewed together in one part.

Moreover, as Andrew Louth shows in Chapter 4, disputes about doctrine went on being fought out by churchmen under the emperor's eye in the mid-seventh century and an ecumenical council was convened in his City

---

[26] *Doctrine of Jacob the Newly Baptised*, ed. and French tr. Dagron and Déroche, p. 168. On the drastic measures apparently needed in the 630s to pay troops in Palestine and Syria with revalued copper coins, see Schulze *et al.* (2006), pp. 17–24.

[27] Cameron, Averil (1992b), pp. 85–6, 104.

near that century's end (see below, pp. 234–5); difficult to cross in its lower reaches, the Danube continued to act as barrier, if not formal border, until the Bulgars installed themselves south of the river in the early 680s; and Carthage, an imperial administrative centre and strategic key to the central Mediterranean, only fell to the Arabs in 698. Until around that time, imperial statesmen may well have reckoned that the Arabs' extraordinary advances would eventually be repulsed, or would ebb away.

It therefore seems defensible to bracket the seventh century together with the sixth as the time when the Christian empire first demonstrated its capacity to go through massive earthly vicissitudes, military triumphs and sudden reversals. For all the sense of imperial Roman continuity that Justinian's propaganda conjured up, his genius lay in providing for conditions of incessant change.

PART II: THE MIDDLE EMPIRE c. 700–1204

The course of events: Byzantium between shocks and rebounds
(Chapters 5–6, 13, 16–17)

Any boundary drawn across conditions of flux is arbitrary, and several chapters in Part II delve back into seventh-century events, as background to the problems facing emperors once warfare on their eastern approaches became unremitting. Armies had to be stationed across the Anatolian plateau, combat-ready yet potentially self-sufficient, and emperors needed to forestall defections to the Arabs by those forces' commanders. The balance between maintaining military effectiveness and ensuring trustworthiness already coloured Byzantine political thinking and strategy in Justinian's era. But the problem gained a new edge from the Arabs' ongoing challenge and, as Walter Kaegi shows, emperors were very fortunate that comparable tensions dogged the Muslim leadership and stymied its capacity for major invasions (see below, pp. 365, 373, 375, 392). By around 700 the Muslims were tightening their hegemony over Armenia after a brief revival of imperial influence there (see below, pp. 345–6). And in 705, Justinian II (685–95, 705–11) forcibly regained his inherited throne in Constantinople, aided not by a 'Roman' army, but by the Bulgars, now installed in the former province of Moesia. The emperor's special relationship with barbarians as an alternative to his own forces would become a hallmark of the medieval empire.

The deep-seated state of emergency is set out in detail by Marie-France Auzépy, who shows how Leo III (717–41) and Constantine V (741–75) recast the formula for state survival set out by the first Justinian. Through reforming the army and identifying it very closely with their own regime, the Isaurian emperors allayed risks of a *coup d'état* and provided a strong right arm for state power, even while recognising the limits of the material defences affordable for Romans living in the provinces. They also provided the wherewithal, in the form of lower-denomination silver coins, for greater recourse to taxes raised in money (see below, p. 270). The sweeping powers of the *autokratōr* and his agents were tempered by concern for justice, providing a vent for the aggrieved through the channel of the emperor's courts, but also ruthless punishment for proven malefaction (see below, pp. 275–7). The spiritual welfare of the emperors' subjects was also catered for systematically, with numerous new sees founded. Furthermore, the 'idols' deemed to have incurred God's wrath – and consequent disasters for the empire – were denounced and, eventually, destroyed. Thus iconoclasm is fitted by Auzépy within a broader context of crisis, and her chapter as a whole illustrates the imperial order's capacity for renewal.

The fruits of this renewal ripened in the decades following the rulers' final abandonment of iconoclasm in 843, while the Abbasid caliphs no longer led or funded massive incursions into Asia Minor. The need to purge contaminating idols had lost its urgency, while devotion to images for accessing the divine was fervent in some quarters of the church. Shaun Tougher's chapter demonstrates the standing of churchmen after the restoration of icon-veneration. Patriarchs could still be unseated from their thrones, like Photios (858–67, 877–86) in 867 (see below, p. 301). But churchmen and monks had stood up for icons, some earning the status of 'confessors', persons who had suffered persecution for true belief, albeit not death. One such churchman was Theophanes Confessor, the author of a chronicle that is one of our main sources for eighth- and early ninth-century Byzantine history. Commemoration of the restoration of icons to favour was celebrated annually at the Feast of orthodoxy (see below, p. 290).

The gradual expansion in the material and demographic resources available to the emperors from the mid-ninth century onwards was therefore tempered by the *esprit de corps* and general repute of churchmen as orthodoxy's guardians. The limits of the emperor's 'space' were symbolised in the routes he did, and did not, take on his way to the liturgy in St Sophia.[28] It may be no accident that one of the earlier – and victorious – eastern expeditions launched by Basil I (867–86) was directed against dualists, the Paulicians, as if to demonstrate his orthodox credentials in the drive against heretics. Basil's expeditions against the Muslims of Melitene and Tarsus were, however, less successful, and his parading of his piety and generalship was at least partly designed to camouflage humble origins and a blood-soaked throne (see below, pp. 294–6). Equally, Byzantine defence installations could do little to curb the depredations of Muslim raiders who had the nearby island of Crete as a safe haven and potential emporium for slave trading from the 820s on (see below, pp. 499–500). Yet their ability to

[28] Dagron (2003), pp. 95–114.

sustain themselves through raiding implies fairly rich pickings to be had. This accords with other hints of economic vitality, for example the code for officials supervising trading and craft activities in the capital – the *Book of the eparch*, issued or reissued under Leo VI (886–912).[29]

Nonetheless, Byzantium's armed forces were fully stretched in containing Muslim land raids. And the Christianisation of the Bulgars in the Balkans from *c.* 865 onwards rendered their polity more cohesive and militarily formidable than ever, even if their receipt of baptism from Byzantine priests made them nominally 'spiritual sons' of the Byzantines, and notionally deferential.[30] With valuables and manpower leeching away to Muslim land raiders and pirates, Byzantium was hard put as ever to conduct large-scale campaigns on two fronts at once (see below, pp. 498–500). Even after the death of Symeon of Bulgaria in 927 eased Byzantine concerns about its western neighbour, offensives to the east were limited in scale and largely confined to removing thorns from the flesh. A kind of equilibrium prevailed, compounded by the emperors' reluctance to entrust their generals with armies of full-time soldiers schooled in aggressive warfare.

Such an army could easily be turned against an emperor and this was, in effect, what happened after the rampages of the amir of Aleppo, Saif al-Dawla, became insufferable. Within a few years of the codification of the status of theme-soldiers' military holdings,[31] the raising of more full-time soldiers and switching of tactics to full-scale offensives, Crete was regained – and its conqueror, Nikephoros II Phokas (963–9), was sitting on the imperial throne. There is little doubt that the army's size increased markedly in the later tenth century.[32] This reinforced the challenge which ambitious army commanders posed to the young emperors claiming the right to rule through birth in the purple, Basil II (976–1025) and Constantine VIII (1025–8).

Basil eventually quelled the revolts of his generals and associated his regime with the army to an extent unparalleled since the iconoclast soldier-emperors. The protracted resistance of the Bulgarians to his attempts to impose hegemony provided opportunities for the exercise of war leadership in person. While the epithet of 'Bulgar-slayer' was only applied to Basil much later,[33] his Bulgarian wars enabled him to square the circle and maintain larger armed forces, spectacularly intimidating neighbours on all sides, without falling prey to rebellion (see below, fig. 37 on p. 523). And the continually mounting agrarian and commercial prosperity and

[29] See below, p. 497.   [30] Dölger (1940); see below, pp. 299, 318–20.
[31] Haldon (1979), pp. 45–65.   [32] Haldon (1999a), pp. 84, 103–5.
[33] Stephenson (2003a), pp. 81–96.

population size of the enlarged empire was most probably sufficient to sustain this army.

What is less clear is whether the empire's customary methods of painstaking tax-collecting and transmuting of revenues into soldiers' pay were well geared for the armies that Basil II amassed. Such negotiable fiscal transactions required very many officials, and a significant increase in their numbers is suggested by the profusion of their seals in this period. Moreover, Basil set a precedent as 'happy warrior' and expansionist, without providing a male heir: his successors had to cope with a certain legitimacy deficit as well as with broader issues of strategy, the role of the armed forces and finding means of paying for them.

The vitality, wealth, yet vulnerability of eleventh-century Byzantium is brought out in Michael Angold's chapter. Culturally the empire was a hive of creativity, from the visual arts to literature. The volume of law-cases concerning money, property and inheritance is registered in a textbook assembled from a senior judge's rulings and opinions, the *Peira* (literally, 'trial, experience').[34] And Constantine IX Monomachos' (1042–55) institution of a law school at Constantinople represented an attempt to ensure well-trained jurists and administrators for state service in an era of widespread litigation (see below, pp. 598–9). Byzantium had not seen such a pitch of general material well-being and diversity of faiths and cultures beneath the imperial aegis since the seventh century. The analogy holds good in strategic terms, too. In the mid-eleventh century, as in the 630s, the emperor could justifiably believe that his foes were subjugated or reduced to virtual impotence (see below, pp. 227–8).

Yet then, without much warning, emperors found themselves combating raiders on three fronts: although the Pechenegs were more or less absorbed into the Balkans, the Normans in the west and above all the Turks in the east were not so amenable. In default of an incontestably legitimate dynasty ruling in Constantinople, several generals fancied for themselves the role of imperial saviour, for which there was pressing need. Disagreements over strategy and uncertainty as to the nature or intentions of the enemy were compounded by rivalries between generals and within the now labyrinthine Constantinopolitan court establishment.

That Byzantium lacked flexibility in its response to external challenges at a time of internal tensions and inflated bureaucracy is not so surprising. More striking is the alacrity with which Alexios I Komnenos (1081–1118) recovered from the strategic mistakes of his early years as emperor and learned from them. He proceeded to reorganise his army, abolish many court titles and effectively debase the coinage. The empire had, after all,

[34] *Peira*, ed. Zacharia von Lingenthal, pp. 11–260.

lost control of much of Anatolia to the Turks and was correspondingly impoverished: in cutting his imperial coat to fit diminished cloth, Alexios was pragmatically responding to severely reduced circumstances. There were precedents from earlier reigns for such economies and recourse to 'flat-management' style, as there were for the simultaneous emphasis on piety and plain living that Alexios made a hallmark of his regime (see below, p. 618).

The empire's material losses made correct worship all the more important, and although the church was now vocally resistant to emperors' tampering with doctrine, Alexios and his descendants still saw themselves as guardians of doctrine, shepherds of their subjects' souls (see below, pp. 617–18 and fig. 46). This was also the case with Manuel I Komnenos (1143–80). Manuel displayed prowess in astrology, jousting and war in equal measure.[35] His virtual 'cult of personality' included placing Christ Emmanuel on his earliest coins, a visual pun on Manuel's name, while the list of subjugated peoples associated with Manuel on an inscription in St Sophia evoked the titulature of Justinian's era.[36]

In emphatically aligning his regime with doctrinal purity and regularity of worship, Manuel resembled Justinian. The blend of expansionist bravado and inspired opportunism with tacitly defensive measures and *ad hoc* fortification-work belonged to a great tradition (see below, pp. 637–9, 642–4, 684, 685). And the Komnenian empire's reversion to a pattern of far-flung strongholds and outer and inner zones of imperial orthodox order in some respects evokes the state of emergency of the late seventh and eighth centuries (see below, pp. 261, 264, 653–4). In the twelfth century, too, the imperial presence could be concentrated in 'hot-spots', the more fertile lands and strategically important points, where protection and exactions were more intensive, in contrast to those districts, maritime or inland, that were left exposed to barbarian incursions or occupied by outsiders. Manuel Komnenos still had formidable armed forces[37] and a navy at his disposal, and these could well have helped him and also his successors gain new vantage-points, tap the burgeoning commerce of the eastern Mediterranean and forge alliances (see below, pp. 638–9, 645).

Two twelfth-century developments complicated matters. Firstly, the political stability and administrative workings of Byzantium were now entwined with the extended family of the Komnenoi, together with a number of related families (see below, pp. 657–8). Lands, fiscal privileges and senior military posts were gathered in their hands, and for all the resultant advantages of cost-cutting and political cohesiveness, the expectations of individuals and branches of the family were high, mutually competitive, and

---

[35] See below, pp. 637, 644, 646; Jones and Maguire (2002), pp. 113–18, 136–9.
[36] *DOC*, IV.1, pp. 281, 296; Mango (1963a), pp. 324 (text), 330.   [37] Birkenmeier (2002).

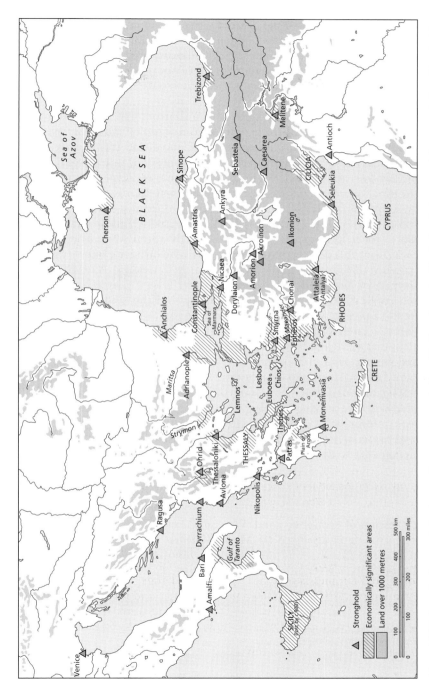

Map 2 Middle Byzantine 'hot-spots': sketch map of key strategic strongholds and fertile, well-populated lands of particular economic interest to the imperial authorities, yielding revenues or other material benefits; few were under continuous imperial control throughout the middle Byzantine period, and some outliers were then ruled by local elites

proliferating. This lessened the flexibility that the imperial administration had traditionally shown in attuning tax assessments to a property's current capability to pay them.[38] The effect of extensive tax exemptions, piling tax burdens on those left unprotected by privileges of one sort or another, was neither healthy for state finances nor conducive to longer-term political stability.

Secondly, the twelfth-century imperial authorities had to contend with western Europeans of a different stamp from those of the earlier middle ages. The westerners were themselves fragmented and many individuals were primarily concerned with trading opportunities or a career rising high in the *basileus'* service. Yet the intimacy of some western venturers with the Komnenoi and their successors paved the way for displaced members of the imperial family or pretenders to seek aid from western potentates and from causes with agendas of their own. Alexios Angelos' fateful bid in 1201–2 for help from western leaders, one of whom was his brother-in-law, was from this perspective nothing out of the ordinary, but it triggered the capture of Constantinople by the Fourth Crusaders. Already in 1185 a kinsman of Manuel I Komnenos, together with a pretender claiming (falsely) to be Alexios II, Manuel's son, had given King William II of Sicily (1166–89) a pretext for sending an expedition that easily took Thessaloniki and only failed to reach Constantinople through overconfidence.[39] Around 1184 another authentic Komnenos, Isaac, had taken control of Cyprus and started issuing coins in his own name, and it was a western crusader, King Richard I of England (1189–99), not the Constantinopolitan emperor, who eventually dislodged him. Thus some of the empire's choicest lands and fortified towns were proving to be highly vulnerable, or self-sufficient imperial entities, a foretaste of conditions after 1204, and indeed after the restoration of imperial status to Constantinople at the hands of Michael VIII Palaiologos (1258–82).

Taking stock: the economy, religious missions, border regions and significant others (Chapters 7–12, 14–15, 18–19)

The question of economic conditions on the eve of the Latins' seizure of Constantinople is discussed by Mark Whittow in one of the ten topic- or region-specific chapters in Part II. Byzantine economic history has undergone intensive enquiry, and *The economic history of Byzantium: from the seventh through the fifteenth century* published in 2002 provides an authoritative summing up.[40] The work's three volumes contain (besides

---

[38] That there should be regular, even equitable procedures at a time of maximal exactions was still a concern of the Komnenoi: Magdalino (1994), pp. 107–14; see below, p. 63.

[39] Brand (1968), pp. 161–71; Angold (2003a), pp. 40–1, 84; Phillips (2004), pp. 90–4. See also below, p. 687.

[40] *EHB.* For a concise yet informative and wide-ranging overview, see now Laiou and Morrisson (2007).

much else) syntheses on economic and non-economic exchange, the role of the state in the economy, and the periodisation of Byzantine economic history, as well as studies on the urban economy, both in Constantinople and in the provinces, and also surveys of economic life in the countryside, and of prices and salaries.[41]

Taking account of all this, Whittow shows that there remains room for discussion over the main lines of Byzantium's economic development. In particular, our ever-expanding archaeological database suggests that the material impoverishment and demonetarisation of the provinces in the seventh and eighth centuries may not have been quite as drastic as often supposed, and thus that the undeniable economic recovery of the ninth and tenth centuries may have started from a higher base-line (see below, pp. 478, 483–4). Whittow reopens the question of the relationship between this recovery and the condition of peasant-proprietors. Such proprietors could be of substance, and imperial *novellae* referring to them as 'poor' (*penētai*) denote their vulnerability to encroachments by the well-connected rather than material penury (see below, p. 489). Imperial pronouncements concerning their vital benefit to the state had their rationale, whereas the eventual amassing of prime properties by a few well-connected and privileged families was of questionable compatibility with the state apparatus' longer-term workings (see below, pp. 490–1).

Unlike economic affairs, Byzantine missions received limited scholarly attention in the twentieth century. Sergei Ivanov's chapter is the first survey in English of the full sweep of missionary activity from Justinian's time to the Palaiologan period.[42] Ivanov questions the strength of the Byzantines' impulse to spread the word to peoples beyond their borders, and shows that the initiative for missions often came from external potentates. The Byzantine state seems to have been better geared to the Christianisation of individuals or groupings of non-Romans now seeking careers in its service, or who had settled *en masse* within its environs. By contrast, Byzantine-born churchmen such as Theophylact of Ohrid assigned to far-flung sees were at their most eloquent in expressing discomfort with their barbarous surroundings.[43]

The emperor's role of indomitable defender of 'the Christians' was projected in court ceremonial as vividly as his image of being the equal of the apostles, and here at least, as Walter Kaegi shows, rhetoric bore some resemblance to reality. The forces of Islam were arrayed against the once mighty Christian empire, which they claimed to have superseded. Devising administrative means of coping with Muslim incursions was of paramount

---

[41] Laiou (2002c); Oikonomides (2002); Laiou (2002d); Dagron (2002); Matschke (2002a); Lefort (2002); Morrisson and Cheynet (2002).

[42] See also Ivanov (2003).

[43] John Mauropous, *Letters*, ed. and tr. Karpozilos; Theophylact of Ohrid, *Letters*, ed. and French tr. Gautier; Mullett (1997); see also below, pp. 321, 672–3.

concern for Constans II (641–68) and subsequent emperors. Warfare with the Muslims was unremitting for centuries, the orthodox Christian convictions of the majority population in Asia Minor supplementing the Taurus mountain range and cold winters in discouraging permanent Arab occupation of Anatolia. Iconoclast emperors repeatedly led expeditions against the Muslims in person; and the early Abbasid caliphs, in contrast to their immediate Umayyad predecessors, were also intent on leading expeditions against the Byzantines themselves (see below, p. 388). The raiding and counter-raiding between the arch adversaries came to form a rhythm, even if the caliphs could still deal knock-out blows to imperial prestige as late as the mid-ninth century (see below, pp. 391–2).

The Byzantines' caution in exploiting the caliphate's internal difficulties with large-scale military initiatives was matched by the Armenian princes, generally wary of bringing down the wrath of their Muslim overlords. Yet, as Timothy Greenwood shows, the boundaries between Byzantine and Armenian faith and church organisation were more fluid than Armenian narrative historians lead one to suppose. While Photios' project for formal union between the churches in the ninth century came to nothing, the Constantinopolitan patriarchate extended its organisational reach into what had been the preserve of Armenian churchmen during the tenth century, and writers on behalf of princes not subscribing to the Chalcedonian line on Christ's nature could still show fulsome admiration for the *basileus* (see below, p. 357). Such intermingling was not to the emperor's unmitigated advantage: the ties between leading Byzantine generals and Armenian princes brought them additional military manpower, and Basil II's involvement with Caucasian affairs was impelled partly by considerations of self-defence (see below, pp. 358–9).

The emperor's interest in the Latin Christians of the central and western Mediterranean regions was likewise stimulated partly by their capacity to intervene in his own affairs, especially as the pope's spiritual standing entitled him to pronounce on even fairly minor disputes concerning elections within the Constantinopolitan patriarchate. Beneath the formal ecclesiastical boundaries, exchanges between Greek-speaking eastern orthodox populations and communities in Sicily, southern Italy and the Byzantine lands remained active even after the Muslim conquest of Sicily. The prospect of southern Italy succumbing to Sicily's fate in the later ninth century and becoming a springboard for Arab incursions into Dalmatia and the Aegean prompted Basil I's decision to restore the southern Adriatic ports and strategically significant inland power-nodes to imperial dominion.[44] For almost 200 years, strongholds and eventually extensive tracts of territory on the peninsula came under Byzantine administration. The population of regions

---

[44] Shepard (1988b), pp. 70–2.

such as Apulia was mostly Latin-speaking, its ultimate spiritual head being the pope, while Lombard customs prevailed in the courts.[45] This hardly disqualifies southern Italy from attention and yet, as has justly been remarked, the source-material for this part of the empire has still to be fully exploited in many works on Byzantium.[46]

The seepage of imperial elements and eastern Christian culture into many strata and spheres of Italian life, from the papacy downwards, is demonstrated in Thomas Brown's chapter. The trajectory of imperial power can only be described as 'recessional', and local elites and the papacy had to fend for themselves against Lombards and later Muslim maurauders. But, as Brown shows, 'le snobisme byzantinisant' was current among some leading families irrespective of their ethnic origins; commercial ties linked other points with the eastern empire; and even as the papacy aligned its own ideology with Frankish *imperium*, 'Rome remained within the Byzantine cultural orbit' (see below, p. 448). All this had to be taken into account by the Carolingians when trying to bring northern and central Italy within their dominions, as rightfully part of their empire.

Many elements in Byzantine religious culture were of interest to churchmen hailing from north of the Alps, not least the utility of Greek for clarifying phrases in the Bible or of the church fathers. As Michael McCormick shows, the militarily robust iconoclast emperors provided a foil for Carolingians and their counsellors, intent on framing an empire to their own specifications yet impeccably Christian (see below, pp. 417–18, 424–5, 431). The working model of such an empire to the east could hardly fail to excite in them emulation, and occasional adaptations. The phenomenon of Frankish arms, letters and church organisation stimulated the papacy to take a firmer, more confident, line in its own dealings with the Constantinopolitan patriarchate and emperors. Things came to a head when in 863 Pope Nicholas I (858–67) took against Photios; the ensuing rift was both symptom of, and further stimulus to, the Byzantine church's sense of its own exalted status.[47]

The Frankish behemoth that loomed behind the papacy's fulminations was, however, disintegrating by the 880s, whereas Byzantium's naval vessels could still sail to relieve Rome from Muslim raiders. Byzantine dominion began to coagulate and then extend northwards from the heel of Italy. As is pointed out in Chapter 14, the Byzantine expedition to oust Muslim pirates from the Garigliano valley south of Rome in 915 was mounted in tandem with warriors supplied by local magnates and with the papacy's cooperation. A century later, the *katepanō* Basil Boioannes managed to intervene in the Garigliano valley and destroy the fortress of a papally backed magnate off his

[45] Martin (1993), pp. 48–53, 531–2, 709–11.   [46] Morris (1995), pp. 5–6.
[47] See below, pp. 420–1; Dagron (1993); Chadwick (2003).

own bat (see below, pp. 538, 558). Emperor Henry II (1002–24) retaliated in 1022 but his attempt to cut the Greeks down to size was no more lastingly effective than his recent predecessors'. The resuscitation of the western empire in 962 by the Ottonian dynasty from Saxony had unleashed challenges, explicit and implicit, to Byzantium, but Liudprand of Cremona's pronouncements on the subject strike a note of defiance rather than full-throated confidence. In fact the Ottonian emperors found many uses for Byzantine luxury goods and authority symbols in devising a political culture for their newly amassed dominions (see below, pp. 546, 549–50, 554–5).

The Ottonians provided the princes of Capua-Benevento and other potentates in south-central Italy with a powerful, yet fitful, counterforce to the Byzantine presence in the peninsula. The principalities of Capua-Benevento and Salerno, and the duchies of Naples, Gaeta and Amalfi seem to have been quite stable through the first two-thirds of the tenth century. They were, however, vulnerable to wrangles over the succession and other disputes within the respective ruling families, and power and resources were becoming diffused among the families of counts and other masters of *castelli* (see below, pp. 571–2, 579–80). In the case of these principalities and duchies, as with so many other elites and political structures bordering on Byzantium, their amoeba-like characteristics and the highly personal nature of leadership placed them at a disadvantage compared with the continuity of a unitary state. The *basileus'* strongholds ensured his potential military presence, while through diverse diplomatic devices, operated by his indigenous officials and local sympathisers and also at his own court, he kept tabs on established leading families and forged ties with significant newcomers.

The power-play of Byzantine Italy is fairly well documented and bears comparison with that in the middle Byzantine Balkans, for which archival evidence is poor. There, too, the imperial government maintained its interests with the help of centrally appointed agents, local elites, potentates ensconced in discrete political structures and mobile groupings whose military capability could be temporarily harnessed. Paul Stephenson's chapter illustrates the traditional workings of steppe-diplomacy and shows how imperial strategy after Basil II's conquest of Bulgaria envisaged hegemony over the Balkans: a network of routes and a series of zones, with the innermost receiving fairly intensive administration, fiscal exactions and protection, while the outer ones were left more to their own devices, under local notables (see below, pp. 664–9, 670, 673–5). Imperial attention and resources could be devoted to those zones where external threats or internal rebellions arose, and in many ways this flexible arrangement worked. Defensive measures and diplomacy succeeded in repulsing or deterring Norman incursions into Dalmatia and beyond for some time after their seizure of southern Italy. Byzantine emperors also exploited divisions within the

Hungarian royal family to curb rising Hungarian power. Manuel I Komnenos even appropriated a strategically significant portion of the Hungarian lands for a while (see below, pp. 642, 684–5).

Yet as Stephenson shows, the emperors' hold over much of the Balkan interior was loose-meshed, and Manuel's preoccupation with the intentions of well-resourced Latin potentates and crusading ventures reflects awareness of this. But diplomatic démarches cost gold, and westerners were no longer bought cheaply or lastingly. The Byzantines generally tried to reconcile non-Greek-speaking populations to their rule by keeping taxes low. But in 1185–6, resentment over higher taxes fuelled an uprising of ethnic notables and provincial Greek-speakers, which took on separatist tendencies and transmuted into the resurrection of an independent Bulgarian power (see below, pp. 656, 687–8).

The outlook for Byzantium's eastern provinces was transformed abruptly by the coming of the Turks. By the mid-eleventh century, there was quite heavy reliance on local elites in the borderlands and a not unreasonable assumption that military threats from Islamic regions could be contained.[48] The vigorous opportunism of Turkish chieftains and individual war-band leaders offset their lack of military cohesiveness and of regularly raised revenues. The drastic reform of military organisation needed to cope with the Turks was beyond the capacity of mid-eleventh-century Byzantine regimes (see below, pp. 600–1, 603, 607). Not that the empire was lacking in a series of outer zones on its eastern approaches any more than it was in the Balkans, as Dimitri Korobeinikov shows: Armenian local notables and the king of Georgia could still be enlisted to the imperial cause, George II (1072–89) being swayed by a sizable concession of strongholds and territories (see below, p. 705). Manuel I Komnenos was also adept at local-level diplomacy in Asia Minor and his personal ties with Turkish dynasts furthered stabilisation of the borders. Stability, however, made established rulers such as Kilij Arslan II (1156–92) even more militarily formidable, and Manuel's attempt to overturn the Seljuq Turkish powerbase at Ikonion (Konya) led to crushing defeat at the battle of Myriokephalon in 1176 (see below, p. 716).

Fortunately for the empire, the Seljuqs and other more established Turkish leaders showed little inclination to descend from their abodes 1,000 or so metres above sea-level in the Anatolian plateau. Not even the dissipation of imperial power after 1204 changed this state of affairs. The imperial Byzantine 'rump state' that formed around Nicaea co-existed fairly easily with the Seljuqs of Rum. It was the Mongols' arrival and pressure in eastern Asia Minor that precipitated a chain reaction of migration among the Turcoman nomads and, in the early 1300s, the breakdown of residual Byzantine

---

[48] See below, pp. 600, 607–8, 674; Haldon (2003b), pp. 60–74.

defences in the western coastal plains (see below, pp. 723–4, 726). This is yet another example of how far-away events could have drastic repercussions, upsetting the best efforts of the empire's guardians.

PART III: THE BYZANTINE LANDS IN THE LATER MIDDLE
AGES 1204–1492

Embers of empire (Chapters 20–24)

By the time Byzantium's defences in Bithynia in north-west Asia Minor succumbed to the Ottoman Turks, an 'emperor of the Romans' had once again been resident in Constantinople for some fifty years. To perceptive contemporaries, Michael VIII Palaiologos' seizure of Constantinople from the Latins appeared ill-starred (see below, pp. 753, 804), and they would seem to have had a point. Recovery of the traditional seat of empire may have brought Michael personal prestige, but organising its defence and everyday maintenance proved to be heavy burdens on state finances and diplomacy. His son and heir, Andronikos II (1282–1328) had neither strategic flair nor trustworthy generals to cope with affairs in Asia Minor or the repercussions of the Mongols' inroads there (see below, p. 726), and he anyway lacked resources to fund a navy. The vicissitudes of Constantinople-based regimes, whether of Latin or Byzantine emperors, reflected the demise of the command economy which had made the City such an omnivorous centre of consumption up to 1204. Thereafter its rulers were unable to collect taxes from numerous far-flung provinces, or to orchestrate a wide range of manufacturing and trading activities to their regimes' advantage.

The City's inherent geographical advantages now provided it with economic buoyancy, in default of overriding state power. Constantinople became a meeting-point of externally based trading enterprises, mainly Italians'. Their self-interest drove the exchanges and determined the alignment of trade routes, and they pocketed the profits.[49] The reinstallation of a 'Roman' *basileus* in Constantinople in 1261 might change the dominant outsiders from Venetians to Genoese, but not the dynamics of a now almost 'globalised' economy: the leading Italian commercial families and enterprises were not amenable to control by any one territorial state, and the Constantinopolitan emperor's ability to rake off proceeds through taxing goods or transactions was gravely impaired. Across the Golden Horn from the City, in Pera (also known as Galata), the Genoese ran their own, fortified, trading centre. The Genoese and Venetians alike were prominent in fourteenth-century Constantinopolitan court ceremonial, a mark of their involvement in the latest permutations of empire.

---

[49] Jacoby (2005a); see below, pp. 776–7.

Byzantine emperors, wherever they were now installed, would never again be able to amass resources or exercise purchasing power on a scale that made state service the main route to status and wealth. Their ability to reward and to coerce was correspondingly diminished and empire became more 'virtual', a matter of voluntary adherence and belief, than had been the case before 1204. But this did not put paid to the idea of empire, and in fact demographic trends, agricultural production and commercial activity seemingly continued on an upward course throughout the lands of the former empire until the mid-fourteenth century (see below, pp. 818, 820–2). These provided material supports for a variety of political structures, under the leadership of scions of what had been imperial, or imperially-connected, families in Constantinople before 1204. So long as they resisted the temptation to make a name for themselves by recovering the City, they could enlist local elites, sport imperial trappings and count on a measure of popular acceptance and even armed backing in what had been outlying provinces, for example, Epiros.

In addition, ambitious leaders of non-Greek-speaking Christian polities in Caucasia and the Balkans sought to legitimise and enhance the standing of their regimes, emphasising the sanctity of members of their dynasty or of other local saints and shrines close-linked with their rule. They, too, tried to make their respective realms coterminous with a church province or patriarchate. And a Greek-speaking *basileus* established himself in distant Trebizond and managed to stay aloof from bids for the throne in Constantinople.[50]

The kaleidoscopic swirl of Byzantine-born claimants to empire, splinter groups of Greek-speaking communities, orthodox Slav nation-builders and Frankish warlords does not lend itself to neat narrative rendition. Full treatment of all the different local situations would require a volume to itself. This is one reason why the conditions of flux following Constantinople's fall in 1204 tend to be set apart from the general history of the Byzantine empire. The chapters in Part III offer an outline of political events in the main Byzantine dominions (except Trebizond) up to the fifteenth century, but no attempt is made to replace or duplicate detailed narratives already available in English.[51] Instead, chapters are devoted to some of the principal beneficiaries from the events of 1202–4: the western European conquerors and colonisers; Italian and other merchants in the Aegean; Serbian and Bulgarian rulers contending for control of the Egnatian Way and outlets to the sea; and Albanian chieftains. Quite extensive coverage is given to matters of trade, emporia and trade routes. These illustrate the volatile nature of the commerce that yielded the most spectacular wealth. Several elites,

---

[50] See below, pp. 731, 779; Bojovic (2001); Eastmond (2003a); Eastmond (2004).
[51] See, in particular, Nicol (1993).

would-be imperial Greek dynasts in the Balkans, Serbian and Bulgarian potentates and Latin men-at-arms, did business with, as well as competing against, one another, making military and marriage alliances in numerous permutations.

At a time when few boundaries were really closed, or power centres firmly rooted, the prospects for a regime or simply a local family could be transformed by appropriation of a prosperous port, or a new deal with the Venetians or the Genoese. If this seldom made for stable political structures, it tended to stimulate rather than stifle new trading nexuses. New axes also formed directly between the former provinces of Byzantium, and Greek-speaking traders and sailors played a significant part in developing and operating these networks, albeit on a secondary plane to westerners.[52] The new conditions prompted local, lower-value commerce and offered opportunities for other forms of intercourse between Greek-speaking imperial subjects or their descendants and Latins in Aegean coastal towns. This spectacle, together with fear for their orthodox souls, may well have stimulated the movement towards extreme asceticism and a hardening of the line against the Latins discernible in some Latin-frequented commercial centres, for example fourteenth-century Thessaloniki, a city in socio-cultural ferment (see below, pp. 47, 820, 823–4, 857–8).

One region that temporarily insulated itself against such cultural contamination was that of Nicaea under the Lascarid emperors, in the first half century or so following Constantinople's fall. They eschewed lavish consumption and ruled in a style somewhat reminiscent of the soldier-emperors of the eighth century.[53] Restrictions against trading with the Latins were enforced and the state's objective was self-sufficiency. Nicaea's mostly agrarian economy and its character of a frontier society facing the Turks made for an effective fighting force, while also sustaining a robust and variegated court culture (see below, pp. 739, 751). Under the capable generalship of Michael Palaiologos, warriors from Nicaea defeated what was, in a sense, their opposite number among the Latins, the Franks of Achaia, at the battle of Pelagonia in 1259 (see below, p. 749). The Nicaeans' victory is the more striking for the fact that their adversaries, under the leadership of the Villehardouin family, included the best-organised among the Frankish occupiers of the Byzantine lands.

The qualities of the Villehardouin regime are brought out in David Jacoby's chapter. The Villehardouin princes' dealings with the Italian entrepreneurs were sometimes fraught and at first they had their differences with other Frankish lordships. But they came to arrangements of mutual advantage with, for example, the Venetians, while also courting the cooperation of Greek-speaking landowning elites and leaving

---

[52] Morrisson (2005); see below, pp. 818, 820–1, 842–3.
[53] Angold (1975a); see also below, pp. 739–40.

orthodox churches and churchmen mostly unmolested, a prudent stance given their own limited numbers. However, the demands placed on peasants were less constrained by law: most tenants on estates became legally unfree, and their disputes could now usually be heard only in seigneurial courts. They lacked access to public courts proceeding by Romano-Byzantine law, which seem to have functioned right up to 1204 (see below, pp. 772–3). The Villehardouin leadership deliberately fostered a sense of regional identity, accommodating indigenous *archontes* within their political culture, and members of these families fought on their side at Pelagonia. Nonetheless, the Villehardouins continued to lose ground to the Palaiologoi in the later thirteenth and earlier fourteenth centuries.[54]

The importance of the Peloponnese to the Palaiologoi is shown by the fact that their territories there were usually allocated to the sons of the emperor. The 'despotate of the Morea' is not recorded as being of much fiscal value to the Constantinopolitan government, but its long-term economic viability and the cultural vitality maintained at the despots' court in Mistra made this more a beacon than an outpost of the orthodox Roman empire. The despotate has been described as a 'success story' of late Byzantium (see below, p. 860), and part of its buoyancy came from the agreements that were made with Latin powers and trading interests. Essentially, the Byzantines marketed their wheat, honey and other primary produce to Italian traders ensconced on the coast, and catered efficiently for newly established trading posts such as Clarence (Glarentza) (see below, pp. 835, 841, 845). In doing business with the westerners without losing political autonomy or doctrinal orthodoxy, the despotate improved upon the example of Nicaea, demonstrating the resilience of 'virtual empire'.

Another success-story, likewise rather undersung in relation to the empire because unchronicled by Byzantine narrative historians, is that of the heterogeneous monks of Mount Athos in this period. Copious writings flowed from the pens of ascetics who resided for a while or were trained there, for example Gregory of Sinai, Gregory Palamas, Evtimii (a future Bulgarian patriarch) and Kallistos, a future patriarch of Constantinople. They recounted the lives and miracles of one another, composed texts for use in worship, denounced the Latins or polemicised with fellow orthodox over other theological matters such as the possibility of experiencing the Divine Light, a basic tenet of the hesychasts.[55] The heavenly kingdom and the means by which individuals could train themselves for exposure to the divine – through prayer, contemplation and abstinence – were of paramount concern to these monks, transcending earthly dangers and

---

[54] Shawcross, 'The Chronicle of Morea' (DPhil thesis, 2005); Shawcross (forthcoming b); see below, p. 772.

[55] See below, pp. 823, 857; Meyendorff (1964); Meyendorff (1974c); Krausmüller (2006).

Figure 1 The Holy Mountain, Athos

powers. Yet the Holy Mountain also acted as a focal point for orthodox potentates: the orthodox emperors in Constantinople and Trebizond, as well as Georgian, Bulgarian and Serb rulers, believed that veneration of Athonite monks in general, and patronage of individual houses in partic- ular, offered them a means of gaining both God's favour and their own subjects' respect (see map 50 below, p. 873).[56] If this polycentric orthodox world was riven by fierce political, territorial and ethnic rivalries, common religious beliefs, saints' cults and axioms of church discipline maintained strands of unity. Athos and affiliated monasteries served as a 'workshop of virtue'.[57]

The frequency of contacts between far-flung monasteries[58] was facilitated by the proliferation of routes and affordability of travel that followed on from the Latins' dominance of the Aegean and the Black Seas. The capacious

[56] See the emperor of Trebizond's explanation for founding a house on Athos in 1374: *Actes de Dionysiou*, ed. Oikonomides *et al.*, p. 60. See below, p. 791.
[57] *Register des Patriarchats*, ed. Hunger *et al.*, II, no. 56, pp. 428–9; *Régestes des actes du patriarcat*, ed. Grumel *et al.*, no. 2309; Nicol (1979), p. 19; Meyendorff (1981), pp. 115, 128–30; Krausmüller (2006); below, pp. 827, 831.
[58] Evans (ed.) (2004), pp. 11–12 (introduction); Gothóni (2004), pp. 60–4; Shepard (2006c), pp. 17– 18, 36–40.

ships of Italian merchants could ferry sizable parties of Rus churchmen from the lower Don to Constantinople, or on to Thessaloniki and thus the neighbourhood of Athos. And the wanderings of holy men such as Gregory of Sinai from Thessaloniki to Chios and beyond may well have been made in Italian vessels.[59] Thus, paradoxically, a community of faith and spiritual role models gained in intensity and range both from the weakness of polities unable effectively to regulate sea traffic, and from the ubiquitousness and drive of Latin merchants and their trading partners in quest of profits.

Not that many senior churchmen in the Constantinopolitan patriarchate or Athonite leaders saw merit in the fragmentation of earthly powers. Besides seeking individual emperors' support in wrangles over hesychasm, church appointments and property-ownership, these churchmen upheld the idea of empire as an article of faith. It was more than a matter of finding a compliant figurehead at a time when the patriarchate's own stock and organisation were riding high. Allegiance to a Christian Roman emperor on earth, and specifically in the 'holy city'[60] of Constantinople, was a characteristic that distinguished true Romans from mere Latins, whose brand of Christian observance seemed to bring them so many material advantages and sharp debating points. The empire that Constantine the Great had instituted was, after all, part of God's design for the redemption of mankind, and those who stayed loyal to the idea were at the same time 'true believers', *orthodoxoi*.

More positively, and less time-specific, senior orthodox churchmen could hold up the imperial order projected in Constantinople through ceremonial and liturgical worship as a kind of 'icon', prefiguring the divine order in heaven. Even if the late Palaiologan empire appeared to be confined within the City's walls, the capital's endurance of siege conditions had venerable precedents.[61] The empire had repeatedly survived almost total submersion beneath alien occupiers and invaders, its enclaves standing out above the flood as a kind of archipelago (see below, pp. 226–7, 255–7, 259–60, 610–12). The successive phases of fragmentation and territorial reconfiguration gained meaning and purpose from a standpoint attuned to liturgy, the constant re-enactment of sacred time by means of key texts and symbols in a church building, a miniaturised heaven (see above, p. 8). This perspective enabled churchmen and laity alike to see beyond current setbacks and material want to the ultimate victory of the emperor and all he stood for. Patriarch Antony IV (1389–90, 1391–7) voiced it in his letter to Grand Prince Vasilii I of Moscow (1389–1425) in 1393, when he insisted on the 'commonality' of the church and 'the natural emperor, whose legislations

[59] Kallistos, *Life of Gregory of Sinai*, ch. 15, ed. Pomialovsky, p. 33; Balfour (1982), pp. 44–7, 52–3; Majeska (1991), pp. 36–7.
[60] MM, II, p. 361; *Régestes des actes du patriarcat*, ed. Grumel *et al.*, no. 3112.
[61] Cameron, Averil (1979b).

and regulations and ordinances are held in regard across all the inhabited world', in contrast to 'particular local rulers', like Vasilii, 'besieged by the unbelievers and himself taken captive', a dig at Vasilii's recent spell as a hostage of the Golden Horde.[62] By this line of thinking, which many on Athos shared, church and empire stood for ethical and political principles of universal validity, and Constantinople was still their exemplary centre.

Whether Rus and other Slavic-speaking potentates fully subscribed to this line is questionable, but one should not underestimate the readiness of some of their clergy, at least, to put an exceptional valuation on the liturgical rites in St Sophia or to associate them closely with the emperor. Thus Ignatius of Smolensk wrote a detailed eyewitness account of the coronation there of Manuel II Palaiologos (1391–1425) in 1392. He interrupts his description of the liturgy to ask 'who can express the beauty of this?' in terms akin to those of Rus emissaries who had reported back to Vladimir of Kiev after witnessing a service in St Sophia some 400 years before: 'We knew not whether we were in heaven or on earth . . . We only know that God dwells there among men.'[63]

For even the most educated Rus churchmen, Byzantine political culture was only a remote aspiration, but south Slav potentates were eager to appropriate details of Byzantine inauguration ritual to sacralise their own regimes. Translated texts containing the basic prayers and procedures are known from fourteenth- and fifteenth-century manuscripts: the translations into Slavonic were probably carried out in the fourteenth century, if not earlier.[64] While these appropriations signal Bulgarian and Serb leaders' ambitions to gain divine sanction for their own authority and for the right solemnly to delegate to subordinates in the manner of the *basileus*, they also imply a kind of gold-standard status for the rites of rulership celebrated at his court. This did not stop them from doing battle with the *basileus*' armies or occupying his former territories and provincial towns, as the Bulgarian Ivan II Asen (1218–41), and the Serb rulers Stefan Uroš II Milutin (1282–1321) and Stefan Dušan (1331–55) did with panache.[65]

Divinely sanctioned authority was not, however, gained quite so straightforwardly. Overweening as individual potentates' personal pretensions might be, many of their churchmen and subject populations still saw in the tsar's court in Constantinople a model of legitimate monarchical rulership, even a reflection of the celestial order. As Alain Ducellier notes, the victorious Milutin effectively remodelled his court ceremonial and panoply of authority symbols on Byzantine lines at the time of marrying

[62] MM, II, pp. 191, 192; tr. in Barker (1969), pp. 108, 109; Crummey (1987), p. 58; see below, p. 852.
[63] Ignatius of Smolensk, tr. in Majeska, *Russian travelers*, pp. 104–5, 110–11; *PVL*, p. 49; *RPC*, p. 111.
[64] Biliarsky (1993), pp. 125–7, 133, 139; Biliarsky (2001), pp. 72–4, 85–8.
[65] See below, pp. 788, 790–2, 801–2; Soulis (1984), pp. 6–11, 25–7, 35–47.

Simonis, daughter of Andronikos II Palaiologos (1282–1328), in 1299.[66] Already wealthy, Milutin could now legitimately bedeck his wife and selected nobles in 'imperial garments and gold belts' and in imperial purple, sending them on progresses through his lands.[67] The belief that preeminence rightfully belonged to the 'emperor of the Romans' resonated among the monks of Athos and even the most ambitious of Serbian predators, Stefan Dušan, had to take heed while appropriating Byzantine-ruled towns in Macedonia and claiming to be chief protector of the Holy Mountain.[68]

Stefan Dušan's conquests and prestige owed much to the military failings and penury of the Byzantine empire. As Angeliki Laiou shows, these weaknesses were partly self-inflicted, a consequence of bitter divisions within the Palaiologan dynasty and civil war between the regents of a minor, John V Palaiologos (1341–91), and a formidable figure who for a while took the helm, John VI Kantakouzenos (1347–54) (see below, pp. 809, 810–11, 822–4). The mid-fourteenth century saw an unmistakable turn for the worse in the empire's fortunes, as pressures from Turks, Serbs and other external powers mounted, while revenues fell far short of the emperor's outgoings. One symbolic indignity was the cessation of issues of gold coins from some point between 1354 and 1366 onwards: striking gold coins bearing his image had been a prerogative of the emperor in the New Rome's heyday (see below, pp. 809–10). A mid-fourteenth-century observer bemoaned the loss of territories: 'Now it is we who are enslaved by all those people who were . . . [formerly] . . . under our sway.'[69] The Ottomans, in contrast, conducted a war-machine formidably well calibrated for continual operations. The Byzantine emperor became a tribute-payer and thus vassal of Sultan Murad I (1362–89), but this bought only temporary respite, and for nearly ten years from 1394 Constantinople was under siege (see below, pp. 827–8, 832). Deprived of a forceful legitimate monarch by Dušan's untimely death in 1355, the Serbs' new polity itself fell prey to internal dynastic rivalries and regional secessions, while the Serbs' defeat at the battle of Kosovo in 1389 might suggest that the Ottomans were all but unstoppable (see below, p. 852); likewise with the Turks' annihilation of a large crusading army at Nikopolis in 1396 under the leadership of Murad's son and heir Bayazid I (1389–1402). The survival of the Byzantine empire into the fifteenth century could plausibly be put down to luck and its very harmlessness in Ottoman eyes.

Yet the loose-knit, almost federal, empire of the Palaiologoi was not necessarily worst-adapted for obstructing the Ottomans. A case may even

---

[66] See below, pp. 801–2; see also Malamut (2000), pp. 500–5; Ćirković, (2004), pp. 49–52.
[67] Danilo II *et al.*, *Životi kraljeva*, ed. Daničić, pp. 96–7; Malamut (2000), p. 503.
[68] Obolensky (1971), pp. 255–6.
[69] Ševčenko, 'Alexios Makrembolites', p. 213 (text), p. 225 (tr.).

be made for its resilience. From behind his Roman walls, the emperor could still seek out his enemy's enemy in the diplomatic tradition of Justinian. The arrival of the Central Asian conqueror, Timur, in Anatolia in 1401 probably owes something to Manuel II's démarches towards him in conjunction with western emissaries.[70] Timur's crushing of Bayazid's army at the battle of Ankara in 1402 and the subsequent squabbles between Bayazid's sons eased the pressure on Byzantium, and some Byzantines invoked another equally venerable tradition, the intervention of the Mother of God. The despatch of icons and relics – 'reliquary diplomacy' – was pursued with as much vigour by emperors and senior churchmen after Nikopolis as before 1396; their efforts were directed at both western and eastern sympathisers, potential providers of military manpower or treasure.[71] Institutionalised links were forged in the late fourteenth century with the church organisations of nascent Wallachian and Moldavian principalities beyond the lower Danube, and as late as the 1430s the Serbian despot George Branković (1427–56) constructed a fortified residence at Smederevo on the lines of one recently built in the City walls at Constantinople by, most probably, his father-in-law, Theodore Palaiologos Kantakuzenos.[72] Other marriage-ties bound the Serbian political elite with that of the empire of Trebizond, and this network was, towards the mid-fifteenth century, extended to the Ottoman ruling family, too (see below, pp. 872, 874).

Given the Ottomans' problems with finding military manpower for the Balkans, and the limited number of Muslims residing west of the Aegean and the Bosporus in the later fourteenth and earlier fifteenth centuries, it was conceivable that the strands and strongholds of orthodox dynasts and supporting populations might be tweaked together in such a way as to thwart the 'Ishmaelites', denying them sufficient captives, plunder or revenues to maintain their war machine. If the Turks proved ultimately unstoppable, this owed much to the Ottomans' methods of 'harvesting' Christian children and firing the 'new army' of janissaries with zeal for further conquests (see below, p. 858). The underlying ties of faith and allegiance between emperor, Greek-speaking Romans and even sometimes the Slavonic-speaking orthodox had survived earlier inundations and, when occupying elites and armies faltered, resurfaced with a vengeance (see below, pp. 785, 798–9). The empire without frontiers lost vital nutrients at grass-roots with each successive 'child levy' and *sürgün*, haemorrhaging as debilitating as the holes blasted in Constantinople's walls by Turkish guns in 1453.[73]

[70] Obolensky (1963), pp. 47–52; Barker (1969), pp. 183, 504–9; Jackson (2005), pp. 238–40.
[71] Barker (1969), p. 408; Mergiali-Sahas, (2001a), pp. 56–9; Baronas (2004), pp. 85–7; Vassilaki (2005); Baronas (2007).
[72] Shepard (2006c), pp. 26–8; Peschlow (2001), p. 401 and illust. 19.
[73] Runciman (1965), pp. 97, 99, 104, 116–17; see below, pp. 858–9.

The care the Ottomans showed in drawing on the human resources of the empire's former provinces is as revealing about Byzantium as it is about their own organisational talents. The Ottoman war machine was vastly more formidable than the one that had enabled the Fourth Crusaders to seize the City and, unlike the Crusaders, the Turks had long dominated its hinterland. But they needed to draw heavily and confidently on their Balkan possessions for revenues and manpower before taking on the task of capturing Constantinople and administering in and from it. They were not going to repeat the experience of the Crusaders, who had had to contend with Greek and Slav populations of, at best, uncertain loyalty, to the west and south-west of Constantinople. The forbearance of the sultans and their counsellors from attempting a direct assault in the first half of the fifteenth century was partly due to internal political tensions. But it also suggests that the Byzantine empire had other strengths besides the near-impregnability of its 'reigning city'. Embers could still flare up in unlikely places and outliers metamorphose into new centres, as Mistra showed signs of doing with the help of its commercial and cultural ties with the Italian world.[74] The sultans were assiduous in courting acceptance from Athonite monasteries by confirming their landed possessions and right to go their own spiritual way and, as Bryer shows, once Mehmed II (1444–6, 1451–81) had captured the City, he showed ambivalence in his quest for cooperation from senior churchmen, from the patriarchate downwards (see below, pp. 869, 871–2). At a material level, he confirmed the Genoese trading privileges within days of Constantinople's fall (see below, fig. 65 on p. 867).

The Genoese deal can, like Mehmed's compact with the orthodox church, be viewed as a measure of the old empire's decomposition, its unravelling into discrete ecclesiastical, monastic, regional and commercial sectors. Yet to dwell only on these negatives would be to overlook the variable geometry that had long been characteristic of the *empire sans frontières* (see above, p. 3). Middle Byzantine emperors had mostly managed the balancing act between Greek-speaking religious orthodox insiders and other princes, populations and powers until the preponderance of western resources and organisational skills made the balance virtually unsustainable. The loose-knit, dynastic mini-empires emerging after the catastrophe of 1204 were structured differently from their illustrious predecessor, and the 'emperor of the Romans' reinstated in Constantinople in 1261 could not call up the administrative or military apparatus of the past. In fact the malfunctioning of late imperial governance was the despair of some of those who sought to operate it or who had written on its behalf,[75] while from

---

[74] On the 'half-way house between a Greek polis and an Italian renaissance seigniory' envisaged by its leading thinkers, some of whom hoped for military aid from the west, see Ronchey (2006), pp. 321–2.

[75] See, e.g. Ševčenko, I. (1961); Nicol (1979), pp. 75–83; Kolbaba (1995).

the end of the fourteenth century, numerous craftsmen – goldsmiths, gold wire-drawers, shipwrights and also medical doctors – saw better prospects in the west and set up successful enterprises as far afield as London.[76] The imperial order did not, however, survive by institutions alone. In its capacity to engage the sympathies, belief or commercial concerns of quite disparate, scattered groupings the Palaiologan empire showed a certain continuity with its earlier incarnation. Not for the first time the patchwork qualities of the Byzantine empire made outright conquest and long-term occupation by even the most resolute outsiders an expensive, potentially self-defeating business. The Ottomans' step-by-step approach to the conquest of the Byzantine empire and its affiliates bears witness to this. So do the studied ambiguities and concern for legitimacy in the eyes of their new subjects of Mehmed the Conqueror and his immediate successors.

[76] Harris (1995a), pp. 156, 164–88.

OTHER ROUTES TO BYZANTIUM

JONATHAN SHEPARD

Our chapters touch on many matters and subject-areas handled at greater length elsewhere and, without aiming to be comprehensive, some of the more important alternative approaches to Byzantium are outlined below. For the most part, only fairly recent publications will be mentioned, as their bibliographies usually cite earlier studies.

CHURCH HISTORY

The Byzantine church's history has been expounded by scholars in connection with ideology, political affairs and relationships with other churches, the church being considered as administrative institution and more generally, as element in urban and rural society.[1] Likewise monasteries great and small, together with monks as individuals and as groups, have been studied from numerous angles: as property-owners, spiritual oases in provincial and Constantinopolitan society, sober counsellors or individual troublemakers. Besides the useful general introductions to the editions of documents from the archives of Mount Athos, collections of studies on Athos, saints and individual monasteries have been published; and monographs have been dedicated to holy fools and to the relationship between monks and laymen.[2]

The broader spectrum of eastern Christian belief, worship, everyday experience and expectations is also receiving scholarly attention, and contributions relating to the Byzantine world feature in volumes dedicated to medieval Christianity in general.[3] An entire volume of the *Cambridge history of Christianity* is dedicated to eastern Christianity after *c.* 1050.[4]

---

[1] Dvornik (1966); Runciman (1977); Nicol (1979); Hussey (1986); Herrin (1987); Angold (1995); Morris (ed.) (1990); Dagron (2003).

[2] See the series of publications of the archives of the individual monasteries on Athos, e.g. *Actes de Lavra*, ed. Lemerle *et al.*, I, pp. 13–48 (introduction); *Actes du Protaton*, ed. Papachryssanthou, esp. pp. 17–109 (introduction); Hackel (ed.) (1981); Mullett and Kirby (eds.) (1994); Mullett and Kirby (eds.) (1997); Morris (1995); Bryer and Cunningham (eds.) (1996); Ivanov (2006).

[3] See Dagron *et al.* (eds.) (1993); Vauchez *et al.* (eds.) (1993); Mollat du Jourdin *et al.* (eds.) (1990); Krueger (ed.) (2006); Noble and Smith (eds.) (2008).

[4] Angold (ed.) (2006).

Congregational worship, priest-led ways of communicating with God, entering into His presence and gaining the intercession of the saints, were of vital concern to the Byzantines, from emperors to provincial peasants, and there are authoritative guides to the liturgy and church services.[5] But individuals – whether monks or laypersons – also sought immediacy with the holy for themselves, and relics and icons offered access: pilgrimages to shrines were a feature of Byzantine life, and relics and relic-containers of one sort or another were prized in the imperial palace and at grass-roots, whether to bring spiritual fulfilment, physical salvation or simply material wellbeing.[6]

VISUAL MEDIA

Icons – more or less formulaic likenesses of otherworldly beings, sacred events and scenes – offered the Byzantines access to the holy *par excellence*, and although reviled as idols by some emperors (see below, pp. 278–84), they became engrained in private piety and collective imprecation. After the Mother of God's protection of her City of Constantinople in the seventh century, icons representing her were revered and, eventually, panel icons were processed regularly through Constantinople's public spaces, helping to render them and the City yet more sacred.[7] Icons were deemed truer than words in conveying the divine. The sense that their contrasting brightness and shade, yet stable basic forms, could relay sacred happenings and communicate spiritual essentials was strong; it is notable in, for example, late Byzantine art, when directly experiencing the energies and uncreated light of God was the ambition of prominent ascetics.[8]

Integral to private devotions, ritual routines and theological truths, icons were painted on wood or walls, or portrayed in mosaics, ivory or metalwork, and from the ninth century onwards the beings on them were generally identified by inscriptions.[9] Significantly, they were not sharply distinguishable in style from images of emperors, past and present, and an emperor

---

[5] Taft (1978); Taft (1992); Taft (1984).

[6] Horníčková (1999); Durand and Lafitte (eds.) (2001); Durand and Flusin (eds.) (2004); Wolf *et al.* (eds.) (2004); proceedings of a symposium on 'Pilgrimage in the Byzantine empire, 7th–15th centuries', published with an introduction by A.-M. Talbot, *DOP* 56 (2002), pp. 59–241; Lidov (ed.) (2003); Klein (2004); Grünbart *et al.* (eds.) (2007).

[7] Ševčenko, N. P. (1991); Ševčenko, N. P. (1995); Angelidi (1994); Angelidi and Papamastorakis (2000), Weyl Carr (2000) and other contributions in Vassilaki (ed.) (2000); Papaioannou (2001); see below, n. 46, p. 129); Vassilaki (ed.) (2005); Gerstel and Talbot (2006), p. 87; Lidov (2006).

[8] See below, p. 823; James (1996), pp. 80–5, 96–101, 117–23, 139–40; Cormack (2000); Franses (2003), p. 823; contributions in Evans (ed.) (2004).

[9] On icons and the Byzantines' ways of painting and viewing them and relating them to texts, see Mango (1963b); Mango, *Art of the Byzantine empire*; Talbot Rice (1968); Maguire (1981); Maguire (1996); Belting (1994); Cormack (1985); Cormack (1997a); Cormack (2000); Rodley (1994); Cutler and Spieser (1996); Lowden (1997); Mathews (1998); Brubaker (1999a); Barber, C. (2002).

could be shown in the company of Christ or a saint (see below, fig. 33, p. 154). A particularly fine mosaic of Christ graced St Sophia from soon after Michael VIII Palaiologos (1258–82) restored empire to Constantinople (see below, fig. 58, p. 826), while Michael demonstrated the imperial presence at newly regained points through wall-paintings, as at Apollonia, south of the strategic base of Dyrrachium (Durazzo) on the Adriatic coast (see below, fig. 57, p. 800).

Michael VIII's projection of his authority far and wide through visual media belongs to a great tradition, involving coins, seals and the minor arts, reaching back beyond Justinian to the heyday of imperial Rome. The ways in which the emperor and his order were portrayed and idealised are discussed and illustrated in specialised but accessible studies as well as in more general works.[10] That beauty and superlative technical expertise should be attributes of imperial power was a tenet of Byzantine thinking until virtually the end. Constantine VII Porphyrogenitus (945–59) could claim that 'all beauty and adornment had been lost to the empire' for want of due attention to ceremonial. He was in fact taking a sideswipe against his detested former co-emperor, who had manipulated political imagery against him.[11]

The grand halls for the reception of visitors, the gardens, feasts, exotica and religious rites experienced, and the 'diplomatic gifts' presented at court or sent to notables and potentates further afield have enjoyed considerable scholarly attention.[12] The Constantinopolitans' penchant for dignifying workaday or dilapidated buildings with silks and other splendid hangings has also been noted. Wealth in this flexible – and portable – form became the hallmark of the elite. The minor arts and ceremonial could cover for the limitations and condition of structures of brick and stone. This held true not only of the capital but also of citadels in ancient cities and strongholds in outlying regions, which could be reoccupied and refurbished when threats loomed.[13]

The authorities' alertness to the impact of sights on outsiders is registered in a text for receiving envoys in the capital: if they came from greater powers, they were to be shown the 'masses of our men, good order

[10] See below, pp. 111, 207, 273–4, 501–3. See also, beside the classic work of Grabar (1936), Spatharakis (1976); Walter (1978); Magdalino and Nelson (1982); Cormack (1985), pp. 179–214; Brubaker (1985); contributions in Evans and Wixom (eds.) (1997); Ousterhout (2001); Grierson (1982); contributions to the series *SBS*; Cheynet (2005).

[11] *DC*, preface, ed. Reiske, p. 4; ed. and French tr. Vogt, I, p. 1; see below p. 509 and fig. 32.

[12] Cormack (1992); Lowden (1992); Maguire (ed.) (1997); Cutler (2001), pp. 261–4; Schreiner (2004); Littlewood *et al.* (eds.) (2002); Anca (2005); Prinzing (2005); Reinsch (2005); Tinnefeld (2005a); Bardill (2006); Bauer (2006); Featherstone (2006); Klein (2006); Luchterhandt (2006); Schreiner (2006); Maguire and Maguire (2007), pp. 29–57.

[13] Holmes (2002a), pp. 97–9, 103–4; Morris (2003), pp. 244–9; Haldon (2005c), pp. 77–8; Featherstone (2006); see also below, p. 486.

of our weaponry and the height of our walls'.[14] In the empire's later years, mosaicists could still portray in St Sophia the emperor wearing a crown and vestments replete with gemstones. Yet, as Nikephoros Gregoras deplored, his actual crown and vestments were 'make-believe (*phantasia*)', 'made of gilded leather . . . and decorated with pieces of glass of all colours'. Here again, one art or craft could substitute for another in the imperial kaleidoscope, to keep up appearances. A peculiarly Byzantine blend of faith, self-belief and expectations of ultimate vindication underlay such improvisations.[15]

The choicest of the visual arts, crafts and architecture were reserved to display imperial majesty, superlative craftsmanship and beautiful artefacts denoting possession of supernatural powers and legitimate authority. Some of the highest-quality imperial silks named their place of manufacture near the Great Palace or the emperor reigning when they were made.[16] Such association of extraordinary skills, technical and aesthetic, with hegemony is characteristic of numerous pre-industrial societies,[17] and to many Byzantines reverence for the emperor appeared interwoven with service of God, however firmly churchmen drew the line.

By and large the imperial authorities and the leading monks and churchmen were, from the mid-ninth century onwards, in alignment as to what was acceptable 'official' and religious art. Their command of skills and resources meant that they could set the tone and contents of the more elaborate, public examples of the visual arts. The forms, decorative programmes and ritual significance of ecclesiastical and monastic buildings have received scholarly attention, and the prominence of churches in studies on Byzantine art and architecture is not wholly an accident of survival: the empire was well- (if not over-)stocked with churches and monasteries from at least the time that Justinian was building more churches in Constantinople than strictly pastoral needs warranted.[18] But not all buildings were commissioned by churchmen or the imperial authorities. Private secular architecture after the seventh century is known to us only from occasional mentions in literary sources and from archaeology. Further excavations should shed light on the material facts of life in Byzantine towns and even, eventually, in rural settlements, which have mostly as yet only been identified from field

[14] *Peri strategias* ('Strategy'), ch. 43, ed. and tr. Dennis, *Three Byzantine military treatises*, pp. 124–5; tr. in Lee and Shepard (1991), p. 30.

[15] NG, XV.11.4, ed. Schopen and Bekker, II, pp. 788–9; German tr. van Dieten, III, pp. 170–1; Hetherington (2003), pp. 164–5.

[16] Lopez (1945), p. 7; Muthesius (1995), pp. 56–64; Muthesius (1997), pp. 34–43.

[17] Helms (1993); Trilling (1997).

[18] Mango (1990), p. 52. See also Talbot Rice (1968); Beckwith (1979); Krautheimer and Ćurčić (1986); Mango (1979); Lowden (1997); Rodley (1985); Rodley (1994); Freely and Çakmak (2004); Cutler and Spieser (1996); Mathews (1998); Ousterhout (1999); Cormack (2000).

Figure 2 The walls of Constantinople, often repaired but basically late Roman in design and technique

surveys.[19] Likewise collation of excavated artefacts with long-studied *objets d'art*, wall-paintings or even manuscript illuminations is beginning to highlight other kinds of subject-matter in the representational arts, unofficial visual statements which could veer far from the 'party-line' of court orations, sermons and other literary set pieces. Ceramics can be particularly eloquent in revealing the fancies, fantasies and humour of Byzantines having little or no connection with the imperial-ecclesiastical establishment.[20]

LITERATURE

We do not glean very much about society or life in general in towns and settlements outside the capital from surviving literature, that is, from writings in Greek composed for more than ephemeral purposes. No term in use among the Byzantines corresponds precisely with our 'literature' and what they wrote has been termed a 'distorting mirror', designed to reflect other than reality.[21] Works recounting the deeds and reigns of emperors could amount to extended narratives, purporting to be 'Histories' while retaining strong rhetorical traits, for example the *Life of Basil* (see below, pp. 292, 294). Such works tended to emanate from court circles, whereas chronicles, less polished presentations of events, often from a religious angle, were less committed to an establishment viewpoint, and were much read (see below, pp. 82, 103).

The Byzantines' writings vary greatly in intricacy of style and in the kind of Greek they use, and fashions and preoccupations changed over time. Rhetorical and grand historical works were written in classical – 'Attic' – Greek, for reading or declaiming primarily among members of the metropolitan elite. Thanks to private secondary schooling, the handful of senior officeholders, churchmen and scholars were at home with an all but dead language far removed from the everyday Greek spoken in the countryside or even in the capital's streets.[22] Authors writing in these circles presupposed familiarity with the antique world[23] but could cross-cut to figures or themes from the Scriptures or to sayings from the church fathers. The collections made of these sayings, like the full-length chronicles, some sermons and many saints' *Lives*, tended to be written in plainer Greek,[24] more akin to the spoken word.

---

[19] Whittow (1995); Whittow (1996b); Bouras (2002); Sanders (2003), pp. 396–7; Bakirtzis (2003), pp. 54–6, 64; contributions to Dark (ed.) (2004); Dark (2004); Dark (2005); see also below, pp. 477–8.

[20] Maguire and Maguire (2007). Marginal drawings and paintings in manuscripts could also convey orthodox messages vividly, even grotesquely: Corrigan (1992).

[21] Mango (1975b).

[22] See below, pp. 86, 212, 238, 511–12. See the letter-collection of a tenth-century Constantinopolitan teacher: *Anonymi professoris epistulae*, ed. Markopoulos (contents summarised by Browning (1954), pp. 402–25). See also Lemerle (1986); Constantinides (2003).

[23] Hunger (1969–70).   [24] For saints' *Lives*, see Pratsch (2005a), pp. 405–7.

This sprawling, still partly unpublished, body of literary materials is not easy to categorise, and perhaps the most authoritative general history of Byzantine literature remains that of Karl Krumbacher.[25] Nonetheless, several histories of branches of Byzantine literature are available, as are histories of particular periods,[26] and the later twentieth and early twenty-first centuries saw studies on the subject burgeoning. Some are wide-ranging survey projects, or introductions,[27] while others examine Byzantine rhetoric, poetry and letter-writing,[28] besides more technical issues such as palaeography, epigraphy and the nature and uses of Byzantine books (codices) and libraries.[29] Byzantine literature and texts written in Byzantine Greek are more approachable by students, now that the classical *Greek–English Lexicon* of Liddell and Scott is reinforced by such works as the *Lexikon zur byzantinischen Gräzität*.[30]

It is becoming clear that poems such as the tale of the border-lord *Digenis Akritis* (in its surviving versions) are the product of complex interplay between *littérateurs* in the capital and the composers of stories and ballads and reciters of songs at popular level.[31] Some acquaintance with letters might be expected at village level, and while the priest was likeliest to be capable of functional literacy, laypersons could have reading skills, or access to social superiors possessing them, for example through confraternities.[32] It was perhaps partly via confraternities or comparable groups that texts in everyday Greek recounting visits to the next world and visions of the wicked receiving punishment circulated. It is quite possible that they were countenanced by churchmen, venting grievances about the workings of church and secular administration, yet counteracting dissidents overtly opposed to the imperial order.[33] Such a cellular structure of orthodoxy has to be deduced, and is not directly attested in our sources, yet it probably constitutes an important strand in the fabric of Byzantine society. Such

[25] Krumbacher (1897).

[26] Beck (1959); Beck (1971); Politis (1973), pp. 1–43; Hunger (1978); Kazhdan and Franklin (1984); Kazhdan (1999).

[27] Agapitos (1991); Littlewood (ed.) (1995); Beaton (1996); Odorico and Agapitos (eds.) (2002); Odorico and Agapitos (eds.) (2004); Rosenqvist (2007).

[28] Hatlie (1996); Hörandner and Grünbart (eds.) (2003); Alexiou (1982–3); Alexiou (1986); Lauxtermann (2003–7); Maguire (1981); Mullett (1997); Mullett (2003); Dennis (1997); Littlewood (1999); Jeffreys, E. (ed.) (2003); Jeffreys, E. (2007).

[29] Wilson (1996); Cavallo *et al.* (eds.) (1991); Cavallo and Mango (eds.) (1995), De Gregorio and Kresten (eds.) (1998); Waring (2002); Ševčenko, I. (2002).

[30] *LBG*.

[31] Politis (1973), pp. 23–5; Beaton and Ricks (eds.) (1993); *Digenis Akritis*, ed. and tr. E. Jeffreys, pp. xiv–xviii, xli–xlix, liv–lvii (introduction).

[32] Browning (1978); Holmes (2002b); Holmes and Waring (eds.) (2002); Jeffreys, E. (2007), pp. 169–70; *Confraternity of Thebes*, ed. and tr. Nesbitt and Wiita, pp. 373–9; Horden (1986); Ševčenko, N. P. (1995).

[33] Baun (2000); Baun (2007); Baun (2008).

hidden strengths of the empire are what Byzantine literature in its broadest sense can intimate.

ARMY AND ADMINISTRATION

The institutions comprising the army, tax-collection and other administrative apparatus and the law are more familiar. Some deliberately evoked ancient Rome, and inscriptions on coins – themselves a clear symbol of continuity – styled rulers 'emperors of the Romans' from around 812 onwards (see below, fig. 28 on p. 418). The organisation and role of the Byzantine navy have been set out in authoritative works.[34] But the army has received the lion's share of scholarly attention, in part reflecting the coverage of military matters in Byzantine literary sources. Military history features in many of our chapters, and the tactical manuals available in translation are noted below (see below, pp. 87–9). The formal units, prescribed methods of fighting and even some pay rates are known from snapshots in particular sources, and certain developments, the metamorphoses of the seventh and eighth centuries and the revival of large-scale offensive warfare in the tenth, are beyond reasonable doubt.[35] Likewise with the retrenchment carried out by Alexios I (1081–1118); the capability of Manuel I Komnenos' (1143–80) forces; and the robustness of the armed forces in Lascarid Nicaea and during Michael VIII's Constantinopolitan regime.[36]

Nonetheless, major questions about the army remain unresolved and sometimes contentious. Aspects of the arrangements for maintaining a pool of operational and potential military manpower in the provinces are opaque, probably because of their flexibility and the late date when they were formally codified. But it is clear that for a full-time core force, iconoclast emperors and their successors relied on 'Byzantine praetorians', elite units generally stationed in or near the capital; and to be enrolled in the military registers in the provinces brought remuneration and status as well as potentially heavy obligations.[37]

More controversial is the question of the armed forces' size in the medieval period. The figures provided by contemporary Arabic writers and occasional Byzantine references would suggest operational field armies of 80,000 or more. But such figures jar with Byzantine chronicles' assumptions about the difficulty of campaigning on more than one front at

---

[34] Ahrweiler (1966); Pryor (1988); Pryor (2002); Pryor (2003); Pryor and Jeffreys (2006).

[35] See below, pp. 236–7, 239–41, 266–9, 517–18. See also McGeer (1988); McGeer (1991); McGeer (1995); Kühn (1991). See also, more generally on the earlier and middle Byzantine army, Treadgold (1992); Treadgold (1995); Scharf, (2001); Haldon (1999a); Haldon (2001a); Haldon (ed.) (2007).

[36] Bartusis (1992); Birkenmeier (2002). See also below, pp. 612, 619–21, 716–17, 747, 749.

[37] Haldon (1979); Haldon (1984); Haldon (1993); see also below, pp. 268–9.

a time, and an abiding imperial concern was to impress upon outsiders that Byzantine armies were larger than in fact they were.[38] The discrepancies in figures probably reflect not only imperial disinformation, but also actual fluctuations of various kinds – in the empire's population size; in the number of units of outsiders employed for short-term campaigning; and in the authorities' resort to *ad hoc* call-ups of all remotely serviceable males. Such call-ups might be made in dire emergencies, or even for occasional offensives.[39] Arms-bearers originating from societies attuned to violence played an important part in maintaining the empire's security from Justinian's era onwards, the Armenians being pre-eminent.[40] They seldom receive extensive attention in Byzantine narratives; even the 6,000 or so Rus warriors sent to the aid of Basil II *c.* 988 are known to us mainly from non-Byzantine sources (see below, p. 525). This was an era of imperial expansionism, but in earlier periods, too, externally based warriors were employed for specific operations, temporarily swelling the ranks of imperial forces.

The question of the figures for the Byzantine armed forces bears heavily on the history of the empire's administration. The forces were the largest item of expenditure, providing much of the *raison d'être* for the apparatus for raising revenue and spending it. If, as seems likely, the empire could get by with modest-sized, highly disciplined armed units for much of the time, counting on a modicum of cooperativeness from eligible military manpower, suppliers and carriers in those places under threat, financial outlay was correspondingly limited. This combination of cost-effectiveness and reliance on cooperative locals lessened the need for a sizable administrative apparatus. Direct supervision from the capital could be focused on the districts that were more fiscally lucrative or the most strategically important, a form of 'hot-spots' and 'cold-spots' or inner and outer zones of governance discernible in varying permutations and regions throughout Byzantium's history (see below, pp. 498–501, 653–4, 664–5, 668, 827–8).

The outlines of central administration from the late seventh and eighth centuries on are only dimly discernible. They seem to comprise departments of senior officials dedicated to particular tasks such as revenue-raising or expenditure, but with overlapping functions and without a firmly cast hierarchy of great offices of state.[41] Their activities could be readily scrutinised by the emperor and his closest associates and counsellors, a cost-effective form of flexible 'flat-management' provided that the volume of business was fairly limited, the emperor or his closest associates reasonably

[38] Compare Treadgold (1995), pp. 64–78 with Haldon (1995b); Haldon (1999a), pp. 101–6; see above, pp. 55–6 and n. 14.

[39] See below, pp. 265–9, 502; Haldon (1993); Haldon (1999a), pp. 105–6, 234–7.

[40] Charanis (1961); see below, pp. 124, 168, 337, 357–8, 364, 665.

[41] See below, pp. 238–9, 273; Brandes (2002a); Haldon (2003a).

assiduous. The names of the higher or more durable offices are known to us. But details come mainly from the orders of precedence of title- and office-holders at palace receptions, and we lack texts clearly setting out functions and lines of accountability in full.[42]

This deficiency is partly made up for by the survival of many lead seals belonging to senior officeholders. A major step towards matching such seals with what else is known of the central administration was made by Vitalien Laurent, followed up by other sigillographers, and the series *Studies in Byzantine sigillography*, notably volumes 7 and 8, offers useful additions and updates. Work on the prosopography of the middle Byzantine period is collating seals with what the written sources relate about individuals' career patterns. This can yield statistical data as well as case studies of individuals working in the administration, and the online database is designed to offer means of access to non-specialists.[43]

The forementioned orders of precedence also list the *stratēgoi* and other senior officials serving in the provinces but expected to attend court functions quite regularly. Collation of these with Byzantine narratives and Arabic sources yields a rough picture by the ninth century. The *stratēgoi* were military commanders at the head of armed units. Their judicial, levying and requisitioning powers were sweeping but did not permanently supplant other, more painstaking forms of tax-collection: this was primarily the task of officials answerable to the administration in Constantinople.[44] The scope of the *stratēgoi* within their respective themes is not wholly clear, and the territorial extent of the themes is seldom delineated precisely, perhaps because they were slow to assume fixed, territorial form.

One clear development is the creation of smaller command units, known as *kleisourai* (literally, 'passes'), to firm up defences in the Taurus mountain regions.[45] Towns and other fortified population centres were fixed points in later seventh- and eighth-century administration, being also the likely sites of *apothēkai*, state depots for storing revenue proceeds such as grain, and for issuing supplies and probably also equipment to soldiers.[46] But the dealings, formal and informal, of state agencies with outlying country-dwellers emerge from our sources only fitfully. The authorities could seldom

---

[42] *LPB* (containing an extensive commentary); useful tables of functions in Haldon (2005c).

[43] Laurent (ed.), *Corpus des sceaux*, II (= *L'Administration centrale*) is a collection of seals of central officeholders; *DOS*; Seibt and Wassiliou, *Byzantinischen Bleisiegel*, II; *SBS* 7–8; *PMBZ*, I (for prosopography to 867) and II (to 1025, forthcoming); *Prosopography of the Byzantine world* (http://www.pbw.kcl.ac.uk).

[44] See below, pp. 269–71; *JG*, tr. McGeer (introduction); Oikonomides (1996a); Oikonomides (2002), pp. 995–1004; Brandes (2002a), pp. 505–10; Haldon (2003a).

[45] *ODB*, II, p. 1132 (A. Kazhdan); *Skirmishing*, ed. and French tr. Dagron and Mihăescu, pp. 219, 240–3 (commentary); Haldon (1999a), pp. 79, 114.

[46] On the role of the *apothēkai* between *c.* 650 and *c.* 730, see below, pp. 271–2; Brandes (2002a), pp. 300–5, 418–26, 505.

guarantee full protection to those far removed from strongholds or fortified refuges.[47]

LAW AND JUSTICE

Something of the way in which peasant-proprietors were expected to resolve issues of property-ownership, animal husbandry, theft, injury or damage emerges from the *Farmer's law* (or *Nomos georgikos*), a text whose date of composition and status remain open to discussion. At any rate, the *Farmer's law* seems to have long been a working document, laying down norms for dispute settlement within local communities. The prescriptions are detailed and presuppose regular taxation, implying governance that was loose-meshed but under the authorities' ultimate oversight. The text was later translated into Slavonic.[48] It is in key with procedures set out in two tax-collectors' handbooks, and is not inconsistent with the texts concerning methods of measuring land for purposes of tax assessment. The latter seem to have been at their most accurate in measuring smaller plots.[49]

The handbooks imply that the individual contributions towards the tax burden imposed on a fiscal unit were ultimately for its members to determine among themselves. The government's concern was that the tax be paid, due allowances being made for lands devastated by enemy raids and abandoned by their owners: these were eventually – usually after some thirty years of non-payment of taxes – declared *klasmata* and they could be reallocated by the state, through sale, renting-out or gift. The productive value of these lands was reviewed from time to time, keeping the central administration abreast of changes – and potential gains for its coffers: *klasma*-land could be sold by the state to new, tax-paying proprietors.[50] The texts relating to taxation offer the viewpoint of officialdom, but the dynamics of the middle Byzantine economy and society glimmer through their assertions and prescriptions.

The quality of justice and the workings of the law in Byzantium are no less murky, but modern studies shed some light.[51] Here, too, affairs in the capital are far better illuminated than elsewhere, and while the *Basilika*

---

[47] See below, pp. 265–6, 498–9, 502.

[48] *Farmer's law*, ed. and Russian tr. Medvedev *et al.*; ed. and tr. Ashburner; see below, pp. 264, 488–9; *ODB*, II, p. 778 (A. Kazhdan); Lefort (2002), pp. 279–81; Górecki (2004).

[49] Dölger, *Beiträge*, pp. 114–23; tr. in Brand (1969), pp. 48–57; Karayannopulos, 'Fragmente', pp. 321–4; tr. in Brand (1969), pp. 57–60; *Géométries du fisc byzantin*, ed. and French tr. Lefort *et al.*, pp. 223–4, 235, 252–5, 263–5 (commentary); Lefort (2002), p. 272; Oikonomides (2002).

[50] On *klasmata* and the government's concern with restoring cultivation and revenue yield from unproductive lands, see Górecki (1998), pp. 244–54; *JG*, tr. McGeer, p. 14 (introduction); Lefort (2002), pp. 281–3; Oikonomides (2002), pp. 995–6; Morris (2006b), pp. 25–30.

[51] Laiou and Simon (eds.) (1994); Karlin-Hayter (1990); Stolte (1998); Macrides (1999); Stolte (2003–4 [2005]).

project of revising Justinian's corpus of laws begun in Basil I's reign laid down markers for the entire empire, some *novellae* issued by Leo VI were primarily concerned with Constantinople, as was the *Book of the eparch* (see below, pp. 301–2, 497–8). That written rulings were being issued by senior officials according to principles of Romano-Byzantine law in distant borderlands is indicated from southern Italian materials, and Athonite beneficiaries of tax exemptions and other imperial privileges were, in the eleventh century, taking care to have them confirmed by successive new regimes.[52]

How disputes were settled among peasants at grass-roots, and the redress available to them in the event of unlawful actions by the well-connected 'powerful', are harder to track down. This bears on the general question of the mesh of imperial administration at grass-roots.[53] There is reason to think that in some borderlands and newly acquired regions in the tenth and eleventh centuries power structures were left largely intact, with local elites or administrators raising exactions and resolving disputes with few departures from past practice.[54] A degree of devolution was customary in the Greek-speaking zones of the empire, too, and diverse rivalries were played out among members of local elites. The already well-connected could pull strings at provincial level or in the imperial court in Constantinople; the newly well-to-do could purchase them, with an eye to further enhancing their local position. Or the rights and possessions of lesser folk could be overridden roughshod, without judges or other officials lifting a finger.[55]

Loose-meshed as local self-governance may have been, courts of justice and other embodiments of imperial solicitousness were not invariably beyond the reach of provincial smallholders with a grievance or under unlawful pressure. The fertile lands of the western Asia Minor theme of the Thrakesioi long remained largely the preserve of smaller proprietors, and the prosperous region of Thebes, while partly in the hands of substantial landowners, still accommodated proprietors of more modest means in the eleventh century (see below, p. 489). We lack direct evidence that this was due to legal process and regard for the spirit of the laws. But where archival evidence survives, in the form of the deeds involving Mount Athos' monasteries, there are indications that communities of peasants did not always complain in vain.[56] The Athonite monks became major landowners in eastern Macedonia from the tenth century onwards, enjoying direct access to imperial circles. Yet the tax exemptions and other privileges for their properties which emperors issued did not spare them judicial investigations and

[52] Morris (1986), pp. 135–7, 143–6; Morris (1995), pp. 140–2, 296–7.
[53] The breadth of the mesh is emphasised in Neville (2004). See, however, Morris (2006a).
[54] Stephenson (2000); Holmes (2001); Holmes (2005), pp. 368–91, 440–7; see below, pp. 570, 668–70, 706.
[55] Neville (2004), pp. 105–18, 136–56.
[56] Morris (1986), pp. 131–5, 141–6; Morris (2006a). See also Magdalino (1994).

hearings, conducted by local judges or at Constantinople. Findings did not always favour the well-connected.[57]

Comparable patterns may emerge from further investigation of the eleventh-century *Peira*. Peasants and other unprivileged persons are depicted as vulnerable to encroachments and unlawful seizure of their lands, animals or chattels from the 'powerful'. But the judge Eustathios Rhomaios' rulings document how he sought to adjudicate disputes over crops and boundaries between what were sometimes quite small-scale proprietors, applying principles of Romano-Byzantine law to current circumstances. The well-connected or well-to-do had the advantage, but the courts could redress the balance.[58] The *Peira*'s rulings were expected by its compiler to apply throughout the empire and the text seems to have been much consulted. This may corroborate the impression that reports of the demise of peasant-proprietors are much exaggerated; *novellae* declaring the worth of a prosperous peasantry to fisc and army were not necessarily dead letters.[59]

These issues are material not just to legal or economic history, but also to the empire's capacity to continue raising taxes on lands and possessions through thick and thin. The unchronicled majority of the population, peasant-proprietors raising livestock and growing wheat and other crops, were the source – by way of land taxes – of the greater part of the state's regular incomes. Equally, chronicles and saints' *Lives* depict fertile regions like, for example, Asia Minor's Aegean coastal areas as vulnerable to external raiders in the earlier tenth century, while Thessaly's plains and other 'hotspots' underwent Hungarian and Bulgarian incursions through the later years of that century. And yet, as Rosemary Morris observes, 'Byzantine bureaucrats in Constantinople and their provincial representatives soldiered on',[60] tax assessments were negotiated, and revenue streams trickled in. The unarticulated nexuses of local pride, peer-group pressure and religious belief accompanying this anomaly underpinned the empire and those who – voluntarily, habitually or perforce – maintained them made up Byzantium's 'silent majority'. They are not treated in detail here, but their existence underlies the chapters that follow.

SOCIETY: GENDER AND EUNUCHS

The social fabric to which Byzantium owed its resilience drew on diverse human resources and the nature of that diversity is worth considering. An

---

[57] Morris (1986), pp. 146–7; Morris (2006b), pp. 34–7.

[58] *Peira*, XL.12, XLII.18–19, XL.1–4, ed. Zacharia von Lingenthal, pp. 167, 177–8, 165–6. For a less sanguine interpretation of the *Peira*, see Litavrin (1977), pp. 179, 187–90, 193. See also Oikonomides (1986b); *ODB*, III, pp. 1617, 1793 (D. Simon); Magdalino (1994), pp. 102–5.

[59] See below, pp. 489, 492; *JG*, ed. Zepos and Zepos, I, p. 209; ed. Svoronos, no. 3, p. 85; tr. McGeer, p. 55.

[60] Morris (2006b), p. 23; see below, pp. 500, 525–7.

elemental difference is that between men and women. The Byzantines' assumptions and demarcations on matters of gender are now receiving attention, as are the specific experiences and activities of women.[61] In some respects, such as life expectancy at birth, their condition seems to have resembled men's – living to between their late twenties and early thirties – with expectancy rising markedly (to perhaps their late forties) for those surviving their first five years on earth.[62] These estimates apply, however, to the early fourteenth century. Demographic and other social and economic data for the middle empire, from the eighth to the thirteenth centuries, is scanty for men and women, while the data available for the early period is not really comparable.[63] Exegesis and comparison of the roles of men and women in Byzantine society and culture with due allowance for all the variations in class, place and time is correspondingly difficult.

In the fifth and sixth centuries, women of wealth, status and also position in public life are quite well attested,[64] and it is no accident that Theodora is portrayed with her female retinue on one side of the sanctuary of the church of San Vitale in Ravenna, in equal majesty to her husband (see below, fig. 8b, p. 211). But for subsequent centuries, the picture darkens in nearly every sense. Already under Justinian, the church's influence on imperial laws was becoming marked, with a ban on the performance of judicial duties by women and abandonment of divorce by mutual consent.[65] Thereafter, little evidence survives for verification of the restrictions on women imposed by canon law, or the idealised portrayals of holy women in their *Lives*.[66]

Not that the picture is wholly dark. Women retained the right to own extensive landed properties as well as chattels during the middle Byzantine period, and strong-minded individuals of substance occasionally surface in narrative sources, for example the widow Danelis.[67] Lower down the social scale, scraps of archival information such as tax registers take for granted the role of women – often but not invariably widows – owning land in peasant communities, heading households and paying taxes.[68] Women in the capital had important economic roles in crafts and trades, including weaving and silk-working, could walk freely in the streets and occasionally joined with menfolk in rioting against unpopular regimes.[69] In the better-attested sphere of religious life, there is evidence of women as writers of hymns, and founders of nunneries in their private houses, and they probably

---

[61] See, for example, the AHRB Centre for Byzantine Cultural History's Gender Project (http://www.byzantine-ahrb-centre.ac.uk/Projects/Gender.htm); Talbot (1997); Smythe (2005).
[62] Dennis (2001a).   [63] Laiou (2002b), pp. 51–2.
[64] Brubaker (2005). On the legal background to women's status, property and the family, see Arjava (1996); Giardina (2000).
[65] Stolte (1999); Humfress (2005), p. 181.   [66] *Holy women of Byzantium*, ed. Talbot.
[67] Laiou (1992b); Cheynet (2000); see above, pp. 19–20; below, pp. 294–5.
[68] Neville (2006), pp. 77–83.   [69] Garland (2006).

played a distinctive part in maintaining the veneration of icons.[70] Most prominent of all were the women occupying or close to the throne who saw to the restoration of icon-veneration.[71] In addition to the *augusta*, women had a formal part to play in court ceremonial.

Nonetheless, the bias of middle Byzantine normative texts, political narrative and even the tax registers is against the independent status of women as individuals, acting in their own right. Empresses who lost their husbands usually remarried, were sidelined (as in the case of Zoe (see below, pp. 504, 505–6)), or eventually were themselves dethroned (as with Irene (see below, pp. 277–8)). The sense that a woman's place is in the home is taken for granted in the *Strategikon* of the eleventh-century general Kekaumenos. Wife and daughters should be kept in their chambers if a man's friend comes to stay because he will seduce them, given the chance.[72] Perhaps significantly Kekaumenos, so free with his advice for men, does not seem to have followed up his stated intention of writing a text on how women should conduct themselves. His world is state-centred: serious money, top jobs and social status come from the public sector. Those prepared to apply themselves to military matters or judicial duties will go far – posted to successive places dotted across the empire. A wife is, at best, an adjunct in one's career.

So long as career structures and spectacular riches revolved around state service and access to the court, the role of 'high-fliers' was reserved for men. But one might expect a change when the state's role as employer and determinant of rank began to fray. One straw in the wind may be observed at the very top, from the late eleventh century onwards. The Komnenoi ceased to rely on an elaborate hierarchy of court-titles, and family ties became more important as bonds of governance. It is no accident that women become more prominent in the new regime of households and affinities, starting with Anna Dalassena, who 'drove the imperial chariot' while her son Alexios I was absent on campaign.[73] During the twelfth century several women of the Komnenian clan and its affiliates exercised extensive powers of literary patronage; some were themselves accomplished *littérateurs*. While this was partly a measure of the wealth and opportunities ever available in Constantinople, it also reflected the enhanced role of the family in high politics, and the multifarious influences that a woman could exercise on behalf of her children or other relatives. The daughter of Manuel I, Maria Komnena, 'reckless and masculine in her resolution', took the initiative

[70] Silvas (2006); Herrin (2006); Herrin (1982); Herrin (1994); Cormack (1997b); Herrin (2000a), pp. 4–5.
[71] See below, pp. 287–91; Herrin (2001).   [72] Kek., ed. and Russian tr. Litavrin, pp. 218–21.
[73] *Al.*, VII.1, ed. Reinsch and Kambylis, I, p. 103; ed. and French tr. Leib, I, p. 123; tr. Sewter, p. 118; see also below, p. 612.

in an attempted *coup d'état* against her stepmother, also named Maria.[74] Anna Komnena, herself blessed with outstanding literary talents, also had a taste for power. She was allegedly 'chief instigator' of a plot to dethrone her younger brother John II (1118–43) in favour of her own husband. Anna's *Alexiad* was itself one more round in the power-play, looking back in anger long after her plot's failure.[75]

The dynamics of power shifted again in the thirteenth and fourteenth centuries, and economic activity proliferated across the imperial or formerly imperial lands. Resources were now diffused in a medley of political centres, aristocratic households and commercial concerns, while laws upheld the legal rights of widows, and dowries were increasingly convertible into liquid assets. It is in this period that Byzantine women's initiatives and activities are documented most fully, whether as founders of long-lasting convents, managers of commercial enterprises, money-lenders, midwives or medical practitioners.[76] It may well be that the shrinking of resources and career opportunities in the emperor's palm had favourable repercussions for certain classes of women. Widows of substance or good family enjoyed considerable independence while the lives of elite women in general were now less geared to spouses' careers and itinerancy in the emperor's service. Familial ties no longer had to compete so hard with the alternative prospects of drastic enrichment or social advance through office. Matriarchs such as Theodora Synadene could, in the thirteenth and fourteenth centuries, make elaborate provision for the women of their family by way of *typika* for the convents they founded.[77]

Another category of difference was imposed by human hands rather than nature, the act of castration that created eunuchs. Eunuchs were not unreservedly admired in Byzantium, and could be denounced as 'ignoble', unfit to govern (see below, p. 519). But individual eunuchs feature in many episodes narrated below, from Justinian's general Narses onwards. The office of 'chamberlain' (*parakoimōmenos*) was usually pivotal in the government and, like other senior posts involving the emperor's bedchamber, it was reserved for eunuchs.

Eunuchs were employed by noble families in their households and some eunuchs were, in the twelfth century, themselves of good family. But they were associated most prominently with the emperor's cause, dedicated to state service rather as monks were to the service of God. In fact some monks and churchmen were eunuchs, gaining renown for their piety,

---

[74] NC, ed. van Dieten, I, pp. 230–2; tr. Magoulias, pp. 130–1.

[75] NC, ed. van Dieten, I, pp. 10–11; tr. Magoulias, p. 8. On Anna, see contributions in Gouma-Peterson (ed.) (2000). On female patrons and connoisseurs of the arts in Komnenian circles, see Laiou (1981), pp. 253–4; Jeffreys, E. (1982); Jeffreys and Jeffreys (1994); Jeffreys, E. (1998); Garland (ed.) (2006).

[76] Laiou (1981), pp. 234–47; below, pp. 814–15, 830; Connor (2004), pp. 263–77.

[77] Connor (2004), pp. 266, 277–308.

especially in the tenth to twelfth centuries.[78] Intimate with the imperial house and presumed (quite often wrongly) to have forsaken all familial and carnal ties, eunuchs symbolised a hierarchy revolving around the emperor. As counsellors-cum-agents of policy, they also suited the kind of 'flat-management' that became characteristic from the seventh century on. Power nodes might form around them, but these did not harden into hereditary coteries even in the case of Basil Lekapenos, the veteran *parakoimōmenos* (see also below, pp. 238–9, 277, 295–6, 505, 519–20, 524, 531–2).

It is probably no coincidence that eunuchs lost their prominence as trusty servants after Alexios I Komnenos called upon his extended family to fulfil the most pressing imperial needs. Members of the Komnenos clan, starting with Alexios' own mother, combined domestic ties with governance and military and civil commands, maintaining the semblance of a unitary state. Manuel I Komnenos did, it should be noted, reverse the trend and brought eunuchs back into governance. But in the late empire eunuchs mostly had lowlier ranks in the imperial and patriarchal households.[79]

SOCIETY: DISSIDENCE AND OUTSIDERS

Men,[80] women and eunuchs answered the description of 'Romans' comfortably enough provided that their religious faith and ritual were orthodox, they acknowledged themselves to be the emperor's *douloi* (a somewhat ambiguous term),[81] and they could manage spoken Greek. A ranking order of precious vestments distinguished the upper echelons of members of the Byzantine empire, while certain conventions of clothing were observed by non-elite men and women for most of its history.[82] There were, however, other types of person who, whether tacitly, through open dissent, or through living in discrete groupings, diverged from religious, ethical or social norms.[83] Some had valuable contributions to make to the empire

---

[78] Ringrose (1999); Sidéris (2002); Tougher (1997a); Tougher (2002); Ringrose (2003), pp. 117–27; Smythe (2005), p. 164; Tougher (2006).

[79] Gaul (2002), pp. 200–1, 208–9; see below, pp. 612, 657.

[80] On notions of masculinity and what was expected of men in Byzantine society, see Barber, C. (1997).

[81] In the sixth century, an imperial official working at Corinth could style himself on inscriptions the emperor's 'faithful servant' (*pistos doulos*; *gnēsiōs douleuōn*) as a measure of his own status, and *doulos* retained connotations of access to the emperor throughout the medieval period: Feissel and Philippidis-Braat (1985), 279–81; Gregory (1993), pp. 12–14; Pazdernik, 'A dangerous liberty' (PhD thesis, 1997); Pazdernik (2005), pp. 203–5. However, *doulos* had other connotations, from 'slave' to non-Roman princes beyond the borders who 'in servitude' (*doulikōs*) acknowledged the emperor's hegemony, for example the Serbs and the Croats: *DAI*, chs. 31, 32, pp. 150–1, 160–1. See also Treitinger (1956), p. 227 and n. 84; *ODB*, I, p. 659 (A. Kazhdan); *LBG*, p. 407 (*douleia, douleusis*); glossary below, p. 888.

[82] Lopez (1945); Maguire (1997); Ball (2005), pp. 37–56, 79–89, 102–4.

[83] For surveys of some alternatives to orthodox society and thought, see contributions to Garland (ed.) (1997); Smythe (ed.) (2000).

in the economic sphere, while the presence, real or supposed, of the un-Roman in the Byzantines' midst had its ideological uses, providing the emperor with vivid foils. Not all these categories of nonconformists – usually minorities within the empire – were self-declared or acting in open concert.

Homosexuality fell foul of Roman and church law and its practice is unlikely to have found very much sympathy in rural communities. Emperors were occasionally accused of homosexual tendencies by contemporaries or by later historians: Michael III (842–67) was one such (see below, p. 295 and n. 23). The monastic vocation and its extensive network of remote, male-dominated communities beckoned to those seeking to sidestep their family's expectations of marriage and to escape from the things of this world; for very many, they offered access to the divine. Nonetheless, some rule-books of monasteries forbade beardless youths and even eunuchs from approaching their houses, for fear of the temptations they might pose.[84]

One form of unacceptable difference virtually endemic in Byzantium's political and religious culture was heresy. Generally this charge of dissidence or error (from *haeresis*, 'sect') was levelled by monks or members of the imperial-ecclesiastical establishment against those held to be breaching orthodox doctrine or ritual; the charge could serve as the small change of political discourse. Several chapters of this book recount how successive earlier emperors sought to reconcile churchmen who disagreed profoundly over the finer points of defining the nature of Christ, only themselves to be accused of heresy. Then, in the eighth and earlier ninth century, the emperors' efforts to purge the empire of 'idols' – icons – aroused opposition and they themselves were styled arch-heretics after icons were reclassified as orthodox in 843 (see below, pp. 117–19, 122–3, 228–9, 231–2, 287–91).

Communities of heretics could, however, profess an alternative creed in certain contexts, especially where the Roman orthodox were thin on the ground. For example Paulician dualists were transplanted from eastern Anatolia to the Thracian borderlands and, in the later tenth and eleventh centuries, Syriac and Armenian monophysites were encouraged to settle in newly won Byzantine territories (see below, pp. 288–9, 297, 532–3, 677, 783 and n. 25). These monophysites formed their own church organisation, the catholicos of the Syriac Jacobites being encouraged to base himself in imperial territory.[85] The sovereign confidence of Basil II (976–1025) and his immediate successors that these heterodox could be brought beneath their imperial umbrella says something for Byzantium's vibrancy at that time. But it is consistent with a tradition whereby the emperor had discretion

---

[84] Galatariotou (1987), pp. 121–2; *ODB*, II, pp. 945–6 (J. Herrin); Smythe (1999); Smythe (2005), pp. 164–5; Tougher (1999); Jordan (2000), pp. 67–71; Ringrose (2003), pp. 112, 126.
[85] Dagron (1976), pp. 187–93.

to license certain forms of diversity: he thereby demonstrated the universal reach of his rule, while himself remaining a paragon of orthodoxy.

Incoming aliens who accepted orthodox Christianity could be assigned fertile lands to work, pay taxes or perform military service from, as with the Pechenegs in the 1040s.[86] Longer-term organised communities of heretics, non-believers or other aliens were left to areas of little economic consequence to the government, for example the warlike Melingoi in the Taygetos mountains of the southern Peloponnese, who still spoke Slavonic and maintained a distinct identity in the thirteenth century, or the Vlachs, Romance-speaking pastoralists of the uplands.[87] Not all of them were confined to the empire's 'cold-spots', however. The Jews occupied a district across the Golden Horn from Constantinople itself and some resided in provincial towns and Cyprus.[88]

The Jews were a special case, anomalous remnants of a faith that Christians thought their religion had superseded; learned proponents of an earlier version of monotheism and priesthood; and a convenient scapegoat for the empire's woes in times of adversity as, for example, in the seventh century when Heraclius launched a drive against them.[89] Unlike some unorthodox, the Jews were not predisposed to proselytise and they lacked powerful co-religionists beyond Byzantium's borders. So while subjected to occasional drives for purification, they were seldom suspected of being actively hostile towards the empire.

The Jews are, then, an example of how minorities of the unorthodox and alien could define the essence of empire through exemplifying error and its price. But the history of the Jews in Byzantium is far from static. Jewish goldsmiths, silk-dyers and other craftsmen were an asset, not least because of their ties with co-religionists across the Muslim world, commercial nexuses at once detectable and taxable.[90] In fact the Jews' fortunes amount to a barometer of Byzantium's general well-being. Jewish immigrants offer examples of a different breed of outsider that rising prosperity in the medieval era attracted, firstly to Constantinople and later to provincial towns. It is no accident that, despite individual Jews' initial dismay at the Byzantines' conquest of Crete in 961, subsequent decades saw many Jews drawn to the empire by the prospects of security and favourable trading conditions it held out.[91] From around the tenth century onwards, various other groups of outsiders were frequenting the capital, travelling mostly by

---

[86] Skyl., ed. Thurn, p. 459; French tr. Flusin and Cheynet, p. 380; see also below, pp. 328, 674.

[87] See below, pp. 258, 664, 687; Ahrweiler (1962b), pp. 3–4, 7–10; Winnifrith (1987).

[88] Starr (1939); Sharf (1971); Jacoby (1995); de Lange (1992); *Greek Jewish texts from the Cairo Genizah*, ed. and tr. de Lange.

[89] See below, pp. 116, 241, 247; Sharf (1971), pp. 107–12, 116–21; Bowman (1986); Maas (1990); Cameron, Averil (2002a); de Lange (2000); de Lange (2005a); de Lange (2006), pp. 172–7.

[90] Goitein (1967–93), I, pp. 42–63, 211–14, 266–72; Muthesius (1995), pp. 245–53; below, p. 474.

[91] Holo (2000); Jacoby (2000a); Ankori (1959), pp. 163–4; Sharf (1971), pp. 107–27.

sea and staying more or less in touch with home ports. 'Syrian' and other Muslim traders, Bulgarians and Rus from the north, and merchants from Italian towns such as Venice and Amalfi frequented the capital.[92]

In presiding over this process, emperors showed characteristic flexibility, alert to the benefits which the outsiders' activities could reap for their own treasury coffers and also to the leverage that could be exerted on outsiders once they had a stake in the empire's economy. These externally based traders were, almost literally, paying tribute to the resources and purchasing power concentrated at the imperial capital from the tenth century on. Their presence was yet another token of the *basileus'* worldwide sway. His toleration of them in the capital was akin to his role of lord and ringmaster of exotic creatures, symbolised by the mechanical birds and lions at receptions for outsiders in the Great Palace.[93] This, however, presupposed a fixed ring, whose creatures would neither evolve nor multiply beyond measure, a presupposition undermined by events unfolding in the wider world. The mounting engagement of external traders with Constantinople's markets and the rising volume and value of transactions there were not necessarily harmful to the empire's interests. Through the eleventh and twelfth centuries emperors showed astuteness and ingenuity in harnessing outsiders' specialist talents and economic dynamism to their own advantage. But the emperors' balancing act between, on the one hand, guarding doctrinal and ritual purity, security and well-being for the 'silent majority' and, on the other, licensing the presence and idiosyncrasies of aliens living within or frequenting the capital was a delicate one. The balancing act presupposed pliability on the outsiders' part, and that the emperor was master in his own house. Such balancing also called for outstanding qualities of statecraft from each successive emperor in turn.

OUTSIDERS WITHIN

From the mid-eleventh century on, the foresaid preconditions began to change as the wealth and numbers of outsiders frequenting Constantinople rose, while some orthodox churchmen and, especially, monks took exception to the rites and ways of western Christians. First hints of what was to come include the outbreak around 1042 of violence between Constantinople's citizens and Arab, Jewish and other non-Roman traders, followed by the emperor's ban on their residence inside the City; and the popular support Patriarch Michael I Keroularios (1043–58) mustered in taking his stand against the papal legates in 1054. Whether or not Keroularios physically

---

[92] Magdalino (2000a), pp. 219–21; Balard (1976); Reinert (1998); Shepard (2006b).
[93] Liudprand, *Antapodosis*, VI.5, ed. Chiesa, p. 147; tr. Wright, pp. 206–7; Brett (1954); Trilling (1997), pp. 222–30; Maguire and Maguire (2007), pp. 41–5, 54–5.

closed the Latin churches in Constantinople, it is likely that an increase in their numbers, itself a register of Latins' commerce there, made their distinctive rites more of an issue than had previously been the case.[94] Ample reserves of authority – material and moral – remained within a manipulative emperor's grasp, and the Latin west's multifarious facets could be kept in play yet apart from one another, as Manuel I Komnenos showed.[95] Nonetheless, western naval capability, martial adventurism and papal aspirations to Christian leadership coalesced in the events culminating in the capture of Constantinople by crusaders in 1204. This was, in part, a matter of long-privileged outsiders who could be deemed 'insiders' – the Venetians – vindicating their rights within the empire.[96]

Intensive intermingling of outsiders' affairs with Byzantium's, and emperors' familiarity with western churchmen would still further characterise the empire Michael VIII Palaiologos restored to Constantinople in 1261. His pressing forward with the Union of Lyons is understandable in light of the threat that Charles of Anjou appeared to pose to his regime, but it earned him execration from orthodox monks and many churchmen.[97]

In the aftermath of 1204, Byzantine clerical writers were voluble in denouncing their western counterparts and warning orthodox lay folk of the impious conduct and unhallowed rituals of Latin Christians in general. Lists describing 'the errors of the Latins' had begun to circulate in the era of Michael Keroularios, and became fuller in the later twelfth century, and more numerous. But it was the thirteenth century that saw the lists lengthen and proliferate.[98] This bespeaks a hardening of the line against outsiders. The church filled the vacuum once the emperor proved wanting in the role of upholder of religious orthodoxy. One may therefore view the orthodox church's anti-Latin stance as a reaction to the experience of, in effect, being colonised by western Christians. This was, after all, the period when Marino Sanudo expressed concern that populations under Latin rule were still, at heart, given up to 'Greek matters' and hostile to their new masters (see above, p. 8).

Yet the very proliferation of the 'lists of the errors of the Latins' suggests that orthodox writers may then have been engaging in a competition for souls whose outcome was not utterly assured. The faithful might yet succumb to Latin ways out of ignorance or lack of clarity as to the points

---

[94] Bar Hebraeus, *Chronography*, tr. Wallis Budge, I, p. 203; Runciman (1955), p. 52–67; Shepard (1978–9), p. 174; Kaplan (1997), pp. 170–1; Kolbaba (2005), pp. 40–1; see below, pp. 601–2. The events of 1054 did not gain a place in Byzantine historiography and, under the Komnenoi, the church leadership was on too tight an imperial rein for Keroularios' stand to be held up as exemplar: Kolbaba (2003). This, however, suggests how potentially provocative the presence of westerners was becoming at street level.

[95] See below, pp. 644–5; Magdalino (1993a).

[96] Angold (2003a), pp. 50–8, 75–101; Magdalino (2007a).   [97] See below, pp. 752–3, 755–8, 803–4.

[98] Kolbaba (2000), pp. 15–16, 25–9, 170, 173–88; Kolbaba (1997).

of difference, or they might be tempted deliberately to opt for a western affiliation, on material or intellectual grounds. The very stridency of the condemnations of the association or marriage of orthodox with Latins in the 'lists' suggests that day-to-day contacts between orthodox lay persons and Latins were not uncommon, at least in the towns.[99] In other words, dividing lines may not have been so clear-cut or so uncrossable as one might at first sight suppose. One can reasonably treat the 'lists' as a sign of new uncertainties and opportunities available following the dissolution of the imperial envelope that had contained the orthodox for so long. Political boundaries were now fluid in the thirteenth century and the empire had anyway long ceased to be more or less coterminous with the faith-zone it had effectively been in the early middle ages. From this point of view the 'lists' represent the justified apprehensions of rigorist orthodox churchmen and their elaboration of culturo-religious identity, in default of the *taxis* provided by the imperially guided state.[100] Yet the 'lists' also suggest how loose-knit the identity of the medieval Byzantines had actually been hitherto or rather how little was spelled out in writing or tabulated, and how much was a matter of liturgical rituals and ceremonies revolving round a few core values, beliefs and traditions. In other words, even the more or less unthinking 'conformists', faithful subjects of the emperor, were perhaps a more variegated bunch than they themselves were fully aware. Beneath the imperial umbrella and the outward and visible symbols of religious orthodoxy, a medley of assumptions, local customs and religious devotions could comfortably co-exist.[101]

UNDERCURRENTS OF BYZANTIUM

This matches the impression given by other scraps of evidence concerning the subjects of the middle Byzantine *basileus*: of undercurrents at various depths of society uncharted even by surviving tax registers and treatises.[102] These points of view, assumptions and practices were not necessarily consciously contradictory to the tenets of the ruling establishment, while even outright dissenters might have no conception of a viable alternative to the apparently irreversible scheme of things. But this very lack of elaborate

---

[99] See also Kolbaba (2000), pp. 17, 28, 38–9, 139–40, 152; Kolbaba (2006), pp. 209–12. See above, pp. 43–4, 45, 46–7.

[100] For the apparent mutual compatibility of Greek and Latin liturgical music and the use, in the fourteenth century, of the scholastic method of argument by orthodox writers, see respectively Lingas (2005); Russell (2006).

[101] Beck (1978), pp. 103–6; Kolbaba (2000), pp. 46, 69–72, 95, 104–17; Cameron, Averil (2006b), pp. 96–8, 112–15, 121–5, 129–32.

[102] Maguire and Maguire (2007); Baun (2007a); Shepard (2007). See also Beck (1978); Mango (1980), pp. 88–104.

definition of 'orthodoxy' was what made it so necessary for writers to spell out the rites, the do's and don'ts of orthodoxy and 'the errors of the Latins' once the imperial order slackened and variants were to hand.[103] All this suggests the multiplicity of approaches that the modern enquirer may take towards the empire, and how much of importance, at once mutable and elusive, remains to be uncovered behind the Roman façade.

[103] On differing conceptions of religious orthodoxy among intellectuals, see Magdalino (2006).

SMOOTHING THE WAY AND SHORT-CUTS TO BYZANTIUM: TEXTS IN TRANSLATION

JONATHAN SHEPARD

Byzantium at first sight looks inaccessible to those approaching for the first time, especially without Greek or Latin, or one of the modern languages spoken in regions closely associated with the empire. Native English-speakers may feel like 'barbarians' before the walls of Constantinople, excluded and daunted. Yet as with the great City, so with the subject, portals and gateways are available and the newcomer can reach some of the landmarks surprisingly fast, arriving at positions not all that much inferior to those of life-long devotees. The reasons are at once straightforward and specific to some of the main types of the surviving literary and other source-materials. Nothing like a full guided tour of sources available in English translation is attempted here, but the curious should be able to follow the directions towards more detail about them. Some of the more general introductions to the subject are noted below (pp. 90, 94).

SOURCEBOOKS

Straightforward considerations first: there are several collections of excerpts from sources, providing historical introductions as well as translations. They make a good first port of call for students, or for teachers who are themselves non-specialists but are thinking of offering a class or two on Byzantium. The earlier period, roughly corresponding to our Part I, is well served by sourcebooks. Michael Maas covers most aspects of life in the Byzantine sphere from the era of Constantine the Great's conversion until the Arab invasions of the seventh century, general remarks being interwoven with extracts from relevant texts.[1] Maas gives details of websites dedicated to more specialised source-guides and collections of texts. A wide-ranging assortment of texts bearing on religion, whether Christian or non-Christian, is provided by Douglas Lee with substantive introductory paragraphs,[2] and collections of texts relating to doctrine and the disputes and councils arising

---

[1] *Readings in late antiquity*, ed. Maas. (This work, like most others cited in this section, features in our bibliography of primary sources; the remainder are in the bibliography of secondary works.)

[2] *Pagans and Christians*, ed. Lee. See also the texts with multi-authored introductions in *Religions of late antiquity*, ed. Valantasis.

therefrom are available.[3] The empire's eastern frontier is the subject of a very full narrative sourcebook.[4]

The middle and later Byzantine periods – effectively our Parts II and III – are covered in their entirety by very few sourcebooks. The contrasting civilisations of Byzantium and Islam are presented by Charles Brand, while Deno Geanakoplos supplies a broad overview of the Byzantine world from Eusebius' time until the Italian Renaissance.[5] Sourcebooks focusing on particular themes are more plentiful, for example the well-chosen collections of saints' lives in *Byzantine defenders of images*, and in *Holy women of Byzantium*.[6] The former is devoted to the iconoclast controversy, for which other translations and authoritative guidebooks exist.[7] Fields in which the Byzantines had close dealings with other peoples have generated source-collections, for example, on medieval trade,[8] the Christianisation of the Slavs,[9] the world of Islam,[10] the Normans or crusading.[11] These can be illuminating, even while offering different perspectives, often hostile towards the Byzantines.

The loss of so many written source-materials from Byzantium is one reason why we depend heavily on outsiders for knowledge of, for example, the layout of Constantinople itself, fortunately a subject of keen interest to pious Rus travellers.[12] But there is something about Byzantium, whether as political structure or cultural atmosphere, that resists categorisation or orderly review in the manner of, say, imperial Rome. And now both sourcebooks and general guides to sources in translation have rivals on the internet. A reliable general guide to printed translations was provided by Emily Hanawalt,[13] but future guides and source-collections will probably appear mainly in cyberspace. Online guides offer accessibility together with high-quality scholarship, as witness the collections of Paul Halsall and Paul Stephenson.[14] An authoritative online survey of translations of saints' *Lives*

---

[3] For the era from the death of Constantine the Great to the council of Chalcedon: *Creeds, councils and controversies*, ed. Stevenson and Frend; coverage up to the eighth century in *Nicene*, ed. Wace and Schaff.

[4] *The Roman eastern frontier*, ed. Lieu *et al.*

[5] *Icon and minaret*, ed. Brand; *Byzantium*, ed. Geanakoplos.

[6] *Byzantine defenders of images*, ed. Talbot; *Holy women of Byzantium*, ed. Talbot.

[7] *Icon and logos*, ed. Sahas; clear, detailed guidance to all forms of source-material in Brubaker and Haldon (2001).

[8] *Medieval trade*, ed. Lopez and Raymond.

[9] *Medieval Slavic lives*, ed. Kantor; *Kiril and Methodius*, ed. Dujčev; *Monumenta Bulgarica*, ed. Butler.

[10] *Islam*, ed. Lewis.

[11] *Normans in Europe*, ed. van Houts; *First Crusade*, ed. Krey; P. Halsall's *Crusade sources in translation* (www.fordham.edu/halsall/source/cdesource.html). See also contributions to Whitby, Mary (ed.) (2007).

[12] *Russian travelers*, ed. and tr. Majeska.

[13] Hanawalt, *Annotated bibliography of Byzantine sources*.

[14] For the collection of translations (into western languages) made available by Halsall in the Internet Medieval Sourcebook, see: www.fordham.edu/halsall/byzantium. For the collection made by

in print is also provided by a bastion of Byzantine studies in the Anglo-phone world, the Dumbarton Oaks Research Center in Washington, DC.[15] Internet guides are open to constant updating, an asset that may have its disadvantages. But they are well suited to Byzantium, in their ability to bring together sources and resources widely scattered across disciplines and geographical space, ready for use by newcomers or by long-time scholars. And, as a medium, the internet offers direct and flexible access to important source-materials, since the visual arts and archaeological data can be presented in various degrees of detail, in high definition but at minimal cost.

ART AND VISUAL MEDIA

The electronic medium is all the more important for introducing students to sources because Byzantium was such a self-consciously 'visual' culture. For the ruling elite, display and portrayal were invaluable in projecting imperial ideology. And in the religious sphere, accurate representation of Christ, the saints and sacred scenes conveyed doctrine, provided instruction and edification, but also transmitted the divine in most truthful form.[16] Certain icons were, from the middle Byzantine period onwards, venerated for themselves working miracles, and ordinary icons were often supposed to possess special powers. Partly for this reason, the veneration of icons became the subject of controversy (see below, p. 282). The polemics generated reveal the many shades of Byzantine thinking on the question. Besides the works already noted, excerpts from texts concerning the iconoclast controversy are provided by Cyril Mango's *The art of the Byzantine empire*. This magisterial collection covers most aspects of the visual arts, including buildings and building-works, and the pithy commentary offers a guide to the Byzantines' writings about imagery.[17] The writings, like the images themselves, usually tell us more about the Byzantines' beliefs and ideals, their notions of what religious doctrine should be, or the awe that buildings or mosaics ought to inspire, than they disclose of ordinary people's reaction to them or of how things actually were. The writings were mostly penned by the more learned members of society. Likewise the political imagery and the court ceremonial represent the order of things as projected by the ruling elite, its agents and aficionados, rather than political realities, everyday affairs or

---

Stephenson, with links to other sites, see: http://homepage.mac.com/paulstephenson/trans.html. For the earlier period, the Society of Late Antiquity's site makes a good starting-point: www.sc.edu/ltantsoc.

[15] The regularly updated survey of Byzantine saints' *Lives* available in translations into English and other western European languages may be found at http://www.doaks.org/research/byzantine/translations_byzantine_saints_lives.html.

[16] See above, p. 54. For example, Photios, *Homilies*, ed. Laourdas, pp. 167, 170; tr. Mango, pp. 290, 293–4; Barber, C. (2002), pp. 135–7; James (1996); see now James (ed.) (2007).

[17] Mango, *Art of the Byzantine empire*.

the living conditions of the unprivileged. This is the case even if details of, for example, ordinary people's clothing can be gleaned from study of the paintings in churches.[18]

With visual imagery, then, as with a great deal of surviving Byzantine literature, one often encounters an ideal scheme of things, what leading lights in the Byzantine church and empire wanted to be seen, rather than a wide range of witnesses as to what actually happened.[19] But these representations are at least approachable by newcomers, whether through looking at religious and political imagery or through reading in translation the prescriptive works, idealised portrayals of saintly lives, and orations and histories emanating from the imperial-ecclesiastical circles. Various possible readings and interpretations are possible, with nuances and allusions being more apparent to the learned, or to those steeped in eastern orthodox religious traditions and practices. But first impressions of these portrayals are not necessarily far removed from those which their creators sought to evoke, while the message of the directly prescriptive texts is often plain enough.

LAWS, *TYPIKA* AND SAINTS' *LIVES*

Imperial laws were systematised by Justinian. His *Institutes* and *Digest* are available in translation, as are several important later legal texts or decrees, including the *Book of the eparch* issued under Leo VI's auspices and the *novellae* of tenth-century emperors on peasant landholdings.[20] The concept of legislation informed works of administrative regulation such as the *Book of the eparch*, and these in turn shade into detailed administrative prescriptions or treatises, such as two texts for tax-collectors.[21] Regulations governing church life were issued by church councils and patriarchs as well as by individual emperors, and the acts of the ecumenical councils are available in translation.[22]

Collections of the rules and regulations issued in the medieval period by Byzantine churchmen and specialists in church law – canonists – have

---

[18] Ball (2005); see also Parani (2003).

[19] Unauthorised tastes and subject-matter are, however, discernible in some visual forms: Maguire and Maguire (2007).

[20] For fuller details of the works cited in this and subsequent footnotes, see Abbreviations or Bibliography of Primary Sources. Justinian, *Corpus iuris civilis*, tr. Birks and McLeod, *Institutes*; tr. Watson, *Digest*; *Ecloga*, tr. Freshfield; *Ecloga privata aucta*, tr. Freshfield; *Farmer's law*, ed. and tr. Ashburner; *Eparch*, tr. Freshfield; *JG*, partial tr. McGeer; *Rhodian sea-law*, tr. Freshfield.

[21] The two handbooks are tr. in Brand (1969), pp. 48–57, 57–60. See further, on the concept of regulations having the force of law: Magdalino (1997).

[22] *Nicene*, ed. Wace and Schaff, XIV. The highly problematic text of the acts of the seventh council (Nicaea 787) is partially available in a more recent translation: *Icon and logos*, ed. Sahas. See also Brubaker and Haldon (2001), pp. 233–7.

not received English translations.[23] However, the regulations for monasteries' administration and liturgical observances, *typika*, are well served by translators. Together with the surviving order for the liturgy prescribed for the monastery of Theotokos Evergetis in Constantinople, they set out in varying degrees of detail what founders envisaged for their monasteries.[24] Considering the broad cross-section of laypersons concerned with monks and monasteries during the middle Byzantine empire and beyond,[25] the *typika* are of great historical importance. They present a spectrum of spiritual aspirations that were widely respected, if seldom fully attained, among the Byzantines.

So, in their way, do the *Lives* of saints, with due allowance made for their authorial agendas, literary genres, frequent aversion to specifics of place and time, and conceptions of truth other than the literal or earthly. The *Lives* were widely appreciated for their transcendent spiritual examples and instruction, and were intended to convey a higher reality than life as actually lived. But one should note that some give details of persons and events verifiable from other sources, and the very desire of the hagiographer to make the case for his (or her) subject could entail reference to their actual situations and the problems they faced. For example, in his *Life* of Lazaros, a stylite for forty years on Mount Galesion, the contemporary author Gregory the Cellarer gives evidence of hostility towards his hero among members of the church hierarchy, 'and even within his own monastic community'. The *Life* also makes 'important allusions to historical events and personages in the world outside the monastery', and offers an at least plausible portrayal of men, women and everyday country matters in eleventh-century Asia Minor.[26]

SERMONS AND ORATIONS

Besides the idealised lifestyles of hagiography,[27] sermons provided the Byzantines with guidelines for praying, living in this world, and enduring. Some, composed by church fathers such as Gregory Nazianzen, became elements in the liturgy, read out during services, while others from

[23] This is scarcely surprising, seeing that the *Nomokanones*, compilations of secular laws (*nomoi*) and ecclesiastical regulations (*kanones*), did not amount to a system of canon law. Important collections were, however, made, notably the *Nomokanon of fourteen titles*, and magisterial commentaries were written, for example by the *nomophylax* of St Sophia, Theodore Balsamon in the twelfth century: see *ODB*, I, pp. 372–4 (A. Schminck), pp. 248–9 (A. Kazhdan); *ODB*, II, pp. 1490–1 (A. Schminck); Macrides (1990); see below, pp. 616–17. See also pp. 241, 245.

[24] Complete translation of extant texts in *Byzantine monastic foundation documents*, ed. Thomas and Hero. See also *Synaxarion of the monastery of the Theotokos Evergetis*, ed. and tr. Jordan (2 vols. to date).

[25] Morris (1995).

[26] Gregory the Cellarer, *Life of Lazaros*, tr. Greenfield, pp. 4, 69 (introduction).

[27] See above, n. 15; see also Pratsch (2005a).

antiquity remained familiar to the Byzantines.[28] New sermons continued to be composed in Attic style and kept, and a few of those designed for special occasions or recounting specific events have been translated.[29] A translation has yet to be made of the sermons written and delivered by Leo VI, who approached his pastoral duties as ruler with high-minded diligence. But a full exegesis of their form and contents is available.[30]

Leo's sermons were delivered before his court, the setting for the delivery or performance of many of the Byzantine elite's literary creations. The sermons, orations and verse-poems furnished a steady, solemn, usually upbeat note to proceedings. Some were written for recurrent religious festivals. Others marked state occasions or recent events, and orations could be more or less unsolicited, currying favour or – more especially during the later empire – advocating a policy, seeking to persuade. Only a tiny proportion of these presentations survives – and not necessarily in the form in which they were first delivered. The little that has been translated into English tends to celebrate specific recent events, for example, the rededication of St Sophia in 562; the building of a palace bathhouse for Leo VI; the treaty with Bulgaria in 927; or Manuel II Palaiologos' funeral oration on his brother, Theodore.[31] Nine orations of Arethas, some after-dinner speeches, others solemnly welcoming the arrival of relics in Constantinople, have been edited with English summaries.[32] And a career-making speech in praise of Nicaea delivered before Andronikos II by the young Theodore Metochites in 1290 has been translated, together with one composed by a future Nicaean emperor, Theodore II Laskaris (1254–58).[33]

One of court oratory's functions was to review current affairs and the recent past, accentuating the positive and setting ups-and-downs within the empire's long history and manifest destiny. It is no accident that some men of letters prominent as speech-writers and -givers at court also composed for the historical record, notably Michael Psellos, Eustathios

[28] See, e.g., John Chrysostom, *Homilies*, tr. Hill; Gregory Nazianzen, *Select orations*, tr. in *Nicene*, ed. Wace and Schaff, VII; tr. Vinson.

[29] Photios, *Homilies*, tr. Mango; Nicholas I Mystikos' sermon lamenting the sack of Thessaloniki (904), in his *Miscellaneous writings*, ed. and tr. Westerink, pp. 9–17. See Sironis (1998) and other contributions in Cunningham and Allen (eds.) (1998); Cunningham (2003).

[30] Antonopoulou (1997).

[31] Paul the Silentiary, *St Sophia*, partial tr. Lethaby and Swainson; Leo Choirosphaktes, 'On the bath', ed. and tr. Magdalino; Dujčev, 'Treaty of 927 with the Bulgarians'; Manuel II Palaiologos, *Oration*, tr. Chrysostomides. See also Magdalino (1993a), pp. 413–70; Dennis (1997); Webb (1999); Jeffreys, E. (2007), pp. 172–4. See also on public uses of rhetoric, Hörandner (2003); Jeffreys, M. J. (2003) and other contributions in Jeffreys, E. (ed.) (2003).

[32] Arethas, *Orations*, ed. (with English summaries) Jenkins *et al.*

[33] Theodore Metochites, 'Nicene oration'; Theodore Laskaris, 'In praise of the great city of Nicaea'. Excerpts from orations and other works relating to political economy are translated in *Social and political thought in Byzantium*, ed. Barker; see below, n. 49.

of Thessaloniki and Niketas Choniates. Unfortunately their orations lack English translations, unlike their histories of reigns or events of their own times.[34]

HISTORICAL WRITING IN AND OUT OF COURT

A few other grand presentations of imperial deeds from insiders at court are – or soon will be – available to Anglophone readers, for example the *Life of Basil*, Anna Komnena's highly personal portrayal of her father Alexios I (the *Alexiad*), and the grand logothete George Akropolites' account of events between the fall of Alexios III in 1203 and Michael VIII's restoration of Constantinople to Roman imperial status in 1261.[35] Anna, however, carried out her work after leaving court life, Niketas Choniates revised his history shortly after Constantinople's fall, and in fact major historical compositions often come from the fringes of the court, from writers formerly at the centre, or ensconced in administrative, legal or ecclesiastical niches rather than at the dizziest heights. A slight distancing from the very top facilitated composition of well-informed, more or less ostensibly favourable presentations of current emperors' deeds or the reigns of an ongoing dynasty.

This generally holds true of historians of the era of Justinian and his successors – Procopius, Agathias and Theophylact Simocatta – and also holds for the period when the empire's fortunes were once again related in formats reminiscent of classical historians, as by Leo the Deacon and John Kinnamos. All these have English translations.[36] Adding the translations of church histories and works generally labelled chronicles, with their diverse priorities and perspectives – for example, the works of John Malalas, Evagrius Scholasticus, the *Paschal chronicle*, Theophanes the Confessor, Patriarch Nikephoros I (806–15) and John Skylitzes – one obtains a continuous account of the earlier and middle empire's history available in English.[37]

---

[34] Psell., tr. Sewter; Eustathios, *Capture of Thessaloniki*, tr. Melville Jones; NC, tr. Magoulias. Substantive extracts from the orations of Eustathios are translated, with exegeses, in Stone (2001); Stone (2003a); Stone (2004). The original version of Niketas' *History* was probably written 'upon the request of the court circle of Alexios III': Simpson (2006), p. 203.

[35] *Life of Basil*, ed. and tr. Ševčenko; *Al.*, tr. Sewter; GA, tr. Macrides.

[36] Pr *W*, ed. and tr. Dewing; Agathias, *Histories*, tr. Frendo; TS, tr. Whitby and Whitby; Leo the Deacon, *History*, tr. Talbot and Sullivan; John Kinnamos, *History*, tr. Brand. Certain histories now available in English did enjoy direct imperial patronage, e.g. Marcellinus, *Chronicle*, tr. Croke; Menander the Guardsman, *History*, ed. and tr. Blockley; see Rapp, C. (2005). See also Treadgold (2007), pp. 227–30, 293–5.

[37] John Malalas, *Chronicle*, tr. Jeffreys *et al.*; Evagrius Scholasticus, *Ecclesiastical history*, tr. Whitby; *Paschal chronicle*, tr. Whitby and Whitby; Theoph., tr. Mango and Scott; Nikeph., ed. and tr. Mango; Skyl., tr. Wortley (in preparation). See also *Life of Basil*, ed. and tr. Ševčenko.

LETTERS, POEMS AND LAMPOONS

To some extent, then, the non-specialist is quite well served, and translated letter-collections or poems of major figures or government employees occasionally supplement the forementioned narratives. Letters collected for publication were partly intended to show their authors' membership of the politico-religious elite and their familiarity with both the scriptures and classical lore. But their stylised qualities and contrived archaisms do not necessarily void them of straightforward historical content. This is especially so with the collected letters of the patriarchs Nicholas I Mystikos (901–7, 912–25) and Athanasios I (1289–93, 1303–9) and of Emperor Manuel II Palaiologos, while other writers such as Leo of Synada, John Mauropous and Gregory Akindynos disclose something of the goings-on in the imperial-ecclesiastical complex.[38]

One 'statesman by day, scholar by night', the grand logothete Theodore Metochites, sought consolation for loss of effective power through his *Poems 'to himself'*.[39] There are no worthy successors to Procopius' *Secret history*,[40] but the pomp and pieties of court provided an arena for political differences, personal rivalries were keen, and undercurrents of criticism and satire flowed on. The currents occasionally surface, as in Psellos' pen-portraits in *Fourteen Byzantine rulers*, where Psellos states that all emperors' actions are 'a patchwork of bad and good', and proceeds to lampoon emperors such as Constantine IX whom his orations had praised to the skies.[41] Former emperors' foibles and misdeeds were fair game after a change of dynasty, as Michael III's (842–67) posthumous reputation attests (see below, pp. 292, 295–6). And whole dynasties of emperors are castigated by iconodule writers such as Patriarch Nikephoros and Theophanes the Confessor.

ACCOUNTS OF THE CHRISTIAN EMPIRE AND ITS PRECURSORS; OTHER 'CHRONICLES'

Theophanes' work exemplifies the rather different perspective of those writers whose main concern was God's plan for mankind since the creation, and matters bearing directly on faith and the church. The realms of the ancient Persians, Assyrians and Macedonians played a part in their story, as did all the vicissitudes of Israel, and the deeds of early Christian Roman emperors were of interest. But these authors' approach to the latter was coloured by

---

[38] NM, ed. and tr. Jenkins and Westerink; Athanasios, *Correspondence*, ed. and tr. Talbot; Manuel II Palaiologos, *Letters*, ed. and tr. Dennis; Leo of Synada, *Correspondence*, ed. and tr. Vinson; John Mauropous, *Letters*, ed. and tr. Karpozilos; Gregory Akindynos, *Letters*, ed. and tr. Hero. For the letters of Theophylact of Ochrid, as yet untranslated into English, see above, n. 43 on p. 37.

[39] Theodore Metochites, *Poems*, ed. and tr. Featherstone.

[40] Procopius, *Secret history*, ed. and tr. Dewing; tr. Williamson.

[41] Psell., tr. Sewter, p. 167; Dennis (1997), pp. 134, 138.

their maintenance of what the authors deemed to be orthodoxy: heretical or simply immoral emperors were condemned and their deviation might be expected to incur God's wrath; the author's task was, in that case, to chronicle their misdeeds, and the consequent disasters.

Theophanes' composition covers the period from the reign of Diocletian (284–305) until 813, but he was finishing off the opus of George Synkellos, whose universal chronicle had aspired to an accurate continuous chronology of events since Genesis.[42] Eusebius and John Malalas had also traced events from the beginning, with somewhat different agendas, and this form of broad-sweep writing was popular with the Byzantines. Later writers such as the twelfth-century John Zonaras continued the tradition, tacking on synopses of events closer to their own time (albeit without yet gaining English translators).[43] Thus the recording of political and ecclesiastical occurrences was partly done by churchmen or pious laymen who accepted the empire as divinely instituted but whose standpoint towards individual emperors was semi-detached, when not rather hostile.

A different perspective comes from works focused on the empire's earthly fortunes, but likewise drawing on heterogeneous texts over a lengthy period. One such is that of John Skylitzes, covering the period from Michael I's accession in 811 until the later eleventh century. Skylitzes recast a medley of earlier works, including part of the text known as Theophanes Continuatus and, probably, the memoirs of a general, written in his disgruntled retreat and recounting his exploits from Armenia to Sicily.[44]

Thus events of the earlier and middle empire are relayed by a variety of voices now available in English. Their coverage is, admittedly, mainly of politico-military and ecclesiastical affairs, and the variations all pay at least lip service to the idea that the ideals of orthodoxy and empire were interdependent, although not all writers considered them identical.

NON-'ROMAN' ACCOUNTS AND DIDACTIC TEXTS

The non-specialist, forewarned, will probably find the differences in nuance between historical accounts written from court and from severely Christian perspectives more illuminating than confusing. Two other types of evidence supply contrasts or supplements to what is on offer from Byzantine narratives. Firstly, accounts penned by persons with no ambition whatsoever to be considered 'Roman' reveal much about Byzantine history, as the frequent citations from them in chapters below will attest. Here one may note that several conflicts or confrontations between the empire and external

---

[42] George Synkellos, *Chronography*, tr. Adler and Tuffin, pp. xxxv–xlii, xlvi–xlviii.
[43] John Zonaras, *Annales* [*Epitomae historiarum*], ed. Pinder and Buttner-Wöbst. See *ODB*, III, p. 2229 (A. Kazhdan); Mango (1988/89).
[44] Skyl., tr. Wortley (in preparation); Holmes (2005), pp. 125–52; Shepard (1975–6).

forces are related from the opposing sides' viewpoints, or in contemporary sources that were composed by third parties. A prime example is the
Arab conquests in the seventh century, recounted by an eyewitness Egyptian bishop, John of Nikiu, and by the contemporary Armenian author
now known as Sebeos, as well as by later Byzantine and Muslim writers.[45]
Other examples might include the encounters, diplomatic and military,
between Byzantine emperors and the emergent German and Rus leader-
ships of the second half of the tenth century,[46] while the First and Fourth
Crusades each inspired a classic Byzantine set piece as well as vivid eyewitness accounts from westerners.[47] Adversarial situations and battles are the
stuff of narrative, and outside observers or travellers – other than ninth-
and tenth-century Muslim writers[48] – have less to say about peaceful forms
of exchange between Byzantium and its neighbours, or about the internal
structure of the empire.

This brings us to a second type of evidence that may draw the newcomer closer to the inner workings of the empire. It is neither narrative nor
descriptive of Byzantium, but consists of didactic texts ranging from general
theoretical considerations, maxims and counsel to precise technical instructions. In some ways these texts resemble the Byzantine source-material discussed above, seeing that they could be termed idealising or aspirational.
They prescribe how things ought to be done, rather than describing things
as they were. They do not amount to archival data, functioning organs of
the empire in use. But the durability of some of the texts suggests that they
appeared relevant, of potential invocation or practical application. The for-
mat could also allow a writer to voice opinions on contemporary issues of
politics and society as well as on the abstract or the technical. This in itself
gives them historical source value. Furthermore, some touch on issues of
life and statecraft that seldom ranked as suitable subject-matter for formal
historical compositions. Only a few examples will be cited here, not least
because the Byzantines closely followed – and copied – the instructions of
the ancients on so many subjects, grammar, mathematics, medicine and
warfare among them. Attempts were, however, made to update received

---

[45] John of Nikiu, *Chronicle*, tr. Charles; Seb., tr. Thomson and Howard-Johnston, I; Theoph., tr.
Mango and Scott; Nikeph., ed. and tr. Mango; al-Tabari, *Ta'rikh*, tr. Yarshater *et al.*

[46] Leo the Deacon, *History*, tr. Talbot and Sullivan; Skyl., tr. Wortley (in preparation); *Leg.*, tr. Scott;
RPC, tr. Cross and Sherbowitz-Wetzor.

[47] The set piece by Anna Komnena (*Al.*, tr. Sewter) may be compared with the *Gesta Francorum*,
ed. and tr. Hill, composed by a First Crusader. For the Fourth Crusade, compare NC, tr. Magoulias
with western participants: Villehard., tr. Shaw; Robert de Clari, *Conquest of Constantinople*, tr. McNeal;
Gunther of Pairis, *Capture of Constantinople*, tr. Andrea. The Second and Third Crusades also receive
lively treatment from (Second Crusade): Odo of Deuil, *Expedition*, ed. and tr. Berry; Kinn., tr. Brand;
(Second and Third Crusades): NC, tr. Magoulias. A relatively temperate account of Crusaders' dealings
with the Byzantine government is supplied by the Latin archbishop of Tyre: William of Tyre, *Chronicon*,
tr. Babcock and Krey. See also Whitby, Mary (ed.) (2007).

[48] El-Cheikh (2004a).

wisdom in light of changing circumstances; occasionally a wholly new text was composed. Fortunately, the Byzantines' more original texts and major revamps tend to attract English translators.

A notable example of political thought couched as recommendations to an emperor dates from Justinian's era, Agapetus' *Mirror of princes*. Ernest Barker translated extensive sections, together with excerpts from orations and other texts bearing on political thought for eras up to the last decades of the Byzantine empire. Among the works translated and commented on by Barker are Gemistos Plethon's 'Address to Manuel Palaiologos on affairs in the Peloponnese', and his 'Treatise on laws'.[49]

One duty of the emperor himself was to set a moral lead, and his injunctions could have the status of solemn precepts or law. Leo VI expanded on this notion not only with his sermons, but also with other writings, including two treatises on military tactics, drawn largely from earlier texts. One of his main sources, the *Strategikon* of Emperor Maurice, is available in English as is the 'constitution' on naval warfare taken from Leo's *Tactica*, but the rest of Leo's oeuvre awaits its translator.[50] Leo's son Constantine went further still, commissioning a lengthy series of excerpts from classical and early Byzantine historical texts, each collection devoted to one topic, for example 'plots against emperors', 'virtue and vice' and 'instructive sayings'. Constantine thereby displayed his unique access to book-learning, but his preface is addressed to 'the public'. The texts are mostly in fairly straightforward Greek, and the lists of excerpted authors provided at the start of, probably, each set will have facilitated quick consultation. The 'public' probably consisted in practice mainly of persons in state service, who might benefit from picking up guidebooks, user-friendly both for practical expertise and for the broader ethical and cultural hinterland of empire. One of the few extant sets of excerpts is devoted to 'embassies', presumably being designed for persons involved with diplomacy in one way or another. The lengthy excerpts from a sixth-century historian of diplomatic exchanges are coherent enough for them to have been published in translation, partially reconstructing the now-lost original.[51]

Constantine VII's regard for the written word as a means of enhancing good form and order is shown by the compilation on court ceremonies he commissioned. His sideswipe at Romanos I Lekapenos (920–44) for shortcomings in ceremonial (see above, p. 19) hits on a fundamental question: how to maintain stately continuity while accommodating the dynamics

---

[49] Agapetus, *Mirror of princes*, partial tr. Barker; Gemistos Plethon, 'Address to Manuel Palaiologos' and 'Treatise on laws', partial tr. Barker.

[50] Maurice, *Strategikon*, tr. Dennis; see below, pp. 498–9. For this 'constitution' (or chapter), see Leo VI, *Naumachica*, ed. and tr. in Pryor and Jeffreys (2006), pp. 483–519.

[51] Men., ed. and tr. Blockley. No set of excerpts has been translated as such, but see on them Hunger (1978), I, pp. 244, 310–12, 326, 361–2; Lemerle (1986), pp. 323–32; below, pp. 511–12.

of power shifts, finding room for one-off events and exceptional circumstances. The *Book of ceremonies*, while invoking the harmony of movement that God gives to all creation, draws partly on memoranda arising from particular occasions. Scholars have detected the layers of adaptation and improvisation underlying this, and the English translation now in preparation should make this plain.[52] Constantine's concern to uphold imperial decorum and exclusivity at all events emerges equally from the treatises on imperial expeditionary forces compiled for him.[53] Most striking of all, however, are the prescriptions for divide-and-rule and other techniques of statecraft in his *De administrando imperio*.[54] Romilly Jenkins' translation conveys the generally plain style both of the source-materials assembled by Constantine and his aides, and of the emperor's own written 'doctrine'. We glimpse the *Realpolitik* behind the scenes, the presupposition that the barbarians for whom the grand receptions were staged were driven mainly by greed, fear and mutual rivalries. A ruler's personal assumptions and calculations about his polity are captured, albeit in snapshot form, to a degree virtually unparalleled among pre-modern states. And all in the name of *taxis*.

ENCYCLOPAEDIAS AND LEXICONS

Constantine VII's significance in commissioning digests of useful knowledge from ancient texts is generally acknowledged, but he was tapping into and trying to direct an intellectual trend under way long before his time, which Paul Lemerle has termed 'encyclopedism'.[55] A collection of late antique texts on the care and medical treatment of horses that Constantine had revised has been expounded in detail, although not yet translated into English.[56] A major compilation made shortly after Constantine's time was a lexicon, the *Suidae lexicon*, containing entries on a variety of words, names and subjects, mostly classical and scriptural, in alphabetical order. This is being translated online.[57]

MILITARY AND OTHER INSTRUCTIVE MANUALS

Several texts dealing with military matters have been translated into English, and their varying degrees of indebtedness to ancient tactical manuals assessed. Essentially, the Byzantines borrowed extensively but made

---

[52] *DC*, tr. Moffatt and Tall (in preparation); for the translation of an important chapter, see Featherstone, '*Di' endeixin*', pp. 81–112. See McCormick (1985); McCormick (1990); Dagron (2000); Morris (2003).
[53] Constantine Porphyrogenitus, *Three treatises*, ed. and tr. Haldon.
[54] *DAI*, tr. Jenkins.   [55] Lemerle (1986), pp. 309–46; *ODB*, I, pp. 696–7 (A. Kazhdan).
[56] McCabe (2007).   [57] www.stoa.org/sol.

adjustments to fit current circumstances, with Emperor Nikephoros II Phokas issuing fresh prescriptions on, for example, equipping, training and deploying heavy cavalry and other, lighter categories of cavalrymen.[58] Another work, on siege warfare, makes classical techniques of building and operating siege-engines readily visualisable and applicable for present-day operations against the Arabs.[59] These texts mostly date from the decades following Constantine VII's reign, registering the switch towards more sustained offensive warfare on enemy territory. The change is signalled in the preface to the manual on *Skirmishing* commissioned by Nikephoros II: the tactics prescribed here 'might not find much application in the eastern regions at the present time', now that the Muslims are being driven back; but a written record is desirable, in case 'Christians need this knowledge' again, and have to contend with raiders ranging freely across Asia Minor.[60] Another shift in priorities features in *Campaign organization*, a work envisaging warfare in Bulgarian territory and assuming that the emperor will be in command. It probably dates from the earlier part of Basil II's reign.[61]

Similar provision for new circumstances is made in Nikephoros Ouranos' *Taktika*, written while he was military governor of Antioch in the early eleventh century. Ancient military texts together with Leo VI's and Nikephoros Phokas' treatises are supplemented by chapters on, for example, cavalry warfare and sieges. These chapters, which have been expertly translated, cover 'the full range of contemporary Byzantine military operations' in the region of occupied Syria.[62]

Prescriptive handbooks could be more discursive. One such, conventionally termed the *Strategikon* of Kekaumenos, we have noted above (p. 67). This contains edifying maxims, tips on household management and social relationships, and counsel about serving as a judge in the provinces. Kekaumenos' bias is, however, towards officers' training: he had himself been a senior commander in the mid-eleventh-century army. An English translation is in preparation, supplementing the Russian translation.[63] No precise analogy to Kekaumenos' work is known. But it survives in just one manuscript. Similar sets of instructions could well have been composed by commanders or civilian officials, without the good fortune of manuscript

[58] Nikephoros II Phokas, *Praecepta militaria*, ed. and tr. in McGeer (1995), pp. 12–59 (text); pp. 181–8, 211–17, 226–9 (commentary).

[59] 'Heron of Byzantium', *Parangelmata poliorcetica – Geodesia*, tr. in Sullivan, *Siegecraft*, pp. 26–151 (text), pp. 1–24 (introduction); see also *De obsidione toleranda*, ed. van den Berg, tr. Sullivan, pp. 150–263.

[60] *Skirmishing*, ed. and tr. Dennis, p. 147.

[61] *Campaign organization*, ed. and tr. Dennis, pp. 289, 291, 305 (text), pp. 242–3 (introduction).

[62] Nikephoros Ouranos, *Taktika*, chs. 56 through 65, ed. and tr. McGeer (1995), pp. 89–163 (text); p. 81 (introduction).

[63] Kek., ed. and Russian tr. Litavrin; tr. Roueché (in preparation).

survival. In fact, comparable stylistic traits, rhetorical devices and didactic tone characterise some of the military treatises discussed above; they are also discernible in Skylitzes' chronicle. Kekaumenos dismisses unnamed rivals in stressing that his work stems from 'authentic experience', presenting 'things not in any other *Strategikon* or any other book'.[64] At the same time he presupposes readers' familiarity with heroes such as Scipio Africanus and Belisarius. His work opens a window on under-chronicled Byzantine officialdom, on men educated in grammar and rhetoric, but not to the highest level. Opinionated and idiosyncratic Kekaumenos may have been, but his value-system was probably common to many of the empire's servants. They were interested in relating recent developments to the classical past, preoccupied with issues of technique and policy, yet also disposed to pass useful knowledge, topped with pieties and worldly wisdom, on to their juniors in age or status.[65]

This political culture could act as a bonding mechanism, providing middling officials scattered across outposts of empire with a common stock of know-how, anecdotes and semi-learned allusions. A certain *esprit de corps* was thereby fostered. But this was no closed body. The military manuals and other practical works imply concern to introduce newcomers or successors to the systems they will have to operate. Most also place present-day norms and practices within the framework of the ancients, still deemed past-masters. The very fact that the counsel was set down in writing suggests that processes of training and dissemination went on beyond the confines of formal education. The attempts at spelling out military techniques in plain words, simplifying classical terminology, also bespeak ambitions for learning, for self-improvement, on the part of individuals coming from outside the gilded circles.

In other words, the instruction manuals themselves constitute evidence of the means whereby the upwardly mobile could hone their military and other skills, gain a certain polish, and ultimately rise higher in the empire's service, especially during its era of expansion, the tenth and eleventh centuries. They would need Greek to understand the manuals and most would be Byzantine-born. But individuals among neighbouring elites, or visitors to the empire, could manage some Greek, written as well as spoken. Didactic texts would have been of use to, for example, the young Norman noble who learnt not only Greek at court but also veterinary medicine for horses and birds in the mid-eleventh century.[66]

[64] Kek., ed. and Russian tr. Litavrin, pp. 172–3, 164–5.

[65] Roueché (2003), pp. 27–8, 33–7; Roueché (forthcoming); seminar paper by Catherine Holmes, 'Literacy and written culture in Byzantine political culture' (17 June 2005, Oxford).

[66] *Chronique de Sainte-Barbe-en-Auge*, ed. Sauvage, pp. 56–7. The information about this visitor to Constantinople is contained in a commemorative note added at the end of the (uncompleted) chronicle. See also Ciggaar (1996), p. 180; Amsellem (1999).

Paradoxical as it might seem, texts covering military matters could become available to outsiders. In fact a section in Kekaumenos' *Strategikon* directly addresses a toparch, a local potentate in the borderlands. He is advised to be wary of the emperor's blandishments, paying just one visit to Constantinople if he values his independence. The fate of an incautious toparch is recounted, by way of warning, and another section features the wiles of one of Kekaumenos' own ancestors, a toparch in the Armenian borderlands who outwitted imperial commanders.[67] Thus a senior military officer could proudly recall Armenian family roots and envisage sympathetically a contemporary toparch's viewpoint. There is no reason to doubt Kekaumenos' overriding loyalty towards the emperor, or that his prime self-identification was Roman. But Kekaumenos had not wholly relinquished ties with another culture, an alternative identity, and in that sense he exemplifies the multiple or mutable personae of many serving in the empire's higher echelons, especially the armed forces. His 'life and opinions', while personal to the point of idiosyncrasy, do much to explain Byzantium's sinews of governance (see above, pp. 15–16). Kekaumenos' injunctions, with other more technical treatises, are now becoming available to Anglophones; in reading these works, the newcomer to Byzantium can gain a direct impression of what it was to make oneself a Roman.

SHORT-CUTS TO BYZANTIUM

There are many forms of short-cut to the study of Byzantium, literally so by way of atlases. Most aspects of its historical geography are authoritatively covered by John Haldon in *The Palgrave atlas of Byzantine history*,[68] and the early phases of the empire and of the Christian church are charted in detail in *The Barrington atlas* and *The atlas of the early Christian world*.[69] Detailed historical atlases of neighbouring peoples and regions are also available in English;[70] likewise with the religious and other movements from outside that had some bearing on the empire's fate.[71] Online guides are likely to extend horizons further, in terms not only of geography but also of art and visual culture.[72]

The Oxford dictionary of Byzantium covers virtually every aspect of Byzantium across the ages, from the spiritual to the archaeological, while a broad canvas is presented in *The Oxford handbook of Byzantine studies*.[73] Several

---

[67] Kek., ed. and Russian tr. Litavrin, pp. 316–19, 186–7.   [68] Haldon (2005c).
[69] Talbert *et al.* (eds.) (2000); van der Meer and Mohrmann (1966).
[70] Hewsen (2001); Rapp and Awde (eds.) (forthcoming).
[71] Kennedy (ed.) (2002); Riley-Smith (ed.) (1991).
[72] See, for example, Byzantine Links listed on the website of the Society for the Promotion of Byzantine Studies (www.byzantium.ac.uk).
[73] *ODB*, 3 vols.; Jeffreys *et al.* (eds.) (2008, forthcoming).

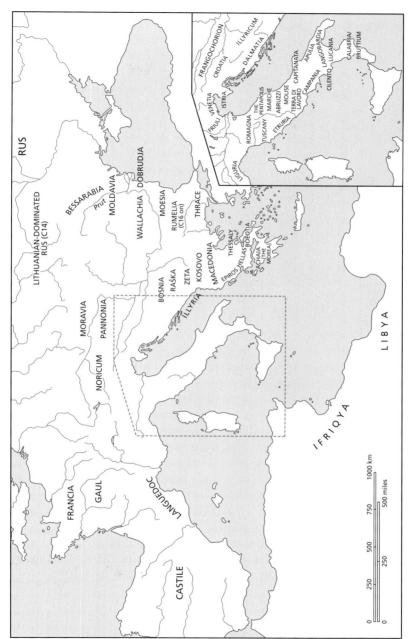

Map 3a Archaic, and other less familiar, names: the central Mediterranean world

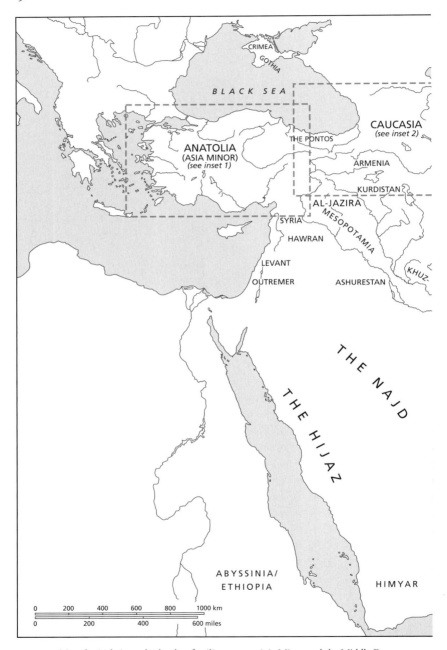

Map 3b Archaic, and other less familiar, names: Asia Minor and the Middle East

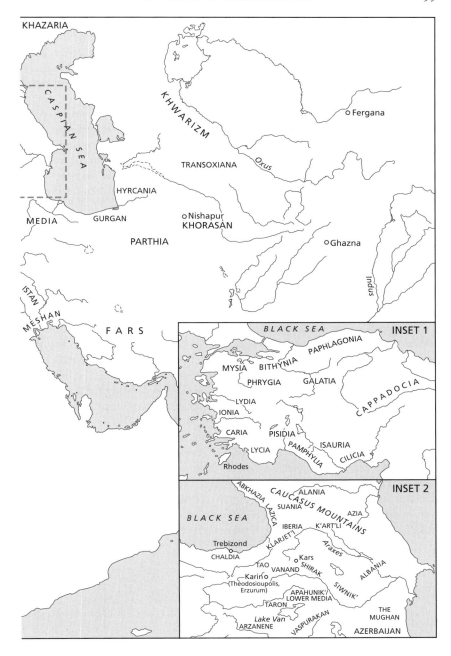

KHAZARIA

CASPIAN SEA

KHWARIZM

○ Fergana

TRANSOXIANA

Oxus

HYRCANIA

MEDIA GURGAN ○ Nishapur
KHORASAN

PARTHIA ○ Ghazna

Indus

ISTAN

MESHAN

FARS

INSET 1

BLACK SEA

PAPHLAGONIA

MYSIA BITHYNIA

PHRYGIA GALATIA

CAPPADOCIA

LYDIA

IONIA

CARIA PISIDIA

ISAURIA

LYCIA PAMPHYLIA CILICIA

Rhodes

INSET 2

ABKHAZIA LAZICA CAUCASUS MOUNTAINS

ALANIA

SUANIA

AZIA

BLACK SEA

IBERIA K'ART'LI

Trebizond KLARJET'I Araxes

CHALDIA

TAO ○ Kars

Karin ○ VANAND SHIRAK ALBANIA

(Theodosioupolis,
Erzurum) SIWNIK'

APAHUNIK'/
LOWER MEDIA

TARON THE
MUGHAN

Lake Van

ARZANENE VASPURAKAN AZERBAIJAN

other introductory multi-authored works or broad synopses appeared early in the twenty-first century.[74] The main papers and abstracts of the Twenty-first International Congress of Byzantine Studies (2006), together with other proceedings published shortly afterwards, summed up the scholarly state of play across the field, the greater part of these papers having been presented in English.[75]

The economic history of Byzantium, covering the Byzantine world from the seventh to the fifteenth centuries, has already been mentioned (see above, pp. 36–7). So have the many accessible introductions to the art and archaeology of Byzantium, the introduction to alternative forms of imagery by Maguire and Maguire (2007) among them (see above, n. 19 on p. 79). Entries on all forms of Byzantine art history (in German) are supplied by the *Reallexikon zur byzantinischen Kunst*,[76] while studies in English as well as other western languages on virtually every aspect of late antique history and culture are published in the compendious *Aufstieg und Niedergang der römischen Welt*.[77] A pithier synopsis emerges from the thematic essays and articles in Bowersock *et al.* (eds.) (1999), covering the antique Christian and Islamic worlds from the mid-third century until the end of the eighth. A chronology of salient political, military and ecclesiastical events year by year from 330 until 1461 is provided by *A chronology of the Byzantine empire*.[78]

These works can be supplemented in highly flexible ways by the online *Prosopography of the Byzantine world*.[79] This offers a full, reliable chronology for most of the eleventh and twelfth centuries and gives details about individuals eminent or obscure. Its gateways also open up to the enquirer a range of thematic topics: for example, 'murder' will bring up a list of all those persons said to have been murdered during that period. Traditional reference works for the cultures and religions most closely linked with Byzantium remain of value as introductions and suppliers of background information, notably *The Oxford classical dictionary, The Oxford dictionary of the Christian church* and *The early Christian world*.[80] The revised edition of *The encyclopedia of Islam* contains many entries on places within the Byzantine empire, encompassing the period before they came permanently under Muslim rule.[81] The *Dictionnaire d'histoire et de géographie ecclésiastiques* contains entries on places, rites and persons of significance

---

[74] Angold (2001); Mango (ed.) (2002); Morrisson *et al.* (eds.) (2004); Harris (ed.) (2005); Gregory (2005); Cameron, Averil (2006b); James (ed.) (forthcoming); Cheynet (ed.) (in preparation); Laiou (ed.) (in preparation); Stephenson (ed.) (in preparation). See also above, nn. 1–3 on p. 22.

[75] *ACIEB* 21 (3 vols.). Other publications include Litavrin (ed.) (2006); Franklin and Mavroudi (eds.) (2007); *SBS* 10 (forthcoming); Whittow (ed.) (forthcoming).

[76] *RbK*.   [77] *ANRW*.   [78] Venning (ed.) (2005).

[79] *PBW*. For the earlier period of 641–867, see Martindale (2001); *PMBZ*, I.

[80] Hornblower and Spawforth (eds.) (2003); Cross and Livingstone (eds.) (2005); Esler (2000).

[81] *EI*.

in the eastern church, while the *Lexikon des Mittelalters* gives balanced treatment in depth of Byzantium as well as the west.[82]

Those wishing to follow the short-cuts through to the point of learning something of the language as written and spoken by the Byzantines have a number of choices. They may start with the classical Attic Greek to which members of the elite aspired, or with New Testament Greek, which is not so far removed from the everyday language of the earlier medieval Byzantines. Standard grammars and self-help courses offer instruction in these forms of Greek. Good introductions are also available for persons wanting to trace the historical connections between Byzantine Greek and the Greek in use today, or to learn something of the grammar of the modern language.[83] The Greek script is explained in detail for newcomers as well as specialists by contributions to *Greek scripts*, while the new lexicon of Byzantine Greek, supplementing the classical dictionary of Liddell and Scott, is nearing completion.[84]

Finally, those who embark on systematic self-tuition or who contemplate offering a lecture or two or even a course on Byzantine history may turn to offerings in the online 'overnight expert' series. One of these is dedicated to the teaching of Byzantium by non-specialists. It provides some suggestions for essay questions or coursework, together with reading lists, and it points out where a Byzantine dimension can usefully be added to standard western medieval teaching topics. The closely related history of the Armenians is also covered in this series.[85]

The short-cuts mentioned in this section should help make basic facts and historical issues reasonably clear and communicable to and by non-specialist teachers. They and their students have online access to sources in English translation and to guides to those sources (see above, pp. 77–8 and nn. 14, 15), while Byzantine landscapes, buildings and imagery can be accessed cheaply and accurately. In that sense, the many roads to Byzantium are wide open to travellers as never before.

---

[82] *DHGE*; *LexMA*.

[83] Browning (1983); Farmakides (1983); Horrocks (1997); Holton *et al.* (2004) (with references to other coursebooks).

[84] Easterling and Handley (eds.) (2001); *LBG*; see also above, p. 59.

[85] http://www.heacademy.ac.uk/hca/resources/detail/teaching_byzantium; http://www.heacademy. ac.uk/hca/resources/detail/teaching_medieval_ paper_armenia.php

PART I

THE EARLIER EMPIRE *c.* 500–*c.* 700

CHAPTER 1

JUSTINIAN AND HIS LEGACY (500–600)

ANDREW LOUTH

AN EMPIRE OF CITIES

The beginning of the sixth century saw Anastasius (491–518) on the imperial throne, ruling an empire that was still thought of as essentially the Roman empire, coextensive with the world of the Mediterranean. Although Anastasius ruled from Constantinople over what we call the eastern empire, the western empire having been carved up into the 'barbarian kingdoms', this perspective is ours, not theirs. Through the conferring of titles in the gift of the emperor, and the purchasing of alliances with the wealth of the empire – wealth that was to dwarf the monetary resources of the west for centuries to come – the barbarian kings could be regarded as client kings, acknowledging the suzerainty of the emperor in New Rome, and indeed the barbarian kings were frequently happy to regard themselves in this light (see below, p. 198). The discontinuation of the series of emperors in the west, with the deposition of Romulus Augustulus in 476, was regarded by very few contemporaries as a significant event; the notion that east and west should each have their own emperor was barely of a century's standing, and the reality of barbarian military power in the west, manipulated from Constantinople, continued, unaffected by the loss of an 'emperor' based in the west.

The empire that Anastasius ruled was still the Mediterranean world as it had been since classical times in more than just a political sense: it consisted of a world whose basic unit was the city which, with its hinterland, formed a self-sufficient economic and even cultural unit. Although shorn of the political powers of the old city-state, the notables of the city still exercised considerable political influence and the provincial governors, appointed from the same social class as these notables, frequently found it more effective to recognise local influence than to challenge it. The cities – with fora, theatres, courts and opportunities for education – formed the seedbed for the educated elite who held posts in the imperial administration, often returning to the cities to enjoy the essentially rural wealth generated by their country estates. All this was to change from the sixth century onwards, though there is a good deal of debate about the rate at which this change took place.

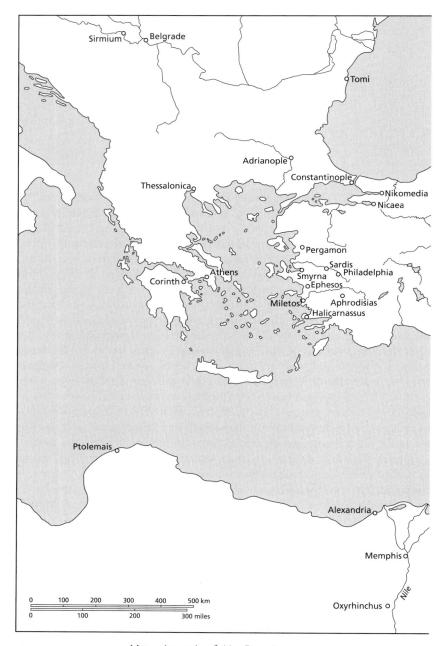

Map 4 An empire of cities: Byzantium *c.* 500

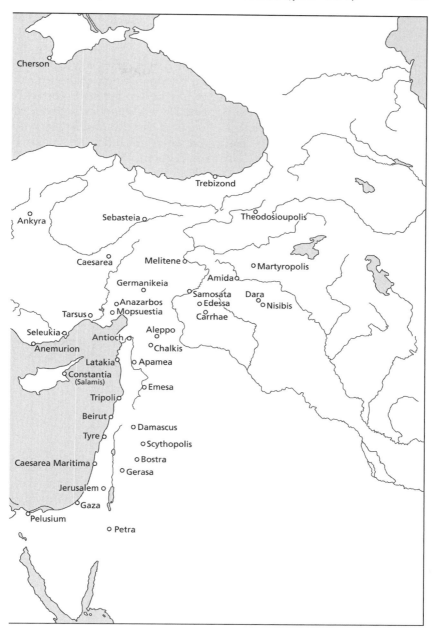

Cherson

Trebizond

Ankyra   Sebasteia   Theodosioupolis

Caesarea   Melitene   Martyropolis

Germanikeia   Amida

Anazarbos   Samosata   Dara
Mopsuestia   Edessa   Nisibis
Tarsus   Carrhae

Seleukia   Aleppo
Anemurion   Antioch
                    Chalkis
Latakia   Apamea
Constantia
(Salamis)

Tripoli   Emesa

Beirut

Tyre   Damascus

          Scythopolis
Caesarea Maritima   Bostra
                    Gerasa
Jerusalem

Gaza
Pelusium

Petra

The city was also the basic unit of the Christian church. From the end of the second century Christianity, which from the start had been a predominantly urban phenomenon, had developed an organisation based on the city and its hinterland; it was led by a single officer, called a bishop, who was appointed for life.[1] With the gradual Christianisation of the Roman empire from the fourth century onwards, the bishop became a considerable figure among the notables of the city. He was sometimes appointed *defensor civitatis*, that is the leader or 'judge' of the city, and he regularly exercised the functions of this post, even when not officially appointed to it. Despite the decline of the city as an economic and cultural entity,[2] the link between bishop and city was to continue. Christianity had never been a particularly peaceful religion, and the importance it attached to correctly formulated beliefs, combined with its increasing social influence as fewer and fewer inhabitants of the empire resisted the pressure to embrace Christianity, meant that well before the sixth century Christian belief had become both a cause of social, political and cultural divisions, and a means of articulating them. Modern historians are shy of regarding religious belief and practice as the reason for social and political divisions, and in general they may well be right, but it is undeniable that in this period division was often expressed and understood in religious terms. As we shall see, issues of religious difference are woven into the narrative of sixth-century history. It is important to understand the basis for these differences before going on to consider other explanations for social, political and cultural divisions that were expressed in these terms. Religious conflict is a theme to which we shall often return.

RELIGIOUS DIVISIONS AND OUR SOURCES FOR THE SIXTH CENTURY

Anastasius inherited, and promoted, religious divisions that were to cast a long shadow over the Christian Roman empire. These religious divisions derived in the first instance from the council of Chalcedon (451), which attempted to settle long-standing differences about how godhead and manhood were united in Christ. The fathers of the council were almost entirely Greek, while the pope of the day, Leo I (440–61), played an important role through his legates. A formula acceptable to the papal legates was eventually agreed, which they regarded as endorsing the teaching of Cyril, the great

---

[1] Translation from one city to another was forbidden by canon 15 of the council of Nicaea, although there were rare exceptions.

[2] The question of the decline of the late antique city, and how such decline is to be interpreted, really becomes critical in the seventh century: see below, pp. 221, 224. For two general accounts, see Mango (1980), pp. 60–87; Liebeschuetz (1992).

patriarch of Alexandria (412–44), who was held in the highest regard by all but a small minority of the eastern bishops. But as a hard-won concession to the papal legates, Chalcedon recognised the unity of Christ's person 'in two natures'. This is not a phrase found in Cyril, but was taken from a papal letter – the so-called '*Tome* of Leo' – which was received by the council. This concession spoilt the achievement of Chalcedon; many Christians, especially in Syria and Egypt, felt that the council had betrayed, rather than endorsed, Cyril.

Rejection of the decision of Chalcedon often took violent forms: Juvenal, bishop of Jerusalem, needed imperial troops to make a safe entry into his episcopal city; and Proterios, appointed to replace Cyril's successor who had been deposed by the council, was murdered by the mob. The violence that often accompanied these religious differences was regularly fostered by monks, who were increasingly becoming a force to be reckoned with in the Christian empire. After unsuccessful attempts to enforce Chalcedon, in 482 Emperor Zeno (474–91) issued a statement of belief with the intention of securing unity (called the *Henotikon*), which disowned Chalcedon, though it fell short of condemning the council. The *Henotikon* was the work of Acacius, patriarch of Constantinople (471–89), and Peter Mongos 'the Hoarse', patriarch of Alexandria (477, 482–89). However Rome, and the Latin west in general, was not willing to disown what it regarded as the council of Pope Leo; the promulgation of the *Henotikon* thus provoked the Acacian schism with Constantinople, named after its patriarch, which lasted until the death of Anastasius. For the *Henotikon* remained imperial policy during the reign of Anastasius who, if anything regarded the edict as too moderate, since he promoted those who rejected the *Henotikon* for not explicitly condemning Chalcedon.

Our sources for the sixth century, although on the face of it plentiful, leave much to be desired. Histories on the classical model survive intact, in contrast to the fragmentary fifth-century histories, and these include Procopius' *Wars*, the *Histories* of Agathias and Theophylact Simocatta, and substantial extracts from the *History* of Menander the Guardsman. These are complemented by chronicles – a new form of history writing of Christian inspiration – such as those by John Malalas (which only survives in an epitomised form) and Marcellinus, as well as the later *Paschal chronicle* (630) and the *Chronicle* of Theophanes (dating from the early ninth century, but incorporating earlier material). Church histories evolved from the form of the chronicle, and the main sixth-century example is that of the Antiochene lawyer, Evagrius Scholasticus. Such Christian history writing regarded the traditions of saints' *Lives* as important, and there is a good deal of hagiographical material relating to the sixth century. Much of this is valuable for the social, as well as the religious, history of the period, notably the collections by Cyril of Scythopolis and John Moschus, together with the lives of individual saints (for example of the stylites or Theodore of Sykeon).

To these can be added texts that are written, or survive, in Syriac, representing the views of those non-Chalcedonian Christians (monophysites) excluded from the imperial church by the drive towards a form of Chalcedonian orthodoxy promoted by Justinian and his successors. These include saints' *Lives* by Zacharias of Mytilene, which were originally written in Greek, although his *Church history* does not advance into the sixth century; and a collection of saints' *Lives* and a *Church history* by John of Ephesus, who wrote in Syriac.[3] There is also an anonymous eighth-century chronicle, attributed to Pseudo-Dionysios of Tell-Mahre, and the twelfth-century chronicle of Michael the Syrian.

Traditionally, the tendency has been to take the classicising histories at face value as a basic record, to be supplemented, with varying degrees of caution, from the chronicles and ecclesiastical sources.[4] The trend of recent scholarship, however, has been to pay much more attention to the intentions and bias of the classicising historians, with the result that we now see in these sources a variety of sharply defined perspectives on the sixth century, rather than a straightforward narrative record that can be used as a basic framework.[5] Archaeology is an important resource, not least over major imponderables, such as the decline (or survival) of the city, economic prosperity and climatic change. In addition we can also draw information from epigraphy, coins and seals, and make use of the evidence (still little used) that remains embedded in the conservative, yet developing, liturgy of the churches.

Accounts of the second half of Anastasius' reign indicate mounting popular unrest, ostensibly because of the emperor's religious policy. Behind this may lie growing economic difficulties and an increasing sense of insecurity within the empire. At the beginning of the sixth century the long peace with Persia, the traditional enemy of the Roman empire, and indeed of its predecessors, came to an end. The Persians' failure to restore Nisibis to the Roman empire, in accordance with a treaty made with Emperor Jovian in the fourth century, led the East Romans to withhold tribute payments; this, in turn, prompted the Persians to invade the Roman empire in 502 and they quickly took a number of frontier towns, including the city of Amida (see below, p. 135). To begin with, Roman resistance was weakened by a divided command, and it was not until 505 that the Romans recovered Amida. The weakness of the Mesopotamian frontier revealed by this war was remedied by the building of the fortress at Dara, close to the frontier and a few

---

[3] The third part of John of Ephesus' *Historia ecclesiastica* survives in a single manuscript, while the first two parts survive in fragmentary form, incorporated into later Syriac chronicles.

[4] This is Gibbon's method (1776–88), still used by Bury (1923) and even Jones (1964).

[5] See, notably, Cameron, Averil (1985).

miles from Nisibis; it was called Anastasiopolis, after the emperor. In the north, too, there were threats from invaders in the early sixth century, and archaeological evidence suggests that the fortresses which Procopius says were built along the right bank of the Danube in the reign of Justinian (527–65) were at least begun by Anastasius.[6]

The riots venting opposition to Anastasius' religious policy were triggered by a matter of liturgy. From the middle of the fifth century, the chant called the *Trisagion* ('holy God, holy strong, holy immortal, have mercy on us') had become a popular part of the liturgy in the east. In Syria this chant was understood to be addressed to God the Son; in order to underline the belief of those rejecting Chalcedon's distinction between the two natures in the Incarnate Son, the phrase 'who was crucified for us' was added to the chant, affirming their conviction that in Christ, God himself had embraced human suffering (a doctrine called theopaschism). In Constantinople, however, the chant, with its triadic form, was understood to be addressed to the Trinity, so such an addition seemed to imply that the divine nature itself was subject to suffering. Behind the differing texts of the chant, there lay genuine mutual misunderstanding, but that only made each side's sense of the other's error more acute. When Anastasius directed that the theopaschite addition should be included in the *Trisagion*, it provoked a riot between non-Chalcedonian monks chanting the amplified form and the clergy and people of Constantinople. This led to popular demands for the deposition of the emperor, demands only quelled by the emperor himself facing the mob in 512, without his diadem, and inspiring an acclamation of loyalty. In the following year the emperor faced a further challenge to his authority from Vitalian, a military *comes*, who claimed to represent the reaction of the orthodox to the policies of the emperor. Although unsuccessful in his challenge to the throne, he outlived the emperor.

THE RISE OF JUSTINIAN AND THE QUESTION OF HIS 'GRAND DESIGN'

Anastasius died in 518, leaving the question of his succession undecided. He was succeeded by Justin I (518–27), a peasant from Illyria, who had risen through the ranks to become count of the excubitors. He was uneducated, perhaps even illiterate, and Procopius would have us believe that the real power behind the throne was Justin's nephew, Peter Sabbatius, who took the name of Justinian; Justin had earlier brought him to the capital and lavished an expensive education on him. It is hard to say how true this is, for there is no independent evidence to support the claim.[7]

---

[6] Poulter (1983), p. 97, cited by Cameron, Averil (1985), p. 220, n. 90.   [7] Honoré (1978), p. 7.

Justin's first act was to repudiate his predecessors' attempts to achieve unity among the Christians by ignoring, or even implicitly condemning, the council of Chalcedon: the *Henotikon* was revoked and Chalcedonian orthodoxy became imperial policy. Justin announced his election and religious policy to Pope Hormisdas (514–23), who sent legates to Constantinople; a council was held there to confirm the ending of the Acacian schism and to condemn those who had promoted it. These included not only Acacius and those successors who had agreed with him, but also – and in this exceeding papal demands – the emperors Zeno and Anastasius. Prominent non-Chalcedonian monophysites, including Severus of Antioch and Philoxenos of Mabbug, were deposed and exiled. Reconciliation with Rome only reopened the wounds that the *Henotikon* had tried to heal, but very soon a refinement of Chalcedonian orthodoxy was put forward that was to become the focus of Justinian's endeavours to achieve religious unity. A group of monks from Scythia, led by John Maxentius, brought their proposal to Constantinople: it involved supplementing the Chalcedonian definition with the affirmation that 'one of the Trinity suffered in the flesh'. This affirmation would appeal to the monophysites' conviction of the indivisible unity of Christ, which had found expression in the theopaschite addition to the *Trisagion*. Justinian was attracted by this proposal and sent the monks off to Rome, where they failed to convince Pope Hormisdas, though others found it acceptable, notably Dionysius Exiguus and Boethius. The proposal remained dormant until the 530s, when Justinian's religious endeavours began in earnest.

In spring 527 Justin fell ill, and Justinian was proclaimed *augustus* in April; four months later Justin died, and Justinian succeeded him. His reign lasted until 565, thirty-eight years in all – or forty-seven, if one includes his stint as the power behind Justin's throne. This was an exceptionally long reign and its duration would have been an achievement in itself. But there was much else besides: reform of the legal code; reconquest of Roman territories in North Africa, Italy and Spain; grandiose rebuilding projects, notably the rebuilding of the centre of Constantinople, including the Great Church of the Holy Wisdom, St Sophia; the closure of the Platonic Academy in Athens; and a religious policy culminating in the fifth ecumenical council, held at Constantinople in 553 (or, to adopt a different perspective, in his lapse into heresy in his final months). The temptation to see all these as parts of a jigsaw which, when correctly fitted together, yield some grand design is hard to resist. And then there is glamour, in the person of Theodora, the woman he married. In doing this, Justinian circumvented the law forbidding marriage between senators and actresses; even Procopius acknowledges her beauty, while regarding her as a devil incarnate. He wrote a malicious account of Theodora's meddling in the affairs of state in his *Secret history*. Procopius also relates how during the so-called Nika riot in 532, when Justinian was terrified by the rioting against his rule and was contemplating flight, Theodora persuaded him to stay and face either death or victory with the dramatic words, 'the empire is a fair winding-sheet.' All this prepares the way for assessments of Theodora that rank her with Byzantine empresses like Irene or Zoe, both of whom (unlike Theodora) assumed imperial power in their own right, albeit briefly.[8]

The 'grand design' view of Justinian's reign sees all his actions as the deliberate restoration of the ancient Roman empire, though a Roman empire raised to new heights of glory as a Christian empire confessing the orthodox faith. According to this view, reconquest restored something like the traditional geographical area of the empire; law reform encapsulated the vision of a Christian Roman empire, governed by God's vicegerent, the emperor; the capital's splendid buildings, not least the churches, celebrated the Christian court of New Rome, with the defensive buildings described by Procopius in the later books of his *Buildings* serving to preserve in perpetuity the newly reconquered Roman world. The defining of Christian orthodoxy, together with the suppression of heterodoxy, whether Christian heresy or pagan philosophy, completes the picture.

In discussing Justinian's reign it is therefore difficult to avoid the notion of a grand design. Virtually all our literary sources reflect something of this idea. It is there in Procopius (even the *Secret history* sees Justinian as a grand designer, albeit malign), in the legal texts and even in the ecclesiastical texts written by those who experienced persecution at Justinian's hand: the monophysites shared with those who embraced imperial Christianity the vision of a Christian empire ruled by a Christian emperor.[9] It is hardly to be denied that there were moments when Justinian fancied he was fulfilling some such grandiose design. In 536, after reconquering Sicily, Justinian affirmed, 'we have good hope that God will grant us to rule over the rest of what, subject to the ancient Romans to the limits of both seas, they later lost by their easy-going ways.'[10] Whether we should think of Justinian's reign as the fulfilment of a consciously preconceived grand design is another matter. This raises two interrelated questions: do all the above-mentioned elements fit together into some grand design; and, even if they do, did Justinian really have the means to bring this grand design to fruition? As we shall see, neither of these questions can be answered in the affirmative without heavy qualification.

---

[8] For a cool appraisal of such accounts, see Cameron, Averil (1985), pp. 67–83. See below, p. 277 (Irene), p. 588 (Zoe).

[9] Fowden (1993).

[10] Justinian, *Corpus iuris civilis, novella* 30, ed. Krueger *et al.*, III, p. 234; tr. in Honoré (1978), p. 19.

Perhaps the most convincing evidence for such a grand design, at least at the beginning of Justinian's reign, is found in his revision of Roman law. Justinian set this in hand as soon as he could, strikingly fulfilling one of the recognised roles of a ruler: that of ultimate judge and legislator. This was a task especially associated with the Roman emperor, for Romans prided themselves on living under the law, something given signal expression in Priscus' account of the embassy to the court of Attila in the fifth century.[11] Within months of assuming sole rule, Justinian had announced to the senate in a formal legal enactment (a 'constitution') his intention of having a new law-code prepared, that would bring matters up to date, reconcile contradictions, winnow out irrelevant legislation, and introduce clarity. He set up a ten-man commission, led by the *quaestor* Tribonian, which completed its work in little over a year. This code no longer survives, but five and a half years later, in 534, it was issued in revised form, arranged in twelve books and containing constitutions from the intervening period; it is this edition that has survived to exercise such an influence on subsequent European law. By the time of the second edition, there had been a further contribution to the work of legal revision, the publication of the *Digest* or *Pandects*, which reduced to order the legal opinions of centuries of Roman lawyers. This was published in December 533. A further part of the legal reform was the publication of the *Institutes*, a revision of the Commentaries of the second-century jurist, Gaius, which was to be the official textbook for students of law at the two official schools of law, in Constantinople and Beirut. This revision and clarification of Roman law was complemented by the later laws of Justinian, the *novellae*. Whereas the main body of Tribonian's work was in Latin, most of the *novellae* are in Greek, for the reign of Justinian marks a watershed between the Roman empire with Latin as the official language and the so-called Byzantine empire, in which Greek was the principal and eventually the sole language.

The purpose of this legal reform should be seen as twofold. It was practical: the code and the *novellae* provided legal norms to be interpreted by judges with the use of the *Digest*. It seems, however, that this function was not to continue much beyond the middle of the next century. But its other purpose was to delineate a world-view, enshrining the inheritance of Roman civilisation, the embrace of Christian orthodoxy, and the paramount position of the emperor. This was an enduring legacy, and at its heart was a vision of the complementarity of empire and priesthood, *basileia* and *hierosynē*, *imperium* and *sacerdotium*. This is expressed nowhere better than in *novella* 6 (535):

The greatest of God's gifts to men, given from on high in accordance with his loving kindness, are priesthood and empire; the one ministers to things divine,

---

[11] Priscus (fragment 11) in Blockley (ed.), *Historians*, II, pp. 242–81, esp. pp. 270–3.

the other rules and cares for matters human, both proceed from one and the same source, and set in order human life. So nothing is more sought after by kings than the dignity of priests, if they beseech God continually on their behalf. For if the one is always unblemished and has open access to God, while the other rightly and fitly orders the received form of government, then there will be a fair harmony, and everything that is good for the human race will be granted. We therefore have the greatest care for the true dogmas of God, as well as for the dignity of the priests, which we believe cares for them, as through it good gifts are given us from God, so that what we have we possess securely, and what we have not yet attained we shall come to acquire. Thus everything will be done rightly and fitly, if the beginning of everything is proper and acceptable to God. We believe that this will be so, if the observance of the holy canons is preserved, which has been handed down by the apostles, who are rightly praised and venerated as eyewitness and ministers of the word of God, and which has been safeguarded and interpreted by the holy fathers.

Such comprehensive legislative activity can hardly be regarded as other than part of a grand design of imperial rule.

The next essential ingredient, reconquest of lost imperial territory, as we have seen above (p. 107), also inspired in Justinian the conviction that he was the divine agent in reconstituting the Roman empire in a Christian form. But was this a settled conviction, or a passing hope? The facts about Justinian's reconquest of North Africa, Italy and Spain are not in doubt, although we are poorly informed about the Spanish expedition; their interpretation is much more hazardous. In 533, Justinian despatched his general Belisarius to North Africa with an impressive force of 10,000 infantry and 5,000 cavalry.[12] However, the reasons for his determination that this enterprise should not fail are perhaps more down-to-earth than the fulfilment of some grand design of imperial restoration. Justinian had only just recovered from the Nika riot, and Emperor Leo's disastrous attempt in 468 to dislodge the Vandals made it imperative that Belisarius' expedition should succeed if Justinian's credibility as emperor were to recover. Even Procopius' celebratory account seems to depict Belisarius' swift success as fortuitous. The Italian expedition, which followed up this success, seems to have been a much more modest affair: only 7,000 troops were involved, compared to the 6,000 sent with Narses in the same year to Alexandria, to protect the monophysite patriarch Theodosius (535–6). At this stage it would seem that the expedition was little more than a matter of showing the flag, even if its early successes, following so closely on the victory over the Vandals, conjured up in Justinian's mind ideas of a grand design, as witness the *novellae* of the period. In reality, the reconquest of Italy proved to be a long-drawn-out affair, during which Italy itself was devastated.[13] By 554, however, when Italy was formally restored to Byzantine rule (by a 'pragmatic sanction'),

---

[12] See below, p. 202; Barbero and Loring (2005), pp. 182–3.   [13] See below, pp. 205–9.

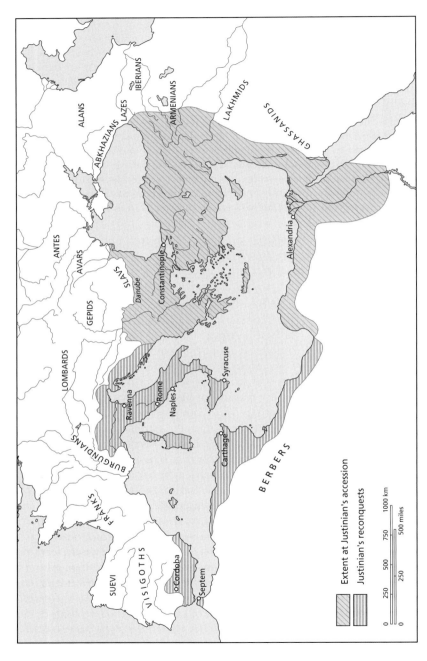

Map 5 East Rome into west: Justinian's expansion of imperial borders, and neighbouring peoples

ALANS

ABKHAZIANS
LAZES
IBERIANS
ARMENIANS
LAKHMIDS
GHASSANIDS

ANTES

AVARS

SLAVS

Danube

Constantinople

GEPIDS

Alexandria

LOMBARDS

Syracuse

Ravenna
Rome
Naples

BURGUNDIANS

Carthage

BERBERS

FRANKS

SUEVI

VISIGOTHS

Córdoba
Septem

Extent at Justinian's accession

Justinian's reconquests

0   250   500   750   1000 km

0   250   500 miles

most of the Mediterranean littoral belonged to the Roman empire once more.

Justinian's rebuilding programmes likewise fit uneasily into the idea of a grand design. Our principal source for Justinian's extensive building activity is Procopius' *Buildings*, which takes the form of a panegyric and consequently presents the fullest and most splendid account, drawing no distinction between new building work, restoration or even routine maintenance. As we saw earlier, the building of fortresses along the frontier, along the Danube and in Mesopotamia, to which Procopius devotes so much space, should not all be attributed to Justinian himself: as archaeological surveys have shown (and indeed other contemporary historians assert, even Procopius himself in his *Wars*),[14] much of this was begun by Anastasius. And the great wonders with which Procopius begins his account, when describing the reconstruction of the centre of Constantinople, were consequent upon the devastation wrought by the Nika riot of 532, which Justinian can hardly have planned. But however fortuitous the occasion, the buildings erected in the wake of the riot are works of enduring magnificence, none more so than the church of the Holy Wisdom, St Sophia. Contemporary accounts are breathtaking. Procopius says:

The church has become a spectacle of marvellous beauty, overwhelming to those who see it, but to those who know it by hearsay altogether incredible. For it soars to a height to match the sky, and as if surging up from amongst the other buildings it stands on high and looks down on the remainder of the city, adorning it, because it is a part of it, but glorying in its own beauty, because, though a part of the city and dominating it, it at the same time towers above it to such a height that the whole city is viewed from there as from a watch-tower.

He speaks too 'of the huge spherical dome which makes the structure exceptionally beautiful. Yet it seems not to rest on solid masonry, but to cover the space with its golden dome suspended from heaven.' Contemporaries were struck by the quality of light in the Great Church: 'it abounds exceedingly in sunlight and in the reflection of the sun's rays from the marble. Indeed one might say that its interior is not illuminated from without by the sun, but that the radiance comes into being within it, such an abundance of light bathes the shrine.'[15] Paul the Silentiary, speaking of the church restored after the collapse of the dome in 558, says 'even so in the evening men are delighted at the various shafts of light of the radiant, light-bringing house of resplendent choirs. And the calm clear sky of joy lies open to all driving away the dark-veiled mist of the soul. A holy light illuminates all.'[16] This

---

[14] See Cameron, Averil (1985), pp. 104–10.
[15] Pr *B*, I.1.27, 45–6, 29–30, tr. Dewing and Downey, pp. 12–13, 20–1, 16–17.
[16] Paul the Silentiary, *St Sophia*, ll. 902–6, ed. Friedländer, p. 252; tr. Trypanis, p. 418.

Figure 3 The interior of St Sophia, Constantinople

stress on light as an analogy of divinity chimes in well with the vision found in the writings ascribed to Dionysius the Areopagite (commonly known as Pseudo-Dionysius); a fact surely with bearing on the huge popularity these writings were soon to assume.

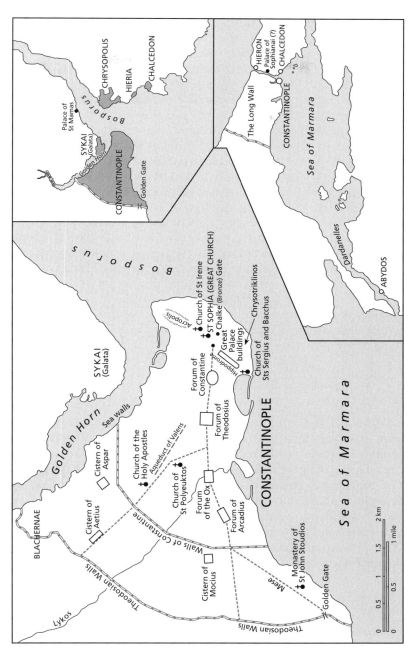

Map 6 Constantinople in the earlier Byzantine period

The novel design of the church, with its dome forming an image of the cosmos, was immensely influential: there are many smaller Byzantine imitations of St Sophia, and the suggestion of the church as a *mimēsis* of the cosmos influenced later interpretations of the liturgical action taking place within (see the *Mystagogia* of the seventh-century Maximus the Confessor and the commentary on the liturgy ascribed to the eighth-century patriarch of Constantinople, Germanos).[17] But it may not have been novel: recent excavations in Istanbul have revealed the church of St Polyeuktos, built by the noblewoman Anicia Juliana in the late 520s, which seems in many respects to have foreshadowed Justinian's Great Church.[18] Original or not, St Sophia and Justinian's other buildings in the capital created a public space in which to celebrate a world-view in which the emperor ruled the inhabited world (the *oikoumenē*), with the support of the court, the prayers of the church and to the acclamation of the people. These buildings included more churches, the restored palace (in front of which, in a kind of piazza, was erected a massive pillar surmounted by a bronze statue of an equestrian Justinian), an orphanage, a home for repentant prostitutes, baths and, finally, a great cistern to secure an adequate water supply in summer. According to Procopius' description of the mosaic in the great Bronze Gate forming the entrance to the palace, there, amid depictions of Justinian's victories achieved by his general Belisarius, stood Justinian and Theodora, receiving from the senate 'honours equal to those of God'.[19]

JUSTINIAN'S DRIVE AGAINST PAGANS AND QUEST FOR CHRISTIAN UNITY

The world-view that Justinian's achievements – whether part of a grand plan or not – were seen to support set great store by an unblemished priesthood offering pure prayer to the true God, the God of the Christians. Unlike other religions of late antiquity – whether the varieties of what Christians called paganism, Judaism, or even (although yet to evolve) Islam – for Christianity, 'purity' or being 'unblemished', embraced not just moral (and especially sexual) purity, but also the correctness of a considerably elaborated system of belief. For most Christians of the sixth century, this system of belief had been defined at councils regarded as universal, or ecumenical, although there were differences, as we have seen, as to whether the council

---

[17] *Mystagogia* in Maximus the Confessor, *Opera, PG* 91, cols. 657–717. The text of Germanos' commentary in *PG* 98, cols. 384–453, is poor, but Meyendorff offers a critical edition with translation: Meyendorff, *On the divine liturgy*, pp. 56–107.

[18] See Harrison (1989).

[19] Pr *B*, I.10.15–19, ed. and tr. Dewing and Downey, pp. 84–7. Rousseau detects irony in Procopius' account here: Rousseau (1996), p. 19.

of Chalcedon was to be regarded as the fourth ecumenical council. Emperor Justin's embrace of Chalcedonian orthodoxy had healed the long-standing schism between the east and Rome, but left unresolved the disagreement between those who accepted Chalcedon (with whatever refinements) and those who rejected it as a betrayal of Cyril of Alexandria, the 'seal of the fathers'.

But all Christians, whatever their differences, were opposed to what they had come to call the 'exterior wisdom', the learning of the classical philosophers. As Romanus the Melodist, the Christian poet who spent most of his life in Constantinople during Justinian's reign, put it:

> And why do the fools outside strive for victory?
> Why do the Greeks puff and buzz?
> Why are they deceived by Aratos the thrice accursed? Why err like
>   wandering planets to Plato?
> Why do they love the debilitated Demosthenes?
> Why do they not consider Homer a chimera?
> Why do they go on about Pythagoras, who were better muzzled?[20]

This antipathy had been returned in kind, and some adherents of Neo-platonism, loftily indifferent to the new-fangled teachings of the 'pale Galilean', developed a world-view that openly ignored Christianity and through their religious practices sought to revive traditional paganism. A notable Neoplatonist was the deeply learned philosopher Proclus, who lived the life of an ascetic, pagan holy man, with an especial devotion to the sun. For fifty years, until his death in 485, he taught in Athens as head (*diadochos*) of the Academy that had been founded by Plato in the fourth century BC. Part of Justinian's commitment to Christian orthodoxy was expressed in his closing of the Academy in 529. The closure, however, did not take place before much of the pagan language and intellectual structures had found Christian expression in the writings ascribed to St Paul's Athenian disciple, Dionysius the Areopagite; these began to make an impact in the 520s, very shortly, it is thought, after they had been written. The philosophers made their way to Persia in 532, led by Damascius the last *diadochos*; but they returned after a few years, Damascius going to Emesa where he seems to have continued to teach.[21] Neoplatonism continued to thrive in Alexandria for another century, where it was not stridently anti-Christian. Indeed most, if not all, of the Alexandrian philosophers were Christian. But the closure of the Academy meant the end of any institutional expression of intellectual opinion.

---

[20] *Kontakion* 33 ('On Pentecost'), stanza 17: Romanus the Melodist, *Cantica*, ed. Maas and Trypanis, p. 265; *Kontakia*, tr. Lash, p. 215 (the Greek original is full of untranslatable puns).
[21] Cameron, Alan (1969).

Alongside the suppression of pagan Neoplatonism, there was suppression of other forms of heterodoxy. In various parts of the empire we learn of more vigorous attempts to suppress survivals of traditional paganism.[22] In the 540s, the monophysite bishop John of Ephesus embarked on a missionary campaign in western Asia Minor with imperial support. He claimed to have converted 70,000 souls there, destroying many temples and founding ninety-six churches and twelve monasteries. In Egypt, too, we know of the destruction of temples. Other forms of heterodox opinion fared no better. The dualist doctrine Manichaeism, whose founder Mani had died in Persia in 276, dogged the Christian church through its years of growing success and was an offence punishable by death. The Samaritans embraced what was perhaps a primitive form of Judaism; their revolt against repression was savagely suppressed in 529. Ancient Christian heresies like Montanism also suffered repression under Justinian. The monophysites, who were both more numerous and closer in belief to the imperial church, are a special case to be dealt with presently.

The Jews formed a relatively privileged group of second-class citizens. In contrast to heretics and pagans, who had no rights and no civil status, Jews were allowed to exist and their existence was protected. Jews were allowed to practise circumcision and to observe the Sabbath; their synagogues were protected from violence or desecration, although not always effectively; they kept their Rabbinic courts of law and were not to be molested. But they were to exist as 'living testimony' to the truth of Christianity, living testimony to the wretchedness of those who had deliberately rejected their Messiah. So the laws protecting their existence also enshrined the principle that Jews must never enjoy the fruits of office, but only suffer its pains and penalties. They were not to expand, so no new synagogues were to be built, and difficulties were often raised over repairing existing ones. The Jews were to be encouraged to convert, but it was to be from a genuine change of heart; they were not to be coerced. They were thus allowed to exist, with rights and civil status, but in a permanently inferior state.[23]

In the 530s, in parallel with the furthering of legal reform, *reconquista* and rebuilding, Justinian sought to achieve a reconciliation between orthodox Chalcedonianism and monophysite anti-Chalcedonianism. The basis for this reconciliation was the doctrine of theopaschism. Brought to Justinian's attention by the Scythian monks a decade or so earlier, this was now part of a wider theological movement usually known as neo-Chalcedonianism, or Cyrilline Chalcedonianism – after Cyril of Alexandria. This theological movement, which was quite independent of Justinian, seems to

---

[22] It is probably misleading to regard as paganism the continuation of traditional religious practices by people who supposed themselves Christians: see Haldon (1997a), pp. 327–37, with literature cited.
[23] Sharf (1971), pp. 19–41.

have been inspired by attempts to counter the attack by the great non-Chalcedonian theologian Severus, patriarch of Antioch (512–18), on the definition of Chalcedon as being incompatible with the teaching of Cyril. Those eastern Christians who had accepted Chalcedon were by no means a minority and did so believing that it endorsed Cyril's teaching. Cyrilline Chalcedonianism sought to interpret Chalcedon in the light of Cyril's teaching, believing (not unreasonably) that this represented the mind of the fathers of the council. It was based on three clarifications of the council's definition: first, that the 'one person' of the Incarnate Christ is the second person of the Trinity; second, consequent acceptance of the theopaschite formula 'one of the Trinity suffered in the flesh'; and third, agreement that one of Cyril's favourite ways of describing the Incarnate Christ ('one incarnate nature of God the Word') was acceptable and only verbally appeared to contradict the doctrine of one person and two natures. This phrase is the source of the term by which the non-Chalcedonians have come to be called: monophysites, believers in (only) one nature. Notable adherents of Cyrilline Chalcedonianism included John of Caesarea and Leontius of Jerusalem. Justinian was convinced that this provided a way of reconciliation and at a conference held in Constantinople in 532, a large measure of theological agreement was reached; however, discussions faltered over practical arrangements for reinstating non-Chalcedonian bishops.[24] Thereafter Justinian resorted to persecution, thwarted by the protection given to the monophysites in the palace itself by Theodora. But he never gave up his attempt to promote Cyrilline Chalcedonianism, which culminated in the fifth ecumenical council, held in Constantinople in 553.

The fifth ecumenical council was concerned with two issues: the condemnation of the so-called Three Chapters, and the condemnation of Origenism.[25] The condemnation of the Three Chapters was part of Justinian's attempt to achieve reconciliation between the orthodox and the monophysites, for they were the writings of three bishops who were particularly obnoxious to the monophysites: Theodoret of Cyrrhus; Ibas of Edessa; and Theodore of Mopsuestia, who died in 428. Theodore was regarded as the inspiration behind Nestorius, patriarch of Constantinople (428–31). The emphasis in his teaching about Christ on the separate integrity of his two natures, divine and human, and especially his consequent denial (or at least heavy qualification) of the title *Theotokos* ('Mother of God') of the

<hr />

[24] Brock (1980).
[25] Because of the silence of western sources about the condemnation of Origenism (including, crucially, the council's *Acta*, which only survive in Latin (tr. in *Nicene*, ed. Wace and Schaff, XIV, pp. 302–16)), some scholars still maintain that Origenism was not dealt with at the council. The arguments of Guillaumont (1962), pp. 133–6, however, seem conclusive. On the western reaction, see also below, p. 213.

Virgin Mary, had provoked the wrath of Cyril of Alexandria, who secured his condemnation at the third ecumenical council, held at Ephesus in 431. Theodoret and Ibas had been condemned at the 'robber council' of Ephesus of 449, but reinstated two years later by the council of Chalcedon. There was considerable resistance to the condemnation of the Three Chapters in the west, where it was regarded as an attempt to interfere with Chalcedon, Pope Leo's council. Pope Vigilius was forcibly summoned to attend the council called by Justinian in Constantinople, where he was held under house arrest until he accepted the condemnation of the Three Chapters, and his successors were required to accept his action, although Pope Gregory the Great only ever speaks of 'four councils'. But others in the west were not so pliant: the pope was excommunicated by bishops in North Africa and northern Italy, and the schism between Rome and Aquileia was not healed until 700.

The condemnation of Origenism has often been regarded as a counterbalance to the condemnation of the Three Chapters, but there seems no reason to accept this. There was nothing monophysite about Origenism: its condemnation really belongs with Justinian's attack on pagan Neoplatonism, for Origen and the Origenists were regarded as deeply indebted to Platonism. Indeed, Origen had been a disciple of Ammonias Saccas, the master of Plotinus. For this reason, it was an action for which Justinian could count on the applause of most Christians, despite Origenist ideas remaining popular among some more intellectually inclined monks.

All these attempts to achieve reconciliation amongst the Christians of the empire achieved nothing. By the time the fifth ecumenical council met, the schism had already become irrevocable. Some ten years earlier, in 542, Theodosius, the exiled monophysite patriarch of Alexandria, had secretly consecrated Jacob Baradaeus in Constantinople as bishop of Edessa; Jacob was responsible for the Ghassanids, an Arab realm allied to the empire (see below, p. 188). Once ordained, he set about ordaining bishops for monophysite congregations throughout the east, thus providing a parallel hierarchy to that of the orthodox church of the empire. Imperial attempts to crush this rival church through persecution met with little success.

On the face of it, Justinian's religious policies look to be a downright failure. This is true, if his endeavours are simply regarded as attempts at healing the schism in the church, especially in the east. But these endeavours can be viewed from another perspective: that of leaving the emperor's mark on the orthodox church of the empire. From this perspective his success was real. The reception of the council of Chalcedon in the sixth century took place along the lines that Justinian promoted: the Christology of the council was henceforth to be interpreted in the east along the lines of Cyrilline Chalcedonianism, and a theopaschite understanding of the Incarnation became accepted, with implications beyond the narrowly theological. By the ninth century the hymn 'Only-begotten Son', ascribed to Justinian, formed a regular part of the eucharistic liturgy. Whether or not the literary composition was Justinian's, the theopaschite theology of the hymn is certainly his ('you were crucified, Christ God . . . being One of the Holy Trinity'), and such theopaschite devotion, flanked by the development of angelology and Mariology, found expression in the flourishing iconographic tradition of the eastern church.

The answer to the first of the questions raised earlier about understanding Justinian's reign in terms of a grand design would seem to be negative, although in the first decade of his sole rule Justinian may have entertained some such idea. But when we consider the second question – whether Justinian had the means to implement a grand design – even had its components fitted together as well as has often been maintained (legal reform, reconquest, rebuilding and the furthering of orthodoxy), there are other factors in Justinian's reign that would have prevented any such grand design from reaching fruition.

ENEMIES OF JUSTINIAN AND OTHER BLOWS

One of the obstacles to any grand design was the Persians, traditional enemies of the Roman empire. After a period of peace in the latter half of the fifth century, war had broken out again in the reign of Anastasius. This led to the building of the fort at Dara shortly after 505 (see above, pp. 104–5 and below, p. 135). It was twenty years before war broke out again between the Roman and Persian empires, partly over Justinian's decision to reinforce the fort at Dara. The initial battles took place in Lazica, an important buffer zone for the Romans, both against the barbarians north of the Caucasus and against a Persian advance through Iberia. One of the Persian generals on this occasion, Narses, defected to the Romans after having inflicted defeat on them. But the main part of Justinian's first Persian war took place in Mesopotamia, and this was the theatre in which another of Justinian's generals, Belisarius, rose to prominence. The Romans held their ground, and the war was concluded with a 'perpetual peace', negotiated with Khusro I (531–79), who had become shah after the death of his aged father on 13 September 531. This peace gave Justinian the resources for the North African and Italian campaigns of the 530s.

Khusro would reign for nearly fifty years and in Persian historiography he is depicted as one of the greatest of the Sasanian shahs.[26] But the 'perpetual peace' negotiated at the beginning of Khusro's reign was not typical of his relations with his western neighbour. In 540 a territorial dispute between two Christian Arab kingdoms, the Nestorian Lakhmids, clients of Persia,

---

[26] See Frye (1983a); see also below, pp. 149–51.

and the monophysite Ghassanids, clients of the Roman empire, provided an opportunity for Khusro to respond to pleas from Witigis, the hard-pressed Ostrogothic king of Italy, and from the Armenians, suffering from their incorporation into the Roman empire through the 'perpetual peace': Khusro invaded the empire. The war was fought on several fronts – in Syria, Mesopotamia and Lazica – and Antioch was seized by the Persians. A truce was called in 545, but fighting went on in Lazica until 557. In 561 a fifty-year peace was negotiated, restoring the status quo; the Romans agreed to pay tribute at the rate of 30,000 *solidi* a year for the whole period.[27] Persia was once again a force to reckon with, and would remain so, until it succumbed to the Arabs in the seventh century, together with much of the Roman empire itself.

Persia was clearly one obstacle standing in the way of any initiatives undertaken by Justinian. Another constraint on his plans, much harder to assess, is the effect of natural disasters and climate change. The chronicles paint a vivid picture of recurrent earthquake, famine and plague, as well as events recorded as harbingers of disaster, such as eclipses and comets. Malalas, for instance, records ten examples of Justinian making grants for the reconstruction of cities devastated by war or natural disaster.[28] Collation of scientific with literary studies suggests that the early years of Justinian's reign saw extreme climatic conditions,[29] whose cause is not yet determined; the years 536–7 saw what is called a 'dust-veil event', recorded in the chron-icles as a kind of perpetual solar eclipse. One can only speculate about the impact of such phenomena, but it is hard not to think that they led to the disruption of traditional patterns and a growing sense of insecu-rity, not to mention a drain on finite resources caused by the need for reconstruction.

It was in this context that the Nika riot of 532 occurred. Tension between the circus factions, the Blues and the Greens, erupted spectacularly: Jus-tinian was nearly toppled, and much of the palace area, including the churches of St Sophia and St Irene, was destroyed by fire. Popular anger against hate-figures was appeased by the dismissal of the City prefect Eudae-mon, the *quaestor* Tribonian, and the praetorian prefect John of Cappado-cia. The riot continued for several days and was only eventually quelled by the massacre of 30,000 people, trapped in the Hippodrome, acclaim-ing as emperor the unfortunate Hypatius, a general and one of Emperor Anastasius' nephews. Afterwards Hypatius was executed as a usurper.

The reaction of some Christians to the whole sequence of disasters is cap-tured in the *kontakion* 'On earthquakes and fires', composed by Romanus the Melodist. Romanus wrote and performed this *kontakion* one Lent while

---

[27] Men., 6.1, pp. 60–3, 70–5.   [28] Scott (1996), p. 25, n. 37.
[29] Farquharson (1996); Koder (1996); Stathakopoulos (2004), pp. 265–9. See also below, pp. 478–9.

Figure 4 Pedestal commissioned for an Egyptian obelisk by Emperor Theodosius I (379–95) in the centre of the Hippodrome of Constantinople, showing the emperor with his family and dignitaries, seated in higher places than the common people, waiting for the start of a race; seating plan and ceremonial were similar in middle Byzantium

the Great Church of St Sophia was being rebuilt (i.e. between February 532 and 27 December 537). It is a call to repentance after three disasters that represent three 'blows' by God against sinful humanity: earthquakes (several are recorded in Constantinople and elsewhere between 526 and 530), drought (recorded in Constantinople in September 530), and finally the Nika riot itself in January 532.[30] These repeated blows were necessary because of the people's heedlessness. Repentance and pleas for mercy begin, Romanus makes clear, with the emperor and his consort, Theodora:

> Those who feared God stretched out their hands to Him,
> Beseeching Him for mercy and the end of disasters,
> And along with them, as was fitting, the ruler prayed too,
> Looking up to the Creator, and with him his wife,
> 'Grant to me, Saviour,' he cried, 'as to your David
> To conquer Goliath, for I hope in you.
> Save your faithful people in your mercy,
> And grant to them
> Eternal life.'

[30] For this analysis see Koder (1996), pp. 275–6.

When God heard the sound of those who cried out and also of the rulers,
He granted his tender pity to the city . . .[31]

The rebuilt city, and especially the Great Church, is a sign of both the care
of the emperor and the mercy of God:

In a short time they [the rulers] raised up the whole city
So that all the hardships of those who had suffered were forgotten.
The very structure of the church
Was erected with such excellence
As to imitate heaven, the divine throne,
Which indeed offers
Eternal life.[32]

This confirms the picture of recurrent adversity, found in the chroniclers
and, it is argued, supported by astronomical and archaeological evidence.
But it also indicates the way in which religion attempted to meet the needs
of those who suffered – a way that evoked and reinforced the Byzantine
world-view of a cosmos ruled by God, and the *oikoumenē* ruled, on God's
behalf, by the emperor. But a study of Romanus' *kontakia* also reveals the
convergence of the public and imperial apparatus of religion, and private
recourse to the Incarnate Christ, the Mother of God and the saints; it
also reveals the importance of relics of the True Cross and of the saints as
touchstones of divine grace. It is in the sixth century, too, that we begin
to find increasing evidence of the popularity at both public and private
levels of devotion to the Mother of God, and of religious art – icons – as
mediating between the divine realm, consisting of God and his court of
angels and saints, and the human realm, desperately in need of the grace
which flows from that divine realm; icons become both objects of prayer
and veneration, and a physical source of healing and reassurance.

But if the 530s saw widespread alarm caused by natural and human disasters, the 540s saw the beginning of an epidemic of bubonic plague that
was to last rather more than two centuries. According to Procopius it originated in Egypt, but it seems very likely that it travelled from the east along
trade routes, perhaps the silk roads. Plague appeared in Constantinople in
spring 542 and had reached Antioch and Syria later in the same year. Huge
numbers died: in Constantinople, it has been calculated, around 250,000
people died, perhaps a little over half the population. Few who caught the
disease survived (one such being, apparently, Justinian himself); those who
died did so quickly, within two or three days. Thereafter the plague seems to
have declined somewhat in virulence, but according to the church historian

---

[31] *Kontakion* 54 ('On earthquakes and fires'), stanzas 18–19: Romanus the Melodist, *Cantica*, ed.
Maas and Trypanis, pp. 468–9; see also tr. Carpenter, II, pp. 245–6.
[32] *Kontakion* 54 ('On earthquakes and fires'), stanza 23: Romanus the Melodist, *Cantica*, ed. Maas
and Trypanis, pp. 470–1; see also tr. Carpenter, II, p. 247.

Evagrius Scholasticus, there was severe loss of life in the years 553–4, 568–9 and 583–4. Historians disagree about the probable effect of the plague on the economic life of the eastern empire: some take its impact seriously;[33] others, following a similar revision in the estimate of the effects of the Black Death in the fourteenth century,[34] think that the effect of the plague has been exaggerated.[35]

In the final months of his life, Justinian himself succumbed to heresy, the so-called Julianist heresy of aphthartodocetism, an extreme form of monophysitism named after Julian, bishop of Halicarnassus who died *c.* 527, and which Justinian promulgated by an edict. This is recounted both by Theophanes and by Eustratius, in his *Life* of Eutychius, patriarch of Constantinople, who was deposed for refusing to accept Justinian's newly found religious inclination, and has been generally accepted by historians. However, it has been questioned by theologians, who cite evidence for Justinian's continued adherence to a Christology of two natures, together with evidence that he was still seeking reconciliation between divided Christians: not only with the Julianists themselves, which might indeed have led to orthodox suspicion of Julianism on Justinian's part, but also with the so-called Nestorians of Persia. The question is complex, but seems to be open.[36]

JUSTINIAN'S HEIRS COPE WITH HIS LEGACY

Justinian died childless on 14 November 565. The succession had been left open. One of his three nephews, called Justin, secured election by the senate and succeeded his uncle; he had long occupied the minor post of *cura palatii* but he was, perhaps more significantly, married to Sophia, one of Theodora's nieces. The only serious contender was a second cousin of Justinian's, also called Justin: one of the *magistri militum*, he was despatched to Alexandria and murdered, reportedly at the instigation of Sophia. Justin II (565–78) continued, or reinstated, Justinian's policy of religious orthodoxy, though he – or at least his wife, Sophia – had earlier inclined towards monophysitism. In renewing his uncle's religious policy, Justin restored religious harmony between east and west, and he affirmed this shared orthodoxy by a gift to the Frankish queen Radegund of a splendid enamelled crucifix containing a relic of the True Cross. This inspired the greatest Latin hymns in honour of the cross, Venantius Fortunatus' *Pange lingua* and *Vexilla regis*. But at the same time Justin sought reconciliation with the monophysites. This attempt at reconciliation ended in 572, with the monophysites' rejection of Justin's so-called second *Henotikon*; this rejection resulted in the

[33] Patlagean (1977); Allen (1979).   [34] See for example Hatcher (1994).
[35] Whittow (1996a), pp. 66–8. See also Stathakopoulos (2004), pp. 277–94. On the mid-eighth-century plague, see below, pp. 255, 260.
[36] See discussion in Grillmeier (1976–96), II.2, pp. 467–73.

persecution of the monophysites which John of Ephesus recorded in his *Church history*.[37]

But Justin is remembered chiefly for his ill-advised foreign policy: by refusing to maintain alliances with barbarian tribes, not least the Avars, or to preserve peace with Persia, he gravely weakened the empire's position. Throughout the century, the Romans had been concerned for the security of the Danube frontier. Both Anastasius and Justinian had invested a good deal in building a line of forts and fortifying cities close to the frontier. In addition to this, Justinian had established alliances with various of the barbarian groupings – the Antes around 545 and the Avars in 558 – and had used them to check other barbarian peoples north of the Danube. Another set of barbarians, which proved a constant concern, was the Slavs: by the middle of the sixth century they were established along the north bank of the Danube, from where they made raids across the river into Byzantine territory, and from around 560 they began to winter on Byzantine territory. Within a few days of Justin's accession, an embassy arrived from the Avars, requesting the tribute they had been accustomed to receive from Justinian in return, they claimed, for not invading the empire and even for defending it against other barbarians. Justin haughtily rebuffed them, but since the Avars were more concerned with the Franks at this stage, Justin's action provoked no immediate response.

Two years later, Justin was able to benefit from war between the barbarians. When the Lombards and the Avars formed an alliance to crush the Gepids, another barbarian group who occupied Pannonia Secunda and held the city of Sirmium, he was able to seize Sirmium, and held on to it during the war with the Avars that followed. The fall of the Gepids had further consequences for the empire, as the Lombards, who were occupying the borders of Noricum, now had the Avars as immediate neighbours. To avoid this they headed south and invaded northern Italy, with which many of them were familiar, having served there as allies of Narses in 552.[38] Under their king, Alboin, the Lombards took most of Venetia in 568 and most of Liguria in the following year, including Milan; Pavia offered more resistance but it, too, fell in 572. Elsewhere barbarians made inroads. Moorish revolts in North Africa caused the death of a praetorian prefect in 569 and two *magistri militum* in the next couple of years. In Spain, the Visigoths attacked the Byzantines, taking Asidona in 571 and Cordoba in 572.[39]

It would therefore seem that 572 was not a propitious year in which to provoke the Persians. However, that was the year when Justin refused the first annual tribute under the fifty-year peace negotiated by Justinian, having evidently paid the three-year tribute due in 569. The Christians

---

[37] On this see Cameron, Averil (1976).   [38] See below, p. 208.
[39] See Barbero and Loring (2005), p. 183.

of Persian Armenia had risen in revolt against their governor's (*marzban*) attempts to impose Zoroastrianism on them and appealed to Justin. Justin not only refused the tribute due in 572, but also threatened to invade Persia and depose Khusro if attempts to turn the Armenians from Christianity persisted. The Armenian revolt was successful, and they were joined by the Iberian kingdom. Justin ordered an invasion of Persia. His cousin Marcian, appointed *magister militum per Orientem* in 572, attacked Arzanene on the southern border of Persian Armenia, and the next year attacked Nisibis. The Persian response, once they had overcome their surprise at the Roman attack, was devastating: they invaded Syria and took Apamea, then relieved Nisibis before besieging and capturing the fortress of Dara.

News of the fall of Dara drove Justin mad, and his consort Sophia took the reins of power. She negotiated a one-year truce with the Persians for which the Romans paid 45,000 *solidi*, half as much again as had been due; this was later extended to five years, at the old rate of 30,000 *solidi* a year. But as a woman, Sophia could not rule as regent herself, and in December 574 she persuaded Justin to promote Tiberius, the count of the excubitors, to the dignity of caesar. Although Justin lived on until 578, government was effectively in the hands of Sophia and Tiberius. Sophia is, in fact, a somewhat neglected Byzantine empress. Though far less famous than her aunt, unlike Theodora she played a direct role in Byzantine politics, securing the succession both of her husband and of Tiberius II (578–82), whom she vainly hoped to make her second husband. She is the first empress to appear on Byzantine coins together with her husband.[40] Theophanes the Confessor, who clearly disliked women with pretensions to power, paints an ugly picture of Sophia and her meddling in imperial matters, as he did of Irene, the first Byzantine empress to rule in her own name. It may be significant that he has comparatively little to say about Theodora.

Tiberius became emperor in 578, but by then had already effectively been governing for four years. In many respects he was the opposite of his predecessor: whereas Justin was financially cautious to the point of being regarded as miserly, but militarily ambitious, Tiberius bought popularity by reducing taxes, but in military matters exercised caution. He also called a halt to the persecution of the monophysites, on which Justin had embarked. Tiberius quickly realised that the empire did not have the resources to engage with its enemies on all fronts. He thus secured the support of the Avars on the Danube frontier by paying them tribute of 80,000 *solidi* a year. This gained not just a respite from hostilities, but Avar support against the Slavs: with Byzantine backing, the Avar cavalry devastated the Slavs' territories on the banks of the Danube. However, this truce with the Avars did not last long. In 580 they attacked Sirmium, and after a lengthy siege

---

[40] For Sophia, see Cameron, Averil (1975).

the city was ceded to the Avars in 582 under an agreement which allowed the garrison and population to withdraw to Roman territory in return for 240,000 *solidi*, the sum total of the tribute not paid since the Avar attack. During the siege of Sirmium many Slavs crossed the Danube and invaded Thrace, Macedonia and what is now Greece: they would eventually settle throughout the Balkans, although there is no evidence for Slav settlements (called *Sklaviniai* by the Byzantines) until the next century.[41]

The attempt to buy off the Avars and secure peace on the Danube frontier was to enable Tiberius to concentrate on the Persian frontier, where his aims seem likewise to have been modest: building up enough strength to re-establish the peace that had been broken by Justin. The one-year truce negotiated by Sophia needed to be extended, but the five-year truce that had later been negotiated seemed to Tiberius too long. On his accession as caesar this truce was set at three years, on the understanding that in the meantime envoys would seek to establish a more enduring peace. At the end of the extended truce, the Byzantine army in the east was in a position to make inroads on the Persians, and had occupied Arzanene; the army was led by Maurice, who had succeeded Tiberius as count of the excubitors on Tiberius' elevation to caesar. Negotiations were underway for a peace that would restore the fortress of Dara to the Byzantines, but in the course of these negotiations – in 579 – Khusro died. His son Hormizd IV (579–90), who succeeded him, broke off negotiations, and war continued. In August 582 Tiberius himself died, having crowned Maurice *augustus* the previous day.

Maurice (582–602) was an effective general, who had already achieved military success under Tiberius before becoming emperor himself. Even if he is not the author of the military treatise called the *Strategikon*, such an attribution is not inappropriate. The treatise certainly reflects late sixth-century Byzantine military practice, with its stress on the importance of cavalry in warfare and provision for campaigning across the Danube.[42] Like his predecessor, Maurice initially concentrated his military efforts on the Persian front, and sought to deal with the other threats to the empire by diplomacy and tribute. At the beginning of his reign he paid the Frankish king Childebert II (575–95) to attack the Lombards in northern Italy, which he did in 584, securing the submission of the Lombard dukes. This was repeated in 588 and 589. Maurice had less success on the Danube frontier. Two years after his accession, the Avars demanded an increase in their tribute from 80,000 to 100,000 *solidi*, and when Maurice refused, they seized Belgrade (then known as Singidunum) and attacked other cities in

[41] See also, on the Slavs' numbers, Curta (2001a).
[42] Maurice, *Strategikon*, II, III, IX, XI.4, ed. Dennis and German tr. Gamillscheg, pp. 108–91, 302–35, 370–89; tr. Dennis, pp. 23–51, 93–105, 120–6. See also Haldon (1999a), pp. 139–40, 195–203.

the surrounding region. Maurice had to pay the extra 20,000 *solidi* in order to recover Belgrade and secure peace. But the Avars soon allowed the Slavs to overrun and ravage Thrace; the Slavs reached Adrianople and the Long Wall before they were driven back. After that, the Avars themselves crossed the Danube and made for Constantinople. Having easily defeated a Byzantine force of 10,000 sent against them, the Avars crossed the Haemus mountains, invaded Thrace and besieged Adrianople; they were only defeated in 586 by Droctulft, a Lombard duke, who came to the service of the empire. In the same year Thessalonica was besieged by the Slavs and was only saved, so its citizens believed, by the intervention of their patron saint Demetrius.[43]

On the Persian front the war dragged on inconclusively. There was a mutiny in the army when Maurice attempted to cut pay by a quarter, to alleviate the drain on the treasury, and Martyropolis, in Arzanene, was taken by the Persians in 590. Soon, however, there was a dramatic change of fortune. The Persian shah, Hormizd IV (579–90), was killed in a rebellion led by one of his satraps, Bahram. His son Khusro fled to the Byzantines and with their help in 591 crushed Bahram's rebellion and secured the Persian throne. In return for the help of the Byzantine emperor, Khusro II (590–628) gave up his claim to Armenia and Arzanene, and restored Martyropolis and Dara to the empire (see below, pp. 169, 337). After twenty years, there was once again peace between the Byzantine and Persian empires. Maurice now turned his attention to the Danube frontier. In 592 the khagan of the Avars demanded an increase in the tribute paid him. With his troops transferred from the now quiet eastern front, Maurice responded by confronting the Avars, who were obliged to abandon their attempt to occupy Belgrade. This did not stop them from invading Thrace, but they left abruptly under the impression that their homeland in Pannonia was in danger.[44]

However, the real object of Maurice's military policy seems to have been the Slavs: in the interests both of preserving resources and of effective military strategy, Maurice ordered the Byzantine troops to engage with the Slavs in their settlements beyond the Danube. The army, accustomed to rest during winter, threatened to mutiny. The next year another measure was introduced, aimed at increasing efficiency and saving money: instead of receiving cash allowances for their military equipment, they were to be issued with it directly. This was deeply unpopular. The Avars made further attacks, being rebuffed in their attack on Belgrade and Dalmatia in 598,

---

[43] Lemerle (ed.), *Miracles de saint Démétrius*, I, pp. 130–65; on St Demetrius, see also below, pp. 856–7. On the emergence of the Slavs in the Byzantine sources, see Kobylinski (2005); Curta (2001a).

[44] Theophylact presents this as a cunning Byzantine ruse, but the twelfth-century Syriac chronicler Michael the Syrian invokes fear that the Turks were threatening their homeland: see TS, VI.5.16, ed. de Boor and Wirth, p. 230; tr. Whitby and Whitby, p. 166 and n. 33; MS, X.21, ed. and French tr. Chabot, II, p. 363.

and failing to take Tomi on the west coast of the Black Sea in 599. Later they threatened Constantinople itself, but a bout of plague in the Avar camp led the khagan to withdraw and agree a treaty in which the Danube was recognised as the frontier. Maurice quickly revoked the treaty and in 600 the Byzantine army defeated the Avars. The next year was quiet, but in 602 the Byzantines made successful attacks on the Slavs north of the Danube. Maurice gave orders for a winter campaign in Slav territory. This time there was open mutiny: the commander of the army fled, and under a new commander called Phocas the troops advanced on Constantinople. Maurice, who had made himself unpopular with his economies, found himself defenceless in his capital. After a bungled attempt to seize his son's father-in-law, Germanus – to whom the troops had offered the crown – Maurice found himself facing a popular riot and the palace of the praetorian prefect of the east was burned down. Maurice fled, and Phocas was proclaimed emperor on 23 November 602. A few days later Maurice was executed, after his sons had been slain before his eyes. The death of Maurice and the accession of the usurper Phocas I (602–10) left the empire in a fragile state: civil war weakened the empire within, and external enemies took advantage of the weakness thus revealed. As the seventh century advanced matters looked very black indeed.

FIN DE SIÈCLE: FAITH, CITY AND EMPIRE

At the end of the sixth century the East Roman empire was, as we know with hindsight, on the brink of dramatic transformation: the rise of Arab power would rob it of its eastern and southern provinces; the settlement of the Slavs in the Balkan peninsula would deprive the eastern empire of those provinces and isolate New Rome from Old Rome; the last vestiges of a traditional city-based society seem to have crumbled in an empire now barely capable of defending its capital, or regenerating itself after natural disaster or epidemic. It is difficult not to see seeds of all this as we survey the history of the sixth century. The idea of an orthodox Christian empire did cause both divisions between Christians in the east, and tensions between the increasingly Greek Christianity of the empire and the Latin Christianity of Rome and the west; the public spaces of the city ceased to be used, and were left to decay or be encroached upon by more private activities.

Although all this is true, to think in terms of decline is to look at only part of the picture. The public life of the cities may have declined, but it yielded to the demands of the Christian church for space for its activities: increasingly the urban rituals that expressed such sense of civic identity as survived became Christian rituals. The church buildings themselves became increasingly important as public places and moved from the urban periphery to dominate the centre, while the episcopal offices grew in size, in parallel with the developing role of the bishop. The growth in devotion to icons, for which our evidence increases dramatically in the latter half of the sixth century, has been plausibly attributed to 'the continuing needs of the ancient city'.[45] Such Christianisation is neither a vampirish corollary of decline nor evidence of the success of Christian mission; it is rather evidence for change and needs to be evaluated on its own terms. What was taking place at the level of the city had a parallel in, and may have been inspired by, transformation of imperial ritual. In the latter part of the century, we see a growing tendency to underwrite the imperial structures of authority by appeal to Christian symbols: the court of the emperor is presented as reflecting the heavenly court, Constantine's *labarum* is joined by icons of Christ and His Virgin Mother.[46] While this transformed society may have come close to disaster in the seventh century, it contained seeds of survival and renewal. What survived was, however, a significantly different society from that of the Roman empire at the beginning of the sixth century.

[45] Brown, P. (1973), p. 21.
[46] For this interpretation see Cameron, Averil (1979a). See also Pentcheva (2002); Speck (2003c).

EASTERN NEIGHBOURS: PERSIA AND THE SASANIAN MONARCHY (224–651)

ZEEV RUBIN

ROMANS AND SASANIANS

A chapter dealing with Iranian feudalism in a distinguished series dedicated to *The rise and fall of the Roman world* bears the title 'Iran, Rome's greatest enemy.[1] This title is more than merely a justification for the inclusion of a chapter on Iran in a work devoted to the history of the East Roman empire. It also reflects a host of fears and prejudices fostered for long centuries in the Roman world, since the trauma of Crassus' defeat by the Parthians at Carrhae. Not even extended periods of decline and internal disarray within the Parthian monarchy, during which it was repeatedly invaded by the Roman army, could dispel the myth of the uncompromising threat posed by Iran to the Roman order. The replacement of the Parthian Arsacid dynasty by a vigorous new one, based in Fars, namely the Sasanian dynasty, at a time when the Roman empire itself was facing one of its severest crises, only aggravated its inhabitants' deeply rooted fear of Iran. Ancient writers in the Roman *oikoumenē* passed on this attitude to modern western scholars.[2]

It is the Sasanian bogeyman which has left a deep imprint in modern historiography. The Sasanian state is widely regarded as a much more centralised and effective political entity than its Parthian counterpart, with a far better army. The great pretensions and aspirations of its monarchs are believed to have been fed by the fervour of religious fanaticism, inspired by the Zoroastrian priesthood, which is commonly depicted as a well-organised state church. No wonder that such a state posed the gravest threat to its greatest rival – the other great power of late antiquity.[3] Each of these accepted beliefs raises a multitude of problems, and a fundamental revision is called for. Only a few of the more salient points can be dealt with here.

---

[1] 'Iran, der grosse Gegner Roms': Widengren (1976).

[2] Widengren (1976). In general, see the contributions in Yarshater (ed.) (1983); also Schippmann (1990), Herrmann (1977), Christensen (1944). There are detailed bibliographic essays in Wiesehöfer (1996), pp. 282–300.

[3] Howard-Johnston (1995a); Lee (1993), pp. 15–25.

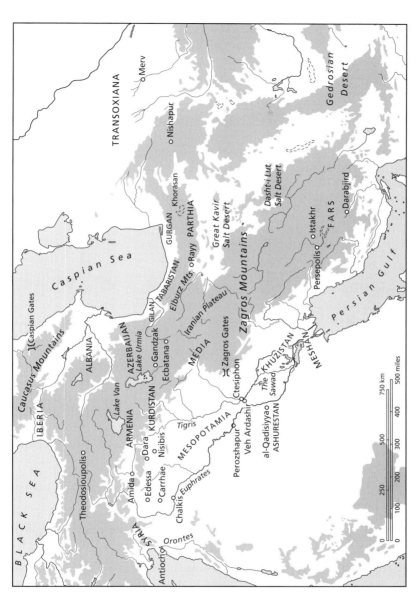

Map 7 Sasanian Persia

The Sasanian empire embraced two distinct geographical areas, the very fertile lowlands of Mesopotamia and the Iranian uplands, which were separated from each other by the mighty Zagros chain stretching from the Kurdistan highlands to the fringes of the Persian Gulf in the south.[4] Mesopotamia, where a complex irrigation system permitted dense settlement, was the economic heart of the Persian realm. Its rich agriculture generated the largest part of the Sasanian state's tax revenues and supported a network of major cities: Ctesiphon, the capital; Veh Ardashir, on the west bank of the Tigris opposite Ctesiphon, which was founded by the first Sasanian monarch; Perozshapur on the Euphrates, which commemorated the site of Shapur I's victory over Gordian and exploited the large number of Roman captives secured then; and Veh Antiok Khusrau, which was a similar foundation by Khusro I to celebrate his capture of Antioch-on-the-Orontes and to provide a home for the captives and booty from his successful 540 campaign (see above, p. 120).

By contrast, the Iranian plateau was sparsely settled, with its main centres of habitation clustered around the sources of water emerging from the Zagros. Rainfall on the plateau is low and beyond the rivers and *qanats* (underground water channels) lies desert: the Gedrosian to the south-east, where much of Alexander's army perished in 324 BC, and to the north the salt desert of the Great Kavir. On the fringes of the Sasanian world were areas of considerable military importance. In the north-west, Iran competed for influence with Rome among the nobilities of Armenia, Lazica, Iberia and Albania, and attempted to control movements across the Caucasian passes. In the wide expanses of Transoxiana, Iran confronted its traditional enemies: the succession of nomadic confederations of the Central Asian steppes. These included the Hephthalites or White Huns, who dominated the frontier in the fourth and fifth centuries; and the Turks, who cooperated with Khusro I in the elimination of their mutual enemy, the Hephthalites, in the 550s, but then rapidly emerged as a much more powerful threat during the rest of the sixth century. The vast barrier of the Zagros restricted communications to a limited number of major passes, so that the structural backbone of the empire was simple: from the economic and political heartland of lower Mesopotamia, routes up the Tigris led to the area of conflict with Rome in the north and north-west; while the road to the east crossed the Zagros into Media and then continued along the southern flanks of the Elburz range, another major defining mountain range, towards Khorasan and the frontier.

The Sasanian heartland was located in Fars, the relatively fertile region at the south-western end of the Iranian plateau, where the family combined positions of religious authority (the chief priesthood of the temple

---

[4] Comprehensive discussion of all aspects of Iranian geography in Fisher (ed.) (1968).

of Anahita at Istakhr) and secular power (governorship of Darabjird). After two decades in which a strong local power base was transformed into authority over the Iranian plateau, Ardashir descended to the Mesopotamian lowlands, overthrew the Arsacid monarch and was crowned 'king of kings' at Ctesiphon in 226. Military success, and in particular conflict with Rome, was an important mechanism for demonstrating the legitimacy of the new regime. The initial thrusts of the two first Sasanian monarchs, Ardashir I (224–40) and Shapur I (240–70), against the Roman east turned out, in the long run, to be little more than a series of wars of plunder: the Romans were defeated three times in the field, with Emperor Valerian being captured at Edessa in 260; the great cities of Nisibis, Carrhae and Antioch were sacked; and ravaging extended into Cappadocia and Cilicia as well as Syria – but there were no permanent gains.[5] Under their immediate successors, the initiative seems to have passed momentarily to the Romans. The conflicts between the two empires at that time brought the problem of Armenia to the fore, and this was to be a major bone of contention for most of the following century (see below, pp. 156–7). The attempt of Shah Narseh (293–302) to regain the upper hand ended in humiliating defeat by the Romans in 297, followed by a no less humiliating treaty. The tide was partly reversed during Shapur II's long reign (309–79). The wars fought between the two powers at the time were largely over contested frontier lands – first and foremost Armenia and northern Mesopotamia. Stability began to emerge after Julian's invasion in 363 permitted the Persians to regain Nisibis and other territories in upper Mesopotamia, and this was reinforced by the treaty between Shapur III (383–8) and Theodosius I in 384, which arranged the division of Armenia.[6]

This ushered in a long period of relative quiet in relations between the empire and Persia, apart from two brief conflicts in 421–2 and 440–1. On the first occasion, the dispute was caused by the Roman reception of Christian fugitives, especially from the Arab tribes allied to Persia. Yazdgard I (399–420) had been favourably disposed towards Christians and other minority religious groups within his kingdom, but energetic Christian missionary activity seems eventually to have forced him to permit persecution; an Arab chief, Aspabad, was instructed to prevent the flight of Christian converts to the Romans, but he proceeded to join the exodus, converted and, now renamed Peter, became bishop for the wandering tribal groups in the desert.[7] Persian demands for subsidies towards the cost of defending the Caspian passes (the so-called Gates) caused the second conflict,

[5] Sources in *The Roman eastern frontier*, ed. Lieu *et al.*, I, pp. 9–67.

[6] Rubin, Z. (1986); Frye (1983), pp. 153–70; Blockley (1992), pp. 39–45; Whitby, Michael (1988), pp. 197–218.

[7] Cyril of Scythopolis, *Life of Euthymius*, ch. 10, in Cyril of Scythopolis, *Saints' lives*, ed. Schwartz, pp. 18–21; tr. Price, pp. 14–17. On this see Rubin, Z. (1986), pp. 679–81; Blockley (1992), p. 199, n. 28.

when Yazdgard II (438–57) attempted to exploit Theodosius' concern over
the Vandal capture of Carthage. On each occasion Roman armies checked
Persian attacks and peace was rapidly restored, with renewed treaties that
contained clauses to regulate the alleged origins of the war.[8]

A plausible explanation for the change from persistent warfare in the
third and fourth centuries to peaceful relations in the fifth is provided by
the other external problems which faced successive rulers. Developments
in the west and the Balkans, as well as internal problems in Isauria, commanded the attention of the emperor at Constantinople, while Sasanian
shahs had to contend with the equally serious threat posed by the Hephthalites on their north-east frontier. This Sasanian problem is not regularly
reported in our sources. The succession of Greek classicising historians from
Priscus of Panium through to Theophylact Simocatta narrate diplomacy
and warfare that involved Romans and Sasanians, but seldom extend their
horizons further east.[9] Sasanian sources are mostly preserved for us through
compilations from the Islamic period, of which the most important are the
Ta'rikh of al-Tabari in Arabic and the *Shahnama* (*Book of kings*) of Firdausi
in New Persian. Both date from the tenth century and depend on lost Iranian sources, in which anecdotal material had substantially ousted reliable
information, so that the resulting narratives are dominated by charming
and exotic stories. Though al-Tabari attempted to cut his way through the
more sensational of his source materials and to produce a sober historical
narrative, he still incorporated two parallel versions of Sasanian history: it
is not safe to trust his information uncritically.[10] Furthermore, these Iranian sources are more informative for the royal court and internal affairs
and, like their Roman counterparts, are silent about a difficult frontier
relationship in which the Persians were often at a disadvantage. Only for
the reign of Peroz (459–84) is there substantial information about Perso-
Hephthalite relations, partly because Peroz was defeated in 464–5 when
the Roman ambassador Eusebius was accompanying the royal army, and
partly because two decades later Peroz perished with much of his army in
a catastrophic attempt to reverse the previous humiliation.[11]

The death of Peroz was followed by a period of dynastic weakness in
Iran. Peroz's brother Valash ruled for four years (484–8) before being overthrown by Peroz's son Kavad I (488–96), who relied on Hephthalite support. Kavad, however, was in turn ousted by the nobility and replaced by his
brother Zamaspes (Jamasp); but he was returned to power (498–531) with
Hephthalite assistance, after marrying their ruler's daughter. Kavad's reign

[8] Blockley (1992), pp. 56–61; Frye (1984), pp. 320–1.
[9] Discussions in Blockley, *Historians*; Cameron, Averil (1969–70); Cameron, Averil (1985); Men.,
pp. 1–30 (introduction); Whitby, Michael (1988).
[10] Howard-Johnston (1995a), pp. 169–72.
[11] Pr *W*, I.3–4, ed. and tr. Dewing, I, pp. 12–31.

witnessed the rise of the Mazdakite 'movement' (see p. 149 below), which advocated communal rights over property, and perhaps also women. It appears to have received some support from the shah, and can be interpreted as an attempt to undermine the entrenched power of the hereditary aristocracy. An indirect consequence of Kavad's dynastic problems was resurgence of warfare with Rome: Kavad undoubtedly needed money to repay the Hephthalites and to enhance his position as supreme patron within Persia, and this led him to ask the Romans for contributions towards the costs of defending the Caspian Gates. Anastasius' refusal provided a pretext for war (502–5), and although Kavad's first campaign secured considerable prestige and booty – with the capture of both Theodosioupolis and Amida – the Roman generals gradually stabilised matters after that.[12]

Sixth-century Romano-Persian relations are characterised by two opposing tendencies: a recollection of the relatively harmonious fifth century, when elaborate diplomatic practices for managing relations had emerged; and international rivalry, caused both by weakness in the Persian shah's position and by mutual suspicion of each other's intentions. In 527, towards the end of Kavad's reign, war broke out again (see above, p. 119). Tension had risen as the empires competed for the allegiance of the principalities around the Caucasus, where acceptance of Christianity by local rulers threatened to weaken loyalties to Persia. However, the flashpoint came when Justin I (518–27) refused to cooperate with Kavad's plans to ensure the succession of his third son, Khusro. Although the Persians took the offensive, a series of invasions failed to capture any major Roman city, and two pitched battles – at Dara in 530 and at Callinicum in the following year – resulted in a victory apiece. Hostilities were concluded with the 'perpetual peace' of 532, when the new Persian shah, Khusro I (531–79) accepted a lump sum of 11,000 pounds of gold in lieu of regular contributions for the defence of the Caucasus.[13]

Peace did not last. Justinian (527–65) exploited the quiet on his eastern frontier to launch the reconquest of Africa and Italy, but his startling victories were brought to Khusro's attention; jealousy fuelled suspicions about Justinian's long-term intentions, and Khusro exploited a dispute between client Arab tribes to attack in 540. After spectacular Persian successes in this first campaign, the Romans organised their defences and a truce confined fighting to Lazica after 545. However, their Arab allies went on fighting (see below, p. 188). This ended with a decisive victory for the Ghassanid allies of

[12] Joshua the Stylite, *Chronicle*, chs. 54–83, ed. and tr. Wright, pp. 51–78, 43–66; tr. Trombley and Watt, pp. 63–101; Pr *W*, I.7–10, ed. and tr. Dewing, I, pp. 48–83; Theoph., ed. de Boor, I, pp. 144–9; tr. Mango and Scott, pp. 222–8; Zacharias of Mytilene, *Chronicle*, VII.3–5, tr. Hamilton and Brooks, pp. 151–64; Blockley (1992), pp. 89–96.
[13] Pr *W*, I.11–22, ed. and tr. Dewing, I, pp. 82–209; John Malalas, *Chronicle*, XVIII.4–69, ed. Thurn, pp. 355–94; tr. Jeffreys *et al.*, pp. 246–74.

Byzantium in 554 near Chalkis, when the Lakhmid ruler al-Mundhir III –
scourge of imperial provinces for the previous half-century – was killed.
Peace finally came in 562 with an agreement that was intended to last for
fifty years; the detailed terms illustrate the range of disputed issues that
could provoke conflict, and are preserved in an important *Fragmentum* of
Menander the Guardsman.[14] Peace lasted for a decade, but on this occasion
the Byzantines were the aggressors: Justin II (565–78) objected to paying
for peace (at the rate of 30,000 *solidi* per year) and believed that he could
count on the support of the Turkish confederation in Central Asia, which
had replaced the Hephthalites as Persia's north-eastern neighbours, to crush
their common enemy. Two decades of fighting ended when Khusro I's son
and successor, Hormizd IV (579–90), was overthrown in a palace coup;
Hormizd's son, Khusro II (590, 591–628), was almost immediately challenged by Bahram Chobin, who had gained great glory from defeating the
Turks and was the first non-Sasanian to seize the throne (590–1). Khusro
sought assistance from Emperor Maurice (582–602), was reinstated by a
Roman army in 591, and peace was again arranged.[15]

The final conflict of the two great rivals of the ancient world broke
out in 602, when Khusro took advantage of the murder of his benefactor
Maurice and the arrival in Persia of Maurice's eldest son Theodosius (or at
least a plausible impersonator); Khusro could shed the image of imperial
client, present himself as the supporter of international ties of gratitude
and friendship, and obtain significant booty and military glory into the
bargain. For twenty-five years the conflict ranged across the entire Middle
East, from Chalcedon on the Bosporus to Gandzak on the Iranian plateau,
until a daring counter-offensive by Heraclius (610–41) prompted the Persian
nobility to overthrow Khusro in 628.[16] Once more peace was restored,
but the defeated Sasanian dynasty lapsed into a rapid turnover of rulers
(eight within five years, including, for forty days, the Christian and non-
Sasanian Shahrvaraz). The last Sasanian ruler Yazdgard III (633–51) had
only just ascended the throne when he had to confront Islamic attacks;
the diminution of royal prestige and the weakness of his armies after a
quarter of a century of unsuccessful warfare against Byzantium made Persia
particularly vulnerable, and Yazdgard was forced to flee to the north-east,
where he was eventually killed.

Wars and animosity loom large in the record of the relations between
Byzantium and Persia, both of which laid claim to universal ascendancy.
The imprint they have left on the Byzantine sources tends to obscure the
fact that both sides could also exploit a rhetoric of peace and co-operative

[14] Pr *W*, II, ed. and tr. Dewing, I, pp. 260–557; Men., 6.1, pp. 70–3.
[15] TS, I–V, ed. de Boor and Wirth, pp. 36–220; tr. Whitby and Whitby, pp. 17–157; Whitby, Michael (1988), pp. 250–304. See also above, p. 127.
[16] Howard-Johnston (1994); Stratos (1968–80), I.

relations. The Sasanians, who had to contend with a succession of nomadic and semi-nomadic powers along their extensive frontiers, tried to impress on the Byzantines that they were defending these frontiers for their mutual benefit. This claim justified repeated demands for diplomatic subsidies, but Sasanian internal propaganda depicted these as tribute, which aggravated imperial resistance to paying up:[17] international prestige was one of the factors that individual Sasanian monarchs used in order to balance the divergent constituencies within their realm and preserve their own supreme position.

ROYAL LEGITIMATION

The best evidence about Sasanian royal ideology comes from the first century or so of the dynasty, and although it is possible to detect developments thereafter, the basic principles apply throughout the regime's history. Shapur I was the first to claim the title 'king of kings of Iran and non-Iran', whereas his father, Ardashir, had contented himself with the title 'king of kings of Iran' only. The legitimation of the new royal dynasty in its own realm was the immediate task the early Sasanians had to face. The great official state inscriptions from the early Sasanian period do not conceal the newness of the dynasty. The *Res gestae divi Saporis* is a list of the exploits of Shah Shapur I on the so-called Ka'ba of Zardusht,[18] and traces the royal genealogy back three generations, through his father Ardashir to his grandfather Papak. On the Paikuli inscription, set up by Shah Narseh to commemorate his successful bid for supreme power and his victory over his nephew Bahram III (293), there is only one significant addition. The dynasty is called 'the seed of the Sasanids', elucidating to some extent the role of 'the lord Sasan', mentioned in the *Res gestae divi Saporis* as recipient of an honorary cult, but not explicitly as a forebear of the dynasty. None of the other remaining six inscriptions that allude to the genealogy of the Sasanian shahs adds anything of significance.[19]

The great pictures that accompany many of these inscriptions present the key elements of legitimate royal authority. In some, the shah and his entourage unseat their rivals in a dramatic joust; or foreign enemies demonstrate their submission – including in some scenes the Roman emperor, who arrives at speed to acknowledge Sasanian mastery, kneels before his conqueror or lies prostrate at his feet. The proper transfer of power at each accession is symbolised by grand ceremonies involving shah and court; and

[17] Rubin, Z. (1986); Braund (1994), pp. 270–1.

[18] The Ka'ba of Zardusht (Cube of Zoroaster) was an Achaemenid tower at Naqsh-i Rustam, a royal burial-ground near the ancient capital of Persepolis. See below, p. 139.

[19] On the *Res gestae*, see Back (1978), pp. 284–371; Huyse, *Dreisprächige Inschrift Šaburs I.*; on the Paikuli inscription, see Humbach and Skjaervø (1978–83), III.1.

Figure 5 Portrayal of Shah Peroz being invested with two diadems by a god and goddess, Taq-i-Bustan, Iran

in some pictures, divine investiture is symbolised by the figure of Ahura Mazda or of Anahita handing over a diadem to the shah.[20] The monuments present a self-fulfilling legitimation. Supernatural sanction for the Sasanian house is demonstrated by the sequence of royal victories through which the Sasanians have achieved power; royal gratitude for this divine support is displayed by the establishment of a series of ritual fires. No attempt is made to conceal the shah's bellicosity, and this self-glorification in divinely sponsored aggression is repeated three times in the *Res gestae divi Saporis*. According to the ideology enunciated in this document, wars of conquest are the duty of a good shah and military success proves legitimacy.[21]

---

[20] Pictures in Ghirshman (1962), pp. 135–201.   [21] Whitby, Michael (1994).

Externally, or at least with regard to the Roman empire, the only area for which we have evidence, Sasanian strategies for legitimation were slightly more complex. Victory was still crucial, but warfare ought to have some justification. In his *Res gestae*, two of Shapur's three expeditions against the Romans are presented as responses to Roman aggression; one of the three versions of the inscription is in Greek, and its contents were probably proclaimed to the inhabitants of the Roman empire, or to its former inhabitants resettled in Iran.[22] More significantly, three historians writing in the Roman empire – Cassius Dio (LXXX.3.3) and Herodian (VI.2.1–5) from the third century, Ammianus Marcellinus (XVII.5.3–8) from the fourth – record how Sasanian envoys presented territorial demands on the Romans in terms of the revival of the old Achaemenid empire.[23] The repeated Roman refusal to return what rightfully belonged to the new dynasty was sufficient justification for war.

If the Achaemenid heritage was important in their western diplomatic dealings, there is no evidence that it was significant for internal legitimation. Although Ardashir and Shapur I chose to glorify themselves at Naqsh-i Rustam, near Persepolis, a site rich in Achaemenid associations,[24] the possible connection is not voiced in their public inscriptions. The site was chosen for its monumental and awe-inspiring nature; there is no evidence that those who beheld these monuments were aware of their specific Achaemenid associations, or indeed of the pristine greatness of the Achaemenids themselves. The modern name of the site, Naqsh-i Rustam, with its reference to the hero of Iranian epic tradition, indicates the extent to which folk memory can misrepresent the true nature of such sites. When Shapur I refers to his ancestors' domain in his *Res gestae*, this is merely to state that exiles from the Roman empire were settled in Iran on crown lands – in Fars, Khuzistan and Ashurestan. Again, this is neither evocation of the Achaemenid empire nor a claim to legitimation as their heirs.[25]

It has been alternatively suggested that the Sasanians' claims to legitimation harked back not to the Achaemenids but to the Kayanids, the heroic mythical rulers of Iran long before the historical Achaemenids.[26] However, this hypothesis is not supported in the inscriptions: Shapur I only traced his genealogy back to his grandfather Papak, and did not claim universal kingship before his own reign (he is the first 'king of kings of Iranians and non-Iranians'). More striking is the absence of any allusion to the dynasty's

---

[22] English translation, based mainly on the Parthian and Middle Persian versions, in Frye (1984), pp. 371–3.

[23] Whitby, Michael (1988); Potter (1990), p. 373 argues that Persian demands were reshaped to fit the presuppositions of Roman historiographical traditions.

[24] Wiesehöfer (1996), pp. 27–8, 154–5; Lee (1993) pp. 21–2.

[25] As suggested by Wiesehöfer (1996), pp. 155, 223; see also Lukonin (1961), p. 23 for a less extravagant interpretation of this passage.

[26] For a full development of this hypothesis, see Yarshater (1971).

Kayanid origin in Narseh's Paikuli inscription, precisely the context where self-designation as 'the seed of the Sasanians' invited a link with a more glorious house. Kayanid names such as Kavad and Khusro only enter royal nomenclature in the late fifth century and probably reflect a change at that time in strategies for dynastic legitimation. Furthermore, it is the mythological Kayanid link which eventually introduces into royal genealogies an Achaemenid element that had not been present before. This Achaemenid link was clearly derived from the *Alexander romance*, which became popular at the Sasanian court in the first half of the sixth century. The Sasanian genealogies relayed through Arabic and New Persian sources deriving from lost Pahlavi historiography reflect, as often, the conditions and traditions of the last century of Sasanian rule; little genuine knowledge was preserved.[27]

SASANIAN SHAHS AND THE ZOROASTRIAN PRIESTS

Divine sanction was an important part of royal legitimation, and one must therefore investigate the relations between monarchs and the Zoroastrian priesthood, the repository of pristine mythological traditions. The established view that the Sasanian shahs relied on the Zoroastrian priesthood's support, and as a consequence actively encouraged their beliefs and enhanced their power, has been largely modified in recent decades.[28] Although the term *mazdesn* (Mazda-worshipping) recurs frequently on Sasanian monuments as a royal epithet, this need not imply automatic recognition of one organised priesthood as sole exponent of this deity's cult. Shahs could perhaps best consolidate royal power by fostering variety, both inside the Zoroastrian church and between different religions.

The traditional view encounters difficulties even with the dynasty's founder, Ardashir I. According to the *Denkard* – the post-Sasanian Zoroastrian encyclopedia – Ardashir should be considered as the great restorer of the Zoroastrian faith: it was under his aegis that the priest Tansar allegedly collected the scattered remnants of the Avestan books, which had survived since Alexander's conquests.[29] However, the picture that emerges from the *Res gestae divi Saporis* is rather different: it makes no mention of Tansar or any member of the Zoroastrian priesthood other than Kirder, whose appearance is rather muted. Ardashir himself can reliably be described as a worshipper of Anahita of Stakhr, whereas evidence of his attachment to Ahura Mazda is more equivocal. As worshipped by the early Sasanians, Anahita was the goddess of victory at whose shrine the severed heads of vanquished enemies were habitually dedicated. If the devotion of Ardashir and his immediate successors to Anahita can be considered as part and

---

[27] Nöldeke (1887b), pp. 87–8; Nöldeke (1920), p. 13.
[28] For a survey of views, see Schippmann (1990), pp. 92–102.   [29] Shaki (1981).

parcel of a Zoroastrian orthodoxy, then this orthodoxy must have been entirely different from the kind of orthodoxy assumed in his glorification in the *Denkard*.[30]

The absence of any clear reference to an organised clergy in the *Res gestae divi Saporis* is at odds with the role ascribed by modern scholars to a 'Zoroastrian church', at least under the early Sasanians. This gap is not filled by the far-reaching claims made in four inscriptions celebrating the career of Kirder, the one priestly character who does figure on Shapur's monument. Kirder was promoted within the Zoroastrian priesthood from a mere *herbed* under Shapur I to the rank of a *mobed* (chief *magus*) under his immediate successors, Hormizd I (270–1), Bahram I (271–4) and Bahram II (274–93). Bahram II bestowed additional honours and supposedly authorised Kirder to enforce Zoroastrianism and persecute heresies and other religions. This only indicates that this shah was attached to the kind of Zoroastrianism preached by Kirder, which is more than can be said of Shapur I.[31]

The extent of Shapur I's Zoroastrian piety as it emerges from his own *Res gestae* is not entirely clear. He was indeed the founder of many fire-temples throughout his realm, according to his own testimony as well as to Kirder's. Yet fire-temples were sacred not only to Ahura Mazda but also to Anahita, and Shapur's favourable attitude to Zoroastrianism should be conceived in the framework of a religious eclecticism that could also accommodate Manichaeism.[32] Furthermore, the fact that he granted Kirder sweeping powers to conduct religious affairs, without matching these powers with the appropriate title – whatever its meaning, *herbed* appears to be a rather modest rank – suggests that Kirder was more a court priest than the designated head of a powerful church. We cannot rule out a degree of tension between Kirder in this function and some of his brethren. Reiterated as a refrain on his inscriptions, Kirder's statement that under his leadership *many* of the *magi* (not all of them) were happy and prosperous implies an attempt to mute some opposition voices. The early Sasanian monarchs, far from depending on an already powerful organisation for vital support, may rather have helped Zoroastrian clergy to improve their position in a fluid and competitive religious milieu.

It is usually assumed that under Narseh the influence of the Zoroastrian priesthood declined, but that it regained much of the lost ground under Shapur II. The figure of Aturpat, son of Mahrspand, looms large in post-Sasanian Zoroastrian literature: he is depicted as a model of Zoroastrian orthodoxy who submitted himself to the ordeal of molten metal to refute heretics whose precise doctrine is disputed. It is natural enough to suppose

---

[30] Chaumont (1958); Duchesne-Guillemin (1983), pp. 874–97.

[31] Back (1978), pp. 384–488; Duchesne-Guillemin (1983), pp. 878–84.

[32] Wikander (1946), pp. 52–124; Chaumont (1958), pp. 162–3. For Manichaeism in the Sasanian empire: Lieu (1994), pp. 24–5, 35–6.

that Aturpat stood at the head of a mighty Zoroastrian hierarchy, authorised by the shah himself to administer the institutions of the only fully
recognised official state religion. However, the hierarchy of what tends to be
conceived of as 'the Zoroastrian church' did not in all probability become
fully established until much later. It is only under Yazdgard II (438–57) that
the high priest Mihr-Shapur, who had already distinguished himself under
previous reigns as a persecutor of Christians, is called *modaban mobad*,
the earliest reliable attestation of this title. But even then the relative position of *mobeds* and *herbeds* in the organisation of Zoroastrian clergy is not
entirely clear. The title *herbedan herbed*, conferred upon Zurvandad, the
son of Yazdgard's powerful prime minister, Mihr-Narseh, has been interpreted as evidence for a hierarchy distinct from that of the *mobeds* within
the Zoroastrian church.

The Zoroastrian priesthood appears to have gained a truly undisputed
position as the sole representative of the one and only state religion in
the course of the fifth century. It is precisely at this time that Avestan
names suddenly proliferate among members of the royal house, and the
title *kavi* or *kay* appears on its coins, marking a crucial stage in the fabrica-
tion of the Kayanid genealogy as a source of legitimation of the Sasanian
dynasty. Yet the Zoroastrian priesthood was soon to suffer a severe blow
under Kavad I (488–96), during the Mazdakite revolt (see below, p. 149).
The reign of Khusro I (531–79) appears to have been a period of harmony between the monarchy and the Zoroastrian priesthood, but it was
a priesthood restored by the shah following the Mazdakite debacle, and
consequently more dependent on the shah than before. Under Khusro's
successors, Zoroastrian influence seems to have declined. Khusro II (590–
628), rather than follow his predecessors in the large-scale establishment
of fire-temples staffed with a vast multitude of *herbedan*, relied heavily on
Christians, including his favourite wife, his finance officer and his chief
general (see below, p. 144); Zoroastrian tradition, as reflected in the apocalyptic composition *Jamasp namagh*, branded him an unjust and tyrannical
shah.[33]

The figure of Mihr-Narseh, Yazdgard II's prime minister, illustrates the
problem of Zoroastrian orthodoxy and heterodoxy in the Sasanian period.
From Armenian sources recounting the persecution he launched against
the Christians in Armenia, it is clear that Mihr-Narseh was an adherent of
Zurvanism (belief in Zurvan i Akanarag or Infinite Time).[34] His son Zurvandad bore a name celebrating this rather shadowy divine personification,

[33] Text in *Ayatkar i zamaspik*, XVI.30, ed. and Italian tr. Messina, pp. 70–1 (text), p. 115 (tr.), where
aparvez ('the victorious') is an unmistakable allusion to Khusro II; see also Duchesne-Guillemin (1983),
p. 896; Boyce (1983), p. 1160.
[34] Elishe, *History*, tr. Thomson, pp. 77–80; French tr. in Langlois, *Historiens de l'Arménie*, II,
pp. 190–1; see also Eznik of Kolb in Boyce, *Zoroastrianism*, pp. 97–8.

and such names seem to have been common among Iranian nobles under the Sasanians. The role of Zurvan in the Zoroastrian pantheon is much disputed, but it represents a trend in Zoroastrianism which sought to provide a unifying monistic framework for its fundamentally dualist theology: Ohurmazd, the good principle, and Ahriman, the evil principle, were depicted as the twin sons of Infinite Time. However, there is little reliable information. Whereas contemporary non-Sasanian and non-Zoroastrian sources suggest that this monistic doctrine was the orthodoxy endorsed by the Sasanian shahs, the Pahlavi Zoroastrian literature of the post-Sasanian era is virtually silent on this.[35]

Various attempts have been made to explain this discrepancy. One suggestion is that the dualist orthodoxy reflected in the surviving Zoroastrian literature only triumphed after the collapse of the Sasanian monarchy: that the former monistic orthodoxy was deliberately suppressed by supporters of the old national religion, in the face of the new Islamic monotheism.[36] According to another view, the story of Zurvanism is one of intermittent success: whereas under some shahs it was indeed the accepted orthodoxy, under others the pendulum swung in the opposite direction and the dualist trend became dominant. Dualism was finally triumphant in the mid-sixth century under Khusro I, whose reign also constitutes a decisive stage in the establishment of a canon of the Zoroastrian scriptures, the Avesta, and in the development of Zoroastrian theological literature. Attempts have also been made to play down the significance of Zurvanism, either as a fad entertained by the upper classes or as a popular version of Zoroastrianism: nothing tantamount to a heresy in its familiar Christian sense.[37]

Perhaps the best way of approaching a solution is to get rid of the notion of a Sasanian Zoroastrian church, analogous in its position to that of the Christian church in the late Roman empire and intent upon using secular support to impose a uniform doctrine within its ranks. The truth may well have been that although the early Sasanian shahs found Zoroastrianism, as represented and propounded by the estate of the *magi*, the most potent religious factor in many of their domains, they were not always prepared to allow it to become the sole officially dominant state religion. Thus, for example, Anahita, who seemingly fades out after the reign of Narseh, springs again into prominence under the last Sasanians, from Khusro II to Yazdgard III.[38]

Furthermore, the fact that some Sasanian shahs, like Shapur I, were prepared to unleash the Zoroastrian priesthood against the Christians in

---

[35] Christensen (1944), pp. 149–54; Boyce (1979), pp. 112–13, 160–1.
[36] Boyce (1979), pp. 160–1; see also Boyce, *Zoroastrianism*, pp. 96–9.
[37] Zaehner (1955); reaction in Boyce (1957); Boyce (1990); Frye (1959); Frye (1984), p. 321 with n. 27; *Denkard VI*, tr. Shaked, p. xxxiv (introduction).
[38] Wikander (1946), pp. 55–6; Duchesne-Guillemin (1983), p. 897.

the service of their own policies does not mean that they themselves subscribed to any version of Zoroastrianism as the binding orthodoxy. Attitudes towards this religion appear to have varied according to circumstances
and the tempers of individual rulers. A sober monarch like Shapur I was
quite capable of striking an alliance of convenience with the Zoroastrian
clergy, while keeping his options open by toying with Manichaeism. Shapur II, a notorious persecutor of the Christians, may well have played
off dualism against Zurvanism precisely in order to check the growth of an
excessively strong, unified priestly caste. Yazdgard I was favourably inclined
towards Christianity and Judaism for most of his reign.[39] On the other hand,
such shahs as Bahram I and Bahram II may be described as truly pious followers of the form of Zoroastrianism propounded by Kirder: probably, but
not certainly, dualism.

The Sasanian monarchs' attitude towards Nestorian Christianity is
another consideration against interpreting their religious policy exclusively
in terms of their Zoroastrian piety. After this creed had been condemned
as a heresy at the council of Ephesus in 431, believers found a relatively safe
haven in the Sasanian empire. In 457, a Nestorian school was founded in
Nisibis by Bar Sauma and Narsai, fugitive Nestorian teachers from Edessa; it
flourished there, particularly under Shah Peroz (459–84), when the Zoroastrian priesthood appears to have been at the peak of its power. There was
no danger in a policy of toleration towards a religious sect now banned
within the Byzantine empire, whose rulers were either Chalcedonian or
inclined to monophysitism. However, even a shah such as Khusro I – who
could afford to be tolerant without marring his relations with a Zoroastrian priesthood firmly under his control – could or would not prevent
persecution, even of Nestorians, after war against Byzantium flared up in
540. Khusro II is often described as sympathetic to the Christians, but the
picture is more complex: he astutely played off monophysites (whose cause
was advocated at court by his favourite wife, Shirin, and her influential
physician, Gabriel) against Nestorians (who found a faithful champion in
his powerful finance minister, Yazdin). Towards the end of his reign, when
his empire succumbed to a Byzantine invasion, Khusro reversed his policy
of general toleration and threatened a wave of persecutions.[40]

SHAHS AND NOBLES

The Sasanian monarchy has a reputation for being better organised and
more centralised than its Arsacid predecessor. But the notion that the

---

[39] Widengren (1961), pp. 139–42; Rubin, Z. (1986), pp. 679–81.
[40] Duchesne-Guillemin (1983), pp. 889–90; *Khuzistan chronicle*, German tr. Nöldeke, pp. 9–13, 18–22,
28; tr. Lieu *et al.*, pp. 230–1, 232–4, 236.

Arsacid kingdom was in essence a cluster of largely independent political entities, held together in little more than a semblance of formal allegiance to a shadowy central royal authority, may have its roots in tendentious Sasanian traditions. These treat the whole of the Seleucid and Arsacid periods as that of the 'petty shahs' or 'tribal shahs' (*mulūk al-tawā'if*) and, in sharp contrast, depict the monarchy established by Ardashir as a coherent and effective political and military power. In the Sasanian sixth-century historical romance, the *Karnamag Ardasher i Papakan*, the fragmentation of Alexander's empire into 240 small states is the foil to Ardashir's expoits; the impression produced by the *Khwaday-namag* tradition of national historical writing, as reflected principally by al-Tabari, is that Ardashir's rise to power was in effect a long succession of wars for the unification of Iran.[41]

Greek and Latin sources give the point of view of contemporary outside observers and help to modify this distorted picture, especially with regard to the Parthian empire. However, even these sources suggest that the establishment of the Sasanian monarchy was a dramatic development, for the drive of a rising new power is all too easily contrasted with the lethargy of the *ancien régime*. The result is a widespread consensus among modern scholars that the Sasanian state was more highly centralised and advanced than its Arsacid predecessor. A more balanced picture emerges from an examination of Sasanian institutions, allowing for the distorting vein of propaganda that runs through many of our surviving sources: the dynasty was new, but many of its structures were inherited. Careful analysis of the epigraphic monuments reveals a strong Parthian inheritance, notably an indomitable nobility whose power was only inadequately matched by a somewhat flimsy central administration. Even the question of the genesis of so monumental an inscription as the *Res gestae divi Saporis* can be misrepresented when coloured by the presupposition of a central royal government controlling every aspect of its erection. A more realistic view would allow for the employment of the remnants of a Parthian chancellery whose execution of the shah's instructions was not always in perfect accord with his intentions.[42]

The territorial extent of the Sasanian empire was vast, but the control exercised by central government was not uniformly effective.[43] Evidence for the foundation of cities by the Sasanian monarchs after Ardashir, based

---

[41] *Karnamak Artakhshir-i Papakan*, ch. 1, ed. and tr. Antia, pp. 1–5; German tr. Nöldeke, pp. 35–8; al-Tabari, *Ta'rikh*, ed. de Goeje *et al.*, I, pp. 813–21; tr. Bosworth, V, pp. 1–18; German tr. Nöldeke, pp. 1–22.

[42] On the genesis of the *Res gestae divi Saporis*, see Rubin, Z. (2002), pp. 291–7.

[43] The efficacy of royal control is stressed by Howard-Johnston (1995a), but his model is based on a hypothetical interpretation of archaeological finds rather than the more explicit literary evidence. Limitations on ability to tax: Altheim and Stiehl (eds.) (1954), pp. 47–8.

chiefly on the detailed data preserved by al-Tabari, indicates that their
activity was confined to a fairly limited area – the provinces of Fars, Meshan,
the Sawad and Media – which were basically the territories conquered by
Ardashir I during his wars against the Arsacids and the *mulūk al-tawā'if*
under their aegis. As a general rule, the Sasanian shahs did not encroach on
those territories held by the great lords of the realm, some of whose lineages
reached far back into the Parthian era. The one exception to this rule was the
occasional establishment of cities in newly acquired border zones, where
the shah's lordship by right of conquest could not be contested; or in
remote provinces where royal authority was being re-established. Examples
of this exception are the cities founded by Peroz following his war against
the Hepthalites: Ram Peroz in the region of Rayy; Roshan Peroz on the
border of Gurgan and the Gates of Sul; and Shahram Peroz in Azerbaijan.[44]
Foundation of a city represented a substantial investment of manpower and
resources, and shahs only undertook this in places where it would benefit
them, and not one of their overmighty nobles.

The picture of a well-ordered hierarchical society, controlled and regulated by a strong monarchy, needs to be reassessed. It emerges from later
literary sources of the Islamic period, such as al-Tabari, al-Mas'udi, Pseudo-
al-Jahiz[45] and *The letter of Tansar*. The latter is attributed to the powerful
third-century *herbed* Tansar, but was probably composed three centuries
later and is preserved in Ibn Isfandyar's *Ta'rikh-i Tabaristan*, a problematic
source.[46] However, these complex issues can be avoided, as the epigraphic
sources from the earlier Sasanian period – notably the third century and first
half of the fourth – anticipate and corroborate our later literary sources. The
inscriptions suggest that the framework of a social hierarchy had already
been formally established under Shapur I.

The highest rung, immediately below the 'king of kings', was that of the
shahrdaran. These virtually independent shahs, whose numbers seem to
have been much lower under the Sasanians than the Arsacids, tended to be
senior members of the royal dynasty and officially ruled their kingdoms as
royal appanages. Below them ranked the *vaspuhragan*, apparently princes
of the royal family who held no official post in the royal court. Third in
rank were the *vuzurgan*: members of the great noble houses, including
Suren, Karin and the Lords of Undigan, among others. As late as *c.* 500,
the unruly heads of these houses admitted only a nominal allegiance to the
central power, and were virtually independent in their hereditary territorial

[44] Altheim and Stiehl (eds.) (1954), pp. 12–18; see also Lukonin (1961), pp. 12–19, specifically on the
foundations of Ardashir I and Shapur I.
[45] al-Tabari, *Ta'rikh*, ed. de Goeje *et al.*, I, p. 821; tr. Bosworth, V, pp. 18–20; German tr. Nöldeke,
p. 22; al-Mas'udi, *Muruj al-dhahab*, chs. 581–8, ed. Pellat, I, pp. 287–91; rev. French tr. Pellat, I, pp. 218–
20; Pseudo-al-Jahiz, *al-Taj*, ed. Zaki, pp. 21–8; tr. Pellat, pp. 51–6.
[46] *Letter of Tansar*, tr. Boyce.

domains. The fourth and the lowest rung documented in the inscriptions was the *azadan*, minor gentry of free status, and distinct from the other nobility, but probably also dependent on them in many cases. From this lesser nobility were recruited the mounted warriors, *asavaran*, who made up the core of the Sasanian army.[47] These may be identical with another category, that of the *kadxvadayan*, who occupy a place above the *azadan* and below the *vuzurgan* in the lists of the Paikuli inscription. On the other hand, they may be an especially favoured group among the *asavaran*, perhaps akin to enfeoffed 'knights' in medieval Europe.[48]

The stratification that emerges from the later literary sources is more general and reflects the (post-Sasanian) Avestan concept of social stratification. The priests (*asronan*) appear at the top of the ladder. They are followed by the military estate (*artestaran*). The third estate is that of the royal bureaucracy (*dibiran*, i.e. scribes). Finally, the commoners are enumerated, subdivided into peasants (*vastaryoshan*) and artisans (*hutuxshan*). If the two hierarchies, inscriptional and literary, are to be amalgamated, the inscriptional hierarchy of nobility should be seen as an expansion of the second estate in the literary sources; on the other hand, the literary hierarchy may not be contemporaneous, since there is no evidence for a separate priestly caste in the early period.

Royal power and influence depended to a large degree on effective control of the *shahrdaran*, as well as on the active support of the majority of the *vuzurgan*, or equivalent groups, whatever their names in later periods. Their cooperation would be needed for the recruitment of the *asavaran* who owed them allegiance, and their consent would be required for the imposition of royal taxation within their domains. Sasanian military organisation has been described as feudal, basically similar to its Arsacid predecessor, and this definition may help us to understand how the Sasanian regime worked. From our meagre information about remuneration for the professional core of soldiery, we may conclude that it was supported through land-grants rather than paid in money or kind. Thus it is tempting to accept the notion of enfeoffment, which by its very nature entails bonds of trust and dependence that may be described as ties of vassalage. Yet, if this picture provides a fairly accurate idea of the relationship between the shah and warriors conscripted in his own domain, as well as of that between the grandees and their own warriors, it does not reveal the realities of the links between shah and grandees. The grandees' domains might have been deemed fiefs granted by the shah, but in most cases this status would only have been theoretical, since forfeiture of such fiefs to the crown could hardly be enforced by means of a simple legal procedure, without recourse to arms:

---

[47] For these ranks, see Schippmann (1990), p. 82; see also Wiesehöfer (1996), pp. 171–82.
[48] See Humbach and Skjaervø (1978–83), III.1, pp. 33–4.

as in any feudal monarchy, there was no guarantee that every Sasanian shah could control all the grandees all the time.

There are clear signs that the great nobles of the Sasanian kingdom developed their own concept of legitimation. It was one of basic loyalty to the royal dynasty, but this by no means entailed unconditional loyalty to the individual seated on the throne at any given moment. The shah in power might be replaced by another member of the dynasty if a significant body of nobles found his reign unjust and tyrannical. The nobles likewise did not consider themselves utterly bound to abide by a reigning shah's own choice of successor. A more suitable candidate might be substituted for his appointee, provided that he came from among the members of the royal house.[49]

TAXATION AND MILITARY ORGANISATION

In an empire which minted a stable silver coinage, the *drahm*, throughout most of its history, the continuing resort to land-grants in return for military service calls for an explanation. The *drahm* was the only denomination in constant circulation, raising the question whether such a simple economic system can be described as a truly advanced monetary economy. Gold dinars were issued occasionally – not, it seems, for purposes of monetary circulation, but rather in commemoration of solemn events. Bronze change seems to have been issued only very intermittently, perhaps in response to specific demands, as at Merv; the volume progressively decreased, posing problems for the mechanics of everyday economic exchanges.[50] The assumption that Arsacid copper coinage was still used in many parts of the Sasanian kingdom is unconvincing,[51] and the conclusion must be that much economic activity was based on barter.

This situation explains a good deal about the Sasanian system of taxation before the beginning of the sixth century. It was based on crop-sharing, the exaction of agricultural produce proportionate to annual yield, as assessed by royal tax-collectors on the spot, and levied in kind. In addition, a poll tax was imposed on most subjects, which may largely have been paid in money, though part was perhaps commuted to goods. The system was inefficient and wasteful, especially with regard to the land tax; it was subject to frequent fluctuations, and allowed little scope for advance financial planning. The necessity of waiting for the tax-collector with the crops untouched in the field or on the tree meant that some might be damaged

---

[49] Rubin, Z. (2004), esp. pp. 263–72.

[50] See Göbl (1954), pp. 96–9; see also Göbl (1971), pp. 25–30; Göbl (1983), pp. 328–9. On Merv, see Loginov and Nikitin (1993a); Loginov and Nikitin (1993b); Loginov and Nikitin (1993c).

[51] Göbl (1954), p. 98; also Göbl (1971), where continued circulation is suggested only for the earlier period, with no explanation offered for the subsequent mechanics of exchange.

or destroyed before being enjoyed by farmers or the shah. Only lands held directly by the shah could be taxed in this manner effectively, but even on royal domains the avarice of corrupt tax-assessors will have hampered collection.[52]

Towards the end of the fifth century, the burden of taxation on the peasantry seems to have become increasingly oppressive: the complex relations with the Hephthalite khanate, looming in the east, resulted in heavy demands at a time when recurrent famines compelled shahs to grant occasional – and somewhat measly – tax relief. This oppression contributed significantly to the popularity of Mazdak, a heretical Zoroastrian priest, who advocated the economic equality of all human beings and regarded the higher classes of the Sasanian kingdom as the worst enemies of his doctrines. For some time he managed to enlist the support of Shah Kavad I himself: Kavad appears to have used this movement precisely in order to humble his recalcitrant nobility.[53] When eventually he turned his back on the movement and allowed his son to put it down, the battered nobles needed royal support to recuperate and regain a fraction of their former grandeur. They were obviously in no position to form a viable opposition to the one serious attempt to introduce a tax reform in the Sasanian realm, begun apparently towards the end of Kavad's reign (531) and continued by his son Khusro I.[54]

On the basis of a general land survey, a new system for exacting the land tax was devised. Fixed rates of tax were imposed on agricultural land according to its size and according to the kind of crops raised. The tax was calculated in *drahm*s, although at least some was probably still levied in kind, calculated according to the current value of the produce in *drahm*s. This new system, efficiently applied, would enable a monarch to anticipate incomes and budget expenses. It might be seen as harsh on the peasantry, primarily because the fixed *drahm* rates apparently disregarded fluctuations in agricultural yield caused by drought, other natural calamities or war. But this is to ignore the best testimony about the reform: if a distinction is drawn between the reform's institution and operation in Khusro's reign, and the way it subsequently worked, the system appears reasonably efficient and fair. It considerably augmented crown revenues, but also included a mechanism for constant revision, making tax rebates and remissions possible when and where necessary.

The fiscal reform was accompanied by agricultural reform. Dispossessed farmers were restored to their lands, financial help was available to enable them to restart cultivation, and a mechanism was instituted to assist farms

[52] For a very different picture, see Howard-Johnston (1995a), who postulates an efficient tax-raising system not unlike that in the Roman empire.

[53] For summary and bibliography on Mazdak, see Guidi (1991); Crone (1991).

[54] For more detailed discussion of sources, see Rubin, Z. (1995).

affected by natural disasters. The overall result should have been to maintain a system of small farms that could be taxed easily, and to prevent the growth of huge estates whose powerful owners might accumulate privileges and immunities, and obstruct effective taxation.

Khusro's reform was meant to have a lasting impact on Sasanian military organisation by providing the shah with a standing army of crack units of horsemen (*asavaran*), under his direct command and permanently at his disposal, who received a salary, at least while on foreign campaign. This body of palace guards was recruited from among young nobles, as well as the country gentry who wished to start a military career. On the frontiers, troops recruited from the nomadic periphery, such as Turks, as well as from semi-independent enclaves within the empire – for example, Daylam in the mountainous region of Gilan – might be employed to repel invasions or hold them up until the mobile crack units arrived.

Khusro's system appears to have enjoyed moderate success for a few decades, until the difficulties that beset the Sasanian monarchy exposed its weaknesses. In the fiscal area, its proper functioning depended on internal stability, external security and continuing financial prosperity, backed up by revenues other than the land and poll taxes – such as taxes on international trade, especially the silk trade, booty from foreign wars, tribute and diplomatic subsidies. These supplementary sources of income were necessary to ensure the smooth running of the control mechanism that was integral to Khusro's system. However, its stability as a whole depended too much on a delicate balance which only a very powerful monarch could maintain at the best of times, and in the vast Sasanian monarchy, with its long frontiers, it was exposed to the dangers that threatened the empire itself. Growing military commitments increased the financial demands and pressure on tax-payers, thereby threatening the system; if central government lost effective control, abuse and corruption might swamp arrangements.

A neglected source which appears reliable on this issue – the *Sirat Anushirwan*, embedded in Ibn Misqawayh's *Tajarib al-umam* – indicates that towards the end of his reign, Khusro struggled to keep his system functioning.[55] The control mechanism proved to be as susceptible to corruption as the taxation machinery it was supposed to regulate. Furthermore, the strained relations between soldier and civilian, especially in the remoter zones, took their toll. In effect, the shah could restrain only those soldiers under his direct command from despoiling the rural tax-payers, as is shown by the restrictions imposed by Hormizd IV on a journey to Media. It is probable, however, that even during the last days of his father many of the cavalrymen no longer owed direct allegiance to the shah, and had reverted to

---

[55] Discussion in Rubin, Z. (1995), pp. 237–9, 279–84.

being retainers of the great, virtually independent landlords. A brief glance at the aftermath of Khusro's military reforms may help us to understand what happened.

The fragility of the financial arrangements underpinning the standing army militated against enduring success for Khusro's reforms. If, as suggested above, the Sasanian economy was never fully monetarised, the need to provide for the army's everyday needs, at times mostly in goods, will have encouraged the reintroduction of enfeoffment as the standard military contract, even among the lower ranks. Following a short period when Khusro made serious attempts to sustain his new standing army, even in his own lifetime the *asavaran* increasingly reverted to an enfeoffed estate, despite such fiefs' tendency to become hereditary and the consequent problems of alienation.[56] Khusro's reforms were, at best, of such limited duration and impact that their scope and intent might be questioned.

From the royal perspective, the higher nobility posed even more serious problems than the cavalrymen. The Mazdakite revolt and its aftermath made possible a feudal system more directly dependent on the shah than ever before. The nobility restored by Khusro was firmly beholden to the shah, so there could be no doubts about the origin of its estates or the nature of the services it owed the crown. But the nobility soon returned to its former position of power. The notion that the supreme military commanders and ministers of state were now salaried civil servants is contradicted by the limited evidence available. Thus, for example, Khusro's nominees as *spahbads* – the four supreme military commands he created to supersede the old office of the *artestaransalar* – can only have been mighty territorial lords from the start, as the very territorial nature of their command suggests. The same goes for the *marzbans*, the commanders of the frontier provinces.

The supposition that direct dependence on Khusro as restorer and benefactor would make his nobility more tractable and obedient to the shah in the long term is not sustainable, in view of the role played by the nobility under subsequent reigns, quite apart from the revolts in Khusro's first decade. Bahram Chobin of the noble house of Mihran, the first serious pretender outside the royal house since the establishment of the Sasanian dynasty, was supported by many disgruntled nobles. Khusro II overcame him in 591 with great difficulty, and only with the expensive support of the Byzantine emperor Maurice.[57] Later, the Sasanian monarchy was rocked

[56] TS (III.15.4, ed. de Boor and Wirth, p. 141; tr. Whitby and Whitby, p. 96) states that Persian troops did not receive a proper salary during service within the kingdom's borders, but had to rely on 'customary distributions' from the shah. This contradicts the hypothesis of a salaried standing army in Howard-Johnston (1995a).

[57] TS, IV–V, ed. de Boor and Wirth, pp. 149–220; tr. Whitby and Whitby pp. 103–57; Whitby, Michael (1988), pp. 276–308.

by other major revolts, such as those of Bistam and Bindoe – Khusro's relatives and allies turned foes – and of his powerful general, Shahrvaraz, who was to depose his grandson Ardashir III (628–9) and claim the throne.[58] By the time of the Arab conquest local rulers, especially in the east and in the Caspian provinces, had become virtually independent. The same is indicated by the confused Arabic traditions concerning Yemen after its conquest by the Persians in the last decade of Khusro I's reign. The growing independence of the great landlords meant that sooner or later they would inevitably control not only their own retinues of fighting men but also independent taxation in their domains. Thus, for example, according to Dinawari, the future rebel Bistam, upon his nomination as governor by Khusro, instituted taxation in the territories under his rule (Khorasan Qumis, Gurgan and Tabaristan) and in the process remitted half of the tax.[59] Other potentates, not in direct or prospective revolt against the shah, may have acted less openly but may not have been impelled by the requirements of war propaganda to be so generous.

Under Khusro II, oriental sources record impressive data about royal revenues, which might suggest that the machinery devised by Khusro I was still operating smoothly, and that Khusro II made even better use of it than his grandfather.[60] But the full narrative of al-Tabari gives a different impression: the revenues were not the product of *regular* taxation and should be explained in part by the influx of booty from Byzantine territories (the rich spoils of Alexandria and Jerusalem), and in part by extreme measures of extortion.[61] It was primarily as an efficient operator of the taxation machinery that Khusro's Nestorian finance minister (*vastaryoshansalar*), Yazdin, endeared himself to his lord; the favourable *Khuzistan chronicle* insists on the vast amounts of money that he sent to the treasury from the sunrise of one day to the sunrise of the next.[62] Such extortions seem to have involved not only an unbearable burden on tax-payers in the royal domain but also an attempt to reintroduce direct royal taxation in the domains of grandees, who had by now come to regard this as a blatant encroachment upon their privileges: the nobles proved ultimately to be his downfall. Thus Khusro II's riches cannot be attributed to the tax reforms of Khusro I.

---

[58] Whitby, Michael (1994), pp. 252–3.   [59] al-Dinawari, *al-Akhbar*, I, p. 102.

[60] Altheim and Stiehl (eds.) (1954), pp. 41–2; Altheim and Stiehl (1957), pp. 52–3.

[61] al-Tabari, *Ta'rikh*, ed. de Goeje *et al.*, I, p. 1042; tr. Bosworth, V, p. 377; German tr. Nöldeke, pp. 354–5. Al-Tabari might give the impression that the enormous sums referred to derived exclusively from taxation; this holds true only if one ignores the other sources of income which he mentions and if the words concerning spoils of war as a source of income subsequently put into Khusro's own mouth are disregarded: al-Tabari, *Ta'rikh*, ed. de Goeje *et al.*, I, p. 1056; tr. Bosworth, V, pp. 392–3; German tr. Nöldeke, pp. 376–7.

[62] *Khuzistan chronicle*, German tr. Nöldeke, p. 22; tr. Lieu *et al.*, p. 234; al-Tabari, *Ta'rikh*, ed. de Goeje *et al.*, I, pp. 1041–3; tr. Bosworth, V, pp. 375–8; German tr. Nöldeke, pp. 351–6.

SASANIAN COLLAPSE

The last decades of the Sasanian dynasty are the story of a chain of violent upheavals, exposing all the inherent weaknesses of the huge empire. The reforms of Khusro I did constitute a serious attempt to cope with these weaknesses and to re-establish the shah's position on a firmer basis. They failed in the long run because they strove to superimpose the framework of a fully centralised state, with a salaried civil bureaucracy and army, financed by an efficient and easily manageable taxation apparatus, on a realm which proved too weak to bear these heavy burdens. The political and military organisation of its vast territories was too flimsy, the economic infrastructure too primitive, and the social structure hidebound by traditions that could not be easily transformed. Khusro's own conservatism was a characteristic reflection of these traditions, for it was Khusro who did much to restore the battered nobility to its traditional powers after the Mazdakite interlude.

Warfare had always been the primary activity of the Sasanian state, but even by its own standards the last century of its existence witnessed a sustained intensity of campaigning that may have weakened the structures of society. After war broke out against Justin I in 527, there were only twenty-eight years of formal peace with Byzantium until the conclusive victory of Heraclius in 628 – and this is to ignore the recurrent tensions enmeshing the Arab satellites of the rival empires, Sasanian involvement in the affairs of the Arabian peninsula and the struggle to maintain control in Caucasian principalities such as Suania and Albania. We know much less about the sequence of campaigns on the north-eastern frontier, but these were probably more debilitating. Khusro's apparent triumph over the Hephthalites in the 550s was only achieved through alliance with the rising Turkish confederation, which now replaced the Hephthalites as Persia's neighbours and soon constituted a far more powerful threat during the 570s and 580s.[63] No less than Justinian, Khusro was repeatedly involved in wars on more than one front, and the expenses of eastern campaigning probably proved much heavier than the gains from spoils, ransoms and payments stipulated in his treaties with Byzantium.

The success of the state depended ultimately on the character and reputation of the shah, and there was a recurrent danger that such a personal monarchy would experience bouts of severe dynastic competition: thus, the long reigns of Shapur I and Shapur II were both followed by shorter periods of instability. This danger may have been increased in the sixth century by the withdrawal of Persian shahs from regular active participation in warfare, a move which fundamentally changed the nature of royal legitimation.

---

[63] Men., 10.3, 13.5, pp. 116–23, 146–7; TS, III.6.9–14, ed. de Boor and Wirth, pp. 121–2; tr. Whitby and Whitby, pp. 80–1.

Early rulers from the house of Sasan had demonstrated divine favour for their rule through personal victories, but the successors of Khusro I relied on others to win their wars.[64] From the royal perspective, legitimacy ran in the family, but the nobility and armies might prefer to give their loyalty to a successful commander such as the non-Sasanian Bahram Chobin or Shahrvaraz. The existence of substantial minority religious groups, Jews as well as Christians, allowed an established ruler to secure his position by balancing their different claims against the majority Zoroastrians. But it also meant that a rival could promote himself by seeking the support of one particular group: Bahram Chobin is known for his links with the Jews.

In spite of the attempted reforms of Khusro, the Sasanian state remained a fairly simple structure in which much economic and military power rested with the feudal nobility. Royal authority was bolstered by a supremacy of patronage, but this presupposed regular inflows of wealth for redistribution. Wars against the empire provided considerable short-term gains, and Byzantine peace payments under the 'perpetual peace' (532) and the fifty-year peace (562) were also important, but it is impossible to calculate how much of this wealth drained eastwards, almost immediately, to the Hephthalites or the Turks. The monetarised heartland of the Sasanian state (as of its Achaemenid antecedent) lay in the rich agricultural lands of Mesopotamia and lower Iraq, areas susceptible to attack from the west, and it seems to have been impossible to increase their tax revenues in the long term.

It is ironic that the most successful Sasanian conqueror, Khusro II, must also bear responsibility for the monarchy's subsequent rapid collapse. In the first decade of his reign, his status as a virtual puppet of Constantinople must have contributed to support for the long-running rebellion of Bistam in the east.[65] The overthrow of his patron Maurice in 602 gave Khusro an opportunity to assert his independence, and the disorganisation of Byzantine defences, particularly during the civil war between supporters of Phocas and Heraclius in 609–11, permitted Khusro to transform a sequence of traditional lucrative frontier campaigns into a massive expansionist thrust towards the west. But whereas a war of pillage replenished royal coffers, the annexation of territories reduced the inflow of funds and meant that the newly acquired resources had to be devoted to maintaining troops in remote regions. Furthermore, Khusro's successful armies had little direct contact with their distant monarch, being tied more closely to their victorious commanders; as a result, the soldiers of Shahrvaraz supported

[64] Whitby, Michael (1994).

[65] *Nihayat al-arab*, ed. Danish-Pazhuh, p. xx; summarised in Browne (1900), p. 240; Firdausi, *Shah-nama*, lines 2791–6, ed. Nafisi, IX, pp. 2791–6; French tr. Mohl, VII, pp. 143–50; tr. Warner and Warner, VIII, pp. 306–11.

their general when he was threatened by the shah. In the 620s, Heraclius' campaigns into the heart of Persia exposed the fragility of Khusro's achievements, prompting a palace coup that introduced the most severe bout of dynastic instability the Sasanian state had ever known. The return of booty to the Byzantines together with the destruction caused by campaigns in Mesopotamia left the monarchy short of wealth and prestige at the very moment when the Arabs started to raid across the Euphrates. Yazdgard III was forced to abandon Iraq in 638–9 and thereafter lacked the resources and reputation to challenge the new Islamic superpower. The Iranian nobility abandoned the Sasanians and transferred their allegiance to the Muslim rulers, who offered stability, while the rural majority went on paying their taxes – to support a new elite.

EASTERN NEIGHBOURS: ARMENIA (400–600)

R. W. THOMSON

INTRODUCTION

Armenia has always had an ambiguous place between the major powers, be they the East Roman empire and Sasanian Iran, the Byzantine empire and the caliphate, or the Ottoman empire and the Safavids. Armenian loyalties have not been consistent, either in support of a coherent internal policy or with regard to external diplomacy. The very definition of Armenia highlights the problem. Does the term refer to a geographical entity – and if so, what are its borders? Or does it refer to a people with common bonds – and if so, are those bonds linguistic, religious, cultural or political?[1]

---

[1] The emphasis in this chapter will be on Armenian reactions to events as expressed by the native historians. The principal Armenian sources for the period are:

Agathangelos: an anonymous history, written at the end of the fifth century, which gives the traditional account of the conversion of King Tiridates and the missionary activity of Gregory the Illuminator at the beginning of the previous century. Although replete with legendary tales and hagiographical commonplaces, it is important for the Armenian Arsacid reaction to the overthrow of the Parthian Arsacid dynasty by the Sasanians.

The *Buzandaran*: this traces the history of Armenia from the death of King Tiridates *c.* 330 to the division of the country into Roman and Iranian spheres *c.* 387. The author is unknown. The work is a compilation of epic tales describing the feats of the Arsacid dynasty, the noble house of the Mamikonean family (which played the leading role in the fourth and fifth centuries), and the descendants of Gregory in the office of catholicos. It is the last witness to the disappearing Iranian traditions of Armenia, although the Christian author did not himself comprehend the original significance of all the aspects of social and political life which he described.

Koriwn: a disciple of the inventor of the Armenian script, Mashtots'. His biography of the master is probably the earliest original composition in Armenian.

Moses of Khoren: author of a history of Armenia from the days of Noah to the death of Mashtots', whose pupil he claims to be. Very important as the first account of Armenian origins, in which oral traditions are integrated into the schema of Eusebius of Caesarea's *Chronicle*, it is the most learned of early Armenian histories. Moses used many Greek, Jewish and Syriac sources (via Armenian translations). But his strong pro-Bagratuni bias and his clear distortions of previous writers suggest a later authorship than that claimed. The date and authenticity are hotly contested. But it is significant that the Bagratuni did not gain their ultimate prominence until the eighth century, and Moses' history is not quoted until the tenth.

Elishe: unknown author of a history describing the revolt against Shah Yazdgard II in 450–1, the defeat of the Armenian army led by Vardan Mamikonean at Avarayr, and the ensuing imprisonment of surviving Armenian nobles. This is probably not an eyewitness account as claimed, but a rewriting of the shorter version of these events in Lazar. Its great importance is the adaptation of the story of the Maccabees to the Armenian situation, and the identification of Christian with patriotic

Despite the conversion of King Tiridates IV (*c.* 283–330) to Christianity, probably in 314,[2] and the establishment of an organised church, the continuing strength of Iranian traditions and the cultural and kinship ties of the Armenian nobility to Iran made Armenia an uncertain ally for the Romans. Yet since the Armenian monarchy was a branch of the Arsacid dynasty which had been overthrown by the Sasanians in 224, relations between Armenia and Iran were already strained. Tiridates' conversion compounded an already difficult situation, for the shahs naturally became suspicious of the future loyalty of Armenians to their Iranian heritage.[3] In the fifth century, attempts by the shahs to impose Zoroastrianism led to armed conflict – while to the west, the Armenians found their relationship with fellow Christians increasingly marred by their involvement in the struggles over orthodoxy. The division of Armenia *c.* 387 into two monarchies and two spheres of influence – a large Iranian sector east of a line running from Sper to Martyropolis (see map 8), and a much smaller Roman sector west of that line up to the Euphrates – did not solve 'the Armenian question'.[4] Both powers were to find Armenia a difficult neighbour.

CHRISTIAN ARMENIA BETWEEN PERSIA AND BYZANTIUM

The ruler of the Roman sector (Inner Armenia) King Arshak III, died in 390. His subjects were immediately placed under direct imperial rule through a *comes Armeniae*; on the other hand, the traditional rights of the Armenian princes in that area were not abrogated.[5] They enjoyed immunity from

virtues. A sophisticated literary work, it shaped Armenian attitudes towards the interaction of religion and politics down to the present time.

Lazar of P'arp: author of a history of Armenia from 387, picking up where the *Buzandaran* ends, to the appointment of Vahan Mamikonean as governor of Persian Armenia in 484. His history is an encomium of the Mamikonean family. Despite its bias, it is valuable as an account by someone who knew the major participants, as most other early Armenian histories are by unknown authors and of uncertain date.

Sebeos: a 'History of Heraclius' by a bishop Sebeos is mentioned by Armenian authors of the tenth and later centuries, but their quotations do not match the untitled text discovered in the early nineteenth century and published as the work of Sebeos. This anonymous work is important, nonetheless, as a product of the seventh century by an author familiar with events in the milieu of the Armenian catholicos. The emphasis is on Armenia in the context of Byzantino-Iranian rivalry from the time of Maurice (582–602) to the accession of Mu'awiya as caliph in 661.

Book of letters: a compilation of documents dealing with ecclesiastical matters from the fifth to the thirteenth century. Of particular importance are the letters exchanged between official representatives of the Armenian church and foreign dignitaries of the Greek-speaking imperial church, the Syriac-speaking church in Iran and the church in Georgia.

[2] This is the usually accepted date for the consecration of Gregory at Caesarea, which marks the beginning of the formal organisation of the church in Armenia. For the origins of Christianity in Armenia, see Thomson (1988–9); Seibt (ed.) (2002).

[3] For the Iranian heritage in Armenia: Garsoïan (1976); for the religious background: Russell (1987).

[4] On this division and the geographical setting: Adontz (1970), pp. 7–24; Hewsen (2001), map no. 69, p. 90.

[5] Toumanoff (1963), pp. 133–4.

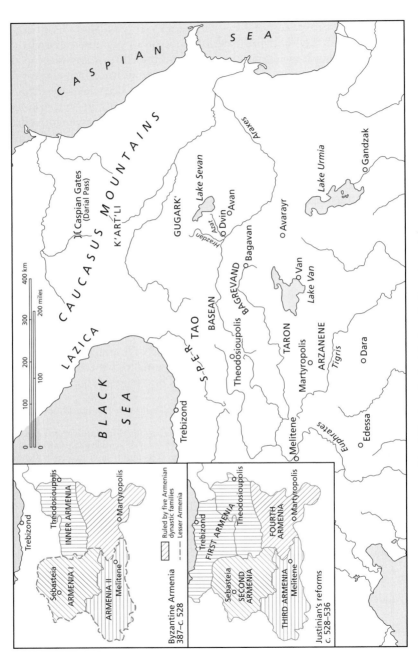

Map 8 The Armenian lands in the earlier Byzantine period

taxation, and no military garrisons were imposed. Procopius claims that it was this military weakness that later led Justinian to tighten his control. He observed that 'Armenia was always in a state of disorder, and for this reason an easy prey for the barbarians.'[6] He might have added that social, religious and cultural ties with their kinsmen across the border could not enhance security. Not until the sixth century did Justinian do away with the traditional rights of the Armenian princes in a series of moves between 528 and 535. Armenian lands west of the border with Iran were then fully integrated into the empire as the four provinces of Armenia (see below pp. 167–8).

It was in eastern Armenia – the sector under Persian suzerainty, which composed about four-fifths of the earlier kingdom – that the major cultural and religious developments of this period had their origin. Yet the border between the two sectors was no solid wall. Although Armenian writers rarely refer explicitly to the border, through the communities in the west contacts between the imperial capital and Persian Armenia were promoted and sustained.

In eastern Armenia the centrifugal tendencies of the leading princely families rapidly overcame the weakened monarchy. The rights and privileges of the noble families, jealously guarded over generations and considered more fundamental than royal authority, had been recognised by the Arsacids and legitimised. The office of chief military officer (*sparapet*), for example, was the perquisite of the Mamikonean family, which played the leading role in politics during the fifth and sixth centuries. Their principal rivals, the Bagratuni – who did not attain the leading role until the eighth century – held the hereditary right to crown Armenian rulers (see below, p. 348).

In Arsacid Armenia there were some fifty noble families of varied size and power, each with its own military forces.[7] Cities played little political or cultural role, despite their economic significance.[8] The focus of noble life was the family holdings. The Mamikonean territories were in Tao, Bagrevand and Taron – i.e. much of north-central Armenia. The Bagratuni homeland was in Sper, but they gradually acquired territories to the south-west. A branch of this family was established in eastern Georgia ('Iberia' to the Greeks, 'K'art'li' to the Georgians). To the south-east of Lake Van another family, the Artsruni, were settled. They acquired land between Lake Van and the Araxes, and were later to become the principal rivals of the Bagratuni. After the demise of the royal line, these families pursued their own interests with regard to Rome or Persia, conducting, as it were, an individual foreign policy. Eastern Armenia was thus not a stable unity.

---

[6] Pr *B*, III.1.16, ed. and tr. Dewing and Downey, pp. 182–3.
[7] Toumanoff (1963), pp. 147–259.
[8] Garsoïan (1984–85). For the economic situation: Manandian (1965), pp. 67–127.

This traditional pattern of society was reinforced by the growth of an organised Armenian church. Armenian historians of the fifth and sixth century often stress the 'national' role of the church and the leadership of the catholicos. But they do not explain that the bishoprics were established within the princely families, reinforcing the authority of the princes. This Armenian pattern, reflecting Armenian society of the time, was very different from that in the empire, which was based on the relative importance of the cities where the bishops resided. Furthermore, the Armenian office of catholicos until the death of Sahak in 439 was itself regarded as a hereditary perquisite of the Pahlavuni family, just as were other offices of state in other families.[9]

Unhappy with any diminution of their privileges, the magnates of eastern Armenia quarrelled with their king Khusro IV (who had been installed in 387 when Arshak III moved to western Armenia) and succeeded in having him deposed in favour of his son Vramshapur (389–417). The weaker the monarchy – from their point of view – the better, and soon the princes came to regard the Persian shah himself as their immediate sovereign. On Vramshapur's death his father was briefly reinstated; then Shah Yazdgard I (399–420) appointed his own son, Shapur. On Yazdgard's death Shapur failed to win the succession to the Sasanian throne. Shah Bahram V (420–38) permitted Vramshapur's son Ardashir to reign, but he too was unpopular. In 428 Bahram agreed to accept the direct submission of the Armenian princes. The monarchy was abolished, and a Persian governor, the *marzban*, installed at Dvin.[10] The *marzban* was responsible for collecting taxes; the princes provided military service to the shah in person with their private armies. In their own lands they were autonomous.

In this way, the shah took advantage of age-long Armenian practices to increase Persian control of Armenia. Recognising the importance of the church in that valuable province, he attempted to strengthen his hand even more by deposing the catholicos Sahak (*c.* 390–438), who represented continuity with the past through his descent from Gregory the Illuminator and whose outlook allied him to Greek cultural interests. Sahak was replaced by an insignificant appointee, to be succeeded by two Syrians.[11] Bahram's policy with regard to the political administration of Armenia was moderate and successful. But his interference in ecclesiastical affairs was less well received. And his successor's harsher measures, aimed at integrating Armenia more closely into the Sasanian empire, eventually sparked outright rebellion. The passion of those who resisted – and resistance was by no means unanimous – reflects the increased Armenian allegiance to the church and to Christianity as their birthright. The terms 'patrimonial' or

---

[9] Garsoïan (1983), pp. 233–5.   [10] On this office: Christensen (1944), pp. 131–9.
[11] On these three – Surmak, Brkisho and Shmuel: *Narratio de rebus Armeniae*, ed. Garitte, pp. 99–102 (commentary).

'ancestral way of life' originally used for the secular realm – where they applied to personal estates or the monarchy – were adapted by early Armenian historians to the religious sphere, where they now defined Christianity and the church within an Armenian context.

Yet Christianity was hardly 'an ancestral way of life' in fifth-century Armenia. The anonymous historian known as Agathangelos, who gives the standard account of the conversion of the country, claims that Gregory visited the whole Caucasus, baptised millions of Armenians and established hundreds of bishoprics.[12] Agathangelos was too optimistic. The process of conversion took many generations, and the church met with opposition on many fronts. The *Buzandaran* paints a vivid picture of the pro-Iranian tendencies of many noble families, whose allegiance to the shah was strengthened by acceptance of Zoroastrianism. For many the Christian message, which reached Armenia from Syria in the south and from Asia Minor to the west, was a foreign faith.[13] The fact that no written medium for the Armenian language existed in the fourth century added to the difficulty of strengthening the church's position and overcoming resistance to this alien innovation. So the invention by Mashtots' of a script for the native tongue *c.* 400 marked a very significant stage in the conversion of Armenia to Christianity, though it was not in itself the last step in that process (see fig. 6 below).

Mashtots' had received a Greek education and rose to a prominent position in the royal chancellery, but withdrew in order to lead a hermit's life. In due course he attracted disciples and, with support from Catholicos Sahak and King Vramshapur, formed a script based on the Greek model – i.e. a fully alphabetical script with separate characters for each consonant and vowel. With only minor modifications, it has remained in continuous use down to the present day. His disciples were sent to Syria and Asia Minor to learn Syriac and Greek and to make translations of books needed for the church. Rapidly a corpus of biblical, liturgical, theological and historical texts was made available. The circle around Mashtots' began to create original works as well, and their interests soon extended to secular studies as pursued in the contemporary schools and universities of the eastern Mediterranean – they produced works of philosophy, grammar and rhetoric, and of scientific enquiry.[14]

The development of a specifically Armenian literature – in the broadest sense of the term – brought several consequences: an increasing sense of solidarity among Armenians on either side of the Byzantine–Iranian border, a

---

[12] For a comparison of the various recensions and versions of this history see Agathangelos, *History*, tr. Thomson, pp. xxi–xcvii (introduction).

[13] There is no general study in a western language of the impact of the Syrian strain in Armenian Christianity more recent than Ter-Minassiantz (1904). Aspects of Syrian liturgical influence are brought out by Winkler (1982) and Winkler (2000), with good bibliographies.

[14] Renoux (1993). Survey of the early period: Thomson (1982); detailed bibliography of sources: Thomson (1995); Thomson (2007).

Figure 6 Inscription dated to 668 from the church of St Gregory at Aruch; a fine example of the uncial script invented by Mashtots' *c.* 400 AD

stronger voice in national affairs for church authorities as a body that spoke for interests broader than those of individual families, and greater involvement in the ecclesiastical questions that were shaking the East Roman empire. Armenia's liturgical practice was greatly influenced by Jerusalem. Many from Armenia and Georgia made pilgrimages to the Holy Land, some staying on as monks. The theological exegesis of Syria made a great impact, and the Greek fathers of the fourth century were well-known. As the Armenians forged their own traditions in matters of practice, their attitudes with regard to matters of faith were sharpened by involvement in the burning issues of the day. This heightened sense of commitment to a faith associated with the empire could only be regarded with concern by the rulers of the Sasanian world in which most of Armenia lay.

The attempt of Yazdgard II (438–57) to impose a form of Zoroastrianism by force in 450 prompted immediate resistance by the church authorities; popular resentment coalesced around the prince of the Mamikonean family, Vardan. He was related by marriage to Catholicos Sahak, whose daughter his father had married, and his family played the leading role in contemporary Armenian politics. Like many other Armenian princes, Vardan had earlier temporised by submitting to Zoroastrianism when summoned to court. But he agreed to lead the revolt, and one of his brothers went with a delegation to seek aid from Theodosius II. The latter died in July, and Marcian refused to become involved in Armenia, having many distractions closer to home in the Balkans.[15]

For that first year the Armenians held off the Persian forces. But faced with dissension in their own ranks, they could not resist a large Persian army sent to Armenia in 451. In June, Vardan and many nobles met their deaths on the field of Avarayr in eastern central Armenia; other leaders, both clerical and lay, were taken in captivity to the region of Nishapur. Resistance in a military sense was thus ended. But Armenia was a valuable asset to the Sasanian empire, and calmer views prevailed. Forced conversion to Zoroastrianism was dropped, and an uneasy peace marked the next generation. During the reign of Peroz (459–84) the imprisoned leaders of the rebellion were released.

The close ties between Armenia and Georgia were the indirect cause of the next attempt to loosen Iranian control. A daughter of Vardan Mamikonean, Shushanik, had married Vazgen, governor of the neighbouring province of Gugark'. But he accepted Zoroastrianism, in return for which he was given a royal princess to wife. His first wife, Shushanik, died of subsequent ill-treatment, and was to become a martyred saint revered on both sides of the Armenian–Georgian border.[16] Her *Life* is the first original composition in Georgian. The Georgian king, Vakhtang-Gorgasal, eventually put Vazgen to death in 482, thereby incurring the immediate wrath of his lord, Shah Peroz. In this emergency Vakhtang sought aid from Huns beyond the Caucasus and from his Christian neighbours to the south. Vardan's nephew, Vahan Mamikonean, now the leading prince of that family, thus found himself at the head of the Armenian forces engaged in another rebellion, thirty-one years after his uncle's death.

Military success was no more possible now than it had been earlier. Armenian–Georgian co-operation was marred by mutual antagonisms, brought out clearly by the historian Lazar, who describes this period in detail – Vahan being the patron and hero of his *History*. The Armenian troops were forced to withdraw to the mountains of north-western Armenia. They were rent by internal dissensions, the Persians always finding supporters among the Armenian nobility. On the other hand, the Persian forces were not at full strength, since Peroz had taken a large army to attack the Hephthalites (see above, p. 134). His unexpected defeat and death on the battlefield in 484 changed the situation entirely. Anxious to placate their fractious subjects, whose Christian ties to the empire were a potential source of danger, the Persians removed their governor. In his place, the prince of the most prominent local noble family was appointed *marzban*.

[15] This revolt is not mentioned in contemporary Greek sources. For the date of Elishe's classic description and its relation to the version of Lazar: Elishe, *History*, tr. Thomson, pp. 23–9 (introduction).

[16] For discussion of the original text by Jacob of Tsurtav and later versions in their historical setting: Peeters (1935).

Thus Vahan Mamikonean gained the measure of internal autonomy for which his uncle Vardan had died in 451.

The attention of Armenian historians moves rapidly from Vahan's success to the involvement of Armenia in the Byzantine–Persian wars of the late sixth and early seventh centuries. In doing so, they ignore the growing estrangement of the Armenian from the imperial church – a rift with cultural and political consequences of the first magnitude.

THE ARMENIAN CHURCH AS RALLYING-POINT AND RELATIONS WITH THE IMPERIAL CHURCH

The increasing importance of the church as a cultural institution following the abolition of the monarchy in 428 is not of itself surprising. It was the only institution that cut across factional lines, and it was the only medium through which literary and artistic endeavours could be realised on any meaningful scale. Individuals with financial backing would still attend the universities of the eastern Mediterranean; Greek and Syriac as well as Armenian sources attest the presence of Armenian students in Antioch, Beirut, Alexandria, Athens and elsewhere. But government service as a career for the educated was no longer an option after 428; the only major patron of education and learning was the church, and only the church could offer advancement for the ambitious and a haven for the studious. The complaints of Anania of Shirak in the seventh century that his fellow countrymen did not admire learning suggest that without patronage a teaching career was difficult.[17] There were cities in Armenia, but they did not play the cultural role of an Antioch or an Athens, with organised schools and subsidised professorial chairs.

The relationship of the Armenian church to the larger Greek-speaking world was thus of importance. Armenians were always admirers of Greek learning, but their attitude to Constantinople was ambivalent. In part, such an attitude reflected the political situation; a pro-Greek attitude could arouse suspicions of disloyalty to the shah. Some part was played by the very different backgrounds of Armenians and Greeks – and, not least, the strong Syrian strain in Armenian ecclesiastical life, church ritual and theological exegesis prevented any automatic acceptance of things Greek. An official break between the churches was long in coming. But the steps leading to that eventual rupture deserve a brief review.

Luckily, the Armenian reaction to the theological questions that divided the Greek *oikoumenē* – debates which gave the Armenians an opportunity to define more carefully their own position – is well documented in the *Book of letters*. The first three sections of this unique collection of official documents

---

[17] His short *Autobiography* is a unique document in early Armenian literature. See Berbérian (1964).

comprise exchanges of letters between Armenian ecclesiastical authorities and members of the Greek-speaking imperial church, representatives of the Syriac-speaking church in Iran, and ecclesiastics in Georgia, covering the fifth, sixth and seventh centuries. The earliest is a letter by Acacius, bishop of Melitene, written soon after the council of Ephesus, held in 431.[18]

Melitene had been one of the cities where the pupils of Mashtotsʻ pursued their study of Greek. Acacius had met Mashtotsʻ on the latter's travels in Roman territory, and was well informed of events in Armenia. He had recently played a significant role in the council of Ephesus, where Nestorius, patriarch of Constantinople (428–31) and other Antiochene theologians had been condemned. So he took alarm when he heard that works by Theodore of Mopsuestia were being read in Armenia. For Theodore was a prominent biblical exponent of the Antiochene school, whose interpretation of the Incarnation had been rejected at Ephesus. But Armenian interest in Theodore was not surprising, since the tradition he represented had been strong in Edessa, the centre of Syriac-speaking Christian culture. It was to Edessa that Mashtotsʻ had gone in his search for an Armenian script, and it was in Edessa that many of his pupils studied. The reply to Acacius' letter, signed by Sahak as head of the Armenian church, was polite but guarded, denying any Armenian involvement in heresy yet not specifying any heresy by name. A second letter was sent by Acacius to the secular authorities of Armenia. It had been prompted by Syrian priests who reported that the influence of Nestorian ideas in Armenia was continuing. But it passed without response.

Of greater impact was a letter from the patriarch of Constantinople, Proclus (434–46). This time it was not foreign Syrians, but two pupils of Mashtotsʻ who had taken the initiative. While in the capital to translate Greek texts, they approached the patriarch for an authoritative interpretation of the doctrine of the Incarnation. That this was not an official solicitation by the Armenian authorities is clear from an apology by a third Armenian disciple, Eznik, who had studied in Edessa before going to Constantinople. Proclus responded by addressing a detailed exposition of the matter to the bishops of Armenia. The Armenian reply was signed by both Sahak and Mashtotsʻ. After defining their own faith, they assured the patriarch that no heretical ideas attributable to Theodore were circulating in Armenia. The letter of Proclus, however, was to remain a keystone of Armenian orthodoxy, and this early emphasis on the council of Ephesus had a profound impact. Ephesus, rather than the council of Chalcedon, held twenty years later, would be the rallying-cry of Armenian theologians.

---

[18] For the Armenian correspondence with Acacius and Patriarch Proclus: *Book of letters*, French tr. Tallon, pp. 29–44, 53–77; for the Armenian reaction to the theological disputes: Sarkissian (1975); and in much greater detail with French translations of the documents: Garsoïan (1999a); for the debates within the Eastern Roman empire: Grillmeier (1975–96).

The fourth ecumenical council – held beside the Bosporus in Chalcedon in 451 – did not bring peace to the warring parties or solve the theological question of defining the Incarnation in a manner satisfactory to all. The catholicos of Armenia was not represented at Chalcedon, though bishops from Armenian provinces on the Roman side of the frontier were in attendance.[19] Somewhat surprisingly, the early Armenian historians pass over both the second ('robber') council of Ephesus in 449 and that of Chalcedon in 451. It was the *Henotikon* of Emperor Zeno (474–91), promulgated in 482, which Armenians emphasised as orthodox.[20] Bypassing the recent divisive council of Chalcedon, in their official pronouncements the Armenians were happy to pledge their allegiance to the councils of Nicaea (325) and Ephesus. As they developed their own traditions in ecclesiastical architecture and moulded an individual Armenian literature, they were not at the turn of the century acting in deliberate opposition to what was then the orthodoxy of the empire.

At a council held in 505–6 in Dvin, the residence of the *marzban* and the main city of Persian Armenia, a group of Syrians from the Persian empire appeared, requesting episcopal consecration for one of their monks, Symeon. These Syrians were not members of the church in Persia which enjoyed the shah's official recognition, but were monophysites. The Armenian bishops consecrated Symeon and recognised the orthodoxy of these Syrians as being in conformity with their own faith and that of the Greeks. But the zealous Symeon, an opponent of the official church in Persia, persuaded the Armenians to anathematise the council of Chalcedon as expressing the views of Nestorius.[21] The Armenians did not anathematise the imperial church as such; the *Henotikon* of Zeno was still in force, and he was regarded by the Armenians as 'the blessed emperor'.[22]

But this apparent unanimity of the imperial and Armenian churches was short-lived. Zeno's policy of compromise with the opponents of Chalcedon was reversed on the accession of Justin I (518–27). After 518 the imperial church of Constantinople made peace with Rome and stood firmly behind the definitions of Chalcedon. As the sixth century progressed, the monophysites in Syria and Egypt became more coherently organised, thanks mainly to the labours of Jacob Baradaeus (see above, p. 118), while their

---

[19] Garsoïan (1988); Garsoïan (1999a), pp. 127–9. See also above, p. 102.

[20] As noted above (p. 163), Vahan Mamikonean was then engaged in open rebellion against the shah, a situation resolved by his eventual appointment as *marzban*.

[21] On Symeon's career: Shahid (ed. and tr.), *Martyrs of the Najran*, pp. 159–79.

[22] In the *Book of letters*, Zeno is called 'blessed' (ed. Izmireants', pp. 49, 140, 268; ed. Pogharean, pp. 159, 284, 112; French tr. Garsoïan (1999a), pp. 448 (but Garsoïan here translates as 'pieux'), 539); 'pious' (ed. Izmireants', pp. 141, 142, 328; ed. Pogharean, pp. 286, 504; French tr. Garsoïan (1999a), pp. 540, 541); 'orthodox' (ed. Izmireants', pp. 126, 262, 277; ed. Pogharean, pp. 266, 105, 144); 'benevolent' (ed. Izmireants', pp. 266, 267, 269; ed. Pogharean, pp. 109, 111, 114). On this council in Dvin: Sarkissian (1965), pp. 196–213; Garsoïan (1999b).

theology found definite expression in the works of Severus of Antioch. The differences apparent at the time of Chalcedon had now become quite clear-cut, and compromise was increasingly difficult.[23]

RELATIONS WITH THE SYRIANS, JUSTINIAN AND HIS SUCCESSORS

The Armenians do not seem to have taken any definite steps to repudiate the Byzantine return to Chalcedonian orthodoxy until they were prompted to do so by another Syrian delegation from Persia, which appeared at another council held in Dvin in 555, again requesting consecration for one of their company. These Syrians were members of a splinter group within the monophysite church, the Julianists, who held that Christ's body had remained 'incorruptible'.[24] The Armenian catholicos Nerses II (548–57) and his bishops found the Syrians' profession of faith orthodox and consecrated Abdisho. The impact of Julianist ideas was not the most important result of this encounter in 555; in later years there was no unanimity among Armenian theologians on that issue. The significant fact was that the Armenians not only rejected Chalcedon again; they also, for the first time, specifically anathematised the imperial church for upholding that council – which to Armenian eyes had approved the ideas of Nestorius.[25]

Despite these important developments, whose significance was perhaps not obvious at the time, Armenian historians have remarkably little to say about Armenian affairs during the reigns of Justin and Justinian (527–65). The first Persian war, which ended in 532, brought no change to the frontiers or the status of the divided country. Even the reorganisation of the Armenian territories within the empire by Justinian is passed over by Armenian sources. In 528 the right of Armenian princes to maintain their private military forces was abrogated when the office of *magister militum per Armeniam* was created. The civil standing of the princes was diminished when their traditional rights of inheritance were brought into line with imperial practice. In 536 Armenian territory was reorganised into First, Second, Third and Fourth Armenia at the expense of neighbouring land in Cappadocia. The use of the name 'Armenia' is an indication of the strongly Armenian presence west of the Euphrates, which had been increasing rather than diminishing. Now, not only were the Armenians inside the imperial borders deprived of their long-standing rights and governance by

---

[23] Frend (1972), pp. 201–20 (on Severus); pp. 284–7 (on Jacob Baradaeus). See also Kennedy (2000), p. 594 and above, p. 118.

[24] For this controversy: Draguet (1924).

[25] On this second council of Dvin and the correspondence in the *Book of letters*: *Narratio de rebus Armeniae*, chs. 60–76, ed. Garitte, pp. 34–6 (text), pp. 130–75 (commentary); French tr. Mahé, pp. 433–4.

traditional princely families (which had been guaranteed in the original treaty), but this significant portion of the total Armenian population was lost to Armenia proper. Imperial authorities did not speak Armenian or encourage allegiance to the Armenian church, as Justinian attempted to impose imperial orthodoxy on his realms. Armenians were useful to the empire in many ways, especially in the army. But an individual Armenian culture flourished henceforth only on the Persian side of the frontier.

Justinian's treatment of his Armenian nobles led to complaints to the shah[26] and Armenian involvement in war plans against the emperor.[27] In 540 hostilities between Byzantium and Persia reopened. Antioch was captured, but Dara resisted the invading Persians. Military operations were confined to Mesopotamia and Lazica during the war, save for an encounter at Dvin in 543. The peace of 545 was one of many made during the long confrontation, which continued into the following century (see above, pp. 120, 135–6).

There was no overt sign of unrest in Persian Armenia until the latter part of the sixth century. When trouble did break out, it seems to have been caused by the attitude of the Persian *marzban* of the time, Suren, not by the official policy of the shah. In 571 Suren set up a fire-temple in Dvin and attempted to impose Zoroastrianism on the country. The reaction was parallel to that of 450. Led by Vardan, prince of the Mamikoneans (not to be confused with the leader of the fifth-century revolt), the Armenians rebelled. When Suren returned the following year with reinforcements, he perished in the encounter. However, the Persians retook Dvin, and Vardan fled to Constantinople. Now, for the first time, the consequences of the religious differences became clear. Vardan had to accept communion with the imperial church, while Catholicos John II (557–74), who had fled with him, remained at Constantinople under the cloud of submission to Chalcedon until his death in 574.[28]

Justin II (565–78) gave Vardan military forces, and Dvin was retaken. But Byzantine success was not lasting. In 576 Persian forces under Khusro I (531–79) crossed Armenia but failed to capture Theodosioupolis. After advancing as far as Sebasteia, Khusro withdrew and sacked Melitene, but after a confrontation there, he fled back to Persia in confusion. During negotiations the following year, the Byzantine general Justinian was defeated by Khusro in Basean and Bagrevand,[29] and the Persians retained the frontier fortress of Dara, which they had captured in 573.[30]

[26] Toumanoff (1963), p. 175; Pr *W*, II.3.31–3, ed. and tr. Dewing, I, pp. 278–9.
[27] Adontz (1970), pp. 160–1; Pr *W*, II.3.53, ed. and tr. Dewing, I, pp. 284–5.
[28] On this rebellion and the 'union' of 572: *Narratio de rebus Armeniae*, ed. Garitte, pp. 183–225 (commentary).
[29] Seb., ch. 71, tr. and comm. Thomson and Howard-Johnston, I, p. 11.
[30] Whitby, Michael (1988), pp. 264–7.

Imperial fortunes revived in 590 when the general Bahram Chobin seized the Sasanian throne upon the murder of Shah Hormizd IV (579–90). The legitimate heir, Hormizd's son Khusro II, appealed to Emperor Maurice for help, promising in return to cede to the empire all Armenia as far as Lake Van and Dvin, plus part of Georgia. The offer was accepted, and the Armenians under Mushegh Mamikonean sided with Khusro and the Byzantines. Their combined forces defeated Bahram the following year at Gandzak in eastern Armenia. Installed as ruler of Persia, Khusro II (591–628) fulfilled his promise: Armenia west of the Hrazdan and Azat rivers passed to Byzantium (see above, pp. 127, 136).

This success for the Roman empire was fraught with a number of consequences for the Armenians. Maurice attempted to integrate Armenia more securely into the empire. He deported significant numbers of Armenians to the Balkans to strengthen his borders there and weaken resistance to imperial rule among Armenians now incorporated into the empire. The Armenian general Mushegh Mamikonean was killed in Thrace.[31] But Maurice sometimes encountered resistance by Armenian soldiers. The Bagratuni prince Smbat rebelled and was condemned to the arena. Saved by his strength, according to the Armenian historian (by the clemency of the empress, according to a Greek source), he was exiled to Africa.[32] But it was not long before he was back east, serving the shah.

The plight of the Armenians between shah and emperor is well expressed in an apocryphal letter which the Armenian historian known as Sebeos claims was sent by Maurice to Khusro:

They are a perverse and disobedient nation, who stand between us and disturb us. I shall gather mine and send them off to Thrace. You gather yours and order them to be sent to the east. If they die, it is our enemies who die. If they kill, they kill our enemies. Then we shall live in peace. For if they remain in their own land, there will be no repose for us.[33]

But the most significant aspect of his policy was the attempt to enforce imperial orthodoxy in the newly acquired territories. The Armenian catholicos was summoned to a synod where the union of the churches might be effected – that is, where the Armenians would accept Chalcedon and take communion with the Byzantines. Catholicos Moses II (574–604) refused to go and remained in Dvin, just across the border. On this occasion he is credited with a riposte that clearly expressed Armenian resistance to assimilation. It is preserved in a rare pro-Chalcedonian document of Armenian

---

[31] Seb., chs. 90–1, tr. and comm. Thomson and Howard-Johnston, I, pp. 35–6; Whitby, Michael (1988), pp. 127–8, notes that Sebeos' account seems to conflate several campaigns.

[32] Seb., ch. 93, tr. and comm. Thomson and Howard-Johnston, I, pp. 39–40; Whitby, Michael (1988), p. 127.

[33] Seb., ch. 86, tr. and comm. Thomson and Howard-Johnston, I, p. 31.

origin: 'I shall not cross the Azat; I shall not eat bread baked [in the oven];
I shall not drink warm water.' The Azat was the river marking the border
and is a pun, the word meaning 'free'. The other two comments refer to the
differing practices of the liturgy, since Armenians used unleavened bread
and did not mix warm water with the wine.[34] Matters of doctrine may figure more prominently in the written records of historians and theologians,
but the development of different rituals was no less potent a factor in the
estrangement of the churches.

Nevertheless, the Armenian bishops in Byzantine territory did go to Constantinople and accept communion, thus causing a schism in the Armenian church. But once Byzantine forces withdrew, then Armenian unity
was restored. This pattern recurred in the time of Heraclius (610–41) and
again under Justinian II (685–95), but proved no more lasting than under
Maurice. Despite the fact that many sympathised with the position of
the imperial church – and significant groups of Chalcedonian Armenians
existed in the succeeding centuries[35] – reunion between the Byzantine and
Armenian churches was never achieved.

Yet the time of Maurice was remembered as a time of peace. The curious
text known as 'Pseudo-Shapuh' – a medley of tales dating from the ninth to
the twelfth century, and not the lost work of the ninth-century historian –
refers to the proverb: 'as in the time of Maurice, when one lived untroubled'.
It also reports that when Maurice summoned his father David, who lived
in Armenia, the latter said: 'I cannot come. I prefer my small garden to the
Roman empire.' But by cutting off the heads of the largest beetroots in his
garden, he indicated to his son's messengers how Maurice should treat his
magnates.[36]

Just as Maurice used Armenian arms in the Balkans, so did those Armenian princes on the Persian side of the border continue to provide military
service to the shah. The most notable example is the career of Smbat,
prince of the Bagratuni, who served at different times both emperor and
shah – Armenian loyalties being rarely unequivocal and permanent. Just
as Maurice settled colonies of Armenians in the west, so did Smbat find
Armenians, Greeks and Syrians deported to Hyrcania when he was serving
as governor there for Khusro II. Sebeos notes that the Armenians had even
forgotten their own language, and that Smbat remedied this by arranging
for the ministry of a priest.[37] The role of language and religion as a means of

---

[34] On the 'union' of 591 and Moses II's comments: *Narratio de rebus Armeniae*, ed. Garitte, pp. 225–54
(commentary); for the border running between Dvin and Avan: Hewsen (2001), p. 90.

[35] For Chalcedonian Armenians in later centuries: Arutiunova-Fidanian (1980). See also below,
pp. 333–64.

[36] Pseudo-Shapuh, chs. 49, 51, tr. Thomson, p. 185; see also Adontz (1934), pp. 1–9.

[37] Seb., chs. 96–7, tr. and comm. Thomson and Howard-Johnston, I, pp. 43–4.

preserving Armenian identity in colonies outside the homeland was already clear.

At the same time, the Armenians were estranged from their northern neighbours. The Georgians under their catholicos Kyrion disavowed the Armenian rejection of Chalcedon and henceforth remained firmly committed to the orthodoxy of Constantinople. The final rupture occurred after a series of bitter exchanges. At another council held in Dvin in 608, the Armenians excommunicated the Georgians.[38] But contacts between the two peoples could not be stopped by fiat, not least because of the extensive bonds of consanguinity linking noble families on both sides of the frontier. Pro-Chalcedonian Armenians were particularly numerous in Tao and Gugark', where the two peoples mingled. Maurice's downfall in 602 gave Khusro II an opportunity to recover the Armenian lands ceded to his earlier supporter. The reign of Heraclius would see the final defeat of Sasanian Persia and the rise of a new power in the Middle East. But already by the turn of the sixth century the building-blocks of an independent Armenian culture had been formed.[39]

CONCLUSION

Many years earlier in his *Annals* (II.56; XIII.34) Tacitus had referred to the ambivalent role of Armenia and the Armenians between Rome and Parthia: 'a people from the earliest times of equal ambiguity in character and geography . . . placed between two great empires, with which they differ frequently'. He described their dealings with both sides, and he knew that fundamentally the Armenians were closer to Iran than to Rome. In Sasanian times as well, the value of Armenia as a vassal state was recognised by the two sides: the East Roman empire and Sasanian Iran both sought to control Armenia, to engage its troops and to profit from its gold mines and other natural resources. After the division of the country and the abolition of the monarchy, attempted control became attempted integration – more successful in Roman Armenia than in the much larger eastern sector.

The conversion of the Armenians to Christianity gradually changed their relationship with Iran, but slowly and painfully. The various strands of Christian practice from Jerusalem, Syria and Asia Minor were moulded into a national tradition. But their faith and practice kept the Armenians apart from the imperial church of Constantinople. Armenian scholars created a national literature that was overtly patterned on the Christian literatures

---

[38] The Armenian–Georgian correspondence in the *Book of letters* has been translated into French in Garsoïan (1999a), pp. 516–83. Many of the documents are also quoted by the tenth-century historian Ukhtanes, *History of Armenia.*

[39] Mahé (1997); Garsoïan and Mahé (1997). See also below, pp. 333, 335–6.

in Syriac and Greek, reflecting also the influence of late antique culture which Armenians of the fourth and later centuries absorbed in the schools of the eastern Mediterranean. But the Iranian background was not easily shaken off, and Persian motifs reappeared throughout the centuries. Many Armenians found fame and fortune in the Byzantine empire,[40] but Armenia as a whole was never integrated into the Greek-speaking empire.

When Armenians later reflected on their individuality and the formation of their unique culture, they concentrated on a few specific episodes: the conversion of King Tiridates, the invention of the Armenian script and beginnings of a literature in the vernacular, and the heroic resistance to Sasanian attempts to impose Zoroastrianism. The interpreters of those events, no matter how far removed or tendentious, became the classic authors *par excellence*. And the images of those events as expressed in the classic histories gave meaning to succeeding generations who sought to understand the role and fate of Armenia in an unfriendly world.

Armenia may have played a larger role in the politics of the Middle East in the time of Tigran the Great, as Moses of Khoren rightly stated: 'He extended the borders of our territory, and established them at their extreme limits in antiquity. He was envied by all who lived in his time, while he and his epoch were admired by posterity.'[41] Yet Tigran and military success were not the typical models in terms of which Armenians thought of their present and future. Imagery of a 'golden age' described the harmony of King Tiridates and Gregory the Illuminator, while wishful prophecies foresaw the eradication of present woes by the restoration of the descendants of the one to the Arsacid throne and of the descendants of the other to the office of catholicos. More powerful than the memory of the heroic Tigran was the model of the Maccabees, whose defence of ancestral customs and an individual religious culture evoked a strong response in Armenian minds.[42] So in the fifth and sixth centuries the image of an Armenian 'classical' age was created. Perhaps exaggerated in retrospect, it nonetheless depicted a people who could not be assimilated into either of the imperial powers.

---

[40] Charanis (1961); Kazhdan (1975) for middle Byzantium.

[41] Moses of Khoren, *History*, I.24, tr. Thomson, p. 113 – though he has dated this Tigran far too early.

[42] See Elishe, *History*, tr. Thomson, pp. 11–18 (introduction). Such imagery was applied by the tenth-century Thomas Artsruni to the Muslim rulers, and is frequently found in later Armenian writers. See also below, p. 336.

CHAPTER 2c

EASTERN NEIGHBOURS: THE ARABS TO THE TIME OF THE PROPHET

LAWRENCE I. CONRAD*

INTRODUCTION: THE QUESTION OF SOURCES

In the present state of our knowledge it is not difficult to describe the physical setting for pre-Islamic Arabian history, and new archaeological discoveries in Saudi Arabia, Yemen, Jordan and the Gulf are producing much valuable evidence. Over the past century a vast body of epigraphical material – some 50,000 north and south Arabian inscriptions and the inscribed sticks now emerging by the hundreds in northern Yemen – has provided a wealth of information on the societies of the peninsula, especially the bedouins.[1] But all this seldom provides a coherent picture of the course of events, as opposed to vignettes and bare details, and thus does not replace a literary historical tradition. There are external epigraphic records of the Arabs and Arabia, and historical sources – especially in Greek and Syriac – are often helpful.[2] But this information too is profoundly discontinuous, and in any case represents the perspective of outsiders who regarded the Arabs as barbarian marauders and most of Arabia as a menacing wasteland.[3]

There is voluminous material on the subject in the Arabic sources, but herein lies the problem.[4] The relevant accounts include a vast bulk of poetry and are frequently attributed to the pre-Islamic period, or are presented as describing events and conditions of that time; but – apart from the Koran – the sources containing these accounts date from at least two centuries later. In times past it seemed reasonable simply to compare the various accounts to determine which seemed most likely to be true. More recently, however, it has become clear that the Arabic sources on the Arabs in pre-Islamic Arabia – and indeed, on the first century of Islamic history as a whole – represent a fluid corpus that adopted a range of argumentative views on issues important at the time when the accounts were being transmitted and

---

* I would like to thank Fidelity and William Lancaster and Michael Macdonald for their valuable comments and suggestions.
[1] See, e.g., Robin (1991); Macdonald (1995a).
[2] Papathomopoulos (1984); Segal (1984); MacAdam (1989).
[3] On the distorted image of bedouins among settled folk: Shaw (1982–3).
[4] Two still valuable overviews are Olinder (1927), pp. 11–19; Caskel (1927–30).

the sources compiled; the result was the colouring and reshaping of much early and possibly genuine material and the creation of many new accounts.[5] Most importantly, pre-Islamic Arabia played an important role in early Islamic preaching of the Word. In explaining the success of Islam and the Arab conquerors, scholars and commentators interpreted Islam's emergence from Arabia as part of God's divine plan.[6] This involved presenting the pre-Islamic Arabs as naive barbarians – ragged ignorant nomads and eaters of snakes and lizards – and Arabia as a quintessential wasteland. This was in sharp contrast with the powerful, sophisticated peoples of the empires to the north and the richness and fertility of their lands: clearly, Arab victories against such formidable foes could only have been won with God's permission and as part of his plan for mankind.[7] This paradigm manifestly proclaims a religious truth, and while it may at various points correspond to historical reality, it does not spring from that reality. In each case, then, we must judge – often on insecure grounds – the extent to which the motifs and stereotypes of this story of the spreading of the Word have affected our sources.[8]

THE ARABS IN LATE ANTIQUITY[9]

Extant references to 'Arabs' begin in the ninth century BC,[10] and in ensuing centuries attest their presence in Arabia, Syria and Iraq, and their interaction with the peoples of adjacent lands. This interaction was encouraged in part by the Roman and Persian policy of using Arab groupings to protect their desert flanks and to perform military functions as confederates and auxiliaries. In Syria, an Arab presence was prominent all along the fringe between the desert and the sown,[11] and inscriptions and literary sources confirm that many Arabs took up settled life in rural villages.[12] The hinterlands of inland Syrian cities were partly populated by Arabs, and major cities such as Damascus and Aleppo had significant Arab populations. In such situations Arabs certainly knew Greek or Syriac – possibly both – and

---

[5] Ahlwardt (1872); Husayn (1927), pp. 171–86; Caskel (1930); Blachère (1952–66), I, pp. 85–127, 166–86; Birkeland (1956); Arafat (1958); Caskel (1966), I, pp. 1–71 (with the review in Henninger (1966)); Crone (1987), pp. 203–30.

[6] See the discussion in Conrad (2002).

[7] Conrad (1987b), pp. 39–40 and n. 46; Conrad (1998), p. 238.

[8] The gravity of the source-critical problems is stressed in Whittow (1999), a detailed critique of the volumes on *Byzantium and the Arabs* by Irfan Shahid (specifically Shahid (1995)) which, though full of valuable information, pose serious problems and need always to be used with caution. See also Shahid (2000).

[9] For recent research on this, see Hoyland (2001); Retsö (2003).

[10] Eph'al (1982), pp. 75–7; Macdonald (1995a).

[11] Dussaud (1955), pp. 51–161; Mayerson (1963); Sartre (1982).

[12] MacAdam (1983); Millar (1993b), pp. 428–36.

perhaps as their first languages.[13] Arabs were also to be found throughout the pastoral steppe lands of northern Mesopotamia, where monks in the Jacobite and Nestorian monasteries occasionally mention them.[14] In Iraq there were large groupings of Arabs; settled Arabs lived as both peasants and townsmen along the western fringes, and al-Hira, the focus of Arab sedentary life in the area, was deemed an Arab town (see map 9). Most were converts to Christianity, many spoke Aramaic and Persian, and they were largely assimilated into Sasanian culture.[15]

The sources referring to the Arabs describe them in various ways. In Greek and Syriac they were most usually called *Sarakēnoi* and *ṭayyāyē*, terms which refer to their tribal origin or to their character as travellers to the inner desert.[16] In Arabic, interestingly enough, the terms *'arab* and its plural *a'rāb* are generally used to refer to tribal nomads. Although the settled folk of Arabia shared much in common with the nomads, they nevertheless drew a sharp distinction between themselves and the bedouins; and rightly so, for a tribesman is not necessarily a nomad. It is true that by the sixth century the Arabic language had spread through most of Arabia – if not so much in the south – and engendered a common oral culture based largely on poetry of often exceptional quality.[17] But in none of this should one see evidence of a supposed archetype for Arab unity in any ethnic, geographical or political sense.

The basis for Arab social organisation was the tribe.[18] Genealogical studies in early Islamic times were already elaborating the lineages and interrelationships of the tribes in great detail. The Arabs comprised two great groupings, northern and southern; the former were traced to an eponymous founder named 'Adnan and the latter to a similar figure called Qaḥtan, and both were further divided into smaller sections and sub-groupings. Ancient Arab history is routinely presented in the sources as determined by these tribal considerations,[19] but modern anthropology has cast doubt on this and has raised the question of whether such a thing as a 'tribe' even exists. While the term is problematic, it seems excessive to resolve a conceptual difficulty by denying the existence of its object.[20] The notion of the tribe, however ambiguous, has always been important in traditional Arab society;

[13] Nau (1933), pp. 19–24; Trimingham (1979), pp. 116–24; Shahid (1989), pp. 134–45.
[14] Nau (1933), pp. 15–18, 24–6; Charles (1936), pp. 64–70; Trimingham (1979), pp. 145–58.
[15] Charles (1936), pp. 55–61; Morony (1984), pp. 214–23.
[16] Macdonald (1995b), pp. 95–6. Other views: Christides (1972); Graf and O'Connor (1977); O'Connor (1986).
[17] Fück (1950), pp. 1–28; Blachère (1952–66), I, pp. 66–82; Gabrieli (1959b); von Grunebaum (1963).
[18] See Caskel (1962); and for modern parallels: Musil (1928), pp. 44–60; Jabbur (1995), pp. 261–8, 286–306.
[19] Caskel (1966), I, pp. 1–71.
[20] *Inter alios*, Schneider (1984). Discussion in Crone (1986), pp. 48–55; Crone (1993), pp. 354–63; Tapper (1990), pp. 60–4.

in pre-Islamic Arabia there can be no doubt that kinship determined social organisation.[21] The problem can perhaps best be formulated as revolving around the questions of how far back this was meaningfully traced, and how stable perceptions of kinship were.

Individuals were very often aware of their primordial tribal affiliations, and took pride in the achievements, glories and victories of their ancestors. Similarly, personal enemies often vilified the individual by calling into question his tribe as a whole. In practice, however, the vast tribal coalitions rarely acted as a unified whole, and the socially meaningful unit was the small tenting or village group tracing its origins back four or five generations at most. The perception of common descent was not unimportant to the cohesion of such groups, but even more vital were considerations of common interest. In order to maintain itself, the group had to be able to defend its pasturing grounds, water supplies and other resources from intruders, and its members from injury or harm from outsiders. Dramatic changes in kinship affiliations could occur when, for example, the requirements of contemporary alliances or client relationships dictated a reformulation of historical genealogical affinities.[22] Such shifts could even occur at the level of the great tribal confederations,[23] and were facilitated by the fact that no loss of personal or legal autonomy was involved – a 'client' tribe was not in the state of subservience implied by the western sense of the term.[24]

Through most of Arabia, the welfare of the individual was secured by customary law and the ability of his kin or patron to protect him. If a member of a group were molested or killed, this dishonoured the group as a whole and required either retaliation or compensation. Individuals thus adhered to at least the minimum standards required to remain a member of their group, since an outcast could be killed with impunity.[25] This system provided security and guaranteed the status of tradition and custom.[26] Violence in the form of warfare, feuding and raiding did occur, but the last of these has given rise to much confusion, and its scope and scale have often been exaggerated:[27] there was no glory in raiding a weak tribe or ravaging a defenceless village, and fatalities on either side posed the immediate risk

[21] Even with respect to Arabs from south Arabia, where Dostal's hypotheses (1984) would lead us to expect social organisation along other lines. Note that in all three of the early Arab urban foundations in Egypt and Iraq, the Arab conquerors – even Yemeni contingents – organised themselves according to tribe. See Pellat (1953), pp. 22–34; Djait (1986), pp. 73–135; Kubiak (1987), pp. 58–75.

[22] Ibn Khaldun, *Muqaddimah*, ed. Quatremère, I, p. 238; tr. Rosenthal, I, pp. 266–7.

[23] Goldziher (1967–71), I, pp. 92, 96; Caskel (1953), pp. 8, 15; Caskel (1966), I, pp. 31–2, 43–4; II, pp. 22–3, 72, 448; Lancaster (1997), pp. 16–23, 32–4, 151–7. See also Gellner (1973).

[24] Lancaster (1997), pp. ix, 73, 128–9.

[25] Musil (1928), pp. 426–70, 489–503; Farès (1932), pp. 44–101; Chelhod (1971), pp. 231–341; Stewart (1994), pp. 130–44.

[26] See Stewart (1994), pp. 139–43.

[27] Most notoriously in Lammens (1928), pp. 181–236; see also Meeker (1979), pp. 111–50.

of a blood feud. Prowess in battle was without doubt a highly esteemed virtue, and Arabian society was imbued with a martial spirit that elevated the raid (*ghazw*) to the level of an institution.[28] Still, this usually involved one powerful tribe raiding another for their animals,[29] and the violence involved was limited by considerations of honour, by the ordinarily small size of raiding parties, and – where weaker groups were concerned – by networks of formal arrangements for protection.

Headship of a tribal unit was vested in a sheikh ('chief' or 'elder', although other terms were also used), but the powers of this office were seriously limited, and the sheikh remained in power as long as the tribe felt this was to their benefit. He was expected to lead the tribe, protect its prerogatives and interests, mediate among its members and with other tribes, and serve as an exponent of *muruwwa*, an ethic of masculine virtue bound up in such traits as courage, strength, wisdom, generosity and leadership.[30] While the chief had no power to enforce his decisions, it was not in the group's interest to maintain a leader in power and yet regularly defy his decisions. The sheikh led by example and by exercise of a quality of shrewd opportunistic forbearance (*ḥilm*): he was a mouthpiece of group consensus whose reputation required assent to his judgement.[31]

The exception to all this was the south, where plentiful rainfall, carried by monsoon winds, allowed for levels of agriculture, population and sedentary development not possible elsewhere. The numerous small towns of the region thrived on the spice trade and enjoyed the stability of a highly developed agrarian economy with extensive terrace farming and irrigation. The towns were closely spaced settlements of tall tower-dwellings, often with a distinct 'centre', and their organisation tended to promote commercial and professional bonds at the expense of large-scale kinship ties. Out of this stability there arose a number of coherent regimes with identifiable political centres: Maʿin, Sabaʾ, Qataban and Hadramawt, based respectively at Qarnaw, Maʾrib, Tamnaʿ and Shabwa. The most dynamic of these was Sabaʾ, which by the third and fourth centuries had managed to annex the territories of all the others.

The early south Arabian entities were ruled by figures called 'federators' (*mukarrib*s). It has long been held that this office was hereditary and had a distinctly religious function, but this now seems unlikely.[32] Not unexpectedly, social differentiation reached levels unknown in lands to the north. The sedentary tribes were led by powerful chieftains known as *qayl*s, and at the other end of the spectrum both serfdom and slavery were well-established institutions. Nomads were held in check by granting them lands

---

[28] Musil (1928), pp. 504–661; Jabbur (1995), pp. 348–55; Lancaster (1997), pp. 140–5.
[29] Sweet (1965), pp. 1138–41.   [30] Goldziher (1967–71), I, pp. 11–44.
[31] See Pellat (1962–3); Pellat (1973); Lancaster (1997), pp. 87–9.   [32] Robin (1991), pp. 52, 55.

in exchange for military services, thus rendering them dependent upon the regime.

ARABIAN RELIGIOUS TRADITIONS

The social organisation of pre-Islamic Arabia was closely bound up with considerations of religion, and it is in this area that problems of methodology and source criticism are most acute. Issues such as borrowing from more advanced civilisations, the starting-points and relative antiquity of religious forms, the roles of animism and totemism, and differences between sedentary and nomadic peoples have been and remain highly controversial. In many cases important arguments involve value judgements about nomads and, similarly, supposed distinctions between 'high' and 'low' forms of religious expression. There is also the problem that the Arabic sources, where the vast bulk of our source material is to be found, can hardly be said to offer an objective view of pre-Islamic religion. The folly of idol-worship and the credulity of its adherents are routinely stressed in stereotyped ways. One tale describes how a tribe fashioned an idol out of dried curd mixed with dates and clarified butter (*ḥays*) and worshipped it for a time, but eventually devoured it during a famine, leading to a poet's wry comment:

> The tribe of Hanifa ate their lord
> When dearth and hunger swept the land,
> Fearing naught for consequences
> From their lord's avenging hand.[33]

Inspired by Koranic criticisms,[34] Arabic sources also present bedouins as indifferent to matters of faith.[35]

Arabian polytheism took several forms,[36] one of which was stone-worship. Greek and Syriac sources presented this as adoration of lifeless rocks, but such objects were not deities in themselves, but their dwelling-places or the focus of the rituals of the cult. Offerings were made at the site, and ritual observances included circumambulation of the stone. The best-known example is of course the Ka'ba in Mecca, but we are told that other places had such cultic foci.[37] These foci were often surrounded by a sacred territory, usually called *ḥaram* in the north and *ḥawa* in the south. These were precincts associated with the sanctity of worship and sacrifice;

---

[33] Ibn Qutayba, *Ma'arif*, p. 621.

[34] *Koran*, Surat al-Tawba, IX.90, tr. Arberry, pp. 189–90 (on procrastinators, liars, malingerers); IX.97–8, 101, tr. Arberry, pp. 190–1 (on hypocrites, stubborn in unbelief, opportunists); Surat al-Fath, XLVIII.11, tr. Arberry, p. 532 (on dissemblers, malicious, corrupt); Surat al-Hujurat XLIX.14, tr. Arberry, p. 538 (on superficial in belief).

[35] Bashear (1997), pp. 7–14.   [36] Arafat (1968).

[37] This is made especially clear in Lughdah al-Isfahani, *Bilad al-'arab*, p. 32.

violence and killing, including hunting, were forbidden there. Holy men were in charge of these precincts, and their descendants enjoyed special religious esteem.[38] Also prominent was religious observance revolving around idols – again, with the idol probably representing the deity being worshipped. The names of many idols are known from ancient poetry and from later prose works drawing on this verse. Important new details pertaining to Yathrib (Medina) may be indicative of a more general pattern: there, clans each had an idol in a room belonging to the whole clan, where the idol was venerated and sacrifices made to it. People also had wooden idols in their homes, making similar observances at that level. To offend the idol was an offence against the honour of the head of the house and a matter for retaliation, and there is some evidence that these idols were intended to be figures of ancestors. There was thus a hierarchy of idols, corresponding to the social status of their owners.[39]

There is good evidence of star-worship and astral divinities as well. The widely venerated al-Lat (a sky goddess) and al-'Uzza (possibly the morning star) may have been representations of Venus, and Byzantine polemics against Islam claim that the Islamic slogan *Allāhu akbar* ('God is great') has as its origin a cry of devotion in astral religion.[40] The worship of astral divinities has also been connected with the veneration of idols.

The attitude of the ancient Arabs towards their gods was entirely empirical and pragmatic. Although they did consider problems of human existence and the meaning of life,[41] they did not look to their deities for the answers. They regarded their gods as the ultimate sources of worldly phenomena beyond human control, such as disease, rain, fertility, and personal and communal adversities of various kinds; they worshipped the gods in expectation of their assistance, but they did not revere them or consider that they owed unwavering commitment to them.[42]

Monotheistic religion was also known in Arabia from an early date. The influx of Jews into Arabia is difficult to trace, but probably had much to do with the failure of the Jewish revolt and the destruction of the Temple in AD 70, and the gradual spread of Christianity over the next three centuries. In south Arabia, Judaism enjoyed considerable success in the fifth and early sixth centuries, and to the north there were various important Jewish communities, notably at Yathrib. Judaism seems to have had deep and powerful roots there, judging from reports that in pre-Islamic times the Jews there had three times as many fortified compounds (*quṣūr*) as all the

---

[38] Serjeant (1962).   [39] Lecker (1993).

[40] On this see Rotter (1993); Hoyland (1997), pp. 105–7.

[41] For example, the ephemeral joys of youth and the ultimate fate of either death or senility: Zuhayr, *Sharh Diwan*, p. 29; al-'Askari, *al-'Awa'il*, I, p. 57.

[42] Wellhausen (1897), pp. 213–14; Crone (1987), pp. 237–41.

other non-Jewish clans combined,[43] and that in the latter half of the sixth century the Jewish clans of Qurayza and al-Nadir collected taxes from the other tribes.[44] The question of Jewish influences in Arabia and on Islam has become highly sensitive in modern scholarship, but there can be no doubt that such influences were profoundly important; the Koran itself contains many tales and accounts of Jewish origin, as also do early Islamic religious lore and scholarship.[45]

The Christianisation of the Roman empire in the fourth century opened the way for the large-scale spread of the faith along and beyond the empire's frontiers, including Arabia.[46] Along the Syrian desert fringe from the Red Sea to the Euphrates, it spread to the Arab tribes via monasteries and wandering missionaries, primarily monophysite. In some cases, as with the Banu Taghlib and Ghassanids, entire tribes converted; some tribal settlements such as al-Jabiya and Jasim, south of Damascus, also became ecclesiastical centres. These tribes were familiar with at least basic observances, yet remained completely within Arab tribal culture as well.[47] Along the Iraqi frontier the spread of Christianity was somewhat slower, perhaps because a network of Nestorian monasteries in the area took longer to appear than had been the case among the monophysites.[48] Still, the Lakhmid base of al-Hira was the seat of a bishopric by 410.[49] Further south, there were major Christian communities at such centres as Najran and Sanaa, and small ecclesiastical outposts along the Arabian coast of the Persian Gulf. Specifically monophysite or Nestorian forms of Christianity were practised in such centres, but elsewhere the Arab tribesman's main contact with the faith was through individual monks and hermits, and there confessional boundaries may have been less sharply drawn.[50]

Two other beliefs – which were influenced by Judaism and Christianity, yet remained distinct from both – revolved around a 'high god' and around ḥanīfiya. Little can be said about belief in a 'high god' in ancient Arabia, apart from the fact that, as elsewhere in the Middle East,[51] some held that a god called Allah had a certain dignity and status above the other deities of

[43] Ibn al-Najjar, Al-Durrah al-thaminah, II, p. 325; Conrad (1981), p. 22.

[44] Ibn Khurradadhbih, al-Masalik, ed. and French tr. de Goeje, p. 128 (text), p. 98 (tr.); Yaqut, Mu'jam al-buldan, IV, p. 460; Kister (1968), pp. 145–7.

[45] On the Jews of pre-Islamic Arabia, see Newby (1988), pp. 14–77; and on influences, Geiger (1833); Rosenthal (1961), pp. 3–46; Nagel (1967); Rubin, U. (1995), pp. 32, 217–25.

[46] For an overview, see Charles (1936); Trimingham (1979).

[47] For a valuable anthology of the verse of early Arab Christian poets, see Cheikho, Shu'ara' al-Nasraniya; also Conrad (1994), pp. 30, 31, 51.

[48] Brock (1982).   [49] Synodicon orientale, ed. and French tr. Chabot, p. 36.

[50] On the Koranic evidence, see Ahrens (1930); Michaud (1960); Parrinder (1965); Bowman (1967); Robinson (1991). The relevant Koranic verses, with the commentaries from many tafsīrs, are assembled in Abu Wandi et al. (1996).

[51] Teixidor (1977), pp. 17, 161–2.

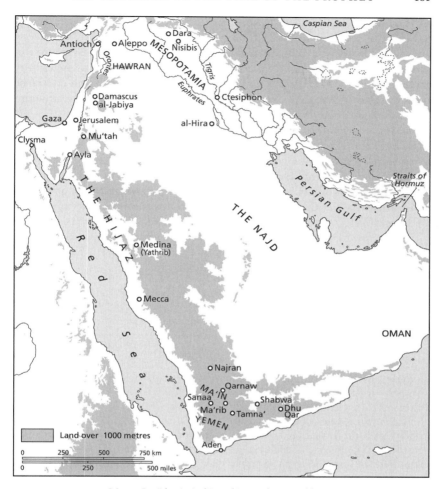

Map 9 Pre-Islamic Arabia and its northern neighbours

the Arabian pantheon and was extolled as a god to whom one could turn in case of particular need.[52] On *ḥanīfiya* there is more information.[53] The Koran makes it the religion of Abraham and associates it, on the one hand, with belief in a single God and, on the other, with rejection of idolatry and repudiation of worship of the sun, moon and stars. In particular, and most importantly, *ḥanīfiya* reflects not the pragmatic attitude towards religion described above – in which the god(s) were worshipped in expectation

---

[52] Watt (1979); Welch (1979); Rubin, U. (1984).
[53] For differing interpretations, see Gibb (1962); Rubin, U. (1990); Rippin (1991).

of help with worldly needs beyond an individual's control – but rather a submissive devotion to and faith in God for his own sake. Nevertheless *ḥanīfiya* is distinct from Judaism and Christianity: in several passages of the Koran, its adherent (a *ḥanīf*) is equated with a Muslim, and in one variant to the Koranic text, *ḥanīfiya* replaces Islam as the 'true religion'.[54] Other sources suggest that there were *ḥanīfs* in various parts of Arabia, that the movement was one of individuals rather than religious communities, and that Mecca was important to its adherents. Other details are less reliable, and there is no evidence to link *ḥanīfiya* with south Arabian inscriptions attesting to worship of a god called al-Rahman, 'the Merciful', one of the Islamic names for God. But the fact that the tradition on the *ḥanīfs* makes some of them doubters or enemies of Muhammad suggests that it should not be dismissed entirely as later prophetic annunciation or the tidying up of a pagan past.

Of interest in this respect is the testimony of Sozomen, who died before 448; writing from the vantage-point of Gaza in southern Palestine, he offered the following comments on Arab religion:

It seems that the Saracens were descended from Ishmael, son of Abraham, and hence were originally called Ishmaelites. Their mother Hagar was a slave, so in order to hide the shame of their origin they took the name of Saracens, pretending to be descended from Sarah, the wife of Abraham. As such is their descent, they practise circumcision like the Jews, abstain from eating pork, and adhere to numerous other Jewish observances and practices. In so far as they in any sense diverge from the observances of that people, this arises from the passage of time and their contacts with other neighbouring peoples . . . It seems likely that with the passage of time their ancient customs fell into disuse as they gradually took to observing the customs of other peoples. Eventually, when some of their tribe came into contact with the Jews, they learned from them the facts of their true origin and returned to observance of Hebrew custom and law. In fact, even at the present time there are some of them who live their lives in accordance with the Jewish law.[55]

The connection with Judaism may reflect an inclination to associate false belief with the machinations of Jews.[56] As to the Abrahamic religion attested in the text, while the connection is circumstantial and Sozomen wrote long before the testimony of the Koran, the Islamic scripture may refer to continuing monotheistic trends in Arabia that it wishes to distance from earlier monotheistic faiths now viewed as rivals.

---

[54] Jeffery, *Text of the Qur'an*, p. 32; *Koran*, Surat al-'Imran, III.19, tr. Arberry, p. 47.

[55] Sozomen, *Church history*, VI.38.10–14, ed. Bidez and Hansen, p. 299. See Cook (1983), p. 81; Millar (1993a), pp. 42–4.

[56] On scheming Jews as a cliché, see Schafer (1997).

ECONOMIC LIFE IN ARABIA

It is difficult to generalise on the notion of an Arabian 'economy', since the internal economic situation in the peninsula varied from place to place and depended on whether a community was settled or nomadic. As noted above, the south had a lively village economy based on terraced farming and irrigation; but even here, production was primarily limited to foodstuffs and use-value goods. South Arabian spices and incense were much sought-after items for centuries, and undoubtedly fortunes were made from trade in them,[57] but overland trade in such goods appears to have collapsed by the first or second century AD.[58]

In the rest of the peninsula the economy was far more rudimentary. The interior of the peninsula consists of various types of steppe lands where lack of water makes major cultivation unsustainable in most years. Reliable water supplies come from wells and oasis springs, and it was around these that Arabia's towns developed. The date palm dominated agriculture in many places, and this and other crops were often cultivated in large walled gardens (*ḥawāʾiṭ*) scattered over whatever patches of arable land there were in or around a settlement. Goats and sheep were kept, and items produced for sale included hides and leather, wool, cloth, dairy products, raisins, dates, wine, and utensils and weapons of various kinds. Gold and silver were mined, but often figured as a replacement for currency rather than as an export item; perfume was produced, especially in Aden and Najran, but beyond the Arabian and Syrian markets it could not compete with the cheaper products of Byzantine centres such as Alexandria.[59] Arabian traders in late antiquity were thus known to their neighbours – in Palestine, for example – as bearers not of costly luxury items, but rather of animals, wool, hides, oil and grains.[60]

Bedouins, on the other hand, were largely herders and pastoralists, though members of many tribes settled for varying periods of time and others engaged in opportunistic agriculture – for example by sowing on a fertile watered plot on their way somewhere else, and then reaping when they returned. Tenting groups travelled in recognised tribal territories, their schedules and movements (and willingness to encroach on the lands of other tribes) largely dictated by the needs of their animals. Those who lived along the desert fringes tended sheep and goats, as well as the single-humped dromedary camel; groups venturing into the depths of the Arabian

[57] Groom (1981).

[58] The last reference to it is in the *Periplus Maris Erythraei*, ch. 27, ed. and tr. Casson, pp. 66–7.

[59] Dunlop (1957), pp. 37–40; Crone (1987), pp. 87–97.

[60] Krauss (1916), pp. 335–6; *Excavations at Nessana*, ed. Kraemer, pp. 251–60 (no. 89). The Palestinian church at Dayr al-ʿAdasa, dedicated in 621, has a mosaic floor bearing various rural scenes, including one of a caravan of camels carrying oil or wine jars: Balty (1989), pp. 149–51.

steppe lands did best with camels, but on occasion are known to have taken goats and sheep as well. For barter or sale, nomads could offer such animal products as hides, leather, wool and dairy products.

The symbiosis between village-dwellers and nomads was important to the whole economic structure of Arabia. Leather, for example, was an extremely important product and was the plastic of its day; everything was made from it, from buckets to items of clothing, and agriculture could not have been maintained without huge supplies of leather for ropes, irrigation equipment, harness and so forth. Apart from often quite complex exchanges of goods and services, bedouins played a major role in economic development. There is evidence, for example, that parts of different tribes concluded share-cropping agreements and worked together to promote and protect agriculture.[61] Certain villages also specialised in serving the needs of nomads, and oases and springs where herds could be watered attracted settlements that thrived on trade with the nomads. Relations were further dictated by the need of settled merchants to move their goods through lands controlled by nomads, and hence to remain on good terms with the tribes.[62]

Arabian domestic trade thus consisted of caravans of camels organised by settled merchants and protected and guided by bedouins who controlled the lands through which the caravans passed. Seasonal fairs were often held, especially around religious shrines, and security at such important times was guaranteed by the declaration of sacred periods during which no raiding or fighting was to occur.[63] The goods being traded were for the most part not costly items, but rather the basic goods and commodities that people needed to live. This in turn limited the distance and duration that the caravans could travel, since the longer the journey, the more expensive the goods would be at their destination;[64] that is, the longer the contemplated journey was in both distance and time, the more precious the goods being carried would have to be in order to generate sufficient income to make the journey economically feasible. The internal trade of Arabia thus seems to have involved the transport of goods on short or medium-length journeys, and it is probably this factor that accounts for the proliferation of market centres. The sources present a picture of lively markets dotting the steppe landscape of the peninsula; wells, springs and small villages were all attractive sites for established market activities, though the scale of such

---

[61] al-Bakri, *Mu'jam ma sta'jam*, I, pp. 77–8. See also Kister (1979), p. 70 on similar arrangements at the time of the Prophet. The same system is still widespread today.

[62] See Simon (1989), pp. 78–86; Morony (1984), pp. 218–19; Donner (1989), pp. 77–8; and for modern examples, Jabbur (1995), pp. 1–2, 5–8, 32–8, 250. See also Nelson (1973).

[63] Wellhausen (1897), pp. 84–94; Brunschvig (1976a), pp. 113–18; Crone (1987), pp. 87–108.

[64] Jones (1955), p. 164; Hendy (1985), pp. 556–7; Crone (1987), p. 7. Not all trade was profit-driven, however: Villiers (1940).

operations was probably small.[65] In some cases, commerce was encouraged by banning private land ownership within the market precinct, thus preventing dominance by a few successful merchants, and suspending taxes and fees on traders and visitors.[66]

IMPERIUM AND IMPERIAL POLITICS

It will be seen from the above that there was little in Arabia to attract the attention of the great powers of late antiquity, and at first it was only Arabia's role athwart the route to the east that lent it any importance to them. This factor alone was sufficient to make Arabia a focus of imperial manoeuvring and power politics, but trade operated in conjunction with other factors as well. The spread of Christianity and to a lesser extent Judaism in Arabia reflects the interest of external powers from an early date. In fact, it was the great triad of politics, trade and religion that determined the course of events there from late antiquity onwards, with trade providing an imperial momentum later transferred to the other two factors.

All around the peripheries of Arabia the impact of *imperium* was being felt. Behind the Roman presence advancing in the north came Roman roads, way-stations and forts, reflecting an increasing interest in control of what lay beyond. Far more vigorous, however, were the inroads by the Sasanians: they had a more immediate stake in Arabia, with their capital at Ctesiphon, the rich agricultural alluvium of Iraq, and the Persian Gulf trade to consider. Settlements were founded up and down the Gulf, and Oman was annexed by Shapur I (240–70). In the fourth century, Arab raids provoked a punitive expedition that reached as far as the Hijaz. Discovery of silver and copper in the Najd led to the foundation of a Sasanian outpost at Shamam.[67]

Several factors exacerbated the rivalry between the two imperial powers. The establishment under Constantine of a Christian empire based at Constantinople made competition with Persia more immediate and provided yet another arena for intrigue and dispute. But more important by far was the evolution of the rival polities themselves. From largely decentralised and culturally diverse empires, tolerant of a broad range of contradictory ideologies and traditions, both developed into world powers; they used political, economic and military strength to pursue imperial aims that were justified by elitist ideologies, spurred by aspirations to universal dominion,

---

[65] Lughdah al-Isfahani, *Bilad al-'arab*, for example pp. 224, 227, 243, 333–4, 335, 345, 358, 361, 397; Muhammad ibn Habib, *al-Muhabbar*, pp. 263–8; al-Marzuqi, *al-Azminah*, pp. 161–70. See also al-Afghani (1960); Hammur (1979).

[66] Kister (1965); Dostal (1979); Lecker (1986).

[67] al-Tabari, *Ta'rikh*, ed. de Goeje *et al.*, I, pp. 838–9; German tr. Nöldeke, pp. 54–7; tr. Bosworth, V, pp. 54–5; Dunlop (1957), p. 40; Crone (1987), p. 46.

and increasingly dictated from the capital. The Byzantine and Sasanian empires competed for control of western Asia and adopted more global strategies in efforts to promote their own interests and undermine those of their rival.[68] Thus, while the rise of Christianity led to the collapse of the market for the incense consumed so massively and ostentatiously by pagan Rome,[69] the demise of this formerly crucial aspect of the eastern trade was more than replaced by new rivalries of unprecedented intensity.

The new level of conflict generated by escalating competition between the two great powers manifested itself in several ways where Arabia and the Arabs were concerned. Firstly a pronounced religious element was introduced into the struggle, primarily in the southern part of the peninsula and surrounding lands. Monophysite missionary activity[70] led to the conversion of Ethiopia to Christianity in the fourth century and the spread of the faith in Yemen and elsewhere in south Arabia. The Christian presence noted frequently in the Koran was probably the result of commercial contacts with Syria. The Sasanians, on the other hand, supported the spread of the rival confession of the Nestorians and also encouraged the Himyarites, a predominantly Jewish regime which ruled most of south Arabia and had influence elsewhere. Religious rivalries played an instrumental role in an Ethiopian invasion of Yemen in about 518 and shortly thereafter in a Himyarite civil war between Christian and Jewish factions. This struggle led to a persecution of Christians in south Arabia under the last Himyarite ruler Dhu Nuwas, culminating in the 520s with the massacre of the Christians of Najran. Ethiopia responded with a second invasion, killing Dhu Nuwas and once again installing a puppet regime in Yemen. The power of the Ethiopian governor, however, was soon usurped by a certain Abraha, who established himself as the paramount authority in the south; the Meccans viewed his expedition of 552 as directed against themselves, but it was in fact a move against tribal forces to the east.

Secondly, external forces gradually encircled and penetrated the peninsula. The Sasanians established trading posts beyond the Straits of Hormuz as far as Aden and in the sixth century occupied Yemen. Persian authority extended as far as Yathrib, where taxes collected by the Jewish tribes of Qurayza and al-Nadir were sent on in part to a Persian 'governor of the desert' (*marzubān al-bādiya*).[71] Byzantium, on the other hand, still had trade through Clysma and Ayla to protect,[72] and sought a sea route to the

---

[68] Fowden (1993), pp. 24–36, 80–137, though the focus on monotheism and the stress on premeditated planning from the centre seem overstated. See also Crone (1987), p. 47; above pp. 135–7.

[69] Müller (1978), pp. 733–64; Groom (1981), p. 162; Crone (1987), p. 27.

[70] Altheim and Stiehl (1971–3), I, pp. 393–431; Shahid (ed. and tr.), *Martyrs of Najran*, pp. 252–60. See below, p. 308.

[71] Christensen (1944), pp. 373–4; Altheim and Stiehl (1957), pp. 149–50; Whitehouse and Williamson (1973); Frye (1983a).

[72] See, for example, *Jerusalem pilgrims*, tr. Wilkinson, pp. 147–8.

east that would not be subject to Persian taxes and interference. It thus tried to extend its influence down the Red Sea and battled against pirates and adventurers to maintain control of ports and customs stations; epigraphical evidence places Byzantine forces nearly a thousand kilometres south of Damascus in the mid-sixth century.[73] It also used its new Christian ally, Ethiopia, to pursue its economic interests and intervene militarily in the affairs of the south, encouraging the Himyarites to attack Persian interests.[74]

Thirdly, both powers used tribal allies in Arabia to further their own interests, protect their Arabian frontier zones, and confront the tribal forces of the other side. Such a tactic was not new. Rome and Persia had routinely used tribal auxiliaries in various capacities,[75] and in the late fifth and early sixth centuries the Himyarites in Yemen coopted the great north Arabian tribal confederation of Kinda into acting in their interest and controlling caravan traffic along the routes from Yemen to Syria and Iraq. Kinda eventually extended its control across central Arabia, as well as part of the Hijaz and areas along the Persian Gulf coast, and in the early sixth century it was attacking both Byzantine and Sasanian targets along the desert fringes of Syria and Iraq. Seeking to avoid further incursions and to gain a strong tribal ally against forces acting for the Sasanians, the Byzantines reached an understanding with the confederation and on several occasions sent embassies to promote good relations. Kinda thus became an ally of Byzantium; turning against the Sasanians, it gained considerable authority in the hinterlands of south-western Iraq and even occupied al-Hira for a time.[76] However, its primary sponsors remained the Himyarites in Yemen, and as this regime declined, so did the fortunes of Kinda.

The Sasanians' main tribal ally was the Lakhmids, a tribe that had established itself in north-eastern Arabia by the fourth century and founded a stable base at al-Hira. There had been contacts and relations between the two sides in the past, but the combination of deteriorating relations with Byzantium and the spectre of powerful Kinda forces allied to Byzantium and positioned within easy striking distance of Ctesiphon and the agricultural plains of Iraq led the Sasanians to support and encourage the Lakhmids with renewed vigour. The latter had long been subordinate to Kinda, and double marriages between them had been arranged at least twice in the past. Nevertheless, by about 504 the new Lakhmid chieftain, al-Mundhir III (504–54), was able to rid himself of Kinda suzerainty and launch operations against the confederation with a well-organised army.[77]

[73] See Abel (1938); Seyrig (1941); Simon (1989), p. 34.   [74] Smith (1954), p. 427.

[75] On Rome, see Shahid (1984), pp. 52–63; and on the fifth-century Salihids in particular, see Shahid (1958); Shahid (1989).

[76] Olinder (1927), pp. 32–93; Simon (1989), pp. 42–6; Lecker (1994); Shahid (1995), I, pp. 148–60.

[77] Rothstein (1899), pp. 134–8; Altheim and Stiehl (1957), pp. 117–23; Kister (1968), pp. 165–7.

Fighting over the next two decades ended with the utter disintegration of Kinda and the extension of Lakhmid authority over their rival's former clients among the Arab tribes. By the 540s the Lakhmids held sway over many of the tribes of central Arabia and over towns as far west as Mecca.[78]

Byzantium was thus forced to turn to other Arab clients for the protection of its position and interests. Its choice fell on the Ghassanids, a south Arabian tribe closely related to Kinda, that had migrated to northern Arabia and Syria in the fifth century and established itself as the pre-eminent power on the desert fringe there. The Ghassanids were a more nomadic group than the Lakhmids; although they were often associated with the camping-ground called al-Jabiya 65 kilometres south-west of Damascus, they had no real fixed centre comparable to that of the Lakhmids at al-Hira. Their influence was not as broad-ranging as that of the Lakhmids, and although they had trading connections with Iraq through Nisibis and Dara, their control over the relevant routes was tenuous. Nevertheless, Byzantium granted the Ghassanid sheikh the title of phylarch and showered him with honours, privileges and money. In return, it was expected that the chieftain would keep his own tribe under control and protect imperial interests from other tribes as well.[79]

The Ghassanids and Lakhmids, confronting one another across the Syrian desert, were thus drawn into the series of great Byzantine–Persian wars that began in 502 and ended with a decisive Byzantine victory in 628 (see above, pp. 119–20, 124–7, 135–6). Significant fighting between them began in the 520s and continued sporadically for sixty years, with dire consequences for the agricultural infrastructure of both Syria and Iraq. Several observers describe the destruction in Syria,[80] and whatever survived the passage of raiding parties and military expeditions was exposed to the brigands and outlaws hovering around such forces.[81]

This military conflict tends to overshadow other developments in which the two sides were variously involved. The Ghassanids were responsible for the establishment of several small towns in the hinterlands south of Damascus and perhaps also for some of the so-called 'desert palaces' of the Syrian steppe.[82] Sponsors of monophysite Christianity, they also erected

[78] Rothstein (1899); Simon (1967); Simon (1989), pp. 27–30, 42–6, 55–8, 149–52; 'Abd al-Ghani (1993), pp. 11–23.

[79] Nöldeke (1887a); Simon (1989), pp. 27–32, 55–8; Sartre (1982); Peters (1984). On the term phylarch, which originated as a post in the provincial administration, not necessarily relating to nomads, see Macdonald (1993), pp. 368–77.

[80] John Moschus, *Pratum spirituale*, chs. 99, 133, 155, cols. 2957–8, 2995–8, 3023–4; *Life of John the Almsgiver*, ch. 9, ed. Delehaye, pp. 23–4; tr. Dawes and Baynes, pp. 203–4; al-Tabari, *Ta'rikh*, ed. de Goeje et al., I, p. 1007; German tr. Nöldeke, p. 299 and n. 4; tr. Bosworth, V, pp. 326–8; al-Washsha', 'Kitab al-fadil', fol. 105r. See also Foss (1975); Foss (1977b), pp. 68–71; Schick (1995), pp. 25, 31–3.

[81] Abu al-Baqa', *al-Manaqib*, I, pp. 105–6. Early Islamic works on jihad also mention the problems posed by these elements.

[82] Gaube (1984).

numerous churches and monasteries. In Iraq, al-Hira grew from a camp (which is what the name means in Arabic) into a lively Arab town, noted for its churches and monasteries, impressive residential compounds and taverns. Persian Gulf shipping could sail up the Euphrates as far as al-Hira, and Lakhmid income included proceeds not only from raids but also from agricultural rents and produce, trade, and taxes from tribes they controlled. There also seems to have been a nascent literary tradition emerging there.[83] Both sides, especially the Lakhmids, were also major patrons of Arab oral culture, and some of the most important poets of pre-Islamic times gained generous support from Ghassanid or Lakhmid sheikhs.[84]

The history of the Arab client regimes is important, but they were not central in the imperial planning of either Byzantium or Persia, in which they figured mainly as threats that had to be countered.[85] Little is known from the Lakhmid and Persian side, but Byzantine emperors, political strategists and historians such as Procopius certainly held the Ghassanids in low esteem. The Byzantines had little faith in the abilities, motives or intentions of their Arab allies. The treaty of 561, for example, expresses dissatisfaction with Saracen adherence to treaty terms in the past, comes close to calling them smugglers and traitors, and warns of harsh punishment for lawbreakers.[86] When Ghassanid phylarchs refused to adhere to Chalcedonian orthodoxy, they were exiled. Byzantium made overtures to the Lakhmids when it was expedient, and the lack of trust and commitment worked both ways: the capture of Dara by Khusro I probably involved some negotiations with the Ghassanid phylarch al-Mundhir (569–82).[87]

Neither side survived the manoeuvrings of their patrons or the broader conflict which engulfed the Middle East in the sixth century. In 581 al-Mundhir was arrested by Emperor Tiberius I (578–82) and exiled to Sicily in a religious dispute, and in 584 his son and successor al-Nuʿman joined him. The Ghassanid phylarchate rapidly fell apart, fragmented by Emperor Maurice (582–602) into a host of smaller entities and riven with dissension and conflict over the deposition of two leaders within four years. Forces from the tribe are mentioned in accounts of the Arab conquest of Syria, but not in a leading role.[88] The Lakhmids survived a while longer, but during the reign of Shah Khusro II (591–628) they were displaced in favour of a similarly decentralised system. The Sasanians also promoted the position

[83] Much valuable material is collected in ʿAbd al-Ghani (1993), pp. 25–138.

[84] Nicholson (1907), pp. 38–54; Blachère (1952–66), II, pp. 293–356; ʿAbd al-Ghani (1993), pp. 365–469.

[85] Important discussion in Whitby, Michael (1992).

[86] Men., 6.1, pp. 70–3. See also above, p. 124.

[87] Whitby, Michael (1988), pp. 257–8. The Nemara inscription of AD 328 has Arabs in the eastern Hawran in contact with both the Romans and the Persians: Bowersock (1983), pp. 138–47; Bellamy (1985).

[88] Nöldeke (1887a), pp. 33–45; Shahid (1995), I, pp. 455–71, 634–41, 648–51.

of the Banu Hanifa, who roamed in the desert on their southern flank.[89] Later, when a force of Persian troops and Arab auxiliaries sought to quell a desert revolt in about 610, their army was beaten at Dhu Qar; this was the first time the tribes had been able to defeat the Sasanians in battle.[90] It also illustrates how the demise of the Arab client regimes marked not the shift from one system of frontier defence to another, but rather the opening of a great power vacuum extending from the desert fringes of Syria and Iraq all the way to central Arabia. Inhabitants of the peninsula remembered that they had once been 'trapped on top of a rock between the two lions, Persia and Byzantium'.[91] But as the next decade was to reveal, those days were gone forever and the Persian setback at Dhu Qar was but a hint of things to come.

MECCA, MUHAMMAD AND THE RISE OF ISLAM

In about 552[92] a boy named Muhammad bin 'Abd Allah was born into a minor clan of the tribe of Quraysh, which was settled in and around the shrine centre of Mecca in the Hijaz, about 900 kilometres south of Syria. A trader by profession, he participated in the caravan trade of Arabia and visited Syria on several occasions. In about 610 he began to preach a monotheistic faith called 'submission to God', or Islam, and summoned his fellow Meccans to prepare for the Last Judgement. By 622 difficulties in Mecca and the erosion of vital support had reached the point where he was obliged to move to Yathrib, 300 kilometres to the north. This migration (the *hijra*)[93] proved to be of crucial importance: for in Yathrib, henceforth called Medina,[94] the ranks of his followers increased dramatically. Raids on enemy caravans, camps and villages met with success and further expanded his support. Muhammad returned to Mecca in triumph in 630, and by the time of his death two years later his authority extended over much of Arabia. The rest was brought under control by the first caliph, Abu Bakr (632–4), and Muslim forces went on to campaigns of conquest that, in less than a century, created an empire extending from Spain to Central Asia.

How all this occurred and why it focused on Muhammad, Mecca and the late sixth century are questions that early Muslims took up themselves,[95] and they are a major concern of modern historical research. In the 1950s William Montgomery Watt proposed a socio-economic solution. Mecca

---

[89] al-A'sha, *Diwan*, pp. 72–87, no. 13, esp. 86 vv. 47–9; al-Isfahani, *al-Aghani*, XVII, pp. 318–22.

[90] al-Tabari, *Ta'rikh*, ed. de Goeje *et al.*, I, pp. 1029–31; German tr. Nöldeke, pp. 332–5; tr. Bosworth, V, pp. 358–61; Rothstein (1899), pp. 120–3.

[91] Qatada (died 735) in al-Tabari, *Tafsir*, ed. 'al-Ghumrawi *et al.*, IX, p. 145; *Koran*, Surat al-Anfal, VIII.26, tr. Arberry, p. 172. See also Kister (1968), pp. 143–4.

[92] For the date, see Conrad (1987a).   [93] Crone (1994).

[94] al-Madina, probably referring not to 'the city', but to the Prophet's house.

[95] But not immediately: Donner (1998), pp. 75–85.

was a major centre for overland caravan trade, and its merchants and others grew wealthy on the profits from commerce in such precious items as incense, spices, gemstones and gold. This widened the gap between rich and poor and led to social malaise as crass materialism eroded traditional values. Muhammad's message was essentially a response to this crisis.[96] More recently, however, serious challenges have been made to the notions of a lucrative Arabian trade in luxury items, of Mecca as an important entrepot, and hence of some serious crisis provoking a religious response.[97]

Mecca is not mentioned in any non-Arabic source of the pre-Islamic period, and does not lie on the main communication routes in western Arabia. The site itself is barren, inhospitable and incapable of sustaining agriculture for more than a minuscule population. Even had there been a lucrative international trade passing through the Hijaz in the sixth century, it would not have found an attractive or logical stopping-point at Mecca, which owed its success to its status as a shrine and pilgrimage centre. As at certain other shrines in Arabia, pilgrims came to circumambulate a rock – in this case associated with an unroofed building called the Ka'ba – and to perform religious rituals with strong affinities to those of Judaism: these included offerings and animal sacrifice, washing and concern for ritual purity, prayer and recitation of fixed liturgies.[98] There are indications that, early on, few people were resident at the site: 'People would perform the pilgrimage and then disperse, leaving Mecca empty with no one living in it.'[99]

The success and expansion of Mecca were due to the administrative and political skills of its keepers, the tribe of Quraysh. The Ka'ba seems to have been a shrine of the god Hubal,[100] but in the religiously pluralistic milieu of pagan Arabia it must not have been difficult to promote it as a place where other deities could be worshipped, too. A greater achievement was convincing other tribes to honour the sanctity of the *ḥaram* of Mecca and to suspend raiding during the sacred months when pilgrims came. As agriculture was not possible at Mecca, Quraysh had to bring in food from elsewhere and so was at the mercy of nearby tribes in any case. The very fact that Mecca survived, much less prospered, thus reflects the diplomatic skills of Quraysh. The Islamic tradition, of course, makes much of the *a priori* importance of Quraysh, but this is surely something that emerged within the paradigm of a sedentary tribe seeking to protect and promote its

---

[96] Watt (1953), pp. 1–29 and in numerous publications of his thereafter. See the review by Bousquet (1954).
[97] Simon (1989); Peters (1988); Crone (1987). See review of Crone in Serjeant (1990) and reply in Crone (1992).
[98] Hawting (1982); Rubin, U. (1986).
[99] al-Bakri, *Mu'jam ma sta'jam*, I, p. 89, citing al-Kalbi (died 763).
[100] Wellhausen (1897), pp. 75–6; Crone (1987), pp. 187–95.

interests through skilful manipulation of relations with the nomadic tribes around it. There was mutual advantage in the prosperity of Mecca: trade with pilgrims, import and marketing of foodstuffs and other necessities, and collection and distribution of taxes levied in kind for feeding and watering pilgrims.[101] It may even be that Quraysh was able to organise a profitable trade with Syria, perhaps as a result of disruption to the agricultural productivity of the Levant caused by the destruction of the Persian wars, numerous droughts in Syria,[102] and the repeated visitations of bubonic plague after 541.[103]

The message that Muhammad preached in the milieu of a prosperous Mecca was in many ways a familiar one, and in others quite a novelty.[104] His summons to the worship of one God recalled the notion of a 'high god', and his identification of Islam as the religion of Abraham had important associations with the doctrines of *ḥanīfiya*. As can be seen from the testimony of Sozomen, his call for the restoration of a pristine faith, free from the corruptions that had crept into it, was already a time-honoured tradition in Arabia. The observances he advocated were also well known from either pagan Arabian or Jewish practice: prayer and Friday worship, fasting, pilgrimage, ritual purity, almsgiving, circumcision and dietary laws.[105]

Where Muhammad broke with tradition was in his insistence on absolute monotheism and his advocacy of a relationship with God that abandoned traditional pragmatic views of religion and summoned man to unconditional commitment and faith in response to God's creative munificence and continuing solicitude. The rejection of pagan eclecticism, however, threatened the entire social and economic position of Quraysh and thus earned him the enmity of their leaders. Among the public at large his message – with its corollaries of reward and punishment in the hereafter – seemed extreme and delusory and evoked little positive response.[106] In order to gain support Muhammad had to prove that his God was a winner, and this he achieved by moving to Medina, where he used his expanding following to disrupt Meccan commerce and food supplies.[107] His military success made him a force to be reckoned with: the tribal arrangements so carefully nurtured by Mecca over the years soon fell apart in the face of this challenge, while the victories of the new religion provided the worldly success which Arabs demanded of their gods and also appealed to the Arabs' warrior ethic. Islam also had a broad appeal on other grounds. The Koran presented itself as a universal scripture 'in clear Arabic speech',[108] and thus took advantage

---

[101] For example, Ibn Hisham, *Sirat Rasul Allah*, ed. Wüstenfeld, I.i, p. 83; tr. Guillaume, pp. 55–6.
[102] Butzer (1957), p. 362.   [103] Conrad (1994); Conrad (1996b).
[104] Cook (1983), pp. 25–60.
[105] Goitein (1966), pp. 73–125; Bashear (1984), pp. 441–514; Rippin (2005), pp. 103–17.
[106] See Izutsu (2002), pp. 45–54.   [107] Discussion in Donner (1977).
[108] *Koran*, Surat al-Nahl, XVI.103, tr. Arberry, p. 270; Surat al-Shu'ara', XXVI.195, tr. Arberry, p. 379. See also Surat Ibrahim, XIV.4, tr. Arberry, p. 246.

of the position of the Arabic language as the common cultural tongue of Arabia and a basis for common action.[109] Arabs could also identify with one another, despite their tribal distinctions, on the basis of a shared participation in Arabian tribal organisation and custom, a heritage of similar cultural and religious experience in pagan systems and folklore, and a long history of trade and commerce, revolving around fairs and religious shrines, that engendered a certain feeling of familiarity around the peninsula.

It has often been asserted that the Arab conquests were of essentially Islamic inspiration. The Islamic tradition of spreading the Word sees things this way, and the Armenian chronicle, written in the seventh century and attributed to Bishop Sebeos, also has Muhammad urging his followers to advance and claim the land promised to them by God as the descendants of Abraham.[110] It therefore seems probable that there was a religious agenda to the conquests from the start, and it is certainly true that without the unifying factor of Islam there would probably have been no conquest at all.

But the arguments of leaders and advocates are one thing, and the response of the fighters themselves is another. Even in Mecca and Medina the teachings of Muhammad and the text of the Koran were still known in only fragmentary fashion, and it is difficult to see how most tribesmen elsewhere could have had more than a vague and trivial knowledge of either so soon after the Prophet's death. Many warriors who joined the conquest forces had only recently fought against the Prophet himself, or had resisted the efforts of the first two caliphs to bring Arabia under their control. It is also implausible that tribal warriors all over Arabia could so quickly have abandoned the pragmatic and worldly attitude towards religion that had prevailed for centuries, in favour of one that expected genuine commitment to the one God. There is, in fact, good evidence on the conquests showing that this was not the case at all.[111]

This is not to detract from the centrality of the message of Islam to Muhammad's own sense of mission and purpose, and probably to that of others around him. One may also concede that Islam enabled the Muslim leadership to mobilise warriors in a way that transcended important differences, and it is likely that Islamic slogans and admonitions of various kinds were often inspiring to fighters on the ground. But if the faith played

[109] Blachère (1952–66), II, pp. 230–41; Blachère (1956); von Grunebaum (1963); Bashear (1997), pp. 54–5.

[110] Seb., ch. 135, tr. Thomson and Howard-Johnston, I, pp. 95–6. See also the quotations from Dionysios of Tell-Mahre in MS, XI.2, ed. and French tr. Chabot, II, pp. 403–5 (tr.); IV, pp. 404–8 (text); *Chronicon ad 1234*, ed. Chabot, I, pp. 227–30 (text); I, pp. 178–80 (tr.); tr. in *Syrian chronicles*, tr. Palmer *et al.*, pp. 129–32. Discussion in Crone and Cook (1977), pp. 8–10; Hoyland (1997), pp. 124–30.

[111] For example al-Walid ibn Muslim (died 810) in Ibn 'Asakir, *Dimashq*, ed. al-Munajjid, I, pp. 461–2; al-Tabari, *Ta'rikh*, ed. de Goeje *et al.*, I, p. 2922; tr. Humphreys, XV, pp. 125–6; al-Maqrizi, *al-Mawa'iz*, I, p. 75.

an important role in uniting and mobilising the tribes, it was nevertheless waves of tribal forces, motivated primarily by traditional tribal ambitions and goals, that broke over Syria, Iraq and Egypt from the 630s on.

It is unlikely that either Syria or Iraq could have withstood the advance of forces of this kind, given the state of their defences after the end of the last Persian war in 628, only six years before the first Arab advance. The Arab armies were not simply marshalled in Medina and then sent forth with the caliph's instructions; providing food, fodder and water for an army of thousands of men and animals would have been extremely difficult. The norm was rather for small contingents to expand as other groups gradually joined them on the march; the sources make clear that commanders were expected to engage in such recruiting along the way, to ensure that the newcomers were armed and equipped, and to 'keep each tribe distinct from the others and in its proper place'.[112] In this way a small force could soon swell to thousands as warriors joined its ranks in expectation of adventure, fighting and plunder.

The situation was made more difficult by the fact that confronting the Arabs on this scale posed entirely new military problems. Both imperial powers were accustomed to dealing with Arabs as bands of raiders, and had planned their frontier defences accordingly. Watch-towers and forts, many of them abandoned for centuries in any case, were inadequate to deter the forces that now swept past them, and whereas the old Roman system had anticipated incursions by single uncoordinated bands, it was now confronted by penetration at many points simultaneously. It was probably also difficult to determine exactly where the enemy was at any given time, for when battle was not imminent an Arab army tended to fragment into bands of warriors roaming the countryside.

Finally, and as the above example shows, Arab strategy was often highly reactive and thus difficult to counter or predict. Incursions into Iraq, for example, seem to have begun when drought in Arabia obliged the tribe of Rabi'a, of the Banu Shayban, to migrate into Iraqi territory, where the Sasanian authorities permitted them to graze their herds on the promise of good behaviour. But the presence of these tribal elements eventually led to friction, which the Rabi'a quite naturally interpreted as unwarranted reneging on an agreed arrangement. When they called on their kinsmen elsewhere for support, the crisis quickly escalated into full-scale conflict between Arab and Persian forces.[113]

It is difficult to guess whether either of the great powers would have been able to stem the military momentum that was building in Arabia, even had they correctly gauged the threat it posed. With Kinda, the Ghassanids

---

[112] Ibn 'Asakir, *Dimashq*, ed. al-Munajjid *et al.*, I, p. 446.
[113] Ibn A'tham al-Kufi, *al-Futuh*, I, pp. 88–9.

and the Lakhmids all in a state of either collapse or disarray, the growing strategic power of Islam was able to develop in what otherwise amounted to a political void; the real source of the danger confronting the empires was effectively beyond their reach from the beginning. Byzantium and Persia could fight armies that violated their frontiers, but could not stop the process that was generating these armies in the first place. Initial victories over the Arabs at Mu'tah in Syria in 632 and the battle of the Bridge in Iraq in 634 thus proved no deterrent, as in earlier times would have been the case.[114]

What overwhelmed the Byzantines and Sasanians was thus the ability of the message and charismatic personality of Muhammad to mobilise the tribal might of Arabia at a level of unity never experienced among the Arabs either before or since. Unprepared for defence on the scale required to counter this new threat and unable to marshal tribal allies of their own to strike at their foe in his own heartlands, both were forced to fight deep within their own territories and suffered defeats that simply encouraged further incursions on a larger scale. Greek and Persian field armies were crushed in one disastrous battle after another, leaving cities to endure sieges without hope of relief and encouraging resistance everywhere else to evaporate in short order.[115]

---

[114] Donner (1981), pp. 105–11, 190–202; Kaegi (1992), pp. 71–4, 79–83.
[115] Donner (1981), pp. 119–220; Kaegi (1992), pp. 88–180.

CHAPTER 3

WESTERN APPROACHES (500–600)

JOHN MOORHEAD

THE CONTINUING UNITY OF THE POST-ROMAN WORLD

Throughout the political history of western Europe, there have been few periods of such dramatic change as the fifth century. In 400 the borders of the Roman empire in the west, by then distinct from the eastern empire which was governed from Constantinople, stood reasonably firm. They encompassed all of Europe south of the Antonine wall in Britain and the Rhine and Danube rivers on the continent, extending eastwards of the Danube's confluence with the Drava; they also included a band of territory along the African coast, stretching two-thirds of the way from the Straits of Gibraltar to the Nile. But within a hundred years this mighty entity had ceased to exist. North Africa had come under the power of groups known as Vandals and Alans; Spain of Visigoths and Suevi; and Gaul of Visigoths, Franks and Burgundians. The Romans had withdrawn from Britain early in the century, leaving it exposed to attacks from the Irish, Picts and Anglo-Saxons, while in Italy the last emperor, Romulus Augustulus, was deposed in 476 by a general, Odovacer. The supplanter of Romulus was himself deposed and murdered in 493 by Theoderic the Ostrogoth (493–526), who established a powerful kingdom based on Italy. While the empire had weathered the storms of the fifth century largely unscathed in the east, in the west it had simply ceased to exist. Western Europe, one might be excused for thinking, had moved decisively into a post-Roman period, and the middle ages had begun.

However dramatic these events may have been, they did not constitute a definitive parting of the ways between the west and what we may now call the Byzantine east. Long-distance trade continued throughout the Mediterranean and beyond, as research on African pots found across a wide area is increasingly making clear.[1] Consuls were being appointed for the west in the year 500 and when, a few decades later, the western consulship lapsed, some in the west still dated documents with reference to the eastern consuls who continued to be appointed. The Mediterranean

---

[1] See Loseby (2005), pp. 621–3. See also Ward-Perkins (2005), pp. 87–106.

Map 10 Lands of the empire in the west in the sixth century

was traversed by members of the intelligentsia and diplomats, such as a legate of Theoderic who made twenty-five trips from Italy to Spain, Gaul, Africa and Constantinople. The west was awash with doctors from the east, among them Anthimius, who lived in Italy and wrote a fascinating book on diet for a Frankish king in which he recommended the use of such foods as leavened bread, beer and mead made with plenty of honey. Another eastern doctor was Alexander of Tralles, brother of the well-known architect Anthemius. Alexander practised medicine in Rome and his *Therapeutica* was translated into Latin in the sixth century.[2] On the other hand Priscian, who was probably an African, was in Constantinople when he wrote what were to become standard works on Latin grammar;[3] we know that Africans in Constantinople were renowned for their Latin accent, but reviled for their poor Greek. Latin manuscripts were copied in Constantinople and Greek ones in Ravenna, the Gothic capital in Italy. Furthermore, despite the political changes in the west, the new rulers there were keen to represent themselves as in some way subservient to the Roman emperors who still ruled in Constantinople. Theoderic the Ostrogoth wrote to Emperor Anastasius that 'our kingdom is an imitation of yours . . . a copy of the only empire' and Sigismund the Burgundian informed him that, while he gave the appearance of ruling his people, he believed himself to be merely the soldier of the emperor.[4] In these and many other respects, the post-Roman west remained firmly part of the Roman world.

THE SUCCESSOR STATES IN THE WEST

Nevertheless, there had been changes, and seen from Constantinople the political situation of the west in 500 cannot have given cause for joy. Developments in the west had not passed unnoticed by the emperors of the east, amidst the other internal and external problems besetting them in the fifth century. The last decade of the western empire had seen the despatch of new emperors and armies from the east, and Romulus Augustulus' deposition in 476 was recorded by sixth-century Byzantine authors in terms which suggest they saw it as marking a major change: according to the *Chronicle* of Marcellinus, Rome was founded 709 years before Octavian Augustus held power, and he died 522 years before it perished in 476.[5] Constantinople became a centre for refugees who fled the new kingdoms in the west. African catholics were prominent among these, including a widely reported group who miraculously found themselves able to speak after King Huneric had ordered that their tongues be cut out. There were also people from Italy who were said, early in the sixth century, to have received a warm welcome at the court of Anastasius (491–518), and in one of his works Priscian expressed the hope that Rome and Constantinople would both come to be under the emperor.[6] Indeed, emperors who had traditionally had pretensions to rule over the whole known world could not have looked with complaisance on the loss of the western provinces, which constituted the greater part of the territory over which their predecessors had ruled.

---

[2] Alexander of Tralles, *Therapeutica*, ed. Puschmann.   [3] Priscian, *Grammatici Latini*, ed. Keil.
[4] Theoderic, in Cassiodorus, *Variae*, I.1.3, ed. Fridh and Halporn, p. 9; Sigismund, in Avitus of Vienne, *Epistulae* 93, ed. Peiper, pp. 100–1; tr. Shanzer and Wood, pp. 146–7.
[5] Marcellinus, *Chronicle*, ed. Mommsen, p. 91; tr. Croke, p. 27.
[6] Priscian, *De laude Anastasii imperatoris*, lines 242–7, 265, ed. and tr. Coyne, pp. 48–9, 60–1.

When the Byzantines looked westwards they saw a world dominated by the Mediterranean, and by the year 500 almost all of its coastline formerly within the western empire was under the control of three barbarian kingdoms. Vandals had occupied the bulk of Roman Africa where they proved stern rulers, whose expropriation of the landowning class and persecution of catholics made them unpopular. Using their powerful navy, the Vandals sacked Rome in 455 and withstood major Byzantine attacks in 460 and 468. They faced two other barbarian kingdoms on the opposite shores of the Mediterranean. The Visigoths, originally settled as Roman *foederati* around Toulouse, had gradually gained control of most of Gaul south of the Loire and begun moving into Spain, while Italy and some adjacent lands were under the control of Ostrogoths.[7] They had made their way there in accordance with an agreement concluded with Emperor Zeno (474–91). Although in 497 Zeno's successor, Anastasius, returned to Italy the palace ornaments, which Odovacer had sent to Constantinople after deposing Romulus Augustulus, this degree of recognition does not imply that the Byzantines were happy to accept the Ostrogothic state.

The Vandals, Visigoths and Ostrogoths had far more in common than possessing adjacent kingdoms around the Mediterranean. They were all Arian Christians, adherents of a heresy which denied that the Father and the Son were of one substance as taught by the council of Nicaea (325); this marked them off from both the Byzantines and the great mass of the people among whom they settled. The Byzantines regarded them as speaking a single language and looking the same; together with the Gepids, they were viewed from Constantinople as nations distinguishable in name only.[8] They were connected by a system of marriage alliances: one of Theoderic's daughters had married the Visigothic king Alaric and his sister married the Vandal king Thrasamund, a web of relationships which may have been anti-Byzantine in purpose.

Of these three states, that of the Ostrogoths was by far the most dangerous. To the east it included Dalmatia, which gave it a border with the empire hundreds of kilometres long: even if the Ostrogoth ruler had no expansionist designs in the east, he was well placed to influence developments there in turbulent times. So it was that a Byzantine rebel had already sought the aid of the Italian-based Odovacer in 486, a circumstance which may have helped prompt the emperor's despatch of Theoderic and his Ostrogoths to Italy to discipline Odovacer shortly afterwards; and when, towards the end of Anastasius' reign, the *magister militum* Vitalian rebelled against the emperor, he was believed to have sought Theoderic's

---

[7] On the Vandals, see Courtois (1955); on the Goths, Wolfram (1988); Heather (1991); on the kingdom of Toulouse, Barbero and Loring (2005), pp. 167–71, 174.

[8] Pr *W*, III.2.1–6, ed. and tr. Dewing, II, pp. 8–11.

assistance. Some decades earlier, before moving into Italy, Theoderic had intervened when a rebellion threatened to unseat Zeno, for which the grateful emperor rewarded him with a consulship. An early sixth-century Italian author, apparently referring to these events, spoke of Theoderic as having bestowed the diadem on Zeno and compelled his love, with the implication that he was superior to the emperor.[9] It was a perspective unlikely to have been shared in Constantinople. If this were not enough, in 504 one of Theoderic's generals gained control of Sirmium, a city in Pannonia formerly part of the eastern empire. The Ostrogoths not only kept the city; they went on to advance further into imperial territory. Following a decisive defeat of the Visigoths at the hands of the Franks in 507, Theoderic ruled part of their kingdom as well as that of the Ostrogoths. Constantinople had reason to look with fear on the mighty Ostrogothic kingdom, in particular, from among the states that had emerged around the western Mediterranean.

These, however, were not the only successor states to the empire in the west. To the north were territories that had come under the control of other peoples, notably Franks and Burgundians.[10] Like the Goths, they had found homes within the borders of the old empire, and they had been integrated into the system of alliances set up by Theoderic; he himself had married the sister of Clovis, king of the Franks (*c. 481–c. 511*), and one of his daughters had married Sigismund, heir to the Burgundian throne. But around the end of the fifth century Clovis had adopted catholicism, and whatever his motives may have been in taking this step, it is clear that he saw himself as accepting the religion of the emperor. Catholic influence was also strong at the Burgundian court, where Sigismund was converted. More importantly, from a Constantinopolitan perspective the impact of the Frankish and Burgundian intruders on the Roman world would have seemed less than that of the Goths and Vandals: their capacity to harm imperial interests was slight, and with judicious encouragement they could be made to serve imperial policy. According to a strange story told in a seventh-century text, the Frankish king Childeric (*c. 463–82*) went to Constantinople, where he sought the emperor's agreement that he should go to Gaul as the emperor's servant.[11] Hence it is not surprising that when conflict broke out in 507 between the Franks under Clovis, who enjoyed Burgundian support, and the Visigoths and Ostrogoths, Anastasius

[9] Ennodius, *Panegyricus*, ch. 14, ed. Vogel, pp. 211–12; ed. and German tr. Rohr, pp. 246–9. On the interpretation, see MacCormack (1981), p. 230.

[10] The Byzantines distinguished the Franks and Burgundians from the Goths by calling them 'Germans', a shorthand way of indicating that they had come from the lands east of the Rhine, which the Romans had failed to conquer.

[11] Fredegar, *Chronicle*, III.11, ed. Krusch, pp. 95–7. The story gains in plausibility if one takes the name of the emperor which is supplied, Maurice, to have been a slip for Marcian.

intervened on behalf of the Franks. He dispatched a fleet which ravaged part of the coast of Italy and prevented Theoderic from intervening in Gaul as early as he would have wished; he also made Clovis an honorary consul.

It is clear that Constantinople viewed the west in a differentiated way. The Mediterranean lands were occupied by powers that threatened Byzantine interests, but the empire could sometimes act to destabilise its enemies. Theoderic's last years were clouded by accusations that a group of Roman senators was treasonably corresponding with the emperor, and by his possible over-reaction to reports that Arians were being persecuted in the east. These two issues were recurrent in the history of the Gothic and Vandal states. The Vandal king Huneric had been concerned at the possibility that catholic clergy were sending letters overseas – presumably to the empire – about the succession to the throne; and on one occasion Theoderic acted to stop correspondence from Burgundy reaching the emperor. The Vandals also felt that religious persecution was a tool that could be employed for reasons of diplomacy. The position of the emperor vis-à-vis catholics in the west had been strengthened by the healing in 519 of the Acacian schism, which had divided the churches of Rome and Constantinople since 484.[12] The last years of Theoderic therefore manifested some of the tensions implicit in the relationship between Constantinople and the successor states to the empire around the western Mediterranean. To the north, on the other hand, were powers from whom good could be expected. It was a basic distinction, and its application became clear during Justinian's military ventures.

THE VANDAL WAR

On 19 May 530, the Vandal king Hilderic was deposed by another member of the royal family, Gelimer. Hilderic had enjoyed close relations with Justinian, who was therefore presented with an excellent opportunity to declare war on the Vandals. The deposition of the emperor's ally was, however, merely a pretext for intervention. According to the African writer Victor of Tunnuna, Justinian's decision to invade was prompted by the vision of a martyred African bishop, while a passage in the *Codex Iustinianus* of 534 – which may well have been written by the emperor himself – is eloquent as to the persecution of catholics by the Vandals. It describes their sufferings in language reminiscent of the account written by the African Victor of Vita in the 480s. We have no reason to doubt that Justinian's invasion, like so many of his activities early in his reign, was motivated by

[12] See above, pp. 106, 114–15.

religion rather than by any ideology of imperial renewal.[13] We are told that
the plan to invade Africa was opposed by his advisers. But the imperial
will was not to be trifled with, especially when a bishop reported a vision
in which success was promised. In 532 a peace was concluded with Persia,
enabling resources to be directed towards the west. Justinian prepared a force
which put to sea at about the summer solstice in 533 under the command of
Belisarius, a general who had recently risen to prominence in campaigning
against the Persians and in putting down a rebellion in Constantinople. The
religious nature of the enterprise was highlighted as the patriarch prayed
over Belisarius' ship and placed on one of the vessels a soldier who had
recently been baptised.

We can follow the Vandal war in some detail, through the eyewitness
account of Belisarius' legal assistant, Procopius. The arrival of the Byzantine forces in Africa occurred in excellent circumstances: Gelimer, unaware
of their approach, had sent part of his forces to Sardinia. The invaders
landed unopposed south of Carthage at Caput Vada, whence they proceeded towards the capital. They kept close to the shore for some distance before they turned inland and marched to Decimum, some fifteen
kilometres outside Carthage. Here Gelimer met them, but after a short
encounter he fled, and two days later, on 15 September 533, the Roman
army marched into Carthage. Belisarius dined on food that had been prepared for Gelimer, while his soldiers, behaving with remarkable restraint,
are said to have bought food in the market. Gelimer summoned forces
from Sardinia, but at the battle of Tricamarium, thirty kilometres outside
Carthage, the Vandal army was again turned to flight, and Gelimer took
up residence among the Berbers on a mountain where he consoled himself
by composing sad verses before surrendering.

Having quickly gained control of Sardinia, Corsica, the Balearic Islands
and Septem, a fort adjacent to the Straits of Gibraltar, Belisarius returned
to Constantinople with booty which included the treasures of the Jews that
Titus had taken from Jerusalem to Rome in the first century and which
the Vandals in turn had taken to Africa in 455. The victorious general
paraded through the streets of Constantinople in triumph, and both he
and Gelimer performed *proskynēsis* before Justinian. The defeated king
was provided with estates in Galatia in Asia Minor, and Belisarius went
on to hold a consulship in 535; the largesse he distributed included spoils
won on this campaign. Justinian saw to the making of gold plates that
depicted the history of his triumphs and legislated for the return of property
the Vandals had taken from its rightful owners. In a matter of months

---

[13] On the martyr's visions, see Victor of Tunnuna, *Chronicle*, ed. Mommsen, p. 198; ed. Cardelle
de Hartmann, ch. 118, p. 38; ed. and Italian tr. Placanica, pp. 38–9; on the persecution of catholics,
see Justinian, *Corpus iuris civilis*, II, *Codex Iustinianus*, 1.27.1, ed. Krueger *et al.*, p. 77. See also above
p. 109.

the kingdom of the Vandals that had seemed so strong had collapsed, and Africa found itself governed by a praetorian prefect appointed by the emperor. We have no reason to doubt that its inhabitants approved of these developments.

Nevertheless, there was still fighting to be done. The nomadic Berbers had been pressing increasingly on the Vandal kingdom, and they were to pose a major problem to Byzantine Africa, for their practice of lightly armed and mobile combat made them difficult opponents. A series of fortifications was quickly erected to deal with them, of which the impressive ruins at Thamugadi still stand, with walls averaging 2.5 metres in thickness and rising to over fifteen metres in height (see figs. 7a and 7b). Archaeological and literary evidence both indicate that, contrary to Justinian's expectation, the Byzantines never succeeded in occupying all the territory held in Roman times, but the number and extent of the defences they erected makes it clear they planned to stay in Africa. There were also internal troubles, for many of Belisarius' soldiers married Vandal women, only to see the property they hoped to gain through their wives threatened by Justinian's legislation for the return of property held by Vandals. They mutinied in 535, and more seriously in 544, after the *magister militum* and praetorian prefect Solomon had been killed fighting the Berbers. But the ringleader of the rebels was murdered in 546 and towards the end of that year a new general, the energetic John Troglitas, arrived. An expedition led by him in the spring of 548 was crowned with success, and Africa knew peace.

THE GOTHIC WAR: EARLY SUCCESSES

Justinian can only have been delighted at Belisarius' triumph in 533, and his thoughts naturally turned to a more ambitious project. Imperial legislation of April 535 referred to the recovery of Africa and the imposition of servitude on the Vandals, but added that the emperor now hoped to receive from God things greater than these.[14] As it happened, it was a propitious time to intervene in Italy. Following the death of Theoderic in 526, his successors had found it hard to step into his shoes, and both his daughter, Amalasuntha, and the man who came to be her rival, Theoderic's nephew Theodahad, entered into negotiations with the emperor. In the spring of 535 Amalasuntha was murdered, so providing a *casus belli*.[15] The reason Justinian gave for intervening in Italy was different from that provided for the war in Africa; whereas the Vandals had been attacked for their outrageous treatment of the catholic provincials, the Ostrogoths were assaulted because of the weakness of their claim to hold Italy. They had done well, it was

[14] Justinian, *Corpus iuris civilis*, III, *Novellae*, 8.10.2, ed. Krueger *et al.*, p. 74.
[15] See Moorhead (2005), pp. 148–9.

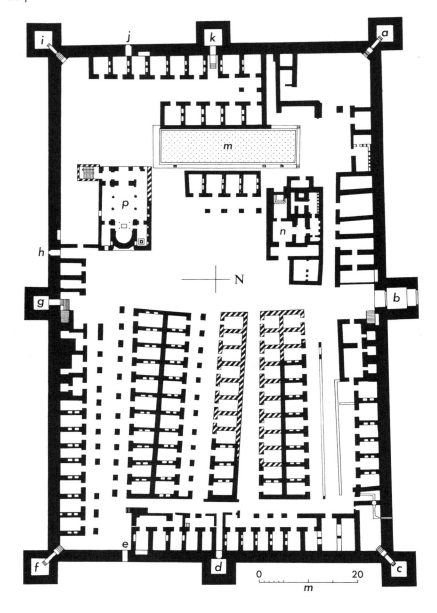

Figure 7a Plan of fort at Timgad (Thamugadi) in North Africa, as an example of careful organisation of defences

Figure 7b Justinianic fort at Timgad

now asserted, to defeat the tyrant Odovacer, but their proper course should have been then to hand Italy back to the empire, rather than keeping it for themselves. As we have seen, the ending of the line of emperors in the west in 476 had not escaped notice in Constantinople.

The initial attack on Italy took place from two directions.[16] One army occupied Dalmatia, which thereafter remained under almost unbroken imperial control, while Belisarius, at the head of a small force, easily gained control of Sicily in 535. From there he could launch an attack on the Italian mainland which the resources of the Goths were ill-equipped to deal with, concentrated as they were in the north. Theodahad, by then sole ruler, offered to resign his kingdom, a proposal he subsequently retracted, and early in 536 Pope Agapetus arrived in Constantinople to hold discussions with Justinian on Theodahad's behalf. But the emperor was in no mood for discussion. A law of 536 refers to the regaining of territory from one ocean to the other, an ambition not hinted at in earlier sources, which indicates that imperial designs had become larger.[17] In the same year Belisarius crossed to the Italian mainland. The Goths, discontented at Theodahad's failure to lead effectively, raised on their shields Witigis, a man of modest family but of proven fighting ability, and Theodahad was

[16] The account of Procopius again constitutes a detailed primary source, closely followed by e.g. Bury (1923); Stein (1949–59), II. However, Procopius was probably not in Italy after 540, and as time passed he came to look on the war with less favour: Hannestad (1961).

[17] Justinian, *Corpus iuris civilis*, III, *Novellae*, 30.11.2, ed. Krueger *et al.*, p. 234.

murdered. The new king left Rome for Ravenna, taking hostages and an oath of loyalty from Pope Silverius, who had succeeded Agapetus, and on 9 or 10 December 536 Belisarius occupied the eternal city. In the following February a large Gothic force arrived and laid siege to it, cutting the aqueducts which supplied the city with water and ravaging Christian burial grounds outside the walls, but to no avail. In March 538 Witigis withdrew. Fighting spread in the north of Italy, and the Byzantines enjoyed the initiative, gaining much territory in 539. The Goths counter-attacked in Liguria and razed the great city of Milan to the ground; we are told that the men were killed and the women handed over to the Burgundians. The Frankish king Theudebert intervened, seeking to benefit no one but himself, and by the end of 539 the Gothic capital, Ravenna, was besieged by imperial forces.

In his hour of need Witigis asked Khusro I, the shah of Persia, to break the treaty he had concluded with Justinian in 532 and distract him in the east, a ploy which made the emperor incline towards offering the Goths generous terms.[18] But Belisarius was confident, and when the Goths offered to accept him as 'emperor of the west', an office obviously prejudicial to Justinian's position, he feigned consent.[19] In May 540 he marched into Ravenna, but refused to honour his agreement with the Goths. Before long he returned to Constantinople, taking with him Witigis and his wife Matasuentha, various Gothic notables and at least part of the Gothic treasure. The reception he received from Justinian was cool, the emperor possibly having been disquieted by the title his general had pretended to be willing to accept. Nevertheless in 540 the mighty state founded by Theoderic had apparently collapsed.

The historian Procopius observed that when Belisarius entered Rome in 536, 'Rome became subject to the Romans again after a space of sixty years',[20] and one gains the impression of a smooth imposition of Byzantine power. In March 537 Pope Silverius, who had owed his appointment to Theodahad and had subsequently sworn loyalty to Witigis, was deposed by Belisarius and replaced by Vigilius, a protégé of the powerful empress, Theodora. By early 537 Belisarius had appointed one Fidelis praetorian prefect, and by the end of the year a *comes sancti patrimonii per Italiam*, an official with competence in financial matters, seems to have been functioning in the conquered lands. Fidelis' tenure of the prefecture would have overlapped with the end of that of Cassiodorus, who had been appointed to the post by the Goths in 533 and whose last letters on behalf of Witigis were written towards the end of 537. By the end of 539 a scribe at Ravenna

---

[18] On Perso-Byzantine relations in the sixth century, see above, pp. 104–5, 119–20, 135–6.

[19] Pr *W*, VI.29.17–29, ed. and tr. Dewing, IV, pp. 128–33; but see also Pr *W*, III.11.18–21, ed. and tr. Dewing, II, pp. 106–7 (misleadingly translated in the Loeb edition).

[20] Pr *W*, V.14.14, ed. and tr. Dewing, III, pp. 146–7.

employed in a document the formula *chi-mu-gamma*, in accordance with Byzantine practice.[21] As early as 535 there had been signs in Rome of discontent with the Gothic government, and the people of Italy, quickly putting aside positive memories they may have had of the reign of Theoderic, accepted the advent of imperial power.

In 540 it must have seemed that the Gothic war, like the Vandal war, had come to a wished-for conclusion. In Constantinople, Justinian had a mosaic placed in the ceiling of the Bronze Gate of the palace, showing Belisarius winning victories for him. In the middle of the composition stood Justinian and Theodora, the kings of the Vandals and Goths approaching them as prisoners, and around them the members of the senate who 'rejoice and smile as they bestow on the emperor honours equal to those of God, because of the magnitude of his achievements'.[22] It was the optimism of a golden moment, such as would never again be possible.

THE GOTHIC WAR: THE RESISTANCE OF TOTILA

As it turned out, the war with the Goths was by no means over. Justinian, perhaps afraid of the threat a mighty general could pose, failed to replace Belisarius, and rivalry and corruption became endemic among the Byzantine commanders left in Italy. They showed little inclination to attend to the Gothic resistance that continued north of the Po, and with the coming to power in 541 of King Totila (or Baduila, as his name was spelt on coins) the Goths gained a leader of outstanding calibre. Totila's attitude to Justinian was expressed in his coinage, on which the portrait of the current emperor was replaced by that of Anastasius, who had recognised the kingship of Theoderic in 497; if Justinian challenged the Goths on the basis of legitimacy, Totila was prepared to dispute his claim.

Before long war was raging again. In the spring of 542 the new Gothic king defeated the imperial army at Faenza and captured its standards, before proceeding to the south and taking Benevento, Cumae and Naples. Belisarius was sent back to Ravenna in 544 to deal with the deteriorating situation, but found himself powerless to stop the Gothic advance. Indeed, his conduct of the war in this period displays an uncharacteristic passivity. This may owe something to a severe outbreak of plague afflicting the empire at the time, with its consequent impact on manpower resources. In December 545 Totila besieged Rome and twelve months later entered it. He immediately visited St Peter's to pray, an act calculated to suggest continuity with Theoderic, who had himself made devotions at the basilica on his one

---

[21] It probably stood for *Christon Maria genna*, 'Mary bore Christ': *Die nichtliterarischen lateinischen Papyri*, ed. Tjäder, II, p. 60, line 75; p. 259 (commentary).
[22] Pr *B*, I.10.19, ed. and tr. Dewing and Downey, pp. 86–7.

known visit to Rome, and, beyond him, with the emperors whose conduct
Theoderic had imitated. But the act was hollow. There were few people left
in the city, and Totila made no secret of his animosity towards the senate.
In fact, he planned to raze the walls of the city, but Belisarius wrote warning
him of the harsh judgement of posterity were he to proceed with this course.
Perhaps Belisarius was able to play on the vanity of the Gothic king; in any
case, Totila behaved foolishly and abandoned Rome, taking members of
the senate as hostages. For forty days the city was home to neither man
nor beast, but by April 547 Belisarius had moved in and begun work on
restoring its defences. During the spring Totila tried to wrest control of the
city from him, but failed.

Nevertheless, the Goths were still masters of much of Italy, to the extent
that Belisarius tended to travel from one place to another by ship rather than
overland, and when Justinian recalled his great general to Constantinople a few years later Belisarius felt much more subdued than he had on
his returns in 534 and 540. In 549 an Ostrogothic fleet ravaged the coast
of Campania and Rome was again besieged; in the following January it
fell. Totila established a mint in the city, held races and, in the words
of a contemporary, lived there 'like a father with his children'.[23] With
Ravenna still in Byzantine hands, Rome came to hold a political significance to which it had long been unaccustomed. Totila moved to Sicily
and ravaged it in 550, whereupon the Franks occupied parts of northern
Italy.

A full decade after Belisarius had seemed to bring the war to a successful
end, the situation in Italy was parlous, and Justinian decided to commit
resources on a scale never entrusted to Belisarius. An enormous army was
placed under the command of the *patricius* Germanus. He was an impressive figure, for not only was he a cousin of Justinian but he had married
Matasuentha, the granddaughter of Theoderic and former wife of Witigis,
a tie which allowed him to anticipate limited resistance from the Goths in
Italy. Indeed, the birth of a baby son to the couple allowed the historian
Jordanes to be hopeful of a future union of the families of Germanus and
Matasuentha.[24] But Germanus died while preparations for the expedition
were still underway, and in 551 the general Narses was appointed to finish
the job.

The great army set off overland for Italy in April 552. Franks who had
settled in Venetia sought to deny it passage on the grounds that it included a
large contingent of Lombards, their traditional enemies. The Goths tried to
make the road impassable, but Narses was able to make his way to Ravenna,

[23] *LP*, LXI.107, ed. Duchesne, I, p. 298; tr. Davis, I, p. 60.
[24] Jordanes, *Romana et Getica*, ch. 314, ed. Mommsen, p. 138; tr. Mierow, p. 141; Momigliano (1955)
provides a rich but inconclusive discussion.

occupying it on 6 June 552. Totila marched out of Rome, and at the end of June or beginning of July the two forces encountered each other at Busta Gallorum, a site in the Apennines.[25] Before the troops of both armies Totila performed a stylish war dance on his charger, but the Goths were heavily outnumbered, and the outcome of the battle was inevitable. The Gothic cavalry could not withstand the enemy archers, and both cavalry and infantry fled, Totila dying of a wound received in flight. Numerous Gothic strongholds surrendered as Narses advanced on Rome, which his enemies were no longer strong enough to defend effectively. The city was easily captured and its keys despatched to Justinian. In their despair the Goths put to death senators they found and 300 children they were holding as hostages, but their cause was now hopeless, and the Franks refused to intervene on their behalf. In October a Gothic force did battle with Narses in the south of Italy at Mons Lactarius, near Nocera, but it was defeated, and Narses gave the surviving Goths permission to return to 'their own land'. Some continued to resist on a local basis until the capture of Verona in 562 or 563, but by the time Narses was recalled, probably not long after the accession of the emperor Justin II (565–78), Italy seemed stable. The Gothic war had lasted far longer than the Vandal war, but its outcome was the same.

A puzzling feature of the Gothic war is the failure of the Visigoths to become involved. For much of the war their king was an Ostrogoth, Theudis (531–48), and at one stage his nephew, Ildibad, was prominent in the resistance in Italy, but we have no reason to believe that help from the Visigoths reached Italy. We do know, however, that around 544 a Visigothic force was defeated at Septem, across the Straits of Gibraltar, which suggests an attempted thrust from Spain into what was by then Byzantine Africa. But in 552 a Byzantine force, purporting to answer an appeal for help from a Visigothic rebel, set out for Spain and succeeded in gaining control of a slice of its south-east coast around Cartagena and Malaga. The area has a mountainous hinterland and looks across the sea to Africa, and the defence of Africa may have been the true reason for Byzantine involvement in Spain.[26] In any case, this modest success was the culmination of an extraordinary expansion of Byzantine power in the west. Within a few decades Africa and Italy, together with the large islands of the western Mediterranean, Dalmatia and part of Spain had been reintegrated into the empire, so that the poet Agathias could legitimately claim that a traveller could go as far as the sandy shore of Spain where the Pillars of Hercules lay and still tread imperial territory.[27]

---

[25] For a detailed account, see Roisl (1981).   [26] See also Barbero and Loring (2005), p. 184.
[27] *Anthologia graeca*, IV.3, lines 83–7, ed. and tr. Paton, I, pp. 120–1.

Figure 8a Justinian, Bishop Maximianus, clergy, officials and soldiers, mosaic from San Vitale, Ravenna; Justinian is, symbolically, centrepiece of the group

CONSTANTINOPLE AND THE WEST IN THE MID-SIXTH CENTURY

We may take the years on either side of 550 as constituting a high water mark of Byzantine influence in the west. Economic links between east and west were strengthened; the export of African pottery to the east, which had declined during the Vandal period, seems to have grown during the early period of Byzantine rule. Byzantine relations with the west were particularly in evidence in Ravenna, the capital of Italy, where Bishop Maximianus obtained from Justinian the title of archbishop and relics of St Andrew, a saint whose cult could be seen as constituting a possible rival to that of St Peter in Rome. It is possible that Maximianus' splendid ivory throne, now to be seen in the Museo Arcivescovile in Ravenna, was made in Constantinople, and it was he who consecrated the church of San Vitale, with its glowing mosaics of Justinian and Theodora. Justinian failed to visit the west, but no one could doubt that the mosaics of San Vitale, whatever the precise liturgical significance of the scenes they portray, were powerful statements of imperial power in the conquered territories.

Figure 8b Theodora and her courtiers, mosaic from San Vitale, Ravenna

Strange as it may seem, the clearest sign of the centrality of Byzantium in western affairs in the mid-sixth century is to be seen in Constantinople itself and in the variety of westerners, the influential, the ambitious and the captive, who were there. Liberius, whom Theoderic had successively appointed praetorian prefect of Italy and praetorian prefect of Gaul, had defected while on an embassy to Constantinople shortly before the Gothic war. He later participated in Byzantine campaigns in Italy and Spain, and returned to Italy, where he was buried at Rimini. During the war, and in particular after Totila's capture of Rome in 546, many Roman aristocrats made their way to the royal city. These included Cassiodorus, formerly prominent in Theoderic's administration, and the leader of the senate, Cethegus; in 554 Justinian gave senators permission to live in Constantinople. The Roman deacon Vigilius was on hand in Constantinople in 537, well placed to become pope when Silverius fell out of imperial favour; when Vigilius died in 555, his successor Pelagius was likewise there, standing in the wings. From the time of Vigilius, imperial confirmation of the election of a pope was needed before he could be consecrated; this accounts for the long intermissions between pontificates that characterised the following period of papal history. Pope Gregory the Great had served as papal legate in Constantinople (c. 579–c. 586) before being appointed as pope in 590.

His two successors would likewise serve in this position before becoming pope. Clearly, after the conquest of Italy, a stint in Constantinople was a valuable item in the *curriculum vitae* of prospective popes. Maximianus was appointed to the see of Ravenna while at Constantinople in 546 and he was to travel there again, while in 552 the clergy of the province of Milan asked a legate travelling to Constantinople to see what he could do to secure the return of bishop Datius; he had been absent from his see for fifteen or sixteen years, and in the royal city for much of the time. One of Gregory the Great's acquaintances while he was in Constantinople, the Milanese deacon Constantius, was appointed bishop of his city in 593, while another, the Spaniard Leander, was to become bishop of Seville. In 551 Reparatus of Carthage and other African bishops were summoned to Constantinople; in the following year Justinian exiled Reparatus and replaced him, against the will of the clergy and people of Carthage, with Primosus, his former legate in Constantinople. Members of various Germanic royal families, such as the Ostrogoth Amalasuntha, were also on hand. An eye could be kept on their activities in the City, and they could be called into action as imperial needs required.

No less striking is the centrality of Constantinople in the intellectual life of the west. A large volume of literature in Latin was produced there during, and immediately after, the reign of Justinian. It was in Constantinople that the Illyrian, Marcellinus, and the African, Victor of Tunnuna, wrote their chronicles; and although the chronicle of the Spanish Goth, John of Biclaro, was produced in Spain, he wrote it after spending some years in the City. It was in Constantinople that the Goth, Jordanes, wrote his histories of the Romans and the Goths. Cassiodorus worked on his *Expositio psalmorum* in the City, and it was there that the African, Junillus, wrote his introduction to the study of the Bible, while another African, Corippus, witnessed the accession of Justin II, which he described in a panegyric; and it was from Constantinople that various African theologians came to operate. Somewhat later, the future pope Gregory delivered there the talks which formed the basis of his massive *Moralia in Job*. Scholars have sometimes doubted Gregory's assertion that he did not know Greek, on the basis that it would have been difficult for the representative of the pope to have functioned in Constantinople without knowing the language. However, given the flourishing and influential community of Latin-speakers there, Gregory may not have found a command of Greek necessary.

THE THREE CHAPTERS

But at this very time of the centrality of Constantinople in western affairs, events were under way which threatened its position and, as often happened in late antiquity, tensions were expressed in disputes over religion.

Imperial policy had long sought to bring together adherents of the council of Chalcedon (451), who recognised the 'unity of Christ's person in two natures', and their monophysite opponents, and Justinian made an important attempt to bring about reconciliation between the disputing parties.[28] He asked the five patriarchs of the church to anathematise the person and works of Bishop Theodore of Mopsuestia, some of the writings of Bishop Theodoret of Cyrrhus, and a letter attributed to Bishop Ibas of Edessa. These three theologians, all long dead, were held to show Nestorian tendencies, and Justinian believed that their condemnation would be a painless way of conciliating the monophysites, who held an opinion contrary to that of the Nestorians. But the council of Chalcedon had accepted the orthodoxy of Theodoret, and the letter of Ibas had been read out there, so an attack on these thinkers could be construed as an attack on the council. Pope Vigilius refused to accept Justinian's proposal, whereupon, to the astonishment of the populace of Rome, he was arrested in a church in 545 and conveyed to Constantinople. Years of intrigue followed, in which Vigilius was alternately vacillating and resolute. Finally, in 553, the council of Constantinople condemned the Three Chapters, as they came to be called, and Vigilius accepted its decision. In 554 he set out to return to Rome, but died at Syracuse in June 555, a broken man.

As it turned out, Justinian's efforts did nothing to reconcile the monophysites and the adherents of Chalcedon, but there was an immediate hostile reaction in the west, where it was felt he had gone against the position adopted by the council. So intense were feelings in Italy that it proved difficult to find bishops prepared to consecrate Vigilius' successor, Pelagius, and a schism broke out in northern Italy (see above, p. 118). There was considerable disquiet in Gaul, and throughout the Visigothic period the Spanish church failed to accept the council of Constantinople. Opposition was, however, strongest in Africa where an episcopate which had seen off the persecuting Arian Vandals was in no mood to be dictated to by a catholic emperor, and the African church flung itself into the controversy with the learning and vigour which had characterised it for centuries. As early as 550 a synod excommunicated Vigilius, and a series of authors wrote attacking Justinian's position; it was an African chronicler who observed that the council of Constantinople was followed by an earthquake in that city![29] Small wonder that a bishop from northern Gaul, Nicetius of Trier, wrote a strongly worded but theologically incoherent letter to the emperor, reporting that all Italy and the entirety of Africa, Spain and Gaul wept

---

[28] For a more detailed discussion of Christological disputes in sixth-century Byzantium, see above pp. 116–19.

[29] Victor of Tunnuna, *Chronicle*, ed. Mommsen, p. 203; ed. Cardelle de Hartmann, ch. 147, p. 49; ed. and Italian tr. Placanica, pp. 52–3.

over him: 'O sweet Justinian of ours, who has so deceived you, who has persuaded you to proceed in such a way?'[30]

Early Christian history is full of controversies on issues apparently so abstruse that modern scholars have often felt they were really about subjects far removed from the matters being overtly debated, and the controversy over the Three Chapters in the west may have been one where the real issue was unstated. It is possible to interpret the strong stance the west took against Justinian's line as constituting a response to the impact of his wars of conquest. Doubtless the heads of churches in Africa and Italy sincerely welcomed the coming of Justinian's armies, but while governed by non-Roman Arians, they had come to enjoy *de facto* independence from imperial oversight, which they would not surrender willingly. It is no coincidence that one of the most famous assertions of ecclesiastical power ever made vis-à-vis the emperor was enunciated by Pope Gelasius (492–6) during the period of Ostrogothic power in Italy. The wars created a situation in which an emperor, for the first time in a long while, was able to attempt to impose his will directly on western churches, and some of the opposition to Justinian's policies may simply have been a reaction against the new reality. But it may also be that opposition to the Three Chapters was a vent for hostility towards, or disillusionment with, the outcome of the wars in the west. If we accept this, we will not be surprised to find Cassiodorus, the best-known collaborator with the Goths among the Romans, writing towards the middle of the century in terms which suggest sympathy for the theologians whose condemnation Justinian was seeking. Nor are other indications of western coolness towards Byzantium lacking in the period after the conquests.

The indigenous inhabitants of Africa and Italy initially welcomed the Byzantine armies. In Italy the Gothic government was worried about the loyalty of the populace even before the war began, and the detailed narrative of Procopius makes it clear that its fears were justified. Yet early in the war a Gothic spokesman told the people of Rome that the only Greeks who had visited Rome were actors, mimes or thieving soldiers, suggesting there was already some resentment towards the Byzantines, which the Goths sought to exploit. We are told that during the pontificate of Pope John III (561–74) the inhabitants of the city maliciously told the emperor that 'it would be better . . . to serve the Goths than the Greeks'.[31] The use of

---

[30] *Epistulae Austrasicae*, no. 7, ed. Gundlach, p. 417. There is a reminiscence here of St Paul (Gal. 3:1). The answer to Nicetius' questions is 'the Devil'.

[31] Gothic spokesman: Pr *W*, V.18.40–1, ed. and tr. Dewing, III, pp. 182–3; message to the emperor: *LP*, LXIII.10, ed. Duchesne, I, p. 305; tr. Davis, I, p. 62.

the term 'Greeks' is interesting, for in Procopius it is a hostile word placed in the mouths of non-Romans. Perhaps the Romans had come to accept, or at least pretend to accept, the barbarians' assessment of the easterners. The dire state of the Italian economy after the long war, and the corrupt and grasping nature of the Byzantine administration imposed in both Africa and Italy, made imperial government unpopular. Further, Italy's integration into the empire did not imply reversion to the position of independence from the east which it had enjoyed before the advent of barbarian power, nor were its Roman inhabitants able to enjoy the positions of influence they had held under the Goths; Italy was now a minor part of an empire governed by a far-away *autokratōr* who never troubled to visit the west. Power in Africa and Italy passed to Greek-speaking incomers, and we have evidence for cults of eastern saints, which they presumably brought with them. Needless to say there were loyalists and careerists who supported the Byzantine regime, for example the African poet Corippus, whose epic *Iohannis* was partly an attempt to justify the imperial cause to his fellow Africans;[32] but these represented minority opinion.

If this were not enough, opposition to Justinian's wars even developed in the east. This can be traced through the works of Procopius, which move from a sunny optimism in describing the Vandal war to the sombre tone which increasingly intrudes in the Gothic war and the animosity towards the emperor displayed in the *Secret history*; but one can also deduce from other sources a feeling that resources had been committed in the west to little profit. However impressive their outcome in bringing Africa and Italy back into the empire, Justinian's wars had in some ways the paradoxical result of driving east and west further apart.

BYZANTINE MILITARY DIFFICULTIES IN THE WEST

Throughout Justinian's reign, that part of the empire south of the Danube had been troubled by incursions, in particular those of the Turkic-speaking people known as Bulgars and groups of Slavs whom contemporaries called Antes and Sclaveni. The government dealt with the threat as best it could by building forts and paying subsidies, but following Justinian's death in 565, the situation deteriorated rapidly. His successor Justin II adopted a policy of withholding subsidies, and in particular he refused a demand for tribute made by Avars, who had recently made their way into the Danube area. The Avars soon showed their mettle. In 567 they joined forces with the Lombards living in Pannonia to crush the Gepids, a victory that signalled the end of the Germanic peoples along the middle Danube. In the following year the Lombards left Pannonia for Italy, whereupon the Avars occupied

---

[32] Cameron, Averil (1985).

the lands they had vacated, the plain of modern Hungary. From there they launched attacks deep into imperial territory, and the renewal of war with Persia in 572 made the Byzantine response to these developments the less effective. In 581 Slavs invaded the Balkans, and before long it became clear that they were moving in to stay.

These events had a major impact on the west. The attention of the authorities was now diverted from the newly won provinces, and direct land access to Italy was rendered difficult. Moreover, it may well have been the rise of the Avars that impelled the Lombards to launch in 568 their invasion of Italy where they quickly gained control of the Po valley and areas of central and southern Italy. The Byzantine administration, under the successor of Narses, the praetorian prefect Longinus, proved embarrassingly ill-equipped to cope, and a force eventually sent from the east under Justin's son-in-law Baduarius was defeated. In 577 or 578 the Roman *patricius* Pamphronius, who had gone to Constantinople seeking help, was sent away with the 3,000 pounds of gold he had brought with him and told to use the money to bribe some Lombards to defect or, failing that, to secure the intervention of the Franks. In 579 a second embassy was fobbed off with a small force and, we are told, an attempt was made to bribe some of the Lombard leaders. Perhaps we see here the reflection of a change in imperial policy, for while Justin had behaved in a miserly fashion, his successor Tiberius I (578–82) was inclined to throw money at his problems. However, neither strategy succeeded, and it was all too clear that the situation in Italy was desperate. It was time for Constantinople to play the Frankish card again.

For the greater part of the sixth century the Franks had steadily been growing more powerful. Their defeat of the Visigoths in 507 was followed by expansion from northern into southern Gaul, while the weakening of the Burgundians and Ostrogoths in the 520s and 530s saw further gains.[33] In the early stages of the Gothic war they were in the happy position of being able to accept the payments that both sides made seeking their assistance, but when King Theudebert marched into Italy in 539, he was acting solely in his own interests. Theudebert issued gold coins displaying his own portrait rather than that of the emperor and bearing legends generally associated with emperors rather than kings. He responded to an embassy from Justinian in grandiloquent terms, advising him that the territory under his power extended through the Danube and the boundary of Pannonia as far as the ocean shores.[34] Towards the end of Theudebert's life his forces occupied Venetia and some other areas of Italy, and it was rumoured that he planned to march on the City: such was the fear he inspired in

---

[33] See Barbero and Loring (2005), pp. 173–4; Van Dam (2005), p. 200.
[34] *Epistulae Austrasicae*, no. 20, ed. Gundlach, pp. 438–9.

Constantinople. The settlement of the Lombards in Pannonia by Justinian in about 546 may have represented an attempt to counter the Franks. Following the death of Theudebert in 547, Justinian sent an embassy to his heir Theudebald proposing an offensive alliance against the Goths, but he was turned down and Frankish intervention in Italy continued to be a problem throughout the Gothic war. The advent of the Lombards, however, placed the Franks once more on the far side of an enemy of the Byzantines and they could again be looked upon as potential allies. But the attempts made to gain their help occurred against a highly complex political and military background.

It is difficult to reconstruct the web of alliances and animosities that lay behind relations between Constantinople and the disparate parts of the west towards the end of the sixth century. In 579 Hermenigild, the elder son of the Visigothic king Leovigild, revolted against his father. After the rebellion's suppression, Hermenigild's wife (the Frankish princess Ingund) and son Athanagild fled to the Byzantines; Athanagild was taken to Constantinople, and his Frankish relatives were unable to secure his return to the west, despite their efforts. A few years later one Gundovald, who claimed to be the son of a Frankish king, arrived in Marseilles. He had been living in Constantinople, but had been lured back to Francia by a party of aristocrats. The emperor Maurice (582–602) gave Gundovald financial backing, and one of his supporters in Marseilles was later accused of wishing to bring the kingdom of the Franks under the emperor's sway. This was almost certainly an exaggeration, and Gundovald's rebellion came to naught, but again we have evidence of imperial fishing in troubled western waters.[35] In 584 the Frankish king Childebert, the uncle of Athanagild, having at some time received 50,000 *solidi* from Maurice, sent forces to Italy, but the results were not up to imperial expectations and Maurice asked for his money back. Other expeditions followed, but little was achieved. Finally, in 590 a large Frankish expedition advanced into Italy and made its way beyond Verona, but failed to make contact with the imperial army. This was the last occasion when Constantinople used the Franks in its Italian policy. The fiasco of 590 may be taken as symbolising a relationship which rarely worked to the benefit of the empire. While it may often be true that the neighbours of one's enemy are one's friends, Byzantine attempts to profit from the Franks had persistently failed.

By the last years of the century the Byzantines were in difficulties throughout the west. Most of Italy was under Lombard control, and severe losses had also been sustained in Africa, although the latter can only dimly be perceived. In 595 Berbers caused alarm to the people of Carthage itself, until the

---

[35] On Gundovald see Gregory of Tours, *Libri*, VI.24, VII.10–14, VII.26–38, ed. Krusch and Levison, pp. 291–2, 332–6, 345–62; tr. Thorpe, pp. 352–3, 394–8, 407–23.

exarch tricked them into defeat. A geographical work written by George of Cyprus early in the seventh century indicates that the imperial possessions in Africa were considerably smaller than those which the Vandals had controlled, themselves smaller than those which had belonged to the Roman empire.[36] The establishment of exarchs in Ravenna and Carthage indicates a society that was being forced to become more military in orientation, and while the Byzantine possessions in Spain are not well documented, it is clear that they tended to diminish rather than grow.

EAST AND WEST: CONTINUING LINKS AND GROWING DIVISIONS

Paradoxically, despite the waning of Byzantine power in the west, the latter continued to be vitally interested in the east. A ready market remained for imported luxury items; goods of Byzantine provenance were included in the early seventh-century ship burial at Sutton Hoo in East Anglia and Radegund, the founder of a convent at Poitiers, petitioned Justin II and his wife Sophia for a portion of the True Cross, which she duly received in 569 (see above, p. 123). At the end of the century, the letters of Pope Gregory the Great reveal a man who saw the empire as central to his world and who had a penchant for wine imported from Egypt, surely one of the few Italians in history of whom this could be said. Byzantine legislation was followed with attention. The Frank Chilperic I did not merely rejoice in the possession of gold medallions that Tiberius I sent him: an edict he issued shows an apparent dependence on a *novella* of the same emperor.[37] Eastern liturgical practice was imitated; on the recommendation of the newly converted Visigothic king Reccared, the third council of Toledo prescribed in 589 that the creed was to be sung before the Lord's Prayer and the taking of communion 'according to the practice of the eastern churches', apparently in imitation of Justin I's requiring, at the beginning of his reign, that the creed be sung before the Lord's Prayer. This is one of a number of indications of the increasingly Byzantine form of the public life of Spain towards the end of the sixth century. The chronicle of Marius of Avenches, written in Burgundy, is dated according to consulships and indictional years, until its termination in 581. Inscriptions in the Rhône Valley were still being dated according to consulships or indictional years in the early seventh century, and coins were being minted in the name of the emperor at Marseilles and Viviers as late as the reign of Heraclius (610–41). Whatever may be the merits of thinking in terms of 'an obscure law of cultural hydraulics', whereby streams of influence were occasionally

---

[36] George of Cyprus, *Descriptio orbis Romani*, pp. x–xi, 33–4.
[37] Stein (1920).

released from the east to water the lower reaches of the west,[38] there can be no doubt that the west remained open to Byzantine influence, nor that western authors such as Gregory of Tours and Venantius Fortunatus sought to keep abreast of eastern material in a way that few easterners reciprocated.

Emperors, moreover, gave indications that they still regarded the west as important. The marriages which the emperor Tiberius arranged for his daughters are strong evidence of this, for whereas one of them married Maurice, the successful general who was to succeed Tiberius, another married Germanus, the son of the *patricius* whom Justinian had nominated to finish the war against the Goths in 550, and of his Gothic wife Matasuentha. Tiberius made each of his sons-in-law caesar and, given the strong western associations of Germanus, it is tempting to see the emperor as having thought of a *divisio imperii* into east and west, something that never seems to have crossed Justinian's mind.

If this was Tiberius' plan, nothing came of it; but his successor, Maurice, drew up a will appointing his elder son Theodosius as lord of Constantinople with power in the east, and his younger son Tiberius as emperor of old Rome with power in Italy and the islands of the Tyrrhenian Sea. Again, nothing came of this plan, but it was from Carthage that Heraclius, the son of an exarch, launched his successful rebellion against Phocas in 610. It was later believed that at a difficult point in his reign the emperor Heraclius planned to flee to Africa, only being restrained by an oath the patriarch forced him to take. In the mid-seventh century Maximus the Confessor, a complex figure who in various ways links east and west, was accused of having had a vision in which he saw angels in heaven on both the east and the west; those on the west exclaimed 'Gregory Augustus, may you conquer!', and their voice was louder than the voices of those on the east.[39] Surely, it may appear, relations between Byzantium and the west remained strong.

But although the west retained a capacity to absorb Byzantine influences, and emperors after Justinian continued to think in terms of controlling the west, in other ways the sixth century saw the two parts of the former empire move further apart. Justinian's wars had over-extended the empire, entailing a major weakening of its position on the northern and eastern frontiers, and as warfare continued against the Slavs, Avars and Persians there were few resources to spare for the west, where the territory controlled by Constantinople shrank to scattered coastal fringes. By the end of the century there was little trade between Carthage and Constantinople. East

[38] See the memorable characterisation of this view in Brown, P. (1976), p. 5.
[39] Mansi, XI, cols. 3–4. The Gregory referred to was an exarch of Carthage who had rebelled against Emperor Constans II. On Maximus, see below pp. 231–2.

and west were drifting apart linguistically: there are no counterparts to a Boethius in the west or a Priscian in the east towards the end of the century. In his correspondence as pope, Gregory the Great complained of the quality of translators out of Latin in Constantinople and Greek in Rome: both sets translated word for word without regard for the sense of what they were translating.[40] Byzantine historians after Procopius rapidly came to display a lack of knowledge of, or interest in, western affairs. Evagrius Scholasticus, writing towards the end of the sixth century, argued in favour of Christianity by comparing the fates of emperors before and after Constantine, a line of argument that could only be sustained by ignoring the later western emperors.[41] The sources available to Theophanes, when he wrote his *Chronicle* in the early ninth century, allowed him to note the accession of almost every pope from the late third century to Benedict I in 575, but not of subsequent ones. Meanwhile Paul the Deacon, writing in the late eighth century, seems to have regarded Maurice as the first Greek among the emperors.[42] One has the feeling that towards the end of the sixth century the west simply became less relevant to easterners.

Meanwhile, the west was going its own way. The discontent manifested in Africa and Italy over the condemnation of the Three Chapters may plausibly be seen as reflecting unhappiness at the situation following the wars waged by Justinian. Increasingly, the Italians came to see their interests as not necessarily identical with those of the empire. In Spain, Justinian's activities left a nasty taste in peoples' mouths: the learned Isidore of Seville, writing in the early seventh century, denied not only ecumenical status to the council of 553, but also a place among Roman lawgivers to Justinian and patriarchal rank to the see of Constantinople. In Africa, the government's inability to deal with the Berbers prepared the way for the loss of the province to the Arabs in the following century. It is hard to avoid the conclusion that in the sixth century Byzantium and the west moved significantly apart; one cannot but see the emperor Justinian as being largely to blame.

---

[40] Gregory I, *Letters*, VII.27, ed. Ewald and Hartmann, I, p. 474; tr. Martyn, II, pp. 482–3.

[41] Evagrius Scholasticus, *Ecclesiastical history*, III.41, ed. Bidez and Parmentier, pp. 141–4; tr. Whitby, pp. 189–92.

[42] 'Primus ex Grecorum genere in imperio confirmatus est': Paul the Deacon, *Historia Langobardorum*, III.15, ed. Bethmann and Waitz, p. 100; tr. Foulke, p. 113.

CHAPTER 4

BYZANTIUM TRANSFORMING (600–700)

ANDREW LOUTH

INTRODUCTION

Most centuries can be said to have been, in one way or another, a watershed for Byzantium, but the case for the seventh century is particularly strong. At the beginning of the century, the Byzantine empire formed part of a political configuration that had been familiar for centuries: it was a world centred on the Mediterranean and bounded to the east by the Persian empire, in which most of the regions surrounding *mare nostrum* formed a single political entity – the Roman (or Byzantine) empire. It was a world whose basic economic unit was still the city and its hinterland; although it had lost much of its political significance, the city retained the social, economic and cultural high ground.

By the beginning of the seventh century, this traditional configuration was already being eroded: much of Italy was under Lombard rule, Gaul was in Frankish hands and the coastal regions of Spain, the final acquisition of Justinian's reconquest, were soon to fall to the Visigoths. By the end of the century this traditional configuration was gone altogether, to be replaced by another which would be dominant for centuries and still marks the region today. The boundary that separated the Mediterranean world from the Persian empire was swept away: after the Arab conquest of the eastern provinces in the 630s and 640s, that boundary – the Tigris–Euphrates valley – became one of the arteries of a new empire, with its capital first in Damascus (661–750) and then in Baghdad (from 750). By the mid-eighth century this empire stretched from Spain in the west to the valleys of the Oxus and the Indus in the east, far larger than Justinian's Byzantine empire or even the Roman empire had ever been, and hugely richer than any of its neighbours. The new empire caused Europe, East Asia and North Africa to be reconfigured around it, forcing the Byzantine empire – and the emergent Frankish kingdoms – into virtual satellite status. This radical upheaval, together with the persistent aggression of the Arabs against the remaining Byzantine lands and the incursion of Slavs and peoples hailing from the central Eurasian steppe into the Balkans, accelerated the transition of the cities of the eastern Mediterranean world that was already well under

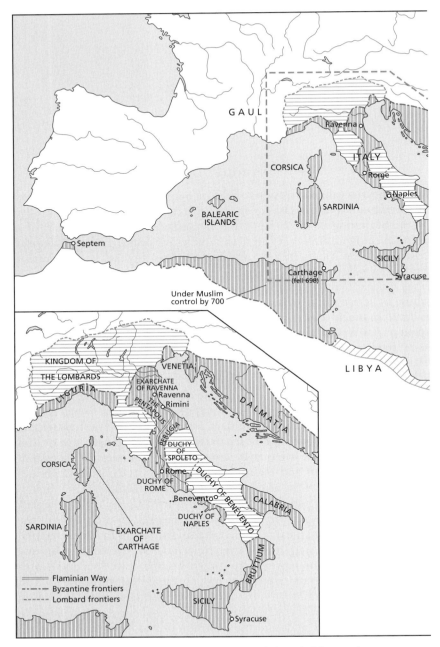

Map 11 Byzantium transforming: the empire towards the end of the seventh century

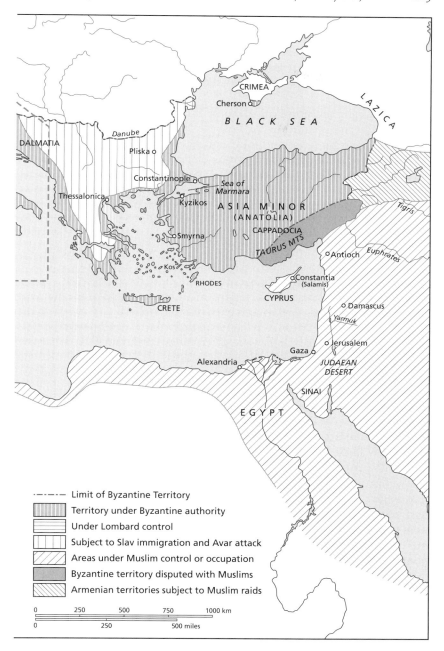

CRIMEA

Cherson ○

BLACK SEA

LAZICA

Danube

DALMATIA

Pliska ○

Constantinople ○

Sea of
Marmara

Tigris

Thessalonica ○

Kyzikos ○

ASIA MINOR
(ANATOLIA)

CAPPADOCIA

○ Smyrna

TAURUS MTS

○ Antioch

Euphrates

○ Kos

RHODES

○ Constantia
(Salamis)

CYPRUS

○ Damascus

Yarmuk

CRETE

Gaza ○

○ Jerusalem

JUDAEAN
DESERT

Alexandria ○

SINAI

E G Y P T

- – · – · – Limit of Byzantine Territory

Territory under Byzantine authority

Under Lombard control

Subject to Slav immigration and Avar attack

Areas under Muslim control or occupation

Byzantine territory disputed with Muslims

Armenian territories subject to Muslim raids

0   250   500   750   1000 km

0   250   500 miles

way. By the end of the century the cities had lost much of their social and cultural significance, and survived as fortified enclaves, if often as market centres, too.[1] The only place approximating to the traditional city was Constantinople, and that largely because of the presence of the imperial court; but even Constantinople barely survived, and did so in much reduced circumstances.[2]

This dramatic transition caused something of a crisis of confidence and even identity for Byzantium. At least twice the emperor entertained the notion of deserting Constantinople and re-establishing the capital of the empire closer to its traditional centre in Rome: in 618 Heraclius (610–41) thought of moving to Carthage, and in the 660s Constans II (641–68) settled in Sicily. In both cases we can see how the traditional idea of a Mediterranean empire still haunted the imagination of the Byzantine rulers. In fact, despite the dramatic and permanent changes witnessed by the seventh century, Byzantine reactions can be seen as attempts to preserve what was perceived as traditional. But as always with the Byzantines, one must be careful not to be deceived by their rhetoric. This rhetoric – and, as we shall see, administrative changes that were more than rhetorical – spoke in terms of centralisation, an increasing focus on the figure of the emperor and the court, and a growing influence of the patriarch and clergy of the Great Church of St Sophia in religious matters. In reality, however, events and persons on the periphery were often more important than what was going on at the centre. The transition that started in the seventh century was not completed in that century: not until the late eighth and ninth centuries, when Arab pressure on the Byzantine empire eased after the capital of the caliphate moved eastwards from Damascus to Baghdad, did Byzantium finally complete the transition begun in the seventh. What emerged was an empire and culture focused on emperor and capital; but much of what the centre now stood for was, in fact, worked out not in Constantinople itself, but at the periphery.

The history of the Byzantine empire in the seventh century is difficult to reconstruct. Traditional sources are sparse and mostly late.[3] We can draw on Theophylact Simocatta's *History* and the *Paschal chronicle*, both of which were probably written at the court of Patriarch Sergius around 630 during the euphoria caused by Heraclius' triumph over the Persians. The celebrations of Heraclius' Persian victories by George of Pisidia also belong to this period but history writing in Byzantium stops thereafter until the end of the eighth century. For the political history of the seventh century our

---

[1] The pace of this change in the cities and its interpretation is the subject of an ongoing debate. See Foss (1975), Foss (1977a), emphasising the impact of the Persian invasion in the first quarter of the seventh century; Haldon (1997a) pp. 92–124, 459–61; below, pp. 261, 264, 483–5.

[2] For Constantinople, see Mango (1990).

[3] On the problems of the literary source materials, see *BEINE*, I.

principal sources are thus two later works: Nikephoros I, patriarch of Constantinople's *Brief history*, composed in the late eighth century and intended as a continuation of Theophylact Simocatta; and the early ninth-century *Chronicle* ascribed to Theophanes the Confessor. To some extent the dearth of writing from the period 630–790 may be seen to be a consequence of the collapse of much of traditional Mediterranean society. The demise of the ancient city meant the collapse of the educational system's traditional base: there were fewer and fewer people to write for.[4] There was also less to write about: details of the fall of the Byzantine eastern provinces to the Arabs and subsequent defeats and losses would not be welcome material for Byzantine writers, and are either omitted by Nikephoros and Theophanes, or drawn from Syriac or Arab sources. Like these Byzantine historians, we can supplement our sparse resources with oriental historical material. There is an anonymous history of Heraclius ascribed to the Armenian bishop Sebeos and dated to the latter half of the seventh century (see above, n. 1, p. 157). There is also a world chronicle, written in Egypt at the end of the century by Bishop John of Nikiu; however, this only survives in mutilated form in an Ethiopic translation. There are in addition several contemporary and later Syriac chronicles: besides anonymous works, there are those compiled by Elias bar Shinaya, the eleventh-century metropolitan of Nisibis, and Michael the Syrian, the twelfth-century Jacobite patriarch of Antioch, both using earlier sources. Legal sources are also sparse for this period, but the *Farmer's law* (*Nomos georgikos*) probably belongs to the seventh or eighth century, as may the *Rhodian sea-law* (*Nomos Rodion nautikos*).

Traditionally, therefore, the seventh and eighth centuries have been regarded as the Byzantine 'dark ages', though historians have begun to recognise that it is only in respect of traditional historical literary material that one can speak of a paucity of sources for the period. For in fact it was an immensely fruitful period for Byzantine theology, dominated by the figure of Maximus the Confessor, perhaps the greatest theologian of the orthodox east and certainly the greatest Byzantine theologian.[5] To make full use of these 'untraditional' sources would, however, involve writing a different kind of history, beginning not from the institutional and political, but rather working outwards from the deeply-considered worldview to be found in such writings.[6] But one should note that there is a notable lacuna in the theological sources themselves. They are all from the periphery: Maximus writing mostly from North Africa, Anastasius of Sinai and John Klimakos ('of the Ladder') from Sinai. Elsewhere, Cyprus

---

[4] See Whitby, Michael (1992).

[5] The contemporary accounts of the legal process he underwent, with some other documents, are edited in Maximus the Confessor, *Scripta saeculi*, ed. and tr. Allen and Neil.

[6] For a notable attempt by a historian to use these theological sources, see Haldon (1992a).

and Palestine were homes to a good deal of writing, polemical and hagiographical for the most part. We know almost nothing of theology in Constantinople between the middle of the sixth century, such as came from the circle of Justinian, Leontius of Byzantium and Leontius of Jerusalem, and the ninth-century revival of learning – that of the iconodule theologians Nikephoros I, patriarch of Constantinople, Theodore the Stoudite, Patriarch Photios and others. The only exceptions are the Constantinopolitan opponent of iconoclasm, Patriarch Germanos I, and some traces of the theology of the iconoclasts preserved by their opponents. Virtually all the theology that survives from this period of transition belongs to the periphery.

This chapter will firstly give an outline of the political history of the period, and will follow this with some account of the transition that the seventh century witnessed. To do otherwise would be nearly impossible, as the elements of the transition – the transformation of the city, the administrative and the religious changes – are not easily datable, and consequently would find no natural place in the narrative history.

EVENTS: PERSIANS DEFEATED, ARABS TRIUMPHANT, CHURCHMEN AT ODDS

The century began with Maurice (582–602) on the imperial throne, urging his army to resist the incursion of Slavs who were seeking to cross the Danube from the north bank. Growing discontent culminated in mutiny when Maurice ordered the army to continue their campaign against the Slavs into the winter months, when bare trees would provide less cover for the marauders. Led by Phocas, a relatively minor officer, the army marched on Constantinople and deposed Maurice. Phocas was proclaimed emperor, but was never very secure and faced a number of revolts. More seriously the Persian shah Khusro II (590–628) used Maurice's murder as a pretext to declare war on the empire, to avenge his former protector (see above, pp. 127, 128). With the invasion of Syria, there began a war that would last until 626–7. In 610 Phocas was deposed by Heraclius, son of the exarch of Carthage, who, according to Theophanes, seized the throne at the invitation of the senate in Constantinople. Heraclius' ships displayed reliquaries and icons of the Mother of God on their masts: a sign of the continuing authentication of political authority by supernatural means seen in the later decades of the sixth century. Phocas was swiftly overthrown and executed, and Heraclius acclaimed as emperor and crowned by the patriarch in St Stephen's chapel in the palace. On the same day he married his betrothed, Eudocia, whom he crowned *augusta*.

The situation Heraclius faced was grim. The Persians were now advancing into Asia Minor, taking Caesarea in Cappadocia in 611, and to the north from across the Danube the Avars were once again a serious menace: in 615 both enemies would make a joint assault on Constantinople. Attempts were made to negotiate a peace treaty with the Persians – immediately, according to the eastern sources; according to the Greek sources, in 615, once the Persian forces had advanced as far as Chalcedon. Anyway the peace efforts were repudiated, as the Persians were convinced that the Byzantine empire lay at their mercy. The war took on the character of a holy war between a Christian army, using icons of Christ and the Virgin as banners, and the predominantly Zoroastrian army of the Persians. Besides advancing into Asia Minor, the Persians invaded Palestine, taking Jerusalem in early May 614, and then Egypt and Libya. The fall of Jerusalem, by now regarded by Christians as their Holy City, was a catastrophe for Byzantium as a Christian empire, and for the emperor as God's vicegerent on earth. Still worse was the seizure of the relic of the True Cross, which was taken back to the Persian capital, Ctesiphon, along with Zacharias, patriarch of Jerusalem, and those Christian notables who survived the sack of the city; tens of thousands are said to have been killed.[7]

It was not until Heraclius had managed to negotiate a truce with the Avars that he was able to make a serious attempt to defeat the Persians. From 622 onwards he conducted a series of campaigns against them. In 626, while Heraclius was on campaign, the Persians joined forces with the Avars to besiege Constantinople. Heraclius himself did not return, but sent a contingent of the field army to reinforce the City's defenders, who were under the leadership of the two regents, Patriarch Sergius and the *magister officiorum*, Bonus. Constantinople was besieged for ten days by a huge army of various peoples under the command of the khagan of the Avars, while the Persian army under Shahrvaraz held the Asian shore of the Bosporus. The siege failed when the fleet of Slav boats was destroyed by the Byzantine fleet in the Golden Horn, just across from the Church of the Virgin at Blachernae. The success of the Constantinopolitans' defence of their city was ascribed to the Virgin Mother of God, and it is likely that the famous troparion 'To you, champion commander' was composed by Patriarch Sergius to celebrate her victory. Heraclius pressed his attack into the Sasanians' heartland. The Persians were demoralised by their troops' failure under Shahrvaraz to secure the City; they were also smarting at the destruction by the emperor's brother Theodore of another contingent destined for Constantinople. Heraclius' successes provoked a palace revolt in which Khusro was murdered, and the Persians sued for peace. All the territory they had taken was restored to the Byzantine empire, and the Tigris–Euphrates valley became the frontier once again. Heraclius recovered

---

[7] For the most thorough examination of the various sources for the taking of Jerusalem by the Persians, see Flusin (1992); see also Kaegi (2003a), pp. 78–80.

the True Cross, and celebrated his triumph by taking the relic on a tour of the restored Byzantine territories, before returning it to Jerusalem on 21 March 630.[8]

It would seem to be at this stage that Heraclius began to face the religious problems that had plagued the Byzantine empire since the council of Chalcedon in 451.[9] The schism between those who supported Chalcedon and those who repudiated it, whom their enemies called monophysites, had become institutionalised with a separate monophysite episcopal hierarchy since the consecration of Jacob Baradaeus in 542. The monophysites had their greatest support in the eastern provinces, especially Syria and Egypt; many Christians in Armenia also declined to acknowledge the council of Chalcedon (see also below, pp. 333, 335). After conquering the eastern provinces, Khusro had sought to strengthen his hold over his new subjects by exploiting the Christians' schisms. At a meeting held in Ctesiphon, Khusro met with leaders of the monophysites, the Armenians and also the Nestorians, the main Christian group established in Persia. These last had rejected the condemnation of Nestorius at the third ecumenical council of Ephesus in 431 and fled to Persia to escape persecution in the Byzantine empire. It was agreed that the Nestorians should retain their position within the traditional Sasanian territories, but that the Persian authorities would support the monophysites in Armenia and those former Byzantine provinces where the monophysites were in a majority, that is, Syria and Egypt. The monophysites welcomed this agreement, their patriarch of Antioch, Athanasius 'the Camel Driver', rejoicing at the 'passing of the Chalcedonian night'.

If Heraclius was to be secure in his regained eastern provinces, he needed to gain the support of the monophysites. The policy he pursued was proposed by his patriarch Sergius, who had foreseen this problem and had already begun negotiations with monophysites: Sergius was himself Syrian, possibly with a monophysite background. The proposal was to seek union on the basis of the doctrine of monenergism, i.e. that Christ, while he had two natures, as Chalcedon had affirmed, possessed only a single divine-human activity. This policy achieved some success in Armenia, but the Syrian monophysites (Jacobites) were not amenable and required an explicit repudiation of Chalcedon. Monenergism's greatest success was in Egypt, where Cyrus of Phasi, appointed patriarch and augustal prefect in 631, reached an agreement with the main monophysite group, the Theodosians.[10] On 3 June 633 a solemn eucharist celebrated the union with the Theodosians, on the basis of a carefully phrased pact of union in nine

---

[8] For the date and the literature cited, see Flusin (1992), II, pp. 293–309.
[9] For the earlier religious problems, see Meyendorff (1989), pp. 333–73; above, pp. 99–129.
[10] Named after Theodosius, the sixth-century patriarch of Alexandria.

chapters; this placed monenergism in the context of the Cyrilline Chalcedonianism that had been espoused by Justinian and endorsed at the fifth ecumenical council in 553.[11]

But it was not only some of the monophysites who refused to accept monenergism. As Cyrus was about to celebrate his triumph of ecumenism, also present in Alexandria was the learned and highly respected abbot, Sophronius. To him, the nine chapters amounted to monophysitism. He protested to Cyrus, to no avail, and took his protest to Patriarch Sergius in Constantinople. Sergius was sufficiently alarmed by Sophronius' protest to issue a ruling on the matter (the *Psephos*) in which he forbade any mention of either one or two activities in Christ. But that scarcely satisfied Sophronius, who took his complaint to Pope Honorius I in Rome. He seems to have had no success with the pope either, and from Rome he made his way to Palestine, where he was elected patriarch of Jerusalem in 634. In his synodical letter Sophronius exposed the heresy of monenergism, though without explicitly breaching the terms of the *Psephos*. Before Sophronius' arrival in Constantinople, Sergius had already communicated the success of the doctrine of monenergism in Alexandria to Honorius, who in his reply used the phrase that was to lead to the refinement of monenergism into the doctrine of monothelitism. That phrase was 'one will'. Monothelitism, the doctrine that Christ had only one divine will, was proclaimed as imperial orthodoxy in the *Ekthesis* issued by Heraclius in 638, although this was doubtless composed by Sergius.

However, by 638 the immediate purpose of this religious compromise was being overtaken by events, for Heraclius' triumph over the Persians proved a pyrrhic victory. Even while it was being celebrated, Palestine and Syria began to experience attacks from Arab tribes that within barely more than a decade would lead to the loss of the Byzantine empire's eastern provinces – this time for ever – and the complete collapse of the Sasanian empire. In 633 there were Muslim attacks on garrisons in Gaza, and the Arab armies soon moved further north, although there is considerable confusion in the sources about the sequence of events thereafter.[12] Heraclius mustered an army and sought to defeat the Arabs. The decisive battle took place at the river Yarmuk in 636, when the much larger Byzantine force was routed. Heraclius abandoned the eastern provinces in despair. The year before, Damascus had already fallen to the Muslims – or more probably had been surrendered – and in 638 Patriarch Sophronius surrendered Jerusalem to Caliph 'Umar bin al-Khattab. Alexandria was taken in 642, and though the

---

[11] See above, pp. 117–18.

[12] For the standard account, see Donner (1981); Kaegi (1992). For the difficulties inherent in using the Arab sources, see Leder (1992); Conrad (1992). For a revisionist account of the Arab conquests, see Cook and Crone (1977); Crone (1980); Crone (1987). For a lucid account of the whole controversy over the value of early Islamic sources, see Humphries (1991), pp. 69–103; see also below, pp. 365, 367.

Byzantines recaptured it, in 645 it finally fell. By that time Mesopotamia had already fallen, and with it the Sasanian empire. The speed with which the eastern provinces of the Byzantine empire succumbed to the Arabs remains to be explained by historians. However attractive at first sight, the idea that these provinces, with their attachment to monophysitism, were already culturally lost to the empire does not seem to be borne out by the evidence we have: on the contrary, there is much evidence for the continuing power of Hellenism in the eastern provinces well into the seventh century – evidence suggesting that Hellenic culture was more potent there than in the empire's capital itself.[13]

When Heraclius died in 641, his death precipitated a dynastic struggle. He was succeeded by two of his sons: Constantine, by his first marriage to Eudocia; and Heraclius, known as Heracleonas, by his second wife Martina, who was also his niece. Martina herself was given a special role to play as *augusta*. Heraclius' marriage to his niece after the death of Eudocia had met with opposition at the time, and there was also opposition to the association of Martina as empress with the two emperors. Constantine's death – the result of poisoning according to a rumour reported by Theophanes – only increased the opposition to Martina and Heracleonas; there were demands that the imperial dignity should be shared with Constantine's son, also called Constantine, but usually known as Constans. As troops from the Anatolian armies appeared at Chalcedon in support of these demands, Heracleonas seems to have acceded to them. Nevertheless, Heracleonas and his mother were deposed and exiled, together with Martina's other two sons, and Constans II became sole emperor.

Constans inherited the continuing collapse of the eastern provinces to the Arabs: Egypt was slipping away and Muslim raids into Armenia began in 642–3. In 647 the future caliph Mu'awiya (661–80) led a raiding party into Anatolia and besieged Caesarea, and from there they penetrated further still into Anatolia. The Arabs made no attempt to settle, but huge amounts of booty were taken back to Damascus. Mu'awiya also realised the need for the Muslims to develop sea power, and in 649 he led a naval expedition against Cyprus, in which Constantia was taken. In 654 Rhodes was laid waste, Kos taken and Crete pillaged. The following year, in an attempt to remove the threat from the sea, the Byzantine fleet under the command of Constans himself engaged with the Arab fleet, but was defeated and Constans barely escaped with his life.

The death of Caliph 'Uthman in 656 precipitated a civil war (*fitna*) amongst the Arabs: one faction was led by Mu'awiya, proclaimed caliph in Syria, the other by 'Ali, son-in-law of the prophet Muhammad. The civil war ended with the death of 'Ali and the establishment of the Umayyad

---

[13] See Mango (1989); Cameron, Averil (1991a).

dynasty under Mu'awiya in 661/2 – events provoking the schism in Islam between Sunni and Shiite that still endures. However, those years of civil war provided valuable respite for the Byzantines. Constans was able to turn his attention to the Balkans, where the power of the Avars had waned, and in 658 he led an expedition into the regions settled by the Slavs (*Sklaviniai*). There he met with considerable success, according to Theophanes, and was able to use the Slavs he captured to repopulate areas in Anatolia that had been devastated or depopulated. This policy of repopulating Anatolian regions by Slavs was to be continued by his successors, Constantine IV (668–85) and Justinian II (685–695/705–711).

Constans also inherited his grandfather's religious policy. By the early 640s, opposition to monothelitism had grown. Behind this opposition was the monk Maximus, known to later ages as 'the Confessor'; he had been a close associate of Sophronius, who had originally stirred up opposition to monenergism. Maximus found support in Palestine and Cyprus, but more importantly in Italy and North Africa, where he had been in exile since the late 620s. These were areas which, in the sixth century, had protested against Justinian's condemnation of the Three Chapters as compromising the decisions of Chalcedon.[14] In North Africa a number of synods condemned monothelitism, and Maximus pressed home the attack in a series of skilfully argued tracts and letters. In 645 the former patriarch Pyrrhus arrived in North Africa; as a supporter of Empress Martina he had shared her fall. In July that year a disputation between the monothelite Pyrrhus and Maximus was held in Carthage, before the exarch Gregory, in which Pyrrhus admitted defeat and embraced orthodoxy.[15] It was perhaps the strength of feeling against monothelitism that led Gregory to allow himself to be declared emperor in opposition to Constans in 646–7, but his rebellion was short-lived; he died the following year defending his province against Arab raiders. Meanwhile, Pyrrhus had made his way to Rome to declare his new-found orthodoxy to the pope, followed closely by Maximus. In 648, in a vain attempt to prevent further controversy, the famous *Typos* was issued in the name of the emperor by Patriarch Paul, forbidding discussion of the number of activities or wills in Christ.

In Rome, Maximus prepared for a synod, together with other Greek monks who had fled west in the face of the Arabs or the heresy of the empire. This was finally held in 649 in the Lateran Palace in Rome, under the newly elected Pope Martin I (649–55): both the *Ekthesis* and the *Typos* were condemned, together with the patriarchs Sergius, Pyrrhus and Paul. The extent to which this synod was of Greek inspiration has become clear

---

[14] See above, pp. 117–18.
[15] The record of the dispute is preserved as *Opusculum* 28 in Maximus the Confessor, *Opera*, PG 91, cols. 287–354.

from recent research, which has shown that the Greek *Acta* of the synod are the original, the Latin version being a translation.[16] Such open defiance of the imperial will could not be ignored. Olympius, exarch of Ravenna, was ordered to arrest Martin and compel the bishops gathered in Rome to accept the *Typos*. When he arrived in Rome, Olympius discovered that, despite his best efforts, Pope Martin's popularity made it hazardous to try and arrest him. In defiance of the imperial will he made his peace with Martin and departed for Sicily to deal with Arab raiders. There, like Gregory the exarch of North Africa, he may have been proclaimed emperor. But he died in 652. In the following year a new exarch arrived with troops and succeeded in arresting the pope. Martin was brought to Constantinople and tried for treason, with Olympius' rebellion being cited as evidence. Although condemned to death, Martin's sentence was commuted to exile and, already ailing, he was sent to Cherson in the Crimea, where he died in 655. Martin felt abandoned by those who should have supported him; his successor had been elected more than a year before his death. By that time, Maximus had already been arrested, likewise tried for treason and sent into exile in Thrace, where attempts were made to break his opposition to monothelitism. When that failed, he was brought back to Constantinople for trial. He was condemned as a heretic, mutilated and exiled to Lazica, where he soon died on 13 August 662.

By the time Maximus died in exile, the emperor himself was in self-imposed exile from Constantinople. Around 662 Constans II and his court moved to Syracuse in Sicily. This attempt to abandon the beleaguered Constantinople and re-establish the court closer to the centre of the truncated empire recalls earlier plans by Heraclius, and shows that there was no sense that the Byzantine empire was now confined to the eastern Mediterranean. From his base in Sicily, Constans clearly intended to liberate Italy from the Lombards; before arriving at Syracuse, he had led a campaign in Italy. This had met with some success, though he failed to take Benevento and soon retired to Naples, from where he made a ceremonial visit to Rome. However, his residence in Sicily was extremely unpopular, imposing as it did an unwelcome financial burden on the island. There was also fierce opposition in Constantinople to the loss of the court, and in 668 Constans was assassinated by a chamberlain.

Constans II was succeeded by his son Constantine IV. It was during Constantine's reign that the Umayyad caliph Mu'awiya made a serious attempt to complete the Arab expansion begun in the 630s, aiming to take Constantinople and with it destroy the only serious opposition to Muslim rule in the Mediterranean. After his victory over 'Ali in the *fitna*, Mu'awiya renewed his offensive against the Byzantine empire. By 670 the islands of

---

[16] Riedinger (1982); see also below, p. 402, n. 29.

Cyprus, Rhodes and Kos, and the town of Kyzikos on the southern coast of the Sea of Marmara, had all been occupied by Arab naval forces. In 672 Smyrna was taken, and in 674 the main attack on Constantinople began. A large Muslim fleet blockaded the city, and for the next four years the same fleet was to blockade Constantinople, retiring in the winter to shelter off Kyzikos. Each year the defences of Constantinople held firm, and in the final naval battle, the Byzantines secured a major victory with the help of Greek fire. First mentioned in the sources on this occasion, Greek fire was a highly inflammable, crude oil-based liquid that was shot out at enemy ships, setting them ablaze.[17] At the same time as this naval victory, the Byzantine army was able to surprise and defeat an Arab army contingent in Anatolia. Mu'awiya was forced to break off his attack on Constantinople and sue for peace. This major victory for the Byzantines proved to be a turning point: the Arab threat to Constantinople receded for the time being and Byzantium's prestige in the Balkans and the west was enhanced. Embassies from the khagan of the Avars, now restricted mainly to the Hungarian plain, and from the Balkan Slavs arrived in Constantinople, bringing gifts and acknowledging Byzantine supremacy.

However, the situation in the Balkans was about to change. The Slavs based there had never formed any coherent political entity, though their presence confined imperial authority to Thessalonica and other coastal settlements. The Bulgars, a Turkic-speaking group whose homeland was to the north of the Sea of Azov, had long been a power among the nomadic peoples of the Eurasian steppes. The Byzantines had maintained friendly relations with them, and had supported them against the Avars. But with the arrival of another people – the Khazars – the Bulgars' khanate began to split up, and one group led by Asparuch arrived at the Danube delta around 680, intending to settle south of the river in traditionally imperial territory. The Byzantines saw no threat in the Bulgars, but were unwilling to allow them south of the Danube. A Byzantine fleet arrived at the river mouth and troops moved up from Thrace, intending to expel the Bulgars. The Bulgars avoided open battle but, as the Byzantine forces withdrew, took them by surprise and defeated them. Constantine IV concluded a treaty with Asparuch, granting the Bulgars the territory they already held. As a result of this presence, several Slav tribes hitherto loyal to Byzantium recognised the overlordship of the Bulgars and became their tributaries, and a Bulgaro-Slav political structure started to develop, with its capital at Pliska. This independent, periodically hostile presence so close to the City, in principle able to control the route from the Danube delta to Constantinople, would prove a long-standing threat to the stability of the empire.

---

[17] Haldon and Byrne (1977); Haldon (2006a).

Figure 9a The imperial fleet burns the ships of Thomas the Slav with discharges of Greek fire (illustration from the Madrid Skylitzes, an illuminated manuscript copied in mid-twelfth-century Sicily)

Figure 9b Twenty-first-century Greek fire: experiment by John Haldon and colleagues to re-create Byzantium's most feared weapon

The enforcement of monothelitism as imperial policy, though it secured papal acquiescence in the years immediately following Martin's arrest and exile, was bound to prove ultimately unacceptable to the west, which saw the council of Chalcedon as endorsing the Latin Christology of Pope Leo I (440–61). By 680 Constantine had come to the conclusion that religious unity with the west was more important than the fragile possibility of union with the monophysites – now mostly lost to the Umayyad caliphate – offered by monothelitism. He proposed to Pope Agatho (678–81) the calling of an ecumenical council to condemn monothelitism. Agatho enthusiastically concurred, and held synods in Italy and England to prepare for the coming ecumenical council. Armed with these synodical condemnations of monothelitism, the papal legates arrived in Constantinople. The sixth ecumenical council met in Constantinople from 3 November 680 until 16 September 681. Monenergism and monothelitism were condemned, and the patriarchs Sergius, Cyrus, Pyrrhus, Paul and Peter anathematised, together with Pope Honorius. There was no word, however, of the defenders of the orthodoxy vindicated by the council, Martin and Maximus, who had suffered at the hands of Constans; nor were the emperors Constans or Heraclius mentioned. Constantine IV himself was hailed, at the final session, as a 'new Marcian' and a 'new Justinian'.

The latter part of Constantine's reign saw the Byzantine empire regain a certain stability. In 684–5 he led a successful military expedition into Cilicia, forcing Caliph 'Abd al-Malik to sue for peace and pay tribute to the Byzantines (see below, pp. 344, 381–2). Religious reconciliation with Rome led to peace with the Lombards in Italy, brokered by the pope. In North Africa, the Byzantines were able to halt the advance of the Arabs through alliances with Berber tribes, though this only bought time until the Berbers themselves converted to Islam.

Constantine IV died in 685 and was succeeded by his son, Justinian II. It is worth noting that both Constantine IV and Constans II had deposed their brothers in the course of their reigns – in Constantine's case, despite open opposition from senate and army – in order to secure the succession of their eldest sons. Justinian sought to build on the relative stability achieved by his father, leading an expedition into the Balkans and reaching Thessalonica. He continued the policy of both his father and his grandfather of transporting Slavs into Anatolia. He also transported some of the population from Cyprus to Kyzikos, depopulated during the siege of Constantinople, and ferried Mardaites from northern Syria and Lebanon to the Peloponnese and elsewhere. Whether or not Justinian was responsible for the breach of the truce with 'Abd al-Malik in 692, he suffered military disaster when his Slav troops deserted. As a result, several Armenian princes once again acknowledged Muslim suzerainty.

In 692 Justinian called a council, known as the quinisext or fifth-sixth council (see below, pp. 244–7). In so doing, he followed both his father's example and that of his namesake, declaring his credentials as emperor and guardian of orthodoxy. This was also manifest in his coinage: the image of the emperor was displaced from the obverse of the coin to the reverse, and replaced with an image of Christ, the source of his authority as emperor.

Figure 10 *Nomisma* of Justinian II, showing bust of Christ on the obverse for first time on gold coins (left); the emperor is shown on the reverse (right)

In 695, Justinian was overthrown in a palace coup and replaced by Leontius (695–8), the recently appointed *stratēgos* of the theme of Hellas. Justinian had his nose slit and was exiled to Cherson, where his grandfather had earlier exiled Pope Martin. Leontius' reign lasted three years, during which he witnessed the end of Byzantine rule in North Africa. That defeat, and the consequent loss of Carthage, provoked another rebellion in which Leontius was deposed in favour of Apsimar, the *droungarios* of the Kibyrrhaiotai fleet, who changed his name to the more imperial-sounding Tiberius. Tiberius II reigned from 698 to 705, during which time Asia Minor was subjected to continual Arab raiding. He was replaced by Justinian II, who returned with the support of the Bulgar khan Tervel, slipping into the City through one of its aqueducts. Justinian's final six years were ones of terror and vengeance, brought to an end by a military coup; thereupon three military leaders succeeded one another for short and inglorious reigns, until the accession in 717 of Leo III, the emperor who subsequently introduced iconoclasm.[18]

ADMINISTRATIVE CHANGE

At the beginning of the seventh century the administration of the empire, both civil and military, was essentially what had emerged from the reforms of Diocletian and Constantine in the late third and early fourth centuries. By the end of the eighth century quite different forms of administration were in place. Although we have a fairly clear picture of early seventh-century Byzantine administration, for the late eighth century the picture is less clear; and because the evidence is both sparse and open to diverse interpretations, the nature and pace of administrative change in this period is still a matter of debate. However, in general terms the change can be described as follows: at the beginning of the seventh century the empire

---

[18] The emperors were: Philippikos (711–13), Anastasios II (713–15) and Theodosios III (715–17). On Leo III's religious policy, see below, pp. 279–82.

was divided into provinces ruled by civil governors who, though appointed by the emperor, were responsible to the relevant praetorian prefect (the provinces being grouped into four prefectures), and the army was organised quite separately; at the end of the eighth century the empire was divided into districts called themes (*themata*), which were governed by a military commander (*stratēgos*) who was responsible for both the civil and military administration of the province, and directly responsible to the emperor. Let us now look at the changes involved in more detail.[19]

Civil administration

In the civil administration inherited from the reforms of Diocletian and Constantine, alongside the administration of the empire through the prefectures, there were also departments called *res privata* and *sacrae largitiones*, administered by counts (*comites*), who belonged to the imperial court (the *comitatus*). The *comes rei privatae* was responsible for all land and property belonging to the state, including the collection of rents and claiming for the state all property that lapsed to it. Originally the *comes rei privatae* had been concerned with the emperor's private property, as the name suggests, but the distinction between that and state property had long been elided. The *comes sacrarum largitionum* controlled the mints, the gold (and probably silver) mines and the state factories in which arms and armour were decorated with precious metals. He was also responsible for paying periodic donatives in gold and silver to the troops, and dealt with the collection or production of clothing and its distribution to the court, the army and the civil service. The praetorian prefects were responsible for the fiscal administration of the prefectures into which the empire was divided. These prefectures consisted of provinces, governed by governors (with various titles), and were themselves grouped into dioceses, governed by *vicarii*. The praetorian prefects were responsible for the rations, or ration allowances (*annonae*), which formed the bulk of the emoluments of the army and the civil service, and also for the fodder, or fodder allowances, of officers, troopers and civil servants of equivalent grades. They had to maintain the public post, and were responsible for public works, roads, bridges, post-houses and granaries which did not come under the care of the urban prefects in Rome and Constantinople, the city authorities in the provinces, or the army on the frontiers. In order to do all this, the praetorian prefects had to estimate the annual needs of their prefecture and raise the money through a general levy, or tax, called the indiction. The whole operation of raising this tax and servicing the running of the empire was overseen by the praetorian prefects,

---

[19] What follows is deeply indebted to Haldon's subtle and powerfully argued account of the administrative changes: Haldon (1997a), pp. 173–253. See also below, pp. 266–7.

who delegated it to their *vicarii* and governors. Only the praetorian prefect in whose prefecture the emperor and his court were located was attached to the court; once the court was permanently settled in Constantinople, this meant the praetorian prefect for the east (*Oriens*). Also influential in the *comitatus* were senior officials of the *sacrum cubiculum*, the eunuch chamberlains (*cubicularii*).

By the end of the eighth century, the fiscal administration was organised rather differently. The distinction between the public and the 'sacred' (i.e. pertaining to the person of the emperor) had gone, and instead of the *res privata*, the *sacrae largitiones* and the prefectures, there were a number of departments, or *sekrēta*, of more or less equal status. Besides the *sakellarios* and the heads of the three great departments – the logothete of the Drome (*tou dromou*), the general logothete (*tou genikou*) and the military logothete (*tou stratiōtikou*)[20] – there were several other senior administrators. Among these were two treasurers, the *chartoularios* of the *sakellion*, in charge of cash and most charitable institutions, and the *chartoularios* of the *vestiarion*, in charge of the mint and the arsenal. Other heads of state establishments included the great curator (*megas kouratōr*), in charge of the palaces and imperial estates, and the *orphanotrophos*, in charge of orphanages. In addition there was an official called the *prōtasekrētis*, in charge of records. Directly responsible to the emperor were the principal magistrates, the City prefect (responsible for Constantinople), the *quaestor* (in charge of the judiciary) and the minister for petitions (who dealt with petitions to the emperor).

A rather obvious, and superficial, change is that of language: whereas the older system used Latin titles, the new system used predominantly Greek titles. This reflects the change in the official language of the empire from Latin, traditional language of the Roman empire, to Greek, language of Constantinople and the Hellenistic east; a change dating from the time of Justinian. More deeply, it can be seen that the change involved a reshuffling of tasks, so that they all became subject to a fundamentally civil administration based on the court. The *genikon* and *stratiōtikon* derived from the general and military departments of the prefectures (in fact, the prefecture of the East, as we shall see); the *sakellion* from the *sacellum*, the personal treasury of the emperor within the *sacrum cubiculum*; and the *vestiarion* from the department of the *sacrum vestiarium* within the *sacrae largitiones*.

The position of the *sakellarios* perhaps gives a clue to the nature of the changes. In charge of the emperor's personal treasury, this official's eventual rise to pre-eminence was a function of his closeness to the emperor and suggests a shift from an essentially public administration, its structure determined by the need to administer a far-flung empire, to an

---

[20] On these officials, see below, p. 273.

administration focused on the court, in which the empire is almost reduced to the extent of an imperial command. The background to this is the dramatic shrinking of the empire in the first half of the seventh century. The loss of the eastern provinces followed by North Africa and, by the end of the eighth century, Italy too, together with the Slavs' occupation of the Balkans and the emergence of the Bulgar realm south of the Danube, meant that the Byzantine empire had shrunk to the rumps of two prefectures, of the East and Illyricum. Reorganisation of the civil administration took the form of Constantinople incorporating the administrative offices of the empire into a court structure. The growing power of the *sakellarios* can be traced back to the time of Justinian; by the mid-seventh century, judging from the role he played in the trial of Maximus the Confessor, he was a powerful courtier who took personal charge of matters of supreme importance to the emperor. Logothetes also feature in the sources from the early years of the seventh century, but officials bearing traditional titles, such as praetorian prefect, not to mention civil governors of provinces, continue to appear in the sources well into the eighth century. This would suggest that there was a substantial period of overlap, with the new administration emerging while the old administration still retained some of its functions. However, the full picture only emerges when we consider the changes in the military administration.

Military administration

The reforms of the Roman army by Diocletian and Constantine separated it from the civil administration, so that governors of provinces no longer commanded a provincial army, although they were still responsible for raising funds to support it. The army was divided into two parts: there were troops protecting the borders, the *limitanei*, under the command of *duces*; and there was a field army, the *comitatenses*, which was mobile and organised in divisions under the command of the *magistri militum*. In addition there were the palace troops and the imperial bodyguard, whose titles changed throughout the fifth and sixth centuries.

By the ninth century a quite different system had emerged, with the army divided into divisions called themes, based in provinces also called themes (*themata*), each under the command of a *stratēgos*. There is no general agreement about how quickly this change took place, or why: was it the result of some planned reorganisation, or simply a fumbling reaction to the problems of the seventh and eighth centuries? There is, however, general dissent from the theory which once commanded much support, and is associated with the name of the great Byzantinist George Ostrogorsky, which saw the thematic army as the result of a deliberate reorganisation of army and empire by Heraclius. The result, supposedly, was a peasant army, based in the themes, in which land had been allotted to peasant families as small holdings, in return for each family providing and equipping a soldier.[21] This somewhat romantic idea of the middle Byzantine empire resting on the popular support of a free peasantry has been generally abandoned. The transition is now thought to have occurred after Heraclius' reign, and change was probably gradual.

Part of the problem is terminology. The word theme originally meant a military unit, and references to themes in sources relating to the seventh century may refer to military units, rather than to the land where they were stationed. But even if it seems that the reference is to territory, we cannot be sure that such a reference is not an anachronism, since our sources date from the ninth century when territorial themes were in place. As with the changes in civil administration already discussed, it is possible – indeed likely – that the two sets of arrangements overlapped; even though there are references to *stratēgoi* and themes in the seventh century, there is still mention of provinces (*eparchiai*), governors, and use of such titles as *magister militum* well into the eighth century. While it is impossible to provide a detailed timescale, one can reasonably suggest that the themes developed in the following way. After the Byzantine army was defeated by the Arabs, the troops retreated over the Taurus mountains into Anatolia. The years following the defeat saw continual raiding by Muslim forces into Anatolia, leading finally in the 660s and 670s to a concerted attempt by Mu'awiya to advance across Asia Minor and take Constantinople (see above, pp. 232–3 and below, p. 372). In this prolonged crisis, the Byzantine armies were stationed in the provinces of Asia Minor. They would have been provisioned in the traditional way, by a levy raised by the local governors from the civilian population. The areas that came to be called the themes of the Armeniakoi and the Anatolikoi were the groups of provinces where the armies commanded by the *magistri militum per Armeniam* and *per Orientem* took up their stands. The theme of the Thrakesioi covered the provinces in western Anatolia to which the army of the *magister militum per Thraciam* withdrew after the Arab victories in Syria and Palestine. The theme of the Opsikion was made up of the armies of the *magistri militum praesentales*, some of which had probably long been established in the area just across the Bosporus from Constantinople. The name derives from the title of the officer (*comes Obsequii*) who, during the reign of Heraclius, was appointed to command the praesental armies on the emperor's behalf. The Karabisianoi, the fleet, formed part of the old *quaestura exercitus*, probably based at Samos (see also below, p. 267). It seems likely that the army corps took up the positions into which they would become embedded sometime

---

[21] Brief account in Ostrogorsky (1968), pp. 95–8. More detail in Ostrogorsky (1958). The romanticism of Ostrogorsky's vision emerges more clearly in Ostrogorsky (1962). See also below, p. 266.

around the middle of the seventh century. Why and at what stage the civil administration declined, to be replaced by the military government of the *stratēgoi*, is much less clear. Presumably the overriding need to supply a standing army, together with the decline of the ancient, city-based economy, meant that the *stratēgoi*, backed up by the increasingly powerful officials forming part of the imperial court, gradually assumed the functions of the old governing elite. The elite lost much of its *raison d'être* because of the court-centred nature of the civil administration.

Legal administration

Given the profound changes in civil and military administration beginning in the seventh century, at first sight it is surprising that so little legislative activity seems to have occurred in this century. One has nothing to set beside the major attempts at legislative reform of the fifth and sixth centuries, embodied in the *Codex Theodosianus* and the *Codex Iustinianus*. Apart from the *Farmer's law*, whose date is disputed and which is anyway a compilation of materials from Justinian's era and before, the emperors seem to have initiated very little legislation; what remains is primarily ecclesiastical in nature, for example Heraclius' edict of 632 requiring the compulsory conversion of the Jews, his *Ekthesis*, and Constans II's *Typos* (see above, pp. 229, 231). In contrast, the quinisext council called by Justinian II represents a major recapitulation of canonical legislation, which can be compared with the law-code of Justinian II's great predecessor (see above, p. 108). The explanation for the lack of legislative activity in the secular sphere is probably to be found in the dual nature of Roman legislation. Legislation was not only a body of rules governing day-to-day behaviour, but more importantly a way of enunciating the world-view and set of values embraced by the Roman – or Byzantine – empire. As John Haldon has put it:

Seen from this perspective, the legal 'system' became less a practical instrument for intervening in the world of men in order to modify relationships or individual behaviour, but more a set of theories which represented a desired (if recognisably not always attainable) state of affairs. Emperors needed to issue no new legislation, therefore, but rather to establish (or to re-establish) the conditions within which the traditional system would once again conform to actual practice.[22]

RELIGION AND THE CHURCH

It is generally recognised that from the later sixth century onwards there was an increasing desire to have direct access to the power of the holy.

[22] Haldon (1997a), p. 259.

Again, this cannot be demonstrated beyond peradventure, since the means of access – cults of saints and their relics, and perhaps even the veneration of icons – were already well established by the sixth century. Traditionally, imperial authority had been justified by the divinely protected status of the emperor, expressed through an imperial cult. The Christianisation of the imperial cult tended rather to enhance its authority than to diminish it, since the representative of the only God was hardly reduced in status in comparison with a divine emperor holding a relatively lowly position in the divine pantheon.[23] It seems to be demonstrable that this Christian imperial authority and that of the hierarchy of the Christian church, which was closely bound up with it, were reinforced by holy men and holy images claiming immediate access to supernatural power. It seems, too, that even traditional imperial authority was increasingly expressed through images that spoke of a more immediate sacred authority. This becomes evident at the beginning of the seventh century from the use of icons of Christian saints as military banners, especially of the Mother of God; from the way in which Christian armies are seen as fighting for the Virgin, with her protection and even her assistance; and from the role claimed for the Virgin as protector of the city of Constantinople. A sacralisation of authority is also manifest in the increasing significance attached to coronation by the patriarch in the making of an emperor; this was always conducted in a church from the beginning of the seventh century, and in the Great Church of St Sophia from 641. The institutional church, indeed, may well have felt itself threatened by the proliferation of the holy in the seventh century: the church in the Byzantine east certainly failed to establish the kind of control over the holiness present in saints, their images and their relics, that the popes and bishops had won in the western church.[24]

But if there is little evidence of tension between the proliferation of the holy and the church hierarchy in the Byzantine east in the seventh century,[25] there is certainly evidence of tension between the centre and the periphery in geographical terms. Despite the wealth of theological literature that survives from the seventh century, we know little about theology at the capital, for the simple reason that by the ninth century no one in Constantinople wanted to be reminded of it. Theology in Constantinople was subservient to the emperor, and to the politically inspired doctrines of monenergism, monothelitism and, in the next century, iconoclasm. Resistance to all of these – a resistance that was finally recognised as 'orthodoxy' – came from the periphery, and in the long term especially from the monks of Palestine, who had long been known for their commitment to Chalcedonian orthodoxy. This fact had curious long-term consequences for orthodox

---

[23] See Dagron (2003).   [24] See Brown, P. (1976).
[25] In the eighth century, the ready support the iconoclast emperors seem to have found among the higher clergy may possibly be evidence of a reaction on the part of the church hierarchy.

Byzantium, and is worth pursuing briefly here. Resistance to monenergism began with Sophronius, who had been a monk in Palestine and later became patriarch of Jerusalem; resistance to monothelitism was led by Sophronius' disciple Maximus, whose impact on the orthodox in Palestine was such that they were called Maximians by the monothelites in Syria and Palestine.[26] In the second half of the seventh century dyothelite ('orthodox') Christians in Palestine found themselves in a new situation. Previously they had been adherents of an imperial orthodoxy that had been backed up, in the last resort, by force. Now they found themselves in a situation where their religious position was opposed by other Christian groups – monophysite, monothelite and even Nestorian – and by non-Christians like Jews, Samaritans, Manichees and, eventually, by Muslims. They had both to defend what they believed in and to work out exactly what their faith amounted to. In order to do this, they had to pay attention to matters of logic and definition, for the only way to defend and commend their position was by convincing others; they could no longer appeal to the secular arm.

One element in this refining of the presentation and understanding of the Christianity of the ecumenical councils was dialogue with – or polemic against – the Jews. After a long period when there was scarcely any dialogue with Jews, or even simple refutation of Judaism, the second half of the seventh century witnessed an extraordinary burgeoning of such works. Most come from the provinces seized by the Arabs: Syria, Palestine, the Sinai peninsula and Cyprus. It is clear from some of these works that Jews themselves took the initiative, forcing Christians to produce fresh defences of doctrines such as the Trinity and practices such as veneration of saints, relics and icons.[27] Alongside such doctrinal clarification there was also celebration of the doctrines of Christianity in liturgical poetry, which came to form the backbone of monastic worship and again stemmed principally from Palestine. This eventually became the worship of the orthodox – that is Byzantine – church, and of those churches which learnt their Christianity from Byzantium. The crucial century for this definition, defence and celebration of orthodoxy was the period from 650 to 750. It is epitomised in the works of John Damascene, an Umayyad civil servant turned Palestinian monk, who thought of himself as a Byzantine Christian. Its first test was the iconoclasm of Byzantine emperors, beyond whose political reach these Christians lived.[28]

---

[26] The view that Maximus was himself a Palestinian, propounded in the Syriac *Life* (Maximus the Confessor, *Syriac Life*), seems to be losing credibility among scholars.

[27] See Déroche (1991); Cameron, Averil (1996a).

[28] For these developments and John Damascene's part in them, see Louth (1996b). See also below, p. 283.

As we have seen, this form of Christianity was called Maximianism by its enemies, but it owed more to Maximus than simply its attachment to dyothelite Chalcedonianism, as declared at the Lateran synod of 649 and vindicated at the sixth ecumenical council of 680–1 (see above, pp. 231, 235). For Maximus' genius as a theologian was to draw together the several strands of Greek theological reflection into an imposing synthesis. One strand in this synthesis was the dogmatic theology of the great patriarchs of Alexandria, Athanasius and Cyril, which formed the basis for the dogmas endorsed by the ecumenical councils from the fourth to the sixth centuries. Another strand was the Christian Hellenism of the fourth-century Cappadocian fathers, Basil of Caesarea, Gregory Nazianzen and Gregory of Nyssa. A further strand was constituted by the ascetic wisdom of the fourth-century Egyptian desert fathers; and of their successors in the Judaean desert to the east of Jerusalem, in the coastal desert of Gaza and the barren mountains of the Sinai peninsula. These three strands Maximus wove together, the final tapestry being shot through with the Neoplatonic metaphysics of Pseudo-Dionysius the Areopagite, believed to be in reality an early sixth-century Syrian monk (see above, pp. 111–12). It was this theological vision of Maximus which inspired the more soberly expressed, even dry doctrinal synthesis that we find in John Damascene. Maximus' vision, in which humankind, the cosmos and the scriptures themselves were all interrelated, was reflected in the domed interior of the Byzantine church. In that space, as Maximus explained in his reflections on the divine liturgy called the *Mystagogia*, the liturgical ceremonies involving the clergy and the people celebrated the whole unfolding of the Christian mystery, from creation to Christ's second coming, in a way that probed the depths of the human heart and illuminated the mysteries of the cosmos.[29]

But to turn from what may seem giddy heights – albeit expressed in such gesture, movement, melody and colour as to impress the simplest of Byzantine Christians – we see a more detailed picture of the life of the Byzantine church in the seventh century emerging from the 102 canons of the quinisext council, called by Justinian II in 692.[30] Like his predecessor and namesake, Justinian II wished to mark his reign and manifest his exercise of imperial power by calling an ecumenical council. Hitherto, all councils regarded as ecumenical had been called to deal with some pressing doctrinal issue, but with the monenergist/monothelite controversy now settled, there was no doctrinal issue to provide occasion for an ecumenical council. However, the previous two ecumenical councils, the second and third of Constantinople, had issued only doctrinal canons, whereas all the

---

[29] For an introduction to the theology of Maximus, see Louth (1996a).

[30] *DGA*, ed. and French tr. Joannou, I.1, pp. 98–241; tr. in Nedungatt and Featherstone (eds.) (1995), pp. 41–185.

earlier ones had dealt with both doctrinal and disciplinary issues. Thus the council Justinian eventually called, which issued only disciplinary canons, was regarded as finishing off the work of the previous two councils (the fifth and the sixth ecumenical councils) and was therefore called the quinisext council. It is also known as the Trullan council (*in Trullo*) from the domed chamber (*troullos*) in the palace where proceedings took place.

The 102 canons issued by the council cover many aspects of the life of Christians, both their religious duties and their behaviour in secular life. The first two canons affirm and define the existing tradition, of which the rest of the canons constitute a kind of completion: canon 1 affirms the unchanging faith defined at the previous six ecumenical councils; and canon 2 confirms the body of disciplinary canons already accepted by the church.[31] The rest of the canons complete this body of canonical material, and the whole body of legislation constituted by this council can be compared in some ways to Justinian's code, in that it is intended as the final statement of an ideal of Christian life, expressed through much quite detailed legislation. It remains the foundation of the canon law of the orthodox church. In this context it is worth drawing attention to the last canon, which affirms that the administration of penalties in accordance with the canons must take account of the quality of the sin and the disposition of the sinner, for the ultimate purpose of canon law is to heal, not simply to punish. This canon reaffirms a principle already expressed in earlier canons,[32] usually called the principle of 'economy' (*oikonomia*). It is not unlike the way in which in seventh-century secular law used Justinian's code as an ideal, trying to fit the ideal to concrete issues rather than promulgating fresh legislation (see above, p. 241).

One guiding principle of the canons of the quinisext council was to define the practices of the Byzantine church in conscious opposition to the developing customs of the Latin west. For instance, canon 55 forbids fasting on Saturdays and Sundays, except for Holy Saturday, and is explicitly directed against the practice of fasting on Saturdays during Lent found in the city of Rome. More important are the canons that allowed for a married pastoral clergy. Although restricted to priests and deacons – since on appointment to the rank of bishop, a married man had to separate from his wife, who took the veil (canons 12 and 48) – this too is in conscious opposition to the Roman canons; it would be some centuries, however, before a celibate priesthood was strictly enforced in the western church. A similar independence of Rome is manifest in canon 36. This prescribed the order of the patriarchates and, following the canons of the first ecumenical council of Constantinople (canon 3) and the ecumenical council

---

[31] For a succinct account of the development of Christian canon law, see Louth (2004).
[32] Canons of St Basil, no. 95, *DGA*, ed. and French tr. Joannou, II, pp. 193–8; see also no. 3, *DGA*, II, pp. 100–1; Canons of St Gregory of Nyssa, no. 1, *DGA*, II, pp. 203–9.

of Chalcedon (canon 28, which had been repudiated by Rome), ranked
Constantinople second after Rome, with equal privileges. Although the
papal legates accepted the canons, Pope Sergius I (687–701) refused to sign
them and Justinian's furious attempt to enforce papal consent only exposed
the limits of his power in Italy. Sergius' introduction of the singing of the
Agnus Dei into the mass at Rome is perhaps to be seen as a snub to the
council (see canon 82, discussed below).[33] Although Pope John VII (705–7)
seems to have accepted the canons of the council in 705, when Justinian was
restored to the imperial throne, this represented no lasting endorsement of
them by the western church.

Other canons regulated the life of the local church, still understood
as essentially an urban church ruled by a bishop although, as we have
seen, the reality of the city was fading fast. Urban churches were grouped
into provinces, under the leadership of a metropolitan bishop, and these
provinces were to convene once a year (canon 8). Bishops were to live in
their sees, and must return to them as soon as possible if they fled during
'barbarian' raids (canon 18). This anxiety that the bishop should stick to his
city was partly to ensure his continuing pastoral care, but also his control of
the church's financial interests; the local churches were frequently considerable landowners with their estates being administered by the bishop. The
requirement that bishops reside in their own sees was taken seriously, as is
evident from the more abundant later evidence, especially from the Komnenian period, when the empire was even more focused on Constantinople
and provincial sees were regarded as exile by their bishops.[34] There are also
canons against selling the sacraments and purchasing church office (what
the west later called simony: canons 22–3). Legislation concerning monasticism, like much earlier legislation, attempted to confine monks to their
monasteries and control the power of holy men (canons 40–9). Legislation
concerning the laity forbade various entertainments, such as playing dice
(canon 50); watching mimes, animal fights or dancing on stage (canon 51);
the observance of civic ceremonies such as the *Calends, Vota* or *Brumalia*,
which had pagan associations, as well as female dancing in public, dancing
associated with pagan rites, cross-dressing, the use of comic, satyr or tragic
masks, and the invocation of Dionysus during the pressing of grapes for
wine (canon 62). All of this the church regarded as 'paganising', though
such practices should probably not be thought of as the survival of paganism outright, but rather the continuance of traditional forms of worship
involving the laity.[35]

Canons also forbade the confusion of traditional liturgies with the Christian sacraments – for example canon 57 forbidding the offering of milk and

[33] *LP*, LXXXVI.14, ed. Duchesne, I. p. 376; tr. Davis, I, p. 89.
[34] See Angold (1995), pp. 139–262.   [35] See Haldon (1997a), pp. 327–37.

honey on Christian altars – and others regulated the institution of marriage and the circumstances of divorce (canons 53, 54, 72, 87, 92 and 93). Several canons dealt with relations between Christians and Jews. Canon 11 forbade eating unleavened bread with Jews, making friends with them, consulting Jewish doctors or mixing with Jews in the baths; canon 33 forbade the 'Jewish' practice of ordaining only those of priestly descent. Both these canons illustrate the way in which Jews were permitted to exist, but separately from the orthodox society of the empire. In fact, the seventh century had seen the beginning of a more radical policy towards the Jews: forced baptism on pain of death. Maximus the Confessor expressly objected to such a policy introduced by Heraclius in 632,[36] and the policy was introduced again in the eighth and tenth centuries, by Leo III (717–41) and Romanos I Lekapenos (920–44) respectively. But the more normal Byzantine attitude to the Jews, to be preserved as a standing witness to the truth of Christianity with limited civil rights, is that envisaged by the canons of the Trullan council.[37]

Two canons bear witness to the place of religious art in the Byzantine world. Canon 100 forbids pictures that excite immoral pleasure, and emphasises how easily the bodily senses move the soul. Canon 82 is concerned with religious paintings and forbids the depiction of Christ as a lamb, a popular form of religious art that picked up the words of John the Baptist about Jesus as the 'lamb of God who takes away the sin of the world' (John 1: 36). However, the canon argues, such symbolism has been fulfilled since God has come in human form; now the reality of the Incarnation is to be expressed by depicting the Incarnate Word as a man. Such concern for the content of religious images, expressed in theological terms, prefigures the controversies of the next two centuries caused by iconoclasm.

The comparatively settled picture of Christian life in the Byzantine empire presented by the canons of the quinisext council is not, however, the whole story. The second half of the seventh century saw the production of apocalyptic texts, composed in Syriac. One of these, soon translated into Greek and subsequently into Latin, was ascribed to the early fourth-century bishop Methodius (of Olympus, according to the Syriac original; of Patara, according to the Greek translation).[38] The *Apocalypse* of Pseudo-Methodius responds to the loss of the eastern provinces to the Arabs – termed Ishmaelites or 'wild ass of the desert' – by recounting the history of the Middle East since biblical times. It predicts the final overthrow of the Ishmaelites at Jerusalem by the king of the 'Greeks' (so the Syriac; 'Romans' in the Greek version), whose victory will usher in the end of the world.[39]

[36] See Devreese (1937).   [37] See above, p. 116.
[38] This confusion as to his see is also found in manuscripts of authentic writings by Methodios.
[39] See Alexander (1985); *Syrian chronicles*, tr. Palmer *et al.*, pp. 222–50.

The emergence of such apocalyptic hopes and fears at the end of the seventh century contrasts sharply with the spirit of the early sixth-century *Chronicle* of John Malalas, written partly to demonstrate that the world had survived the transition from the sixth to the seventh millennium from the creation (i.e., *c.* AD 500) without disaster.

The end of the seventh century saw the Byzantine empire still in a process of transition and redefinition: the Arab threat to Constantinople would continue well into the eighth century, and iconoclasm is probably to be seen as a further stage in the empire's search for its identity and ways of expressing this in the aftermath of the crisis of the seventh century.[40] But there were scarcely any signs of incipient iconoclasm at the end of that century. The quinisext council invested a clearly articulated theological significance in religious art, and the process observed since the end of the sixth century of authenticating political authority by imagery invoking the supernatural was taken a stage further at the end of the seventh century: Christ's image appeared on the obverse of imperial coinage, the imperial image being consigned to the reverse (see fig. 10 above, p. 236). But the structures of the society that would eventually emerge from this period of crisis can already be seen, albeit in inchoate form; so too can some of its limitations, when compared with Justinian's vision of the Roman empire which it claimed to embody. Already there is a sense in the legislation of the quinisext council that the customs of those Christians who looked to Constantinople were different from those who looked to Rome: a gap that would widen as Rome moved from the Byzantine emperor's sphere of influence to that of the Franks. The Mediterranean Sea was no longer to unite the territories that bordered it, but would come to separate the several societies which claimed the heritage of that lost unity.

---

[40] Not all scholars accept that the seventh century should be regarded as a crisis for the Byzantine empire: see Treadgold (1997), pp. xvi, 287–413; Treadgold (1990). On iconoclasm, see below, pp. 278–84.

PART II

THE MIDDLE EMPIRE *c.* 700–1204

CHAPTER 5

STATE OF EMERGENCY (700–850)

MARIE-FRANCE AUZÉPY

AN IMPENETRABLY DARK AGE?

The so-called Byzantine iconoclast period is a 'dark age' whose obscurity is only randomly illuminated by the few remaining sources, and even these are difficult to interpret. Apart from in Italy, no archives have been preserved. The contemporary sources comprise two chronicles – that of Theophanes the Confessor, covering the period up to 813, and the *Breviarium* of Patriarch Nikephoros, which stops at 769 – and an account of Leo V's reign whose author is known as the 'Scriptor incertus'. The only near-contemporary chronicle for the reigns of Michael II and Theophilos is that of George the Monk, probably completed in 846 and reworked in 871–2,[1] with Theophanes Continuatus being the most important of the later chroniclers to cover this period. Other sources include the *Acts* of the second council of Nicaea (787); these contain several extracts from the ruling of the iconoclast council of Hieria (754), which they set out to refute. Further sources include a legal code called the *Ecloga* (741); the *Farmer's law* (or *Nomos georgikos*) – though this is not dated with precision; the *Taktikon Uspensky* (842–3); the correspondence of the monk Theodore the Stoudite, and of Bishop Ignatios of Nicaea (known as Ignatios the Deacon) from the first half of the ninth century; numerous saints' *Lives*; and the polemical anti-iconoclast literature.[2] We can add to these sources others of Arab, Syriac, Armenian and Greek origin from the caliphate, as well as several inscriptions and numerous seals.

This slightly simplified overview of the internal, written sources for the 150 years of iconoclasm reveals both the paucity of material, and how inadequate it is for understanding the profound transformation of the empire in this period – a transformation demonstrated by the fact that, from the 850s onwards, nothing was 'as before', even if it is difficult to date the reforms whose effects historians observe. This lack of source-material forces us either to project forwards, based on the situation in the seventh century, or backwards, from the state of affairs in the second half of the

---

[1] Afinogenov (2004).
[2] Introduction to the sources: *PMBZ, Prolegomena*; Brubaker and Haldon (2001).

Map 12a The empire in the eighth and ninth centuries: key towns in the Balkans

ninth, and the history of eighth-century Byzantium tends to be highly hypothetical, an overlapping of past and future, rendering the period itself virtually non-existent. As a result, while recognising that the period was one of profound institutional restructuring, historians are hesitant about gauging the continuity or discontinuity of these institutions from the late Roman to the medieval empire.[3]

[3] Oikonomides (1996a); Oikonomides (2002); Haldon (1999a), pp. 107–11; Brandes (2002a), pp. 480–98; Haldon (2003a), pp. 727–8.

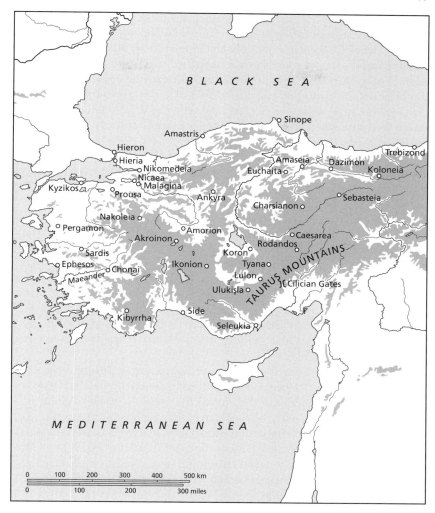

Map 12b The empire in the eighth and ninth centuries: key towns in Asia Minor

This period of history is further obscured by the shadow of religion, to the extent that it takes its name from imperial religious doctrine – iconoclasm – rather than from the Isaurian or Amorian dynasties. Thus our sources are not only sparse, they are also biased; with the exception of juridical or administrative documents, they were written by the iconoclasts' enemies, the iconodules, and they are all of clerical or monastic origin. They paint a picture of a period in which religious questions obscure everything else, and the Isaurian emperors Leo III (717–41) and Constantine V (741–75), who initiated and championed iconoclasm, are subject to virtual *damnatio memoriae*.[4] No pro-Isaurian texts remain, apart from prescriptive ones, and our information about them is both minimal and hostile. All this conspires to make the eighth century not only an empty period, but also off-putting; nothing positive could possibly have happened then. Although Theodora's defence of her husband Theophilos helped mitigate the *damnatio memoriae* imposed on the Amorian emperors Michael II (820–9) and Theophilos (829–42) because of their iconoclasm, nonetheless the sources – all written under their successors, the Macedonians – are highly critical of them simply for being predecessors of Basil I.

This negative presentation has had a lasting effect on historical writing about the period, especially the eighth century; for example, archaeological finds from these dark centuries were, until recently, dated either to the seventh or the ninth century, exaggerating the dearth of sources for the intervening years. Most important of all, however, has been the presentation of the period's historical narrative in terms of a history of the church: essentially the heretical emperors' persecution of the church for venerating icons, and the valiant defence of the institution by monks and patriarchs. Modern historiography has tended not to question this presentation or the periodisation it imposes. 'Iconoclasm' (730–843) has been broken down into two periods, the first (730–87) mainly covering the Isaurian dynasty, and the second (815–43) the reigns of Leo V (813–20) and his Amorian successors, separated by an iconodulic interval which began with the second council of Nicaea in 787.

Although this division should be questioned for imposing a religious frame of reference on a period characterised principally by a struggle for survival against enemies who threatened the empire's very existence, it is nevertheless consistent with the course of events. Against the background of long-term structural reforms of domestic policy, one can indeed distinguish three different epochs: the first, under the great Isaurians Leo III and Constantine V, one of violence when the empire was saved from destruction; the second, under Irene and her successors, a time when the earlier period's gains dwindled away and war loomed large; and finally, in the early ninth century, an era of returning prosperity, when the spectre of war receded. At the same time the empire's geopolitical situation changed completely. Whereas at the end of the seventh century the empire could still, albeit with difficulty, lay claim to being universal, by the mid-ninth century it had become a Balkano-Mediterranean state. Even if throughout this period, those whom we call the Byzantines continued to call themselves Romans, others began calling them Greeks.[5]

---

[4] Rochow (1994), pp. 123–71.

[5] *Opus Caroli*, IV.28, ed. Freeman and Meyvaert, p. 557; Paul the Deacon, *Historia Langobardorum*, IV.46, V.10–11, VI.57, ed. Bethmann and Waitz, pp. 135, 149–50, 185; tr. Foulke, pp. 200, 223–5, 303.

EARTHQUAKE, PLAGUE AND CONTINUOUS WARFARE

The eighth century was not only a time of obscurity, but also one of adversity, when man and nature conspired to bring the empire almost to the point of extinction. A series of natural catastrophes afflicted Constantinople and its hinterland in the middle of the century. An earthquake brought down the walls of the City on 26 October 740. The Justinianic plague (see above, p. 123; below, pp. 478–9) returned one last time; starting in Mesopotamia and travelling through Sicily and the Peloponnese, the epidemic reached the capital in 747, emptying the City of its inhabitants.[6] The winter of 763–4 was so harsh that the Black Sea and the Sea of Marmara froze, with huge icebergs on the Bosporus threatening the City's sea walls during the thaw. In 766, a drought affected Constantinople's water supply.[7]

As if nature's depredations were not enough, man brought incessant warfare to the empire. At the beginning of the eighth century the Arabs were waging a war of annihilation against the empire. Enormous Arab land and sea forces encircled Constantinople in 717, attempting unsuccessfully to seize it, and this operation was repeated at Nicaea in 727.[8] There followed almost ritualised warfare in Asia Minor, with annual raids by the caliph's armies; although they seldom succeeded in capturing Byzantine cities, they ravaged the countryside and carried off the population and livestock. The Arabs could also mount both large-scale invasions – Harun al-Rashid's expedition in 782 reached as far as Chrysopolis, opposite Constantinople[9] – and sea raids, such as those launched on the Sicilian coast by ships from Ifriqya.

The Isaurians managed to save the empire by raising an army which could go to the aid of besieged cities, but which was also capable of defeating enemy armies in open country, as it did at the battle of Akroinon in 740 (see below, p. 386).[10] During the upheavals caused by the transition of power from the Umayyads to the Abbasids, the Byzantines took the offensive. They raided beyond the Taurus in 751 to Melitene and in either 754 or 755 to Theodosioupolis, transplanting these cities' populations.[11] The offensive also took place by sea. The fleet of the Kibyrrhaiotai destroyed an Arab fleet

[6] Nikeph., ch. 67, ed. and tr. Mango, pp. 138–41; Theoph., ed. de Boor, I, pp. 422–4; tr. Mango and Scott, pp. 584–6; Stathakopoulos (2004), pp. 382–5.

[7] Theoph., ed. de Boor, I, pp. 434, 440; tr. Mango and Scott, pp. 600–1, 607–8.

[8] Mango (2005).

[9] Theoph., ed. de Boor, I, p. 456; tr. Mango and Scott, pp. 628–9; Brooks (1900), pp. 737–9.

[10] Nikeph., ch. 61, ed. and tr. Mango, pp. 130–1; Theoph., ed. de Boor, I, pp. 405–6, 411; tr. Mango and Scott, pp. 559–62, 570–2.

[11] Nikeph., chs. 70, 73, ed. and tr. Mango, pp. 142–7; Theoph., ed. de Boor, I, pp. 427, 429; tr. Mango and Scott, pp. 589–91, 592–4; Lilie (1976), pp. 164–5.

off Cyprus in 748;[12] and the organisation of a Sicilian fleet during the 750s put paid to half a century of incessant Arab raiding on Sicily.[13] Even after the empire had been saved from annihilation and a lasting border between the two empires had been drawn at the Taurus, warfare continued: but now it was waged by new enemies.

On the Arab side, the annual raids in Asia Minor continued to ravage Cappadocia and were particularly dangerous when the empire was weak, or the caliphate in a strong position. Such was the case under Empress Irene (797–802) when, in 798, a detachment got as far as Malagina and stole a saddle from the imperial stables. And during the revolt of Thomas the Slav in 823, Thomas' supporters allowed Arab raiders to reach Bithynia.[14] Finally, there were two such emergencies under Theophilos: when Caliph al-Ma'mun (813–33) led successful raids in person from 830 to 832, capturing Lulon and Tyana; and again in 838, when Caliph al-Mu'tasim (833–42) responded to the emperor's attack on Sozopetra in Syria in the previous year, defeating him roundly at Dazimon and capturing Amorion, capital of the theme of the Anatolikoi and cradle of the ruling dynasty.

In the 150 years of conflict, only two major truces were concluded – in 782 and 806; both imposed humiliating terms on the Byzantines, who had to pay tribute, and altogether they suspended the fighting for fewer than five years. The chain of signal-towers functioning by the ninth century, possibly even by the eighth, shows the permanent nature of the conflict with the caliphate. The towers ran from the northern entrance of the Cilician Gates, on the border at Lulon (near Ulukişla), to the Pharos of the imperial palace in Constantinople, and signals alerted the emperor to Arab incursions within the hour.[15] But in the ninth century it was attacks by sea, independent of the caliphate, which did most harm. Euphemios, turmarch of Sicily, summoned the Aghlabids of Kairouan to help him in his rebellion against Michael II, and in 827 they landed and besieged Syracuse (see below, p. 462). Thus began the conquest of Sicily which was to drag on for the rest of the century. It was probably in this same year that Crete was attacked and soon taken by exiles from Cordoba; they had captured and subsequently been driven out of Alexandria by the caliph's army.[16] Crete and Sicily served as bases for raids on the islands and the Aegean littoral, now under constant threat; so, too, were the coasts of southern Italy, and Bari was captured around 842.

---

[12] Nikeph., ch. 68, ed. and tr. Mango, pp. 140–1; Theoph., ed. de Boor, I, p. 424; tr. Mango and Scott, pp. 586–7; Lilie (1976), p. 164, n. 9.

[13] McCormick (2001), pp. 865–72.   [14] Theo. Stud., no. 475, ed. Fatouros, II, p. 683.

[15] Pattenden (1983); Zuckerman (1994); SD, ed. and French tr. Auzépy, p. 238, n. 282; Constantine Porphyrogenitus, *Three treatises*, ed. and tr. Haldon, pp. 132–5 (text), 254–5 (commentary).

[16] Tsougarakis (1998), pp. 30–41; Malamut (1988), I, pp. 72–6.

On the northern border a new front was opened in 754 against the Bulgars in Thrace. Constantine V had made Thrace more secure through repeated campaigning in the last fifteen years of his reign, particularly with his victory at Anchialos in 763. On Constantine's death, Thrace enjoyed a state of peace, with its network of *kastra* where garrisons were stationed[17] and its renovated roads.[18] This is illustrated by Empress Irene's progress in 784 when she went as far as Beroia and Anchialos, which she 'ordered to be rebuilt'.[19] Relations with the Bulgars were in fact so close that in 776–7 Khan Telerig sought refuge in Constantinople, where he was baptised in the presence of Leo IV (775–80) and married one of Empress Irene's relations.[20] But under Irene and Constantine VI (780–97) the northern border became very dangerous once again. The Bulgars crushed the armies sent against them – as at Markellai in 792 – and their power increased still further under Khan Krum (*c.* 803–14). The efforts of Nikephoros I (802–11) to get the better of them ended in disaster in 811. The Bulgars annihilated the imperial army after it had seized their capital Pliska; Nikephoros was killed and his skull was used by Krum as a drinking goblet.[21] This disaster was compounded two years later by the defeat at Bersinikia near Adrianople; the resulting fall of the Byzantine towns and fortresses of Beroia, Probaton, Anchialos and Mesembria allowed the Bulgars to devastate Thrace and Macedonia. The state of emergency which arose after Bersinikia led to the seizure of the throne by Leo 'the Armenian', *stratēgos* of the theme of the Anatolikoi; he organised the defence of Constantinople, while the people assembled at Constantine V's tomb, crying: 'Arise and help the state which is perishing!'[22] The death of Krum and the victory of Leo V in 816 changed the situation once again; a treaty was signed that same year and brought peace for more than three-quarters of a century, allowing for the reconstruction of the region.[23]

One portion of the empire which saw little warfare in this period was mainland Greece and the Peloponnese, following massive Slavonic immigration there in the seventh and eighth centuries; occasional Byzantine military expeditions were sufficient to ensure continued overlordship. Constantine V subjugated the *Sklaviniai* of Macedonia around 759;[24] and in

---

[17] Theoph., ed. de Boor, I, p. 447; tr. Mango and Scott, pp. 617–18.
[18] Mango and Ševčenko (1972).
[19] Theoph., ed. de Boor, I, p. 457; tr. Mango and Scott, pp. 630–1.
[20] Theoph., ed. de Boor, I, p. 451; tr. Mango and Scott, p. 622.
[21] Theoph., ed. de Boor, I, pp. 489–91; tr. Mango and Scott, pp. 671–4; *Chronicle of 811*, ed. and French tr. Dujčev, pp. 210–17; tr. Stephenson (2006), pp. 87–90. On the settlements at Pliska, see Henning (2005), pp. 42–3 and nn. 11–14 on p. 50.
[22] Scriptor incertus, *De Leone Armenio*, ed. Bekker, pp. 338–40; Theoph., ed. de Boor, I, pp. 496, 498–503; tr. Mango and Scott, pp. 679–80, 682–6.
[23] Treadgold (1984).
[24] Theoph., ed. de Boor, I, p. 430; tr. Mango and Scott, pp. 594–6; Ditten (1993), pp. 234–5.

783 Staurakios the eunuch, logothete of the Drome under Irene, led an expedition against the *Sklaviniai* in Macedonia (or Thessaly[25]), Greece and the Peloponnese, returning victorious with booty and captives. Although previously considered of great importance, this expedition has recently been re-evaluated so far as the Peloponnese is concerned, with archaeological and sigillographic records showing the claims of the so-called *Chronicle of Monemvasia* to be exaggerated. According to the *Chronicle*, the Peloponnese had been abandoned to the Avaro-Slavs for 218 years – from the sixth year of the reign of Maurice (582–602) to the fourth year of Nikephoros I's reign – with the exception of the eastern part, from Corinth to Cape Malea, where the emperor sent a *stratēgos*.[26] In reality, the Slavs were never completely beyond imperial control in the eighth century. In Thessaly, the seals of Slav *archontes*[27] attest imperial recognition, and even in the less politically organised Peloponnese, the Slavs came into contact with the Greek population, which was more numerous in the eastern part of the peninsula. This contact occurred not only at the level of military administration, as shown by seals of *stratēgoi* and *droungarioi* found around Argos, but also of church administration, as shown by seals and the presence of bishops at the second council of Nicaea.[28] Two revolts by the Slavs in the Peloponnese had to be put down by military force in the course of the ninth century. First came the rebellion of the Slavs of Patras in the reign of Nikephoros I, recounted by Constantine VII Porphyrogenitus (945–59); this eventually led to the appropriation of both them and their property by the archbishopric of Patras, which was then asserting its independence from Corinth. Secondly, in 842 the Melingoi and Erizites further to the south rose in revolt and, once suppressed, were subjected to tribute.[29]

War was not only caused by enemy attacks on the empire; imperial succession could also lead to bloody civil war. On the death of Leo III on 18 June 741, his son Constantine V had to put down a revolt led by his brother-in-law Artabasdos; Constantine was supported by the fleet of the Kibyrrhaiotai and the armies of the Anatolikoi and the Thrakesioi, while the Opsikion, Thrace and the Armeniakoi backed Artabasdos. In the summer of 742 Artabasdos was proclaimed emperor in Constantinople, which was then besieged and, on 2 November 744, captured by Constantine.[30]

[25] Oikonomides (1999–2000), p. 62.

[26] Lemerle (1963), pp. 10, 16–17; Lampropoulou *et al.* (2001), pp. 206–8, 220; Turlej (2001), pp. 125–58.

[27] Seibt (1999); Seibt (2003a).   [28] Avramea (1997), pp. 86–104; Avramea (2001).

[29] *DAI*, chs. 49, 50, pp. 228–45; Turlej (2001), pp. 93–111.

[30] Nikeph., chs. 64–6, ed. and tr. Mango, pp. 132–7; Theoph., ed. de Boor, I, pp. 413–15, 419–21; tr. Mango and Scott, pp. 572–6, 580–4; Speck (1981); *PMBZ*, #632; Rochow (1994), pp. 21–9; Stathakopoulos (2004), pp. 377–8. For the most recent discussion of the debate over the chronology of the siege of Constantinople, see Nichanian, 'Aristocratie et pouvoir impérial' (PhD thesis, 2004), pp. 519–44.

Some eighty years later, Thomas the Slav, turmarch of the *foideratoi* in the Anatolikoi, rebelled against Michael II on Christmas Eve 820; Michael was Leo V's successor and was generally considered to have been responsible for his murder.[31] The rebellion lasted three years and nearly succeeded, for Michael could only count on Constantinople and its fleet and the themes of Opsikion and the Armeniakoi, whereas Thomas controlled everything else, including the tax revenues, and had been crowned emperor at Antioch. Thomas laid siege to Constantinople in 821–2, but was foiled by a Bulgar attack and Michael's destruction of his fleet using Greek fire. In the end he took refuge in Thrace, where he was captured by Michael at Arkadiopolis in October 823.[32] The battle fought against the army of the Armeniakoi in 793 by Constantine VI at the head of all the other armies might also be considered a struggle for the succession. The Armeniakoi did not want Irene to be co-ruler with her son Constantine, who had been reconciled with her after a spell of sole rule (790–2). They wanted to remain loyal to him alone and to their *stratēgos* Alexios Musele(m), who had been blinded for alleged complicity in a plot in favour of the caesar Nikephoros (son of Constantine V and uncle of the emperor) after the debacle at Markellai at the hands of the Bulgars in 792. Although this third civil war was apparently confined to the army, the other two, which both lasted over two years and involved sieges of the capital, also affected the civilian population.

Thus, war dominated the eighth and early ninth centuries. Under the Isaurians it was a war of survival which overshadowed society as a whole and still threatened the empire's very existence at the beginning of the ninth century, as can be seen from the Constantinopolitans' reaction in 813 at the tomb of Constantine V. After 830, however, war affected mainly the armed forces in operations on the border with the caliphate, on the islands and in Italy; and even in these far-flung areas, its impact varied. Thrace, a land of reconquest and colonisation from 750, was ravaged by the enemy during the years 811 to 813, but regained its peace and prosperity after 816. Asia Minor suffered heavy but uneven losses. As the caliphs abandoned hopes of conquering the empire, a border gradually emerged between the Aegean and the Black Sea, along a line from Seleukeia to Trebizond; this became a sort of no-man's-land, frequently changing hands, and studded with nineteen fortresses, according to Ibn Khurradadhbih.[33] Regions close to the border were particularly exposed, such as Cappadocia and the Pamphylian and Lycian coasts; so too were the Anatolikoi, Armeniakoi and Opsikion, which bore the brunt of the Arab attacks. In contrast, the inhabitants of the Thrakesioi and the Black Sea coast were largely spared.[34] The Kibyrrhaiotai

---

[31] See Afinogenov (2001) for the argument that the revolt began under Leo V, as against Lemerle (1965).
[32] Lemerle (1965).   [33] Haldon and Kennedy (1980), pp. 85–6.
[34] Lilie (1976), pp. 169–78 and map, p. 186; Haldon (1997a), pp. 106–7.

successfully protected the Aegean islands in the eighth century, but after the Arab conquest of Crete in the 820s they became front-line targets. At the same time Sicily, after fifty years of peace following an earlier fifty years of raids, also came under attack. Finally, Constantinople itself was besieged four times, twice by foreign armies, in 717–18 and 813.

It is difficult to determine the precise impact of both plague and continuous warfare on population figures; however, this was already being felt in the seventh century, and the population level seems to have reached its nadir in the eighth,[35] although the situation was not uniform. Greece and the islands appear to have been more densely populated than the rest of the empire in the eighth century, but this changed after a century of Arab raiding. In Constantinople, the low point was the plague of 747–8; according to Patriarch Nikephoros, plague emptied the City of its inhabitants, and although it is difficult to give precise figures for the surviving population, estimates vary from 40,000 to 70,000.[36] Constantinople was a case apart; while greatly affected by the plague, it also profited from war in demographic terms, thanks to the influx of refugees into the capital – a topic rarely studied.[37]

DEPOPULATION AND RURALISATION

The overall demographic decline had two important consequences: shortage of manpower became a principal factor in imperial policy, and this in turn transformed the landscape of the empire. Human spoils, the captives who followed in the train of victorious armies, were a constant feature of the wars against the Arabs, Bulgars and Slavs. Prisoner exchanges and the refusal to hand over fugitives are more often mentioned in Arabic sources than in Byzantine ones, but show that manpower had become a precious commodity; the withholding of captives led to the disastrous campaign against the Bulgars at Bersinikia in 813.[38] The emperors conducted a veritable settlement policy. Constantine V and Leo IV settled prisoners taken on the Arab border – from Germanikeia, Melitene and Theodosioupolis – in newly-constructed *kastra* in Thrace.[39] Constantine repopulated Constantinople in 756 with natives of Greece and the islands,[40] and in the 760s he installed migrant Slavs on the Asiatic coast of the Black Sea near

---

[35] Laiou (2002b), p. 50.   [36] Mango (1990), pp. 51–62; Magdalino (1996a), p. 18.

[37] Theoph., ed. de Boor, I, p. 397; tr. Mango and Scott, p. 546.

[38] al-Mas'udi, *al-Tanbih*, ed. de Goeje, pp. 188–92; tr. Carra de Vaux, pp. 255–8; Theoph., ed. de Boor, I, pp. 498–9; tr. Mango and Scott, p. 682–3; Skyl., ed. Thurn, p. 12; French tr. Flusin and Cheynet, pp. 12–13.

[39] Nikeph., chs. 70, 73, ed. and tr. Mango, pp. 142–5; Theoph., ed. de Boor, I, pp. 427, 429, 451; tr. Mango and Scott, pp. 589–94, 621–3; Lilie (1976), pp. 164–5.

[40] Nikeph., chs. 67–8, ed. and tr. Mango, pp. 138–41; Theoph., ed. de Boor, I, pp. 422–4, 429; tr. Mango and Scott, pp. 584–5, 592–4.

the Bosporus.[41] But it was Nikephoros I who pursued a settlement policy most vigorously. According to Theophanes' *Chronicle*, in 807 he began by moving to Thrace people in Asia Minor found to be without fixed homes, and in 809–10 he settled impoverished soldiers from the themes of Asia in the *Sklaviniai* of Greece and Macedonia. The so-called *Chronicle of Monemvasia* corroborates Theophanes' information for the region of Sparta.[42] Later, according to the *Life* of Athanasia of Aegina, manpower shortages forced Theophilos to issue an edict requiring Roman widows to marry barbarian immigrants.[43] Likewise, Theophilos adopted the policy of settling defectors from the caliphate in Asia Minor: initially the Banu Habib of Nisibis were installed as freebooters on the border, and the famous Persian unit commanded by Theophobos was transferred to the regions of Sinope and Amastris, later to be dispersed throughout the themes (see below, p. 393).[44] The empire required men, both to join the army and to pay the taxes which provided for its upkeep: this could explain both the forced conversion under Leo III of the Jews and Montanists,[45] and also the persecution of monks by Constantine V between 767 and 770, forcing them to return to lay status and marry.[46]

The scarcity of men also transformed the landscape and economy of the empire between the end of the sixth century and the seventh. Certain regions, such as Mount Athos, were abandoned and would not be repopulated until the ninth century.[47] The empire was no longer a network of cities, but rather a rural state supervised from Constantinople, the metropolis which survived behind its walls. The fate of the cities of antiquity has been much studied[48] and there is agreement that the standard model – that of cities being abandoned for fortresses or refuges built on higher ground – needs refining. To begin with, a large number of cities were abandoned outright – including Anemurion[49] and Tyana – even if some, such as Pergamon, revived in the tenth century.[50] However, despite frequent examples of refuges built beside an ancient city – in Calabria one

---

[41] Nikeph., ch. 75, ed. and tr. Mango, pp. 148–9; Theoph., ed. de Boor, I, p. 432; tr. Mango and Scott, pp. 597–9.

[42] Theoph., ed. de Boor, I, pp. 482, 486; tr. Mango and Scott, pp. 661–3, 666–8; *Chronicle of Monemvasia*, ed. Lemerle, p. 10.

[43] *Life of Athanasia of Aegina*, ed. Halkin, ch. 2, p. 181; tr. Sherry, pp. 143–4.

[44] Ibn Hawqal, *Surat*, ed. Kramers, I, pp. 211–13; French tr. Kramers and Wiet, I, pp. 205–6; French tr. in Vasil., pp. 419–21; al-Tabari, *Ta'rikh*, ed. de Goeje *et al.*, III, p. 1235; tr. Bosworth, XXXIII, p. 85; French tr. in Vasiliev (1935), I, p. 294; Cheynet (1998a).

[45] Through baptism, they became eligible for enrolment in the army: Theoph., ed. de Boor, I, p. 397; tr. Mango and Scott, p. 546; Rochow (1991), p. 104; Haldon (1999a), pp. 260–2.

[46] Nikeph., chs. 80, 83, ed. and tr. Mango, pp. 152–3, 156–9; Theoph., ed. de Boor, I, pp. 437–9; tr. Mango and Scott, pp. 604–5; SD, ed. and French tr. Auzépy, pp. 36–7 (introduction).

[47] Lefort (1991), pp. 67–8.

[48] Kirsten (1958); Brandes (1989); Foss (1996a); Brandes and Haldon (2000). See also below, pp. 470–2, 482–5.

[49] Russell (2002).   [50] Rheidt (2002), p. 624.

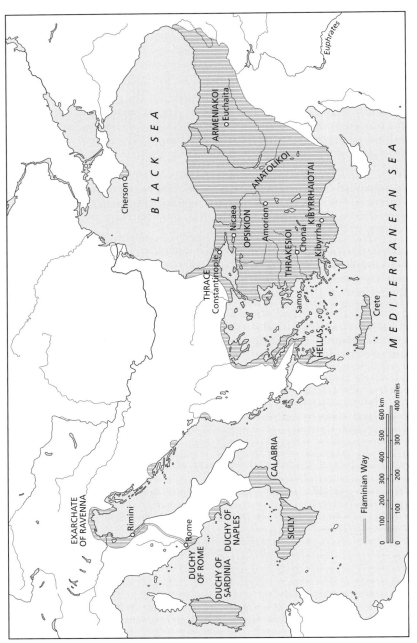

Map 13 The empire under militarised rule: army units and embryonic themes, earlier eighth century

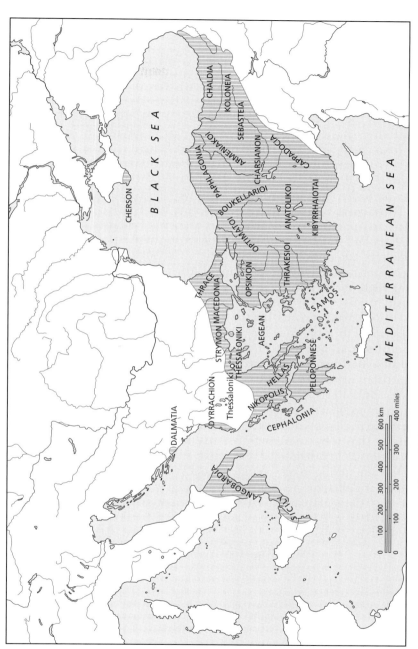

Map 14 Administrative organisation: themes in the later ninth century

could cite the case of Locri, abandoned for Gerace (Hagia Kyriake) before 787[51] and examples from Asia Minor are legion[52] – the inhabitants often remained inside the ruined city, even when they had no means of rebuilding it: they withdrew to a defensive position, fortifying only a small part of the city with materials from the ruins. Such was the case at Ankyra,[53] Amorion,[54] Side[55] and Sardis.[56] Ephesos combines the two patterns: one small part of the ancient city surrounding the port was reused and fortified, and a fortress was built on higher ground nearby, around the cathedral of St John (now Selçuk).[57] Furthermore, fortifying a reduced space was in no way incompatible with small groups living in other districts inside the perimeter of the ancient city, as at Amorion, or with the presence of a *kastron* on higher ground further off, as is well illustrated by the *Miracles* of St Theodore at Euchaita under Constantine V.[58] Finally, there were the cities created on virgin sites or on the sites of ancient fortresses, strongholds on high ground which contained the newly constituted civil, ecclesiastical and military administration within their walls. Such were the Thracian *kastra* of Probaton and Bulgarophygon constructed under Constantine V,[59] ranking high on the list of bishoprics, or Santa Severina (Nikopolis) in Calabria.[60]

There were many variants, but the essential pattern was that cities shrank to a quarter of their previous size; all of them – whether old or new – were now fortified and their main function had changed. The city had become above all a local branch of the state; both from a military point of view – as garrisons or refuges for the surrounding rural population – and from an ecclesiastical perspective – as the residence of the bishop. However, it should be noted that the economic function of the city as a place for markets and fairs did not disappear. In the context of the demographic and economic depression shown by numismatic records, the written sources sometimes give paradoxical information; one example is the remission by Constantine VI of fees amounting to 100 pounds of gold (7,200 *nomismata*) for the fair of St John at Ephesos in 795 – an enormous sum which continues to puzzle historians.[61] One explanation might be the industry of local peasants, whose villages (*chōria*) had become the basic unit of the fiscal system, so vividly pictured in the *Farmer's law*.[62] Indeed, the Arabic geographers describe the

[51] Prigent (2002), p. 938; Noyé (1998), p. 234.
[52] Brandes (1989), pp. 111–20; Haldon (1997a), p. 108.   [53] Foss (1977a).
[54] Lightfoot (1998).   [55] Foss (1996b), pp. 24–46.   [56] Foss and Scott (2002).
[57] Foss (1979a), pp. 103–15.   [58] Zuckerman (1988), pp. 198–9.   [59] Kountoura-Galake (1997).
[60] Prigent (2002), pp. 939–46.
[61] Theoph., ed. de Boor, I, p. 469; tr. Mango and Scott, pp. 644–5.
[62] *Farmer's law*, ed. and Russian tr. Medvedev *et al.*; ed. and tr. Ashburner; Lemerle (1979), pp. 35–51; Brandes and Haldon (2000), pp. 148–9. See also, pp. 487, 488–9.

empire as having no cities and being made up of prosperous districts with fortresses and villages, often in caves or underground.[63]

THE ARMED FORCES

The emperors in the eighth century confronted an empire that had been ruralised and depopulated, and teetered on the brink of ruin. The situation was particularly dire when Leo III took power in 717, as Constantinople was besieged by land and sea by enormous Arab forces. Leo followed a succession of emperors – six in the twenty-two years following the first deposition of Justinian II in 695 – which marked a crisis for the empire.[64] The failure of the siege in 717 had considerable repercussions; this was the first major setback in the Arab conquest which had begun in the 630s and had continued unrelentingly ever since (see below, pp. 370–7; above, p. 221). However, it did not guarantee the security of an empire still very much under threat. It was because of this threat that the Isaurian emperors and their successors, with the exception of Irene, introduced reforms designed to strengthen the empire against its enemies. It is often difficult to unscramble the Isaurians' reforms from the attempts of Heraclius and his successors to cope with the Arab invasions and the loss of the eastern provinces; only in the ninth century do we become better informed about the state of play. But there is now a tendency to reassess the role played by the Isaurians, long minimised because of their discredited religious policies. The threat which hung over the empire explains why absolute priority was given to the army. Organising the army and maintaining it well required that the state apparatus be placed under direct authority of the emperor; victory depended on the purity of faith of the Christian people.

The empire's defences were fragmented into small units stationed in fortresses, so that walls became as important as men (see above, fig. 2 on p. 57). Repair of the walls went on incessantly, the unrivalled champion in this being Michael III (842–67), at the very end of the period. In Constantinople after the earthquake of 740 Leo III paid for the restoration of the walls, previously the inhabitants' responsibility, out of the imperial treasury, raising the City taxes by $8\frac{1}{3}$ per cent (a tax of one *miliarēsion* per *nomisma*, called the *dikeraton*). Inscriptions on the land walls near the Sea of Marmara record this work.[65] Theophilos, for his part, repaired the walls near the Blachernae district and large sections of the sea walls.[66] At Nicaea

[63] *Hudud al-'alam*, tr. Minorsky, ed. Bosworth, pp. 156–7; Ibn Hawqal, *Surat*, ed. Kramers, I, p. 200; French tr. Kramers and Wiet, I, pp. 194–5; Haldon (1997a), p. 112.

[64] Haldon (1997a), pp. 74–82.

[65] Nikeph., ch. 63, ed. and tr. Mango, pp. 130–3; Theoph., ed. de Boor, I, p. 412; tr. Mango and Scott, p. 572; Meyer-Plath and Schneider (1938–43), II, nos. 7, 12, 13, 16, 24, 29a, 32, pp. 124, 127, 130–2.

[66] Meyer-Plath and Schneider (1938–43), II, no. 61, p. 141; van Millingen (1899), pp. 183–4.

the walls were restored by Leo III and Michael III.[67] Leo III (or Leo IV) sent a *spatharios* to repair the walls of Rodandos on the Arab border, and Leo IV sent the *stratōr* Isaac, better known as Theophanes the Confessor, to repair those of Kyzikos.[68] Following the pattern at Constantinople, these repairs were paid for by the local inhabitants, though carried out under the orders of an imperial official.

The human element of the empire's defence is more complicated than that of the physical walls, and many points remain unclear. At the beginning of the eighth century the army was based in the provinces and made up of different corps redeployed throughout Asia Minor after 636, following their withdrawal from the east. The troops of the *magister militum per Orientem* were stationed in central Asia Minor, their name Hellenised to Anatolikoi (from the Latin Orientales) and *magister militum* being translated to *stratēgos*. The troops of the *magister militum per Armeniam* were deployed in northern Asia Minor and took the Greek name of Armeniakoi; those of the *magister militum per Thracias*, which had been sent as reinforcements to the east, were pulled back to the west coast of Asia Minor and took the name of Thrakesioi. Finally, that part of Asia Minor closest to Constantinople had remained the quarters of the imperial guard, the Opsikion (see above, p. 240). These army units became known as themes (*themata*), a generic name whose etymology is disputed. By the beginning of the ninth century, theme had come to mean the territory on which a corps was stationed, with each unit's *stratēgos* based in the theme's capital: Amorion in the Anatolikoi, Euchaita in the Armeniakoi, Chonai in the Thrakesioi and Nicaea in the Opsikion. Similarly, at the end of the seventh century new army corps were installed in Sicily, Hellas and Thrace, each commanded by a *stratēgos*. This currently accepted model for the emergence of the themes has replaced that suggested by George Ostrogorsky.[69]

A further development saw the subdivision of the existing army corps, or themes, for tactical reasons; at the beginning of the ninth century the theme of Cappadocia was created in the Anatolikoi, with its capital at Koron; and in the Armeniakoi, the themes of Paphlagonia and Chaldia were established. But themes could also be subdivided for political reasons, as was the case with the Opsikion. All too often involved in plots, it was broken up into the Boukellarioi (768) and Optimatoi (*c.* 775) and these were simultaneously demoted from combat to rearguard units. The Opsikion theme proper retained only the western part of its former territory (Phrygia, the Hellespont and western Bithynia). Moreover, several new themes were created: in Crete, probably in the eighth century, and

[67] Schneider and Karnapp (1938), nos. 29, 36, pp. 49, 51–2.
[68] Grégoire (1908); Methodius, *Life of Theophanes*, IX.15, ed. Latyshev, pp. 10–11.
[69] Haldon (1997a), pp. 208–20; Haldon (1999a), pp. 71–4; Ostrogorsky (1968), pp. 95–8. See also above, pp. 239–40.

in Macedonia, the Peloponnese and Cephalonia in the ninth century. As regards the fleet, the Kibyrrhaiotai (from the city of Kibyrrha in Caria) had reinforced the Karabisianoi at the end of the seventh century and then replaced them to ensure protection of the southern coasts of Asia Minor, which were also guarded by the fleet of the Aegean Sea in the eighth century.[70] Access to the western Mediterranean was controlled by the fleet of the Helladikoi, which revolted in 727, and a fleet of Sicily also appeared in the 750s.[71]

In organisational terms, themes were subdivided into *tourmai, droungoi* and *banda*. The *tourma*, at the head of which was a turmarch, and the *bandon*, under the orders of a count (*komēs*), were assigned to a territory, whereas the *droungos* was a tactical unit, under the orders of a *droungarios*.[72] The numbers of men in a unit varied by region and over time, and figures suggested for individual themes are no more than rough estimates.[73] According to Theophanes, Constantine V mobilised the entire Byzantine army against the Bulgars in October 773 (or 774); this totalled some 80,000 men, drawn both from the provincial – thematic – units and from the elite regiments stationed in the capital (*tagmata*). This figure is considered reasonable by some scholars, but far too high by others,[74] and should be compared with information given at the end of the ninth century by Leo VI in his *Tactica*: according to Leo, the cavalry themes had 4,000 men each, 2,000 per *tourma*.[75]

From the mid-eighth century on, the *tagmata* stationed at Constantinople consisted of the Schools (*scholai*) and excubitors (*exkoubitoi*), old guard units which over the centuries had become largely ceremonial. Constantine V made them operational again and it was these *tagmata* who surrounded the emperor on the battlefield and whose arms were provided by the state.[76] The *tagmata* – who prefigured the professional army of the tenth and eleventh centuries – were reinforced by Constantine V's successors, though the Schools were demoted for a time under Irene, punishment for their fervent iconoclasm in hindering the meeting of the iconodule council in 786; they were replaced by another *tagma*, the *Arithmos*, formed out of *banda* from various themes.[77]

---

[70] For a summary: Haldon (1999a), pp. 86–7 and table 3.1.

[71] McCormick (2001), pp. 865–972; Theoph., ed. de Boor, I, p. 405; tr. Mango and Scott, pp. 559–60; Avramea (1997), pp. 101–4.

[72] Haldon (1999a), pp. 110–14.

[73] Treadgold (1995), pp. 64–75; Haldon (1999a), pp. 113, 314, n. 68.

[74] Theoph., ed. de Boor, I, p. 447; tr. Mango and Scott, p. 617; Treadgold (1995), p. 64; Haldon (1999a), p. 102.

[75] Haldon (1999a), p. 110.

[76] First mentioned in the sources by Theoph., ed. de Boor, I, p. 442; tr. Mango and Scott, p. 610.

[77] Theoph., ed. de Boor, I, p. 462; tr. Mango and Scott, pp. 635–7; Haldon (1984), pp. 239–42.

Unlike the troops of the *tagmata* who were full-time, those of the provinces were only mobilised for campaigns during the summer months and sometimes served outside their theme; natives of the Asia Minor themes might even be employed in Europe.[78] However, some thematic soldiers were permanently on duty if they guarded a fortress, since fortresses had standing garrisons. The conditions under which soldiers were recruited is a question upon which much has been written; however, it remains an open question, involving as it does the entire system of taxation, an understanding of which, in turn, depends on one's interpretation of the empire's monetary circulation. There is agreement on some points: that thematic soldiers were based throughout the whole territory of a theme; that they were responsible for their own maintenance, since they had to present themselves for service with their equipment;[79] and that the administration provided for their needs on campaign.

Various suggestions have been put forward as to how soldiers paid for their equipment and how their service was remunerated. One is that the tenth-century system – that military service was inextricably linked with the holding of inalienable, exempted land – had, in fact, been in place since the seventh-century withdrawal of troops from the east: in effect, troops whom the state could no longer pay in cash were paid in land. Based on the numismatic records available before *c.* 1980[80] and on the disappearance of imperial estates between the sixth and tenth centuries,[81] this interpretation is intellectually tempting and has been favoured by those who consider military service as a fiscal obligation, bound up with a plot of exempted land.[82] However, as has often been noted,[83] such an interpretation jars with the fact that those few contemporary sources which mention soldiers contain no evidence of compulsory military service in connection with land; these sources include the *Ecloga*, the *Chronicles* of Theophanes and Nikephoros, the *Lives* of Philaretos and Euthymios the Younger, and the letters of Theodore the Stoudite.

Chapter Sixteen of the *Ecloga*, often cited but yet to be examined in detail, gives an idea of the position of soldiers under the Isaurians. When soldiers (*stratiōtai*) were enrolled (*strateuomenoi*), their name and place of origin were inscribed on the theme's military roll, as well as on that of the central office of the *stratiōtikon* in Constantinople. Enrolment entailed military responsibilities: going to war, when called up, fully equipped with horse, harness and arms. It also entailed benefits: soldiers received a regular

[78] Theoph., ed. de Boor, I, p. 462, 470–1, 491; tr. Mango and Scott, pp. 635–7, 645–8, 673–4; *Life of Philaretos the Merciful*, ed. Rydén, pp. 72–5.
[79] *Life of Philaretos the Merciful*, ed. Rydén, pp. 72–5; Lemerle (1979), pp. 59–60.
[80] Hendy (1985).   [81] Treadgold (1983a), pp. 628–31; Treadgold (1995), pp. 171–6.
[82] Oikonomides (1988a); Oikonomides (1996a), pp. 37–40.
[83] Lemerle (1979), pp. 59–64 ; Haldon (1993), pp. 20–9.

wage, which was paid whether or not they were on campaign, as well as extra wages during combat, booty, and bonuses from the emperor or *stratēgos*. The regular wage (*roga*) was an annuity due to those who held the office of soldier, the so-called *strateia*. The household (*oikos*) in which an enrolled man lived, and which he could leave for another, was also probably exempt from supplementary taxes and impositions, although there is no mention of this in the *Ecloga*. Furthermore, the term *strateia* was not confined to soldiers. Under the Isaurians, every individual inscribed on the administrative roll by virtue of his office – in effect, everyone in imperial office, including ecclesiastical office – was deemed to hold a *strateia*, and thus entitled to receive a *roga* 'from the hand of the emperor', as well as rations in kind. *Strateiai* could either be bought or granted out by the emperor.[84] The ways in which military *strateiai* changed hands are not altogether clear. Elderly soldiers might be taken off the rolls and thus forfeit their *strateia*; but on the other hand, soldiers' widows had to furnish a fully equipped soldier – or the equivalent sum – if they wanted to keep the *strateia*, i.e. to continue receiving the *roga* and, perhaps, tax exemptions for the household. This latter practice was abolished under Irene, but it must subsequently have been re-established, as we find it in use around 840 in the *Life* of Euthymios the Younger.[85]

Irene's measure forced her successor Nikephoros to make up for the soldiers who had thus been lost to the army, giving rise to the second in the list of this emperor's 'vexations' decried by Theophanes. Nikephoros decreed that the poor from the villages should be enrolled as soldiers (*strateuesthai*); they were to be equipped at the expense of their fellow villagers who, in addition, were to pay $18\frac{1}{2}$ *nomismata* for each poor man so enrolled. The latter sum has generally been understood to be the price paid for the equipment.[86] But it could also be understood as the price of the soldier's *strateia*. This would imply that the enrolled man's *roga* was paid not directly to him – though he retained any extraordinary earnings – but to those who had jointly bought the *strateia* for him (the *syndotai*) and who, according to article 18 of the *Farmer's law*, paid his taxes and had the use of his land.

TAXATION AND THE PROVINCES

The debate over the arrangements for recruitment of the army is connected with the debate over whether the tax system worked in cash or in kind; and

---

[84] *Ecloga*, XVI.3–4, ed. and German tr. Burgmann, pp. 222–5; tr. Freshfield, pp. 102–3; Nikeph., ch. 80, ed. and tr. Mango, pp. 152–3.

[85] Nikephoros, *Antirrhetici*, III.62, cols. 491–2; French tr. Mondzain-Baudinet, pp. 268–9; Theo. Stud., no. 7, lines 61–3, ed. Fatouros, I, p. 26; *Life of Euthymios the Younger*, ed. Petit, p. 18.

[86] Theoph., ed. de Boor, I, p. 486; tr. Mango and Scott, pp. 666–8; Lemerle (1979), pp. 62–3; Haldon (1993), pp. 25–6; Oikonomides (1996a), p. 39.

this, in turn, depends on how one believes money circulated. It is unanimously agreed that circulation dwindled between 650 and 850. However, recent studies have drawn attention to the vitality of Sicilian gold coinage, as well as to the role played by the *miliarēsion* – the silver coin worth $\frac{1}{12}$ of the *nomisma*, introduced by Leo III in 721. The latter innovation helps explain the great importance of the fortress of Lulon, located on the border with the caliphate at the heart of a mining region. The circulation of copper coins has also been reassessed; this had previously been assumed to be non-existent, as account had not been taken of the many anonymous *folleis* preserved among archaeological finds in Turkish museums, notably at Ankyra.[87]

Availability of money was vital for the army, in order to pay the *rogai* of the officers and men. The enemy was well aware of this and the 'Wells Fargo' wagon of the *rogai*, accompanied by the *stratēgos*, was a key target for attack. In 809 the Bulgars seized the *rogai* of the army on the Strymon, totalling 1,100 pounds of gold, or 79,200 *nomismata*. Two years later, the Arabs captured the *rogai* of the theme of the Armeniakoi, which amounted to 1,300 pounds, or 93,600 *nomismata* – over three times the annual tribute of 30,000 *nomismata* paid to the Arabs by Nikephoros I in 806.[88] It is generally thought that the *roga* was paid every four years, though no contemporary text declares as much.[89] The state also needed to issue allowances in kind to maintain the army on campaign. The system described in the military *Treatise* compiled under Constantine VII Porphyrogenitus, but based on documents of the Isaurian period,[90] was probably at least partially in place from the eighth century. Under this system, the *prōtonotarios* of the theme – the highest civilian official in the thematic administration, first mentioned in the ninth century – would supply each military staging-post (*aplēkton*) with barley for the horses and other necessities; these outgoings would be recorded in and deducted from the theme's account in the *eidikon*, the central office of the tax administration.[91] We can see this supply system at work in 782 under Irene. According to al-Tabari, she supplied Harun al-Rashid 'with guides and markets' for his journey back from Bithynia to the caliphate, after he had negotiated a peace treaty in which this featured as one of the clauses.[92]

---

[87] Morrisson (1998); Morrisson (2001); Pitarakis (1998), p. 170; Lightfoot (2002). See also below, pp. 469, 470, 483–4.

[88] Theoph., ed. de Boor, I, pp. 482, 484, 489; tr. Mango and Scott, pp. 661–5, 671–2; see also TC, p. 11.

[89] Haldon (1999a), p. 124; Treadgold (1988), p. 352.

[90] Constantine Porphyrogenitus, *Three treatises*, ed. and tr. Haldon, pp. 96–7.

[91] Constantine Porphyrogenitus, *Three treatises*, ed. and tr. Haldon, pp. 116–17.

[92] al-Tabari, *Ta'rikh*, ed. de Goeje *et al.*, III, p. 504; tr. Kennedy, XXIX, p. 221; cited by Brooks (1900), p. 736.

The sources do not really allow us to decide between the two interpretations of the tax system currently on offer. Those who argue that taxes were paid in cash do so mainly by reference to the tax on Constantinopolitans for repairs to the City's walls; they maintain that the hearth tax, the *kapnikon*, as well as the property tax, described by the *Farmer's law* in a village context, were paid in cash from the time of Constantine V.[93] This would indeed appear probable for the *kapnikon*, which Nikephoros I extended to the inhabitants of church lands – those belonging to bishoprics, monasteries and pious foundations – and we even know the rate at which the *kapnikon* was paid under Michael II: two *miliarēsia* per household.[94] But it is harder to say the same of the property tax.

Two contemporary letters support the idea of a property tax called the *synōnē*, paid in kind: both were written between 820 and 843 by Bishop Ignatios of Nicaea to the *prōtonotarios* Nicholas, complaining on behalf of the men of his church. Although these men were theoretically exempted from the *synōnē*, as they were from forced labour and other impositions – and despite having already sent the grain of the *synōnē* to the public granaries that year – the *synōnē* was still being demanded of them, together with an additional six *modioi* per male inhabitant. Opinions as to whether the property tax was paid in cash or kind depend on whether one interprets the word *synōnē* as a property tax or as a requisition; it was originally the Greek translation of the Latin *coemptio*, the compulsory, fixed-price sale to the state of goods needed for the army.[95] One might also take into account the case, under Theodora and Michael III, of the poor who were imprisoned by the *dioikētēs* of Prousa for non-payment of taxes; the abbot of Agauroi gave them 100 *nomismata*, which had been earmarked to pay the taxes of his own monastery.[96] It is not clear, however, which tax was involved here.

This debate is compounded by another concerning the *kommerkiarioi*, whose numerous seals have been found for the period between 650 and 730, dated by indiction and stamped with the emperor's effigy. Their legends also mention warehouses (*apothēkai*) and the names of several provinces. There is general agreement that the *kommerkiarioi* reported to the central office of finances in Constantinople, the *genikon logothesion*. Those who believe taxes were paid in kind argue that the *kommerkiarioi* were responsible for depositing the tax proceeds needed for the year's campaigns in the *apothēkai*; and there is undeniably a certain correspondence between the dates and provinces mentioned on the seals and military expeditions.[97] On the other

[93] Oikonomides (1996a), pp. 29–39; Oikonomides (2002), pp. 980–1.
[94] Theoph., ed. de Boor, I, pp. 486–7; tr. Mango and Scott, pp. 666–8; *Life of George of Mytilene*, ed. Phoutoules, ch. 5, p. 35; TC, p. 54.
[95] Ignatios the Deacon, *Correspondence*, ed. and tr. Mango, nos. 7, 8, pp. 38–45; Kazhdan (1992); Oikonomides (1996a), pp. 70–2 as against Haldon (1994a); Kaplan (2001).
[96] *Life of Eustratios of the monastery of Agauroi (Abgar)*, ch. 15, ed. Papadopoulos-Kerameus, p. 378.
[97] Brandes (2002a), pp. 281–426.

hand, those who argue that taxes were paid in cash see the *kommerkiarioi* as private entrepreneurs who controlled the silk trade for a fixed period in the provinces where they managed the *apothēkai* for the state.[98] After 730 the seals of the *kommerkiarioi* disappear for about a century and are replaced by impersonal seals 'of the imperial *kommerkia*' from one city or province or another. This implies reform under Leo III, the exact terms of which are unknown. However, this might explain the appearance in our sources of the *kommerkion*, or indirect tax on transactions. The *kommerkion* is mentioned under Constantine VI in connection with the fair at Ephesos, and under Irene and Nikephoros I in connection with the customs offices on the Bosporus (Hieron) and the Dardanelles (Abydos).[99] At the beginning of the ninth century the *kommerkiarioi* reappear in the Balkans and even in the Danish port of Hedeby, where seals of the *kommerkiarios* Theodore have been found.[100]

This survey of the army and the tax system needed to maintain it, to ensure the empire's survival, can only be fragmentary and provisional, and our knowledge is constantly being expanded with the publication of new sources, such as seals. However, the most important fact remains the Isaurians' mobilisation of all the empire's resources for the army, and the resultant militarisation of society, which also has the effect of obscuring civilian life. We know little about the civil administration of the provinces before a thematic civil administration under the authority of the *prōtonotarios* was installed at the beginning of the ninth century. All we know is that it was carried out by *chartoularioi* and eparchs, who had a role in the tax system, and by the *dioiketai* 'of the provinces' who were the collectors of taxes.[101]

Another consequence of this militarisation was the creation of a military aristocracy, whose titles were reward for senior command. The Isaurians surrounded themselves with men who often had their origins outside the empire: for example under Leo III the *patrikios* Beser, or Artabasdos, *stratēgos* of the Anatolikoi and later brother-in-law of the emperor; and under Leo IV, the five *stratēgoi* appointed after the expedition of 778, four of whom were Armenian. Leo V, himself of Armenian origin, was the son of a *patrikios* named Bardas – perhaps the *stratēgos* of the Armeniakoi in 771. Leo married the daughter of the *patrikios* Arsavir, also an Armenian and probably the nephew of Bardanes Tourkos (i.e. Khazar), the *stratēgos* of the Anatolikoi who revolted against Nikephoros I in 803. It is also under the Isaurians that

---

[98] Oikonomides (1986a); Oikonomides (2002), pp. 983–8.

[99] Theoph., ed. de Boor, I, pp. 469–70, 475, 487; tr. Mango and Scott, pp. 644–7, 653–4, 668; Brandes (2002a), pp. 583–9.

[100] Brandes (2002a), pp. 562–64; McCormick (2001), p. 227; Cheynet (2003), p. 51.

[101] Oikonomides (2002), p. 989; Brandes (2002a), pp. 195–225; Brandes and Haldon (2000), pp. 169–71.

family names first make an appearance – most often as sobriquets applied to the iconoclasts – and aristocratic families were constituted. Several of the latter, such as the Kamoulianoi and the Melissenoi, who appeared under Constantine V, were to have a long history. A good part of the aristocracy of the ninth century owed its standing to the brilliant military career of an ancestor in the previous century.[102]

CENTRAL ADMINISTRATION AND IMPERIAL IDEOLOGY

The state of emergency in the empire also led to a tightening up of the administration and a change in the emperor's role. The departments established in the seventh century remained in operation – the *logothesia*, each under the direction of a logothete – and we know about their organisation in detail from the *Taktikon Uspensky*. The general (*genikon*) *logothesion* was a sort of finance ministry, collecting taxes and distributing money. The *stratiōtikon logothesion* was the department managing the army. The *logothesion* of the Drome (*tou dromou*) managed the roads, intelligence and diplomacy. Other departments or functions grew in importance during this period, and there has been considerable debate as to their continuity from Roman institutions. The *sakellarios*, originally a eunuch who kept the emperor's purse, became a key figure who, by the end of Theophilos' reign, was the chief organiser of expenditure and had more authority than the general logothete himself. Likewise, the office of the *eidikon*, a treasury whose functions are unclear, makes its appearance in the ninth century.[103]

The tightening up of the administration around the emperor enabled him to govern more directly, especially since the offices of the logothetes were located in the Great Palace. This immediacy of power is also a feature of the military sphere: from the time of Heraclius, emperors had led their armies into battle in person. This was particularly true under the Isaurians and Leo V, who went on campaign nearly every year. This tradition of the warrior emperor makes Irene's reign even more anomalous: as a woman, she could not lead the army.

In diplomatic relations with newer, neighbouring states, the emperors continued a policy of impressing their subjects with the empire's superiority and prestige. Theophilos adorned the reception hall of the Magnaura with a throne surrounded by automata of roaring lions and chirping birds in a plane tree, which Liudprand of Cremona described in the tenth century.[104] John the Grammarian's embassy to Baghdad on behalf of Theophilos was

---

[102] Cheynet (2000), pp. 288–302; Kountoura-Galake (2004); *PMBZ*, #4244.
[103] Brandes (2002a), pp. 106–72, 427–79.
[104] Lemerle (1986), p. 178 and n. 27; Liudprand, *Antapodosis*, VI.5, ed. Chiesa, p. 147; tr. Wright, pp. 207–8.

celebrated for its richness and splendour. The organ which Pepin the Short received as a gift from Constantine V also contributed to the empire's renown amongst the Franks (see below, p. 414).

Imperial building projects had the same goal and here, too, Theophilos was a master. He remodelled the Great Palace where, it is thought, Constantine V had built the church of the Mother of God of the Pharos in the previous century;[105] of the many buildings added by Theophilos, the best-known are the Triconch of the Sigma and the Sigma itself. Across the Bosporus Theophilos constructed the Palace of Bryas, which has yet to be identified with certainty, and he adorned St Sophia with the bronze doors that are still in place.[106]

This restructuring of the emperor's image went hand in hand with the reinforcement of dynastic rule. From Heraclius on, rulers crowned their eldest sons as co-emperors, although the form of coronation sometimes varied. In 776 Leo IV added to the ceremony an oath of loyalty to both emperors, which civilian and military officials, as well as notables, had to swear; this vow not to accept any emperor other than Leo's newly crowned son Constantine was signed by all and deposited in St Sophia.[107] The gold coinage gives an excellent example of the insistence on dynastic rule under the iconoclast emperors, for on their coins both the Isaurians and Theophilos showed images not only of their descendants, sometimes including their daughters, but also of their ancestors. So Constantine VI's father, grandfather and great-grandfather are all squeezed in on the reverse of his *nomisma*.[108] In this as in other areas, Irene is an exception; she was the only sovereign in the history of the empire to put her bust on *both* sides of the *nomisma*.

The Isaurians appear to have done most to boost the dynastic aspect of the imperial office. Indeed, it was Constantine V who created the legitimising concept of *porphyrogenitus* for his son Leo; being born-in-the-Porphyra – the chamber in the imperial palace covered with red marble – would become a prerequisite for the Macedonian emperors.[109] At the Easter ceremonies in 769, Constantine V made official the hierarchy of court titles given to members of the imperial family: his sons were given the titles of caesar and *nobelissimos*, as recorded in the *Book of ceremonies*.[110] Indeed the emperor's reception for the poor – given on the eighth day after Christmas in the Hall of the Nineteen Couches – should be dated to Constantine's period

---

[105] Theoph., ed. de Boor, I, p. 444; tr. Mango and Scott, pp. 612–14; Jenkins and Mango (1956), pp. 134–5; Magdalino (2004), pp. 20–3.

[106] Ricci (1998); Treadgold (1988), p. 323; Mango (1967).

[107] Theoph., ed. de Boor, I, pp. 449–50; tr. Mango and Scott, pp. 619–21.

[108] *DOC*, III.1, pp. 292, 406–10; Morrisson, *Catalogue des monnaies byzantines*, II, pp. 466, 514–15.

[109] Dagron (1994), pp. 112–13.

[110] *DC*, I.43, 44, ed. Reiske, pp. 217–29; Diehl (1905), pp. 269–302; Mango and Ševčenko (1972), p. 390.

Figure 11a Gold coin of Constantine VI
showing his ancestors squeezed onto the
reverse of the *nomisma* (below)

of rule, since a token of a 'pauper of the Nineteen Couches' dating from
his reign has been found.[111]

OATHS AND THE EMPRESS IRENE

Besides insisting on dynastic rule, the iconoclast emperors made other
innovations in the imperial office: they were keen on justice, and their
personal relations with their subjects were marked by the intensive use
of oaths. In fact, it would appear that by use of *silentia* they somehow
sought approval of their decision-making from the elite, and even from the
people. So far as justice is concerned, later chroniclers have given Leo V and
Theophilos the reputation of emperors close to their people, eager to right
the wrongs committed by their officials; and the Isaurians, who were accused
by their opponents of being litigious and fond of trials, demonstrated in
both the prologue and the text of the *Ecloga* just how much they considered

---

[111] Bendall and Nesbitt (1990).

Figure 11b Gold coin of Irene, portray-
ing her on *both* sides of the coin

good justice to be a vindication of their imperial office.[112] Its clear style,
easily comprehensible and focusing on the practical essentials of civic life,
ensured that this Isaurian compendium would long remain in use. Another
innovation of the *Ecloga* was to institute salaries for judges, so that their
decisions no longer depended on gifts offered by those on trial.[113]

The widespread use of oaths as a political instrument also appears to
be an iconoclast novelty, and Constantine V was probably the instigator.
According to Agapius of Membij he used oaths to reinforce the hereditary
transmission of imperial power, thereby binding his subjects to his son
Leo. According to Theophanes, Constantine also invoked the protection
of his other sons,[114] and as we have seen, Leo IV made taking an oath of
loyalty to his son into a ceremony involving the army and the entire body
politic. The swearing of loyalty oaths was subsequently taken to extremes
by Constantine VI and Irene; they demanded that oaths be sworn to both
of them, but on several occasions ordered further oaths to the exclusion

---

[112] TC, pp. 30–1, 87–8, 93–4; Nikephoros, *Antirrhetici*, III.62, cols. 487–8; French tr. Mondzain-
Baudinet, p. 267; Simon (1994), pp. 12–16.

[113] *Ecloga*, preface, lines 96–109, ed. and German tr. Burgmann, pp. 166–7; tr. Freshfield, p. 70.

[114] Agapius of Membij, *al-'Unwan*, ed. and French tr. Vasiliev, *PO* 8.3, p. 544; Theoph., ed. de Boor,
I, p. 450; tr. Mango and Scott, p. 621; Svoronos (1951), pp. 109, 119–21.

of one or the other, thus provoking the revolt of the Armeniakoi in 793. Constantine V put oath-taking to even broader use. In 766 he commanded that his subjects swear an oath not to bow down before religious images, and this was one of the points which made it difficult for the bishops to renounce iconoclasm twenty years later: they feared – rightly – the accusation of perjury, a crime for which the *Ecloga* prescribes the cutting out of the tongue.[115] It appears that the swearing of oaths was practised widely in this period, so much so that Theodore the Stoudite and the patriarch Nikephoros complained, and Irene sought to limit it.[116]

Another innovation under Leo III was the use of the *silention*; under Justinian I this had been a restricted council, but under Leo it became a type of special assembly in the Great Palace, convened by the emperor when he wanted to announce a particularly solemn decision. According to the *Life* of Stephen the Younger, a *silention* could even involve assembling all the people, when it was convened in the Hippodrome.[117] The populist tendencies of the iconoclast emperors, remarked upon by Nikephoros, are also evident in their use of mockery as a political weapon: under Constantine V the conspirators of 766, as well as the monks and Patriarch Constantine II, were all subjected to public ridicule in the Hippodrome; likewise, under Michael II, Thomas the Slav was mocked by the army before his execution.[118]

The characteristics of the iconoclast emperors – warlike, just and close to the people – bring a certain coherence to their reigns in the eighth and ninth centuries, in contrast to that of Irene. Perhaps because she was a woman and her position as *basileus* was in the strict sense exceptional, she took exactly the opposite course from her predecessors in every sphere. By blinding her son she made the dynastic transmission of power impossible; she abolished iconoclasm; she got rid of the elite corps of soldiers; she sued for peace when the battle was nearly won; she chose a patriarch from among the laity; and she set up an intermediary power between emperor and administration, entrusting the latter to her close advisers, the eunuchs of the Bedchamber. Thus Staurakios, logothete of the Drome in 782, remained in office until his disgrace in 800 and played a dominant role in Byzantine politics for twenty years.

---

[115] Theoph., ed. de Boor, I, p. 437; tr. Mango and Scott, pp. 604–5; Nikeph., ch. 81, ed. and tr. Mango, pp. 154–5; Mansi, XIII, col. 61; Ignatios the Deacon, *Life of Tarasios*, ch. 14, ed. and tr. Efthymiadis, pp. 86, 177; Nikephoros, *Refutatio*, ch. 23, ed. Featherstone, pp. 49–50; *Ecloga*, XVII.2, ed. and German tr. Burgmann, pp. 226–7; tr. Freshfield, p. 106.

[116] Nikephoros, *Antirrhetici*, III.62, cols. 487–8; French tr. Mondzain-Baudinet, p. 267; Theo. Stud., no. 7, lines 37–41, ed. Fatouros, I, p. 25; Burgmann (1981).

[117] Christophilopoulou (1951); SD, ch. 40, ed. and French tr. Auzépy, pp. 139–41, 235–7.

[118] Nikephoros, *Antirrhetici*, III.64, cols. 493–4; French tr. Mondzain-Baudinet, pp. 270–1; Theoph., ed. de Boor, I, pp. 437–8; tr. Mango and Scott, pp. 604–6; Rouan (1981), pp. 425–8; TC, p. 69.

The imperial office as reinforced by Constantine V was proof against this singular reign. It withstood both the diplomatic failures which led to the establishment of a rival empire in the west, and the military failures in the face of the caliphate's renewed offensive in Asia Minor; but in the end it was laxity in financial matters that led to Irene's downfall. The revolt against her came not from the army but from the offices of finance; Irene was deposed and replaced by the minister of the treasury, the general logothete Nikephoros, who had to reimpose the taxes which the empress in her benevolence had abolished.

CULTURE, PURIFICATION AND THE DRIVE AGAINST IDOLATRY

The religious policy of the period has deliberately been left until last, to prevent it eclipsing all other aspects, as so often happens. In fact, the religious direction taken is hardly surprising, inspired as it was by the misfortune of the times and the need to save the empire. However, it has been completely distorted by the violence of the anti-iconoclast polemics, transforming a well-thought-out and sound decision into the deranged impulse of ignorant men inspired by Satan. Iconodule propaganda is now being subjected to closer scrutiny. One example is the allegation that the iconoclasts were lacking in education (*amathia*). Because the chroniclers Theophanes and Nikephoros maintain that classical culture was dead at the beginning of the eighth century – for which Theophanes holds Leo III directly responsible[119] – and because polemical works accuse the iconoclasts of ignorance, it is generally considered that Byzantine society under the iconoclast emperors lost access to classical culture. This accusation is not altogether unfounded; with the disappearance or drastic contraction of towns, and the ruralisation of Asia Minor and the Balkans, there must have been an equivalent reduction in the number of books. Even in Constantinople, books became rare. A work such as the *Parastaseis*, in which self-styled philosophers show their non-comprehension of the masterpieces of classical art surrounding them in the capital, proves that there was no great flourishing of classical culture in the eighth century.[120] However, texts written in refined Greek started to emerge in the second half of the ninth century, presupposing continuity of literary studies during the eighth and ninth centuries, and there are several indications of such continuity. The saints' *Lives* of the period attest a functioning elementary and secondary educational system,[121] and there were some deeply learned men of letters of the beginning of the ninth century, including George Choiroboskos, deacon of St Sophia,

---

[119] Theoph., ed. de Boor, I, p. 405; tr. Mango and Scott, pp. 559–60; Nikeph., ch. 52, ed. and tr. Mango, pp. 120–1.
[120] Mango (1975a); *Parastaseis syntomoi chronikai*, ed. Preger; tr. Cameron and Herrin.
[121] Lemerle (1986), pp. 81–2, 108–15.

John the Grammarian, patriarch of Constantinople (837–43) and Leo the Mathematician. The Isaurians' reputation for ignorance has been reinforced in a sort of vicious circle by the fact that, at first sight, no manuscript of a scholarly nature has survived from this period. The famous uncial manuscript of Ptolemy's 'Handy Tables' with its miniature of the zodiac was attributed to the ninth century until it was demonstrated that the astronomical calculations it contains could only have been done during the reign of Constantine V.[122]

The accusation of *amathia* brought against the iconoclasts must be considered in its ideological context. In characterising the iconoclasts as ignorant, the iconodules certainly wanted to accuse them of grammatical ignorance; but above all they wanted to accuse them of ignorance of divine truth and thus blindness to the reality of the Incarnation, which had made representation of Christ possible. It is unlikely that the appearance of minuscule – a highly important development for Greek letters – could have occurred in a world devoid of culture, and its replacement of uncial script might almost be compared to the invention of the printing press. Minuscule's use of ligatures, accents and punctuation made it far quicker to write, easier to read and more economical in its use of paper and ink. Codicologists now date the use of minuscule in manuscripts to sometime around the 780s, in two distinct geographical areas: Constantinople and Palestine.[123] The earliest extant minuscule manuscript with a precise date is the 'Uspensky Gospels', dated to 835 by a notice of the scribe Nicholas, a monk of the Constantinopolitan monastery of Stoudios.[124] Exactly where minuscule writing originated remains unknown, but it is curious that the imperial palace has never been considered.

The religious policy of the iconoclast emperors Leo III, Constantine V and Leo IV in the eighth century, and of Leo V, Michael II and Theophilos in the ninth, should be understood as just one aspect of their struggle to ensure the empire's survival. Various explanations have been offered for Leo III's sudden ban on venerating icons in 730. The apparent aniconism of the eastern part of the empire is one suggestion. This was Leo's birthplace and seat of Bishops Constantine of Nakoleia and Thomas of Claudiopolis; according to Patriarch Germanos' letters read out at the second council of Nicaea, these two bishops had forbidden veneration of icons in their sees even before 730. Another suggestion is the supposed influence of Islam and Judaism; early in the 720s Caliph Yazid II (720–24) issued an edict banning Christian images, and the iconoclasts invoked the Old Testament ban on pictorial representation (Exodus 20:4). But the argument of eastern

---

[122] Ptolemy, 'Handy Tables', Biblioteca Apostolica Vaticana, MS. gr. 1291 (see fig. 12); Lemerle (1986), pp. 83–4; Wright (1985). See fig. 13.
[123] Fonkič (2000), pp. 181–2.
[124] 'Uspensky Gospels', St Petersburg, Rossiiskaia Natsionalnaia Biblioteka, RNB gr. 219 (see fig. 13).

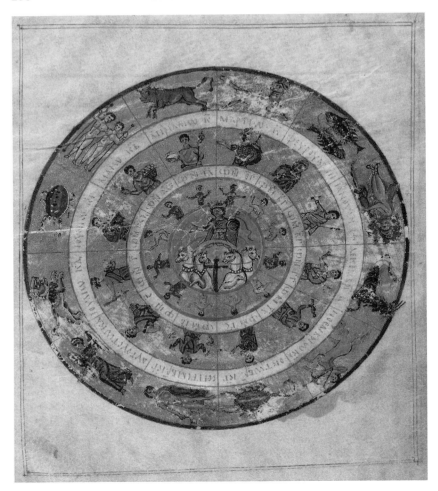

Figure 12 Zodiac from Ptolemy's 'Handy Tables' – a hint of intellectual life continuing in the eighth century

aniconism does not stand up to scrutiny, and Jewish and Muslim influences were only indirect.[125] The chroniclers do offer one plausible explanation for Leo III's decision: that iconoclasm was triggered off by Leo's false interpretation of the terrifying volcanic eruption at Thira in 726 as a manifestation of the wrath of God. He thought, wrongly they say, that God's wrath had been caused by the idolatry of the empire's subjects in venerating religious

---

[125] Auzépy (2004), pp. 135–42.

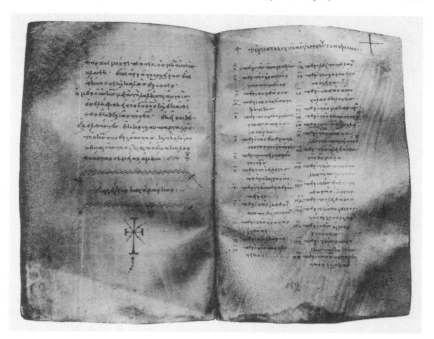

Figure 13 Manuscript of the Uspensky Gospels, dated to 835 – the earliest dated example of the new 'speed-writing' in minuscule, easier to read as well as faster to write than the previous form, uncial

images.[126] According to Theophanes, Leo launched a propaganda campaign in 725, and in the following year, the icon of Christ said to have been situated above the Great Palace's bronze gate (Chalke) was reportedly destroyed.[127] This culminated on 7 January 730 with Leo's declaration against icons, during a *silention* in the Hall of the Nineteen Couches. Patriarch Germanos refused to subscribe and was forced to resign, and opponents of the decisions taken at the *silention*, clerics and laymen alike, were persecuted.[128]

This explanation given by the chronicles is plausible enough. An emperor who considered himself divinely commanded to 'tend the most Christian people' in a manner pleasing to God, thereby obtaining military victories and domestic peace,[129] would understandably be concerned by such violent and repeated manifestations of God's wrath against his people. In the

---

[126] Nikeph., chs. 59–60, ed. and tr. Mango, pp. 128–9; Theoph., ed. de Boor, I, pp. 404–5; tr. Mango and Scott, pp. 558–60.

[127] Theoph., ed. de Boor, I, p. 405; tr. Mango and Scott, pp. 559–60; Auzépy (1990); Auzépy (2004), pp. 133–4.

[128] Nikeph., chs. 60, 62, ed. and tr. Mango, pp. 128–31; Theoph., ed. de Boor, I, pp. 404–5, 407–9; tr. Mango and Scott, pp. 558–60, 562–7.

[129] *Ecloga*, preface, lines 21–31, ed. and German tr. Burgmann, pp. 160–1; tr. Freshfield, pp. 66–7.

Bible, the reason why God abandons his people to the point where they are vanquished and led off to captivity in Babylon – a prospect anything but theoretical in Byzantium of the 720s – is none other than idolatry. Iconoclasm, in banning the veneration of religious images through such gestures and ritual as bowing down (*proskynēsis*), kissing (*aspasmos*), and the burning of lights and incense, is in fact nothing but a rejection of idolatry.[130] In all probability, Leo III aimed to please the Almighty by choosing iconoclasm; by banning idolatry, he might induce God to stop granting victories to the enemy and avert the threat of defeat and captivity from his people. And this choice might be considered a good one, seeing that God's wrath did in fact subside. The danger from the Arabs, and then from the Bulgars, abated and Isaurian propaganda was, according to Patriarch Nikephoros, able to ascribe these successes, as well as the longevity of the emperors, to iconoclasm.[131] Furthermore, it was precisely the renunciation of iconoclasm that coincided with defeat and then, under Nikephoros and Michael I, military disaster; and its reinstatement by Leo V in 815 was followed a year later by victory over the Bulgars. Thus, iconoclasm could well be considered as the religious component of the overall strategy for the empire's survival.

It is difficult to assess the cult of images at the beginning of the eighth century and to determine whether the Isaurians' charge of idolatry was justified. Scholarly opinion is divided, particularly as to when this cult arose.[132] At the council of Hieria in 754, the Isaurian bishops maintained that worship of images became widespread after the sixth council in 680.[133] This is possible, though it has not been proved. What we know of devotional practices would suggest that Leo III's diagnosis was not exaggerated. At the second council of Nicaea in 787, the bishops cited a passage from the *Miracles* of Cosmas and Damian as an authority favouring icons and their cults: this tells of a woman who was cured by drinking the scrapings from a fresco representing the saints.[134] And, in a letter to Louis the Pious (814–40) seeking to justify his attachment to iconoclasm, Michael II listed the practices he considered inadmissible: fragments of icons mixed in the eucharist, icons which served as altar tables, or as sponsors in baptism or monastic tonsure.[135]

The popularity of icons and their cult might also be explained by the misfortunes of the times. Icons were a refuge when daily life was disrupted and institutions no longer worked; they permitted a direct relationship

---

[130] Mansi, XIII, cols. 221C, 277D, 353C.

[131] Nikephoros, *Antirrhetici*, III.70, cols. 503–4; French tr. Mondzain-Baudinet, p. 278.

[132] Brubaker (1998) as against Delierneux (2001); Auzépy (2004), pp. 152–6.

[133] Mansi, XIII, cols. 217A, 221C, 225D; *Adversus Constantinum Caballinum*, ch. 13, col. 329. See also p. 235.

[134] Mansi, XIII, col. 68A–D; van den Ven (1955–7), no. 57, p. 356.

[135] Michael II and Theophilos, *Letter to Louis I*, pp. 478–9; McCormick (1994a), pp. 145–9.

with an intercessor, an individual devotion which did not need any church or clergy.[136] This would explain why Leo III's decision in 730 met with resistance – perhaps amplified by iconodule propaganda at the beginning of the ninth century, but still historically certain. Leo III overrode Patriarch Germanos' opposition, replacing him with Anastasios, his *synkellos*, but then came up against the patriarchs of Rome and Jerusalem. John of Jerusalem, with the support of John Damascene, virulently opposed the imperial policy of iconoclasm and sent round a synodal decision hostile to the emperor's proposition. This synodal decision, with later modifications, was transformed into a pamphlet entitled *Adversus Constantinum Caballinum*.[137] For his part, Pope Gregory II (715–31) rejected the synodal decision of Anastasios and wrote Leo letters of reproach. The only version we have of these is one revised and corrected by later polemicists, who put into Leo's mouth the famous saying: 'I am emperor and priest.'[138] Gregory's successor, Gregory III (731–41), condemned iconoclasm in November 731 at a provincial council whose acts have been lost.[139] There appears to have been no further debate on iconoclasm after this, even though Artabasdos authorised the cult of images while he held Constantinople.[140]

Constantine V finally decided to legitimise iconoclasm throughout the church by summoning a council; although this purported to be the seventh ecumenical council, it is generally known as the iconoclast council of Hieria. Judging by the quotations from his writings by Patriarch Nikephoros, collected under the title *Peuseis*, Constantine was himself a good theologian. He prepared the ground for the assembly with a public awareness campaign similar to that of his father before the *silention* of the Nineteen Couches. Constantine timed the council to coincide with the vacancy in the see of Constantinople following the death of Anastasios, assembling 338 bishops in the palace of Hieria on the eastern shore of the Bosporus from February to August 754.[141] This council must have had a disciplinary aspect, for it issued numerous (non-extant) canons, but its main decision was to ban the making and venerating of religious images upon pain of punishment. The argument hinged on the portrayal of Christ: this was rejected on Christological grounds, since Christ (being God and man) could not be delimited in a material figure without falling into the error of Nestorianism or into the confusion of monophysitism.[142] Unlike the decisions of the *silention* of

[136] Brown, P. (1973); Haldon (1997a), pp. 356–62.   [137] Auzépy (1995a).

[138] *LP*, XCI.24, ed. Duchesne, I, p. 409; tr. Davis, II, p. 16; Gouillard (1968), pp. 253–76; Pseudo-Gregory II, *Letters*, ed. and French tr. Gouillard, no. 2, pp. 298–9; Dagron (2003), pp. 158–66.

[139] *LP*, XCII.2–3, ed. Duchesne, I, pp. 415–16; tr. Davis, II, pp. 19–20; McCormick (2001), pp. 867–8.

[140] Theoph., ed. de Boor, I, p. 415; tr. Mango and Scott, pp. 575–6; Nikeph., ch. 64, ed. and tr. Mango, pp. 132–5; Gero (1977), pp. 15–19 as against Speck (1981), pp. 127–32.

[141] Nikeph., ch. 72, ed. and tr. Mango, pp. 142–3; Theoph., ed. de Boor, I, pp. 427–8; tr. Mango and Scott, pp. 589–92; MS, XI.24, ed. and French tr. Chabot, II, p. 520.

[142] Council of Hieria (754), *Horos*, Mansi, XIII, cols. 241, 244, 245, 252, 256.

the Nineteen Couches, the council of Hieria appears at first to have been accepted without demur. Iconoclasm became the orthodoxy of the empire, if not the *oikoumenē*. The papacy waited fifteen years before condemning the imperial policy of iconoclasm and the council of Hieria at the Lateran council of 769.

It was an internal crisis in the empire that brought Constantine V to violent action in the summer of 766, when a plot against him was thwarted. In fact the trouble began in November 765 with the execution of the monk Stephen the Younger, a friend of the conspirators. Stephen's execution was followed by the persecution of officials and a compulsory oath for all imperial subjects, abjuring veneration of saints' images. The climax came in August 766, when ceremonies of ridicule were organised in the Hippodrome – on 21 August against the monks, and four days later against the conspirators. Finally, there was a purge of those in positions of command. New *stratēgoi*, faithful to the emperor and his doctrines, were named to the themes of the Anatolikoi and Thrakesioi. Patriarch Constantine, suspected of complicity in the plot, was replaced by Niketas on 16 November 766, before undergoing cruel and humiliating punishment almost a year later in October 767. The *stratēgos* of the Thrakesioi, Michael Lachanodrakon, conducted a virulent campaign against both icons and monks in his theme, burning the former and forcing the latter to discard their monastic habits. Betrayal by the men he had trusted led the emperor to harden his policy. The persecution he launched against the monks was peculiar, aimed not at making them iconoclasts – which they had been since 754, like all imperial subjects – but at making them renounce their monastic state and take up clerical, civil or military positions. However, not all were affected, for Leo IV later named monks to the highest episcopal sees.[143]

REVITALISING THE CHURCH OF CONSTANTINOPLE

The Isaurians' religious policy was not limited exclusively to iconoclasm, although this was its major feature. It also had international ramifications, defending and extending the rights of the church of Constantinople. Thus, relations with the pope were always connected with imperial policy in Italy; Rome was subject to the empire, at least until 751, when the exarchate of Ravenna was seized by the Lombards. Indeed, according to Theophanes, Leo III's iconoclasm was the reason why Italy seceded.[144] But the Roman *Liber pontificalis* reports that Gregory II was initially opposed to the emperor's attempt to bring the taxes of the province of Rome into line with

---

[143] Nikeph., chs. 79–84, ed. and tr. Mango, pp. 150–61; Theoph., ed. de Boor, I, pp. 436–43, 449, 453; tr. Mango and Scott, pp. 603–12, 619–21, 625–6; SD, ed. and French tr. Auzépy, pp. 21–42 (introduction).
[144] Theoph., ed. de Boor, I, p. 413; tr. Mango and Scott, pp. 572–3.

those of the other provinces, particularly those payable by the churches; it was only later – at some indeterminate date after 725 – that Gregory refused the emperor's demand that he should accept iconoclasm.

The reaction of Leo III to papal opposition, which stiffened after the *silention* of the Nineteen Couches and Germanos' resignation, was highly effective. The church of Rome was deprived of the patrimony of St Peter both in Sicily, where imperial *stratēgoi* had been sent since the end of the seventh century, and in Calabria, which was dependent on the *stratēgos* of Sicily.[145] Thus after 732–3 the income from certain estates traditionally allocated to the church of Rome for, amongst other things, the lighting of places of worship and maintenance of the poor, reverted to the central tax administration – a hefty annual sum of some 350 pounds of gold, or 25,200 *nomismata*.[146] This measure perhaps explains the relatively high number of issues from the mint at Syracuse, in a period of general monetary restriction. The mint never struck silver coins, only copper and gold, and in fractions of the *nomisma* that had disappeared in the rest of the empire; although devalued after 820, this coinage circulated throughout Europe as far as the Crimea.[147] In 743, Constantine V partially compensated Gregory III's successor, Zacharias (741–52), for the loss incurred by the reallocation of these revenues by granting him the estates of Ninfa and Norma to the south of Rome. Lying between the hills of Volsci and the sea, they were not far from Terracina and Gaeta which were later claimed by the duchy of Naples, when it was an ally of the Byzantines.[148]

Finally, Leo III decided to harmonise political and ecclesiastical structures – probably in tandem with the measures of 732–3, and in any case before 754 – by placing such regions as were under the direct or indirect authority of the eastern empire beneath the patriarch of Constantinople's jurisdiction. The bishops of Illyricum, Crete, Sicily, Calabria and of the duchy of Naples, formerly subordinate to Rome, found themselves under the authority of Constantinople – although in the case of Naples, this lasted only until 769.[149] The transfer of these regions to Constantinople was probably accompanied by the confiscation of possessions from the church of Rome, such as happened in Istria in the 770s.[150]

[145] *LP*, XCI.16, 17, ed. Duchesne, I, pp. 403, 404–5; tr. Davis, II, pp. 10, 11–12.

[146] Theoph., ed. de Boor, I, p. 410; tr. Mango and Scott, pp. 567–70; Hadrian I, *Letter*, Mansi, XII, col. 1073; Noyé (1998), p. 233.

[147] Morrisson (1998); Morrisson (2001).

[148] *LP*, XCIII.20, ed. Duchesne, I, pp. 433, 438 and n. 45; tr. Davis, II, pp. 20, 46 and n. 78; Saxer (2001), p. 531; *CC*, no. 64, ed. Gundlach, p. 591; partial tr. King, pp. 289–90; McCormick (2001), p. 878. See also p. 443.

[149] Hadrian I, *Letter*, Mansi, XII, col. 1073; Anastos (1957).

[150] Saxer (2001), p. 531; *CC*, no. 63, ed. Gundlach, p. 590; partial tr. King, p. 289; McCormick (2001), p. 878.

The popes never accepted this reorganisation at patriarchal level, which was coupled with an adjustment of ecclesiastical structures to match the military situation. This entailed a similar reorganisation at episcopal level, disregarded until recently because of scholarly doubts about the source-value of the list of bishoprics known as the *Notitia* of the iconoclasts (*Notitiae episcopatuum*). Recent study, however, has shown that on several points this text gives an accurate picture of the church in the eighth century.[151] In Calabria and Thrace, the *kastra* built to accommodate the military and administrative authorities received the status of both city and bishopric from the emperor; the imperial right to bestow such status had been acknowledged at the council of Chalcedon (canon 17) and incorporated into canon 38 of the council *in Trullo*. Calabrian examples include Gerace, sometime before 787,[152] and the creation of the archbishopric of Santa Severina, probably after 736.[153] In Thrace, *kastra* such as Bulgarophygon, Skopelos and Develtos, which had been built or renovated by Constantine V and settled with captives taken on the Arab border, were made bishoprics, as their bishops' presence at the second council of Nicaea shows.[154] In Greece the bishoprics of Epirus Primus encircled the Peloponnese from Cephalonia to Aegina. They were sometimes located on smaller islands such as Orobe, which also served as relays for the fleet, as the numerous seals found on them attest.[155] The route to Italy was thus guarded by a military as well as an ecclesiastical network. This use of the church provides the background to Constantine V's policy towards the monasteries. His persecution cannot be described as bloody, seeing that it caused only two deaths, but he lifted previous exemptions from both individuals and property, reimposing liability to contribute to the state: monasteries and monastic lands as well as episcopal estates were sold, confiscated for military purposes or reallocated to the armed forces.[156]

The Isaurians saw the church as a reputable institution for which they were responsible, and the patriarchs as enforcers of the imperial will in ecclesiastical matters. Their expectations of subordination could sometimes be harsh and humiliating, as when Anastasios was paraded round the Hippodrome on an ass after the defeat of Artabasdos and then restored to the patriarchal throne; but the gift of the extension of jurisdiction westwards was ample compensation. The later iconodule patriarchs never questioned this gift to their institution made by an iconoclast emperor whom they had anathematised. In the *Acts* of the second council of Nicaea, Patriarch Tarasios (784–806) omitted translating into Greek the passages of

[151] Kountoura-Galake (1996b), pp. 121–43; Prigent (2002).
[152] Noyé (1998), p. 234; Prigent (2002), p. 938.   [153] Prigent (2002), pp. 939–46.
[154] Kountoura-Galake (1997); Darrouzès (1975), p. 54; Lamberz (2004), pp. 74–5.
[155] *NE*, no. 3, p. 245 (text); Darrouzès (1975), p. 37–8; Lamberz (2004), pp. 62–3; Avramea (1997), p. 99.

Pope Hadrian I's letter demanding the restitution of the patrimony of St Peter.[157]

Bishops formed the most important rank of the ecclesiastical hierarchy, residing in their sees and taking responsibility for charitable works, amongst other things. Judging by iconoclast-linked hagiographical sources, the bishop was deemed a model of holiness even worthier of emulation than the monk. However, it is possible that the episcopal office was the equivalent of a *strateia*, which could be purchased and which carried with it rights to the bishopric's revenues. In the *Ecloga* clerics are sometimes described as *strateuomenoi*, and even Tarasios admitted after the second council of Nicaea that most of the bishops present had bought their office, leaving them open to charges of simony by the monks.[158]

Iconoclasm provided the cement for the edifice, with duly anointed clergy delivering the people from idolatry through celebration of the eucharist. Constantine V sought to spread the doctrine adopted at Hieria throughout Christendom (see above, pp. 283–4) and conducted a vigorous diplomatic campaign aimed at Pippin the Short (751–68), sending numerous embassies and, it would seem, several eastern patriarchs. This campaign, whose success Pope Paul I briefly feared, finally ended in failure in the wake of the crisis of 766. The council of Gentilly (Easter 767) ratified the Carolingian rejection of iconoclasm, making possible its subsequent condemnation by the papacy at the Lateran council in 769; meanwhile, at least some of the eastern patriarchs sent a written condemnation of iconoclasm to Rome, which arrived in August 767.[159] The church of Constantinople was thereupon cut off from the other churches, and this probably explains Irene's desire to put an end to the situation.

FROM THE SECOND COUNCIL OF NICAEA (787) TO THE *SYNODIKON OF ORTHODOXY* (843)

The switch in imperial religious policy was the work of Irene and of Tarasios, the patriarch whom she had chosen after the death of his predecessor, Paul IV. Formerly head of the imperial chancellery (*prōtasekrētis*), on Christmas Day 784 Tarasios was elevated from layman to the patriarchal throne – a step frowned upon by Pope Hadrian I, as the Lateran council had banned this type of episcopal election.[160] Irene and Tarasios sought to give their new

---

[156] SD, ed. and French tr. Auzépy, pp. 36–7 (introduction).   [157] Lamberz (2001).

[158] *Life of George of Amastris*, chs. 16, 23–4, pp. 26–7, 36–7; Auzépy (1992), pp. 60–2; Mansi, XIII, col. 474E; Auzépy (1988), pp. 18–19.

[159] McCormick (1994a), pp. 113–32; Auzépy (1999), pp. 215–28.

[160] Ignatios the Deacon, *Life of Tarasios*, chs. 8–17, ed. and tr. Efthymiadis, pp. 78–91, 174–8 and p. 14 (introduction); Theoph., ed. de Boor, I, pp. 458–61; tr. Mango and Scott, pp. 631–5; *LP*, XCVI.20, ed. Duchesne, I, p. 476; tr. Davis, II, p. 99.

policy a solemnity comparable to that of the council of Hieria by calling an ecumenical council, and they gained the support of the pope, who sent two legates. However, this abrupt change in position did not go unopposed. The council first assembled on 1 August 786 in the church of the Holy Apostles in Constantinople, but was dispersed by soldiers of the *tagmata* – the schools and excubitors – who had the backing of several of the bishops taking part.[161] This did not discourage the empress. That autumn she tricked the soldiers of the *tagmata* into dispersing, by sending them to Asia Minor in response to an alleged Arab attack. She then had them disarmed, and reconstituted the City units with soldiers taken from the thematic army corps.[162] Tarasios, for his part, disarmed episcopal opposition; his first, novel, strategy was to invite the monks – possibly a group opposed to the bishops – to participate in the council, while allowing the bishops to keep their posts only on condition that the most notorious iconoclasts among them made a public admission of error. He also passed off two eastern monks as official envoys from the patriarchates of Antioch and Alexandria, so as to justify the council's claim to ecumenical status.[163] Finally, it was not in Constantinople but at Nicaea – a place full of symbolism for Christendom – that the 365 bishops and 132 monks assembled from 11 September to 1 October 787, and declared the making and venerating of religious images an article of faith.[164]

Christological arguments were abandoned in favour of other, less substantial ones, or even for unproven affirmations: the antiquity of icons and their cult; the impossibility of idolatry – necessarily pagan – after the coming of Christ; insistence on the incarnation of Christ, which rendered acceptable representation of that which had been seen; dismissal of the charge of idolatry by virtue of the name inscribed on the icon. The council's ruling that icons should receive *proskynēsis*, after thirty years' prohibition as idolatry, was not accepted as easily as iconodule propaganda would have us believe. The *Libri Carolini* mention civil war, and many of our early ninth-century sources – which are admittedly iconodule – deplore the number of people, clergymen included, who remained convinced iconoclasts, even if they stopped short of considering Constantine V a saint.[165] During the reign of Michael I (811–13), Theophanes' *Chronicle* mentions the heretics known as Athinganoi in Phrygia – probably the successors of the

[161] Mansi, XII, cols. 990B–991D, XIII, col. 459C; Ignatios the Deacon, *Life of Tarasios*, ch. 26, ed. and tr. Efthymiadis, pp. 100–1, 183; Theoph., ed. de Boor, I, pp. 461–2; tr. Mango and Scott, pp. 634–7.
[162] Theoph., ed. de Boor, I, p. 462; tr. Mango and Scott, pp. 635–7; Haldon (1984), pp. 239–42.
[163] Auzépy (1988); Auzépy (1999) pp. 211–28.
[164] Darrouzès (1975); Lamberz (2004); Janin (1975), pp. 427–41; Herrin (1987), pp. 417–23.
[165] *Opus Caroli*, II.24, III (*praefatio*), ed. Freeman and Meyvaert, pp. 282, 329; SD, ch. 38, ed. and French tr. Auzépy, pp. 137–8, 232–4; Theoph., ed. de Boor, I, pp. 488–9, 496–7; tr. Mango and Scott, pp. 668–72, 679–82; Nikephoros, *Antirrhetici*, III.69, cols. 501–4; French tr. Mondzain-Baudinet, pp. 277–8.

Montanists whose forced conversion under Leo III had failed – as well as the Paulicians. The latter had been active in the region of the Pontus since the end of the seventh century and under Theophilos and especially under Michael III, they became a military threat to the empire on the borders with the caliphate.[166] They were persecuted at the instigation of Patriarch Nikephoros, who pressed for capital punishment for them as well as for iconoclast abbots.

Religious policy changed again in 815 when Leo V (813–20), raised to the throne to save the empire, reinstated iconoclasm. Much like Leo III before him, he was unable to convince his patriarch, who was sent into exile. The change in policy was formalised by a provincial council assembled after Easter by the new patriarch, Theodotos Kassiteras; Theodotos was of the Melissenoi family and, like his predecessor, was a layman promoted overnight to the patriarchal throne. Hieria was re-established and the second council of Nicaea overturned. The cult of icons was forbidden, but this new iconoclasm was less intransigent: there was no longer any question of idols or idolatry, and images which were not actively venerated, for example those suspended high up, were permitted. New emphasis was laid on the argument that, since man is made in the image of God, any additional material image is superfluous.[167] In its preliminary stages between Christmas 814 and Easter 815, this new position initially met with staunch opposition from the patriarch, Nikephoros; from the bishops who had supported Tarasios or who had been trained by him, such as Euthymios of Sardis, Michael of Synada and Theophylact of Nikomedeia; and from many monks who had received their instruction during the iconodule interval. Foremost among the rebellious clergymen was Theodore, head of the great Constantinopolitan monastery of Stoudios. Theodore had already distinguished himself by his intransigence both to imperial power and to the patriarch, notably when Tarasios acceded to Constantine VI's second marriage. Theodore went into exile for a second time in 815, and was followed by other bishops and abbots who rejected the return to iconoclasm, notably Theophanes the Confessor, Makarios of Pelekete and Niketas of Medikion from Bithynia. This generation of anti-iconoclasts is well known, for it was celebrated in numerous saints' *Lives*.[168] Nevertheless, they were kept on the sidelines and iconoclasm remained the religious law of the empire under Michael II – who continued Leo V's policies, despite arranging his murder – and Theophilos. Michael II recalled those who had been exiled, but did not restore them to their positions, and the persecution under Theophilos,

---

[166] Theoph., ed. de Boor, I, p. 495; tr. Mango and Scott, pp. 678–9; Gouillard (1965), pp. 307–12; Lemerle (1973), pp. 75–90.
[167] Alexander (1953); Alexander (1958b).
[168] Alexander (1958a), pp. 136–55; *Byzantine defenders of images*, ed. Talbot.

Figure 14 The emperor who resumed the drive against 'idols' and his fellow iconoclasts were execrated by iconodules after the restoration of icon-veneration in 843 and throughout the later history of Byzantium and orthodoxy: this miniature from the Theodore Psalter of 1066 from the Stoudios Monastery in Constantinople shows Theodore the Stoudite in discussion with Leo V and Patriarch Nikephoros, beside iconoclasts defacing the image of Christ

denounced in the hagiographic texts, seems to have been motivated more by political than by religious considerations.[169]

Theophilos' death when his son was barely two years old brought about a final change in religious policy, less well documented than the earlier ones. Yet again the patriarch was got rid of: John the Grammarian (837–42) was replaced by Methodios, an iconodule monk with so much influence that Theophilos had preferred to keep him close at hand in the palace. But this time the re-establishment of images was definitive; it was not only the result of a decision by an assembly of church authorities, but also took liturgical form on 11 March 843, the first Sunday of Lent. This Sunday became a celebration of the re-establishment of images and was soon named the Feast of orthodoxy, when the *Synodikon of orthodoxy* was read out. This document, celebrating the triumph over the iconoclasts' heresy, has become the symbol of the orthodox faith, receiving successive additions over the centuries concerning other heresies.[170]

From the 850s iconoclasm belonged to the past in so far as Patriarch Methodios had purged the clergy, but the repeated 'U-turns' in religious policy over more than a century had lasting consequences. With the victory of iconodulism the patriarchate was able to affirm the church's autonomy from imperial power, which was accused of encroaching on its domain by imposing religious norms, as encapsulated in the celebrated phrase put in Leo III's mouth: 'I am emperor and priest.' Moves towards an independent sphere for the church had begun in Rome in the seventh century with the monothelite crisis. The pope then affirmed his autonomy in the eighth century by associating himself with the Carolingians and creating his own temporal base. In the ninth century it was the patriarch of Constantinople who, through opposing the imperial policy of iconoclasm with the help of unprecedentedly vehement texts, excluded the emperor from questions of dogma and assumed the position of head of the church. This new

[169] Dagron (1993), pp. 143–7; Auzépy (2003), pp. 432–9.
[170] Gouillard, 'Synodikon de l'Orthodoxie', pp. 120–33, 161–8.

equilibrium between church and imperial power – albeit unequal because the emperors still named the patriarchs – was expressed in the *Eisagōgē*; probably drawn up by Photios, this described the patriarch as the 'image of Christ', whereas the emperor is only the 'legitimate authority'.[171]

By the end of the iconoclast period the empire had been transformed. Henceforth it would be characterised by religious peace; by a new orthodoxy now fixed in liturgical and iconic repetition; by a provincial administration structured by war around the theme, which had become the sole civil and military administrative unit; and by a central administration regrouped around the emperor but divided into large departments. The shock of the invasions had passed and, owing in part to the survival of its capital, the empire metamorphosed into a great Balkano-Anatolian power, administered coherently and financed through an effective tax system. This transformation made possible the initiatives and achievements of the period that followed.

---

[171] Auzépy (1999), pp. 300–11; Afinogenov (1994); Afinogenov (1996); Dagron (1993), pp. 202–7; Dagron (2003), pp. 223–35.

CHAPTER 6

AFTER ICONOCLASM (850–886)

SHAUN TOUGHER

INTRODUCTION

Two emperors dominate the generation or so following iconoclasm, Michael III the Amorian (842–67) and Basil I the Macedonian (867–86).[1] The story of this pair is intimately intertwined, although it climaxed with the assassination of the former at the instigation of the latter on the night of 23 September 867 in Michael's bedroom in the palace of St Mamas. Thus began the long ascendancy of the Macedonian dynasty, which witnessed the peak of Byzantium's power. A clear understanding of the reigns of Michael and Basil is, however, fraught with difficulty given the nature of our main narrative sources. These are both late – dating to the mid-tenth century – and polarised.[2] The Macedonians were naturally keen to justify the ousting of Michael III, so he is depicted in Theophanes Continuatus and Genesios as unworthy of imperial power and deserving of his fate.[3] The Macedonians were also concerned to present Basil in the best possible light, as God-favoured and preordained to rule.[4] The most famous expression of this is the *Life of Basil* (which forms book five of Theophanes Continuatus' chronicle), written in the reign of his grandson Constantine VII Porphyrogenitus (945–59), though we also have Leo VI's *Funeral oration for Basil I* (dated to 888) and poems and artefacts from Basil's reign.[5] However, a hostile view of Basil is provided by the chronicle of Symeon the Logothete, which also treats Michael more ambiguously.[6] Despite these sources'

---

[1] There is still no monograph on Michael III, but see *PMBZ*, #4991. For Basil I we have Vogt (1908); see also *PMBZ*, #832.

[2] For the narrative sources in general see Markopoulos (2003) with bibliography; for Michael's reign: Karlin-Hayter (1971).

[3] For the *Chronographia* of Theophanes Continuatus see Nickles (1937); Jenkins (1948); Jenkins (1954). On Genesios, see the introduction to Gen., tr. and comm. Kaldellis.

[4] See Agapitos (1989).

[5] On the authorship of the *Life of Basil* see Ševčenko, I. (1992a). For the funeral oration: Leo VI, *Funeral oration for Basil I*, ed. and French tr. Vogt and Hausherr; Adontz (1933). For other sources and artefacts see e.g. Markopoulos (1992); Magdalino (1987); Brubaker (1999a), pp. 147–200.

[6] On the chronicle of Symeon the Logothete: Bury (1912), pp. 455–9; Jenkins (1965); Karlin-Hayter (1991a); Wahlgren (2001). See now Symeon [Magister] the Logothete, *Chronicle*, ed. Wahlgren.

polarity and emphasis on court politics it is clear that there was continuity in the goals of the two regimes. The security of the east was paramount, although the west was still of concern. The government also had to cope with the Arab naval menace and the potential Bulgar threat from the north. New opportunities were seized when they arose, among Moravians, Armenians and the Rus. Such were the achievements of an era that it is usually characterised as a decisive turning-point, if not a *belle époque*. But it is clear that they followed upon an already advancing recovery, as much a cultural as a political revival. One should also recognise that this was not a period of unbroken success.

COURT POLITICS 842–867

The elimination of Michael III was the culmination of a power struggle that had been going on for most of his reign. When Michael succeeded his father in 842 he was only a child, probably two years old.[7] This necessitated the establishment of a regency headed by his mother, Empress Theodora (842–56).[8] The dominant force, however, appears to have been the eunuch Theoktistos, who was logothete of the Drome and *epi tou kanikleiou*, and a key agent of the Amorian dynasty.[9] Theoktistos appears to have had no love for the empress' brother Bardas, who found himself excluded from political power. When Michael approached adulthood, but was still constrained by the wishes of Theodora and Theoktistos – who arranged his marriage to Eudocia Dekapolitissa despite his supposed attachment to Eudocia Ingerina – it seems that Bardas seized the moment and persuaded his nephew to consent to a plot to remove Theoktistos. In 855 the eunuch was murdered in the palace and Theodora soon found herself formally barred from government. She still appears to have hankered after position and influence, for she was implicated in a plot against Bardas. He, however, was firmly in the ascendant, and is credited with running the empire until his death in 866. Bardas' government is often glowingly praised, as is his fostering of intellectual life by the establishment of the school of the Magnaura.[10] His importance is reflected by his developing career as well as the careers of those close to him. He served as domestic of the Schools and rose through a series of titles, eventually attaining the honour of caesar. His brother Petronas replaced him as domestic of the Schools. Photios, a relative of the Amorian house[11] and a close ally of Bardas, became patriarch of Constantinople in 858 on the deposition of Ignatios, who had opposed Bardas.

---

[7] Mango (1967).   [8] On Theodora: Garland (1999), pp. 95–108; Herrin (2001), pp. 185–239.

[9] For a positive assessment of Theoktistos: Grégoire (1966), pp. 105–8.

[10] Bury (1912), pp. 161, 439; Jenkins (1966), pp. 160, 164; Ostrogorsky (1968), pp. 223–4. On the school: Lemerle (1986), pp. 183–5.

[11] Mango (1977), esp. pp. 9–12.

What the ultimate ambitions of Bardas were is a moot point; his career was cut short in 866 when he was murdered while preparing to embark on an expedition to Crete. Afterwards the reason given for his death was that he had been plotting to overthrow Michael, but it is possible that Bardas had simply fallen victim to the ambitions of others, not least the emperor's favourite, Basil the Macedonian.

The origins of Basil the Macedonian are obscure and the story of his rise to prominence and power is spiced with colourful episodes, still the stuff of analysis and debate.[12] Basil's sobriquet, 'the Macedonian', is thought to refer to his provenance from the theme of Macedonia, not Macedonia itself, although the *Life of Basil* asserts that his ancestors were originally settled in Macedonia. The Macedonian claim recalled the famed figures of Philip and Alexander the Great.[13] Basil seems also to have had Armenian blood in his veins,[14] and the dynasty was to claim descent from the Arsacids.[15] Our narrative sources relate that the infant Basil was among the citizens of Adrianople seized and transported across the Danube by the Bulgar khan Krum (*c.* 803–14), and Symeon the Logothete specifies that he was born in the reign of Michael I (811–13).[16] While some scholars accept this date of birth, estimating that Basil was fifty-five years old when he became emperor,[17] others are less sure.[18] Certainly the narrative sources also depict Basil as still a young man when he made his way to Constantinople to make his fortune in the mid-850s. The stories about Basil's developing career, dependent on the favour of a variety of patrons, suggest a lowly background, undermining the *Life of Basil*'s assertion of his not undistinguished ancestry. His peasant origins are not contested by modern historians, and are in fact supported by the Davidic imagery embraced by Basil.[19] Having been taken in by Nicholas, keeper of the church of St Diomedes – in whose porch Basil had slept on his first night in Constantinople – Basil soon moved on to the service of Theophilitzes; he ended up working for Michael III himself, having cemented a social relationship with the wealthy Peloponnesian

[12] Moravcsik (1961).

[13] Schminck (2000), pp. 67–8, argues that this is why Basil was fancied to be a Macedonian, rejecting the view that Adrianople was in the theme of Macedonia. The *Life of Basil* claims that Basil's mother was descended from both Alexander the Great and Constantine the Great: *Life of Basil*, pp. 215–16. On the Macedonian link with Constantine, see Markopoulos (1994).

[14] Adontz (1933–4). Ostrogorsky (1968), p. 232, n. 2, and Schminck (2000), pp. 64–7, are sceptical, but most seem happy with Basil's Armenian origin, e.g. Treadgold (2001), p. 133.

[15] Markopoulos (1994), p. 163. According to the *Life of Ignatios* (cols. 565, 568) and Pseudo-Symeon (*Chronicle*, p. 689) Photios invented a genealogy for Basil which made him a descendant of the Armenian king Tiridates.

[16] GMC, p. 817. On the Bulgarian episode see Kislinger (1981).

[17] Treadgold (2001), p. 133.   [18] For example Brooks (1911); Adontz (1933–4).

[19] See Markopoulos (1992), pp. 227–8; Markopoulos (1994), pp. 161–2; Brubaker (1999a), pp. 183–93; Dagron (2003), pp. 199–200.

Figure 15 Illustration from the Madrid Skylitzes: Michael III racing near the church of St Mamas

widow Danelis along the way.[20] Genesios relates that Michael first met Basil after hearing of his participation in a wrestling match and summoning the wrestlers to come before him; but our other sources assert that the encounter occurred when Basil managed to break in one of the emperor's horses. This episode has suspicious overtones of Alexander and Bucephalus,[21] but it does tie in with Basil's subsequent career. He was enrolled among the imperial grooms, and after the failure of Theodora's plot against Bardas he was made head groom (*prōtostratōr*); the previous incumbent of the post had been executed as a conspirator. Perhaps Basil's equine skills endeared him to Michael, since the emperor's passions included hunting and chariot-racing; his enthusiasm for equestrian pastimes is also conveyed by his construction of luxury stables.

Our narrative sources make clear that there was an intense bond between Michael and Basil.[22] It has been suggested that there was in fact a sexual relationship between the two men, although some scholars have no truck with this hypothesis.[23] The appointment of Basil as *parakoimōmenos* (after the fall of his predecessor Damian) does suggest an unusual state of

[20] After becoming emperor, Basil rewarded Nicholas, his family and the institution. On Theophilitzes: Tougher (1999), p. 154. For Danelis: Tougher (1997b), pp. 27–8, 129–30, with bibliography.

[21] Gen., IV.26, ed. Lesmüller-Werner and Thurn, p. 78; tr. Kaldellis, p. 98 makes explicit the echo, and also recalls Bellerophon and Pegasus.

[22] For example, the strong language used to describe their relationship: e.g. GMC, pp. 825, 832; Gen., IV.27–8, ed. Lesmüller-Werner and Thurn, pp. 78–80; tr. Kaldellis, pp. 98–9.

[23] For discussion: Tougher (1999). For acceptance of Michael's homosexuality, see Schminck (2000), pp. 61–4; for rejection, Treadgold (1997), p. 943, n. 11.

affairs, seeing that the position was normally assigned to eunuchs.[24] The name of the post itself, though generally understood as 'chief eunuch' or 'grand chamberlain', literally means 'sleeping beside' and thus indicates close physical proximity. The question of the relationship between Michael and Basil is further complicated by the fact that Basil married Eudocia Ingerina. Symeon the Logothete provides further information about this union: Michael arranged for Basil to marry Eudocia, having separated him from his first wife Maria. However, Eudocia was to remain as the emperor's mistress, while Basil was to have Michael's sister Thekla in recompense. Some historians have accepted these details, as well as Symeon the Logothete's report that the future Leo VI (886–912) was Michael's son.[25] The account and its interpretation can, however, be questioned.[26] The hostility of the Logothete should not be overlooked, nor should details be cherry-picked.[27] It is perfectly possible that Leo was a son of Basil.

Whatever the truth about the relationship between Michael, Basil and Eudocia, it is clear that the two men were still close in 866 when Bardas was assassinated. Following their return to Constantinople after aborting the Cretan expedition, Basil was adopted by Michael, given the title of *magistros* and then quickly crowned as co-emperor. Since Basil had Michael murdered in his bedchamber just over a year later, their relations obviously deteriorated. Perhaps Basil had always set his sights on sole power, or perhaps Michael and Basil simply lost trust in one another. The sources present alternatives according to their biases, and we must judge for ourselves. Clearly Michael suffers from receiving negative treatment, and some have sought to defend his reputation, even to the extent of claiming him as a great emperor.[28] Others have recognised the hostility of the Macedonians but have felt that to reinterpret Michael as great is going too far, and that the sources' calumny contains a grain of truth.[29] It is acknowledged, too, that whatever one thinks of Basil's motives his reign was generally successful, even if the *Life of Basil* exaggerates his greatness. Certainly Basil built on the achievements of the age of Michael III, and it is salutary to turn from court conflicts to the continuities of foreign policy.

---

[24] Tougher (1997a), pp. 171–2.

[25] The classic interpretation is Mango (1973a). Treadgold (1997), p. 453 accepts Mango's case.

[26] E.g. Kislinger (1983), pp. 128–32; Karlin-Hayter (1991b); Tougher (1997b), pp. 43–5.

[27] For instance Symeon the Logothete declares that Constantine, too, was a son of Michael. This is argued away by asserting that Constantine was a son of Basil and Maria (e.g. Adontz (1933), p. 509); but there is no Byzantine testimony to this effect. It is possible that Constantine was a son of Basil and Eudocia.

[28] On Michael's image: Kislinger (1987); Liubarsky (1987). Henri Grégoire was a notable champion of Michael, e.g. Grégoire (1966), pp. 105–15; see also Karlin-Hayter (1989).

[29] E.g. Bury (1912), p. 162; Jenkins (1966), pp. 156–7; Ostrogorsky (1968), p. 223. Treadgold (1997), pp. 450–5 accepts the negative image of Michael.

EXTERNAL AFFAIRS 850–886

The main concern of Byzantium was the Muslim threat.[30] The focus fell naturally on the eastern frontier, beyond which lay the Abbasid caliphate. By the mid-ninth century, however, the caliphate was no longer launching full-scale invasions, and the raids into Byzantine territory were largely headed by the amirs of Tarsus and Melitene. The reign of Michael III was marked by a series of successes against the Arabs on land: there were Byzantine victories in 855 and 859, the latter led by the emperor himself. Inscriptions at Nicaea and Ankyra from this period recording their fortification by Michael are suggestive of a concerted effort.[31] However, 863 is the famous date, often seen as a turning-point in the Byzantine–Arab conflict on the eastern frontier; thereafter the Byzantines were able to go on the offensive, eventually triumphing in the tenth century.[32] In this year Michael's uncle Petronas defeated the army of the amir of Melitene, who was killed in the engagement.[33] During Basil's reign, however, the Byzantines were preoccupied with crushing the Paulicians. The Paulicians were a religious group of Armenian origin deemed heretical by orthodox Byzantines, and they formed distinctive communities in the eastern borderlands.[34] Following the restoration of icons under Theodora they were severely persecuted, but found sanctuary on the upper Euphrates, and Tephrike became their power centre. The Paulicians joined the Byzantines' enemies on the eastern frontier, assisting the raids of the amir of Melitene. Their leader Karbeas died in 863, but his nephew and successor Chrysocheir appears to have been even more formidable, penetrating into Asia Minor. It was the domestic of the Schools and relative of Basil, Christopher, who managed to defeat the Paulician leader in 872, though Tephrike was only taken in 878. Basil's efforts against Arab targets had more limited success, and his reign witnessed defeats such as the failed attack on Tarsus in 883. It seems that the reorganisation of the eastern frontier in the second half of the ninth and early tenth centuries was as important as military victories for increasing Byzantium's strength.[35]

The Byzantines did not just face land war in the east; the Arabs were also a potent naval threat. The struggle for security at sea had intensified after Muslims originally from Spain had seized Crete, a vital strategic location, in the 820s (see above, p. 256). The Byzantines tried to rectify this situation. In the first year of the regency Theoktistos led an expedition to Crete, and Michael and Bardas were preparing to sail there when the caesar was

---

[30] For Byzantium and the Arabs, see below, ch. 9; Vasiliev (1935–68). See also the translation of al-Tabari, *Ta'rikh*, general ed. Yarshater.
[31] Grégoire (1966), p. 110. See also above, p. 265.   [32] Whittow (1996a), p. 311.
[33] Huxley (1975).   [34] See Lemerle (1973); Ludwig (1998); above, p. 289.
[35] Whittow (1996a), p. 315.

murdered in 866. The reoccupation of Crete was clearly a consistent goal, but one only achieved in 961. The Byzantines are, however, credited with a successful assault on Damietta in Egypt in 853.[36]

A naval response was also called for in the case of Sicily, as the Arabs extended their control of the island and threatened southern Italy: their castle-by-castle advance culminated in the fall of Syracuse in 878.[37] Despite this event Basil I launched a concerted effort to maintain Byzantine power in the west.[38] When the Arabs threatened Ragusa in 867, the emperor responded emphatically, no doubt as concerned to stem the expansion of the Arabs as to tackle the specific problem of southern Italy and Sicily. To address the latter situation in 868 Basil entered into alliance with the Frankish emperor Louis II (855–75), who was campaigning against the Arabs in southern Italy on his own account, with the Byzantines supplying naval assistance. This arrangement was cemented with the engagement of Basil's eldest son Constantine to Louis' daughter. However, the alliance foundered, and Louis' ambitions faltered and then died with him in 875.[39]

Despite this setback Basil maintained his aspirations. Otranto was occupied in 873, and three years later Bari was regained, as was Taranto in 880. In the closing years of Basil's reign the general Nikephoros Phokas (grandfather of the future emperor of the same name) was active in southern Italy, and increased Byzantine control of Apulia and Calabria.[40] It appears that the successes of the early Macedonians were assisted by the revival of the imperial fleet and the creation of new naval themes.[41] Basil was well served by admirals such as Niketas Ooryphas and Nasar (anticipating Himerios under Leo VI), who were active throughout the Mediterranean; one success was the temporary occupation of Cyprus. Thus although Sicily slipped inexorably from Byzantine control, the empire did provide some response to the Arab naval threat. Yet this remained intractable, persisting into the reign of Leo VI (see below, pp. 499–500). A strong presence was, however, re-established in southern Italy, and was soon enhanced. Byzantine ambitions there remained live down to the twelfth century.

Besides the Muslims, the Byzantines' other major bugbear had been the Bulgars on the northern frontier, with their centre near the lower Danube at Pliska.[42] As recently as 811 Nikephoros I (802–11) had been killed on campaign against them. Khan Krum subsequently ventured against Constantinople, only to die in 814 (see above, p. 257). Following his death there was an extended phase of peace between Byzantium and the Bulgars.

[36] Grégoire (1966), pp. 106–7.   [37] See below, p. 462.
[38] See Gay (1904), pp. 79–145; Kreutz (1991), pp. 41–7, 62–3.   [39] See below, p. 419.
[40] On Nikephoros Phokas: Grégoire (1953); Tougher (1997b), pp. 204–7; below, pp. 504, 560.
[41] Ahrweiler (1966), pp. 96–9. See also above, p. 286.
[42] Fine (1983); Whittow (1996a), pp. 262–85.

For the mid-ninth century the key issue was religion. Under Khan Boris (*c.* 852–89) Christianity was spreading in the Balkans, and Boris contemplated conversion. He sought missionaries from the Franks, but Byzantium was probably uneasy at Frankish interference so close to Constantinople. The exact course of events is controversial, but whether or not Boris was threatened by a Byzantine invasion, Boris turned to Byzantium for a Christian mission.[43] In the mid-860s Boris was baptised, taking the Christian name of his godfather, Michael III himself. Thus it looked as if Byzantine cultural influence in Bulgaria was assured. However, in 866 Boris turned to the papacy, seeking advice and an archbishop from Pope Nicholas I (858–67), who was then happy to score points against Constantinople.[44] Papal missionaries replaced Byzantine ones. But Boris found his plans for the Bulgarian archbishopric thwarted, and in 870 cannily returned to the Byzantine fold; he procured an archbishop by skilful manoeuvring at the time of the 869–70 church council in Constantinople. Byzantine cultural influence was secured, although this also fuelled the political ambitions of Bulgaria, which were to burst forth under Boris' even cannier son, Symeon (893–927). For the reigns of Michael III and Basil I, though, the relationship between Byzantium and Bulgaria was remarkably peaceful, and this probably freed up military energy for release elsewhere.

For Byzantium the traditional concerns in the sphere of foreign affairs were the Arabs and Bulgaria, but new problems arose. The most dramatic came from the north.[45] In 860 a Rus fleet suddenly appeared before Constantinople, having sailed across the Black Sea, though probably not from Kiev, which was yet to develop as a political centre. The raiders subjected the suburbs around the imperial city to plunder. Michael III was away on campaign, but he hurried back when informed of the assault. However, the fleet soon departed, perhaps simply through having amassed enough booty rather than being driven away by an act of God. While it seems that the Rus were already known to the Byzantines, the events of 860 made a deep impact. Byzantium responded to the Rus' subsequent request for a mission, although this mission does not seem to have lasted long (see below, p. 320). The relationship remained mixed, with further Rus raids in the tenth century but also trading treaties and Rus serving with the imperial forces. Diplomatic and cultural contacts intensified, leading ultimately to the conversion of Prince Vladimir of Kiev and his people *c.* 988 (see below, pp. 325–6).

[43] For traditional acceptance of a Byzantine invasion see e.g. Whittow (1996a), p. 282. For the view that Boris freely turned to the Byzantines: Shepard (1995a), pp. 239–40; Zuckerman (2000a), pp. 118–200.

[44] On the conflict between Rome and Constantinople under Photios: Dvornik (1948); Dagron (1993); pp. 169–83; Simeonova (1998a). See also below, pp. 318–19.

[45] On the Rus: Franklin and Shepard (1996); Whittow (1996a), pp. 241–62. For the raid of 860 see also Vasiliev (1946).

Soon after the Rus raid, another avenue for Byzantine cultural influence opened up, when Prince Rastislav of Moravia (846–70) requested churchmen.[46] It is likely that Rastislav, sandwiched between Franks and Bulgars, turned to Byzantium in the hope of securing a political counterweight. The Byzantines embraced the opportunity, despatching in 863 the famous brothers Constantine and Methodios. They hailed from Thessaloniki, and Constantine had especially strong bonds with the court and intellectual circles of Constantinople.[47] To pursue their mission in Moravia they sought to spread the word in the language of the Slavs, and to this end developed a Slavic alphabet, the first of its kind, and translated many religious texts into the literary language they coined. Their mission dissolved after the death of Rastislav and disengagement of other Slav princely patrons, who came under Frankish pressure. But their disciples had an impact in the newly Christianised Bulgaria of Boris, where they ended up as refugees after being expelled from Moravia in 885. Installed at Ohrid and Pliska, they were entrusted with the creation of a Slavic clergy and expounding Christianity in comprehensible Slavic, lessening the need for Byzantine-born clergy; but Greek remained the language of court ceremonial and, probably, the liturgy.[48] Thus the outcome of the mission to Moravia had unintended consequences, not necessarily advantageous to Byzantium in so far as they nurtured the aspirations of Symeon, Boris' son.

A final development lay to the east.[49] Armenia had fallen under Arab overlordship from the end of the seventh century, and the leading Armenian families (the Bagratuni and the Artsruni) had assisted in the Arab sack of Amorion in 838. But with the decentralisation of the Abbasid caliphate there came the opportunity for greater independence, and this was exploited by Ashot I Bagratuni ('the Great'), prince of princes, who in 884 was crowned king of Armenia. Under Michael III and Basil I political relations with Armenia were fostered, Basil recognising Ashot as prince of princes (*archōn tōn archontōn*).[50] These friendly relations persisted into the tenth century, and assisted in Byzantium's expansion eastwards.

COURT POLITICS 867–886

Compared with the shenanigans of the court politics of Michael III's reign, court politics in the reign of Basil I seem relatively tranquil. Turbulence is concentrated at the extremes of his period of rule. Following the assassination of Bardas and the elevation of Basil, one of the main conspirators,

---

[46] For the mission to Moravia and its aftermath, see below, pp. 316–18; Dvornik (1970); Tachiaos (2001).

[47] Constantine had already been on a mission to the Khazars: see below, p. 315.

[48] See Goldberg (2006), pp. 270–1, 280–1; Hannick (1993), pp. 930–4.

[49] For Armenia, see below, ch. 8; Whittow (1996a), pp. 195–220; Grousset (1947).

[50] On ecclesiastical relations between Armenia and Byzantium under Photios, see below, pp. 351–2.

Bardas' son-in-law Symbatios, felt sidelined and came out in revolt. This was apparently aimed at Basil, not Michael, but was anyway suppressed, and Symbatios and his accomplice Peganes found themselves mutilated and forced to beg in the streets of Constantinople. With the assassination of Michael, Basil clearly had to justify himself, and judging by the amount of propaganda produced under the new regime much energy was devoted to this task. Following the murder, one of Basil's first main steps was to depose Patriarch Photios (858–67, 877–86) and reinstall Ignatios.

These acts of Basil have been viewed in the light of ecclesiastical politics, namely the tensions between Rome and Constantinople that had set in during the patriarchate of Photios and the supposed internal division between 'extremists' and 'moderates'. The existence of these opposing 'politico-religious' groups was formulated by Francis Dvornik, who saw them as competing for control over church and state in Byzantium.[51] The extremists were identified as traditional and conservative Christians, mainly monks and their supporters. The moderates were considered those more in touch with the realities of earthly life, and more willing to compromise in the matter of Christian ideals. Amongst their number Dvornik included the secular clergy and intellectuals. Basil's ousting of Photios and favouring of Ignatios was read by Dvornik as signifying that the emperor threw in his lot with the extremists in a bid to secure support for his regime. Even if one accepts the existence of these two factions in Byzantine society – and surely such a formulaic reading of history is open to question – it is perfectly possible that Basil was simply motivated by the desire to eliminate a political rival: Photios had close connections with the Amorian dynasty and could have headed opposition to the usurper.[52] However, Photios later returned to favour, taught Basil's children, and became patriarch again upon Ignatios' death in 877.[53]

Ironically, it seems that the rehabilitated Photios had a part to play in contributing to, and even shaping, the ideology of the new regime.[54] Basil was cast as the legitimate God-favoured restorer of the Roman empire. The appeals to Armenian ancestry and Davidic imagery appear to have had some input from Photios, even while he was still in exile.[55] The dynasty's ideological concerns, including devotion to the prophet Elijah and the archangel Gabriel, are reflected in the illustrated copy of the homilies of Gregory Nazianzen presented to Basil c. 880, the commissioning of which has been attributed to Photios (see fig. 16).[56] Photios' fingerprints have also

---

[51] Dvornik (1948), pp. 9–18.   [52] Tougher (1997b), pp. 76–8.
[53] On Photios' fall, exile and rehabilitation see e.g. Dvornik (1948), pp. 136–7, 161–73; Dagron (1993), pp. 176, 180–1; Simeonova (1998a), pp. 247–8, 280–91.
[54] Tougher (1997b), pp. 32, 70–1.
[55] See Ciccolella (1998), esp. pp. 325–8; Markopoulos (1992), pp. 226–9; Magdalino (1987), p. 58.
[56] See Brubaker (1999a), esp. 147–200; Dagron (2003), pp. 193–9.

been detected on Basil's legislative work, which was to culminate in the issuing under Leo VI of the *Basilika*, a revised Greek version of the Justinianic corpus.[57] The model of Justinian, the 'great restorer' of the sixth century, seems to be evident in other spheres of Basil's activity, too. Basil's interest in the empire's western approaches is notable, and the example of Justinian's reconquest may have influenced him. Basil also has the reputation of being a great builder, particularly in the *Life of Basil*.[58] While it is possible that this text overplays the emperor's architectural achievements, as did Procopius those of Justinian in *The Buildings*,[59] it is clear at least that Basil was responsible for a new complex in Constantinople, encompassing a polo ground, gardens, a courtyard, and the Nea Ekklesia ('new church'), which celebrated the dynasty.[60]

The difficult court politics towards the end of the reign revolve around Basil's heir Leo, but can perhaps be opened up to reveal larger issues. Basil's intended successor was his eldest son Constantine, but he died from a fever in 879. As next oldest, and already a co-emperor, Leo became heir apparent. The future of the dynasty looked assured, as Leo was duly married to Theophano Martinakia, a relative of both the Amorians and Eudocia Ingerina.[61] However, relations between Basil and Leo were strained.[62] A common explanation for this is that Basil disliked Leo because he was Michael III's son, but perhaps the answer lies more in a clash of personalities and wishes. Leo was not content with Theophano. The *Life of Euthymios* has Leo vividly recall how Basil threw him to the floor and beat him when Theophano told him that Leo was having an affair with Zoe Zaoutzaina.[63] Relations deteriorated to the point that Leo was suspected of plotting against Basil, and was shut up in the palace apartment of the Pearl, a confinement that is thought to have lasted for three years, from 883 to 886.[64] It is evident that Leo had formed his own group of supporters, such as Andrew the domestic of the Schools and Stephen *magistros*, but it is not certain that they had hatched a plot. Indeed the narrative sources depict Leo as victim of the machinations of Photios' circle. It looks as if towards the end of Basil's reign the Amorians were preparing to stage a comeback. It has been suggested that this move was also inspired by discontent with Basil's western initiatives, which seem to have incurred some internal opposition.[65] That a major plot against Basil headed by John Kourkouas was exposed in March 886 adds to the air of political crisis. Maybe from realisation that Leo had been innocent, or perhaps simply because difficult circumstances required a show of dynastic unity, Basil restored Leo on 20 July 886, the feast day of Elijah, one of the patrons of the Macedonian

---

[57] See e.g. Fögen (1998), esp. pp. 11–12.   [58] *Life of Basil*, pp. 321–41.
[59] See e.g. Ousterhout (1998), esp. p. 129. See also above, p. 111.   [60] See Magdalino (1987).
[61] Tougher (1997b), pp. 134–40.   [62] Tougher (1997b), pp. 42–67.
[63] *Life of Euthymios*, ed. and tr. Karlin-Hayter, p. 41.   [64] Jenkins (1965), pp. 101–2.
[65] Vlysidou (1991).

Figure 16 Basil I being crowned by the Angel Gabriel, who flanks him together with the Prophet Elijah

dynasty.[66] This event was followed by Basil's death just over a month later, and Leo was thrust to sole power. The question of his complicity in the demise of the dynasty's founder remains open.

[66] See for instance Magdalino (1987); Magdalino (1988a); Dagron (2003), pp. 192–8.

CONCLUSION

It is clear then that the period *c.* 850–*c.* 886 was one of great moment in the recovery and advance of the Byzantine empire. Whether this was due to individuals such as Theoktistos, Michael, Bardas and Basil, or to favourable conditions such as an already progressing revival and altered international circumstances, is a matter for debate. Probably there is an element of both. However, the failures of the period and the persistent problems, such as the Arabs' occupation of Sicily and naval threat, should not be overlooked, nor should the uncertainties of the evidence. But whatever overall verdict is reached on this phase of the empire's life, it surely qualifies as one of the most intriguing periods of Byzantine history.

CHAPTER 7

RELIGIOUS MISSIONS

SERGEY A. IVANOV

INTRODUCTION

Although Christianity would seem by its very nature to be a missionary religion, both the sense of what 'mission' means and the specific motivations of missionaries have varied as each generation reads afresh the Gospels' injunctions. Early Christians were keen to stress the 'international' character of their religion and the primordial equality of all peoples, yet a different conceptual system was embedded in the very language in which the early Christian apologists wrote. St Paul already uses the term barbarian, with its implicit contrast between 'us' and 'them'. Early Christians also appropriated the discourse of the Roman world, which was similarly permeated with the spirit of empire. If the empire was 'the world', then those beyond the imperial borders were automatically assigned to an 'other' world, not inhabited by real people. Primitive Christianity opposed this kind of logic. St Christopher, for example, was – according to his *Life* – 'from the race of dog-heads, from the land of cannibals';[1] but this did not prevent him becoming a Christian martyr. Does this imply that natural savagery could be eradicated? An answer can be found in another legend – the 'Tale of St Christomeus' – one of the apocryphal stories of the wanderings of the apostles Andrew and Bartholomew. The legend tells how a certain cannibal was visited by an angel, who breathed grace into him and ordered him to assist the apostles. When the inhabitants of 'the city of the Parthians' incited wild beasts against the preachers in the circus, Christomeus asked God to give him back his former nature: 'and God heeded his prayer and returned his heart and mind to their former savagery'. This monster then tore the beasts to pieces, whereupon many of the pagans died of fright. Only after this did Andrew come up to Christomeus and say: '"the Holy Spirit commands that your natural savagery should leave you" . . . and in that moment his good nature returned'.[2] The legend is clearly designed to

---

[1] *Acta sanctae Marinae et sancti Christophori*, ed. Usener, p. 57.

[2] 'Tale of St Christomeus', Cod. Hier. Sab. 373, fols. 117–29, Jerusalem; Cod. Brescian A III 3, fols. 142–5, Brescia. I am grateful to A. I. Vinogradov for allowing me access to this text (*BHG* 2056), which he is preparing for publication.

Map 15 Byzantine religious missions

glorify Christomeus and its superficial message is that even a cannibal can become a Christian. Yet the deeper message – which perhaps reveals itself despite the author's best intentions – is precisely the opposite: that there is always a beast sleeping within any barbarian.

By taking the first step, by assimilating the discourse of barbarism, early Christians were also well on the way to assimilating a Roman conceptualisation of barbarians.[3] In Christian apologetics one increasingly finds the idea that Christianity was useful to the empire because it could help in moderating barbarian savagery; not, one might think, a matter of prime concern for persecuted Christians. This notion is already fully formed in the writings of Origen. It could have prompted missionary undertakings, but in fact did not. From a Christian viewpoint, conversion was something so fundamental that it could not depend on the paltry efforts or specific initiative of mere humans. Oddly, not even the apostles in their apocryphal wanderings were portrayed as missionaries in the proper sense of the word.

Among the agents of the initial Christianisation of the barbarians we find merchants, mercenaries, hostages and political exiles: that is, missionaries without a mission as such. If priests travelled to barbarian lands, it was only in order to minister to Romans in foreign captivity.[4] The Syrian monks probably constituted the only group of deliberate propagandists for the faith.

STATE-SPONSORED MISSIONS IN THE AGE OF JUSTINIAN

During the sixth century Christian space was very significantly expanded, thanks above all to centralised missionary policies.[5] Emperors began to receive state visits from barbarian rulers, showering them with gifts and baptism. In 522 Justin I (518–27) baptised Tzathus, king of Lazica, gave him a Byzantine bride and declared him his own son. In 527, Justinian (527–65) baptised Grod, prince of the Bosporan Huns, and Grep, ruler of a Germanic people, the Heruli. Justinian was also active beyond the empire's borders, and his missionary initiatives extended in several directions. Thus, in Abkhazia many new churches were constructed at a fair distance from the sea. These churches were clearly intended for the barbarians; they contain baptisteries suitable for adult baptism. The expensive building materials and the high quality of the construction-work suggest that the empire was footing the bill.

---

[3] For more details see Ivanov (2002).
[4] Seminal articles on Byzantine missionary activities in general include: Beck (1967); Hannick (1978); Ševčenko, I. (1988–9); Shepard (2002a). The only monograph is Ivanov (2003).
[5] For a detailed account of the main missionary undertakings of the sixth century see Engelhardt (1974).

Justinian's aims were purely political, as is clear from the account of the baptism of the Abkhazians by Procopius of Caesarea. The empire began to intervene in the internal affairs of this barbarian tribe so as to counter the influence of Sasanian Persia. This political pressure had a mildly civilising tinge. From an attempt to persuade the barbarians to renounce their 'savage' rituals it was but a short step to full-scale Christianisation. This in turn led to the overthrow of the authorities associated with the pagan religion and from there it was another small step to attempted colonisation. Such a policy could also have unforeseen consequences: the repudiation of Christianity because of its association with imperial expansionism.[6]

The Caucasian Tzani also became the targets of a state mission.[7] The principal agent of the dual policy here – combining threats and Christian proselytism, church building and deforestation – was the Byzantine commander Sittas. Where Byzantium had no direct political interest, it likewise had no active interest in missions. The sincerity of the conversion was of no concern. According to Procopius, Justinian:

persuaded all [the Heruli] to become Christians. Thus, having exchanged their way of life for one more mild, they resolved in all things to adopt Christian customs and on the basis of a treaty of alliance to cooperate with the *Romaioi* (Romans). Yet among themselves they are fickle, and adept at doing harm to their neighbours. And they engage in indecent intercourse even with donkeys. They are the most disgusting of all peoples.[8]

For the Byzantines, barbarian 'mildness' and 'Christianity' meant only one thing: forbearance from attacking the empire.

We should not imagine, however, that every mission in this period was accomplished by armed force or with narrowly political aims. Missionary activity in Abyssinia was different. Unfortunately, Greek authors say not a word about it, and we shall encounter such silences again, many times. Yet the local Ethiopian sources are far from reticent. They tell us that a group of monks from Byzantium settled in the region of modern Akale Guzay. These 'righteous men from Baraknakh' were murdered by locals during a pagan uprising, and thereby became the first Abyssinian martyrs. Another group of seven or nine 'Roman saints' arrived in Axum and yet another missionary was Michael Aragawi, whose Ethiopian *Life* reveals a few details of his preaching.[9] Although the chronological indicators in the 'Roman

---

[6] PR *W*, VIII.3.18–19, 21; VIII.9.10–12; I.12.3; VIII.2.17; II.29.15, ed. and tr. Dewing, V, pp. 80–1, 132–5; I, pp. 96–7; V, pp. 68–9; I, pp. 532–3. See also Evagrius Scholasticus, *Ecclesiastical history*, IV.22, ed. Bidez and Parmentier, p. 170; tr. Whitby, p. 221.

[7] PR *W*, I.15.24–5, ed. and tr. Dewing, I, pp. 136–7; PR *B*, III.6.6–8; III.6.11–12, ed. and tr. Dewing and Downey, pp. 206–7, 208–9.

[8] PR *W*, VI.14.33–6, ed. and tr. Dewing, III, pp. 410–13.

[9] *Life of Michael Aragawi*, ed. van den Oudenrijn, p. 19.

saints' file are contradictory, scholars usually date them to the late fifth and early sixth centuries.

Around the end of the 530s the southern Arabian state of Yemen broke free of Ethiopian patronage and established close links with Byzantium. A sign of the strengthening of Yemen's religious contacts with the Byzantines was the construction of a large church in Sanaa, built in red, yellow and black marble and adorned with mosaics in the Constantinopolitan manner.[10] It is not clear exactly when or by whom the Byzantines were asked to send a teacher of Christianity for the re-Christianised country; it may have been the occupying Ethiopian authorities or, more logically, the local inhabitants themselves. We have only one text, and a dubious one at that: the *Life* of Gregentius, bishop of the Homerites (Himyarites). In the story of Byzantine missions, Gregentius is as significant as he is mysterious. No reliable data about him has survived. His extant *Life* is late and most likely fictitious.[11] Appended to it is a text known as the *Laws of the Himyarites* which, even if it is not an authentic piece of legislation, remains an example of Byzantine missionary thinking, albeit abstract and from a later period. The striking feature of the *Laws* is that their rules for the newly converted Arabs are much stricter than the rules in force in the Christian empire itself (see also above, pp. 186–7). The *Laws* turn practically every civil offence into a criminal one, and virtually all private law becomes public law. The Romans themselves would never have dreamed of abiding by such ferocious requirements.[12] Overall, the *Laws of the Himyarites* represent a totalitarian missionary utopia. As for the Arab tribes immediately bordering Byzantium to the east, conversions of pagan bedouin to orthodox Christianity were rare. Here, as so often, the empire was more preoccupied with averting heresy than with making Christian converts.[13]

Travelling up the Nile, Justinian's emissaries reached a multi-confessional sanctuary on the island of Philae, at the outer limits of the imperial possessions. The temple was converted into a church of St Stephen. The first extant inscription left by a native is dated as early as 537: 'I, Theodosius the Nubian'.[14] The history of the mission to Sudan is much better known than any other, because it involved the rivalry between Justinian and his wife Theodora, patrons of Chalcedonism and monophysitism respectively. The main source – virtually our only source – is John of Ephesus, himself a monophysite. In John's account, the idea of a mission to Sudan was conceived in the circle of the monophysite patriarch of Alexandria, who lived in exile in Constantinople under the patronage of Theodora. Theodora

---

[10] al-Tabari, *Ta'rikh*, ed. de Goeje *et al.*, I, pp. 934–6; tr. Bosworth, V, pp. 217–21.
[11] *Life of Gregentios*, p. 107; Berger (2001), pp. 57–61.   [12] Papathanassiou (1996).
[13] Evagrius Scholasticus, *Ecclesiastical history*, VI.22, ed. Bidez and Parmentier, p. 238; tr. Whitby, p. 314.
[14] *Fontes historiae Nubiorum*, ed. Eide *et al.*, III, no. 325, p. 1181.

turned to her husband for support, but he had his own plans to dispatch a
Chalcedonian embassy to Sudan from Egypt. John's subsequent narrative
unfolds like a thriller. The imperial couple sent two missions, racing each
other, but Theodora's cunning ensured that her own mission, headed by
Julian, arrived first:

> [Julian] handed over the empress' letters . . . And [the Nubians] also received mag-
> nificent gifts, many baptismal garments and all in abundance. And they immedi-
> ately . . . believed in the Christian God . . . Then he taught them . . . and also
> intimated to them the following: 'Be forewarned that among Christians there are
> disputes concerning the faith . . . *for this reason* the empress has sent us to you.'[15]

Julian then explained to the Nubians how they should respond to the
emperor's mission. On arrival, Justinian's envoy immediately handed over
the emperor's letter and gifts to the Nubians, and then his missionaries
'began to teach them as they had been ordered, and they said, "Our Roman
emperor has instructed us to propose that, if you become Christians, you
should join the church and those who adhere to it, *and not those who have
been cast out.*"'[16] However, according to John of Ephesus, the barbarians
firmly rebuffed him. The intrigue here revolved less around conversion than
around the rivalry between monophysitism and Chalcedonism. Yet after
the expulsion of Justinian's embassy, Julian stayed in Sudan for two more
years, showing great zeal and instructing the barbarians in Christianity
daily: from nine in the morning until four in the afternoon he would
conduct his lessons naked, sitting up to his neck in water in a cave, because
of the unbearable heat: 'Yet he endured this, and instructed and baptised
the king, his magnates, and many people with them.'[17]

  The initial baptism of Sudan took place between 537 and 539, whereupon
Julian returned to Byzantium. In 565 Theodosius, Patriarch of Alexandria,
had his protégé Longinus ordained as the new bishop of Nubia. Longinus was immediately arrested by Justinian and imprisoned for three years;
but eventually he managed to escape to Sudan, where he spent some six
years. According to John of Ephesus, Longinus 'taught, enlightened and
instructed them anew, and he built a church there, and appointed clergy,
and taught them the entire order of the services and all the rules of Christianity.'[18] It would appear that Longinus' major achievement was the training
of local clergy. This enabled the new religion to put down roots in Sudan,
where it survived for many centuries.[19]

---

[15] JE, IV.7, ed. and Latin tr. Brooks, II, p. 138.   [16] JE, IV.7, ed. and Latin tr. Brooks, II, pp. 138–9.
[17] JE, IV.7, 49, ed. and Latin tr. Brooks, II, pp. 139, 175–6.
[18] JE, IV.8, ed. and Latin tr. Brooks, II, p. 140.
[19] Excavations at Faras have revealed the tomb of Bishop John who died in 606, aged eighty-two:
presumably he was one of Longinus' trainees.

The fashion for the new religion spread further still, and Longinus was invited to a tribe further south, the Alodians. It is curious, however, that John of Ephesus says nothing about any mission to the Makurrah, though their land lay between Sudan and Alodia. Only the Latin chronicle of John of Biclaro mentions the conversion of the Makurrah, which he dates to the year 569;[20] we can surmise that they were converted by the Chalcedonian patriarch of Alexandria, with the aim of annoying his monophysite rivals. In the ruins of Dongola, capital of Makurria, the remains of several 'Byzantine' churches have been identified. We do not know how long the Makurrah remained Chalcedonian. At some time in the late sixth or early seventh century they joined up with Sudan and accepted monophysitism. No Greek source contains even a single word about this rich and dramatic story of the Byzantine mission to the middle Nile: again we come up against silence.

Justinian's successors could be as ambitious as he was. According to John of Biclaro the Garamantes, Berbers living in the Libyan desert, were baptised under Justin II (565–78),[21] while Maurice (582–602) is associated with an attempt to Christianise Byzantium's great eastern rival, Persia. Christianity had been known in Persia from a very early period. After Christianity became the Roman empire's state religion, any deterioration in the relations between the two superpowers would lead to persecution of Persian Christians. As divisions within Christianity deepened, the Persian authorities began to encourage Nestorianism, and this gradually expanded to become the second religion of Iran (see above, p. 144). The Persian ruler Hormizd IV (579–90) was notably tolerant of all Christians in Persia, including Chalcedonians, and this gave rise to a legend about the Persians' own conversion.[22] This legend, preserved only in Latin tradition, probably reflects hopes generated in the empire by developments in Persia.

In 590 the shah was deposed and his son, Khusro II (590, 591–628), fled to Byzantium. The prince regained the throne with the aid of troops provided by Maurice. According to the *Shahnama* (*Book of kings*), in this new spirit of friendship the emperor sent Khusro 'a cross ornamented with jewels' and garments embroidered with crosses.[23] During this period, the Chalcedonians were in favour. Here too, we learn of Byzantine activities from all kinds of sources, but with one conspicuous exception – the Byzantines themselves. Why does Theophylact Simocatta, who recounts

---

[20] John of Biclaro, *Chronicon*, ed. Mommsen, p. 212; ed. Cardelle de Hartmann and Collins, p. 61; tr. Baxter Wolf, p. 60.

[21] John of Biclaro, *Chronicon*, ed. Mommsen, p. 212; ed. Cardelle de Hartmann and Collins, p. 61; tr. Baxter Wolf, p. 60. Christian features in the language of the Garamantes' descendants, the Tuareg, suggest that their forebears had contact with Latin-speaking missionaries.

[22] Fredegar, *Chronicle*, IV.9, ed. Krusch, pp. 125–6; tr. Wallace-Hadrill, pp. 7–9.

[23] Firdausi, *Shahnama*, French tr. Mohl, VII, pp. 145–6; tr. Warner and Warner, VIII, pp. 307–8.

Maurice's dealings with the Persians in great detail, not say a word about his Christianising activities? However, these achievements were short-lived: in 602, as soon as Maurice was murdered, Khusro launched an attack on Byzantium, and 'from the Euphrates to the east, the memory of the Council of Chalcedon was obliterated utterly'.[24]

The sixth century was an age of grandiose missionary undertakings, but there were also smaller-scale ones. The 'Legend of seven bishops of Cherson', for example, reflects local hagiographical tradition. One version of this legend, which probably originated in the sixth century, includes a certain Ephraim among the Christian missionaries in Cherson. According to this variant, Ephraim had been sent to convert 'the land of the Tauroscythians which borders on Cherson'. It is noteworthy that in later centuries this mythical Ephraim was recast as having converted a number of barbaric tribes: Turks, Huns and Hungarians.[25]

The sixth century was also the age of the parting of ways between Chalcedonian and 'heretical' Christianity (see above, pp. 116–18, 212–13). The subsequent large-scale missions of the Nestorian and monophysite churches, involving conversions in Central Asia and China, had nothing to do with Byzantium. Henceforth only a 'heretic' could allow himself an elevated, 'pan-Christian' attitude towards missions. One such champion of unalloyed apostolic evangelism was the sixth-century Alexandrian traveller Cosmas Indicopleustes. In his *Christian topography*, Cosmas presents a kind of bird's eye view of world-wide evangelisation.[26] This sense of universality was all but lost by the imperial church.

THE LULL IN MISSION WORK

A policy of 'state Christianisation' persisted into the seventh century. Heraclius converted a 'Hunnic' leader in 619 and Caucasian Albania in 628.[27] Not until the ninth century do we hear of any further centralised initiatives on the part of the imperial authorities to convert distant barbarian tribes.[28] Yet this very decline created substantial scope for local and personal initiatives of a kind which had perhaps existed before, but which the large-scale state ventures had overshadowed.

---

[24] Pigulevskaia (1946), p. 262.   [25] Ivanov (2003), pp. 82–3, 192.

[26] Cosmas Indicopleustes, *Christian topography*, III.65–6, ed. and French tr. Wolska-Conus, I, pp. 502–7; tr. McCrindle, pp. 117–21.

[27] There is also an unreliable later tradition that Heraclius converted the Croats: *DAI*, ch. 31, pp. 148–9; see also Konstantin Bagrianorodnyi, *Ob upravlenii imperiei*, ed. and tr. Litavrin *et al.*, p. 376 (commentary).

[28] Note, however, the baptism of the Bulgar khan Telerig in 777: Theoph., ed. de Boor, I, p. 451; tr. Mango and Scott, p. 622.

Apart from cursory allusions to certain exiles who carried out pastoral work in the Crimea and Khazaria,[29] we have the *Life* of Stephen, bishop of the Crimean city of Sougdaia. The Greek version of this *Life* is very brief, although slightly fuller versions exist in Slavonic and Armenian. Stephen was born in Cappadocia and received his bishopric in Sougdaia. The establishment of an episcopal see at a place like Sougdaia, on the edge of the barbarian world, is noteworthy in itself, since the town had only been founded in the later seventh century. Sougdaia was home to pagans (Khazars and Circassians) as well as Christians, and Stephen was an active preacher: 'When the pagans heard that he worked wondrous miracles, they believed in the Lord, and a countless multitude was baptised. And he appointed many presbyters and deacons for them.'[30] The missionary had established good relations with the local Khazar commander (the *tarkhan*), who 'while exercising his power would regularly come to St Stephen and would listen and do as [Stephen] told him. And the saint instructed him much on the path to salvation.'[31] Stephen died in office at the end of the eighth century.

In the second quarter of the seventh century, a new and fearsome enemy appeared on Byzantium's eastern borders: the Islamicised Arabs. Preaching Christianity to them directly was difficult in the extreme, except in the case of prisoners-of-war. Yet already by the eighth century we find instances of Arabs voluntarily converting to orthodoxy, as in the *Life of Stephen Sabaites*.[32] What we have here, for the most part, is the apostasy and subsequent reconversion of Christians who had accepted Islam while in Arab captivity. One of the preachers to such people was Romanos the Neomartyr, executed in 778.[33] According to the legendary *Life of Theodore of Edessa*, who most likely lived between 776 and 856, this bishop baptised none other than Mu'awiya, 'caliph of Baghdad', at the caliph's own request! Another missionary among the Arabs was Elias the Younger, a Sicilian who was shipped off to North Africa in the mid-ninth century.[34] All these missionaries preached at their own risk. They would never have counted on support from Byzantium.

The system of bishoprics in the Balkans virtually collapsed with the incursions of the Slavs. The Byzantine reconquest began in Greece in the eighth century and was followed by the Christianisation of the Slav groupings that had settled there. The *Chronicle of Monemvasia* relates how Emperor Nikephoros I 'concerned himself with rebuilding churches and with

---

[29] *Menologion of Basil II*, col. 181.
[30] *Life of Stephen of Surozh*, ch. 15, ed. Vasilievsky, p. 86 (longer *Life*).
[31] *Life of Stephen of Surozh*, ch. 30, ed. Vasilievsky, p. 95 (longer *Life*).
[32] *Life of Stephen Sabaites*, pp. 544–6.
[33] *Life of Romanos the Neomartyr*, ed. and Latin tr. Peeters, pp. 422–3.
[34] *Life of Elias the Younger*, ed. and Italian tr. Rossi Taibbi, pp. 24–6, 32–4.

turning the barbarians themselves into Christians'.[35] The emperor's methods are interesting: 'He installed [the fugitive inhabitants of Patras] where they had been before, together with their own pastor . . . and he offered Patras the status of a metropolitanate . . . Therefore the barbarians, too, were instructed in the faith and baptised, and they joined the Christian faith.'[36] The chief prerequisite for the baptism of the barbarians on reconquered imperial lands was thus the organisation of a network of bishoprics.

THE MID-NINTH-CENTURY UPSWING

A notable upswing in the empire's missionary activities may be observed around the turn of the ninth century. A growing interest in converting the barbarians is traceable in the *Life of Andrew the Apostle*, written by the monk Epiphanios. The author made his own journey in the footsteps of the apostle, and his narrative combines hagiographic commonplaces with first-hand observations: 'And from there he went to Bosporus . . . where we ourselves found Bishop Kolymbadios, who knew ten languages.'[37] The emphasis which Epiphanios places on the bishop's polyglot skills could reflect his own interest in the apostolic succession from St Andrew. Thus the 'first-called' apostle is regarded not just as a miracle-worker (his main characteristic in the apocryphal 'Wanderings') but as a practising missionary. Epiphanios' text is also important as the first, albeit timid, attempt to describe a missionary as he 'really' was: 'Seeing that the apostles were unselfish, exhausted, pallid, without even sandals on their feet and dressed only in tunics, and that despite this divinely inspired words issued forth from them – seeing this, people did not wish to part from them.'

The role attributed to Patriarch Photios (858–67, 877–86) in ninth-century Byzantine missionary activity is usually exaggerated;[38] we lack firm evidence as to any deliberate plans he might have had to convert the barbarians. However, several of the missionary undertakings of the period were initiated by Emperor Michael III (842–67). If we believe Niketas Byzantinos,[39] Michael was associated with some kind of coordinated religious work among the Muslim Arabs.[40] The ninth century also saw the beginning of missionary progress on the empire's northern periphery. This is indicated by the celebrated episcopal notice outlining the 'see of Gothia': 'The metropolitanate of Doros: [bishops] of the Chotziroi, Astel, Chwales, the

[35] *Svod drevneishikh pis'mennykh izvestii o slavianakh*, ed. Gindin *et al.*, II, p. 330; Kislinger (2001), p. 202. See also above, p. 258.
[36] *Svod drevneishikh pis'mennykh izvestii o slavianakh*, ed. Gindin *et al.*, II, p. 330; Kislinger (2001), pp. 202–3. However, see the doubts voiced by Turlej (2001), pp. 109–11.
[37] Vinogradov, 'Grecheskie zhitiia apostola Andreiia' (PhD thesis, 2001), pp. 152–3; *Greek traditions*, ed. Vinogradov, p. 145. See also Mango (2002a).
[38] Hurbanič (2005).   [39] Niketas Byzantinos, *Confutatio*, col. 672.
[40] See the *Life of Peter of Argos*, ed. Kyriakopoulos, pp. 244–5.

Onogurs, Reteg, the Huns, Tamatarcha'.[41] At the end of the notice, unconnected with the previous text, we find additional information: 'the eparchy
of Gothia: [the bishop of] the Chotziroi near Phoullai and near Charasion,
which is called Black Water. [The bishop of] Astel: Astel is the name of
a river in Khazaria, and there is a fortress there.'[42] The metropolitanate
of Doros, as described in the notice, encompassed an enormous territory
including part of the Crimea, the northern Caucasus and the north-eastern
Caspian region – that is, all the territory of the Khazar khaganate. Even if
this list of bishoprics is in fact merely a rough draft, it is extremely revealing;
its compilation implies expansive missionary ambitions on the part of the
church of Constantinople. Hopes of converting the khaganate apparently
rose in Byzantium at the start of the ninth century, in the course of a
multifaceted diplomatic offensive to the north.[43]

Around 860, as part of the same initiative, Michael III sent Constantine
the Philosopher (the future St Cyril) on a mission to Khazaria. Constantine
saw it as an evangelising opportunity, if we may believe his *Life*. He said to
the emperor:

'If you command, lord, on such a mission I shall gladly go on foot and unshod,
lacking all the Lord forbade His disciples to bring.' The emperor answered, saying:
'Well spoken, were you to do this [on your own]! But bear in mind the imperial
power and honour, and go honourably and with imperial help.'[44]

This discussion neatly encapsulates two views of missionary activity: Constantine's remark alludes to Christ's instructions to his disciples (Matthew
10:9–10), whereas the emperor counters to the effect that a missionary from
Byzantium is at the same time an ambassador, and so the Gospel's insistence
on simplicity does not apply to him. Here mission manifestly merges with
diplomacy. In the event, the results of Constantine-Cyril's work among
the Khazars were not particularly impressive: 'about two hundred of these
people were baptised, having cast off heathen abominations and lawless
marriages'.[45] Soon afterwards the Khazar khaganate adopted Judaism as its
state religion. The *Life of Constantine-Cyril* also relates how the saint took
time out from his Khazarian diplomacy to mount, at his own initiative, a
missionary raid on the people of Phoullai in the Crimea, felling their sacred
oak tree.[46]

---

[41] *NE*, no. 3, pp. 241–2 (text). See also above, p. 286.
[42] *NE*, no. 3, p. 245 (text). 'Astel' is identifiable as the Khazar capital, Itil.
[43] Shepard (1998), pp. 19–20.
[44] *Life of Constantine-Cyril*, ch. 8, ed. Angelov and Kodov, p. 95; ed. Floria, pp. 148–9; tr. Kantor,
p. 43.
[45] *Life of Constantine-Cyril*, ch. 11, ed. Angelov and Kodov, p. 102; ed. Floria, pp. 163–4; tr. Kantor,
p. 61.
[46] *Life of Constantine-Cyril*, ch. 12, ed. Angelov and Kodov, p. 103; ed. Floria, pp. 165–6; tr. Kantor,
pp. 63–5.

Later Michael III ordered the brothers Constantine and Methodios to create a Slavonic alphabet for the translation of the Scriptures (see below, fig. 19). It was Michael who sent Constantine and Methodios to Moravia and who initiated the baptism of both the Bulgars and the Rus. Michael's role in these missions has been somewhat overshadowed by Basil I's subsequent successes, as Basil appropriated his predecessor's initiatives for himself. However, Basil the Macedonian (867–86) seems to have been the first Byzantine emperor seriously to consider himself on a par with the apostles in missionary matters.[47] It was during Basil's reign that the feast of Pentecost acquired missionary connotations. In mosaics in the church of the Holy Apostles, which Basil extended and decorated, the apostles were clearly represented as missionaries. Similar representations can be found in miniatures[48] and frescoes[49] of the period. It is interesting, for example, that in the frescoes of the Tokale Kilise church in Cappadocia, the 'peoples', 'tribes' and 'tongues' who turn to the apostles are virtually obscured by huge depictions of emperors in Byzantine imperial ceremonial dress (fig. 17). In this sense the emperors are indeed 'equal to the apostles'.[50] The sources consistently stress the role of the emperor in the conversions of the Bulgars, Rus and the north-western Balkans.[51]

Byzantium's religious embassy to Moravia in 863 and the activities of Constantine and Methodios laid the foundations of Slav written culture. Yet in no way does this justify the oft-made claim that the Moravian mission was the high-point of Byzantine missionary activity. Although the brothers are frequently labelled 'apostles of the Slavs', Moravia had in fact received Christianity without Byzantine involvement. True, Prince Rastislav's letter to the emperor mentions that the Moravians had been visited by 'many preachers . . . from the Greeks',[52] which might be taken to imply that there were Byzantine missionaries in Moravia before Cyril and Methodios. However, this phrase's context undermines such an interpretation: the Byzantines are contrasted with all previous missionaries to Moravia, including 'Greeks'; the implication is that these particular Greeks were not reckoned 'Byzantines'. The Cyrillo-Methodian embassy itself should be viewed more as a unique event than as an integral part of an overall missionary strategy. The brothers from Thessaloniki did not undertake it as churchmen; when they did acquire ecclesiastical office, they observed the Latin rather than the Greek rite; and, yet again, the most striking feature of contemporary Greek sources is their total silence about the mission.

Left to their own devices, lacking imperial assistance, the orthodox teachers also came into conflict with the German clergy – 'the Franks' – who

[47] TC, p. 341. See also above, p. 301.   [48] Brubaker (1999a), pp. 238–45.
[49] Epstein (1986), p. 77, fig. 99.   [50] Jolivet-Lévy (2001), pp. 259, 261, plates 31, 33.
[51] See *DAI*, ch. 29, pp. 124–7.
[52] *Life of Methodios*, ch. 5, ed. Angelov and Kodov, p. 188; ed. Floria, p. 186; tr. Kantor, p. 111.

Figure 17 Fresco from Tokale Kilise church in Cappadocia, showing emperors between apostles and 'the nations'

were supported by the neighbouring east Frankish realm. The work of Methodios and his followers in Moravia can be pieced together from the *Lives* of Methodios and Clement of Ohrid, and also from the legal code known as the *Court law for the people*, which the Byzantines helped compile. These sources make clear that, although the brothers lacked political support for their activities in Moravia, from the start they made the same demands on the barbarians as they would have made on subjects of the empire. This concerned, above all, the laws of marriage: polygamy was forbidden, as was marriage to any relative, to godparents, and so forth.

The Byzantine missionaries were admirably consistent: they made no distinction between the elite and the masses, between neophytes and Byzantines. Such an attitude was bound to make the Slav elite wary of orthodox
churchmen.

This was one of the reasons for the ultimate failure of the Cyrillo-
Methodian mission. After Methodios' death some of his followers were
expelled from Moravia, others were sold into slavery. The empire, for
its part, showed no interest in the fate of the enterprise. Constantinople made no attempt to absorb Moravia into its own sphere of ecclesiastical
jurisdiction; it did not quarrel with Rome about the introduction of the
Latin rite into Moravia; nor did it intervene to defend its own envoys from
harassment by the Franks.

In the late seventh century, the Bulgars had seized much of the Byzantine
province of Moesia south of the lower Danube. The conquests of Khan
Krum (c. 803–14) greatly extended their dominions to the south, bringing
a sizeable number of Greek-speaking Christians under Bulgar sway (see
above, p. 257). The influence – including religious influence – of these
Greek-speaking Christians on the incoming Bulgars can be traced in sources
from the early ninth century. As usual, missionary activity was initiated by
captives as well as by local Christians. The *Life of Blasios of Amorion*[53] and the
tale of Prince Enrabotas illustrate this.[54] The conversion of the Bulgars took
place in the mid-ninth century in several stages and in complex competition
with the church of Rome. Theophanes Continuatus claims that Boris of
Bulgaria (c. 852–89) was coaxed towards Christianity both by his sister, who
had spent some time in the empire as a hostage, and also by a Byzantine
captive, a monk named Theodore Koupharas; however, he also alleges that
Boris' final decision to convert was made after a severe drought in 864
or 865.[55] All the sources on the conversion of Bulgaria[56] tend to stress the
wonder of divine intervention, the role of famine, the emperor's diplomatic
skills or the persuasiveness of Boris' entourage, but nowhere do we find a
word about Byzantine missionaries. Indeed, the Greek sources make plain
that the Bulgars would never have accepted Christianity were it not for
exceptional circumstances. Photios himself calls the conversion of Bulgaria
'improbable',[57] which supports the impression that it was not a pre-planned
action.

The first attempt to establish Greek Christianity in Bulgaria was a failure. The Greeks were obviously unprepared for the methodical persistence of missionary work. The extent to which the two sides spoke, as it
were, different languages can be seen from the long letter sent by Patriarch

[53] *Life of Blasios of Amorion*, pp. 660–1.   [54] Theophylact of Ohrid, *Martyrium* , cols. 193–7.
[55] TC, pp. 162–3.   [56] See Speck (2000), pp. 342–61. See also above, p. 299.
[57] Phot., no. 2, ed. Laourdas and Westerink, I, p. 51.

Photios to the newly baptised Prince Boris.[58] Photios' arrogant tone, wholly unsuitable for a missionary epistle, reflects the general attitude of the Greek clergy in Bulgaria. Boris found the behaviour of the empire's minions so irritating that as early as 866 he rejected their ministrations and turned instead to the Roman church.

Vacillating between Constantinople and Rome, playing off one Christian centre against the other, Boris sent an extensive set of questions to Pope Nicholas I (858–67) in Rome. Boris' letter has not survived, but we do have the pope's answers. This document is in striking contrast to Photios' epistle. The papal letter is respectful and specific. Through it, by inference, we can see which of the Byzantine demands the newly baptised barbarians had found most irksome. The Greeks fussed about Bulgarian marriage ritual;[59] they forbade visits to the baths on Wednesdays and Fridays;[60] they required worshippers to stand in church with their arms crossed over their chests; those without their belts fastened were banned from receiving communion,[61] and so on. In some cases, Nicholas indicates that he understands the principles laid down by the Greeks, but that he disagrees with their rigorist approach which could scare neophytes away from Christianity altogether. He proposed distinguishing the essential from the secondary. Such flexibility was alien to the Byzantines of the ninth century.

After an elaborate contest in ecclesiastical politics, Bulgaria returned once more to the fold of the Constantinopolitan church. Theophanes Continuatus writes that:

through the emperor's continual admonition, through formal receptions and still more through magnanimous generosity and gifts, [Basil I] made them accept an archbishop and agree to their land being filled with bishops. And through them, and also through the pious monks whom the emperor summoned from the mountains and from the caves in the earth and sent thither, this people . . . allowed itself to be caught in Christ's net.[62]

Such meticulousness in carrying out a programme of conversion is due, above all, to the Byzantines' strong sense that the Bulgarian land was originally theirs and must inevitably be returned to them in time.

The Bulgarians were well aware how their country was viewed by its mighty neighbour, and they understandably regarded Byzantine Christianity as a potential threat. That is why in the 880s Boris was happy to receive

---

[58] Photios, *Letter to Khan Boris*, ed. Laourdas and Westerink; tr. White and Berrigan.
[59] Nicholas I, *Responsa*, ch. 3, ed. Perels, pp. 569–70; German tr. Heiser, pp. 403–5. See also above, p. 299.
[60] Nicholas I, *Responsa*, ch. 6, ed. Perels, p. 572; German tr. Heiser, pp. 409–10.
[61] Nicholas I, *Responsa*, chs. 54, 55, ed. Perels, p. 587; German tr. Heiser, pp. 450–2.
[62] TC, p. 342.

Methodios' followers after they were expelled from Moravia. The problem was that the Greek clergy did not know the Slavonic language. The training of local clergy reduced the Bulgarian church's dependence on Byzantium.

In 860 a people called Rus mounted an attack on Constantinople (see above, p. 299). And 'soon', according to Theophanes Continuatus 'an embassy came from them to the ruling city, asking that they be brought into communion through divine baptism; and thus it came to pass.'[63] In his circular to the eastern patriarchs, Photios depicts the Rus as under Byzantium's spiritual authority; despite their previous reputation for savagery, the Rus were now 'subjects and friends',[64] and had received a Byzantine bishop. A century later, a different version was concocted by Constantine VII Porphyrogenitus:

through generous distribution of gold, silver and silk garments [Basil] also inclined towards compliance the invincible and godless people of the Rhos [Rus]. He concluded peace treaties with them and persuaded them to join in the salvation of baptism and to accept an archbishop ordained by Patriarch Ignatios; and the archbishop appeared in their country and the people loved him.[65]

Then we read of how the bishop was asked by the Rus to cast the Gospel into the fire, but the book would not burn.

One mission is more likely than two; the embassy travelled to the Rus under Michael III, but Michael's achievements were later attributed to Basil I. Whether this short-lived conversion occurred in 863 or 867, this is the earliest surviving Greek account of a religious mission dispatched to distant barbarians in the name of the central authorities in Constantinople. The mission brought no perceptible long-term results; in the tenth century, when Byzantine sources again begin to speak of the contemporary Rus, there is not the slightest hint of any 'baptism'.

MISSIONS TO THE ALANS, HUNGARIANS AND RUS

Deliberate Christianisation of Alania – a barbarian power stretching from the Kuban to the Terek – began during the second patriarchate of Nicholas I Mystikos (901–7, 912–25), more precisely between 914 and 918. We possess an invaluable source for this mission in the form of the patriarch's letters. The attempt to convert the northern Caucasus had been instigated by the Abkhazian principality rather than directly by Byzantium, but Nicholas was personally responsible for several significant initiatives. In the first place, he sent missionaries to Alania drawn from his own closest associates (whereas Constantine and Methodios had held no ecclesiastical office); secondly, he did not send and then ignore them, but kept continual watch

---

[63] TC, p. 196.   [64] Phot., no. 2, ed. Laourdas and Westerink, I, p. 50.   [65] TC, p. 342.

over their activities (again in contrast with Constantinople's indifference to the brothers from Thessaloniki); finally, Nicholas set in motion a process which soon led to the inclusion of the see of Alania within the Constantinopolitan patriarchate. In the context of Byzantine traditionalism, this was revolutionary. Dioceses had been founded before, even in foreign realms – Bulgaria, for example – but always within the historical boundaries of the Roman empire. The lands to the north of the Caucasus were completely 'other', and their entry into the patriarchal ambit, followed by the vast lands of Rus, opened a new page in ecclesiastical history.

The missionaries to Alania give us the first intimations of just how difficult it was to convert barbarians. Peter, archbishop of Alania, complained to Nicholas that his 'sorrows are many and great is the affliction of [his] evils'.[66] He added that Nicholas, who had never been in exile, could not hope to understand his torments. In reply, the patriarch objected, '. . . your wisdom was not being sent out for your comfort . . . but to labours and toils and distresses', before advising him to 'consider the blessed heralds of the Gospel, in whose number you have been found worthy to be enrolled . . . and cease to lament and to be dismayed because human affairs do not run as we would have them!' Nicholas then consoled him, declaring that '. . . your portion of honour [is] equal to that of the apostles' own'.[67]

Peter and another envoy, Euthymios, are the first Byzantine missionaries, in the proper sense, whose names survive in a Greek source. For the first time we read of the conversion of pagans not as an act of divine providence but as hard and often thankless work. And we read of missionaries as real people: self-sacrificing, perhaps, but also prone to despair. The appearance of such figures in Byzantine writings is an important sign that the culture of the *Romaioi* was developing a rather more realistic view of barbarians. This development is particularly evident in the advice which Nicholas gives to his missionaries. In a letter to Peter, the patriarch formulates his position on marriage among the Alans:

As for what you write of matters respecting marriage which are opposed to the church order, and of other habits which give a more pagan character to those practising them, your wisdom is aware that so sudden a conversion of pagan life into the strictness of the Gospel is not easily achievable. You should therefore continually apply your doctrine and salutary exhortation in a paternal and generous spirit . . . and where you find them recalcitrant, bear it with long-suffering, especially if the disobedient belong to the upper class of this nation and are not governed but governors. Towards their subjects you may perhaps be able to behave rather more austerely and despotically . . . but towards the powerful ones, who are quite capable of counteracting the salvation of the whole nation, you must reflect whether, if we behave too harshly to them, we may not unawares exasperate them the more, and thus turn everything upside down.[68]

[66] NM, no. 135, pp. 436–7.   [67] NM, no. 135, pp. 438–41.   [68] NM, no. 52, pp. 284–7.

Thus the Byzantines softened their previously inflexible stance on polygamy, especially among the nobility. The failure of the Cyrillo-Methodian mission in Moravia had been to a large extent caused by missionary rigour on precisely this issue (see above, pp. 317–18). Apparently the Greeks had learned useful lessons from their Latin rivals in Bulgaria and Moravia.

And yet the fruits of the mission of Euthymios and Peter were not long-lasting; al-Mas'udi relates that after 932 the Alans 'turned away from their new beliefs and expelled the bishops and the priests who had been sent by the emperor of Rum'.[69] We do not know the circumstances in which the Byzantine church reappeared in Alania, although recent research has shown that this could have been as early as the 960s,[70] and we shall return to the Christianisation of Alania below.

After half a century of Byzantino-Hungarian military clashes and political contacts, around 948 envoys of Fajsz, prince of the Magyars, arrived in Constantinople. A few years later there came Bulcsu, who was baptised by Constantine VII Porphyrogenitus, and his example was then followed by Gyula. According to John Skylitzes, the latter 'took with him a monk by the name of Hierotheos, renowned for his piety. Theophylact [patriarch of Constantinople] consecrated him bishop of Tourkia [Hungary]. Once there, Hierotheos converted many people from their barbarian errors to Christianity.'[71]

The metropolitanate of Tourkia appears in none of the official lists, but it probably existed until at least the mid-eleventh century.[72] Archaeological evidence suggests that the Byzantine mission was especially active in the region of Szombor.[73] Finds of Byzantine reliquary crosses in Hungary are distributed along the course of the Danube and the Tisza. They number about forty, with fifteen dating from between the mid-tenth and the mid-eleventh century (fig. 18). The ruling family from Géza I (972–97) onwards accepted the Latin rite, although Greek clerics remained in the southern Hungarian lands well into the twelfth and even thirteenth centuries.

Around the turn of the tenth century Niketas the Paphlagonian compiled a cycle of panegyrics in honour of the apostles. He depicts Andrew,[74] Bartholomew[75] and Matthew as thoroughgoing missionaries; Matthew is even said to have preached to the 'Ethiopians . . . in their own language'.[76] Unlike his predecessors writing on similar themes, Niketas shows awareness of a clash of cultures, though he decides not to describe how his protagonists overcame it. Thomas the Apostle, for example:

---

[69] al-Mas'udi, *Muruj al-dhahab*, ch. 479, ed. Pellat, I, pp. 228–9; rev. French tr. Pellat, I, p. 173.
[70] Beletsky and Vinogradov (2005).
[71] Skyl., ed. Thurn, p. 239; French tr. Flusin and Cheynet, pp. 201–2.
[72] Oikonomides (1971), pp. 527–31.   [73] Györffy (1976), pp. 175–8.   [74] NP, cols. 64–5, 68.
[75] NP, col. 208.   [76] NP, cols. 280–1.

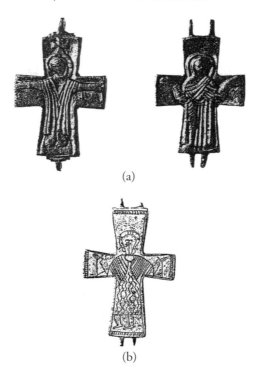

Figure 18 (a) Reliquary pectoral cross found in Hungary, with Christ crucified on obverse and the Virgin with her arms raised in prayer on the reverse (b) Reliquary pectoral cross found in Orosháza, Hungary; the poorly rendered figure is of the Virgin or an unidentified saint

. . . arrived among these people who are revolting in appearance but even more repulsive in their disposition. What was it like for him to associate and converse with them on questions of piety! He complained quietly about the burdensomeness of associating with these peoples, and suddenly the solution to all his difficulties appeared.[77]

As far as the eulogist is concerned, relief comes in the form of intervention by Christ, so he does not delve into the specific techniques of apostolic missionary practice.[78]

Another indication of the Byzantines' growing interest in missionary activity can be seen in the *Life* of the apostle Thomas, contained in the late tenth-century collection of reworked saints' *Lives* of Symeon Metaphrastes. All the early versions of Thomas' acts derived from Gnostic accounts which – contrary to official Christianity – emphasise the harmfulness of

[77] NP, col. 136.   [78] NP, col. 140.

marriage and wittily describe miracles and transformations. In these earlier versions, the problems of mission as such merit just one phrase: Thomas complains that, as a Jew, he cannot preach to the Indians. Nowhere do these versions explain how Thomas managed to solve his problems. Yet when Symeon Metaphrastes embarked on writing a commentary on Thomas' acts, missionary problems become a central theme:

Thomas was sent to India, which was utterly barbaric . . . That which is rooted over the course of a prolonged period turns into habit, which is stronger than any arguments of reason. Arriving in such a country, the apostle did not behave arrogantly and provocatively, did not start talking grandly and boastfully, and refrained from many things which might have made him seem haughty, insufferable and smug . . . With dirty hair, a pallid face, dry and thin . . . dressed in a dirty threadbare cloak, he prepared himself . . . for meek and humble behaviour. He did not immediately start criticising them, did not reproach them with anything, and decided not to resort to such devices as severity. For he knew: what has become fixed in our souls through long habit cannot easily be eliminated, but is more likely to be changed by persuasion than force. Therefore he resorted more to gentleness, to kind manners and pleasant words . . . He came before them not with arrogance and superciliousness, and not with grandiloquence, but with deeds and signs . . . The Indian people were inducted into the mysteries and the seed of the Word was implanted in their souls. Thomas' preaching [was disseminated] to such an extent that it reached the king himself, though it did not enter deeply into his consciousness.[79]

In Metaphrastes' work Thomas is transformed from the showy magician of earlier tradition into a modest, industrious missionary. Interestingly, Metaphrastes' ideal preacher conducts his propaganda 'from below'. The text of the 'Commentary' is an implied polemic with those who deal with barbarians without bothering to conceal their contempt.

Such an attitude in no way abrogated the imperial conception of barbarians as targets for conquest. In real life these two types of discourse – the imperial and the missionary – coexisted. In Constantine VII Porphyrogenitus' *Book of ceremonies* we find the following paean to God: 'He has enlightened the peoples . . . [and] glorifies imperial benefactors with victories and subjects barbarians to their right hand.'[80] Elsewhere in the same work Constantine introduces chants that are to be performed at Pentecost: 'God, who tamed the godlessness of the nations with tongue-like manifestations of flame, promises through you, brave lords, to conquer and annihilate pagan godlessness. The emperor So-and-So, the joy and reviver of the *Romaioi*, will force the alien tongues to become of one tongue in

---

[79] Symeon Metaphrastes, *Life of Thomas the Apostle*, pp. 156–67.
[80] *DC*, I.9, ed. Reiske, I, p. 59; ed. and French tr. Vogt, I, p. 54.

faith.'[81] The inner contradictions of these passages are self-evident to us, but not to the Byzantines.

After the first 'baptism' of the Rus in the 860s, there is a long gap in the sources. The only references to Byzantium's attempts at Christianisation are to be found in the *Rus primary chronicle* where, after the conclusion of the peace treaty of 911, the emperor provides the Rus envoys with an escort 'so as to show them the beauty of the churches . . . and to instruct them in their [i.e. the Byzantines'] faith'.[82] That there were Christians in the Kievan elite is shown by the fact that a priest called Gregory went to Constantinople as part of Princess Olga's entourage. The first extensive evidence, however, is provided by the stories of the baptism of Olga in 954–5[83] or 957,[84] as told by the Rus chronicler and by Skylitzes. Despite the detailed account in the Rus chronicle,[85] we cannot be certain when or even where Olga was baptised. There is no doubt, however, about the fact that the princess accepted Byzantine orthodoxy; she took the baptismal name of Helena in honour of the empress, who thereby became her godmother. Yet her relations with her godparents soon deteriorated to such an extent that in 959 she requested bishops from the Saxons.

The conversion of the princess did not in itself lead to the Christianisation of Rus. This process was instigated in 988 by her grandson Vladimir. Unfortunately not a word about the conversion of Rus can be found in the works of contemporary Byzantine authors; the details have to be extrapolated from Rus, Arabic and western sources and, once again, we encounter the extraordinary silence of the Greek sources. What, for all this, do we know about the Byzantines' involvement in the conversion? The *Rus primary chronicle* states that, following envoys from the Muslims, the 'Germans' and the Jews, 'the Greeks sent a philosopher to Vladimir'.[86] Scholars have speculated as to who this anonymous 'philosopher' might have been. Most likely he is merely the chronicler's generalised representation of a Byzantine missionary, and the term 'philosopher' harks back to Constantine-Cyril the Philosopher. The chronicle puts a long speech into this philosopher's mouth.[87] The speech, supposedly delivered in Vladimir's presence, is overburdened with names and details that were hardly central to the teaching of Christianity. It is ponderous in the extreme, and hardly likely to have attracted and held the attention of a curious pagan. We cannot treat it as a standard missionary text, routinely regurgitated by Greek missionaries for the conversion of barbarians.

---

[81] *DC*, I.9, ed. Reiske, I, p. 59; ed. and French tr. Vogt, I, pp. 54–5.

[82] *PVL*, p. 20; *RPC*, pp. 68–9.

[83] Litavrin (1999), pp. 435–6. See also the arguments for 946 in Zuckerman (2000b).

[84] Nazarenko (2001), pp. 285–6. For detailed surveys of other hypotheses on the time and place of Olga's baptism, see Nazarenko (2001), pp. 219–310; Featherstone (2003); Tinnefeld (2005b).

[85] *PVL*, p. 29; *RPC*, p. 82.

[86] *PVL*, p. 40; *RPC*, p. 97.   [87] *PVL*, pp. 40–8; *RPC*, pp. 97–109.

Although the episode with the 'philosopher' has clearly been inserted into the chronicle from some other work unconnected with Vladimir, it is not pure fantasy. Aspects of the philosopher's conduct remind us of other missionaries. For example, a painting of the Last Judgement is shown by the philosopher to Vladimir,[88] just as a painting of the Last Judgement had figured in the conversion of Boris of Bulgaria by the Byzantine missionary Methodios; and the reliance on citations from the Old Testament is reminiscent of Constantine-Cyril's speech to the people of Phoullai. Be that as it may, in the chronicle's account none of these ploys impressed Vladimir. He refused to be baptised, and said: 'I will wait a little more.'

Next, according to the chronicle, the prince sent his own embassies to various countries in order to 'test the faiths'. In Constantinople the emperor and patriarch did everything possible to impress the envoys with the pomp of the service in St Sophia, and 'they were astonished'.[89] Yet despite the envoys' warm reception in Constantinople, and despite their very positive reactions, Vladimir attacked and captured the Byzantine city of Cherson. We need not enter into the scholarly debates and attempt to explain this extraordinary turn of events. Vladimir's baptism, according to the *Rus primary chronicle*, was merely a corollary to the negotiations about the return of Cherson, a precondition for receiving the emperor's sister Anna as his bride;[90] the negotiations concluded, Anna travels to Cherson not with a metropolitan for Rus, nor even with a staff of missionaries, but merely with the clergy of her personal entourage. It is left to Vladimir to say: 'let those who have come with your sister baptise me'; so 'the bishop of Cherson together with the emperor's sister's priests instructed Vladimir in the faith and baptised him.'[91] After his baptism Vladimir 'took his imperial bride, and Anastasios [the Chersonite who had betrayed the town to the Rus] and priests from Cherson ... and he also took ecclesiastical vessels and icons.'[92] This suggests that providing liturgical vessels had not been reckoned a missionary responsibility of the princess' entourage, nor had anyone had the foresight to bring vessels from Constantinople in anticipation of the baptism of Rus; instead they were simply trophies plundered by Vladimir in Cherson. Although the Rus metropolitanate most probably existed from around 990, nothing is heard about it until 1039.

Later Russian chronicles attempted to fill this lacuna with tales of local conversions,[93] and even with the story of a certain 'philosopher' named Mark the Macedonian, who was allegedly sent by Vladimir on a

---

[88] *PVL*, p. 48; *RPC*, p. 110. See also Ševčenko, I. (1988–9), pp. 25–6.
[89] *PVL*, p. 49; *RPC*, p. 111.
[90] *PVL*, p. 50; *RPC*, p. 112.   [91] *PVL*, p. 50; *RPC*, p. 113.   [92] *PVL*, p. 52; *RPC*, p. 116.
[93] *Nikon chronicle*, *PSRL* 9, pp. 63–4; tr. Zenkovsky and Zenkovsky, I, pp. 110–11.

mission – in the event unsuccessful – to the Volga Bulgars in 990.[94] But this is highly dubious information from a late source. We learn something of the activity of senior Byzantine clergy in Rus from the series of questions that were put to Metropolitan John II. On the one hand, the metropolitan's general approach is plain enough in his injunction to 'adhere to strictness rather than to the custom of the land'.[95] He rejects anything that is 'far from present-day piety and the becoming way of life of the *Romaioi*'.[96] Yet in two of his responses John shows a degree of tolerance: firstly he urges that sorcerers and magicians should not be punished with mutilation;[97] and secondly, he allows priests to wear animal skins under their robes 'because of the terrible cold and frost'.[98] But such concessions to local conditions are rare.

Besides the metropolitanate at Kiev, in the eleventh century there were bishoprics in perhaps as many as eight other towns, including Chernigov, Pereiaslavl', Polotsk and Novgorod, and in the twelfth century in at least three more. The prelates in all these towns were Greek-born, but the only detailed information comes from the *Life* of an eleventh-century bishop, Leontios of Rostov (though the text was composed in the twelfth century, some time after the death of its hero). According to his *Life*, Leontios had been preceded by Theodore and Ilarion, Byzantines who, 'unable to endure the abuse and persecution, fled home to the [land of the] Greeks'.[99] Initially Leontios, too, had little success; driven out by the pagans, he moved to the edge of the town and built himself a hut. Children began to visit him and he gave them instruction, and then adults, too, would come. Eventually Leontios was invited back to the citadel, where he set about cautiously instilling Christianity, with encouragement and gentleness. Leontios' success was again brief: he died in a pagan uprising. Although its 'facts' are probably fictitious, the *Life* of Leontios reflects contemporary Byzantine missionary practice; or at any rate it reflects the impressions of such practice that were formed in Rus.

One serious problem for Byzantine churchmen was their ignorance of the local language. Metropolitan Nikephoros addresses the Kievans thus: 'I have not been granted the gift of tongues, like the divine Paul, so as to carry out my tasks in that language [i.e. Slavonic], and therefore I stand amongst you voiceless and am much silent.'[100]

---

[94] *Nikon chronicle, PSRL* 9, pp. 58–9; tr. Zenkovsky and Zenkovsky, I, p. 109; see also *Kniga stepennaia*, I, pp. 111–13.

[95] John II, *Canonical responses*, ed. Beneshevich, p. 109. The text survives in Greek and in Slavonic versions, though the two do not always coincide. Here we draw on both versions.

[96] John II, *Canonical responses*, ed. Beneshevich, p. 110.

[97] John II, *Canonical responses*, ed. Beneshevich, pp. 110–11.

[98] John II, *Canonical responses*, ed. Beneshevich, p. 114.

[99] *Life of Leontios of Rostov*, ed. Titov, p. 4.

[100] Text in Nikephoros, *Sermon*, ed. Nazarenko, p. 569; Nikephoros, *Works*, ed. Polianskii, p. 186.

LATER BYZANTINE MISSION-WORK

From the eleventh century onwards[101] Byzantium's only remaining pagan neighbours were the nomadic peoples of Asia Minor and the Black Sea steppes. Missions sent to them typically achieved swift successes which could just as easily be reversed. In 1048 the Pecheneg leader Tyrach was converted.[102] Several years earlier Kegen, leader of a Pecheneg splinter-group, had 'received holy baptism, himself and those with him. And a certain pious monk named Euphemios was sent, who set up a sacred font beside the Danube and provided holy baptism for all.'[103] This conversion provoked a certain amount of controversy in Byzantium. John Mauropous viewed it with great enthusiasm,[104] his friend Michael Psellos was quite sceptical,[105] while Michael Attaleiates was downright hostile: 'there is no point in trying to bleach the Ethiopian.'[106]

Alexios I Komnenos (1081–1118) was praised for his missionary endeavours:

> For the emperor . . . was fond of teaching our doctrines and was a real missionary by choice and in his manner of speech; he wanted to bring into the fold of our church not only the Scythian nomads, but also the whole of Persia, as well as the barbarians who inhabit Libya and Egypt and follow the rites of Muhammad.[107]

Anna Komnena returns to this theme elsewhere: 'I for my part would call him "the thirteenth apostle".' In contrast with the church fathers, who had reckoned the world already baptised or about to be baptised, Alexios took a realistic view both of the extent of the unbaptised world and of the complexity of the task before him. We should note, nevertheless, that there is no firm evidence that Alexios ever dispatched any religious missions beyond the old limits of the empire.

Theophylact, archbishop of Bulgaria two generations after its conquest by Byzantium, spent the first half of his life – until 1092 – at the Constantinopolitan court, and the second part in provincial Slav Ohrid. He composed the extended *Life of Clement of Ohrid*, his remote Slav predecessor in his see. Theophylact's missionary principle, as it emerges from the *Life*, may be formulated thus: when helping barbarians adapt to Christianity, one should take them as they are, and one should simplify Christianity to make

---

[101] For more detail on Byzantine missions of the second millennium, see Ivanov (2007).
[102] Skyl., ed. Thurn, p. 459; French tr. Flusin and Cheynet, p. 380.
[103] Skyl., ed. Thurn, p. 456–7; French tr. Flusin and Cheynet, pp. 378–9.
[104] John Mauropous, *Quae . . . supersunt*, no. 182, ed. de Lagarde, pp. 143–6.
[105] Michael Psellos, *Orationes panegyricae*, ed. Dennis, p. 63.
[106] Attal., ed. Bekker, pp. 30–1; ed. and Spanish tr. Peréz Martín, p. 25.
[107] *Al.*, VI.13.4, ed. Reinsch and Kambylis, I, p. 199; ed. and French tr. Leib, II, p. 81; tr. Sewter, pp. 211–12. See also XIV.8.8, ed. Reinsch and Kambylis, I, p. 457; ed. and French tr. Leib, III, p. 181; tr. Sewter, p. 466.

it accessible to their understanding. He praises Cyril and Methodios for creating 'an alphabet which matched the coarseness of the Slavonic tongue' (see fig. 19).[108] He likewise appreciates the flexibility of his own hero, Clement, in dealing with the barbarians: 'Knowing the coarseness of the people and their extraordinary obtuseness in mastering Scripture, [Clement] . . . devised the following scheme: for every festival he composed sermons that were simple, clear, containing nothing deep or subtle, the type of sermon that could not escape the comprehension of even the dullest of Bulgarians.'[109] Theophylact explains that in Bulgaria only 'wild' trees had grown, bearing no 'cultured' fruit; but Clement 'ennobled the wild plants through grafts, in order (as I think) thus to nurture human souls.'[110] What we have here is not so much a narrative of Clement's specific missionary activity, but more of a parable: Byzantine culture cannot be forced on the barbarians; it must be carefully grafted onto their own culture.[111]

With few exceptions, the emphasis shifts in the twelfth century from the conversion of barbarians to their subjugation. In the abundant panegyrical literature, emperors' victories wholly overshadow their missionary achievements. One of the period's few known preachers to the barbarians was Nicholas Hagiotheodorites, metropolitan of Athens, who died in 1175.[112] Moreover, according to Euthymios Tornikes, in this period Byzantium reestablished bishoprics in the cities that had been captured by the Seljuqs, but not, he stresses, in new places.[113]

The work of Byzantine missionaries in Alania continued, although we have no direct sources on the subject. The seat of the metropolitanate of Alania is thought to have been a town in the vicinity of modern Nizhnii Arkhyz, but we do not even know the town's name. Active church-building continued in the northern Caucasus, although the architecture of the extant churches is more reminiscent of Abkhazia than of Byzantium. A few dozen Greek inscriptions attest the presence of Greeks. Apparently there was an attempt to adapt the Greek alphabet so as to render local languages. Vestiges of Byzantine orthodoxy, albeit sometimes in heavily distorted form, have been detected in the pagan beliefs of the modern inhabitants of the northern Caucasus, especially the Ossetians. There exists a unique written document, a report by Theodore, metropolitan of Alania. In 1225 Theodore sent to the Nicaean patriarch, Germanos II, a report on his journey to the Caucasus. The report's general conclusion is that Christianity in Alania has withered: 'Alas, on apostolic foundations there was built a house of straw and cane,

[108] Theophylact of Ohrid, *Life of Clement*, II.7, ed. Milev, p. 80; ed. Iliev, p. 82.
[109] Theophylact of Ohrid, *Life of Clement*, XXII.66, ed. Milev, p. 132; ed. Iliev, p. 101.
[110] Theophylact of Ohrid, *Life of Clement*, XXXIII.68, ed. Milev, p. 134; ed. Iliev, p. 102.
[111] Floria *et al.* (2000), pp. 202–3, 208.
[112] Euthymios Tornikes, *Syngraphai*, ed. Papadopoulos-Kerameus, pp. 159–60.
[113] Euthymios Tornikes, *Syngraphai*, ed. Papadopoulos-Kerameus, p. 183.

Figure 19 Early example of the Glagolitic script invented by Constantine-Cyril to cater for the Slavonic language

and it has fallen victim to fire';[114] 'the Alans are Christians only in name.'[115] Theodore complains at the lack of proper missionary experience, though at the same time he is proud of his own modest successes in this area.[116]

---

[114] Theodore of Alania, *Alanikos*, col. 400.   [115] Theodore of Alania, *Alanikos*, col. 409.
[116] Theodore of Alania, *Alanikos*, cols. 405, 409.

Figure 20 Early example of Cyrillic script: an early eleventh-century inscription in Bitola, commissioned by John Vladislav (see below, p. 529); although now bearing the name of Constantine-Cyril, this form of writing was a pragmatic adaptation of the Greek alphabet to accommodate the Slavonic language's distinctive sounds and gradually replaced the brand-new, accurate, but intricate script devised by Constantine-Cyril himself

State missionary activity limped on after the restoration of Greek power in Constantinople, but a weakened empire and the strengthening of her Islamic neighbours forced the emperors to show extreme caution.[117] However, centres of orthodoxy in close contact with the barbarians, for example in the Crimea, were active in conversion-work. Late Byzantine baptisteries suitable for the baptism of adults have been found at several Crimean sites, suggesting possible missionary activity on the part of the local cave monasteries.

In the late Byzantine period some new ecclesiastical provinces were created on barbarian territory. Among them was a bishopric instituted at Sarai, capital of the Golden Horde. In 1276 Bishop Theognostos of Sarai sent the patriarch of Constantinople, John Bekkos (1275–82), a list of questions arising from his pastoral work. Many questions reveal the missionary character of his concerns.[118] The patriarch's answers display considerable tolerance. In its final period the empire was eventually able to work out an integral and flexible ideology of mission. Realism characterises the missionary activity of the patriarchate in general. Thus in September 1365 a new bishopric of

---

[117] Duc., XX.4, ed. Grecu, p. 135; tr. Magoulias, p. 112.
[118] Theognostos of Sarai, *Questions*, col. 136 (Slavonic version); appendix 1, col. 10 (Greek text).

Achochia is mentioned in a patriarchal document.[119] The bishopric was perhaps created for the migrant Abkhazian population. Around 1317, arch-bishoprics were founded in Lithuania and the Caucasus,[120] although an attempt to convert the Lithuanian prince Olgerd ended in failure.[121] As an example of this more practical approach to mission one might point to Gregory Palamas: while in Muslim captivity in 1354, Gregory conducted religious disputations, and in Nicaea he preached Christianity in the streets, on his own initiative.[122] And yet, even on the eve of its downfall, Byzantium could not fully shed its cultural snobbery or arrogance.

The very term barbarian refers to a political discourse dominated by Roman imperial rhetoric in which Christianity does not fit comfortably. Missionary ideas are also the losers at the level of folkloric discourse. Thus among the Byzantines there was a widely held belief that the northern tribes of Gog and Magog had been locked behind iron gates by Alexander the Great. No writer from among the *Romaioi* ever took the trouble to consider whether Gog and Magog might be baptised. For the Greeks, the cultural stereotype was stronger than the religious principle: speaking in terms of Gog and Magog they could indulge themselves, lumping together all barbarians as a seething, subhuman mass.

In the Byzantine mind the concept of universal Christianity was linked to the idea of world empire, which the Byzantines never entirely aban-doned. This aspect of their outlook could easily be dubbed expansionism. Dimitri Obolensky proposed that Byzantium maintained an enormous, highly complex and diffuse system of international ties, which he called the 'Byzantine commonwealth'. However, if we look closely at the fabric of the relations between the *Romaioi* and the world around them, we see that there was as much isolationism as there was expansion. In Byzantine missionary activity we find a paradoxical yet characteristic instance of isolationism, in the form of barbarians being converted by a stylite.[123] The image of a static, lone missionary contradicts the basic concept of activism that the idea of proselytising normally implies. Yet in this image we can see the distillation of a specifically Byzantine perception of mission.

---

[119] MM, I, p. 477.   [120] *NE*, no. 17, pp. 399–400 (text), 182 (commentary).
[121] NG, XXXVI.40–1, ed. Schopen and Bekker, III, pp. 520–1.
[122] Philippidis-Braat, 'La Captivité de Palamas', p. 161.
[123] *Life of Symeon Stylite the Younger*, ed. van den Ven, I, p. 112.

CHAPTER 8

ARMENIAN NEIGHBOURS (600–1045)

T. W. GREENWOOD

INTRODUCTION

Anyone wishing to unravel the history of the relationship between Byzantium and Armenia from late antiquity into the eleventh century has to confront a series of historical and historiographical challenges. The most immediate, and intractable, of these is one of definition: what does 'Armenia' mean? Although Armenia is used to express a territorial entity in contemporary texts, both Armenian and non-Armenian in origin, its precise meaning varies according to the date and the context in which it is used. Far from finding a single, stable definition of Armenia, one discovers multiple 'Armenias'.[1] Thus a seventh-century Armenian geographical compilation depicts 'Great Armenia' as comprising not only regions currently recognised as Armenian but also those with historic associations.[2] Successive provinces of Armenia were imposed and superimposed by external powers, each with a particular scope. The kingdom of Armenia, re-established in 884, bore little relation to its Arsacid precursor and increasingly represented only the Bagratuni kingdom centred on Ani, excluding rival kingdoms in Vaspurakan, Siwnik' and elsewhere.

Given the absence of stable territorial boundaries and in the light of significant Arab settlement in certain districts from the end of the eighth century, there have been attempts to construct Armenian identity in terms of a blend of confessional, linguistic and cultural features. Once again the evidence supports a plural and inclusive definition. Instead of a community of believers, united around a single confession and recognising the spiritual authority of a single leader, the Armenian church embodied a spectrum of doctrinal interpretations, revolving largely, but not exclusively, around the acceptance or rejection of the council of Chalcedon.[3] This interpretation is at odds with the conventional outline of Armenian church history supplied by the majority of the Armenian sources, which advertise a pronounced anti-Chalcedonian, monophysite character after 600. Yet the faint

---

[1] Hewsen (2001) offers a comprehensive sequence of maps.
[2] Anania of Shirak, *Geography*, ed. Soukry, pp. 29–35; tr. Hewsen, pp. 59–70.
[3] Garsoïan (1999a) to 700; thereafter Mahé (1993).

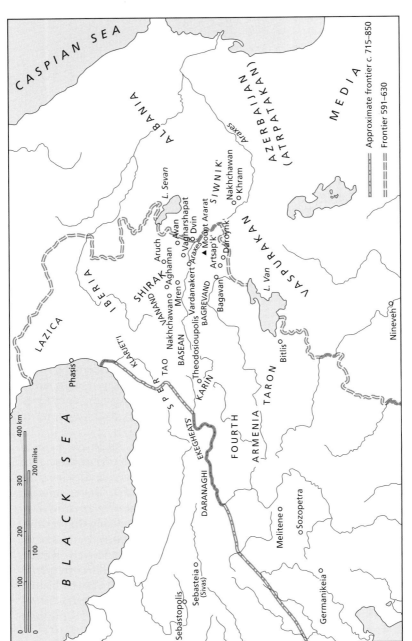

Map 16 Armenia 591–850

Figure 21 View from within the walls of Ani, looking south across what was the heart of the flourishing eleventh-century city to the ruined cathedral and beyond to the hills in the Republic of Armenia

impression of a pro-Chalcedonian, and arguably pro-Byzantine, party may still be traced and other schismatic traditions may have survived long after their suppression elsewhere.[4] Nor is there good evidence for either linguistic or cultural uniformity. Whilst the written form of the Armenian language may once have possessed such a quality, it seems inherently unlikely that contemporary speech was ever uniform. An eighth-century cleric, Stephen of Siwnik', identified seven dialects, all associated with remote, mountainous districts.[5] As for cultural uniformity, one has only to think of the selective histories, sponsored by princely houses to their own glory and the denigration of others, the multiple versions of the *History* of Agathangelos describing the conversion of Armenia or the different traditions surrounding the relics of Gregory the Illuminator, to appreciate that the past was essentially plastic, at the disposal of contemporary writers to develop and rework as they thought fit.[6]

When one considers the fragmented, isolating topography of the central Caucasus region, the individual districts of varying size, wealth and potential, the harsh continental climate, the dispersed settlement pattern focused upon the village, the frontier status of the region through the period, partitioned between Rome and Persia and then Byzantium and the caliphate,

[4] Garitte (1960); Arutiunova-Fidanjan (1988–9).
[5] Stephen of Siwnik', *Meknut'iwn*, ed. Adontz, p. 187.
[6] See respectively TA; van Esbroeck (1971a); van Esbroeck (1971b).

the lack of organic national political institutions, the long-standing doctrinal divisions within the Armenian church, the presence of different dialects and languages, even the potential for different interpretations of the past, one can only conclude that 'Armenia' and 'Armenian identity' are complex and elusive terms defying concrete definition and characterised by fluidity and plurality. Instead of maintaining the fiction of a united Armenia or a singular Armenian identity, Armenian diversity and incongruity deserve to be highlighted.

A second challenge is the uneven treatment in the primary sources of the relationship between Armenia and Byzantium. At times, it receives significant coverage but more often it remains frustratingly obscure, the periods between 730 and 850, and between 925 and 980 being particularly opaque. This may reflect a genuine lack of engagement. But it is also possible that the outline of Armenian history presented by the majority of Armenian sources is intentionally partial. Arguably, Armenian authors anticipated a similar collective historical experience to that of the people of God in the Old Testament and therefore stressed those contexts which replicated the biblical paradigm, including valiant but ultimately unsuccessful resistance against an oppressive and impious empire, exile and return. A neighbouring Christian polity, particularly one which adhered to a rival confession of faith, did not sit comfortably with this model and its influence was therefore downplayed or ignored. Armenian histories are much more than simple vehicles for the preservation of factual information; rather they are complex compositions which need to be handled with care and exploited only after careful textual criticism. Silence on the subject of Byzantium and the imperial church should not be mistaken for lack of contact.

Finally, insofar as the literary sources record the development of Byzantium's relationship with Armenia, they tend to do so in terms of the principal Armenian political and ecclesiastical leaders. As we shall see, Byzantium cultivated multiple ties with several noble houses at the same time. In a society characterised by intense competition between and within princely families, in which those with ambition and ability attracted followers, acquired lands and amassed wealth at the expense of those who did not, it paid to develop links with as many potential clients as possible. Some of this evidence survives only through contemporary Armenian colophons and inscriptions, sources whose historical potential has not been fully exploited. By drawing on these materials, as well as the twin disciplines of numismatics and sigillography, a more complex, nuanced picture of their relationship begins to emerge.

POLITICAL AND CONFESSIONAL FLUX (591–661)

In 590 the fugitive Sasanian king Khusro II (590, 591–628) appealed to Emperor Maurice (582–602) for military assistance against the usurper

Bahram Chobin, offering generous terms, including substantial territorial concessions in Armenia. These were accepted by Maurice, and after the defeat of Bahram in 591 the frontier shifted eastwards.[7] The following decade witnessed unprecedented cooperation between the two 'great powers' across Armenia. Maurice and Khusro II set out to strip their respective Armenian sectors of soldiers for service in distant conflicts. Two rebellions from the middle of this decade attest the resulting sense of bewilderment among the Armenian elite.[8] Only the uprisings in the 770s and the resistance to the forces of Michael IV (1034–41) in 1041 outside Ani reveal a similar desperation. The first of the two rebellions collapsed when threatened by imperial and Persian forces acting in concert. The second ended in bloodshed. An army under the general Heraclius and Hamazasp Mamikonean defeated the rebels, killing the majority and capturing the remainder who were taken back to Theodosioupolis and executed. The only rebel to escape fled to Khusro II but was returned, tortured and killed.

The role of Hamazasp Mamikonean challenges the standard picture of Armenian helplessness in the face of implacable imperial oppression. Here is an Armenian noble serving imperial interests inside Armenia. The suspicion must be that there were other Armenian princes prepared to work with the new regime. When war with Persia broke out after Maurice's assassination in late 602, as Khusro II sought to recover those districts previously ceded, several Armenian princes fought for Byzantium. In 605, the Byzantine forces defending the district of Bagrevand against Khusro were led by the local Armenian lord Theodore Khorkhoruni who entered into negotiations with the Persians only after Byzantine forces had withdrawn.[9] Significantly, it took at least five seasons of campaigning for the Persians to expel the Byzantine forces from Armenia (603–7). Moreover, the fighting was not restricted to those western districts which had been under imperial control for generations but was concentrated further east, across the districts recently acquired by Byzantium. Such a holding strategy would have been inconceivable without local support.

The decade after 591 also witnessed pressure upon those districts now under imperial control to conform to imperial orthodoxy. Although Catholicos Moses II (574–604) refused to attend a council in Constantinople convened to establish union between the churches and remained in the Persian sector at Dvin, Maurice ordered the council of Chalcedon to be preached in all the churches of the land of Armenia, threatening 'to unite them in communion through the army'.[10] A second catholicos, John

[7] Whitby, Michael (1988), pp. 297–304. See above, p. 169.
[8] Seb., chs. 15–18, ed. Abgaryan, pp. 87–90; tr. and comm. Thomson and Howard-Johnston, I, pp. 32–5.
[9] Seb., ch. 32, ed. Abgaryan, pp. 109–10; tr. and comm. Thomson and Howard-Johnston, I, pp. 60–2.
[10] Seb., ch. 19, ed. Abgaryan, p. 91; tr. and comm. Thomson and Howard-Johnston, I, p. 37. See also above, pp. 169–70.

of Bagaran, was established at Avan, provocatively situated just across the border. John is usually titled 'anti-catholicos' and dismissed as little more than the creature of Maurice with an ephemeral influence upon Armenia. However, there is good evidence for a sizeable body of support for John, at and below diocesan level. After the election of Abraham as catholicos (perhaps in 606, probably in 607), five bishops and nineteen leaders of religious communities, including those linked to the 'holy cathedral' and the church of St Hrip'sime in Vagharshapat, acknowledged their error and returned to the anti-Chalcedonian party.[11]

Moreover, there were repeated attempts at ecclesiastical reconciliation. In 604, the Byzantine commander in Armenia, Sormen, wrote to the temporary head of the monophysite party, Vrt'anes, noting that they had met and corresponded on this subject many times. Sormen expressed a hope that they could meet 'like fellow brothers, joint heirs in baptism and sons in the faith of our father St Gregory', revealing thereby his own Armenian ancestry.[12] This spirit of compromise, which was not reciprocated, seems to find an echo in the remarkable *karshuni* version of Agathangelos.[13] This transposes the key events in the original narrative of the conversion of Armenia to different, contemporary locations. Thus of the seventy-seven virgins who accompanied St Hrip'sime, forty are assigned to Dvin and thirty-seven to Avan, thereby establishing the equal sanctity of both sees. Gregory the Illuminator baptises in the western district of Ekegheats'; he meets King Tiridates fifteen kilometres from Theodosioupolis; and he dies in Daranaghi. This radical revision represents a rare witness to the intellectual tradition of the pro-Chalcedonian party in Armenia after 591 and a very subtle development – or rather, subversion – of Armenian tradition.

Even the Byzantines' defeat at Persian hands in Basean, probably in 607, and their subsequent loss of key fortresses, including Theodosioupolis, did not mark the end of operations in Armenia. The following year, a Byzantine counter-attack in the district of Theodosioupolis was repulsed, whilst in 610 the city's inhabitants were transferred to Ecbatana in Persia, suggesting an ongoing threat. In 613, another Byzantine army marched through these districts. When Heraclius (610–41) launched a significant campaign in 624 against Theodosioupolis and then Dvin, he was advancing through districts which had been incorporated into provincial and episcopal structures for generations. Evidently he was looking to attract additional support. In autumn 624, Heraclius appealed to the princes and leaders of the lands of Albania, Iberia and Armenia by letter, urging them to come and serve

---

[11] *Book of letters*, ed. Izmireants', pp. 151–2; ed. Pogharean, pp. 298–9; French tr. Garsoïan, pp. 514–15.
[12] *Book of letters*, ed. Izmireants', p. 90; ed. Pogharean, p. 231.
[13] van Esbroeck (1971a); Cowe (1992).

him together with their forces but threatening reprisals and subjugation if they refused.[14] It is impossible to gauge the response to his appeal but it seems that many Armenian princes preferred to support Khusro II.[15] Only one late source refers explicitly to Armenians being attracted into imperial service before Heraclius' defeat of the Persian army at the battle of Nineveh on 12 December 627.[16]

The years between 624 and 628 witnessed a complex series of military manoeuvres and engagements in the Transcaucasus.[17] Three primary strategic considerations seem to have guided Heraclius. He courted potential allies across the Transcaucasus and from the steppe world to the north. The decisive impact of Turkic forces in 627 and 628 cannot be exaggerated. Secondly, such a strategy drew Persian armies away from Constantinople and into an environment in which logistical pressures dictated that possession of the larger army was no guarantee of success. Thirdly, whether or not instructed by his father, Heraclius had recognised the potential for striking at the centre of the Sasanian kingdom from the north, using Armenia as a bridgehead.[18] Such considerations go a long way towards explaining why Armenia continued to command such attention from successive emperors throughout the seventh century and beyond.

When Byzantine forces were expelled in 607, the monophysite party in the Armenian church was already in the ascendant and remained so throughout the reign of Khusro II. The latter began to favour the expanding monophysite confession across his dominions in preference to the Nestorian church of the east. In the aftermath of Heraclius' triumph and the return of the True Cross to Jerusalem on 21 March 630, the fissures within the Armenian church were reopened. The recently appointed catholicos Ezra (630–41) was invited to attend a church council at Theodosioupolis, probably in early 631, and under threat of the creation of a second catholicos he accepted union. Statements that Ezra was 'a humble and gentle man' and that 'no indecorous word ever passed from his mouth' reflect a partisan opinion.[19] In reality his accommodation with Heraclius is likely to have provoked considerable antagonism, an echo of which may be found in the exile of John of Mayragom, an ardent monophysite whose own catholical ambitions had been thwarted by Ezra's election.[20] An inscription commemorating Ezra, partly in Greek and partly in Armenian cryptograms, has been unearthed at Avan; evidently Ezra wished to associate himself

---

[14] *HA*, II.10, ed. Arak'elyan, p. 132; tr. Dowsett, pp. 79–80. The *History of the Albanians* has been variously, and wrongly, attributed to Moses Daskhurants'i or Moses Kaghankatuats'i; the identity of the compiler is unknown.
[15] Theoph., ed. de Boor, I, p. 311; tr. Mango and Scott, p. 443.
[16] *Chronicon ad 1234*, ch. 99, ed. Chabot, I, pp. 233–4; *Syrian chronicles*; tr. Palmer *et al.*, p. 137.
[17] Howard-Johnston (1999).   [18] Kaegi (2003a), pp. 22–3.   [19] Greenwood (2002), pp. 360–3.
[20] Yov., XVIII.15–30, ed. Emin, pp. 77–80; tr. Maksoudian, pp. 99–100.

with the church founded there by John of Bagaran and the confessional tradition espoused by him.[21]

Ezra's choice of Avan was also dictated by political circumstance, since Dvin still lay in the Persian sector. The deposition of Khusro II did not give Heraclius possession of the whole of Armenia. In 628, Khusro II's successor, Kavad II, appointed Varaztirots' Bagratuni as governor (*marzban*) of Armenia. Only under the terms of a subsequent treaty in the summer of 630, between Heraclius and the latest claimant to the Sasanian throne, Boran (630–31), were those districts ceded to Maurice returned to Byzantine control. Even then, Persian influence over eastern and southern Armenia persisted. In autumn 637, the leading Armenian prince, Mushegh Mamikonean, responded to a Persian call-to-arms, raising 3,000 troops whilst Gregory, lord of Siwnik', contributed 1,000.[22] Both fell at the battle of al-Qadisiyya on 6 January 638. With the benefit of hindsight, such loyalty to the Sasanian cause might seem misguided, but the success of the Arab conquest of Persia was still far from assured at that time.

The loyalty of Varaztirots' Bagratuni and Mushegh Mamikonean to Sasanian Persia may also explain the promotion of 'new men' to the office of 'prince of Armenia' in the Byzantine sector of Armenia after 630, a title used to denote the principal client. Mzhezh Gnuni and his successors, David Saharuni and Theodore Rshtuni, all came from minor noble houses. Although the narrative sources reveal little beyond this sequence, epigraphic evidence supports the proposition that this decade saw an intense Byzantine campaign to attract a broad spectrum of support. Three inscriptions, recording the foundation of churches at Aghaman (completed 636/7), Bagavan (August 639) and Mren (between 638 and mid-640), all give a regnal year of Heraclius and accord him a laudatory epithet.[23] Contemporary regnal formulae and protocols used in imperial documents and legislation repeat this combination. These inscriptions therefore attest an otherwise lost body of correspondence between Byzantium and Armenia.

The inscriptions at Aghaman and Mren also confirm that imperial honours were distributed and were prized by their recipients. The founder of the small church at Aghaman chose to define himself as Gregory *elustr* – i.e. *illustris*, no more than a middle-ranking imperial title by this time. This reveals a considerable down-reach on the part of the imperial authorities into individual Armenian districts, for Gregory was not the lord of the district in which he sponsored his church. The founder of the church at Mren, David Saharuni, is titled *patrikios, kouropalatēs* and *sparapet* of Armenia and

---

[21] Greenwood (2004), inscription A.6 and p. 41.
[22] Seb., ch. 42, ed. Abgaryan, p. 137; tr. and comm. Thomson and Howard-Johnston, I, pp. 98–9.
[23] Greenwood (2004), inscriptions A.4, A.5 and A.7 and pp. 43–7, 62–78.

Syria. His remit encompassed all Armenia and must postdate the death of Mushegh Mamikonean at al-Qadisiyya in 638. The extension of his command beyond the boundaries of Armenia into Syria is unprecedented and suggests that Heraclius was prepared to make remarkable concessions in his efforts to forge an effective opposition to the Arab invasions after the fall of Syria, one in which Armenian military resources had a leading role to play.

The contention that Heraclius invested heavily in a network of Armenian clients is supported by the numismatic evidence. Seven different issues of silver hexagrams from the reign of Heraclius and four issues of Constans II (641–68) have been discovered in hoards or during excavations in Armenia, the latest issue being struck between 654 and 659.[24] This flow of Byzantine silver into Armenia has traditionally been linked to the presence of Byzantine forces; however, in light of the epigraphic evidence and the elite's prosperity, reflected in the numerous church foundations, one is tempted to speculate whether this silver was minted for, and paid to, Armenian clients. Armenia had been integrated into the Sasanian silver-based monetary system for centuries and silver coins would have been familiar to Armenians.

This strategy proved effective during the following decade. When an Arab raiding party advanced from northern Syria through the Bitlis pass in autumn 640 and sacked Dvin, Theodore Rshtuni ambushed the invaders during their retreat, albeit without much success.[25] A second Arab raid, attacking from the south-east through Azerbaijan in summer 643, encountered stiff resistance. One of its divisions, numbering about 3,000, was heavily defeated by Theodore Rshtuni outside the fortress of Artsap'k'. The major centre of Nakhchawan in the Araxes valley held out. These operations showed the offensive and defensive potential of Armenia and may have deterred further attacks.

Armenia was not insulated from the political turmoil engulfing Constantinople after the death of Heraclius. The failed coup by Valentinus in 645 seems to have prompted widespread changes in the military hierarchy across Armenia. The new commander, Thomas, was anxious not to damage the agreement established with Khorokhazat, leader of continuing Persian resistance against the Arabs in Atrpatakan (Azerbaijan). Thomas visited him and promised that Theodore Rshtuni would be taken to Constantinople.[26] This episode illustrates how the interests of two clients did not necessarily coincide. Khorokhazat faced growing recalcitrance from Albania

[24] Mousheghian et al. (2000a).

[25] Seb., chs. 42, 44, ed. Abgaryan, pp. 138–9, 145–7; tr. and comm. Thomson and Howard-Johnston, I, pp. 100–1, 109–11.

[26] Seb., ch. 44, ed. Abgaryan, pp. 142–3; tr. and comm. Thomson and Howard-Johnston, I, pp. 106–8.

and was looking for assistance in deterring Armenian support for dissident elements. In choosing to back Khorokhazat, Byzantium precipitated a crisis in Armenia.

Theodore Rshtuni was soon restored to his command but the relationship was clearly strained. In 652 the governor of Syria (and later caliph) Mu'awiya (661–80) induced him to switch sides, promising *inter alia* that Armenian forces would not be employed in Syria and that Arab forces would not be stationed in Armenia unless invited to repel a Byzantine attack.[27] In response, Constans II travelled to Armenia to shore up his support and undermine his erstwhile client. He advanced to Theodosioupolis and there received the submission of a disparate group of Armenian princes and their armed forces. Evidently they believed that it was in their long-term interests to return to imperial service. Constans II moved on to Dvin and stayed with Catholicos Nerses III (641–61). He attended a service with his host in the cathedral church of St Gregory, during which the liturgy was celebrated in Greek and the council of Chalcedon was proclaimed. Only one anonymous bishop refused to participate but this tells us little about the ongoing confessional tensions within the Armenian church; presumably anti-Chalcedonians did not attend.

Constans II did not remain in Armenia long, being forced to return and defend Constantinople in 654. Thereafter Byzantine fortunes fluctuated, imperial forces being driven out of Armenia twice, but by the first half of 656, Hamazasp Mamikonean was securely installed as *kouropalatēs* and prince of Armenia.[28] At the same time, honours were distributed to the other princes and treasures to the soldiers, confirming that the benefits of imperial service were not confined to a few but were spread broadly among the elite. Nerses III returned from exile in Tao after 'the lord of Rshtunik' had died and the Arab invasion had come to an end', indicating an earlier date, perhaps 656, than is generally admitted.

Constans II was determined to exploit the unexpected breathing space afforded by the outbreak of civil war or *fitna* across the caliphate. He sought to establish a broad network of clients across the Transcaucasus. Juansher, prince of Albania, and the princes of Siwnik' quickly submitted.[29] In autumn 659, the emperor undertook a second progress eastwards lasting several months.[30] He ventured into Media, meeting and rewarding loyal clients including Juansher, who requested and received a fragment of the

---

[27] Seb., chs. 48–9, ed. Abgaryan, pp. 164–8; tr. and comm. Thomson and Howard-Johnston, I, pp. 135–42.
[28] Seb., chs. 50–2, ed. Abgaryan, pp. 169–77; tr. and comm. Thomson and Howard-Johnston, I, pp. 143–53.
[29] Seb., ch. 52, ed. Abgaryan, p. 175; tr. and comm. Thomson and Howard-Johnston, I, p. 153; *HA*, II.19–21, ed. Arak'elyan, pp. 180–2; tr. Dowsett, pp. 115–17.
[30] *HA*, II.22, ed. Arak'elyan, pp. 183–6; tr. Dowsett, pp. 118–20.

Figure 22 The southern façade of the palatine church of Aruch, built by Mu'awiya's principal Armenian client, Gregory Mamikonean, and his wife Heline in 670. A columned palace has been excavated immediately to the south of the church, attested by the capital in the foreground

True Cross. Constans was also seeking to attract others, including Persians who wished to fight on against the Arabs. He was still in Armenia in spring 660, at Vagharshapat, where he rewarded Juansher a second time. A later text suggests that the emperor was present at the inauguration of the impressive church of Zvart'nots'.[31] Whilst this cannot be proved, his involvement would have done much to bolster the standing of its founder Nerses III and the pro-Chalcedonian party across Armenia. Intriguingly, the terse inscription commemorating Nerses' role is in Greek rather than Armenian.[32]

In the event, Constans II's vision of a chain of clients did not survive beyond the conclusion of the *fitna*. As the lynchpin of the network, Hamazasp was swiftly removed and replaced by his brother Gregory Mamikonean, previously a hostage of Mu'awiya. Juansher transferred his allegiance to the 'king of the south [Mu'awiya]', when 'the emperor of the Romans [Constans] took the dregs of his forces and hastened across sea and land to cross to the . . . distant islands of the west'.[33] It seems very likely that the principal Byzantine clients had been displaced or turned by late 661 or early 662.

---

[31] *HA*, III.15, ed. Arak'elyan, p. 317; tr. Dowsett, p. 207.
[32] Greenwood (2004), inscription A.18 and p. 41.
[33] *HA*, II.27, ed. Arak'elyan, p. 193; tr. Dowsett, pp. 124–5.

INDEPENDENCE AND INTEGRATION UNDER ISLAM (661–850)

After 661, the limitations of the primary sources make it much harder to trace the interaction between Byzantium and Armenia. The conventional approach has been to treat this dearth of information as evidence for the exclusion of Byzantine influence. Armenian colophons and inscriptions together with isolated textual references collectively support an alternative view, of persistent, wide-ranging Byzantine engagement until 730 but a more limited focus thereafter, concentrated on and operated through those districts bordering imperial territory.

The second sustained period of civil war across the caliphate after 680 afforded a fresh opportunity for Byzantine intervention. According to Lewond's *History*, Armenia repudiated Arab sovereignty by refusing to pay tribute, probably in 682, but it is impossible to prove Byzantine influence lying behind this decision.[34] A later Armenian source records how an Iberian prince, Nerses, massacred the Arab forces in Armenia during the time of Catholicos Israel I (667–77).[35] The Arab blockade of Constantinople between 674 and 678 supplies an appropriate historical context for just such a diversionary campaign but a Byzantine connection remains conjectural (see also pp. 233, 372).

Constantine IV (668–85) was eager to exploit contemporary disorder across the caliphate. In 685, he invaded Cilicia and threatened northern Syria, compelling the new caliph, 'Abd al-Malik (685–705) to sue for peace on very generous terms on 7 July 685.[36] This campaign may have been coordinated with the devastating Khazar raid into Armenia during which Gregory Mamikonean and Nerses were killed in battle on 18 August 685.[37] According to Theophanes the Confessor, Justinian II (685–95, 705–711) ratified the truce with 'Abd al-Malik soon after his accession although its term was extended to ten years and an additional provision was inserted, requiring the parties to share the tax revenue of Cyprus, Armenia and Iberia.[38] A subsequent passage under the same year entry adds that Justinian II despatched a *stratēgos*, Leontius, into Armenia. He subjugated Armenia, together with Iberia, Albania, Boukania (probably Vaspurakan) and Media, imposed taxes on those countries and remitted a large sum to Justinian. The changes to the treaty make sense when viewed in the aftermath of this raid. The revenue arrangements may reflect a more fundamental partition, of sovereignty. Gregory Mamikonean's successor as prince of Armenia was Ashot Bagratuni, titled *patrikios*. Since he also brought an icon of the

---

[34] Lew., ch. 4, ed. Ezean, p. 15; tr. Arzoumanian, p. 54.
[35] Yov., XX.18–19, ed. Emin, p. 93; tr. Maksoudian, p. 106.
[36] Theoph., ed. de Boor, I, p. 361; tr. Mango and Scott, pp. 503–4.
[37] Lew., ch. 4, ed. Ezean, pp. 15–16; tr. Arzoumanian, pp. 54–5.
[38] Theoph., ed. de Boor, I, p. 363; tr. Mango and Scott, pp. 506–7.

incarnation of Christ 'from the west' for his church at Daroynk', forty kilometres south of Mount Ararat, it seems likely that he was a Byzantine client.[39]

After Ashot's death – confronting Arab raiders in the Araxes valley in 689 – a number of Armenian princes switched allegiance. This prompted Justinian II to travel to Armenia in person, as his grandfather Constans II had done in similar circumstances. Justinian summoned the princes to him, taking some of their sons hostage, while rewarding others: he raised Nerses Kamsarakan, the lord of Shirak, to the rank of prince of Armenia and the *patrikios* and exarch Varaz(tr)dat was made prince of Albania.[40] He then returned to Constantinople, taking with him Catholicos Sahak III (677–703) and five bishops. Theophanes likewise reports Justinian's visit to Armenia although he places it too early, in his second year, and wrongly associates it with the Mardaites.[41] A remarkable, pro-Chalcedonian account of Armenian ecclesiastical history, which survives only in Greek, records that Sahak and his bishops accepted Chalcedon at a council convened in Constantinople in the fifth year of Justinian II, although on their return to Armenia and under pressure, they reneged.[42]

This revival in Byzantine fortunes occurred in the context of the second *fitna*. Even before his final victory over his main rival in 691, Caliph 'Abd al-Malik was turning his attention to Byzantium. Contrary to the traditional view, it seems very probable that it was 'Abd al-Malik, not Justinian II, who broke the ten-year truce.[43] The heavy Byzantine defeat in 692 at Sebastopolis occurred deep inside newly secured Byzantine territory, indicating an Arab offensive (see below, p. 384). Several Armenian clients promptly transferred allegiance but the Byzantine position did not collapse overnight. A colophon confirms that the principal Byzantine client in 689, Nerses Kamsarakan, was still alive in 696 and in contact with Constantinople.[44] The region of Fourth Armenia also resisted. Although Muhammad bin Marwan, the governor of al-Jazira, campaigned there in 694/5, evidently it had not been subjugated in 701/2 when Baanes 'Heptadaimon' switched sides.[45] Perhaps most surprisingly, in 702 Smbat Bagratuni rebelled and defeated an Arab force at Vardanakert, being rewarded with the title *kouropalatēs*.[46] A

[39] Lew., ch. 5, ed. Ezean, p. 16; tr. Arzoumanian, p. 55.

[40] ST, ed. Malkhaseants', p. 101; French tr. Dulaurier, p. 129.

[41] Theoph., ed. de Boor, I, p. 364; tr. Mango and Scott, pp. 507–8.

[42] *Narratio de rebus Armeniae*, chs. 144–5, ed. Garitte, pp. 46–7 (text), pp. 350–6 (commentary); French tr. Mahé, p. 437.

[43] Proposed by James Howard-Johnston in a seminar paper, 'Byzantium and 'Abd al-Malik' (11 March 2003, Oxford).

[44] Mat'evosyan (ed.), *Hishatakaranner*, no. 28, pp. 21–2; Socrates Scholasticus, *Ecclesiastical history*, pp. 9–13, 35–40.

[45] Theoph., ed. de Boor, I, pp. 368, 372; tr. Mango and Scott, pp. 514, 519.

[46] Lew., ch. 10, ed. Ezean, pp. 31–5; tr. Arzoumanian, pp. 64–6.

parallel account of this uprising, but with a Kamsarakan spin, affords useful corroboration.[47]

The aftermath of this rebellion remains confused. Lewond maintains that Smbat withdrew into Tao and that Catholicos Sahak III negotiated a three-year peace. According to the *History of the Albanians*, however, military operations continued.[48] Dvin fell to a joint Byzantine-Armenian force whilst the Arabs captured a fortress in Sevan only after a three-year blockade. Both sources agree that a Byzantine force then suffered a heavy defeat. Lewond adds that this occurred in Vanand in the first year of Caliph al-Walid I (705–15). The Byzantine troops fled and the Armenian rebels suffered severe reprisals, with 800 men in Nakhchawan and 400 in Khram being imprisoned in churches and then burnt alive. Ominously, the lord of Shirak, Nerses Kamsarakan, was summoned to Syria in 705; his fate is not recorded. Smbat *kouropalatēs* escaped into Byzantine territory and was settled in the city of Phasis in Lazica. This sequence of events – a rebellion by Armenian princes, contact with Emperor Tiberius II Apsimar (698–705), the despatch of Byzantine forces, a successful counter-offensive by Muhammad bin Marwan followed by the burning alive of Armenian princes – is corroborated by Theophanes.[49] The only significant difference is chronological. Theophanes records this sequence of events under one year, AM 6195 (702/3) but it seems more likely that they were spread across several years (702–5).

Aside from the failed attempt at union in the time of Justinian II outlined above, relations between the churches after 661 are almost entirely obscure. In 719, however, Catholicos John III (717–27) stated unequivocally that the six catholicoi after Komitas (between 628 and 705) were all Chalcedonian, exempting only his immediate predecessor Elias (703–17) from criticism.[50] As outlined previously, Ezra, Nerses III and Sahak III all engaged in discussions with the imperial church but none of their correspondence or other writings survives. Indeed the only extant letter between 628 and 705 is a draft Armenian 'Defence' of the monophysite position, prepared in 649 for despatch to Constans II.[51] Arguably, no records or letters associated with these catholicoi survive precisely because of their confessional perspective. An exchange between Patriarch Germanos I (715–30) and Catholicos John III from the 720s does survive, defining and defending their respective positions in great detail.[52] Conceivably this correspondence marks the

[47] Yov., XXI.1–5, ed. Emin, pp. 95–8; tr. Maksoudian, pp. 107–9.

[48] *HA*, III.16, ed. Arak'elyan, pp. 317–18; tr. Dowsett, pp. 207–8.

[49] Theoph., ed. de Boor, I, p. 372; tr. Mango and Scott, pp. 519–20.

[50] *Book of letters*, ed. Izmireants', pp. 221–2; ed. Pogharean, pp. 475–6. See now Greenwood (2008).

[51] Seb., ch. 46, ed. Abgaryan, pp. 148–61; tr. and comm. Thomson and Howard-Johnston, I, pp. 114–32; Thomson (1998).

[52] *Book of letters*, ed. Izmireants', pp. 358–95; ed. Pogharean, pp. 414–66.

final breach between the churches and was preserved because it articulated the differences. Confessional tensions at the highest level need not have deterred other contacts. Colophons reveal that four patristic works were translated into Armenian in Constantinople between 713 and 717 by David *hypatos* and Stephen of Siwnik'.[53]

After 730, Byzantine influence persisted but on a more limited scale. An inscription on a tombstone located in a crypt at Nakhchawan in Shirak commemorates 'the blessed lord Artawazd Kamsarakan *apo hypatōn patrikios* and prince of Armenia, son of Hrahat *patrikios* lord of Shirak and Asharunik''.[54] Artawazd was the grandson of Nerses Kamsarakan mentioned previously. Evidently Byzantine titles continued to be awarded during the eighth century to Armenian princes. Artawazd does not feature in any other source, which is surprising given his rank of 'prince of Armenia'. His omission is hard to explain unless one views him as a second, rival prince of Armenia and client of Byzantium.

When the third *fitna* erupted, two groups of Armenian princes may once again be discerned. One party, under Ashot Bagratuni, remained loyal to Caliph Marwan II (744–50); the other under Gregory Mamikonean, looked to Constantine V (741–75). Having taken refuge in Tao, 'they relied upon the forces of the king of the Greeks, who were in the regions of Pontos, because there was a treaty of peace between them, at the command of the emperor Constantine'.[55] After blinding Ashot Bagratuni, perhaps in 748, Gregory went to Theodosioupolis and broadcast news of his victory. Evidently Theodosioupolis was under his, or Constantine's, control and he was attempting to attract further support. His success or otherwise in this initiative is not recorded by Lewond, who simply notes that he died in agony at an unspecified date and was replaced for a short time by his brother.[56] Whether Lewond's hostility stems from a political (anti-Mamikonean) or confessional (anti-Chalcedonian) perspective is unclear. Again this temporary Byzantine revival in Armenia was halted by the resolution of the strife within the caliphate. In 754, Constantine V transferred the population of Theodosioupolis to Thrace. Lewond adds that many from the surrounding districts also left and 'placed themselves on the side of the pious king', a rare favourable view of Constantine V.[57] This transfer may represent a tactical withdrawal at the end of a series of initiatives in Armenia rather than the original goal.

Armenian princes did not risk rebellion against the dominant, controlling power without support, or expressions of support, from a rival power

[53] Mat'evosyan (ed.), *Hishatakaranner*, nos. 31–4, pp. 24–6.
[54] Greenwood (2004), inscription A.13 and pp. 75–6.
[55] Lew., ch. 26, ed. Ezean, p. 123; tr. Arzoumanian, p. 120.
[56] Lew., ch. 26, ed. Ezean, pp. 123–4; tr. Arzoumanian, pp. 120–1.
[57] Lew., ch. 29, ed. Ezean, p. 129; tr. Arzoumanian, p. 124.

other than in exceptional circumstances. At first sight, the complicated series of rebellions across Armenia in the 770s fall into that category. At no stage do the narrative sources indicate any Byzantine involvement.[58] Two of the rebel leaders, Artawazd and Mushegh Mamikonean, are said to have begun their uprisings by killing local Arab tax-collectors. New administrative arrangements and fiscal burdens at district level may have precipitated their actions. On the other hand, Artawazd moved into Iberia and later reappears as *stratēgos tōn Anatolikōn* whilst Mushegh's rebellion apparently took the form of a prolonged, and ultimately unsuccessful, siege of Theodosioupolis. This strategy is hard to fathom unless one accepts that Byzantine support was anticipated. No Byzantine campaign is recorded but it may have been planned; in 777 a large Byzantine army, under Armenian commanders, attacked Germanikeia and devastated the surrounding region.[59]

For the following five decades, there is very little evidence for Byzantine involvement in Armenia. In 788 as many as 12,000 people under the leadership of Shapuh Amatuni, his son and other Armenian nobles were granted refuge within the empire by 'the emperor Constantine'. Lewond portrays this as a reaction to hardships inflicted by the caliph and his representatives, specifically the seizure of land.[60] It is in the last quarter of the eighth century that several quasi-independent Arabic emirates emerged, ruling districts previously under Armenian control.[61] At the same time, members of the Bagratuni princely house exploited their status as preferred Abbasid clients to secure a dominant position. After 775, Byzantine attention was concentrated on potential clients in those districts of Iberia which abutted imperial territory. Ashot Bagratuni, established in neighbouring Klarjet'i, was appointed *kouropalatēs* before 826.[62] Byzantine strategy towards Armenia came to operate on and through the remote district of Sper which bordered the theme of Chaldia. The first ninth-century Armenian prince known to have been accorded an imperial title was another Ashot Bagratuni, prince of Sper; he was appointed *patrikios* and *apo hypatōn* by Theophilos (829–42).[63] Intriguingly, his appointment is recorded in the context of Byzantine operations against Theodosioupolis, Basean and Vanand, all to the south and east of Sper. Although these operations have been compressed into a single campaign and linked to a major Byzantine offensive against Sozopetra, Melitene and Fourth Armenia undertaken in 837, they could equally comprise separate campaigns spread over a number of years.[64]

---

[58] Lew., ch. 34, ed. Ezean, pp. 137–52; tr. Arzoumanian, pp. 129–38.

[59] Theoph., ed. de Boor, I, p. 451; tr. Mango and Scott, p. 623.

[60] Lew., ch. 42, ed. Ezean, pp. 168–9; tr. Arzoumanian, p. 149.

[61] Ter-Ghewondyan (1976).

[62] Martin-Hisard (2001); Martin-Hisard (2002); Abashidze and Rapp (2004).

[63] ST, ed. Malkhaseants', p. 144; French tr. Dulaurier, p. 171.

[64] Laurent (1980), pp. 249–52.

This targeting of Theodosioupolis and its surrounding districts mirrors the pattern of Byzantine offensives outlined previously, whilst the Khurramite rebellion under Babek afforded a suitable opportunity (see below, p. 390).

Caliph al-Muʻtasim (833–42) responded swiftly to this Byzantine threat. In 838, his forces inflicted a heavy defeat upon Theophilos at Dazimon and captured Amorion. Genesios reports that Armenian forces under the 'Vasparakanites' (presumably the leading Artsruni prince) and the prince of princes (probably Bagarat Bagratuni, prince of Taron) participated in these campaigns.[65] This represents a rare instance of active service by Armenian forces against Byzantium. It illustrates how closely the leading Armenian princes now identified with caliphal interests and the degree to which Byzantine influence over them had waned.

ARMENIA RESURGENT, BYZANTIUM EXPECTANT (850–1045)

In 850, Caliph al-Mutawakkil (847–61) sent Abu Saʻid Muhammad bin Yusuf to Armenia to collect the so-called 'royal taxes'. Although these were apparently paid, relations between representatives of Abu Saʻid and the principal Artsruni and Bagratuni princes deteriorated rapidly and all parties took up arms.[66] In 852, Bugha al-Kabir embarked on a series of ruthless campaigns to quash Armenian resistance. The principal noble families were targeted and many leading members were either killed or captured and despatched to the Abbasid capital, Samarra. A few, however, escaped. In 853 or 854, Gurgen Artsruni sought refuge with Gregory Bagratuni, prince of Sper.[67] Gregory had recently captured an unidentified Byzantine fortress called Aramaneak. When the Byzantine 'general of the east' – an Armenian rendering of *stratēgos tōn Anatolikōn* – attempted to recover Aramaneak, both princes opposed him. He was so impressed by Gurgen's courage that he informed Michael III (842–67), who invited Gurgen to Constantinople. Gurgen declined but he did persuade Gregory to return the fortress and also fought against Bugha's troops when they attacked 'the Greek forces in their fortresses'. This is the first recorded contact between an Artsruni prince and Byzantium for many generations. Significantly it took place in Sper while Armenia was in turmoil.

Nor was this the limit of Byzantine ambitions. In 858, after Gurgen had returned to Vaspurakan, he was confronted by Gregory Artsruni at the head

---

[65] Gen., III.13, ed. Lesmüller-Werner and Thurn, p. 47; tr. Kaldellis, pp. 62–3. The prince of princes could have been Bagarat Bagratuni's brother, Smbat Abu'l ʻAbbas, at this time.

[66] TA, ed. Patkanean, pp. 106–212; tr. Thomson, pp. 173–275; Yov., XXV–XXVII, ed. Emin, pp. 113–35; tr. Maksoudian, pp. 116–26.

[67] TA, ed. Patkanean, pp. 194–5; tr. Thomson, pp. 258–9.

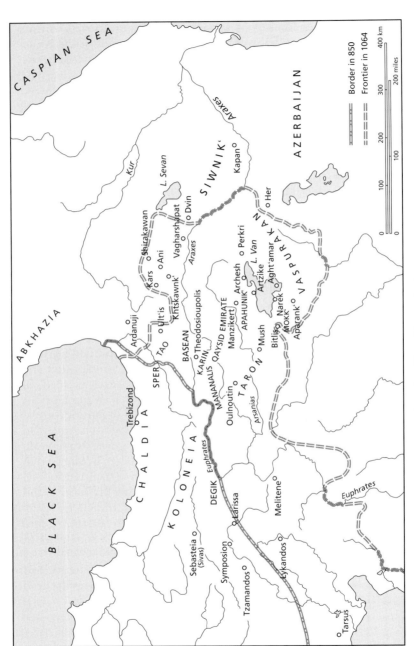

Map 17 Armenia and imperial expansion 850–1045

of Abkhazian and Iberian troops.[68] Having failed to attract Gurgen, it seems that Byzantium had switched its attention to a second displaced Artsruni prince and backed his bid to seize Vaspurakan. Although Gregory was unsuccessful, the imperial administration evidently had a strategic vision which extended far beyond those districts adjacent to imperial territory.

Therefore when Photios became patriarch of Constantinople in 858 and re-established contact with the Armenian church, he did so in the context of renewed Byzantine engagement across Armenia. The sequence and chronology of the letters exchanged between Photios (858–67, 877–86) and several Armenian correspondents, including Catholicos Zacharias (855–76), remains contentious, as does the authenticity of one of Photios' letters to Zacharias.[69] Collectively the correspondence attests Photios' determination to heal the long-standing confessional breach. The council of Shirakawan, convened in 862 by Zacharias, represents the first fruits of Photios' initiative.[70] Canons 13 and 14 respectively condemn two groups: firstly, convinced monophysites who masquerade as Chalcedonians, for personal gain; and secondly, those who have apparently accepted Chalcedon, but still cannot help themselves from adopting the traditional Armenian charge – that the council's ruling on the unity of Christ's person was, in fact, Nestorian. As Jean-Pierre Mahé puts it, 'le cas prévu était la conversion de monophysites au dyophysisme et non l'inverse.'[71] The aftermath of this council is unknown but just before his deposition in 867, Photios observed in an encyclical letter that 'today, the covenant of the Armenians worships purely and in orthodox fashion the Christian faith.'[72]

By the time Photios was reappointed patriarch on 26 October 877, conditions had altered dramatically. His 'spiritual brother' Zacharias had died and the prince of princes, Ashot Bagratuni, was now entrenched as the pre-eminent client of the caliph and wary of Byzantine initiatives. Although Photios made considerable efforts to engage with Ashot, sending conciliatory letters addressed to 'your most eminent piety', despatching a relic of the True Cross and even reporting that relics of the three most revered Armenian saints had been found in Constantinople, he was unable to recover lost ground.[73] The final letters chart the breakdown in discussions with Ashot and his spiritual advisers. Both sides reverted to their traditional positions, defining and rebutting in meticulous detail the doctrinal errors of the other. Although these letters are not dated, the heavy defeats suffered

---

[68] TA, ed. Patkanean, pp. 198–9; tr. Thomson, pp. 262–3.
[69] See Dorfmann-Lazarev (2004) and Greenwood (2006a) for opposing views.
[70] Akinean and Ter-Pawghosean (1968a), cols. 261–6; Maksoudian (1988–9).
[71] Mahé (1993), p. 495.
[72] Phot., no. 2, ed. Laourdas and Westerink, I, p. 41, lines 43–4.
[73] On the letter, see Akinean and Ter-Pawghosean (1968b), col. 439. On the True Cross, see Mat'evosyan (ed.), *Hishatakaranner*, no. 50, pp. 40–3. On the relics, see van Esbroeck (1971b), pp. 401–4; Greenwood (2006b).

by the Byzantine forces at Melitene in 882 and Tarsus in 883 provide a likely *terminus ante quem* (see above, p. 297). Around 925, Patriarch Nicholas I Mystikos (901–7, 912–925) reflected that Photios had pursued ecclesiastical reconciliation with Armenia without success, implying no correspondence on this subject between the churches in the intervening forty years.[74]

Frustratingly there is no evidence for contacts with the feuding members of the Artsruni house in Vaspurakan after 858. A little more is known about relations with the extended Bagratuni family. Photios acknowledged Ashot Bagratuni's concern for his recent travails and joy at his restoration in 877, suggesting contact before he had regained the patriarchate. Moreover Ashot learned about the discovery of the Armenian relics during an embassy from Basil I (867–86) in 878. In spite of these initiatives, it was not Ashot, prince of princes, who was appointed *kouropalatēs* but his cousin Ashot, prince of Taron, at an unspecified date before 878.[75] In a final letter, Photios described the Taronites who inhabited Fourth Armenia as orthodox.[76] It may well be the case that Ashot was rewarded for his orthodoxy. Alternatively the relative proximity of Taron to imperial territory may have influenced the appointment. Either way, Byzantium developed ties simultaneously with several Bagratuni princes.

Three decades of ambitious military and ecclesiastical initiatives beyond the eastern frontier, lasting from 854 to 883, were followed by an era of consolidation. Little-known figures, controlling districts much closer to imperial territory, were induced to acknowledge imperial sovereignty. After the accession of Leo VI (886–912), Manuel, lord of Degik, was given a written guarantee of immunity, taken to Constantinople and appointed *prōtospatharios*.[77] At the same time, other Armenians were appointed to separate commands along the frontier, usually organised around individual fortresses, and encouraged to expand into adjacent districts. Thus Melias (or Mleh in Armenian) was first appointed turmarch of Euphrateia and Trypia.[78] In 908, he captured the *kastron* of Lykandos and became its kleisouriarch. He then advanced to Tzamandos and constructed a *kastron*. Later he annexed Symposion. In 915 he was appointed *stratēgos* of the newly-created theme of Lykandos. Melias' lordship thereby gained an administrative and legal identity within the Byzantine state. The network of themes created piecemeal along the eastern frontier reflected the local achievements of men such as Melias. Inevitably there were losers as well as winners. For every Melias, there were figures like Ismael 'the Armenian', kleisouriarch of Symposion, who was killed by raiders from Melitene.

It would be wrong, however, to assume that this time of consolidation on the frontier coincided with any break in relations with Armenian princes

---

[74] NM, no. 139, pp. 450–1. [75] TA, ed. Patkanean, pp. 218–24; tr. Thomson, pp. 282–8.
[76] Phot., no. 284, ed. Laourdas and Westerink, III, p. 94, lines 3194–6.
[77] *DAI*, ch. 50, pp. 238–9. [78] *DAI*, ch. 50, pp. 238–41.

beyond the frontier. Again, several isolated references indicate continued contact with key Bagratuni princes. After Ashot, prince of princes, had been crowned king on 26 August 884 by Catholicos George II (877–97) using a crown brought from the caliph, Basil I acknowledged him as his 'beloved son'.[79] Leo VI addressed Ashot I's son Smbat I Bagratuni ('the Martyr') (c. 890–913) in the same way after he succeeded his father in about 890, sending him 'fine weapons and ornaments and clothing embroidered with gold and cups and chalices and golden belts studded with gems'.[80] In 892 Smbat captured the city of Dvin and sent its commanders to the emperor in chains, although it seems that this campaign was his own initiative rather than a joint operation.[81] When the prince of Taron, Krikorikios ('little Gregory'), captured his two cousins in battle in the mid-890s, Smbat wrote to Leo VI, interceding for their release.[82] Evidently he believed that the emperor could influence the actions of Krikorikios and in this he was proved right.

This incident is reported in chapter forty-three of Constantine VII Porphyrogenitus' *De administrando imperio*, whose importance has long been recognised.[83] It describes how several members of the princely family of Taron across two generations were drawn into the political and cultural orbit of Byzantium; the titles, marriages and properties variously granted to them; and the consequences of such engagement for the very existence of the principality. The chapter ends with the *patrikios* Tornikios offering to cede his territories to the emperor, Romanos I Lekapenos (920–44). Although Tornikios died before completing this transfer of sovereignty, he left a will – a Byzantine rather than an Armenian custom – devising the same. His cousins complained to Romanos, who agreed to exchange his inheritance for Oulnoutin, a strategically placed *kastron* in the west of Taron. This chapter reveals much else besides, not least the collection and retention of information gained during diplomatic exchanges; a legal dispute between different members of an Armenian family over title to their property in Constantinople, encouraged if not inspired by the imperial authorities; and complaints to Romanos from three other Armenian princes over payments made to Krikorikios. It is worth remembering, however, that this chapter affords a partial view of diplomatic relations with one particular princely house and the territorial rights conceded to Romanos. The following three chapters trace imperial claims to the Qaysid emirate of Manzikert, to specific districts and *kastra* around Theodosioupolis and to the *kastron* of Ardanuji in Klarjet'i; they do not supply an exhaustive account of relations with every Armenian princely house.

[79] Yov., XXIX.13, ed. Emin, p. 140; tr. Maksoudian, pp. 129, 272–3.
[80] Yov., XXXI.2, ed. Emin, p. 158; tr. Maksoudian, p. 138.
[81] Yov., XXXI.9-13, ed. Emin, pp. 160–1; tr. Maksoudian, pp. 138–9.
[82] *DAI*, ch. 43, pp. 188–91.   [83] Shepard (2001).

A better impression of the range of Armenian contacts is supplied by the protocols for imperial correspondence preserved in the *Book of ceremonies*.[84] The list, which has been dated to between 918 and 922, identifies not only the prince of princes of Greater Armenia and the prince of Vaspurakan, 'who now is honoured as prince of princes', but also seven other Armenian princes. Yet arguably even this list does not do justice to the range of potential correspondents. It identifies only the leading representative of each princely house, but, as we have seen in respect of Taron above, several members of the same house could be in direct relationship with the emperor.

In addition to the activities of Armenian commanders on the frontier, and diplomatic links, Byzantium could also intervene directly using its military forces. A Byzantine force attacked Theodosioupolis as early as 895, whilst in 915 Ashot II Bagratuni ('the Iron') (914–c.928), son of King Smbat I 'the Martyr', returned from exile in Constantinople at the head of a Byzantine army, intent on re-establishing himself in the districts previously held by his father.[85] In the event, neither campaign was followed up but such apparently isolated actions need to be placed in the context of heavy Byzantine defeats in the Balkans, at Bulgarophygon in 896 and Anchialos in 917. Only after peace had been achieved in 927 were Byzantine forces redirected to the east.[86] Thereafter key fortresses under Arab control were systematically targeted. Melitene capitulated in 934 and Theodosioupolis in 949, both after years of persistent pressure and blockade. At the same time, every effort was made to ensure that neighbouring Armenian or Iberian princes were not antagonised. Conceivably this strategy was devised after two early reverses. In 922 when a Byzantine army attacked Dvin, it was opposed by the same Ashot II 'the Iron' who had benefited from imperial support seven years before.[87] Only in exceptional circumstances did an Armenian prince fight against imperial troops. Arguably his own interests had been prejudiced by this advance. Secondly, an attempt was made in 923 to seize control of Ardanuji, located beyond the frontier in Klarjet'i, by infiltrating troops under the guise of a visiting diplomatic mission.[88] Although this *kastron* had been offered to Romanos I Lekapenos by its prince, the threat by neighbouring Iberian princes to make common cause with local Arabs precipitated a rapid withdrawal.

Frustratingly it is at this very moment, with Byzantium poised to utilise all three approaches – administrative, diplomatic and military – that our source-material peters out. There is sufficient evidence, however, to confirm

---

[84] *DC*, II.48, ed. Reiske, I, p. 687; Martin-Hisard (2000).
[85] *TA*, ed. Patkanean, p. 231; tr. Thomson, pp. 294–5; Yov., LVI.1–4, ed. Emin, p. 292–3; tr. Maksoudian, pp. 201–2.
[86] Whittow (1996a), pp. 316–17. See also below, p. 509.
[87] *ST*, ed. Malkhaseants', p. 170; French tr. Macler, pp. 24–5.   [88] *DAI*, ch. 46, pp. 214–23.

that the eclipse in Bagratuni power – epitomised by Smbat I's murder in 913 and perpetuated by the long confrontation between Ashot II 'the Iron' and Smbat's nephew, also called Ashot – forced Byzantium to reappraise its position and recognise Gagik Artsruni as the pre-eminent figure.[89] Shortly after the death of Catholicos John V in 925, Gagik I Artsruni (908–c.943) wrote to Nicholas I Mystikos, seeking to secure the succession for his preferred candidate through a ceremony in Constantinople. Nicholas' reply, addressed to Gagik 'prince of princes', was uncompromising in its defence of orthodox belief, maintaining that Gagik's candidate would need to be instructed in sound doctrine and ecclesiastical government.[90] At the same time Nicholas noted the 'confession of friendship' by which Gagik was 'attached to our Christ-loving emperor and to our most holy church of God'; his own orthodoxy was not at issue. This relationship had practical implications. According to Ibn al-Athir, in 931 the lord of Vaspurakan, Ibn al-Dayrani (the Arabic version of [Gagik] son of Derenik) proposed and participated in a joint campaign with Byzantine forces against the Qaysid amirs.[91]

During the Artsruni ascendancy, Byzantium retained ties with other noble houses. The leading Bagratuni after 929, Abas, held the title of *magistros*, reflecting both the continuing demise of his family's fortunes and a closer link to Byzantium than many commentators have credited.[92] A letter written in about 933 by Theodore Daphnopates to the bishop of Siwnik', reprimanding him for teaching monophysite doctrine, reveals the spread of Byzantine interest eastwards.[93] Yet it is clear that Byzantium did not enjoy a monopoly of influence across Armenia. Mindful of recent Sajid intervention and devastation, Armenian princes remained wary of Muslim powers to the east and south, however ephemeral these proved to be. Thus when Saif al-Dawla, the future Hamdanid amir of Aleppo, marched north through the Bitlis pass to Lake Van in 940, several Armenian princes responded to his summons and submitted, including one of Gagik's sons and Ashot, son of Krikorikios, prince of Taron.[94] Although the sources contradict one another over the course of his campaign and the identity of the Artsruni client, they confirm that Armenian princes were prepared to recognise the sovereignty of an enemy of Byzantium if they believed this would serve their own interests. Ibn Hawqal offers a second example, listing those Armenian princes who paid tribute to the Sallarid ruler of

---

[89] *DC*, II.48, ed. Reiske, I, p. 687.
[90] NM, no. 135, pp. 446–51. A second, unrelated letter from Gagik to the patriarch and the emperor survives: *Book of letters*, ed. Izmireants', pp. 295–301; French tr. Garsoïan, pp. 540–9.
[91] Ibn al-Athir, *al-Kamil*, in Vasil., p. 153.   [92] *DAI*, ch. 44, pp. 198–9.
[93] Theodore Daphnopates, *Correspondance*, ed. and French tr. Darrouzès and Westerink, no. 10, pp. 108–41. Intriguingly the original letter from the bishop was in Armenian.
[94] *DAI: Comm.*, p. 169; Whittow (1996a), pp. 319–20.

Figure 23 The southern façade of the palatine church of Aght'amar, constructed by the architect Manuel for King Gagik I Artsruni of Vaspurakan between 915 and 921 on an island in Lake Van. The external walls are lined with figural and decorative sculpture, inspired by biblical and Artsruni history; frescoes, now badly damaged, cover the interior

Azerbaijan, Marzuban, in 955 and the considerable amounts due.[95] It is unclear whether such sums were actually remitted or whether this liability lapsed after Marzuban's death in 957, but the principle, however short-lived, seems established. By contrast, there is no evidence that Byzantium imposed any financial burdens upon its Armenian clients.

In the event, Saif al-Dawla did not develop a bloc of Armenian support. His victories over Byzantine forces provoked a series of counter-offensives. The successes enjoyed by Nikephoros Phokas after 955 drew Byzantium southwards, into Cilicia and northern Syria, away from active military engagement in Armenia (see below, p. 517). As observed above, campaigns across Armenia had been directed against those emirates and their bases which historically had posed the greatest threat. This strategy concluded with the capture of Theodosioupolis in 949. Although the military focus shifted south, it seems that the nexus of relationships with Armenian princes and clerics continued to be maintained and developed. Admittedly there is very little evidence of Byzantine involvement in Armenia between 935 and 976, but it is during this period that significant confessional tensions emerged within the Armenian church. Catholicos Anania I (943–67) reasserted

[95] Ibn Hawqal, *Surat*, ed. Kramers, II, pp. 354–5; French tr. Kramers and Wiet, II, pp. 347–8; Minorsky (1953), pp. 519–20.

his authority over the dissident see of Siwnik' at the council of Kapan in 958, but was succeeded by Vahan I of Siwnik' who 'wished to develop friendship and agreement with Chalcedonians'.[96] Vahan I was deposed in 968 by the council of Ani and sought refuge with the king of Vaspurakan, Apusahl Hamazasp (953/8–72). Byzantine influence in these events may be inferred. A colophon records the visit of a priest named Pantaleon to Constantinople in January 966 at the command of Apusahl Hamazasp, 'king of kings of the house of Armenia'.[97] The colophon adds that this occurred in the time of Nikephoros, 'emperor of the Greeks, valiant and virtuous, victorious in battles against the heathens'. Pantaleon returned safely 'through the power of the Holy Cross and the prayers of the Holy Apostles and the grace of both our kings, Nikephoros and Hamazasp'. Not only was Apusahl in direct contact with Constantinople; in the eyes of the author, Nikephoros II Phokas (963–9) enjoyed joint sovereignty with the Artsruni king.

Nor is this the only evidence of continued Byzantine engagement. Whilst the four chapters devoted to Armenian and Iberian affairs in the *De administrando imperio* largely recount past episodes rather than present circumstances, their very inclusion is significant. In 966 or 967, after the death of its prince, Ashot, Taron came under Byzantine control. Two years later, Bardas Phokas, nephew of Nikephoros and *doux* of Chaldia and Koloneia, advanced to Manzikert and destroyed its walls.[98] Thus within fifteen years of the compilation of this work, Taron had been incorporated into the empire and the potential threat posed by Manzikert neutralised.

In 974, John I Tzimiskes (969–76) travelled to Armenia. According to our only source, the twelfth-century Armenian historian Matthew of Edessa, King Ashot III Bagratuni ('the Merciful') (953–77) assembled all the leaders of the countries of the east, including Sennacherim, lord of Vaspurakan, and their forces.[99] Having opened lines of communication with Ashot, the emperor advanced to Mush in Taron and camped outside the fortress of Aytsik'. His forces came under overnight attack, although the circumstances and outcome are obscure. At some point thereafter, Tzimiskes was handed a letter, apparently from Catholicos Vahan I. This detail is hard to interpret, given Vahan's deposition six years before. The two leaders then made a treaty whereby Ashot III 'the Merciful' supplied 10,000 troops in return for notable gifts. Several elements in this account – specifically the leadership role accorded to Ashot, the skirmishes at Aytsik' and Vahan's letter – may reflect a Bagratuni spin or a conflation of different episodes. Scholars have generally interpreted Ashot's attendance upon the emperor at the head of a large army as a defensive precaution. Yet his conduct also befits a loyal client,

[96] ST, ed. Malkhaseants', p. 181; French tr. Macler, p. 41.
[97] Hovsep'yan (1951), no. 51, cols. 117–20.
[98] ST, ed. Malkhaseants', p. 183; French tr. Macler, p. 44.
[99] ME, I.17, ed. Melik'-Adamean and Ter-Mik'ayelean, pp. 22–4; tr. Dostourian, pp. 27–8.

responding to an imperial summons and supplying military assistance at a designated location. Tzimiskes' subsequent letter to Ashot 'shahanshah [originally a Persian royal title, 'king of kings'] of Great Armenia and my spiritual son', describing his victorious campaign of 975 into Syria and Lebanon, then becomes apposite.[100]

The degree to which Armenian princes had been drawn into the orbit of Byzantium can be seen through their involvement in the rebellions which erupted against Basil II (976–1025) and Constantine VIII (1025–8) after 976. Bardas Skleros had the support of Gregory and Bagarat, sons of Ashot, prince of Taron, and Zap'ranik, prince of Mokk', whilst Bardas Phokas exploited his relationship with the Iberian prince David of Tao – forged while he was *doux* of neighbouring Chaldia – to win him to Basil II's cause.[101] In addition to the title of *kouropalatēs*, David received substantial territorial concessions, including the districts of Karin and Apahunik', recently prised from Arab control. The personal ties with Bardas Phokas which caused David to fight for Basil II later prompted him to join Phokas when he rebelled against Basil in 987. All three survived these confrontations. Gregory Taronites, *doux* of Thessaloniki and *magistros*, fought against Samuel of Bulgaria (987/988–1014) after 991 and was killed in 995.[102] Zap'ranik *manglabitēs* was charged in 983 by Basil II and Constantine with transporting a relic of the True Cross from Constantinople to the monastery of Aparank'.[103] David *kouropalatēs* retained possession of all the lands granted to him previously although these now reverted to the emperor after his death.[104] It is striking, however, that neither Gregory nor Zap'ranik remained in their ancestral districts and that David continued to exercise authority only in the knowledge of inevitable imperial intervention.

Contemporary relations between the churches reveal a similar pattern of increased engagement. As Byzantium pushed eastwards, and significant numbers of Armenians came, or were transferred, within its borders, the respective hierarchies increasingly overlapped. An exchange between Metropolitan Theodore of Melitene and Samuel of Kamrjadzor, responding at the behest of Catholicos Khach'ik I (973–92), confirms that confessional tensions were developing at a local level.[105] Another exchange, between Khach'ik I and the metropolitan of Sebasteia, occurred in 989.[106] Complaints of oppression and torture in Sebasteia were combined with

---

[100] ME, I.19-20, ed. Melik'-Adamean and Ter-Mik'ayelean, pp. 24–32; tr. Dostourian, pp. 29–33.
[101] ST, ed. Malkhaseants', pp. 191–2; French tr. Macler, pp. 56, 59–60.
[102] Skyl., ed. Thurn, p. 341; French tr. Flusin and Cheynet, p. 285, n. 121.
[103] Gregory of Narek, *Discourses*, ed. Awetik'ean, pp. 9–36; Mahé (1991); Gregory of Narek, *Book of lamentations*; tr. Mahé and Mahé, pp. 78–83.
[104] Skyl., ed. Thurn, p. 339; French tr. Flusin and Cheynet, p. 283, n. 108; ST, ed. Malkhaseants', p. 275; French tr. Macler, p. 162.
[105] *Book of letters*, ed. Izmireants', pp. 302–22; French tr. Garsoïan, pp. 550–79.
[106] ST, ed. Malkhaseants', pp. 201–44; French tr. Macler, pp. 76–123.

observations that the Armenian bishops of Sebasteia and Larissa, and other priests, had removed themselves from the Armenian church and accepted Chalcedon. Yet neither of these sees had previously been described or treated as Armenian. By contrast eleven new suffragan bishops under the metropolitan of Trebizond had been created by the 970s, including those of Mananalis, Oulnoutin and Basean, confirming a simultaneous extension eastwards by the imperial church.[107] This fluidity was recognised by contemporaries. Sargis was appointed catholicos of Armenia in 992 at a council convened by King Gagik I Bagratuni ('the Great') (989–c. 1017) at which there were bishops 'from this country of Armenia and from the side of the Greeks'.[108]

Little is known about the contemporary actions or attitudes of leading members of the Bagratuni and Artsruni houses. Significantly, however, the deposit of the relic of the True Cross at Aparank' during Easter 983 was attended by the three Artsruni brothers then ruling Vaspurakan, Ashot-Sahak, Gurgen-Khach'ik and Sennacherim-John. Their presence at this isolated, mountainous site so early in the year for the arrival of an imperial donation implies respect for – and close relations with – Byzantium. Gregory of Narek asserted in his description of the ceremony that

the divine will is clear: it is that the empire of the Romans, spread out like the sky across the vast surface of the whole world, will gather in its ample bosom innumerable multitudes, as a single flock in a single place, a single synod and a single church, the one bride in the bridal chamber, the one beloved in the single dwelling place . . . the one spouse under the one tent of the Covenant.[109]

His support for Basil II seems unequivocal.

David *kouropalatēs* of Tao died on Easter Sunday, 31 March 1000. Two sources allege that he was poisoned when receiving the eucharist, although one adds that he survived this attempt and was smothered instead.[110] Arguably this reflects a confessional spin, since David 'died' in a spiritual sense when taking wine mixed with water in the eucharist. Basil II was quick to take advantage.[111] He marched north from Tarsus, meeting and rewarding several prominent princes, including Sennacherim-John of Vaspurakan. He then moved east to the plain of Vagharshapat, but Gagik I 'the Great' failed to attend, 'reckoning it a diminution', and Basil thereupon returned via Ult'is in Tao and Theodosioupolis to Constantinople. Gagik

[107] *NE*, no. 9, pp. 296–306 (text).

[108] ST, ed. Malkhaseants', p. 259; French tr. Macler, p. 144.

[109] Gregory of Narek, *Discourses*, ed. Awetik'ean, p. 11. A colophon of Gregory expresses identical sentiments: Gregory of Narek, *Book of lamentations*; tr. Mahé and Mahé, pp. 777–8.

[110] Arist., ed. Yuzbashian, pp. 22–3; French tr. Canard and Berbérian, pp. 2–6; ME, I.33, ed. Melik'-Adamean and Ter-Mik'ayelean, p. 44; tr. Dostourian, p. 39.

[111] ST, ed. Malkhaseants', pp. 275–8; French tr. Macler, pp. 162–5; Arist., ed. Yuzbashian, pp. 23–4; French tr. Canard and Berbérian, pp. 3–6.

may have viewed David's death as an opportunity to revive Bagratuni hegemony, an ambition that submission to Basil II would have compromised, if
not thwarted; other princes had been compelled to lead or contribute large
numbers of troops for operations against Bulgaria. Alternatively he may
have been influenced by ecclesiastical opinion; both Catholicos Khach'ik
and his successor Sargis I (992–1018) were steadfast in their opposition to
the imperial church. Whatever the cause, Basil II was prepared to consolidate his gains and bide his time. After more than a century of regular
dealings with Armenian princely houses, Byzantium was keenly aware that
times of political flux after the death of the leading prince offered the best
opportunity for direct intervention, as the rival claimants looked for outside
support. Basil could afford to wait.

When George I (1014–27) succeeded his father Bagrat III as king of
Georgia in 1014, Basil II asserted his claim to certain districts previously
ceded to David of Tao and then Bagrat.[112] George rejected this claim and
resisted an attempt to occupy them. Basil waited until Bulgaria had been
pacified. In 1021 he travelled east, expecting to receive George's submission;
but George did not attend. Further negotiations failed and both sides took
up arms. Although there is no evidence that any Armenian princes joined
George in defying Basil II, he had arbitrated between John-Smbat III and
Ashot IV Bagratuni ('the Brave') following the death of their father, Gagik
I 'the Great', probably in 1017, and had intervened in their subsequent
confrontation.[113] Arguably John-Smbat now saw an opportunity to gain
imperial backing. In January 1022, Catholicos Peter I (1019–58) attended
upon Basil II at his winter quarters in Trebizond, bringing with him a will
from John-Smbat III appointing him as his heir.[114] This underpinned the
Byzantine claim to Ani after his death in 1041.

John-Smbat and Ashot were therefore pulled back into the imperial orbit
indirectly through the conduct of King George I of Georgia. Sennacherim-
John Artsruni, however, exchanged his ancestral lands of Vaspurakan for
territories in Cappadocia, including the cities of Sebasteia and Larissa, after
being attacked by Turkish forces from Azerbaijan. Although conventionally
dated to 1016 or early 1017, it may have occurred as late as 1021. After the
collapse of a rebellion by Nikephoros Phokas and Nikephoros Xiphias in late
summer 1022, it is significant that Basil II campaigned beyond Vaspurakan,
attacking the city of Her.[115]

---

[112] Arist., ed. Yuzbashian, p. 25; French tr. Canard and Berbérian, p. 7. Bagrat III became the ruler of
Kartli in 975 and Abkhazia three years later. Under his direction the kingdom of Georgia was established
between 1008 and 1010.

[113] Arist., ed. Yuzbashian, p. 27; French tr. Canard and Berbérian, p. 10; ME, I.10, ed. Melik'-Adamean
and Ter-Mik'ayelean, pp. 12–14; tr. Dostourian, pp. 22–3.

[114] ME, I.50, ed. Melik'-Adamean and Ter-Mik'ayelean, pp. 56–8; tr. Dostourian, p. 46.

[115] Arist., ed. Yuzbashian, p. 38; French tr. Canard and Berbérian, pp. 23–4; ME, I.51, ed. Melik'-
Adamean and Ter-Mik'ayelean, p. 58; tr. Dostourian, p. 47. See also, p. 696.

Although both Sennacherim-John Artsruni and John-Smbat III had come to terms with Basil II by January 1022, this did not deter Nikephoros Phokas from soliciting support from other family members. It is unclear, however, how far they responded to his appeal.[116] In the event, Phokas was assassinated on 15 August 1022, possibly by the son of Sennacherim-John Artsruni. Basil then moved quickly, inflicting a sharp defeat upon George I on 11 September 1022 and coming to terms with him shortly afterwards. Evidently Abkhazian, Georgian and Armenian princes were still tempted to participate in a rebellion fomented in the east by a member of the Phokas family. Basil II was aware of the threat. His persistent involvement with Armenia, and the extension of the empire's frontiers to incorporate first Vaspurakan and ultimately Ani, should be seen in the context of, and as a response to, these rebellions.

During the tenth century, a large number of small 'Armenian' themes were created, consisting essentially of a fortress and its surrounding district.[117] By contrast, the themes of Taron (966 or 967), Vaspurakan (c.1021) and Iberia (1022) were organised around existing Armenian principalities ceded to the empire. Tellingly, these were not broken up. Whilst the sigillographic evidence reveals considerable fluidity in the combination of high military commands across these themes during the eleventh century, there is presently little evidence for sustained administrative down-reach within them.[118] No more than a skeleton administrative structure can be traced, suggesting that existing social and political structures continued to be employed.[119] This 'slim-line' Byzantine presence would prove to be inadequate when faced by sustained Turkish assault after 1045.[120]

Basil II's campaign of 1022 did not mark an end to military operations. In 1023 or 1024 the fortified town of Archesh on Lake Van was captured by Nikephoros Komnenos whilst nearby Perkri was taken in 1035.[121] These were both granted separate thematic status but this is unsurprising, seeing that they had never formed part of Vaspurakan and had been captured from the 'Persians'.[122] Separate themes of Manzikert (after 1000) and Artzike had also been created.[123] This string of small themes fulfilled a long-cherished strategic aim, expressed in the *De administrando imperio*, that if these *kastra* were in imperial control, 'a Persian army cannot come out against

---

[116] ME, I.51, ed. Melik'-Adamean and Ter-Mik'ayelean, p. 58; tr. Dostourian, pp. 46–7.

[117] *LPB*, pp. 264–8, 355–63; Yuzbashian (1973–4), p. 169.

[118] On Taron, see Yuzbashian (1973–4), pp. 140–54; on Iberia: Kühn (1991), pp. 187–204; on Vaspurakan: *Zacos*, ed. Cheynet, pp. 93–4.

[119] *DOS*, IV, nos. 57.1, 75.2, 75.3, 75.4, 76.1, pp. 148, 166–9; *Zacos*, ed. Cheynet, nos. 37a, 37b, pp. 72–4.

[120] Holmes (2001), p. 56; Holmes (2005), pp. 538–41; see also, p. 698.

[121] On Archesh, see Arist., ed. Yuzbashian, p. 41; French tr. Canard and Berbérian, pp. 26–7; on Perkri: Arist., ed. Yuzbashian, pp. 48–9; French tr. Canard and Berbérian, pp. 38–40; Skyl., ed. Thurn, p. 388; French tr. Flusin and Cheynet, p. 322.

[122] On Archesh, see *Seyrig*, no. 168, p. 123.

[123] On Manzikert, see *DOS*, IV, no. 67.1, pp. 156–7; on Artzike: Oikonomides *et al.* (1998), p. 44.

Romania'.[124] They also deterred Ashot IV 'the Brave' from expanding south-wards into former Artsruni territory.

The literary sources reveal almost nothing about the reigns of John-Smbat III Bagratuni and Ashot IV 'the Brave' between 1022 and 1041. Contemporary inscriptions and colophons, however, confirm ongoing relations with Byzantium, and the numismatic evidence is persuasive. From the reign of Nikephoros II Phokas, Armenia switched from a silver-based coinage to a gold- and copper-based coinage, using exclusively Byzantine issues. During the excavations at Ani, several thousand Byzantine copper coins were found, both loose and in hoards.[125] In 1979, some 3,539 of Constantine VIII's *nomismata*, equivalent to almost 50 pounds of gold, were unearthed at Nouchevan, near Dvin.[126] The epigraphic evidence is no less valuable in the historical reconstruction. An inscription at Khtskawnkʻ, dated 1033, refers to 'the reign of Smbat *shahanshah*, son of Gagik *shahanshah*, who had adopted the beloved boy Sargis, during the time of the three kings of the Romans, when he received the triple honour *anthypatos, patrikios, vestēs* and *doux* of the east'.[127] Aristakes records that John-Smbat's son, Erkatʻ, died young.[128] This inscription confirms that he had designated Sargis as his successor, and that Sargis had received imperial sanction.

By the time of his death, however, John-Smbat III had apparently changed his mind. A colophon dates the completion of a Gospel book to 1041, 'when Yov[h]an[n]ēs [that is, John-Smbat III] king of Armenia was translated to Christ and gave his kingdom to his nephew Gagik'.[129] The complex sequence of events between 1041 and 1045, concluding with the Byzantine occupation of Ani, therefore originated in a familiar context, a time of political transition.[130] Instead of developing ties with both Sargis and Gagik, however, Byzantine policy after 1022 seems to have antic-ipated only the succession of Sargis. Gagik's unexpected accession thwarted these plans and with Constantine IX Monomachos (1042–55) embroiled in George Maniakes' rebellion (see below, pp. 599–600), Gagik II Bagratuni enjoyed two years' respite.[131] In 1044, however, he was induced to visit Con-stantinople where he was detained and offered Melitene in return for Ani.[132] Initially he refused but when the forty keys of Ani were produced, proving treachery on the part of Catholicos Peter, he abdicated and received lands in Cappadocia. Although the leaders of Ani then resolved to entrust their city either to Gagik's brother-in-law, David Dunatsʻi or to Bagrat IV, king

[124] *DAI*, ch. 44, pp. 204–5.   [125] Mousheghian *et al.* (2000b), p. 38.
[126] Mousheghian *et al.* (2000a), p. 149.   [127] Kostaneantsʻ (1913), pp. 17–18.
[128] Arist., ed. Yuzbashian, p. 32; French tr. Canard and Berbérian, p. 16.
[129] Matʻevosyan (ed.), *Hishatakaranner*, no. 105, p. 86–7.   [130] Shepard (1975–6).
[131] Arist., ed. Yuzbashian, pp. 57–8; French tr. Canard and Berbérian, p. 46; ME, I.77–8, ed. Melikʻ-Adamean and Ter-Mikʻayelean, p. 96; tr. Dostourian, p. 67.
[132] Arist., ed. Yuzbashian, pp. 61–2; French tr. Canard and Berbérian, pp. 50–1; ME, I.84, ed. Melikʻ-Adamean and Ter-Mikʻayelean, pp. 102–4; tr. Dostourian, pp. 71–2.

Figure 24 Part of the southern façade of the cathedral church of Ani, begun in 989 under King Smbat II Bagratuni ('Master of the Universe') (977–89) but completed in 1001 by Queen Katrinide, wife of King Gagik I Bagratuni. It was designed by the architect Trdat who was also commissioned to repair St Sophia in Constantinople following earthquake damage in 989. Katrinide died in 1012 and was buried in a mausoleum close to the church

of Georgia (1027–72), the approach of another Byzantine army precipitated the final surrender of the city.[133]

CONCLUSION

Although the relationship between Byzantium and Armenia changed repeatedly across these centuries, three particular features stand out. In the first place, relations were continuous – only the period between 790

---

[133] Arist., ed. Yuzbashian, p. 62; French tr. Canard and Berbérian, p. 52.

and 830 lacks evidence for any direct contact, but this mirrors the dearth of information about any aspect of Armenia during these decades. Secondly they were multi-layered. The sources tend to focus upon high-level contacts involving the leading Armenian clerics and princes and treat these as exclusive or representative. In fact, it seems very likely that lesser lords and individual bishops were also in contact with Byzantium throughout this period, although such ties are usually hidden from view. Thirdly they were reciprocal. Byzantium was eager to secure its eastern flank and therefore sought to attract Armenian clients into its service. At the same time, Armenian princes looked to Byzantium to bolster their own status within Armenia through the concession of titles, gifts and money. In a highly competitive, militarised society, there were obvious advantages in gaining recognition from a neighbouring polity, not least in the event of attack, when Byzantium could serve as a far more effective refuge than any mountain redoubt or individual fortress. It is no coincidence that the Byzantine army – and then the state – came to be filled with men of Armenian origin or descent. That, however, is another story.[134]

[134] Garsoïan (1998). See also above, pp. 272, 300.

CHAPTER 9

CONFRONTING ISLAM: EMPERORS VERSUS CALIPHS (641–c. 850)

WALTER E. KAEGI

INTRODUCTION[1]

Two features characterise Byzantine–Muslim relations between the seventh and ninth century: a finely tuned link between domestic strife and the external fortunes of war and diplomacy; and the fitful involvement of both polities' leaders with their armed forces, without exercise of personal command. The Arabs' dramatic conquest of Byzantium's eastern territories in the 630s was followed by four further periods of Muslim expansion; by gradual stabilisation; and then by Byzantine strengthening and eventual territorial recovery. The four periods of Muslim expansion were all brought to an end by bouts of civil war (*fitna*) among the Muslims, the first lasting from 656 until 661. The second expansionary period under the Sufyanid Umayyad caliphs was followed by almost ten years of civil war, from 683 until 692; the third, under the Marwanid caliphs – the final branch of the Umayyad dynasty – was broken by infighting for some two years between 718 and 720, only to be followed by a twenty further years or so of aggressive campaigning. The violent replacement of the Umayyads by the Abbasids in the mid-eighth century owed nothing to Byzantium, nor did it halt military and diplomatic interaction between the two polities; but it did transform Arab–Byzantine relations.

THE PARAMETERS OF CONFLICT

The most vulnerable period for Byzantium came immediately after the disastrous battle of the river Yarmuk in 636, during the imperial succession crisis triggered by Heraclius' death in 641 and in the earliest years of his successor Constans II (641–68) (see above, pp. 230–1). After the withdrawal of their armies from Syria and northern Mesopotamia, the Byzantines had managed to regroup by the late 630s and early 640s and create new Anatolian defences, taking advantage of the Taurus mountains and key fortified points in the interior. Although limited truces had previously been struck

---

[1] I should like to thank Paul Cobb for his advice and clarification on a number of points.

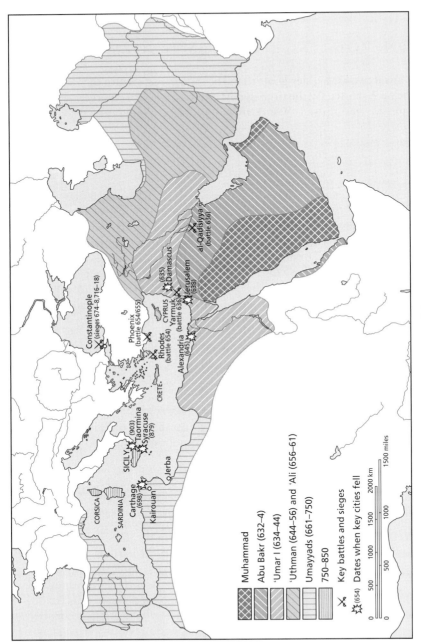

Map 18 The expansion of Islam 632–850

Legend:

- Muhammad
- Abu Bakr (632–4)
- 'Umar I (634–44)
- 'Uthman (644–56) and 'Ali (656–61)
- Umayyads (661–750)
- 750–850

⚔ Key battles and sieges

☆☆(654) Dates when key cities fell

Scale: 0 – 500 – 1000 – 1500 – 2000 km
0 – 500 – 1000 – 1500 miles

Labels on map:

- al-Qadisiyya (battle 636)
- Damascus (635)
- Jerusalem (638)
- Yarmuk (battle 636)
- CYPRUS
- Phoenix (battle 654/655)
- Rhodes (battle 654)
- Alexandria (645)
- Constantinople (sieges 674–8, 716–18)
- CRETE
- SICILY
- Taormina (903)
- Syracuse (879)
- Jerba
- Kairouan
- Carthage (698)
- CORSICA
- SARDINIA

with the Arabs, no formal, linear frontier was ever established and hostilities persisted. Fortunately for the Byzantines, the Muslims had priorities elsewhere. They needed to consolidate their vast territorial gains in Syria and northern Mesopotamia and to complete their conquest of Egypt, both more attractive and easier goals than the continued seizure of territory in Byzantine Anatolia. By the time that Mu'awiya (661–80) emerged as caliph, the Muslims had missed their chance of outright conquest of Byzantium: the empire was stabilising, as Constans II rapidly gained military experience and judgement, and developed his defences against the Arab threat from Syria.

Caliph 'Umar (634–44) reportedly believed that the Muslims needed to consolidate their territorial expansion of the 630s before pursuing further conquests at the expense of Byzantium. Tradition has it that during his caliphate 'Umar restrained Mu'awiya from attempting an invasion of the island of Cyprus.[2] This is plausible, and consistent with the well-known story that 'Umar also tried to restrain the very able military commander 'Amr ibn al-'As from invading Egypt.[3] Mu'awiya only succeeded in implementing his far more aggressive policy towards Byzantium after 'Umar's death, prompted no doubt in part by a calculation of his own interests, as well as of the advantages he believed such a policy would gain for Islam.

Political, topographical and logistical impediments combined with Byzantine military resilience to halt major Arab advances into Anatolia in the seventh century, even though the Arabs made significant territorial conquests in the central and western Mediterranean at Byzantium's expense. They initially used a combination of force and diplomacy to overcome the Byzantine defences, being prepared to engage in fierce combat, while also negotiating separate terms with both local civilians and military commanders. However, these tactics ceased to be effective once the Muslim armies tried to penetrate and establish permanent control north of the Taurus and Anti-Taurus mountains in Asia Minor.

It is difficult to define the style of Arab–Byzantine warfare in the seventh century. Muslim methods involved a broad conformity to Islamic principles, including the spreading of the faith by force, together with use of combined military and political initiatives. The Muslims would divide their opponents both on and off the battlefield, identifying those willing to conclude separate peace terms and then allowing them to negotiate their submission, thus reducing the likelihood of costly, bloody resistance. However, using political pressure to control the Byzantine civilian population was not inconsistent with fighting Byzantium's forces and demolishing their strong points, destroying their opponents' equilibrium. There tended to be

---

[2] al-Baladhuri, *Futuh al-buldan*, ed. de Goeje, p. 152; tr. Hitti and Murgotten, I, p. 235.
[3] al-Baladhuri, *Futuh al-buldan*, ed. de Goeje, p. 212; tr. Hitti and Murgotten, I, p. 335.

close consultation, as far as was practicable, between field commanders and the highest Muslim leadership. The Arabs generally tried to avoid positional warfare, such as slow-moving sieges, except when they were forced onto the defensive; their strategy was to drive their opponents into decisive battle, with an eye to exploiting military victories to the full. The Byzantines, for their part, tended to avoid the risk of major land battles after their defeat at Yarmuk, preferring to seek refuge in fortified positions. They made cautious efforts to identify, cut off, attack and destroy smaller detachments of Muslim raiders, using relatively modest-sized mobile units.

Concepts of holy war and crusade did not dominate Byzantine warfare between the seventh and ninth century.[4] It is similarly hazardous to superimpose later concepts of jihad onto seventh- and eighth-century Arab–Byzantine warfare, as both jihadi practices and concepts in this period are poorly documented. They become better documented with the expansion and stabilisation of the Muslim territories, when communal obligation to perform jihad was increasingly focused on the frontier regions, and it was in areas such as northern Syria and upper Mesopotamia that the most zealous Muslim soldiers tended to be concentrated. Areas further back from the frontiers, although theoretically supportive of military expansion, were in practice less involved on a daily basis. It became increasingly difficult to engage the whole Muslim community actively in the process of jihad.

Between the late 630s and 650s both empire and caliphate periodically created zones of devastation between their territories. Local inhabitants would occasionally be allowed to stay, but only if they agreed to act as informers and refused to help the enemy. However, these more charitable arrangements do not appear to have been successful: both powers expelled inhabitants they regarded as hostile, leaving either a total wasteland, or settling their own armed troops and loyal populations. 'Umar reportedly wanted to create at least a temporary zone of destruction between Byzantium and the caliphate, just as Heraclius (610–41) had done in the remaining imperial territories after the Arabs overran Syria. According to al-Ya'qubi, whenever 'Umar spoke of the Byzantines, he voiced the hope that God would 'turn the passes between us and them into burning coals; this side [of the passes] for us and what is behind [the passes] for them'.[5] The ninth-century historian al-Baladhuri reports that 'Umar ordered that Arabissos be destroyed and its inhabitants forcibly removed, after learning of their refusal to give information on Byzantine troop movements to the Muslims, while continuing to act as informants for the empire.[6] The inhabitants of

[4] On the question of these concepts' existence in Byzantium, see Oikonomides (1995); Kolbaba (1998); Dennis (2001b); Stephenson (2007).

[5] al-Ya'qubi, *Ta'rikh*, II, pp. 178–9.

[6] al-Baladhuri, *Futuh al-buldan*, ed. de Goeje, pp. 156–7; tr. Hitti and Murgotten, I, pp. 241–2; on Arabissos see Hild and Restle (1981), pp. 144–5; Kaegi (1992), p. 244; MS, X.21, ed. and French tr. Chabot, II, p. 359; al-Tabari, *Ta'rikh*, ed. de Goeje *et al.*, I, p. 2349; tr. Friedmann, XII, p. 134.

nearby Duluk and Raban, in northern Syria, apparently honoured a similar arrangement with the Muslims.[7] And while governor of Syria in 649, Mu'awiya forced the Cypriots to stop giving aid to the Byzantines and to inform on them, an arrangement which they failed to respect.[8]

Byzantine and Muslim governing circles thus had an equal interest in creating zones of devastation. The resulting attempts to tighten governmental control on either side of the *de facto* border, to counteract the emergence of independent borderland powers, helped to strengthen state-building for both caliphate and empire. From Heraclius' reign onwards, the Byzantines started to appoint military commanders in place of those civil governors who proved too willing to come to terms with the Muslims. Through such appointments, the Byzantines hoped to concentrate power in the hands of military leaders who were dependent on the emperor: they would therefore make no local settlements with the Muslims without having received explicit imperial authorisation and approval.[9]

Not all early Arab–Byzantine contacts were violent, and despite extensive military engagement, limited maritime trade, exchange and travel – especially pilgrimages – persisted. Some Christian churchmen and ascetics managed to cross the frontiers at transit points such as Cyprus, and smugglers and renegades played their part in creating a porous frontier. Diplomacy coexisted with warfare. Prisoner- and hostage-exchange was a complex challenge for both Byzantine and Muslim authorities in the seventh and eighth centuries. Diplomatic negotiations generally took place either at Damascus or Constantinople at the highest level and were conducted by the caliph and emperor – or their envoys – but *ad hoc* exchanges could also occur occasionally between local commanders.[10] Accommodating such political realities committed neither side to any fundamental theoretical or religious concessions. Diplomatic protocol was highly formalised by the tenth century, as witness Constantine VII Porphyrogenitus' *Book of ceremonies*, but it is likely that this protocol owed its origins to seventh- and eighth-century practices.

MU'AWIYA VERSUS CONSTANS II: BYZANTIUM UNDER PRESSURE

Byzantine Anatolia quickly became the target of Muslim expeditions after the Byzantine evacuation of Syria and northern Mesopotamia in the mid-seventh century. Muslim historical traditions disagree on who led the

---

[7] al-Baladhuri, *Futuh al-buldan*, ed. de Goeje, p. 150; tr. Hitti and Murgotten, I, p. 231.

[8] al-Baladhuri, *Futuh al-buldan*, ed. de Goeje, p. 153; tr. Hitti and Murgotten, I, p. 236. See also *ibid.*, pp. 153–8; tr. Hitti, and Murgotten, I pp. 236–43; Ibn Sallam, *al-Amwal* (1968), pp. 248, 253; repr. 1986, pp. 184–5, 187–8, citing the scholar al-Awza'i as his authority.

[9] Haldon (1993), pp. 1–47.   [10] See Kaegi (1992), pp. 250–2; Kaplony (1996).

earliest Arab raids through the mountain passes into Anatolia and the 'land of the Romans'. Ibn 'Abd al-Hakam's *Futuh misr* reports the earliest Muslim expedition against Amorion in 644 (AH 23), when Constans II was still too young to be capable of developing his polity's defences.[11] These early raids penetrated deep into Byzantine territory. Mu'awiya had already commanded an incursion into Asia Minor in 643, and he probably led another expedition against Amorion in 646. His expeditions disrupted the Anatolian interior, forcing the Byzantines into defensive countermeasures.

The antecedents of later Muslim warfare and diplomacy can be traced back to Mu'awiya's governorship of Syria, and to the period after he became caliph in 661.[12] Summer raids (*saifa*) began from around 640. The raids of the 640s were often launched from Mesopotamian and Syrian towns such as Homs and Antioch, and the raiders entered Anatolia by way of passes such as the one at Hadath (between Germanikeia and Melitene) and the Cilician Gates (using bases such as Mopsuestia and Tarsus once these were in Arab hands). Whether or not Mu'awiya himself went on the important early expedition against Amorion in 644,[13] he led a number of other campaigns into Anatolia at a time when Byzantine resistance was beginning to harden. As Constans II tried to fortify Byzantine cities and strongholds and to develop a coherent resistance, Mu'awiya gained experience in how to fight and to negotiate with the Byzantines, becoming familiar with the problems and challenges of their Anatolian terrain, climate and logistics. Probably no other caliph had as much personal military experience against the Byzantines as Mu'awiya did.

Despite this, Mu'awiya's offensives against Byzantium did not result in any lasting Muslim conquests in Anatolia between 643 and his death in 680. Muslim raids became an almost annual event, penetrating up to 1,000 kilometres into the Anatolian plateau. They were not restricted to summer, and a winter raid would sometimes follow hard upon a summer one.[14] The raids contributed to Mu'awiya's prestige, helping to enrich the Muslims and attracting ever more tribesmen to take part, while the Muslim casualties probably remained relatively modest. However, this persistent raiding seriously damaged the empire's infrastructure: the Byzantines' territories were devastated; they lost property and human lives; many were taken captive; and their commerce and agriculture were destroyed. The raids also kept Byzantium off-balance, forcing them onto the defensive and preventing them from launching major offensives of their own against Muslim Syria.

---

[11] Kaegi (1977).   [12] On Mu'awiya, see *PMBZ*, #5185 and below, n. 35.

[13] Kaegi (1977). See also the eighth-century scholar Layth bin Sa'd's account in al-Fasawi, *al-Ma'rifah*, III, p. 307; Ibn Hajar al-'Asqalani, *Kitab al-Isabah*, II, p. 533.

[14] See Brooks, 'Arabs in Asia Minor' for a collection of translated fragments now in need of major revision.

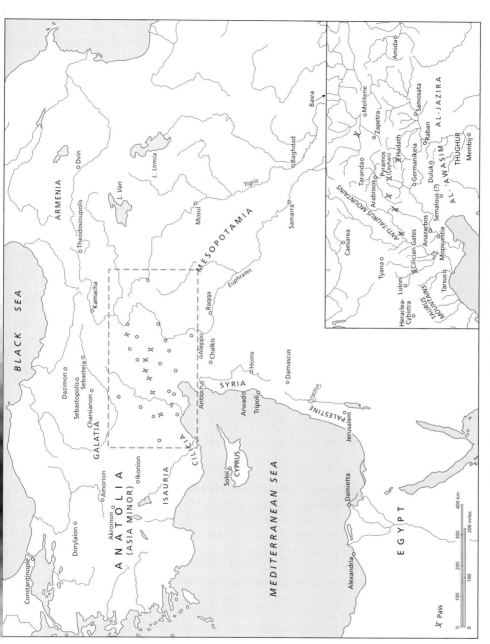

Map 19 Byzantium versus Islam: the zone of direct confrontation

Inset (upper right):

Amida

Melitene
Basra
Samosata
AL-JAZIRA
Zapetra
Raban
THUGHUR
Tarandao
Arabissos
Pyramos ()(Ceyhan)
Hadath
Germanikeia
Duluko
Membij
Anti-Taurus Mountains
Semalous (?)
AL-'AWASIM
Caesarea
Anazarbos
Cilician Gates
Tyana
Mopsuestia
Heraclea-Cybistra
Lulon
Tarsus
TAURUS MOUNTAINS

Main map:

BLACK SEA

ARMENIA
Theodosioupolis
Dvin
L. Urmia
L. Van
Kamacha
Dazimon
Sebastopolis
Sebasteia
Charsianon
GALATIA
Mosul
MESOPOTAMIA
Samarra
Baghdad
Tigris
Euphrates
Raqqa
Aleppo
Chalkis
Amorion
Akroinon
Okonion
Dorylaion
ANATOLIA
(ASIA MINOR)
ISAURIA
CILICIA
Antiocho
SYRIA
Homs
Damascus
Arwado
Tripoli
PALESTINE
Jerusalem
Constantinople
CYPRUS
Soloi
MEDITERRANEAN SEA
EGYPT
Damietta
Alexandria

0 100 200 300 400 km
0 100 200 miles

)(Pass

Under Mu'awiya's able command, the Muslims were innovative and capable of taking their opponents by surprise. Despite a lack of any Arab seafaring tradition, they embarked on combined land and naval operations, highlighting their readiness to adopt new strategies and techniques of warfare. Although the literary evidence about naval expeditions against Byzantine-controlled islands such as Arwad and Rhodes is contradictory and impossible to verify, epigraphic evidence confirms an intensification of Muslim military and naval activities, including devastating Muslim raids on Byzantine Cyprus in 649 and 650 at Soloi.[15] Some 120,000 Cypriots are said to have been deported, marking a serious change in the island's fortunes. Although the Byzantines did receive forewarning of the Arabs' preparations for some of these naval expeditions, the raids further reduced Byzantine resources and naval capabilities in the Mediterranean, jeopardising yet more of the empire's coastline and islands. Muslim power was proving capable of extracting financial concessions from regions hitherto beyond its reach.

In 654 or 655, Mu'awiya's naval forces decisively defeated Constans II at the battle of Phoenix off the south-western Anatolian coast, also known as the 'battle of the masts'. The late seventh-century ascetic Anastasius of Sinai testified to the shock of this Byzantine naval defeat.[16] Ibn Abi Sarh, governor of Egypt, commanded the Arab fleet, and its crew members may have included many Christian Egyptians. The Muslims then mounted a threatening but brief and abortive combined land-and-sea operation, reaching almost to Constantinople itself.[17] The seventh-century Muslim naval offensives culminated in their costly and disastrous assault and naval blockade of Constantinople from 674 to 678. The Arabs failed to plan adequately and they also encountered a new Byzantine weapon, Greek fire, which devastated their warships and inflicted heavy casualties (see above, p. 233).

Mu'awiya's governorship of Syria and his caliphate extended Arab territorial control, with Cyprus and most of Armenia falling under Muslim influence. The period of Mu'awiya's ascendancy also saw larger-scale expansion in North Africa, as Muslim military pressure on Anatolia reduced the Byzantine government's ability to reinforce and defend vulnerable positions in the empire's western approaches. Mu'awiya's prestige derived from his military victories; from the fact that he received recognition from the Byzantine emperor; from his control of the holy places of Christianity and Islam; from the line of successors from the Prophet Muhammad; and also from the messianic attributes of his leadership. His aggressive, risky and unpredictable strategies challenged a number of arrogant assumptions of the Byzantines

[15] Feissel (1987), pp. 380–1.
[16] Anastasius of Sinai, *Sermons*, ed. Uthemann, pp. 60–1.   [17] O'Sullivan (2004).

about the Arabs: as with their earlier stereotypes about the Persians, they assumed that the Arabs could not fight in cold weather and instead became lethargic.[18] Muslim winter expeditions into Anatolia brought home to the Byzantines just how wrong their notions about Muslim warfare could be. Winter campaigns were costly to both sides; it was gambling with the lives of Muslim soldiers to keep them in such a totally hostile environment for long periods, but they unquestionably disrupted the Byzantines' way of life in Asia Minor and kept them on the defensive.

So why did rapid Muslim expansion not continue northwards under Mu'awiya, in the wake of the extraordinary early successes? Although no explicit treatise outlining Mu'awiya's strategy exists, the failure does not seem to lie in flawed tactics, nor can it be put down to Byzantine policy or military victories. The harsh Anatolian climate and terrain played their part, as did the sheer logistical complexity of mounting lengthy, long-distance raids into the interior. The Muslims encountered tougher resistance, the closer they penetrated to the rather more ethnically and religiously homogeneous core areas of the empire; there could be no realistic expectation of winning over many converts to Islam there. Resources for potential Arab expansion were also squandered on the ill-fated naval siege of Constantinople itself (see above, pp. 232–3) and, above all, on the first and second Muslim civil wars. Muslim leaders started to see the sense in exploring temporary arrangements with the Byzantines, rather than engaging in perpetual warfare.

Another complication worked to the Byzantines' advantage and helps to explain the caliphate's reluctance and inability to provide whole-hearted commitment to invading and fully subjugating Anatolia: the Arab incursions were frequently undermined by rivalry and envy among their leaders. One of the most daring Muslim commanders, Khalid bin al-Walid, was much admired 'because of his usefulness to the Muslims in Byzantine territory, as well as his bravery'.[19] However, his fame and success appeared to threaten other military leaders, and the caliph himself allegedly contrived al-Walid's poisoning in 666/7, on his return to Homs after a raid into Anatolia: Mu'awiya feared his growing prestige among other Syrian Arabs. Although al-Walid's death may perhaps signal other problems, including tensions between Muslims and Christians at Homs, the reports of his death there highlight the rivalries and tensions among Muslim commanders.

As Byzantine intelligence on Muslim strategy and tactics improved, so did their response to Muslim aggression. Byzantine resistance began to take shape, notably during the reign of Constans II, who inherited sole rule at the age of eleven in 641.[20] Constans faced various hurdles, including

---

[18] See Dagron (1987), p. 222.
[19] al-Tabari, Ta'rikh, ed. de Goeje et al., II, p. 82; tr. Morony, XVIII, p. 88.
[20] PMBZ, #3691. See also above, p. 230.

factional and dynastic infighting, the need to justify his authority and policies, and internal military strife.[21] Yet his military and diplomatic activities
in Anatolia between 641 and 663, and in the central and western Mediterranean between 663 and his assassination in Syracuse in 668, present us
with something of a riddle.

The last memories of military victories – especially in the east – were
those of Constans II's grandfather, Heraclius, who had personally risked his
life and reputation in campaigning, even if his efforts against the Muslims
had failed catastrophically. Constans went out on campaign in Armenia and
in Anatolia, and this pleased his troops. His Armenian campaign of 652/3
was an unsuccessful attempt to restore his claim to authority, faced with
the prospect of the Armenians becoming clients of the caliph, although
virtually no Armenian conversions to Islam took place at this time (see
above, p. 342). The emperor's presence in person was needed to make the
military system work, as would still be the case many hundreds of years
later.[22] This obviated the risk of disobedience or incompetence on the part
of his commanders, but it was not always practicably possible.

Echoes of earlier Heraclian accusations of betrayal resound in the accusations made by Constans II's courtiers' against Maximus the Confessor and
Pope Martin I (649–55).[23] It was difficult for his officials to explain Byzantine
disasters at Arab hands. Heraclius and Constans both resorted to public
accusations, ridicule and the denunciation of those whom they charged
with harming the empire and the dynasty. When Constans received a letter
from Caliph 'Uthman (644–56), summoning him to Islam and proposing
that he become the caliph's subject, his reaction was to have it deposited on
the altar of St Sophia and to invoke a passage from Isaiah.[24] Here Constans
acted as both head of state and mediator to the deity.

Constans II ruled at a time when the balance of military power between
empire and caliphate was fundamentally unfavourable to the former and
when a Byzantine collapse was not out of the question. This obliged him to
enter into diplomatic relations with the Muslims in the form of embassies.[25]
In 650 the Muslim commander Busr bin Abi Artat led a raid into Isauria and
netted 5,000 prisoners. Constans requested and received a two- or three-
year truce in return for his payment of tribute. However, with the impact
of the Arab conquests of Syria, Palestine, Egypt and upper Mesopotamia

[21] Kaegi (1981), pp. 154–80; Kaegi (2003a), p. 313.   [22] Birkenmeier (2002), p. 235.
[23] On the accusation against Pope Martin I for allegedly engaging in correspondence and financial
contacts with the 'Saracens', see Anastasius Bibliothecarius, *Correspondence of Martin I*, col. 587. See
also Maximus the Confessor, *Scripta saeculi*, ed. and tr. Allen and Neil, pp. 49–51; Brandes (1998). See
also above, pp. 231–2.
[24] Seb., ch. 50, tr. and comm. Thomson and Howard-Johnson, I, pp. 144–5; see also *ibid.* ch. 38, I,
pp. 79–81 on the Persian siege of Constantinople, comparable to the subsequent Arab attempts.
[25] Beihammer (2000), pp. 259–323; Kaplony (1996), pp. 48–9.

still reverberating in imperial circles, Constantinople remained highly suspicious of anyone who made – or who was in a position to make – unauthorised, local contacts with Muslims, whether commander or churchman.[26] The imperial administration was equally suspicious of anyone who dissented from imperial policy, whether civil or religious, and Constans II's attempts to censure Pope Martin I for unauthorised contacts with the Arabs are comparable with those of his grandfather Heraclius: he, too, had tried to prevent unapproved negotiations between local leaders and Muslim commanders. By the ninth century, however, it would be impractical to enforce such rigid policies along the border.

Although not providing the only explanation, the *fitna*s were as important a factor in the Muslims' inability to crush the Byzantine empire in the Umayyad period as was Byzantine institutional restructuring.[27] The first Muslim *fitna*, fought between Mu'awiya and 'Ali, son-in-law of the prophet Muhammad, from 656 to 661, forced Mu'awiya to purchase an expensive temporary peace with Byzantium in 657,[28] and he had to keep this until his decisive victory over 'Ali in 661 or 662. Only then was Mu'awiya free to turn his and his armies' attention to the situation on the northern approaches of Syria, although even then the Kharijite rebellion remained a formidable problem for them.

According to Ibn Sa'd's *Kitab al-tabaqat al-kabir*, a Muslim army first established its winter quarters in Anatolia, 'in the land of the Romans' (*'ard al-Rum*) in 662/3,[29] but Ibn Sa'd does not identify the expedition's leaders, the number of raiders or their provenance, nor exactly where they wintered. Arab winterings in Byzantine Anatolia were more perilous for local life and disruptive to agriculture than were their summer raids. But they were also risky for the Arabs,[30] for they prompted the Byzantines to strengthen their defences in Asia Minor.[31] It is noteworthy that the earliest references to some form of thematic units in Byzantine Anatolia occur only a few years after the initial Muslim winterings there, whether or not these units as yet had any of the social or economic ties with particular areas that they would eventually form (see above, pp. 239–41, 266–7).

The campaign theatre of Anatolia does not seem to have been a priority for the early Muslim historians. Those records which do survive come

[26] Kaegi (2003b).

[27] Kaegi (1967), pp. 43–9; Lilie (1976), pp. 68, 103, 110, 164. See above, pp. 265–6.

[28] The terms included payment of 1,000 dinars, one slave and one horse per day or week.

[29] 'And the Muslims wintered in the land of the Byzantines in the year AH 42 and this was the first winter quarters/camp (*huwa awwalu mashtan*) they set up there': Ibn Sa'd, *al-Tabaqat*, ed. Sachau, V, p. 166; Ibn Sa'd, *al-Tabaqat al-kubra*, V, p. 224; Ibn 'Asakir, *Dimashq*, ed. 'Amrawi, XXXVII, p. 114; al-'Azimi, *Ta'rikh Halab*, p. 177.

[30] For a survey of raids, although to be used with caution, see Lilie (1976), esp. pp. 63–155, 346–51. See also Kaegi (1978); Kaegi (2003b).

[31] Brandes (2002a); Haldon (1993), pp. 1–47. See also Lampakes (ed.) (1998); Vlysidou *et al.* (eds.) (1998); Tsiknakis (ed.) (1997).

from Iraq, an area from which relatively few raids into Anatolia originated, because of the formidable logistical hurdles such as distance, heat and supplies.[32] We have no source-material comparable to the extensive narratives on other regions; this may simply not have survived, or details of the Anatolian conquests were either unavailable, or deemed unworthy of historical attention by al-Tabari and other later historians.[33] The brevity of allusions in the extant Muslim histories to seventh-century raids into Anatolia may well owe at least something to the following considerations. Firstly, many raids started out from Homs or points further north, where there were few Muslim scholars in the mid- and late-seventh century. The surviving raiders were probably often some distance away from historical writers or their copyists who might have been in a position to record information about them and pass it on to later generations. Secondly, in Syria, Egypt, Iraq and Africa there eventually arose issues of tax and property rights which, although they might contaminate the source-materials, at least gave reason to put on record details about relations with the local inhabitants. There was no such incentive in the case of Anatolia, for it had not been conquered by the Muslims. A third possible reason for the lack of source-material on the early Anatolian raids is that the motive for recording such expeditions was the pious commemoration of the names of participants, including those who perished, partly so as to add fame and distinction to their families, groups and clans back in Syria, Iraq and even in Egypt. But all that was needed for this purpose was the lists of their names and the dates – whether accurate or not – for those events. A fourth and final possible reason for the dearth of Muslim source-material about the early raids into Anatolia may be that it concentrates so heavily on the house of Mu'awiya, the Umayyad caliph, celebrating its feats.[34]

The cessation of the first *fitna* was not the only factor behind Mu'awiya's adoption of a more active approach towards Byzantine Anatolia.[35] Another likely catalyst was Constans II's departure for Italy and Sicily in 662/3 in an attempt to strengthen military defences in the west: this coincided with the ending of the *fitna* and the release of extensive Muslim resources – both human and material – for offensives against the empire.[36] The date for the first Muslim wintering was neither accidental nor random.[37] Although the military situation in Anatolia worsened for the Byzantines after 663,

[32] Kaegi (2003b), pp. 269–82.   [33] Paul Cobb helped clarify this issue for me.

[34] Bonner (1996), pp. xi–xii, 139–42.

[35] For recent studies on Mu'awiya, see Keshk, 'Depiction of Mu'awiya in the early Islamic sources' (PhD thesis, 2002); Cook, 'Beginnings of Islam in Syria' (PhD thesis, 2002); Polat (1999).

[36] Beihammer (2000), pp. 313–14; see also Kaplony (1996), pp. 48–9. Beihammer's analysis of this dispute seems the most plausible. See also Corsi (1983), pp. 85–96, 117–18; Kaegi (forthcoming); Kaegi (in preparation). Constans II failed in his campaign in Armenia in 660–1: see Greenwood (2004), p. 73, n. 215, in contrast to Zuckerman (2005), pp. 80–1.

[37] Cheïra (1947), p. 113 believed that the first wintering occurred in 663.

the Arabs failed to establish any permanent base north of the Taurus mountains. Indeed, the series of Muslim raids from that time onwards could even be seen as indirectly attesting the overall effectiveness of the Byzantine defensive system. However awkward the Muslim winter campaigns made the situation for the Byzantines in Anatolia, the raids were, from the Byzantines' point of view, preferable to irreparable Muslim conquest.

If Constans' move westwards offered the Arabs an opportunity, the fates of Asia Minor and the more distant Mediterranean were now more closely intertwined. Exchanges between Damascus and Constantinople intensified during the mid- to late seventh century, and Muslim officials and military commanders were not infrequently switched between Anatolia and North Africa. To take just one example, Fadhala bin 'Ubayd was transferred from campaigning in the east to join Ruwayfi bin Thabit al-'Ansari in the major raid on the North African island of Jerba; this raid probably occurred in 677/8.[38]

Constans II lacked the skills that Heraclius had shown in exploiting his domestic and Persian enemies' internal strife, and it was internal discord that ultimately overwhelmed Constans and led to his murder. He also lacked his grandfather's skills in identifying external enemies' weak points and then applying pressure to them, and he did not have his sense of timing in battle: Constans was able neither to divide the Muslims, nor to decapitate or neutralise their leadership.

BYZANTINE RESPONSES TO THE SUSTAINED MUSLIM OFFENSIVES: THE ROLE OF SENIOR *STRATĒGOI*

Byzantine military effectiveness against the Arabs was mixed. The imperial government found no sure means of checking or reversing their early territorial gains, and there is no evidence to suggest that any major administrative measures to redress the problem were taken specifically between 659 and 662.[39] The very ease with which Mu'awiya's forces penetrated Anatolia in the mid-650s indicates that, in the first fifteen years following the early Islamic conquests, the government in Constantinople failed to mount effective resistance against the Muslims on the Anatolian plateau. Of events in 653/4, Sebeos writes: 'When he [Mu'awiya] penetrated the whole land, all the inhabitants submitted to him, those on the coast and in the mountains and in the plains.'[40] Mu'awiya's armies were able to range

[38] al-Maliki, *Riyad al-nufus*, ed. Mu'nis, p. 53; al-Dabbagh in Ibn Naji, *Ma'alim*, I, pp. 122–3; al-'Usfuri, *al-Tabaqat*, I, p. 193 (from Tripoli); Ibn 'Asakir, *Dimashq*, ed. 'Amrawi, XLVIII, p. 296; al-Bakri, *al-Mughrib*, p. 19; Taha (1989), pp. 59–60.

[39] For a different view, see Treadgold (1995), pp. 25, 156, 180, 207; Treadgold (1997), pp. 314–18; Treadgold (2002), pp. 132–3. See also Brandes (2002b), pp. 722–3; Kaegi (1999).

[40] Seb., ch. 50, tr. and comm. Thomson and Howard-Johnston, I, pp. 144–5.

far and wide, devastating Anatolia, and they could hardly have achieved this level of military activity had an effective Byzantine defence system been fully in place then.

By the end of the seventh century, both states found it necessary to tighten control over the frontier zone, leaving no scope for the local populations to decide on their orientation for themselves. The Muslims even gave up the policy of allowing Cyprus to remain independent during the reign of Caliph 'Abd al-Malik (685–705), although they soon reversed this particular decision,[41] and it was difficult for any region close to Syria to maintain neutrality between the two powers. The two central governments could either introduce garrisons, as the Muslims reportedly did for a while in Cyprus, or they could evacuate the entire local population from a border zone and destroy what was left of the cities, as was the fate of Arabissos. None of these acts created hermetically sealed borders, but they did help enhance the manipulative powers of the empire and caliphate, and neither polity wanted independent buffer states to emerge between Byzantium and Umayyad Syria.

Despite reports of Byzantine mobilisation during Mu'awiya's caliphate, it is highly unlikely that the Byzantines could have managed major military expeditions reaching into Syria. They could and did threaten Germanikeia and Melitene, and they used the Mardaites as valuable allies or surrogates, even as far afield as Lebanon. But they lacked the means and the resolve to attempt the reconquest of Antioch or other major strongholds in northern Syria, such as Chalkis, let alone any points further south. It is unclear how quickly the Byzantines' familiarity with conditions in Syria faded after their withdrawal from there in the later 630s.

A tradition has it that when Caliph Mu'awiya was informed of a string of calamities – one of his governors had run off, various prisoners had escaped and the Byzantines were raising a fresh army – the commander 'Amr bin al-'As advised him not to worry: 'This is not much [trouble] for you. As for the Byzantines, satisfy them with a few concessions with which you can restrain [dissuade] them . . . And Mu'awiya followed his advice.'[42] This may be a hostile tradition, intended to malign the allegedly easy-going ways of the Umayyads, but it may also reflect a general sense among the Muslims that Byzantine threats did not need to be taken too seriously; that it was possible to reach negotiated settlements with them, without resorting to arms.

The abortive rebellion of Saborios, *stratēgos* of the theme of the Armeniakoi, illustrates the benefits to both empire and caliphate of direct diplomacy between Constantinople and Damascus, and Mu'awiya's response

[41] al-Baladhuri, *Futuh al-buldan*, ed. de Goeje, pp. 155–8; tr. Hitti and Murgotten, I, pp. 238–43.
[42] al-Baladhuri, *Ansab al-ashraf*, ed. 'Abbas et al., IV.1, p. 47; ed. Schloessinger and Kister, IV.A, p. 36.

neatly sums up Muslim strategy in the face of Byzantine internal strife. The well-publicised failure in 667/8 of Saborios' rebellion – for all his negotiations with Mu'awiya[43] – underlined the terrible fate awaiting those Byzantines who attempted private or personal diplomacy with Damascus. According to the chronicler Theophanes:

> the general of the Armeniakoi, Saborios – who was of the Persian race – rebelled against the emperor Constans. Saborios sent his general Sergios to Mu'awiya, promising to subject *Romania* to Mu'awiya if he would ally with Saborios against the emperor. When the emperor's son, Constantine IV, learned of this, he sent Andrew the *koubikoularios* to Mu'awiya with gifts so that he would not cooperate with the rebel.

Mu'awiya reportedly declared: 'You are both enemies, I will help him who gives the most,' to which Andrew replied: 'You should not doubt, caliph, that it is better for you to get a little from the emperor than a greater deal from a rebel.' Although the revolt enabled the Muslims to capture Amorion, the administrative centre of the Anatolikoi theme, and to raid as far as the Bosporus, the Byzantines soon seized the city back, annihilating the Muslim garrison that had been installed there.[44]

Saborios' revolt marked a high point in Umayyad diplomatic attempts to win control of the Byzantine empire through negotiations with the local Byzantine commanders. The Muslims hoped to peel away segments of the empire by convincing local Byzantine (or Byzantino-Armenian) border commanders to break away, perhaps to found neutral buffer states or even to switch allegiance outright, allowing the Muslims to occupy these border areas and raise tribute from them. The miserable fate of Saborios and his supporters reinforced imperial authority, strengthening the belief that revolt against Constantinople or direct negotiations with the Muslims would only result in death and destruction.[45]

Despite a few early, encouraging examples of local Byzantine towns in Syria and Egypt surrendering to the Muslims, this did not become a trend.[46] While Mu'awiya hoped to exploit tensions between Greeks and Armenians on the Byzantine side of the frontier, Constantinople employed a range of policies and techniques to enforce the emperor's authority there. These

[43] Kaegi (1981), pp. 166–7, 182, 201, 234. For another interpretation of seventh-century Byzantine military revolts, see Haldon (1986a).

[44] Theoph., ed. de Boor, pp. 350–1; tr. Mango and Scott, pp. 489–90; see also al-Tabari, *Ta'rikh*, ed. de Goeje *et al.*, II, pp. 84–6; tr. Morony, XVIII, pp. 91–4.

[45] Yet there continued to be numerous military revolts after the failure of Saborios: Kaegi (1981), pp. 186–208.

[46] On a civilian governor's negotiations at Chalkis, see Theoph., ed. de Boor, p. 340; tr. Mango and Scott, p. 472; MS, XI.7, ed. and French tr. Chabot, II, p. 426; Agapius of Membij, *al-'Unwan*, ed. and French tr. Vasiliev, *PO* 8.3, pp. 476–7. On Egypt, see Theoph., ed. de Boor, p. 338; tr. Mango and Scott, p. 470; Agapius of Membij, *al-'Unwan*, ed. and French tr. Vasiliev, *PO* 8.3, pp. 471–2.

included appointing skilful and ruthless eunuchs to punish and put to death anyone who attempted to become separatists, or who toyed with coming to terms with the Muslims on their own.

Constantinople's efforts paid off: the core areas of Byzantine Anatolia lacked commanders who would find it in their best interests to switch sides between Constantinople and Damascus. Mu'awiya and his successors failed to find a single *stratēgos* or senior officer within the all-important theme of the Anatolikoi who would be willing to betray his command to the Muslims. The best-known example of Muslim attempts to subvert a Byzantine border commander are the negotiations in 717 between the commander-in-chief of the great expedition against Constantinople, Maslama bin 'Abd al-Malik, his field commander, Suleiman bin Mu'ad, and Leo 'the Isaurian', the wily *stratēgos* of the Anatolikoi. Leo reportedly parleyed with Suleiman for several days near Amorion. But for all his show of readiness to offer tribute and even reportedly to discuss with Muslim emissaries ways of handing the empire over once he had ensconced himself in Constantinople, Leo never intended to submit to the Umayyads: his was a long-drawn-out ruse, as Suleiman and Maslama learned to their bitter regret. These negotiations helped Leo to gain the throne, but they brought only embarrassment and defeat to the Muslims.[47]

The utmost care was taken by the emperor in selecting commanders of the theme of the Anatolikoi. This was the most powerful field command, and despite occasional rebellions, the *stratēgoi* of the Anatolikoi never betrayed their commands to the Muslims. Had they done so, the overland road to Constantinople would have lain open to the enemy. Although Umayyad Damascus and its court continued to hope for such an opportunity, it eventually became apparent that the problem of Syria's northern borders would not be resolved by Byzantine commanders' switching sides. The empire proved resilient, as it restored a degree of control over its borders and peripheral regions. There was also an inherent contradiction between the desire of some Muslims to amass booty for themselves from Anatolian raiding and Damascus' need to reach a *modus vivendi* with the local inhabitants and leaders in the border regions.

Greek and Roman military maxims shaped how the Byzantines saw the warfare against Muslim Syria, and it is unclear how successfully they digested their own, much more recent experience of military catastrophe there. Until about 711 the reigning Heraclian dynasty may well have made it awkward for anyone to offer a written historical analysis of events. Such inhibitions would have eased from 711, but by then Byzantine Syria had

---

[47] Theoph., ed. de Boor, pp. 386–91, 395; tr. Mango and Scott, pp. 536–42, 544–5; al-Tabari, *Ta'rikh*, ed. de Goeje *et al.*, II, pp. 1314–17; tr. Powers, XXIV, pp. 39–41. On Leo III, see Schenk (1880), pp. 13–21; Gero (1973), pp. 32–4 and n. 7, 182, n. 25; Kaegi (1981), pp. 193–5, 204–13, 224–35; Haldon and Brubaker (forthcoming).

more or less passed from living memory, except among a small number of renegades and refugees. Despite recent warfare, the borders were now gaining durable, albeit still uncertain, parameters.

As with the caliphate, the empire suffered from acute internal rivalries, discouraging the emperors and their advisers from giving adequate resources or total confidence to the best military commanders. There was a deep-seated fear in Constantinople that well-resourced generals might be able to exploit newly won military victories to overthrow the government. As long as the empire's Armenians were less than reliable in their loyalties, any long-term offensive against Umayyad Syria was impractical, no matter how much money Byzantium might extort from Damascus under *fitna*-induced truces. Only the Armenians could provide enough hardy military manpower for the Byzantines, yet the imperial government's relationship with the Armenians living in Caucasian regions under Muslim control was ambivalent and many-stranded (see above, ch. 8).

Finally, it is worth noting that seventh- and earlier eighth-century Byzantines and Muslims lived in a mental environment of eschatological, indeed apocalyptic expectations, although they were not explicitly linked with the approach of any specific millennium. Those fears and hopes remained strong throughout the seventh century and were to be found in many regions, both east and west. They affected and nurtured a number of religious manifestations and movements within Greek, Armenian, Syriac monophysite and Muslim communities. Apocalyptic expectations soared in the middle of the seventh century, perhaps peaking in the reign of Leo III (717–41), as the centenary of the appearance of Islam approached.[48]

THE ERA OF ʿABD AL-MALIK: MUSLIM CONSOLIDATION AND RENEWED OFFENSIVES

The failure of the siege of 674–8 marked the high point in Muʿawiya's efforts to seize Constantinople and for some Muslims this episode became the stuff of legend.[49] There followed the second Muslim *fitna*, which provided a welcome breathing space for the Byzantines. The years 678–9 marked a turning-point in the earliest Muslim–Byzantine encounters. The failure of the blockade of Constantinople, followed by the civil war, caused Caliph Muʿawiya to purchase a suspension of hostilities from Constantine IV (668–85) in 680: he had to offer an annual payment of 3,000 gold pieces, together with fifty slaves and the same number of horses. The Byzantine empire observed these terms throughout the caliphate of Yazid I (680–3),

---

[48] Magdalino (1993b), pp. 18–23; Reinink (2002); van Bekkum (2002); Drijvers (2002); Kaegi (2003a), p. 314; El-Cheikh (2004a), pp. 66–9.
[49] El-Cheikh (2004a), pp. 62–3.

and early in 685 Caliph ʿAbd al-Malik requested renewal of the truce for several reasons. These included the ongoing *fitna*, the Khazars' pressure on Armenia and Constantine IV's offensive which regained Mopsuestia for the Byzantines.[50] The cost of a truce was now huge, amounting to 365,000 gold pieces, 365 slaves and an equal number of horses. Constantine did not seize the opportunity to push deeper into Muslim Syria, or even to try and win it back, at this very vulnerable moment for ʿAbd al-Malik. Maybe Constantine himself was in poor health or the plague raging in Muslim territories at the time could have acted as a disincentive. A second truce on similar terms was negotiated at the end of 689 or at the beginning of 690 (see above, p. 235).

Another instrument of Byzantine diplomacy took the form of the unruly bands of Mardaites that Constantine IV unleashed to raid along the north Syrian coast and to infest its hills. The hardy Mardaites were few in number, and proved disproportionately successful in disrupting Muslim control over northern Syria. A troublesome and temporary Byzantine tool of the late 680s and early 690s, they were probably of Armenian origin. Their operations on behalf of the Byzantines were all the more effective thanks to the protracted second *fitna*, which lasted from 683 until 692: the Muslim authorities found it difficult to check the Mardaite raids while they were seriously distracted by their own internal strife. Justinian II (685–95, 705–11) withdrew the Mardaites from the mountainous regions around Antioch and the north Syrian coast sometime around 687, shortly before sending Leontius to Armenia in command of a strong expeditionary force; in 690 Caliph ʿAbd al-Malik restored Antioch to Muslim rule. The city may have slipped out of Muslim hands because of the Mardaite raiding and the distractions of the *fitna*.

Caliph ʿAbd al-Malik achieved many of his objectives against Byzantium, although he did not radically shift the borders; these remained roughly where they had been at the beginning of the 640s, following the line of the Taurus and Anti-Taurus mountain ranges. Although the end of the second *fitna* was a significant turning-point, it would not be until Caliph ʿUmar II's reign (717–20) that another major effort was launched against central Byzantine lands, reaching as far as the capital itself and making use of both naval and land forces. ʿAbd al-Malik's armies were unable to accomplish the sort of deep penetration of Byzantine Anatolia that Muʿawiya had achieved. His military actions were fairly effective but limited in scope; they concentrated on the border areas, in contrast to the sweeping Muslim gains made in the western Mediterranean region in this era.

---

[50] On Constantine's expedition to Mopsuestia in 684/5 and the town's general strategic importance, see Hild and Hellenkemper (1990), I, pp. 353, 356–7.

Figure 25a Dinar of 'Abd al-Malik, showing a
standing caliph, issued before his coin reform

Figure 25b Dinar of 'Abd al-Malik, having no images at all, only writing, and
in Arabic not Greek or Pahlawi (Persian): proclaiming that there is only one
God, and Muhammad is his messenger 'whom He sent with guidance and the
religion of truth to make it supreme over all others whether the polytheists like
it or not' (Koran, 9:33)

'Abd al-Malik's Byzantine strategy fits well with his domestic policies.
These included the Arabising of both his bureaucracy and the coinage,
while the coin reforms involved the polemical rejection of the types of coin
struck by his adversary, Justinian II. The monumental construction of the
Dome of the Rock in Jerusalem (see fig. 26) reinforced Umayyad assertions
of their right to control the holy places and to the heritage of Abraham. But
'Abd al-Malik and his armies and subjects also benefited from the internal
tensions and strife of the reign of Justinian II. The kaleidoscopic changes
of emperors in the two decades or so following Justinian's initial overthrow
provided ample opportunities for bolder Muslim initiatives (see above,
p. 236).

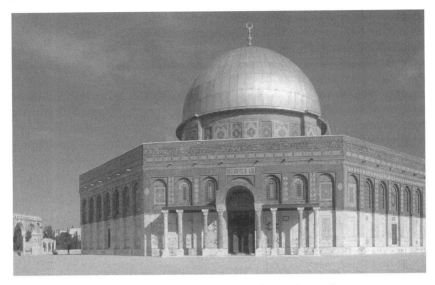

Figure 26 A general view of the Dome of the Rock, Jerusalem

Arab–Byzantine warfare intensified. By 691/2 the truce had been broken and Justinian II suffered a sharp defeat at the Muslims' hands at Sebastopolis, north-west of Sebasteia, after his Slavic recruits defected to the Muslims en masse.[51] Serious Arab invasions of Byzantine Anatolia followed in 695 and 696, reaching as far as Mopsuestia and Melitene. By 695 the Muslims were raiding the region of Fourth Armenia, and by 697 they were marauding elsewhere in Anatolia and taking large numbers of prisoners. Exploiting the instability of the Byzantine throne after the overthrow of Justinian II, Muslim expeditions reached Theodosioupolis in 700, Samosata by 701 and the fortress of Taranda in 702. They succeeded in gaining control of the region of Fourth Armenia, but raiders in Cilicia met with defeat in 704 (see also above, p. 346). From 705 onwards Maslama began to lead expeditions into Anatolia in person.

The early eighth century saw an intensification of Arab offensives while the Byzantines were distracted by internal upheavals.[52] Under Caliph al-Walid I (705–15), Maslama captured Tyana in 707/08; in 713 Antioch-on-the-Maeander in Pisidia fell; and in 714 Maslama managed to reach Galatia, bringing back many captives. Maslama's brother, the caliph Suleiman, put him in command of the great expedition to capture Constantinople in 716–18. This unwieldy force allegedly numbered more than 100,000 warriors and it is said to have had a supply train of some 12,000 men, 6,000 camels

[51] Theoph., ed. de Boor, p. 366; tr. Mango and Scott, pp. 511–12.   [52] Cobb (forthcoming).

and a similar number of donkeys. The venture turned out to be a costly and embarrassing fiasco for the Arabs and a morale-booster for the Byzantines. Serious logistical challenges faced the attackers while Leo III's shrewd bargaining skills and talent for deception contributed to the Byzantines' repulse of this assault on their capital. Immediately thereafter, the Kharijite rebellion in Iraq distracted the attention of Maslama and the caliphal government. Later Umayyad raiders mostly sought to obtain booty, rather than attempting to acquire territory for good.

LEO III, CONSTANTINE V AND FALTERING MUSLIM OFFENSIVES

The Byzantines failed to take advantage of their repulse of the Muslims' second siege of Constantinople. The Arab raiders retained the military initiative throughout the 720s, penetrating more effectively into Anatolia than they would manage to do again in the remaining years of the Umayyad dynasty. However, although they retained the initiative, their objectives were mostly limited to the capture of Byzantine fortresses that lay near the frontier.

'Umar II's caliphate showed the beginnings of defensive thinking and political retrenchment in the Muslim leadership. But although 'Umar wanted to withdraw from frontier positions in Cilicia, including Mopsuestia, other Umayyad leaders stationed as many troops as possible on the frontiers so as to keep them preoccupied with fighting and contented with the proceeds of raids. During the caliphate of Yazid II (720–4), al-'Abbas bin al-Walid invaded Paphlagonia where he reportedly captured 20,000 prisoners and took Dabasa (probably Thebasa) in 721. In the same year, 'Umar bin Hubayra defeated the Byzantines in Fourth Armenia and took 700 prisoners, and many Byzantine captives from these raids were resettled in Syria. Further Muslim raids followed over the next three years, and in 724 the Arabs briefly took Ikonion and the frequently disputed fortress of Kamacha on the upper Euphrates. Under Caliph Hisham (724–43), Muslim expeditions intensified and Maslama's final major summer raid in 726 resulted in his temporary capture of the key Byzantine fortified town of Caesarea in Cappadocia.[53]

In the late 720s and early 730s, the pendulum was swinging back in the empire's favour. Leo III's formidable military skills and personal familiarity with local topography and living conditions in the foothills of the Taurus Mountains helped him counter Arab incursions and strengthen the empire's defences. Apart from their fleeting capture of the nodal stronghold of Charsianon in 730,[54] the Arabs suffered various checks or reversals and by

---

[53] On Caesarea, see Hild and Restle (1981), pp. 193–6.
[54] On Charsianon, which had not previously fallen to the Arabs, see Hild and Restle (1981), pp. 164–5.

732 Byzantine resistance on the Anatolian frontier had hardened. Between 733 and 740 the Muslims tried to maintain their rhythm of campaigning against the Byzantines, but to little effect. Byzantine defensive tactics improved and despite limited victories in 738 and 739, the Muslims made very few permanent territorial gains.

The greatest military initiative during Hisham's caliphate was a summer expedition in 740, led by two of his sons, Muhammad and Maslama, and under the supreme command of a third son, Suleiman, which culminated in the battle of Akroinon. However, both the governor of Melitene, Malik bin Shu'ayb, and the Arabs' commander, Sayyid al-Battal, fell in the battle, together with perhaps as many as 13,000 Arab warriors, and the Byzantines took many prisoners. Akroinon was a great victory for Leo III and a disaster for the Umayyads, opening them up to a major Byzantine expedition against Melitene; although they failed to take the town, the Byzantines laid waste to the surrounding countryside.[55] The civil war which followed Leo III's death in 741 allowed the Muslims to resume their Anatolian raiding and the seizure of captives. But there were no brilliant naval successes and Umayyad armies would never penetrate as deeply into Anatolia as they had done in the early years of Hisham's caliphate;[56] the Byzantines for their part began to raid more boldly into Muslim territory.

In no sense can Byzantium be described as a satellite of the caliphate during the eighth century, whether under the Umayyads or their successors, the Abbasids, who had overthrown the Umayyads by 750. The suggestion made by some scholars that the Muslims played a decisive role in the development of Byzantine iconoclasm appears to be unsubstantiated (see above, pp. 279–80). The *fitna* that destroyed the Umayyads temporarily eased the Arab pressure on Emperor Constantine V (741–75), but he did not succeed in exploiting this civil war to recover significant swathes of former Byzantine territory in Syria. In 746 and in 747 Constantine campaigned in northern Syria, and then along the upper Euphrates and into Armenia. He managed to capture Germanikeia and carry away many of its inhabitants. However, after the Abbasids' overthrow of the Umayyads, Constantine made peace with the Muslims in 752.

THE ABBASIDS' BUILDING OF BAGHDAD AND
SPONSORSHIP OF JIHAD

From al-Mansur to Harun al-Rashid

This regime change in the Islamic world had very important consequences for Byzantium. The dynamics of the relationship between the two central

---

[55] On the strategic importance of Melitene as a communications hub, see Hild and Restle (1981), pp. 233–6; *EI*, VI, p. 230 (E. Honigmann).
[56] Blankinship (1994).

governments changed, as the Abbasids initially sought to consolidate their own leadership through championship of the jihad against Byzantium. Late in the reign of their first caliph, al-Saffah (749–54), the large army that had been mustered for use against Byzantium was diverted by its commander, 'Abdallah bin 'Ali, in an attempt to seize power for himself. His efforts were thwarted,[57] but this abortive *coup d'état* diverted Muslim resources at a time when logistical considerations were making it increasingly difficult for the Abbasids to wage war on Byzantium from their new capital under construction at Baghdad. Under Caliph al-Mansur (754–75) the Byzantine frontier was regarded as an area for Muslim settlement and fortification rather than a theatre for major campaigning. Warfare became positional, while the borders were now relatively static; some would argue that the raiding became virtually ritualised.[58]

The Abbasid leaders had to reckon with possible Byzantine invasions, and they also had to keep a close eye on the Muslim armies from northern Mesopotamia, who still maintained their loyalties to the Marwanids. Various border warlords also gave them cause for concern, particularly those from the region of Samosata. To counter all these threats, al-Mansur tried to coopt supporters of the last Umayyad caliph, Marwan II (744–50), and he also imported troops from Khorasan. The result, however, was chaos and anarchy on the borders. The caliph was forced to call on Abu Muslim – who had led the Abbasids' revolt against the Umayyads in 747, establishing al-Mansur's predecessor al-Saffah on the throne, and who was now governor of Khorasan – for support to crush the rebellion of 'Abdallah bin 'Ali. Al-Mansur proceeded to develop his own network of border commanders, of disparate origins, to serve as a counterbalance to the warlords. No single Muslim commander was to lead an expedition against Byzantium more than twice in succession. This rotation system was designed to prevent any border commander from gaining control of really substantial human and material resources. Yet it was also a precarious system, provoking jealousy and competition among the local commanders and it did not make for maximum military efficiency against the Byzantines. The rotation system had been dropped by 769, towards the end of al-Mansur's caliphate, and thereafter al-Mansur sought to control the frontier regions from a distance. Expeditions and leaders of expeditions had proliferated because anyone with sufficient resources could try to mount an expedition against Byzantium. The Abbasids now attempted to make permission from the imam a necessary precondition for embarking on an expedition against Byzantium.

---

[57] 'Abdallah bin 'Ali was the uncle of the second Abbasid caliph, al-Mansur (754–75). See Cobb (2001), pp. 23–6.

[58] Haldon and Kennedy (1980), pp. 114–15; see also Vaiou, 'Diplomatic relations between the 'Abbasid caliphate and the Byzantine empire' (DPhil thesis, 2002); Ibn al-Farra, *Rusul al-muluk*, ed. and tr. Vaiou.

During the caliphates of al-Mahdi (775–85), al-Hadi (785–86), and
Harun al-Rashid (786–809) warfare against the Byzantine empire became
a priority for the leadership. Al-Mahdi ordered the stationing of 2,000 new
troops at Mopsuestia, to be maintained by stipend, and his first campaign
against Byzantium was launched with aplomb in 776, with the caliph lend-
ing his symbolic presence to the proceedings. In 778 the Byzantines, under
the Isaurian dynasty's favoured commander Michael Lachanodrakon, penetrated the Hadath pass and attacked Germanikeia. Eventually the siege
was lifted (through the garrison commander's bribery of Lachanodrakon,
according to Theophanes),[59] but not before the Byzantines had deported
many Jacobite Christians to reside on the other side of the empire, in
Thrace. Emperor Leo IV (775–80) celebrated a triumph for his generals at
the palace of Sophianai on the Bosporus, distributing rewards. In the following year, the Byzantines again penetrated to the Hadath pass, provoking
a Muslim counter-expedition under Hasan bin Qahtaba, which reached –
but failed to capture – Dorylaion.

Henceforth Caliph al-Mahdi appointed frontier regional commanders
from his own household and family, aiming to raise them above the level
of the local border warlords. He accompanied an expedition as far as the
frontier region in 780 and from there he sent on his son, Harun al-Rashid,
who penetrated Byzantine territory and managed to besiege and capture
Semalous. In 781/2 al-Mahdi sent Harun to engage the Byzantine forces at
the head of a huge force, allegedly some 100,000 strong. After penetrating to
Chrysopolis, on the Asiatic side of the Bosporus opposite Constantinople,
and after seizing many captives, Harun imposed expensive and embarrassing terms on Empress Irene in 782: the truce was to last for three years, and
involved an annual tribute payment by the Byzantines of 100,000 dinars; in
addition, Harun's army kept its prisoners and considerable booty.[60] Warfare against the Byzantines now counted for more than it had done at any
time since the Umayyad caliphate of Hisham.

Harun al-Rashid resumed military operations in 785–6, in response to
an alleged violation of the truce in 785 and the Byzantines' seizure and
destruction of the fortress of Hadath. From the Abbasids' point of view,
the frontier system was not working very well and the Barmakid family
gained effective control of the caliphate's north-west frontier provinces.
Nonetheless, Byzantium faced a formidable opponent when Harun al-
Rashid became caliph in 786; he had won great renown for his personal
participation in the jihad against Byzantium, and he had taken shrewd
advantage of Empress Irene's weakness and her serious problems with her

---

[59] Theoph., ed. de Boor, p. 451; tr. Mango and Scott, p. 623. On Michael Lachanodrakon, see *PMBZ*,
#5027; see also above, p. 284.
[60] Tritle (1977).

military units (see above, p. 270). Around the time that Constantine VI (780–97) was reigning in uneasy equilibrium with his mother, Harun chose to make Raqqa his residence in order to control access to the frontier. In 797/8 Harun led the expedition that captured the Byzantine fortress at Safsaf, not far from the Cilician Gates. The Muslims are even said to have reached the Bosporus again, and Harun appointed commanders for further raids. He agreed to negotiate with Byzantium only because of the pressure he was coming under from the Khazars to his north. The caliph led expeditions in person against Irene's successor Nikephoros I (802–11) in 803 and 806; during the latter expedition, Harun's forces captured Heraclea-Cybistra and Tyana, and the emperor was compelled to accept peace and to pay a humiliating poll tax on himself and his son (see above, p. 256).

Harun took institutional measures to strengthen the caliphate's position against Byzantium in the long term. In the very first year of his caliphate, he created a new frontier district called al-'Awasim with Membij as its centre. This marked the beginnings of a new system of frontier organisation. Opposing the Byzantines along a straggling line from Tarsus north-eastwards as far as Theodosioupolis were the strongholds of the *thughur*, subdivided into the *thughur*s of Syria and of the al-Jazira.[61] These fortifications ran through mountainous country from the Taurus in Cilicia towards Germanikeia, and then on to Melitene. In 799 Harun built the town of Haruniyya, named after himself, between Germanikeia and Anazarbos, as part of his programme to organise and improve the defences of the northern Syrian frontier. These strongholds on the front line were the culmination of a long process that had already been underway before Harun's caliphate. But behind them Harun instituted the *'awasim*; these formed a second, more compact buffer zone between northern Syria and the Cilician *thughur*, extending from Antioch to Membij. Harun sought to break up the conglomeration of north-west frontier provinces and to impose his own personality directly on the frontier area and on the waging of jihad, thus cutting down to size the figures of the local commanders and warlords.

The frontier became a centre of unprecedented attention in part because of the accession to the throne of Nikephoros I in 802. Harun al-Rashid was provoked by an insulting letter from Nikephoros, demanding the return of the tribute that Irene had paid, but more important may have been a Byzantine raid against Anazarbos and Kanisa al-Sawda. There was an exchange of prisoners in 805 but, as mentioned above, in the following year Harun imposed tribute of 30,000 dinars on Byzantium, in addition to the poll tax that was payable by Nikephoros and his son. In 808 an exchange of prisoners and a summer expedition into Byzantine territory took place,

---

[61] On the *thughur*s in the Arab–Byzantine frontier region, see *EI*, X, pp. 446–7 (C. E. Bosworth).

but no further major Muslim expeditions into Byzantine territory would occur until 830.

Harun's commitment of so much energy and so many resources to his wars against the Byzantines reflected his sense of duty, although some scholars see his warfaring primarily as propaganda intended for internal consumption.[62] His wars brought few concrete territorial gains, but demonstrated his personal involvement with the jihad. Harun may be characterised as the first *ghazi*-caliph.[63] For Hisham and the Marwanids, military service had been a personal obligation, but Harun adopted the role of *ghazi*. He owed his accession to the power base that he and his supporters controlled in the north-western frontier regions, facing the Byzantines. He held himself out as a ruler whose power was coterminous with Islam and also as an imam-volunteer. Irene and Nikephoros I could not match him as commanders themselves and they lacked generals who were capable of resisting such an effective leader.[64] In this period some Muslim scholars and saints also settled on the frontier, a trend that had not been typical of the Umayyad era. Tarsus and Melitene emerged as the principal centres of the *thughur* by the mid-ninth century, and part of their population was made up of *ghazi*-volunteers. Some commercial goods passed through these strongholds to and from Byzantine territory, and professional military men tried to wield power there.

Al-Ma'mun and al-Mu'tasim

Muslim–Byzantine warfare abated after the death of Harun al-Rashid in 809. Prolonged internal troubles within the caliphate limited the ability of Harun's successors to take the offensive against Byzantium. This period also saw bands of autonomous, armed Muslims marauding into Anatolia. In Byzantium, too, internal conflicts – notably the revolt of Thomas the Slav (see above, pp. 258–9) – severely limited the ability of Emperor Michael II (820–29) to wage war on the Muslims in the east in the early 820s. Thomas' revolt received additional impetus and reinforcements from diehard followers of the defeated al-'Amin, brother of Caliph al-Ma'mun (813–33). Among these were Zawaqil bedouin from Syria, who had no other refuge as they fled from the manhunts and reprisals carried out by the caliph's soldiers. But they were unable to give Thomas' insurgency enough additional resources to bring him victory. Internal violence in the caliphate brought further reinforcements into the Byzantine empire, of rather mixed value. After the crushing in 838 of Babek's Khurramite rebellion, which may have received Byzantine support, the remaining rebels fled into Byzantine territory where

---

[62] Bonner (1996), pp. 96–106, 144–7.   [63] Kennedy (1981); Kennedy (2001); Kennedy (2004b).
[64] On Irene's and Nikephoros' lack of military skills and 'clout', see above, pp. 256–7, 259, 269, 277.

they were incorporated into the armies of Emperor Theophilos (829–42) and placed under the command of the controversial Theophobos. These separate armed bands of Khurramites brought to Byzantium not only experienced manpower but also valuable information about Muslim military matters. Their relative prominence in the course of events testifies to the shortage of adequate Byzantine soldiers to fight the Muslims. However, these recruits, who are termed 'Persians' in the Byzantine sources, did not necessarily make for stability. They were liable to switch sides and so could, in their turn, provide important intelligence back to the Muslims.[65]

Caliph al-Ma'mun assigned northern Mesopotamia, and the border fortress districts of the *thughur* and the *'awasim* to his son al-'Abbas, together with the sum of 500,000 dinars. The civil war between al-Ma'mun and his brother al-'Amin had significantly weakened the Abbasids' position vis-à-vis Byzantium. Nevertheless, al-Ma'mun was determined to redress the balance and in 830 he launched a series of offensives, invading Cappadocia in response to Emperor Theophilos' attack on Mopsuestia and Tarsus. He captured and fortified the city of Tyana, and even claimed that he would conquer Constantinople itself. A second campaign into Asia Minor was mounted the following year. In 832, al-Ma'mun forced the major border fortress of Lulon to surrender, and in 833 he tried, albeit unsuccessfully, to capture Amorion. He died while planning further offensives against the Byzantine frontier regions: having recaptured Tyana, al-Ma'mun was preparing an expedition to implant Arab tribesmen in Anatolia.

Al-Ma'mun was succeeded by his brother al-Mu'tasim, who ruled from 833 to 842. His caliphate marks the end of the pivotal period of Byzantine–Muslim relations that followed the death of Harun. Al-Mu'tasim abandoned Tyana soon after assuming power, but his anger was roused by the Byzantines' capture of Samosata and Zapetra in 837, and he succeeded in fulfilling the ambitions of his brother by organising a massive three-pronged invasion of Anatolia. His forces crushed the armies of Theophilos at the battle of Dazimon and then besieged and briefly occupied Amorion in 838, not only an important military base, but also the ancestral home of the Amorian dynasty. He thereby dealt a massive blow to the resources and prestige of Theophilos and his dynasty – and to Byzantium in general – and a number of Byzantine prisoners were executed. Although al-Mu'tasim's armies were obliged to withdraw to caliphal territories in order to suppress worrisome insurgents, the campaign of 838 revealed major weaknesses in Byzantine military capacity. Al-Mu'tasim's newly recruited elite Turkish forces proved their archery skills against the Byzantine soldiers to deadly effect, and the Byzantines were initially unable to resist them.[66] Al-Mu'tasim's forces also

---

[65] See Cheynet (1998a).   [66] Kaegi (1964).

demonstrated their ability to undertake and bring to a successful conclusion sieges of large, well-fortified Byzantine cities such as Amorion.[67]

Once again, internal Muslim political, religious and military strife rather than Byzantine institutions or imperial decisions brought respite for Byzantium, just as the Byzantines' mood was turning to despair. The 838 campaign marked the zenith of caliphal expeditions across the Taurus mountains into Anatolia. Theophilos and al-Mu'tasim made peace in 841. The shift of the Abbasids' main residence from Baghdad to their huge new city of Samarra and the emergence of a powerful separate unit of Turkish guards changed the dynamics of Abbasid power for the worse.[68] No future Abbasid caliph would lead in person an invasion from Iraq into Anatolia. Nor would any Abbasid expedition manage to assemble troops on the scale of that of 838. The death of al-Mu'tasim in 842 marks a turning-point in the caliphate's offensive capability against Byzantium. His new commanders based at Samarra regarded volunteers for the jihad as a nuisance. In 857 Caliph al-Mutawakkil (847–61) abolished all the fiscal immunities that the *thughur*s had enjoyed. He did try to mount a huge show-piece campaign when he moved his army and much of the administration westwards to Damascus in 858, but military unrest thwarted his efforts. The assassination of al-Mutawakkil in 861 triggered what is sometimes termed the spell of 'anarchy' at Samarra, and Byzantium's military situation benefited accordingly.[69]

THE EASING OF JIHAD: DIPLOMATIC AND CULTURAL CONTACTS BETWEEN BYZANTIUM AND THE MUSLIM WORLD

Summer raids into Byzantine Anatolia diminished in intensity once Abbasid power began to fragment both on the periphery and in the central cities during the internal conflicts of the middle decades of the ninth century. A slave revolt broke out in southern Iraq in 869 and the rebels, mostly of east African origin and known as the Zanj, took over Basra and even started striking their own coins before eventually being overwhelmed in 883. Then, from the 890s onwards for almost a century, the Carmathians (Qaramita) backed by bedouin tribes posed a constant challenge, sometimes amounting to a serious threat to the state. Even before inner turmoil diverted the caliphate's resources, growing military and economic power enabled Byzantium to undertake offensive actions. One Byzantine expeditionary force penetrated to Amida, where it took many prisoners in 851, and a Byzantine fleet raided the Egyptian port of Damietta in 853 (see above,

---

[67] On material evidence from Amorion, see Lightfoot (1998).
[68] Gordon (2001).   [69] Kennedy (2004b), p. 169.

p. 298). The central government in Samarra or Baghdad could do little effectively to deter this.

Ninth-century Byzantine–Muslim diplomatic practices and protocols are well documented in the Greek and Arabic sources. Muslim geographical texts such as that of Ibn Khurradadhbih, with its itineraries and other data concerning the empire, also testify to growing contacts and exchanges.[70] Famous Byzantine embassies to Baghdad include those in the reigns of Leo V and Theophilos.[71] Two of the most important missions were those of John the Grammarian of 829 and 831: returning from his first mission, John is said to have advised the emperor Theophilos to build the palace of Bryas 'in imitation of those of the Saracens'.[72] Not all the information passed through formal channels. Members of Syrian Christian communities, some of whose members also knew Greek, were important intermediaries between the two empires and cultures. They could carry out translations of ancient texts[73] and they could also transmit intelligence of vital relevance to contemporary politics, war and commerce. The frontiers were not tightly sealed between Byzantium and the lands under Abbasid rule. In fact, in every century renegades fled from one side to the other: many of them were neither Greek nor Armenian by origin, and some moved repeatedly to and fro. The migrants included the Banu Taghlib in the seventh century, Tatzates in the late eighth century, Theophobos in the ninth century, Samonas in the early tenth century and Bardas Skleros in the late tenth century.[74] Such defections reveal the potential for the movement of individuals and even, occasionally, of whole groups or communities across the frontiers. Precisely for this reason, attempts were made by the respective authorities to keep vigilant watch over the border zones. It is probable that the Byzantines had developed techniques for reporting and tracking, and for mobilising their own military forces to cut off and destroy enemy raiders in Anatolia, by the late seventh or earlier eighth centuries. Documentation of these practices exists from the tenth century, but the basic military defence measures were most probably in place much earlier.[75]

[70] See Ibn Khurradadhbih, *al-Masalik*, ed. and French tr. de Goeje, pp. 100–13 (text), 73–86 (tr.). For ninth- and tenth-century Muslim information about Byzantium, see El-Cheikh (2004a), pp. 8–9, 139–56.

[71] Vaiou, 'Diplomatic relations', pp. 102–31.

[72] TC, pp. 98–9; Ricci (1998); Magdalino (1998), pp. 196–9, 206–10.

[73] On the role of Syrian Christians as intermediaries, see the various studies in Griffith (1992); also Griffith (1996). On the broader movement to translate Greek texts into Arabic, which was triggered by the foundation of Baghdad and the patronage of courtiers and scholars as well as caliphs such as al-Ma'mun, see Gutas (1998), pp. 7, 11–34, 53–4, 61–104; El-Cheikh (2004a), pp. 103–4.

[74] On defectors, see Mansouri (2000), pp. 242–3. The aim of John the Grammarian's first embassy to Baghdad was partly to persuade a prominent defector, Manuel the Armenian, to return home. See also pp. 273–4, 503, 524–5.

[75] For discussion of the tactics recommended in *Skirmishing*, ed. and tr. Dennis, see pp. 138–9 (introduction); ed. and French tr. Dagron and Mihăescu, pp. 214–25, 235–7, 245–8 (commentary).

CONCLUSION

Emperors, caliphs and amirs took responsibility for major operations on the Byzantine–Arab frontiers intermittently between the seventh and the mid-ninth century, but none persisted in campaigning in person. Too many other priorities and pressures were in play, and important as the frontier was, it did not monopolise their attention. Constans II spent much of his time on or near scenes of military campaigning; the state of emergency required the emperor's continuous personal involvement. Leo III and Constantine V managed to lead far more effectively than their seventh-century predecessors had done (see above, pp. 265–6, 273, 277), but only a few of the earlier ninth-century emperors came from a military background and those who scored significant successes did so in fighting the Bulgars, not the Arabs (see above, p. 257). So far as the Muslims were concerned, no leader after their campaigns of conquest in the seventh century, and occasional expeditions of the eighth and earlier ninth centuries, managed to assemble sufficient human and material resources to undertake further major offensives or to conquer fresh territories. The personal presence of a sovereign was necessary to make the respective military systems function effectively on both sides of the frontier, yet neither caliph nor *basileus* could long give the Byzantine–Muslim frontier his full attention in the light of pressures elsewhere. No single campaign, battle or other brilliant tactical or political feat could resolve the underlying military challenges and political tensions in northern Syria and upper Mesopotamia. Processes of political and military deterioration undermined Muslim strength in the area, but limited resources, the cost and complexity of mobilisation and fear of military coups continued to frustrate the Byzantine emperors, too. Internal conflicts greatly complicated the conduct of warfare and diplomacy on their eastern frontier. No systematic institutional solution showed signs of emerging there for either Byzantines or Muslims, and indecisive if incessant warfare and diplomacy remained the norm. The approximate limits of Byzantine control to the south-east in the mid-ninth century were not radically different from those which had emerged some two centuries earlier, in the aftermath of the earliest Muslim conquests. Decisive change could wait.

CHAPTER 10

WESTERN APPROACHES (700–900)

MICHAEL McCORMICK

INTRODUCTION

The early medieval societies of Byzantium and western Europe that emerged from the late Roman world shared more than a few institutions, traditions and religious experiences. They sometimes rubbed shoulders in ways we overlook. Rome's clerical elite was so hellenised that the pope who reigned at Charlemagne's birth spoke Greek as his mother tongue. Under Charlemagne's grandsons, members of the Byzantine missionary Methodios' entourage wrote Greek majuscules in the memorial book of a German monastery to record their stay; Methodios was himself a native of Thessaloniki, formerly a Byzantine imperial official in Macedonia and a monk in Bithynia (see above, p. 300). Conversely, Franks served in the Byzantine emperor's military household and figured at palace banquets.[1]

Facts like these raise the broader question of how the two main entities of Christendom interacted over the six or seven generations from c. 700 to c. 900. The historical problem is not without snares. 'Influence' can be misleading: interaction between cultures rarely has one society passively undergoing the active influence of another. Once something is available, the borrowing civilisation must take the initiative in appropriating it from the other culture. So when, where and how Byzantium and the west came into direct or indirect contact needs clarifying. Moreover, though these early medieval societies evolved away from their late antique roots, those common roots are everywhere discernible, and it is easy to mistake residual for recent borrowing. Indeed, the shared matrix could give rise to structural parallels, that is, similar developments that arose independently in each culture.[2] And, even over seven generations, patterns of interaction changed. Byzantium took as well as gave.

Around 700, a kind of community of imagination preserved lingering mental links where real ones had lapsed. In England, Bede still synchronised his universal chronicle with contemporary Byzantine regnal

---

[1] *Verbrüderungsbuch Reichenau*, 53D4–5; compare Zettler (1983); Philotheos, *Kletorologion*, p. 177. On Methodios, see above, pp. 316–18.

[2] McCormick (1987); McCormick (1997).

Map 20 Western neighbours *c.* 700–*c.* 1025

years.[3] Frankish celebrants, eager to use the authoritative new texts of the mass that had been imported from the Byzantine duchy of Rome, sometimes seem scarcely to have noticed that they were still praying for the Roman emperor.[4] Anglo-Saxon missionaries, heirs of the easterners Theodore and Hadrian, who had come to them from Tarsus and Africa via Rome, encouraged obedience to St Peter and a fascination with Italy that

[3] Bede, *De temporum ratione*, pp. 534–5; tr. Wallis, pp. 236–7. Compare Bede, *De temporibus*, ch. 22, pp. 609–11; Bede gives mainly the eastern, not the western Roman imperial succession.

[4] Tellenbach (1934), pp. 19–21. On Byzantium's nominal rule over Rome, see below, pp. 444–6.

fostered face-to-face meetings with Byzantine provincial civilisation. They also copied the Antiochene biblical exegesis transmitted to them by their Byzantine teachers.[5]

Paradoxically, by 900 actual contacts had increased and the old imaginary links were gone. In Byzantine eyes western Europeans' Christianity still created the basis for special relations with the empire. Traditional barbarian stereotypes still prevailed at Constantinople: the Franks were brave but stupid fighters, emotional and undisciplined; recent experience confirmed their avid corruptibility.[6] If eighth-century Byzantines imagined Rome as a typical Byzantine town and the popes as obedient functionaries reverently storing imperial communiqués near the tomb of Peter or routinely transmitting them to western barbarians, ninth-century strains induced an angry emperor to brand the pope and his Latin language as 'barbarian'.[7] 'Byzantines', of course, never existed as such: the empire of Constantinople was known to inhabitants and enemies alike as Roman, a usage into which even a hostile Einhard slips.[8] Its subjects might simply identify themselves as 'Christians'.[9] Westerners might lump the empire's inhabitants together under the simplistic linguistic heading *Graeci*, particularly when they wished to ignore the uncomfortable political implications of eastern imperial continuity. Beneath the uniformity of its Greek public language and tax payments to the emperor in Constantinople, the empire was multi-ethnic: Armenians, Syrians, Slavs, Italians, Istrians all swore allegiance to the Roman emperor, and as cultivated a man as Einhard casually identifies a eunuch with a Slavic name as a 'Greek'.[10] But the ancient empire had changed since the days of Justinian's reconquests.

EARLY MEDIEVAL BYZANTIUM: THE 'NEW ROME' TRANSFORMED

The upheavals of the seventh century had transformed Byzantium. The old urban fabric of the Roman empire largely gave way. Though the precise causes and chronology remain controversial, archaeological evidence shows that, in the long run, the cities of Asia Minor and the Balkan peninsula fared little better than those of western Europe.[11] Despite streams of refugees, even the capital of Constantinople shrank dramatically in population.[12]

[5] Bischoff and Lapidge (1994); for the distinctively Byzantine identity of various regions of Italy in this period, see McCormick (1998b).

[6] Leo VI, *Tactica*, XVIII.77, 85–9, cols. 963–4, 965–8; see also Dagron (1987), pp. 217–18.

[7] Pseudo-Gregory II, *Letters*, ed. and French tr. Gouillard, no. 1, pp. 276–97; arguments assigning these texts to Rome have left me unconvinced. For Michael III on Latin, see Nicholas I, *Epistulae*, no. 88, p. 459.

[8] Einhard, *Life of Charlemagne*, ch. 28, ed. Waitz *et al.*, pp. 32–3; tr. Dutton, pp. 33–4.

[9] Mango (1980), p. 31.   [10] Einhard, *Translatio*, IV.1, p. 256 ; tr. Dutton, p. 111.

[11] Biraben and Le Goff (1969); Conrad, 'Plague in the early medieval Near East' (PhD thesis, 1981); Sarris (2002). See also pp. 122–3, 478–9.

[12] Haldon (1997a), pp. 92–124; Mango (1990), pp. 51–62. See also above, p. 260.

To the north, the old Danube frontier and much of the Balkans were overrun by Slavs, Avars and Bulgars, although the imperial government still clung to coastal strongholds like Thessaloniki or Monemvasia. The closing of the old military roads across the Balkans effectively sundered Byzantine Italy from the imperial centre in the winter months, when sailing was difficult.[13] To the south, Rome and Ravenna hung by a thread as the Lombards expanded their power from the Po basin down Italy's mountainous spine. The bold attempt of Emperor Constans II (641–68) to defend the empire's southern flank by transferring his imperial headquarters back to Italy around 662 collapsed with his murder.[14] At the same time, a cash-strapped government intensified the fiscal yield of its western provinces.[15] That pressure may have reinforced tensions which had started over religious issues.

For a government whose professional bureaucracy and military forces were sustained largely by a land tax levied on the provinces, the fiscal implications of such territorial losses were devastating, amounting to as much as three-quarters of revenues.[16] Defeat and the fiscal crunch forced radical administrative and military reconfigurations in the empire's besieged remnants. And conjugated disaster opened more than a political crisis in a society which lived and breathed its religious sentiment: the challenge of Islam was ideological no less than political and military. Was the sect in whose sign the Roman empire had conquered since Constantine's conversion no longer stamped with God's seal of success?

Lifestyle and mental attitudes underwent a sea change as the amenities of late Roman daily life became a thing of the past outside the court's island of archaism.[17] By the seventh century, Greek had supplanted Latin as the characteristic language of the central administration. Outside the Latin-speaking outposts of Dalmatia and Italy, only the Latin lettering of coins and imperial documents, a few fossilised acclamations and the massive presence of Latin loan words in the technical jargon of the state offered a faint linguistic echo of the old Roman past.

Byzantine culture no longer coincided with the Byzantine polity. For a few generations, Constantinople ceded Hellenic cultural leadership to the empire's geographic edges. John Damascene, the greatest Byzantine thinker of his time, wrote his Greek theological treatises under the Arab caliphs; the best Byzantine art adorned the shrines and pleasure palaces of the new Islamic empire, while remarkable Byzantine hagiography of the eighth century was produced in Italy or Palestine.[18]

Small wonder that one of the few pieces of contemporary Byzantine literature translated into Latin around 700 is an apocalyptic vision of the Arab

---

[13] McCormick (2002), pp. 25–8.   [14] Corsi (1983). See also above, p. 232.

[15] McCormick (1998a), pp. 78–80. See also below, pp. 433, 436.

[16] Hendy (1985), p. 620. See also above, pp. 269–71.   [17] Mango (1981a).

[18] Mango (1991); Kazhdan (1999), pp. 75–94, 169–81. See also above, pp. 242–3.

conquest, the last Byzantine emperor's return to Jerusalem and the impending end of the world![19] But events would follow an unforeseeable path. Transformed and reorganised, Byzantium was about to begin a remarkable resurgence. Bede, who had earlier succumbed to optimistic reports of the Roman reconquest of Africa, accurately reported the successful defence of Constantinople from the final Arab siege of 717–18.[20] That victory inaugurated an era whose scarce sources cannot obscure the renewal of Byzantine civilisation which, by 900, stood on the threshold of its great medieval expansion.

The changes that produced this revamped empire are much debated. The Byzantines themselves located the defining moments of their history in dynasties and doctrines, a vision which says as much about emperor and faith in Byzantine mentality as about historical trends. By these lights, confusion and usurpation followed the toppling and execution of Heraclius' last descendant, Justinian II (685–95/705–11), until the usurper general Leo III (717–41) defended the capital from the Arabs and launched the 'Isaurian' or Syrian dynasty. The victorious Leo promoted a new cult practice whose affinity with Islam many observers feel is undeniable: he proscribed most religious images and their veneration as a form of idolatry. His dynasty championed iconoclasm almost to the end, uncovering powerful stresses within the Byzantine ruling class which succeeding generations memorialised as religious persecution (see above, pp. 279–84).

Three generations later, the regent empress Irene recruited the support of Pope Hadrian I (772–95) to overturn the imperial doctrine at the second ecumenical council of Nicaea in 787 (see above, pp. 287–8). Charlemagne's ambassadors witnessed the palace coup that ended Irene's independent rule and the Isaurian dynasty in 802. This spell of short reigns, involving a toned-down reversion to iconoclasm, led to a coup by Michael II (820–9) who established the Amorian dynasty, named after his home town in Asia Minor, where excavation has uncovered the material face of the age.[21] Another regent, Empress Theodora (842–56), finally abolished iconoclasm in 843. Her son Michael III (842–67) and the Amorian house were overturned by a palace parvenu, Basil I (867–86). Down to Michael III's time, soldier emperors predominated: Leo III and his son Constantine V (741–75) were particularly successful commanders.

Reorganisation and re-establishment of control characterise this era. Survival required first and foremost the military stabilisation of the eastern front, where Arab incursions into the empire's new agrarian heartland of western Asia Minor were increasingly checked thanks to new provincial defence systems, known as themes. These *themata* spread sporadically as

---

[19] Pseudo-Methodius, *Apocalypse*; see also Prinz (1985).
[20] Bede, *De temporibus*, ch. 22, p. 611; Bede, *De temporum ratione*, pp. 534–5; tr. Wallis, pp. 236–7.
[21] Gill (2002); Lightfoot (2003).

events dictated. The word's derivation is contested but it refers simultaneously to autonomous military units and to the large territorial districts in which they were permanently stationed and of which the empire was composed. They may have been inspired at least in part by the western exarchates, earlier administrative and military structures elaborated in reconquered Italy and Africa. By the time of Charlemagne and his son, themes and the generals or military governors (*stratēgoi*) who headed them had everywhere ended the late Roman tradition that strictly separated civil and military administration, and government had shifted to a permanent war footing.[22]

The mighty themes of Asia Minor helped slow the Arab advance. The European themes straddled the capital's western approaches and defended Constantinople from the rising power of the Bulgars. But the very concentration of power that facilitated the generals' defensive tasks complicated the political structure of the empire, since *stratēgoi* like the future Leo III often challenged the emperor resident in Constantinople (see above, p. 380). The last great revolt of the themes in particular had serious consequences. The civil war between Michael II in Constantinople and Thomas the Slav in 821–3 and the ensuing disarray contributed to the empire's greatest territorial losses in our period: the Arab conquest of Crete (*c.* 824–8) and the beginning in 826 of the fall of Sicily, both of which had implications for imperial communications with western Europe.

To counter their own provincial armies, the Isaurian emperors created a new, imperial army of cavalry and infantry, known simply as 'the regiments' (*tagmata*) and headquartered in the capital. The *tagmata* spearheaded offensive operations and played a key role in the Isaurians' notable successes in the Balkans and Asia Minor. At sea, the seventh-century Karabisianoi fleet, essentially conceived to defend the central coastal areas and sea approaches to Constantinople, was superseded by provincial fleets organised as maritime themes in the course of the eighth and ninth centuries. An imperial fleet equipped with Greek fire was stationed at Constantinople and chiefly destined for long-range intervention, flanked by elements of the thematic fleets.[23] On the empire's western flank, a naval squadron based in Sicily brought enhanced security to Italian waters in the 750s.[24] Despite occasional setbacks, the new military apparatus proved effective in preserving the empire. As surviving inscriptions attest, the emperors began refurbishing critical infrastructures across territories that had slipped out of their control in the seventh century. Whatever local discomfort the return of imperial tax-collectors may have brought to any provincial landowners who might have survived the century of storms, the centripetal dynamic was probably

---

[22] Lilie (1984a); Haldon (1993), pp. 7–11. See also above, pp. 266–8, 272.
[23] Ahrweiler (1966), pp. 7–107.   [24] McCormick (2001), p. 872, no. 159.

powerful: imperial armies brought coinage, administrators and bishops, who sent back to Constantinople the newly restored tax revenues; these, in turn, reinforced the imperial treasury which financed the bureaucracy and military apparatus and enabled the empire to extend its reach even further.[25]

In the capital, the few great late Roman ministers like the praetorian prefects or the masters of the offices, into whose offices various vertical chains of administrative institutions formerly converged, had disappeared. They were replaced by the omnipresent 'accountants' or logothetes ever vigilant for income and expenditure of a state straining against the abyss. These new sub-ministers reported directly to the emperor and so brought more direct lines of authority into his hands (see above, pp. 238–9, 273). Administrative structures were far more institutionalised than in the west, as professional bureaucracies looked after imperial finances and justice. Whatever survived or now emerged as a ruling class owed much to government service as the source and sign of its wealth and power. The stresses of a ruling class in the making mark the top echelon of society: frequent *coups d'état*, political shake-ups and church schisms start to stabilise only in the tenth century. From *c.* 800, Byzantine and Frankish sources yield the earliest glimpses of family names and clans like the Phokai or the Argyroi who would dominate the social scene at Byzantium's apogee and who seem to ride a rising tide of economic and demographic recovery.[26] A state hierarchy structured this emerging power elite, as imperial promotion granted life-long, non-hereditary state dignities like patrician or *prōtospatharios* and salaries to leading officials who trumpeted their titles on numerous surviving lead seals. Each official's place in the hierarchy was communicated by his position in imperial ceremonies and delineated in official lists of precedence, the earliest surviving example of which (the *Taktikon Uspensky*) dates from 842–3.[27] For all its factions, the power of this senatorial order was such that a prudent pope might demand that it confirm by oath guarantees issued to his legates by a shaky regency, and it is this social group that supplied most of the challenges to imperial authority, whether they came in the form of conspiracies, usurpations or doctrinal dissidence.[28]

---

[25] On the recovery, see Hendy (1985), pp. 77–85, 90–1; the basic picture is confirmed by the seal evidence: see, e.g. *DOS*, I, pp. 40, 46, 104; II, pp. 1, 22, 89; IV, p. 107. On population transfers organised by the government, see Lilie (1976), pp. 227–54; for inscriptions: e.g. Mango and Ševčenko (1972), pp. 384–93; for provincial town walls: Ivison (2000).

[26] On elite factionalism, see Winkelmann (1987), pp. 75–7; on families: Kazhdan and Ronchey (1999), pp. 248–9, 256, table 2, and esp. Cheynet (2000), pp. 285–92.

[27] For seals, an essential source for prosopography and institutional history, see *DOS*, I; for the precedence lists: *LPB*; for dignities and precedence and how they worked in this period: Kazhdan and McCormick (1997), pp. 195–7; Oikonomides (1997a).

[28] Mansi, XII, col. 1073B.

Iconoclasm, the most lasting and disruptive doctrinal quarrel of the era, had many consequences. Resistance to the imperial heresy challenged the emperor's power in matters of doctrine and, implicitly, in other matters as well. The considerable efforts subsequently devoted to restoring the emperor's prestige and redefining relations with the ruling class are most visible in the refurbishing of imperial ceremonial. Iconoclasm affected the institutional history of the church even more deeply. The patriarchs resided only a stone's throw from the imperial palace and were often under the emperor's thumb. The secular church's relative tractability with respect to imperial doctrinal shifts fostered internal conflict. Churchmen who sought to resolve conflict without throwing the ecclesiastical hierarchy into chaos clashed with zealots. A monastic party centering on the great cenobitic reformer Theodore the Stoudite (759–826) burned to root out any who had temporised with what had been the empire's official doctrine over nine of the last twelve decades, factionalising the church in ways which paralleled and were perhaps connected with fissures in the lay aristocracy (see also above, pp. 288–9). In any case conflict spilled over into other issues and spawned a series of bitter schisms from the Moechian controversy – a dispute centering on Emperor Constantine VI's decision to divorce and remarry in 795 – to the 'Tetragamy' in which the Italian-born patriarch and former imperial adviser, Nicholas I Mystikos (901–7, 912–25) bitterly opposed Emperor Leo VI's (886–912) fourth marriage (see below, p. 503). Since partisans of each faction challenged their opponents' ecclesiastical appointments, Byzantine bishops' careers seemed noticeably unsettled in this era.

Factionalism in the upper echelons of church and state provoked sudden political shifts which affected relations with the west. Since the days of Pope Leo I (440–61), whose memory the iconophile hero Theodore Graptos still celebrated, the Roman see and its doctrinal rectitude had enjoyed great prestige in the Constantinopolitan church. This prestige was only enhanced by Rome's role in the earlier monothelite controversies and Pope Martin I's (649–55) resistance, arrest and death in imperial custody which led the Byzantine church to venerate him as a martyr (see above, pp. 231–2). A Greek account of his suffering was composed in eighth-century Jerusalem or Rome, an alternative which is itself revealing. Rome had become the authority to which Byzantine religious thinkers under pressure appealed for support. That the duchy of Rome was slipping out from under the emperor's effective administrative reach only increased its attractiveness, hence efforts to persuade western authorities to curtail the activities of eastern émigrés at Rome.[29]

---

[29] The attribution of the *Life of Martin I* (*BHG* 2259) to eighth-century Greeks at Rome (see Mango (1973b), pp. 703–4; Sansterre (1983), I, pp. 138–9) has been seriously challenged in favour of Jerusalem

Figure 27 Mosaic of Theodore the Stoudite from the monastery of Nea Moni on Chios; this seems to have the features of a character portrait and probably belongs to a type ultimately deriving from the funerary portrait of Theodore in the Stoudios monastery

Culturally, four generations of theological debate for and against icons spurred renewed examination of the Hellenic theological and cultural heritage. The hunting out and recopying of old books – to uncover or rebut authorities on icons – marks the earliest stages in the birth of Byzantine humanism, the encyclopaedic movement. The political and economic recovery of a society based in large part on written administration equally invigorated literary culture. Imperial bureaucrats like the future patriarch

by Conte in *Sinodo lateranense dell'ottobre 649*, ed. Riedinger, comm. Conte, pp. 238–49. This text appears to have abbreviated and combined the Greek text of several of the documents transmitted in Latin in Anastasius' *Collectanea*: Devreesse (1935), esp. pp. 54–5, n. 1. See in general on these texts Chiesa (1992); on efforts to curtail émigrés at Rome, see Michael II and Theophilos, *Letter to Louis I*; Phot., no. 290, ed. Laourdas and Westerink, III, pp. 137–8.

Nikephoros I (806–15) figure prominently in the early phases of the revival.[30] They were reinforced by intellectuals and others like Michael Synkellos or Patriarch Methodios (843–7) who migrated back to a recovering imperial centre from Arab-controlled Palestine or the Italian borderlands. As in the west so in Byzantium a new minuscule book script was the tool and hallmark of the new culture.[31] So too the new Greek writing required and conditioned the phenomenon of transliteration. Ancient exemplars in the old script were sought out, compared and copied in the new script. That new writing has preserved in such Byzantine 'editions' most of what has survived of classical Greek and patristic literature.

In the capital, the receding danger of Arab siege was replaced by the imminent menace of Bulgar attack. Repairs were made to the city walls.[32] Behind their protective bulk, renewal stirred in a city where nature had reconquered much of the urban fabric. Though on a much smaller scale and with a more religious focus than the colossal monuments of the old Roman state, construction and redecorating were nonetheless significant by recent standards and invite comparison with contemporary western efforts. In 768, Constantine V restored the aqueduct of Valens, which had been interrupted since 626 and was essential to the water-starved site of Constantinople. Numerous churches were remodelled in the ninth century. Theophilos (829–42) built a new suburban palace, 'Bryas', modelled, significantly, on the Arab caliphs', the new standard-bearers of luxury. Basil I constructed a splendid new chapel, the Nea, for the Great Palace, and the ebb and flow of icon veneration required redecoration of religious shrines according to the dictates of the moment.[33]

It was, then, a changing Byzantium which bordered on western Christendom. As the threat of political extinction receded, the reorganised empire reasserted control. The progress of imperial administration allied with an improving general situation and sporadic disarray amongst the empire's most lethal enemies to allow renewed, if staccato, campaigns of intervention at the empire's extremities, which despite all setbacks and reversals steadily extended outwards from Constantinople.

BYZANTINE–WESTERN TRADE?

Broad economic structures had once spanned the Mediterranean and fostered Byzantine commercial interaction with the west. The sweeping changes of the seventh century naturally affected communications between

---

[30] Mango (1975a).
[31] Cavallo (1997); McCormick (1997). See also above, p. 279.
[32] Müller-Wiener (1977), pp. 288, 293, 303, 308; see also p. 313 and above, p. 265.
[33] See in general Mango (1990); Magdalino (1996a), pp. 17–50; Brubaker and Haldon (2001), pp. 3–30.

the two former halves of the empire. The occasional western shipwreck and growing ceramic evidence of imports confirm that, although dwindling, economic links to Byzantine Africa and the eastern Mediterranean persisted well into the seventh century, perhaps reinforced by supply efforts to the last garrisons perched along the Ligurian coastline.[34] But even the trickle of sea communications between Constantinople and the west seems almost to dry up towards 700.[35] A high-status ecclesiastical community whose traces have been recovered at Crypta Balbi in Rome was still importing some luxury wares from Byzantine Africa and the Islamic Middle East in the late seventh century. But the imports practically ceased early in the eighth century, if one can judge from their absence and a turn towards recycling and away from Levantine raw materials in glass manufacture.[36] Long-distance shipping routes declined in importance, and regional shipping networks emerged as characteristic.[37]

The reasons for all this remain controversial; certainly the causes were multiple. Networks of easterners trading with the west may have withered under the cyclical plagues, whose contagion contemporaries linked with shipping. Declining economic fortunes presumably shrank western purchasing power even before the Islamic conquests redistributed eastern wealth and reorganised macro-economic structures, fanning demand in the east. To grant Henri Pirenne his due, warfare around the Mediterranean rim probably played a role. The final fall of Byzantine Carthage in 698 disrupted a crucial pivot for shipping linking the eastern and western Mediterranean.[38] Even before it came to conflict, the rapid build-up of Arab and Byzantine fleets will – initially at least – have competed with merchant ventures for such sailors and ships as were available.[39] Greek and Coptic papyrus archives of 698–711 from the inland town of Aphrodito on the Nile paint an astonishing picture of how the new rulers mobilised local wealth and conscripted landlubbers for sea raids (*koursa*) launched from Africa, Egypt and the east.[40] Land travel too was disrupted: Byzantine loss of control in the Balkans blocked the old Roman overland routes to the west, essentially cutting Italy off from Constantinople during the winter months.[41] The structure of exchange within the territories that remained Byzantine took

[34] For a ship from Constantinople that sank off Narbonne *c*. 630–1, see Solier *et al.* (1981), pp. 26–52; the most recent appraisal allows a date later in the seventh century for the Saint-Gervais 2 wreck off the Merovingian customs port of Fos-sur-Mer, originally dated *c*. 600–25: Jézégou (1998); for imports at Marseilles: Bonifay *et al.* (1998), pp. 377–8; for Italy: McCormick (2001), pp. 110–11.

[35] Claude (1985), pp. 303–9; Panella (1989), pp. 138–41; McCormick (2001), pp. 115–19.

[36] Panella and Saguì (2001); Mirti *et al.* (2001).

[37] McCormick (2001), pp. 537–47; see also Wickham (2000a); Horden and Purcell (2000), pp. 160–72.

[38] McCormick (2001), pp. 106–8. [39] McCormick (2001), p. 113.

[40] *Greek papyri*, IV, pp. xxxii–xxxv; see also e.g. *ibid*. no. 1350 (AD 710), pp. 24–5.

[41] McCormick (2001), pp. 68–73.

new shapes, as the shrunken fiscal component, formerly dominated by massive northbound shipments from Egypt and Africa, sought new bases. And, it has been argued, very differently administered economic zones emerged in the capital and the provinces.[42] Byzantium's own long-distance trade in the eighth century seems to have been reorientated along a new axis linking the Aegean and the Black Sea.[43]

Direct documentary evidence of trade between Byzantium and the west is slim, and complicated by the ambiguity of the notions of trade and 'Byzantine'. Should we classify as 'Byzantine' middlemen the Venetian merchants who recognised Byzantine sovereignty and sailed between Italy and Africa, Egypt and Palestine? In any event, over the next two centuries the old infrastructures of travel gradually recovered or were replaced. After the nadir of the earlier eighth century, communications and also commerce rebounded smartly in the final quarter of the century; they continued to climb into the reign of Louis the Pious (814–40) and, after a period in which they leveled out, growth resumed in the later ninth century.[44] Although the structures and volume of trade differed greatly from those of the late Roman period, communications and commerce were again significant factors in the relations between western Europe and the Middle East.

Practically in the shadow of the Alps, the more or less autonomous Byzantine outpost of Venice rose out of the Adriatic mists from insignificance to embody this change. The ancient trunk route linking the Tyrrhenian coast with the Middle East via the straits of Messina, around southern Greece and across the Aegean had never ceased completely to function. Indeed, in 746–7, it transmitted *eastwards* to the Byzantine capital the last major seaborne outbreak of the bubonic plague (until 1347), even though the epidemic had begun in the Levant.[45] But over the next century, branch routes sprouted again on the Adriatic or through the Gulf of Corinth, feeding piracy along the coast. The old Balkan and Danubian overland routes, including the Egnatian Way, returned to activity, even if the Hungarians were to make the Danube corridor short-lived.[46]

The rare data on Venetian shipping between *c.* 750 and 850 point mostly to trade between Italy and the Islamic world. Muslim traders show up at Rome around 800. Slave trading ran along the west coast of Italy and involved Rome and the shipment to Africa of enslaved Europeans by Venetian and Greek merchants *c.* 750–75; and Emperor Leo V (813–20) was eager to block Venetian commerce with the caliphate.[47] Further west, it may be

---

[42] Oikonomides (1993); Oikonomides (1997b); Patlagean (1993); Haldon (2000a).

[43] Lilie (1976), pp. 276–9; McCormick (2001), pp. 543–7, 600.

[44] McCormick (2001), pp. 437–43, 786–93.

[45] Pryor (1988), pp. 93–111, 137–49; Biraben and Le Goff (1969), p. 1497.

[46] McCormick (2001), pp. 523–37, 548–69.

[47] McCormick (2001), pp. 618–30; *CC*, no. 59 (from AD 776), ed. Gundlach, pp. 584–5; tr. King, p. 286 (paraphrase); *LP*, XCIII.22, ed. Duchesne, I, p. 433; tr. Davis, II, p. 47; Dölger, *Regesten*, no. 400.

more than coincidental that all four of the tenth-century shipwrecks discovered off the French Riviera were carrying goods from the Islamic world.[48] At the head of a reinvigorated Adriatic shipping route, Arab gold and silver coins competed with Byzantine and Frankish money, to judge from the way coins found in the earth converge with those mentioned in contemporary records. They testify in their way to intensifying economic links between the Islamic world and eighth-century Italy. That people involved in this sort of contact also frequented at least Byzantine provincial centres is also suggested by finds of Byzantine bronze coins. Although these coins never served as a medium of international exchange, their presence in western Europe nevertheless indicates that the people who lost them had direct or indirect contacts with the Byzantine world.[49]

Merchants make only sporadic appearances in Carolingian sources, and 'Greeks' are rarest among them. Traders who do show up tend to be Frisians, Anglo-Saxons, Jews or Italians, and only rarely can we discern the horizons of their activities.[50] Some Jews and Italians may have been subjects of the Byzantine emperor; in any event commercial contacts with Byzantium may have been realised through non-Greek intermediaries. Thus, in 885–6, an astute observer in the caliphate described the trading patterns of Jewish merchants who alternated their export voyages of eastern luxury wares, travelling one year to Constantinople, and the next, to the Frankish court. One of their main western routes probably ran through Venice.[51]

A few 'Greek' merchants do crop up in the eighth-century Tyrrhenian Sea. Towards the tenth century, some Italo-Byzantines imitated their neighbours in Amalfi, Naples and Gaeta, such as the Greek slave trader from Armo near Reggio di Calabria who would not sacrifice his trade's superior profits for less reprehensible commercial ventures. A near-contemporary life of a Sicilian saint compared his crossing from Africa back to Sicily *c.* 880 to 'some huge ship filled with all kinds of merchandise'. Such hints perhaps explain the concession of a landing for Greek merchants to the church of Arles by one of the last Carolingians, Louis the Blind who, as we shall see, had other connections with Constantinople.[52] The account of the North African crossing underscores that Greek merchants, like their Venetian peers, might have found more profit linking western Europe with the huge Islamic economy than with Constantinople. In other words, western contacts with Byzantine merchants may have been an indirect result of commercial relations with the Islamic world. But this does not diminish the

---

[48] McCormick (2001), p. 599, table 20.4.
[49] McCormick (2001), pp. 319–87.   [50] McCormick (2001), pp. 614–69.
[51] Ibn Khurradadhbih, *al-Masalik*, ed. and French tr. de Goeje, pp. 153–5 (text), 114–16 (tr.); as discussed in McCormick (2001), pp. 688–91.
[52] On eighth-century 'Greek' merchants, see: *CC*, no. 59, ed. Gundlach, p. 585; tr. King, p. 286 (paraphrase); on the slave trader: *Life of Elias the Speleote*, III.18, p. 855; on the crossing from Africa: *Life of Elias the Younger*, ch. 25, ed. and Italian tr. Rossi Taibbi, pp. 36–7; on Louis the Blind: Poupardin, *Recueil des actes*, no. 59, p. 108.

significance either of the intermediaries or of the overall growth in infrastructures which permitted and channelled relations between Byzantium
and the west.

Underlying ideas and realities

Constantinople took the diplomatic initiative in order to defend its own
vital interests on its western flanks, especially in Italy. Over time both Franks
and Byzantines expanded their imperial reach, and their concerns converged
or collided in other regions as well. Thus Charlemagne's destruction of the
Avars in central Europe opened a power vacuum into which the dynamic
Bulgar realm expanded from its headquarters at Pliska some 300 kilometres north of Constantinople. Bulgaria's Greek inscriptions and inhabitants make its Byzantine cultural cachet unmistakable, and it may have
acted occasionally as an intermediary.[53] Ninth-century Franks and Byzantines shared powerful and dangerous neighbours in the Bulgars. Wherever its political centre lay, the new Slavic society of the Moravians which
sprang up between the destruction of the Avars and the Hungarians' arrival
would greatly concern the eastern Franks and allow Byzantium to cultivate
yet another power situated to Bulgaria's rear. Finally, tenth-century links
between Byzantium and northern Europe were foreshadowed by the Scandinavians' appearance on the Black Sea, a fact perhaps not unconnected
with the new north-eastern axis of Byzantine shipping, and the coalescence
of a 'northern arc' of traders, linking the Baltic to the Middle East. In 839
Emperor Theophilos sent with his ambassadors to Louis the Pious some
mysterious newcomers called 'Rhos'. Louis knew a Viking spy when he saw
one and so informed his Byzantine colleague.[54] A couple of years later, the
Byzantine ambassador to the Franks and to the Venetians communicated
with the Baltic trading emporium of Hedeby, if we may judge from the
excavators' recovery there of his seal. The idea that this may have been
connected with his known mission to recruit warriors for Byzantium is not
weakened by the recent discovery of a second seal in another Scandinavian
trading settlement.[55]

   Ideas as well as realities conditioned Byzantium's approach to the west.
Byzantines viewed Constantinople as the capital of the Roman empire, a
unique historical entity established by God to foster the spread of Christianity. Various barbarians had occupied parts of the whole but the empire

---

[53] Venedikov (1962), pp. 273–7; Shepard (1995a), p. 238.

[54] *Annales Bertiniani*, ed. Grat et al., pp. 30–1; tr. Nelson, p. 44; McCormick (2001), pp. 918 (no.
944), 606–12.

[55] Stiegemann and Wemhoff (1999), I, pp. 375–6, nos. VI.78 and VI.79; see also McCormick (2001),
pp. 227, 920 (no. 455).

retained theoretical claim to territories which were, for the time being, not effectively administered. This attitude affected imperial ideas about Italy, for example in Constantine V's pressure on Pippin the Short, king of the Franks (751–68) to restore the exarchate of Ravenna to Byzantine control.

A second idea conditioned Byzantine policy and was linked with the first: just as the Roman empire was a unique historical entity, so its ruler, the *basileus* – the Greek word had come gradually to occupy the semantic zone of the Latin word *imperator*, triumphing officially by 629 – was God's lieutenant on earth and incomparably superior to other terrestrial rulers (*archontes*) or kings (*reges*). A family hierarchy of powers projected onto foreign relations the conceptions that structured domestic society. The Roman emperor reigned supreme as the father of all other rulers, although the exception once made for the Persian shah was now extended to the caliph, who was reckoned worthy of fraternal status. This would give a particular edge to the Frankish imperial usurpation, as viewed from Constantinople.[56]

The means by which Constantinople sought to effect its aims ranged from carefully calibrated gifts to armed intervention. Religious cooperation or conversion, subsidising potential rivals and cultivating satellite powers as buffers worked as well as dangling prospects of marriage with the imperial family. A favourite tactic was to encourage hostile action by the enemies of Byzantium's enemies.[57] All these approaches featured in the diplomatic dialogue with the west.

Geographically and historically, a fragmented Italy and its complicated local politics held the key to Byzantine dealings in the west. The Lombard principalities of the Po basin, Spoleto and Benevento pressed against the increasingly autonomous Byzantine coastal areas stretching from Ravenna to Naples via Rome. At the extreme south of the Italian boot, first Sicily and later Calabria and Apulia anchored Constantinople's power in Italy. The loss of Rome to the barbarians – for this is how Constantinople viewed the papal alliance with the Franks – and Carolingian ascendancy in Italy inevitably intensified Byzantine interest in the new transalpine power, especially when the Arabs of Africa surged across the Mediterranean to assault Byzantine Sicily and southern Italy.[58]

Rome as a 'Byzantine province'

Three successive trends characterised the political situation. As elsewhere in its former dominions, Constantinople sought in the early eighth century

---

[56] See Ahrweiler (1975a), esp. pp. 129–47; *ODB*, I, p. 264 (M. McCormick, A. Kazhdan); III, p. 1945 (M. McCormick); Grierson (1981), pp. 890–914.

[57] Obolensky (1963).   [58] von Falkenhausen (1978–9), p. 152.

to reintegrate Italy into the imperial structure, and so to restore late antique patterns of political domination. But local and distant forces conspired to loosen Constantinople's grasp on the Italo-Byzantine societies. From the north, expanding Lombard power absorbed Ravenna in 751 and menaced Rome. The Franks would soon swallow the Po kingdom and extend the Lombard pattern into an attempt to restore a Roman empire in the west. They forcibly removed northern Italy from the Byzantine sphere and so strengthened its transalpine political, cultural and economic links that it looked much like the southernmost extension of northern Europe. The even greater vitality of the Islamic world capitalised on the complexities of southern Italy to drive Byzantium from Sicily and establish toeholds on the Italian mainland. Finally, the collapse of the Frankish empire combined with the resurgence of Byzantine power to shift the dynamics in a new direction so that, as far north as Rome, the late ninth-century peninsula again appeared as the northwestern edge of a southeastern Mediterranean world.

If Italy was the key to Byzantine and western interaction, Rome was the key to Italy. The city's cultural and religious significance outweighed its economic or strategic importance, although the wealth of its churches would tempt Arab and Frankish looters alike, and great prestige accrued to its master. It was uniquely suited to intensive cross-cultural contacts. Politically it lay on the fluctuating frontier of Byzantine and northern power zones. Culturally, it attracted pilgrims from all parts of the Christian world: Irish, Anglo-Saxons, Franks, Lombards, Byzantines, even Arabs made their way to its fabled shrines.[59] Economically, the restored finances of the Roman church and wealthy pilgrims created a market for expensive imported goods that began flowing again on the main trunk routes. From 700 to 900, the elite culture of the ancient city changed.

Around 725, the church of Rome was nearing the last generation of its 'Byzantine period', under the powerful influence of immigrants from the lost eastern provinces. The papal bureaucracy, the lay elite and the monasteries all show signs of Greek predominance, as some befuddled Anglo-Saxons learned in 704 when the papal advisers they were meeting began joking and discussing the matter among themselves in Greek.[60] The city produced Greek literature, including a papal translation of Gregory the Great's *Dialogues*, and the *Miracles of Anastasius*, while surviving fragments suggest that Greek inscriptions were not uncommon.[61] The public face of

---

[59] On Byzantine pilgrims, see von Falkenhausen (1988), pp. 644–6; see also the semi-fabulous description associated with Harun ibn Yahyah: Ibn Rustah, *Al-A'laq al-nafisah*, tr. Wiet, pp. 144–6. On Frankish establishments, see Stoclet (1990).

[60] Eddius Stephanus, *Life of Wilfrid*, ch. 53, ed. Levison, p. 247; ed. and tr. Colgrave, pp. 112–13.

[61] In general, see Sansterre (1983); Sansterre (2002). Pope Zacharias' translation of Gregory's *Dialogues*: *PL*, 77, cols. 147–8; see also Photios, *Bibliotheca*, cod. 252, ed. Henry, VII, p. 209; tr. Wilson, pp. 228–9. On Anastasius the Persian, see *Miracles of Anastasius*. On inscriptions, see Cavallo (1988), pp. 484–92.

the papal court owed much to Byzantine provincial officialdom, naturally enough given the prominence of descendants of refugees from the eastern upheavals. Although the process is difficult to track, such families must increasingly have assimilated the local language, even as innovations rooted in the immigration flourished: the name stock of the Roman elite, new saints' cults and liturgical feasts like the Assumption are all imports from the east.[62] From about the middle of the eighth century Latin prevails, but a Greek heritage perdured: the person who forged the *Donation of Constantine* wrote a Greek-accented Latin, and Pope Paul I (757–67) supplied Pippin the Short with Greek books.[63]

Two or three generations later, the Greek presence at Rome appears to have been concentrated in the monasteries, which had received fresh reinforcements fleeing the upheavals in the Byzantine church. Papal distributions to the monastic establishments of the eternal city reveal that in 807, six of the most important monasteries and one convent were Greek.[64] A fragment from their liturgical services shows that one community used the Greek liturgy associated with Jerusalem when praying for Pope Hadrian I (772–95).[65] Around the same time, a native Greek speaker who probably resided in one of those communities contributed to Byzantine literature a remarkable hagiographical novel set in Rome and Sicily in the days of Gregory the Great (590–604).[66] In the later ninth century, some Roman aristocrats may still have felt nostalgia for Byzantine rule, Anastasius Bibliothecarius may have been able to compare different manuscripts of Pseudo-Dionysius the Areopagite in Rome, and the occasional Greek monk might work purple cloth or copy texts there. But the instruction in and use of Greek were becoming rarer and more private.[67] As Roman ambassadors insisted in Constantinople in 870, some churches under Roman jurisdiction were Greek in language, and clergy appointed to them were chosen for their linguistic qualifications.[68] But Anastasius, with his command of both languages, stands head and shoulders above his contemporaries. By 900 immigration from the east had shrunk to undetectable levels and the old Greek monasticism of Rome was entering its final decline even as Byzantine power surged in the south.[69]

In some ways, the very recovery of the imperial centre distanced the two societies; a reorganising empire sought to tighten slackened links with

---

[62] On provincial ceremonial, see McCormick (1990), pp. 252–9; on names: Llewellyn (1981), pp. 360–1; on saints: Sansterre (1983), I, pp. 147–9; Detorakès (1987), pp. 94–6.

[63] On the *Donation of Constantine*, see Loenertz (1974). For the gift of books, see *CC*, no. 24, ed. Gundlach, p. 529.

[64] *LP*, XCVIII.76–81, ed. Duchesne, II, pp. 22–5; tr. Davis, II, pp. 212–18; Sansterre (1983), I, pp. 32–4, 90–1.

[65] Sansterre (1984).   [66] 'Leontius of St Sabas', *Life of Gregory of Agrigento*.

[67] On nostalgia, see Brown, T. S. (1988a), pp. 39–44; on Anastasius' manuscripts: Chiesa (1989), p. 198; on cloth and calligraphy: *Life of Blasios of Amorion*, ch. 14, p. 663; on the changing character of Greek learning: Cavallo (1988), pp. 490–2.

[68] *LP*, CVIII.51, ed. Duchesne, II, p. 183; tr. Davis, III, p. 285.   [69] Sansterre (1988), pp. 709–10.

provincial society by restoring old standards of political, fiscal and religious integration and subordination long in abeyance and now newly resented. A carrot and stick approach seems unmistakable: *c.* 710 Justinian II violently repressed a rebellion in Ravenna and blinded and exiled its archbishop Felix; later the same prelate was restored and enriched. Pope Constantine (708–15) and his entourage were summoned to Constantinople for a year-long consultation and celebration of unity, during which the future Pope Gregory II's theological expertise impressed the emperor, who confirmed earlier privileges of the Roman church, while imperial envoys arrested and executed the papal officials who had stayed behind in Rome.[70]

Lombard perils

Some time between *c.* 724 and 755, a series of distinct developments coalesced to undermine the old assumptions which governed the church of Rome's thinking about the empire. They did so at about the time trans-Mediterranean communications in general reached their lowest ebb and direct overland travel had ceased. The precise chronology and relative weight of each development is disputed, but the overall result is clear. As Constantinople reorganised, it increased the tax burden on the lands of the Roman church. The papal establishment resisted paying. Despite imperial efforts to stabilise the Arab threat from the south, expanding Lombard power menaced Rome and Ravenna ever more acutely, even as pressing military threats closer to home kept Constantinople from shoring up Italy's defences. Leo III's new doctrine of iconoclasm met papal opposition. The imperial government responded to papal tax delinquency by confiscating the papal properties in Sicily and Calabria; then or somewhat later, the emperor transferred ecclesiastical jurisdiction over southern Italy and Illyricum from Rome to the patriarch of Constantinople.[71]

According to their loyal biographers, the popes vociferously protested at doctrinal and administrative measures of which they disapproved even as they dutifully represented imperial power in security matters. Thus in 713 Pope Constantine intervened to quell a murderous riot against an official who had accepted an appointment in the name of Emperor Philippikos (711–13), whose orthodoxy the pope himself had challenged.[72] Gregory II

---

[70] Agnel., chs. 137, 143–4, ed. Holder-Egger, pp. 367–8, 371–2; ed. Mauskopf Deliyannis, pp. 313–16, 321–4; tr. Mauskopf Deliyannis, pp. 259–61, 266–70; *LP*, XC.1–7, XCI.1, ed. Duchesne, I, pp. 389–91, 396; tr. Davis, I, pp. 91–3, II, p. 3; Todt (2002); see also McCormick (2001), p. 860, no. 73, and below, pp. 438, 440.

[71] On the stabilised Arab threat, see Leo III, *Epistolae*, no. 7, p. 98; see also Amari (1933–9), I, pp. 350–1; on taxes, see *LP*, XCI.16, ed. Duchesne, I, p. 403; tr. Davis, II, p. 10; Theoph., ed. de Boor, I, pp. 404, 410; tr. Mango and Scott, pp. 558–9, 567–9; see also Sansterre (1983), II, p. 165, nn. 176–7. On the date of the transfer, see von Falkenhausen (1978–9), pp. 151–5; see also Schreiner (1988), pp. 369–79. See above, p. 285.

[72] *LP*, XC.10, ed. Duchesne, I, p. 392; tr. Davis, I, p. 94. See also below, p. 440.

(715–31) is supposed to have quashed an Italian plan to elect a rival emperor to oppose Leo III's iconoclasm and attack Constantinople, despite purported Byzantine plots on his life.[73] Pope Zacharias (741–52) intervened twice with the Lombard kings to protect Ravenna. Despite recognising the usurper Artabasdos (see above, p. 258), he even obtained the imperial estates of Ninfa and Norma in Campania from Constantine V.[74]

To judge from the imperial largesse, papal opposition sounded louder locally and beyond Byzantine borders than it did inside the Great Palace in Constantinople. Nonetheless, the pope had held a local synod in 731 to clarify his position against iconoclasm. Roman links with the Greek milieux of Jerusalem, which were ardently defending icons from the safety of the caliphate, and with monks fleeing from Constantinople, perhaps stiffened papal attitudes. The emperors' appropriations of papal patrimonies and jurisdiction were certainly not tailored to soften the papal stand on doctrine.

Doctrinal and administrative differences might have remained just that, as they had in far more dramatic circumstances a hundred years earlier, were it not for the inexorable Lombard threat. This pressure produced a triangular relationship between Constantinople, Rome and whoever controlled the Po valley, in which every rapprochement between two of the partners might threaten the third. When Rome urged Constantinople to check the Lombard threat, it nonetheless dreaded that Constantinople might sacrifice Rome to accommodate the Lombards. So, too, when the popes entered their alliance with the Franks, Constantinople attempted to bind the Carolingian kings to Byzantium – to the popes' detriment. Paradoxically, when Rome seemed strictly subordinated, relations between the Franks and Byzantines were on the best footing, for instance immediately after Pope Leo III's restoration by Frankish arms in 799.

In its last century of existence, the Lombard kingdom centred on Pavia must have had fairly intensive contacts with Byzantium, not least because of its ongoing absorption of the exarchate of Ravenna. But records are rare. Diplomatic exchanges, for instance, are known only in so far as the papacy was involved. The extent of contacts is suggested by a few hints: a Byzantine jester named Gregory entertained the court of King Liutprand (712–44); Lombard royal charters emulated Byzantine models; and in 750, King Aistulf forbade business with the Byzantines during periods of conflict.[75]

The same pope who convened the council condemning iconoclasm in 731 had secretly invited the Franks to attack the Lombards in what was, after all, only a classic manoeuvre of Byzantine diplomacy. In 732, a Roman

[73] *LP*, XCI.14–20, ed. Duchesne, I, p. 403–7; tr. Davis, II, pp. 10–13.

[74] Bertolini, O. (1968), II, pp. 695–701: compare the different interpretation of Speck (1981), pp. 114–22.

[75] Lounghis (1980), pp. 133–4; *Urkunden Pippins*, ed. Mühlbacher *et al.*, no. 183, p. 247; Brühl (1977), pp. 9–10; Aistulf, *Leges*, no. 4, ed. and German tr. Beyerle, pp. 360–1.

council very publicly ignored imperial sovereignty. A decade or two after the fact, a member of the Carolingian family remembered that the pope had promised to defect from Byzantium if Charles Martel helped him. True or not, it shows that under Pippin the Short the Carolingian clan fully grasped the Byzantine implications of intervening in Italy.[76]

The coming of the Franks and the crowning of Charlemagne

Theological tension probably converged with Lombard military pressure to drive the papacy into the arms of the Franks: Pope Stephen II's trip across the Alps to seek Frankish intervention effectively put him and his chief advisers out of Byzantine reach for the iconoclast council scheduled in Constantinople for February 754. In any event, Pippin the Short's twin invasions of Italy in 754 and 756 signalled to Constantine V that his power counted in the ancient territories over which Constantinople was reasserting control (see below, p. 444). That Byzantium viewed the Franks in the light of Italy emerges from every aspect of its diplomatic démarche to the west: the embassy to Pippin followed his first intervention in Italy; John *silentiarios*, one of the ambassadors, had headed previous negotiations with the Lombards; he stopped at Rome to liaise with the pope before heading on to Pippin's court.[77] Papal assertions to the contrary notwithstanding, Constantine V's efforts to woo the Franks for his version of an anti-Lombard alliance clearly tempted the Franks and frightened the Romans. In May 757, Byzantine ambassadors pressed their case and presents, including an organ, on Pippin's court at a general assembly at Compiègne. More than simply symbolising superior technology, a Byzantine organ was a strictly secular instrument used chiefly in ceremonies glorifying the emperor. Its ostentatious presentation to the usurper king at the gathering of his unruly magnates suggests that Byzantium curried royal favour by supplying the means to magnify a nascent monarchy.[78]

In the last twelve years of his reign, Pippin's frequent diplomatic contacts with Constantinople provoked papal anxiety; the papacy tried to examine Frankish correspondence with Byzantium and stressed the heretical character of imperial theology. This explains for instance the staging of a theological debate between imperial and papal representatives at Gentilly in 767. The popes supplied Pippin's court with specialists who could advise him on

---

[76] Mordek (1988); Fredegar, *Chronicle continuation*, ch. 22, ed. Krusch, pp. 178–9; tr. Wallace-Hadrill, p. 96; compare Classen (1983), pp. 102–3.

[77] *LP*, XCIV.8, 17–23, 43–5, ed. Duchesne, I, pp. 442, 444–6, 452–3; tr. Davis, II, pp. 56, 59–61, 70–1. On diplomacy between the Franks and Byzantines in general, see Nerlich (1999); embassies between Byzantium and western Europe are catalogued in McCormick (2001), appendix 4, pp. 852–972; for Carolingian attitudes towards Constantinople, see Wickham (1998); compare Sansterre (1996).

[78] *ARF*, s.a. 757, ed. Kurze, p. 15; tr. Scholz, p. 42. See also above, p. 274.

the Byzantines. To papal horror, Pippin solidified his Byzantine relations by betrothing his daughter Gisela to Constantine V's son.[79] But the fragile Frankish political consensus which had allowed intervention in Italy disintegrated with the king's death. The Frankish aristocracy turned inwards to the succession of Pippin the Short's sons, Charlemagne and Carloman, as Italy and Byzantium receded to the far periphery of Carolingian politics.

Yet this very succession issue triggered decisive Frankish intervention in Italy. Among the reasons spurring Charlemagne to invade the Lombard kingdom in 773, the escape of Carloman's wife and sons to her father's capital of Pavia after Charlemagne pounced on his dead brother's kingdom was critical. Carloman's kin residing at the Lombard court in Pavia constituted a permanent threat to Charlemagne. The papacy's position appears ambivalent. It had worked hard to foster warm relations with the Carolingians and benefited from the virtual Frankish protectorate in northern Italy. But for all its differences with the emperors, Rome continued formally to recognise imperial sovereignty.[80] In fact, the year before Charlemagne's invasion, Pope Hadrian I was comfortable enough with the iconoclast regime to send his political enemies to Constantinople for safekeeping.[81] In any event, Charlemagne's conquest of Pavia brought renewed relations with Constantinople. A marriage alliance was resurrected and formally concluded in Rome in 781; the eunuch official Elissaios was dispatched to Charlemagne's court to prepare his daughter Rotrud for her new life as a Byzantine empress.[82] Rome again faced the disturbing prospect of its two major partners making arrangements over its head, when Pope Hadrian responded cautiously but positively to Empress Irene's overtures in 784 and 785 about restoring icons and doctrinal – and therefore political? – unity.[83]

The second Frankish–Byzantine entente was short-lived. Why it collapsed is unclear. Einhard claims that Charlemagne simply could not bear to lose his daughter and torpedoed the alliance. It is no less likely that the Franks had inherited the Lombard kingdom's conflicts with Constantinople – notably in the Adriatic, where Venice already presented an inviting target – and the Lombard assimilation of Byzantine Istria was pursued.[84] To the south, the allegiance of the powerful duchy of Benevento oscillated. Charlemagne's efforts to impose his overlordship met with patchy success, and the policies of the dukes there and in Bavaria – both of whom

---

[79] On papal anxiety see, for example, *CC*, nos. 11, 30, ed. Gundlach, pp. 505–7, 536–7; on Gentilly: *ARF*, s.a. 767, ed. Kurze, p. 25; tr. Scholz, p. 46; on specialists: McCormick (1994b); on Gisela: *CC*, no. 45, ed. Gundlach, p. 562; tr. King, p. 272; Auzépy (1994a).

[80] Deér (1957).   [81] *LP*, XCVII.13–14, ed. Duchesne, I, p. 490; tr. Davis, II, p. 129.

[82] *Annales Mosellani*, s.a. 781, p. 497; Theoph., ed. de Boor, I, pp. 455–6; tr. Mango and Scott, pp. 628–30.

[83] Dölger, *Regesten*, no. 341 (= Mansi, XII, cols. 986B–C); *Régestes des actes du patriarcat*, ed. Grumel et al., no. 352.

[84] Bullough (1955), pp. 161–6.

had married sisters of Adelchis, the Lombard co-king who had escaped to Constantinople – were unpredictable. Hadrian's growing disillusionment with Frankish domination can be read in his constant, vain entreaties to Charlemagne to fulfil his part of the bargain struck by his father.[85]

The break came early in 787, when Charlemagne met with Byzantine ambassadors at Capua, even as he reasserted his authority over the Beneventans. Hadrian frantically relayed reports of Beneventan collusion with an impending Byzantine invasion which would restore Adelchis. The invasion occurred early in 788; it coincided – perhaps not coincidentally – with attacks by the Bavarians and Avars. The Byzantine expeditionary force expected aid from Benevento. But the new duke sided with the Franks and the imperial troops were crushed in Calabria. Alcuin of York boasted that 4,000 Byzantines were killed and another 1,000 captured. Among the latter was Sisinnios, Patriarch Tarasios' (784–806) brother, who would spend the next decade in western captivity. The Byzantine defeat secured the Frankish position in Italy and left relations with Constantinople at a standstill.[86]

There was a complication. Even as Byzantine forces and the Lombard king were disembarking to drive the Franks from Italy, Hadrian's ambassadors were en route or just back home from Constantinople with their copy of the *Acts* of the second council of Nicaea (787). The Greek text of the proceedings proclaimed the perfect unity of the Byzantine rulers and the pope on icon-veneration, punctuated by the usual acclamations of imperial power; the whole, of course, signed and approved by papal legates. To make matters worse, the Greek text had silently excised references to Charlemagne (and the papal patrimonies) from its quotations of Hadrian's correspondence with the emperors.[87] Exactly when Charlemagne and his advisers learned about all this is unclear. Their reaction is not: it can be read in the enraged pages of the *Libri Carolini*. Although papal opposition ultimately forced the Frankish court to abandon the treatise, more accurately called the *Opus Caroli regis contra synodum*, this theological assault on the second ecumenical council of Nicaea was clearly about more than pure doctrine.[88]

Hadrian's relations with Charlemagne survived this crisis, but the Frankish court persisted in a modified version of its iconoclast views as the council of Frankfurt (794) shows, and the court of the next pope, Leo III (795–816),

---

[85] *CC*, nos. 49, 53–6, ed. Gundlach, pp. 568–9, 574–81; tr. King, pp. 277–9, 281–5 (partial tr. and paraphrase).
[86] *ARF*, s.a. 786, 798, ed. Kurze, pp. 73–5, 104; tr. Scholz, pp. 63–4, 76–7; Theoph., ed. de Boor, I, pp. 463–4; tr. Mango and Scott, pp. 637–8; *CC*, nos. 80, 82–4 and App. 1–2, ed. Gundlach, pp. 611–14, 615–20, 654–7; tr. King, pp. 295–303 (partial tr.); Alcuin, *Letters*, no. 7, ed. Dümmler, p. 32; tr. Allott, p. 42; Classen (1985), pp. 28–34; *PMBZ*, #6794.
[87] Mansi, XII, cols. 1075C–6A; see also Lamberz (1997). See also above, pp. 286–7.
[88] *Opus Caroli, praefatio*, ed. Freeman and Meyvaert, pp. 97–102.

made its differing opinion known to the Roman public and visitors by raising huge icons in the city's main pilgrim shrines. In the south, Byzantium
recouped its position somewhat by marrying the emperor Constantine VI's
sister-in-law Evanthia to the duke of Benevento.[89] Starting again in 797,
Byzantium attempted to normalise relations with the increasingly powerful Charlemagne, whose contacts with the caliphate and Byzantine milieux
in Palestine could scarcely have escaped Constantinople's notice.[90] Two
more legations had arrived at the Frankish court by late 798. But the crisis in Rome pre-empted whatever was cooking between the two courts,
and Charlemagne's actions in subsequent months appeared hostile. The
Frankish crackdown which restored Pope Leo III was soon followed by the
famous visit to Rome at Christmas 800.[91]

In Constantinople, Charlemagne's coronation as emperor naturally
appeared as the latest in a long series of Italian usurpations, the most recent
of which had occurred only nineteen years before, and it was believed an
invasion of Sicily would soon follow.[92] When this did not materialise,
Irene (797–802) continued her contacts and two of Charlemagne's right-
hand men travelled to Constantinople, according to a Byzantine witness,
in order to discuss a marriage between the new emperor and the increasingly beleaguered empress.[93] Irene was toppled, however, and subsequent
contacts led nowhere, as Charlemagne's imperial pretensions poisoned an
atmosphere of increasing hostility. Again Italy supplied the kindling, as an
internal power struggle in Venice spilled over into Frankish politics: the new
Venetian leaders and two key officials of Byzantine Dalmatia shifted their
allegiance to Charlemagne in 805. The result was Charlemagne's second
war with Byzantium, which ended only when the Franks, whose Adriatic
successes were mitigated by naval defeat and the death of Charlemagne's
son, renounced their claim to Venice. In return Byzantine ambassadors
acclaimed Charlemagne as *basileus* – without specifying of what or whom –
in the new chapel of Aachen. Byzantine silver coins henceforth entitled
their rulers *basileis Romaion:* 'emperors of the Romans' (see fig. 28).[94] This
compromise would govern the two powers' basic *modus vivendi* for over a
quarter of a century.

The compromise facilitated some military co-ordination in Italy. Arab
raids increasingly menaced the peninsula's western coast, and the pope was
able to act as intermediary between the Byzantine governor of Sicily and
Charlemagne. Border disputes along the western Balkans were the subject

[89] On the council of Frankfurt, see Hartmann (1989), pp. 108–10; Auzépy (1997); on icons: *LP*,
XCVIII.3–5, ed. Duchesne, II, pp. 1–2; tr. Davis, II, pp. 180–1; on Evanthia: Classen (1985), p. 33.
[90] Borgolte (1976), pp. 46–58; *DAI*, ch. 26, pp. 108–13.
[91] Becher (2002). See below, p. 447.   [92] Classen (1983), pp. 34, 40–1.
[93] Grierson (1981), pp. 906–8; however, compare Classen (1985), pp. 83–6.
[94] Classen (1985), pp. 91–7; Grierson (1981), pp. 910–11.

Figure 28 Silver coin of Michael I bearing the inscription '*basilis* [=*basileus*] *Romaion*' ('emperor of (the) Romans') in the bottom two lines (left); on the reverse, a 'cross potent' affirms his faith and power (right)

of two Byzantine missions in 817. But the crisis of the Carolingian political structure that overtook Louis the Pious' court interrupted the progress realised by the missions of 824 and 827, aimed at a deepened diplomatic and theological union. Further embassies in 833, 839 and the early 840s found the Franks enmeshed in civil war and a looming succession crisis, which dashed Theophilos' hopes of Frankish military support.[95]

Carolingians in Italy, papal ambitions in the Balkans and Byzantium's resurgence

By the middle of the ninth century, the context had changed dramatically. The Frankish empire had fragmented even as Mediterranean infrastructures recovered and ramified. The duchy of Rome was regaining autonomy, Venice grew in wealth and power, while Arab attacks on the coasts intensified and Sicily slowly slid under Arab control, perhaps encouraging Venice to focus its future on the Levant and Constantinople. Yet Byzantine power was on the upsurge at home and abroad. Between the Frankish kingdoms and Constantinople, new centres of power were emerging among the Moravians and the Bulgars. These changes combined with the recent past to shape the final phase of Byzantine–Carolingian interaction. Frankish imperial ambitions continued to irritate the Roman emperors of Constantinople. And the old papal claims to jurisdiction in the Balkans lost none of their relevance as that area figured anew on the historical stage.

---

[95] On the pope as go-between, see Leo III, *Epistolae*, nos. 7, 8, pp. 97–100 and compare with nos. 1, 6, pp. 87–8, 96–7; on the Byzantine missions of 817, see *RKK*, nos. 642b, 655a; on those of 824 and 827: *RKK*, nos. 793a, 842b as well as McCormick (2005); on the missions of 833 and 839, see *RKK*, nos. 926a, 993b; Gen., III.16, III.18, ed. Lesmüller-Werner and Thurn, pp. 50, 51; tr. Kaldellis, pp. 66, 67–8; TC, p. 135; compare Dölger (1953), pp. 330–1; McCormick (2001), p. 920, no. 455.

The installation of Arabs on the Italian mainland from 838 combined with their sack of St Peter's to dramatise the need for cooperation. The residence of the Frankish emperor, Louis II (855–75) in Italy deepened his involvement in the complex politics of Rome and southern Italy, and consequently with Constantinople. At least two more marriage alliances were contracted between members of the Frankish emperor Lothar I's (840–55) family and its Constantinopolitan counterpart, although again the marriages never took place.[96] Cooperation focused on the key strongholds of Apulia, where the complementarity of Frankish land forces and the Byzantine navy was obvious. Bari had been an Arab emirate for decades; its coastal site counselled a land and sea operation. Joint Byzantino-Frankish operations were foreseen in 869 and 870 but coordination broke down. In 871 Louis II finally captured Bari in an operation in which the Byzantine sources claim they participated. He then failed to take Taranto.[97] It was in this context that Louis II sent his famous letter to Basil I, composed probably by Anastasius Bibliothecarius, newly returned from a Frankish mission to Constantinople. The letter responded vigorously to Basil's criticism of the Carolingian imperial title, even as Louis requested more naval support and suggested that he and Basil had agreed to liberate Sicily once Calabria was rid of Arabs.[98]

The ambivalent tone of Louis' letter foreshadowed how interests which had converged at Bari now collided. Both powers aimed to control southern Italy and both focused on Benevento in this respect. Louis II had turned Bari over to the duke of Benevento rather than the Byzantine admiral. But the duke soon turned on him, capturing and humiliating the Frankish ruler. Louis' further efforts to subdue the duke were frustrated in part because of the duke's new alliance with Constantinople.[99] Louis' subsequent death without an heir precipitated a struggle over northern Italy which Charles the Bald's short-lived success failed to resolve, even as the pace of Byzantine intervention accelerated in the south. Already in 872 the Byzantine fleet had scored one success off the Campanian coast to the relief of Pope John VIII (872–82).[100] When Rome itself was occupied by the duke of Spoleto early in 878, John VIII felt himself driven into the arms of Constantinople. As his letter to Basil I shows, the Roman see was now led to look with a different eye on the latest in the Byzantine church's continuing upheavals and to seek resolution of its own bitter conflicts with recent patriarchs.[101]

[96] Dölger (1953), pp. 334–7.
[97] TC, pp. 292–4; DAI, ch. 29, pp. 122–39; DT, II.11, ed. Pertusi, pp. 97–8; see also Dölger (1953), pp. 337–8.
[98] Amari (1933–9), I, pp. 518–23; RKK, nos. 1242a, 1246abc, 1246ef, 1247; Gay (1917), pp. 84–96; Louis II, Epistula ad Basilium.
[99] RKK, no. 1261a.   [100] John VIII, Fragmenta registri, no. 5, p. 276.
[101] John VIII, Epistulae, nos. 72, 69, pp. 67, 64–5.

These conflicts had arisen despite the final restoration of icons and the appointment as patriarch of Methodios, a Sicilian who had been ordained during the few years he had lived in Rome. In fact, however, the papacy's resentment over its jurisdictional losses had not disappeared. It was exacerbated by the expansion of Bulgar power in the Balkans, that is Illyricum. Papal suspicion of the patriarchate was plain to see right from 787, when Hadrian had qualified his cooperation by repeating long-standing papal objections against the patriarchal title *oikoumenikos* or *universalis*, as well as against Tarasios' elevation from lay official to patriarch.[102] Two generations later new developments were to mix different sources of contention in explosive fashion: Roman primacy, lost jurisdiction over southern Italy and Illyricum, growing awareness of disciplinary divergences and the factionalisation of the Byzantine elite.

Monastic pressure on Patriarch Methodios to purge all bishops compromised under the second spell of iconoclasm was given new life by his rigorist successor, the monk Ignatios (847–58, 867–77), a castrated son of Emperor Michael I (811–13). For reasons that are unclear, Ignatios deposed one of Methodios' close associates, Gregory Asbestas, archbishop of Syracuse, who appealed to Rome. While this case was pending, Ignatios himself was swept away by a political crisis and replaced by the head of the imperial chancery, the great lay intellectual Photios (858–67, 877–86), who was consecrated by none other than Gregory Asbestas. In spring 859, the deposed Ignatios' supporters met in Constantinople and claimed to depose Photios; Photios retorted with a synod which attacked Ignatios (see above, p. 293).

At this point, the opposing factions seemed to stall in stalemate. Photios and Michael III sent an embassy to the new pope, Nicholas I (858–67), seeking his support for a council which would deal finally with iconoclasm and the current schism within the Byzantine church.[103] Bishops Radoald of Porto and Zacharias of Anagni, the papal legates, apparently exceeded their mandate at the ensuing council held at Constantinople in April 861, by approving the deposition of Ignatios; but they failed to recover Illyricum.[104] The remaining Greek monastic communities in Rome again added an internal dimension to papal relations with Constantinople. Ignatios clearly had vociferous supporters there, particularly the monk Theognostos. Pope Nicholas I convened a council which repudiated his legates' actions and declared Photios and Asbestas deposed, eliciting from

---

[102] Mansi, XII, cols. 1074A–1075B. See also above, pp. 287–8.

[103] Nicholas I, *Epistulae*, no. 82, pp. 434–7; compare Dölger, *Regesten*, no. 457; *Régestes des actes du patriarcat*, ed. Grumel *et al.*, no. 467 [464].

[104] Deusdedit, *Collectio canonum*, IV.428–31, pp. 603–10; compare e.g. Beck (1969), p. 178; see also Shepard (1995a), pp. 238–41.

Michael III the famous and contemptuous letter about the barbarity of Latin Rome.[105]

On an already complex situation, further complications now obtruded, as the Bulgar ruler Boris (c. 852–89) was having second thoughts over his contacts with Constantinople and approached Louis the German about converting to Frankish rather than Byzantine Christianity.[106] At about the same time Constantinople dispatched two veteran diplomats and missionaries to the edges of East Francia, in response to the Moravians' expression of interest in conversion. It is a sign of the rapid development of both Bulgar and Moravian societies that they now looked to conversion and therefore cultural integration with the dominant neighbouring cultures. It is a measure of their political astuteness that each explored the advantages of converting to the church most removed from their respective borders. The Bulgar initiative, which was soon notified to the pope, opened up the unexpected prospect of recovering jurisdiction over Illyricum regardless of the Byzantine emperor's attitude. In 866, the Bulgar ruler expressed dissatisfaction with the Greek missionaries working in his kingdom by approaching Pope Nicholas I, who answered with legates and a remarkable document responding to the khan's queries about Byzantine criticism of Bulgar customs. The pope expressed a fairly enlightened attitude towards Bulgar practices even as he slammed the customs of rival Constantinople (see above, p. 319). Photios retorted by enumerating western doctrinal and disciplinary deviations in an eastern encyclical. He convoked a council which deposed Nicholas I and dispatched emissaries to Louis II to solicit his help in toppling the pope, even as Nicholas sought theological support from the dynamic cultural centres of the Frankish kingdoms.[107]

At that very moment, the power constellation with which Photios was identified crumbled when Basil I had Michael III assassinated. The new emperor soon restored Ignatios and requested papal support, offering to have the rival patriarchal parties submit to the pope for judgement. Only Ignatios' legation made it to Rome intact, and Nicholas I's successor, Pope Hadrian II (867–72), unsurprisingly found for Ignatios. Papal legates then travelled to Constantinople for a council convened over the winter of 869–70 to sort out the implications of the recent upheavals. At the same time, Louis II's ambassadors – including Anastasius Bibliothecarius – were busy in Constantinople discussing a marriage alliance and the military cooperation

---

[105] Dölger, *Regesten*, no. 464; Nicholas I, *Epistulae*, no. 88, p. 459; *ODB*, III, p. 2055 (A. Kazhdan); for the intricacies of the Photian schism, see Hergenröther (1867–9), I, pp. 357–9; see also Dvornik (1948), which must be used with caution. Compare Beck (1969).

[106] On the nature of Byzantine missionaries, see Ševčenko, I. (1988–9). See also above, ch. 7.

[107] For Nicholas' advice to Boris, see Nicholas I, *Responsa ad consulta Bulgarorum*, on which compare *ODB*, III, p. 1785 (A. Kazhdan); for the pope's attempts to rally support from churchmen and kings, see Nicholas I, *Epistulae*, nos. 100–2, pp. 600–10. For Photios' encyclical: Phot., no. 2, ed. Laourdas and Westerink, I, pp. 40–53; compare p. 424 below.

we have already noted. The intractable papal legates imposed their own views on the council. But afterwards, they were confronted and confounded by Bulgarian ambassadors and a Byzantine hierarchy led by Ignatios, backed by Basil and supported by the eastern patriarchates, which forcefully denied Roman claims in Bulgaria. The resulting strain would endure until events in Italy drove Pope John VIII in 878 to seek political rapprochement with Byzantium.[108]

Ignatios had died in 877 and Photios resumed the patriarchal office. The pope allowed his legation to participate in another winter council in 879–80. The text of the Roman documents presented there appears to have been toned down; Photios emphasised that he had never opposed Roman jurisdiction over Bulgaria; he had only bowed to the imperial will in the matter. Concord of a sort was re-established. Although Roman jurisdiction over Bulgaria would never become a reality, old and new Rome were again in communion and the way was open for military cooperation.[109]

The need was great: the Byzantine stronghold of Syracuse had fallen to the Arabs a few weeks after John VIII wrote to Basil seeking his support, and Constantinople reacted vigorously. In 879, the Byzantine navy attacked the Arabs off Naples, and the pope complained that the detachment had not continued up the coast to receive his blessing and defend Rome. After the latest council in Constantinople the pope received the seemingly good news about Bulgaria, the loan of several warships and the restoration of Roman rights over the elegant Justinianic church of Sts Sergius and Bacchus next door to the Great Palace.[110] A powerful military force from the western themes reconquered Taranto, even as a Byzantine fleet won an important victory off the northern coast of Sicily. Basil I's hold on Calabria expanded considerably, as the Byzantines occupied some strongholds while others recognised eastern overlordship.[111] Charles the Fat now claimed his family's inheritance in Italy; he rightly feared that Rome – and even the Frankish family who ran the duchy of Spoleto – was turning away from the Carolingians to Constantinople. Duke Wido had in fact sent his own embassy to Byzantium.[112]

As post-Carolingian chaos descended on the north of Italy, the Byzantines briefly occupied Benevento from 891 to 895, organised the new theme of Langobardia and seemed more significant to Italy's fate than ever.[113] That significance expressed itself in the dating formulae of local charters or the

[108] Mansi, XVI, cols. 1–208; *LP*, CVIII.32–64, ed. Duchesne, II, pp. 179–85; tr. Davis, III, pp. 274–91; see also Stiernon (1967); John VIII, *Epistulae*, nos. 69, 72, pp. 64–5, 67. See also above, p. 299.
[109] Mansi XVII, cols. 373–526; Dvornik (1948), pp. 159–201.
[110] John VIII, *Epistulae*, nos. 245, 259, pp. 214, 229–30.
[111] von Falkenhausen (1967), pp. 19–20.
[112] On Rome, see *RKK*, no. 1639e; on Wido: Hiestand (1964), pp. 27–9.
[113] Brown, T. S. (1993).

dispatch of Venetian bells to adorn Basil I's splendid new palace chapel of the Nea. Monasteries scurried to obtain Byzantine confirmations of their privileges and local Italian aristocrats flaunted Greek court titles. Reinforced by population transfers from the east, the Byzantine south became increasingly active in the renewed writing and copying of Greek texts.[114] Italians made pilgrimages to St Demetrios' shrine in Thessaloniki and Leo VI invited to his court holy men from Italy, even as Eugenius Vulgarius sent him fawning panegyrical poems in Latin.[115]

Presumably in anticipation of the impending Carolingian succession in Italy, in 872 and 873 Basil I had reopened diplomatic contacts with a northern Frankish court by concluding an alliance (*amicitia*) with Louis the German.[116] Italy motivated, at least in part, the Byzantine envoy who travelled to Regensburg in 894 for an audience with King Arnulf of Carinthia after his Italian expedition. So too another embassy in 896 followed Arnulf's imperial coronation.[117] Pope John IX's ambassadors to Constantinople in 899 consecrated the renewed harmony between Rome and the east and may have played a hand in arranging the betrothal of Louis III, king of Provence – whose mother Ermengard had once been promised to the Byzantine emperor – to Anna, daughter of Leo VI (see below, p. 541). The question of whether the betrothal was followed up by actual marriage is controversial. If the marriage did take place, Louis III the Blind, who sporadically controlled areas of northern Italy between 900 and 905, sired the only Carolingian also descended from the Byzantine Macedonian house, Charles-Constantine, count of Vienne. Such a union might perhaps clarify the mention of Greek merchants in Louis' privilege of 921.[118] In any event, Rome's relations with Constantinople and renewed Byzantine power in Italy would soon be symbolised by the victorious joint operation against the Arab colony on the Garigliano river in 915.[119]

CULTURAL INTERACTION BETWEEN BYZANTIUM AND THE WEST

Diplomatic interaction had cultural ramifications. The several dozen embassies which travelled between Constantinople and western courts

---

[114] On dating, confirmations, titles and transfers, see von Falkenhausen (1967), pp. 10–12, 21–4, 31–7; on bells: John the Deacon, *Cronaca*, p. 126; on manuscripts, see Irigoin (1969).

[115] *Miracles of Demetrius*, chs. 222–6, pp. 192–4; *Life of Elias the Younger*, ch. 66, ed. and Italian tr. Rossi Taibbi, pp. 104–7; compare with the *Life of Blasios of Amorion*, ch. 19, p. 666; on Eugenius, see *ODB*, II, p. 744 (M. McCormick).

[116] *RKK*, no. 1490b, with Dümmler (1887–8,) II, pp. 336–7; Dölger, *Regesten*, nos. 489, 491.

[117] Dölger, *Regesten*, nos. 525, 533; *RKK*, no. 1922a; Hiestand (1964), pp. 70, 75–6.

[118] See p. 407 above; Hiestand (1964), pp. 90–107. On the question of whether Anna actually married Louis, see Kresten (2000a), pp. 200–7; Thompson, 'The kingdom of Provence' (PhD thesis, 2001), pp. 208–11.

[119] Gay (1917), pp. 147–55. See also below, pp. 538, 562–3.

constituted privileged intermediaries, and much cultural exchange bears their stamp. Men of great influence led them: for instance Charlemagne's ambassador Count Hugh became father-in-law of Lothar I. Some, like Amalarius of Metz or Anastasius Bibliothecarius, were distinguished intellectuals. Amalarius, for example, used his experience of the Greek liturgy in his own commentaries and wrote a poem about his trip to Constantinople.[120] The numbers involved are surprising: at least fifty-five diplomats travelled between the Frankish court and Constantinople between 756 and 840. What is more, the structure and size of the parties they led means that the heads of embassies – whose names alone the sources usually supply – were only the tip of the iceberg; thus these ambassadors were probably accompanied by a very large number of attendants of varying status.[121]

Byzantine gifts were carefully chosen for their impact, as the ceremonial organ presented to Pippin suggests. The manuscript of Pseudo-Dionysius the Areopagite offered to Louis the Pious' court in 827 was tailored to the pretensions of Louis' adviser, Hilduin, abbot of St Denis, who identified the Areopagite with his abbey's patron saint. Diplomatic contacts required translators; we have already noted how the Roman church supplied Pippin the Short with Byzantine experts. One product of such contacts survives in the Latin translation of Michael II and Theophilos' letter to Louis the Pious.[122] In the eighth century, Byzantine relics from the Black Sea area reached the royal convent of Chelles, and it is likely that the short-lived betrothal to Constantine V's son of Gisela, its abbess, clarifies their unexpected presence there.[123] The embassies help explain why transalpine interest in Byzantine culture clustered around the Frankish courts.

Because of its diplomatic implications, the Frankish court mediated western discussion about religious images. Launched by the debate on iconoclasm between representatives of Constantine V and the Roman church at Gentilly, the discussion echoed across the sea through the court-produced *Opus Caroli regis* and the councils of Frankfurt (794) and Paris (825). Frankish theologians joined the Photian fray when, at Pope Nicholas I's request, Hincmar of Rheims raised the matter before Charles the Bald's court over Christmas 867. The result was that at Paris and Corbie, Bishop Aeneas and the monk Ratramnus refuted Byzantine objections against the *filioque*, papal primacy and various disciplinary issues. The East Frankish bishops offered their own response in a council held at Worms in 868.[124]

So too the Byzantine practice of inviting foreign ambassadors to witness important state rituals explains western court familiarity with some

[120] *ODB*, I, pp. 72–3 (M. McCormick).   [121] McCormick (1994b).
[122] Michael II and Theophilos, *Letter to Louis I*.   [123] McCormick (2001), pp. 309, 312.
[124] On iconoclasm, see *CC*, no. 36, ed. Gundlach, p. 546; Haendler (1958); McCormick (1994a); on Hincmar, see Devisse (1975–6,) II, pp. 628–31; on Aeneas and Ratramnus, see Bouhot (1976), pp. 60–7; on the council of Worms, see Hartmann (1989), pp. 301–9.

Byzantine ceremonies: Count Hugh and Bishop Haito's embassy of 811 accounts for Charlemagne's crowning of his son Louis the Pious in 813 in a manner resembling Emperor Michael I's crowning of his own son, Theophylact, in 811. Notker the Stammerer claims that a Byzantine delegation's sweet chanting prompted Charlemagne to obtain an isosyllabic translation, the antiphon *O veterem hominem*, so that it could be sung in his chapel, and independent Byzantine evidence appears to bear him out.[125] Hilduin of St Denis' and John the Scot's translations of Pseudo-Dionysius both show court connections and used the manuscript conveyed in 827. Conversely, the eastern missions to the court of Louis the Pious resulted in Byzantine translations of Latin hagiography. Hilduin's fantastic *Passion of St Denis* was rendered into Greek soon thereafter, while the Latin *Passion of St Anastasia* was translated during the Roman leg of the embassy of 824.[126] Outside the royal courts, sustained Byzantine cultural contacts north of the Alps were rarer. Two exceptions were Reichenau and, especially, St Gall: religious houses which, not coincidentally, lay where a great complex of Alpine passes met the Rhine, Francia's main north–south axis.[127]

Even left to their own devices, Carolingian scholars needed to understand the Greek expressions which littered St Jerome's letters or Priscian: hence the collection of lists of Greek terms organised by the Latin authors where they occur.[128] The drive to comprehend the Bible deepened interest in Greek. Bilingual psalters like those connected with Sedulius Scottus' circle did double duty. The prophetic character that Christian exegesis recognised in the Septuagint gave its Greek text great prestige, while the fact that the psalms were often known by heart allowed them to serve as a crude dictionary in which Greek equivalents for Latin phrases might be hunted down. Although not every Carolingian crumb of Greek need reflect a personal contact with Byzantines, such encounters may have played a larger role than usually suspected. So Thegan claims that Charlemagne consulted Greeks and Syrians about the text of the Gospels.[129] Northern scribes who delighted in spelling their names with Greek letters may strike us as superficial pedants, but they were perhaps inspired by Italians from Byzantine borderlands who had been using Greek letters for Latin subscriptions since the days of Justinian.[130] The lists of Greek numbers frequently found in

---

[125] On Michael's crowning of Theophylact, see Wendling (1985), pp. 207–23; Notker, *Gesta Karoli*, II.7, ed. Haefele, p. 58; tr. Thorpe, pp. 142–3; compare Strunk (1964).
[126] Hilduin, *Passion of St Denis*; Loenertz (1950); Loenertz (1951), pp. 228–37; *Passion of St Anastasia*, pp. 86–7 (introduction), 131 (text).
[127] Kaczynski (1988); compare the Rhenish connections of the Hiberno-Greek data in Bischoff (1977), pp. 51–3.
[128] Dionisotti (1988), pp. 13, 49–50.
[129] Thegan, *Deeds of Louis*, ch. 7, ed. and German tr. Tremp, pp. 186–7.
[130] von Falkenhausen (1968–9), pp. 177–80; compare the somewhat different interpretation of Luzzatti Laganà (1982 [1983]), pp. 740–7.

Carolingian manuscripts give the modern rather than the classical names, and so derive from early medieval Greek speakers.[131] Linguistic contacts left tangible traces in Lupus of Ferrières' comment on the accent of a Greek loan word or in bilingual phrase collections for travellers. The St Gall–Angers list has useful Greek expressions like 'do me a favour'; one at Monza in early Italian and Greek may have been connected with an early tenth-century travelling doctor.[132]

Outside Europe, the Greek-speaking church of Jerusalem offered a privileged place for cross-cultural encounter. Royal involvement with Christians there is documented by an extraordinary Frankish administrative roll indicating revenues, personnel and languages of prayer of the church of Palestine. Alcuin sought a prayer association with the Greek patriarch of Jerusalem and, by Charlemagne's last years, seventeen nuns and many monks from the Frankish empire had established communities in the Holy City, one of which survived for at least another half-century, when its members were still displaying the splendid bible, presumably from Charlemagne's court school, sent to them by the emperor. They formed a natural focus for contacts among western pilgrims, Italian merchants and the Greek clergy, which explains why the *filioque* controversy over the wording of the creed arose there, when Greek monks heard Latins chanting the offending passage.[133]

But like political ones, cultural contacts between Byzantium and the west pivoted on Italy. As far back as the Lombard court's Greek jester, the Po basin had channelled western encounters with Byzantine civilisation. Declining shipping to the Rhône corridor and the rise of Venice only reinforced the Po's prominence. Although Ravenna's gateway role in our period has perhaps been overrated, Agnellus' historical memory and Charlemagne's export of Ravennate artwork testify to its enduring Byzantine after-life. If it is genuine, Charles the Bald's mention of the Greek liturgy to the clergy of Ravenna need not reflect its performance there. Already in 826, a Venetian came to Louis the Pious' court, promising to construct a Byzantine organ. Across the Adriatic, Carolingian *missi* grappled with the intricacies of Byzantine provincial administration during an inquest into the Frankish absorption of Istria.[134] Some slight evidence for translations in the Po

[131] Bischoff (1966–81), II, p. 264.

[132] Lupus of Ferrières, *Letters*, no. 20, ed. Marshall, p. 27; tr. Regenos, p. 22; on St Gall, see Kaczynski (1988), pp. 70–1; on Monza, see Aerts (1972); compare Bischoff (1984), p. 255.

[133] On the roll, nuns, etc., see *Commemoratorium de casis Dei*, esp. p. 302; see also Borgolte (1976), pp. 45–107; Alcuin, *Letters*, no. 210, ed. Dümmler, pp. 350–1; on the splendid bible, see *Itinerarium Bernardi*, ch. 10, p. 314; on Italian merchants, see *Miracles of Genesius*, ch. 2, ed. Waitz, pp. 170–1; on the *filioque*, see Peri (1971); *Konzil von Aachen 809*, ed. Willjung.

[134] For the argument that Ravenna has been overrated as a conduit for Hellenic 'influence', see Brown, T. S. (1988b), pp. 131–41; compare Sansterre (1992); on Agnellus, see *ODB*, I, p. 37 (M. McCormick); on the grant of Ravenna artwork to Charlemagne, see *CC*, no. 81, ed. Gundlach, p. 614; on Charles the

basin anticipates the Monza glossary, and Anastasius Bibliothecarius found a Greek manuscript of the *Translation* of St Stephen in Mantua.[135] The controversial Gottschalk of Orbais drew on his experience in Byzantine Dalmatia and Venice when delineating the semantic fields of key words in his defence of predestination.[136]

Rome was a propitious place for translations. Pope Hadrian I ordered a Latin translation of the Greek Acts of the second council of Nicaea brought back by his legates.[137] The Roman translator Anastasius Bibliothecarius was Carolingian Europe's pre-eminent Byzantine specialist. He translated the usual fare of hagiography and councils, but Anastasius' interest in 'modern' Byzantine literature is even more noteworthy, since he rendered into Latin the most outstanding chronicle of the period, a sermon by Theodore the Stoudite and a work by his own contemporary and acquaintance Constantine-Cyril.[138] A fellow papal emissary, Bishop John of Arezzo – precisely one of the legates who presided over Charles the Bald's experiment in Byzantine ceremonial at Ponthion in July 876 – may have translated a Byzantine text on the Assumption.[139] Rome is virtually unique in so far as it was also a centre for translation from Latin into Greek. Thus Pope Zacharias' rendering of Gregory the Great's *Dialogues* was perhaps intended for circulation at home as well as abroad: a manuscript probably copied at Rome survives from *c.* 800 (see fig. 29); the Greek translation of the *Passion of St Anastasia* mentioned above used a Latin manuscript at the saint's Roman shrine.[140]

Latin speakers rubbed shoulders with hellenophones in the south. Late ninth-century Taranto, for instance, had Latin bishops but counted many Greeks among its elite.[141] The renewal of Byzantine power and culture helps explain the sudden bloom of Latin translations along the Campanian frontier. The church of Naples fostered rather superior translations. For instance, the Neapolitan deacon Paul sought to capitalise on Charles the Bald's enthusiasm for things Greek by dedicating to the Frankish ruler his translations of the *Life* of St Mary the Egyptian and the Faustian forerunner, the *Penance* of Theophilus. Both works enjoyed enormous success north of

---

Bald, see Jacob (1972); on the Byzantine organ, see *ARF*, s.a. 826, ed. Kurze, p. 170; tr. Scholz, p. 120; on the inquest, see Margetić (1988).

[135] Chiesa (1989), pp. 173–5.

[136] Gottschalk of Orbais, *De praedestinatione*, IX.6, ed. Lambot, p. 208.

[137] *LP*, XCVII.88, ed. Duchesne, I, p. 512; tr. Davis, II, pp. 168–9; compare Freeman (1985), pp. 75–81; see in general Chiesa (2002).

[138] *ODB*, I, pp. 88–9 (M. McCormick).

[139] Philippart (1974); Schieffer (1935), pp. 16–25. See also below, p. 448.

[140] Gregory I, 'Dialogues', Vat. gr. 1666. On the manuscript available to the learned Byzantine envoy who was in Rome in 824, see *Passion of St Anastasia*, ed. Halkin, pp. 86–7 (introduction) and above, p. 425.

[141] von Falkenhausen (1968), p. 149.

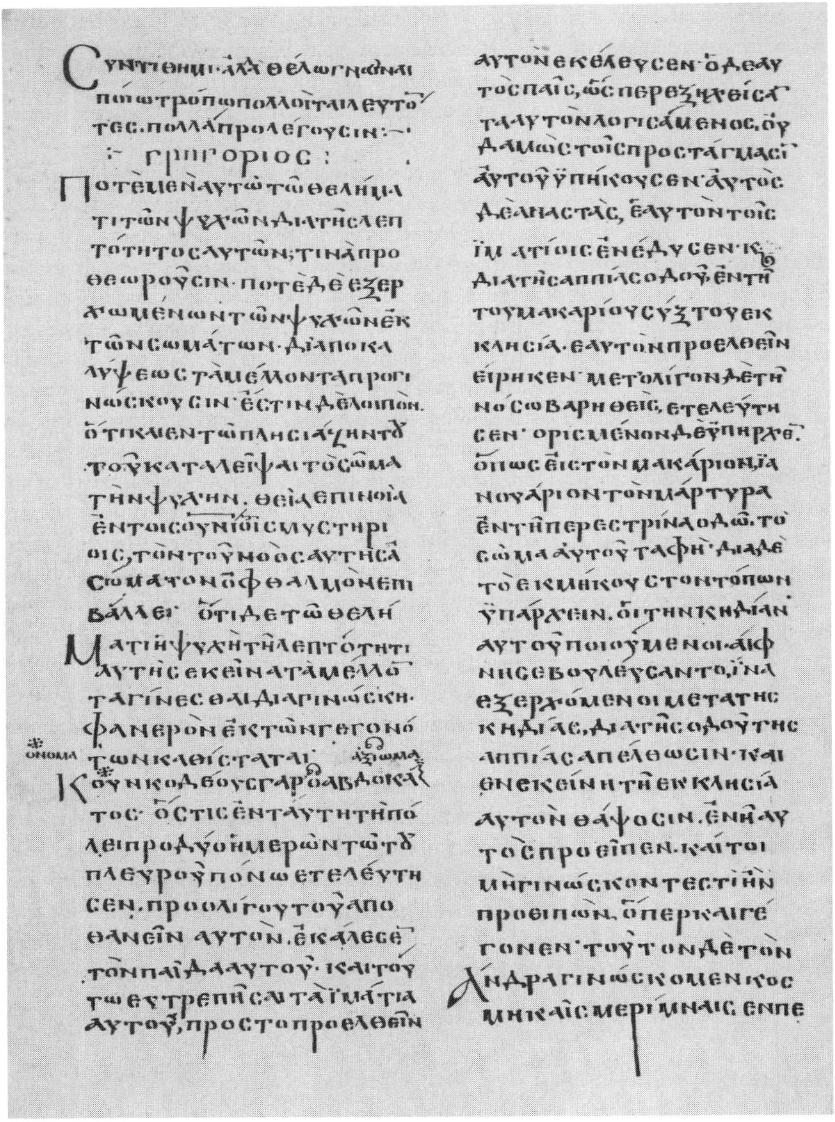

Figure 29 Latin into Greek: from a manuscript of the Greek translation of Gregory the Great's *Dialogues*, probably copied at Rome *c*. 800 (Vat. MS gr. 1666, fol. 154v)

the Alps and fuelled the veneration of Mary as an intercessor for sinners.[142] John, deacon of Naples, who wrote a continuation of his diocesan history around 900 and enjoyed the patronage of the bishop and the abbot of St Severinus, also collaborated with a Greek speaker to produce Latin adaptations of hagiographical classics like Cyril of Scythopolis' sixth-century *Life of Euthymios* as well as Patriarch Methodios' *Life* of Nicholas.[143]

Not a few instances of apparent western appropriation of Byzantine iconography and style have been challenged. Even when derivation from 'Byzantine' style or iconography is uncontested, it is often unclear whether we have a direct appropriation from a contemporary Byzantine exemplar, or a residual rather than recent borrowing from Byzantium. The art-historical problem is only complicated by the scarcity of securely dated and localised surviving eastern items for comparison.[144]

Some Byzantine models were nonetheless certainly available for imitation in the west: *c.* 850 a party of Irish pilgrims to Italy jotted down a description of a Greek gospel cycle and left the codex at St Gall. Even its sophisticated Islamic neighbours appreciated ninth-century Byzantium's outstanding metalwork and locks. Diplomacy documents the dispatch of Byzantine luxury products like the bejewelled gospel book and chalice conveyed to Pope Benedict III (855–8). Nor were such gifts destined only for papal and royal treasure hoards; Constantinople had a shrewd grasp of the power structure at a western court and, as the lists of presents intended for Hugh of Arles, king of Italy (926–47), and his court in 935 reveals, imperial diplomacy distributed its gifts accordingly, placing Byzantine prestige items in the hands of key royal associates who were no less active than the kings as patrons of art. A prominent early ninth-century traveller and diplomat proudly bequeathed to the churches of Grado expensive reliquaries purchased in Constantinople. Nor was the traffic exclusively one way: we have already noted Basil I's bells from Venice, while the technique of making cloisonné enamel may have travelled from the west to Byzantium around the same time, and a high Byzantine official acquired religious art at Rome late in the eighth century.[145] Conversely, an important technology transfer in the opposite direction occurred at Rome a few decades earlier, when local

[142] Kunze (1969), p. 40; Meersseman (1963).
[143] *Life of Euthymios the Younger*, ed. Dolbeau; *Life of Nicholas*, ed. Corsi; Chiesa (1989), pp. 183–5.
[144] Brubaker (1997a).
[145] On the gospel cycle, see Mütherich (1987); on metalwork: Pellat (1954), p. 159; compare on the date Lewis (1977), p. 13; on the gifts to Benedict III, see *LP*, CVI.33, ed. Duchesne, II, pp. 147–8; tr. Davis, III, pp. 185–6; on Hugh of Arles, see *DC*, II.44, ed. Reiske, I, pp. 661–2; on Fortunatus of Grado's will: *Documenti relativi alla storia di Venezia*, ed. Cessi, I, no. 45, pp. 76–7; on enamel, see Buckton (1988); on Roman religious art: *Life of Niketas Patrikios*, ed. and French tr. Papachryssanthou, ch. 3, pp. 324–5.

kilns started making glazed ceramic of a type that archaeologists believe was inspired by similar Byzantine wares.[146]

Linguistic evidence yields some tentative insights into technology transfers and material culture, since words could be borrowed with the thing they designated. Of course the problem of residual borrowings is compounded by the potential lag between the borrowing and a word's earliest attestation in the rare written records. Still, Byzantium's apparent linguistic impact in this period does not contradict the picture derived from the other evidence. Most securely identified Byzantine loan words relate to expensive items associated with the lay or clerical elite; virtually all of them seem to enter usage through Italy, whether via the Po basin or Rome. Byzantium's impact on religious life and art is suggested by the Italian Latin loan words *olibanum* for incense (< *[t]o libanon*) and *icona* (Gr. *eikōn;* acc. *eikona*). At Rome, Byzantium appears as the west's intermediary with the Islamic world with *magarita* and *magarizare* ('apostate', 'to convert to Islam') from Arabic *muhadzhir* ('Muslim Arab settler in newly conquered territory') via Greek *mōagaritēs* or *magaritēs.* On the other hand, *cendatum*, a word from the good life ('fine silk cloth', 'brocade'), probably derives from Persian *sundus* via Byzantine Greek *sendes* and shows up almost simultaneously in milieux connected with the Carolingian court and northern Italy. Military contacts such as we have seen in southern Italy can be traced in words for 'catapult' which seem to have been borrowed at this time, and the Byzantine term *chelandion*, perhaps derived from the Greek word for 'eel', designated Constantinople's sleek warships in Latin. Technology is probably represented by the ancestors of the modern English words 'bronze' and 'varnish'.[147] Transfers in the other direction seem rarer, but so are the sources. One very likely candidate for our period is *kortēs* (Latin *cortis*) apparently in the sense of 'royal tent'.[148]

CONCLUSIONS

Despite the renewed dynamism of the Byzantine south, Italy from Rome northwards was now fastened to transalpine Europe to an extent and in ways no one could have imagined in 700. Venice was well on its way to becoming a distinctively Italo-Byzantine amalgam and a gateway city to the populations of the Po basin and across the Alps. The issue of the imperial legacy and legitimacy was posed and would rarely leave the forefront of diplomatic relations. Rome's paper victory in defending its ecclesiastical claims to Illyricum would be swept aside by the Bulgaro-Byzantine

---

[146] Paroli (1992a), pp. 44, 57; Paroli (1992b), p. 356–9.
[147] McCormick (2001), pp. 708–9, n. 53; Kahane and Kahane (1968–76), cols. 368–71, 380, 385, 412.
[148] For example, Theoph., ed. de Boor, I, pp. 467–8; tr. Mango and Scott, pp. 642–4.

confrontation and the Hungarian attacks. While Greek monasticism in the environs of Rome would not cease altogether, the dynamic provincial society of Byzantine Calabria probably provided a more characteristic note than Constantinople.

Byzantium's interaction with the west appears chiefly political and cultural. Economic links to the imperial metropolis seem distinctly secondary. But whatever the kind of interaction, Italy was pivotal, simultaneously a privileged locus of encounter and the stakes of competition. Three essential zones appeared there: the Po–Adriatic basin; Rome and vicinity; and the Byzantine south. Other secondary, eccentric zones of encounter followed the itinerant human networks that were the Frankish courts; farther afield, significant contacts certainly occurred between westerners and Byzantines in Jerusalem.

Generally speaking, the extent to which transalpine Europe controlled parts of Italy was the chief factor affecting the intensity of political and direct cultural interaction north of the Alps. Such contacts first peaked between 756 and 768. They intensified again in the 780s and once more in the first three decades of the ninth century. After that, the possibility for Constantinople to deal directly with a Carolingian ruler in Italy made this kind of contact more sporadic.

The sociology of interaction suggests mostly an affair of elites. But this social slant may in part be the product of our aristocratically minded source material. The content of exchanges is pretty clear. Elite lifestyle concerns played an important role; westerners imported eastern political rituals and symbols, liturgical pieces, theological treatises, and political and military support where Byzantium's capacities complemented but did not threaten their own. Constantinople was interested in obtaining political support on its own terms, as well as western warriors. The religious traditions of Rome provided useful sanctions to competing factions of the Constantinopolitan elite, while the inability of Constantinople to project its power there made it a safe haven for dissidents. Both societies avidly discovered each other's saints and the texts describing their wonders. The Greek church of Jerusalem sought Frankish wealth for its own local purposes, even as the semi-autonomous Byzantine outposts of Italy provided inoffensive go-betweens linking the huge economy of the house of Islam, a resurgent Byzantium and a recovering west.

In this crucial period of some seven generations, communications began picking up again, as Byzantium and the west began again to know one another. In so doing, each began to discover with amazement how different the sibling had become. Like the creed, once-identical shared traditions had begun to show slight variations which were all the more disturbing for the substantial sameness of their backgrounds. The Photian schism had been overcome, but these centuries' interaction left scars; the issues of papal primacy, the *filioque* and disciplinary divergences between Rome and Constantinople were so many ticking time-bombs, awaiting future moments of tension. And the Carolingian claim to have restored the Roman empire, despite brief periods of mutual acceptance, constituted a permanent challenge to all that was essential to the Byzantine identity. The stage was set for the cooperation and competition that would mark the future of Byzantium's interaction with the west.

CHAPTER 11

BYZANTINE ITALY (680–876)

THOMAS S. BROWN

BYZANTINE ITALY IN 680

By the last quarter of the seventh century the Byzantine areas of Italy had experienced over a century of upheaval. Within decades of their first invasion of Italy in 568 the Lombards had established a powerful kingdom consisting of the territories north of the river Po, Tuscany and the two outlying duchies of Spoleto and Benevento. The empire was confined to the areas of Rome and its duchy, Ravenna, and the neighbouring areas of the exarchate and the Pentapolis, approximating to the present-day Romagna and Marche, and a few coastal areas elsewhere. The Byzantines had only been able to hold on to their possessions by initiating a thoroughgoing militarisation of society, which involved the concentration of land in military hands and the concentration of authority in the hands of the commander-in-chief in Ravenna (the exarch) and his subordinates *(duces* and *magistri militum* at a provincial level and *tribuni* in the localities). In many areas, such as the Roman Campania, this process was accompanied by a steady shift of population, as settlement became concentrated on military strongholds and refuges, usually located on promontories. Although the pressure eased somewhat in the seventh century, Liguria and most of the remaining settlements on the Venetian mainland were lost to the Lombards in the reign of King Rothari (636–52), and the duchy of Benevento made continual encroachments in the south, accelerating after the unsuccessful expedition of Emperor Constans II (641–68) to southern Italy in 663–8. Internal tensions were reflected in a series of revolts, the determined opposition led by the papacy to Constans II's monothelite doctrines and a bitter conflict between the sees of Rome and Ravenna over the same emperor's grant of ecclesiastical autonomy (*autokephalia*) to the latter in 666.[1] In two letters addressed to his successor, Pope Agatho (678–81) bemoaned the dislocation

---

[1] On Lombard–Byzantine relations, see Delogu *et al.* (1980); on the Byzantine territories: Guillou (1969); Brown, T. S. (1984); Ferluga (1991); Ravegnani (2004); on the movement of settlement to defensive *castra*: Brown and Christie (1989); on Pope Martin I's exile to Cherson, see above, p. 232. Useful surveys of the Byzantine territories' relations with a wider world, especially in the economic sphere, can be found in: Horden and Purcell (2000); McCormick (2001); Wickham (2005).

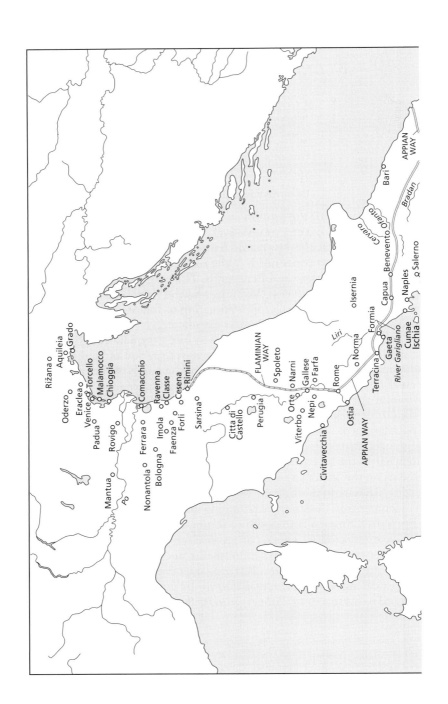

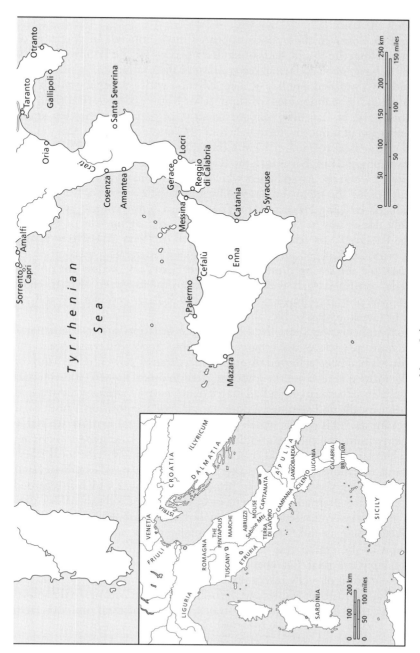

Map 21 Italy 700–900

Otranto
Gallipoli
Taranto
Santa Severina
Oria
Crati
Locri
Gerace
Cosenza
Amantea
Reggio di Calabria
Sorrento
Amalfi
Capri
Messina
Catania
Syracuse
Tyrrhenian Sea
Cefalù
Enna
Palermo
Mazara

0   50   100   150   200   250 km
0   50   100   150 miles

LIGURIA
FRIULI
VENETIA
ISTRIA
CROATIA
DALMATIA
ILLYRICUM
ROMAGNA
THE PENTAPOLIS
MARCHE
TUSCANY
ETRURIA
ABRUZZI
MOLISE
Sabine Mts
CAPITANATA
APULIA
TERRA DI LAVORO
CAMPANIA
LANGOBARDIA
CILENTO
LUCANIA
CALABRIA
BRUTTIUM
SARDINIA
SICILY

0   100   200 km
0   50   100 miles

caused by the 'gentiles' and complained that lack of food forced the clergy to work the land.[2]

By 680, however, the outlook appeared more hopeful. In that year, or shortly before, the empire had concluded a treaty with the Lombards which seems to have involved formal recognition of their kingdom.[3] Constantine IV (668–85) pursued a policy of reconciliation with the papacy which was reflected in his abandonment of support for Rome's ecclesiastical rival, the archbishopric of Ravenna; reduced taxation of papal patrimonies; and a renunciation of monotheletism in favour of Chalcedonian orthodoxy at the sixth ecumenical council, held in Constantinople in 680–1.[4] The process of absorbing the Lombards into the Roman and Christian mainstream was facilitated when the Arian beliefs which had long served as an anti-Roman rallying-point for many Lombard kings and their followers were finally repudiated by King Perctarit (661–2, 671–88). Complete unity within the catholic ranks was at last achieved when the damaging schism over the Three Chapters was resolved by the council of Pavia in 698 (see above, pp. 117–18, 212–14). Byzantine influence was considerable in many respects, for example the strong presence of eastern clerics and artists not only in imperial territories such as Rome, but also in the kingdom of Italy; eight of the nine pontiffs who sat on the throne of St Peter between 676 and 715 were of Greek, Syrian or Sicilian origin.

Any euphoria was short-lived because the situation within the remaining Byzantine enclaves was inherently unstable. Successful resistance to the Lombards had been achieved through concentrating power in the hands of locally formed elites from the imperial garrison units (*numeri*). Bureaucrats and soldiers of eastern origin had married into native families, accumulated property locally and assumed a dominant hereditary position within their communities. This group, which probably included some more adaptable elements from among the middle-ranking civilian landowners surviving from the late Roman period, came to identify strongly with local interests and traditions; it was in a position to flex its muscles whenever it saw its position threatened by an imperial government which it regarded as remote and alternately impotent or oppressive. As a result of this process, and of the empire's preoccupation with more immediate threats from the Arabs, Bulgars and Slavs and its consequent shortage of resources, the position of the exarch and other officials sent out from the east became increasingly marginal. Exarchal power was further limited in the early 690s by the elevation of Sicily into a theme, whose governor (*stratēgos*) was also granted authority over Naples and the other imperial territories in the southern mainland.[5] In this context the transformation of the Lombards from

---

[2] *PL* 87, cols. 1164, 1219, 1220.   [3] Dölger, *Regesten*, no. 240. The precise date is uncertain.
[4] Dölger, *Regesten*, no. 238 and references; Dölger, *Regesten*, no. 250; Mansi, XI.
[5] Oikonomides (1964). For details of officials throughout Byzantine Italy, see Cosentino (1996–2000).

barbarian bogeymen to Romanised catholics served to weaken allegiance to the empire further.

THE LAST DECADES OF BYZANTINE RULE

The late seventh century also saw a crisis in the economic position of the Byzantine territories of Italy. The loss of Carthage to the Arabs and the general weakening of imperial power led to a dramatic decline in imports such as pottery from Africa and the east, and to an increase in the importance of local Italian centres of production. This readjustment is reflected in finds from recently excavated sites such as Crypta Balbi in Rome, although luxury imports from the east remained important, and building activity, particularly of churches, continued at a significant level.[6]

On a political level, the delicate equilibrium was soon upset by the autocracy and impetuosity which the youthful Emperor Justinian II displayed in his first reign (685–95). After a brief honeymoon period with the papacy,[7] in 691–2 the emperor convoked a council in Constantinople, the quinisext, or council *in Trullo*, which promulgated a number of canons in conflict with the customs of the Roman church (see above, p. 245). Faced with resistance from Pope Sergius I (687–701), Justinian resorted to the same strong-arm tactics which his grandfather had attempted against Martin I (649–55) (see above, p. 232). On this occasion, however, military contingents from Ravenna and the Pentapolis intervened to prevent Sergius' arrest by the *prōtospatharios* Zacharias.[8] The antagonism of Ravenna towards Justinian found expression in 695, when a number of its citizens resident in Constantinople joined in the emperor's deposition and mutilation.[9] Italian hostility to the empire was visible again in 701, when 'the army of all Italy' moved to protect Pope John VI (701–5) against the newly appointed exarch Theophylact, who had presumably been sent to Rome by Emperor Tiberius II Apsimar (698–705) to pressurise the pontiff into accepting the quinisext decrees.[10]

The situation deteriorated further when Justinian recovered his throne with Bulgar help in 705. The chronology and motives of imperial policy are far from clear. However, it is likely that while he harboured plans for revenge

---

[6] Zanini (1998), pp. 320–32; Wickham (2005), pp. 728–41. On Crypta Balbi, see Manacorda (2001). Coates-Stephens (1997) argued for continuous building activity in Rome, with an increase in quantity and quality from the mid-eighth century. See also above, p. 405.

[7] A continuation of his father's pro-papal policy is demonstrated by a letter of 687 asserting Justinian's adherence to Chalcedonian orthodoxy (Dölger, *Regesten*, no. 254), and by a reduction of taxation on papal patrimonies in Sicily and southern Italy (Dölger, *Regesten*, nos. 255, 256).

[8] *LP*, LXXXVI.7–9, ed. Duchesne, I, pp. 373–4; tr. Davis, I, pp. 86–7.

[9] Agnel., ch. 137, ed. Holder-Egger, p. 367; ed. Mauskopf Deliyannis, p. 312; tr. Mauskopf Deliyannis, p. 259. Although Agnellus' account has many legendary elements, support for this episode is offered by the known presence of Italian troops in Constantinople (Mansi, XI, col. 737).

[10] *LP*, LXXXVII.1, ed. Duchesne, I, p. 383; tr. Davis, I, pp. 89–90.

against Ravenna, his approach to Rome was more accommodating. Papal support was seen as crucial to the emperor's desire for political and religious unity, and the see of Rome appears to have enjoyed enhanced power as the representative of imperial authority in Rome.[11] Pope John VII (705–7), the son of a Greek official, was offered a compromise over the quinisext decrees, which he refused. The pope then proceeded to establish a papal palace on the previously imperial preserve of the Palatine hill, and carried out a lavish programme of artistic production, best reflected in the superb frescoes of the church of Santa Maria Antiqua (fig. 30).[12] The strongly 'Byzantine' character of John's programme lends support to the notion of a positive element to relations between Justinian and the pope. For example, the emperor appears to have sided with Rome in a renewed conflict with its fractious suffragan, Ravenna. At his ordination in 709 the city's archbishop, Felix, refused to offer the traditional pledges of loyalty to the pope, and with the support of the (by now independent-minded) Ravenna officials (*iudices*) submitted his own version. The emperor's despatch of a punitive expedition led by the patrician Theodore, *stratēgos* of Sicily, can best be seen as retribution for the snub to papal authority, rather than vengeance for Ravennate opposition to the emperor in 693 or 695.[13] By a ruse Theodore succeeded in arresting Felix and the leading citizens of Ravenna, who were taken to Constantinople and tortured.[14] In fear of further moves by Justinian the remaining citizens organised an elaborate local defence force under an elected duke named George.[15] It is probable that this new force caused the 'revolting death' suffered by John Rizokopos when he sought to take up his post as exarch in Ravenna late in 710.[16] The whole episode led to a turning-point in Ravenna's relations with the empire: the general allegiance associated with

[11] Llewellyn (1986). Noble (1984) approaches the question from a different perspective (of increasing tension and papal independence), but his interpretation is broadly compatible for the position between *c.* 680 and the outbreak of iconoclasm.

[12] Nordhagen (1988), pp. 600–10 and more recently Osborne *et al.* (eds.) (2004). On the Palatine in the Byzantine and post-Byzantine periods, Augenti (1996).

[13] My interpretation of this episode differs radically from that of Guillou (1969), pp. 211–18, who argues that the Ravenna *iudices* forced Felix to climb down and places Theodore's expedition after the murder of John Rizokopos. The latter chronology runs counter to the contemporary account in the *Liber pontificalis* (*LP*, XC.2, ed. Duchesne, I, p. 389) and my interpretation of the phrase 'sed per potentiam iudicum [Felix] exposuit ut maluit' is supported by Davis' translation (I, p. 92). On Justinian II's relations with Ravenna: Brown, T. S. (1995).

[14] The outlines of the dramatic account in Agnellus of Ravenna, *Liber pontificalis* (Agnel., chs. 137–8, ed. Holder-Egger, pp. 367–9; ed. Mauskopf Deliyannis, pp. 313–16; tr. Mauskopf Deliyannis, pp. 259–63) can probably be accepted because (a) the episode clearly loomed large in Ravenna folk memory and the traditions of Agnellus' family and (b) it is broadly confirmed by the *Liber pontificalis*' account.

[15] Agnel., ch. 140, ed. Holder-Egger, pp. 369–70; ed. Mauskopf Deliyannis, pp. 317–19; tr. Mauskopf Deliyannis, pp. 263–5. George was the son of Iohannicius, a learned secretary at the exarch's court who had served for a time in the capital before becoming one of the unfortunates arrested by Theodore.

[16] The account in the *Liber pontificalis* is vague: 'suis nefandissimis factis iudicio Dei illic [sc. Ravennae] turpissima morte occubuit' (*LP*, XC.4, ed. Duchesne, I, p. 390; tr. Davis, I, p. 92).

Figure 30 Fresco showing a Seraph's head from the church of Santa Maria Antiqua, Rome, commissioned by Pope John VII

benign imperial *laissez-faire* in the late seventh century turned to marked antipathy and an even more marginal role for the exarchs in the eighth. It is hardly surprising that there was rejoicing in Ravenna when the emperor was deposed and his severed head was transported to Italy.[17]

---

[17] Agnel., ch. 142, ed. Holder-Egger, p. 371; ed. Mauskopf Deliyannis, p. 320; tr. Mauskopf Deliyannis, pp. 266–7; see also Nikeph., ch. 45, ed. and tr. Mango, pp. 112–13; Theoph., ed. de Boor, I, p. 381; tr. Mango and Scott, p. 529.

A rapprochement between Rome and the empire was achieved in early 711, when Pope Constantine I (708–15) visited Constantinople, being honourably received by Justinian II and accorded privileges. However, Justinian appears to have been playing a double game: during the pope's absence the newly appointed exarch John Rizokopos had executed four prominent papal officials, presumably to punish advisers considered anti-imperial and to intimidate the pope.[18]

Justinian was assassinated in December 711 and relations between Rome and Constantinople deteriorated during the short reign of his successor, Emperor Philippikos (711–13), who was refused recognition in Rome on the grounds of his monophysite sympathies. As the *de facto* authority in the city, Constantine had to make peace between the warring factions.[19] An improvement in relations followed Philippikos' deposition in 713, but once again events made this short-lived. After years of instability the Lombard kingdom became a potent force under King Liutprand (712–44), who adopted a policy of unifying the peninsula under Lombard rule. Meanwhile the empire came under renewed pressure from the Arabs, culminating in a year-long siege of Constantinople. In Sicily the *stratēgos* Sergios, in apparent despair of the empire's survival, rebelled and proclaimed a certain Basil Onomagoulos emperor. Emperor Leo III (717–41) responded by sending an expedition under a replacement *stratēgos*, Paul, and Sergios was forced to seek refuge among the Lombards of southern Italy (see below, p. 461).

More serious was the Lombards' exploitation of the empire's difficulties. In 717 the duke of Benevento seized Cumae, the duke of Spoleto occupied Narni, and the king himself invaded the exarchate and occupied Classe. Although the loss of Narni proved permanent, Liutprand promptly withdrew from Classe and the Roman pontiff Gregory II (715–31) was able to recover Cumae. Once his position in the east was secure, Leo III attempted to reassert the empire's authority in Italy. In 724 or 725 the emperor imposed an increase in taxation which hit the papal patrimonies particularly hard; they had hitherto been exempted from fiscal burdens by a privilege of Constantine IV.[20] In the light of Gregory's opposition, a plot to kill the pontiff was hatched by imperial *duces* in collaboration with papal officials. When this failed, the exarch Paul sent forces backing another plot on the pope's life. However, the Romans, together with the Lombards of Spoleto and Benevento, rallied to the pope's defence and forced the exarch's troops to withdraw.

Stronger resistance arose to Leo III's publication of decrees prohibiting the veneration of icons in 727. Gregory II's vehement reaction is reflected

---

[18] *LP*, XC.4, ed. Duchesne, I, p. 390; tr. Davis, I, p. 92.

[19] *LP*, XC.8–9, ed. Duchesne, I, p. 391; tr. Davis, I, pp. 93–4.

[20] *LP*, XCI.16, ed. Duchesne, I, p. 403; tr. Davis, II, p. 10; on the circumstances see Marazzi (1991), pp. 231–46.

in the words of both the *Liber pontificalis* – 'he took up arms against the emperor as if against an enemy'[21] – and the Byzantine chronicler Theophanes – 'he removed Rome and all Italy from his [Leo III's] rule'.[22] In areas such as Venetia and the Pentapolis this dispute reinforced existing discontent and prompted local army units to revolt and elect their own *duces*. When the notion was mooted of electing a rival emperor and setting him up in Constantinople, however, Gregory refused his support in the hope that Leo could still be won back to orthodoxy, and urged the empire's subjects 'not to renounce their love and loyalty to the Roman empire'.[23] Serious divisions soon appeared within the Byzantine provinces. While in Rome the population killed one pro-imperial duke and blinded another, in the duchy of Naples iconoclasm appears to have attracted widespread support;[24] in the exarchate there was serious conflict between pro- and anti-Byzantine factions, costing the exarch Paul his life.[25] Gregory's position reflects not only the durability of the imperial ideal in the absence of any ideological alternative, but also his need to retain a protector against the Lombards, still regarded as barbarians intent on exploiting the situation to dominate the peninsula. In fact, while the dukes of Spoleto and Benevento showed solidarity with the pontiff, King Liutprand seized western portions of the exarchate.

Later in the same year (727) a new exarch, Eutychios, disembarked in Naples but was unable to enter Rome or to enforce his authority there.[26] When Liutprand moved south to establish control over Spoleto and Benevento, he and Eutychios found it expedient to make a surprising alliance against the pope. However, Gregory was able to play upon the king's catholic piety to induce him to leave for the north, and a revolt in Roman Etruria in 728 gave Gregory an opportunity to demonstrate his continuing loyalty to the imperial ideal. The pope encouraged the exarch to defeat and capture the usurper, Tiberius Petasius, and Eutychios then also headed north in order to reimpose imperial control over Ravenna.

The empire's position was soon undermined by Leo III's promulgation of stronger decrees against icons in 730 (see above, p. 279). After diplomatic remonstrations failed, the new pope, Gregory III (731–41), summoned a

---

[21] *LP*, XCI.17, ed. Duchesne, I, p. 404; tr. Davis, II, p. 11: 'contra imperatorem quasi contra hostem se armavit'.

[22] Theoph., ed. de Boor, I, p. 409; tr. Mango and Scott, p. 565.

[23] *LP*, XCI.20, ed. Duchesne, I, p. 407; tr. Davis, II, p. 13.   [24] Bertolini, P. (1974).

[25] *LP*, XCI.18, ed. Duchesne, I, p. 405; tr. Davis, II, p. 12. The view of Guillou (1969), p. 220, that Leo responded by sending a punitive expedition, is based on a misunderstanding of Agnel., ch. 153, ed. Holder-Egger, p. 377; ed. Mauskopf Deliyannis, pp. 330–1; tr. Mauskopf Deliyannis, pp. 276–7. The expedition referred to was probably intended to recover the city after its capture by the Lombards (see also Bertolini, O. (1967), pp. 35–49); but Agnellus may also have confused it with the attack of the *stratēgos* Theodore in 710. See also Brown, T. S. (1995).

[26] *LP*, XCI.19, ed. Duchesne, I, pp. 405–6; tr. Davis, II, p. 13.

council in Rome in December 731 which resolutely upheld the iconodule position. Leo III responded by transferring the papal provinces of southern Italy, Sicily and Illyricum to the jurisdiction of the patriarch of Constantinople. However the attitude of the pope and the imperial authorities in Italy was surprisingly conciliatory. While Gregory took a principled stand in opposing iconoclasm and imperial persecution in the east, in practice he cooperated with Eutychios in defending the Italian provinces against the Lombards. In turn the exarch appears to have made no attempt to impose the iconoclast decrees in Italy and even sent the pope a gift of onyx columns for St Peter's. Eutychios' alliance with Liutprand had proved short-lived, and imperial forces even attempted to recover some of the Lombard conquests. Lombard forces occupied Ravenna at an uncertain date in the mid- or late 730s, forcing Eutychios to flee to Venice. Possibly after the failure of an imperial expedition to recover the city, Pope Gregory III wrote to the duke of Venetia and the patriarch of Grado requesting their help in restoring Ravenna 'to the holy republic and the imperial service of our sons Leo [III] and Constantine [V]'.[27] A Venetian fleet duly recovered the city.

In 739 Thrasamund II, duke of Spoleto, captured the stronghold of Gallese from the duchy of Rome. Gregory III resorted to negotiation to recover it for 'the holy republic and the Christ-loved Roman army'.[28] Thrasamund then rebelled against King Liutprand and, when ejected from his duchy by royal troops, sought refuge in Rome. In his fury the Lombard king then devastated the area around Rome and seized four strategic strongholds on the Flaminian Way, prompting Gregory to appeal to the Frankish mayor of the palace, Charles Martel. When Liutprand returned northwards, Thrasamund was able to recover his duchy with Roman support.

Gregory's successor, the Greek-born Zacharias (741–52), had to deal with another period of uncertainty when the more militantly iconoclast Constantine V (741–75) was faced with a revolt by his brother-in-law Artabasdos. Liutprand appeared characteristically opportunistic in applying renewed pressure against both Spoleto and Rome. Zacharias resumed negotiations, obtained the four disputed *castra*, together with lost papal patrimonies in the Pentapolis and the duchy of Spoleto, and concluded a treaty of twenty years' peace with the Lombard kingdom in 742. In the following year Liutprand prepared to attack Ravenna again, and in alarm the exarch Eutychios and the city's archbishop appealed to the pope to intervene. Zacharias set off for Ravenna, where he was received with great honour by the exarch and population; he went on to Pavia, where in the summer of 743 he persuaded

[27] *Epistolae Langobardicae collectae*, ed. Gundlach, p. 702 (= *Regesta pontificum romanorum*, I, no. 2177).

[28] '. . . in conpage sanctae reipublicae atque corpore Christo dilecti exercitus Romani annecti praecepit': *LP*, XCII.15, ed. Duchesne, I, pp. 420–1; tr. Davis, II, p. 28.

Liutprand to return most of the territories seized from the exarchate. The pope acted independently of the empire, and appears for the first time to have staked the kind of proprietorial claims to the exarchate he had already made to the duchy of Rome. Soon afterwards, in 743, Constantine V granted the pope two estates south of Rome, probably in order to restore the pope's allegiance to his rule and to offer compensation for the loss of papal jurisdiction and property in 732/3 (see above, p. 285).

751 AND ITS CONSEQUENCES

In early 744 Liutprand died, and Zacharias was able to confirm the twenty-year treaty with his successor-but-one, Ratchis (744–9). For obscure reasons Ratchis abandoned his pro-Roman policy in 749 and launched a campaign against the Pentapolis. Zacharias met the king and prevailed upon him to renounce his conquests, but within a short time Ratchis became a monk and was succeeded by his brother Aistulf (749–56). Aistulf adopted a more aggressive policy, including attacks on Istria, Ferrara, Comacchio and Ravenna itself, which was in his hands by 4 July 751. The ease with which the capital was finally taken may in part be explained by the exarch Eutychios' realism in surrendering the city in the face of considerable odds. The existence of a pro-Lombard party among its citizens – hostile to the only viable alternative, papal overlordship – may also help explain the city's defeat: this group may have included the city's archbishop, Sergius, who, according to Agnellus, had aspirations to rule the area 'just like an exarch'.[29] Certainly Aistulf showed himself aware of Ravennate sensibilities by observing the forms and titles of Roman rulership, patronising the city's churches and showing deference to its patron, St Apollinaris. Nor did he attempt a military occupation of the exarchate, relying on control exercised on its border through the foundation of the royal monastery of Nonantola and the foundation of the duchy of Persiceto under a loyal Friulian noble.

The long-term consequences of the fall of Ravenna in 751 proved dramatic for the papacy and for the Lombard and Frankish kingdoms, especially since the same *annus mirabilis* saw the deposition of the last Merovingian king with the sanction of Pope Zacharias, and the anointing of Pippin the Short (751–68) as king of the Franks by the Frankish bishops. Ironically the fall of the capital with more of a whimper than a bang had little direct effect on the remaining territories of Byzantine Italy. The process of decentralisation had been underway for decades, with effective power in the hands of local elites led by *duces*. Nevertheless the history of the surviving provinces is best studied by examining them in three separate blocks, since

---

[29] Agnel., ch. 159, ed. Holder-Egger, p. 380; ed. Mauskopf Deliyannis, p. 337; tr. Mauskopf Deliyannis, p. 284.

in each the relatively uniform social structure of the imperial period was gradually transformed by particular local factors. In the north, Venetia and Istria retained their imperial allegiance; in the south, Sicily and the duchies of Calabria, Otranto and Naples continued to come under the authority of the *stratēgos* of the Sicilian theme;and in central Italy the exarchate, the Pentapolis and the duchies of Perugia and Rome were the subject of a tug-of-war between the Lombards, the papacy and entrenched local elites.

ROME AND ITS DUCHY

Zacharias' successor, Pope Stephen II (752–7), was alarmed when Aistulf followed up his conquests by demanding a tribute from the duchy of Rome, and sought help from Constantine V. At the emperor's behest, he entered into frantic negotiations with the Lombard court at Pavia, but to no avail. As Lombard pressure on Rome increased in 753, the pope made overtures to Pippin the Short, paid a fruitless visit to Pavia on imperial orders, and then proceeded to cross the Alps to meet Pippin at Ponthion in January 754. The upshot was that Stephen granted Pippin the title *patricius Romanorum* (with its echoes of the rank held by the Byzantine exarch), a Frankish army was sent to besiege Pavia, and Aistulf was compelled to hand territories formerly belonging to the exarchate over to Stephen II. When these promises were broken, the Frankish king returned to Italy in 756 and conceded all the exarchate's territories to the pope through the 'donation' of Pippin. Although this represented a serious snub to imperial claims, an overt divergence between the papacy and the empire cannot be postulated before at least the 770s, when the pontiff's name replaced that of the emperor on Roman coins and documents. In practice, however, ties between the papacy and the Franks became increasingly close, and it is also to this period (between 752 and 771) that most recent scholars would date the forging of the 'donation of Constantine' (*Constitutum Constantini*) by a Roman cleric working in the Lateran chancery. Although it is doubtful that this document can be seen as an official production intended to legitimise papal claims to Byzantine territory, it appears to reflect the predominant ideology of clerical milieux in Rome who were working towards a wholly independent status for the 'patrimony of St Peter'.

The following years were ones of uncertainty. Widespread fears of Byzantine attempts to recover their territory failed to materialise, while the new Lombard king Desiderius (757–74) showed himself at first conciliatory, but later hostile, to papal claims. Although after Stephen II's death in March 757 Desiderius failed to deliver all the areas he had promised and Pippin was too preoccupied with other concerns to intervene, an uneasy *modus vivendi* was achieved between the Lombard king and Pope Paul I (757– 67). Following Paul's death, however, the duchy of Rome sank into bitter internal conflicts, whose key element appears to have been a struggle between an elite of military officials with their power base in the country and the clerical bureaucrats of the Lateran Palace in the city. One of the military officials, Toto, duke of Nepi, succeeded in having his brother Constantine 'elected' as anti-pope in June 767, but the clerical party, led by an influential Lateran bureaucrat the *primicerius* Christopher and his son Sergius, soon regained power; with Lombard help, they had their candidate elected as Pope Stephen III in August 768. However, serious difficulties continued, including anti-papal activity in the exarchate and dissension among the papacy's Frankish allies, and in 771–2 a coup staged against Christopher and Sergius' clerical regime led to the rise to power of Paul Afiarta, the pro-Lombard papal chamberlain. After the death of the vacillating Stephen III (768–72), a new pope from a leading Roman family was elected as Hadrian I (772–95), and he proved no mere tool in Afiarta's hands. He had Paul Afiarta arrested in Ravenna and resisted Desiderius' attempts to enter Rome and to have his protégés, the sons of the Frankish king Carloman, anointed there. When Desiderius proceeded to occupy strategic towns in the exarchate, Hadrian prevailed upon the new Frankish king Charlemagne to order their return. When Desiderius refused to comply, Charlemagne led an army into Italy, besieged Desiderius in Pavia and took over the Lombard kingdom (see above, p. 415).

In Hadrian's pontificate, the papacy's alliance with its Frankish protectors grew increasingly close and cordial, especially after Charlemagne conquered the Lombard kingdom in 774 and renewed the grants made by his father, Pippin the Short. Hadrian went to the length of addressing Charlemagne as a new Constantine in 778.[30] Ties with the eastern empire were not formally broken – in 772 criminals were sent to Constantinople for punishment – but in practice turned to hostility. The pope's implicit claim to independence is evident in a letter addressed to Constantine VI (780–97) in which Hadrian wrote of how Charlemagne had 'restored by force to the apostle of God the provinces, cities, strongholds, territories and patrimonies which were held by the perfidious race of the Lombards'.[31] Hadrian's letters reflect his constant fear of a *reconquista* led by the Greeks in alliance with Arichis, duke of Benevento (759–87) and Desiderius' exiled son Adelchis, but the pope was unable to prevail upon Charlemagne to intervene militarily against Benevento. In Rome and its hinterland Hadrian I established new levels of prosperity and stability, largely as a result of his personal position as a powerful family magnate with influential relatives and allies among both the Lateran bureaucracy and the secular aristocracy. Hadrian also succeeded

---

[30] *CC*, no. 60, ed. Gundlach, p. 587; tr. King, p. 287. The passage appears to be based on the *Actus Sylvestri*, the main source of the forged 'donation of Constantine'.

[31] Mansi, XII, cols. 1075–6 (= *Regesta pontificum romanorum*, I, no. 2442).

in strengthening papal authority in the countryside around Rome by setting up six papal estate complexes known as *domuscultae* such as Santa Cornelia, 25 kilometres north of Rome. Here he was continuing a policy initiated by Zacharias, who had set up five such complexes, and more estates were set up by his successor, Leo III. These had a number of purposes, including the securing of food supplies for the city at a time when it had lost its traditional sources of provisions in Sicily and southern Italy. However the primary role of the *domuscultae* was to strengthen papal control in the face of endemic disorder in the countryside, and to serve as papal strongholds against local warlords such as Toto of Nepi. The peasant workforce was organised into a loyal *familia Sancti Petri*, and furnished militia contingents which were used to suppress a *coup d'état* in 824 and to fortify the area around St Peter's in 846.[32]

Hadrian, however, experienced continuing difficulties in enforcing his authority over the wider complex of cities, villages and patrimonies often anachronistically termed 'the papal state'. These were particularly acute in areas where the papal claim to be heir of the Roman state was somewhat dubious, such as the Sabine territories around the monastery of Farfa, which had been held by Lombard settlers for generations.[33] Even in the exarchate and the Pentapolis, although opposition to papal rule subsided somewhat with the death of Archbishop Leo of Ravenna in 778, Hadrian complained in 783 that lay officials from Ravenna had appealed directly to Charlemagne, and in 790–1 elements in the city were denying the pope's legal authority. The pope did, however, receive additional territories on the occasion of Charlemagne's visit to Italy in 787 when the king made over a grant of part of Lombard Tuscany stretching from Città di Castello in the north to Viterbo and Orte in the south and a number of towns in the duchy of Benevento. The pope also had problems in establishing his rights to various papal patrimonies in the duchy of Naples, and it was probably to apply pressure for their return – as well as to secure the southern flank of the duchy of Rome – that papal troops seized Terracina from the Neapolitan duchy in 788.[34]

Hadrian's successor, Leo III (795–816), was a less powerful character from a non-aristocratic background. As a result his position was much weaker, and his dependence on the Franks for protection even greater. His first action was to treat Charlemagne in the manner that preceding popes had adopted towards their Byzantine sovereigns by sending him the protocol of his election, together with a pledge of loyalty and the keys and banner of the city of Rome. Matters were brought to a head by a coup in 799, when aristocratic elements associated with Hadrian I accused Leo of various

---

[32] Christie, Neil (ed.) (1991), pp. 6–8. [33] Costambeys (2007).
[34] *CC*, nos. 61, 64, ed. Gundlach, pp. 588, 591–2; tr. King, pp. 288, 289–90.

offences and sought to arrest and mutilate him. Leo fled first to Spoleto and then across the Alps where he met Charlemagne at Paderborn. He then returned in the autumn with an investigating commission of bishops and officials in order to restore his position in Rome. In the following November Charlemagne visited Rome and was crowned emperor in St Peter's on Christmas Day 800. The intentions of the parties involved in this event are the subject of considerable scholarly debate. We will merely note that the papacy's action represents the culmination of a long process of distancing from the Byzantine empire, and that one possible motive for Charlemagne may have been to win support in the 'Roman areas' of Italy such as the exarchate and Rome by exploiting vestigial nostalgia for the Roman imperial title.[35]

As a result of the events of 800, Rome burnt its boats with the Byzantine empire on a political level. An alternative ideological model was instituted, clerical control of the government was enhanced, and Frankish influence became more marked. The pope adopted a strongly pro-Frankish policy – as long as the Carolingian empire lasted, until 888 – and the chronicler Theophanes the Confessor wrote, 'now Rome is in the hands of the Franks'.[36] Thus in 817 Louis the Pious (814–40) issued the privilege known as the *Ludovicianum*, in which the grants of his father and grandfather – Charlemagne and Pippin the Short – were tidied up and made more precise on terms favourable to the papacy.[37] In 824, however, a less generous line was taken by the *Constitutio Romana*, which weakened the papacy's independence by setting up two *missi* in Rome – one papal and one imperial – and by demanding from the Romans an oath of loyalty to the western empire.[38] Byzantium remained a factor, but only of limited importance, in the first half of the ninth century. Fears were expressed of plans for a Byzantine *reconquista*, and there may well have been links between the eastern empire and elements of the secular aristocracy nostalgic for the Byzantine period and eager for an end to the influence of the 'barbarian' Franks. Certainly in 853 a *magister militum*, Gratian, was accused of accepting Byzantine bribes. The situation changed, however, as a result of the growing threat of Muslim naval power to the coasts of Italy, especially after the Muslims' occupation

---

[35] Classen (1952). Such a policy certainly appears to have had the desired effect in Ravenna since the normally xenophobic local writer Agnellus accepted the legitimacy of Charlemagne's imperial title: Agnel., ch. 94, ed. Holder-Egger, p. 338; ed. Mauskopf Deliyannis, p. 259; tr. Mauskopf Deliyannis, p. 207; see also Brown, T. S. (1986), pp. 109–10; above, pp. 417–18.

[36] Theoph., ed. de Boor, I, p. 472; tr. Mango and Scott, p. 649.

[37] Louis I, *Pactum Ludovicianum*, ed. Sickel. Louis promised not to interfere in papal jurisdiction or to intervene in papal elections.

[38] *Constitutio Romana*, ed. Boretius. Noble (1984), p. 308, argues that the traditional contrast between the two documents is exaggerated and that the *Constitutio* was a logical extension of the *Ludovicianum*. Useful as this corrective view is, it has to be remembered that from 822 Italy was under the direct rule of Lothar I who in general took a firmer line with the papacy than his father, Louis the Pious.

of Bari and their sack of St Peter's in 846. Although the papacy looked primarily to the Frankish emperor Louis II (855–75) to deal with the Saracen danger, it supported his attempts to secure Byzantine naval cooperation, and when Louis' efforts in southern Italy proved a failure, Pope John VIII (872–82) resorted increasingly to diplomatic overtures to Byzantium aimed at involving the empire in a Christian enterprise against the infidel. These papal efforts were not crowned with success, however, before the early tenth century.[39]

On an ecclesiastical level, relations with Byzantium were strained by the second wave of iconoclasm in the east (815–43) and even after the restoration of icons, contentious issues remained. The transfer of jurisdiction and patrimonies in southern Italy and Illyricum to the patriarchate of Constantinople and the closely associated problem of authority over missions to the Balkans proved sources of conflict, especially during the pontificate of Nicholas I (858–67) (see above, p. 299). Nevertheless the papacy retained its claims to primacy over the eastern as well as the western churches, and Rome remained a magnet for eastern pilgrims and exiles. In many respects Rome remained within the Byzantine cultural orbit. Eastern artistic influence on the city remained strong, expressed through a flow of liturgical objects and in all probability also an influx of artists. A number of Greek monasteries continued to flourish in the city, and Rome became a major centre of translation activity, best exemplified by the Latin versions of Greek historical and hagiographical texts produced by the papal librarian, Anastasius Bibliothecarius (see above, p. 427).

On an institutional level, the extent and durability of the Romano-Byzantine inheritance in the duchy of Rome has been a subject of controversy, mainly because of the paucity of evidence for the ninth century. Certain titles from the imperial period continue, such as consul, *dux* and *magister militum*, while others, such as *tribunus*, disappear. There is similar uncertainty over whether the apparently lay judges known as *iudices dativi* constitute a survival from the Roman period. It is clear that any notion of a strong centralised secular authority on the traditional Byzantine model has to be rejected. This had already broken down in the last decades of imperial rule, to be replaced by a decentralised power system in the hands of local warlords. On the other hand, it is likely that most of the families to which the latter belonged established their position in the Byzantine period, and they remained deeply attached to the old imperial titles, even though these were used in an increasingly vague and debased way. In the city of Rome certain institutions persist which can be traced to the imperial past, such as the local militia units (*scholae*) and the strong sense of

---

[39] Brown, T. S. (1988a), p. 38. See also below, pp. 538, 563. Rome's continuously complex and dynamic relations with Byzantium are reflected in many of the studies in Smith (ed.) (2000).

public rights and property, but these were taken over and transformed under papal control. The papal bureaucracy modelled its workings and titles on that of the Byzantine empire. In certain respects the popes themselves can be seen behaving in self-conscious imitation of emperors, as with Gregory IV's (827–44) naming of the refortified Ostia as Gregoriopolis and Leo IV's (847–55) short-lived foundation of Leopolis following the Arab attack on nearby Civitavecchia. In general there appears to have been a striking nostalgia for all things Byzantine, especially in the sphere of titles, names and dress. This became if anything stronger as the century progressed, with growing disenchantment at Frankish barbarism and impotence. Northern writers pointed to the resemblance between the Romans and the Greeks, especially in the pejorative sense of their effeminacy and cowardliness.[40] The impact of 'une sorte de snobisme byzantinisant'[41] proved more than a passing fashion, since it helped to build support for renewed political relations between the Roman elite and Byzantium in the tenth century.

THE EXARCHATE AND THE PENTAPOLIS[42]

The other major area within the central bloc of formerly Byzantine territories – the exarchate and the Pentapolis – was also claimed by the popes after 751, but their authority there was always much less effective. These two closely related areas had developed such strong local institutions in the last decades of imperial rule that the area's takeover by Aistulf had little effect. Ravenna remained dominant as the political and economic centre of the whole region, but power became concentrated in the hands of the city's archbishop, whose church controlled extensive patrimonies from Ferrara to Perugia and whose patronage secured him the allegiance of local elites throughout Romagna and the Marche. The short-lived Lombard overlordship appears to have been benign, and the king was compelled to hand over both areas to papal authority in 755, in accordance with a peace agreement made at Pavia.[43] This settlement aroused bitter opposition in Ravenna and, when Pope Stephen II decided to visit Ravenna in that year in order to make the necessary administrative arrangements, he was refused admission into the city by the local lay and clerical aristocracy, with the apparent connivance of Archbishop Sergius (744–69). A second Frankish expedition proved necessary to make Aistulf fulfil his promises, and a commission of Frankish officials led by Abbot Fulrad was sent to the exarchate.

---

[40] For references, see Toubert (1973), II, p. 1007.

[41] The phrase is that of Toubert (1973), I, p. 697, n. 1.

[42] For valuable studies, which deal at length with these areas before and after 751, see Berardi *et al.* (eds.) (1990–6), II.1, II.2 (ed. A. Carile) and *Atti* 17.

[43] The tangled history of the early years of papal rule over the exarchate has been convincingly clarified by Bertolini, O. (1950) and a number of other articles republished in Bertolini, O. (1968).

Stephen II despatched two influential Romans, the priest Philip and Duke Eustachius to assume authority in his name; they succeeded in sending the leaders of the local opposition to Rome, where they were imprisoned. Papal administrators such as a *vestararius* were then sent to the area, but it is unclear how much practical power they were able to exercise. Certainly they faced widespread obstruction and hostility from the local population, and considerable *de facto* power remained in the hands of the archbishop, whom Agnellus of Ravenna describes as ruling the areas 'just like an exarch' and 'arranging everything as the Romans [i.e. the Byzantines] were accustomed to doing'.[44] When Archbishop Sergius entered into negotiations with Aistulf to re-establish Lombard rule, he too was arrested and sent to Rome for trial by a tribunal of judges. At that moment Stephen II died, and his successor as pope, his brother Paul I, considered it expedient to reach a compromise, possibly out of fear of a Byzantine attempt to reconquer the exarchate. Sergius was therefore sent back to his city with the right to conduct the day-to-day administration while the pope's overall authority was upheld.

This arrangement seems to have worked relatively well until Sergius' death in 769. The Lombard king Desiderius then joined forces with local military elements led by Maurice, duke of Rimini, to impose a strongly anti-Roman cleric named Michael as archbishop, but he was deposed after a year as a result of popular outrage at his avarice and the arrival of Frankish *missi*. However, the next, legitimately elected, archbishop, Leo (771–8), was equally hostile to papal claims and proceeded to send an embassy to Charlemagne, much to the anger of Pope Hadrian I. The pope complained to Charlemagne that Leo had taken over the cities of Faenza, Forli, Cesena, Sarsina, Comacchio and Ferrara and expelled papal officials in them and in Ravenna itself. Charlemagne took no immediate steps against Leo, who went on a personal visit to Francia to defend his position in the spring of 775. Charlemagne's reactions are unclear, but Leo certainly behaved as if he had independent control of the exarchate. He claimed that King Desiderius had granted him Bologna and Imola, had prevented papal representatives from obtaining oaths of loyalty to St Peter, had expelled papal officials and had imprisoned a certain Dominicus, appointed count of Gavello by the pope.[45]

After the bitter resistance to the papacy led by Archbishops Sergius and Leo, the situation appears to have become more settled for the greater part of Charlemagne's reign, probably as a result of a compromise agreement.[46] The popes retained overall political authority, together with extensive but imprecisely known rights and lands. At the same time practical power was largely

[44] Agnel., ch. 159, ed. Holder-Egger, p. 380; ed. Mauskopf Deliyannis, p. 337; tr. Mauskopf Deliyannis, p. 284. In general, see Fasoli (1979).

[45] *CC*, no. 54, ed. Gundlach, p. 577; tr. King, pp. 282–3.

[46] Noble (1984), pp. 172, 251 terms this arrangement a 'double dyarchy'.

in the hands of the archbishop by virtue of his vast patrimonies, his close political and economic ties with the local aristocracy, and his traditional role as focus for the exarchate's traditions and aspirations. The details of these rights and powers cannot be reconstructed from the very patchy sources; even the lively, contemporary local writer Agnellus (*fl. c.* 840) is of little help, since the biographies of most of the bishops of this period are missing in the one surviving manuscript of his work. In addition, the presence of the Frankish rulers as kings of Italy complicated matters; even though most of them respected papal claims, they were susceptible to the imperial associations of Ravenna and aware of the strategic importance of the area with its seaports on the Adriatic and its proximity to the Byzantine possessions in Venetia. Frankish *missi* were also active in the area; Pope Leo III shows awareness of this in letters addressed to Charlemagne: he complains of scandalous utterances made to visiting *missi* by Archbishop Valerius (806–10); and judgements made by *missi* in favour of the papacy were being flouted.[47] This interest of the Franks in the region was exploited with some success by the archbishops of Ravenna in order to obtain privileges.[48]

The rule of Pope Leo III appears to have been particularly unpopular in Ravenna and encouraged the archbishops to solicit Frankish support. Charlemagne seems to have turned a deaf ear to such requests, but the strongly anti-Roman Archbishop Martin (810–17) apparently had success in winning Frankish support against papal claims through a mixture of sycophancy and bribes. The line taken by his successor, Petronax (817–34) was arguably more pro-papal, to judge from critical allusions in Agnellus' work and the privilege which he received from Pope Paschal I (817–24) in 819. When Louis the Pious' son Lothar I took effective control as king of Italy in 822, he seems to have built up strong links with major sees such as Ravenna. The next archbishop, George (834–846), attempted to exploit Lothar's poor relations with Rome to undermine the papal position, and his policy may have been to seek a return to the autocephalous status granted by Constans II rather than the more limited autonomy sought by Sergius and Leo.[49] Certainly the gradual penetration of Frankish authority continued within the exarchate, as is demonstrated by a legal case brought about by the *advocatus* of the archbishop and decided by imperial *missi* at Rovigo in 838.[50] However, George incurred the opposition of his clergy through his personal greed and his costly recourse to bribery of his royal benefactors.[51]

---

[47] Leo III, *Epistolae*, nos. 2, 9, pp. 91, 101: the expression used in the former is *turpitudo*.
[48] For details of what follows, see Brown, T. S. (1990).
[49] The suggestion is that of Fasoli (1979), p. 102.
[50] *Placiti del 'Regnum Italiae'*, ed. Manaresi, I, no. 43, pp. 139–44.
[51] George's personal visit to Lothar in 841 ended in fiasco when his imperial patron was defeated by his brother, Louis the German, and half-brother, Charles the Bald, at the battle of Fontenoy and the see's treasures were plundered: Agnel., ch. 174, ed. Holder-Egger, pp. 389–91; ed. Mauskopf Deliyannis, pp. 354–7; tr. Mauskopf Deliyannis, pp. 301–4.

Even more bitter hostility to papal overlordship broke out under arch-bishops Deusdedit (846–50) and John VIII (850–78). The latter dominated the exarchate in conjunction with his brother Duke Gregory and displayed his independence at the time of his consecration by altering the pledges of loyalty to the papacy and Frankish empire which new prelates were expected to sign. He cooperated closely with Louis II, who may have been attempting to incorporate the exarchate within the kingdom of Italy. Unfortunately, like other ambitious Ravenna prelates, he appears to have feathered his own nest and alienated local interests in his opposition to Rome. In February 861, Pope Nicholas I responded to complaints against John by summoning a council in Rome. There the archbishop was excommunicated for heresy, violation of the rights of his clergy, especially his suffragan bishops, and interference with Roman rights in the exarchate. John's appeals to Louis for help proved fruitless, and in a second council of November 861 John acknowledged his guilt and suffered the humiliation of receiving back his see from the pope on strict conditions. Nevertheless, he continued to make trouble for Nicholas I's successors, and was roundly denounced in Pope John VIII's (872–82) letters for usurpation of papal property.[52] The crisis over the succession to the Frankish empire which followed the death of Louis II in 875 gave Archbishop John new opportunities. He sided with the Roman faction led by Formosus, bishop of Porto, which supported Louis the German and Charles the Bald, and in 876 armed pro-Formosan elements sacked the property of papal followers, seized the keys of Ravenna from the papal *vestararius* and handed them over to the archbishop.[53]

Despite their difficulties, the popes had some success in countering this separatist feeling through the backing of their officials and pro-Roman elements in the exarchate and by holding regular councils in Ravenna, as in 874, 877 and 898. Thus Archbishop Romanus (878–88) was excommunicated for his anti-Roman policy in 881 and failed in his attempt to appoint his successor. However, an important change in the balance of forces occurred towards the close of the ninth century. The rule of the Carolingian emperors was replaced by that of local Italian monarchs, who visited the exarchate more often and held assemblies representing their whole kingdom in Ravenna. As a result the exarchate and the Pentapolis became more integrated into the kingdom of Italy, as is reflected in the dating system of documents from Ravenna from around 898 on. Since royal authority was weak, the main beneficiaries were the archbishops who retained their metropolitan status and great prestige, wealth and patronage networks.[54] By the end of the ninth century, however, the area had lost

[52] Belletzkie (1980).   [53] John VIII, *Fragmenta registri*, no. 62, p. 312.
[54] Fasoli (1979), pp. 106–9. The exact date and significance of the exarchate's incorporation within the kingdom of Italy is the subject of debate. Some ties with Rome remained, as is shown by Archbishop John IX's election as Pope John X (914–28).

much of its traditional Romano-Byzantine character; a centralised administration system had been replaced by family and patrimonial ties between the Ravenna elite and local elements, and dynastic links were beginning to be forged with neighbouring Germanic families from Tuscany and the Po valley.[55]

The nature of the Byzantine legacy in the exarchate is difficult to assess despite the comparative wealth of evidence, furnished especially by Agnellus and the papyrus and parchment documents preserved by the church of Ravenna.[56] The evidence of the documents reveals remarkable continuity in the Greek and Roman names employed, in the use of Romano-Byzantine titles such as *magister militum, dux, tribunus* and consul, in the division and management of land, and, most significantly, in the close relations of the lay military elite with the see of Ravenna. This nexus was cemented through the leasing out of church land on generous terms, a practice deriving from an officially encouraged policy of the imperial period.[57] Paradoxically, clear Greek cultural elements were limited in Ravenna, the residence of the emperor's representative. Although there is some evidence for the continued existence of Greek monasteries after 751, it is very limited compared with Rome, and the liturgical or other influence from the east on the see was slight. Nor is there any trace of the translation activity or literary composition in Greek so evident in Rome.[58] Although Agnellus' work includes a sizeable number of Greek terms, his attitude to the Byzantines is one of contempt, and this view was apparently shared by most of his compatriots.[59] A letter which Patriarch Photios (858–67, 877–86) addressed to the archbishop of Ravenna is likely to have been less a reflection of the traditional links between Ravenna and the east than a desire to cause difficulties for the pope with a prelate known to be independent-minded.[60] Even so, there may have been a vestigial attachment to the eastern empire in certain outlying areas of the exarchate, especially those close to the Byzantine province of Venetia; thus a document from Rovigo near Padua was dated by the regnal years of the Byzantine emperors as late as 826.[61]

[55] Fasoli (1979), pp. 110–11; Curradi (1977).

[56] See Agnel., and also *Die nichtliterarischen lateinischen Papyri*, ed. Tjäder, which includes documents up to 700. The collection known as the *Codex bavarus*, ed. Rabotti, records transactions as early as the seventh century. The parchment documents (rare for the eighth century and before, more numerous for the ninth century) are published in *Chartae Latinae antiquiores*, ed. Cavallo and Nicolaj: for the ninth-century ones, see pt. 54 (Italy XXVI, Ravenna I, 2000) and pt. 55 (Italy XXVII, Ravenna II, 1999).

[57] Brown, T. S. (1979).

[58] Brown, T. S. (1988b), pp. 148–9; Sansterre (1983), I. Translation activity, especially of medical works, had been common in the sixth century.

[59] See for example Agnel., ch. 140, ed. Holder-Egger, p. 369; ed. Mauskopf Deliyannis, p. 317; tr. Mauskopf Deliyannis, p. 264.

[60] Phot., no. 267, ed. Laourdas and Westerink, II, pp. 217–18.

[61] The document is referred to in a Frankish *placitum* of 838: *Placiti del 'Regnum Italiae'*, ed. Manaresi, I, no. 43, p. 142.

VENICE AND ISTRIA

In the early stages of imperial rule in Italy *Venetia et Istria* constituted a single province but at some stage in the seventh century it was divided in two. Istria embraced most of the peninsula, but its northern limits are uncertain, since it came under continual pressure from Lombards, Avars and especially Slavs. Extremely little is known of it during the imperial period, and it fell into Lombard hands for brief periods in or soon after 751 and again between 768 and 772. By 774 it was once more in the eastern emperor's possession, but at some stage in the late eighth century it was conquered by the Franks, possibly at the time of Charlemagne's victory over the Byzantines in southern Italy in 788.[62] It is all the more ironic that the most informative document on the society of Byzantine Italy survives from this obscure region and from the period immediately after imperial rule. In 804 three Frankish *missi* met at Rižana with the patriarch of Grado, the duke of Istria, the local bishops and 172 representatives of the local towns to examine the rights and exactions customary in the times of the Greeks. The resulting report, known as the Plea of Rižana (or Risano) reveals the considerable local power exercised by the landowners and their leaders (*primates*); their attachment to their military offices (such as tribune) and to the titles obtained from the eastern empire (*hypatos* or consul); and the relatively low level of taxes paid to the empire.[63]

Istria's neighbour to the west, Venetia, remained under Byzantine authority and experienced the most dramatic development in our period. The area also presents serious problems because the evidence is scanty and often late and unreliable. The islands of the lagoon from Chioggia in the south-west to Grado in the north-east had received an influx of refugees at the time of the Lombard invasion of 568 and became the predominant element of the Byzantine province of Venetia when the mainland city of Oderzo fell to the Lombards and the residence of the *magister militum* or governor was transferred to Eraclea (also known as Cittanova). The area followed the general pattern of Byzantine Italy, with political and economic power concentrated in the hands of a local elite drawn from the ranks of the imperial garrison but increasingly identified with local interests. Within the islands, however, economic activity must have been based on fishing and local trade as much as agriculture. It was probably as a result of its growing trading role that the duchy was able to make an agreement with the Lombard king Liutprand which defined its boundaries on the mainland.[64] The area's distinctiveness

---

[62] Ferluga (1988), pp. 174–5; Carile (1996). See also above, p. 426.

[63] *Plea of Rižana*, ed. Manaresi, I, no. 17, pp. 50–6; ed. and Italian tr. Petranović and Margetić, pp. 56–69; Guillou (1969), pp. 294–307. The tax paid by nine towns amounted to 344 *solidi mancosi* in addition to levies in kind and labour exacted by the duke and various obligations to the church, over which there was an argument. See also McCormick (1998b), pp. 47–51.

[64] Referred to in *Pactum Lotharii*, ch. 26, p. 135.

was fostered by the existence of its ecclesiastical structures separate from the mainland under the authority of the patriarch of Grado.

According to later tradition, a period of a century and a half of rule by the indigenous nobility of *tribuni* was followed by the election of the first local doge or duke, supposedly in 697 or *c.* 715.[65] In reality this event only occurred in 727, with the election of the Eraclean leader Ursus, and it was part of a more general process. As we have seen, many provinces elected their own *duces* that year as a result of general discontent with the policies of Emperor Leo III (see above, p. 441). The step also turned out not to denote a decisive break with the empire, since Ursus was soon recognised by the Byzantines as an autonomous *dux* with the title of *hypatos*, and the area's continued loyalty to the empire was demonstrated by the help given to the exarch Eutychios in recovering Ravenna in the 730s. As elsewhere, the decline of imperial authority and mounting pressure from the Lombards led to an increase in conflict between local factions. The details of these are obscure, but they appear to have stemmed from rivalries between different families and islands, as in 742 when Malamocco revolted against the capital, Eraclea, and elected as duke Deusdedit, the son of Ursus. These internal pressures were exacerbated by the powerful presence of the Franks in the region from the 770s on. Venetia and Istria were not included in the papal claims to former imperial territories expressed in the 'donations' of Pippin from 754 and 756 (see above, p. 444), but they did figure among the lands promised to Pope Hadrian I by Charlemagne in 774.

Loyalty to Byzantium nevertheless remained paramount, and was reflected in the use of imperial titles and customs. For example, the family of Maurizio Galbaio was probably following imperial practice when the founder's son and later his grandson were coopted as dukes. Meanwhile Frankish power in the region was further enhanced by Charlemagne's takeover of Friuli and Istria and defeat of the Avars, and certain factions found it expedient to side with the new western empire. Such a pro-Frankish group seized power in the person of Obelerius in 802. When Charlemagne recognised Venice as a Frankish fief under his son, Pippin, king of Italy, Nikephoros I (802–11) retaliated by sending a fleet under the command of the *patrikios* Niketas. A compromise was reached whereby Obelerius' position as doge was confirmed and he accepted the title of *spatharios* as an imperial official. A truce between the two empires was signed in 807. However, hostilities broke out again when Obelerius showed renewed signs of disloyalty to the empire and a second Byzantine fleet came into conflict with the Franks. Pippin intervened and sacked several of the settlements of Venice shortly before his death in July 810.

---

[65] Andrea Dandolo, *Chronica*, ed. Pastorello, pp. 105–6; John the Deacon, *Cronaca*, ed. Monticolo, p. 91.

In the face of this crisis the Venetians sank their differences and established a new centre of settlement and administration at Rialto under a
new doge, Agnello Partecipazio (or Particiaco). Local opinion had shifted
decisively in favour of attachment to Byzantium,[66] and Venetia was recognised as Byzantine territory by the treaty agreed between the Frankish
and eastern empires in 812. Venice benefited from its new-found stability to develop into an important emporium – trading in the luxury items
of the east; exporting western timber, slaves, salt and fish; and serving
as the empire's listening post in the west. The growth and sophistication
of Venice's commercial role is reflected in the will of Doge Giustiniano
Partecipazio, who died in 829: in addition to extensive property-holdings,
it lists investments in long-distance trading ventures.[67] Venice's relations
with Byzantium remained cordial, with widespread use of Byzantine titles
and fashions, but in practice the province was increasingly independent.

The doges also wished Venice to enjoy ecclesiastical independence, especially after the suffragan sees of the patriarchate of Grado were placed under
the patriarch of Aquileia by the council of Mantua of 827. In the following
year the body of St Mark was seized in Alexandria by Venetian seamen and
deposited in a new basilica adjoining the ducal basilica in Rialto. The city's
new patron rapidly became a symbol of Venetian pride and independence.

The middle years of the ninth century were a period of both danger
and opportunity for Venice. The Byzantine and western missions to the
Slavs helped open up new areas to Venetian enterprise, but also led to new
tensions which complicated Venice's position as a middleman. Even more
serious was the wave of naval raids launched by the Arabs of North Africa.
Venice's growing naval strength was called upon by the Byzantines to help
combat these attacks on Sicily in 827 and in the Adriatic in the 830s and 840s.
In 840 a treaty was signed with Lothar I, guaranteeing Venice's neutrality,
boundaries and right to trade freely. Frankish recognition of Venice's power
and independence was reflected in confirmations of the agreement in 856
and 880 and by a state visit by Louis II to the city in the former year. At the
same time Venice faced new dangers from Slav disorder and piracy within
its Istrian and Dalmatian spheres of influence and from the reassertion of
Byzantine power in the Adriatic following the reconquest of Dalmatia in
868 and of southern Italy from 876 onwards. Yet Byzantium continued to
recognise the need for Venetian naval assistance, especially when a planned
alliance with the Franks against the Arabs fell through. In 879 an imperial
embassy travelled to Venice to confer upon Doge Ursus I Partecipazio gifts
and the title of *prōtospatharios*. Ursus I's dogeship also saw the creation

---

[66] According to Constantine Porphyrogenitus (*DAI*, ch. 28, pp. 120–1), the Venetians told Pippin
they preferred to be subjects of the emperor of the Romans. The best survey of early medieval Venetia
is now Azzara (1994).
[67] *Documenti relativi alla storia di Venezia*, ed. Cessi, I, no. 53, pp. 93–9.

of *iudices* as magistrates and advisers to curb the doge's authority and the establishment of new bishoprics, including Torcello. From the late ninth century, therefore, many of the characteristic features of medieval Venice were in place, including some distinctive constitutional arrangements, a marked independence in outlook and government, and wide-ranging naval and commercial activities. Yet the city retained its powerful if ambiguous links with the east.

The duchy of Naples included the coast and islands of the Bay of Naples, the Terra di Lavoro inland and the outlying towns of Sorrento, Amalfi and Gaeta. Little is known of its history in the seventh century, and the traditional view that its first local *dux* was Basilius, confirmed by Constans II around 661, is now rejected. Its institutions followed the usual Italian model, with a concentration of power and property in the military elite of the *exercitus*, but its loyalty to the empire was consistently greater than that of the territories to the north, probably because of its maritime links with the east and the need for imperial protection against the constant threat posed by Lombard Benevento. Thus the Neapolitans allowed the exarch Eutychios to disembark in their city in 727, when most of Byzantine Italy was in revolt. The duchy was also sympathetic to the Isaurian policy on images, to the extent that the episcopal see was held by an outright iconoclast, Calvus, between 750 and 762. The duchy was unaffected by the fall of Ravenna in 751, having come under the nominal authority of the *stratēgos* of the theme of Sicily for several decades.

Nevertheless, Naples experienced the same trend towards increased autonomy as other areas, and by 755 it had its first locally elected *dux*, Stephen. After his election as bishop in 767, Stephen was able to pass on the ducal office to his two sons, Gregory and Caesarius, in succession, and then to his son-in-law Theophylact. As in Venice, relations with the empire oscillated considerably, probably as a reflection of the ascendancy of rival factions. While the duchy supported the *stratēgos* of Sicily in opposing papal claims to Campania in 779/80, in 812 Duke Anthimus refused to send his fleet to help his nominal superior, the *stratēgos*, fend off an Arab raid on Ischia. In 818 the citizens of Naples petitioned the *stratēgos* of Sicily to appoint a *dux* to govern them, but in 821 one such imperial appointee was deposed in favour of a candidate from the family of Stephen. However, the decisive stage in the detachment of Naples from the empire came with the Arab invasion of Sicily in 827, when the *stratēgos* was too preoccupied to intervene in the duchy and Naples was left to its own devices to resist the growing pressure from the Arabs by sea and the Lombards on land. As an example of the delicate balancing act required, Duke Andrew employed

Muslim mercenaries in 835 against Prince Sicard of Benevento (833–9) and then gave his allies help in conquering Messina from the empire in 842/3. Although Naples attracted considerable criticism for these opportunistic alliances with the infidel, the strengthened position thus attained enabled Andrew to conclude a favourable treaty with the Lombards in 836 (the *pactum Sicardi*), and in 839 Lombard pressure was for a time alleviated by the civil war which split the Lombard principality into two parts, Benevento and Salerno. Later, in the 840s, Duke Sergius, together with his son, the consul Caesarius, turned against the Arabs and won a series of victories culminating in the battle of Ostia in 849. Later, however, the Neapolitans established friendly relations with the Saracens, perhaps in order to prevent raids from Muslim strongholds such as Taranto. These tactics, while necessary to safeguard the duchy's political survival and commercial interests, drew bitter denunciations from the papacy. Once again outside intervention served to foment internal factional strife. Duke Sergius II was deposed and replaced by his brother, Bishop Athanasius II, in 877. *Realpolitik*, however, obliged the new duke to make a new deal with the Arabs, thus earning excommunication by his former patron, Pope John VIII.

Already in the ninth century Naples began to assume an important role as a centre of translation activity from Greek into Latin, although this reached its height in the tenth century. Other evidence shows that the cultural and economic influence of Byzantium was pervasive. Imports of pottery from the east were numerous, signatures to documents in Greek characters were common and a penchant for Byzantine titles such as consul (*hypatos*) remained strong.[68]

To the north, Gaeta had become increasingly important as a centre of communications after Formia was destroyed by the Arabs and its bishopric transferred to the nearby port in the eighth century. It remained nominally part of the Neapolitan duchy until 839, although in practice it often had to align itself with the papacy, whose territories surrounded it. On occasion Gaeta acted independently of Naples, as when it responded to a request from a *stratēgos* of Sicily for help against Muslim raiding parties.[69] From around 839 Gaeta's greater measure of independence is reflected in the title of *hypatos* held by city leaders such as Docibilis I. Although its continuing ties with the Byzantine empire were reflected in the dating of documents by the regnal years of emperors and by the elite's custom of signing their names in Greek characters, the town was forced to adopt policies favourable to the Muslims. In the 880s Aghlabid raiders were allowed to set up a pirate nest at the mouth of the nearby Garigliano river – a move which provoked bitter denunciation on the part of Pope John VIII.[70]

---

[68] Luzzati Laganà (1983); Brown, T. S. (1988a), p. 34; Arthur (2002).

[69] Leo III, *Epistolae*, no. 6, p. 96.

[70] Merores (1911), esp. p. 15, but see also the comments of von Falkenhausen (1983), p. 348 and Skinner (1992), pp. 353–8.

To the south was the non-Roman settlement of Amalfi, first recorded in 596 as a *castrum* populated by refugees from the Lombards. By the eighth century it was recorded as a naval base used in conflicts with the Lombards, Franks and Arabs, and it assumed increasing importance as a trading centre, while remaining part of the duchy of Naples, perhaps because of the continual pressure it faced from the Lombards. Although its population was temporarily transferred to Salerno after it was sacked by Prince Sicard of Benevento in 839, Amalfi soon after achieved independence from Naples under its own leaders (*comites* and later *praefecturii*). By the late ninth century its tiny territory consisted of a small coastal strip (see fig. 41), the Monti Lattari in the hinterland and the isle of Capri, and a dynasty was established by the *praefecturius* Manso which lasted for seventy years (see below, p. 577). Although the Greek element was never as strong as in Naples and its foreign policy became steadily more independent of the empire, Amalfitan trading links with the east became increasingly important.[71]

THE DUCHIES OF CALABRIA AND OTRANTO

The term Calabria was originally applied to a late Roman civilian province corresponding to the Terra d'Otranto. In the mid-seventh century the imperial possessions underwent a severe crisis with the civilian administration finally breaking down and the Lombard dukes of Benevento capturing large areas. It is likely that, as a result of an administrative reorganisation in the late seventh century, the name was applied to a duchy ruled from Reggio and covering both those areas remaining under Byzantine rule, the Terra d'Otranto and southern Calabria (i.e. the lands south of a line running from the Crati river – to the south of Cosenza – to Amantea on the Tyrrhenian coast).[72] This period marked an important stage in the hellenisation of both areas, probably largely as a result of immigration from Greece and Sicily rather than settlements of refugees from the Muslim invasions further east or official transfer of soldiers or peasants. In the early eighth century Otranto was lost to the Lombards and the term 'duchy of Calabria', which previously included present-day Apulia, was confined to the old civilian province of Bruttium in the south-west toe of Italy, which came under the authority of the *stratēgos* of Sicily. The duchy is mentioned in the *Taktikon Uspensky* (842–3) but does not appear in the *Kletorologion* of Philotheos of 899, presumably because it became the main power base of the *stratēgos* of Sicily, when most of Sicily had fallen to the Arabs.[73] Disappointingly little is

---

[71] Schwarz (1978), especially pp. 16–17.

[72] von Falkenhausen (1978), p. 7; the boundary with the Lombards can be reconstructed from the *divisio* of the principality of Benevento: *Divisio ducatus Beneventani*, ch. 9, ed. Bluhme, p. 222; ed. Martin, p. 205.

[73] *Taktikon Uspensky*, p. 57; see also *ibid.*, pp. 351, 356 (commentary). von Falkenhausen (1978), p. 7, suggests that after 843 Calabria became a *tourma* within the theme of Sicily.

known of the duchy in this period from written sources, but archaeological research has pointed to a move away from settlements on the plains and coast towards hilltop sites and to fairly widespread circulation of eastern goods such as pottery.[74] Only after 885–6, when Lombard Calabria was conquered by Nikephoros Phokas (see above and below, pp. 298, 560) does the position become clearer.

Even less is known of Calabria's imperial neighbour on the heel of Italy, the duchy of Otranto. Otranto and Gallipoli remained Byzantine at the time of the Lombard advances of the late seventh century, but some time after 710 Otranto was lost. It was restored to the empire in 758 by King Desiderius in return for Byzantine help against a rebel duke of Benevento. The case for the area's status as a separate duchy depends on a seal of uncertain date, and the duchy's non-appearance in the *Taktikon Uspensky* (842–3) suggests that at some stage it was reincorporated in the duchy of Calabria.[75] The boundaries of imperial rule are uncertain; the duchy may have been confined to the dioceses which clearly came under the jurisdiction of Constantinople, Gallipoli and Otranto, or it may have included all the Terra d'Otranto including Oria. Excavations have suggested that Otranto was a rich centre, probably thanks to its strategic importance as the main point of entry for imperial troops and officials sent to the west.[76] However, following the swift *reconquista* of Lombard Apulia from 876 the capital became Benevento and later Bari.

SICILY

In radical contrast to the separatism evident in most of the Byzantine territories in the Italian peninsula, Sicily assumed a more central place within the imperial orbit from the seventh century. In the first half of the century it appears to have been a prosperous backwater, secure from the Lombard assaults which devastated much of the mainland, and retaining civil government under a *praitōr* and resilient elements of civilian society. Following the first major raid by the Arabs in 652, repulsed by an expedition led by the exarch Olympius, it assumed a more central role on the political stage. After Constans II's decision to abandon Constantinople in 661 and his unsuccessful campaigns against the Lombards of southern Italy, the imperial court moved to Syracuse (see above, p. 232). Although the emperor was murdered in 668, the island gained new importance as a naval base used to oppose Muslim advances in North Africa, and Justinian II elevated it into a theme in the early 690s. Its *stratēgos* came to assume authority over imperial territory in southern Italy, and after the fall of the exarchal

---

[74] Noyé (1988); Noyé, (1998), pp. 233–43; Dalarun (ed.) (1991).
[75] See also von Falkenhausen (1978), p. 9.
[76] Brown, T. S. (1992), pp. 27–30. On Apulia in general, see Martin (1993).

government in 751 he came to play a leading role in diplomatic negotiations with the Franks, the Lombards and the papacy.[77]

The effects of these changes were mixed. The influx of officials and soldiers from the east accelerated a wide-scale process of hellenisation. The origins of this are uncertain, but there is evidence that a dual Greek and Latin culture existed in the Roman period and that the Greek substrata were reinforced by immigration, most notably from Greece and the Balkans, by the early seventh century. The church remained under the jurisdiction of the see of Rome, but the hellenisation, reflected in the Greek monks encountered by eastern visitors such as Maximus the Confessor and by the Greeks from Sicily who ascended the papal throne, is in sharp contrast to the impression of Latin predominance given in the letters of Pope Gregory the Great (590–604). On the other hand, the militarisation and decentralisation involved in theme organisation must have served to strengthen local elements. One reflection of this was the revolt of the *stratēgos* Sergios in 717–18 (see above, p. 440): he responded to the Arab siege of Constantinople by crowning one of his subordinates, Basil Onomagoulos, as emperor. However, after his defeat of the Arabs, Leo III had no difficulty in quelling the rebellion, executing Basil and forcing Sergios to seek refuge with the Lombards across the Straits of Messina.

The new emperor was prompt to recognise the economic as well as political and military value of the island. He ordered that the vast revenues previously paid to the Roman church should be transferred to the imperial fisc, and Sicily was one of the areas transferred from papal jurisdiction to that of the patriarch of Constantinople (see above, p. 285). Partly as a result of these moves, the Latin element virtually disappeared and the process of hellenisation continued apace, as is demonstrated by a number of important saints' *Lives* and the prominent Greek scholars and churchmen from Sicily of the eighth and ninth centuries, for example Gregory Asbestas, Joseph the Hymnographer, Constantine the Sicilian and the patriarch Methodios (843–7). The dominant Greek culture, with its strong cosmopolitan links with the capital, appears to have been largely confined to elite groups and was limited in its local impact and character. Although several iconodules were sent into exile on Sicily and its neighbouring islands, there appears to have been no large-scale migration as a result of iconoclast persecution. In general the iconoclast crisis seems to have had little impact on the island, apart from the execution of the *stratēgos* Antiochos together with eighteen other iconodule officials in Constantinople in 766, and the appointment of the strongly iconoclastic Theodore Krithinos as archbishop of Syracuse during the second wave of the movement.[78] Rather, the island's attachment to icons and to Greek saints helped to bind it more closely to the empire.

---

[77] See now Nichanian and Prigent (2003). [78] Gouillard (1961).

Nevertheless, unrest was clearly growing by the eighth century, although the pattern of this was different from the mainland. One likely factor here was economic decline. Although a full picture is only gradually emerging from archaeological surveys,[79] the island's prosperity was probably adversely affected by the increasing frequency of Arab raids and by the severe plague of 745–6 (see above, p. 256).

The island's ties with the centre were so strong that revolts seem to have reflected personal ambition, or the political and religious conflicts of the capital, rather than local separatism. A case in point is the crisis of 781, when the *stratēgos* Elpidios was accused by the empress Irene of conspiring with her brother-in-law, and the Sicilian *exercitus* prevented his arrest. Irene responded by sending an expedition, which defeated Elpidios' forces and compelled him to seek refuge in Africa, where he had himself crowned emperor with Arab support.[80] Unlike the mainland provinces of Italy, Sicily lacked one dominant political and cultural centre analogous to Ravenna, Rome or Naples, or an independent-minded military elite with a strong sense of local collective identity and a tradition of autonomy. As a result, the population's reaction to the upheavals of the 820s was divided and in some respects passive.

Discontent broke out early in the decade, possibly sparked off by the revolt of Thomas the Slav in the east. An attempt by Michael II (820–829) to raise taxation from the island triggered a rising by an anti-imperial faction. By 826 this faction was led by the ambitious commander of the Sicilian fleet, the turmarch Euphemios, who had led successful raids against North Africa.[81] When the *stratēgos* Constantine moved to arrest him, probably for his disloyalty rather than as result of the romantic excesses ascribed to him by later legend,[82] Euphemios responded by seizing Syracuse, proclaiming himself emperor and then defeating and killing Constantine in Catania. However, some of Euphemios' supporters then switched their loyalty to the imperial government and he was forced to flee to Africa, where the Aghlabid amir Ziyadat Allah I recognised his title and granted him a fleet to attack the island. In June 827 the predominantly Arab force landed at the western port of Mazara and soon afterwards defeated the Byzantine *stratēgos* Plato. Despite fierce resistance and some Byzantine successes, the Arabs gradually extended their hold over the island, conquering Palermo in 831, Cefalù in 857 and Enna in 859. A decisive blow was struck when the capital, Syracuse, fell after a nine-month siege in 878 and its population was massacred.[83] A few outposts, however, survived into the tenth century.

---

[79] See Wickham (2005), p. 737 and references in n. 91.
[80] For details, see Treadgold (1988), pp. 66–7.   [81] Alexander (1973), pp. 9–14.
[82] Later accounts claim that Euphemios had abducted his niece from a nunnery and forced her into marriage.
[83] For a contemporary, if melancholy and impersonal account, see Theodosios the Monk, *Letter*, ed. Zuretti.

SARDINIA

The worst-documented Byzantine province in the Italian theatre is Sardinia. In the seventh century it had close administrative ties with the exarchate of Africa, although ecclesiastically it came under the see of Rome. It suffered from Lombard naval attacks, but these appear to have been successfully repulsed, to judge from an inscription attributing victories to the emperor, whether he was Constans II, Constantine IV or even Constantine V.[84] After the fall of the exarchate of Carthage in 698, imperial rule over the island became increasingly nominal. However, Byzantine-style institutions and Greek titles survived in the eighth and ninth centuries. By the latter century numerous attacks from the Arabs further weakened links with Constantinople and power became concentrated in the hands of locally appointed officials (*iudices*).

CONCLUSION

Over the two centuries Byzantium's position in Italy had turned virtually full circle, from the outwardly hopeful but in practice precarious position of 680, to the verge of a new period of power and influence in the late ninth century. Despite, and in some measure because of, the short-lived political and ecclesiastical peace which prevailed at the beginning, discontent and separatist feeling had grown rapidly. As a result of the election of local military leaders as *duces*, the power of the emperor and his representative, the exarch, had become marginal from the late 720s. The fall of Ravenna in 751 was only one stage in the fragmentation of the Byzantine territories, but it did promote distinct development in each area. Only in the theme of Sicily and the associated duchies of Calabria and Otranto was traditional imperial control effective, assisted by a steady process of hellenisation. In Venetia and the various component parts of the duchy of Naples, nominal loyalty to the empire survived side by side with growing economic sophistication and political independence under leaders chosen locally from the traditional military elite. Elsewhere, as in the exarchate, the Pentapolis and duchy of Rome, the predominant power came into the hands of senior churchmen, but these had to work out a *modus vivendi* with lay aristocratic families, and with the Frankish rulers of the kingdom of Italy after 774. In each area, however, developments were conditioned by the decentralisation underway as early as the seventh century; and distinctive traditions and institutions, more often Roman than strictly Byzantine, remained powerful, as can be seen in the persistence of titles, names and legal institutions.

If Byzantium's power and influence were in decline for most of the period, it remained a force to be reckoned with, as can be seen in its successful

---

[84] Mazzarino (1940). A dating to Constantine V's reign has been proposed by Fiori (2001). In general on Sardinia, see Spanu (1998).

defence of its interests in Venetia, and the preoccupation of both the Franks and the popes with their relations with the empire. In the economic, artistic and literary spheres, Byzantium's impact was as considerable as ever, and was channelled through Rome as much as through the nominally Byzantine centres. Byzantine naval power was always significant, and it is this which especially enabled the empire to come into its own again as a player on the Italian scene in the second half of the ninth century. Byzantium's position was reinforced by the devastation of the Arab raids; by disenchantment with Frankish political and military weakness; and by the aggressive yet pragmatic policy pursued by Michael III (842–67) and Basil I (867–86). The reconquest of much of the Lombard territories in Apulia, Calabria and Lucania, including Bari and Taranto (retaken in 876 and 880 respectively) ushered in a new era of Byzantine domination in southern Italy.

CHAPTER 12

THE MIDDLE BYZANTINE ECONOMY
(600–1204)

MARK WHITTOW

INTRODUCTION

The Byzantine economy is an important subject on a number of grounds. It is arguably the key to the history of the Byzantine state, society and culture; it forms part of the picture of a transition from the ancient world to the middle ages – and part of the debate as to whether those are meaningful concepts at all; it is a test case for whether we should be talking about particular regional economies, such as the 'Byzantine economy', or whether we should instead be thinking in terms of a general pre-modern Mediterranean economy, of which the economic activities of the Byzantine world were merely a part. It is a subject, too, upon which there was once considerable agreement among scholars, but there is now some uncertainty. The recent publication of *The economic history of Byzantium*, a substantial multi-authored work in three volumes, has been a major achievement and it serves as an important reference work and body of data; it does not represent an end to debate.[1]

THE BYZANTINE ECONOMY: LATE ANTIQUITY TO 1204

All that said, there are considerable areas of scholarly agreement and it is the aim of this section to set these out. It is also worth saying that the volume and quality of evidence available has improved markedly, particularly since the 1980s. The study of Byzantine coins, the excavation of Byzantine sites, including underwater archaeology, the study of pottery types and the publication of texts and associated linguistic studies have all made great advances. But it is also important to recognise that Byzantium is not a well-documented society. Late antique Egypt provides an exception, but it was lost to the Muslims by the mid-seventh century. The rich materials from the Cairo Genizah will be referred to later, and the vivid picture they give of Mediterranean commerce in the eleventh and twelfth centuries is a reminder of what we are missing. The masses of largely monastic documentation that underpin so much of traditional economic history in the

---

[1] *EHB*; see now also Laiou and Morrisson (2007).

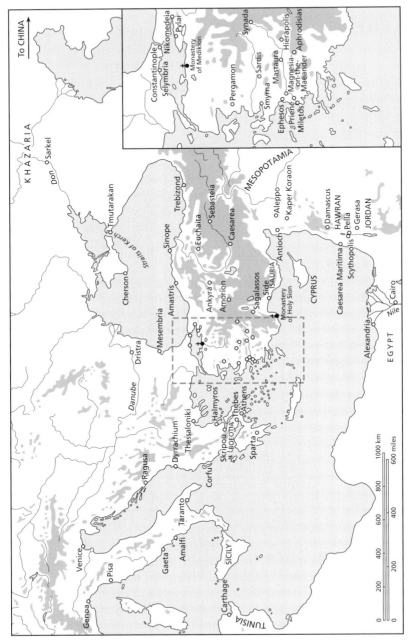

Map 22 The Byzantine economic world

To CHINA

KHAZARIA

Sarkel
Don

Tmutarakan
Straits of Kerch
Cherson

Sinope
Amastris
Trebizond
Euchaita
Sebasteia
Caesarea

MESOPOTAMIA

Ankyra
Amorion

Aleppo
Kaper Koraon

Side
ISAURIA
Sagalassos
Antioch
Monastery
of Holy Sion

Damascus
HAWRAN
Pella
Gerasa
JORDAN
Scythopolis

Caesarea Maritima

CYPRUS

Alexandria
Cairo
Nile

EGYPT

Mesembria
Dristra
Danube

Ragusa

Venice
Pisa
Gaeta
Amalfi
Taranto

SICILY

Carthage
TUNISIA

Genoa

Dyrrachium
Thessaloniki
Corfu
Skripou
Halmyros
Thebes
BOEOTIA
Athens
Sparta

0   200   400   600   800   1000 km
0   200   400   600 miles

Constantinople
Selymbria
Nikomedeia
Pylai
Monastery
of Medikion

Pergamon

Sardis

Smyrna
Mastaura
Magnesia
on-the-
Maeander
Ephesos
Priene
Miletos

Synada

Hierapolis
Aphrodisias

west do not exist for the Byzantine world. After 1204, Latin documentation will make a significant difference, not only by reason of its quantity, but because we are talking of new types of evidence: commercial documents preserved in secular archives. This material begins to appear before 1204, but its real contribution comes later (see below, pp. 843–4).

This would not matter so much if the lack of documents were offset more fully by archaeology. Recent advances in our understanding of the economy of western Europe during this period have come as much from this direction as any other. Pottery studies, for example, have shown that even remote villages were involved in networks of exchange. Pollen studies have shown both the early date and ultimately the permanent effects of medieval agricultural expansion. Similar work has been done for the Byzantine world, but it lags behind what has been achieved in western Europe.[2] Even so, there are considerable areas of scholarly agreement and the story of Byzantine economic history over the last thirty years has been one of solid achievement.

The late antique inheritance

A once widespread picture of late antique decline has been replaced by an appreciation of the wealth and complexity of the late antique economy. Throughout the territories of the Roman empire in Egypt, the Levant, Asia Minor, the Aegean world and Africa, the general picture is of a monetarised and commercial world, where agricultural expansion in some areas had reached its pre-modern peak. Much of the Balkans and Italy are exceptions to this rosy picture. Military insecurity in the one case and the aftermath of the Justinianic reconquest in the other appear to have had disastrous effects (see above, pp. 214–15). But these are exceptions. The rule in the eastern empire is of late antique prosperity.

The basis of this rosy picture lies in archaeology. In particular, Georges Tchalenko's publication between 1953 and 1958 of the extraordinary villages and monasteries of the limestone massif between Antioch and Aleppo in northern Syria compelled historians into a new view of the late antique economy.[3] These for the most part fifth- and sixth-century structures, that now strike us as vivid testimony to a prosperous rural world, had been partly published by the Princeton expeditions at the beginning of the century. But their significance was overlooked. At that date they were seen as material for art history rather than as evidence for the economy. Tchalenko was explicit. His book is illustrated with village plans that mark fields, pasture and tree crops, and his thesis is that the rise and fall of the economy of the limestone massif is explained by the production of olive oil for export; but

---

[2] Pals (1987); Durand (1998); Geyer (2002); Argant (2003).   [3] Tchalenko (1953–8).

it took until the 1970s or even the 1980s before the message sank in. Their
eyes opened, archaeologists and historians have come to see the evidence
for late antique prosperity everywhere.[4]

Recent work throughout the Levant, in Libya and along Turkey's southern shore has produced more well-preserved sites to match those of the
limestone massif. Tchalenko's villages now seem part of a pattern and
exceptional only to the extent that the recent remoteness of these limestone
hills has saved the stones from modern reuse. Survey projects that draw
on newly gained knowledge of late antique pottery types to identify settlements where no standing remains survive have made it clear that fifth- and
sixth-century Syria, Palestine, North Africa and parts of Greece too, shared
in the rural prosperity.[5]

Towns, too, have been approached in a new light. Rich citizens of late
antiquity did not build theatres, public baths or gymnasia, in the same way
that their ancestors had in the second or even third century AD, but they did
build churches, houses, private baths and city walls. They spent money on
marble and mosaic. If one judges late antique urbanism by the standards of
the richest sites of the first century AD, it may appear a fallen world; by other
standards, those of the long-term history of urbanism in the Middle East
or Mediterranean, for example, it appears thriving.[6] Hierapolis in Phrygia,
now famous as Pamukkale, a key site of the Turkish tourist industry, is
a case in point. In AD 60 the city was destroyed by an earthquake and
then lavishly rebuilt with imperial funding. In the mid-fourth century an
earthquake struck again. This time the emperors were not interested. The
city was rebuilt from local resources. Columns were patched and re-erected,
damaged buildings made good. Compared with the first-century work it is
a come-down; in the long-term history of Anatolian urbanism, late antique
Hierapolis appears an example of robust local prosperity.[7]

New knowledge of late antique pottery types has already been mentioned as a tool for survey projects, but in its own right this knowledge
has transformed our picture of the late antique economy. We can now
identify the amphorae that carried oil and wine around the Mediterranean
and the distinctive forms of red-slip pottery that went on the same boats
and so can be treated as trace elements for goods not carried in amphorae.
Tchalenko is now generally thought to have overstated the dependence
of the limestone massif on the production of olive oil for export, but a
lively Mediterranean exchange economy is an undoubted fact. The best-
known types of red-slip pottery are those made in Tunisia (African red-slip)

    [4] Foss (1995), pp. 213–23.
    [5] Recent surveys include Ward-Perkins (2000a), pp. 315–32; Ward-Perkins (2000b), pp. 350–61;
Morrisson and Sodini (2002); Chavarría and Lewit (2004); Wickham (2005), pp. 443–65; Foss (1994).
    [6] Recent surveys include Ward-Perkins (1998), pp. 403–9; Lavan (2001); Wickham (2005), pp. 609–
35.
    [7] Whittow (2001), pp. 140–2.

and western Turkey (Phocaean red-slip).[8] They are found throughout the Mediterranean basin and beyond. More recently, Sagalassos in west-central Anatolia has been identified as a major centre of red-slip pottery production too. The implications are intriguing. The city of Sagalassos is separated from the sea by 100 kilometres and a mountain range. What else was the Sagalassos region exporting that involved its pottery in a complex network of exchanges across these roads to the wider world? Timber, pitch and wool, either as a raw material or as finished cloth, have all been suggested. Whatever the answer, the Sagalassos pottery is proof that late antique trade was not bound to the shores of the Mediterranean and its immediate hinterland. The vitality of the late antique economy was a far-reaching phenomenon.[9]

Coinage tells the same story. Since the fourth century the empire's monetary system had been based on the gold *solidus* or *nomisma*, supplemented by a copper coinage, based since 498 on the *follis*, whose value fluctuated against that of the gold coin. A *nomisma* was a coin of high value used for paying salaries and making capital purchases. Day-to-day payments involved *folleis*, and it is the ordinariness of late antique copper coins which attracts attention. Stray copper coins are common finds all over the empire and on all sorts of sites, villages as well as cities like Ephesos, Antioch, or Constantinople itself. This was a world where money was a normal part of almost everyone's lives.[10]

Silver was not minted in the late antique east. But it was an important part of the late antique economy. Made into dishes and bowls, jugs and lamp-stands and marked with date stamps that guaranteed its precious metal content, silver was a vital means of storing and displaying wealth. What is striking is the ordinariness of so much late antique silver. There are stunning fifth- and sixth-century silver treasures, but many such objects clearly belonged to people who did not rank among the super rich. The church silver from Kaper Koraon in the limestone massif, or that from the monastery of Holy Sion in south-western Turkey, make the same point as the Sagalassos pottery, or the copper coins.[11] The late antique economy was doing well, for a comparatively large number of people.

The 'dark age'

If the idea of late antique prosperity in the east has become generally accepted, so too has that of the seventh century marking the onset of a 'dark age', at least in the Byzantine world. Those areas fortunate enough to have been conquered by the Muslims prospered. In Syria, Palestine and

---

[8] The classic study of this material is Hayes (1972).   [9] Poblome and Waelkens (2003), pp. 185–6.
[10] Morrisson and Sodini (2002), pp. 212–19.
[11] Boyd and Mundell Mango (eds.) (1992); Mundell Mango (1986).

Egypt, the picture appears very much one of business as usual. Not just for the inhabitants of Damascus which became the new Islamic capital (see above, p. 221), but for many provincial cities too the seventh century was a 'good' period. The buildings, public and private, the coinage, the pottery and the small finds from such well-excavated sites as Pella and Gerasa (Jerash) in Jordan, or Scythopolis (Bet Shean/Baysan) and Caesarea Maritima in Israel tell a clear story. For the villagers of the limestone massif too, recent work has done much to show that life carried on much as before, and field survey projects throughout the region give the same picture.[12] But for the rump of the Roman east, those territories that stayed under the rule of Constantinople and made up the world of Byzantium, this period was grim. Anatolia and the remaining territories in Greece and the Balkans experienced recession on a scale that justifies the description 'the collapse of the ancient economy'.

The evidence is seemingly incontrovertible and rests on the same sorts of indices that have been used to show the dynamism and vitality of the late antique economy: buildings, pottery and coinage. In a series of seminal publications Clive Foss looked at the evidence coming from a number of excavated ancient cities in Turkey. At Pergamon, Ephesos, Sardis, Magnesia-on-the-Maeander, Priene, Miletos and Aphrodisias on the west coast, at Side on the south coast and from Ankyra in the interior of Anatolia the same picture emerged. A centuries-old urban economy came to a halt. The construction of public buildings, which in late antiquity may have shifted from theatres and baths to churches, was now limited to defensive walls and minimal repairs. The amphorae and red-slip pottery characterising late antique sites disappear – to be replaced by local, hand-made products. Copper coins, the loose change of late antique urban life, similarly vanish. The graphs of stray coin finds on these sites make the message plain. Once common, their number falls to almost nothing for the seventh and eighth centuries. Ephesos, one of the great cities of the late antique east, contracted to a walled settlement around the harbour. The decline of Sardis was starker still. The seventh century saw it transformed into a hilltop fortress, with a few knots of primitive dwellings on the plain beneath (fig. 31a). More or less the same can be said for the other sites too. Hierapolis, the city that had recovered robustly from a fourth-century earthquake, was struck again in the seventh century. There was no rebuilding this time. Hierapolis survived as a scatter of very basic farmhouses.[13]

Even Constantinople appears not to have been immune. There was certainly more coinage available in the imperial capital. A graph of stray coin

[12] On Syria, see Foss (1997); Walmsley (2007); on Palestine and Arabia: Tsafrir and Foerster (1994); Zeyadeh (1994); Walmsley (2000); Walmsley (2005); Hamarneh (2003); on Egypt, see Wickham (2005), pp. 132–44.
[13] Foss (1975); Foss (1976); Foss (1977a); Foss (1977b); Foss (1979a); Foss (1996b); Brandes (1989); Brubaker and Haldon (2001), pp. 146–56; Wickham (2005), pp. 626–35.

Figure 31a The Byzantine hilltop fortress of Sardis, viewed from the Temple of Artemis

finds from the city-centre excavation of the church of St Polyeuktos shows a rate of coin loss that continued at a steady level right through these centuries. Similarly, although in Constantinople as elsewhere late antique pottery types had disappeared by the end of the seventh century, what replaced them is much clearer here. Constantinopolitan white ware, a type of glazed pottery made from local clay, appears in the seventh century to fill the gap left by the end of the red-slip tradition.[14] Yet, even in the capital there is no doubting the basic trend. Late antique Constantinople was a boom town with a major building industry, capable of carrying out such huge projects as the long-distance water supply of the city, six kilometres of the Theodosian land walls, and 45 kilometres of the Anastasian long walls of Thrace, as well as erecting Justinian's massive church of St Sophia in under five years. Projects like this, which in turn are only a fraction of the total number of houses, palaces, churches, cisterns, colonnades and monuments put up during these years, required brick production on an industrial scale. Recent work on the stamp markings of Constantinopolitan bricks has shown as much.[15] All this came to a halt in the seventh century. For the following two centuries one has the impression of a huge salvage site. The paltry new building-work done in these years employed reclaimed bricks and marble

---

[14] Hendy (1986); Harrison and Hayes (1986–92), II, pp. 12–18.   [15] Bardill (2004), I, pp. 28–39.

Figure 31b Marble column drums, probably from the Temple of Artemis, reused for the walls of the Byzantine hilltop fortress at Sardis

and was decorated with reused mosaic cubes. Medieval Constantinople, like medieval Rome, would seem to have been living amidst the ruins left by giants.[16]

Recent work at Sagalassos tells the same story. The prosperous city of late antiquity came to an end in the seventh century. The tradition of public building and the Sagalassan pottery industry stopped. Hannelore Vanhaverbeke's survey shows that neither the city nor the surrounding countryside were deserted; rather, life continued, but with fewer people and on a simpler scale. Pollen analysis suggests the disappearance of olives as a major crop, a decline in cereal production, the spread of woodland and perhaps a shift to pastoralism. What we seem to see is a society and economy top-sliced: deserted by its elites, leaving a poorer, tattier, rural world.[17]

[16] Mango (1990), pp. 51–62; Magdalino (1996a), pp. 17–50.
[17] Vanhaverbeke and Waelkens (2003), pp. 285–315; Vermoere *et al.* (2003); Vanhaverbeke *et al.* (2004).

The middle Byzantine revival

By the tenth century at latest it is clear that the Mediterranean economy was reviving and, equally, that the Byzantine world shared in this process. Using the same indices that plotted the decline of the late antique economy – buildings, pottery, coinage, settlement surveys and pollen analysis – a new prosperity can be seen emerging.

One rough-and-ready index is provided by church-building. While there is very little to show for the seventh and eighth centuries, from the ninth century onwards the numbers of urban and rural churches rise and continue to go up through the tenth, eleventh and twelfth centuries. Byzantine church architecture achieves its classical form during these years, characterised by small domed buildings, their interiors covered in wall-paintings or mosaic, their exteriors enlivened by decorative brickwork.[18] Similarly Byzantine glazed pottery, jars and amphorae become much more common. Likewise with coinage: the graphs of stray coin finds that 'flatline' for the seventh and eighth centuries take off again from the ninth century onwards, slowly at first, but on a steepening gradient. By the eleventh century, stray finds of copper coins are commonplace.[19] Pollen analysis and patterns of alluviation can also be brought into play. The clearest pictures to date come from Greece and Crete, where from the ninth century onwards tree pollens decline and those from plants associated with agriculture and deforestation go up; a cycle of erosion and the silting-up of coastal plains appears to have been triggered by growing exploitation of fragile hill-slopes.[20]

Survey projects in central and southern Greece, on Cyprus and Crete and now in Turkey too, all point towards middle Byzantine rural growth. Everywhere there are more sites with more things; and the more we can identify middle Byzantine pottery types, the more obvious does this trend appear.[21] Cappadocia is perhaps the most striking example, since there the rock-cut churches, houses, store-rooms and water-systems actually survive as visible structures and the churches can be dated by their wall-paintings. New caves were being dug in the later ninth century. Numbers increase through the tenth, and the region was clearly thriving in the eleventh.[22] Towns follow the same pattern. The excavation of middle Byzantine towns may not have revealed anything very photogenic, but the houses, churches, workshops, alleys, yards, cisterns and rubbish dumps

---

[18] Mango (1976).   [19] Spieser (1991); François and Spieser (2002); Dark (2001); Morrisson (2002).
[20] On Greece, see Bellier et al. (1986), p. 104; van Andel et al. (1986), p. 122; Atherden and Hall (1994), pp. 118–20; Zangger et al. (1997), pp. 594–5; on Crete, see Atherden and Hall (1999), p. 190.
[21] Projects include those on Greece: Cavanagh et al. (1996–2002); Bintliff (1996); Bintliff (2000); on Cyprus: Given and Knapp (2003); on Crete: Watrous et al. (2004); Nixon et al. (2000); on Turkey: Baird (2000).
[22] Thierry (2002); Ousterhout (2006).

of Athens, Corinth and Sparta in Greece, Amorion, Aphrodisias, Pergamon and Sardis in Turkey show much more happening than had been
the case in the seventh century. The story of Byzantine Constantinople is
obscured by the fact that modern Istanbul lies on top of it, and the record
of urban archaeology in the city is patchy at best; but the basic trend shows
through.[23]

Written sources confirm this picture. Merchants, craftsmen and markets
are a commonplace in middle Byzantine texts. The *Book of the eparch*, dating
from the late ninth or early tenth century, regulates the commercial world
of Constantinople. We hear about guilds and money-dealers, merchants
coming with silk from Syria and the trade that brought sheep, pigs and cattle
to feed the city. Much of this trade in livestock had its roots in Anatolia.
In the eleventh century, John Mauropous described his see of Euchaita in
Anatolia as the centre for an important annual livestock market. One of
the termini for the drove-roads heading to the imperial city was Pylai on
the Gulf of Nikomedeia. Leo, metropolitan of Synada, banned from the
capital in the late tenth century, could grumble that there was an express
service for animals to the imperial city, but not for him. Boats appear in
documents from the monasteries of Mount Athos, as do shops, acquired
as investments. Jewish merchant communities are known, not just from
Constantinople, but from Mastaura, a small town in western Turkey, 100
kilometres from the sea. The *Life of Metrios* describes the saint picking up
a bag of gold coins dropped by a merchant, heading for market in the next
small Paphlagonian town. Agricultural expansion, too, is well attested. The
Athos archives talk of the opening up of new land and the planting of
new vineyards and olive groves. Michael Psellos talks about doing much
the same for the monastery of Medikion which he had acquired on the
shore of the Sea of Marmara. Eustathios Boilas' will shows him opening
up extensive new farmland near the empire's eleventh-century borders.[24]
These references could easily be multiplied, but to count them up would
have no statistical value. They are cited as examples of the ordinary, and to
illustrate the fact that in town and country, commerce, manufacture and
agriculture, the middle Byzantine empire appears to have been a prosperous
world.

[23] Bouras (2002); Magdalino (1996a), pp. 51–90.
[24] *Eparch*, II–III, V, XV, ed. and German tr. Koder, pp. 84–91, 94–7, 122–5; tr. Freshfield, pp. 10–
15, 19–20, 38–9 (repr. pp. 230–5, 239–40, 258–9); John Mauropous, *Quae . . . supersunt*, no. 180, ed.
de Lagarde, p. 135; Leo of Synada, *Correspondence*, ed. and tr. Vinson, no. 54, pp. 86–7; on Athos
boats, see *Actes du Protaton*, ed. Papachryssanthou, no. 8, pp. 226–7; *Actes de Lavra*, ed. Lemerle *et
al.*, I, no. 55, pp. 282–7; on shops: Oikonomides (1972); on Jews at Mastaura: Reinach (1924); *Greek
Jewish texts from the Cairo Genizah*, ed. and tr. de Lange, no. 1, pp. 1–10; Barnes and Whittow (1993),
pp. 130–1; on Metrios: *Synaxarion of Constantinople*, cols. 721–2; on land clearance: *Actes de Xénophon*,
ed. Papachryssanthou, I, no. 1, pp. 70, 72; *Actes de Lavra*, ed. Lemerle *et al.*, I, no. 26, p. 178; Michael
Psellos, *Letters*, ed. Sathas, no. 29, pp. 263–5; Eustathios Boilas, *Testament*, ed. Lemerle, pp. 21–2. See
also below, pp. 532–3, 673–4.

During the later decades of the eleventh century the empire suffered a profound and prolonged crisis. By the later 1080s most of Anatolia had slipped from imperial control, the south Italian provinces were lost, and it appeared likely that the Balkan provinces would go the same way. Under Alexios I Komnenos (1081–1118), his son and grandson, the empire pulled back from the brink, but much was lost for good (see below, pp. 610–12, 629–46).

The crisis' economic consequences are palpable. The Cappadocian rock-cut building boom came to an end; in the central Anatolian theme of the Anatolikoi, the bustling – if not very smart – eleventh-century town of Amorion survived only as a small village, the former cathedral becoming a storehouse and stable.[25] Cappadocia and the Anatolikoi were lost to the Turks, but the effects were no less profound in what remained of imperial territory. Constantinople as a centre of demand and population inevitably dominated the Byzantine economy more fully than it had done before; at the same time, even if not severed by a strict frontier, the imperial city was now separated from much of its natural hinterland. The Anatolian drove-roads, the livestock markets, the new farms of Eustathios Boilas' eastern estates would never be Byzantine territory again.

The loss of territory entailed loss of tax revenue. The empire had until now paid its servants in gold coin, in an annual ceremony that saw the highest earners drag bags of gold coin across the palace floor. This cash fuelled demand for land, services and goods. The system was showing signs of strain under Isaac I Komnenos (1057–9), but under Nikephoros III Botaneiates (1078–81) it went bankrupt and under Alexios I Komnenos was permanently pruned. The Byzantine state still raised taxes and still paid some of its servants in gold coin; but it could no longer do so for them all. The twelfth-century empire saw a great deal more tax farming, in cash and kind; and many more of the state's servants were now rewarded with land not gold.[26]

Yet, although in some respects these years of crisis were a watershed, in others they were clearly not. As Michael Hendy pointed out,[27] in those areas remaining under Byzantine rule (in other words Greece, the Balkans and, after the reconquests of the early twelfth century, most of the coastlands of Asia Minor) the tenth- and eleventh-century trend seems to have continued, if anything on an increased scale. Hierapolis has been cited twice already, as an example of late antique provincial prosperity and as one of subsequent urban collapse. Growing again from the ninth century on, it was in the twelfth century very much in the empire's 'wild east', a frontier territory where a deacon could be described as an expert sheep-rustler and Turkish raiders could be seen from the city walls. Yet even here the ruins

[25] Lightfoot *et al.* (1998), pp. 325–6.   [26] Oikonomides (1997a), pp. 207–10; Harvey (2003).
[27] Hendy (1970).

of the ancient baths were reoccupied as workshops for potters and black-smiths, and excavation has uncovered quantities of good-quality glazed pottery for which there was clearly a market.[28] Similar evidence could be cited from town and country, from all parts of what was left of Byzantine territory. Despite the changes brought about by the late eleventh-century crisis, Byzantium did not enter a renewed 'dark age'. Rather, the evidence points to the twelfth century as actually the peak of the middle Byzantine revival.

The coming of the Latins

The other uncontroversial story of the Byzantine economy is that of the Latin take-over of the Mediterranean. Latin sailors, traders and travellers came from the west to Byzantium throughout the period and Michael McCormick's recent collection of data on eighth- and ninth-century Mediterranean travellers would suggest that even in the 'dark age' they did so in significant numbers.[29] But by the mid-twelfth century it is clear that the Latin presence was on a new scale and a large proportion of Byzantium's internal and external trade was in Italian hands. A crucial factor in this take-over were the treaties made by Alexios I Komnenos and his successors with first the Venetians, then the Genoese and Pisans, offering commercial privileges in exchange for military support. The terms varied, but essentially those so favoured gained a 10 per cent reduction in costs against their competitors, including of course their indigenous Byzantine competitors. No wonder that by the second half of the century the pro-visioning trade of Constantinople was largely in Italian hands and with it much of the carrying-trade of the Aegean.[30] Halmyros, on the Aegean coast in central Greece, is not even mentioned before 1108, but thereafter the fact that Venetian, Pisan and Genoese merchants had made it their base for buying Thessaly's agricultural produce, above all grain, ensured its rapid growth at the expense of older regional centres.[31] Further south, Thebes tells a similar story. By the mid-1140s this hitherto unremarkable provincial town had become a major centre for the production of high-quality silk cloth, so much so that in 1147 it was sacked by the forces of Roger II of Sicily (1130–54) and its expert silk-workers taken as booty. Despite this, the town soon recovered and by 1162, when the Jewish traveller Benjamin of Tudela was there, its silk industry seems to have been thriving as ever. On one level the prosperity of middle Byzantine Thebes is just another example of what

[28] NC, ed. van Dieten, I, p. 197; tr. Magoulias, p. 111; Böhlendorf-Arslan (2004), I, pp. 258–60; Şimşek (1995).
[29] McCormick (2001), pp. 123–8.
[30] Laiou (2002a), pp. 749–54; Magdalino (1993a), pp. 142–50; Lilie (1984b).
[31] Harvey (1989), pp. 221–2; Koder and Hild (1976), pp. 170–1.

was described above: a prosperity which reached out into the provinces; but it is clearly more than that. The silk industry was a particularly high-value business that needed a stable market of wealthy consumers. Provincial aristocrats and clergy no doubt wore silk, but the chief centre of consumption in the Byzantine world was inevitably Constantinople. The rise of this particular industry in Thebes, some 600 kilometres from the imperial city, therefore suggests its chief market was not Constantinople, but the west.[32]

The rise of the Latins certainly does not mean that there were no Byzantine merchants; but by the end of the twelfth century, the Italians had taken a commanding position in the Byzantine economy. The rulers of Genoa, Pisa, and above all Venice, drew large profits from the eastern trade. Many of them spent much of their lives in Byzantine territory, either in the privileged Italian enclaves along the Golden Horn in Constantinople, or in places like Halmyros or Thebes. They built family houses and churches, where they buried their relations.[33] Like the British East India Company in the eighteenth century, they had not come to conquer, but by the end of the twelfth century they had too much invested to leave its management in wayward local hands.

INTERPRETING THE EVIDENCE: DOUBTS AND DISAGREEMENTS

So far, so uncontroversial, for most scholars at least. To go beyond what has been said above is to run into problems, but it is also to open up the debates that make the economic history of Byzantium a lively, and intellectually vibrant, area of research. The problems are essentially two: our lack of documents and the underdeveloped state of middle Byzantine archaeology.

The first point is less true of the period up to the early seventh century when to some extent the ancient practice of inscribing texts on stone continued, and when Egypt remained part of the empire and hence the mass of Egyptian evidence preserved on papyrus is still relevant. But after that date there is no avoiding the fact that Byzantium is an ill-documented world. The same could be said of seventh- and eighth-century western Europe, but thereafter monastic and cathedral documents survive in increasing quantities, making possible the sort of detailed regional studies of the agrarian economy that cannot be written for Byzantium. From the twelfth century onwards additional types of evidence become available in the west: fiscal records, rent rolls, notarial registers. None of these are available for Byzantium in anything more than a few fragments.

The second problem, the condition of middle Byzantine archaeology, is more remediable, in fact already changing, but this is still an

---

[32] Louvi-Kizi (2002); Koder and Hild (1976), pp. 269–71.
[33] Magdalino (2000a), pp. 223–6; Magdalino (1996a), pp. 85–90; Jacoby (2005c), pp. 13–19; Maltezou (1995).

under-exploited source. Throughout the territories of the former Byzantine world urban development too often goes ahead with inadequate archaeological record, the less glamorous deposits attracting least attention. Considering how much of our knowledge of the western medieval economy comes from rubbish dumps, it is clear how much we have lost and are still losing for Byzantium. Furthermore, until recently, survey projects tended to neglect the middle Byzantine period, with very few of them looking at Turkey. Even in Greece the coverage was patchy. Things are now changing. Current survey projects in Boeotia in central Greece, the Sagalassos region and the Ikonion plain in Turkey are among those taking the middle Byzantine period seriously and using the full range of available techniques to explore the past landscape.[34] But there is a great deal to be done and archaeology is a cumulative discipline. Patterns emerge in one project that can be tested in another; questions are asked that lead to the collection of data that would otherwise have been destroyed. The outlook is hopeful, but the fact remains that archaeological evidence which has the potential to transform our picture of the middle Byzantine economy is still to a large extent untapped.

That said, going beyond the bounds of consensus is what makes the subject interesting and important. The study of any medieval economy gains from being an exercise in economic anthropology, with the potential to ask fundamental questions about the nature of production, growth, access to resources and their relationship to forms of society and culture. The study of the middle Byzantine economy raises particular questions because of the contrast with the west. Above all, how is a pre-modern economy shaped by the existence of a powerful state? Was Byzantium a rich society, ultimately plundered by Latin and Turkish predators? Or was it a comparatively poor world, where the distribution and exploitation of resources was skewed by its political superstructure?

LATE ANTIQUITY: 'CRISIS? WHAT CRISIS?'

If the late antique economy was so robust, why did it not ride out the troubles of the seventh century? One answer would be that it was already in difficulty by the mid-sixth century. The plague which hit the Mediterranean world in 541 cut the population by perhaps as much as half, and in a pre-industrial economy, the number of people is the basic factor which underlies output and growth. Climate change may have been a factor, too, possibly involving a shift to a warmer and drier phase. There is also evidence from tree rings for a 'dust-veil event' – in other words an event sending dust into the atmosphere sufficient to reduce the amount of sunlight reaching the

[34] Bintliff (1996); Vanhaverbeke and Waelkens (2003); Baird (2004).

earth – in 536–7, caused either by a massive volcanic eruption, or a comet hitting the earth. The sources seem to suggest more frequent earthquakes and famines in these years too. Military defeat by the Persians and Arabs may therefore have simply been the factor tipping an already fragile economy into profound recession.[35]

These arguments attract considerable support, but equal criticism. Many familiar with the relevant evidence are not convinced that it shows an economy in trouble after 550. In Syria, Jordan, Palestine and Egypt it is easy to find evidence that suggests continuing prosperity right through the sixth century and beyond. Coinage remains common and on sites such as Pella and Gerasa in Jordan, or Caesarea Maritima and Scythopolis in Israel, the ceramic record carries on unbroken through the sixth century and through the seventh too. On the limestone massif in northern Syria it appears that the building boom had halted after 550, but dated silver treasures from the area imply no lack of resources, and the villages appear to have been occupied much as before for centuries to come. Further south, in the Hawran and the Jordan valley, building-work continued. Investment in fine mosaics and new churches could be seen as a fearful response to a worsening world, but most historians would be happier to see these buildings, more prosaically, as a sign of people with resources to spare.[36]

The plague is equally problematic. Assuming that its mortality was as high as usually supposed, comparison with the impact of the Black Death on fourteenth- and fifteenth-century Europe would not necessarily suggest disastrous economic consequences. High mortality is likely to benefit survivors, who can take advantage of higher wages and more available land. Unless there is some other factor regulating numbers at a lower level – as seems to have happened in fifteenth-century England for example – populations will tend to bounce back to their previous level.[37]

The same sort of points can be made about earthquakes, famines and dust-veil events. Things happen; and life goes on. If 536–7 was a 'year without summer', then so too was 1816.[38] Both Justinian and his critics saw plague, famine and earthquake as events of cosmic significance. It is not necessary that we should feel the same.

In many ways we know more about the late antique economy than we do about that of the middle Byzantine period that followed. Yet the evidence is still too patchy and imprecise to settle these arguments, and that is particularly true for those territories of the late antique world that came to form medieval Byzantium. We know more about areas such as the Levant or Egypt, which in the seventh century were to pass under Muslim rule,

[35] Koder (1996); Meier (2003), pp. 45–55, 359–87; Gunn (2000); Keys (1999); Baillie (1999). See also above, pp. 120–3.
[36] Whittow (1990); Walmsley (1996).   [37] Horden (2005); Whittow (2001), pp. 149–51.
[38] Stommel and Stommel (1983).

than we do about Asia Minor, the Balkans, or Constantinople itself. Even
the evidence from sites such as Aphrodisias, Sardis and Ephesos, which do
not have modern cities on top of them and which have undergone decades
of excavation, is ambiguous. On each of these sites, opinion is divided
as to whether the evidence shows continuity through the sixth and into
the early seventh century, or a down-turn after 550.[39] And since everyone
would agree that a city needs to be seen as a single economic unit with
its rural hinterland, the lack of any survey looking at the hinterland of
these sites is a drawback. At Sagalassos, Marc Waelkens' Belgian team is
pointing the way with an integrated programme of urban excavation and
rural survey, but even here the implications are debatable. If investment in
substantial new buildings seems to have stopped after 550, Sagalassos was
still occupied up to the seventh. Is this evidence of a widespread 'crisis' in
sixth-century Anatolia, or the local consequences of an earthquake in 518
that had deprived Sagalassos of a suitable water supply?[40]

Another approach to the late antique economy is to examine its relationship with the state. It is beyond question that in pre-modern terms
the Roman empire was a powerful state, capable of having a major impact
upon its citizens' lives. What effect did the state have on the economy? Did
the state's collection of goods in kind through taxation and their transport
across the empire by means of subsidised shipping – in other words the
annona system (see above, p. 11) – subvert the market to such an extent that
when the state collapsed, the late antique economy went with it? Or should
we be looking at the economic impact of state salary payments, skewing
investment and development in peculiar ways? In any case, was the apparent prosperity of the late antique world effectively a creation of the state
and hence vulnerable to the political and military crisis that unfolded in
the seventh century?

The scale and archaeological visibility of the *annona* makes the first
an attractive argument. We know that Rome and Constantinople were
fed substantially on grain, wine and oil imported from Africa and Egypt.
More than a century's work dating and identifying the amphorae that
carried the oil and wine, and the identifying of the huge harbour facilities
built to receive the annual grain fleets, combine with the evidence of the
Codex Theodosianus and the *Codex Iustinianus* to make this clear. The
annona's impact on the wider economy is at first sight obvious enough too.
Throughout late antiquity, pottery types carried in the state-subsidised
ships that transported these foodstuffs appear to dominate Mediterranean
markets. Private shipping and alternative centres of production could not
compete. Such a system fed first Rome and then Constantinople effectively,
but it starved other centres of investment and diverted more natural patterns

of exchange. When crisis struck the *annona* system in the early seventh century, there was no lively network of private and inter-regional trade to take its place.[41]

Twenty years ago this was a more convincing argument. Since then, however much remains obscure, it has become clear enough in the Levant and Egypt that the late antique economy was much more various and complex than once seemed the case. Whereas identifiable late antique pottery once meant in effect imported red-slip wares and amphorae, now a number of regional pottery types have come to light; and significantly, where the data has been collected, it is these regional types that dominate the ceramic assemblages. As usual, we know less about Anatolia and the Balkans, but the identification of Sagalassos ware should serve as a warning that there are likely to be many centres of regional and local late antique pottery production still to be discovered. To talk of 'an economy dominated by *annona* transport' may be overstating the case.[42]

The second and more recent suggestion, that we should be looking at the economic impact of state salary payments, has been made by Jairus Banaji and Peter Sarris and it fits more easily with the emerging picture of a complex late antique economy, where inter-regional and local trade was as important as what was carried on the *annona* trunk routes. Compared with its first- to third-century predecessor, the late antique empire was characterised by far greater numbers of official posts. The late antique aristocracy, particularly in the east, were holders of imperial office. The monetary economy of the earlier empire had been based on silver; that of the late antique empire was based on gold, specifically the *solidus*, struck from 309 onwards at seventy-two to the pound. It was a high-value and stable currency, and was used to pay official salaries. A middle-ranking official in the praetorian prefecture in Constantinople could earn 1,000 *solidi* a year and aristocratic fortunes were calculated in tens of thousands of *solidi*.[43]

To put this in context, the number of copper *folleis* to the *solidus* varied during the sixth century between 180 and 480, the former a short-term revaluation in the wake of the plague, the latter being the mode.[44] Bare survival was possible on a couple of *folleis* a day; a workman might earn between five and twelve *folleis* a day. A *solidus* might buy a pig, three *solidi* a donkey, fifteen a camel, thirty a skilled slave. Forty *solidi* was the dowry for the daughter of an army veteran living in a Palestinian village. It might cost 400 *solidi* to build a village church.[45]

By the sixth century, the papyri evidence shows that much of the Nile valley was organised into great estates owned by this gold-rich aristocracy,

---

[41] McCormick (2001), pp. 27–114; Wickham (2005), p. 72.   [42] McCormick (2001), p. 116.
[43] Banaji (2001), pp. 213–21; Sarris (2004), pp. 290–5; Kelly (2004), pp. 138–85.
[44] Morrisson (1989), pp. 244–51.   [45] Morrisson (1989), pp. 252–6; Morrisson and Cheynet (2002).

who ran them as commercial enterprises, producing primarily for the market. That in turn fuelled further commercial activity and economic growth. All the indications are that late antique Egypt was highly monetarised and market-oriented.[46]

The papyri are effectively unique to Egypt, but the archaeological evidence cited above for late antique prosperity suggests that the Egyptian pattern held true for the sixth-century east as a whole. If this interpretation is right – and it seems to fit the evidence better than the alternatives – the state's contribution to the success of the late antique economy was threefold. It provided a stable gold currency; it organised the fiscal system that underpinned the stability of that currency; and through official salaries it channelled wealth into the hands of the aristocracy, whose activities in turn fuelled prosperity. Such an economy could have ridden out climate change, dust-veil events and plagues – and the Egyptian evidence suggests strongly that it did – but it would have been vulnerable to political and military crisis, and that was what it faced in the seventh century.

A dark age?

Why was the Byzantine empire, which survived the rise of Islam and continued to rule relatively extensive territories in Anatolia and the Balkans, apparently so much poorer than its late antique predecessor, or indeed than its Muslim neighbour? Some believe the answer lies in plague or climate change; others, as we have seen, do not. A more straightforward answer would be to cite Persian and then Arab devastation. But Anatolia, in particular, is a large place. Would it not have required remarkably Stakhanovite raiders to have had this sort of global economic impact? The poorer and more primitive world revealed by the Sagalassos survey seems to require a more complex explanation than direct enemy action.

One approach, casting back to what has been said above about the late antique economy, is to look to the economic role of the state; but, not surprisingly in view of the disagreements about that role before the seventh century, there is no more unanimity for the period that follows. Was the Byzantine empire of the seventh and eighth centuries a weak state? If the late antique economy was dominated by the demands of the *annona*, or even if the state's role was more a matter of organising taxation and a stable currency, did the weakening of the state in the seventh century lead to economic collapse? The persistence of a monetary economy in Constantinople and its apparent withering elsewhere could be seen as fitting this model rather well. The Byzantine state clearly survived and where it had real control, a more complex economy survived too, but its reach did

---

[46] Banaji (2001), pp. 39–88, 134–70.

not extend far into its nominal territories and so neither did a monetary economy. On the other hand, one might think about Byzantium during these centuries in terms of a powerful state, which survived the early middle ages by becoming a highly militarised society, based upon efficient and ruthless exploitation of its resources. This was not so much a poor world, as one where resources were focused on a very particular end.[47]

Comparison with the caliphate does not answer these questions, but it underlines their significance. Recent research has made the wealth of the Islamic world during these centuries steadily more obvious. This was a society with a prolific silver coinage, with a standard of living certainly no lower than that of late antiquity and capable of undertaking at Baghdad and Samarra building projects on a scale that makes the Byzantinist, let alone the historian of the early medieval west, boggle. Was the caliphate fulfilling the economic role once played by the late antique empire and no longer provided by its Byzantine successor? Or was the wealth of this world due to the fact that the caliphate could afford to be less intrusive? To find high-quality seventh- and eighth-century church architecture, it is interesting that one needs to look outside Byzantium: to Syria, Palestine and, above all, to Armenia (see above, pp. 340–1, 344–5 and fig. 22). Is that because of the paradoxical survival of the late antique state in the form of the caliphate, or is it because the church-building classes outside the empire were able to spend their resources on fine architecture rather than footing tax bills?[48]

Behind these uncertainties is the fact that written evidence for the seventh- and eighth century economy is virtually non-existent and the archaeological evidence, at first sight so secure, is not. Current interpretations rest, as explained in the first section of this chapter, on treating stray coin finds, pottery and buildings as proxy indices of economic activity. But in each case there are grounds for caution.

Copper coins of the seventh and eighth century collected as stray finds from the excavations of ancient city sites in western Turkey and Greece are certainly very rare, but the same coins seem not to be so rare when Turkish villagers show what they have picked up from their fields. Is this because cities were no longer so important as central places, and transactions were taking place at other sites, possibly rural fairs?[49] The very fact that the empire continued to mint gold throughout this period is worth noting. To do so required taxation in gold and that in turn depended upon the fact that tax-payers could obtain gold coins through trade. Even if most gold coin passed rather as tokens from the emperor to his servants and back again, it

[47] Haldon (2000a); Whittow (2003), pp. 410–14.
[48] Hodges and Whitehouse (1983), pp. 123–57; on Samarra, see Northedge (2001); on church architecture, see Mango (1979), pp. 89–107; Schick (1995), pp. 119–23; Piccirillo (1993), pp. 196–201, 218–31, 234–5, 238–9, 266–7.
[49] Whittow (2003), pp. 411–12; Lightfoot (2002).

must have been supplemented by gold reaching tax-payers by other means. In the west, minting in gold had to be abandoned in the eighth century. Its continued minting in Byzantium may have been largely due to the survival of the tax system, but it presumably also indicates a more than minimal monetary economy.

The same inference may be drawn from the survival in Byzantium of a multi-denominational coinage. From the eighth century to the thirteenth, western mints produced only single-denomination silver coins. The emergence of a more complex system in the west was a response to economic growth and the consequent demand for something more practicable and flexible. A two-tier coinage in Byzantium might be explained as a simple consequence of the need to keep minting the ideologically critical gold *solidi*, while at the same time providing some other lesser-value coin; but the emergence of a successful three-tier system from the 720s, with the silver *miliarēsion* (worth twelve to the *solidus*) supplementing the existing gold and copper coins, likewise suggests a more than minimal monetary economy. It equipped Byzantium with a highly flexible system of coinage.[50]

The pottery, too, tells an ambiguous story. Certainly an ancient tradition of manufacturing red-slip pottery and distributing it across the Mediterranean world came to an end in the seventh century. The standard types of late antique amphorae similarly disappear during these years. Constantinopolitan white ware, which certainly dates from this period, is neither common nor widely distributed. But the problem is as much an inability to identify seventh- and eighth-century pottery as it is one of absence. The excavations of the Saraçhane site in the middle of Istanbul produced a continuous sequence of coins through the dark age; John Hayes' study of the ceramics has produced a similarly continuous sequence of tableware, cooking pots and carrying vessels. Large water jars commonly found on sites in western Anatolia were certainly in production by the eighth century. Hannelore Vanhaverbeke's impression from the Sagalassos survey coincides with that of others: that much of the unidentified pottery found on Anatolian sites is locally or regionally produced, some likely dating to the seventh and eighth centuries. In the Levant, the study of local wares has helped transform the picture of the early Islamic centuries. The same may be about to happen for dark age Byzantium.[51]

Ceramics are manufactured objects; they are also trace elements for trade. If we cannot recognise seventh- and eighth-century pottery we lose this

---

[50] Morrisson (2002), pp. 920–30; see above, p. 270.

[51] In general, see Brubaker and Haldon (2001), pp. 148–56; Vroom (2003), pp. 229–32; Vroom (2005a), pp. 30–66; on Constantinople, see Hendy (1986); Harrison and Hayes (1986–92), II, pp. 12–18, 41–3, 55–7, 71–3; on water jars from western Asia Minor, see Whittow (2003), pp. 413–4, and figs. 1 and 2; Arthur (1997); on Sagalassos: Vanhaverbeke *et al.* (2004); on the Levant: Sodini and Villeneuve (1992); Watson (1992); Magness (1993); Magness (2003).

means of plotting movement and have tended to assume the minimal worst. But there are other trace elements. Michael McCormick has assembled the evidence for journeys of all sorts in the dark age Mediterranean and what he has found suggests much more activity during this period than has generally been imagined. Peregrine Horden and Nicholas Purcell note the evidence for dark age piracy and point out that piracy will only occur when there is something to steal. These are straws, but they need to be taken into account.[52]

With buildings too, there is a danger that we currently underestimate the evidence already to hand. Seventh- and eighth-century Ephesos, for example, was not on the same scale as its late antique predecessor, yet the huge church of St John was kept standing and the cut-down church of St Mary remained in use. In any case the largest building project of these years was not a church but the circuit of walls. Although they enclose only a small part of the ancient city, at something over 2.5 kilometres long and 3.4 metres thick they were a major undertaking in themselves, and more so when seen as part of programme of fortification which covered the empire's territories with castles.[53] When in 766 Constantine V (741–75) wanted to restore the aqueduct of Valens in Constantinople, 'he collected artisans from different places and brought from Asia and Pontos 1,000 masons and 200 plasterers, from Hellas and the islands 500 clay-workers and from Thrace itself 5,000 labourers and 200 brickmakers.'[54] The building industry was not on the late antique scale, but it did exist.

Constantine's activities are a reminder of the continuing importance of Constantinople itself. No doubt much smaller than it had been in the sixth century and far smaller than Abbasid Baghdad, the Byzantine capital was still a large city with, for example, over eighty churches built before 600 and kept in repair through the following centuries. One of Cyril Mango's many contributions to Byzantine studies has been to pour cold water on over-optimistic interpretations of all sorts. His vision of Constantinople is of a city whose population plummeted in the seventh century from perhaps 400,000 to 40,000. Others would be more optimistic. Paul Magdalino suggests a population of not less than 70,000; Michel Kaplan talks of not less than 150,000. For any of these figures the supporting evidence is slight. Until recently the same could be said of early medieval Rome and an equally depressing picture was drawn. But medieval archaeology has come of age in Italy and the remains of early medieval Rome are beginning to receive proper attention. A new picture of the city is emerging, certainly far smaller-scale even than its late antique predecessor, but by the criteria of the early middle

---

[52] McCormick (2001), pp. 852–972; Horden and Purcell (2000), pp. 157–8.
[53] Foss (1979a), pp. 103–15; Müller-Wiener (1961), pp. 89–91.
[54] Theoph., ed. de Boor, I, p. 440; tr. Mango and Scott, p. 608; see above, p. 274.

ages a large and prosperous place. For the moment one can only speculate, but it is at least quite likely that when comparable archaeological work is done in Istanbul, the same sort of positive re-evaluation will follow.[55]

If seventh- and eighth-century Byzantium was incontestably a poorer society than in late antiquity, or than its contemporary Muslim neighbour, we need to be careful before coming to bleakly minimalist conclusions (see above, pp. 469–70, 472). This was a world that increasingly looked to the steppes and Turkic central Asia for cultural models. Constantine V married a Khazar bride and by such routes was a new material culture introduced to Byzantium, a culture that displayed wealth in textiles and in metalwork. Wealthy Byzantines of the new age wore turbans and kaftans, prayed on carpets, reclined on cushions, dined off silver. Not-so-wealthy Byzantines likewise wanted to emulate the east. The disappearance of red-slip pottery is a fact about production; it is also a matter of cultural choice, as consumers took to green- and brown-glazed wares, a fashion that ultimately had its origins in China. The wealth of late antiquity is obvious to us because it was still spent in the ancient manner on buildings and marble. By contrast much of the wealth of Byzantium was spent on perishable textiles and recyclable silver. We have hints in the texts, but little survives.[56]

Although 'dark age' Byzantium is a term that some find jarring, it has its uses. The term does not necessarily imply that seventh- and eighth-century Byzantium lapsed into prehistoric poverty – which would certainly be over-drawn – but it does carry a message that this period is obscure, with much resting on assumption and more research needed. The currently available evidence strongly suggests a poorer society with fewer resources than its late antique predecessor; beyond that much remains obscure. There is a case, sketched out above, that dark age Byzantium was less poor and more economically active than we have come to believe. The thesis will have to be tested in the years ahead, but at the least it opens interesting perspectives. If the economy of dark age Byzantium was more active than tends to be supposed, this would have implications, not just for the seventh and eighth centuries, but for what followed in the ninth to twelfth and more generally for the grand narrative of middle Byzantine economic history.

---

[55] On Constantinople, see Mango (1990), pp. 51–62 ; Magdalino (1996a), p. 18; Kaplan (1992), p. 446, n. 5; on Rome: Wickham (2000b), pp. 162–4; Paroli (2004).

[56] On links between Byzantium, the steppe world and China, see Noonan (2000), pp. 286–8; Bálint (2000); Vaissière (2004), pp. 213–28; on Constantine V and his Khazar bride, see Whittow (1996a), pp. 225–6; on turbans and carpets: Mango (1981b), pp. 51–2. The implications of glazed ceramics for the orientation of Byzantine culture remain valid even if the lead-glaze technology used by Byzantine potters came from Mesopotamia via Italy and not from central Asia or the far east: François (2005), pp. 211–13.

The middle Byzantine revival: a 'feudal revolution'?

The mounting prosperity of the Byzantine world from the ninth century is a phenomenon common to the contemporary west; this encourages one to look for explanations valid for both. Two potentially global explanations are the end of outbreaks of the Justinianic plague in the eighth century or a shift to a more favourable climate, in either case triggering population growth. Although both theses attract support, most scholars consider the evidence too slight and inconclusive. As with the arguments that invoke the impact of plague in late antiquity, comparison with the Black Death tends to be discouraging. In the sixteenth-century west and in the Ottoman empire the economy and also population levels recovered long before the outbreaks of the plague abated; in fact they coincided with a period of worsening climate.[57]

Improved security was certainly a factor. In Byzantium it is obvious that economic growth and the end of Arab raiding roughly coincide, and that will have encouraged investment in provincial property. Cappadocia is a case in point. The excavation and decoration of new cave complexes begins just as the region ceases to be an exposed frontier zone. In the west the argument works less well. The end of Viking, Hungarian and Arab raiding probably has a bearing, but in general violence and economic growth seem to go hand in hand. Historians have therefore tended to look elsewhere.

Since the 1950s and Georges Duby's seminal work on the Mâconnais, an explanation that envisages aristocratic demand pushing reluctant peasants onto the market has been widely favoured, and for Byzantium this 'feudal revolution' model now underlies the prevailing narrative. The great estates of late antiquity, according to this thesis, broke up in the seventh century, leaving an economically static peasant economy, as pictured in the *Farmer's law* of the seventh or eighth century. The ending of Arab raids encouraged a new generation of aristocratic landowners to emerge from the later ninth century onwards; this is reflected in the body of land legislation from the tenth century, through which successive emperors tried and failed to halt the trend. The eleventh century was a new era of great estates and these survived the crises of the later eleventh century to flourish in the twelfth. They provided the motor of Byzantine economic revival. The land legislation was not only a failure, it was misconceived, being set against the very process that was enriching Byzantine society as a whole. Emperors might regret the loss of independent peasant farmers and the potential political unreliability of this new aristocratic class; but the richer material culture attested by field surveys and excavation-work, especially in

[57] Yun (1994), p. 126.

Greece, suggests an economy where a broad section of the population was benefiting.[58]

What limited the success of the Byzantine economy was not the rampancy of its landlords, but the immobility of its peasants. When Michael Choniates, the metropolitan of Athens and brother of the historian, complained in the late twelfth century about the injustice of already privileged landowners gaining further exemptions while the poor were ruthlessly fleeced, he may have been morally right, but his economic diagnosis was wrong. The Byzantine economy needed not more protection for peasants, but less.[59]

Up to a point this looks a convincing model, but its assumption that peasants are merely a drag on economic growth is now somewhat dated. It also fails to engage with the effects of the late eleventh-century crisis. Recent work by anthropologists and development economists has emphasised the extent to which peasant agriculture can generate growth, not least because self-sufficiency in an uncertain world requires substantial margins of extra production and the most effective way to insure against shortage is engagement with the market. Far from peasants being averse to the market, producing cash crops for the market is essential for their survival. In an even partially monetary economy this allows the building-up of surpluses and hence the creation of an insurance against the inevitable bad years. The chief brake on Byzantine economic activity may not have been peasant immobility, but aristocratic self-sufficiency. Only the rich could afford to be self-sufficient.[60]

Such insights in turn fit with the evidence emerging in various parts of western Europe that suggests economic growth started in some areas as early as the seventh or eighth centuries, rather than the tenth or eleventh, and that the roots of such growth lay in peasant enterprise. Rather than thinking of peasants needing to be forced onto the market and so launching an economic revolution, we should perhaps be thinking of a world where landowning aristocrats hijacked the fruits of pioneering peasant enterprise.[61]

To Byzantinists this will sound curiously like a return to the ideas of an earlier generation. Before the current consensus that the seventh century ushered in a poorer, more primitive world, the seventh to tenth centuries were painted as a golden age for Byzantium, or at least for Byzantine peasants. A contrast was drawn between the evidence from the late antique law

---

[58] On the feudal revolution model, see Duby (1971); Fossier (1999), pp. 50–63; on Byzantium, see Harvey (1989) pp. 244–68; Hendy (1989a); Lefort (2002), pp. 283–308.

[59] Michael Choniates, *Epistulae*, ed. Kolovou, pp. 41, 87. On Michael, see Herrin (1975), pp. 270–1, 274.

[60] Horden and Purcell (2000), pp. 175–230; Kaplan (1992), pp. 521–40; Devroey (2003), pp. 174–5.

[61] Devroey (2003), pp. 30, 38, 129–30.

codes for a semi-free peasantry tied to the land and a picture derived from the *Farmer's law* of independent peasants free from landlordly exploitation, who rebuilt the Byzantine economy on new and healthier foundations. For good reasons it is an idea that has largely fallen out of fashion. It was the product of an intellectual current, widespread in the late nineteenth and early twentieth centuries, that saw an independent peasantry as a moral and economic good in itself, and it was innocent of archaeology. But there is a case for taking its basic thesis more seriously.[62]

The tenth-century land legislation offers clues. It is now usually taken as evidence for the rise of a landed aristocracy, but it is also undeniable evidence for the existence of a free peasantry whom the emperors wanted to protect. The term peasant does not inevitably imply 'very poor'. In fact, as Rosemary Morris pointed out over thirty years ago, the terminology of the land legislation makes plain that the lawmakers were specifically not concerned with a destitute rural underclass, but with the 'powerless'.[63] It has become customary to dwell upon the failure of the land legislation, which makes it a natural progression to link eleventh-century growth with the rise of an aristocracy and to see one as a principal cause of the other. But when one turns to the collection of eleventh-century legal judgements known as the *Peira*, or looks at the contrast between the place of free peasants in Byzantine southern Italy and their position in the same areas following the eleventh-century Norman conquest, or considers the contrast between the status of peasants before and after the Frankish conquest of Greece, what stands out is the *effectiveness* of the land legislation.[64] The legislation did protect the rights of free peasants and it did act as a brake on the expansion of aristocratic estates. The growing economy of the eleventh century took place in a world where a substantial proportion of the empire's output was generated by free peasant farmers responding to their own agenda. Archaeological data from southern and central Greece has been cited already. The many new churches are an obvious feature, and some such as Skripou and Hosios Loukas are undoubtedly evidence of aristocratic expenditure, but what is most striking overall is the *un*aristocratic culture of eleventh-century Greece. The new building revealed at Corinth, Athens or Thebes seems very ordinary. The associated material culture appears to be one that would fit well with a prospering peasant world.[65]

If such a pattern provides a key to the development of the Byzantine economy, a number of implications follow. They would fit with a

---

[62] Ostrogorsky (1966); Górecki (1986); Górecki (2004).

[63] *JG*, ed. Zepos and Zepos, I, pp. 207, 208–9; ed. Svoronos, no. 3, pp. 82, 83–4; tr. McGeer, pp. 53, 54–5; Morris (1976), pp. 17–20.

[64] *Peira*, ed. Zacharia von Lingenthal, pp. 32, 38–40, 52–3, 85–6, 228; on Italy, see Martin (1993), pp. 293–328; on Greece, see below, pp. 772, 773–4.

[65] See above, nn. 21 and 23; on Skripou and Hosios Loukas, see Megaw (1966), pp. 20, 23–5; Connor (1991), pp. 112–21.

reinterpretation of the seventh and eighth century putting a more positive gloss on the cessation of the great aristocratic enterprises of late antiquity; they would highlight the importance of the survival in Byzantium of a flexible monetary system whereby peasant farmers could effectively produce for the market; they might also suggest a less optimistic view of the twelfth century.

Since 1970 most historians have followed Hendy's line that the twelfth century saw a continuation of the growing prosperity of the tenth and eleventh centuries. In terms of its value for the economy, the loss of Anatolia to the Turks did not matter because the most valuable parts of Asia Minor either remained in Byzantine hands, or were soon recovered. Anatolian stock-raisers may no longer have lived under imperial rule, but they would have had little option but to supply Byzantine demand. In other words business as usual; the indices of coins, ceramics and buildings show all was well and, in some areas, better than ever. Michael Choniates was no doubt telling the truth as he saw it when he describes rapacious tax-collectors destroying the poor; but he wrote in the 1180s and 1190s, a time when the empire was ringed by enemies, much territory had been lost and what remained was bound to be taxed hard.[66]

The crucial issue for the twelfth century as a whole is not taxation, but the role of the great landed estates. A number of documentary texts make it plain that vast areas of the Komnenian empire were run as the estates of various Constantinopolitan landlords – a category that includes the emperor, his kinsmen, the church and those monasteries and other pious institutions known as the 'pious houses'.[67] If the economic revival of the tenth and eleventh centuries was driven by aristocratic pressure, this phenomenon does not matter, or can be seen in a positive light, a return to the conditions underlying late antique prosperity. Rather than taking demand out of the system, the bankruptcy of the previous system of remunerating the state's servants in cash would have encouraged aristocratic landlords to put the produce of their estates on the market and indeed run their estates with the market in mind.[68] But if the economic revival of the middle Byzantine period was in fact driven from below, these vast estates might look more like a stifling of Byzantine economic enterprise. Did the great estates necessarily promote local and regional economic enterprise, or did they dampen such activity in favour of self-sufficiency and the provision of goods in kind to feed their dependents in the capital? Is the growth of Latin commerce a sign of the economic vitality of Byzantium, or rather a symptom of an economy where Byzantine traders were disadvantaged in favour of outsiders servicing the great estates? An economy, in other

[66] Hendy (1989a), pp. 46–7.   [67] Magdalino (1993a), pp. 160–71.
[68] Oikonomides (1997a), pp. 210–15.

words, shifting, like that of later medieval eastern Europe, to become one of great estates producing for a profitable export market, but in so doing fundamentally damaging its social base. Good cases can be made on both sides of the argument. For want of sufficient documentary evidence to shed light on how estate and society interacted at local and regional levels, any judgement must ultimately rest on a more general view of the state of the twelfth-century economy. How rich was Byzantium?

1204: A BALANCE SHEET

In 1204 the Crusaders had expected a great deal of the empire. One of their number, Robert de Clari, wrote, 'I do not think that in the forty richest cities of the world there has been so much wealth as was found in Constantinople. For the Greeks say that two-thirds of the wealth of this world is in Constantinople and the other third scattered throughout the world.' But when it was actually counted, two-thirds of the world's wealth only amounted to 300,000 marks.[69]

So perhaps the empire was not as rich as it appeared to be. Its reputation for wealth owed a lot to Constantinople, the tax system funnelling resources into the city, and the court culture that ensured they were spent there, partly on luxury goods manufactured in the city (see below, p. 776). It also owed a lot to deliberate image-making, keeping up appearances of stupendous wealth. Outside the imperial capital, as a succession of Latin and Muslim observers noted, the empire was far less impressive.[70] Athens, Ephesos, Corinth, Sparta, Thessaloniki and the like may have been doing better in the twelfth century than they had in the past, but from a contemporary European perspective, they were not great cities. A comparison between Byzantine and Latin church-building in the twelfth century is telling. Byzantine architecture may have its aesthetic merits, but seen simply in terms of scale and resources, the achievements of the Latin building industry in the age of the Romanesque and early Gothic dwarf those of Byzantium.[71]

To some extent Byzantium was disadvantaged by geography. A great deal of imperial territory was taken up by mountains and arid plateaux, but one should not press that too far. Some of these same areas did very well under other rule. Central Anatolia thrived during the thirteenth century under the Seljuqs; western Turkey prospered in the late middle ages and again in

---

[69] Robert de Clari, *Conquest of Constantinople*, ed. Lauer, pp. 80–1; tr. McNeal, pp. 101–2; Queller and Madden (1997), pp. 199–200.

[70] *Leg.*, ch. 63, ed. Chiesa, p. 216; tr. Scott, p. 55; Ibn Hawqal, *Surat*, tr. Kramers and Wiet, I, p. 192; Odo of Deuil, *Expedition*, ed. and tr. Berry, pp. 88–9; *Hudud al-'alam*, tr. Minorsky, ed. Bosworth, p. 157: 'In the days of old cities were numerous in Rum, but now they have become few.'

[71] Mango (1979), pp. 108–67; Ousterhout (1999), pp. 7, 51.

the eighteenth century; in Greece and the Balkans the later middle ages and the eighteenth century also stand out.

A major achievement of the last half century in studies of the Byzantine economy has been the recognition of the prosperity of the middle Byzantine period and of the fact that in some respects this carried on through to 1204. But it seems equally clear that by 1204, at least, the Byzantine economy was not fulfilling its potential. In 934 Romanos I Lekapenos (920–44) had justified his land legislation to protect the free peasantry on the grounds that it was 'beneficial to the common good, acceptable to God, profitable to the treasury and useful to the state'.[72] Robert de Clari's disappointment in 1204 may go to show that his concerns were not misplaced.

[72] *JG*, I, ed. Zepos and Zepos, p. 207; ed. Svoronos, no. 3, p. 82; tr. McGeer, p. 54.

CHAPTER 13

EQUILIBRIUM TO EXPANSION (886–1025)

JONATHAN SHEPARD

INTRODUCTION: COEXISTENCE WITH THE CALIPHATE

As earlier chapters have shown, the empire's military situation was alleviated by political upheavals in the Muslim world and the abatement of hammer blows directed by the Abbasid leadership. The caliphate itself had more recourse to diplomacy, recognising Ashot I Bagratuni ('the Great') (884–90) as paramount prince among the Armenians and bestowing a crown on him. Soon afterwards, Basil I (867–86) responded with démarches of his own towards Ashot.[1] The later ninth century probably saw the elaboration of the *basileus'* diplomatic web eastwards, drawing in political elites in central and eastern Caucasia such as 'the chiefs of Azia', lords of the Caspian Gates.[2] By the reign of Leo VI (886–912) the court was maintaining well-to-do Turks from the Fergana valley as well as Khazars, and these young men were making substantial down payments of gold in order to receive annual *rogai* as members of a unit of the imperial bodyguard.[3] The chinks in Muslim power were shown up in other forms, such as the prisoners-of-war kept at court. The more prominent among them were enrobed in the white garments of catechumens at the emperor's Christmas and Easter banquets, as if to affirm willingness to adopt the religion of the Christians.[4] Triumphal parades of Basil I, as of Theophilos (829–42), celebrated with spectacular props the emperors' occasional forays into Muslim-held regions, and a poet could write of Basil as a new David, who with God's help will vanquish the enemy hosts.[5]

A triumphalist note is likewise sounded by orators such as Arethas in his praises for Basil's son Leo VI at the turn of the ninth century. However, there is little talk of outright reconquest of lands from the Muslims. Arethas' accent is, rather, on the benefits bestowed by Leo on the city of Constantinople through translation there of the relics of St Lazaros, from

---

[1] See above, p. 353; Shepard (2001), pp. 27–8.
[2] *DC*, II.48, ed. Reiske, I, p. 688; Zuckerman (2000c), pp. 537–9, 542–8.
[3] *DC*, II.49, ed. Reiske, I, pp. 692–3.   [4] Simeonova (1998b), pp. 91–9, 103–4.
[5] McCormick (1990), pp. 147–50, 154–7; Markopoulos (1992), p. 231, lines 212–14, p. 226 (commentary).

Map 23 The empire in the tenth and eleventh centuries: key towns in the Balkans and Asia Minor

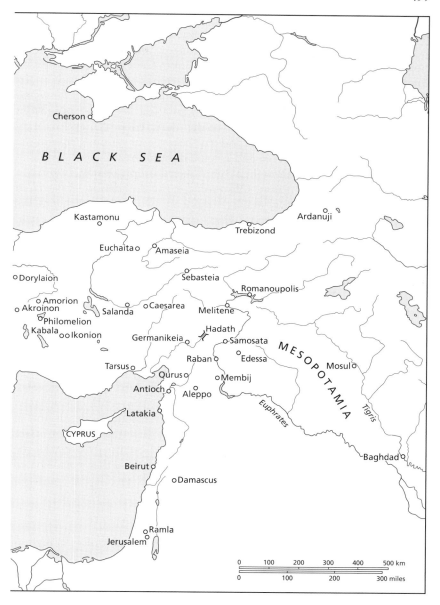

Cherson

BLACK SEA

Kastamonu

Ardanuji

Trebizond

Euchaita o oAmaseia

oDorylaion

Sebasteia

Romanoupolis

o Amorion
o Akroinon   o Caesarea   Melitene
       Salanda
  oPhilomelion   Hadath
Kabala oo Ikonion
                Germanikeia o   o Samosata
                                              MESOPOTAMIA
                    Raban o   o Edessa
Tarsus o   Mosul o
           Qurus o
    Antioch o   o Aleppo
      Latakia o   Euphrates
                                                        Tigris
CYPRUS

                                                      Baghdad o

Beirut o
        o Damascus

           o Ramla
Jerusalem o

0   100   200   300   400   500 km
0   100   200   300 miles

the border-zone island of Cyprus.[6] The humbling of the barbarians was refracted through Constantinopolitan lenses, presenting Basil and his son as, respectively, generals and masters of strategy, gaining spoils and additional supernatural protectors for the City. But in fact Leo was hard-pressed to cope with the repercussions for the border regions of the Abbasids' internal political problems. In many ways the vigorous jihad waged by the *ghazi*s of the Tarsus region,[7] like the burgeoning piratical fleets operating from Syrian and Cretan ports, were signs of the increased wealth and military capability available to freebooters and true believers of various stripes at the interface between the imperial and Islamic dominions.

The dislocation of the resource-rich Abbasid caliphate was, in short, a mixed blessing for Byzantium. Oft-quoted is the declaration of Patriarch Nicholas I Mystikos (901–7, 912–25): 'there are two lordships, that of the Saracens and that of the Romans, which stand above all lordship on earth, shining out like the two mighty beacons in the firmament.'[8] This is a figure of speech, but its context is suggestive. Nicholas was writing to Caliph al-Muqtadir (908–32), urging him in effect to disown the measures taken against the civilian population of Cyprus by Damian, an apostate Christian who had gathered a large fleet and operated semi-autonomously, albeit notionally on the caliph's behalf. Byzantium's state of co-existence with the caliphate was neither peaceful nor wholly stable. But the emperor could exchange embassies, gifts and courtesies with the caliph, thereby maintaining dignity. The numerous humiliating if petty challenges to his authority from pirate fleets could be as politically debilitating as any caliphal hammer blow. From this perspective, there was *Realpolitik* in Patriarch Nicholas' rhetoric concerning 'lordships'. The events of the mid-tenth century tend to bear out the unarticulated grounds for imperial statesmen's caution in exploiting Abbasid disarray. The jihad waged by an ambitious amir intent on legitimising his new regime in Aleppo would eventually overturn the underlying equilibrium, and equilibrium was the best that palace-based emperors could realistically hope for.

IMPERIAL IDEALS, BORDERLAND REALITIES

It is against this background that one should view the various manuals of governance and law-collections dating from Leo's reign. They evince his enthusiasm for order, godliness and good learning. Besides commissioning, compiling or interpolating these works he wrote numerous sermons. He aspired to be acknowledged as the fount of wisdom and pious enlightenment, judging by the description of his bathhouse near the palace complex.[9]

---

[6] Arethas, *Scripta minora*, ed. Westerink, II, pp. 16, 31–4; Shepard (2002b), pp. 67–8.

[7] Bosworth (1992), pp. 274–6, 281–5.   [8] NM, no. 1, pp. 2–3.

[9] Magdalino (1988b), pp. 103–10, 116–18.

Leo's sobriquet, 'the Wise', implied in the bathhouse imagery, acclaimed by contemporary courtiers and derided by Symeon of Bulgaria, was not wholly undeserved. Like his father Basil I, he wished his rule to be associated with illustrious figures of the Christian empire's acknowledged heyday, notably Constantine and Justinian. At the same time he propagated the idea of renewal in, for example, his highly euphemistic version of Basil's accession: the former state of affairs had been removed together with Basil's senior co-emperor, Michael III, 'for the purpose of fresh and well-ordered change'.[10]

The concept of 'cleansing' government and society of the corrupt and the obsolete is threaded through the *novellae* of Leo VI, an assemblage of 113 ordinances, mostly dating from the earlier years of his reign. They are largely concerned with morality and church discipline, and envisage a well-tempered society whose laws apply to all men save the emperor; he has been granted 'discretionary powers' (*oikonomia*) over earthly affairs by God. The laws, it is repeatedly asserted, are to help men, bringing benefits to their souls as well as to their bodies.[11] How far Leo's *novellae* were practicable administrative instruments and how far they were enforced is, however, uncertain.

The *Book of the eparch* was issued in 911 or 912 in the name of Leo VI. Its preface invokes by way of analogy the tablets upon which the Law was disclosed by God's 'own finger' for all mankind,[12] but its scope is confined to Constantinople, whose administration was supervised by the eparch. It regulates the conduct of nineteen guilds, and lays down harsh penalties for those who breach the regulations. General professions of concern for the welfare of the emperor's subjects are here juxtaposed with detailed administrative procedures. The *Book of the eparch* reveals something of the government's assumptions and priorities. It is particularly concerned with top-quality products such as silks, purple dyes, silver- or goldwork and spices. Five guilds connected with the silk industry receive detailed attention, whereas tanners and leather-softeners get cursory treatment and numerous other known guilds are not mentioned at all. The monopolisation and rationing out of luxury goods was the stock-in-trade of imperial statecraft, at home and abroad. Great efforts were made to ensure that the various stages of production and retail of silk remained in the hands of different professions, and dealers in less valuable goods such as groceries, meat and soap were also not to merge their enterprises. Small-scale units could safely be allowed to monitor their own operations and their own tax assessments and collections to a large extent; fewer officials were thus required

---

[10] Leo VI, *Funeral oration for Basil I*, ed. and French tr. Vogt and Hausherr, pp. 56–7. See also Tougher (1997b), pp. 25, 65–7.

[11] Leo VI, *Novels*, ed. Noailles and Dain, pp. 131, 197, 329–31, 345, 361.

[12] *Eparch*, preface, ed. and German tr. Koder, pp. 72–3.

for them. The *Book of the eparch* essentially envisaged self-regulation by craftsmen and traders in conjunction with the City authorities.

A still more urgent priority for the government was provisioning at affordable prices. The heads of the fishmongers' guild were to report to the eparch at dawn on the night's catch, whereupon he set a price. The prices of meat and bread were likewise set by him; rigorous inspection of all weights and measures was enjoined. The drafters or revisers of the *Book of the eparch* assumed that residence in Constantinople was a privilege, and 'exile' was a harsh penalty in itself. No clear distinction was drawn between provincials and foreigners: for example, anyone 'from outside' bringing any kind of merchandise 'into the God-protected city' was to be closely supervised by the eparch's deputy; a list of their purchases was to be made at the end of their stay, 'so that nothing forbidden should leave the reigning city'.[13] The sale of pigs and sheep was regulated in detail; the express aim was cheaper food for the populace, and the interests of provincial producers were secondary.

All this probably had a positive effect on the citizens' well-being, but it also publicised the emperor's solicitousness. An emperor enjoying the citizens' goodwill was screened against would-be usurpers. Leo broadcast his piety and accentuated the mystique of emperors born in the Porphyra (himself and his son Constantine). He maintained the festival celebrating the consecration of the Nea Ekklesia built by Basil I. A dirge composed soon after Leo's death linked Constantinople and the reigning family thus:

> O City, sing, intone the praise
> of Basil's noble offspring,
> For they impart a deeper hue
> To thy imperial purple.[14]

Bread-and-butter issues were at least as important as pomp in winning the sympathies of the populace. Leo seems to have realised this.

Concentration on the emperor's home town rather than the provinces is not particularly surprising. More striking is Leo's assumption, in compiling his *Tactica* in (for the most part) the 890s, that the provinces are vulnerable to enemy attack and that this will continue indefinitely. He states that the work is for fighting the Saracens, who harass his subjects 'day by day'.[15] Warfare is essentially defensive, and commanders must ensure that all necessities

---

[13] *Eparch*, XX.I, ed. and German tr. Koder, pp. 132–3; tr. Freshfield, pp. 44–5 (repr. pp. 264–5); see also XIII.2, ed. and German tr. Koder, pp. 120–1; tr. Freshfield, p. 36 (repr. p. 256); XV.I, ed. and German tr. Koder, pp. 122–3; tr. Freshfield, p. 38 (repr. p. 258); XVII.4, ed. and German tr. Koder, pp. 128–9; tr. Freshfield, p. 41 (repr. p. 261); XVIII.I and XVIII.4, ed. and German tr. Koder, pp. 128–9, 130–1; tr. Freshfield, pp. 41–2 (repr. pp. 261–2).

[14] Ševčenko (ed.) 'Poems', pp. 202 (Greek text), 205 (translation); see also pp. 225, 227.

[15] Leo VI, *Tactica*, XVIII.142, cols. 981–2. Leo's predecessors had had similar concerns; see above, p. 393.

are removed from areas under attack to safe places, livestock dispersed and the population evacuated. The Arab raiders should be attacked only when returning, weary and preoccupied with booty. Here, at least, the emperor was attuned to life as it was lived in the eastern provinces. Much the same tactics are advocated in *Skirmishing*, which drew on first-hand experience of the ninth- and earlier tenth-century borderlands and was composed in the milieu of the Phokas family; it presupposes that humans as well as livestock will be amongst the raiders' encumbrances, and the *stratēgos* is to assume that his troops will be numerically inferior to the raiders.[16]

The subterranean settlements of Cappadocia provide material evidence for the insecurity of the south-eastern provinces. Some predate the Arab invasions, but others, such as Salanda, 80 kilometres west of Caesarea, were created then. Several of the millstones which closed its numerous entrances are still extant, though such ingenuity did not prevent this redoubt from being captured in 898 and again in 906–7. *Skirmishing* sets notably less store by man-made fortifications than by familiarity with mountain heights and natural defences from which observers can gauge enemy numbers and movements.[17] Rapid movement was here at a premium, thus limiting what the mounted raiders could take back. Their numbers seldom exceeded 10,000, and were often far smaller. The brunt of the seasonal land raiding was borne in the south-east borderlands. Nonetheless, *Skirmishing*'s preoccupation with finding out the raiders' targets betrays the difficulty of keeping track of them, let alone of mustering soldiers from widely scattered agricultural holdings. Its detailed provisions for coping with major invasions, replete with siege equipment, bespeak a state of alert and uncertainty as to where the next blow would fall.

No less uncertainty overhung the southern and western coastal districts of Asia Minor. The amir of Tarsus despatched or led naval *razzia*s, and these, like the piratical fleets operating from north Syrian ports, enjoyed a safe haven in Crete, if needed. It was there that the pirate chief Leo of Tripoli withdrew after sacking Thessaloniki, the empire's second city, in 904, and there 22,000 prisoners were counted before being auctioned to the Cretans. For a while Leo's fleet was expected to attempt an attack on Constantinople; it was probably this, rather than just the humiliation at Thessaloniki, that spurred Leo VI into large-scale countermeasures. But a combined land-and-sea operation soon collapsed. The commander of land forces, Andronikos Doukas, had recently led a successful incursion into Cilicia. He now fell under suspicion of rebellion and fled to Baghdad after holding out in the fortress of Kabala for six months in 905.

---

[16] Leo VI, *Tactica*, XVII.76–80, XVIII.126–7, XVIII.134, cols. 931–4, 975–6, 977–8; *Skirmishing*, prologue, chs. 4, 19, ed. and tr. Dennis, pp. 146–7, 156–9, 214–15.

[17] *Skirmishing*, chs. 1–3, 8, 11, 12, ed. and tr. Dennis, pp. 150–5, 164–5, 184–7; Howard-Johnston (1983a), p. 259.

A later, massive task force under the command of a trusted civil servant and relative-by-marriage of Leo VI, Himerios, was directed at least partly against Crete, from which the Byzantines had vainly tried to dislodge the Arabs in the ninth century. Himerios was no more successful in 911–12, even though he seems to have followed the precepts of Leo's *Tactica*, and Leo of Tripoli remained at large in the Aegean for ten more years.[18] Arab raids are quite commonplace in tenth-century hagiography; the tales may be fabulous, but their setting has substance. The sermons of Peter, bishop of Argos (*c.* 852–*c.* 922), and his *Life* concur in suggesting that the locals looked to the saints and to Peter himself, rather than to the emperor, for protection.[19] Peter regularly ransomed captives from pirates who put in at Nauplion; and, reportedly through the miraculous production of flour, he acted to relieve a famine. Peter's ransomings were not far removed from tribute, and it seems that a regular form of tribute was exacted from the inhabitants of southern Aegean isles such as Naxos.

At one level these facts of provincial life make a mockery of the *bien pensant* Leo VI's public pronouncements. Yet the raiding fleets were normally modest, and the boats in everyday piratical use needed to be small and light, to facilitate swift concealment in Aegean coves. So their carrying capacity was restricted. In any case, not even Byzantine or Muslim authorities could achieve high standards of seaworthiness; naval technology did not allow either side to dominate the seas, and vessels of any bulk tended to ply a limited – and predictable – range of routes. The Muslim fleets seldom liaised with one another, being intent on plunder, not conquest. The account of one of Leo of Tripoli's captives of 904 suggests there was more or less covert trafficking between the Muslim and Christian zones, involving redeemable prisoners and other commodities.[20] The smattering of copper coins belonging to Cretan amirs found on the Greek mainland may hint at commercial exchanges. In the border regions, local self-reliance and deals with the men of violence were unavoidable.

Some of the areas most exposed to enemy raids actually showed signs of increasing economic activity and wealth. In Sparta and Corinth the coin sequences which had begun in the mid-ninth century continue uninterrupted through the first half of the tenth. Still more suggestive is the proliferation of painted chapels and churches in the rocks of Cappadocia. Some formed part of monasteries, but most were lay foundations, serving

---

[18] See above, pp. 297–8. It may be that this campaign was an extension of the major raid on the region of Latakia in 910, the Syrian ports and Cyprus being targeted as the ultimate bases of the pirates' operations: Haldon (2000b), pp. 240–3, 339–40.

[19] *Life of Peter of Argos*, ed. Kyriakopoulos, pp. 34–5, 48–9, 174–5 (sermons); 242–3, 244–5, 246–7, 250–1 (*Life*); see also Morris (1995), pp. 113–14.

[20] John Kaminiates, *De expugnatione Thessalonicae*, chs. 70, 73, ed. Böhlig, pp. 59, 63; tr. Frendo and Photiou, pp. 115, 123.

as shrines, marks of piety and oratories. Similar monuments may well have been raised above ground in other provinces, particularly those in north-west Asia Minor, long secure from Arab raids. On the fertile southern shore of the Sea of Marmara lay several large wealthy monasteries, and ports such as Kyzikos, Pylai and Trigleia offered outlets to convey produce and live-stock to the megalopolis. Under intensive police and customs scrutiny, the Sea of Marmara was the inner sanctum of the empire, prosperous and secure. There are signs of economic dynamism at Constantinople itself in the early tenth century. The size of the population remains uncertain, but the number of buildings was apparently increasing. Leo's *novellae* regulate building land and the spaces to be preserved between buildings, in ways not found in the Justinianic planning legislation, and this hints at greater building density.[21]

Yet even in the megalopolis, driver of the Byzantine economy, the scale of activity and growth was modest. The citizens' needs could apparently be met by twenty-four notaries. Five of the nine owners of the shops listed in a mid-tenth-century rental note were officials or title-holders, and only one is identifiable by his trade. The richest pickings came from supplying the state or holding office, and the government was by far the largest employer in Constantinople. The palace complex required many hundreds of servants; eunuchs, pages and foreign bodyguards were reportedly numbered in their thousands. Most of those attending banquets or other ceremonies were holders of offices, heads of guilds or other such city worthies, but persons who held titles yet lacked a state function could attend. A text deriving from Leo VI's reign specifies the sums payable for certain court titles and offices, and indicates the *roga* payable annually by the treasury to title-holders according to their rank. Provided that the purchaser lived on for several years, he could make a profit, but the advantage lay mainly in the conspicuous connection with the imperial court, invaluable given the multifarious dealings which any man of property would have with tax inspectors and other officials.[22]

The purpose of the unremitting palace ceremonial was set out by Con-stantine VII Porphyrogenitus (945–59) in the preface to the handbook on ceremonies he commissioned: 'may it be an image of the harmony of movement which the creator gives to all creation, and be regarded by our subjects as more worthy of reverence and therefore more agreeable and marvellous.'[23] The establishment over which the emperor presided was as just and as immutable as God's, and attempting to overturn it was tan-tamount to challenging God's order of things – and no less wicked or

[21] Leo VI, *Novels*, ed. Noailles and Dain, pp. 257, 373–5.
[22] *DC*, II.49, ed. Reiske, I, pp. 692–4; Lemerle (1967), pp. 80–3, 99–100.
[23] *DC*, preface, ed. Reiske, I, p. 5; ed. and French tr. Vogt, I, p. 2.

futile. The ceremonies also dramatised the emperor's role as the sole source of legitimate authority, and of serious money. Leo VI recommends the appointment as general of a 'good, well-born and rich [man]' even while piously urging a more meritocratic approach.[24] Leo probably appreciated how much the running of his army in the provinces depended on officers' local connections and resources. The rank and file did not receive substantial regular cash wages, and Leo's *Tactica* discusses the problem of ensuring a high turn-out of well-drilled soldiery after a call to arms. His solution is a combination of fiscal privileges for the soldiers with the arousal of religious fervour throughout provincial society, so that non-combatants would be predisposed to contribute unstintingly to the war effort. In this respect, at least, the Muslims' mobilisation of their society to participate in the jihad appeared to Leo a shining example.[25]

The reforms would have to be carried through by one of the army's few full-time components, officers above the rank of *droungarios*. These were appointed directly by the emperor and drew their salaries from him, but their effectiveness would not be the less for their being gentlemen of private means. The *stratēgos* who commanded them had to cope with enemy incursions. He had to take major decisions, and possessed sweeping powers to requisition and to evacuate civilians. He was left largely to his own devices, but the term of office was short and he was forbidden from owning land in the theme he governed, a provision evidently designed to prevent close ties growing up between the governor and local society. It could not always be enforced, especially in the distant south-eastern borderlands. Yet on the whole a balance was struck between affiliations, imperial and local.

Imperial propaganda did not merely proclaim an ideal of good order from the palace. The palace rites nearly all involved prayer or the veneration of the sainted. Many involved liturgical celebrations in St Sophia or churches outside the palace complex. The emperor constantly led his entourage in prayers for the welfare of his subjects, acting together with the patriarch and fortified by the concentration in his palace of Christendom's finest relics, the Instruments of Christ's Passion among them. The rhythmic intercession gained in significance from the disorder which many provincials endured, constituting both an oasis and a clarion call for supernatural aid. Such a combination of imprecation and material splendour amidst all-enveloping turbulence could be found in the west, in Cluny, and the spell which Cluny's sumptuous liturgies cast on the propertied classes of Francia was perhaps akin to that of the *basileus*' festive prayers in Byzantium. His ritual displays of intimacy with God and *philanthrōpia* for his subjects were the

---

[24] Leo VI, *Tactica*, II.25, cols. 687–8.
[25] Leo VI, *Tactica*, XVIII.128–33, cols. 975–8; Dagron (1983), pp. 221–3, 230, 233–9.

visible accompaniment of works of legislation and tabulations of good administrative practice.

Those who did not view their interests or spiritual salvation as best served by the imperial establishment were too poor, localised and ill-equipped to take concerted action; the nearest they came was to respond tardily, if at all, to the general call-to-arms which the authorities periodically issued. Widespread if unchronicled apathy meant that *stratēgoi* had little hope of turning their forces against the government successfully. Their regular soldiers were too few and often too dispersed, and their principal mode of guerrilla warfare was ill-suited for an assault on Constantinople's formidable walls, which were ringed by water.

PALACE INTRIGUES AND COUPS

These underlying stabilisers of 'the great laden ship of the world'[26] pass virtually unnoticed in the chronicles composed in Constantinople, which focus on the colourful factional rivalries between leading courtiers and generals. Thus the eunuch Samonas tried unsuccessfully to flee to the caliphate *c.* 904, but was soon restored to favour in the palace, rising to the position of *parakoimōmenos* in 906. But ultimately he depended on the emperor's favour, and once this was withdrawn, in June 908, Samonas became a political nullity confined to a monastery. The patriarch could sometimes, if determined enough, exert moral pressure on the emperor about matters with some religious or ethical content. In 906–7 Patriarch Nicholas I Mystikos made an issue of the marriage of Leo to his mistress, who had recently borne him a longed-for male heir, Constantine. This, Leo's fourth marriage, flagrantly violated canon law and a recent edict issued by Leo and his father Basil. Nicholas caused the emperor acute political embarrassment, and his involuntary abdication in 907 was galling to many churchmen. But deposed he was. One of the charges laid against him was that he had written a letter to the domestic of the Schools, Andronikos Doukas, urging him to continue with his stand at Kabala (see above, p. 499) and promising that 'the City by our exhortations will soon ask for you'.[27]

Whether authentic or not, the letter touched on the rawest of political nerves. Andronikos belonged to one of the families which had risen to prominence in the army in the later ninth century through martial talents and imperial favour. Andronikos' son, Constantine, who had fled with him to Baghdad, later returned, to be pardoned and even promoted. He became domestic of the Schools in the last years of Leo's reign or during that of Leo's brother, Alexander (912–13). However, the latter's death and

---

[26] *DAI*, ch. 1, pp. 48–9.
[27] Nicholas I Mystikos, *Miscellaneous writings*, ed. and tr. Westerink, p. 16.

the infancy and debatable legitimacy of Constantine VII presented Doukas with an opportunity, and he is alleged to have been 'ever longing for the crown'.[28] His attempt to seize control of the palace met with stiff resistance from the reigning emperor's bodyguards, and in the house-to-house fighting within the palace complex he was killed. After this foiled coup attempt in June 913, the Doukai ceased to hold senior army commands.

The family which became the military mainstay of the Macedonian dynasty was neither illustrious nor particularly wealthy by origin. Its first outstanding member, Nikephoros Phokas, rose thanks to the favour of Basil I. He must have acted largely on his own initiative while domestic of the Schools on the eastern frontier, yet his exploits are approvingly mentioned by Leo VI, who repeatedly calls him 'our general'.[29] Nikephoros was the *prōtostratōr* during Leo's childhood, a post entailing close contact with the emperor. He most probably won Leo's trust then. The emperor on the Bosporus, culling ancient writers on strategy for his generals' benefit, was demonstrating that he was still supreme commander, making his unique contribution to the war effort. The artificial convention of imperial omniscience was one to which the Phokades were normally willing to subscribe. *Skirmishing* cited Leo's work as the source for an exploit of Nikephoros, even though the account given in *Skirmishing* is much fuller than that in Leo's *Tactica*.[30] The two families had risen together and their interests were furthered by mutual praise and material aid. The build-up of lands, wealth and local connections of the Phokades in Cappadocia was set in motion by imperial patronage and office.

Nikephoros' elder son, Leo, was seemingly made *stratēgos* of the single most important theme, the Anatolikoi, in the early tenth century. The post was held subsequently by Leo's younger brother, Bardas. The Doukai were then in the limelight and Andronikos Doukas was clearly regarded by some courtiers as a budding usurper. Perhaps for that very reason ties were kept up with the Phokades. Constantine Doukas' coup attempt appeared to confirm the courtiers' darkest suspicions. It could be a sign of contemporary Byzantine preoccupation with coups that Symeon of Bulgaria's march on Constantinople later that summer was assumed to be aimed at the throne. Nicholas I Mystikos, the chief regent, had no special reason to cherish the boy emperor; his refusal to sanction Leo VI's marriage to Constantine's mother, Zoe, had cost him his patriarchal throne. He regained it only after Leo's death, and upon becoming chief regent in June 913 he expelled Zoe from the palace. Nicholas is not implausibly alleged to have incited

[28] TC, p. 382.

[29] Leo VI, *Tactica*, XI.25, XV.38, XVII.83, cols. 799–800, 895–6, 933–4. See also above, p. 298.

[30] Leo VI, *Tactica*, XI.25, XVII.83, cols. 799–800, 933–4; *Skirmishing*, ch. 20, ed. and Dennis, tr. pp. 218–19, 223, n. 1; ed. and French tr. Dagron and Mihăescu, pp. 167–8. *Skirmishing* was composed in the milieu of Nikephoros II Phokas.

Constantine Doukas' attempted coup. In a letter to Symeon of July 913 Nicholas seems to hint that if only Symeon will stop short of outright usurpation, a role as guardian of the boy emperor may yet be found for him. Nicholas' position was insecure within the palace, understandably enough given his attitude to Constantine VII, and early in 914 the boy's yearning for his mother was cited as grounds for ousting Nicholas from the regency council. Zoe returned to the palace, and took charge.

The following six years are commonly regarded as a break in the generally orderly political history of tenth-century Byzantium. However, the period of overt jockeying for power was relatively brief. Moreover, Zoe seems to have maintained a stable regime for some three years, renewing the imperial axis with the Phokades. Leo Phokas was appointed domestic of the Schools, probably at the same time as or soon after the eunuch Constantine was restored as *parakoimōmenos*, early in 914. Leo is said by the main chronicle to have been endowed with 'courage, rather than a commander's judgement'.[31] A court orator was even less flattering, dubbing him 'the deer-hearted brother-in-law'[32] of the *parakoimōmenos*. But the expeditions sent to distant theatres in Armenia and central Italy were successful, and the government felt confident enough to attempt to 'annihilate' Symeon of Bulgaria (893–927) with a surprise attack.[33] Bitter recriminations followed the disastrous defeat at Anchialos on 20 August 917. An attempt was made to lay heaviest blame on the admiral of the fleet, Romanos Lekapenos, for failing to ferry the nomadic Pechenegs across the Danube to attack Symeon from the north, and also for not picking up survivors. These allegations probably represent an official attempt to exonerate the land army's commander, Leo Phokas. He proceeded to station himself at Constantinople with his surviving soldiers, as did Lekapenos with the imperial fleet.

ROMANOS LEKAPENOS: REGIME, ACHIEVEMENTS AND EXILE

Romanos I Lekapenos (920–44) was a provincial without particularly close court connections, but he exploited the fact that Constantine VII was now too old to be ignored. Romanos struck early in 919, benefiting from surprise, sympathisers in the palace and the apparent paralysis of Zoe and Phokas, once the intelligent *parakoimōmenos* had been seized and stowed aboard one of Lekapenos' ships. Lekapenos claimed to be acting in response to a handwritten appeal from the boy emperor. On the morrow the thirteen-year-old Constantine announced that he would assume imperial power in conjunction with Patriarch Nicholas and a veteran courtier, Stephen

---

[31] TC, p. 388.   [32] Dujčev, 'Treaty of 927 with the Bulgarians', p. 276.
[33] *aphanisai*, TC, p. 388. For the expeditions to Armenia and Italy, see pp. 354, 563. For the 'first strike' against Symeon, see Shepard (1999), pp. 574–5.

magistros. Zoe was to be expelled from the palace – although her tearful pleas at once made her son relent – and Phokas was to be replaced as domestic of the Schools. Remarkably, Phokas' reaction was merely to insist, before leaving the palace, that a brother and nephew of the *parakoimōmenos* be appointed to key commands. Still more remarkably, when these were also immediately expelled from the palace, Phokas turned to Lekapenos for consolation and support. Oaths of mutual assistance were sworn between them. Phokas' prominence at court had not been in reward for political skills. Romanos Lekapenos, in contrast, was a politician to his fingertips, who even capitalised on his status as an outsider to the palace and posed as disinterested arbiter. He made the modest request of access to the palace, the better to guard the *porphyrogenitus*. Although in late March he resorted to a display of force, arraying the entire fleet in the main harbour of the palace, he relied heavily on a small number of active sympathisers in the palace and acceptance by courtiers loyal to the *porphyrogenitus*. He entered the massively fortified precincts with only a few followers 'to perform obeisance' to the emperor,[34] exchange oaths and be appointed commander of the imperial bodyguard.

Once installed in the palace, Romanos Lekapenos acted promptly yet circumspectly. Letters in Constantine VII's name were sent to Leo Phokas, who had withdrawn to Cappadocia, warning him not to contemplate rebellion. Equally promptly, Romanos betrothed his daughter to Constantine. The marriage was celebrated on 9 May 919 and Romanos assumed the title 'father of the palace' (*basileiopatōr*). His rapid rise now alarmed well-wishers of the *porphyrogenitus*; but Lekapenos controlled the fleet and the palace, as well as Constantine's person and thus his validating authority. It was the last of these cards that he played against the large army which Phokas led from Cappadocia to Chrysopolis, across the straits from Constantinople. A letter from the emperor was read out to the rebels, singing Romanos' praises as his most trustworthy guard and denouncing Phokas as a traitor who had 'always' coveted the throne.[35]

Upon hearing this, the soldiers apparently deserted *en masse* and Phokas, who tried to flee, was caught and blinded. These events suggest the focal role of the emperor, in whose cause all parties professed to be acting, even though Constantine VII's forebears had only worn the purple for half a century and even though he had been born out of wedlock. It was Romanos' talent to harness this sentiment to his own interests. More than eighteen months elapsed before Romanos induced his son-in-law and Patriarch Nicholas to crown him co-emperor, on 17 December 920. By mediating between Nicholas Mystikos and his enemies Romanos had given Nicholas a stake in the perpetuation of his rule. Romanos was now about fifty years old and so

[34] TC, p. 394.   [35] TC, p. 396.

Figure 32 *Nomismata* of Romanos I Lekapenos showing the jockeying for power: on Class V of AD 921 (left), Christ crowns Romanos I on the obverse, while Christopher Lekapenos holds the cross with his hand above that of the smaller, beardless, Constantine VII on the reverse; on Class VII (right), Christ reigns on the obverse, while Romanos I Lekapenos and Christopher occupy the reverse, to the exclusion of the *porphyrogenitus* (this type, which is exceedingly common, is datable to 921–31)

he needed to move fast, yet any outright deposition of Constantine would outrage the very sensibilities which he had harnessed to seize power. On 17 or 20 May 921 Romanos induced the *porphyrogenitus* to crown his eldest son, Christopher, co-emperor. The 'unusual profusion of patterns and ceremonial issues'[36] of coins in the 920s reflects Romanos' aspirations, but also his hesitation about promoting Christopher to the exclusion of Constantine VII. On certain classes of *nomisma* Constantine appears smaller than Christopher and (unlike him) beardless, while on the commonest class of the 920s only Romanos and Christopher are depicted. Nonetheless, Constantine retained his formal position as second after Romanos in the palace ceremonies.

In the early 920s Romanos constructed, in effect, an alternative palace with adjoining monastery on the site of his private residence, over one kilometre to the west of the Great Palace. The new complex, although small by comparison, was clearly intended to be the shrine of the Lekapenos dynasty, and Romanos' wife was buried there in 922. The Myrelaion might lack a Porphyra, birthplace of emperors, but the monastery implied that in piety, at least, the new imperials were unimpeachable. Romanos also sought

[36] *DOC*, III.2, p. 529.

to demonstrate his philanthropy to the citizens of Constantinople through charitable foundations.

Even so, Romanos could be branded a 'stranger and intruder' by Symeon of Bulgaria,[37] and charged with imposing himself upon Constantine. The furiousness of Romanos' denial said it all; the Bulgarian had put his finger on the speciousness of the pretext for Romanos' rise to power.[38] However, if Symeon hoped to destabilise Romanos' regime, he was to be disappointed, and his armies' repeated attacks on Constantinople may well have rallied support behind the seasoned naval commander. In autumn 924 Symeon led his host in person, and at a preliminary meeting with Patriarch Nicholas he requested an encounter with Romanos. Romanos is credited with delivering a miniature homily, exhorting Symeon to desist from slaughtering fellow Christians and demonstrate his Christianity by making peace. Symeon is depicted as being shamed by these words and agreeing to make peace, though in reality nothing firmer than an accord was negotiated; the account most probably echoes contemporary imperial propaganda. Romanos also turned the Bulgarian problem to political advantage in 927, when emissaries from Symeon's heir, Peter (927–69), arrived, proposing peace. A treaty was soon ratified and on 8 October the young tsar was wedded to Maria, daughter of Romanos' eldest son, Christopher.

Romanos had his reasons for publicising the wedding. Losses in the Bulgarian war had been substantial, and peace was more than welcome to the citizens and also to the provincials in Thrace who had lived through years of Bulgarian occupation. Romanos also sought to advance his own son's status through the marriage: the Bulgarians were 'barbarians', and Peter's father had styled himself emperor only from, probably, 913, but Peter's family had long been royal. It was most probably at Romanos' prompting that the Bulgarians insisted on Christopher's name being acclaimed before that of Constantine at the wedding, and Romanos bowed to their protests. The predilections, and imperial style, of the Bulgarians could thus be yoked to Lekapenan aspirations. In so far as the interests of these two families converged, the court rhetoric about 'union' and fellowship had an unsuspectedly solid foundation. Christopher's imperial credentials were enhanced and he could be described as revitalising his father's old age through 'flourishing in his turn in majesty, and he nourished [it] with hopes of [his] succession to the throne'.[39]

Romanos Lekapenos is said to have been devastated by Christopher's death in August 931. He does not seem to have had the heart to set

[37] Theodore Daphnopates, *Correspondance*, ed. and French tr. Darrouzès and Westerink, no. 6, pp. 72–3.

[38] Theodore Daphnopates, *Correspondance*, ed. and French tr. Darrouzès and Westerink, no. 6, pp. 70–3.

[39] Sternbach, 'Christophorea', p. 17.

about advancing his younger sons Stephen and Constantine ahead of the *porphyrogenitus*; they were still only boys. Constantine VII was restored to the gold coins, even occupying a position senior to Romanos', a move which reflects the uncertain political outlook. Constantine was neither assured of the succession nor involved in decision-making. His bitter disdain for his father-in-law is patent in his *De administrando imperio*, most explicitly in his dismissal of the Bulgarian marriage arranged by the 'common and illiterate fellow'.[40]

This uneasy *ménage* was upset publicly by Romanos' show of favour towards Constantine VII: he proposed that Constantine's son should marry the daughter of his domestic of the Schools. Stephen and Constantine Lekapenos protested vehemently and the plan was dropped. It is striking that the domestic, John Kourkouas, was brought into play by Romanos to counteract the tensions of court factions, inevitably aggravated by his advanced age. Romanos' alertness to the post's significance is suggested by the brevity of domestics' tenure early in his reign, in contrast with Kourkouas' twenty-two-year stint. Kourkouas was under thirty when appointed in 922, and he had no record of associations with the Macedonian house, probably a prime recommendation in Romanos' eyes; his experience of pitched battles on the eastern borderlands was then minimal. But Kourkouas proved to have military talents. From the later 920s onwards, he was repeatedly sent eastwards and won praise from Byzantine chronicles for all the towns, forts and castles, allegedly numbering over 1,000, that he captured from the Saracens. The troublesome Muslim raiding bases of Melitene and Theodosioupolis were repeatedly attacked. Melitene was finally annexed in 934, and Theodosioupolis was eventually captured in 949. Muslim forts along the upper Euphrates and its tributaries were turned into Byzantine strongpoints. One of them was renamed Romanoupolis, in the emperor's honour. The domestic, who was aptly compared with Belisarius, gained for his sedentary master an aura of expansion. He is credited with having doubly benefited *Romania*, stemming the Muslim raids deep into Asia Minor and extending Roman borders as far as the Euphrates and even the Tigris.[41] More impressive is the fact that Kourkouas' offensives could be sustained for almost twenty years without much overt foreboding of *coups d'état*.

Romanos chose the theatres of operations no less shrewdly. They lay for the most part in Armenia and Mesopotamia. He did not mount ambitious combined operations of the sort that had come to grief in Leo VI's reign, nor was there much concentrated effort in the south-eastern borderlands. Instead, the pressure was applied further north, on Armenia and adjoining regions. Theodosioupolis and Melitene lay in fertile countryside and were

---

[40] *DAI*, ch. 13, pp. 72–3.   [41] TC, p. 427; Savvides (1990), pp. 11–25.

important trading centres. They could yield ample revenues and Melitene was declared an imperial *kouratoreia*, an establishment whose proceeds went straight to the emperor's coffers. The rocky slopes of the Taurus and the Anti-Taurus, by contrast, were neither fertile nor well-populated, while the Cilician plain was studded with Muslim forts. One further advantage of Romanos' eastern strategy was that it did not rely on Byzantine military resources alone. John Kourkouas and his brother Theophilos were able to gain the collaboration or formal submission of certain Armenian princes, while Romanos himself sought to forge bonds with individual princes, offering titles or a residence and estates in Byzantium. He thereby complemented and, at the same time, kept track of Kourkouas' activities. The princes' ties were with Romanos himself.

The most spectacular of Kourkouas' *tours de force* induced the citizens of Edessa to surrender their famed *mandylion*, the cloth with the miraculous imprint of Christ's features. In return, Romanos issued a chrysobull, pledging that Byzantium would never again molest the region of Edessa.[42] Edessa lay little more than 100 kilometres south from Melitene, but was clearly not regarded as a desirable candidate for annexation. The gaining of the relic showed up the caliph's impotence and the *mandylion* was conveyed through the provinces to Constantinople. But the high-pitched celebration of its arrival had much to do with Romanos' domestic problems. Some time earlier he had had to yield to his sons' protests at his scheme to marry Constantine VII's son to Kourkouas' daughter. Now he was too frail for the main procession, from the Golden Gate to St Sophia, and the advent of the image may unintentionally have bolstered the standing of his two unfavoured younger sons; they played a leading role in the celebrations welcoming the image to Constantinople, whereas Kourkouas is not recorded as having been present.[43]

By the autumn of 944, Kourkouas had been dismissed. That same autumn Romanos made another gesture in favour of Constantine VII, issuing a testament declaring him 'the first emperor' and threatening his own sons' imperial status should they attempt anything against Constantine.[44] Acting, presumably, in light of this, the young Lekapenoi struck against their father on 20 December 944. He was secretly abducted to one of the islands in the Sea of Marmara. It is uncertain whether Constantine

---

[42] TC, p. 432; von Dobschütz, *Christusbilder*, p. 75**. The environs of Edessa were traversed by Byzantine forces on several occasions, and as early as 949 Samosata, a city named in the chrysobull, was attacked and, nine years later, devastated. However, these were essentially countermeasures against Saif al-Dawla, who was the first to breach the terms of the chrysobull: Canard (1953), p. 751; Segal (1970), p. 216.

[43] Kalavrezou (1997), pp. 55–6; Morris (2003), pp. 249, 251; Engberg (2004), pp. 132–5. On the relic's later fortunes, see Wolf *et al.* (eds.) (2004); contributions to Durand and Flusin (eds.) (2004); Hetherington (2006).

[44] TC, p. 435.

VII connived with the plotters: what is (and was) clear is his status as the sole adult emperor to have been born in the Porphyra. When a rumour spread that he had been murdered by the two Lekapenoi, the populace gathered outside the palace, calling for Constantine. It was placated only by his appearance, poking his bare head out through a lattice.

The citizens of Constantinople seem to have associated the Macedonian house with their own well-being, just as Leo VI had intended. But the *porphyrogenitus* did not rely on aura alone. He is said to have immediately appointed Bardas Phokas as domestic of the Schools, the brother of the man against whose alleged ambition for the throne Lekapenos had launched his own political career.[45] Bardas' first loyalty was patently to Constantine VII, and the appointment was a first step towards the undoing of the Lekapenoi. They themselves were apparently hatching a plot against the *porphyrogenitus* when they were seized in the palace on 27 January 945. They were, without any reported popular outcry, abducted to the Princes' Islands and a new life as exiles. Had their father backed them whole-heartedly, they might perhaps have supplanted the *porphyrogenitus*. But Romanos had not repeated his efforts to advance Christopher. At home, as abroad, his hard-headed ambition did little more than maintain the status quo.

CONSTANTINE VII AS LEADER

Erudition, education, prayer

The reign of Constantine VII Porphyrogenitus as senior and dominant emperor (945–59) has traditionally been viewed as the apogee of Byzantium as a great power resplendent in culture and learning. It would be more accurate to say that the gathering strength of the economy and manpower began to be harnessed to imperial politics in spectacular ways, in the palace and on the battlefield. Constantine, like his father Leo VI, saw himself as a writer and instructor, and he was interested in many branches of written knowledge. This was partly a matter of theoretical knowledge or erudition about the past, but Constantine regarded the practical experience relayed by writings as indispensable to an emperor, as he stated in his preface to the *De administrando imperio*, a handbook devoted principally to foreign peoples and compiled for the instruction of his young son so that foreign nations 'shall quake before thee as one mighty in wisdom'.[46]

Constantine's public stress on learning reflected his own views and there is no reason to doubt the characterisation by the author of a *Synaxarion*, a history of the saints celebrated through the church year, commissioned by the emperor. Constantine, rising before the birds, was zealous to study

---

[45] TC, p. 436.   [46] *DAI*, preface, pp. 46–7.

'every book' and read through 'the ancient . . . histories' from which one could become 'experienced . . . in all kinds of matters'.[47] This, like the standard preface to the fifty-three instalments of extracts from classical and early Byzantine historical works commissioned by Constantine, asserts the special access of the emperor to wisdom through the books amassed in his palace. An emperor who exploited these reserves of past experience and piety was uniquely wise and reverend. But Constantine was simultaneously offering the 'benefit' of his digests 'to the public', in the words of the preface.[48] This exaltation of book-learning was in the tradition of Constantine's father, Leo 'the Wise'; both were palace-dwellers, and both asserted that the books and learning accumulated behind its closed doors were, through their mediation, relevant and advantageous to their subjects.

Constantine may have been guided partly by the example of another early tenth-century emperor, who had also filled his palace with books and whose reputation for learning was known to the Byzantines: Symeon of Bulgaria. Constantine and Symeon both accepted the ruler's duty to educate his people. This notion had been propounded by ninth-century scholar-ecclesiastics like Photius,[49] and became engrained in the propaganda and self-image of the Macedonian dynasty, although Constantine's education had in fact been very limited. His piety was sometimes patently dynastic. Thus he appropriated the acquisition of the *mandylion* from Edessa; the texts celebrating the event composed in the opening years of his reign represent the arrival of Christ's image as prefiguring and even precipitating Constantine's advance to sole rule.[50] Probably already by January 946 Constantine had brought 'home' to the capital the relics of Gregory Nazianzen; the casket was borne to the palace on purple cloth, restoring the 'sanctity and reverence' of which it 'had previously been deprived'. Subsequently the relics were installed in the church of the Holy Apostles, the burial-place of emperors, and a panegyric extolled the emperor responsible for all this as 'our new Moses'.[51]

Constantine emphasised most prominently his least controvertible qualities, invaluable assets even in his infancy: birth in the purple (declared on his silver coins from 945 onwards); and the supposed link between his well-being and that of the citizens of Constantinople, asserted in the acclamations chanted before large crowds in the Hippodrome. Constantine, by commissioning the *Book of ceremonies*, in large part an almanac of

[47] *AASS Novembris, Propylaeum*, col. XIV; Ševčenko, I. (1992a), p. 188, n. 52.

[48] Constantine VII Porphyrogenitus, *Excerpta de legationibus*, ed. de Boor, p. 2.

[49] See above, p. 301; Shepard (1999), p. 572.

[50] von Dobschütz, *Christusbilder*, pp. 79**, 85**; Morris (2003), p. 251; Engberg (2004), pp. 133–6; Hetherington (2006), pp. 193–7. See also Dubarle, 'L' Homélie de Grégoire le Référandaire.

[51] *AASS Maii*, II, p. 452; Flusin, 'Le Panégyrique de Constantin VII Porphyrogénète', pp. 12, 21–5, 32–7.

the emperor's participation in church festivals and celebration of imperial power, showed his regard for both book-learning and the rhythm of the ritual; he claimed to be both restoring old practices and introducing new ones.[52] The rites he described and prescribed amounted to one long round of intercession, and the relics which Constantine amassed underlined the traditional designation of the palace as 'sacred'. They also enhanced his ability to gain supernatural protection for favoured subjects, such as soldiers out on campaign; the saints, present through their relics, would heed the emperor's prayers, protecting his armies and bringing victories. The power of imperial prayer is stressed in the *Life of Basil*, yet another of the works issued under Constantine's auspices, and the theme is also implicit in three works of art probably emanating from court circles which show Constantine with a relic or in prayer.[53]

Law and property

Yet prayer and book-learning were not enough to sustain a regime. The balance between piety and practicality ascribed to Basil I in the *Life* probably represents Constantine's own line of thinking. One symbol of his concern for those beyond the City walls was the promulgation of laws valid throughout the empire. Eight are extant, at least one more known. A *novella* of 947 survives in versions addressing the themes of the Thrakesioi and the Anatolikoi, strengthening the sanctions and impediments on the purchase of land from 'the poor' by 'the powerful' laid down by Romanos in a *novella* of 934. Another attempts to protect the land-holdings of those enrolled to supply military service in the themes.[54]

There is little doubt that smaller peasant proprietors were increasingly alienating their lands to 'the powerful'. But it is unclear how far they were acting involuntarily and how far they were trying to profit from a more active property market. The two explanations are not mutually incompatible and, taken together, they could imply a gradual increase of population and quickening of commercial transactions (albeit largely in agricultural produce) as Muslim land raids abated. It appears that 'the powerful' of keenest concern to the emperors were those trying to take over lands in the fertile coastal region of western Asia Minor and also in the most strategically

---

[52] *DC*, preface, ed. Reiske, I, pp. 3–4; ed. and French tr. Vogt, I, pp. 1–2; Jolivet-Lévy (1987), pp. 452–4; Moffatt (1995), pp. 379–84.

[53] TC, pp. 299, 315–16; Weitzmann (1971a), pp. 242–6; Weitzmann (1972), pp. 59–60; Jolivet-Lévy (1987), pp. 452–4, 458, n. 68. See figs. 33, 34.

[54] *JG*, ed. Zepos and Zepos, I, pp. 214–17, 222–6; ed. Svoronos, nos. 4, 5, pp. 98–103, 118–26; tr. McGeer, pp. 63–7, 71–6; Lemerle (1979), pp. 87, 94–8, 117–25. See above, pp. 268–9, 489. Lawmaking, often in response to requests for rulings by officials in the provinces, was an important imperial function in the reign of Constantine VII's heir Romanos, too: Fögen (1994), pp. 61–8.

Figure 33 Moscow ivory of Constantine VII being crowned and blessed by
Christ (mid-tenth century)

Figure 34 King Abgar of Edessa, who received the *mandylion* from Christ, shown with features resembling those of Constantine VII

important theme, the Anatolikoi. There is clear evidence of construction-work and economic revival during the tenth century in towns such as Sardis, Amorion (following its sack in 838), and Akroinon on the military highway to Syria.[55] The overwhelming majority of 'the powerful' were themselves office- and title-holders, with a personal stake in the state's welfare, or they were churchmen or members of well-to-do monasteries. It was not diffi-cult to exploit one's position in the 'establishment' to personal advantage, minimising or avoiding one's own tax payments and other obligations to

[55] Foss (1976), pp. 70, 74–5; Lightfoot (1998), pp. 67–70 and table 1 on p. 71; Lightfoot *et al.* (2001), pp. 394, 398; Cheynet *et al.* (2004), pp. 215–17, 226.

the central administration and buying up properties from the hard-pressed peasants who were left to shoulder the burden in their now depleted tax unit (*chōrion*); hence the paradoxical-seeming attempts to hinder the accumulation of landed estates in the hands of persons of influence. This was a problem of success for the empire which would become more acute with the elaboration of the state's apparatus and financial needs, and these, in turn, were driven largely by the demands of the military machine.

Partnership with the Phokades and the shift to the offensive

Constantine VII's legislation registers governmental concern about the material underpinning of the theme army in the wake of Kourkouas' repeated offensives in the east. Constantine's *novella* on 'military lands' was issued not long before the expedition of 949 to reconquer Crete, a cherished project. Extravagant rhetoric celebrated the emperor's supposed victories and his extension of the frontiers. In a poem in honour of Romanos II, Constantine is described as growing weary from writing down the roll of subjugated cities:[56] Tarsus and Crete tremble, as peoples and cities race to submit to the emperor. In reality, though, most of these towns were sacked rather than occupied, and the Cretan expedition ended ignominiously. It was part of the continuity Constantine sought to maintain, especially with his own father's reign; then, too, a Cretan expedition of some sort had been launched and land campaigning concentrated on the south-eastern borderlands. Equally, Constantine looked to the Phokades to provide military leaders, and the poem likens Bardas Phokas, domestic of the Schools since 945, to 'a glittering broadsword or a flame of fire, kindled by thy father's [Constantine's] prayers'.[57] These lines evoke the 'special relationship' between the Phokades and the Macedonian house which Romanos Lekapenos had so dexterously disconnected in 919. Constantine seems nevertheless to have balked at entrusting a major command to any military man of repute. The commander of the Cretan expedition, Constantine Gongylios, had been in charge of the imperial fleet since 945, but was described as 'without experience of war'.[58] Our sole detailed account of the expedition blames him for its failure and alleges that he failed to take the elementary precaution of establishing a secure camp on the island.[59]

Constantine's early years as senior emperor remained within the framework of essentially static, palace-based rule implied by the preface to the *De administrando imperio*. This work, compiled at his command between *c.* 948 and *c.* 952, bears his fingerprints more markedly than any of the other

---

[56] Odorico, 'Il calamo d'argento', p. 91.   [57] Odorico, 'Il calamo d'argento', p. 91.
[58] Skyl., ed. Thurn, p. 245; French tr. Flusin and Cheynet, pp. 206–7; see also TC, p. 436.
[59] Skyl., ed. Thurn, pp. 245–6; French tr. Flusin and Cheynet, pp. 206–8.

works associated with him. Diplomacy was an activity which a sedentary emperor could conduct highly effectively on his own account, and its ceremonial workings were focused on his mystique alone. But even as the compilation got under way, a military crisis developed in the east which was eventually to force Constantine to depart from the strategy of previous generations. The catalyst was Saif al-Dawla, a scion of the Hamdanid clan that had tightened its hold on Mosul and other prosperous parts of Mesopotamia, to the detriment of the caliph of Baghdad. By the end of 947 Saif was in firm control of Aleppo and its commercial wealth. He embarked on a series of devastating, if strategically insignificant, raids into Asia Minor. The Byzantines responded to this energetic warlord on their borders with major reprisals, taking captives and razing the walls of foreposts such as Hadath and Germanikeia. Hadath, a fortress on a key pass leading towards Byzantine-occupied Melitene, was the scene of several battles involving sizable Byzantine armies intent on demolishing the walls and Muslim units no less determined to defend or rebuild them. Bitter as the fighting was, it formed part of a broader strategy. At the same time as attempting to deny Saif secure bases, Byzantium sent embassies proposing truces and prisoner exchanges. However, Saif seems to have taken these as signs of impending Byzantine collapse. He rejected offers of an exchange of prisoners, and the poets in his entourage proclaimed his courage and the imminence of victory.

Saif al-Dawla's militancy and obduracy seem to have persuaded the reluctant Constantine that he would have to be worsted or removed, if his own authority was not to be tarnished. In, probably, 955 Nikephoros Phokas was appointed domestic of the Schools. He is said to have raised his soldiers' morale, training them to attack in good order and to occupy enemy territory confidently 'as if in their own land'; heavy cavalry charges were now central to tactics.[60] The reason for this more aggressive strategy is given by Abu Firas, a member of Saif's entourage: after suffering incessant incursions and after Saif had refused a truce except on extraordinary terms, Constantine made treaties with neighbouring rulers, sought military aid from them and sent out a large and expensive expedition to break Saif's power.[61] In the summer of 958 Samosata, on the Euphrates, was captured and demolished, and Saif was heavily defeated trying to relieve Raban, in October or November. Next spring the Byzantine force reached Qurus, only about 60 kilometres from Aleppo, and took many prisoners. Muslim sources suggest that Byzantium was fielding much larger forces than before, heavily armoured cavalry and units of Rus, Khazar and other foreign fighters.

---

[60] TC, p. 459; McGeer (1995), pp. 179–80, 280–315, 327.
[61] Abu Firas, *Diwan*, French tr. in Vasil., p. 368.

Figure 35 Illustration from the Madrid Skylitzes of Byzantine cavalry pursuing fleeing Muslims

Whether Constantine VII would have refrained from launching a large-scale *reconquista* must remain uncertain; death, on 9 November 959, relieved him of the problems posed by departure from his own model of static, 'Solomonic' kingship. Constantine's right-hand man, Basil Lekapenos the *parakoimōmenos*, was arguing for another assault on Crete during Constantine's last months. Even in court circles, the temptation to put to new uses the military machine assembled to break Saif al-Dawla was growing all but irresistible.

NIKEPHOROS II PHOKAS, JOHN I TZIMISKES AND VICTORIES IN THE EAST

Basil Lekapenos was dismissed by Constantine's heir, Romanos II (959–63), but the new *parakoimōmenos*, Joseph Bringas, also urged an attack on Crete, and Romanos himself seems to have been enthusiastic for military success at the outset of his reign. The greater part of the empire's armed forces embarked for the island in a huge flotilla in June 960. The ensuing hard-fought campaign lasted until March 961. Contemporaries were well aware of the significance of this feat. The author of a poem composed just after Crete's fall looks forward to the invasion of other Muslim lands: the vultures of Egypt will devour the victims of the emperor's sword. As the preface acknowledges, the real hero of the poem is Nikephoros Phokas, for all the dutiful praise awarded to Romanos.[62] Nikephoros was now allowed to strike at Aleppo, from which Saif had continued to harass the empire's borderlands. Saif's army proved no match for the Byzantine heavy cavalry and he fled ignominiously. Byzantine soldiers entered the city on 23 December 962.

---

[62] Theodosios the Deacon, *De Creta capta*, ed. Criscuolo, pp. 1, 36.

Double question-marks now hung over Byzantium: would the offensive against the Muslims be sustained, now that Saif had been humbled? And how would relations fare between Nikephoros and the young emperor, depicted in chronicles as a dissolute youth much given to pig-sticking?[63] The second question was resolved by Romanos' sudden death on 15 March 963, from poison according to some sources, and before the slighting of Aleppo had been celebrated. Phokas was summoned to the capital by Joseph Bringas, was hailed as 'bravest conqueror',[64] a pun on his first name ('victory-bearer'), and then withdrew to the east; but the temptation or pressure to claim the throne was strong. Unlike his uncle Leo Phokas in 919, Nikephoros had a large victorious army at his disposal and the officers seem to have felt prime loyalty to him. If we may believe a source biased heavily in his favour, they proclaimed Nikephoros emperor willy-nilly, maintaining that he, rather than an 'ignoble eunuch with sucklings [the infant *porphyrogeniti*, Basil II and Constantine VIII] should be giving out orders to men of blood'.[65] Nikephoros also enjoyed active support among the Constantinopolitan populace,and whereas Leo Phokas had been opposed by the fleet under Romanos Lekapenos, Basil the ex-*parakoimōmenos* managed to seize the docks and their warships armed with Greek fire. Basil Lekapenos' web of patronage was extensive, while in the palace the mother of the *porphyrogeniti*, Theophano, seems to have been in sympathy with Nikephoros. Basil sent ships, including the imperial yacht, inviting him into the City, and on 16 August 963 Nikephoros made a triumphal entry, receiving such acclamations as 'Nikephoros for emperor the public good demands'.[66] He was crowned in St Sophia. In little more than a decade, the army had become not only a battering-ram against distant Muslim foes but also a sought-after presence in the political life of the capital.

Constantine VII had claimed the inheritance of Constantine the Great through his veneration of the True Cross; Nikephoros bid for the succession by acts of conquest. An inscription on an ivory reliquary from his reign reads: 'Formerly, Christ gave the Cross to the mighty master Constantine for his salvation. But now the lord by the grace of God Nikephoros, possessing this, routs the barbarian peoples.'[67] It fits with the notion that the empire's military fortunes hinged upon Nikephoros' personal survival, expressed in a book of prophecy, the *Visions of Daniel*, shown to Liudprand of Cremona at Constantinople in 968.[68]

[63] TC, p. 472; Skyl., ed. Thurn, p. 248; French tr. Flusin and Cheynet, p. 209.
[64] *andriōtate nikēta*: DC, I.96, ed. Reiske, I, p. 438.
[65] Leo the Deacon, *History*, III.4, ed. Hase, p. 40; tr. Talbot and Sullivan, p. 91. According to Leo, this was the argument put by Phokas' second-in-command, John Tzimiskes, to other senior officers.
[66] DC, I.96, ed. Reiske, I, p. 439.
[67] Frolow (1961), p. 240; Frolow (1965), p. 101.
[68] *Leg.*, ch. 39, ed. Chiesa, p. 204; tr. Scott, pp. 14, 43; Morris (1988), pp. 94–5.

Nikephoros, acclaimed as 'conqueror' at his coronation as well as at his triumphs, kept his forces engaged; in some years there were two or three expeditions in progress on different fronts. The disastrous outcome of the 964 Sicilian expedition did not prevent Nikephoros from reducing the numerous Muslim fortifications beyond the Taurus and Anti-Taurus ranges, in Cilicia and northern Syria. He is plausibly credited with the capture of 'more than a hundred towns and forts'.[69] This was a very fertile, well-populated region which had not suffered ruination from Byzantine campaigning earlier in the century, being studded with 'hard' targets. The forts, most notoriously Tarsus, had served as bases for raids, and in 965 Tarsus itself surrendered. That same year, a Byzantine force occupied Cyprus. Nikephoros commanded an expedition as far as the outskirts of Aleppo in 966 and briefly laid siege to Antioch. Pressure was resumed in the autumn of 968: he initiated another siege of Antioch and then left a blockade under subordinates; almost a year later, on 28 October 969, Antioch surrendered.

The fall of Antioch had considerable *éclat*, for this was an ancient Christian city. The Muslims' execution of its patriarch on a charge of treachery in 967 gave edge to claims that Nikephoros was 'armed with the holy spirit'.[70] Yet the fundamentally defensive cast of his strategy is indicated by the truce which Peter Phokas concluded with the amir of Aleppo in January 970: a blueprint for coexistence and commerce, biased in Byzantium's favour but leaving the emirate as a semi-autonomous power. The amir was to inform the emperor of the military movements of his fellow Muslims, and 'if any Muslim troops arrive to invade the Rum . . . [he is] to hinder them, saying "Pass through other regions and do not come into the land of the truce!"'[71] The terms were probably not very different from those initially offered to the amir of Melitene some forty years earlier (see above, p. 509), and they presupposed that Byzantium would rest content with its gains in Cilicia and along the Euphrates valley.

The terms had almost certainly been approved by Nikephoros, but by the time the truce was made he was dead and headless, murdered during the night of 11 December 969. His fall was a quintessential palace coup; his wife, Theophano, had been attracted to his former right-hand man, John I Tzimiskes (969–76), who personally participated in the killing of Nikephoros and had the severed head displayed to the guards who came, too late, to the rescue. Tzimiskes' first measure, after consultation with Basil Lekapenos the *parakoimōmenos*, was to decree that looting or violence would be punished with death, a stern pronouncement against the lawlessness that had been dogging the City in the later part of Nikephoros' reign.

---

[69] Skyl., ed. Thurn, p. 271; French tr. Flusin and Cheynet, pp. 227–8.
[70] 'Office inédit en l'honneur de Nicéphore Phocas', ed. Petit, p. 401. This comes from an office venerating Nikephoros, written soon after his death.
[71] Canard (1953), pp. 833–4; Farag (1977), pp. 2–3.

Figure 36 Illustration from the Madrid Skylitzes of the head of Nikephoros II Phokas being shown to his supporters outside the palace

This endeared him to the propertied classes, as did his remission of the hearth tax, and he increased the stipends payable to senior officials and title-holders. He was also more attentive to the material needs of ordinary citizens than Nikephoros had been. Reportedly, he had to be restrained by the *parakoimōmenos* from emptying the treasury through distributions to the poor.[72] He took steps to alleviate famine in the countryside, but pacification of the City was probably his first priority. When celebrating a triumph through the streets, he had them bedecked with laurel branches and cloths of gold 'like a bridechamber',[73] thus invoking the emperor's role as bridegroom of the City. The procession was staged to mark his victory over the Rus, thwarting Prince Sviatoslav's attempt to instal himself on the Danube; but it gave Tzimiskes the opportunity to demonstrate to the citizens 'ignorant of military matters' the utility for their own security of large, well-equipped armed forces, and the indispensability of military leadership.[74]

The need to rekindle personal loyalties among the former soldiers of Nikephoros Phokas was one of the reasons for the spectacular campaigns against the Muslims which John I Tzimiskes launched from the autumn of 972 onwards. Byzantine propaganda even claimed that in 974 he led an all-conquering army to Baghdad itself; he certainly levied tribute from the amir of Mosul. In 975 Tzimiskes penetrated as far south as Damascus, levying tribute from its governor and taking Beirut by storm. Relics were

---

[72] Leo the Deacon, *History*, VI.3, ed. Hase, p. 97; tr. Talbot and Sullivan, p. 147.

[73] Leo the Deacon, *History*, IX.12, ed. Hase, p. 158; tr. Talbot and Sullivan, p. 201.

[74] Leo the Deacon, *History*, IV.6, ed. Hase, p. 63; tr. Talbot and Sullivan, p. 112. The 'Bamberg silk', commonly associated with Basil II, may well commemorate this triumph: Prinzing (1993a). On Sviatoslav's campaigns, see Franklin and Shepard (1996), pp. 145–51.

sent back to Constantinople, as they had been by Nikephoros II after several of his campaigns. In a letter to Ashot III Bagratuni ('the Merciful') (953–77), 'king of kings' of Armenia, Tzimiskes claimed to have received tribute from Ramla, Jerusalem and other towns, and that the liberation of Jerusalem was his ultimate goal.[75] Such propaganda was partly for domestic consumption, but it also bolstered the emperor's moral, and eventually political, authority over the Armenian princes.

BASIL II VERSUS REBEL GENERALS

John I Tzimiskes' designs on Armenia had, however, no time for fruition. On 11 January 976 he died of typhoid or poison. The elder son of Romanos II, Basil II (976–1025), was about eighteen years old. No formal regency was required, although his great-grandfather Romanos I's bastard son Basil Lekapenos the *parakoimōmenos* dominated the administration for a further ten years. Basil II's speech was staccato, 'more that of a peasant than a gentleman',[76] a description which would surely have pained his bookish grandfather Constantine Porphyrogenitus. In fact Basil, with his single-minded devotion to his army and preoccupation with drill and military formations, had far more in common with Nikephoros Phokas, another celibate ascetic. The role of war leader, which he assumed in early adulthood, became habitual and congenial and was highlighted in portrayals of Basil. He is depicted in military uniform on the frontispiece of a celebrated psalter, opposite verses explaining such images as the archangel Michael handing Basil a spear.[77] A predominantly martial note was also struck in the verses engraved on his tomb:

> No one saw my spear lie still . . .
> but I was wakeful through all the time of my life
> and guarded the children of the New Rome . . .[78]

Basil's watchfulness was in reality directed as much at his own subjects and officers as at foreign foes. The resentment of the Bulgarians at the dissolution of their ancient state was exploited by four sons of an Armenian officer in the Byzantine occupation army. Soon after Tzimiskes' death, if not before, the Kometopouloi ('sons of the *komēs*') deserted, and they were soon leading Bulgarians in rebellion.[79] More immediately menacing was the revolt of the eastern army within months of Tzimiskes' death. The

---

[75] ME, tr. Dostourian, pp. 30–1; Walker (1977), pp. 319–27.
[76] Psell., I.36, ed. and French tr. Renauld, I, p. 23; ed. and Italian tr. Impellizzeri *et al.*, I, pp. 54–5; tr. Sewter, p. 49.
[77] 'Psalter of Basil II'; Cutler (1984), p. 115 and fig. 412, p. 253; Stephenson (2003), p. 51–2, 61–2. See fig. 37.
[78] Mercati (1970), p. 230.
[79] Shepard (1999), p. 584.

Figure 37 Illustration from the 'Psalter of Basil II', showing Basil II in parade armour, crowned by Christ with defeated foreigners and rebels grovelling at his feet

new claimant was Bardas Skleros, the general upon whom the government had relied to combat the Rus and also to quash the rebellion of Bardas Phokas, a nephew of the emperor Nikephoros II Phokas, in 970. Skleros forced the Taurus mountain passes, and after further battles he gradually closed on Constantinople. Basil the *parakoimōmenos* turned to none other than Bardas Phokas, but the troops which Phokas mustered in his family heartland around Caesarea were no match for the array of regular units which Skleros could field, and Phokas was defeated twice in the summer

Figure 38 Illustration from the Madrid Skylitzes showing intensive negotiations between Bardas Skleros, the caliphate and Basil II, who tried to secure Skleros' handover from Baghdad: (above) Bardas Skleros sends a message to the caliph; (below) the emperor sends a counter-message to the caliph

and autumn of 978. The Macedonians' plight was undoubtedly dire, even though Skleros hesitated to march straight for Constantinople. The day was saved by the arrival of a 12,000-strong force of cavalry despatched by David *kouropalatēs*, the ruler of Tao, the region of western Georgia adjoining Theodosioupolis. The Georgians joined up with the remnants of Phokas' army and surprised and defeated the rebels to the west of Caesarea, in the theme of Charsianon, on 24 March 979. Bardas Skleros fled to Muslim territory and lengthy negotiations about his repatriation ensued between Byzantium and Baghdad.

Skleros eventually returned, but as a claimant to the throne, not a deportee. In 985 Basil II dismissed the *éminence grise* of tenth-century politics, Basil Lekapenos the *parakoimōmenos*, and subsequently exiled him from the City, upon suspicion of plotting with various generals of the eastern army. Basil II resolved to take charge of the army himself and to undertake an operation independently of his overbearing and well-connected generals. Bulgaria offered at once an opportunity and a real threat to his regime. In 985 and early 986 Samuel of Bulgaria (987/8–1014), who was emerging as dominant among the Kometopouloi, was systematically reducing important forts and towns in Thrace and northern Greece. He transplanted the inhabitants of Larissa to Bulgaria and enrolled the males for military service. Basil led a large army to Sofia, a key strategic centre, but he failed to reduce the town and his army was ambushed withdrawing through the pass at Trajan's Gates; Basil himself barely escaped. Basil II's first steps in soldiering thus ended in ignominy and Bardas Skleros seized the opportunity to negotiate his release with the authorities in Baghdad and make his second bid for the throne early in 987. Then, on 15 August 987, Bardas Phokas, to whom Basil had earlier turned for assistance against Skleros, was himself proclaimed emperor: with the help of Maleinos and other Cappadocian notables he had raised local troops, supplementing the *tagmata* already under his command. A pact was negotiated between the two rebel generals, whereby Skleros would become master of Antioch and other recently gained or still unconquered territories to the south and east of that city.

By the end of 987 Bardas Phokas had gained control of most of Asia Minor and was able to send a detachment to Chrysopolis, in the footsteps of his grandfather Leo Phokas in 919. He himself laid siege to Abydos, at the other end of Byzantium's 'inner sea'. Once again, the mystique of imperial authority seems to have dispersed a Phokas-led army, but this time the mystique worked on a distant foreign ruler, and not on rank-and-file Byzantine soldiers. A marriage was negotiated between Basil II's sister, the *porphyrogenita* Anna, and the ruler of the Rus, Vladimir Sviatoslavich of Kiev. In return for Anna's hand, Vladimir would send warriors to the emperor's aid and, according to an almost contemporary Armenian writer, 6,000 Rus arrived at Byzantium. They surprised and routed the rebel force encamped at Chrysopolis.[80] However, they were infantrymen, and probably could not have prevailed over the heavy cavalry of the eastern army. It was hugely to Basil's good fortune that on 13 April 989 his most formidable enemy, Bardas Phokas, died suddenly of a stroke and the rebel army dispersed. Bardas Skleros emerged to make common cause with the dead man's sons. In June, Skleros wrote to the Turkish general in charge of Baghdad, requesting his aid. No prompt aid was forthcoming, and this may well have been one reason why Skleros entered into negotiations with the Byzantine government. Basil granted him an amnesty in the autumn of 989. Only then did

---

[80] ST, French tr. Macler, p. 164; Psell., I.13, ed. and French tr. Renauld, I, p. 9; ed. and Italian tr. Impellizzeri *et al.*, I, pp. 22–3; tr. Sewter, pp. 34–5; Skyl., ed. Thurn, p. 336; French tr. Flusin and Cheynet, pp. 280–1. On the conversion of Rus, which these events triggered, see above, pp. 325–6; Franklin and Shepard (1996), pp. 162–9.

the citizens of Antioch drive Leo Phokas (Bardas' son) out of their city and acknowledge Basil II's regime.

BASIL II'S BULGARIAN WARS

As the ruler of a greatly enlarged empire, Basil became his own general, thereby dispensing with the military 'establishment' which had been the mainstay of governance in the first years his reign. Basil's intimate knowledge of the characters of individual soldiers and his supervision of promotions reduced the risk of plots and coups. He maintained the strictest military discipline. Basil's martinet-like stance probably sprang from a mixture of personal proclivity and political calculation. He had, in any case, little choice but to take up the challenge which Samuel of Bulgaria was posing.

On 14 June 987 or 988 Samuel had his own brother Aaron and most of his family put to death, becoming in effect sole ruler. He was determined to found a new dynasty based in the Macedonian highlands, forswearing Symeon's Preslav. The gain of Dyrrachium – apparently without violence – relieved him of the danger of surprise attacks from the west, and Samuel married Agatha, daughter of Dyrrachium's 'leading man' John Chryselios,[81] who presumably swung the town behind him. Samuel also aspired to control Thessaloniki, the counterpart of Dyrrachium; they stood at opposite ends of the Egnatian Way, where it reached the Aegean and Adriatic seas. There were already a number of significant towns in the *massif* traversed by the Egnatian Way, comprising bishoprics and monastic centres; these stood to benefit from the grain grown in the plains of northern Greece, an area that Samuel was set to dominate. Byzantine and Armenian captives were settled by him in areas adjoining the Egnatian Way and so, probably, were the deportees from Larissa. Samuel made an island on Lake Prespa his principal residence, building an immense cathedral, some forty-four metres long, and also a palace. He installed in the church the relics of St Achilleus, removed from Larissa in 985 or 986. He was thus acquiring for his seat not merely supernatural protection but also legitimacy, for the erstwhile patron and guardian of Larissa would not have allowed an impious usurper to abduct his remains. Samuel could hope to gain through such imperial measures acceptance and even allegiance from his motley assemblage of subjects: Bulgarians, Vlachs, Albanians, Armenians and Greeks.

Samuel's dispositions give no hint of designs upon the Byzantine throne. Nonetheless, an upstart astride the Balkans menacing the emperor's revenues from the fertile Thessalian plain would have been unpalatable even to rulers less martially-minded than Basil, and by about 990 the lower

---

[81] Skyl., ed. Thurn, p. 349; French tr. Flusin and Cheynet, p. 292.

Danube was under Samuel's sway. Basil turned to the Bulgarian problem once he considered the eastern provinces to be quiescent, in early spring 991. Four years of campaigning brought the recapture of Berrhoia, some 60 kilometres south-west of Thessaloniki. Basil had Berrhoia and several other recaptured fortresses demolished, evidently assuming that they could not be held indefinitely against Samuel. In 995, while Basil was away on the eastern front, Samuel counter-attacked, sending patrols up to the walls of Thessaloniki itself. In one clash the *doux* of Thessaloniki himself was killed, and Samuel's raids ranged further south. His incursions were interrupted in the autumn of 997 or the spring of 998, when his army was surprised during withdrawal from a raid on the Peloponnese. Many Bulgarians were butchered in their sleep and Samuel and his son Gabriel-Radomir were seriously wounded.

The general responsible for the victory on the Spercheios, Nikephoros Ouranos, could now undertake bolder forays into enemy territory. Basil himself moved to the eastern borders, taking advantage of the death of David of Tao. David had lent troops to the rebels in 987–9 and had subsequently been overawed into bequeathing his principality to the empire (see above, p. 358). The cavalrymen whom Basil now transplanted from Tao were very probably of assistance to him on his subsequent campaigns. Byzantine authority was reimposed on north-east Bulgaria, and around 1002 Basil exploited his new-found control of the lower Danube to advance upstream. He besieged Vidin, which capitulated after eight months; Basil strengthened the fortifications, clearly intending to establish an outpost to Samuel's north-west. He was allied with a local Hungarian magnate, Ahtum-Ajtony, who is said to have 'received power from the Greeks' and to have been baptised.[82] Basil then drove far to the south and received the surrender of Skopje.

Basil's spectacular circumscription of Bulgaria tipped the strategic balance in Byzantium's favour, but neither side could deliver a knock-out blow. In fact, the gains made by Basil's long march were fleeting: Skopje was back in Bulgarian hands by the time of their final surrender in 1018. Dyrrachium's leading family did transfer its loyalties back to the emperor, John Chryselios' two sons each receiving the title of *patrikios* and an imperial official being admitted to the city. But the date of Dyrrachium's return to Basil's authority is uncertain, and in any case Dyrrachium remained isolated and in 1018 was still open to Bulgarian attack. Furthermore, the ruler of Duklja, the Slav principality north of the city, was endowed by Samuel with 'all the land of the people of Dyrrachium'.[83] The prince, John Vladimir, had been forced to submit to Samuel; but after a spell in detention at Prespa, he had been married to the daughter of a relative of Samuel, one

---

[82] *Legenda S. Gerhardi*, ed. Szentpétery, p. 490. [83] *LPD*, p. 335.

Theodorites. Thus Samuel seems to have felt sufficiently in control of Dyrrachium's hinterland to entrust it to a local prince linked to his own family.

Basil's annual *razzias* in the period following his long march were carefully organised. His insistence on tight formations, 'making his army into a kind of tower',[84] assured it invincibility in open countryside and enabled it to brave mountain passes. But the absence of any known victories between the opening years of the century and 1014 throws into doubt their effectiveness. Basil's adversary did not merely rely on natural defences. He was 'most expert in strategy',[85] and was ultimately responsible for the numerous fortifications which guarded the passes. The large earthwork at Kleidion comprised three lines of ramparts and two ditches aligned with the terrain, and it protected the local population very effectively from Basil's incursions. Until the end of his reign Samuel was able to deploy large armies, 'the numberless Bulgarian phalanx'.[86] There is no sign that the war effort overstrained either the Bulgarians' manpower reserves or loyalty to their new tsar. Samuel presided over various ecclesiastical building works. At Ohrid a large basilica was apparently built or refurbished, and the head of the Bulgarian church installed there. Samuel's relocation of the patriarchal see from Prespa to a place famed for its associations with Sts Clement and Naum reflected his rising confidence that Ohrid was reasonably secure, even though it lay on the Egnatian Way. He made Ohrid his own principal residence and the location of his treasury. Reportedly, 'much money' and 10,000 pounds of 'stamped gold',[87] as well as imperial crowns, were kept in the heavily fortified and extensive citadel. Samuel gained an aura of legitimacy, being called *rex* by a contemporary Italian chronicle,[88] and his descendants enjoyed imperial status in eleventh-century Byzantium.

Samuel's treasury may well have been filled with regular revenues from his southern towns, as well as spoils of war. However, the reconstituted political structure was inevitably shaken by his death on 6 October 1014. Byzantine writers maintain that he was overcome by the spectacle of 14,000 or 15,000 men marching back, most of them blinded, from Byzantine captivity.[89] Undoubtedly, he had suffered a humiliating defeat: an army guarding the Kleidion pass had been surprised and routed by a Byzantine unit, and Samuel himself only just escaped. But it was his demise, not the debacle at Kleidion, that tipped the scales in Byzantium's favour. Samuel's son,

---

[84] Psell., I.33, ed. and French tr. Renauld, I, p. 21; ed. and Italian tr. Impellizzeri *et al.*, I, pp. 48–9; tr. Sewter, p. 47.

[85] '*stratēgikōtatos*', Kek., ed. and Russian tr. Litavrin, pp. 168–9.

[86] *Life of Nikon*, ed. and tr. Sullivan, p. 148.

[87] Skyl., ed. Thurn, pp. 358–9; French tr. Flusin and Cheynet, pp. 298–300.

[88] Lupus Protospatharius, *Annales*, ed. Pertz, p. 57.

[89] Skyl., ed. Thurn, p. 349; French tr. Flusin and Cheynet, p. 292; Kek., ed. and Russian tr. Litavrin, pp. 168–9, n. 178 on p. 368.

Gabriel-Radomir, was bellicose and forceful, but lacked his political skills. Gabriel's first cousin, John Vladislav, begrudged his succession, and on 15 September 1015 he had him assassinated. John became the new Bulgarian tsar. Basil II tried hard to exploit the rivalries of the ruling family, seizing the town of Edessa in Thessaly. He sacked several Bulgarian royal residences and the town – though not the citadel – of Ohrid. However, John Vladislav was able to renovate and strengthen the fortifications of an alternative base, Bitola, commemorating the work with an elaborate inscription (see above, fig. 20 on p. 331). Moreover, Basil's eighty-eight-day siege of Pernik ended in failure and heavy losses, while his siege of Kastoria, in late spring or summer 1017, was also unsuccessful. He seems still to have been unsure of Edessa's loyalty, seeing that he had to 'set everything in order there' on his way back to Constantinople.[90]

The ambivalence of the Edessans was prudent. John Vladislav was still capable of attacking even the hardest targets. After Basil's withdrawal, he resumed personal command at Dyrrachium. In February 1018 a pitched battle was fought before the city walls. John Vladislav was, 'like another Goliath', 'invincible', engaged in single combat when two footsoldiers managed to deal fatal blows to his stomach.[91] This changed everything, as Basil realised. He 'immediately' set forth for Adrianople,[92] but no forcible entry into Bulgaria was necessary. John had not designated an heir and there were tensions between his widow and Samuel's descendants. So the prospects of an agreed succession looked faint. Krakras, the magnate who had defended Pernik for eighty-eight days, now surrendered not only Pernik but also the thirty-five other forts forming an elaborate system round it. Other warlords and community leaders saw that the game was up and, as Basil advanced along the Egnatian Way, their envoys brought offers of surrender. Basil responded with honours, senior court titles and other blandishments, making Krakras, for example, a *patrikios*. Contemporary historians in Armenia and the west show awareness that Basil's triumph owed little to pitched battles.

BASIL VICTORIOUS – AND MAGNANIMOUS TO OUTSIDERS

Basil's settlement of Bulgaria should be viewed against this background. Ohrid and the other residences of Samuel and John Vladislav were divested of their royal trappings. John's widow, Maria, and her children were drawn into Basil's court circle, receiving titles. Several of the males eventually rose to high office in the imperial administration. Basil is credited with the

---

[90] Skyl., ed. Thurn, p. 356; French tr. Flusin and Cheynet, pp. 297–8.
[91] Michael Psellos, *Scripta minora*, ed. Kurtz and Drexl, I, p. 160; Grégoire (1937), pp. 287–90.
[92] Skyl., ed. Thurn, p. 357; French tr. Flusin and Cheynet, p. 298.

desire 'not to innovate at all',[93] letting revenues be raised in grain and wine rather than coin. It is most probable that these and other administrative duties were, in the remoter regions, left to local notables bedecked with titles and offices. Basil had never recognised the patriarchal rank of Bulgaria's head churchman, but now he reaffirmed the special status of the Bulgarian church. Basil's appointee as archbishop was a Bulgarian monk named John, a concession to his new subjects' sensibilities, and his concern for the church's well-being is expressed in three imperial charters confirming its rights. That of 1020 sternly forbids other metropolitans (subject to the Constantinopolitan patriarch) from encroaching into the Bulgarian province. Archbishop John is to have authority over the same number of sees as his precursors in the time of 'Peter the emperor and Samuel'.[94] Imperial officials, including tax-collectors, were forbidden to interfere in the churches' or monasteries' affairs on pain of the 'great and pitiless . . . wrath of our majesty'.[95]

To the north-west, Basil consolidated his possession of Vidin, and pushed further north-westwards. The recalcitrant potentate who controlled Sirmium was assassinated and the town became the headquarters of a new Byzantine theme. Even the Croats, a people hitherto only spasmodically connected with Byzantium, now came within its orbit. The ruling brothers, Gojslav and Krešimir III, formally submitted to Basil and received court titles, thus acknowledging his commanding position in the Balkans and beyond. King Stephen of Hungary was now his ally and may well have taken part in the last stages of the campaign against John Vladislav and the final occupation of Ohrid in 1018. That same year, Doge Otto Orseolo of Venice drove the Croats back from the region of Zara, and imposed tribute on some of the cities on islands off the Dalmatian coast. The Croats were hemmed in by Byzantium's possessions, allies and vassals.

Basil showed no signs of being prepared to let his 'spear lie still' after his subjugation of the Balkans. Although now well into his sixties, he embarked on a massive expedition to Caucasia in 1021 and 1022. He superintended the takeover of the administration of Vaspurakan, whose lord, Sennacherim-John Artsruni, had been induced to cede his realm to Basil (see also pp. 360, 696). He fought a series of engagements against King George I of Georgia, in order to retrieve all the forts and lands claimed as the inheritance of David of Tao. After George had renounced all title to Tao, Basil returned to Constantinople. His energies now swung towards the central Mediterranean and still more aggressive campaigning. He was about to embark with reinforcements for an invasion of Sicily when he fell ill and died, on 13 or 15 December 1025.

[93] Skyl., ed. Thurn, p. 412; French tr. Flusin and Cheynet, pp. 340–1.
[94] Gelzer, 'Orientalischen Kirche II', p. 44; *FHGB*, VI, p. 44.
[95] Gelzer, 'Orientalischen Kirche II', p. 46; *FGHB*, VI, p. 47. See below, p. 671.

BASIL'S 'EXPANSIONISM': ITS POLITICAL RATIONALE AND ITS COSTS

Basil's dominions were half as extensive again as those of Constantine VII. Constantine seems to have had little appetite for direct territorial expansion, preferring like his father to emphasise his pre-eminent role as the wise guarantor of order and justice. Basil, by contrast, appears to have presented conquest as his prime aim, without any palpable regard for the question of who would succeed to leadership over the newly amassed territories after the deaths of himself and his younger brother, Constantine VIII (1025–8). But he had managed to maintain the army's loyalty by becoming its general and personally directing its affairs, a stance which had much in common with Nikephoros II Phokas'.

Basil was contending with the prestige which individual commanders and great military affinities still enjoyed. They were bracketed with other, less politically involved, families whose wealth and influence was liable to occlude imperial authority locally and thus lower the proceeds from taxation at the disposal of central government. Basil, like his grandfather and the soldier-emperors of the eighth century, presented the provision of justice and security of property for the lowliest of his subjects as an essential duty of the ruler (see above, pp. 275–7, 489). Just after his spectacular campaign to rebuff Fatimid attempts at seizing Aleppo while Thessaloniki's outskirts lay exposed to Bulgarian raiders, Basil issued an important *novella* on land law. This in effect abolished the statute of limitations for restitution of property acquired by 'the powerful' from 'the poor', save only for that property covered by legal documents for 934 or earlier; the legal process was, more or less, to be skewed in favour of claims by members of peasant fiscal communities against 'the powerful' who had 'wrongfully deprived and despoiled' them.[96]

Basil was avowedly trying to preserve tax units of property-owning country-dwellers of limited or slender means who had been the subject of imperial legislation earlier in the tenth century and who were described as vital for the empire's well-being (see above, p. 492). His rhetoric of equity was the more strident for his need to rally the war effort against the Bulgarians in hostilities that gave every sign of being protracted and very burdensome for tax-payers. The *novella* of 996 alluded to those who had used their senior positions in the establishment to amass properties and who through their wealth and influence put undue pressure on those small proprietors not yet swallowed up by their estates. One such had risen from humble beginnings to the dignity of *prōtovestiarios*, only to be abruptly divested by the emperor, who 'made him one of the villagers once more'; another

---

[96] *JG*, ed. Zepos and Zepos, I, pp. 264, 265–6; ed. Svoronos, no. 14, pp. 200, 204; tr. McGeer, pp. 116, 118.

eunuch, Basil the *parakoimōmenos*, may well have been the ultimate target of this cautionary tale.[97] But the Phokades and other great military families which had benefited from imperial patronage were probably the target of the *novella*'s allusion to those who, thanks to such positions as domestic of the Schools, could build up and maintain their property empires over seventy or a hundred years (see above, p. 504).

The most active admirers of such tenth-century heroes as Nikephoros II Phokas were themselves in or connected to the army, and it was from their ranks that a coup was attempted during Basil's last Caucasian campaign. A great-nephew, also called Nikephoros, was proclaimed emperor and we are told that 'many of those who were in the camp had walked with their feet behind the emperor [i.e. Basil], but in thought and words they were behind the rebels'.[98] According to Michael Psellos, Basil II treated his subjects as if he had subjugated them.[99] His ability to maintain a large standing army probably owed much to the vulnerability of the well-to-do to his arbitrary seizure of property and commandeering of resources. Such were the dividends of a soldier emperor blessed with the will-power and the energy to march his men from one end of the empire to the other until the death-knock.

Only the patriarch of Constantinople and other senior churchmen and monks seem to have presumed to object to a new measure to make large landowners responsible for the tax liabilities of missing minor landowners. Basil promised Patriarch Sergios (1001–19) that he would lift this obligation 'if' he were to prevail over the Bulgarians.[100] At the same time, Basil seems to have hoped for the gratitude of his non-Greek and non-Chalcedonian subjects in return for his consideration for their rites and customs. They might provide soldiers no less effective, and perhaps actually more loyal, than his Greek troops. In this way, he could turn the 'diversity' of the empire to his advantage, binding 'the elements of power in imperial harmony'.[101] One feature of this policy is the generous scale of the lands and forts granted to eminent Armenian expatriates in Asia Minor.

The expansion was not ruinous in itself. Bulgarians served effectively on the eastern front in the eleventh century, while Armenians fought loyally in Basil's Bulgarian wars. And, if Bulgaria lacked a monetarised economy, some of Armenia's towns and smaller settlements offered important new sources

[97] *JG*, ed. Zepos and Zepos, I, p. 265; ed. Svoronos, no. 14, p. 202; tr. McGeer, p. 118; Holmes (2005), pp. 468–71.

[98] Arist., French tr. Canard and Berbérian, p. 20.

[99] Psell., I.30, ed. and French tr. Renauld, I, p. 18; ed. and Italian tr. Impellizzeri *et al.*, I, pp. 42–3; tr. Sewter, p. 44.

[100] Skyl., ed. Thurn, p. 365; French tr. Flusin and Cheynet, pp. 303–4.

[101] Psell., I.22, ed. and French tr. Renauld, I, pp. 13–14; ed. and Italian tr. Impellizzeri *et al.*, I, pp. 32–3; tr. Sewter, pp. 39–40.

of revenue. The prosperity of towns such as Ardanuji in the Armenian bor-derlands had already attracted the notice of Constantine VII, and they seem to have expanded in the eleventh century. In Cappadocia, a former Byzan-tine border zone, building work and lavish decorative programmes prolifer-ated among the rock chapels and monasteries. The numerous churches and monasteries erected by Syriac Jacobite immigrants in the Euphrates valley south from Melitene and in parts of Cilicia attest their wealth as well as their piety in Basil's time. And Antioch, a *kouratoreia* of the emperor, seems to have prospered. Many Armenians, initially soldiers but probably subse-quently craftsmen and traders too, were settled in its vicinity. The increase in population and in economic transactions involving coin in these newly won regions should have worked to the government's advantage.[102]

However, a major problem was posed by the very instrument of the empire's expansion, the army. Materials upon which a firm estimate of its size and cost to the state might be based are lacking, but the armed forces were certainly very substantially larger than they had been dur-ing the first half of the tenth century, and much more dependent on money for their maintenance and remuneration. More men needed to be employed full-time for Basil's ceaseless campaigning, while key points such as Dyrrachium or Sirmium needed permanent garrisoning, even if less significant strongholds were assigned skeleton crews, or provisionally decommissioned. The fiscal and administrative apparatus responsible for their upkeep was not radically different from the one which had operated the smaller theme armies of the tenth century, and many of the military units were still based on long-established themes in Asia Minor. This was an obstacle to swift, cost-effective deployment of resources to wherever they were most needed, characteristic of the era when Byzantium's armed forces had been smaller-scale and modestly equipped. The adaptability and willingness to devolve administration to local elites and apparatuses shown in the newly conquered regions of the Balkans, eastern Asia Minor and Syria made for prudent, relatively inexpensive governance.[103] Yet it did not resolve the fiscal problem posed by the empire's armed forces.

At the same time, the increasing security of many parts of Asia Minor, mounting prosperity and concern for property boundaries and rights called for larger numbers of non-military officials to assess and adjudicate. By the earlier eleventh century, towns in Greece such as Athens and Corinth,[104] and others in Asia Minor's western coastal plain were witnessing further build-ing development and more intensive use of coin for commercial transac-tions. The towns' purchasing power signalled the emergence of local elites;

---

[102] Dagron (1976), pp. 186–98; Howard-Johnston (1995b).
[103] See Stephenson (2000), pp. 74–80; Stephenson (2003a), pp. 34–47; Stephenson (2003b), pp. 122–7, 130–1; below, pp. 665, 668–9; Holmes (2002a), pp. 91–9, 103–4; Holmes (2005), pp. 321–2, 352–91.
[104] Sanders (2003), pp. 386–7, 390–1, 396–7 and n. 43; Dunn (2006), pp. 38–40, 53–9.

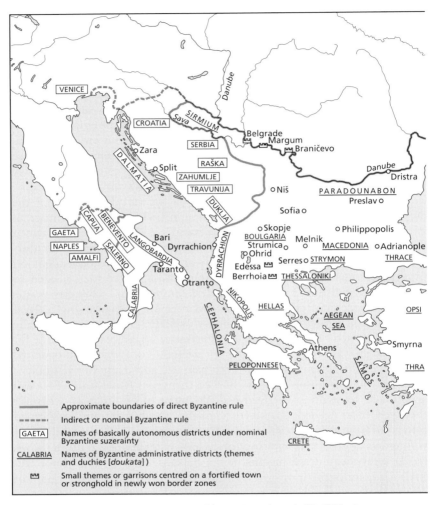

Map 24 Administrative organisation of the empire at the end of Basil II's reign *c*. 1025

local landholders gained opportunities for enrichment through supplying produce to the town-dwellers. The interests of these provincial groupings were not directly opposed to those of central government; in fact their leading members looked keenly to Constantinople for status and some sort of office;[105] for their part the 'professional', expensively equipped soldiers relied more heavily on state pay and other subventions than their early tenth-century precursors had done.[106] But there were burgeoning

[105] Morris (1995); Neville (2004), pp. 37–47, 109–11, 166–7.
[106] Haldon (1999a), pp. 123–34.

conflicts of jurisdiction and fiscal rights between the military's needs and the civilian administrative apparatus; as the eleventh century progressed, labyrinthine nexuses of tax-collectors and imposers of charges and services to the state sprawled across the empire, providing ample opportunities for lucrative careers in legal practice and stimulating legal studies (see below, p. 599).

These tendencies were not necessarily inimical to effective central government. The very care which major landowners took to gain charters exempting them from state charges suggests as much, and the state took steps to increase the number of peasants labouring on its own domain. The overall increase in the population of the empire also potentially swelled the state's tax rolls and revenues. However, this combination of administrative problems with the need to finance and maintain recruitment to a very large standing army was primed by the political threat which the generals seemed to pose. Basil II masked the problem by marrying his army. Booty from foreign campaigning and ruthless seizure of properties brought in enough for him to keep his forces operational and, according to Psellos, to hoard 200,000 gold pieces in his palace treasury.[107] But Basil's strong-arm methods were no substitute for the administrative reform needed to cope with success, and his stance, like that of Nikephoros II, presupposed a situation in which only one enemy, essentially static, needed to be faced at any one time. The Bulgarians had had ample reserves of manpower but a largely agrarian economy, while the Muslims were divided among themselves and their most formidable power, Fatimid Egypt, was not disposed to devote its economic resources to sustained aggression against Byzantium; the rivalry for dominion over Aleppo and northern Syria was keen, but could be conducted as effectively by diplomatic manipulation of local elites and tribes as by outright warfare. Whether the Byzantine state would prove capable of marshalling its resources to address a plethora of enemies, fast-moving and mutating, on several fronts was, however, another question. The militaristic posture struck by Basil II provided no lasting answer.

---

[107] Psell., I.31, ed. and French tr. Renauld, I, p. 19; ed. and Italian tr. Impellizzeri *et al.*, I, pp. 44–5; tr. Sewter, p. 45.

CHAPTER 14

WESTERN APPROACHES (900–1025)

JONATHAN SHEPARD

BYZANTINE LINKS WITH THE WESTERN CHRISTIANS, 900–950

Byzantium's relations with the Latin west in this period have a 'Cheshire cat' character in comparison with ninth-century exchanges. Very little attention is paid to the Christian west by Byzantine writers even when Saxon potentates begin to intervene in Italy and bedeck themselves with imperial trimmings. A memorandum of diplomatic procedures, compiled partly from older materials in the mid-tenth century, lists the standard form of address for letters to various *reges*, of 'Gaul' as well as Bavaria and Saxony: each is to be addressed as 'spiritual brother', unlike the numerous other addressees. But the protocols for receptions of ambassadors make no special provision for western ones: formulaic greetings for envoys from the Bulgarians and eastern Muslims are rehearsed, presumably because their visits were more important or frequent.[1]

A somewhat later compilation would probably have paid western ambassadors little more attention than the *Book of ceremonies* did on the eve of the imperial coronation of Otto I (962–73). For Basil II (976–1025), as for his predecessors, the existence of a rival Bulgarian *basileus* mattered more. But if events beyond the Adriatic were generally of secondary importance to Byzantium's rulers, the very powers which troubled them in the Balkans or hindered communications with the west obliged the empire to maintain far-flung bases from which to disrupt their activities. Byzantine claims in Italy were based on quite recent military actions and not merely on the inheritance of the old Roman empire. The *De administrando imperio* recognises the territorial losses to the Lombards, but stresses the help which Basil I (867–86) had provided against the Arabs, and claims imperial authority over Capua and Benevento on the strength of 'this great benefit rendered to them' then.[2]

Great expectations continued to be vested in Sicily. Byzantine bases there provided platforms for speedy démarches towards any figure of note in Italy or even southern Francia, and a ready means of monitoring and hindering

---

[1] *DC*, II.48, 47, ed. Reiske, I, pp. 689, 681–6. [2] *DAI*, ch. 29, pp. 134–5.

the passage of Arab vessels, a capability not open to Christian magnates lacking fleets. The *De thematibus*, a work commissioned by Constantine VII, claims that Sicily is 'now' under Byzantine rule 'since the emperor of Constantinople rules the sea as far as the Pillars of Hercules'.[3] This should be inverted: a presence in Sicily gave Byzantium disproportionate influence and status in the western Mediterranean world, and to abandon claims to it would have been demeaning. Thus *stratēgoi* residing in Calabria were officially designated governors of 'Sicily' through the first half of the tenth century (see below, p. 568). Sicily was, together with Calabria and Illyricum, under the patriarch of Constantinople, and contacts with orthodox monks and churchmen on the island persisted. Partly because of this, the Byzantine military position was not utterly hopeless: Taormina fell to the Arabs in 902, but was regained by 912–13; it was only fully taken over by the Arabs in 962.

If imperial ambitions showed great resilience, loss of control of the straits of Messina had in reality eroded Byzantium's capacity for intervention in Rome or further north. Expeditionary forces or major diplomatic démarches could no longer be funded from the island, and Calabria was too poor and too harassed by Sicilian Arab *razzia*s to provide much in the way of resources before the end of the tenth century. Byzantium thus had greater need of allies in the west and there were indeed periodic contacts between Constantinople and several western courts. The temerity of Muslim raiders and the existence of stray Arab colonies further north could affront the Christian sensibilities and prestige of enough parties for joint action to be attempted, but actual operations were rare. Those best-placed to provide effective land forces were the very Lombard princes whose patrimonies had been most impaired by the Byzantine recovery in southern Italy. Only after skilful negotiation and manoeuvring by Nicholas Picingli, the *stratēgos* of Langobardia, and by Pope John X (914–28), could the lords of Gaeta and Naples be induced to cooperate with Capua-Benevento, Roman nobles and Picingli's fleet and army to expel the Arabs from the Garigliano valley. The coalition captured the Saracens' base in August 915, but did not long survive its victory. Soon Landulf I of Capua-Benevento (901–43) and other Lombard princes were in 'rebellion', raiding Byzantine possessions in southern Italy and regaining control of much of them (see below, p. 563).

Otherwise, few important western rulers had interests which clashed or converged with Byzantium's strongly enough for intensive relations to be maintained with them. The main fixed points on the Byzantine political map were cities. Venice's interests were aligned quite closely with the empire's and its ruling families were willing to designate themselves as *servi* (*douloi* in Greek), a vague term ranging in meaning from 'slave' to

---

[3] *DT*, II.10, ed. Pertusi, p. 94.

'subordinate' of the emperor. The *basileus* felt no need to show particular favour towards the managers of Venice, being well aware of the Venetians' need of the sea for protection, sustenance and income. Reliance on the import of bulk goods made them vulnerable to famine or financial ruin since merchantmen were small, unwieldy and even in summer scarcely seaworthy. Byzantium was the obvious and most lucrative of the limited outlets available to the Venetians for their re-export of weaponry, wood and slaves, while Byzantine luxury goods were much in demand among the elites of north Italian towns. The deficiencies of navigation and the revitalised Byzantine presence along the island-studded Dalmatian coast-line thus made Venetian maritime communications highly sensitive to the actions of the imperial authorities.

Fortunately for the Venetians, it was in Byzantium's interests to foster a self-financing and largely self-reliant naval capability on the outermost fringe of its Adriatic possessions, since this relieved it from maintaining a significant fleet of its own there. Each party stood to gain from the status quo, in which direct contacts between Constantinople and the northern Adriatic were monopolised by the Venetians, while taxed and supervised by the Byzantine government. The Venetians' returns were substantial, and guaranteed access to secure markets in Constantinople helped to offset the delays and losses of the sea voyage. The Venetians also tended to profit from their ability, very rare among westerners, to monitor events in Constantinople, and some, at least, could speak Greek. Even Venice, however, ranked fairly low in Byzantine priorities and its rulers' compliance was assumed. Of far greater weight was the city of Rome, with its indelible imperial connotations and especially its role as the residence of the pope.

The importance attached to the papacy is demonstrated by the protocols for the reception of envoys: those for 'ambassadors' from the pope feature first, and are detailed and full.[4] Long-standing tradition played its part here, but there was also a more dynamic reason. The pope was the sole western figure who could intervene substantively in the empire's affairs and within its sphere of influence. Apulia's subjection to papal jurisdiction was not formally disputed, and as the population was mostly Lombards under Latin priests and bishops it was imperative for the Byzantine government to keep in touch with its spiritual leader. In the Byzantine 'mainland' the papacy's reputation had been enhanced by its stand against iconoclasm. Orthodox monks and holy men continued to make their way to venerate Rome's churches and the tombs of Sts Peter and Paul; eastern churchmen were in contact with the Greek monasteries – still prominent, although not numerous – in Rome, and also with the curia. Papal verdicts on religious questions mattered; hence emperors, too, looked to the papacy in their

[4] *presbeis, DC*, II.47, ed. Reiske, I, pp. 680–1.

efforts to manage their own patriarchate. Romanos I Lekapenos (920–44) seemingly regarded papal support as pivotal to his plan to impose his son, Theophylact, as the patriarch of Constantinople (933–56), and papal legates carried out the act of enthronement on 2 February 933.

There was another equally cogent reason for the intensity of imperial relations with Rome. The papacy was slow to abandon hopes of Bulgaria. In papal eyes, Bulgaria fell within Illyricum, a province rightfully under its jurisdiction. Symeon of Bulgaria's (893–927) imperial pretensions and his later hostility towards Romanos I may have made him seem amenable to papal overtures, as Patriarch Nicholas I Mystikos (901–7, 912–25) apparently suspected when, in the early 920s, he detained two papal emissaries whose declared aim was to persuade Symeon to make peace with Byzantium. Symeon's proclamation of himself as 'emperor of the Romans' may well have been known to the papacy. The papal legates who mediated between Symeon and Tomislav of Croatia in 926–7 may have investigated a possible accommodation between pope and self-declared emperor.[5] The papacy had originally been responding to an approach from Tomislav, Symeon's enemy, and papal interest in south Slav affairs need not have been wholly repugnant to the imperial government at that time. Nonetheless, the papacy's title to Illyricum could have made for some sort of concordat between Rome and a Bulgarian ruler seeking recognition. All this underlay the golden bulls for, and ritual attention to, 'the spiritual father of our holy emperor'.[6] Formal exchanges were probably accompanied by multifarious unofficial contacts with other churchmen and notables in Rome. The pope might thus be deflected from undesirable initiatives and his undeniable authority put to the emperor's own uses; papal approval of Theophylact's appointment is said to have been bought by Romanos.

The benefits to the emperor of papal cooperation made others' interventions in Rome a matter of some concern, since they might yoke the papacy to their own ambitions, seeking the irritatingly grandiose title of emperor. Yet such interventions might also provide leverage over a recalcitrant pope. A masterful occupant of the Italian kingdom's throne like Berengar of Friuli was uncongenial, but even Berengar's imperial coronation in Rome in December 915 seems to have been received with equanimity on the Bosporus. If Byzantium showed a penchant for closer ties with more distant potentates in southern Francia, this probably sprang from an abiding concern about Sicily as well as from fears that a Lombardy-based 'emperor' might intervene more persistently in Roman affairs. For the *basileus* nurtured a dream of his own: with the cooperation of a southern Frankish

[5] Shepard (1999), p. 578.

[6] *DC*, II.47, ed. Reiske, I, p. 680. The logothete of the Drome termed the pope thus in his greetings for envoys from Rome.

ruler, the chances of driving Arab predators from their bases and eventually isolating and subduing the occupiers of Sicily became slightly less remote. There is suggestive evidence from a mid-tenth-century diplomatic memorandum that the emperor maintained contacts with the *archōn* of Sardinia.[7] Greek inscriptions there suggest that court titles were still being sported by members of the ruling elite towards the end of the century.[8] If, as is likely, Leo VI's (886–912) infant daughter Anna was betrothed to Louis the Blind of Provence around 899–900, shortly before the fall of Taormina to the Arabs, the two episodes may be related. This commitment of the emperor's only daughter to a western spouse may not have led to actual marriage, and anyway did not yield tangible aid for the Byzantines. Relations were distant and Romanos I seems to have responded tepidly to an embassy from Hugh of Arles; upon being crowned king of Italy in Pavia in 926, Hugh 'took care to make his name known even to the Greeks placed far from us'.[9]

Emperor Romanos showed keen interest in the marriage of one of his sons into the leading Roman family which included Pope John XI (931–5) himself, his half-brother and enemy Alberic, and their forceful mother Marozia. An imperial letter of early February 933 offers more warships to ferry Marozia's daughter, the bride-to-be, to Constantinople and shows willingness to entertain John's request for help.[10] But the letter was already out-of-date by the time of writing: Marozia herself had married Hugh of Arles and he had come to Rome, only for them both to be expelled by Alberic and the citizens under his command. Alberic now sought a marriage-tie, but by then Romanos was looking for an ally against the Muslim corsairs and the Lombard princes in southern Italy. A mission acknowledging Hugh as *rhēx Italias* was despatched in 935, with money, dress tunics and *objets d'art* for him and his magnates; in return they were to attack the Lombard 'rebels'.[11] The subsequent operations were successful and Hugh, from his base in northern Italy, established close relations with Romanos. But the commander of the mission had received contingency instructions in case Hugh sent an army without leading it in person; he was also supplied with a reserve of costumes, presumably for others whom he might find serviceable. Such flexibility was of the essence. In late 944 or early 945 Byzantine warships attacked Fraxinetum and destroyed many Muslim boats with Greek fire, acting in response to a request from Hugh. Romanos had made his assistance conditional upon a marriage-tie: Hugh

---

[7] *DC*, II.48, ed. Reiske, I, p. 690.

[8] von Falkenhausen (1978), p. 44 and n. 135; Boscolo (1978), pp. 111–15; Cosentino (2005), pp. 71–3, 75–6.

[9] Liudprand, *Antapodosis*, III.22, ed. Chiesa, p. 76; tr. Wright, p. 119.

[10] Theodore Daphnopates, *Correspondance*, ed. and French tr. Darrouzès and Westerink, p. 14 (introduction); pp. 38–41 (text).

[11] *DC*, II.44, ed. Reiske, I, pp. 661–2.

was to give one of his daughters in marriage to the infant son of Constantine VII Porphyrogenitus, also called Romanos, the future Romanos II (959–63). Liudprand of Cremona regarded the threat to the Byzantine south from the Lombard princes as underlying Romanos' request.[12] Hugh, lacking a legitimate daughter, sent Bertha, his child by a concubine. She was brought to Constantinople in the late summer of 944 and the two children were married; Bertha was given the new eastern Christian name of Eudocia.

There is a tone of family feeling and pride in the sketch of Bertha-Eudocia's lineage provided in the *De administrando imperio*, a work commissioned and partly written by her father-in-law, Constantine VII.[13] In 948, after the death of Hugh, Constantine wrote to Berengar of Ivrea, urging him to act as faithful guardian of the late king's son, Lothar. But at the same time he wrote another letter, urging Berengar to send an ambassador who would return with proof of Constantine's love for Berengar.[14] Constantine was discreetly shifting towards the more important figure in Italy: Berengar was already sidelining Lothar. Even the injunctions to protect Lothar – who might, at around twenty years of age, have been expected to fend for himself – were somewhat double-edged. The emperor had to preserve decorum but also to do business with whoever prevailed in northern Italy or Rome, so long as they did not persistently offend against his interests. His main concern at that time was the reconquest of Crete; elsewhere in the Mediterranean he sought tranquillity. Liudprand, who had travelled with an envoy of Otto I, reached Constantinople during or just after the expedition, and the diplomatic activity he records turned essentially on Crete. Constantine's sense of kinship with Hugh's family could not outweigh the requirements of Crete. Any possible tensions between sentiment and strategy were relieved by the timely deaths of Bertha-Eudocia in 949 and Lothar in 950.

BYZANTIUM AND OTTO I

Although Byzantium's most active concerns lay in the Balkan and Mediterranean worlds, the empire also maintained some contacts with potentates based north of the Alps. The Greek embassies which visited Otto I in 945 and 949 may be the tip of an otherwise unrecorded iceberg of diplomacy, and the 'pallia graeca' presented by King Edmund of Wessex to the shrine of St Cuthbert in 944 could have been brought directly by emissaries of the *basileus*; indeed, West Saxon kings from Æthelstan (925–39) onwards sometimes bore the title *basileus* in their charters. Increased Byzantine attention to Otto during the late 940s may have been induced by recent Bavarian victories over the Hungarians. Constantine VII, was interested too, in this still

[12] *Leg.*, ch. 7, ed. Chiesa, p. 190; tr. Scott, p. 30.   [13] *DAI*, ch. 26, pp. 108–9, 112–13.
[14] Liudprand, *Antapodosis*, VI.2, ed. Chiesa, p. 146; tr. Wright, p. 206.

Figure 39 Ivory of Romanos II and Bertha-Eudocia being crowned by Christ (mid-tenth century)

semi-nomadic people; he devoted three chapters of the *De administrando* almost exclusively to the Hungarians' history, and saw to the baptism and investiture with the title of *patrikios* of at least two of their chieftains.[15]

In September 951 Otto I led an army across the Alps. Probably in the same year Constantine requested the hand of his niece Hadwig, daughter of Duke Henry of Bavaria (947–55), for his widowed son Romanos. He may have reckoned that Hadwig's uncle would one day reign as *imperator*: and Otto did, while in Italy, sound out the pope about a possible imperial coronation, albeit to no effect. But Constantine may also have envisaged Henry as a prospective in-law because of his occupation of Aquileia, which bridged Byzantine interests in Venice and the Dalmatian coast. Around this time Henry went on the offensive against the Hungarians and captured 'much booty' from them,[16] which cannot have escaped Byzantine notice. Allegedly, however, Hadwig herself refused the match and Byzantine bids lapsed. Instead, Constantine intervened directly in the central Mediterranean. In 956 he sent a large expeditionary force to overawe rebels in Calabria and Apulia, reduce Naples to submission and attack the Saracen raiders in their Sicilian base (see below, p. 564). This was for the most part accomplished, but the underlying purpose was apparently the defensive one of relieving southern Italy of Muslim pressure.

Substantive change in the tempo and tenor of east–west relations was, however, imminent. Other westerners were trying to correspond with Byzantium, judging by a decree issued by Doge Peter IV Candiano in June 960. This implies that the Venetians' carriage of letters from northern Italians, Bavarians, Saxons and others to the emperor was increasing and bans the delivery of letters other than those customarily passing 'from our palace'.[17] Byzantium soon began to deploy its newly enlarged armed forces in theatres other than those for which they had originally been mobilised, notably in Sicily. Taormina fell to the Muslims for a second time in 962. A huge Byzantine force including heavy cavalry landed on Sicily in the autumn of 964, but was soon crushed at Rametta; the fleet was destroyed in a subsequent action. An attempt to assemble another, more modest, task force in Calabria in 965 was abortive. Byzantium was nevertheless better placed and disposed to flex muscles in the west than it had been since the seventh century, and the later 960s saw some administrative reorganisation (see below, pp. 567–8); the newly instituted *katepanō Italias* was of high rank and may have had some supervisory duties over all Byzantium's possessions on the peninsula. It was more coincidence than cause and effect that the two leading Christian powers simultaneously turned their attention towards

---

[15] *DAI*, chs. 38–40, pp. 170–9; Skyl., ed. Thurn, p. 239; French tr. Flusin and Cheynet, pp. 201–2.

[16] Widukind, *Res gestae Saxonicae*, II.36, ed. Hirsch and Lohmann, p. 95; ed. and German tr. Bauer and Rau, pp. 118–19.

[17] TT, I, p. 21.

parts of Italy. Already in the late 950s some Byzantines had envisaged the reconquest of Crete as the prelude to victory in Sicily, while Otto I's intervention in Italy came in response to appeals from nearly every prominent figure, including Pope John XII (955–64). Although it is difficult to assess Otto's understanding of his title of *imperator*, his crowning by the pope in 962 or the relevance to this rite of the city of Rome, these steps gave him good reason to care about the pope's future allegiance. John XII soon tried to make contact with Constantinople and so did Berengar of Ivrea's son, Adalbert. Otto was well aware of John's appeals for Byzantine assistance, judging by the allegations which Liudprand puts into his mouth.[18]

Several other issues troubled relations between the new *imperator* and his eastern counterpart. These were probably not all clearly understood at the time, and this and the delays caused by distance made the course of events still more tortuous. Firstly, there was the question of the interrelationship between two empires, each of which had some call on the imperial Roman past. One of the foundation stones of Byzantine imperialism was that Constantine the Great had by God's will moved legitimate leadership from 'old Rome' to 'the reigning city' on the Bosporus. The *De thematibus* – not a work of propaganda – states flatly that the city of Rome has 'put aside' imperial power and is mainly controlled by the pope;[19] and the mid-tenth-century Arabic scholar, al-Mas'udi, noted that the city's ruler had neither worn a diadem nor called himself emperor until shortly before the time of writing.[20] The Byzantine government can hardly have been unaware that Louis the Blind and Berengar of Friuli had both called themselves *imperator* following a papal coronation, and Berengar's realm is even termed a *basileia* by Constantine Porphyrogenitus himself.[21] But if Byzantium did not actively oppose the western warlords' pretensions, neither did it actively encourage them. Hugh of Arles adapted various Byzantinising modes of depicting his majesty, such as gold bulls and documents written in gold on purple parchment, and his daughter married a *porphyrogenitus*. This rendered Hugh's status comparable to that of the *basileus*, and Bertha's large dowry was probably meant to indicate parity. It was perhaps in deference to Byzantine sensitivities that Hugh abstained from the imperial title itself. That these could be awakened is shown by Leo Phokas' qualification of Liudprand's master in 968: Otto was not an *imperator*, but a *rex*.[22] Nikephoros II Phokas (963–9), like most tenth-century *basileis*, had personal grounds to be vigilant about unauthorised use of the imperial title; he was himself an intruder in the palace, while even Constantine VII deemed

[18] Liudprand, *Liber de rebus gestis Ottonis*, ch. 6, ed. Chiesa, p. 172; tr. Wright, pp. 219–20; Hiestand (1964), p. 219 and n. 129.
[19] *DT*, II.10, ed. Pertusi, p. 94.
[20] al-Mas'udi, *al-Tanbih*, French tr. Carra de Vaux, p. 246; Vasil., p. 404.
[21] *DAI*, ch. 26, p. 110, line 37.   [22] *Leg.*, ch. 2, ed. Chiesa, pp. 188; tr. Scott, p. 28.

it necessary to flaunt his purple birth. Moreover, the Saxon *arriviste* Otto was a different class of *imperator* from his earlier tenth-century predecessors. He showed himself both more blind to the Greeks' concerns and less pressed to gain their recognition of his title than Charlemagne had been in 800 (see above, p. 417).

A second potential source of tension was the developing Christianisation of eastern Europe. In 961, on the point of departure for Italy, Otto I sent a religious mission to Princess Olga of Kiev. A few years earlier she had been baptised in Constantinople and had taken the Christian name of Helena, after the emperor's wife, and a significant proportion of the Rus elite were beginning to show interest in Byzantine Christianity. The German mission folded almost immediately and does not feature in Byzantine sources, but it displayed a certain readiness to intervene in the Byzantines' patch. Not that Byzantium was wholly inert: a Bishop Hierotheos had been sent to Tourkia (Hungary) with the chieftain Gyula *c.* 948, and ecclesiastical ties were subsequently put on a permanent footing (see above, p. 322). A metropolitan of Tourkia was in office in 1028 and the see remained in existence throughout the eleventh century. The papacy was also interested in Hungary, and in 965 John XII was accused of trying to send two emissaries there among the envoys destined for Byzantium. More alarmingly for Byzantium, the appearance of Bulgarian envoys at Otto's court in 961 or 965/6 and in 973 suggested that the Hungarians were ceasing to act as a barrier between the east Franks and the Balkans.

Otto's actions in Italy touched on some of these sore points. In December 967 he came to terms with Venice, largely renewing earlier *pacta* between rulers of the Italian realm and Venice (see above, p. 456). Doge Peter IV (959–76) was married to a niece of the emperor. Otto had already gained the fealty of Pandulf I Ironhead (961–81) of Capua-Benevento, the leading power in south-central Italy. At the same time, the Greeks' very ability to make trouble in Rome confronted Otto with their continuing presence in the peninsula. There were also some more positive reasons for an accommodation with the *basileus*. A Greek marriage alliance would not merely demonstrate that Otto's predominance in the west was acknowledged by the other outstanding Christian ruler; it would also transfuse purple-born blood into his own descendants' line, enhancing their imperial status. Moreover, the connection would open up the *basileus'* store of portrayals, emblems of authority and valuables. After Otto's imperial coronation in 962, his seals began to show him frontally, wearing a cross-topped crown and holding an orb and a sceptre, echoing although not slavishly copying contemporary Byzantine coins and imperial seals.

There were thus strong reasons for Otto to regularise his relations with the eastern emperor. The build-up of Byzantine armed forces in the central Mediterranean need not preclude an accommodation. Judging by one interpretation of a prophecy then current in Constantinople, some Byzantines viewed Otto as a promising future junior partner in the coming fight-to-the-death with the Saracen 'wild ass'.[23] Yet the negotiations reached an impasse with the visit of Liudprand to Constantinople in 968. It seems clear that Otto I, after Otto II's coronation as co-emperor, was impatient for a number of objectives: a fittingly purple-born bride for Otto II (973–83); the destruction of the Muslims' notorious lair in Fraxinetum as a demonstration of his God-given invincibility; and his own return to his northern power base. Most of these aims are enumerated, and the impatience evinced, in a letter dated 18 January 968. Time spent away from Saxony probably seemed time wasted, and this, rather than any positive desire to conquer the Byzantine south, probably made for Otto's threatening tone towards the eastern empire. In the letter, Otto asserts that the Greeks 'will [be forced to] give up Calabria and Apulia . . . unless we consent' [to their remaining];[24] he had already given a hostage to fortune by publicising his bid for a purple-born bride for his son, 'the step-daughter of Nikephoros himself, namely the daughter of Emperor Romanos [II]'.[25] Otto's close counsellor Adalbert, archbishop of Magdeburg, penned these words in, most probably, early 968, when Otto still publicly aspired to a top-ranking bride for his son. Otto II's coronation on 25 December 967 may well have originally been planned as a preliminary to the wedding. Otto I's exasperation is understandable if, as is likely, his envoy Dominicus had returned with the news that Nikephoros was favourably disposed; for the Byzantine embassy which arrived on Dominicus' heels brought words of peace, but no *porphyrogenita*. Otto miscalculated badly in supposing that he could jolt the Greeks into compliance by launching an assault on Bari. Soon afterwards, Liudprand was despatched at his own suggestion to finalise a marriage agreement and, seemingly, to fetch the bride. Otto probably planned to use Bari as a bargaining chip, while demonstrating to regional magnates such as Pandulf Ironhead, whom he had recently invested with the duchy of Spoleto, his ability to better the *basileus*.

Liudprand's mission was no more effective than Otto I's assault on Bari had been. The venomous *apologia* for failure which he wrote soon afterwards, the *Legatio*, registers a certain pattern of development. Dominicus had sworn that Otto would never invade imperial territory and according to Nikephoros II Phokas he had given a written oath that Otto would never cause any 'scandal' (*scandalizare*) to the eastern empire.[26] This sweeping undertaking had been flagrantly violated by Otto's simultaneous attack and

---

[23] *Leg.*, ch. 40, ed. Chiesa, p. 204; tr. Scott, p. 43.
[24] Widukind, *Res gestae Saxonicae*, III.70, ed. Hirsch and Lohmann, pp. 146–7; ed. and German tr. Bauer and Rau, pp. 174–5.
[25] Adalbert, *Reginonis continuatio*, p. 178.
[26] *Leg.*, ch. 25, ed. Chiesa, p. 198; tr. Scott, p. 37; see also ch. 31, ed. Chiesa, p. 200–1; tr. Scott, p. 40.

styling of himself as emperor. Then Nikephoros proceeded to demand that Otto relinquish his bonds of fealty with the princes of Capua-Benevento, Pandulf and his brother Landulf. Nikephoros reiterated that they were rightfully his *douloi* and demanded that Otto 'hand them over',[27] but he may essentially merely have been seeking a disclaimer to these borderlands. That these were Nikephoros' top priority is shown by a subsequent proposal: even if a 'perpetual friendship' was no longer in play,[28] Liudprand could at least ensure that Otto would not aid the princes, whom Nikephoros said he was planning to attack. At the eleventh hour the prospect of a 'marriage treaty' to confirm 'friendship' was dangled before Liudprand;[29] the price would presumably have been an undertaking on Otto's behalf concerning the Lombard princes. Thus Liudprand's fulminations do not quite conceal the Byzantines' continued willingness to negotiate, and indeed he returned with official letters for emperor and pope. Otto's was sealed with a gold bull whereas the pope was only accorded silver, against custom. It may be that one, perhaps the principal, purpose of the *Legatio* was to counteract such emollient effects as the letter might have on Otto.

In the short term Liudprand's militancy was in key with Otto I's. Otto invaded southern Italy again and in an Italian charter of 2 November 968 was represented as seeking the reconquest of all Apulia.[30] Otto's advance was, however, hindered by the numerous *kastra* whose construction Nikephoros and earlier emperors had encouraged. In 969 Byzantine forces went on the offensive. Pandulf Ironhead was captured while besieging Bovino and shipped to Constantinople. In 970 Otto sent another mission to the new *basileus*, John I Tzimiskes (969–76); one of the envoys may have been none other than Liudprand. The eventual outcome was a marriage agreement. Princess Theophano was sent to Italy, and married to Otto II on 14 April 972. Soon afterwards, Otto and his father returned to Germany. Otto I had stayed on in the south four years longer than his letter of January 968 intimated. If the main reason for the delay was his quest for an imperial bride for his son, it is at first sight surprising that Theophano was not in fact a *porphyrogenita* but 'the most splendid niece' of Tzimiskes, as Otto II's dowry charter terms her.[31] More than forty years later a chronicler could comment openly that she was *non virginem desideratam*; all the Italian and German magnates mocked at the match, while some urged that she be sent home.[32] There was an authentic *porphyrogenita* available, but Tzimiskes apparently

---

[27] *Leg.*, ch. 27, ed. Chiesa, pp. 198–9; tr. Scott, p. 38. Pressing geopolitical concerns underlie the prominence of these princes in Liudprand's account of his exchanges with Nikephoros. That they were the primary audience intended for Liudprand's tract was advocated by Mayr-Harting (2001).

[28] *Leg.*, ch. 36, ed. Chiesa, p. 202; tr. Scott, p. 41.

[29] *Leg.*, ch. 53, ed. Chiesa, pp. 210; tr. Scott, p. 49.

[30] Otto I, *Diplomata*, no. 367, p. 504.   [31] Otto II, *Diplomata*, no. 21, p. 29.

[32] Thietmar, *Chronicon*, II.15, ed. Holtzmann, p. 56; tr. Warner, p. 103.

did not feel sufficiently threatened or tempted by Otto to offer her up, and many years later Princess Anna would be wedded to the Rus prince, Vladimir (see above, p. 525). Otto, for his part, could see that the Greeks' presence in the south was ineradicable. Moreover, his former adjutant, Pandulf Ironhead, now urged peace, and although he remained Otto's vassal, he could no longer be counted on in future hostilities. Otto probably concluded that some sort of 'royal' 'from the palace of the Augustus' was better than none.[33] The other issues do not seem to have carried the same weight with him. His very insistence on retaining Pandulf as his vassal suggests this; he was essentially trying to provide for his own inevitably prolonged absences from Rome, by forging close personal bonds with the leading potentate to the south. These alarmed the *basileus*, but really they signalled the marginal role which the city of Rome and central Italy played among Otto's concerns. Once Pandulf had been neutralised, Otto let other Mediterranean matters rest and returned to his Saxon grassroots.

OTTO III, ROME AND BYZANTIUM

The nature and extent of the impact of Theophano on Ottonian court culture is controversial and ambivalent.[34] The many Byzantine *objets d'art* datable to the late tenth or early eleventh century still extant in German cathedral treasuries and museums probably arrived by a variety of routes, not merely from Theophano's sumptuous dowry. The emperor, however, remained the principal distributor. Some of the works had important symbolic functions beyond conspicuous display. Otto II is shown on an ivory – most probably Italian-carved and now in the Musée de Cluny – wearing an imperial *loros* (a richly embroidered pendant sash) and other ornamented vestments. Theophano also wears Byzantine imperial vestments and the couple are being crowned with *stemmata* by Christ (fig. 40). Such depictions were in use in contemporary Byzantium; in Germany they counter-balanced the fact that Theophano had needed to be crowned by the pope before her wedding to Otto. The Byzantine origins of this visual statement – diffused among the Saxons' Nordic neighbours through crude lead medallions[35] – may have been lost on most of Otto's subjects. But one should not underestimate the comprehension of the political elite; in 984 Gerbert of Aurillac could assume that Archbishop Egbert of Trier would be familiar with the Greeks' custom of associating 'a new man' on the throne as 'co-emperor'.[36] It was probably in such matters that Byzantium had most

---

[33] *Life of Mathilda*, ch. 15, ed. Schütte, p. 141; tr. Gilsdorf, p. 87. See also Leyser (1995), p. 19.
[34] See Wentzel (1971); Leyser (1995), pp. 19–27; Westermann-Angerhausen (1995); Erkens (2000).
[35] Schramm and Mütherich (1962), p. 144 and plate 74.
[36] Gerbert of Aurillac, *Letters*, no. 26, ed. and French tr. Riché and Callu, I, pp. 52–3. Theophano's own uncle, Tzimiskes, was one such 'new man'.

to offer the Ottonians. Its arsenal of symbols could help each ruler pass on the imperial crown – itself partly of Byzantine inspiration – to his chosen son. For a family with pretensions to being the *beata stirps* ('blessed family'), readily recognisable emblems of long-established authority were of inestimable value.

Otto II, for his part, seems to have been more positively interested than his father in the imperial Roman past and its Italian foundation stones; the use by his Italian chancery of the title of *imperator Romanorum augustus* from March 982 signalled a much keener commitment to Italian affairs. He tried to subjugate Venice, attacked Byzantine Taranto and aspired to the extra moral authority and power which expulsion of the Saracens from southern Italy would bring. In the 980s and 990s their depredations surpassed those of Fraxinetum's Muslims, whom local lords had managed to extirpate *c.* 972. A victorious Otto could have complemented his Roman title through reclamation of Apulia and Calabria, while eclipsing the *basileus* as *pallida Saracenorum mors* ('white death of the Saracens').[37] However, Otto's army was outmanoeuvred by the Saracens near Reggio di Calabria and he himself escaped only by swimming out to a Byzantine warship anchored offshore that was following events. He died fifteen months later, on 7 December 983, and was laid in an antique sarcophagus beneath a porphyry lid in St Peter's, Rome; here too, Byzantine imperial symbolism was echoed.

Considering Otto II's misadventures, his son might be expected to have emerged from his long minority with the limited goal of tightening control over his Teutonic subjects and rebellious Slavs. In fact Otto III showed unprecedentedly fervent attachment to both the city and the imperial mystique of Rome from quite soon after his coronation as emperor in 996 until his death in 1002. He also came to envisage his hegemony as extending spiritually and ecclesiastically as far east as Poland and Hungary. Yet these tendencies did not manifest themselves all at once, and they were neither wholly consistent nor the product of Otto's whims alone. It was most probably his advisers who were responsible for the decision to seek a marriage-tie with Byzantium, only four or five years after Theophano's death in 991. Her presence was evidently remembered as benign; it had presumably inspired the king of France, Hugh Capet (987–96) to seek a Byzantine princess for his son and heir, Robert II (996–1031), already in 988. Gerbert of Aurillac, who had a hand in this démarche, was esteemed by Otto both as counsellor and polymath and brought into his circle of courtly correspondents; Otto expressed the desire that Gerbert would bring out his 'Greek exactitude' while banishing 'Saxon rusticity'.[38] But this serious-minded, highly strung adolescent was also strongly drawn to holy men whose vision was focused

---

[37] *Leg.*, ch. 10, ed. Chiesa, p. 191; tr. Scott, p. 31; Ohnsorge (1983), pp. 199–200, 203–4; Kresten (1975).

[38] Gerbert of Aurillac, *Letters*, no. 186, ed. and French tr. Riché and Callu, II, pp. 482–3.

Figure 40 Ivory of Otto II of Germany and Theophano being crowned by Christ

on God's kingdom or on spreading the Gospel on earth. First among these was Adalbert of Prague, who became Otto's spiritual father in 996. He seems to have aroused in Otto a longing for spiritual regeneration that intensified after Adalbert's martyrdom by the Prussians in the following year. Otto's yearning for personal salvation fused with a general sense of mission to save others, itself a facet of his desire to resurrect the empire. Thus he joined with the ruler of the Poles, Boleslaw I Chobry (992–1025) in venerating Adalbert, personally laying the relics on the altar of Gniezno's cathedral in 1000. Otto came under the influence of other fathers, such as the group of hermits around Romuald whom he met in Rome in 1000; and Nilus of Rossano, the Calabrian Greek holy man who had moved to a monastery near Gaeta and was urged by Otto to come and take charge of any monastery he might wish in Rome. Nilus was later visited by Otto, who is said to have wept and placed his crown in the old man's hands upon departing.[39]

Otto seems to have been able to converse freely with Nilus, and he had a reading knowledge of Greek. Thus one of the most formidable barriers to intercourse between Greek and western courts was, temporarily, lowered. But Theophano's 'splendid retinue'[40] from Constantinople had included no one who emerged as a dominant figure in the Ottonian court or as a special adviser to the young Otto. The one Greek to rise high in Theophano's favour came not from Constantinople but from southern Italy. John Philagathos instructed Otto, his godson, in Greek for several years. In 989 or 990 he was put in charge of the administration at Pavia, overriding entrenched customs and interests there. Subsequently John was sent to Constantinople to negotiate a marriage alliance for his young master. He returned in late 996 without a *porphyrogenita*, but with a Greek envoy, Leo of Synada. Soon, against all Ottonian expectations, he had been acclaimed pope in lieu of Otto III's appointee Gregory V (996–9); but before long John's chief patron, Crescentius, had been beheaded and he himself was blinded, deposed and paraded around Rome by supporters of Otto III, seated back to front on a donkey, in the spring of 998. Leo of Synada claimed a hand in John's elevation, but this cannot have formed part of his original brief, and the key axis was that between John Philagathos and the Crescentii.[41] Nonetheless, Byzantine support for John was probably suspected by contemporaries, as it certainly was by later writers, and the episode can scarcely have encouraged Otto to employ other Italo-Greeks.

[39] *Life of Nilus the Younger*, chs. 92–3, cols. 153–4. On Otto's regard for Italo-Greek holy men, which seems to represent personal predilection rather than later hagiographical confection, see Seibert (2000), pp. 216–20, 223, 242–5.

[40] Thietmar, *Chronicon*, II.15, ed. Holtzmann, p. 56; tr. Warner, p. 103.

[41] Leo of Synada, *Correspondence*, ed. and tr. Vinson, nos. 6, 11, 12, pp. 8–9, 16–17, 20–1; Kolditz (2002), pp. 562–6, 583.

In 1000, after his visit to Adalbert's shrine, Otto had Charlemagne's remains at Aachen exhumed and the body laid on Byzantine silks, evidently acting here as heir. He contemplated making Aachen his most favoured residence, but then chose another city, like Aachen on the periphery of his lands but still more deeply imbued with historical legitimacy. Otto determined in effect to abandon the essentially absentee lordship of Rome practised by his father and grandfather. He would make Rome a 'royal city' as a conscious riposte to the papacy's self-proclaimed 'apostolic' status and to self-willed local nobles.[42] The phrase was most probably also a conscious evocation of the Byzantines' term for their own 'reigning city'. Otto's choice of site for his residence there is highly significant: the Palatine Hill, where the caesars' palaces had stood from the reign of the emperor Octavian Augustus onwards. The outpourings of Otto's clerical staff reflect his residence there: some sixty-five diplomata were issued in or near Rome between May 996 and February 1001, two of them expressly stating that they were issued *in palatio monasterio*, probably an allusion to the adjoining monastery of San Cesario on the Palatine.[43] Otto's installation of his court there for quite lengthy stretches from 998 onwards blatantly flouted the idea that the area within the city walls had been made over to the papacy by the *Donation of Constantine*.[44] There was no recent precedent for a large-scale secular court in Rome, but a fair proportion of the citizens were acquainted with the luxury products and authority symbols of the Byzantine emperor. Otto's predecessors had used Byzantine-style media, such as the flamboyantly *de luxe* copy of Otto II's dowry charter for Theophano. If Otto III borrowed more extensively, this was because he was trying to root his court in a city where such things clearly appealed to some of the leading families and where at the same time elaborate ceremonial trappings and liturgies daily glorified St Peter and his heir. The Byzantine extravaganza of palace ceremonies and street parades could bring to life the idea that the emperors conferred pre-eminence on the City by residing there and ensured divine favour for it through prayer. The new establishment on the Palatine was intended to be the node of a fresh network of bonds with laymen and clerics.

A farrago of terms for officials emerges from Otto's diplomata. Two are of unmistakably Byzantine stripe, logothete and *protospatharius*. Otto

[42] Schramm (1957), pp. 30–1, 168–9; Brühl (1968), p. 503.

[43] Otto III, *Diplomata*, nos. 383, 384, pp. 812, 814. The term '*urbs regia*' occurs (like '*caput mundi*' – 'head of the world') in the introductory sentences of only one of Otto's diplomata: Otto III, *Diplomata*, no. 389, pp. 819–20; Görich (1993), p. 196. But miscellaneous evidence, notably the building works on the Palatine, signals Otto's expectation that Rome would be conspicuously his residence, in the manner of the ancient caesars. To a youthful seeker after legitimate ascendancy there, the eastern empire offered useful additional stocks of impeccably Christian symbolism and clear-cut notions of imperially driven 'renewal' (see above, p. 497). For western medievalists' views on Otto's conception of his empire and Rome's role in it, see Althoff (2003), pp. 81–9.

[44] Tellenbach (1982), pp. 243–4, 250; Brühl (1989–97), I, pp. 4–6, 19 with n. 82, 24–9. For a different approach, see Görich (1993), pp. 263–7.

began in 998 to call his chancellor for Italy, Heribert, *cancellarius et logotheta* (or *archilogotheta*). The title *protospatharius* is consistently borne by only one individual but he too is associated with the palace, as *comes palatii* in Italy. Most of the other terms come from the contemporary civilian administration of Rome or, as in the case of *imperialis palatii magister*, were Otto's own coinings. They feature principally in his documents issued in or after 998, and exemplify Otto's efforts to represent himself as the legitimate, palace-based master of the city.[45] From 1000 Otto also experimented with his own title, varying it in accordance with his location north or south of the Alps. Very little is known about the ceremonial envisaged for his palace. The descriptions in the *Libellus de cerimoniis aulae imperatoris* are mainly due to Peter the Deacon's mid-twelfth-century fascination with classical Rome, but three protocols most probably date from Otto's time. One of these prescribes how a *protospatharius* should present to the emperor a prospective *patricius*; the emperor will then invest him with a cloak and place a golden 'crown' (*circulus*) on his head.[46] A conspicuous feature of court life was that Otto would sometimes sit at a separate table, elevated above his fellow diners. To dine apart, or with a few guests at a separate, raised, table was also the practice of the *basileus* at certain banquets, and this was probably the chosen model of Otto's dining ritual.

Otto also tried to earn the appreciation of Rome's citizens through his promotion of the cult of the Virgin as protectress of Rome. He even commissioned a hymn in her honour which included the lines: 'Holy mother of God, look after the Roman people and look kindly on Otto!' The Virgin, rather than Sts Peter and Paul, is associated with the City, and Otto is acclaimed by name, a combination also to be found in contemporary Constantinople. The hymn was chanted through Rome's streets by the 'Greek School' on the Vigil of the Assumption in 1000.[47] The impact of such rites was all the greater at a time when there were still a significant number of Greek-speakers in Rome; there were fresh arrivals of monks from the south at that time, refugees from Muslim raiding. Rome was both central to Otto's designs and the haunt of influential persons conversant with Byzantine ways, including Byzantine forms of punishment and degradation for rebels, such as those inflicted on Philagathos.

North of the Alps Otto's experiment with a new political culture could expect fewer sympathisers. The fairly plentiful finds in northern Germany

---

[45] See Schramm (1968–71), I, pp. 288–97, who emphasises the un-Byzantine uses to which the terms *logotheta* and *protospatharius* were put. But that Byzantium's court culture was deliberately evoked is in itself suggestive of its connotations of solemnity and functioning power, and of its uses for Otto's experiments. See also Leyser (1995), p. 27; Kolditz (2002), pp. 533–5, 549–50, 572–4; and below, n. 49.

[46] *Libellus de cerimoniis aulae imperatoris*, ch. 20, ed. in Schramm (1968–71), III, p. 352; Bloch (1984), pp. 87–9, 90–105, 119–27, 141–2; Bloch (1988), pp. 799–800, 823–6.

[47] *Poetae Latini*, ed. Dümmler *et al.*, V, p. 468, line 59; Berschin (1988), p. 185.

of *objets d'art* and silks showing distinctively Byzantine traits or workman-
ship do nevertheless show that some members of the north German elite
had an appetite for eastern luxuries, and there is evidence that they adapted
motifs like the symmetrical double portrait and *proskynēsis* to their own
family needs. Authority symbols such as the *loros* were assimilated by the
reigning family. *Stemmata* of Byzantine design retained a place among the
insignia of Emperor Henry II (1002–24), while other items, such as the orb,
seem to have belonged to an easily comprehensible vocabulary of directly
God-given power common to eastern and western courts. In 1000 Otto III's
newly mounted political culture travelled on show to the Slav north-east,
to Gniezno. Otto is said to have removed a crown from his own head and
placed it on Boleslaw's, rendering him 'brother and partner of the empire'.
Otto also declared him 'friend and ally of the Roman people'.[48] A comparable crown-transfer is attested only once in Byzantine chronicles, but the
emperor was accustomed to crowning junior emperors and caesars personally. Otto seems to have been consciously drawing on Byzantine rites and
terminology to convey his own notion of his relationship with Boleslaw
as a kind of *primus inter pares*. He presented him with a gilded lance; for
Otto and his forebears a 'Holy Lance' – perhaps inspired by Byzantium
and its cult of Constantine the Great – had long been a symbol of imperial authority. Nonetheless, Otto's new political order required frequent
displays of military *virtus* and ample bounty, as well as ceremonial, and
time would have been needed to instil it.[49] Thietmar of Merseburg voices
the incomprehension and dissatisfaction of some northerners in describing
Otto's aim as being to revive 'the ancient customs of the Romans, now
largely destroyed'.[50]

The reaction of the Byzantine government to Otto's experiment was as
mixed as that of the Saxon nobility. Otto's initial attempts to tighten his hold
on Rome are unlikely to have been welcome, but Leo of Synada's embassy
implies at least a willingness to sound out the young ruler; negotiations were
still in progress, and Leo still in the west, in September 998. His observations
of the turmoil in Rome could have persuaded the government that Otto
was too weak to warrant a *porphyrogenita*. Yet only a few years later, in
response to another request or proposal from Otto, Byzantium acceded
and a daughter of Constantine VIII (1025–8) landed at Bari, probably in
February or March 1002, too late to find Otto alive; he had died near
Rome on 23/24 January. Why was the eastern empire now so much more
forthcoming, subjecting a *porphyrogenita* to a winter sea voyage? Otto's

---

[48] Gallus Anonymus, *Chronicae*, I.6, ed. Maleczyński, pp. 19–20; tr. Knoll and Schaer, p. 37.
[49] Intimations of that order, and of the uses of Byzantine authority symbols and iconography in
expressing it, come from the texts and illuminations in Otto's personal prayer book: Hamilton (2001);
Saurma-Jeltsch (2004), pp. 71–4, 82–5.
[50] Thietmar, *Chronicon*, IV.47, ed. Holtzmann, p. 184; tr. Warner, p. 185.

pretensions and claims had grown more sweeping in the meantime, and Gerbert of Aurillac's assumption of the name Sylvester upon becoming pope in 999 signalled that Otto himself was to rank as a new Constantine: the pope in the era of Constantine the Great's adoption of Christianity had been called Sylvester. The signal was aimed mainly at Otto's heterogeneous subjects and the newly Christianised peoples of eastern Europe. But a poem composed soon after Gregory V's return to Rome in 998 claims that 'golden Greece' and the Muslims fear Otto and 'serve [him] with necks bowed'.[51] The poem, probably chanted at a festival in Rome, challenged Byzantine claims to be sole continuators of the *imperium Romanum* and thus the crucible of legitimate earthly authority. Yet these various manifestations of Otto's God-given majesty did not win round all the leading families or the mob in Rome, and his experiment with an *urbs regia* (reigning city) could therefore have been dismissed by the Byzantines as tawdry and ill-starred; Otto had to abandon his residence on the Palatine in 1001. Such things probably did not go unnoticed by easterners passing through Rome. Otto's one foray into southern Italy, in 999, took him only to Benevento and Capua, and was not notably effective, nor is there evidence that he claimed all southern Italy (see below, p. 581).

Otto III did, however, show a pronounced interest in Venice, and visited Doge Peter II Orseolo (991–1009) in April 1001. Already the godfather of a son of Peter named after him, Otto now became godfather to the doge's daughter. His visit may have been viewed with unease from Byzantium; the empire's position in the Adriatic was hard pressed after the loss of Dyrrachium to Samuel of Bulgaria (987/8–1014). Samuel lacked a fleet to reduce Byzantium's subject cities on the Dalmatian coast and his incursions probably ranged no further north than Ragusa. But they may well have occasioned Doge Peter's show of force down the coast in 999, when he received oaths of *fidelitas* from the notables of Zara, Split and most of the other Dalmatian towns.

Whether this operation was undertaken with prior Byzantine approval is uncertain, but Venice's fleet had proved its efficacy in an area where Byzantine possessions were beleaguered. This alone could account for Byzantium's close attention to Venice and to any other power exercising leverage over it. Another, related reason may lie behind Byzantium's readiness to oblige Otto III between 1000 and 1002. Basil II was about to lead his army up the Danube against Samuel. As Samuel was probably linked to Stephen I of Hungary (1000–38) through a marriage alliance, Basil was liable to be attacked by Stephen, and he most probably joined forces with a Hungarian chieftain in the region of Vidin, Ahtum-Ajtony (see above, p. 527). Otto

---

[51] *Poetae Latini*, ed. Dümmler *et al.*, V, p. 479, verse 8 and apparatus criticus. See also Gerbert, *Lettres*, ed. Havet, p. 237.

may have appeared a useful potential restraint on Stephen, for Stephen's wife was sister of Duke Henry of Bavaria, the future emperor Henry II; and through 'the grace and urging' of Otto, Stephen founded cathedral churches and duly received a crown and, most probably, a gilded lance in late 1000:[52] such links gave Otto a certain moral leadership. If word of Otto's démarches towards Hungary reached Byzantium in 1001, while preparations for the daring venture up the Danube were afoot, this could have tipped the balance in favour of Otto's repeated requests for a marriage-tie.

This explanation, though hypothetical, fits the pattern of east–west relations throughout the tenth century. The Balkans, especially Bulgaria, loomed large among the concerns of the Byzantine government; matters further afield were mostly of secondary importance. A well-disposed Otto might do little more than discourage Stephen I of Hungary from attacking Basil's far-reaching Danubian expedition, but Otto will have seemed likely to be a force in east-central Europe for many years to come, and for his good offices a *porphyrogenita* probably seemed a price worth paying.

Otto III's unexpected death and his successor's preoccupation with matters north of the Alps loosened Byzantino-German relations for almost two decades. Basil II for his part was embroiled in the Bulgarian war. It was the Venetians who came to the relief of Bari when it was in danger of falling to the Saracens in 1003, and the Sicilians and North Africans continued to pillage the south Italian coastline through the opening decades of the eleventh century. Imperial authority suffered another blow when an Apulian notable, Melo, instigated a revolt *c.* 1009. This was far from being the first local insurrection (see below p. 570), but it was serious, involving Ascoli as well as Bari. The imperial authorities took several years to suppress it and Melo then fled to the courts of Lombard princes. Subsequently, in 1017, he mounted another challenge to imperial power, relying heavily on a band of Normans, at first exiguous but later reinforced. This is the first occasion when the Normans' armed presence in the south is incontrovertible, although a few Normans had probably found employment at Lombard courts from the opening years of the century onwards. Melo now ventured to fight pitched battles and several important towns such as Trani renounced imperial authority. However, in October 1018 Melo and his Normans were defeated at Cannae by Basil Boioannes, the *katepanō* of *Italia*.

Boioannes was assisted by the fact that Bulgaria was being pacified and manpower and money were now available for operations in Italy. The forces which he led onto the battlefield were like 'bees issuing forth from

[52] Thietmar, *Chronicon*, IV.59, ed. Holtzmann, p. 198; tr. Warner, p. 193.

a full hive'.[53] But he showed great organisational talent, building numerous strongholds in northern Apulia. Several towns were founded in what amounted to a system on the Byzantine side of the River Fortore, including Civitate and Fiorentino. Others were founded in Calabria. Boioannes expressly claimed to be restoring at Troia a town long abandoned; the name and site of Civitate likewise evoked classical antiquity. Troia – 'Troy' – lay only 215 kilometres from Rome.

Boioannes' prime objective was to consolidate Apulia's northern defences and overawe the borderland princelings. But the effect was to provoke the German emperor and aggravate the hostility which Pope Benedict VIII (1012–24) had already shown in granting a fortress on the Garigliano to Melo's brother-in-law, Datto. In 1017 Benedict had probably played a part in encouraging Norman fortune-seekers to join up with Melo and the rulers of Capua-Benevento and Naples. Benedict also looked to the German emperor as a patron of church reform and counterweight to the Crescentii, and it was to Henry II's court that Melo fled after Cannae. In 1020 Benedict himself accepted Henry's invitation and crossed the Alps to Bamberg, where he exchanged the kiss of peace with Henry and celebrated the liturgy using the *filioque* clause in the creed, a heretical interpolation in Byzantine eyes. Henry made his claim to overlordship in the south explicit by conferring on Melo the title of *dux Apuliae*. However, on 23 April 1020 Melo died. The following spring Boioannes suddenly attacked Melo's brother-in-law on the Garigliano. The fortress was handed over to Pandulf IV of Capua, now a Byzantine vassal; Datto himself was paraded through Bari's streets on a donkey, then thrown in the sea. Henry II marshalled a large army and reached Ravenna at the end of December 1021. A detachment was sent to deal with Pandulf and his cousin Atenulf, abbot of Monte Cassino. Henry led the main force towards the base which had assisted Boioannes to operate so effectively on the Garigliano, an area where Picingli had required allies a hundred years earlier (see above, p. 538). Henry besieged Troia for about three months, until his army succumbed to dysentery, the *basileus'* abiding ally against intruders from the north. Henry eventually managed to extract token submission from Troia, but soon after his withdrawal the inhabitants opened the gates to Boioannes. So long as Henry stayed in the south, he could overawe the Lombard princes. Pandulf IV, besieged in Capua, sued for terms and was stripped of his principality; the prince of Salerno, Guaimar III (999–1027), surrendered; and a new abbot was installed at Monte Cassino in lieu of Atenulf. But Boioannes' barrier fortress stood undemolished; Henry's southern foray had made no more impact on Byzantine Apulia than Otto I's or Otto II's expeditions had done.

[53] Amatus of Monte Cassino, *Storia de' Normanni*, I.22, ed. de Bartholomaeis, p. 29; tr. Dunbar and Loud, p. 51.

In 1025 the eastern empire appeared on course towards reconquering Sicily and dominating commercial traffic in the central Mediterranean when Basil II died and his expeditionary force dispersed. But Byzantine Italy was becoming more prosperous and populous than it had been for centuries. Many of its inhabitants seem to have preferred the distant, undemanding *basileus* as the safeguard of their interests, while Byzantine emperors contemplated yet another Sicilian expedition. Byzantium's build-up of power in southern Italy antagonised the papacy and the western emperor, but their retaliatory capability was very limited. It was small groups of alien predators whose energies, greed and organisational skills wore down the Byzantine authorities in the mid-eleventh century. The spoils of the burgeoning towns and, eventually, power over them would go to these self-reliant freebooters, hailing from the shores of a northern sea.[54]

[54] For the Normans' arrival in southern Italy and struggles for mastery there, see Loud (2000a), pp. 67–130.

CHAPTER 15

BYZANTIUM AND SOUTHERN ITALY

(876–1000)

G. A. LOUD

The last seventy years of the ninth century were an era of disorder and continued crisis in southern Italy. The government of the principality of Benevento, which ruled over most of the south of the peninsula, was riven by succession disputes which led to the formal partition of the principality in 849. But far from ending the contention, this division gave only a brief pause in the internecine strife. Muslim attacks from Sicily and North Africa threatened to swamp a feeble and divided Christian defence, and the local rulers were far more intent on their internal power struggles than on making any coherent and effective stand against the invader. However, the years round about 900 marked a very significant change, with regard both to the internal stability of southern Italy and also to its relative freedom from external threat – or at least from the threat of conquest rather than sporadic raiding. For much of the tenth century the land was not exactly peaceful, but freed at least from the dreary litany of civil war and the establishment of territorial footholds for further Muslim advance that had made the previous period a troubled one, the impact of which had been reflected in the pessimism of contemporary chroniclers such as Erchempert, and in the number of charters mentioning relatives or fellow monks captured by the Saracens.

This change was marked by three factors. First, there was the revival of Byzantine power in the late ninth century. Under the governorship of Nikephoros Phokas in the 880s the Byzantines had recovered much of northern Calabria and consolidated their hold in southern Apulia (see above, p. 460). The creation of the new theme of Langobardia in this period was part of the process of consolidation, as was the creation of new dioceses in Calabria after 886. Visits by local rulers to Constantinople, such as those of Guaimar I of Salerno (880–900) in 887 and Landulf I of Benevento in 910, as well as the use once again of the regnal years of the Byzantine emperor in the dating clauses of documents from both the cities of the west coast and in the Lombard principalities, demonstrate the restored

Map 25 Southern Italy in the tenth century

prestige of the empire.[1] Secondly, there was much greater internal stability in those parts of southern Italy not ruled by Byzantium. In 900 a bloodless coup had installed Atenulf I of Capua (900–10) as ruler of Benevento, and a few months later another coup displaced Guaimar I of Salerno, who was despatched to end his days as a monk. But while these events might seem to have been merely a continuation of the ninth-century chaos in the Lombard principalities, in fact they marked its end. The union of the two principalities of Capua and Benevento was to last for eighty-one years, and Guaimar I was merely replaced by his son, who remained as prince, apparently unchallenged, until his death in old age in 946. Thirdly, there was the threat from Islam. The conquest of Taormina, the last major Byzantine bastion in Sicily, early in 902, was indeed the prelude to a renewed invasion of the Calabrian mainland in the late summer of that year. But the death of its leader, Ibrahim 'Abd-Allah, at Cosenza in October marked not just the end of that invasion, but also the end of serious threat for many years; internal instability proved as much of a problem in Islamic Sicily in the tenth century as it had in Lombard southern Italy in the ninth.

Thus from around 900 onwards the political structures of southern Italy remained, at least outwardly, more or less in equilibrium. Apulia and Calabria were ruled by the Byzantine empire, each with its own provincial government, based respectively at Bari and (probably) at Reggio. Southern Campania and the Cilento region formed the Lombard principality of Salerno, which had been created by the division of 849. The central mountain region and the bulk of the Terra di Lavoro – the two principalities of Capua and Benevento[2] – were ruled by the descendants of Atenulf I of Capua, to judge by their surviving diplomata largely from Capua. Three coastal duchies, Gaeta, Naples and Amalfi, retained their independence from the Lombard principalities, as they had always jealously done, but each was really just one city with a very small dependent territory. Given how limited were their hinterlands, their economies were largely dependent on overseas trade.

The effective cessation of Muslim attempts at conquest after 902 still left one very serious problem for the security of the principalities of the west coast unresolved, namely the Saracen colony at the mouth of the Garigliano river, established around 881. From here the north of the principality of Capua and the Abruzzi region lay at the invaders' mercy. Indeed in 881–3 raiders from the Garigliano had destroyed the famous and prosperous

---

[1] Imperial regnal years were used in Gaeta up to 934 and in Naples throughout this period. In Capua and Benevento usage was more sporadic, but the princes referred to their title of *patrikios* up to 920: von Falkenhausen (1967), pp. 32, 37.

[2] Cilento (1966), pp. 149–50 argues that the use of terms like 'the principality of Capua' is anachronistic since the early tenth-century rulers described themselves as prince without any territorial designation; see, however, *CS*, ch. 159, pp. 166–7: 'Atenulfus Beneventanus princeps'; ch. 172, pp. 174–5, 'Beneventi fines'.

inland monasteries of Monte Cassino and San Vincenzo al Volturno, whose surviving monks had had to take refuge in Capua for a generation or more. A first attack on the Garigliano base, launched by Atenulf I of Capua in 903, failed, not least because of support lent to the Saracens by the forces of the duke of Gaeta.[3] Under papal auspices a second, successful attack was made in 915. A prolonged diplomatic campaign by the papacy and the Byzantine government deprived the Muslims of their Christian allies – the coastal cities of Amalfi and Gaeta, whose trading interests had led them to seek accommodation with the Arabs. It also secured the reinforcement of the local armies of Capua and the duchy of Naples by troops from central Italy and from Byzantine Apulia, under the personal command of the *stratēgos* of Langobardia.[4] The destruction of the Garigliano colony ensured that southern Italy was in future free from serious Muslim threat; raids on Calabria continued intermittently for much of the century, but were often bought off by the payment of tribute. Occasionally such attacks also menaced southern Apulia; for example, Oria was sacked in 925 and Taranto a few years later. But these were essentially plundering expeditions, not attempts to establish bridgeheads for further conquest. As such, they were of only very limited significance.

THE BYZANTINE HOLD ON CALABRIA AND APULIA

After 915 the main problem for the Byzantine government was disaffection among their provinces' inhabitants, combined with the ambitions of the princes of Capua to extend their rule towards the Adriatic coast. The *stratēgos* of Calabria, John Muzalon, was assassinated in an uprising near Reggio in 921, and soon afterwards the *stratēgos* of Langobardia, Ursoleon, was killed at Ascoli fighting against the forces of Capua-Benevento, which went on to occupy much of northern Apulia, apparently with the support of the local inhabitants. The fiscal pressure of Byzantine rule was undoubtedly one cause of disaffection, and this was, as the Calabrian revolt shows, by no means confined to the Latin areas under Byzantine dominion.[5] But the desire of the princes of Capua to recover those parts of Apulia which had been under the rule of their predecessors at Benevento until the mid-ninth century, and to secure control of coastal towns like Siponto and Bari which benefited from trade in the Adriatic, should not be underestimated. That this was a very real ambition is clear from the attempt of Landulf I (910–43) after his victory at Ascoli to persuade the Byzantine government

---

[3] *CMC*, I.50, pp. 130–1.   [4] Vehse (1927) remains the best discussion.

[5] Gay (1904), pp. 202–4 shows that the two revolts were separate, despite some confusion in the sources. For a later revolt in Greek Calabria, protesting against exactions for military service, see the *Life of Nilus the Younger*, chs. 60–2, cols. 103–10.

to appoint him as *stratēgos* of Langobardia.[6] Although details are obscure, it seems that the Byzantine position in Apulia was restored for a time after 921, but a second Beneventan invasion in 926, this time with the support of the prince of Salerno – who were apparently not involved in 921 – proved more serious. For some seven years substantial parts of Apulia were in the hands of the princes of Capua-Benevento, and parts of Lucania and northern Calabria were under the rule of the prince of Salerno. The status quo was only restored when the Byzantine government secured an alliance with Hugh of Arles, king of Italy (926–47); combined with substantial military reinforcement from Constantinople, this achieved the withdrawal of the Lombard princes.[7] For more than thirty years from *c.* 934 onwards, the frontier between the principality of Benevento and the Byzantine province of Langobardia remained relatively secure, if not entirely uncontested, especially in the late 940s.

Despite problems on the province's northern border, Byzantine rule in Calabria was largely unaffected by the tense relations with the Lombard principalities. Indeed for some considerable period Calabria was also free from Arab raids. Tribute money paid to Sicily from Calabria apparently ceased after 934, and in the latter part of this decade the island's Muslims were in the grip of civil war. It was only after internal peace was restored in Sicily in 947 that Calabria was once again threatened. Reggio fell in 950 and a further attack took place in 952, but once again the payment of protection money secured a period of truce.

The Byzantines were therefore able to maintain, albeit with some difficulty, their dominions in Italy more or less as they had been secured by the reconquests of the 880s (see above, p. 298). What they were not able to do, more than very sporadically, was to enforce any recognition of their rule in the petty duchies of the west coast, still less so in the Lombard principalities. Only in Naples did documents continue to be dated by the regnal years of the Byzantine emperors, and such links were of far more cultural than political significance. Indeed in 956, when the government in Constantinople was able to release sufficient troops for a major expedition to Italy, the first target of that offensive was apparently Naples; however, their aim may quite possibly have been to secure Neapolitan naval assistance against renewed Arab attacks on Calabria. Furthermore, it would seem that during this period there was once again disaffection in those areas under direct Byzantine rule.[8] Byzantium was a 'superpower', unlike the independent south Italian states. But for its government southern Italy was of far

---

[6] NM, no. 82, pp. 338–42.

[7] The period of seven years is given by *Leg.*, ch. 7, ed. Chiesa, p. 190; tr. Scott, p. 30. From 935 the regnal years of the emperors appeared occasionally in Beneventan charters: Mor (1952–3), I, p. 263. Details of the troops sent to Italy are given in *DC*, II.44, ed. Reiske, I, pp. 660–4.

[8] TC, pp. 453–4.

less moment than either the frontier in Asia Minor or the defence of its European provinces against the Bulgarians. For the most part the defence of its Italian dominions was left to local efforts, and only very occasionally could imperial troops or ships be spared in any numbers. Even in 956 the policy was essentially defensive: to secure a commitment by the Lombard princes not to attack Byzantine territory, to enforce effective government in that territory, and to prevent further raids on Calabria. The one exception to this limited policy came with the launching of a large-scale expedition to Sicily by Nikephoros II Phokas (963–9) in 964, but the disastrous defeat which resulted cannot have encouraged further such ambitious enterprises, and renewed military operations in other theatres anyway prevented a fresh attempt.

Moreover, in 966 the balance of power in southern Italy was to be, for a time, seriously affected by a new player on the stage, the German ruler Otto I (962–73), who in reviving Charlemagne's western Roman empire also revived Carolingian imperial claims to overlordship over southern Italy. The means whereby Otto sought to vindicate his claims were both direct military action and an alliance with the strongest of the local rulers in the south, the prince of Capua and Benevento, Pandulf I Ironhead (961–81). What this meant in practice was that the Capuan pressure on the Byzantine frontier in northern Apulia of the 920s and 930s was once again revived, but with the formidable military assistance of the German emperor.

The alliance with Pandulf Ironhead served a further purpose for the German emperor. By conceding the margravate of Camerino and the duchy of Spoleto to the prince of Capua, Otto secured a vital ally and recognition of his overlordship in the south; he also created a viceregal power in central Italy through which he could the more effectively control the Roman nobility, understandably restive at the prospect of a series of Ottonian clients being placed on the papal throne. The alliance enabled Pandulf to revive his ancestors' ambitions to encroach on Byzantine territory in Apulia, while also protecting his dominions from incursions from the north, such as had apparently occurred in the early 960s.[9] Otto himself paid a brief visit to Benevento in February 967, and in the spring of 968 a full-scale attack was made on Byzantine Apulia which reached as far as Bari before the allies withdrew. A further attack occurred in the winter of that year which took the German imperial army as far south as the Calabrian border. But in the end very little was accomplished. After Otto I had returned to northern Italy, Pandulf was captured while besieging Bovino on the Apulian frontier and sent as a prisoner to Constantinople. It was in good measure due to his intercession, after a further year's inconclusive warfare, that a peace between the two empires was eventually patched up, sealed by the marriage of the

[9] *CS*, ch. 166, p. 170.

young Otto II (973–83) to a Byzantine princess, Theophano (see above, p. 548).

The overwhelming impression given by this period of conflict, as indeed by the sporadic border warfare of the earlier part of the century, is of its essential sterility. Each side was capable of deep penetrations into the other's territory – Byzantine troops briefly got as far as Capua in the summer of 969 – but neither was strong enough to make any permanent impression. While the Byzantines held on to key border fortresses like Ascoli and Bovino the province of Langobardia was essentially safe. Furthermore the enhancement of the prince of Capua's authority was hardly in the interests of the other local rulers; while they had no wish to be Byzantine clients, they were equally unwilling to be clients of Capua and the German emperor. The duke of Naples supported the Byzantine invasion of Capuan territory in 969. Although the prince of Salerno did not, and in fact sent a relieving force to Capua, he seems to have otherwise tried to keep on good terms with the Greeks. Significantly the late tenth-century *Chronicon Salernitanum* took a favourable view of Nikephoros II Phokas, very different from the infamous portrayal of the emperor by Otto's envoy to his court, Liudprand of Cremona.[10] And around 966 the duke of Amalfi was once again, after a long interval, using a Byzantine title, a sign of renewed contact with the government at Constantinople.[11]

CHURCHES AND MONASTERIES IN CALABRIA AND APULIA, AND BYZANTINE ADMINISTRATION

The conflict between the two empires in the 960s had a further aspect, however, and one which was of very considerable significance for southern Italy. In 966, while taking refuge with Prince Pandulf from the hostile nobility of Rome, Otto's client Pope John XIII (965–972) raised the see of Capua to be a metropolitan archbishopric. Three years later, at the height of the military conflict in Apulia, he did the same for that of Benevento. The creation of the archbishopric of Capua should almost certainly be seen as a recognition of Capua's status as Pandulf's *de facto* capital and as an attempt to boost princely authority over the rest of the principality; the first archbishop was Pandulf's younger brother John. However, the creation of the new ecclesiastical province of Benevento was overtly anti-Byzantine and the authority granted to the archbishop stretched deep into Byzantine territory. Among the new suffragan sees to be subject to it were Ascoli and Bovino, the two key border fortresses under siege from Otto's and Pandulf's forces. Since the bulk of the population of Byzantine Apulia were

---

[10] 'Vir bonus et iustus': *CS*, ch. 173, pp. 175–6.
[11] For the dating, see Schwarz (1978), pp. 37, 243, *contra* Gay (1904), p. 321.

Latins, the loyalties of their churchmen were clearly of crucial importance to the Byzantine government; the creation of the new archbishopric of Benevento, which was intended to destabilise northern Apulia, was to have wide-ranging repercussions.

The Byzantines' reaction was to reorganise the church in Apulia, to create new archiepiscopal sees rivalling Benevento, and to ensure that the Apulian church remained loyal to Constantinople. In the 980s, when Otto II tried once again to invade Byzantine territory, the creation of the archbishopric of Salerno by Pope Benedict VII (974–83) was a further anti-Byzantine ecclesiastical measure. The sees of Cosenza and Bisignano in Calabria, previously suffragans of the Greek archbishop of Reggio and in areas clearly under Byzantine jurisdiction, were subordinated to Salerno; but unlike most of Calabria, they almost certainly contained a substantial Latin population.[12] Here too, the Byzantine authorities reacted with ecclesiastical changes of their own, including the creation of an archbishopric at Cosenza in defiance of papal authority.

The ecclesiastical changes after 970 were one aspect of a more general overhaul of the administrative structure of Byzantine Italy. In part a reaction to the renewed threat to its borders, this overhaul also reflected changes in the distribution of the region's population, although quite how extensive these were has been a matter of debate among historians.[13] But it seems clear that Arab raids on Calabria – by no means continuous, but alarming and destructive – encouraged the population both to retreat from coastal settlements to more defensible hill sites inland and, in some cases, to move northwards towards the borderlands with the principality of Salerno. Some Greeks living in Sicily under Arab rule may also have crossed the straits of Messina and moved north, although the evidence for this is almost entirely derived from contemporary saints' *Lives*, and we cannot be certain that the movement of these holy men was accompanied by any substantial numbers of laymen. Christian monks may well have been more obviously at risk in periods of disorder in Sicily, as in the 940s, than the laity who were less of a provocation to the Muslim devout.[14] In any case, nearly all the saints' *Lives* from tenth-century Calabria show their protagonists settling around the northern frontiers of the province, in the regions of Mercourion and, further north still, Latinianon; in the ninth century Latinianon had been a gastaldate of the principality of Salerno. The saints' *Lives* imply that their

---

[12] The earliest evidence for Salerno as an archbishopric comes in a papal bull of 989, which is clearly retrospective. Gay (1904), p. 358 argued convincingly for dating the promotion to the summer of 983 and this has been generally accepted, e.g. by von Falkenhausen (1967), p. 148; Taviani-Carozzi (1991b), p. 673.

[13] Notably between Ménager (1958–9), I, and Guillou (1963).

[14] For example Elias the Speleote (*c.* 865–*c.* 960) left Sicily after his companion at his hermitage was killed by the Arabs: *Life of Elias the Speleote*, I.8, pp. 850–1; Ménager (1958–9), I, p. 763.

heroes were not the only Greeks present in these regions. Luke of Armento, for example, spent some seven years in the Val di Sinni in Latinianon before fleeing to escape a crowd of would-be disciples.[15] Some Greeks, both monks and laymen, crossed into Lombard territory. The most famous example was Nilus of Rossano, who towards the end of the century spent some fifteen years at Valleluce, near Monte Cassino (see above, p. 552). But his was not the only case. In the eleventh century there were at least four Greek monasteries in the vicinity of Salerno, and one as far away as Pontecorvo, near the northern border of the principality of Capua.[16]

The expansion of the Greek population of Calabria into the heel of Italy led to administrative changes both lay and ecclesiastical. From the 880s onwards there had been two separate and apparently independent provinces of Byzantine Italy: Langobardia (that is Apulia) and Calabria (up to the 940s still officially and anachronistically known as the theme of Sicily, although the Byzantines only retained a few isolated strongholds in the north-east of the island). In the reign of Nikephoros II Phokas there came a change. The theme of Langobardia, strategically the more significant of the two since through its ports the mouth of the Adriatic was in Byzantine hands and easy access was possible to the European mainland of the empire, was placed under an official known as the *katepanō*, who was of more senior rank and status than previous governors. It is probable that the new *katepanō* was placed in overall authority over Byzantine Italy, and it is also likely that a new province of Lucania was created at this time, although the dating is far from certain. Lucania incorporated Latinianon, Lagonegro and Mercourion, regions to the north of Calabria into which there had recently been an influx of Greeks, and a new diocese, Tursi, was set up as the bishopric for Lucania.[17] Tursi was made part of a new metropolitan province, subject to the previously autocephalous archbishopric of Otranto. Both these sees had Greek clergy, but four Latin sees in southern Apulia – Tricarico, Acerenza, Matera and Gravina – were also subjected to the archbishop of Otranto. In the next few years two further Apulian sees were raised to the status of archbishoprics: Taranto in 978, and Trani in 987.

The process was continued in the early eleventh century when archbishoprics were created at Lucera, Brindisi and Siponto. The intention here was to bind the Latin clergy of these sees firmly to the Byzantine government, and to combat the claims of the archbishop of Benevento. The policy was not anti-Latin. Given that the majority of the population in all but

---

[15] *Life of Luke of Armento*, ch. 6, p. 338; Ménager (1958–9), I, pp. 767–8.

[16] Borsari (1950–1); Borsari (1963), pp. 58–60, 71–5; Loud (1994a), pp. 38–41. For examples of Greek laymen in the principality of Salerno see *CDC*, II, no. 384 (986), pp. 235–6; III, no. 521 (999), p. 88.

[17] von Falkenhausen (1967), pp. 46–7, 65–8, 104 argues that the theme of Lucania was created in the eleventh century and had only an ephemeral existence, and that Calabria was not subject to the *katepanō*'s authority. Guillou (1965) makes a very convincing case to the contrary.

the extreme south of Apulia was Latin, it could not be, and Liudprand of Cremona's claim that Nikephoros Phokas and Patriarch Polyeuct (956–70) wanted to forbid the Latin rite in southern Italy is clearly ludicrous.[18] Sees with Latin bishops and clergy remained Latin, even in towns like Taranto where most of the population were Greek. But these ecclesiastical changes were clearly political, designed to exclude the influence both of the papacy – which was under Ottonian control – and of the archbishopric of Benevento. The latter was an instrument of Pandulf Ironhead's ambitions and possibly those of his successors, in so far as they had any power. The policy seems to have worked. In 983 the *katepanō* granted a privilege to the bishop of Trani in reward for his support during the recent siege of the town.[19] But no chances were taken. Latin churches in Apulia remained under very tight supervision. Sees were often merged and then split up once again. Officials of the government acted as the advocates (i.e. legal representatives) of churches. Occasional exemptions from taxation given to Latin clergy were specific and highly restricted,[20] although this was part of a more general desire by the Byzantine authorities to preserve the fiscal base of the state.

Despite the continued hazard of Muslim raids on Calabria – a problem which, after a pause, became serious again from the mid-970s – the Byzantine provinces retained their cohesion and even flourished in a modest way. Not only did Greek influence increase and push the border northwards in Lucania – the creation of the theme was a recognition of this; in the last years of the century, after Ottonian policy in southern Italy had collapsed and Pandulf Ironhead's dominions divided, the Apulian frontier also shifted northwards from the River Ofanto to the River Fortore. The area of northern Apulia thus incorporated into the theme of Langobardia became known, significantly, as the Capitanata, i.e. the land of the *katepanō* (or 'captain') – reflecting its incorporation under Byzantine rule after this new title for the governor had been introduced. At the end of the century the Byzantine administration can be seen in full operation as far inland as Tricarico on the Apulia–Lucania border, redefining boundaries and setting up new *chōria* (taxable units).[21] Monasteries were often the focus for the clearance of land and new settlement, particularly in the hitherto underexploited Lucanian region, and the villages which developed around them were then officially incorporated as *chōria*. The population, it would seem, was expanding, although in Lucania migration can explain new settlement

[18] *Leg.*, ch. 62, ed. Chiesa, p. 215; tr. Scott, p. 54. For the ecclesiastical changes generally, see von Falkenhausen (1967), pp. 147–57; Martin (1993), pp. 563–72.

[19] *Carte di Trani*, ed. Prologo, no. 7, pp. 32–5.

[20] See, for example, *Carte di Trani*, ed. Prologo, no. 8, pp. 35–8 to the archbishop of Trani (999), discussed by Borsari (1959), pp. 128–34.

[21] Holtzmann and Guillou (1961).

(see above, p. 567). In a few cases population transfers may have been deliberate, although the evidence for this relates mainly to the reign of Leo VI (886–912), who is known to have sent settlers from the Peloponnese to southern Italy. By the end of the tenth century agriculture was apparently flourishing in at least some parts of Calabria, with extensive vineyards and the beginnings of silk production which had, by the mid-eleventh century, reached a considerable scale. Evidence for the Byzantine provinces' external trade is extremely scanty, but it would appear that in the tenth century Otranto and Brindisi were probably the most important ports, with Bari becoming more important in the eleventh.

While Calabria and Lucania, with a largely, if not exclusively, Greek population, might seem very much like other Byzantine provinces, Apulia was different. The presence of a substantially Latin populace meant that the Byzantine government had to concede a degree of local autonomy, or at least variation, which was inconceivable in entirely Greek parts of the empire. While the provincial governors and some of their more senior officials were Greeks sent out from Constantinople – in the case of the *stratēgoi* and *katepanoi* generally holding office for fairly brief periods, about three years on average – many of the more junior officials were Latins. At Bari in the late tenth and early eleventh centuries eight out of eleven recorded turmarchs were Latins, and only three Greeks; in Taranto, by contrast, all but one of the known turmarchs were Greeks.[22] Such use of locally born Latin officers was probably even more prevalent in inland Apulia, where on occasion they might use titles derived from the Lombard principalities, such as gastald, and in one case at least, from Lucera at the end of the century, model their documents on Beneventan princely charters.[23] Most significant was the widespread sanction given to the use of Lombard law. The growth of a fairly prosperous class of small-scale landed proprietors in Apulia, judged by their own law and with their own Latin churches, approved of but closely supervised by the provincial government, was probably the best guarantee for the stability of Byzantine government in Apulia. But it was by no means infallible. Revolts in the coastal towns occurred a number of times in the tenth century,[24] and intensified after 1000, although contributory factors such as the abnormally harsh winter of 1007–8 should not be underestimated. Nor should the burden of taxation, which in Italy as in the rest of the Byzantine empire probably increased with the ambitious military policy of the late tenth-century emperors. While the Latin chroniclers tend to ascribe instances of disaffection in the Byzantine

[22] Probably by this time, turmarchs were town judges or governors, rather than the immediate deputies of the provincial governor.

[23] von Falkenhausen (1973).

[24] For example at Conversano in 947, Trani in 982/3 and Bari in 986: Lupus Protospatharius, *Annales*, pp. 54–6; *Carte di Trani*, ed. Prologo, no. 7, pp. 32–5.

provinces to the cruelty or demands of particular governors, one might well conclude that it was rather the reaction of the populace to a governmental system which was far more efficient – and thus more oppressive in locals' eyes – than that in the Lombard principalities.

THE PRINCIPALITIES OF CAPUA-BENEVENTO AND SALERNO

These Lombard states, if one can use such a term for markedly inchoate organisations, presented a great contrast to Byzantine Italy. They were undoubtedly much more stable in the first three-quarters of the tenth century than they had been before 900, and whereas in the earlier period the princely office had at times seemed little more than a football to be kicked back and forth among local gastalds and other members of the office-holding aristocracy, by the tenth century hereditary succession was the norm. This was made more certain by the nomination of sons as co-rulers in their father's lifetime, which was also the practice in the duchies of Naples and Amalfi.

In the principality of Capua-Benevento family stability was ensured by joint rule between brothers, as well as between father and son. For one very brief period in 939–40 no fewer than four individuals were using the princely title: Landulf I, two of his sons and his younger brother, Atenulf II (910–40). But generally no more than two princes held office at any one time, and the younger of two co-ruling brothers could not expect to pass the title down to his children. There were never more than two brothers holding the princely title at the same time. Pandulf Ironhead associated only his eldest son with him as co-prince, although he had several younger ones as well, and he did that only after his younger brother's death in the winter of 968–9. It may sometimes have been the case that one, probably the senior, prince held Capua, while the other was associated with Benevento. This seems at first sight to be implied by the *Chronicon Salernitanum*'s account of Pandulf Ironhead abandoning Otto I's army on the Calabrian border upon hearing the news of his brother Landulf's death, and hastening to Benevento to secure his son's enthronement as prince. However, the same chronicle also shows the two brothers acting together at Capua a few months earlier, escorting the prince of Salerno to meet their overlord Otto. The significance of the incident may simply be that the palace church of St Sophia at Benevento remained the traditional place for a new prince to be enthroned, as it had been back in the eighth century.[25] Charters generally show princes acting together, as Pandulf I and Landulf III (961–8/9) invariably did in the 960s. In 943 Atenulf III (933–43), acting

---

[25] *CS*, chs. 169–70, pp. 171–3. It is, however, noteworthy that the Beneventans installed Landulf's son as their chosen prince in 982.

by himself from Benevento, issued a group of charters for Monte Cassino. Although he did this in the name of his absent father and younger brother as well as on his own behalf, his action was almost certainly a symptom of a political crisis; soon afterwards he was expelled from Benevento, according to the *Chronicon Salernitanum* for his 'sins and cruelty', and took refuge with his son-in-law, Guaimar II of Salerno (900–46).[26] It looks as though the attempt to associate several members of the princely family together as co-rulers in the late 930s had not been a success, or perhaps Atenulf was simply displaced by his younger brother, to whose sons the princely title was eventually to pass. But the episode suggests that a division of Capua or Benevento between individual princes was neither normal nor wise.

The association of a son with his father was clearly important in ensuring a smooth succession. Gisulf I of Salerno (946–77) was made co-prince when only three years old.[27] From the few chronicle accounts we have it would seem, however, that whatever the importance of such designation and of the appearance of the co-prince in diplomata, in practice the senior ruler was the effective one who was considered to dictate policy. Only in exceptional circumstances would matters be different, and the most obvious would be when the inheriting prince was still a minor. This was the case with Prince Landenulf of Capua, who succeeded in 982 and was for some years under the tutelage of his mother, Aloara. Similar examples occurred in the duchy of Amalfi in the 950s and at Gaeta in the early eleventh century. But minorities could be very dangerous: the minor duke of Amalfi in the 950s, Mastalus II, was murdered in 958, and his family replaced by a new dynasty.

Yet for the most part princely rule, and that of the dukes in the coastal cities, seems to have been stable in the tenth century – at least up to the 970s in Salerno and the 980s in Capua and Benevento – and certainly when compared with the chaos of the preceding century. But, paradoxically, the foundations of princely authority were being eroded. In the ninth century, the embattled princes of Benevento were careful not to alienate parts of their fisc and regalian rights; they preferred to give out property which had reverted to them either judicially or essentially by accident – for example, from men lacking heirs. Their tenth-century successors were less cautious, particularly after 950. It was under Pandulf Ironhead, when the prince was at least nominally at his most powerful, that the most extensive concessions were made. For example, in 964 Pandulf and his brother conceded the county of Isernia to their cousin Landulf, with an extensive immunity which effectively withdrew the county from their jurisdiction. A similar abdication of public power can be seen in the concessions which Pandulf II (982–1014) of Benevento made to a certain Count Poto in 988 of Greci and regalian rights over its inhabitants, and of Trivento on very similar terms to Count Randisius in 992.[28] It may be that Pandulf Ironhead's ambitious policy made him more reckless than his predecessors in securing support from his nobles, many of whom were relatives, and from churchmen. Certainly more of his diplomata – nearly all embodying grants – survive from the twenty years of his rule as senior prince than for the preceding sixty years, since the union of Capua and Benevento. But it may also be that Pandulf's policy was pragmatic, and that such grants as that to the count of Isernia were not really giving much away, but recognising alienations already made. There could also have been sound reasons for such concessions as that to Count Poto in 988. Greci was on the frontier with Apulia, and the grant of the right of fortification was an obvious security measure, while the generous judicial and financial concessions may have been necessary to persuade an aristocrat to settle an apparently deserted, quite possibly dangerous site.

There was, however, a longer-term process at work in this privatisation of authority. By around 900, gastaldates were in effect probably hereditary, and already in the ninth century the authority of the prince was very obviously ineffectual in the remoter areas of his principality. Furthermore, to judge by the *Chronicon Salernitanum*, by far the lengthiest and most circumstantial historical work of the time, concepts of princely authority were still very personal, rooted in a traditional framework of fraternity, mutual obligation, gift-exchange and condominium of prince and aristocracy. Vassalic links were not so much weak (as for example in tenth-century Francia) as non-existent. *Fidelitas* in Lombard southern Italy implied a contractual relationship, not one of dependence.[29] In Benevento the role of the princely palace as an effective institution of government had probably already begun to diminish *c.* 850; after that date its officials ceased to appear in princely diplomata. By making grants to nobles, the princes were at least making a statement that authority still ultimately came from them, however remotely. They were also creating some sort of short-term link and mutual goodwill, particularly when most of those receiving such concessions were kinsmen, who doubtless came to expect these marks of favour. In the long term, though, such hereditary grants – and there is very little evidence for temporary and revocable concessions – led to a haemorrhage of central authority outside the immediate vicinity of the princely residences.

The symptom, and also one of the causes, of this privatisation of authority was *incastellamento*. The development of private fortifications (in southern Italy fortified villages rather than castles pure and simple) had several functions. It was partly defensive; even after the cessation of the Saracen

[28] Poupardin (1907), nos. 112, 144–5, pp. 105–6, 117–18; Wickham (1981), p. 162 has a useful discussion of the first of these grants.

[29] Delogu (1977), pp. 70–111; Taviani-Carozzi (1980); Taviani-Carozzi (1991b), pp. 686–702.

threat there was still external danger. Hungarian raiders penetrated deep into the principality of Capua in 937, and as far as Apulia in 922 and again in 947. The *castello* was in addition a means of protection against greedy neighbours, especially when central authority was weak or distant. But it was also a means for effective exploitation by patrimonial landowners, attracting new settlers, imposing common rents and services, and providing a centre for collection of such rents and for local judicial authority. The creation of *castelli* and the attraction of immigrants could repopulate areas abandoned or under-exploited, although we should be cautious about taking at face value the claims in monastic chronicles as to the extent of such desertion before the age of *incastellamento*. Concessions by the princes of the regalian right of fortification, largely from the second half of the tenth century, were a symptom of central authority in decline. They were not necessarily the mark of a society in decline. Indeed, the tenth century was an age of growing population and increasing agricultural prosperity, though in southern Italy more than in most areas of Europe there could be striking regional variations. What might hold good for such fertile areas as the Capuan plain or the broad and flat Liri valley in the north of the principality of Capua was not necessarily the case for more mountainous areas like Molise.

There were also contrasts between the different principalities. In Salerno the capital city and the princely court continued to act as a magnet for the nobility in a way that no longer applied in the more decentralised principalities of Capua and Benevento. This was probably a function of the greater size of the city of Salerno, and its correspondingly greater influence, economic and social, within the principality. A mark of the city's development is that in the period 980–1000 twenty-nine notaries, all of them laymen, can be found operating there.[30] Furthermore, the other main centres of habitation within the principality lay relatively close to the city. The prince's kinsmen continued, for the most part, to reside at Salerno, whereas in the other two principalities they lived in their *castelli* and established their territorially based dynasties.

The title of count, which had begun as a personal distinction signifying relationship to the princely family, evolved in Capua and Benevento into a territorial designation. The counts replaced the gastalds as the chief local princely officials. (The gastalds in the ninth century had fulfilled a role which was analogous to that of the counts in the *regnum Italiae*.) But the emergence of the territorial counts in southern Italy signified not merely a change in title, but also one of function, a step along the way to the privatisation of authority. There were far more counts in the principality of Capua in the later tenth century than there had been gastalds in the

---

[30] Taviani-Carozzi (1991b), pp. 541–2.

ninth, as local authority not only became more entrenched but also more fragmented. The process spread eastwards into Molise and the principality of Benevento, although with less density in these more mountainous and sparsely settled regions.[31] The role of princely cadets in this process is clear. Two of Landulf III's sons became counts at Sant'Agata and Larino. Two of Pandulf Ironhead's younger sons in turn became count of Teano, replacing an existing line of counts descended from Atenulf I. In the eleventh century the descendants of one of them were counts at Venafro and Presenzano. This fragmentation of local authority was encouraged by the partible inheritance of Lombard law. The change in usage seems to have occurred particularly in the 950s and 960s, in the years of Pandulf Ironhead's co-rulership with his father and in the early years of his own rule; in one case, that of the creation of the county of Isernia in 964, he can be seen expressly sanctioning this development. Perhaps significantly, the gastalds of Aquino, who were not descended from the Capuan princely dynasty, did not use the title of count until some twenty years later.

In the principality of Salerno the process was much slower and less complete, for the reasons outlined above. It has been suggested that a count had been established by 947 in a territorial lordship at Nocera on the border with the principality of Capua, at a period when relations between the two princes were hostile. But the evidence for such a supposition is at best inconclusive, and it is more probable that the count was simply a princely relative who held property at Nocera. A son of either Atenulf II or the exiled Atenulf III of Benevento was established in a lordship at Conza on the southern border of the principality, facing Byzantine territory; however, he does not appear to have held the title of count, and his relationship with Prince Gisulf later deteriorated to the point that he was once again driven into exile, at Naples.[32] Hence in Salerno the title of count remained a mark of personal status, not of institutional function. Furthermore, the princes retained their control over the church and their monopoly over public justice until well into the eleventh century. Legal cases first heard under local officials in outlying parts of the principality were often concluded at Salerno itself.

The princes of Capua-Benevento sought to bolster their authority in the north of their principality by allying with and favouring the two great monasteries of the region, Monte Cassino and San Vincenzo al Volturno. Both of these were not just major landowners; they also possessed coherent

---

[31] Martin (1980), pp. 573–5 provides a most valuable discussion, on which I have drawn heavily. For Salerno, see Taviani-Carozzi (1991b), especially pp. 449–51, 573–4, 725–7, 769–70.

[32] CS, chs. 161, 175, pp. 168, 177–9; CDC, II, no. 260 (969), pp. 62–3; Mor (1952–3), II, pp. 139–40. The chronicle is infuriatingly vague as to which Atenulf he was son of, and the genealogical charts in Mor (1952–3), I, pp. 294–5, Cilento (1971), table 2, and Taviani-Carozzi (1991b), p. 397, do not agree either. For Nocera, see Taviani-Carozzi (1991b), pp. 492–6; CDC, I, no. 174, pp. 224–5.

blocks of territory, and could serve as counterweights to the local nobility in localities some distance away and geographically separate from the centres of princely authority. Both monasteries had been destroyed by the Arabs – Volturno in 881 and Monte Cassino two years later – and in the early years of the tenth century both communities were still in exile. The monks of Volturno returned to their mother house in 914, but those of Monte Cassino remained in exile, first at Teano and later at Capua, until 949. This long residence at Capua was, to judge both from a contemporary papal letter and from later Cassinese tradition, the result of direct pressure from Landulf I in his greed to exploit the monastery's property.[33] If so, this policy was short-sighted, for the chief profiteers were not the princes but the nobles of the Liri valley, who alienated much of the abbey's land.

Under Landulf II (943–61) and Pandulf I the policy changed. The monks returned to Monte Cassino, and the princes actively supported them, forcing the local nobles to disgorge their stolen property and respect the abbey's lands in future. The gastalds of Aquino were brought to heel by direct military action, and a series of land pleas in the early 960s consolidated this process. Landulf II similarly took action to protect Volturno's territory from the incursions of the counts of Venafro.[34] In the 960s Pandulf Ironhead conceded both fiscal immunities and, in 967, the right to erect fortifications to the monasteries.[35] Admittedly one must not overestimate the extent of the *incastellamento* on the lands of either monastery. Pandulf's charter to Monte Cassino mentioned only two *castelli* by name, and a tower at a third site, and the development of fortified sites on the abbey's lands was gradual. By around 1000 there were no more than half a dozen *castelli* there. The fortification of settlements was largely confined to the central portion of San Vincenzo al Volturno's lands in the immediate neighbourhood of the mother house, and to some eastern parts about which the abbey was in dispute with the counts of Isernia.[36] The beginning of *incastellamento* on these abbeys' lands was more a matter of the reorganisation of their system of land exploitation, rather than being intended for directly military purposes, although those *castelli* founded in the San Vincenzo lands to which the counts of Isernia laid claim were set up primarily to symbolise the abbey's claims to this territory.

The abbeys could, however, rely on princely support, and indeed that of the emperors Otto I and II, in case of difficulty. The princes could use their

---

[33] Agapetus II (*Regesta pontificum romanorum*, I, no. 3664); *Papsturkunden*, ed. Zimmermann, I, no. 109, pp. 191–3; *CMC*, I.59, pp. 147–8, which clearly used this letter.

[34] *CMC*, II.1–3, pp. 166–71; *Placiti cassinesi*, ed. Inguanez; *Chronicon vulturnense*, ed. Federici, II, pp. 64–8.

[35] The latter are edited in *Storia della badia di Monte-Cassino*, ed. Tosti, I, pp. 226–8 and *Chronicon vulturnense*, ed. Federici, II, pp. 162–4; Italian tr. de Benedittis, pp. 364–7.

[36] Wickham (1985), pp. 250–1; Loud (1994b), pp. 54–6. For the social and economic consequences of *incastellamento*, see Del Treppo (1956), pp. 74–100; Toubert (1976).

relationship with these abbeys to validate their rule in the north of their dominions, and to limit the building of local power bases by nobles whose activities they might otherwise find hard to check. After the two principalities of Capua and Benevento separated in 981 the relationship between the prince of Capua and Monte Cassino became closer; Prince Landenulf (982–93) appointed a kinsman, Manso, as abbot of Monte Cassino, and in 1011, while the two principalities were briefly reunited, Pandulf II installed one of his sons as abbot. But by that stage San Vincenzo al Volturno was no longer playing any part in this policy. After 981 there were no further princely diplomata for the monastery, and by the eleventh century Molise had slipped entirely from princely control.

AMALFI, NAPLES, GAETA: MATTERS OF TRADE

The coastal duchies of Amalfi, Naples and Gaeta were very different from the Lombard principalities. For one thing, the small size of their territories meant that they did not face the problems of distance and control which undermined effective government in the principalities. In Naples and Gaeta hereditary dynasties were already established by 900, and in Amalfi a ruling family was in the process of consolidating itself by that date when the city's governor, Manso, associated his son with him in its rule. By 907 the Byzantine government had recognised his position by granting him the rank of *spatharokandidatos*, although the comparatively lowly status of the *parvenu* Amalfitan dynasty is suggested by the fact that at the time of the Garigliano expedition the rulers of Naples and Gaeta were granted the much higher rank of *patrikios*.[37] Manso's family was displaced by a coup in 958, but otherwise the ruling dynasties in the coastal duchies were stable enough to persist unchallenged throughout this period, and indeed well into the eleventh century. The new Amalfitan ruling family lasted until the time of Robert Guiscard in the late eleventh century, and that of Naples until the death of the last duke in 1139.

The economy of all three duchies was based on trade, but not to the same extent. Amalfi, with the smallest and most mountainous territory, was the most active in such trade; Naples, with the largest hinterland, the least. According to Ibn Hawqal, an Arab traveller writing *c.* 975, Amalfi was 'the richest city of southern Italy, the most noble and most illustrious by its condition, the most affluent and the most opulent'.[38] By the 940s Amalfitan merchants were present in some numbers at Constantinople, and by the end of the century in Egypt. But the primary trading destinations were

---

[37] Schwarz (1978), pp. 31–2. See also above, p. 563.

[38] Ibn Hawqal, *Surat*, ed. Kramers, I, p. 202; French tr. Kramers and Wiet, I, p. 197; *Medieval trade*, ed. Lopez and Raymond, p. 54.

Figure 41 View of Amalfi's hinterland

North Africa and Sicily, to which timber, grain, linen and other agricultural products from southern Italy were transported. Naples was a centre for linen production, which was praised for its quality by Ibn Hawqal. Such trade required good relations with Islam, and this explains the reluctance of Amalfi and Gaeta to participate in military operations against the Arabs in the ninth and early tenth centuries; indeed, at times they provided actual assistance to the invaders. That the duchy of Naples played a more active role in combatting the Arabs of the Garigliano suggests that the city's trade was less significant to its well-being than to the other two duchies. But the fact that grain was certainly imported from the interior of southern Italy to Amalfi, and probably also to Gaeta, shows that the economy of the Campanian ports required links with the Lombard principalities as well. Furthermore, the role of Salerno in such trade cannot be entirely excluded. It was Islamic gold that was used to mint imitation quarter-dinar coins called *tarì*, the principal money of southern Italy outside the Byzantine provinces, and from *c.* 1000 these were minted at Salerno as well as Amalfi.

Profits from such trade helped particular families to establish their rule at Gaeta in the mid-ninth century and at Amalfi in the 890s, and to consolidate their regimes thereafter. The surviving wills of two rulers of Gaeta, Docibilis I in 906 and Docibilis II in 954, show the very considerable movable wealth that these men had at their disposal, for which trading profits are the most obvious source.[39] The possession of mills was also an important facet of their power. The duke of Gaeta had a monopoly over mills, which he granted out to others only in exceptional circumstances. In Amalfi the number of mills attested in surviving documents far exceeds what the relatively

---

[39] *Codex diplomaticus cajetanus*, I, nos. 19, 52, pp. 30, 87. For Gaeta, see Skinner (1995), esp. pp. 57–102.

small population of the duchy can have needed for its domestic supply, and yet their value was high. While not possessing a monopoly like their Gaetan counterparts, the Amalfitan rulers held quite a number of mills and could thus benefit from the income that they generated. In these, as in other ways, rule in the coastal duchies was very different from that in the Lombard principalities.

Unlike the Lombard princes, the dukes of Amalfi, Naples and Gaeta could not look to a tradition of rule hallowed by time, nor did they assert the ultimately divinely sanctioned nature of their rule; the exception found in Amalfi from the 950s, the *dei gratia/providentia* style, may well have been an attempt to legitimise the new and usurping dynasty. Rather, their position rested on their wealth, both from the remains of the public fisc and from their private family property, on their role as lawgivers and military leaders, and on their control of the local church, in which their relatives were frequently given high office. In the early part of the century the rulers of Amalfi were often content to refer to themselves as 'judges', while the adoption in the early eleventh century of the title *magister militum* by the rulers of Naples reflects their military role as defenders of their people. Byzantine titles were an important element of legitimisation for the newer dynasties of Gaeta and Amalfi, although their use of such titles might vary depending on how far they felt in need of Byzantine support and alliance. With the coming of the Ottonians in the 960s and their support for Pandulf Ironhead of Capua, the dukes of Naples and Amalfi gravitated once more towards friendship with the eastern empire, and their documents once again made reference to their Byzantine ranks. The duke of Naples actively supported the Byzantine invasion of Campania in 969.

THE BREAK-UP OF CAPUA-BENEVENTO AND THE GENERAL FRAGMENTATION OF AUTHORITY IN THE SOUTH

In the 970s the growing power of the prince of Capua-Benevento was threatening to take over those parts of southern Italy not under Byzantine rule. In 973 there was an abortive coup in Salerno in which the childless Prince Gisulf was packed off to Amalfi as a prisoner. The ringleader of this coup was the former lord of Conza (the son of either Atenulf II or Atenulf III of Benevento) whom Gisulf had expelled many years earlier, but then allowed to return. Swift and decisive action by Pandulf Ironhead restored Gisulf to his throne. However, the price of his restoration was that Pandulf's son be associated with him as co-ruler, and when Gisulf died in 977 that son (also called Pandulf) was his successor. Thus in theory at least the unity of the old principality of Benevento, as it had existed before the division of 849, was restored (see above, p. 560). But such unity proved illusory, for the death of Pandulf Ironhead in 981 was the precursor to the

break-up of his empire. Despite the presence of an imperial army under
Otto II both Salerno and Benevento revolted. The Beneventans installed as
their prince Pandulf's nephew, the son of his brother and co-ruler Landulf
III, who had died in 968/9. The Salernitans turned first to Duke Manso
of Amalfi, and then in December 983 to a palace official, John of Spoleto
(983–99), who succeeded in holding on to the principality and founding a
new ruling dynasty.[40] Thus from 982 on Lombard southern Italy was once
again divided into three separate principalities.

The year 982 also saw the eclipse of Ottonian influence in the south.
Otto II had decided to abandon the peace of 969, and launched a fresh
invasion of the Byzantine provinces. His army marched first into southern
Apulia where it besieged, but failed to take, Matera and Taranto. Then
he marched south into Calabria, which was once again menaced by Arab
incursions from Sicily. Otto's army was defeated in a pitched battle with the
Arab invaders near Reggio and the emperor himself only narrowly escaped.[41]
Landulf IV of Capua (981–2) and his brother Pandulf, the deposed prince
of Salerno, were among the dead.

The defeat in Calabria, followed by Otto II's death little more than
a year later and the resultant minority, meant that there was no further
German intervention in southern Italy for some sixteen years. It also ensured
that there would remain three separate Lombard principalities and that no
ruler would dominate the non-Byzantine south with imperial assistance,
as Pandulf Ironhead had done. His rule over Spoleto and Camerino was
granted to others. The principality of Capua was left in the hands of a
minor, under the tutelage of his mother. And in both Capua and Benevento
the forces of decentralisation, of which *incastellamento* was a symptom,
reduced princely authority little by little. In the principality of Benevento
the development of *castelli* accelerated from around 1000, and the rule of
the prince became limited to little more than the immediate vicinity of
Benevento itself.

The maintenance of central authority was certainly not helped by a
fragmentation of interests within the ruling families. For a time in 985 Duke
Manso of Amalfi was displaced by his brother Adelferius. More seriously,
in 993 Prince Landenulf of Capua was murdered in an uprising in Capua,
and there are some indications that this was with the connivance of his
brother Laidulf (993–9), who succeeded him as prince.[42] Soon afterwards

---

[40] For the dating, see Schwarz (1978), pp. 39–41. The number of Amalfitans living within Salerno
undoubtedly facilitated Manso's takeover.

[41] Thietmar, *Chronicon*, III.20–2, ed. Holtzmann, pp. 122–6; tr. Warner, pp. 143–5. See also above,
p. 550; for the location of the battle, Alvermann (1995).

[42] Otto III justified his deposition of Laidulf in 999 because of his alleged involvement: *CMC*, II.24,
pp. 208–10. A more contemporary Capuan chronicle does not go this far, but describes Laidulf as
'coming joyfully' to Capua after his brother's murder: Cilento (1971), pp. 308–9. Most damning is the
Life of Nilus the Younger, ch. 79, cols. 133–4.

Archbishop Aion of Capua was also murdered, and in 996 Abbot Manso of Cassino – who was, it will be remembered, a princely kinsman – was captured while on a visit to Capua and blinded; this came after a period of virtually open warfare in the north of the principality between the abbey of Monte Cassino and the neighbouring counts of Aquino. Authority within the principality of Capua was seemingly near collapse in the 990s.[43] The intervention of Emperor Otto III (983–1002) in 999 did nothing to cure this. He deposed Laidulf and installed his own nominee as prince. But as soon as Otto's army withdrew his protégé was expelled, and replaced by a brother of the prince of Benevento (whose capital Otto had besieged but failed to capture).

While we have no such spectacular manifestations for other areas as we have for Capua, dissipation of authority would appear to have been a fairly general phenomenon. Even in the minuscule duchy of Gaeta the same fissiparous tendencies as in the Lombard principalities manifested themselves, with cadet branches of the ducal house setting up their own, almost independent, counties in outlying parts of the duchy, at Fondi, Traetto and Suio. The Byzantine dominions in contrast had a strong central administration. But the recurrence of Arab attacks in the 980s and 990s posed serious problems, not least because imperial attention was devoted almost exclusively to more pressing matters elsewhere: revolts in Asia Minor and then war with Bulgaria (see above, pp. 522–7). These Muslim raids penetrated not merely into Calabria, but also deep into Apulia. The outskirts of Bari were ravaged in 988, Taranto attacked in 991, Matera captured after a long siege in 994, and Bari itself besieged for nearly five months in 1003 and rescued only by a Venetian fleet. In northern Calabria, Cosenza was sacked in 1009. If a note of pessimism creeps into contemporary documents this is hardly surprising; Peter, an inhabitant of Conversano, lamented in 992 that he had made suitable provision for his elder sons in a time of peace; but now in 'a time of barbarism' he could not do the same for his younger son.[44]

Nor indeed was the west coast exempt from attack. The duchy of Amalfi, whose trading links had hitherto protected it, was raided in 991. And in 999 the outskirts of Salerno were the victim of a further piratical raid. According to the chronicle of Amatus of Monte Cassino (written some eighty years later) there was general panic before a group of forty pilgrims from Normandy, returning from a visit to Jerusalem, volunteered to combat the invaders, caught them unawares and routed them. Impressed with their prowess, Prince Guaimar III (999–1027) invited them or their relatives to

---

[43] See also Prince Laidulf's unprecedented oath to respect the possessions of Monte Cassino, c. 993: *Accessiones ad historiam abbatiae Cassinensis*, ed. Gattula, pp. 90–1.

[44] *Pergamene di Conversano*, ed. Coniglio, no. 26, p. 55.

enter his service as mercenaries. So at least ran the legend, and perhaps even the sober fact, of the arrival of the Normans in southern Italy.[45] For some years to come they were only minor players in the region's history. But, as the eleventh century wore on, the Normans would change its course for ever.

---

[45] Amatus of Monte Cassino, *Storia de' Normanni*, I.17–19, ed. de Bartholomaeis, pp. 21–4; tr. Dunbar and Loud, pp. 49–50. For the date: Hoffmann (1969); Loud (2000a), pp. 60–6.

CHAPTER 16

BELLE ÉPOQUE OR CRISIS? (1025–1118)

MICHAEL ANGOLD

THE ELEVENTH-CENTURY QUESTION

Basil II died in December 1025 after a reign of almost fifty years. He left Byzantium the dominant power of the Balkans and Middle East, with apparently secure frontiers along the Danube, in the Armenian highlands and beyond the Euphrates. Fifty years later Byzantium was struggling for its existence. All its frontiers were breached. Its Anatolian heartland was being settled by Turkish nomads; its Danubian provinces were occupied by another nomad people, the Pechenegs; while its southern Italian bridgehead was swept away by Norman adventurers. It was an astonishing reversal of fortunes. Almost as astonishing was the recovery that the Byzantine empire then made under Alexios I Komnenos (1081–1118). These were years of political turmoil, financial crisis and social upheaval, but it was also a time of cultural and intellectual innovation and achievement. The monastery churches of Nea Moni, on the island of Chios, of Hosios Loukas, near Delphi, and of Daphni, on the outskirts of Athens, were built and decorated in this period. They provide a glimmer of grander monuments built in Constantinople in the eleventh century, which have not survived: such as the Peribleptos and St George of the Mangana. The miniatures of the Theodore Psalter of 1066 are not only beautifully executed but are also a reminder that eleventh-century Constantinople saw a powerful movement for monastic renewal. This counterbalanced but did not necessarily contradict a growing interest in classical education. The leading figure was Michael Psellos. He injected new life into the practice of rhetoric and in his hands the writing of history took on a new shape and purpose; he claimed with some exaggeration to have revived the study of philosophy single-handed. However, his interest in philosophy was mainly rhetorical and it was left to his pupil John Italos to apply philosophy to theology and to reopen debate on some of the fundamentals of Christian dogma.

Modern historiography has singled out the period from 1025 to 1118 as the watershed of Byzantine history. George Ostrogorsky provided the classic interpretation.[1] He saw the eleventh century as the beginning of

[1] Ostrogorsky (1968), pp. 316–75.

Figure 42 This fine miniature exemplifies those in the Theodore Psalter, copied at the Stoudios Monastery in Constantinople in 1066; in the scene below, Asaph teaches from the book of the law

Byzantium's inexorable decline, which he attributed to the triumph of feudalism. Private interest gained at the expense of the state. Without effective central institutions it was impossible to mobilise the resources of the empire or provide any clear direction. Symptomatic of the decline of central authority was the struggle for power between the civil and military aristocracies. The latter emerged victorious with the accession to the throne of Alexios I Komnenos. But his success was limited and his restoration of the empire superficial, because 'the empire was internally played out'. Ostrogorsky meant by this that the peasantry and their property were coming increasingly under the control of great landowners. He believed that this compromised the economic and demographic potential of the empire.

Ostrogorsky's presentation of the history of the Byzantine empire in the eleventh century has been attacked from two main directions. Paul Lemerle doubted that the eleventh century was a period of absolute decline at Byzantium.[2] There is too much evidence of economic growth and cultural vitality, which he connects with 'le gouvernement des philosophes'. The tragedy was Alexios I Komnenos' seizure of power, which substituted family rule for the state. Robert Browning would add that Alexios damped down the intellectual and religious ferment of the eleventh century through deliberate use of heresy trials.[3]

Alexander Kazhdan takes a rather different view.[4] He agrees that in the eleventh century Byzantium prospered. He attributes the political weakness of the empire to reactionary elements holding back the process of 'feudalisation'. Alan Harvey presses this approach to extremes.[5] He insists that the advance of the great estate was essential for economic and demographic growth. Kazhdan is also struck by the buoyancy and innovation of Byzantine culture. He connects this with a growth of individualism and personal relations. It was a victory for progressive elements, which were promoted rather than hindered by the Komnenian regime.[6]

Such a bald presentation does not do justice to the subtleties and hesitations displayed by the different historians nor to their skilful deployment of the evidence. It makes their views far more schematic than they are, but it highlights differences of approach and isolates the major problems. They hinge on the effectiveness of the state. Was this being undermined by social, economic and political developments? Though their chronology is different Ostrogorsky and Lemerle are both agreed that it was. They assume that the health of Byzantium depended on the centralisation of power. By way of contrast Kazhdan believes that imperial authority could be rebuilt on a different basis and this is what Alexios Komnenos was able to do. The nature of Alexios' achievement becomes the key issue.

A weakness of all these readings of Byzantium's 'eleventh-century crisis'[7] is a willingness to take Basil II's (976–1025) achievement at face value; to see his reign as representing an ideal state of affairs. They forget that his iron rule represents an aberration in the exercise of imperial authority at Byzantium. His complete ascendancy was without precedent. In a series of

---

[2] Lemerle (1977), pp. 249–312.
[3] Browning (1975a).   [4] Kazhdan and Epstein (1985), pp. 24–73.
[5] Harvey (1989), pp. 35–79.   [6] Kazhdan and Franklin (1984), pp. 242–55.
[7] See Angold (1991); contributions to Vlysidou (ed.) (2003); Holmes (2005), pp. 16–35.

civil wars in the early part of his reign he destroyed the power of the great Anatolian families, such as Phokas and Skleros, but only thanks to foreign aid. He used his power to straitjacket Byzantine society and subordinate it to his authority. To this end he reissued and extended the agrarian legislation of his forebears. Its purpose was ostensibly to protect peasant property from the 'powerful' as they were called. It was, in practice, less a matter of the imperial government's professed concern for the well-being of the peasantry, more a way of assuring its tax revenues. These depended on the integrity of the village community which was the basic tax unit. This was threatened as more and more peasant property passed into the hands of the 'powerful'. Basil II followed up this measure by making the latter responsible for any arrears of taxation which had till then been borne largely by the peasantry.

Control of the peasantry was vital if Basil II was to keep the empire on a war footing, while keeping the empire on a war footing was a justification for autocracy. The long war he waged against the Bulgarians only finally came to an end in 1018 (see above, pp. 526–9). It exploited the energies of the military families of Anatolia and cowed the aristocracy of the Greek lands. They were terrified that they would be accused of cooperating with the Bulgarians. The war with the Bulgarians was bloody and exhausting, but it was a matter of recovering lost ground, not of gaining new territory. The Bulgarian lands had been annexed by John I Tzimiskes (969–76) in the aftermath of his victory over the Rus in 971. It was only the civil wars at the beginning of Basil II's reign and the emperor's own ineptitude that allowed the Bulgarians to recover their independence. Basil II's triumph over the Bulgarians gave a false impression of the strength of the empire.

In part, it depended on an absence of external enemies. Islam was for the time being a spent force; thanks to Byzantium's clients, the Pechenegs, conditions on the steppes were stable; the Armenians were divided; and western Christendom was still bedazzled by Byzantium. The Rus officially converted to orthodoxy c. 988. This confirmed their passage into the Byzantine orbit. The Rus were essential to Byzantine greatness under Basil II. They provided Byzantium with soldiers and sailors, and their merchants made Constantinople the entrepot for the products of the Russian steppes and forests and stimulated its commercial role.[8] This was complemented by the growing presence of Venetian merchants at Constantinople. In 992 Basil II encouraged their activities by reducing the tolls on their ships paid for passage through the Hellespont to Constantinople. The effect was to favour Constantinople's role as the clearing house of Mediterranean trade and to underline her position as the cross-roads of the medieval world. Constantinople was, however, disproportionately large and gave a false impression of Byzantine strength. It drew its wealth and population from

[8] Franklin and Shepard (1996), pp. 161–5, 178.

well beyond the political frontiers of the Byzantine empire. Under different circumstances this might leave it vulnerable.

If forced to rely entirely on its own demographic and economic resources, Byzantium would have been condemned to the role of a regional power, at best. But it did not have to do so. The Armenian highlands were always an important recruiting ground for the Byzantine armies, but it went further than this. The Byzantine conquests in the east were followed under Byzantine auspices by Armenian colonisation of Cilicia, the Euphrates provinces and northern Syria. The Rus provided another recruiting ground. Basil II relied heavily on the Varangian guard, which not only formed an elite corps but was also an instrument of his political ascendancy. Reliance on foreigners was a double-edged sword. In the course of the eleventh century relations with the Armenians deteriorated, while those with the Rus began to cool. In 1043 for reasons that remain obscure Iaroslav the Wise, prince of Kiev, sent an expedition against Constantinople. It was easily defeated, but thereafter the Rus played a less prominent role in the affairs of the Byzantine empire. In due course, the Varangian guard would be recruited not from the Rus and Scandinavians but from exiled Anglo-Saxons.

When pondering the collapse of the Byzantine empire in the eleventh century, it must be remembered that Basil II left his successors a poisoned legacy. The empire's apparent strength depended on circumstances beyond its control. Conditions along its frontiers might change radically. Basil II's policy of annexing Bulgaria and Armenia suited his own time, but would produce real difficulties for his successors. His greatest failure, however, lay elsewhere: he neglected to make adequate provision for his succession, and there would be no settled succession to the Byzantine throne for some seventy years until Alexios I Komnenos was securely in control.

POLITICAL INSTABILITY AFTER BASIL II'S REIGN

Basil II never married. The understanding was that the succession would pass to his younger brother Constantine VIII, but he never produced a male heir, only daughters – of whom Zoe was Basil II's favourite. It was clear for many years before his death that succession to the throne would go with the hand of Zoe. Basil considered various matches, but all were rejected, and when he died Zoe was in her early forties, still a spinster and unlikely to bear children. Why Basil II was so negligent about the succession is hard to fathom. It may be that the short-term advantages of leaving the succession in doubt were too tempting. Constantine VIII (1025–8) seemed in no more of a hurry than his brother to marry Zoe off, and it was only on Constantine's deathbed that Zoe was married to Romanos Argyros (1028–34), who then succeeded in the right of his new wife. However, Argyros was already somewhat elderly and unlikely to satisfy Zoe's hopes for children;

increasingly frustrated, Zoe took a young lover, Michael the Paphlagonian, who happened to be the brother of John the Orphanotrophos, one of Basil II's eunuch ministers. When Romanos died in his bath in suspicious circumstances, Michael married Zoe and duly succeeded to the throne. Michael IV (1034–41) was remembered as an effective emperor, but he soon fell sick and his brother John sought to keep the throne within the family by persuading Zoe to adopt one of his nephews, also called Michael, as her son. Michael V came to power in 1041 with no intention of being beholden to his uncle; rather, he wished to rule as an autocrat in the style of Basil II. He drove out John the Orphanotrophos and other members of his family, before packing Zoe off to a convent. This produced a spontaneous uprising on the part of the people of Constantinople, who did not want to be deprived of their 'Mother', as they called Zoe; the emperor was cornered and blinded, and Zoe brought back in triumph to the capital. For a few months in 1042 she ruled jointly with her younger sister Theodora, who had been at the centre of opposition to Michael V's coup. Zoe then married again, this time to Constantine Monomachos, who as Constantine IX (1042–55) became the new emperor. Zoe died around 1050, so Theodora succeeded on Constantine IX Monomachos' death in 1055. Upon Theodora's death in the following year the Macedonian line came to an end, complicating the succession still further.

There is no *prima facie* reason for supposing that a troubled succession would necessarily weaken the fabric of the Byzantine state. After all, the succession was in doubt on many occasions in the tenth century, but this did not prevent Byzantium from going from strength to strength. It might be argued that frequent change of the imperial regime was a positive benefit because it made for a greater flexibility and ability to meet critical situations. The rise to power of Romanos I Lekapenos (920–44) against a background of the threat from the Bulgarian tsar Symeon or the spectacle of Nikephoros II Phokas (963–9) and of John I Tzimiskes (969–76) holding the throne in trust for the young Basil II are cases in point. They gave clear direction to imperial government, as did Basil (see above, pp. 520–2).

Basil II's death, however, was followed by a spate of conspiracies. The uncertainty of the succession provides only a partial answer. The conspiracies had more to do with a rapidly changing elite, and the tensions created found some release in plots against the throne. In the early tenth century the Byzantine elite was a less complicated social group than it was to become. It was divided into a military and a civilian establishment. The former was dominated by the great military families of Anatolia, while the latter could boast a handful of civil service families whose members had held office for generations. The great military families went into decline from the end of the tenth century. The Phokas family, for example, virtually disappears, but others were more fortunate; the Skleroi kept estates in Anatolia, but transferred their centre of operations to Constantinople and gradually abandoned their military traditions. Basil II relied on other families for his commanders, such as the Diogenes, Dalassenoi and Komnenoi. The fortunes of these families were made under him. The military aristocracy was becoming wider and more diffuse. The same could be said of the civilian elite. Alongside the old civil service families, there were others which had made their fortunes in trade, but had converted their wealth into status through education and the purchase of honours. There were many interests to be satisfied. Conspiracy and revolt might become necessary to satisfy supporters and clients or might simply be a gesture of political credibility.[9]

Thus instability came to be built into the political structure. Some modern historians would like to see this as a struggle between the military and civilian elites. There is some contemporary support for this interpretation, but it was a matter of continuing to apply the political divisions of a previous age, which had largely disappeared. The politics of the eleventh century were instead dominated by families that transcended these divisions. They drew their support from the whole spectrum of political society. They were often old military families that had transferred their centre of operation to Constantinople. It comes as no surprise that Romanos Argyros emerged as the successful claimant for Zoe's hand and the imperial throne. His age apart, he was eminently well qualified. He came from one of the most ancient of the Anatolian military families, but one which had long been resident in Constantinople. Romanos Argyros made a career and a name for himself within the capital, becoming the City prefect. He was also related to many of the great families of the capital, including the Monomachoi. Constantine IX Monomachos came from a very similar background to Romanos Argyros and was an obvious candidate for the hand of Zoe and the imperial office. He had already plotted to seize the throne from Michael IV, who was regarded as an upstart, being one of those newcomers who had recently risen to prominence. One of Michael's brothers had been a trusted agent of Basil II and a sister married into the new wealth of Constantinople, her husband having made a fortune out of shipbuilding. It was their son who succeeded as Michael V: indeed, he was known contemptuously as the 'Caulker' in reference to his father's activities.

The snobbery of the Constantinopolitan crowd told against Michael V. The citizens of Constantinople brought about his downfall and, although their rising may have been spontaneous, it showed how powerful a force they were. Thereafter emperors had to placate Constantinopolitan opinion. This was another factor making for political instability in the eleventh century. In the tenth century internal tensions could be absorbed through a policy of conquest and expansion. This became less easy after Basil's death.

---

[9] Cheynet (1990), pp. 157–98.

GOVERNMENT FINANCES AND ECONOMIC GROWTH

Basil II's immediate successors attempted to pursue his policy of expansion and annexation, but with little success. Large and expensive expeditions were mounted against Sicily, Syria and even Egypt. All there was to show for this costly effort was the annexation of Edessa in 1032 by the military commander George Maniakes. Against this, there was a serious revolt by the Bulgarians in 1040. Although it was suppressed, it suggested that Basil II's conquest was not that securely based. It was a watershed; the period of expansion was over. The empire was beginning to turn in on itself and in these circumstances internal divisions would only be magnified.

Keeping the empire on a war footing may explain why the imperial government was faced with increasing financial difficulties after Basil II's death. Tax revolts were a feature of this phase of Byzantine history.[10] Basil must bear some of the blame; at the end of his life, as an act of charity, he remitted two whole years' taxation and his generosity was more than his brother could afford. The new emperor had to rescind the measure and collected five years' taxation within the space of three years. This caused hardship and sparked off at least one tax revolt. The next emperor Romanos Argyros instituted a laxer and more humane fiscal regime. The opening years of his reign coincided with drought and a plague of locusts in Anatolia, forcing the peasants off their land and towards Constantinople. To get them to return to their native villages Romanos Argyros provided each with a donative of three *nomismata*, the rough equivalent of the tax on a substantial peasant holding. He also abandoned Basil II's practice of forcing the 'powerful' landowners to pay any arrears of taxation. Instead he farmed these out, which hints at financial difficulties. His successor Michael IV seemed equally in need of ready cash: he forced the Bulgarians to pay their taxes in coin, despite Basil II's promise that they would be taxed in kind, and this action sparked off the Bulgarian revolt (see below, p. 670). Michael IV was also accused of tampering with the currency, while his brother John the Orphanotrophos exploited the state's right of monopoly over the corn trade.

Modern numismatists have reluctantly exonerated Michael IV from the charge of debasement. It was left to Constantine IX Monomachos to carry out a controlled debasement of the Byzantine gold coinage. It was done quite openly and deliberately. The fineness of the gold coinage was lowered by stages from twenty-four carats to eighteen. Each stage of the debasement was clearly signposted by the issue of different types of coin. This debasement of the coinage is a feature of the history of eleventh-century

---

[10] They are attested at Naupaktos, Nikopolis and Antioch. The Bulgarian uprising of 1040 began as a tax revolt.

Byzantium which has attracted a great deal of attention from modern historians, because it seems to provide a key to the economic developments of the time. There are two major interpretations. The first is straightforward: debasement was a solution to a budget deficit and was a way out of the long-standing financial difficulties of the Byzantine state. The other interpretation is more sophisticated; it sees debasement as a reaction to the problems of rapid economic growth which the Byzantine empire was supposed to be experiencing in the early eleventh century.[11] The argument goes that the Byzantine economy was consequently facing a liquidity crisis: not enough coinage was in circulation to meet demand. Given the inelasticity of the supply of precious metals, the only solution was to debase.

The second of these interpretation has its merits, and indeed some Byzantine civil servants did show a surprisingly advanced grasp of economics. However, even if they had an inkling that an inelastic money supply was a barrier to economic growth, they were not likely to consider this sufficient justification for debasing a coinage that had remained more or less unchanged since the days of Constantine the Great. Budgetary difficulties are surely the only explanation for the debasement carried out by Constantine IX Monomachos. The emperor could cite as a precedent the temporary debasement carried out by Nikephoros Phokas in the tenth century. However unpopular at the time, it had eased a period of financial embarrassment.

Even if budgetary difficulties are the explanation, debasement may still have helped to ease a liquidity problem. But was there economic growth in the early eleventh century on a scale sufficient to create a liquidity problem? There are certainly signs of economic growth, but they mostly relate to the Greek lands, where towns were prospering and becoming centres of trade and manufactures. Thebes, for example, became a major producer of silk, which in the tenth century had been a monopoly of the capital. There are indications that coastal trade round the Aegean was prospering and that the population of the region was growing. But this scarcely represents growth of such an order that it would have induced the imperial government to debase the gold coinage in order to increase the circulation of coinage.

In any case, it would be hard to square the financial difficulties that the imperial government faced from the death of Basil II onwards with rapid economic growth. Would the state not have been the chief beneficiary, given that it imposed a value-added tax of 10 per cent on every commercial transaction? This ought to have gone some way towards balancing the budget. Admittedly, the continuing growth of population was not matched by a corresponding increase in the basic tax yield. The agrarian legislation of the tenth century was applied less stringently. As significant was the extension of tax exemptions for the great estates. Blanket immunities were probably

---

[11] Morrison (1976).

less important than preferential rates of taxation, such as those enjoyed in
the eleventh century by the Athonite monasteries for their estates. This
was all part of the creation of a dependent peasantry, which paid taxes and
owed labour services to a lord. Ostrogorsky connected this manorialisation
of rural society with economic decline. He was certainly wrong, but he was
correct to see it as a drain on imperial revenues (see also above, pp. 488–91).

It seems safe to assume that there was economic and demographic growth
in the early eleventh century, but scarcely on a scale to create liquidity
problems. Debasement was a response to the government's financial problems. Tax exemptions were partly to blame, but these were symptomatic of
financial mismanagement on the part of the imperial government. Michael
Psellos blamed the government's financial difficulties on the extravagance of
Zoe and her consorts. This may have been a little unfair on Zoe. Dabbling
in perfumes and alchemy may have been unnecessary, but was unlikely to
bankrupt the state. It was at best a reflection of lax government. Zoe was not
a great builder, unlike her husbands who expended colossal sums on their
building activities. Romanos Argyros erected the monastery of the Peribleptos to serve as his last resting place and a memorial of his reign. Michael IV
was a patron of the monastery of Sts Cosmas and Damian at Kosmidion,
outside the walls of Constantinople, which he rebuilt on a lavish scale.
Constantine IX Monomachos added the church of St George and other
buildings to the Mangana complex. Accounts by later travellers provide an
impression of the magnificence and scale of these churches, but none of
them survives. Only St George of the Mangana has been partially excavated:
its dimensions were imposing, with a dome of approximately ten metres
in diameter, thus rivalling some of the Justinianic foundations in size.[12]
One of Constantine Monomachos' foundations does survive, however: the
monastery of Nea Moni on the island of Chios. Its intricate planning and
rich mosaics give some idea of the care and money lavished on these imperial
foundations. But the costs did not end with construction and Nea Moni,
like St George of the Mangana, was generously endowed by the emperor.

There had not been building on this scale in the Byzantine empire since
the sixth century. Emperors had mostly been content to restore the public
monuments and churches inherited from the fifth and sixth centuries and
to add to the Great Palace of the emperors. Basil II's main contribution
had been the repair of St Sophia in 989 after it had suffered damage in
an earthquake. The emperors of the eleventh century in good aristocratic
fashion wanted to leave their mark on the capital through their monuments
and used state revenues to this end. Again building even on this grand scale
was unlikely by itself to bankrupt the state, but taken in conjunction with
an extravagant court life it placed a substantial extra burden on the state's

[12] Mango (1976).

Figure 43a General view of the eleventh-century monastery of Nea Moni on Chios

Figure 43b The mosaics of Nea Moni on Chios: Christ raising the dead

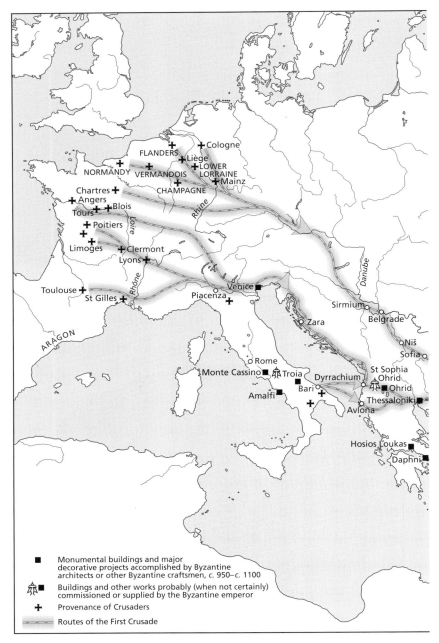

Monumental buildings and major
decorative projects accomplished by Byzantine
architects or other Byzantine craftsmen, c. 950–c. 1100

Buildings and other works probably (when not certainly)
commissioned or supplied by the Byzantine emperor

Provenance of Crusaders

Routes of the First Crusade

Map 26 Cross-currents: Byzantine building- and decorative works in the later tenth and eleventh
centuries, and the course of the First Crusade

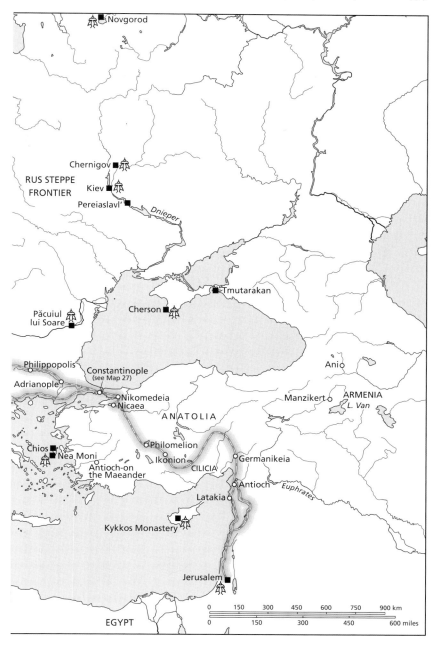

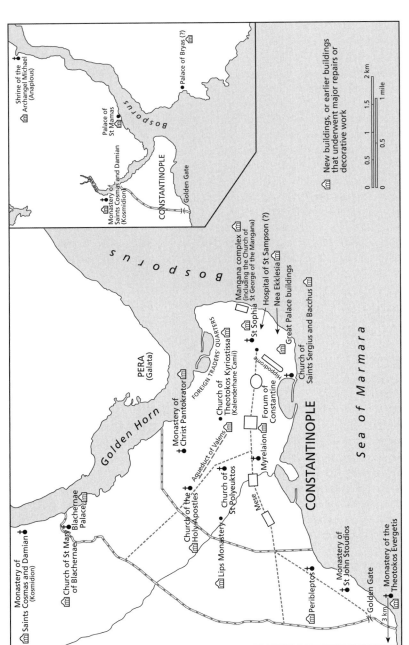

Map 27 Constantinople in the middle Byzantine period: new building-work, major repairs and embellishments

revenues. They were in any case likely to be declining because of Romanos Argyros' decision to abandon Basil II's strict control over the arrears of taxation.

Government expenditure was rising for quite another reason: the civil list was increasing dramatically as more and more honours were granted out. Michael Psellos was of the opinion that the honours system had been one of Byzantium's strengths, but was now being abused. This he singled out as one of the fundamental causes of the decline of the Byzantine state. Byzantium had developed a complicated system of honours with a double hierarchy of office and dignity. Both brought with them pensions and salaries. While sale of office was rare, sale of dignities was an accepted part of the system. If a dignity was purchased, then the holder received a pension at a standard rate. It has been calculated that this brought a return of around 3 per cent, but it was also possible to purchase at an augmented rate which brought a rather higher rate of up to 6 per cent. The state was creating a system of annuities. It almost certainly worked very well while it was properly supervised. The potential cost to the state was also limited by the relatively restricted number of dignities on offer. But this changed rapidly in the eleventh century as new orders of dignities were created to meet a growing demand. It was also the case that they might pass under the control of individuals who could distribute them as they saw fit. They were regarded as an investment which a father might make for his sons. Imperial largesse to monasteries sometimes took the form of a grant in perpetuity of the pensions attached to dignities. It is tempting to connect the debasement of the coinage with the inflation of honours, all the more so because of contemporary criticism of Nikephoros Phokas' earlier debasement of the coinage. One of his purposes was apparently to pay salaries and pensions in debased currency and to collect taxation in the old coinage. The temptation to debase would be all the stronger in the eleventh century as the honours system got out of hand.

However, it is difficult, if not impossible, to establish such a connection on a valid statistical basis. Our evidence is anecdotal. Jean-Claude Cheynet discounts such evidence as unreliable.[13] He contends that the rate of pension for each dignity is a better guide to the costs of the honours system. The very highest dignities were always granted out sparingly. The inflation of honours affected the lesser dignities from *spatharokandidatos* to *vestarchēs*, their pensions ranging from 36 *nomismata* to 1,008 *nomismata* or 14 pounds of gold in weight, which was a considerable sum. But here the argument breaks down; there is simply no way of computing the numbers of office holders. All that remains is the anecdotal evidence. Contemporaries were adamant that by the reign of Nikephoros III Botaneiates (1078–81) the

---

[13] Cheynet (1983).

honours system had broken down, because the state was unable to meet the cost of the pensions involved. The honours system had bankrupted the state. Alexios I Komnenos' reform of the honours system was equally seen as an essential step towards restoring soundness to the body politic. It has to be admitted, however, that complaints about the failure of the honours system coincide with, rather than antedate, the debasement of the coinage. The two worked together to undermine the fabric of the state: the inflation of honours combined with other items of unnecessary expenditure and with various fiscal measures to cause budgetary difficulties, leading to debasement under Constantine Monomachos. Thereafter the combination of debasement and a galloping inflation of honours ensured that the financial position would continue to deteriorate and well-conceived measures of reform had little chance of success.

THE REIGN OF CONSTANTINE IX MONOMACHOS

In the twenty-five years following Basil II's death the Byzantine empire had lost direction and momentum. The policy of military expansionism inherited from Basil II had little to commend it. Keeping the empire on a war footing was expensive. Cutting back on the armed forces was the simplest way of reducing expenditure. The Bulgarian rebellion, followed almost immediately by the 1042 uprising of the citizens of Constantinople against Michael V, was an urgent reminder that a new approach to government was needed. The new emperor, Constantine IX Monomachos, had an agenda: military expansionism seemed out of place at a time when the empire appeared to have secure frontiers, and Monomachos wished to cut back on the military establishment. To carry out his programme of reconstruction he turned to Constantine Leichoudes and the team of clever young men he had assembled about him. These included Michael Psellos, the future Patriarch John Xiphilinos and their teacher John Mauropous. The thrust of their reforms was to strengthen the civil administration of the empire and to simplify its military organisation.[14] In frontier regions the local levies were stood down and defence was left to professional troops stationed at key points. The armies of the themes continued to exist but largely on paper. Provincial administration passed increasingly from the *stratēgos* to a civilian official known as the judge or the *praitōr*. This had been an *ad hoc* development over the preceding fifty-odd years. Monomachos regularised it by creating a new ministry at Constantinople under the *epi tōn kriseōn*, to which the civilian administrators were now responsible. It completed a process of demilitarising provincial government.[15]

---

[14] Lefort (1976).   [15] Oikonomides (1976a).

Constantine IX Monomachos' propagandists presented his reforms in the guise of a *renovatio* of the empire. Imperial revivals punctuated Byzantine history. Normally, they centred on a new codification of the law. The Isaurians issued the *Ecloga* (see above, pp. 275–6), the Macedonians the *Basilika* (see above, pp. 301–2). Monomachos judged the *Basilika* to be more than adequate. What was lacking was an effective legal education. This was either picked up informally or was in the hands of the guild of notaries. Monomachos therefore instituted as the centrepiece of his reforms an imperial law school, placing it under the direction of a new official called the *nomophylax* and appointing John Xiphilinos as the first holder of the office. It was opened in 1047 and attached to the Mangana complex. Monomachos also created the post of consul of the philosophers for Michael Psellos. His duties included supervision of the schools of Constantinople. This measure was designed to bring educational establishments in the capital under more effective government control. Education was at the heart of Monomachos' reforms.[16]

However admirable, Monomachos' reform programme was not carried out in full, for it offended too many existing interests. John Xiphilinos found himself under pressure from the legal establishment and preferred to retire to monastic seclusion on Bithynian Olympus. John Mauropous, appointed bishop of Euchaita in deepest Anatolia, treated this as a form of exile, which indeed it was. At the same time, conditions along Byzantium's borders were changing rapidly. The Pechenegs were dislodged from the Black Sea steppes by the Uzes, nomads from further east. In the winter of 1046–7 the main body of Pechenegs crossed the Danube, seeking refuge on Byzantine soil, somewhat as the Goths had done seven centuries earlier. The settlement of the Pechenegs was equally mishandled. Constantine IX Monomachos was forced to send out a series of expeditions to pacify them. They had little success. The upshot was that the Pechenegs were left in possession of large tracts of the Balkans. Around the same time the Seljuq Turks began to make their presence felt along the eastern frontier. In 1048 they laid siege to Ani, the Armenian capital, which had recently been annexed by the Byzantines. The Turks might have been thwarted on this occasion, but it was a taste of things to come. The tide was also turning against Byzantium in southern Italy, as Norman freebooters harried Byzantine territories from their base at Melfi where they had established themselves in 1041.

The rapidly changing conditions in the empire's frontier provinces meant that Constantine IX Monomachos had to improvise. Experience had taught him that they were danger zones. They had been the launching pad for the two most serious revolts he had to face. The first came early in his reign and was the work of George Maniakes who had been sent as supreme

---

[16] Wolska-Conus (1976).

military commander to Byzantine Italy by Michael V. He was suspicious of the new regime, if only because his great enemy Romanos Skleros was close to Monomachos. He crossed over to Albania in 1043 and advanced on Thessaloniki down the Egnatian Way. His troops brushed aside the imperial armies sent to oppose him, but in the hour of victory he was mysteriously killed and the revolt fizzled out. The centre of the other revolt was the major military base of the southern Balkans, Adrianople. Its leader was Leo Tornikios, a nephew of the emperor. In the autumn of 1047 he advanced on Constantinople and only the emperor's coolness saved the day. There are good reasons to suppose that underlying this revolt was dissatisfaction on the part of the military families of Adrianople with Monomachos' policies. The emperor was cutting back on military expenditure while recruiting detachments of Pechenegs to serve on the eastern frontier.

Constantine IX Monomachos had to devise some way of neutralising the danger from discontented generals. In southern Italy he turned to a local leader called Argyros, who despite his Greek name was a Lombard. He had seized the city of Bari in 1040 and proclaimed himself 'prince and duke of Italy', but he had opposed Maniakes' rebellion. Monomachos was grateful and brought him and his family to Constantinople. Argyros again proved his loyalty to the emperor in 1047 when he helped defend Constantinople against Leo Tornikios. In 1051 Monomachos sent Argyros to Italy as supreme commander, an appointment which showed that Monomachos was willing to work through the local elites, rather than relying on Byzantine governors. Such a policy seemed to offer two advantages: it should have reconciled local opinion to rule from Constantinople, as well as leading to some relaxation of the grip exerted by the imperial administration. This may have been deliberate. The changing political conditions along the Byzantine frontiers would have alerted the imperial government to one of the disadvantages of the military expansionism espoused by Basil II. Byzantium was left exposed to new forces gathering strength beyond its frontiers. Byzantium had been more secure when protected by independent territories in Bulgaria and Armenia, however irksome they could seem at times. By working through Argyros, Monomachos seems to have been trying to shed some of the responsibilities for frontier defence which now burdened his government at Constantinople. He seems to have been trying to do something of the same kind in the Balkans and Anatolia with his attempts at settling Pechenegs and Armenians. But these efforts were mismanaged and only produced friction with the local population. Disengagement is always one of the most difficult political feats to carry off.

Constantine IX Monomachos' reign was pivotal. It is scarcely any wonder that later contemporaries unanimously blamed him for the disasters suffered by the empire later on in the eleventh century. He had a programme for the restoration of the empire and it failed. The programme was well conceived, but was not able to survive a combination of internal opposition and changes occurring along the empire's frontiers, and its failure left the empire adrift. Around 1050 Monomachos dismissed Leichoudes, the architect of his reforms. His last years were characterised by an oppressive fiscal regime in a vain effort to restore the empire's finances.

THE SCHISM WITH ROME

In modern historical writing the schism of 1054 dominates the end of Monomachos' reign. It had little impact at the time, but it was important for the future, because it underlined the unbridgeable gulf that was developing between Byzantium and the west. The background to the schism was paradoxically an alliance between the Byzantine emperor and Pope Leo IX (1049–54). It was directed against the Normans and had been engineered by Argyros. There was an assumption on the part of the papacy that this alliance would promote its claims to jurisdiction over the church in Byzantine Italy. In 1053 the papal forces made contact with the Normans near Civitate. They were expecting to link up with a Byzantine army under Argyros, but it failed to appear. The Normans trounced the papal army and captured Leo IX. This did not prevent him from despatching a delegation to Constantinople in the autumn of 1053 to renew the Byzantine alliance. It was headed by Humbert, cardinal priest of Silva Candida, chief ideologue of the papal reform movement and Leo IX's trusted adviser. By the time the papal legation reached Constantinople the pope was dead, but its members carried on regardless, acting as though their commissions were still valid.

Constantine IX Monomachos gave them much encouragement; the alliance with the papacy remained vital for his Italian policy. Cardinal Humbert followed the instructions he had received from Leo IX. The alliance was to be cemented by a regularisation of relations between the two churches, which had not been in communion for nearly half a century. The discussion revolved around the Latin use of unleavened bread – azymes – in the communion service. The patriarch of the day, Michael I Keroularios (1043–58), had earlier condemned it as a Jewish practice and argued that the Byzantine use of leavened bread had the support of the gospels. Leo IX had taken exception to this and wanted the question resolved. Cardinal Humbert tried to carry out his wishes, but it was difficult because Keroularios refused to acknowledge his presence. Humbert treated this as contumacy. On 16 July 1054 he entered St Sophia with the other papal legates and put on the altar a bull of excommunication directed at Michael Keroularios. The patriarch in his turn placed Humbert and the rest of the papal delegation under anathema. It confirmed an already existing state of schism between the two churches.

What stance did Constantine IX Monomachos adopt? From the out-set he worked for an accord between the two churches. The papal legates came under his protection. He organised two debates between Humbert and a representative of the orthodox church, designed to clarify all the issues separating the two churches. They were conducted in an irenic fash-ion. Monomachos was as frustrated as the papal legates by Keroularios' lack of cooperation. This does not mean that he would have encouraged Humbert to excommunicate the patriarch. The legates' hasty departure from the City suggests that Monomachos had not approved their action. Michael Keroularios insisted that the papal legates should be brought back to Constantinople. The emperor demurred, but the patriarch used popular indignation to get his way. The legates were reprimanded, but punish-ment was reserved for the interpreters and members of Argyros' immediate family, who happened to be resident in the capital. Michael Keroularios blamed the incident on Argyros, who was a personal enemy. He accused him of deliberately misinforming the papacy. By singling out Argyros as the main culprit, Keroularios played down the religious issues. There were still hopes that the differences between the two churches might be resolved, or so it seemed to one of the legates, Frederick of Lorraine, who in 1057 became Pope Stephen IX. He almost immediately despatched a delegation to Constantinople to repair the damage, but it never reached its destination because he died soon after it set out. Other counsels prevailed at Rome. In 1059 the new pope Nicholas II (1058–61) turned to the Normans for support. By this time the events of 1054 had forced a reassessment of papal interests. These were now seen to be better served by an alliance with the Normans rather than with the Byzantines. It was a momentous change which profoundly affected western relations with Byzantium.

THE PATRIARCH AND THE PHILOSOPHER: ELEVENTH-CENTURY CULTURAL VITALITY

At Byzantium the events of 1054 gave Patriarch Michael I Keroularios a prominence which he had neither enjoyed nor sought before. His under-standing with the people of Constantinople gave him immense power. He was on bad terms with Empress Theodora, openly objecting to a woman ruling the empire. On her deathbed she nominated Michael Stratiotikos to succeed her, as Michael VI (1056–7). He came from the distinguished civil service family of Bringas. He was old and was intended as a figure-head for a faction among the bureaucracy which had come to power with Theodora. The new government dealt generously with potential support-ers in the capital, but pleaded poverty when the generals Isaac Komnenos and Katakalon Kekaumenos came seeking promotion and donatives. They were sent packing to their estates in Anatolia. They raised the standard of rebellion and defeated the imperial forces sent against them in a particularly bloody encounter not far from the city of Nicaea. The rebels advanced on Constantinople. Within the capital there was a struggle for power between various factions. Michael VI Stratiotikos hoped to keep the throne by using the good offices of Constantine Leichoudes and Michael Psellos, who had been absent from the political scene and had not crossed the generals. The emperor sent them to the rebels' camp to offer Isaac Komnenos the rank of caesar and eventual succession to the throne. But Michael Keroularios had already taken things into his own hands by having Isaac Komnenos proclaimed emperor in St Sophia. Michael VI backed down; he was not willing to turn Constantinople into a bloodbath by opposing the entry of Komnenos' troops. Isaac I Komnenos (1057–9) owed the throne to Michael Keroularios. The patriarch's reward was the right to appoint to the two most senior posts of the patriarchal administration: those of the *oikonomos* and the *skeuophylax*, appointments which in the past had been in the imperial gift. It marked an important stage in the emancipation of the patriarchal administration from imperial control.

Isaac I Komnenos did not wish to be beholden to the patriarch. He had been impressed by the way Michael Psellos had conducted negotiations, even if they lacked concrete result. Psellos struck him as a man he could trust. Isaac needed an experienced minister to supervise his plans for financial retrenchment. Arrears of taxation were chased up; pensions paid to officials were reduced; grants of property made from the imperial demesne were revoked; and there were restrictions on grants to monasteries in line with the anti-monastic legislation of Nikephoros Phokas. Isaac's intentions were made plain by the iconography of his coinage. It showed the emperor holding an unsheathed sword (fig. 44). He had come to restore the military might of the empire. The essential first step was to impose order on the state's finances. In theory, Michael Psellos approved, but he thought that Isaac acted too abruptly, alienating too many vested interests by his harshness.

Isaac I Komnenos' conduct aroused Patriarch Michael Keroularios' opposition, which Isaac took as a challenge to his imperial authority. Michael Psellos accused the patriarch of 'daring to usurp imperial authority'.[17] The clash of Michael Keroularios and Isaac Komnenos was a *cause célèbre* of the eleventh century, raising real constitutional issues. Keroularios assumed the role of moral arbiter, entitled to discipline emperors if they failed to protect orthodoxy or to decide the succession when this was in doubt. He had popular support which he exploited; but this laid Keroularios open to the charge that he was flirting with democracy. This accusation reflected the uncertainties created by the end of the Macedonian line and for the time being of dynastic succession, provoking a debate on the

[17] Michael Psellos, *Orationes forenses*, ed. Dennis, p. 61.

Figure 44 *Nomisma* (*histamenon*) of
Isaac I Komnenos, showing him stand-
ing, brandishing his sword (reverse);
Christ is enthroned on the obverse

constitutional niceties of selecting an emperor. Michael Psellos looked
back to the Augustan settlement for guidance. He recognised that imperial
authority rested on three factors: the people, the senate and the army. He
objected to Michael VI's accession on the grounds that he only obtained
the consent of the people and the senate, but not that of the army. His
charge against Michael Keroularios was that he was using the voice of the
people to transfer power from one emperor to another. The constitutional
role of the people of Constantinople – the New Rome – was never very
clear. Their acclamation of a new emperor was one – some would claim, in
accordance with Roman practice, the most important – of the constitutive
acts in the making of an emperor. The people might on occasion rise up
against an emperor, as happened with Michael V. This could be construed
as a right to remove tyrants. Another constitutive act was the coronation,
which in times of great political confusion gave the patriarch considerable
leverage. Keroularios exploited the constitutional difficulties produced by
the end of the Macedonian dynasty, seeking to turn the patriarch into the
arbiter of the constitution.[18] This was seen by Psellos as a threat to imperial
authority. Under his prompting Isaac I Komnenos exiled Keroularios from

---

[18] On the ambivalence and diversity of inauguration rituals and on Keroularios' ambitions, see
Dagron (2003), pp. 54–83, 235–8.

Constantinople. Psellos was put in charge of the prosecution, but his speech against the patriarch was never delivered. Keroularios died on 21 January 1059, before he could be brought to trial.

Michael Psellos' evident dislike of the patriarch was something more than a clash of personalities. The two men stood for very different ways of life. Psellos accused the patriarch of being an exponent of the mysticism which was then fashionable in some Constantinopolitan circles. It centred on the cult of Symeon the New Theologian, who died in March 1022. The cult was promoted by Niketas Stethatos, a future abbot of the monastery of St John Stoudios, and Keroularios supported his campaign for Symeon's canonisation. His teachings provided some of the inspiration behind the monastic revival, now associated with the monastery of the Theotokos Evergetis, which was gathering strength at Constantinople.[19]

Psellos spelt out the dangers of mysticism. It exalted ignorance and denied human reason. It was divorced from everyday life. Psellos, for his part, gloried in his own humanity: 'I am an earthly being', he told the patriarch, 'made of flesh and blood, so that my illnesses seem to me to be illnesses, blows blows, joy joy.'[20] Psellos came close to admitting that he believed that 'man was the measure of all things'. He certainly emphasised the primacy of human experience. He saw no contradiction between Christianity and life in society; had not Christ often frequented the market places and much less frequently the mountains? Psellos was preaching a Christian humanism. Society was held together by the bonds of a Christian faith, friendship and reason. It possessed its own logic and justification. However, it was shaped and guided by the 'philosopher', and Psellos set his authority as 'philosopher' on the same level as that of the patriarch. If he did not challenge imperial authority quite so directly, his *Chronographia* dwells on the human frailties of individual emperors. Its message is that without the wisdom of a 'philosopher' to guide him an emperor was incapable of living up to the responsibilities of his office.[21] Niketas Stethatos was less circumspect in his promotion of the mystic. He exalted the primacy of the mystic over 'emperor, patriarch, bishop or priest'.[22]

The emphasis on the role of the mystic and the 'philosopher' devalued traditional authority at Byzantium. They had access to 'knowledge' that was of immediate benefit to a Christian society. Mystical experience opened up direct access to the Godhead. Symeon the New Theologian saw this as a guarantee that Christ's ministry was ever present and not set in some distant past. Psellos had the harder task of explaining the relevance of classical learning in a Christian society. He was not simply content with

[19] On this monastery, see Mullett and Kirby (eds.) (1994); Mullet and Kirby (eds.) (1997).
[20] *MB*, V, p. 232.
[21] On the difficulty of unpicking the strands of Psellos' themes and practical objectives in the *Chronographia*, see Kaldellis (1999).
[22] *Life of Symeon the New Theologian*, ed. and French tr. Hausherr, p. lxxvi (cited in introduction).

Figure 45 A Byzantine view of the world: the notion that the world was encircled by the ocean, with antipodes above and below, derived from classical antiquity, but was acceptable to the Byzantines; the Theodore Psalter was copied at the Stoudios Monastery in Constantinople in 1066

the traditional justification that it was an educational tool, a means of cultivating human reason. Learning made possible an understanding of the natural world, which offered clues to God's existence and purpose. Psellos sought to build on the classical heritage and bring it up to date. His letters and rhetorical works are not redolent of the drab encyclopaedism of the previous century, but are full of emotion and concrete detail. Unlike earlier Byzantine histories, his *Chronographia* is not dominated by the workings of Divine Providence, but emphasises instead the human element as a decisive historical factor. Psellos did not see any contradiction between Christianity and the classical tradition; to his way of thinking the former fulfilled the latter. He liked to think of himself as in the tradition of the Cappadocian fathers who used their profound knowledge of Greek philosophy to deepen understanding of their Christian faith. Psellos never grappled with theology in any systematic way. This task was left to his pupil John Italos, who reopened many of the basic questions of Christian dogma.

The work of John Italos was just one more sign of the cultural vitality of the eleventh century. The decline of imperial prestige raised basic questions about the ordering of a Christian society. The rivalry of mystic and humanist will sometimes have sharpened the edge of debate, but not all agreed with Michael Psellos that they were diametrically opposed. Most saw their approaches as complementary.[23] They gave a new breadth to Byzantine culture. Equally, the claims of mystic and humanist were subversive of traditional authority at Byzantium. Some of the strongest social ties were those that formed around them among their followers. In this way, they gave a Christian society a degree of independence of the

[23] Hussey (1960).

hierarchical authority exercised by emperor and patriarch. The exchanges between Psellos and Keroularios show how traditional assumptions about the ordering of Byzantine life were being reassessed in the mid-eleventh century. Cultural flux mirrored political uncertainties.

CONSTANTINE X, ROMANOS IV AND THE TURKISH CHALLENGE

The attack on Patriarch Michael I Keroularios cost Isaac I Komnenos a good deal of support. Michael Psellos saw which way the wind was blowing. He persuaded the emperor to resign at a time when a bout of illness had left him in a state of depression. The new emperor was Constantine X Doukas (1059–67) who happened to be married to a niece of the patriarch. It was an admission among other things that the reforms initiated by Isaac Komnenos and supervised by Michael Psellos were not working. Constantine X immediately repealed them and restored honours to those who had been deprived of them. Setting out his programme in a speech delivered before the guilds of Constantinople, Constantine X emphasised that truth and justice, and not the sword, were to be the keynotes of his reign. It was a return to the policies that had been tried at the beginning of Constantine IX Monomachos' reign. Constantine X was sensible enough to dispense with Michael Psellos' political services. Less wise was his decision to appoint Psellos tutor to his son and heir Michael Doukas. Contemporaries were unanimous that this rendered the latter unfit to rule.

Constantine X had to all appearances a remarkably successful reign. He was well fitted to be emperor, having good connections with both the military families of Anatolia and the great families of Constantinople. He also anticipated the future in the way he associated his family in government. He relied heavily on the support of his brother John, whom he raised to the rank of caesar. He was later criticised for his overgenerous distribution of honours and pensions to the people of Constantinople and for the way he allowed the military establishment to run down. There was increasing pressure on the frontiers of the empire. The Normans made significant advances in the south of Italy in the wake of their alliance with the papacy in 1059, but Constantine X reacted energetically, despatching a number of expeditions to secure the main Byzantine bases along the Adriatic coast. He himself led the army that mopped up an Uze invasion of the Balkans. Less was done on the eastern frontier. The defences of Melitene were rebuilt in 1063, but Ani – the Armenian capital – was lost to the Seljuqs the next year. Constantine will not have heard of the sack of Cappadocian Caesarea and the desecration of the cathedral of St Basil which occurred around the time of his death in May 1067. Only an emperor as securely in control as Constantine was could adopt such a strategy in the east: a war of attrition. He aimed to hold the key positions and allow the eastern provinces to absorb Turkish pressure. There was increasing agitation for a more aggressive policy (see below, pp. 699, 701).

In the normal course of events Constantine X would have been succeeded by his son Michael, who was aged about sixteen, but he was already seen as something of a liability. Constantine therefore left the regency to his empress Eudocia Makrembolitissa, but she was forced to swear on oath never again to marry.[24] She also undertook to rule with the aid of the caesar John Doukas, until Michael Doukas was capable of carrying out the duties of an emperor. In good dynastic fashion Constantine X Doukas was trying to safeguard the succession for his family. The oath was administered by Patriarch John Xiphilinos (1064–75), who was soon persuaded that the common interest required that Eudocia should be released from her oath. This allowed her to marry Romanos Diogenes, the head of a powerful Anatolian family. He came to the throne on the understanding that he would respect the eventual succession of Michael Doukas.

The chances of this happening soon became remote as Eudocia bore her new husband two sons in quick succession. Romanos IV (1068–71) needed a decisive victory in order to establish himself and his line in power. His efforts to search out and destroy the Turkish bands of marauders left him open to ridicule. The Turks were far too nimble for the lumbering and badly trained troops at his disposal. Romanos changed his strategy. Instead of waiting for the Turks to invade the Byzantine provinces, he decided to engage them at their major point of entry into Byzantine territory. This was the bottleneck to the north of Lake Van, which was commanded by the fortress of Manzikert. In the summer of 1071 Romanos led all the troops he could muster to Lake Van and recovered possession of Manzikert and other strategic points which had been lost to the Turks. The emperor appears not to have known that the Seljuq sultan Alp Arslan (1063–73) was also operating in the area. Once he learned of the sultan's presence he seized on the opportunity to engage him in battle. The combat lasted two days, the Byzantines fighting with surprising tenacity and discipline. They had the better of the battle until towards evening on the second day, when a rumour started to spread that Romanos had fallen. This was the work of Andronikos Doukas, a son of the caesar John Doukas. His motives were political. If Romanos emerged from the battle with credit, the Doukas cause was doomed. Andronikos Doukas was in command of the rearguard and in a position to do maximum damage. He abandoned the field leaving Romanos and his elite troops unprotected. They had fought bravely, but they were now quickly surrounded by the Turks and the emperor was captured.

---

[24] Oikonomides (1963).

In military terms Manzikert was not a disaster; the Byzantine casualties were relatively slight.[25] It should only have confirmed Turkish domination of the Armenian highlands, not that almost the whole of Anatolia would be overrun by the Turks within ten years. Early Turkish settlement was concentrated a thousand miles west of Manzikert along the northern and western rims of the Anatolian plateau. Why should a defeat at the extreme limit of Byzantium's eastern frontiers have opened up Anatolia to Turkish settlement? Part of the answer is weight of numbers. The Turks were a people on the move seeking new pastures. But their penetration of the Byzantine empire was facilitated by the civil wars sparked off by the defeat at Manzikert. Partisans of the Doukas cause at Constantinople, including Michael Psellos, seized control of the government for Michael VII Doukas (1071–78). Romanos IV had not, however, been killed in the battle, as rumour suggested. He was soon released by the sultan and rallied his supporters to his base in Amaseia. Defeated by an army despatched from Constantinople, Romanos retreated to Antioch. The next year 1072 he was again defeated by an army sent out from the capital, commanded by Andronikos Doukas and consisting largely of Frankish mercenaries. Romanos was captured and taken back under safe-conduct. As they were approaching Constantinople the order came that he was to be blinded. This was done so savagely that he died a few weeks later on 4 August 1072. The year of civil war had given the Turks an opportunity to exploit their victory, but it did not end there.

Russell Balliol, a Norman mercenary in Byzantine service, seized the main chance. He had taken part in the opening stages of the Norman conquest of Sicily, and recognised a similar opportunity in the confusion produced by the aftermath of Manzikert. Balliol made Amaseia his centre of operations and soon brought most of the old theme of Armeniakoi under his control. Local people welcomed his presence because he offered some protection from the marauding Turks. The government at Constantinople took the threat from Russell Balliol far more seriously than that presented by the Turks. Its apprehension increased when Balliol captured the caesar John Doukas, who had been sent with an army against him; Balliol proclaimed Doukas emperor and advanced on Constantinople. The Doukas government brought in Turks as the only means of combating Balliol and in the short term it worked. Balliol was defeated, but managed to get back to Amaseia, where he retained his independence. In retrospect, the use of Turks was a miscalculation on the part of the Byzantine government, but at the time the Turks seemed no kind of threat to Constantinople. Cocooned in the capital, Michael VII and his advisers may well have felt that the Turks could be treated like the Pechenegs in the Balkans: given lands and

[25] Cheynet (1980); *EI*, VI, s.v. Malazgird [Manzikert], pp. 243–4 (C. Hillenbrand); below, pp. 702–3. On eleventh-century strategy, see also Haldon (2003b).

a degree of tribal autonomy and in due course absorbed within Byzantine government and society.

Eventually the young Alexios Komnenos was sent to deal with Russell Balliol. It was his first major commission. With the help of a local Turkish chieftain he managed to apprehend the Norman and take him back to Constantinople. He acquitted himself with great skill and assurance, but the result was that much of northern Anatolia fell under Turkish domination. Alexios Komnenos had the greatest difficulty in extricating himself and his prisoner from Amaseia because the whole country was alive with Turks. He made a detour to Kastamonu where he expected a friendly reception, since it was the centre of his family's estates. He found instead his grandfather's palace occupied by Turks and he had to hurry on. This incident reveals how swiftly Byzantine control in the region collapsed. It was largely because of a lack of local leadership.

The story was much the same in other parts of Anatolia. In 1077 Nikephoros Botaneiates – a noted general – abandoned his estates in western Asia Minor and marched on Constantinople with his retinue of 300 men. He left the area unprotected. Still worse, he engaged the services of a Turkish chieftain named Suleiman ibn Qutlumush (1081–6). Botaneiates seems to have been unaware that he was no ordinary warband leader, but a capable and ambitious scion of the ruling Seljuq dynasty. It was a colossal miscalculation on Botaneiates' part, though he might not otherwise have overthrown Michael VII Doukas to become Emperor Nikephoros III (1078–81). Botaneiates in turn would have to face a challenge which compounded his own folly. Nikephoros Melissenos raised the standard of revolt on the island of Kos and he too turned to the Turks for support. The price was the surrender of cities along the western coast of Asia Minor, such as Smyrna. A succession of revolts and civil wars had drawn the Turks westward to the shores of the Aegean and handed them most of the great cities of Asia Minor. Thus was the fate of Byzantine Anatolia sealed. The Turks established themselves in force on the northern and western edges of the Anatolian plateau and proved impossible to dislodge: Suleiman's horde roamed across Bithynia and, after occupying Nicaea and Nikomedeia, he proclaimed himself sultan (see below, p. 708). Behind this shield the much slower process of Byzantine Anatolia's transformation into Turkey could go on more or less unhindered. In retrospect, the loss of Anatolia to the Turks seems to have been folly on a grand scale.

ALEXIOS I KOMNENOS' MILITARY DEFEATS AND POLITICAL SKILLS

Emperor Nikephoros III Botaneiates was an old hero, but incapable of mastering circumstances that were spinning out of control. As if the loss of Anatolia was not bad enough, Robert Guiscard, the Norman leader, was massing his forces in southern Italy for an invasion. The commander of Byzantium's western armies was now Alexios Komnenos, but his abilities, ambition and family connections marked him out as a threat to the regime in Constantinople. The young commander found himself in an impossible position. He struck in the spring of 1081. On 1 April 1081 Alexios with the help of his brother Isaac and the support of the caesar John Doukas seized Constantinople and overthrew the old emperor.

In the meantime Robert Guiscard and his son Bohemond had crossed to Albania and laid siege to Dyrrachium at the head of the Egnatian Way. Guiscard justified his actions by proclaiming that he was coming to restore to the throne of Constantinople the rightful house of Doukas. These dynastic pretensions made him all the more dangerous at a time when the new emperor's hold on power was still shaky. Alexios I Komnenos assembled all available forces and made for Dyrrachium, only to suffer a shattering defeat. His troops were no match for the Normans. In military terms it was a far more serious defeat than Manzikert. While one Norman army advanced down the Egnatian Way to within striking distance of Thessaloniki, another under Bohemond headed south into Greece. The key position was Larissa in Thessaly. If it fell to the Normans, then the rich provinces of Hellas and the Peloponnese were lost. With a scratch force of Turkish archers Alexios marched in 1083 to the relief of Larissa. The emperor was careful not to engage the Normans in open battle, relying instead on skirmishing tactics. He was able to raise the siege of Larissa and forced the Normans to evacuate Thessaly. The Norman threat only ended with the death of Robert Guiscard in 1085, which prompted a succession crisis in southern Italy and the withdrawal of the Normans from their bases in Albania and the Ionian islands.

More by luck than judgement Alexios I emerged from the first test of his reign with his reputation enhanced. His next task was to restore the Danubian frontier. The key this time was the fortress city of Dristra. This was under the control of the Pechenegs, who in 1086 caught Alexios by surprise. Yet another Byzantine army was lost and, once again, Alexios was lucky to escape. The Pechenegs pushed south towards Constantinople. The danger was even more serious because they allied with Tzachas, a Turkish amir who had turned Smyrna into a pirate base. By the winter of 1090–1 Alexios controlled little more than Constantinople itself, with no army to speak of. The force that he led out against the Pechenegs consisted very largely of the retainers of his relatives and supporters. He headed for the port of Ainos at the mouth of the Maritsa, in the hope of preventing the Pechenegs from linking up with their Turkish ally. The situation was further complicated by the appearance of another nomadic people – the Cumans – who had crossed over the Danube into the Balkans.

Their original intention was to cooperate with the Pechenegs, but Alexios succeeded in winning them over to the Byzantine side. Thanks largely to their help, Alexios crushed the Pechenegs at the battle of Lebounion in Thrace. The Pechenegs ceased to count. The Cumans were still a potential threat to Byzantine control of the Balkans, but in 1094 Alexios defeated them outside the walls of Anchialos on the Black Sea. At long last, Alexios was in full control of the Danubian frontier.

Alexios displayed great tenacity in the face of a series of military defeats. But this cannot disguise the fact that they were often of his own making. It was largely his own foolhardiness which had jeopardised Byzantine control of the Balkans. Without the support of his family it is doubtful whether he could have survived his early years as emperor, so patchy was his military record. Alexios had, however, wisely entrusted the running of the government to his mother Anna Dalassena. While he was campaigning, Anna kept control of Constantinople and managed to meet his military requirements. This necessitated a harsh administrative regime.

Alexios' survival also depended on the support of the great families. He came to power as the leader of an aristocratic faction and his overthrow would almost certainly have meant their downfall. The Komnenoi were linked by ties of blood and marriage to all the major aristocratic families. Alexios turned this into a principle of government, accomplishing this very largely through a radical reform of the honours system. His daughter Anna Komnena perceptively singles this out as a major achievement.[26] In the past the honours system had been hierarchical rather than dynastic; membership of the imperial family did not bring rank at court as of right. The inflation of honours over the eleventh century resulted in a collapse of the old honours system. Alexios rebuilt it by creating a series of new ranks that were reserved for members of his family. The imperial epithet *sebastos* was now accorded to the imperial family in its widest sense. The *sebastoi* became a distinct hierarchy with their own gradations. At the top came the rank of *sebastokratōr* which was a conflation of *sebastos* and *autokratōr*. This Alexios created for his elder brother Isaac who shared the burdens of the imperial office. The rank of *prōtosebastos* went to one of the emperor's brothers-in-law. It was normally combined with the position of *prōtovestiarios*. This too marked a profound change in the texture of government. In the past the *prōtovestiarios* had almost always been a eunuch and one of the chief officers of the imperial household. Alexios did away with eunuchs and created an imperial household staffed very largely by members of his family, while the more menial positions went to retainers of the house of Komnenos. The imperial household had always been the instrument for the exercise of

---

[26] *Al.*, III.4.3, ed. Reinsch and Kambylis, I, p. 96; ed. and French tr. Leib, I, pp. 114–15; tr. Sewter, p. 112.

direct imperial authority. Its identification with Komnenian family interest gave it a different quality.

In the past, office and rank brought lucrative salaries. One of the attractions of reforming the honours system was that it provided a way of abolishing these profits of office. Alexios found other ways of rewarding members of his family, granting them administrative and fiscal rights over specific areas. This was the basis of grants that were later known as *pronoiai*. In the past similar grants had been made out of the imperial demesne, but Alexios extended this principle to state lands. In a sense, he was parcelling out the empire among his family and creating a series of appanages. He rebuilt imperial government as an aristocratic connection; family business might be a more accurate description. It was a radical step which would later create tensions, because the theory of imperial autocracy could not easily accommodate the transformation that occurred in practice. But it provided Alexios with the strengths necessary to hold on to power during his difficult early years.

ALEXIOS' PIETY AND PRAGMATISM

Many great families were not included in the Komnenian circle and it was from these that the main opposition to Alexios' regime came. The senatorial families which had run the administration under the Doukai had most to lose. The underlying current of hostility that existed between them and the Komnenoi surfaced during Alexios' seizure of Constantinople. We are told that his supporters deliberately set upon any senators they came across in the streets. Patriarch Kosmas I (1075–81) forced Alexios and members of his family to do public penance for the violence that accompanied their seizure of power. It was one more demonstration of the patriarch's moral authority, which was such a powerful factor in the politics of eleventh-century Byzantium. It was a deliberate humiliation of the imperial family. Alexios' reaction showed his mettle: he procured the dismissal of the patriarch and replaced him by Eustratios Garidas (1081–4), a monk cultivated by his mother. It revealed how ruthless he could be, but it earned him the hostility of a powerful section of the clergy led by Leo, bishop of Chalcedon. Leo objected to the way that Alexios had seized church treasures in order to pay for his first campaign against the Normans, a measure for which there were in fact good precedents. This was, in other words, chosen as a suitable issue through which to attack the emperor. Patriarch Eustratios was not strong enough to defend either himself or the emperor and was replaced in 1084 by Nicholas the Grammarian. Leo of Chalcedon switched the attack to the new patriarch, but Alexios I Komnenos was now sufficiently sure of himself to have Leo exiled.

Figure 46 Alexios I Komnenos (shown far right) receiving as if from the church
fathers (shown above) the *Panoplia dogmatike*, a theological treatise condemning

The emperor's new confidence owed much to the successful outcome of
the trial of John Italos on a charge of heresy. Italos had been a leading figure
at the court of Michael VII Doukas, who entrusted him with negotiations
with Robert Guiscard. He was also a teacher of note. He had succeeded
Michael Psellos as consul of the philosophers and took over his responsibilities for the supervision of education in the capital. Unlike Psellos his bias
was towards Aristotle rather than Plato. His application of philosophical
method to theological questions earned him an enthusiastic following but
also laid him open, like Psellos before him, to charges of heresy. Michael
VII encouraged him to submit a profession of faith to Patriarch Kosmas
as a way of exonerating himself. The patriarch demurred; and there the
matter rested.

The case was reopened by the Komnenian regime in the winter of 1081–
2, when its stock at Constantinople was very low following Alexios' defeat

all heresies past and present, which Alexios had commissioned from the monk Euthymios Zigabenos

at the hands of the Normans. Italos numbered among his former pupils members of prominent Constantinopolitan families who were seen by the Komnenoi as potential centres of opposition to their rule. If successful, an attack on Italos would help to discredit them. After a preliminary hearing before the emperor Italos was passed over to the patriarch, so that his case could come before the patriarchal synod. It duly convened in the church of St Sophia. There was a good chance that Italos would be acquitted, because feeling among the bishops was beginning to turn against the Komnenoi, but before this could happen a mob broke into St Sophia and hunted Italos down. He escaped by hiding on the roof of the Great Church. The patriarch was out of his depth and handed matters back to the emperor, who had Italos condemned as a heretic. On the feast of orthodoxy, which in 1082 fell on 13 March, Italos publicly abjured his errors.

The trial of John Italos was a significant episode. It allowed Alexios I Komnenos to establish an ascendancy over the orthodox church. There were three distinct strands to this process. The first was his use of the mob. The Constantinopolitan mob had proved itself over the eleventh century to be a significant political factor, but had normally been mobilised in support of the church. Now Alexios was able to win it over to his side and deploy it against the church. How and why he managed this has to remain a matter of speculation. The most likely explanation is that the mob responded to Alexios' pose as the guardian of orthodoxy. This receives some support from the timing of Italos' condemnation to coincide with the Feast of orthodoxy, which was a celebration of the victory over iconoclasm in 843 and the occasion on which the *Synodikon of orthodoxy* was read out (see above, p. 290). This statement of faith condemning heresy in general and iconoclasm in particular had remained virtually unchanged from 843 down to the eleventh century. It was Alexios who hit upon the device of bringing it up to date by adding the condemnation of John Italos and, as his reign progressed, that of others condemned for heresy. It was a concrete expression of the emperor's role as the guardian of orthodoxy.

Alexios was not content with the condemnation of Italos alone. He also pursued his pupils: they were forbidden to teach and remained under the shadow of their master's condemnation for heresy. This had two consequences. The first was that it discredited members of families potentially opposed to the Komnenoi. The second, paradoxically, was a rapprochement with the clergy of the patriarchal church. Among Italos' most prominent pupils were a number of deacons of St Sophia. Induced to disown their master, they were not only reconciled with the church but also permitted to continue teaching. One was Eustratios, the future bishop of Nicaea, who was soon to become Alexios' most trusted religious adviser. An understanding with the patriarchal clergy was useful to the emperor because at synod they constituted a counterweight to the episcopal presence. Alexios acted to guarantee the privileges of the patriarchal clergy. He also issued a chrysobull defining the privileges and role of the *chartophylax* of St Sophia. It upheld the precedence of the *chartophylax* over bishops, on the grounds that he was the patriarch's deputy. In practice, the holder of the office came to oversee the patriarchal administration. This was much to the advantage of the emperor because he still controlled appointments to this office.

Alexios' measures went a long way towards neutralising the independence of action which the eleventh-century patriarchs had displayed. They had, for instance, taken the initiative over marriage legislation and litigation, and this produced differences between canon and civil law. Alexios intervened to re-establish imperial control of this important area of law. He re-enacted the *novella* of Leo VI over the age of consent for betrothal and marriage with its important rider that the emperor could use his powers of discretion to ignore the stipulations of the *novella*. Having regained the initiative over legislation, he then conceded that marriage litigation should in normal circumstances go before the ecclesiastical courts.

Alexios' church settlement is among his greatest – and most neglected – achievements. It enabled him to rebuild the moral and spiritual foundations of imperial authority, which had been undermined in the course of the eleventh century. He recovered control over the administration of the patriarchal church and regained the initiative in matters of legislation. He was the guarantor of the privileges or liberties of the church. He assumed the role of *epistēmonarkhēs* or regulator of the church, even if this title did not enter official usage until the mid-twelfth century.

Above all, beginning with the trial of John Italos, he used heresy as a way of establishing his credentials as the guardian of orthodoxy. Under Alexios the suppression of heresy became an imperial preserve and a series of heresy trials contributed to the image Alexios was endeavouring to project, but there were political undercurrents. They were a means of discrediting potential opponents. The most spectacular heresy trial was that of Basil the Bogomil and his followers. The date can only be fixed approximately to *c.* 1100. The Bogomil heresy originated in Bulgaria and was a form of dualism. It is impossible to establish any clear connection between the Bulgarian and Byzantine phases of Bogomilism. It is possible that they arose quite separately and spontaneously and that a connection was only perceived in retrospect. Byzantine Bogomilism had its roots in lay piety. It was transformed by Basil the Bogomil's missionary zeal. He organised his followers around his twelve disciples and was assumed to be aiming at converting the world. It has also been suggested that he was responsible for providing Bogomilism with its theological justification; his dualist teaching transformed unease with the material world into a system of belief. Like other holy men Basil could count some distinguished figures among his followers. He had entrée to the highest circles. There is even a suspicion that Anna Dalassena was a supporter. This would explain the comic scene so graphically sketched by Anna Komnena, which otherwise beggars belief. Alexios Komnenos and his brother Isaac interviewed Basil the Bogomil and pretended to be sympathetic to his teachings. By this means they were able to induce Basil to set out his Bogomil beliefs in full. Behind a screen a secretary was taking down his words, which were then used against him.[27] What distinguishes Basil from other heretics is that he also possessed a large popular following, which meant that he was doubly dangerous.

---

[27] *Al.*, XV.8.3–6, ed. Reinsch and Kambylis, I; pp. 486–8; ed. and French tr. Leib, III, p. 219–21; tr. Sewter, pp. 497–9.

Though this was not necessarily Alexios' intention, one of the consequences of Basil's condemnation was to strengthen imperial authority on the streets of Constantinople. This is apparent from the edict issued in 1107 in the aftermath of the Bogomil trials. Alexios' purpose was to create an order of preachers attached to St Sophia who would tackle the problem of heresy on the streets of the capital and act as the moral policemen of the different neighbourhoods. His edict shows how effective his control over the church had become. The creation of an order of preachers was originally the work of Patriarch Nicholas the Grammarian (1084–1111). It was now taken over by the emperor, who also took responsibility for reorganising the patriarchal clergy.

Nicholas the Grammarian accepted imperial ascendancy. He understood that the church benefited from the emperor's benevolent supervision. He also recognised the emperor's piety. This was best seen in Alexios' patronage of monks and monasteries. This Nicholas the Grammarian would have appreciated; the founder of a Constantinopolitan monastery, he was also famed for his self-denial. Alexios was the heir of his mother's careful cultivation of monks and holy men, and their support had been useful during his difficult early years as emperor. He and members of his family supported the work of monastic figures, such as Christodoulos of Patmos, Meletios and Cyril Phileotes in the provinces. They also founded and refounded monasteries in the capital. Constantinople had been the scene of a strong current of monastic revival from the middle of the eleventh century, associated with the monastery of the Theotokos Evergetis. Its *typikon* or rule provided a guide to a series of Komnenian foundations.[28] Monastic order also provided the inspiration for the reform of imperial court life begun by Anna Dalassena and continued by Alexios' empress Irene Doukaina. Anna Komnena noted that under their guidance 'the palace assumed the appearance of a monastery'.[29] Alexios and his family became exemplars of a piety that drew its inspiration from the monastic revival that gathered strength at Constantinople from the mid-eleventh century. This went a long way towards reconciling the church to the Komnenian ascendancy and gave the new dynasty a moral standing which the emperors of the eleventh century had lacked.

The monastic revival continued, but under Komnenian auspices. This was typical of Alexios' church settlement. His main purpose was to assert imperial control, harnessing new forces and ideas that surfaced in the eleventh century and putting them at the disposal of the imperial dynasty. Alexios' patronage of monastic leaders does not mean that he was therefore

---

[28] *Theotokos Evergetis*, ed. and French tr. Gautier, pp. 14–94; tr. Jordan, pp. 472–500.
[29] *Al.*, III.8.2, ed. Reinsch and Kambylis, I, p. 105; ed. and French tr. Leib, I, p. 125; tr. Sewter, p. 121.

hostile to humanism. If he destroyed John Italos, he rehabilitated his pupil Eustratios of Nicaea, who continued his master's work on Aristotle. The Komnenoi promoted humanist culture. Alexios' daughter Anna Komnena was one of its adornments. The *Alexiad*, her history of her father's reign, owed something to Michael Psellos, whose learning Anna much admired. She was also a patron of Eustratios of Nicaea and Aristotelian scholarship. The *sebastokratōr* Isaac Komnenos, perhaps the brother but more probably the son of Alexios Komnenos, continued Psellos' Neoplatonic interests. Komnenian self-interest meant that the cultural revival of the eleventh century changed its character. It lost much of its effervescence, but it might have fizzled out, or the Komnenoi might have repressed it. Instead, they preserved its essentials and ensured the cultural breadth and vitality that characterises later Byzantine history.

REFORM OF THE COINAGE AND TAXATION

Alexios' achievement was to rebuild the Byzantine empire. The new and the traditional were mixed in equal measure. He restored the traditional role of the emperor in ecclesiastical affairs, but took it further. Caesaropapism is an apt enough description of his supervision of the church. Politically, Byzantium was organised on a dynastic rather than a hierarchical basis. This is perhaps where Alexios was at his most radical because it had far-reaching implications for the organisation of government. It meant that the emperor shared power with members of an extended family. There was, on the other hand, no radical restructuring of government. Alexios was more interested in finding ways of exercising control. His solution was to create coordinating ministries. The civil service was now subordinated to the logothete of the *sekrēta*, later known as the grand logothete; the fiscal services were placed under the control of the grand logariast.

Alexios inherited a bankrupt state. The coinage was miserably debased, with the gold coinage's fineness reduced from twenty-four to eight carats. So desperate was his situation that Alexios had to debase still further, but by 1092 he was able to restore some order to the coinage. He raised the fineness of the standard gold coinage to around twenty carats and kept the debased electrum issues, but stabilising them at around six carats. He also kept the debased silver coinage in the form of a billon coin with a minimal silver content. He issued a new copper coinage. Alexios' reform of the coinage was typical of the measures he took to restore the empire. He imposed order and stability, but his measures had radical consequences. Michael Hendy contends that 'the Alexian coinage reform of 1092 attempted and achieved nothing less than a complete reconstruction of the coinage system on an entirely novel basis; . . . only the Diocletianic reform had been on a similar

(a)   (b)

Figure 47 Alexios I Komnenos' reformed coinage: (a) a *nomisma* with low gold fineness, mainly of electrum (*aspron trachy nomisma*). On the reverse (below) Alexios and Irene are shown full-length, holding the cross between them; on the obverse (above), Alexios' son John II (full-length) is crowned by Christ. (b) a low-value *tetarteron noummion* mainly of billon; this type, showing the emperor on the reverse (below) in traditional pose, holding orb and sceptre topped by crosses, circulated widely

scale.'[30] His innovation was to create a regular coinage based on alloys rather than pure metal. It is likely that the existence of both an electrum and a billon coinage, which took the place of the old silver *miliarēsia*, made for a more flexible monetary system. But the greatest service that Alexios' coinage reform did was to re-establish clear equivalences between the different coinages. Their absence had brought chaos to the fiscal system. In the wake of his reform of the coinage Alexios was able to proceed to a thoroughgoing reform of the collection of taxes – the so-called *nea logarikē*. It was essentially an adaptation of the taxation system to the reformed coinage. It has been estimated that it was done in such a way as to quadruple the tax rate.

Alexios I Komnenos ended the lax fiscal regime of the eleventh century. There are no signs that the Byzantine economy suffered. It quickly recovered from a period of dislocation which lasted for approximately twenty years,

[30] Hendy (1985), p. 513; see also Hendy's account of Alexios' coin reforms in *DOC*, IV.1, pp. 192–201.

from the defeat at Manzikert to Alexios' victory over the Pechenegs in 1091. The manorialisation of the countryside continued with largely beneficial results for the peasantry (see above, pp. 584–5). The towns of Greece and the southern Balkans prospered. Places such as Corinth, Thebes and Halmyros (in Thessaly) benefited from a growing Italian presence and there was an upsurge of local trade around the shores of the Aegean. Constantinople continued to be the clearing house of the medieval world. The empire was far from being 'internally played out'. But there had been a decisive shift in its centre of gravity from Asia Minor to Greece and the southern Balkans, which experienced sustained economic growth. It is not clear, however, that this compensated for the loss of the resources of Anatolia. Its recovery was always Alexios' major task.

THE FIRST CRUSADE

By 1095 Alexios had pacified the Balkans, brought peace to the church and restored sound government. He was in a position to contemplate recovering Anatolia from the Turks. He moved troops across the Bosporus and using Nikomedeia as a base created a defensible zone, but it soon became clear that he did not have the resources to effect a reconquest of Anatolia; his preoccupation with Europe had given the Turks the opportunity to settle key parts of Anatolia in depth. Alexios had made the situation still worse at the very beginning of his reign by withdrawing the remaining Byzantine garrisons from Anatolia. Paradoxically, the only area where there was potential support for a Byzantine reconquest was in the Euphrates lands and Cilicia where the Armenians had retained their independence.

Alexios needed troops. The Byzantines had long appreciated the martial qualities of the Franks, but had reason to fear their indiscipline and ambition. The main recruiting ground had been among the Normans of southern Italy, but a chance meeting in 1089 opened up a new source of Frankish cavalry. Robert I, count of Flanders, was returning overland from a pilgrimage to Jerusalem. He made a detour to pay his respects to Alexios I Komnenos, then in winter quarters in Bulgaria. He offered to send Alexios a force of 500 cavalry and sealed the bargain by taking 'the usual Latin oath' to the emperor. The count was as good as his word and the Flemish cavalry arrived the next year. They were sent to guard the area of Nikomedeia, but were then evacuated in 1091 in order to take part in the campaign against the Pechenegs which culminated in victory at Lebounion. They were an important addition to Alexios' forces at a critical moment. However, Alexios required more than a contingent of 500 Flemish cavalry if he was to have any chance of recovering Anatolia. He turned for help to Pope Urban II (1088–99), with whom he had been conducting negotiations over the reunion of the churches. Their outcome was inconclusive, but relations remained cordial. Urban II knew that his mentor Gregory VII (1073–85) had tried and failed to organise a papal expedition, which was to go to the rescue of Constantinople and then press on to Jerusalem. Whether Alexios knew about this too is another matter, but he was well aware of the importance to Latin Christians of Jerusalem. In the spring of 1095 Urban II held a council at Piacenza. Byzantine envoys were present and made a plea for papal aid against the Seljuqs, although the exact terms in which this plea was couched cannot now be recovered. Urban then held a council at Clermont in November 1095, where he made an appeal to the knighthood of France for an expedition to go to the rescue of eastern Christendom. The pope linked this with pilgrimage to Jerusalem and the attendant spiritual rewards. He fixed 15 August 1096 as the day of departure for Constantinople, which was to be the assembly-point.

The passage of the crusade was to present Alexios with huge problems. The numbers are not easy to estimate. Modern calculations vary from 30,000 to 70,000 soldiers – over 100,000 if non-combatants are included. The first contingents started to arrive in the early summer of 1096 with Peter the Hermit. They were perhaps less of a rabble than Anna Komnena would have us believe. The swiftness of their arrival took Alexios by surprise. He shipped them over to Asia Minor, where many were killed by the Turks. Alexios was better prepared for the crusading armies that followed in the autumn and winter of 1096. These were under the command of western princes, such as the dukes of Normandy and Lower Lorraine, the counts of Toulouse, Blois, Vermandois and Flanders, and worryingly, the Norman Bohemond. Alexios had had time to establish markets along the main routes to Constantinople. As the crusade leaders came one by one to Constantinople he was able to persuade them to take 'the customary Latin oath' to him, as the prospective leader of the expedition against the Turks. Raymond de Saint-Gilles, count of Toulouse, was the leader who gave him most trouble, refusing to take any oath to the emperor. Of all the crusade leaders he was the closest to Urban II. The pope had consulted him before making his appeal at Clermont and he was the first of the princes to take the cross. He also took a vow never to return from the east. The papal legate Adhemar of Le Puy was attached to his contingent. Raymond therefore had some claim to be the military leader of the crusade. The emperor had to be content with an alliance, whereby each agreed to respect the life and honour of the other.

The first task was to conquer Nicaea, now the headquarters of an emirate. The Turks preferred to surrender the city to the Byzantines rather than face the fury of the Franks. The fall of Nicaea opened the road leading up to the Anatolian plateau. Alexios had turned down the proposal made by the crusade leaders that he should take personal command of the expedition.

But he supplied an important contingent under the command of Tatikios, one of his most trusted commanders. Alexios' strategy was to encircle the Turks: the crusaders were to force a passage across Anatolia and establish control over Cilicia, the Euphrates lands and northern Syria, where there was still a reasonable basis for the restoration of Byzantine rule. At first all went according to plan and the crusaders won a great victory over the Turks on 1 July 1097 at Dorylaion on the edge of the Anatolian plateau. By the end of the summer they were encamped in Cilicia and had started to blockade Antioch. Alexios followed up the victory by conquering large parts of western and northern Asia Minor and pushing the Turks back to the Anatolian plateau (see below, p. 710).

But the period of cooperation was soon over. Ostensibly the stumbling block was control of Antioch, but tensions went much deeper than this. The hardships of the passage across Anatolia followed by those of the siege of Antioch transformed the crusade from a joint venture of Byzantium and the west into an ideology that was fixated on Jerusalem and quickly took on an anti-Byzantine stamp. Such was crusader hostility that the Byzantine commander Tatikios abandoned the siege of Antioch and returned to Byzantium. His withdrawal was taken as an act of betrayal. The crusaders' distrust of Byzantine intentions was then reinforced by Alexios' failure to go to their rescue. He had set out and reached Philomelion, a Byzantine outpost on the Anatolian plateau, when he was met by two of the leaders of the crusade who had fled from Antioch in despair. They told the emperor that all was lost. Alexios therefore turned back. This was the sensible thing to do, but in fact all was far from lost. Thanks to Bohemond the lower city was secured at the beginning of June 1098 and on 28 June the crusaders inflicted a crushing defeat on the Seljuq relief force. Bohemond secured possession of the city for himself, while the crusade moved on towards Jerusalem.

BOHEMOND'S EXPEDITION OF 1107–1108

Antioch, traditionally the main Byzantine centre of operations in the east, was vital to Alexios I Komnenos' plans for recovering Anatolia from the Turks. The crusade leaders had given Alexios an undertaking that they would return Byzantine cities and territories. This Bohemond was refusing to do. Alexios therefore set about trying to evict him from Antioch, and his forces had some success. They occupied Cilicia but the key point was the port of Latakia. In 1103 the Byzantines secured the lower city of Latakia and were endeavouring to dislodge the Normans from the citadel. Such was the pressure that in 1104 Bohemond decided to leave his nephew Tancred in charge of Antioch, while he returned to the west for reinforcements.

He won the backing of Pope Paschal II (1099–1118) and the support of the French king Philip I (1060–1108), whose daughter he married.

It remains an open question whether his expedition qualified as a 'crusade'. The final goal was Palestine, and Bohemond was accompanied by a papal legate. The pope presented him with the banner of St Peter and according to a contemporary, Bartolf of Nangis, appointed him 'standard-bearer of the army of Christ'.[31] Bohemond's propaganda stressed the treachery of Alexios towards the crusade as just cause for his invasion. Bohemond's expedition against Byzantium displayed many features of a crusade, but full recognition would depend on its outcome, simply because crusading theory was still in its infancy. But for Anna Komnena it was a different matter. She was clear that Bohemond's invasion not only had papal approval, but had also been accorded the status of a 'just war'.[32] It confirmed Byzantine apprehensions about the dangers that the crusade held in store.

Bohemond landed on the Albanian coast in 1107 and laid siege to Dyrrachium. Alexios deployed his forces in the surrounding mountains. Bohemond soon found himself in an impossible position, isolated in front of Dyrrachium with his escape by sea cut off by the Venetians, and Paschal II withdrew his support. In 1108 Bohemond sued for peace. He recognised Alexios as his overlord, accepting that he held the principality of Antioch from Alexios. On paper Alexios had won what he most wanted: recognition of his claims to Antioch. But the treaty remained a dead letter.[33] Bohemond returned to southern Italy, while his nephew Tancred continued to rule at Antioch and refused to countenance the concessions made to the Byzantine emperor. Alexios was in no position to enforce them. To meet Bohemond's invasion he had withdrawn his forces from Cilicia and Syria. This allowed the Seljuqs to regain the initiative in western Asia Minor. Alexios was unable to mount a major expedition against them until late in his reign. The aim of his expedition to Philomelion in 1116 was to evacuate from central Anatolia the Greek populations still living under Turkish rule. It was a tacit admission of defeat.

ALEXIOS I KOMNENOS' ACHIEVEMENTS AND FAILURE

Alexios' appeal to Urban II was brilliantly conceived, but Byzantium gained very little from the crusade. In its wake Byzantine forces recovered the rich coastlands of western Anatolia, which they might reasonably have expected

---

[31] Bartolf of Nangis, *Gesta Francorum*, ch. 65, p. 538.

[32] *Al.*, XII.8.5, ed. Reinsch and Kambylis, I, p. 380; ed. and French tr. Leib, III, p. 80; tr. Sewter, p. 390.

[33] For the treaty, see *Al.*, XIII.12, ed. Reinsch and Kambylis, I, pp. 413–23; ed. and French tr. Leib, III, pp. 125–39; tr. Sewter, pp. 424–34; Lilie (1993a), pp. 75–81. On the development of crusading ideas and practice, see Riley-Smith (2002); Tyerman (2004), pp. 95–124.

to achieve anyway. The shadow of 1204 looms over Alexios' achievements and calls in question the success of his restoration of the Byzantine empire. His reputation has also suffered among modern historians because of the *Alexiad*, his daughter Anna Komnena's history of his reign. It is judged to lack objectivity, being too obviously an exercise in filial piety and too much of an idealisation. It is all these things, but it also provides a consummate portrait of an age, which, when allowance is made for bias, carries conviction.[34] Anna Komnena's assessment of her father's greatness is borne out by his administrative and fiscal reforms and his church settlement, about which she has relatively little to say. These aspects of her father's reign have to be pieced together from the documentary sources. They provide the best evidence for Alexios' achievement in restoring the empire.

Anna Komnena breathes not a word about her father's appeal to Pope Urban II which triggered the crusade. This may have been because she did not know about it or because she did not connect her father's appeal with the crusade, but more probably, she was trying to protect her father's reputation. By the time she was writing – some thirty years after her father's death – it was apparent that the crusade was the cutting edge of western expansion. It was Alexios' task to come to terms with western encroachment, which had begun to make itself felt from the middle of the eleventh century and which took various forms. Least harmful appeared to be the commercial activities of Venetian and other Italian merchants. They offered a solution to Byzantium's need for naval assistance, and early in his reign Alexios engaged the services of the Venetian fleet. In 1082 he granted the Venetians special privileges in Constantinople and exemption from the payment of customs duties throughout the empire.[35] It appeared a very good bargain. In 1111 Alexios entered into a similar arrangement with the Pisans, reducing their customs duty to 4 per cent. He was angling for their support in his plans – which never came to anything – to bring the crusader states under Byzantine control. Alexios was using the Italians much as the emperors of the tenth century had used the Rus: to strengthen the empire's naval and commercial resources. The appeal to Urban II was intended to complement this by harnessing the military potential of the Franks. Alexios could not have imagined that it would trigger off a crusade, nor that this would cease to be a cooperative venture and be turned against Byzantium.

Within Byzantium the crusade not only hardened attitudes towards the west, it also created tensions. Opinion polarised between those who favoured continuing cooperation with the west and those who rejected this approach, preferring to fall back on 'splendid isolation'. This put added

[34] See the contributions to Gouma-Peterson (ed.) (2000).

[35] Frankopan (2004a) makes a better case that the chrysobull to the Venetians was reissued in 1092 by Alexios Komnenos than that it was originally granted in that year.

pressure on the fault-lines that existed within the Komnenian settlement: between the emperor and church; between autocracy and aristocracy; between the Komnenian ascendancy and the excluded; between the capital and the provinces. Alexios hoped that an understanding with the west would provide Byzantium with the additional resources needed to restore its position as a world power. He could not have foreseen how it would undermine Byzantium from within. This was the true nature of Alexios' failure. It was counterbalanced by his success in restoring the integrity of the imperial office and the soundness of imperial administration. For more than half a century after his death Byzantium remained a great power.

CHAPTER 17

THE EMPIRE OF THE KOMNENOI (1118–1204)

PAUL MAGDALINO

Between the death of Alexios I Komnenos and the establishment of the Latin empire of Constantinople, eight emperors ruled in the eastern Roman capital. Their reigns were as successful as they were long: under John II Komnenos (1118–43) and Manuel I Komnenos (1143–80) Byzantium remained a wealthy and expansionist power, maintaining the internal structures and external initiatives which were necessary to sustain a traditional imperial identity in a changing Mediterranean world of crusaders, Turks and Italian merchants.[1] But the minority of Manuel's son Alexios II Komnenos (1180–83) exposed the fragility of the regime inaugurated by Alexios I. Lateral branches of the reigning dynasty seized power in a series of violent usurpations that progressively undermined the security of each usurper, inviting foreign intervention, provincial revolts and attempted *coups d'état*. Under Andronikos I Komnenos (1183–5), Isaac II Angelos (1185–95), Alexios III Angelos (1195–1203), Alexios IV Angelos (1203–4) and Alexios V Doukas (1204), the structural features which had been the strengths of the state in the previous hundred years became liabilities. The empire's international web of clients and marriage alliances, its reputation for fabulous wealth, the overwhelming concentration of people and resources in Constantinople, the privileged status of the 'blood-royal', the cultural self-confidence of the administrative and religious elite: under strong leadership, these factors had come together to make the empire dynamic and great; out of control, they and the reactions they set up combined to make the Fourth Crusade a recipe for disaster.

The Fourth Crusade brought out the worst in the relationship between Byzantium and the west that had been developing in the century since the First Crusade; the violent conquest and sack of Constantinople expressed and deepened old hatreds, and there is clearly some sense in the standard opinion that the event confirmed beyond doubt how incompatible the two cultures had always been. Yet the Fourth Crusade also showed how central Byzantium had become to the world of opportunity that Latin Europe was

---

[1] For a re-evaluation of twelfth-century Byzantium, see Magdalino (1993a). The classic presentation of a bleaker, long influential view is Chalandon (1910–12), II.

discovering in the east, and how great an effort Byzantine rulers had made to use this position to advantage. Growing estrangement came from growing involvement; the xenophobia which manifested itself in the 1182 massacre of the Latins in Constantinople was the reverse side of the accommodation of westerners and their values taking place at all social and cultural levels. Both sides of the coin are reflected in the main source for the period, the *History* of Niketas Choniates, which combines impassioned outbursts against the Latins with idealisation of individual western leaders and disapproval of his own society in terms which echo western criticism of Byzantium.

SOURCES

Niketas Choniates' *History* covers the years 1118–1206. The author was a contemporary of most of the events he relates, and from about 1175 he was an increasingly close eyewitness of developments at the centre of power, first as a student and clerk in government service, then as a rising government official involved in the making and presentation of imperial policy. Such credentials, together with the power, the nuance, the acuity and the high moral tone of his narrative, make it difficult to resist seeing the period through his eyes. However, there is growing recognition that the very qualities which make Choniates a great literary commentator on his age also make him a sophisticated manipulator of the facts to fit his picture of a decadent society being punished by divine providence for the excesses of its rulers and the corruption of their subjects.[2] For the period 1118–76 his account can be balanced by the *History* of John Kinnamos, which is slightly more critical of John II and much more favourable to Manuel I, whom the author served for most of his reign.[3] Otherwise, as for earlier and later periods of Byzantine history, the picture has to be supplemented and corrected by a wide range of other material – literary, legislative, archival, epigraphic, visual. The balance of this material partly reflects and partly determines what makes the twelfth century look distinctive. It is richer than the preceding century in high-quality information from Latin chronicles, in rhetorical celebration of emperors and in canon law collections which preserve a wealth of imperial and patriarchal rulings.[4] The flow of documentation from Patmos and Mount Athos dries up for much of the period, though some material has been preserved from other monastic archives in Asia Minor and Macedonia, and the archives of Venice, Pisa and Genoa

---

[2] *ODB*, I, p. 428 (A. Kazhdan); Magdalino (1993a), pp. 3–22. See now Simpson (2006).
[3] *ODB*, II, p. 1130 (A. Kazhdan); Magdalino (1993a), pp. 18–20; Stephenson (1996).
[4] For the collections, see Macrides (1990); Macrides (1991) and other contributions to Oikonomides, (ed.) (1991); Macrides (1994). Evaluation of other written sources in Magdalino (1993a).

begin to yield substantial evidence for the movement of their merchants into Constantinople and other markets throughout the empire.[5]

JOHN II KOMNENOS (1118–1143)

Alexios I Komnenos (1081–1118) left his successor with a state in good working order. Territorially it was smaller, especially in the east, than the empire of the early eleventh century, but thanks to Alexios' reforms and good management over a long reign, it was once more an effective financial and military power, and as a result of Alexios' controversial family policy, it had a structural coherence which was largely new to Byzantium. After the failure of numerous conspiracies against Alexios, the ruling family of Komnenos had established itself not only as the unchallenged source of the imperial succession, but also, in association with the Doukai, as the centre of a new princely aristocracy in which wealth, status and military command depended on kinship to the emperor and were reflected in a hierarchy of titles all of which had originally applied to the emperor. The emperor's kinsmen were in such a dominant position, and so widely connected, that for almost the first time in the empire's history the threat to the ruling dynasty from a rival faction was entirely eliminated (see above, pp. 612–13). Instead, competition for power had moved inside the family circle.

The weakness of the system was that it gave the whole imperial family a share and a stake in the imperial inheritance without providing any firm rules of precedence. Thus John II, though Alexios' eldest son and crowned co-emperor in 1092, had to contend with a serious effort by his mother Irene Doukaina to exclude him from the succession in favour of his sister Anna and her husband Nikephoros Bryennios. Only by building up his own group of loyal supporters, inside and outside the family, and making a preemptive strike while Alexios lay on his deathbed did John secure his claim, and only by putting those supporters into key positions did he prevent a conspiracy by Anna within a year of his accession. To gain and maintain power, the emperor had had to create his own faction. He was well served by the members of this faction, especially by John Axouch, a Turkish captive with whom he had grown up and whom he entrusted with the supreme command of the armed forces. But the promotion of these favourites played

[5] For monastic evidence from Asia Minor, see MM, IV, pp. 62–3, 305–8, 317–29; Wilson and Darrouzès, 'Restes du cartulaire de Hiéra-Xérochoraphion', pp. 31–4; Ahrweiler (1965), pp. 5, 100, 127–9. For monastic evidence relating to Macedonia, see Petit, 'Le monastère de Notre Dame de Pitié'; Lefort (1985); Lefort (2005). For Italian evidence, see TT, I, pp. 67–74, 95–8, 109–33, 150–67, 177–203, 206–11, 215–16, 246–81; *Trattati con Bisanzio*, ed. Pozza and Ravegnani, pp. 47–137; *Documenti sulle relazioni delle città toscane*, ed. Müller, pp. 8–10, 11–13, 40–58, 66–73, 74–9; *Nuova serie di documenti sulle relazioni di Genova coll'Impero bizantino*, ed. Sanguineti and Bertolotto.

a part in causing the growth of an opposition at court. Anna and Nikephoros were no longer a threat; Nikephoros served the emperor loyally until his death in 1138, leaving Anna to nurse her grievances in writing the epic biography of her father, the *Alexiad*.[6] However, their place as a magnet for the disaffected was taken by John's brother, the *sebastokratōr* Isaac, who had supported John at their father's death, but in 1130 sought the throne for himself. When his plot was detected, he fled with his son John into exile among the empire's eastern neighbours, moving from court to court until he sought reconciliation in 1138. But his son again defected to the Turks in 1141, Isaac remained a prime political suspect and his other son, the future Andronikos I Komnenos, would later inherit his role.

John II's power base in Constantinople was secure enough to allow him to leave the City on campaign year after year, but this ceaseless campaigning, in which he surpassed most of his imperial predecessors, including his father, is indicative of his need to command the loyalty of the army and prove himself worthy of his inheritance. It was rarely necessitated by emergencies as serious as those Alexios had faced for most of his reign, and it was not clearly dictated by any pre-existing strategy of territorial expansion. Certainly, the recuperation of lost territory was high on the agenda which John took over from his father. The First Crusade had originated in a Byzantine attempt to reverse the Turkish occupation of Asia Minor and northern Syria, and for the last twenty years of his reign Alexios I had expended great military and diplomatic energies in pressing his claims to Antioch and other territories which the crusaders had appropriated (see above, pp. 623–4). Yet over the same twenty years, the empire had learned to live with the eastern borders which Alexios had established in the wake of the crusade and with the new Turkish dynastic states of the Danishmend *malik*s and the Seljuq sultans, which had formed in the lost territories of central and eastern Anatolia. The empire was left in control of the coastal plains and river valleys which were the most valuable parts of Asia Minor to a ruling elite based, more than ever, on Constantinople; the loss of the Anatolian plateau and the frontier regions of northern Mesopotamia, which had been the homeland of many military families, greatly facilitated the integration of the aristocracy into the Komnenian dynastic regime. Alexios' successor thus had to strike a balance between the completion of unfinished business and the consolidation of such gains as had been made. Either way, he was expected to produce victories, and these John delivered consistently. Their propaganda value was their most lasting result, and possibly their most important objective.

The year after his accession, John took and fortified the town of Laodicea in the Maeander valley; the next year he captured and garrisoned Sozopolis,

---

[6] See above, p. 625; contributions to Gouma-Peterson (ed.) (2000).

on the plateau to the east. This might have been the beginning of a campaign of reconquest against the Seljuq sultanate of Rum; on the other hand, both places lay on the land route to Antalya (Attaleia), and John's later interest in this area suggests that he might have been securing his lines of communication for an expedition to Antioch. Yet if Antioch was the goal, it is surprising that John did not simultaneously revive the negotiations for a dynastic union which Alexios had been conducting at the end of his reign, especially after the disastrous battle of the Field of Blood (1119); this first major crusading defeat at the hands of the Muslims provided an ideal opportunity for John to offer imperial protection in return for concessions. There is no evidence that John tried to take advantage of the crisis in the Latin east, as Venice did by joining the crusading movement. Indeed, the fact that John initially refused to renew his father's treaty with Venice, and did not change his mind even in 1122, when a Venetian armada passed through Byzantine waters on its way to Palestine, suggests that the new emperor was pursuing a policy of deliberate isolationism with regard to the Latin world. Only when the Venetian fleet ravaged Chios, Samos and Modon on its return journey in 1125 did John agree to renew the treaty. This he did in 1126, acceding to two further Venetian demands.[7]

Meanwhile, John had been forced to turn his attention from Asia to Europe by an invasion of the Pechenegs which caused great alarm but which he defeated by resolute military action in 1122. No campaigns are recorded for the next five years, during which John became occupied by diplomatic relations not only with Venice but also with Hungary, where he was connected through his wife to the ruling Árpád dynasty. In 1125 he welcomed her kinsman Almos as a refugee from the king of Hungary, Stephen II. Stephen took offence at this support for a political rival, and he may have felt threatened by the Byzantine rapprochement with Venice, which disputed Hungary's dominion over the cities of the Dalmatian coast. There followed a two-year war: Stephen attacked the imperial border fortresses and stirred the Serbs into revolt, while John retaliated by leading two expeditions to the Danube to restore the status quo.

When in 1130 John II returned to campaigning in Asia Minor, it was with a new objective: the northern sector of the frontier, where the imperial position in Bithynia and along the Black Sea was being eroded by the aggressive Danishmend polity, and by the defections of the Greek magnates who controlled much of the littoral. For six years the emperor led expeditions into

[7] Crete and Cyprus were added to the list of places where the Venetians could trade without paying taxes, and Byzantines with whom they did business were now exempted from paying the *kommerkion* or any other taxes on their transactions: TT, I, pp. 95–8. See also Lilie (1984b), pp. 374–5; Nicol (1988), pp. 80–1; Laiou and Morrisson (2007), p. 144.

Paphlagonia. The Byzantine sources highlight the successful sieges of Kastamonu (twice) and Gangra, thus giving the impression that this was a war
of reconquest. But these and other gains in the area were soon retaken after
the emperor's departure and it is difficult to believe that John realistically
expected to be able to hold them with the modest garrisons that he could
afford to leave behind (see below, p. 711). On balance, it seems that the
aim was to make a show of force, to raid the flocks of the Turkish nomads
in retaliation for past depredations and to impress all in Constantinople
and in the imperial entourage whose loyalty was wavering. For John's first
campaign against the Danishmends was cut short by the conspiracy of his
brother Isaac, and it was to these Turks that Isaac fled to avoid arrest in 1130.
A year or two later, John abandoned another campaign in order to deal with
a plot to put Isaac on the throne. In the circumstances, it is not surprising
that the emperor's subsequent successes were advertised to maximum effect
and that he celebrated the taking of Kastamonu by a triumphal entry into
Constantinople, to the accompaniment of panegyrical songs and speeches
(1133). These celebrations set the tone for the extravagant glorification of
imperial achievements that was to characterise the imperial image for the
rest of the century.

Isaac's movements in exile, which took him from Melitene to Armenia,
Cilicia, Ikonion and Jerusalem, help to explain why, from 1135, John II made
larger plans for political and military intervention further east. The opportunity arose when Alice, the widow of Bohemond II of Antioch, offered
their daughter Constance in marriage to John's youngest son Manuel. The
offer was a desperate and doomed attempt to prevent Constance from
marrying Raymond of Poitiers, to whom she had been promised, but it
encouraged John to focus on Antioch as the key to the strategy for dealing
with all the empire's eastern neighbours, Muslim and Christian. Raymond's
marriage to Constance in 1136 provided a justification for military action in
support of imperial claims to Cilicia and Antioch. An imperial expedition in
1137 succeeded in reconquering Cilicia from the Armenian Rupenid prince
Leo I, who held the mountainous areas, and from the Latins, who held the
cities of the plain, Adana, Mopsuestia and Tarsus. John also compelled the
new prince of Antioch to become his vassal, to allow him right of entry
into the city, and to hand it over in return for investiture with the cities of
the Syrian interior – Aleppo, Shaizar, Homs and Hama – once these were
recaptured from the Muslims.

The subsequent campaign to take these cities failed, and so did the
emperor's attempt to use the excuse to take possession of Antioch. But
overall, the performance of the imperial army and the deference shown by
all the local rulers were a triumphant demonstration of the empire's and
the emperor's power. According to Niketas Choniates, it had the effect
of making John II's exiled brother Isaac seek a reconciliation, 'for lacking

money . . . and seeing the emperor John universally renowned for his feats in battle, he found no one who would fall in with his ambitions'.[8] During the following years, John returned to Asia Minor, to strengthen the frontier defences in Bithynia, to strike at Neocaesarea, the town from which the Danishmends threatened the eastern section of the Black Sea coastal strip, and to secure and extend imperial control in the southern sector of the frontier in western Asia Minor. Yet these last operations, in the area where he had conducted his earliest campaigns, were clearly a prelude to the new expedition to Syria which he launched at the end of 1142. He wintered in the mountains of Cilicia, preparing to strike at Antioch in the spring and from there to go on to Jerusalem.

The emperor's death from a hunting accident in February 1143 aborted what looks like the most ambitious attempt at restoring the pre-Islamic empire that any Byzantine ruler had undertaken since the tenth century. John was finally making up for Alexios' failure to take personal command of the First Crusade. With the wisdom of hindsight, we may question whether the course of history would have been very different if John had lived. Constant campaigning and drilling had made the Byzantine field army into a superb expeditionary force with an unrivalled siege capability, but John II had pushed its performance to the limit. It had consistently run into problems when operating beyond the empire's borders and rarely held on to its acquisitions. In addition to the standard logistical constraints of medieval warfare, there was the basic problem that the empire was frequently unwelcome in many of its former territories, even among the Greeks of Turkish-occupied Asia Minor. John had, moreover, developed the army at the expense of the navy. However, Cilicia had remained in imperial control since 1138. If John had succeeded in his aim of welding Antioch and Cilicia together with Cyprus and Antalya into a kingdom for his son Manuel, the benefits to the empire and to the crusader states would have been enormous; at the very least, if the imperial army had remained in Syria throughout 1143, the emperor would have formed a coalition of local Christians that would have checked the Islamic counter-crusade of *atabey* Zengi (1127–46) of Aleppo and thus postponed, or even prevented, the fall of Edessa and the calling of the Second Crusade.

The revival of imperial interest in the crusader states had permanent consequences in that it led to a renewal of Byzantine links with western Europe. During the first half of his reign, John had retreated from the active western diplomacy that Alexios had conducted. But this changed in 1135, when John revived imperial claims to Antioch and sought to cover his back against interference from Roger II of Sicily (1130–54), who also had an interest in the principality. He renewed the empire's treaty with Pisa,

---

[8] NC, ed. van Dieten, I, p. 32; tr. Magoulias, p. 19.

Figure 48 Monastery of Christ Pantokrator, Constantinople

negotiated alliances with the German emperors Lothar III (1125–37) and
Conrad III (1138–52), and sent a very conciliatory letter to Pope Innocent II
(1130–43) on the subject of church union. Most importantly for the future,
the alliance with Conrad III was sealed by the betrothal of Conrad's sister-
in-law Bertha to John's youngest son Manuel. Manuel not only happened
to be available; he had also been proposed as a husband for the heiress to
Antioch, and was the intended ruler of the projected kingdom of Antioch,
Cilicia, Cyprus and Antalya.

Apart from the conspiracies of his sister and brother, the internal history
of John's reign looks conspicuously uneventful. On the whole, it seems
fair to conclude that the paucity of documentation generally reflects a
lack of intervention or of the need for it. As with the frontiers, it was a
case of maintaining internal structures that had stabilised in the last ten
years of Alexios' reign. John's most significant policy change was to reduce
expenditure on the fleet, on the advice of his finance minister John of
Poutza. Although he looked outside his family for individual support, John
upheld the ascendancy of the Komnenoi and Doukai, and continued to
consolidate their connections by marriage with other aristocratic families. In
the church, he was by Byzantine standards remarkably non-interventionist,
apparently because church affairs had settled down after the disputes of
Alexios' reign. He left his mark on them principally through generous
benefactions to churches and monasteries, above all through his foundation
of the monastery of Christ Pantokrator. The foundation charter and the
church buildings provide the best surviving picture of the appearance, the
organisation and the wealth of a great metropolitan monastery and its
annexes, which included a hospital.[9]

---

[9] 'Le Typikon du Christ Pantocrator', ed. and French tr. Gautier, pp. 26–131. See also *ODB*, III,
p. 1575 (A.-M. Talbot and A. Cutler); Ousterhout (1999), pp. 104–8 and figs. 78, 79, pp. 120–1; Freely
and Çakmak (2004), pp. 211–20 and plates XXX, XXXI.

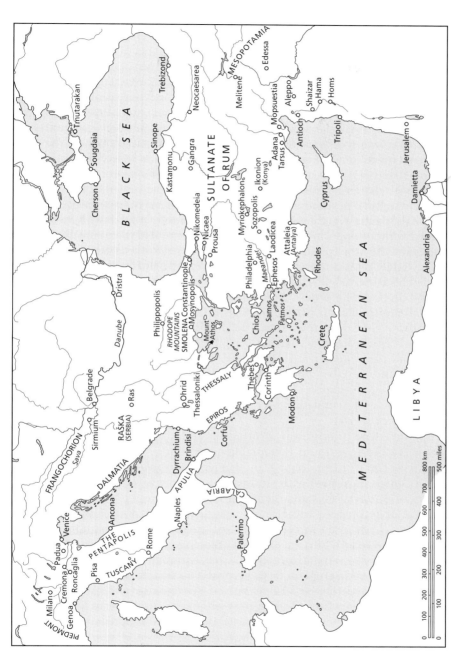

Map 28 The empire and its neighbours in the twelfth century

MANUEL I KOMNENOS (1143–1180)

For most of his reign, John had managed to prevent his own children from being divided by the sibling rivalries which had bedevilled his own succession. Yet in the months before his death, his arrangements were thrown into confusion when Alexios, his eldest son and co-emperor of long standing, fell ill and died, followed shortly by the next son, Andronikos. This left John, on his deathbed, with a highly invidious choice between his older surviving son, Isaac, who was in Constantinople, and the youngest, Manuel, who was with him in Cilicia. John no doubt voiced many of the arguments for Manuel's superiority which the Byzantine sources put into his mouth, but it is hard to fault the explanation of William of Tyre that Manuel was chosen in order to ensure the army's safe return.[10] Prompt action forestalled any attempt by Isaac to take advantage of his presence in the capital. Manuel was thus able to enter Constantinople and have himself crowned without opposition. As the winner, he was able to command or commission the propaganda which represented his election as providential and inevitable. Yet Isaac nursed a legitimate grievance, and his sympathisers included his father's right-hand man, John Axouch. Isaac was not the only one who coveted his brother's throne: their brother-in-law, the caesar John Roger, attempted a coup, backed by a faction of Norman exiles, and their uncle Isaac was believed to be still awaiting his opportunity. Even apparently innocuous female relatives, Manuel's aged aunt Anna and his widowed sister-in-law Irene, were treated as political suspects. The new emperor was unmarried and therefore without immediate prospect of legitimate issue. All in all, the circumstances of his accession put him under intense pressure to prove himself by emulating his father's achievements without putting his inheritance at risk.

The immediate priority was to bring the unfinished foreign business of John II's last years to an honourable conclusion. There could be no question of the emperor leading another grand expedition to Syria, so Manuel contented himself with sending an army and a fleet to ravage the territory of Antioch. This and the fall of Edessa to Zengi in 1144 obliged Raymond of Antioch to come to Constantinople and swear obedience, while Manuel promised to come to the prince's aid. There was also the matter of the German alliance. Manuel's marriage to Bertha of Sulzbach had been negotiated and she had come to Constantinople, before he had any prospect of becoming emperor. It was probably to extract more favourable terms from Conrad III that Manuel put off the marriage and exchanged embassies with Roger II of Sicily, against whom the alliance with Conrad had been directed. When he finally married Bertha, who adopted the Greek

<hr>

[10] William of Tyre, *Chronicon*, XV.23, ed. Huygens, II, pp. 705–6; tr. Babcock and Krey, II, pp. 128–9.

name Irene, in 1146 he had evidently won some sort of unwritten promise from Conrad, possibly to guarantee Manuel a free hand in the east, but more likely to give him a share of the conquests from his planned invasion of southern Italy.

These treaties opened up commitments and prospects which Manuel did not immediately pursue. Instead, he used the security they gave him to revert to the limited-objective campaigning against the Turks which had characterised his father's reign, with even more emphasis on military victory for its own sake. The expedition which he led as far as Ikonion in 1146 was ostensibly in retaliation for the capture of a border fortress in Cilicia. In effect, however, it was a display of the emperor's prowess in leading his army up to the walls of the sultan's capital and then fighting courageous rearguard actions in the retreat. This gratuitous bravery was intended to vindicate Manuel's youthful heroism in the eyes of his critics. It may also have been meant to impress the Latins with the emperor's zeal for holy war. But it did nothing to help the crusader states, and that help now came in a form which exposed Manuel's lack of a strategy for dealing with the fall of Edessa and the repercussions this was bound to have in the wider world of Latin Christendom. The fact that the Byzantine sources fail to mention the event which provoked the Second Crusade suggests that they seriously underestimated its importance.

The Second Crusade would have been a major military and political crisis even if it had been confined to the expedition of Louis VII of France (1137–80), as Manuel was originally led to expect. The size of Louis' army, his royal status, which precluded any oath of vassalage to the emperor, and the ties which bound him and his entourage to the nobility of the Latin east were sufficient to thwart any effective concordance between Byzantine claims and crusader objectives. The problem was more than doubled by the unexpected participation of Conrad III with an equally huge army and an even touchier sense of sovereign dignity. His arrival in the east strained their alliance almost to breaking point, since it brought the German emperor-elect where Manuel least wanted him from where he needed him most, namely as a threat to Roger II of Sicily. Roger now exploited the situation to seize the island of Corfu and launch raids on the Greek mainland, whose garrisons had been redeployed to shadow the crusading armies. It was alarmingly reminiscent of earlier Norman invasions of Epiros, and Manuel responded by calling on Venetian naval help, in return for which he renewed Venice's trade privileges and extended the Venetian quarter in Constantinople.[11]

In these circumstances, it is understandable that Manuel moved the crusading armies as quickly as possible across the Bosporus into Asia Minor, where the treaty of peace that he had signed with the sultan of Rum may

---

[11] TT, I, pp. 109–24; Nicol (1988), pp. 85–9. On the quarter: Jacoby (2001b), pp. 156–8.

well have contributed to the appalling casualties they suffered at the hands of the Turks. These casualties, which rendered the armies largely ineffective by the time they reached Syria and Palestine, earned Manuel a lasting reputation as the saboteur of the Second Crusade. However, they did lead eventually to a renewal of the alliance with Conrad III, who, when he fell ill at Ephesos in December 1147, accepted Manuel's invitation to come and recuperate in Constantinople. Manuel then provided ships and money for Conrad to continue to Palestine and recruit a new army. On his return to Europe late in 1148, the two monarchs met at Thessaloniki to agree on a joint invasion and partition of southern Italy and Sicily. The Byzantine share was to count as the dowry owing to Manuel from his marriage to Bertha-Irene. The alliance was sealed by the marriage of Manuel's niece Theodora to Conrad's cousin Henry of Babenberg.

The renewal of the German alliance determined the principal orientation of Manuel's foreign policy for the rest of his reign. For the next twelve years he remained committed to a partnership with the Hohenstaufen which he hoped would bring substantial territorial gains in Italy. Manuel pursued this goal despite setbacks and distractions, and despite the gradual divergence of interests between the two empires after Conrad III died and was succeeded by Frederick I Barbarossa (1152–90). As soon as Manuel had recovered Corfu from its Sicilian garrison in 1149, he planned to carry the war into Italy. The invasion plan was frustrated, first by bad weather, and then by wars in the Balkans stirred up by the disruptive diplomacy of Roger II. Thus the campaigns which Manuel led from 1150 to 1155 against the Serbian *župans* of Raška and King Géza II of Hungary were essentially diversions, for all the energy he put into them and the considerable publicity they generated. However, the war at sea continued and upon the death of Roger II in 1154 Manuel moved to take advantage of the insecurity and unpopularity of the young William I of Sicily (1154–66), reviving the invasion plan of 1149. Lacking German participation, the campaign eventually came to grief at Brindisi in 1156, and Frederick disowned it as a Greek initiative which interfered with his own programme of Roman imperial renewal. Yet for a time, the Byzantine agents had enjoyed great success, receiving the cooperation of disaffected Norman lords and the submission of many towns throughout Apulia. Manuel did not act as if either the German alliance or the prospect of a Byzantine revival in Italy had been destroyed by the defeat. His agents returned to sow disaffection against William I in 1157, and he continued to seek collaboration with Frederick Barbarossa even after he had concluded a peace treaty with William in 1158. In 1160, they were still exchanging embassies to discuss joint action against Sicily, and a Byzantine request for a share of imperial dominion in the Italian peninsula.

Manuel's basic and consistent objective was the acquisition of the coastal towns of Apulia; they had Greek populations, had belonged to the theme of

Langobardia before 1071, and control of them would prevent the recurrence of invasions like those of Robert Guiscard, Bohemond and Roger II.[12] Beyond that, Byzantine territorial aims in Italy were flexible, and by 1160 it seems that Manuel had traded his empire's historic claims to Calabria and the Naples area in return for the recognition of a right to the Pentapolis, the area comprising the city of Ancona and its hinterland. Ancona was the Byzantine base of operations in 1155–6, and it had been chosen for this purpose in 1149. It may well, therefore, have been designated in the treaty of 1148 between Conrad and Manuel as belonging to the Byzantine sphere of influence. Justification for the Byzantine claim could have been found in the fact that the Pentapolis had been part of the old exarchate of Ravenna (see above, pp. 449–53). While the coastal towns of Apulia were ruled by the king of Sicily, Ancona was the only alternative to Venice as a gateway for Byzantine agents, envoys, troops and subsidies to reach the empire's Italian and German allies – and Venice was basically opposed to any Byzantine revival in Italy. Once the coastal towns of Apulia also reverted to Byzantine rule, possession of the Pentapolis would have given Manuel control of almost the entire east coast of Italy.

The failure of his negotiations with Frederick Barbarossa in 1160 caused Manuel to try an alternative to the German alliance, which was coming under strain for other reasons. Frederick's increasingly strident imperialism made him less receptive to the idea of sharing sovereignty in Italy with the Greek empire. Indeed, his programme of reclaiming imperial rights, which he had stated at the diet of Roncaglia in 1158 and showed every sign of enforcing, threatened to change the balance of power in Italy and make the Hohenstaufen empire the main danger to Byzantium's western flank. At the same time, his quarrel with Pope Hadrian IV (1154–59), and his refusal to recognise the canonical election of Hadrian's successor, Alexander III (1159–81), made him an embarrassment for Manuel's relations with other parts of Latin Christendom, particularly the crusader states. Above all, the bond of kinship between the two emperors was severed when Manuel's German wife Bertha-Irene died in 1159.

From 1161, Manuel aligned himself with Pope Alexander III and all who took his side against Frederick and the antipope elected by Frederick's council of Pavia in 1160. Thus relations between Byzantium and Alexander's main European supporter, Louis VII of France, began to improve for the first time since the Second Crusade. Manuel's main diplomatic priority, however, was to cultivate close relations with all those in the Italian peninsula who, like Alexander, felt threatened by Frederick's expansionism. Chief among them was the king of Sicily, and Manuel twice entered into negotiations with a view to marrying his daughter to William I's son,

---

[12] See Magdalino (1993a), pp. 57–61.

William II (1166–89). But Manuel also poured money into creating an extensive web of potential supporters among the towns and the aristocracy throughout Italy. Byzantine money helped to rebuild the walls of Milan, razed at Frederick's orders in 1162. To the pope himself, Manuel not only gave material support but offered the prospect of reuniting the Greek and Roman churches, and several discussions were held. In return, the pope gave Manuel to understand that he would consider recognising him as sole Roman emperor.[13]

This ambition seems like a vastly unrealistic escalation of Manuel's previous aims, but it is unlikely to have involved any major political changes, other than excluding Frederick Barbarossa from Italy and giving Manuel the senior place among the rulers of Christendom. For the pope to entertain the notion, it must have been predicated on a guarantee to maintain the status quo in Italy: the continued existence of the communes in the north, the papal lordship in the centre and the kingdom of Sicily in the south. It is far from certain that the arrangement would have involved any territorial concessions such as Manuel had sought from the Hohenstaufen. The ulterior aim of Manuel's diplomacy after 1160 may have been to pressurise Frederick Barbarossa into renewing the alliance. The prospect of renewing it in 1170–2 was certainly enough to make Manuel pull out of a marriage treaty with William II of Sicily for what he thought was a better offer from Frederick. The offer did not materialise, and the 'cold war' resumed, but the episode demonstrated that what Manuel sought above all was a partnership with the sovereign powers of the Christian west that would guarantee security for his empire within negotiated territorial limits. In the papal alliance as in the Hohenstaufen alliance, Italy was the focus for negotiation, and Ancona remained the Byzantine gateway to Italy.

The peace of Venice in 1177, in which Frederick Barbarossa and Alexander III settled their differences and Italian affairs without reference to Manuel, put an end to the latter's hopes of either territorial gains in Italy or a western imperial crown. However, it was neither the end of his diplomacy nor of his deeper ambition to align his dynastic programme of imperial restoration with the power structure of Latin Christendom from which his empire had been perilously excluded at the time of the Second Crusade. That ambition was as close to being realised at his death in 1180 as it would ever be. He had failed to secure a working relationship with Frederick Barbarossa, but he remained on good terms with Alexander III, his daughter had married Renier of Montferrat, from the major magnate family of north-western Italy, and his son was betrothed to the king of France's daughter.

On other fronts, while Manuel did not neglect the security and the extension of the empire's borders, his initiatives were ultimately shaped by

---

[13] Further details in Magdalino (1993a), pp. 83–92.

the aim of being taken into partnership by the great powers of the west. The crusader states provided an ideal opportunity for him to enhance his credentials in western eyes. The disaster of the Second Crusade had left them increasingly vulnerable to Zengi's successor, Nur al-Din (1146–74), who had taken over Damascus following the failed crusader offensive, and had made the kings of the west wary of getting involved in a major new expedition to the Holy Land. Although they were responsive to the plight of the Latin settlers, their own domestic problems and mutual rivalries kept them in Europe, while the armed pilgrimages undertaken by some of their vassals did not properly compensate for the lack of a general crusade. In the circumstances, the princes of Outremer turned increasingly to Byzantium for military and financial aid and the Byzantine emperor was only too pleased to avoid the recurrence of a general crusade.[14]

Soon after the Second Crusade, the northern principalities suffered a crisis: Raymond of Edessa was killed in battle in 1149 and Joscelin II of Edessa was captured a year later. Manuel bought the remaining castles of the county of Edessa from Joscelin's wife and attempted to persuade Raymond's widow Constance to marry his recently widowed brother-in-law, the half-Norman caesar John Roger. However, the castles soon fell to the Muslims, and Constance rejected John Roger in favour of Reynald de Châtillon, a recent arrival from France. Neither these failures nor Reynald's subsequent raid on Byzantine Cyprus in conjunction with Thoros II (1148–68), the Armenian prince of Cilicia, drew an immediate response from Manuel, who was occupied with the war with Sicily. Only when this was over did the emperor intervene personally with a show of force. Moreover, his expedition to Cilicia and Syria in 1158–9 was not, despite superficial resemblances, a repeat of those conducted by his father. It followed the conclusion of a marriage alliance with Baldwin III, king of Jerusalem (1143–63), who in 1157 broke with crusader precedent and sought a bride from the Byzantine imperial family. Thus the reassertion of imperial supremacy in Cilicia and Antioch, and the humiliation of Reynald and Thoros, were performed with the full cooperation of the senior potentate in Outremer, who accepted them as the ritual price the Latin settlers had to pay for Byzantine material aid, and as the necessary prelude to joint military action against Nur al-Din by all the local Christian powers.

Although this action was cut short when Manuel was recalled to Constantinople by news of a conspiracy, he continued to work closely with the crusader states. It was to Tripoli, and then to Antioch, that he looked for a new bride after Bertha-Irene's death in 1159. He married Maria of Antioch, daughter of Raymond and Constance, in 1161, and some fifteen years later strengthened his connection with her brother, Prince Bohemond III

---

[14] Phillips (1996).

(1163–1201), by providing the latter with a Komnenian bride. The connection with Jerusalem was briefly interrupted at Baldwin III's death in 1163 but resumed when the king's brother and successor, Amalric I (1163–74), decided he could not do without Byzantine aid and negotiated a marriage to another imperial relative in 1167. Following a treaty in 1168, a Byzantine naval force joined Amalric in an invasion of Egypt in 1169, and the king came to Constantinople to negotiate a fresh agreement in 1171. The resulting plans for further joint operations against Egypt were halted upon Amalric's death in 1174, but were back on the agenda in 1176–7, when a Byzantine fleet was despatched to Palestine. These ventures came to nothing militarily, but they proved that the empire would deploy impressive resources in offensive as well as defensive support of its Latin allies, and thus undoubtedly helped to impede the counter-crusade of Nur al-Din and Saladin. Manuel further bolstered the Latin settlements both by providing their princes with generous subsidies, and by ransoming their knights who were captured in battle. In return, the emperor asked only for due recognition of his overlordship, and for fulfilment of the long-standing treaty agreement to appoint a Greek patriarch in Antioch.

Despite his considerable investment in Latin Syria, Manuel did not revisit the area after 1159. On the other hand, he returned more than once to the Danube frontier after King Géza II of Hungary died in 1161, leaving a disputed succession. The position of Hungary between the German and Byzantine empires, and adjacent to the empire's Serbian vassals, gave it a strategic importance in Manuel's growing conflict of interest with Frederick Barbarossa, which increased his concern to ensure that it was in friendly hands. His kinship with the Hungarian royal dynasty via his mother, and the empire's historic claim to certain frontier areas of the kingdom, also incited his intervention in Hungarian affairs (see below, pp. 684–5). Although Manuel initially failed to install his first candidate, Stephen IV, repeated campaigning from 1162 to 1167 ensured the future succession of his next protégé, Béla III, and the cession to the empire of Béla's patrimony, consisting of the central Dalmatian coast and an area south of the middle Danube known as Frangochorion, which included the old Roman frontier capital of Sirmium. Béla III lived in Constantinople from 1164, where he was betrothed to Manuel's daughter Maria and regarded as heir apparent to the throne until the birth of the emperor's son Alexios in 1169. He took power in Hungary at the death of his brother Stephen III in 1172 and served the empire loyally while Manuel was alive.

On the empire's other land frontier, in Asia Minor, Manuel's preferred policy was similarly one of trying to maintain and improve the status quo by drawing the main regional power, the sultanate of Rum, into the imperial orbit. After some fighting in 1159–60, Manuel welcomed the sultan, Kilij Arslan II (1156–92), to Constantinople in 1161. The two rulers concluded

Figure 49 Manuel I Komnenos and his second wife Maria of Antioch; the shade of Manuel's skin corresponds with contemporary reports concerning his swarthy complexion

a treaty whereby the emperor ritually adopted the sultan as his son and undertook to subsidise his wars against his Turkish rivals; in return, any important cities recovered from the latter were to be surrendered to the emperor, and the sultan promised to prevent raids on the empire's territories. Kilij Arslan did not keep his side of the treaty, which effectively allowed him to unify Turkish Asia Minor under his rule. But it brought peace to western Anatolia for fourteen years, and it set up an effective Islamic rival to the rising power of *atabey* Nur al-Din of Damascus, which helped the crusader states. Only when the death of Nur al-Din in 1174 changed the configuration of power in the Islamic world did Manuel adopt a policy of confrontation with Kilij Arslan, building fortresses on the Anatolian plateau to control the routes to the east in 1175, and then mounting a major expedition to conquer the sultan's capital of Ikonion in the following year.

It is clear from the publicity surrounding Manuel's offensive in Asia Minor that it was not only a belated move from appeasement to reprisal, but also a holy war intended to restore Asia Minor to imperial rule and open up the land route for pilgrims to Palestine. The grand expedition of 1176 was thus, above all, the culmination of Manuel's long attempt to redeem the failure of the Second Crusade, which had come to grief in the borderlands of Asia Minor. It was meant to finish, under imperial leadership, the business that had got out of imperial control in the First Crusade. The resounding defeat which the expedition suffered at Myriokephalon was correspondingly devastating for Manuel's attempt to take over the crusading movement and to reverse a century of Turkish occupation in Asia Minor (see below, pp. 716–17). Yet the empire's army, finances and borders were intact; its power in the Balkans and its influence in eastern Europe had never stood higher. Louis VII of France gave a big vote of confidence by sending his daughter Agnes as a future bride for the young Alexios II Komnenos (1180–3). There is no knowing how things would have developed if Manuel had not died only four years after the battle.

Manuel conducted his warfare and his diplomacy with lavish ceremony and rhetorical publicity which explicitly recalled Constantine and Justinian. This and the autocratic style which he adopted in his legislation and regulation of church doctrine led Niketas Choniates to assert, and modern scholars to accept, that Manuel dreamed the impossible dream of restoring the Roman empire in all its ancient glory. Careful attention to the reality behind the rhetorical and ceremonial image reveals that Manuel's Roman imperialism was more concerned with security than expansion.[15] It is true that at different times he sought the elimination of the two main neighbouring states, the Norman kingdom of Sicily and the Seljuq sultanate of Rum, which had recently been founded at the empire's expense. However, he did not do so consistently and he acted only within the framework of an alliance. Manuel's imperialism only began to depart from tradition after 1160, when he was obliged to seek an alternative to the German alliance. The main departure (though even this had precedents) was that instead of following the time-honoured practice of weakening the empire's neighbours by setting them against each other or destabilising their regimes, Manuel sought to establish a ring of reliable satellite kingdoms which he strengthened against their enemies in return for their support. The kingdom of Jerusalem, Hungary, the sultanate and the kingdom of Sicily were all tried in this role to a greater or lesser extent.

---

[15] NC, ed. van Dieten, I, pp. 100, 159–60; tr. Magoulias, pp. 58, 91. See Magdalino (1993a).

In general, it seems clear that Manuel sought allies and clients more than he sought territories. As we have seen, he hoped that the German alliance would give him control over the Adriatic coast of Italy, while from Hungary he gained Frangochorion and the Dalmatian coast. Otherwise, apart from his rather belated crusade of reconquest in Asia Minor, his main identifiable objective was the coastal area of Egypt, which was to be the Byzantine share in the partition of the country agreed between Manuel and Amalric in 1168 and, presumably, in later renewals of their treaty. This was hardly a programme to restore the empire of Justinian. At the same time, it was more than random opportunism. The Egyptian coast, including the ports of Alexandria and Damietta, was the most sought-after trading destination in the Mediterranean. Possession of the east coast of Italy together with possession of the Dalmatian coast would have given the empire control of the Adriatic and thus of the access to eastern markets from Venice, the main trading city in the Mediterranean.

Realisation of all these territorial goals would have allowed the empire to dominate the commerce of the eastern Mediterranean and thus to renegotiate its treaties with the Italian maritime republics. That this was indeed Manuel's aim is suggested, first, by his considerable investment in the Byzantine navy, and, secondly, by the evolution of his policy towards Venice, an evolution which parallels his adoption of a less indulgent line in dealing with the Byzantine church, the other main beneficiary of economic privilege. In 1148, during the crisis of the Second Crusade, he had extended the already exceptional privileges enjoyed by Venetian merchants throughout the empire, but in 1171 he ordered their arrest and the confiscation of their goods. The Pisans and Genoese to some extent took their place, but not with the same exemption from the 10 per cent sales tax. Pisa was unable to negotiate an improvement to the terms of its original treaty with Alexios I (see above, p. 625), which had allowed a total exemption only on bullion exports, and a 6 per cent reduction on imports of other goods. The Genoese were originally admitted on the same basis in 1155, but had to accept further restrictions on the 6 per cent concession in 1169.[16]

In the light of recent work on Byzantium in the eleventh and twelfth centuries, it is clear that Manuel's power was more impressive and his ambitions more moderate than previously thought. However, his achievements still fell short of his ambitions, and his military failures against Sicily and the Turks were spectacular, perhaps more so than his successes against Hungary. The empire declined so rapidly after his death that historians from Niketas Choniates onwards have sought, and continue to seek, the seeds of its decline in his reign and in his policies. Modern commentators have also

---

[16] Lilie (1984b), pp. 76–8, 84–100; Day (1988), pp. 25–7, 135–8; Magdalino (1993a), p. 94. On the role of Italian merchants in Byzantium, see Laiou and Morrisson (2007), pp. 143–7.

looked for structural weaknesses in the imperial regime of the Komnenian dynasty.

THE LEGACY AND SUCCESSORS OF MANUEL I: 1180–1204

Choniates believed that the empire and its rulers had incurred God's displeasure by their impious behaviour, and he identified the beginnings of this sinfulness in Manuel – in the emperor's belief in astrology, in his jealousy of popular and talented nobles, in his extravagant expenditure, in his favouritism towards kinsmen and foreigners and in his assumption of authority in church matters.[17] These were flaws that Manuel could be seen, with hindsight, to have shared with the emperors who reigned after him with obviously disastrous effect. But in picking on these characteristics, Choniates also undoubtedly echoed criticisms which had surfaced during Manuel's lifetime. His military failures in Italy and Asia Minor, together with his failure to produce a male heir by his first wife or in the first eight years of his second marriage, must have led to speculation that he had offended God by his style of government, and the speculation would have been encouraged by those male relatives, notably Manuel's cousin Andronikos, who were suspected of harbouring designs on the throne. Thus the insecurity which Manuel had faced at his accession stayed with him throughout his reign, and the soundness of his imperial edifice was already under scrutiny during his lifetime. The imperial image projected by the voluminous court rhetoric of his reign seems altogether too confident to be plausible.[18]

Yet on the whole the image commanded respect from foreigners and subjects alike. Manuel controlled his subjects, his resources and his policies as well as any of his imperial predecessors or royal contemporaries. What he did not control was beyond the control of any ruler: the tender age at which his son succeeded him. The crisis of Byzantium after 1180 was in a very obvious way the familiar story of a monarchy thrown into disarray by a minority.

However, Byzantium had experienced minorities in the past without falling apart and falling prey to foreign conquest. Is there a case for thinking that the disasters of the period 1180–1204 were waiting to happen, inherent in the structure of the empire of the Komnenoi? In the mid-twentieth century, the view prevailed that although the Komnenian emperors gave the empire a temporary reprieve by their vigorous military leadership, their aristocratic dynastic priorities undermined the efficacy of the state system

---

[17] NC, ed. van Dieten, I, pp. 143, 154, 179, 204–5, 209–21; tr. Magoulias, pp. 81, 87, 101, 116, 119–24. On Manuel's interest in astrology and his critics: Magdalino (2006), pp. 109–30.
[18] See Magdalino (1993a), pp. 434–70.

that had made Byzantium great in the 'imperial centuries'. According to the classic formulation of George Ostrogorsky,

> in structure the empire now differed considerably from the rigid centralised state of the middle Byzantine period. The age of the Komnenoi saw an intensification of the feudalising process and those very feudal elements in the provinces, against which the tenth-century emperors had battled with such insistence, were to become the mainstay of the new state ... Byzantium had thrown over its once solid foundations and its defences, and its economic and financial strength were greatly diminished. This is the explanation why the successes of the Komnenoi were not enduring and were followed by the collapse of the Byzantine state.[19]

Recently, this view has been replaced by the realisation that the privileges and immunities bestowed by the Komnenian emperors did not in themselves decentralise, weaken or impoverish the machinery of government and warfare. The Komnenian empire had all the apparatus of a fully developed pre-industrial state: a standing army and navy, regular monetary taxation and an elaborate bureaucracy. The armed forces performed indifferently, the taxation was oppressive and iniquitous and the bureaucracy often inefficient and corrupt, but under strong leadership the apparatus worked. Moreover, the resource base on which it worked was not obviously diminished by either the loss of territory in Asia Minor or the granting of exemptions. Rather, all the indications from written and material evidence are that agricultural production and trade intensified throughout the twelfth century, and that the government was reaping the benefits as well as the aristocracy, the monasteries and the Italian merchants.

The most eloquent testimony to the wealth of Byzantium in the late twelfth century comes from the observation of an Anglo-Norman writer, Gerald of Wales, that the revenues of the German and English monarchies were as nothing compared with those of the kingdom of Sicily and the Greek empire before these were destroyed 'by the Latins'; the yearly income from Palermo alone (a smaller city than Constantinople) exceeded that from the whole of England.[20] Interesting here is the coupling of Byzantium and Sicily as wealthy states which were destroyed by northern European conquest. Gerald goes on to recall a remark of Louis VII of France, reported somewhat differently by Walter Map,[21] contrasting the great resources of other kingdoms with the simple self-sufficiency of his own. The king of Germany had many armed men but no wealth, the rulers of Sicily and Greece were rich in gold and silk, but had no men who could do anything but talk, and the king of England had something of both. In the perception,

[19] Ostrogorsky (1968), pp. 374–5.
[20] Gerald of Wales, *De principis instructione*, III.30, ed. Warner *et al.*, VIII, pp. 316–17; tr. Stevenson (repr. 1991), p. 108.
[21] Walter Map, *De nugis curialium*, V.5, ed. and tr. James, rev. Brooke and Mynors, pp. 450–1.

and the reality, of statehood in twelfth-century Europe, strong finances and a strong war machine did not necessarily go together.

Byzantium's problem was one of survival in a world where weak, wealthy Mediterranean societies were in the way of northern warrior aristocracies with slender means and big appetites. Survival lay in the effective use of wealth to manage the bonds which kept the empire together and free from confrontation with potential aggressors. These bonds consisted in three characteristic features of the Komnenian empire which had either not existed or had been less pronounced before 1081: the deep involvement of the empire with the Latin west, the centralisation of power and resources in Constantinople and the emphasis on family, lineage and kinship as the defining elements in the Byzantine political system. The unravelling of all three features is clearly visible in the disintegration of imperial power at the end of the twelfth century.

BYZANTIUM AND THE WEST

The empire's involvement with the west derived partly from its historic interest in the Italian peninsula (see above, chs. 3, 11, 15), and partly from the consequences of its attempt to use western military power to restore its position in Asia Minor. The relationship set up by the First Crusade persisted and intensified throughout the twelfth century, tying the empire's eastern interests to its western relations, and making the viability of its traditional role in the Christian orient dependent upon its standing among the powers of the Latin west. The Second Crusade confirmed what John II had belatedly begun to realise in the 1130s: that to succeed, and even to survive, Byzantium needed to keep one move ahead of the crusading movement in preserving the Latin settlements in Syria; it needed to participate as an inside player in the power politics of western Christendom. In the thirty years following the crusade, Manuel had done all in his power to make the involvement inextricable and irreversible. The proliferation of ties with the Latin world which he cultivated so assiduously at all levels was a natural response to the growing volume of western business and religious interests in the eastern Mediterranean. These would have affected Byzantium regardless of imperial policy.

Yet the period following Manuel's death and the overthrow of the regency government of Alexios II saw reversion to something like the isolationism of John II's early years. Under Andronikos I Komnenos, Isaac II Angelos and Alexios III Angelos, Byzantium opted out of the crusading movement at a time when crusading activity was intensifying, and abandoned the search for a high-level European *entente* with one or more of the major western powers. To some extent this was the result of a backlash against Manuel's expensive Latinophilia, which was carried to even greater excess by the regency government of Maria of Antioch; it proceeded inexorably from the massacre of the Latins in Constantinople, mostly Pisans and Genoese, which accompanied the seizure of effective power by Andronikos Komnenos in 1182, as well as from his liquidation of the key members of Manuel's family through whom dynastic links to the west had been forged: Manuel's widow Maria of Antioch, Manuel's daughter Maria and her husband Renier of Montferrat, and the young Alexios II himself. That Andronikos, who was probably older than Manuel, did not murder Alexios' child fiancée, Agnes of France, but forced her to marry him, can hardly have made her family warm to him. In the circumstances, it is not surprising that when he was threatened with invasion by the king of Sicily, the only western power prepared to ally with him was Venice, whose citizens had been unaffected by the massacre of 1182 and were only too glad to take advantage of the removal of the Pisans and Genoese. Nor is it surprising that Andronikos considered that imperial interests in the east were better served by alliance with the growing power of Saladin rather than with the beleaguered Latin princes of Outremer, who no doubt remembered Andronikos' scandalous sexual adventures in Antioch and Jerusalem in 1166–7.[22]

It is perhaps more remarkable that no realignment was attempted after 1185 by Isaac II Angelos, who otherwise had every reason to reject his predecessor's reign as a tyrannical deviation from the normal course of imperial policy. Isaac was not anti-western. Soon after his accession he took as his second wife Margaret, a daughter of Béla III of Hungary, and he invited Conrad of Montferrat, brother of the murdered Renier, to Constantinople, where he played a large part in defeating a major revolt in 1187. Yet despite receiving the title of caesar, which Renier had held, and the hand of the emperor's sister in marriage, Conrad became dissatisfied and moved on to Syria, where he joined in the defence of Tyre against Saladin and became a candidate for the throne of Jerusalem. Isaac's renewal of Andronikos' alliance with Saladin may have been a factor in Conrad's disenchantment; what is certain is that Saladin's conquest of the Holy Land and the mobilisation of the Third Crusade in response in 1188–9 only confirmed Isaac in the alliance, from which he hoped to gain some sort of Byzantine dominion in Palestine, including the occupation of all the episcopal sees and the Holy Places, in return for obstructing the crusaders' advance. The rapprochement with Saladin should also be seen in the context of Isaac's treaties with Venice, which also took no part in the Third Crusade and stood to gain

---

[22] While *doux* of Cilicia, Andronikos seduced Philippa, the prince of Antioch's sister; subsequently he won over the niece of Manuel and widow of King Baldwin III of Jerusalem, Theodora, siring two children by her: NC, ed. van Dieten, I, pp. 139–42; tr. Magoulias, pp. 79–81; Kinn., VI.1, ed. Meineke, p. 250; tr. Brand, p. 188; William of Tyre, *Chronicon*, XX.2, ed. Huygens, pp. 913–14; tr. Babcock and Krey, II, pp. 345–6.

at the expense of Genoa and Pisa from either a Byzantine or a Muslim occupation of the coast of Palestine. In both alliances, one may detect the influence of Isaac's spiritual mentor, Dositheos, a Venetian-born monk who had predicted Isaac's rise to power and was duly rewarded, being appointed patriarch, first of Jerusalem, and then of Constantinople.[23]

This disengagement from the Latin west – which was not total, since it gave the Venetians an even more privileged position in Byzantine society than they had enjoyed before 1171 – may have seemed more true to the 'national' interest, which was increasingly being seen in terms of Greek as well as orthodox identity, than Manuel's costly commitments to allies with no love for the empire. Indeed, the process of dissolution had been started by one of those allies, Manuel's brother-in-law Bohemond III, who put aside his Komnenian wife well before Andronikos' usurpation. However, the empire paid dearly for its withdrawal. The pirates who terrorised the shipping and the coastal settlements of the Aegean world in the 1180s and 1190s came mainly from Pisa and Genoa, the cities which had suffered most from the massacre of 1182. The Sicilian invasion of 1185, which took Dyrrachium and went on to sack Thessaloniki, could have been prevented if Andronikos had had firm alliances, or at least a proactive diplomacy, in the west. By failing to anticipate the Third Crusade, and by allying with Saladin instead of supporting the crusaders, Isaac II weakened his moral claim for the restitution of the island of Cyprus when Richard I of England (1189–99) conquered it from its self-proclaimed emperor, Isaac Komnenos, in 1191: Cyprus was too important a source of supplies for the crusaders to entrust it to an unfriendly power.

Isaac II also entered into a damaging confrontation with Frederick Barbarossa when the latter came through Byzantine territory on the overland route to Palestine in 1189–90. The damage was not so much in the humiliating defeats inflicted by the German army, or in its systematic plundering of much of Macedonia and Thrace from its base at Philippopolis, as in the manifest contrast between Isaac's inability to obstruct a crusade which he wrongly assumed to be directed against Constantinople and Frederick's ability to threaten Constantinople if Isaac persisted in obstructing him. The contrast was painfully apparent to Niketas Choniates, who was assigned to Philippopolis at the time, and it was much appreciated by the Serbs and Vlachs, then in revolt against Byzantine authority, who offered to join forces with the Germans (see below, p. 688). Nor was the significance of the episode lost on Frederick's son Henry VI Hohenstaufen (1190–7), whom Frederick had charged with collecting money and ships from Italy in preparation for an assault on Constantinople. When Henry succeeded as emperor after Frederick's tragic death by drowning in Cilicia, he inherited

---

[23] See Magdalino (2007a).

Frederick's unfulfilled crusading ambitions and placed them high on his agenda, along with his claim to the throne of Sicily which he derived from his marriage to Constance, the aunt of William II of Sicily; William had died childless in 1189. The danger from Henry VI spurred Isaac II into diplomatic action. In 1192, he negotiated the renewal of the empire's commercial treaties with Pisa and Genoa, the two cities which Henry relied on to provide him with ships for his conquest of Sicily. Isaac also married his daughter Irene to Roger of Apulia, the son of Tancred of Lecce, who had occupied the Sicilian throne in defiance of Henry's claim. But Irene was widowed a year later, and in 1194 she was among the spoils which fell to Henry VI in his violent occupation of the Sicilian kingdom. He married her to his brother Philip of Swabia, thus making her an instrument in his policy of aggression against Byzantium.

It is uncertain whether Henry VI of Hohenstaufen really intended to take over the Byzantine empire by force, but he threatened to do so, and he used the threat, first against Isaac II, and then against Alexios III, to try and extort money and ships for his forthcoming crusade. Alexios accordingly levied an extraordinary tax, the *alamanikon*, to pay the tribute.[24] He was saved by Henry's sudden death in 1197. Yet the episode showed that however much Byzantium wanted to opt out of the crusading movement, the crusading movement would not leave it alone. It had relinquished the initiative, but was still expected to pay the bill. On this point, the western empire and the papacy, although in all other respects implacable enemies, were in agreement. Pope Innocent III (1198–1216) insisted on it in his letters to Alexios III: Alexios ought to model himself on Manuel, whose devotion to the cause of the Holy Land and the unity of the church had been exemplary.[25]

Isolationism still might have worked, and the Byzantine empire might just have been allowed to find a niche as a neutral regional power, if the Fourth Crusade, preached in 1198, had gone according to its original plan of sailing directly against Egypt. The crusade seems to have been intended to bypass Byzantium completely, and the conquest of Egypt would not only have liberated the Holy Land, but made the crusader settlements materially self-sufficient. But the leadership failed to communicate its strategic vision to the majority of crusaders. The army which assembled in Venice was well below the numbers which the Venetians had estimated in building and equipping the fleet. A detour via Byzantium thus seemed an irresistible option, indeed, the only option for keeping the crusade on course, when a pretender to the imperial throne conveniently turned up with a promise

---

[24] On the *alamanikon*, see *ODB*, I, pp. 50–1 (C. M. Brand).
[25] *PL* 214, col. 1125, tr. in Andrea, *Contemporary sources for the Fourth Crusade*, p. 38; *PL* 216, col. 1185.

of rich rewards if the crusaders restored him to what he plausibly claimed was his rightful inheritance. The pretender was Alexios, son of the deposed Isaac II Angelos, who had escaped from custody in Constantinople and gone to join his sister Irene and her second husband, Philip of Swabia; the promise, no doubt formulated on Philip's advice and calculated partly on the basis of the demands made by Henry VI, was to place the empire under the obedience of the Roman church, to pay 200,000 silver marks and supply provisions for every man in the army, to send 10,000 men with the expedition to Egypt and to maintain 500 knights for the defence of Outremer for the duration of his lifetime. As Isaac II later remarked, 'this is a big commitment, and I do not know how it can be kept',[26] especially since Byzantium was to get no share in the conquest of Egypt. Whether or not the crusade leaders knew that the offer was too good to be true, the diversion to Constantinople attracted them for other reasons. It appealed to Boniface of Montferrat, who saw a chance to claim the Byzantine inheritance of which his brothers Renier and Conrad had been cheated. It appealed to Enrico Dandolo, the doge of Venice, which stood not only to recover the costs of the fleet, but also to improve its trading position in Constantinople through the restoration of Isaac II, a much better friend than Alexios III Angelos, who had tended to favour Genoa and Pisa despite his confirmation of Venetian privileges in 1198. It could be made to appeal to the crusaders from northern France by reminding them of the generosity with which Manuel I Komnenos had treated their forebears.

The diversion of the Fourth Crusade was thus a reversion to a prevailing tendency. Now, however, Byzantium had to promise much more than it could expect in return, and Byzantium's weakness could not really help the crusading movement. The problem for both the Byzantines and the crusaders was that the latter came to Constantinople in 1203 at the invitation not of a reigning emperor, but of a rival claimant for power, and that resources were dwindling rapidly. In 1197, Alexios III had only just managed to raise the money to buy off Henry VI. By 1203 Alexios IV had a much smaller resource base from which to make good his promises: Alexios III had emptied the treasury on fleeing from Constantinople, and he and his supporters in the provinces naturally denied the government in Constantinople the provincial revenues which they controlled. Alexios IV made himself unpopular in Constantinople by his demands for money, by resorting to the requisitioning of church valuables and by consorting with the crusaders; he then alienated the crusaders by failing to keep up his payments. His overthrow and murder in a palace coup by Alexios Doukas Mourtzouphlos relieved them of the embarrassment of making war on their

---

[26] Villehard., ch. 189, ed. and French tr. Faral, I, p. 192; tr. Shaw, p. 75. On the promise see, e.g. Brand (1968), pp. 241–2; Angold (2003a), p. 86; Phillips (2004), pp. 127–9.

own protégé and gave their renewed attack on Constantinople the status of a holy war against a traitor and regicide. Alexios V Doukas put up a competent defence, but it could not prevent the Venetians from using their ships to storm the low sea walls on the Golden Horn; and when the crusaders entered the City the defence collapsed. The crusaders were thus able to gorge themselves on the riches of Constantinople, set up a Latin regime and divide up the empire on paper. However, making the division a reality proved much harder, and in the end they held on to only a fraction of the twelfth-century empire (see below, pp. 759, 763–5). The Fourth Crusade never reached Egypt, and the Latin empire of Constantinople operated at a loss.

CONSTANTINOPLE AND THE PROVINCES

The Byzantine state was one of the most centralised in the medieval world, and never more so than in the period 1081–1180, when the loss of central and eastern Anatolia forced the empire's military elite, as well as its bureaucratic elite, to identify with the capital as never before. Territorial contraction thus accentuated the already marked tendency of the Byzantine aristocracy to think fiscally rather than territorially, to invest in office-holding rather than land-holding. Indeed, it is possible to see a correlation between the centralised structure of the Komnenian empire and its territorial limits, which were essentially those of the area within which expeditionary forces mobilised from Constantinople could operate without allied help, and within which the emperor could safely absent himself from Constantinople. By these criteria, the Danube and the Adriatic were within the range of imperial government from Constantinople, but southern Italy, Ikonion and Egypt were not, and the empire was overextended in Dalmatia, Cilicia and Syria. Thus the empire consisted of those territories which a secure, mobile, military emperor could control from Constantinople. Those territories corresponded by and large to the limits of Greek linguistic culture and orthodox Christianity. The main exceptions were, first, in the Balkan interior, where Slavonic, Vlach and Albanian speakers predominated, along with a sizeable, non-integrated Armenian population, and, secondly, in the areas of southern Italy and Asia Minor which had been lost to the empire in the late eleventh century, and in which Greek-speaking orthodox Christians were numerous.

Looked at another way Byzantium – or *Romania* as its inhabitants termed it – corresponded to the area needed to support a large standing army and navy, an expensive international diplomacy and an enormous capital city. There was an outer frontier zone, broad in the Balkans, thin in Asia Minor, which was partly protective shield and partly forward base for imperial operations in Italy and Syria. In this zone, direct imperial administration was limited to a few key strongholds, and local resources were either unexploited (to starve invading forces), untaxed (to secure local loyalties) or used to pay for regional defence and diplomacy (notably the case in Cyprus). Surrounded by this zone, in an area consisting essentially of the Aegean and southern Black Sea hinterland, the core Komnenian empire existed largely to maintain the safety, the opulence and the population of Constantinople.

The pull of Constantinople was due not only to its role as the administrative capital, but also to its status as the 'reigning city' of New Rome, an unrivalled showcase of holy relics, glittering treasures, ancient public monuments and magnificent buildings, a megalopolis with a population somewhere between 200,000 and 400,000 which appears to have been growing steadily throughout the eleventh and twelfth centuries, even as the empire contracted overall in territorial extent. By the late twelfth century, the relationship between the 'reigning city' and the provinces was seen, on both sides, as that of a metropolis to its satellite tributaries, which were inhabited by culturally inferior second-class citizens. Ownership of the empire's prime agricultural land was overwhelmingly concentrated in Constantinople (see above, p. 490).[27]

In the 'outer territories', as opposed to Constantinople, heretics abounded, ignorance of the law was standard, uncanonical, semi-pagan religious customs were practised, people spoke bad Greek and there was no protection against corrupt and brutal officials. Yet this unequal relationship obviously depended on the productivity of the suppliers, on the ability of provincial communities to provide the metropolis not only with money, foodstuffs, manpower and raw materials, but also, increasingly, with manufactured goods, such as silks from Thebes and knives from Thessaloniki. It is abundantly clear that Constantinople was not the only place where urban society was expanding.[28] It is also clear, although documentation is patchy, that revenue could not have been raised or military defence organised in the localities without the cooperation and participation of the local aristocracy, the *archontes*. In frontier cities, such as Dyrrachium, Philadelphia or Trebizond, their loyalty was crucial in keeping invaders out. Equally, in those parts of Asia Minor which had come under Turkish rule, the attitude of the local notables was crucial in the empire's failure to recover lost territory.

The administration of the *pronoia* system, the conditional allocation of state lands and revenues as livings to mounted soldiers, which was greatly extended by Manuel I, must have created opportunities for patronage at the local level.[29] Thus, as Constantinople became more and more self-important, self-centred and exclusive of the 'outer territories', it became

[27] Magdalino (2000b); Magdalino (2007b), no. 10.

[28] Magdalino (1993a), pp. 144–6, 150–60; Laiou and Morrisson (2007), pp. 117–24, 127–33, 136–7.

[29] On *pronoia*, see *ODB*, III, p. 1734 (M. C. Bartusis); Magdalino (1993a), pp. 232–3. See also above, p. 613 and below, pp. 810–11.

increasingly noticeable that Constantinople needed the 'outer territories' more than the latter needed Constantinople. The perception may have existed before 1180, but it found expression in the following years – for the first time in the middle ages – as central government proved less and less capable of protecting the provinces from raiders and invaders. The period 1180–1204 also saw the resurgence of the Constantinopolitan populace as a political factor for the first time since 1082: in changes of regime, in anti-government and anti-Latin riots and in opposition to imperial demands for money to buy off Henry VI and the Fourth Crusade.

Under Manuel I Komnenos' successors, the empire's provinces were lost to imperial control or became centres of opposition to the government in Constantinople. The process began, predictably, in areas of the frontier zone where the empire's hold had been short or shaky, and administration largely in the hands of local potentates. Soon after Manuel's death, Béla III of Hungary seized Byzantine Dalmatia and Sirmium, which he considered to be his own patrimony. Next to secede were the Serbs of Raška and the Armenians of Cilicia, whose princes – respectively, Stefan Nemanja (c. 1165/68–96) and Rupen III (1175–87) – had always been unwilling vassals of the emperor. In the process, Rupen took possession of the last Byzantine cities in Cilicia and captured their governor, Isaac Komnenos.[30] Released upon payment of a ransom by Andronikos I, Isaac promptly spent the money – no doubt with the connivance of Rupen and Bohemond III of Antioch – on making himself lord of Cyprus in 1185, where he ruled independently until dispossessed by Richard I and the Third Crusade. At least initially, Isaac had the support of the local aristocracy. The usurpation of Andronikos also provoked rebellions in two major cities of north-western Asia Minor, Nicaea and Prousa, and dissatisfaction with his rule may have contributed to the ease with which the Sicilian army took Dyrrachium in 1185 and advanced to Thessaloniki unopposed.

The most serious and damaging centrifugal movement, however, was provoked not by the 'tyrant' Andronikos, but by Isaac II Angelos, the emperor who delivered the empire from Andronikos' tyranny. This was the Vlach revolt started by the brothers Peter and Asen and continued by their brother Kalojan. As it spread, the revolt came to resemble the other ethnic separatist movements, those of the Serbs and Armenians. Like them, it occurred in a mountainous frontier area, it was boosted by the Third Crusade and it resulted in the formation of a national kingdom, whose ruler received a crown from the pope. Yet there were differences: the revolt of Peter and Asen involved two peoples, the Vlachs and the Bulgarians, and the kingdom it created was a conscious resurrection of the first Bulgarian empire of the tenth century. Like its predecessor, it was not marginal to the

---

[30] See below, p. 686; Der Nersessian (1969), pp. 643–4; Boase (1978), pp. 14–15.

Byzantine heartland, but encroached significantly on the agricultural hinterland of Constantinople and the northern Aegean. Moreover, it originated in what had been, for almost a century, the most trouble-free sector of the frontier zone, where there were no local dynasties with a history of political insubordination, and contacts with the neighbouring nomads, the Cumans, took the form of peaceful commerce in the cities of the lower Danube. The revolt resulted largely from the complacency that is evident, first, in Isaac II Angelos' failure to prevent, punish or recompense the rapacity of his officials who seized Vlach livestock for his marriage feast; secondly, in his rude rejection of Peter and Asen when they requested a modest benefice; thirdly, in his failure to move quickly to deprive the rebels of their military advantages, their mountain strongholds and their Cuman allies.[31] Peter and Asen were thus local chieftains politicised by the carelessness of central government. In this, they may have had something in common with Theodore Mangaphas, a Greek magnate in Philadelphia, who used his proximity to the Turkish frontier to declare independence from Isaac II. Although eventually subdued by Isaac, Mangaphas re-emerged at the time of the Fourth Crusade, as one of several 'dynasts' who took advantage of the changes of regime in Constantinople to seize power in their localities.[32] By then, many other rebels had more or less successfully defied imperial authority from a variety of provincial power bases.

It is difficult to generalise about the origins and aims of all these figures. Several were from the Komnenian nobility, and ultimately sought power at the centre. Others such as Ivanko and Dobromir Chrysos were by-products of the Vlach–Bulgarian revolt.[33] A certain John Spyridonakes, who followed their example, was a Cypriot immigrant who had worked in the treasury of the imperial household and then been posted as administrator of Smolena in the Rhodope mountains. Aldobrandinus, who ruled Antalya in 1204, may have been a Pisan pirate. The others must have originated among the provincial *archontes*, and notably among the local cadres of military recruitment and defence. They included the least ephemeral of the local lordships to emerge before the formation of the Byzantine successor states: that of Theodore Mangaphas in Philadelphia, the main command centre on the eastern frontier, and those of Leo Sgouros and Leo Chamaretos in the coastal towns of the eastern Peloponnese which contributed contingents to the imperial fleet.[34]

Whatever the specific origins and aims of these individuals, they all shared the conviction that more was to be gained from opposition to central

---

[31] NC, ed. van Dieten, I, pp. 368–9, 371–4; tr. Magoulias, pp. 203–4, 205–6. See below, pp. 687–8.
[32] NC, ed. van Dieten, I, pp. 399–401, 603–4; tr. Magoulias, pp. 219–20, 331. On Mangaphas, see Brand (1968), pp. 85–7, 244; Cheynet (1990), pp. 123, 134–5, 454–5.
[33] On Ivanko and Dobromir Chrysos, see Brand (1968), pp. 125–31; Cheynet (1990), pp. 132–3; Stephenson (2000), pp. 305–8.
[34] Brand (1968), pp. 132–3, 143, 152–4, 244–5; Cheynet (1990), pp. 138–9, 147–8, 152–3, 454–8.

government than from service, and that they could count on provincial support. The trend they represented received spectacular endorsement in 1203, when it was joined by the emperor Alexios III Angelos. Instead of persisting in the defence of Constantinople against the crusaders, he decided to abandon the City to Alexios IV. He established his court at Mosynopolis in Thrace, where he drew on the resources of a rich hinterland extending as far as Thessaloniki.

THE KOMNENIAN FAMILY SYSTEM: BONDS AND FLAWS

The most distinctive, as well as the most fatal, characteristic of the Komnenian empire was the identification of the state with the imperial family; this was the essence of what used to be labelled the feudalism of the Komnenian dynasty. In some ways, Manuel's regime looks less feudal than that of Alexios or John, despite his liking for the culture and the company of western knighthood. As he matured, according to Choniates, 'he ruled more autocratically, treating his subjects not as free men but as if they were servants who belonged to him by inheritance'.[35] His reliance on eunuchs recalls the pre-Komnenian period, as do his attempts to cut back on grants of privilege and immunity. Yet the cut-back was mainly at the expense of the church and the Italian maritime republics. All other indications are that he was at least as indulgent to his extended family as his father and grandfather had been, and that he was scrupulous in maintaining a strict hierarchy by blood-relationship. He created one new title, that of *despotēs*, for Béla-Alexios of Hungary, when designating him as his future son-in-law and heir to the throne; the title lapsed at the birth of Alexios II, but it was revived by later emperors, and it remained the most senior of the three titles (the others were *sebastokratōr* and caesar) which were reserved for the emperor's immediate family, and carried semi-imperial status, allowing their bearers to wear quasi-imperial insignia and to sit with the emperor on ceremonial occasions.

Manuel may also have introduced certain changes to the titulature of the wider circle of imperial relatives. In the earlier years of the dynasty, all relatives by blood or marriage below the rank of caesar had been designated by variants of the title *sebastos* (see above, p. 612). In the ceremonial lists of Manuel's reign, however, the imperial nephews and cousins, who stand next to the enthroned imperial family, have no titles beyond their kinship designation, with the sole exception of the senior imperial nephew, who is *prōtosebastos* ('first *sebastos*') and *prōtovestiarios*, i.e. head of the imperial household. The ranks of the *sebastoi* begin at the next level down and, among them, those who are designated as the emperor's *gambroi*, that is

---

[35] NC, ed. van Dieten, I, p. 60; tr. Magoulias, p. 35.

the husbands of his female nieces and cousins, rank senior to those whose
relationship is too distant to be named. Not only are ranks carefully graded
by degree of kinship to the emperor, and within each degree according
to the seniority of the kinsman through whom the kinship is traced, but
kinship designations begin to take the place of titles.[36]

In addition to this continual articulation of the imperial family system,
Manuel's reign witnessed its further extension downwards from the military to the bureaucracy, and outwards into the sphere of foreign relations.
As the Komnenian aristocracy proliferated, more of its members came to
hold civilian office, while others married into the more illustrious civilian families, one of which, the Kamateroi, was already connected with
the Doukai and well on the way to establishing its later ascendancy in the
church and the bureaucracy. The marriage diplomacy of Alexios I and John
II had created blood lines leading from the Komnenoi to ruling dynasties
in the lands of the Rus, the Caucasus, Hungary and Germany. Manuel
more than doubled the network with marriage alliances that related the
imperial family in Constantinople to royal and princely families in Austria,
Jerusalem, Antioch, Tuscany, Piedmont, northern France and Languedoc.
Marriage alliances were also discussed with Henry II of England (1154–89)
and William II of Sicily. This was perhaps the closest Byzantium came to
being at the centre of an international 'family of kings'; even the sultan of
Rum was included by virtue of his ritual adoption as the emperor's son. That
Manuel saw a close connection between his internal and external families
is evident in the way he interfered with the church's marriage legislation on
the forbidden degrees of kinship and punished men from undistinguished
bureaucratic families who threatened to devalue the status of Komnenian
brides by attempting to marry into noble families.

In 1180, then, the political existence of the Byzantine empire was governed
by kinship and lineage to an unprecedented degree. The future of the system
consisted as never before in the cohesion of the extended imperial family.
For a century that cohesion had been managed by the emperor as head of
the family, but now that the emperor was an eleven-year-old, it depended
on a consensus of loyalty to the young Alexios II among the Komnenian
nobility. Manuel did what he could to create a framework of collective
patriotic and familial responsibility: he set up a regency council, perhaps
based on his inner circle of advisers, comprising his widow, the patriarch
and a number of relatives. The latter were presumably selected on the basis
of seniority, although Niketas Choniates indicates that they participated on
a basis of equality.[37] At the same time, Manuel obtained guarantees from
the sultan, the prince of Antioch, the king of Jerusalem and possibly other

---

[36] For further details see Magdalino (1993a), pp. 181–5, 188–91, 501–9.
[37] NC, ed. van Dieten, I, pp. 224, 253–4; tr. Magoulias, pp. 127, 142.

members of the external 'family of kings' that they would defend Alexios' inheritance.

With hindsight it seems clear, and contemporaries seem to have sensed, that these measures were doomed to failure. The Komnenian family had been prone to factionalism from the time of Alexios I, and its solidarity inevitably weakened as each generation multiplied the number of household units (*oikoi*) with which the imperial *oikos* at the heart of the kin-group (*genos*) had to share the finite resources of an empire which they all still regarded as the Komnenian family patrimony. The accessions of John II and Manuel I had not gone unchallenged, and although Manuel saw off his original challengers, the *sebastokratores* Isaac, his brother and uncle, the latter's place was taken by his son Andronikos, while the former's supporters seem to have gravitated towards Alexios Axouch, the husband of Manuel's niece by the emperor's late brother Alexios.

Axouch's 'conspiracy' in 1167 was quickly disposed of, but Andronikos was a constant worry to Manuel from 1154, almost as troublesome during his long spells in prison, from which he escaped twice, in 1159 and 1164, and in exile among the empire's eastern neighbours (1167–80), as he was during his brief period of liberty. After his return and rehabilitation in Manuel's final year, he was understandably sent – like his father before him – into comfortable internal exile on the Black Sea coast. But this exclusion from Constantinople played into Andronikos' hands, by giving him a provincial power base where he could recruit supporters, and by casting him as an impartial outsider to the selfish intrigues which divided the regency council of Alexios II, to the gross neglect of the boy's upbringing and the public interest.

According to Niketas Choniates, there were those who lusted after the widowed empress and sought to seduce her, those who lusted after money and appropriated public funds to meet their growing expenses and those who lusted after imperial power.[38] Elsewhere he describes them in somewhat different terms: 'Some of his noble guardians winged their way repeatedly like bees to the provinces and stored up money like honey, others like goats hankered after the tender shoots of empire which they continually longed to crop, while others grew fat like pigs on filthy lucre'.[39] The emphasis on money-making is interesting, particularly the implied distinction between the misappropriation of tax revenue from the provinces, and the sordid enrichment from the profits of trade, and possibly of prostitution, in Constantinople. It shows that the search for funds to maintain an aristocratic lifestyle was a constant motivating factor in political loyalty.

---

[38] NC, ed. van Dieten, I, pp. 223–4; tr. Magoulias, p. 127.
[39] NC, ed. van Dieten, I, pp. 227–8; tr. Magoulias, p. 129.

His enforced isolation thus put Andronikos in an ideal position, which he exploited masterfully, to pose as champion of Alexios II's best interests, which the boy's guardians were patently neglecting, and to win the sympathies of the many noble figures in Constantinople: these included Manuel's daughter Maria, who resented the dominance which one of the regency council, Manuel's nephew the *prōtosebastos* Alexios, acquired over the young emperor by forming an amorous liaison with the dowager empress. After the tension between Maria and the *prōtosebastos* broke out in armed conflict, Andronikos' intervention became inevitable. If Andronikos, once in power, had kept his election promises and formed a genuinely inclusive regency government for Alexios II, he might have held the Komnenian nobility together. His programme of administrative reform, admirable in itself, could have won him support even among his peers if he had treated them fairly and generously. But by instituting a reign of terror against all potential rivals for the regency, including the emperor's sister and mother, he provoked a serious revolt in Asia Minor; then, by going on to eliminate Alexios II and settle the succession on his own son John, he removed the only focus of consensus among the Komnenian kin-group, and committed himself to dependence on a faction bound to him by self-interest.

The terror continued, and those who could escaped by fleeing abroad, to the courts of rulers who had had ties or treaties with Manuel and Alexios II. Thus the sultan, the prince and patriarch of Antioch, the king of Jerusalem, the pope, Frederick Barbarossa, the marquis of Montferrat, the king of Hungary and, above all, the king of Sicily were approached by refugees imploring their intervention. It was at the insistence of Manuel's great-nephew, the *pinkernēs* Alexios Komnenos, that William II of Sicily sent the invasion force which took Dyrrachium and Thessaloniki in 1185. The stated aim of the expedition was to replace Andronikos with a young man claiming to be Alexios II: pseudo-Alexioi were the inconvenient but inevitable consequence – for later emperors, too – of the fact that Andronikos had sunk Alexios' body in the Bosporus. The Sicilian invasion thus not only recalled the past invasions of Robert Guiscard, Bohemond and Roger II; it also set a precedent for the diversion of the Fourth Crusade, both by the damage and humiliation it caused, and in the way it involved the external 'family of kings' in the politics of the Komnenian family.

Andronikos would probably have succeeded eventually in repelling the Sicilian invasion, as he succeeded in quelling every organised conspiracy against him, but the very diligence of his agents in hunting down potential conspirators led, quite unpredictably, to the spontaneous uprising which toppled him. When his chief agent went to arrest a suspect who had given no cause for suspicion, the suspect slew the agent in desperation, and then did the only thing he could do in order to avoid immediate execution: he rushed for asylum to the church of St Sophia. A crowd gathered, Andronikos –

evidently feeling secure – was out of town and, St Sophia being also the imperial coronation church, one thing led to another. So Isaac II Angelos became emperor because he was in the right place at the right time, and this had a decisive effect on the course of his reign. His propagandists claimed, and he firmly believed, that his accession was providential, that he was the Angel of the Lord sent by heaven to end the tyranny, so that his whole reign was ordained, blessed and protected by God. He considered his power irreproachable and untouchable, and he exercised it with a mixture of grandiosity and complacency quite inappropriate to his situation.

Other important people did not share Isaac II's belief. His miraculous elevation was not enough to convince Isaac Komnenos in Cyprus, Peter and Asen in Bulgaria, Theodore Mangaphas in Philadelphia or Basil Chotzas at Tarsia, near Nikomedeia, that they owed loyalty to Constantinople, or to prevent two young men from raising rebellions by pretending to be Alexios II. Among his own close family, it did not make up for his lack of seniority, or his military incompetence; he was challenged by his uncle John and his nephew Constantine Angelos. The Komnenian nobility as a whole were not impressed, because many of them had equally good, if not better, dynastic claims in terms of the hierarchy of kinship which had operated under Manuel: Isaac was descended from Alexios I's youngest daughter, but others could trace their descent through the male line, and some could count John II among their ancestors. For several of them, Isaac's success was only an incentive to follow it and turn up at St Sophia in the hope of being acclaimed. The first to try this was Alexios Branas, the general who had halted the Sicilian invasion. Having failed in this first attempt, he waited until he was put in command of the army sent to quell the Vlach revolt. What made his rebellion so dangerous was the fact that he combined good Komnenian lineage with military expertise and strong family connections among the military aristocracy of Adrianople. Isaac was saved only by the loyalty of the people of Constantinople and a bold sortie by Conrad of Montferrat.

During ten years in power, Isaac II faced at least seventeen revolts, a number exceeded in the eleventh and twelfth centuries only by the twenty-one plots that are recorded for the thirty-nine-year reign of Alexios I. Isaac undoubtedly saw something providential in the fact of his survival, but repeated opposition took its toll on the effectiveness of his rule, making it virtually impossible for him to delegate important military commands to highly competent noble commanders. This was probably decisive for the outcome of the rebellion of Peter and Asen. Lack of support among the Komnenian nobility may have prompted what was seen to be Isaac's excessive favouritism to his grand logothete, his non-Komnenian maternal uncle Theodore Kastamonites, and to the latter's successor, Constantine Mesopotamites. It certainly drove the members of five leading Komnenian families, the Palaiologos, Branas, Kantakouzenos, Raoul and Petraliphas, to mount the coup in 1195 which replaced Isaac with his elder brother Alexios III Angelos.

Sibling rivalry had, as we have seen, threatened to destroy the Komnenian system in the past, but it had been kept under control, and its eruption into successful usurpation sealed the fate of the system in its twelfth-century phase. Niketas Choniates saw the overthrow of brother by brother as the supreme manifestation of the moral depravity for which the fall of Constantinople was just retribution.[40] From the deposition of Isaac II proceeded the escape of his son Alexios to the west just when the Fourth Crusade needed an excuse for a detour via Constantinople. In their comeback, the internal and external dimensions of the system fatally converged. Choniates, perhaps looking back to Andronikos and even to his father, saw a pattern:

If anything was the supreme cause that the Roman power collapsed to its knees and suffered the seizure of lands and cities, and, finally, itself underwent annihilation, this was the members of the Komnenoi who revolted and usurped power. For, dwelling among the nations which were unfriendly to the Romans, they were the bane of their country, even though when they stayed at home they were ineffectual, useless and incompetent in anything they tried to undertake.[41]

This retribution apart, however, Alexios III faced relatively little opposition from the Komnenoi. In 1200–1 there were provincial revolts led by his cousins Michael Angelos and Manuel Kamytzes, and a one-day occupation of the Great Palace in Constantinople by a son of Alexios Axouch, John Komnenos the Fat. But otherwise, Alexios enjoyed fairly good support in the bureaucracy and the church through his connection by marriage with the Kamateros family, and the consortium of Komnenian families which brought him to power appear to have been satisfied with his laissez-faire regime, and with his adoption of the name Komnenos in preference to Angelos. All five families flourished after 1204; four were to be prominent after 1261 in the restored empire of the Palaiologoi, and the Palaiologoi gained a head start in their future ascendancy from the marriage which Alexios III arranged between his daughter Irene and Alexios Palaiologos.

The marriage of another daughter, Anna, to Theodore I Laskaris (1205–21) laid the dynastic basis for the empire of Nicaea, the most successful of the three main Greek successor states after 1204. Cousins of Isaac II and Alexios III established the western state which enjoyed brief glory as the empire of Thessaloniki and then survived in north-western Greece as the despotate of Epiros. The empire of Trebizond, which lasted until 1461,

---

[40] NC, ed. van Dieten, I, pp. 453–4, 532; tr. Magoulias, pp. 249–50, 292.
[41] NC, ed. van Dieten, I, p. 529; tr. Magoulias, p. 290.

was ruled by a dynasty calling themselves the Grand Komnenoi, who were descended from Andronikos I.

Under the successors of Manuel I the Komnenian system, centred on Constantinople, was programmed for self-destruction. Relocated to the provinces after 1204 through the leading families of the last twelfth-century regimes, it ensured the survival of the Byzantine empire for another two and a half centuries, while losing none of its divisive potential.

CHAPTER 18

BALKAN BORDERLANDS (1018–1204)

PAUL STEPHENSON

BYZANTIUM'S NORTH-WESTERN APPROACHES IN THE REIGN OF BASIL II AND HIS SUCCESSORS

Byzantine emperors desired stability and security in the peripheral regions of the empire so as to continue controlling and exploiting the productive lands which provisioned the principal cities, most importantly Constantinople; these also yielded tax revenues to support the apparatus of government. In the Balkans the vital regions were the rich lands of Thrace and the hinterland of Constantinople in the east, and Thessaly and the lands around Thessaloniki in the west. Security required direct supervision of major communication routes, by land and water, and of strategic cities across the peninsula, but only a stabilising influence in the mountainous interior, the north-eastern plains and the north-western littoral. Control of the Black Sea ports between Constantinople and the lower Danube, notably Anchialos, Mesembria and Varna, was considered essential, as was command of the major mountain passes through the Haemus mountains. Minor paths remained in the hands of locals, largely Vlachs, whose allegiance was assiduously cultivated.

A similar situation prevailed to the west, where Albanians (*Arbanoi*) and Vlachs (*Blachoi*) had intimate knowledge of the tracks and defiles of mountains known to the Byzantines as the Zygos. Close regulation of the Egnatian Way, the principal land route between Constantinople and Thessaloniki which ran on to the Adriatic coast at Avlona and Dyrrachium, was a priority; so was control over the main land roads to the north, along the course of the Maritsa, Vardar and Velika Morava rivers. This required supervision of such cities as Skopje, Sofia, Niš and Braničevo. However, there was never an attempt to establish a centralised administrative structure across the whole Balkan peninsula: stability was best ensured by retaining the allegiance of regional potentates and populations, including Serbs and Bulgarians, through a combination of force and favour. This would also, in principle, prevent insurrection or defection in the event of foreign invasion.

Basil II (976–1025) was well able to assert his will in the periphery by virtue of the formidable reputation he established through regular campaigning, and by occasional acts of great brutality, for example mass blinding, which instilled fear in those who might contemplate resistance or rebellion. There is little evidence that Basil intended to conquer Bulgaria before 1014; rather, he used it as an arena for exercising his troops and as a source of booty and slaves.[1] Following the death of Samuel of Bulgaria (987/8–1014), no individual was able to dominate the Bulgarian magnates, and the consequent instability forced Basil's hand. In four years of hard, not always successful campaigning, he established his military superiority and received the submission of the magnates.[2] Basil's annexation of Bulgarian lands in 1018 involved primarily the military occupation of strategic towns and fortresses. Civilian administration was left to local potentates, who received stipends and honours from the emperor, and whose sons and daughters were married to those of Byzantine aristocrats. Members of the Bulgarian royal family were taken to Constantinople and absorbed into the hierarchy and ceremonial life of the imperial court. A few powerful chieftains were transferred with their retinues to the eastern frontier. Most of the lesser Bulgarian nobles were left in place, where they continued to levy taxes in grain and wine, now as representatives of the Byzantine emperor. These they passed on, in part, to the local garrisons. In his determination not to innovate in this matter, Basil will have considered the best way to supply an army.[3]

Supreme authority over the Byzantine forces of occupation rested with the *stratēgos autokratōr* of Bulgaria, based in Skopje, the *patrikios* David Areianites.[4] His most important subordinate was the *patrikios* Constantine Diogenes, who from 1018 was designated commander in Sirmium, which he had captured himself, as well as the neighbouring territories.[5] It is possible that Diogenes' title was *stratēgos* of Serbia at this time.[6] Diogenes later bore the elaborate title '*anthypatos, patrikios* and *doux* of Thessaloniki, Bulgaria and Serbia'.[7] Further subordinate *stratēgoi*, stationed in key cities as commanders of garrisons, were responsible for liaising with and monitoring local potentates. George Ostrogorsky noted astutely that '. . . the mention of a *stratēgos* in any particular town by no means implies that this town was the centre of a theme'.[8] We may take this a stage further, as did Hélène Ahrweiler, and state that the presence of a *stratēgos* need not imply the establishment of a theme, except insofar as the term signifies military control

---

[1] Shepard (2002b), pp. 73–6; Stephenson (2003b), pp. 127–33.
[2] Yahya of Antioch, *History*, ed. and French tr. Kratchkovsky, Vasiliev *et al.*, III, pp. 406–7.
[3] Skyl., ed. Thurn, p. 412; French tr. Flusin and Cheynet, pp. 340–1; see above, pp. 529–30.
[4] Skyl., ed. Thurn, p. 358; French tr. Flusin and Cheynet, pp. 298–9.
[5] Skyl., ed. Thurn, pp. 365–6; French tr. Flusin and Cheynet, pp. 303–4.
[6] *DOS*, I, no. 34.1, p. 102; Maksimović (1997), p. 39.
[7] Swiencickyj (1940), pp. 439–40.   [8] Ostrogorsky (1968), p. 311 n. 2.

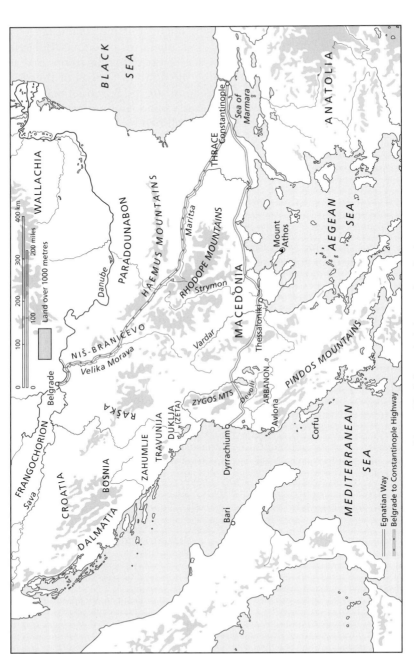

Map 29 The Balkans: physical geography and regions

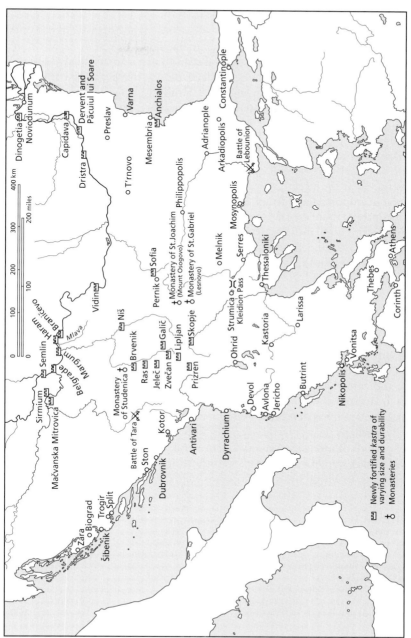

Map 30 The imperial mesh in the Balkans, eleventh and twelfth centuries

of a locality or region. John Skylitzes uses the term in exactly this limited sense.[9]

Basil II's efforts to consolidate military control of the north-western limits of Bulgaria have left clear traces in the archaeological record. At Sirmium renovations were undertaken on the walls, and a garrison installed.[10] On the opposite bank of the Sava, at modern Mačvanksa Mitrovica, a new episcopal church was built, the third on the site.[11] Similarly, a sixth-century church was renovated at Veliki Gradac, some way to the east of Sirmium.[12] The restoration of ramparts, and relatively large number of bronze coins found there, suggest that Basil also installed a garrison at Belgrade.[13] Excavations at Margum, at the confluence of the Velika Morava and Danube, have turned up seals and several coins from Basil's reign.[14] A new fortress was constructed at Braničevo, at the confluence of the Mlava and Danube, and it grew in importance through the eleventh century.[15]

In contrast, there are no clear indications that Basil established garrisons in the interior highlands south of the Danube and west of the Velika Morava, namely in Raška and Bosnia. Instead, a line of small watch-towers studded the passes through the Zygos mountains west of the Velika Morava corridor between Skopje and Niš. Excavations or surveys have identified several fortresses constructed or rebuilt in the eleventh century, including those at, from south to north, Lipljan, Zvečan, Galič, Jeleč, Ras and Brvenik.[16] In the later eleventh century we know that a no-man's-land stretched to the west of these fortresses.[17] Serbia, lying beyond this, was never to become a Byzantine administrative district. A seal struck by a *katepanō* of Ras has been convincingly dated to the reign of John I Tzimiskes (969–76), and may indicate that he enjoyed a brief period of recognition in Raška.[18] This is apparently confirmed by the *Chronicle of the priest of Duklja*.[19] Moreover, a seal has demonstrated that a command known as Serbia existed briefly, perhaps related to the recovery of Sirmium in 1018. However, these brief periods of intensified Byzantine presence never compromised the local Slavic power structures. Instead, Constantinople sought to work through local rulers, to whom titles and stipends were distributed. Thus, in a charter

[9] Skyl., ed. Thurn, p. 363; French tr. Flusin and Cheynet, p. 302; Ahrweiler (1960), pp. 48–52, 78–9. See also above, pp. 240–1, 266–7.

[10] Popović, V. (1978), pp. 189–93. [11] Popović, V. (1980), pp. i–iv.

[12] Janković (1981), pp. 21–3, 41–2, 75–8. [13] Ivanišević (1993); Popović, M. (1982), pp. 42–3.

[14] Maksimović and Popović (1993), pp. 127–9; *DOS*, I, no. 36a, p. 195; Ivanišević and Radić (1997), pp. 133–4, 141.

[15] Ivanišević (1988); Popović and Ivanišević (1988), p. 130.

[16] Popović, M. (1991); Stephenson (2000), pp. 125, 148–50.

[17] *Al.*, IX.4.3, ed. Reinsch and Kambylis, I, p. 266; ed. and French tr. Leib, II, p. 167; tr. Sewter, p. 277.

[18] *DOS*, I, no. 33.1, pp. 100–1; Kalić (1988), pp. 127–40. [19] *LPD*, p. 324.

Figure 50 Seal of Leo, imperial *spatharokandidatos*: his exact relationship with the imperial authorities is uncertain, but he was probably a local Croat notable; the seal is weakly imprinted and the obverse appears to be blank

issued in July 1039, the Slavic ruler of Zahumlje boasted a string of imperial titles: 'Ljutovit, *prōtospatharios* of the Chrysotriklinos, *hypatos* and *stratēgos* of Serbia and Zahumlje'.[20]

Beyond Serbia, in Croatia and Dalmatia, authority was similarly exercised by local notables who were willing to recognise Byzantine overlordship. A seal has come to light which bears the legend 'Leo, imperial *spatharokandidatos* and [*archōn*] of Croatia'.[21] The use of the name Leo may suggest that the Croat in question had taken a Byzantine name, or a bride, or had been baptised by the emperor, or by one of his subordinates. We have examples of all such eventualities in the Balkan lands recovered by Basil II.[22] A certain Dobronja, who also went by the name Gregory, accepted Byzantine money and titles in recognition of his authority in the northern Dalmatian lands. Charters preserved in Zara show that he had been granted the rank of *prōtospatharios* and the title *stratēgos* of all Dalmatia. Kekaumenos records that he travelled twice to Constantinople as *archōn* and toparch of Zara and Split before 1036, when he was taken prisoner and later died in gaol.[23]

[20] von Falkenhausen (1970).   [21] *DOS*, I, no. 16.1, pp. 48–9.
[22] Stephenson (2000), pp. 74–7, 123–30.   [23] Kek., ed. and Russian tr. Litavrin, pp. 316–18.

REBELLIONS AND CULTURAL COMPROMISE IN
OCCUPIED BULGARIA

Dobronja's change of fortunes is likely to have been the result of a change in Byzantine policy towards the western Balkans. Rather than patronise regional potentates and continue to raise taxes in kind, a policy was devised to extract gold from the periphery through taxation in coin. This initiative was taken in response to cash shortages within the state economy generally,[24] and in particular to demands to redirect both coinage and manpower to the north-eastern Balkans, which were threatened by the Pechenegs in the 1030s.[25] While the medium-term result was the increased monetisation of the region, the immediate consequence was a series of rebellions between 1040 and 1042. The first was started by a certain Peter Deljan in Belgrade and Margum. The second was a direct result of the first, and involved the troops raised in the theme of Dyrrachium to fight Deljan. Instead of fighting Deljan, they and their leader Tihomir joined him. The third rebellion was also a response to Deljan's activities: a Bulgarian prince, Alusjan, observed his success with envy from Constantinople and determined to seize control of the rebellion to further his own interests. He succeeded in dividing support for Deljan and, ultimately, replacing him at the head of the rebel army. He then surrendered to the Byzantines.

The fourth rebellion was an entirely distinct affair which arose in Duklja under Stefan Vojislav, who went by the title *archōn* and 'toparch of the *kastra* in Dalmatia, Zeta and Ston'. According to Kekaumenos, Vojislav invited the *stratēgos* of (Ragusa) Dubrovnik, named Katakalon, to act as godfather to his son, but kidnapped him en route to the ceremony.[26] This confirms that a close working relationship – albeit one subject to arbitrary violation – existed between local potentates and Byzantine officers in this peripheral zone of the empire into the 1040s. Eventually, Vojislav's rebellion was crushed with the aid of neighbouring Slavic potentates. If we can trust the *Chronicle of the priest of Duklja*, Ljutovit '*princeps* of Zahumlje' mentioned above, as well as the *ban* of Bosnia and the *župan* of Raška, all welcomed Byzantine ambassadors offering piles of imperial silver and gold in return for military assistance against Vojislav.[27]

After Vojislav's demise, Duklja's loyalty was to be ensured by the marriage of Vojislav's son and successor Michael to a relative of Constantine IX (1042–55).[28] Michael's four sons by this marriage, and seven by another, extended their authority over neighbouring regions, including Zahumlje, Travunija and Raška, without provoking serious complaints or interference from Constantinople. In contrast, an increased Byzantine presence was

[24] Oikonomides (2002), pp. 1019–26.   [25] Stephenson (1999); Stephenson (2000), pp. 130–5.
[26] Kek., ed. and Russian tr. Litavrin, pp. 186–8.
[27] *LPD*, pp. 346–7.   [28] *LPD*, p. 357; Stephenson (2000), pp. 138–41.

Figure 51 Illustration from the Madrid Skylitzes of Peter Deljan being proclaimed ruler by his fellow Slavs

introduced into the lands around Ohrid and Skopje, which comprised the secular and ecclesiastical centres of the theme of Bulgaria. In the 1040s we learn of a *pronoētēs* of (all) Bulgaria, the eunuch and monk Basil, who was also called the *satrapēs* of Bulgaria.[29] Subsequently a *praitōr* operated alongside the military commander, now known as the *doux* of Bulgaria or Skopje. The *praitōr* John Triakontaphyllos held the elevated rank of *prōtoproedros*, which was introduced *c.* 1060,[30] and he may well have been a contemporary of Gregory, *prōtoproedros* and *doux* of Bulgaria.[31]

The autocephalous status of the Bulgarian church, with its prelate in Ohrid, had been guaranteed in directives issued by Basil II in 1019–20. Basil had left the church under a local archbishop, who could conduct services in Slavonic and communicate effectively with his subordinates; the latter were left in post throughout the Bulgarian lands, from the Adriatic to the Danube and Black Sea.[32] In effect, the ecclesiastical jurisdiction of the archbishop of Bulgaria in 1020 matched that of the *stratēgos autokratōr* of Bulgaria in military affairs. And just as the role of the latter diminished over time, so did that of the archbishop. By the mid-eleventh century a metropolitan of Dristra was appointed for the bishoprics of the lower

[29] Kek., ed. and Russian tr. Litavrin, p. 180; Attal., ed. Bekker, p. 37; ed. and Spanish tr. Pérez Martín, p. 29; Schlumberger, *Sigillographie*, pp. 740–1.

[30] Oikonomides (1976a), p. 126; *ODB*, III, p. 1727 (A. Kazhdan, A. Cutler).

[31] *DOS*, I, nos. 29.2, 29.4, pp. 94–5. For further references to officials in charge of Bulgaria, see: Skyl., ed. Thurn, p. 478; French tr. Flusin and Cheynet, p. 394; Kek., ed. and Russian tr. Litavrin, p. 280; Skyl. Con., p. 121; Attal., ed. Bekker, p. 83; ed. and Spanish tr. Pérez Martín, p. 63; Bănescu (1946), p. 144; Hunger (1968), pp. 186–7; Cheynet (1990), p. 409; Prinzing (1995), p. 223; Kühn (1991), p. 230.

[32] Gelzer, 'Orientalischen Kirche II'.

Danube, a parallel to the emergence of a theme known as Paradounabon.[33] In 1037 Leo, a Greek-speaking archbishop, was installed in Ohrid. He conducted services in Greek in the church of St Sophia, a domed basilica named after the Great Church in Constantinople, but whose wall-paintings have parallels in contemporary structures in Thessaloniki,[34] and it has been suggested that 'the program of decoration provides an explicit statement of the imperial agenda for the newly reintegrated province'.[35]

There can be no doubt that the theme of Bulgaria was treated differently from semi-autonomous lands left in the hands of local rulers. However, the extent to which Bulgarian culture was hellenised under Byzantine rule is impossible to quantify, and there is no evidence for systematic suppression of the Slavic language, which continued to exist alongside Greek as a language of worship and literary production. A number of Old Church Slavonic liturgical codices, for example the mid-eleventh-century *Epistolarium eninensis* and twelfth-century *Euchologium sinaiticum*, attest the vitality of the language. Indeed, it is only in the twelfth century, not the tenth, that Slavic appears to have replaced Greek as the principal language of sung liturgies throughout Bulgaria.[36] If the number of original Slavonic works of the highest order was small, translations of Greek works into Slavic continued uninterrupted into the twelfth century, including those of the Cappadocian fathers Basil of Caesarea, Gregory Nazianzen and Gregory of Nyssa. This production suggests an increasingly bilingual community of scholars in the major centres, but also in provincial monastic settings, for example the new Slavic foundations of St Joachim at Mount Osogovo and St Gabriel at Lesnovo.[37] There emerged also, for the first time, a genre with no contemporary parallels in Byzantine Greek: popular Slavic saints' *Lives* composed in a simple style without rhetorical introductions and conclusions or long theological digressions, for example the *Lives* of the forementioned Joachim and Gabriel.[38]

The fifth Greek-speaking archbishop of Ohrid, Theophylact, wrote extensively from and on Bulgaria, elucidating the balance between secular and ecclesiastical affairs. From his letters we learn that taxation and conscription were pursued ruthlessly in the lands around Ohrid, and he appeals on numerous occasions to Byzantine administrators on behalf of locals.[39] Although he often appears scornful of their rusticity, Theophylact took the care of his Bulgarian flock seriously and showed grudging respect

[33] The lands bordering the lower Danube were known as either Paradounabon (literally '[lands] beside the Danube') or Paristrion ('beside the Ister', the ancient name for the Danube).

[34] Zarov (2003), pp. 130–1.   [35] Wharton (1988), p. 106.

[36] Hannick (1988); Hannick (1993), pp. 932–3.

[37] Thomson, F. (1989), pp. 140–4; *pace* Fine (1983), pp. 219–20.

[38] Bojović and Georgiev (1997), pp. 28–31, 43–4.

[39] Theophylact of Ohrid, *Letters*, ed. and French tr. Gautier, pp. 166–9, 194–5, 208–11, 237, 324.

for distinctive Bulgarian institutions in the Cyrillo-Methodian tradition.[40] It would appear that the principal agents of hellenisation, such as Theophylact, had no desire to eradicate Slavonic, but rather allowed it to develop in an enriched cultural context.[41]

WEALTH, MIGRATIONS OF NOMADS AND DISARRAY ON THE LOWER DANUBE

The reorganisation of the western Balkan lands in the mid-eleventh century took place against a background of renewed nomad threats to Paradounabon. Between 1032 and 1036, a series of raids by the Pechenegs penetrated the empire as far as Thessaloniki, laid waste much of Thrace and Macedonia, and sacked a number of the smaller fortified *kastra* on the lower Danube. Excavations at two such fortresses, Dervent and Capidava, have revealed destruction levels dated by coins of Michael IV (1034–41). At Capidava archaeologists have uncovered a pit full of dismembered bodies and burnt debris.[42] The suburbs of Dinogetia show similar signs of a devastating nomad assault, datable by over 100 coins to spring 1036.[43] New houses were subsequently built there; unlike earlier semi-subterranean dwellings, they were erected at ground level on a foundation of small stones and twigs, and the regular pattern of construction suggests this was a coordinated imperial enterprise. A contemporary project saw the construction of similar surface-level houses on the island of Păcuiul lui Soare near Dristra.[44]

Both Dinogetia and Păcuiul lui Soare appear to have flourished as trading posts in the mid-eleventh century, sharing in the remarkable growth in trade between Constantinople and the lower Danube which coincided exactly with the intensification of the Pecheneg threat. This probably reflects a deliberate policy of encouraging the nomads to trade rather than raid. Contemporary written references to this phenomenon are scarce. The *Life* of Cyril the Phileote reveals that the saint was employed as a navigator on board a ship that traded along the Black Sea coast and at the watch-towers of the lower Danube.[45] Michael Attaleiates provides a brief description of these fortified entrepôts, where a myriad of languages could be heard.[46] However, the archaeological record provides greater insights. Finds of amphorae, used to transport a variety of goods including olive oil and wine, have been abundant at sites along the lower Danube, while trade in other ceramics also grew rapidly, most commonly olive-green glazed wares produced in Constantinople.[47] Further evidence for trade links with the imperial capital

[40] Mullett (1997), pp. 272–3.   [41] Thomson, F. (1989).
[42] Diaconu (1970), pp. 48–9; Madgearu (1999), p. 485.   [43] Stefan *et al.* (1967), pp. 22–50.
[44] Diaconu (1970), p. 62.   [45] *Life of Cyril the Phileote*, pp. 63, 284–5.
[46] Attal., ed. Bekker, p. 204; ed. and Spanish tr. Pérez Martín, p. 150.
[47] Diaconu *et al.* (1972–7), I, pp. 71–119; Stefan *et al.* (1967), pp. 229–49.

is provided by a seal discovered at Noviodunum struck by 'Niketas, *notarios*
and *boullotēs*', a Constantinople-based official responsible for oversight of
controlled merchandise.[48]

Large numbers of coins facilitated trade on the lower Danube. Most of
them were struck in Constantinople. To cite just a couple of examples,
over 1,000 eleventh-century Byzantine bronze coins have been discovered
at Păcuiul lui Soare, with a peak under Michael IV (*c.* 200 coins) and Constantine IX (*c.* 300 coins). Of the more than 600 bronze coins discovered
at Dinogetia, 100 represent a single hoard of *folleis* struck by Michael IV.
While such numbers are still modest when compared with extensively excavated sites in the heart of the empire, such as Athens or Corinth, they are
far greater than in previous periods in this region. Significant numbers of
Byzantine precious coins have been found in lands which were then occupied by the Pechenegs, for example in Bessarabia and Wallachia, which
may represent tribute payments.[49] Great care was taken to maintain good
relations with the people who lived alongside the Pechenegs. The citizens
of the towns on the lower Danube were provided with annual stipends
(*philotimiai*) to guarantee their loyalty and to support a substantial local
army.[50]

Payments and opportunities for trade failed to prevent a massive migration of Pechenegs into Byzantine lands in 1043. A feud had erupted between
the Pechenegs' supreme chieftain, Tyrach, and his subordinate Kegen, who
had fled with his followers to an island near Dristra.[51] Kegen was baptised
in Constantinople, awarded the rank of *patrikios* and given command of
three *kastra* on the Danube, whence he provoked Tyrach to launch an invasion across the frozen river in winter 1047.[52] The nomads pillaged widely,
before an outbreak of pestilence forced their surrender. Captives were settled along the main road that ran from Niš to Sofia.[53] Just as all seem settled,
an attack on the eastern frontier by the newly arrived Seljuq Turks inspired
the emperor to raise a force of 15,000 from among the Pecheneg colonists.
Despatched to the east under their own chiefs, the nomads rebelled as
soon as they had crossed the Bosporus. They made their way back into the
Balkans, crossed the Haemus and settled in the vicinity of Preslav. Kegen's
Pechenegs, previously loyal to the emperor, joined the rebellion, and efforts
to crush the rebellions led to a series of imperial defeats.[54] Public reaction
was strong, and the emperor was left with no option but to recognise the

---

[48] Barnea (1983), p. 265; *LPB*, p. 321.
[49] Madgearu (2001b), pp. 207–8; Custurea (2000), pp. 185–95.
[50] Attal., ed. Bekker, pp. 83, 204–5; ed. and Spanish tr. Pérez Martín, pp. 63, 150.
[51] Skyl., ed. Thurn, p. 433; French tr. Flusin and Cheynet, pp. 359–60; Shepard (1992).
[52] Kazhdan (1977). See above, p. 328.
[53] Skyl., ed. Thurn, pp. 455–7; French tr. Flusin and Cheynet, pp. 377–9; Shepard (1975); Malamut
(1995), pp. 118–22.
[54] Kek., ed. and Russian tr. Litavrin, p. 180.

settlement of an independent group of nomads between the Haemus and lower Danube, in a region called the 'hundred hills'.[55] In 1053 he agreed a thirty-year peace treaty, and with 'gifts and imperial titles soothed the ferocity and barbarity' of the Pechenegs.[56]

It is in the context of the Pecheneg wars that we first find mention of an integrated command known as Paradounabon. We have the seals of several *katepanoi* of Paradounabon, which have all been dated later than *c*. 1045.[57] The *magistros* and *doux* Basil Apokapes was probably appointed to command Paradounabon during the brief reign of Isaac I Komnenos (1057–9).[58] In response to a joint assault of Hungarians and Pechenegs, Isaac renewed an aggressive policy. He achieved no substantive success, but returned to Constantinople having destroyed some nomad tents and bearing booty, with 'his head crowned with the garlands of victory'.[59] If the Pechenegs proved unwilling to relinquish territory in Paradounabon it had much to do with the Uzes, or Oghuz, who now occupied their former lands north of the lower Danube. Ominously for both the Pechenegs and Byzantines, in 1064,

when the commanders of the towns of the Danube were the *magistros* Basil Apokapes and the illustrious *magistros* Nikephoros Botaneiates, the entire tribe of Uzes, bringing their possessions, crossed the frozen river Danube in long wooden boats and sharp-prowed vessels made of branches lashed together. They defeated the Bulgarians and other soldiers who attempted to block their passage.[60]

Both Byzantine commanders were captured, and lands were despoiled even beyond Thessaloniki. Fortunately for the Byzantines, like Tyrach's Pechenegs in 1047, the Uzes fell victim to disease. Some survivors were recruited into the Byzantine army, others returned north and were employed as border guards by the rulers of the Rus and Hungarians.

SLAV MALCONTENTS, ARMED HERETICS AND PECHENEGS

The persistent threat posed by the various nomadic peoples led the new emperor and former general Constantine X (1059–67) to believe there could be no effective military solution to the problems in Paradounabon, and

[55] Skyl., ed. Thurn, pp. 465, 467; French tr. Flusin and Cheynet, pp. 384–6; Diaconu (1970), pp. 66–9.

[56] Attal., ed. Bekker, p. 43; ed. and Spanish tr. Pérez Martín, p. 33; Diaconu (1970), pp. 75–6. See also above, p. 600.

[57] Iordanov (2003). See also Banescu (1946), p. 70; Iordanov, 'Neizdadeni vizantiiski olovni pechati', pp. 89–92; Madgearu (1999), pp. 426–9; Zacos *et al., Byzantine lead seals*, II, p. 300.

[58] Iordanov, 'Neizdadeni vizantiiski olovni pechati', pp. 89–92; Grünbart (1998) pp. 37–40; Barnea (1987), pp. 84–5.

[59] Psell., VII.70, ed. Renauld, II, p. 127; ed. and Italian tr. Impellizzeri *et al.*, II, pp. 270–1; tr. Sewter, p. 320; Attal., ed. Bekker, pp. 66–8; ed. and Spanish tr. Pérez Martín, pp. 51–2; Skyl. Con., pp. 106–7.

[60] Attal., ed. Bekker, p. 83; ed. and Spanish tr. Pérez Martín, p. 63. See also Skyl. Con., pp. 113–14.

that security was better achieved by appeasement. However, even this broke down in the fiscal and political crisis of the 1070s, when the empire suffered assaults from all sides. In 1071 Seljuq Turks and Turkoman nomads invaded Anatolia, and in the extended aftermath of the battle of Manzikert bands of Turkoman nomads moved into the interior plateau of Anatolia (see above, pp. 609–10). No decent defence was mounted while the emperor Romanos IV Diogenes (1068–1071) competed with the Doukas family for control of the throne. The Balkan and Italian lands of the empire were no more stable at this time than Anatolia. In 1071, Bari, the last Byzantine stronghold in southern Italy, fell to the Normans. In the same year, the Hungarians and the Pechenegs crossed into imperial lands and plundered throughout Thrace and Macedonia; as a consequence

the Slav people threw off the Roman yoke and laid waste Bulgaria, taking plunder and leaving scorched earth. Skopje and Niš were sacked, and all the towns along the river Sava and beside the Danube between Sirmium and Vidin suffered greatly. Furthermore, the Croats and Dukljans throughout the whole of Dalmatia rose in rebellion.[61]

Skylitzes Continuatus provides a useful account of the Slavs' rebellion. Michael of Duklja, we are told, was approached by Bulgarian chieftains who demanded that he despatch a son 'to deliver them from the oppression and exactions of the Romans'.[62] Michael gladly sent his son Bodin with 300 troops to Prizren, where he was met by the magnates and the leading man of Skopje, George Vojteh, who acclaimed Bodin 'as emperor of the Bulgarians and gave him the new name Peter'. Peter was an imperial name in Bulgaria, recalling the tsar who reigned from 927 to 969. The *doux* of Skopje, Nikephoros Karantenos, marched on Prizren with an allied force of Byzantines and Bulgarians. However, Karantenos was undermined by rumours and replaced by a certain Damian Dalassenos, who taunted and insulted his troops, destroying their morale on the eve of battle; they suffered a bloody rout at the hands of the Serbs. Consequently, the rest of the Bulgarians recognised Bodin-Peter as their emperor, while he set about plundering lands around Niš and abusing the locals.

Vojteh's opportunism in approaching the Dukljans had thus been turned against him, for the new 'Bulgarian emperor' proved to be more avaricious than the Byzantines. Moreover, when a Byzantine army marched on Skopje, Bodin-Peter showed no concern for his 'subjects', obliging Vojteh to surrender without offering resistance. A garrison was installed in Skopje while Byzantine forces turned to Niš and promptly captured Bodin-Peter, who was despatched to Constantinople, and thence to Antioch.[63] Skylitzes Continuatus considered the reason for the rebellions to have been the

---

[61] Nikephoros Bryennios, III.1, *Histoire*, ed. and French tr. Gautier, p. 208–11.
[62] Skyl. Con., pp. 162–3; Stephenson (2000), pp. 141–4.   [63] *LPD*, p. 358.

'insatiate greed' of the treasurer Nikephoritzes, which he compared to the policy that had sparked the rebellions of the 1040s. The burden of taxation caused particular offence to the local leadership in lands around Skopje, at the northern limits of direct Byzantine administration, where Peter Del-jan had initially found his supporters. Such sentiments were not shared by all Bulgarians, and many fought alongside the Byzantine troops against Bodin-Peter.[64]

The turmoil of the early 1070s left Pechenegs in charge of key outposts on the Danube. It also saw the end of the distribution of stipends, forcing the nomads to look elsewhere for booty. Once again they set their sights on the lands south of the Haemus, and in 1077 launched a devastating raid into Thrace.[65] Ominously, the Pechenegs began to forge connections with the Paulicians, a heretical sect settled near Philippopolis, who had taken control of several passes through the Haemus. The fact that the nomads relied on a heretical minority may also suggest that they could expect little assistance from the orthodox majority. From his stronghold at Beliatoba, which dominated a pass of the same name through the Haemus, the Paulicians' leader Traulos controlled access between Paradounabon and Thrace. When Traulos sought to ally himself with the Pechenegs, marrying the daughter of one of their chieftains, the new emperor Alexios I Komnenos (1081–1118) 'foresaw the evil likely to result, and wrote conciliatory letters full of promises. He even sent a chrysobull guaranteeing Traulos an amnesty and full liberty.'[66] The emperor's efforts at conciliation were fruitless, and once again the Pechenegs crossed into Byzantine lands.

Gregory Pakourianos, commander-in-chief of the imperial forces in the west, was given responsibility for resisting the Pechenegs while the emperor campaigned against the Normans at Dyrrachium. Pakourianos prosecuted his war with some success, but died in battle in 1086, riding his horse headlong into an oak tree.[67] In spring 1087, Tzelgu, the supreme chieftain of the Pechenegs who were still settled north of the Danube, launched a devastating invasion. His route, crossing the middle Danube, suggests that he had reached an agreement with the Pechenegs settled in Paradoun-abon not to violate their territory. He had also reached an understand-ing with the Hungarians, and a large force under the former Hungar-ian king Salomon (1063–74) accompanied him. A Byzantine force fell on them in a mountain pass and succeeded in killing Tzelgu. However, those who escaped 'returned to the Danube and made their camp there. Living

---

[64] Fine (1983), p. 214.
[65] Nikephoros Bryennios, III.14, *Histoire*, ed. and French tr. Gautier, pp. 236–7.
[66] *Al.*, VI.4.4, ed. Reinsch and Kambylis, I, p. 174; ed. and French tr. Leib, II, p. 49; tr. Sewter, p. 187.
[67] *Al.*, VI.14.3, ed. Reinsch and Kambylis, I, p. 200; ed. and French tr. Leib, II, p. 83; tr. Sewter, p. 213.

alongside [Byzantine] lands they treated them as their own and plundered with complete licence.'[68]

Groups of nomads on both sides of the Danube had made common cause, forcing Alexios Komnenos to reconsider his northern policy. In an oration delivered in January 1088 by Theophylact, the future archbishop of Ohrid, the emperor's willingness to treat with the Pechenegs is celebrated as a 'bloodless victory'.[69] However, this was ephemeral, and the Pecheneg wars, which are copiously documented by Anna Komnena, reached their bloody conclusion at Lebounion in Thrace on 29 April 1091. This was a magnificent victory for the imperial forces, hence the chant by the Byzantines: 'All because of one day, the Scythians never saw May.'[70] The *Life* of Cyril the Phileote provides a near-contemporary account of the panic before the battle when 'because of the imminent danger all took refuge in citadels', and the relief afterwards when 'the insurmountable turmoil caused by the Scythians was transformed into peace with the aid of God and the perseverance of the emperor'.[71] The victory at Lebounion established the Komnenoi in an unassailable position in Constantinople. Alexios was able to disinherit the son of Michael VII Doukas and appoint his own three-year-old son John – the future John II (1118–43) – as junior emperor.

THE WESTERN BALKANS: THE NORMAN CHALLENGE, AND VENETIAN AND HUNGARIAN ALLIANCES

Peace in the western Balkans was equally hard-won. There the greatest menace was posed by the Normans who had come to dominate southern Italy, and wished to expand across the Adriatic into the theme of Dyrrachium. A Norman invasion, led by Robert Guiscard and his son Bohemond, accompanied Alexios I's accession in April 1081 (see above, pp. 610–11), and the earliest indications for the new emperor were not good. First, the citizens of Dubrovnik and other unspecified 'Dalmatians' provided transport ships for Norman troops.[72] Next, advance forces were handed the citadel at Corfu by its defenders, and proceeded to capture the ports of Vonitsa, Butrint and Avlona without difficulty.[73] Evidently, the greatest concern for the emperor was retaining the loyalty of the native population. Anna Komnena records that 'Alexios sent letters to the leaders (*hēgemones*) of the coastal towns and

---

[68] *Al.*, VII.1.1–2.1, ed. Reinsch and Kambylis, I, pp. 203–4; ed. and French tr. Leib, II, pp. 87–8; tr. Sewter, pp. 217–18.

[69] Theophylact of Ohrid, *Discourses*, ed. and French tr. Gautier, pp. 222–7; Malamut (1995), pp. 138–9.

[70] *Al.*, VIII.5.8, ed. Reinsch and Kambylis, I, p. 249; ed. and French tr. Leib, II, p. 143; tr. Sewter, p. 258.

[71] *La Vie de Sainte Cyrille*, pp. 127, 135.

[72] William of Apulia, *Gesta Roberti Wiscardi*, pp. 210, 220.

[73] William of Apulia, *Gesta Roberti Wiscardi*, pp. 214–17.

to the islanders earnestly exhorting them not to lose heart, nor to relax their efforts in any way.' Guiscard's intention was to secure, through intimidation and persuasion, the support of these same *hēgemones*. Moreover, the Norman had taken a crucial measure to secure their defection: he had in tow a man claiming to be the deposed emperor Michael VII. Clearly, Guiscard was aware that the population of Dyrrachium was loyal to the empire, but not necessarily to the current emperor. The Byzantine *doux* in Dyrrachium, George Palaiologos, kept the emperor informed of developments with regular despatches.[74] From his missives 'the emperor learnt that . . . countless hosts from all directions were rallying thick as winter snowflakes, and the more frivolous folk, believing that the false Michael was in truth the emperor, were joining Robert.'[75]

As he marched to the city Alexios I received news that Palaiologos had lost a pitched battle and been badly wounded. The emperor lost a second battle on 18 October 1081, in military terms a worse defeat for the Byzantines than the infamous rout at Manzikert.[76] Many magnates fell, and the emperor barely escaped, leaving Dyrrachium at the mercy of the Normans. A saving grace appeared to be the retention of the citadel by the Venetians, Alexios' allies who shared the imperial antipathy towards Norman expansion across the Adriatic, and rallied to the Byzantine cause in return for exceptional trading privileges. The Venetian doge Domenico Silvio was granted the title *doux* of Dalmatia and Croatia, and the elevated rank of *prōtosebastos*, placing him fourth in the new imperial hierarchy devised by Alexios.[77]

Venetian support was instrumental in the Byzantine recovery of territory and authority in Dyrrachium after 1082. The doge maintained vigilant guard over the Adriatic sea lanes while the emperor slowly clawed back land. The turning-point came at Larissa, where the emperor took advice from locals and determined to 'lay an ambush there and so defeat the Latins by guile'.[78] Alexios won his first significant victory by avoiding pitched battle, tricking the Norman cavalry into a chase and shooting at their horses from a distance. When Guiscard returned in full force in 1084 he was confronted by the Venetians, who achieved important victories at sea. Then, having landed and advanced into the interior of the theme of Dyrrachium, the Normans were caught between a vigorous naval blockade and the mountains, where the Byzantines vigilantly guarded the passes. Guiscard withdrew to the port of Jericho where he was trapped for two

---

[74] *DOS*, I, no. 12.2, p. 41.
[75] *Al.*, IV.2.1, ed. Reinsch and Kambylis, I, p. 122; ed. and French tr. Leib, I, p. 146; tr. Sewter, p. 137.
[76] *Al.*, IV.6., ed. Reinsch and Kambylis, I, pp. 131–6; ed. and French tr. Leib, I, pp. 157–63; tr. Sewter, pp. 145–9; William of Apulia, *Gesta Roberti Wiscardi*, pp. 224–7.
[77] *Al.*, IV.2.2–3, VI.5.7–10, ed. Reinsch and Kambylis, I, pp. 122–3, 178–9; ed. and French tr. Leib, I, pp. 146–7, II, pp. 53–5; tr. Sewter, pp. 137–8, 190–1. See also p. 625.
[78] *Al.*, V.5.5, ed. Reinsch and Kambylis, I, p. 155; ed. and French tr. Leib, II, p. 25; tr. Sewter, p. 168.

months by adverse winds and the allied ships.[79] Up to 10,000 Normans are said to have starved to death before a withdrawal was effected. Guiscard died the following year, 1085. Alexios had discovered how best to use the natural defences of Dyrrachium and the services of his allies. These tactics would serve him well again, in 1106–7.

The city of Dyrrachium was returned to the empire, and thereafter the command was considered sensitive enough only to be granted to close relatives of the emperor, including Alexios' brother-in-law John Doukas and his nephew John Komnenos, the son of the *sebastokratōr* Isaac.[80] This second John led an unsuccessful campaign against the Dukljans, suffering many casualties through inexperience and impetuousness. However, John retained his command and in 1096 was the Byzantine commander who first encountered an entirely new menace from the west: the First Crusade. It has been demonstrated that during the course of the crusade the emperor enjoyed particularly close ties with Bohemond.[81] In spite of their earlier conflict, indeed probably because of the familiarity that encounter engendered, Alexios had received favourably Bohemond's proposals to act as his intermediary with the crusading leaders, and promised him lands and office in the east. However, the agreement was abandoned at Antioch, where a remarkable victory left Bohemond in command of the city. While in the following years the emperor accepted the crusaders' conquests, and acknowledged their local jurisdiction in exchange for recognition of his overlordship, he would never accept the Norman domination of Antioch. Thus, Bohemond returned to the west in autumn 1104 to recruit new troops, and proposed a crusade directed against his foe in Constantinople. His resolve and status were strengthened when he married the elder daughter of Philip I of France (see above, p. 624).

Alexios I responded swiftly to the Norman's mission: he wrote to potentates throughout Europe denying charges levelled by Bohemond and urging against a second armed pilgrimage. He was peculiarly keen to prevent any alliance that would expose the empire's western flank to attack, and Anna emphasises his concern over approaches to the Italian maritime cities of Venice, Pisa and Genoa.[82] Alexios had a further concern: the possibility of an aggressive Norman–Hungarian alliance. In 1097 Bohemond's cousin, Roger of Sicily, had forged a marriage alliance with the Hungarians. Alexios could not afford to let Bohemond reach a similar understanding, which would expose the empire to a massive invasion through the northern marches. A simultaneous assault on the coast at Dyrrachium would

---

[79] *Al.*, IV.3., ed. Reinsch and Kambylis, I, pp. 124–6; ed. and French tr. Leib, I, pp. 148–50; tr. Sewter, pp. 139–40. Anna incorrectly places these events in her account of the 1082 campaign.

[80] Frankopan (2002), pp. 75–98.   [81] Shepard (1988a).

[82] *Al.*, XII.1.2, ed. Reinsch and Kambylis, I, p. 359; ed. and French tr. Leib, III, pp. 53–4; tr. Sewter, p. 369.

have led to the loss of the whole of the western Balkans. Thus the emperor orchestrated an extraordinary diplomatic initiative. In 1104 an embassy was sent to the court of the Hungarian king, and it was arranged that Piroska, the daughter of the late King Ladislas I (1077–95), should be betrothed to John, heir to the Byzantine throne. Bohemond was left to launch his assault on the southern Adriatic littoral, and the emperor had sufficient time to make suitable preparations.

The emperor had learned from earlier campaigns to use the terrain of Dyrrachium to his advantage, and took great pains to seal the mountain passes to the east of Dyrrachium. Even after Alexios was betrayed by certain *Arbanoi*, who showed Bohemond the mountain tracks, the Normans could neither advance nor easily retreat.[83] An effective naval blockade, mounted with Venetian assistance, prevented further supplies and troops from reaching the invasion force.[84] Norman foraging parties were frequently ambushed and returned empty-handed, if they returned at all. In this way Bohemond's spirit was broken, and he sued for peace, agreeing the treaty of Devol which is recorded in full by Anna Komnena.[85] Bohemond was to receive the elevated imperial rank of *sebastos* and command of the cities of Antioch and Edessa, both of which would revert to imperial control upon his death. However, Bohemond never returned to Antioch, and the carefully constructed clauses of the treaty of Devol were not implemented. Consequently, Alexios and his successor John II (1118–43) were committed to an arduous military and diplomatic struggle to regain Antioch, devoting little attention to the empire's Balkan lands. Into this vacuum stepped two expansionary powers, the Venetians and Hungarians.

The need to secure first Venetian and then Hungarian assistance for wars against the Normans saw the Byzantines delegate authority in Dalmatia and Croatia. As early as 1081–2 the Venetian doge was granted the title 'doux of Dalmatia and Croatia', ostensibly acting for the emperor, but in reality advancing his own interests. The Hungarians did likewise, and in 1102 Coloman completed the annexation of Croatia to his kingdom and had himself crowned King of Croatia in Biograd.[86] The betrothal in 1104 of Piroska and John Komnenos gave this act Byzantine recognition, and also appears to have offered tacit imperial support to a Hungarian invasion of Dalmatia, which took place against Venetian interests in 1105. The inhabitants of the maritime cities surrendered to the Hungarian king

---

[83] *Al.*, XIII.5.2, ed. Reinsch and Kambylis, I, pp. 397–8; ed. and French tr. Leib, III, pp. 104–5; tr. Sewter, pp. 408–9.

[84] *Al.*, XIII.7.4–5, ed. Reinsch and Kambylis, I, pp. 404–5; ed. and French tr. Leib, III, pp. 113–14; tr. Sewter, pp. 414–15.

[85] *Al.*, XIII.12., ed. Reinsch and Kambylis, I, pp. 413–23; ed. and French tr. Leib, III, p. 125–39; tr. Sewter, pp. 424–34. See also above, pp. 623–4.

[86] *Codex diplomaticus regni Croatiae*, II, p. 1; Steindorff (1984), pp. 44, 47–8.

in return for certain privileges, the details of which have been preserved in extant charters.[87] Venetian retaliation was delayed until 1115–16, when the doge recovered the major cities. Despite Hungarian efforts, the Venetians retained control of most of Dalmatia into the 1140s.

During this time John II showed little interest in the northern Balkans. In 1122 he achieved a significant victory over an invading force of 'Scythians', possibly Pechenegs, but probably Cumans. His only subsequent military venture into the region was brief and opportunistic. Niketas Choniates notes that in 1127 the Hungarians sacked Braničevo and Sofia, and in response John sailed 'along the Danube from the Black Sea, falling upon the foe by both land and water . . . captured Frangochorion [between the Sava and Danube] . . . and Semlin, and attacked Haram, from which he wrested great spoils. After further struggles, he offered peace.'[88] For the remainder of John's reign the treaty signed with the Hungarian king was honoured. Furthermore, stability was guaranteed by the good relations John enjoyed with the German rulers Lothar III (1125–37) and Conrad III (1138–52). In 1136 Byzantine troops took part in Lothar's campaign which pressed into Norman-occupied southern Italy. Relations with Conrad were even better, and from 1140 were destined to be cemented by the marriage of John's fourth son, Manuel, to Conrad's sister-in-law, Bertha of Sulzbach (see above, pp. 636–7). Thus John was free to concentrate on his eastern campaigns, and it was in Cilicia in 1143 that he was killed in a hunting accident. The younger of his two surviving sons, Manuel, succeeded.

NORMANS, HUNGARIANS, SERBS AND GERMANS: MANUEL KOMNENOS' BALANCING ACT

In the early years of his reign Manuel I Komnenos (1143–80) remained committed to his father's policies in the east. The crusader principalities, particularly Antioch, were priorities, and he was prepared to tolerate both increased Hungarian influence in Sirmium and the Venetian domination of Dalmatia. However, Manuel's attention was drawn increasingly towards the west, not least when Conrad III led the forces of the Second Crusade through Byzantine lands against his wishes. While the Germans were marching across Bulgaria and Thrace, a Norman fleet seized the island of Corfu and captured Thebes and Corinth. It sailed back to Sicily with great plunder and many captives, retaining control of Corfu, whence attacks on the lands south of Dyrrachium might easily be launched. Manuel turned to the Venetians for naval assistance, and in October 1147 renewed their

---

[87] Steindorff (1984), pp. 11–25; Stephenson (2000), pp. 199–203.
[88] NC, ed. van Dieten, I, pp. 17–18; tr. Magoulias, pp. 11–12. Kinn., I.4, ed. Meineke, pp. 10–13; tr. Brand, pp. 18–19, offers an alternative account. See also Stephenson (1996).

trading privileges. The Venetians were themselves troubled by the Norman occupation of Corfu.

In 1149, while preparing a retaliatory assault on Norman positions in southern Italy, Manuel learned of an uprising by the Serbs of Raška. He marched north, swiftly recovering the fortress of Ras, where around fifty metres of the western ramparts of the city were destroyed in the assault and later rebuilt.[89] The decisive blow was struck with the storming of the fortress of Galič. Manuel took many captives, but failed to capture the elusive *veliki župan* Uroš II. The court panegyrist Theodore Prodromos provides a contemporary account of the campaigns of 1149, when

the supreme ruler of the barbarous Serbs, the *archiserbozoupanos*, this mountain-reared swine, thrice a slave since birth, driven by senseless audacity, rose against us and our lord, having Hungarian forces for allies and thus misled by the Sicilian Dragon [Roger II of Sicily], and he was persuaded by his [Roger's] gifts to enter into treaties to distract the emperor from attacking him.[90]

Evidently the Normans were responsible for inciting the Serbian uprising, and for the deterioration in Byzantino-Hungarian relations. If the Serbs were seduced by gifts, the Hungarians saw in an alliance with the Normans the opportunity to consolidate their interests in Dalmatia. The Normans were the only naval power capable of challenging Venetian domination of the Adriatic. Ominously, the emperor was unable to ensure stability in the region by the distribution of largesse and titles, or through his proxies. Manuel was drawn into more frequent shows of strength in the Balkans.

Manuel I's biographer, John Kinnamos, provides a detailed account of the campaigns of the following year, 1150, which culminated in the battle of Tara. The historian describes a hard-fought battle, the climax of which was Manuel's victorious duel with the commander of the Hungarian attachment, Bakchinus (Bagin). In defeat the Serbian *veliki župan* swore to remain loyal to the emperor, breaking off his alliance with the Hungarians and Normans. However, the emperor determined to punish the Hungarians and set off for the Danube before he had 'even wiped the dust of the battle-field from his face and was still covered in warm sweat'.[91] Thus he was able to devastate the lands between the Sava and Danube rivers and seize tens of thousands of captives before a treaty was agreed. Details of these campaigns are provided by the sycophantic panegyrist Manganeios Prodromos, who delivered at least three orations to praise the emperor as a 'brilliant triple victor'. 'What yearly cycle', he asked, 'ever saw so great a miracle, a terrible bloodless victory, a capturing of prisoners, herds of goats and cattle, many thousands of mares, innumerable flocks of the fattest sheep?'[92]

[89] Popović, M. (1999), pp. 171–85. But see also Kalić (2000).
[90] Theodore Prodromos, *Poems*, p. 354.   [91] NC, ed. van Dieten, I, p. 92; tr. Magoulias, p. 54.
[92] Manganeios Prodromos, *Poems*, nos. 1, 2 and 27.

King Géza II of Hungary (1141–62) came to blows and agreements with Manuel on three more occasions, in 1151, 1153 and 1154. On the first two occasions he was acting as an ally of the Normans, and the third was inspired by secret negotiations with Manuel's cousin, the pretender Andronikos Komnenos. The instability was indicative of the new balance of power that had emerged in the north-western Balkans. Both Hungarians and Normans offered alternative sources of patronage for the Serbs and Dalmatians, even before Venetian interests were considered. This seemed of secondary importance while Byzantium was allied with Germany, for the two imperial powers imagined they might control their neighbours. However, relations with Germany began to worsen, and Manuel felt obliged to strengthen the Byzantine presence in the north-western Balkans. He renovated key fortresses on his border with Hungary, at Belgrade and Braničevo, where larger garrisons were installed.[93] Within the frontier, he staged a trial to arbitrate a dispute between the Serbian *veliki župan* Uroš II and his brother Desa; the latter had ousted the former in the turmoil of autumn 1153. Manuel's judgement in favour of Uroš was carefully orchestrated, 'a statement about the nature of imperial sovereignty, calculated to impress the German, French and Turkish emissaries who happened to be present'.[94] Moreover, it mirrored a similar judgement reached by the new German emperor Frederick I Barbarossa (1152–90) in 1152, arbitrating between two claimants to the throne of Denmark. Manuel, thereafter, was swift to press his claims as suzerain of Serbia. More ambitiously, he also sought to extend his influence beyond the Danube, into Hungary.

Kinnamos states explicitly that 'Manuel wished to establish control of Hungary because it lay in the midst of the western realms'.[95] In fact he wished to secure the loyalty of the Hungarian king and thereby retain a pliant buffer kingdom between his empire and Germany. This is the context for the Hungarian succession disputes of the early 1160s, where both emperors supported rival candidates, exploiting factionalism within the kingdom.[96] Barbarossa and his clients supported Stephen III, while Manuel favoured Stephen IV, and later Stephen III's younger brother Béla; Béla was brought to Constantinople in 1163, betrothed to Manuel's own daughter Maria, and given the name Alexios (see above, p. 642). Before the death of his father, Géza II, Béla-Alexios had been promised a large appanage at the frontier between Hungary and the empire, and it was ostensibly in defence of his rights that Manuel invaded and occupied Sirmium and Frangochorion in spring 1164.[97] It is not clear that these were in fact the lands Béla-Alexios had been promised, but they were certainly the lands

[93] Popović, M. (1982), pp. 49–53; Popović and Ivanišević (1988); Stephenson (2000), pp. 241–5.
[94] Magdalino (1993a), p. 56.   [95] Kinn., V.5, ed. Meineke, p. 214; tr. Brand, p. 163.
[96] Makk (1989), pp. 63–106; Stephenson (2000), pp. 247–61.
[97] Kinn., V.6, ed. Meineke, pp. 217–18; tr. Brand, pp. 164–5.

on which Manuel had set his sights. So much is demonstrated by the reaction in 1165 to an attempt by Stephen III to recover the territory, when the emperor despatched letters and envoys to numerous powers requesting their support for his attack on Stephen III. The Venetians were willing allies, and committed 100 ships for an attack on Hungarian positions in Dalmatia which was launched in May 1165. By the time Manuel arrived on the Danube the whole of central Dalmatia was in Byzantine hands, and the Venetians had recovered Zara. John Kinnamos states that:

> Already [the Byzantine general] John Doukas had subdued Dalmatia and turned it over to Nikephoros Chalouphes, as he had been directed by the emperor, who had previously sent him there to conquer it by force of arms or negotiation. The reason for this was that the Hungarians had designated it in a treaty as Béla's patrimony. . . . At that time Trogir and Šibenik came over to the Byzantines, as well as Split . . . and whatever cities are located in Dalmatia which total fifty-seven.[98]

Manuel took personal responsibility for the recovery of Sirmium, and having obliged Stephen III of Hungary to sign an unfavourable treaty, left generals in the region who showed 'the most earnest concern for the fortifications of Belgrade, built walls around Niš, and brought Braničevo under settlement'.[99] Traces of their efforts to strengthen the established fortifications have been uncovered in excavations.[100] In 1166 the Hungarians launched retaliatory campaigns in both Sirmium and Dalmatia, the latter led by the *ban* Ampud, the former under the count Denis and thirty-seven disgruntled generals which ended with the plains 'almost covered in the carcasses of barbarians'. Five generals were captured, along with 800 men and 2,000 breastplates of the fallen: 'the war on the Hungarians concluded there'.[101] Ampud's attack on Split also failed, but he managed to capture the Byzantine governor, Nikephoros Chalouphes. Extant charters issued in the name of the Hungarian king suggest that Ampud recovered Biograd and possibly Šibenik. However, this was ephemeral. Following the defeat of Denis' army, Manuel enjoyed control of Dalmatia south of Šibenik. As allies who had provided invaluable assistance to John Doukas in 1166, the Venetians maintained control of the lands north of Zara.

The recovery of Dalmatia was considered an essential stepping-stone to extending Byzantine influence in northern Italy, which, like Hungary, was an arena for competition with the German emperor. Immediately before his appointment to command Dalmatia, Nikephoros Chalouphes had travelled to Venice to secure the assistance of the doge in the 1165 campaigns, and had also persuaded 'Cremona and Padua and many other outstanding cities in

---

[98] Kinn., V.17, ed. Meineke, pp. 248–9; tr. Brand, pp. 186–7.
[99] NC, ed. van Dieten, I, p. 136; tr. Magoulias, p. 77.
[100] Popović, M. (1982), pp. 49–53; Popović and Ivanišević (1988).
[101] Kinn., VI.7, ed. Meineke, p. 274; tr. Brand, p. 205.

Liguria to join with the emperor'.[102] The *doux* of Dalmatia was charged with certain responsibilities in northern Italy, just as, after 1071, the Byzantine governor in Dyrrachium was charged with oversight of affairs in southern Italy. Thus, Chalouphes' replacement, Constantine Doukas, was often to be found there distributing money to potential allies, and even commanded a Byzantine garrison during the German siege of Ancona.[103]

The empire's Balkan lands, therefore, drew increased attention as a consequence of anxieties about German imperial ambitions. Manuel advanced the empire's frontiers across the Danube and into Dalmatia, and made inroads into Italy and Hungary through strategic use of force and aggressive diplomacy. Expansionary policies were pursued to prevent the loss of suzerainty over peripheral potentates in the face of interference from the west, and to confront the perceived enemy on safer, more distant ground. Manuel exploited the resources of his rich empire, with an economy expanding throughout his reign, to distribute cash and prestige goods within and beyond his borders, and to bind disparate potentates and peoples to him. Moreover, he quashed rebellions effectively and efficiently, for example bringing the Serbs to heel on numerous occasions. In many ways his policies resembled those of Basil II, although Manuel was remembered for his generosity as much as for his martial capabilities. His legacy also resembled that of Basil, for Manuel's successors lacked his reputation, meticulously constructed through decades, and were unable to impose their authority in the periphery or extend their influence beyond.[104] Indeed, it can be argued that Manuel's expansionary policies were, like Basil's, unsustainable and precipitated the crises that the empire faced after his death.

AFTER MANUEL: SERB SECESSION, VLACH AND BULGARIAN UPRISINGS

As soon as news of Manuel's death reached Serbia, Stefan Nemanja (*c.* 1165/8–96) declared independence. In the following years he annexed Duklja and the southern Adriatic littoral, where there were many Latin bishoprics. This placed 'medieval Serbia on the crossroads of Byzantium and the west', but even as Stefan turned away from Constantinople his faith was increasingly orthodox.[105] He founded four monasteries, the last being Studenica, built after 1183, which became a model for later richly endowed royal foundations. Stefan's youngest son, Rastko, drew Nemanjid patronage to Mount Athos, where he fled *c.* 1191 and took the monastic name Sava. As a monk at the Vatopedi monastery he was visited by his

---

[102] Kinn., V.9, ed. Meineke, p. 231; tr. Brand, p. 174.
[103] Abulafia (1984), pp. 210–11. See also above, pp. 639–40.
[104] Magdalino (1993a), pp. 413–70.   [105] Obolensky (1988a), p. 120.

dying father who brought lavish gifts including horses, mules, and buckets of gold and silver.[106]

Béla III, Manuel I's protégé who had been king of Hungary since 1172, also reacted to Manuel's death with a land-grab, annexing Dalmatia and Sirmium. Furthermore, when Andronikos I (1183–85) usurped the imperial throne, Béla established unopposed his control across the whole of the Niš–Braničevo region, from Belgrade as far as Sofia.[107] That territory, but not Sirmium and Dalmatia, was returned in 1185, when Béla reached an agreement with the new emperor, Isaac II Angelos (1185–95); Isaac agreed to marry Béla's daughter Margaret, who took the name Maria, and to receive as her dowry the region of Niš–Braničevo.[108]

Before this, Andronikos had also to face an invasion by the Normans of Sicily, who brought a character claiming to be the deposed Alexios II (1180–3). This ploy, echoing Guiscard's use in 1081 of the pseudo-Michael Doukas, persuaded the *hēgemones* of Dyrrachium to capitulate before the mountain passes could be blocked or a naval force mustered. Norman forces were able to advance by land and sea, and converged upon Thessaloniki, where a brief but bloody struggle ensued. The city's archbishop, Eustathios, composed an account which devotes long passages to the deaths of citizens, some by the sword, others trampled underfoot in vain attempts to seek the security of the citadel or churches. The Normans' threat to march on Constantinople precipitated the murder of Andronikos I and accession of Isaac Angelos, whose spirited counter-offensive drove the Sicilians from both Thessaloniki and, later, Dyrrachium. Less successful was Isaac II's handling of the Vlachs and Bulgarians settled in and near the Haemus.

To pay for the festivities associated with his wedding to Margaret-Maria, Isaac II Angelos determined to raise money from imperial estates.[109] However, demands were also made on those settled near estates in the region of Anchialos, provoking complaints brought to the emperor by the brothers Peter and Asen, who requested that Isaac grant them an imperial estate in the vicinity of the Haemus 'which would provide them with a little revenue'. Their request was denied, and consequently 'they spat out heated words, hinting at rebellion and the destruction they would wreak on their way home'.[110] Inspired by the sack of Thessaloniki, the brothers announced that St Demetrios had abandoned the Byzantines and claimed him as their own. Support for their rebellion cohered around St Demetrios, and Vlachs and Bulgarians launched assaults on Byzantine settlements, seizing captives and cattle in abundance. Isaac launched a counter-offensive, and recovered much ground. However, thereafter he entrusted the struggle to a series

---

[106] Obolensky (1988a), pp. 124–7.   [107] Makk (1989), pp. 115–19.

[108] NC, ed. van Dieten, I, p. 368; tr. Magoulias, p. 203. See also above, p. 649.

[109] NC, ed. van Dieten, I, p. 368; tr. Magoulias, p. 203; Magdalino (1993a), pp. 134–5.

[110] NC, ed. van Dieten, I, p. 369; tr. Magoulias, p. 204.

of disloyal generals, each of whom launched a bid for the throne rather than prosecuting the war. The Vlachs and Bulgarians were able to forge an alliance with the Cumans and consolidated their control of all the lands between the Haemus and lower Danube.[111]

In 1189 the situation deteriorated still further for Isaac II when Frederick Barbarossa determined to lead the German contingent in the Third Crusade across the Balkans. The passage was long and arduous, exacerbated by mutual suspicion and violence. The Germans believed Isaac had struck a deal with their enemy and target, Saladin. En route Barbarossa was approached by the Serbian *veliki župan*, Stefan Nemanja, and his brothers, who offered to support Frederick's march and provide aid against the Byzantines, and in return sought Frederick's promise to act as guarantor of recent Serbian conquests.[112] Similarly, Peter and Asen sent envoys to the Germans, and when Barbarossa had arrived at Adrianople, they offered 40,000 Vlach and Cuman archers for an assault on Constantinople.[113] Barbarossa's ongoing negotiations with the Balkan peoples provoked Isaac's unease. The German emperor was regarded as an authority who might lend legitimacy to the regimes of autonomous rulers who had until recently owed loyalty to the Byzantine emperor, effectively recognising their permanent detachment from the eastern empire.

The Germans did not sack Constantinople, and Barbarossa died before reaching the Holy Land. In the aftermath of the crusade, in autumn 1190, Isaac II returned to the Haemus, whence the Vlachs with their Cuman allies launched unremitting assaults on imperial lands. Isaac was unable to engage them in pitched battle, and as he withdrew led his army into an ambush in a narrow defile, where many of his troops were crushed by rocks thrown down upon them. The emperor barely escaped and rumours of his death circulated widely as the Vlachs and Bulgarians made unprecedented advances.[114] Whereas previously their assaults had been concentrated on villages and fields, now they advanced against 'lofty-towered cities. They sacked Anchialos, took Varna by force, and advanced on . . . Sofia, where they razed the greater part of the city.'[115]

In the following year the Byzantines recouped some territory, notably Varna and Anchialos. Isaac himself led a campaign against the Vlachs and Cumans from Philippopolis, and from there continued on to confront Stefan Nemanja. After an indecisive battle, Isaac concluded a peace treaty with the *veliki župan*, allowing him to keep much land that he had captured. A contemporary reference to this can be found in an oration of George

[111] Vásáry (2005), pp. 13–56.   [112] Ansbert, *History of Frederick's expedition*, p. 30.
[113] Ansbert, *History of Frederick's expedition*, p. 58.
[114] NC, ed. van Dieten, I, pp. 429–32; tr. Magoulias, pp. 236–7.
[115] NC, ed. van Dieten, I, p. 434; tr. Magoulias, p. 238.

Tornikios, alluding to a marriage between Eudocia, Isaac's niece, and Stefan, the eldest son of Stefan Nemanja.[116] Then, late in 1192, a dispute broke out between Peter and Asen. The former had chosen to reside in Preslav, the imperial capital of his chosen namesake, Tsar Peter of Bulgaria, while Asen was based in T'rnovo.[117] It is likely that Isaac had persuaded Peter to enter into an arrangement, facilitating an imperial campaign against Asen in spring 1193. The emperor did not take the field himself, but preferred to remain in Constantinople where 'he delighted in ribaldries and lewd songs and consorted with laughter-stirring dwarves'.[118] The campaigns against Asen were entrusted to the emperor's young cousin, Constantine Angelos who, like so many before, sought to seize the throne.[119] He failed, was blinded, and the Vlacho-Bulgarians set out with their Cuman allies against Philippopolis, Sofia, and even Adrianople, laying waste the lands en route. Once again the Byzantines had lost the initiative because of the independent ambitions of a general. The imperial campaign of 1194 was equally unsuccessful, and Isaac raised conscript and mercenary forces for a grand campaign to crush the Vlacho-Bulgarians in 1195. However, before this could happen Isaac was blinded and replaced by his brother Alexios III Angelos (1195–1203).

The period 1190–95 was one of lost or scorned opportunities for the Byzantines. Isaac II Angelos seems to have acted rationally in the aftermath of the Third Crusade, accepting that the empire had, for a time at least, to abandon claims to lands beyond the Velika Morava. His alliance with Béla III, and consequent negotiations with Stefan Nemanja, allowed Isaac to concentrate his limited resources on combatting the Vlachs and Bulgarians. In 1193, by winning over Peter, Isaac isolated Asen and weakened considerably his ability to launch raids south of the mountains. However, Isaac's commanders scorned the initiative, placing personal ambition above the good of the empire. More threatening still was the fact that, after Isaac's death, the nature of Vlacho-Bulgarian raids changed. Whereas before 1195 they were content to plunder lands south of the Haemus and around the Black Sea ports, which remained in Byzantine hands, from 1196 the Vlacho-Bulgarians began to contemplate permanent possession of both *kastra* and cities. Moreover, for the first time the new rulers began to strike their own coins. These so-called 'Bulgarian imitative' coins have been found in considerable numbers north of the Haemus in hoards buried between 1195 and 1204.[120]

---

[116] George Tornikios, 'Oratio ad Isaacium Angelum Imperatorem', in *Fontes rerum Byzantinarum*, ed. Regel and Novosadskij, p. 277.

[117] NC, ed. van Dieten, I, p. 470; tr. Magoulias, p. 258.

[118] NC, ed. van Dieten, I, p. 441; tr. Magoulias, p. 242.

[119] NC, ed. van Dieten, I, p. 435; tr. Magoulias, p. 239.   [120] Hendy (1969), pp. 218–22.

After 1196 Byzantine forces were no longer willing to march through the Haemus passes. The empire's frontiers now ran roughly across the Haemus as far as the river Vardar, or in places the Strymon, and the Velika Morava, which together marked the effective western limit of Byzantine authority. And beyond that limit, in Serbia and Bulgaria, the emperor was regarded increasingly with contempt. This is nowhere better illustrated than in the case of Eudocia. By 1198 Eudocia's father, Alexios, was emperor and her husband Stefan had replaced his father as *veliki župan*. Yet so far had Serbian sentiment shifted that Stefan 'stripped [his wife of] her woman's robe, leaving her only with her undergarment, which was cut around so that it barely covered her private parts, and dismissed her thus to go forth as if she were a harlot'.[121] With her, Stefan rejected Byzantine suzerainty. The Byzantine emperor was held in similar disdain north of the Haemus, where Kalojan, who succeeded his brothers Peter and Asen in 1197, sought recognition for his realm from Rome. In a series of letters exchanged with Pope Innocent III (1198–1216) from 1197 to 1204, Kalojan was willing to accept the title 'king (*rex*) of the Bulgarians and Vlachs' and an archbishop's pallium for his chief cleric, Basil of T'rnovo. Thus he rejected an approach from Constantinople offering both imperial and patriarchal titles, having determined that it was better to be a king by papal authority than an emperor by Byzantine (see below, pp. 782–3).[122]

CONCLUSION: THE WANING OF IMPERIAL POWER IN THE BALKANS

At the death of Basil II, Byzantium was the most powerful polity in the eastern Mediterranean. Imperial advances in the Balkans, as in the east, had been consolidated by the construction of fortifications and imposition of garrisons, but stability was ensured by securing the allegiance of peripheral potentates, who lived in fear of imperial retribution should they err, and enjoyed the prestige and prizes of office when they remained loyal.[123] As the eleventh century proceeded, troops were withdrawn from the periphery, and fear of retribution was allowed to dissipate. Moreover, a thirst for gold to service the state economy led bureaucrats in Constantinople to tax subject peoples too harshly, provoking rebellions by the Bulgarians. Authority was recovered, but on each occasion with greater difficulty.

From the middle of the twelfth century the Balkan peoples, courted and threatened from both sides, were offered unprecedented choices. The Dalmatians welcomed the return of Byzantine patronage, which was lavish

---

[121] NC, ed. van Dieten, I, p. 531; tr. Magoulias, p. 292.
[122] Prinzing (2002), pp. 163–74; Stephenson (2000), pp. 309–15.
[123] Holmes (2005), pp. 368–91, 475–87.

compared to that of the Venetians or Hungarians, but the Serbs made overtures on various occasions to the Hungarian and Sicilian Norman kings and
the German emperor, showing an informed preference for a more distant
suzerain. Byzantine efforts to maintain authority in the Balkan periphery
involved balancing a multitude of internal and external interests, forces
and factors. Manuel I Komnenos' policy became increasingly elaborate and
expensive, and his agents roamed ever more widely. After Manuel's death in
1180, the empire was without an emperor able to maintain this delicate balance, and unwilling to commit substantial resources to the periphery. The
empire endured a series of short reigns punctuated by rebellions. Increasingly, Balkan potentates saw no reason to tie their own interests to those
of eastern emperors who were unable even to control their own kin. The
Vlachs, Bulgarians and Serbs all rebelled and resisted attempts to restore
Byzantine suzerainty. The titles and stipends offered by Constantinople,
which had seduced all in the 1020s and 1030s, lacked magnetism in the
1180s and 1190s. After the sack of Constantinople by the Fourth Crusade
in 1204, the emperor in Constantinople would never again enjoy political
control across the Balkan peninsula.

CHAPTER 19

RAIDERS AND NEIGHBOURS: THE TURKS
(1040–1304)

D. A. KOROBEINIKOV

I, Gregory, the priest over the enfeebled people of the Armenians, at the time of our persecutions by the nation of the Ishmaelites who had appeared from eastern lands [wrote this colophon on the Gospels]. We came from Mount Ararat, from the village, which is called Arkuri, following our God-loving king Sennacherim, to dwell in this city of Sebasteia where the Forty Martyrs shed their blood in the battle with bitter-blowing wind and ice-cold water. And there, after five years my many talented and greatly honoured father, the priest Anania passed away, in the royal city of Constantinople[1] ... And [so] we remained [in Sebasteia], two brothers, George and Gregory ...'[2]

This colophon, written in 1066, offers us insight into an Armenian monastery on Byzantine territory. Gregory, the copyist of the Gospel Book, moved to Sebasteia after 1021, when Basil II (976–1025) granted the city to Sennacherim-John Artsruni, in exchange for his native kingdom of Vaspurakan (see above, p. 360). Gregory's colophon is his testament, bequeathing his most valuable possession, the Gospels, to his spiritual son.

The colophon was written at a difficult period for Byzantine Asia Minor. Although primarily concerned with spiritual themes, Gregory mentions 'our persecutions by the nation of the Ishmaelites'. The question arises: who were these 'Ishmaelites'?

THE TURKS' FIRST APPEARANCE

As so often in Byzantine history, a population movement which came to threaten the empire had its origins far beyond its borders. In the mid-sixth century the great Eurasian steppes were occupied by a new people, who spoke Turkic and called themselves Turks, or more precisely Kök Turks ('Blue or Celestial Turks'). They established a Turkic khaganate sometime between 546 and 552 and apart from a short interruption in the later seventh century, this continued in existence until 744/5, when the Uighurs killed the last Turk khagan, Pai-mei, and sent his head to the Chinese court.

---

[1] The colophon contains a gap.
[2] Mat'evosyan (ed.), *Hishatakaranner*, no. 124, p. 105. See figs. 52a and 52b.

Figure 52a Title page of the Armenian Gospel Book of 1066, Sebasteia

Figure 52b Miniature of St Mark writing his gospel from the Armenian Gospel Book of 1066

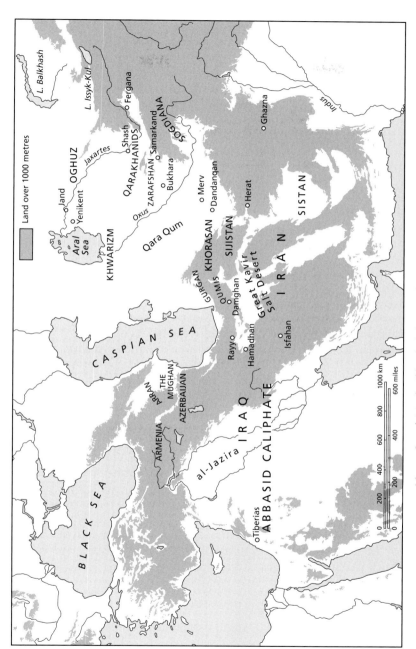

Map 31 Central Asia, the Abbasid caliphate and the emergence of the Seljuqs

The Turkic khaganate became the breeding-ground for other powerful Turkic tribal confederations. The most notorious were the Uighurs, who established their own khaganate over the remnants of the Kök Turk empire from 745 to 840, and, further west, the Qarluqs and the Oghuz. Like the Uighurs, the Qarluqs rebelled against their Kök Turk masters in 744/5. They then migrated west from near the headwaters of the Irtysh to the lands between Lake Balkhash and Lake Issyk-Kul. To the north and west of them, in the steppes between the Jaxartes and the Aral Sea, were the pastures of the Oghuz tribes, who were likewise former members of the Turkic khaganate. Their ruler bore the title of *yabghu* and was based at Yenikent.

The Arabs and the Muslim successor states in Central Asia at first managed to maintain their defences against these nomadic peoples along the Jaxartes river. The Samanids (875–1005), the last Iranian dynasty in Central Asia, built a formidable line of fortresses in Fergana and Shash. The Islamisation of the Turkic peoples along the Jaxartes resulted from their close ties with the Muslims of Transoxiana.[3] But in 999 this period of stability ended. The Qarakhanids, who belonged to the Qarluq confederation, concluded an alliance with Sultan Mahmud of Ghazna (998–1030) and destroyed the Samanids. The victors divided the spoils: Mahmud took Transoxiana, Khorasan and all the territories to the west of the Oxus, including Khwarizm. The Qarakhanids became masters of Sogdiana, Fergana, Bukhara, Samarkand and the lands to the east of the Oxus.

The Iranian barrier in Central Asia had now collapsed, opening up the central Muslim lands to the Turkish hordes. The instability in Central Asia had serious repercussions for Armenia, Arran and al-Jazira, all close to the Byzantine borders. Because the central Iranian plateau – and notably the Dasht-i Kavir (Great Kavir), the greatest salt desert in the world – prevented any migration *en masse* to the south, the nomads took the easier route westwards, along the Caspian's southern shore to the rich pastures of Azerbaijan and the plain of Mughan (see above, p. 132). A horde which had recently moved from Central Asia attacked Sennacherim-John Artsruni's kingdom. The Armenians lost the battle, which probably took place either in 1016 or early 1017;[4] and Sennacherim-John exchanged his kingdom for safer lands in the depths of Asia Minor, under the protection of the emperor. Subsequent events only served to confirm the king's wisdom: in 1021 a new horde of Turks devastated the country of Nig, between Shirak and Lake Sevan. Such were the first signs of the new enemy-to-come.

THE SELJUQ INVASION

However, it was another Turkic group – a branch of the Oghuz named after the founder of their dynasty, Saljuq – who posed the most serious

---

[3] Kennedy (ed.) (2002), p. 41a.   [4] Seibt (1978), cols. 49–56. See also above, p. 360.

threat to the Byzantines. The Turks, as we have seen, did not appear in the Middle East as a *deus ex machina*. By the beginning of the tenth century, the Oghuz occupied the lands along the river Jaxartes and between the Aral and Caspian seas, as far as the northern borders of Khorasan. Their lifestyle was similar to that of other Turkic peoples, but their language differed, having dominant voicing consonants and distinctive grammatical features, notably in its system of declension. They formed a complex hierarchy of tribes, whose common ancestor was a legendary Oghuz khagan, and their short-lived 'state' under their own *yabghu* was neither centralised nor organised as a single political or military unit.

The dynasty's founder, Saljuq, son of Duqaq, was a military commander (*subaşi*) of the Oghuz *yabghu*. At the beginning of the eleventh century he lived in Jand, an important emporium on the Jaxartes, where he had fled from the anger of the *yabghu* who had opposed his conversion to Islam. There, Saljuq began to organise Turkic units of his own. It is important to note that the Oghuz Turks did not unite around Saljuq on a tribal basis. Zahir al-Din Nishapuri, one of the main early Seljuq chroniclers, writing in the twelfth century, listed the five 'pillars' of Seljuq power: 'They [the Seljuqs] were an illustrious family, [which ruled over] a great number [of possessions], with countless riches, well-equipped [military] units (*'iddat*), tribes (*khail*) and retainers (*ḥashamī*).'[5] It was on this basis that the Seljuqs, as one of the richest, most militarily successful clans, came to be recognised as leaders by other Oghuz tribes and finally, in the mid-eleventh century, managed to establish the first great Turkic Muslim state. The nucleus of Seljuq military power, especially at the beginning of their conquests, was their kinsmen, retainers, slaves (*ghilman*) and servants. The early Seljuq army consisted of three types of unit: the *'askar*, cavalry under the command of the sultan himself; the *jund*, auxiliary cavalry of the sultans' retainers, relatives, subordinates or tribal chieftains; and the *mushat*, or infantry. The other nomadic Oghuz made up part of the *jund*, but they were extremely unreliable allies. As we shall see, this helps explain why the conquest of Asia Minor continued even when the Byzantine empire and the Great Seljuq sultanate were formally at peace.

Saljuq had three sons: Mika'il, Musa and Isra'il/Arslan. Mika'il was killed while still a young man, but he left capable sons, two of whom, Tughril-beg (c. 1037–63) and Chaghri-beg, became the founders of the Seljuq state.[6] After breaking away from the *yabghu*, the Seljuqs moved to the Zarafshan valley near Samarkand, becoming subordinate firstly to the Samanids, and then, from 999, to the Qarakhanids. In 1025 'Ali-Tegin, the Qarakhanid ruler of Bukhara, was defeated by Mahmud of Ghazna; Isra'il/Arslan was taken prisoner by the Ghaznavids and imprisoned in India, where he died.

---

[5] Zahir al-Din Nishapuri, *Saljuq'namah*, I.i, ed. Afshar, p. 10; tr. Luther, p. 29; ed. Morton, p. 5.
[6] On Tughril-beg, see *EI*, X, pp. 553–4 (C. E. Bosworth); on Chaghri-beg: *EI*, II, pp. 4–5 (C. Cahen).

The Seljuqs asked Mahmud for new lands, and he granted them the northern borders of Khorasan. However, they proved to be unruly subjects and started to raid Ghaznavid territories; in 1027, Mahmud defeated and scattered them. Without a leader, the Seljuqs fled, some reaching Persian Iraq and Azerbaijan in 1029; these were the first Seljuq Turks to appear in the vicinity of the Byzantine borders in Armenia.

Under pressure from Shah-Malik of Jand, Tughril-beg moved his people – who formed a separate grouping from Isra'il/Arslan's – from their pasturing grounds in Khwarizm to the northern borders of Khorasan in 1034; Shah-Malik was probably an Oghuz *yabghu* and certainly an ally of Sultan Mas'ud I of Ghazna (1030–41). Tughril-beg thus had to seek Mas'ud I's permission for his Turks to live near Nasa and Farava in Khorasan, in the fertile valleys west of Merv, that separated the province from the sands of Qara Qum. The sultan, preoccupied with trying to conquer India, halfheartedly agreed. However, when Tughril-beg boldly claimed lordship over Merv, one of the richest cities of Khorasan, Mas'ud's patience snapped. Open warfare between the Seljuqs and the Ghaznavids ended in the defeat of the latter at the decisive battle at Dandanqan on 23 May 1040. Mas'ud escaped to Ghazna, only to be killed the following year on his way back to India; his state survived, mostly in Afghanistan and northern India, but its Iranian lands, Khorasan and Sistan, were lost forever.

Tughril-beg was proclaimed amir of Khorasan on the battlefield. Possession of Khorasan gave the Seljuqs an excellent opportunity to conquer the other Ghaznavid territories in Iran. Rayy soon fell, becoming a springboard for further conquests, as did Hamadhan in 1043. The newly founded polity was never centralised in the manner of the Ghaznavids or the Samanids. It was, rather, based on the military presence of the Turks in various provinces of Iran, Iraq and later Syria. The Seljuq sultan ruled his vast dominions with the help of his relatives, whom he rewarded with rights, revenues and offices, such as the military command of certain regions. One such region was southern Azerbaijan, which the Seljuq leaders began to occupy from the 1040s onwards, finishing the conquest of the entire province in 1055; and Isra'il's son Qutlumush was granted the provinces of Gurgan, Damghan and Qumis by his cousin Tughril-beg. As the Seljuqs pushed along the southern Caspian shore and through Azerbaijan, their next targets would inevitably be Armenia and Asia Minor.[7]

Once the Seljuqs moved into Azerbaijan and Arran, Turkish incursions into Anatolia gathered pace; indeed, the first was launched from Urmia by the Oghuz Turks in 1038, even before Tughril-beg's arrival in the region. But the most devastating invasions came between the mid-1040s and the early 1050s. In 1045 the Turkish army, probably led by Qutlumush, defeated

---

[7] On reasons for the Seljuqs' interest in Caucasia, see now also Peacock (2005).

Stephen Leichoudes, the governor of Vaspurakan. In 1047 another member of the Seljuq clan, Hasan the Deaf, governor of Herat and Sijistan, invaded Vaspurakan, but was defeated by Katakalon Kekaumenos, the governor of Ani. In September 1048, in response to Hasan's defeat, the Seljuq commander Ibrahim Inal took Artsn, devastated the area around Theodosioupolis and Basean, and won a resounding victory over the Byzantine armies.

The invasion of 1054, led by Tughril-beg himself, engulfed a vast area from Theodosioupolis to Lake Van. But the Byzantines resisted, and Tughril-beg did not dare besiege Theodosioupolis, his primary target. Empress Theodora (1055–6) sent an embassy to the sultan and bought off his claims to Byzantine territory with rich gifts. Tughril-beg's name was proclaimed in the Friday prayer (*khuṭba*) in the mosque of Constantinople between April 1055 and March of the following year, and this represented a form of recognition by the Byzantines that Tughril-beg was now the secular protector and guarantor of the Muslim faithful in Constantinople.[8] A temporary halt to incursions by the sultan and his closest relatives was brought about by this peace agreement, and also by Tughril-beg's preoccupation with Baghdad, which he seized in 1055 and again four years later. But the treaty could not stop repeated raiding by other Turks in the mid- to late 1050s. In the winter of 1057–8 Melitene was taken by a chieftain named Dinar, and Sebasteia, home to our colophon's author Gregory, fell on 6 August 1059. The leaders of these Turkish raids included Samukh, Amr K'ap'r (whose name derives from *amīr-i kabīr*, meaning 'great amir'), Gichachichi and a commander-in-chief (*sipāh-sālār*) of Khorasan.[9] The latter is noteworthy for his raids on Paghin and Arghni in 1062/3 and the area around Edessa in 1065/6.

Tughril-beg died in 1063. His nephew, Alp Arslan (1063–73) became sultan and resumed an aggressive policy towards Byzantium, culminating in the capture of Ani by the sultan himself on 16 August 1064. Through capturing Ani, the Turks secured the left bank of the Araxes, along their chief invasion route into Byzantine territory. One of the reasons for the Turks' success was the direction from which they raided; in the north, ranging along the Araxes from Vaspurakan as far as Theodosioupolis, and also along the Aratsani (eastern Euphrates) in the south. Byzantine defences were traditionally strong in Syria and southern Armenia, where they had withstood the Arabs for centuries. But the Turks came from the Caucasus, where the empire least expected any serious threat. The Byzantine cities

[8] al-Maqrizi, *al-Suluk*, I, p. 32. On the mosque in Constantinople, first reliably attested for the tenth century, see Reinert (1998), pp. 127–8, 137–40.

[9] *Chōrosan tis selarios* or *Chōrosalaris*: ME, II.12, ed. Melik'-Adamean and Ter-Mik'ayelean, pp. 133–5; tr. Dostourian, pp. 94–6; Skyl. Con., pp. 112–13; Attal., ed. Bekker, pp. 78–9; ed. and Spanish tr. Pérez Martín, pp. 59–60. The name 'Gichachichi', with the duplicated syllable 'chi', may have contained a nickname (in Old Turkic) *kiçig, kiçigin*, 'the small one'.

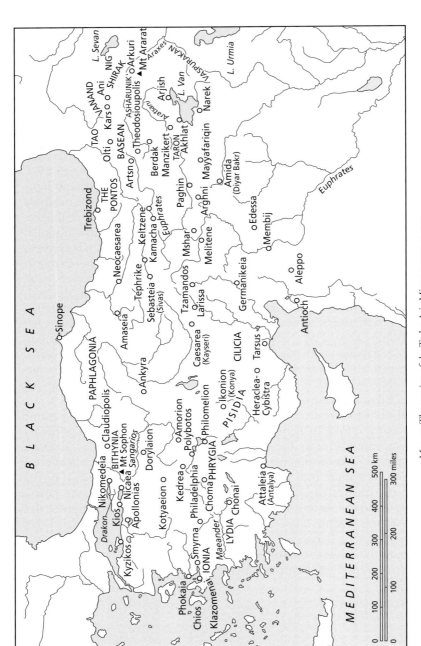

Map 32 The coming of the Turks: Asia Minor *c.* 1040–*c.* 1100

were unprepared for the task of withstanding Turkish attacks; Sebasteia, for example, had no city walls at all. After the fall of Ani, Oghuz hordes could penetrate Byzantine lands with relative impunity and as a result, the Turkish invasions became lengthier and bolder: in 1066/7 they pillaged Caesarea, reaching Cilicia and the environs of Antioch. In the following year, a certain Afshin al-Turki took Neocaesarea and Amorion, and in the winter and spring of 1070–1 he reached Chonai in western Anatolia. Byzantine fortification lines in Armenia were broken.

Nevertheless, one should treat with caution the blood-curdling descriptions of the Turkish invasions found in the Byzantine and Armenian sources. For these incursions had yet to break Byzantine power in Armenia, and extensive areas were more or less unscathed; although the Turks penetrated deeply, they went for the easiest pickings – rich, unprotected towns and cities. Equally, the Byzantines were not sitting idly by; for example, the city walls of Melitene were restored after Dinar's raid of 1057/8.

One set of contemporary sources which are untouched by the rhetorical or didactic pretensions of the larger historical works show an astonishing lack of interest in the Turks. These are the Armenian colophons. Our scribe Gregory asked his teacher Isaac to bring precious bindings from Constantinople to Sebasteia in 1066, even as the Turks were threatening the highways. Another colophon, dated to the following year, is particularly interesting for the almost idyllic picture it paints of a monastery mediating between rival lords over a property at Langnut.[10] What is really striking is the fact that, although Langnut lay in the province of Asharunik' on the Araxes, a border zone raided almost every year by the Turks, the colophon fails to mention them.

These colophons have a double significance. Firstly, they show that the Turkish invasions were neither an ethnic 'avalanche', nor a carefully orchestrated conquest. The Turkish hordes, whose chief weapon was their speed and mobility, destroyed everybody and everything in their path; but many places not on their direct route escaped devastation. Secondly, people did not realise the full scale of the danger at the time. All the sources which describe the 'horrifying' Turkic invasions in the 1050s and 1060s were composed after the battle of Manzikert.

THE BATTLE OF MANZIKERT (1071)

On 1 January 1068, at the invitation of the widowed Empress Eudocia Makrembolitissa, Romanos IV Diogenes (1068–71) was crowned emperor (see above, p. 608). Two months later he set out for Membij in Syria, which he captured. Romanos' next campaign took place between spring

---

[10] Mat'evosyan (ed.), *Hishatakaranner*, no. 125, p. 106.

1069 and the winter of 1069/70. Although he drove the enemy from Larissa in Cappadocia, he did not manage to prevent the Turks from plundering Ikonion (Konya). The main battle, however, took place in 1071. In the spring of 1070 the emperor sent the *kouropalatēs* Manuel Komnenos, nephew of the late emperor Isaac I Komnenos (1057–59), as *stratēgos autokratōr* of the Byzantine eastern army. Manuel had to defend the theme of Chaldia, which was being threatened by a certain Arisghi, brother-in-law of Sultan Alp Arslan. An important battle took place at Sebasteia in the autumn of 1070. The Byzantines were defeated; but then Manuel Komnenos persuaded Arisghi, who was at odds with the sultan, to join the emperor's side.

Meanwhile in August–September, Alp Arslan took Arjish (Archesh) and Manzikert, moving on to Mayyafariqin, Amida and then Edessa, which he besieged but did not manage to take. By April 1071 Alp Arslan was besieging Aleppo. His primary aim, however, was to campaign against the Fatimid forces in Syria. At this juncture a Byzantine embassy arrived, offering Membij in exchange for Arjish and Manzikert. The sultan, who needed to secure his northern flank, agreed to a peace treaty on condition that the emperor paid a yearly tribute. But in the meantime Afshin al-Turki had penetrated deep into the territory of Byzantine Asia Minor (see above, p. 701) taking Chonai and ravaging the environs of Tzamandos. It was at this moment when news of Afshin's audacious raid arrived in Constantinople that Romanos IV decided to declare open war.

In July 1071, the Byzantine army moved across the River Sangarios to Caesarea and the emperor arrived at Theodosioupolis; at this point the sultan was in Vostan, near Narek. By mid-August Romanos had retaken Manzikert. Alp Arslan believed that Diogenes had broken the truce; he abandoned plans to go to Syria and hastened back towards the Byzantine army. However, he offered to sign a peace treaty with Romanos once again. The emperor refused. The battle ended in humiliating defeat for the Byzantines, with Romanos IV being captured and brought before Alp Arslan on 26 August 1071.

The causes of the Byzantine defeat were manifold and complex. The first was Romanos' misjudgement of Alp Arslan's strategy. Had Romanos known that the sultan intended to concentrate on Syria instead of attacking the Byzantine borders, and that he faced serious financial difficulties in paying his own soldiers, the battle could have been averted. Secondly, the Turks employed superior tactics; they were mostly horsemen armed with bows and arrows, capable of striking the enemy while themselves staying out of range, thus rendering the Byzantine army's close formations a disadvantage. Not only did Byzantine tactics fail against the Turks; the action of the imperial army depended far too much on the instructions of its commander-in-chief. Romanos realised too late that the sultan was approaching, and divided his forces by sending large contingents in the direction of Akhlat. Finally, the emperor was betrayed by the *proedros* Andronikos Doukas, whose detachment withdrew when the outcome of the battle was still uncertain (see above, p. 608).

Given the crushing nature of the defeat, the terms of the peace treaty were comparatively moderate. Reparations came to a total of one and a half million dinars: an immediate payment of 300,000 dinars, with the balance to be paid as an annual tribute of 60,000 dinars, implying that the peace treaty was expected to last for twenty years.[11] Romanos was also required to cede four cities in northern Syria and Armenia to Alp Arslan – Edessa, Membij, Antioch and Manzikert – before the sultan would release him. Alp Arslan's intentions remained the same as they had been before the battle: he wanted the empire to be his peaceful neighbour and to keep his flanks in Syria secure for his further advance against the Fatimid caliph in Egypt.

Although in the event the Byzantines only ceded Manzikert, these four cities were the key Byzantine strongholds in northern Syria and Armenia. And although the peace treaty in theory gave the empire a twenty-year respite from attacks by the sultan's army, it could not stop the incursions of the *other* Turks. The bitter experience of the three decades before the battle of Manzikert had shown that the Byzantines' defence of the region relied on a strong field army, working in liaison with the large fortresses' garrisons. After 1071 the main field army was no longer an operational military unit, although the empire still possessed battle-worthy detachments.[12] Had there been a strong government, the army could still have been restored to a level comparable with the enemy's. Instead, the empire plunged into civil war.

THE LOSS OF ASIA MINOR, 1071–1081

Romanos IV Diogenes was released after 3 September 1071. He wrote to his wife, the empress Eudocia, informing her of what had happened. While the letter was still on its way, a *coup d'état* took place in Constantinople. In October 1071 Michael VII Doukas (1071–8) was proclaimed emperor; the son of Constantine X (1059–67), Michael had the support of his uncle, the caesar John. Eudocia was compelled by them to become a nun. Civil war became inevitable (see above, p. 609).

Romanos IV, who enjoyed support in eastern Anatolia, was defeated twice: the first time near Amaseia, and then in Cilicia. He was captured and so cruelly blinded on 29 June 1072 that he died a few weeks later. One

---

[11] 1,500,000 dinars – 300,000 dinars = 1,200,000 dinars: 60,000 dinars per year = 20 years. According to Ibn al-Athir, the treaty was concluded for fifty years: Ibn al-Athir, *al-Kamil*, ed. al-Qadi, VIII, p. 389; tr. Richards, p. 172. Another variant is given by Bar Hebraeus, who states that the total sum of reparations of 1,000,000 dinars was to be paid as an annual tribute of 360,000 dinars: Bar Hebraeus, *Chronography*, ed. Bedjan, p. 249; tr. Wallis Budge, I, p. 222.

[12] Cheynet (1980), pp. 421–34.

of Romanos' commanders, Philaretos Brachamios, refused to recognise Michael VII and sought to create a polity of his own, centred on Mshar, and later on Germanikeia. Meanwhile Romanos' death nullified the peace treaty struck between him and Alp Arslan, who himself perished in Transoxiana shortly afterwards. All our sources agree that it was Romanos' death which gave the Turks the opportunity to invade Byzantine territories and, more importantly, to remain permanently in Anatolia.[13]

In 1073 Michael VII sent Isaac Komnenos against the Turks; Isaac was the new domestic of the Schools of the East, and elder brother of the future emperor Alexios Komnenos. Their expedition ended in disaster; the western mercenaries under the command of Russell Balliol rebelled and abandoned the Byzantine army. Meanwhile Isaac was defeated and taken captive by the Turks near Caesarea; Alexios managed to escape and get as far as Ankara (Ankyra), where he was rejoined by Isaac, who had been ransomed by the Byzantine cities. However, Ankara itself was by no means secure, as the Turks were ravaging the surrounding countryside. Near Nikomedeia the young Komnenoi and their small detachment were attacked by a larger group of some 200 Turks. The brothers barely escaped to Constantinople. This episode vividly illustrates conditions in Asia Minor two years after the battle of Manzikert: the countryside lay open to the Turks, while the fortified towns were still in Byzantine hands. Yet even without a strong field army, the Byzantine defence system disintegrated only slowly.

The Turks managed to make their first, quite small, territorial acquisitions on Byzantine soil only after 1075. The territories conquered were the Pontos and Bithynia, and the loss was as a result of Russell Balliol's revolt in 1073–5. After breaking away from Isaac Komnenos' army, Russell's own detachment of 400 men went to Melitene, where he repulsed the Turkish hordes, then turned to Sebasteia and managed to occupy the theme of the Armeniakoi from the autumn of 1073 onwards. The small and ineffectual Byzantine army under the command of the caesar John Doukas could do nothing to stop him, and Russell reached Chrysopolis in 1074 with an army by then numbering 3,000. Under these circumstances, Michael VII had no choice but to ask the Turks for help. In June 1074 he sent an embassy to the Seljuq sultan Malik Shah (1073–92)[14] but, as time was pressing, the emperor also sought help from the leader of a roving Oghuz band nearby, the tribe known as the *döger*. This band was led by Artuq, founder of the Artuqid dynasty which later based itself in Diyar Bakr (Amida). Artuq heeded the emperor's plea, and in a battle at Mount Sophon some time in the second part of 1074 he defeated and took prisoner both John Doukas

---

[13] See, for example: Skyl. Con., pp. 156–7; MS, XV.4, ed. and French tr. Chabot, III, p. 172 (French translation), IV, p. 579 (Syriac text).

[14] Sibt ibn al-Jawzi, *Mir'at al-zaman*, ed. Sevim, p. 170.

and Russell Balliol. Michael VII ransomed the caesar John, while Russell was redeemed by his wife who had survived the battle in the fortress of Metabole nearby. Then Artuq left Asia Minor, while Russell withdrew to the theme of Armeniakoi.

According to Michael Attaleiates, at this moment

the emperor, . . . enraged against him [Russell], preferred that the Turks should occupy and rule the land of the Romans, rather than that this Latin should withdraw to the previous place [the theme of Armeniakoi].[15]

Indeed, the young Alexios Komnenos is said to have remarked to Tutaq, commander-in-chief of the Seljuq army:

Your sultan and my emperor are mutual friends. However, this barbarian, Russell, raises his hands against them and he has become the most terrible enemy of both. On the one hand, he makes incursions and little by little subdues some parts of the [land of the] Romans; on the other, he seizes [lands] in Persia, which might otherwise have remained Persia's.[16]

Both statements refer to the situation in Anatolia in the second half of 1075, and indicate that in accordance with the treaty of June 1074 – whereby Michael VII and Malik Shah became 'friends' – the Byzantines recognised the Seljuqs' acquisitions east of the Armeniakoi theme, in return for their assistance against Russell.

Important details of how the Byzantines employed the Turks against Russell Balliol are to be found in the Georgian *Royal Annals*, which also describe how the Turkish advance into the Pontos was contained with Georgian help. In 1074 Gregory Pakourianos left his post of commander-in-chief (*zorvari*) of the imperial forces in the east[17] and returned to Constantinople. Gregory gave all the lands under his control (Theodosioupolis, Olti, Kars, Vanand, Karnip'ori[18] and a portion of Tao) to King George II (1072–89) of Georgia. At first, this tactical withdrawal worked well enough: Georgian garrisons were established in the former Byzantine strongholds and Georgian troops cleared the territory of the Turkish war bands in 1075. Although the Turks soon occupied Theodosioupolis, Olti and then Kars, some time passed before they subdued the territory completely. They only made their first full-scale invasion into Georgia in 1080.[19]

---

[15] Attal., ed. Bekker, p. 199; ed. and Spanish tr. Pérez Martín, p. 146; see also Nikephoros Bryennios, *Histoire*, II.17, ed. and French tr. Gautier, pp. 178–9.

[16] *Al.*, I.2.2, ed. Reinsch and Kambylis, I, p. 13; ed. and French tr. Leib, I, pp. 11–12; tr. Sewter, p. 33; see also Nikephoros Bryennios, *Histoire*, II.21–2, ed. and French tr. Gautier, pp. 186–9.

[17] *Zorvari* was a Georgian version of the Armenian title *zawrawor*, the latter being the translation of the Byzantine title *stratēgos autokratōr*.

[18] Between Kars and the river Araxes.

[19] *Georgian royal annals*, ed. Qauxč'išvilis, I, pp. 317–20; ed. and tr. Brosset, I.1, pp. 199–200, 236–7 (Georgian text), I.2, p. 199, n. 2, pp. 345–8 (French tr.); tr. Thomson, pp. 307–11.

Byzantine policy was realistic and flexible. The withdrawal of Gregory Pakourianos' army was caused by Byzantium's desperate need for troops during Russell's revolt and by a fresh influx of Turks into the Pontos in 1073–5. With Russell at their rear, the Byzantines had little hope of standing up to the Turks. It was Georgian military support that restricted the Turks' migration into the Byzantine Pontic provinces in 1075, when Russell's revolt was suppressed with Turkish help.

The Byzantine eastern border zone with its formidable fortifications and huge cities did not collapse as soon as the Turks occupied Theodosioupolis. Sebasteia and its environs, or at least a portion of Sennacherim-John Artsruni's possessions, may have remained in the hands of his sons Atom and Abusahl, who were still alive as late as 1079–80. Maria, the daughter of Gagik-Abas II (1029–64) of Kars, held her father's possessions in Tzamandos in 1077. The Byzantines themselves stood their ground in the strategically important region of Choma, Polybotos and Kedrea as late as 1081.[20] We also read in an Armenian colophon that in 1079 Ch'ortowanel Mamikonean, 'the great prince of Taron and all the lands of the Armenians', gave with the consent of the emperor his ancestral village of Berdak to the monastery (or church) of the Holy Apostles.[21] If this Berdak can be identified as Sewuk Berdak (Maurokastron) on the headwaters of the Araxes, the colophon suggests that an Armenian prince recognising imperial authority retained territory south of Theodosioupolis at the end of the 1070s.

The Turks in the Pontos – hemmed in by Byzantine fortresses to the north, west and south, and by the Georgians to their east – did not pose much of a threat to Byzantine power in Asia Minor. Far more dangerous was another invasion led by Suleiman ibn Qutlumush (1081–6) from Syria in 1074–5.[22] According to Sibt ibn al-Jawzi, Suleiman 'was reported to have come from the Turkmen of [the confederation of] al-Nawakiyya who dwelt in Syria'.[23] Already in 1070, some of the al-Nawakiyya had gone to Asia Minor, under the leadership of Arisghi (see above, p. 702), where first Romanos IV and then Michael VII settled them in western Anatolia; but most made for Syria, which they occupied in 1071–2.

In 1073, northern Syria was caught up in the struggle between the Fatimid caliphate of al-Mustansir (1036–94) and Atsiz, a kinsman or at least a fellow tribesman of Artuq. Atsiz was commander of the largest Turkish band that had been ravaging Syria from 1064 onwards; the al-Nawakiyya Turkmen were another such band. The ensuing chaos led masses of Turks to swarm

---

[20] Cheynet (1998b).   [21] Mat'evosyan (ed.), *Hishatakaranner*, no. 133, pp. 111–12.

[22] *Tarihî takvimler*, ed. Turan, p. 64; Sibt ibn al-Jawzi, *Mir'at al-zaman*, ed. Sevim, p. 173.

[23] Sibt ibn al-Jawzi, *Mir'at al-zaman*, ed. Sevim, p. 243. The name al-Nawakiyya comes from the Persian word *nawak* 'a small arrow', usually used for shooting birds.

into Syria, many of them antagonistic not only to the Fatimids but also to the Seljuq sultan Malik Shah. Despite being themselves of the Seljuq clan, Suleiman ibn Qutlumush and his brother Mansur/Mas'ud[24] were among those Turks who – like the al-Nawakiyya – were hostile to the ruling dynasty of the Grand Seljuqs. Their father Qutlumush, the invader of Vaspurakan in 1045, had rebelled against his cousin Alp Arslan and died in battle near Rayy sometime before 23 January 1064.

Although Atsiz lacked the illustrious pedigree of Suleiman, with Malik Shah's support he grew from strength to strength. Not without reason he became suspicious of the sons of Qutlumush, and open struggle between them ended in victory for Atsiz near Tiberias in 1075. Suleiman and Mansur were then driven off from Antioch by the *doux* Isaac Komnenos and forced to leave Syria for Asia Minor. Suleiman's horde advanced quickly along the Byzantine military road, taking Ikonion and the fortress of Kabala en route.[25] His arrival at Nicaea in the summer or autumn of 1075 transformed the situation in Asia Minor to the Turks' advantage. According to Attaleiates, the Turkish incursions spread as far as the Bosporus at this time.[26]

Suleiman's chance came in October 1077, when Nikephoros Botaneiates – later Emperor Nikephoros III (1078–81) – began his rebellion against Michael VII (see above, p. 610). Arisghi and his al-Nawakiyya Turks at once supported Nikephoros in Phrygia. Suleiman, in command of another grouping of the al-Nawakiyya near Kotyaeion, followed suit at the beginning of 1078. He recognised the new emperor as his suzerain and even helped Nikephoros Botaneiates defeat the rebellion of Nikephoros Bryennios in the spring of 1078. But the main problem for the new emperor was Suleiman's proximity to the Bosporus; his horde roamed the fertile lands of Bithynia, raiding them relentlessly. Neither the expedition of the amir Bursuq, whom Malik Shah had sent in pursuit of Suleiman in 1078, nor the attempts of Nikephoros III himself to restrict his 'allies' could stop the devastating raids. Although, with the exception of Ikonion, the Turks had yet to take any Byzantine cities, they dominated the heart of western Asia Minor. By 1078 Philaretos Brachamios had managed to become master of Edessa, Melitene and Antioch and to halt the influx of Turks from Syria. He also recognised Nikephoros III as his emperor. But even this could not tip the balance in favour of the Byzantines.[27]

---

[24] His name was recorded by Nikephoros Bryennios, *Histoire*, IV.2, ed. and French tr. Gautier, pp. 258–9 as 'Masour'. This could have been either an honorary title *al-Mansur* ('victorious') or a proper name Mas'ud.
[25] *Histoire des Seldjoukides*, ed. Uzluk, p. 36.
[26] Attal., ed. Bekker, p. 200; ed. and Spanish tr. Pérez Martín, p. 147.
[27] On Philaretos, see Yarnley (1972).

THE BYZANTINE RECONQUEST

Alexios I Komnenos

On 1 April 1081, the Byzantine troops who had proclaimed Alexios I Komnenos (1081–1118) emperor entered Constantinople; Nikephoros III was deposed. By this time, Anatolia was a patchwork; Byzantine strongholds held out side-by-side with areas under Turkish control. It was the revolt of Nikephoros Melissenos against Nikephoros III in 1079–81 that gave the Turks access to many Byzantine cities in Phrygia and Galatia (see above, p. 610). The Byzantines still held the Mediterranean coastline of Asia Minor, south of Phokaia.[28] Similarly they still controlled the chief cities in Paphlagonia, while Theodore Gabras had liberated Trebizond by 1081. It was around this time, certainly by June 1081, that Suleiman felt himself strong enough to shake off nominal Byzantine suzerainty. He occupied Nicaea and Nikomedeia and proclaimed himself sultan.

Meanwhile other parts of Asia Minor became subject to new lords: the Danishmends in Sebasteia (Sivas), Caesarea (Kayseri) and Amaseia (Amasya); the Mengucheks in Keltzene, Kamacha and Tephrike (Divriği on the upper Euphrates; and the Saltuqs in Theodosioupolis (Erzurum). Of these, the emirate of the Danishmends was the mightiest. Rivalry, yet sometimes unity, between the Seljuq sultans of Rum and the mighty Danishmends characterised the internal politics of Turkish-dominated Asia Minor from the 1080s until the 1170s. Until the First Crusade, Alexios I's strategy in Asia Minor was to expel the Seljuq Turks from Bithynia; preserve the Byzantine strongholds on the sea coast; and impose imperial authority or at least overlordship, however tenuous, on the motley assortment of warlords – Turkish, Greek or Armenian – who had emerged elsewhere in the peninsula.

Despite his lack of military resources, Alexios I's eastern policy was successful, even in the first fifteen, most difficult years of his reign. Firstly he succeeded in reconquering the coastline of Bithynia from Suleiman, including Nikomedeia. A peace treaty had been signed by 17 June 1081, establishing the Drakon river as the frontier between the empire and the sultanate of Rum. In 1086, after Suleiman's death, Malik Shah offered Alexios an alliance, to be cemented by marriage between Alexios' daughter (and future historian) Anna Komnena and Malik Shah's son Barkyaruq. Although the marriage was never concluded, with Malik Shah's permission Alexios retook Sinope and other Pontic cities from the Seljuqs. The sultan's concession was not particularly generous: both rulers were

---

[28] TT, I, pp. 52–3. The coastal cities between Phokaia and Nikomedeia seemed to have been occupied, or at least seriously threatened, by the Turks.

united in antipathy towards the Nicaean statelet, now ruled by Suleiman's successors.[29]

Some of the Christian lords ruling over the remnants of the Byzantine territories in Anatolia still recognised imperial authority. Philaretos remained Byzantine domestic of the East and *doux* of Antioch until December 1084 when Suleiman seized the city. Gregory Pahlavuni, the nephew of Catholicos Gregory II the Martyrophile (1066–1105), was the Byzantine *magistros, doux* and '*kouropalatēs* of the East' until 1099 when he was killed in the neighbourhood of Ani. Finally, in 1091 Theodore Gabras visited Constantinople and accepted the authority of the emperor.

However, Alexios I's foremost concern upon his accession was the Turkish statelets in western Anatolia. Although Suleiman had proclaimed himself sultan, his power base was far from solid, despite controlling the old Byzantine military road from Nicaea to Ikonion. The situation became even more volatile when he moved his armies back to Cilicia and thence to Syria in 1082–3. Suleiman almost destroyed Philaretos' lordship, taking Antioch and finally Melitene in 1084–5, but he was himself killed in battle against Malik Shah's brother Tutush near Aleppo in May–June 1086. However, Suleiman's departure from Anatolia and subsequent death did not halt the Turkish incursions into Mysia, Lydia and Ionia. At the end of 1083, shortly after Suleiman had withdrawn his forces to Syria, Alexios was forced to repel a series of attacks against the Byzantine cities along the Sea of Marmara by Abu al-Qasim, chief deputy to the sultan of Rum. In 1092, while the rapprochement between emperor and sultan after the death of Suleiman was still in force, Alexios I organised a counter-attack against the Turks in Nicaea; his general Tatikios marched on Nicaea to help the army of Malik Shah's amir Buzan besiege the city, while Manuel Boutoumites destroyed Abu al-Qasim's fleet near Kios in Bithynia. By the end of 1092 or early 1093, Abu al-Qasim was required to sign a peace treaty while receiving imperial hospitality in Constantinople and he accepted the Byzantine title of *sebastos* from Alexios.[30]

Malik Shah died on 19 November 1092 and for two years after his death a struggle raged between the new sultan, Barkyaruq (1094–1105) and his uncle Tutush. In early 1094, Buzan ordered the murder of Abu al-Qasim near Isfahan, and became Barkyaruq's commander-in-chief in Asia Minor; just before Abu al-Qasim was killed, Suleiman's son Kilij Arslan I (1092–1107) entered Nicaea. Alexios I also subdued two other over-active Turkish beys in the early 1090s: Tzachas (Çaka) of Smyrna, who occupied Klazomenai,

---

[29] *Al.*, VI.9.4–5, ed. Reinsch and Kambylis, I, pp. 187–8; ed. and French tr. Leib, II, pp. 65–6; tr. Sewter, p. 200.

[30] *Al.*, VI.10.5–11, VI.12.1–2, ed. Reinsch and Kambylis, I, pp. 190–2, 194; ed. and French tr. Leib, II, pp. 69–72, 74–5; tr. Sewter, pp. 202–5, 206–7; Frankopan, 'The foreign policy of the emperor Alexios I Komnenos (1081–*c*. 1100)' (DPhil thesis, 1998), pp. 327–34.

Phokaia and Chios from 1090 to 1093 (see above, p. 611), and at the end of 1093, a certain Elchanes who, judging by his title, was Buzan's or Kilij Arslan I's deputy in Apollonias and Kyzikos. Around this time Alexios regained Nikomedeia and built some other forts looking onto the Gulf of Nikomedeia.[31]

Yet despite all these measures, the most the Byzantines achieved in Asia Minor between 1081 and 1096 was the temporary halting of Turkish incursions into north-west Anatolia. It was the participants of the First Crusade who destroyed the Turkish statelet in Bithynia. Not only did they besiege and take Nicaea on 19 June 1097; they also defeated the army of Kilij Arslan I at Dorylaion on 1 July 1097 (see above, p. 623). So shattering was this defeat to the Seljuqs of Rum that the sultan, who was later supported by the *malik* known as Danishmend, only managed to organise resistance on the eastern borders of his realm, in Hebraike near Heraclea-Cybistra, at the beginning of September 1097. Once again, the crusaders were victorious.

The Byzantine reconquest of western Anatolia began almost as soon as Nicaea had fallen to the Crusaders. By 28 June 1098 the Byzantine armies had cleared the Aegean coast and the provinces of Phrygia, Ionia and Lydia of the Turks and reached the river Maeander. Sardis, Philadelphia and Laodicea became Byzantine, and imperial troops penetrated as far as Polybotos. At the end of 1099 or early in 1100 General Manuel Boutoumites' expedition to Cilicia brought Antalya back to the Byzantines, although the road between the city and the Byzantine strongholds on the Maeander remained vulnerable to possible Turkish incursions. Antalya (Attaleia) became the springboard for further Byzantine campaigns into Cilicia, where Alexios I established a nucleus for Byzantine administration in 1101. Towards the end of his reign, the emperor succeeded in subjugating the lands around Kotyaeion in the summer of 1113, reaching Kedrea (near Amorion) and Philomelion in the autumn of 1116.

Two 'wings': the strategy of John II Komnenos

When Alexios I died on 15 August 1118, he left his successor John II Komnenos (1118–43) a well-organised and prosperous state, and John continued his father's policy in Asia Minor. Like Alexios, he undertook military operations against Seljuq territory to forestall Turkish invasions and capture strategically important border fortresses. However, there was a difference. John II's military activity was largely focused on the two 'wings' of the Byzantines' territories in Asia Minor: Paphlagonia and the Pontos in the

---

[31] The title of Elchanes is usually translated as 'subject khan' and is the same as the title Ilkhan, later employed by the Mongols of Iran. See *Al.*, VI.10.9–10, X.5.3, ed. Reinsch and Kambylis, I, pp. 191–2, 296; ed. and French tr. Leib, II, pp. 71, 206; tr. Sewter, pp. 204, 308; Foss (1985–96), II, pp. 45–9, 64–9; Shepard (2005), pp. 328–33.

north; and Pisidia, Pamphylia and Cilicia in the south. Despite this, John's diplomatic and military activities were no less successful than those of his father.

Southern Asia Minor was the more important of the two 'wings': the main cities of the Seljuq sultanate of Rum were to be found there, while the lowlands of Cilicia served as a base for Byzantine support for, or military pressure on, the Crusader states in Syria. In 1119 John II took Laodicea and Sozopolis in western Asia Minor from the Turks. He then managed to secure the road to Antalya, occupying the fortresses that protected the port from its hinterland. In 1124 the emperor involved himself in the dynastic struggle between Sultan Mas'ud (1116–55) and his brother Malik 'Arab, ruler of Kastamonu and Ankara. Combining both military and diplomatic pressure, John II forced Mas'ud to become his ally, while holding the defeated Malik 'Arab as a hostage in Constantinople. In spring 1136 John undertook an expedition against the principality of Antioch, whose vassal Count Baldwin of Marash had defeated, imprisoned and then released the Rupenid prince Leo I. By the summer of 1137 John II had conquered both the highlands and the lowlands of Cilician Armenia, including the cities of Tarsus, Adana, Mopsuestia and Anazarbos (see above, p. 632). The unfortunate Leo I was once again imprisoned, this time by the Byzantine emperor, and sent to Constantinople. Although the Danishmendid Muhammad Ghazi (1134–42) soon drove the Byzantine garrisons out of the Cilician highlands, Byzantine administration persisted in Tarsus, Adana and Mopsuestia until 1183, apart from two short intervals in 1152–8 and 1173–5, when the Rupenid princes Thoros II (1148–68) and Mleh successively gained temporary control of the lowlands of Cilicia.[32]

John II was less successful in his northern campaigns. Although his expeditions against Kastamonu and Gangra in 1131–2 and 1134–5 achieved the temporary subjugation of both fortresses, his siege of Neocaesarea (Niksar) in 1139–40 was fruitless. John faced considerable difficulties in Asia Minor after 1130, when the sultan Mas'ud switched his allegiance from the Byzantines to Amir Ghazi Danishmendid (1104–33/4). Another ally of Amir Ghazi was Constantine Gabras, the *doux* of Trebizond, which was effectively an independent polity from 1126. John II's response was to launch military campaigns deep into Paphlagonia and the Pontos. Although he never managed to take Neocaesarea or to break the alliance between Mas'ud and the Danishmends, John nevertheless brought the Pontic provinces to heel in 1140. The furthest-flung 'wings' of Byzantine Asia Minor – the Pontos and Cilicia – became firmly reunited with the main body of the Byzantine state in western Anatolia.

---

[32] Lilie (1993a), pp. 166–8, 176–7, 195–6, 214, n. 300.

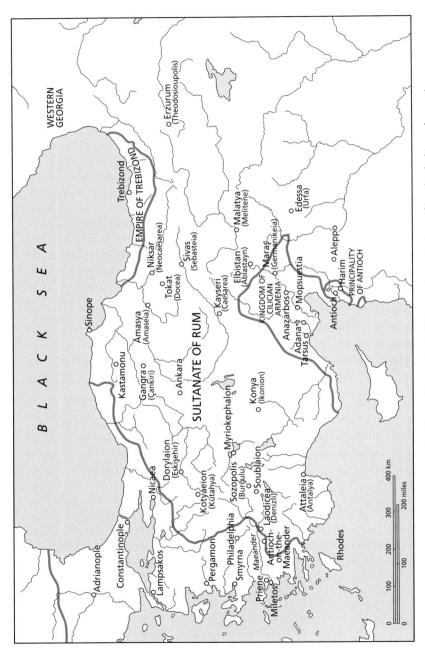

Map 33 Byzantine Asia Minor, the Seljuqs of Rum and other Turks: coexistence in the twelfth and early thirteenth centuries

Manuel I Komnenos and the Turks: triumph, co-existence and tribulation

The long reign of John II's successor Manuel I Komnenos (1143–80) saw the zenith of the recovery of Byzantine power in Asia Minor after 1081. For the first time, imperial diplomacy managed to bring nearly all the Turkish potentates in Anatolia into the Byzantine fold. Circumstances helped the emperor. Muhammad Ghazi died in 1142 and his death triggered the fragmentation of the Danishmend emirate: Sebasteia went to one of his brothers, Yaghibasan (1142–64); Ablastayn and Melitene to another, ʿAyn al-Dawla (1142–52); and his son, Dhu al-Nun (1142–68) became master of Caesarea. The alliance between the Seljuq sultanate of Rum and the Danishmends was finished by 1143, as Sultan Masʿud and his successor Kilij Arslan II (1156–92) were almost always at odds with Yaghibasan, the most powerful of them.

It was Sultan Masʿud who first tried to take advantage of John II's death, seizing Ablastayn in 1143 and besieging ʿAyn al-Dawla's capital, Melitene. Two years later, shortly after *atabey* Zengi (1127–46) of Aleppo had seized Edessa from the crusaders, the sultan captured the Cilician fortress of Prakana, whose ruler Tigran had acknowledged Byzantine overlordship. Masʿud then attacked Germanikeia, one of the remnants of the ever-shrinking county of Edessa. Some time after January 1146 Manuel I launched a full-scale campaign against the Seljuqs; by this stage Yaghibasan had become a subject ally (*hypospondos* and *doulos*) of the emperor, fearful that his emirate might be the next target for the mighty sultan's armies.[33] The Byzantines organised a counter-attack against Konya (Ikonion), which they besieged. A peace treaty concluded in the first half of 1147 restored the status quo on the border, although Ablastayn was to remain in Seljuq hands under the heir-apparent Kilij Arslan. Sultan and emperor joined forces against Thoros II, who was then threatening Byzantine Cilicia; between 1153 and 1155, at Manuel's request and with the support of Yaghibasan, Masʿud tried to force Thoros to return the cities he had recently conquered in Cilicia to the Byzantines.

There is no doubting that the Seljuqs were a formidable foe and the Second Crusade in 1147–8 only showed their strength. They inflicted a severe defeat on the German emperor Conrad III (1138–52) near Dorylaion in October 1147, forcing the rest of his army to join Louis VII (1137–80) of France; Louis had chosen a safer route to Antalya, passing through Byzantine territory and then on to Antioch by sea. The empire and the sultanate had widely different attitudes towards the crusaders; for Masʿud, they were mortal enemies, while for Manuel they were involuntary allies, whom he supported as long as it was in the empire's interests.[34]

---

[33] Kinn., II.5, ed. Meineke, p. 39; tr. Brand, p. 39; Oikonomides (1983), pp. 191–2.
[34] See Magdalino (1993a), pp. 5, 41–53.

Byzantine diplomatic and military pressure steadily increased in Asia Minor, despite Manuel I's preoccupation with western affairs between 1147 and 1159. By 1156 the Seljuqs had reconquered Ankara and Gangra from Yaghibasan, who had taken Ablastayn. However, Sultan Kilij Arslan II did not manage to establish effective control over Turkish-occupied Paphlagonia, which came into the hands of his younger brother Shahinshah. Thus after Kilij Arslan II's accession in 1156 there were no fewer than five Turkish states in central Anatolia: the sultanate of Rum itself, the three Danishmend emirates of Sebasteia, Caesarea and Melitene, and the Paphlagonian appanage of Shahinshah. A peace treaty struck between Kilij Arslan II and Yaghibasan in 1156 was short-lived; although they colluded in raiding Byzantine lands thereafter, they were nevertheless rivals for control of the other three Turkish statelets. In 1158 Manuel forced the sultan to return the conquered Byzantine border fortresses of Pounoura and Sibylla, despite being heavily involved around this time with campaigning against both William I (1154–66) of Sicily and Reynald de Châtillon (1153–60), prince of Antioch.

Manuel I's campaign against Antioch in 1158–9 was a vivid demonstration of residual Byzantine power: he defeated both Kilij Arslan II and Thoros II en route to Cilicia – which reverted to being a Byzantine province – before forcing Reynald to become his vassal. But Kilij Arslan remained hostile, for his state was now surrounded by the territories of Byzantium and her allies, and while Manuel was on his way back from Cilicia he attacked the Byzantine rearguard near Kotyaeion. Most probably in order to contain Yaghibasan, Kilij Arslan also attempted to negotiate a marriage alliance with 'Izz al-Din Saltuq II (1132–68), the master of Theodosioupolis, only to be thwarted when Yaghibasan kidnapped Kilij's bride, who was later married to Dhu al-Nun Danishmendid of Caesarea (see above, p. 642).

The final round in this series of Byzantine initiatives took place in the winter of 1160–1. Manuel I formed a grand coalition with King Baldwin III (1143–63) of Jerusalem, Reynald de Châtillon, Thoros II, Yaghibasan and Kilij Arslan II's brother, Shahinshah, claimant to the Seljuq throne. After he had been defeated in 1160 by the armies of both John Kontostephanos[35] and Yaghibasan,[36] Kilij Arslan swore to be the empire's military ally (*symmachos*); the sultan also swore that he would become Manuel's friend (*philos*), retainer (*oikeios*) and son.[37] Meanwhile Manuel's ally George III (1156–84) of Georgia had defeated the joint forces of Kilij Arslan's supporters Saltuq II of Theodosioupolis, and his son-in-law the Nasir al-Din (Miran) Sukman II,

[35] Kinn., IV.24, ed. Meineke, p. 200; tr. Brand, p. 152.
[36] NC, ed. van Dieten, I, p. 118; tr. Magoulias, p. 67; Ibn al-Athir, *al-Kamil*, ed. al-Qadi, IX, p. 477.
[37] Kinn., IV.24, ed. Meineke, p. 201; tr. Brand, p. 152; NC, ed. van Dieten, I, p. 123; tr. Magoulias, p. 70.

lord of Akhlat. At the end of 1161 both Sukman and Kilij Arslan travelled to Constantinople, where the sultan signed a peace treaty.[38]

This was a triumph for Manuel's policy in Asia Minor, ensuring the safety of Byzantium's borders and allowing Manuel to concentrate on Hungarian affairs.[39] Yet this stability in Anatolia lasted for only fifteen years, as one of its essential elements – the emirate of the Danishmends – suffered a sharp decline after Yaghibasan's death in 1164. Both Manuel and Kilij Arslan had foreseen this: in 1162–3 they negotiated an agreement on how the emirate should be conquered and its lands divided; Sebasteia was to become Byzantine again.

When Yaghibasan died his widow, Kilij Arslan II's sister, became ruler of Sebasteia and married Isma'il ibn Ibrahim, Yaghibasan's nephew; oddly enough, Yaghibasan's three legitimate sons did not inherit the city. In autumn 1164 Kilij Arslan attacked the emirate with Byzantine help, but Isma'il survived. Some five years later in 1169, during Manuel's great naval expedition to Egypt (see above, p. 642) and when the empire had no forces to spare, Kilij Arslan launched a surprise attack on the Danishmends in Caesarea and Tzamandos. Their ruler, Dhu al-Nun, was forced to flee to the powerful *atabey* Nur al-Din (1146–74) of Damascus, and Caesarea became a Seljuq possession. In the same year Kilij Arslan forced Shahinshah to accept his sovereignty.

Manuel did not respond to the sultan's actions. The rationale behind his policy in Asia Minor was in tension with the other goals of his foreign policy, seeing that the Danishmend emirates were under Nur al-Din's protection, and so any Byzantine support for the Danishmends would require the cooperation of Damascus. But Nur al-Din was also the mortal enemy of the crusader states, as whose protector Manuel sought to present himself. In 1164 at the battle of Harim, Nur al-Din had defeated the combined forces of Constantine Coloman, Byzantine governor in Cilicia, Bohemond III (1163–1201) of Antioch and Raymond III (1152–87) of Tripoli.[40] Under these circumstances, Manuel allowed his ally Kilij Arslan to enlarge the sultanate at the Danishmends' expense.

Indeed the primary objective of both rulers – Sebasteia – remained unconquered. In 1172 Isma'il and his wife were killed in a *coup d'état* and Kilij Arslan II immediately invaded the emirate; but Nur al-Din ordered him to stop and his *protégé* Dhu al-Nun entered the city. However, in the

---

[38] ME (continuation), 44, 47, ed. Melik'-Adamean and Ter-Mik'ayelean, pp. 425–6, 428; tr. Dostourian, pp. 277, 279. Matthew of Edessa mistakenly calls Miran (Sukman II) the brother of Nur al-Din; but see also Ibn al-'Adim, *Zubdat*, ed. Dahhan, II, p. 254: Miran was Nur al-Din's cousin. See also above, pp. 642–3.

[39] See above, pp. 684–5. On the forms of co-existence between the Byzantines and the Turks in Asia Minor, see also Lilie (1991), pp. 37–49.

[40] Ibn al-'Adim, *Zubdat*, ed. Dahhan, II, p. 318–22; Lilie (1993a), pp. 190–3.

following year Nur al-Din formed a grand coalition against Byzantium; his allies were Kilij Arslan, Shahinshah of Ankara and the Rupenid prince Mleh, who conquered Adana and Tarsus. Although the sultan did not quite dare proclaim open war against Byzantium, the Byzantine–Seljuq alliance was almost dead. Nur al-Din himself died on 15 May 1174, removing the final obstacle to Kilij Arslan II's conquest of the emirate. He occupied Sebasteia and other Danishmend centres, while driving Shahinshah out of Ankara, and both Dhu al-Nun and Shahinshah fled to Byzantium.

Only then did Manuel realise the scale of the danger. Instead of being able to exploit the divisions among the Turkish states, he now faced a sultanate that had united almost all the Turks in Asia Minor beneath its banner. The emperor acted quickly. In 1175 he sent out two expeditions: one to Amaseia, led by the *sebastos* Michael Gabras, and the other to Seljuq-controlled Paphlagonia, headed by Shahinshah. Both ended in defeat: the Amaseians refused to let Gabras into their city, while the Seljuqs destroyed Shahinshah's army. A further military mission to Neocaesarea, this time led by Andronikos Vatatzes and Dhu al-Nun, also ended in humiliation, for the citizens of Neocaesarea refused to cooperate. Manuel's diplomacy had failed, in that the empire had no allies in Asia Minor, and court orators' lauding of his refortification of Dorylaion could not redeem this.[41]

Manuel's last hope lay in his own army; in the past, the Seljuqs had been no match for it. In spring 1176 the emperor marched to Dorylaion, intending to attack Konya, and he rejected Kilij Arslan's plea for peace. But the situation had changed: the sultan now possessed far greater military resources and he summoned all his troops, including those from the newly conquered lands. On 17 September 1176 the Seljuqs trapped the Byzantine army en route to Konya, in a defile near Myriokephalon, and the imperial army was defeated after a hard-fought battle, with heavy casualties on both sides.

It is easy to list the mistakes of Manuel I that led to the diplomatic and military debacle of 1176: his preoccupation with relations with the crusader states; his long-lasting conflict with Nur al-Din; his Balkan campaigns; and his general absorption in western affairs at the expense of the east after 1161. But the main factor boosting the sultan's chances was the dissolution of the Danishmend emirate, and here Manuel could do very little. John II's expeditions some fifty years before show how difficult it was to reconquer territory from the Turks (see above, p. 711), and several generations after 1081 the central Anatolian lands were going their own way: one in which the Greek inhabitants cooperated with the Turks. This cooperation was first and foremost economic, but it helps to explain the Amaseians' and Neocaesareans' similar decisions in 1176. Myriokephalon did not extinguish

---

[41] Stone (2003a), p. 195.

Byzantine hopes for a military reconquest of Asia Minor – the imperial army was still the strongest in Anatolia – but it was a political watershed. The sultanate was now as powerful as the empire and an equilibrium was established in Asia Minor after 1176 that neither side could overturn.

Given the large number of Greeks (*rumi*) living within the sultanate, an orthodox church with strong links to Constantinople and the presence of Byzantine aristocrats at the Seljuq court,[42] Byzantine diplomacy still stood a good chance of ensuring a friendly sultan. This policy was not entirely new and in fact dated back to the reign of Alexios I, but the personal, 'father–son' relationship between emperor and sultan became more significant after 1176.

BYZANTINE–SELJUQ RELATIONS 1176–1232: THE TIES OF RULING FAMILIES

According to a letter from Manuel I Komnenos to Henry II (1154–89) of England, after the battle of Myriokephalon Sultan Kilij Arslan

> sent to beg our imperial majesty supplicantly, employing the language of entreaty, suing for peace, and promising to fulfil every wish of our imperial majesty, to give us his service against all men, to release all the prisoners who were detained in his kingdom, and in every way to conform to our desires.[43]

In reality Manuel agreed to demolish the fortresses of Dorylaion and Soublaion and to become a Seljuq tributary,[44] although it should be noted that even before 1176, Manuel had paid sums to Kilij Arslan as part of his special relationship with the Seljuqs. The friendship (*philia*) between Manuel and Kilij Arslan continued until Manuel's death in 1180. The sultan's failure to exploit his victory at Myriokephalon and Byzantium's gradual weakening after 1180 are not to be explained entirely in military terms.[45] Kilij Arslan decided to divide the sultanate – most probably in 1187 – between his nine sons, a brother and a nephew. However, soon afterwards he handed the whole realm over to his eldest son, Qutb al-Din, upon which Kilij Arslan's other sons ceased to recognise his authority. Seeking undisputed power, Qutb al-Din arrested his father, but the old sultan escaped and settled in Sozopolis in the 'realm' of his youngest son Kay-Khusraw I (1192–6, 1205–11). Kilij Arslan recognised Kay-Khusraw as his heir before his death in 1192, and that same year Kay-Khusraw entered Konya.

After Qutb al-Din's death in 1195, his brother Rukn al-Din of Tokat gradually occupied almost all the sultanate's lands. Kay-Khusraw I was forced

[42] Turan (1953); Balivet (1994), pp. 47–9.   [43] Vasiliev (1929–30), p. 239.
[44] NC, ed. van Dieten, I, p. 189; tr. Magoulias, p. 107; *Histoire des Seldjoukides*, ed. Uzluk, p. 39.
[45] The military campaigning did not finish in 1176, and Manuel I managed to repulse the Seljuq raid against Claudiopolis at the end of 1179.

to leave his capital in September 1196. After a long journey trekking across Cilician Armenia, Ablastayn and the Pontos, the ex-sultan sailed to Constantinople in 1200, where he was received with great honour by Alexios III Angelos (1195–1203). Kay-Khusraw was wedded to the daughter of Manuel Maurozomes, a member of the Komnenian elite, and was even baptised and adopted by the emperor as his son. He was still in Constantinople when the Fourth Crusaders arrived on 23 June 1203 and he helped his adoptive father, Alexios III, to flee the capital on the night of 17–18 July 1203.

When the crusaders finally took Constantinople in April 1204, the empire broke up into its constituent parts. In Asia Minor, 'Theodore, who was called Morotheodore [i.e. 'silly Theodore'],[46] ruled over the city of Philadelphia; another, Sabbas by name,[47] ruled Sampson and its surrounding territory; and David, brother of Alexios, who had taken over Trebizond and was also known as Grand Komnenos, subdued the whole of Paphlagonia . . .'[48] Others who seized this opportunity to establish local power bases included Leo Gabalas of Rhodes and, on the upper Maeander, Nikephoros Kontostephanos and Kay-Khusraw I's father-in-law Manuel Maurozomes (from 1205). One of the most successful was Theodore I Laskaris (1205–21), founder of what emerged as the Nicaean state; he managed to unite all the Byzantine territories in Anatolia, save those conquered by the Latins or occupied by the empire of Trebizond.

Of all the emperors recognised as legitimate in or just before 1204, none managed to establish himself in Asia Minor after the fall of Constantinople.[49] In 1203–4 Alexios III was in Adrianople, and then he moved to Mosynopolis in Thrace (see below, p. 734). It was his son-in-law, Theodore I Laskaris, who acted as the emperor's chief deputy in Anatolia, where at first his imperial connections offered Theodore little advantage; what he really needed was military help so as to vanquish his rivals.

When help arrived it came in the form of the Seljuqs. In June 1204 Rukn al-Din died and his young son Kilij Arslan III (1204–5) succeeded him as sultan. That summer Kay-Khusraw I and Manuel Maurozomes left the environs of Constantinople and hastened to the sultanate of Rum. They passed through Nicaea, where Theodore and Kay-Khusraw concluded an agreement. With the sums advanced by Theodore, Kay-Khusraw was able to depose Kilij Arslan III in March 1205; in return, the sultan gave Theodore a military force to help him subdue his main rivals – Theodore Mangaphas, Sabbas Asidinos and probably also Nikephoros Kontostephanos – and to reconquer some of the lands occupied by the Latins. Only two Greek rivals remained: Manuel Maurozomes, now himself at large in Laodicea, and the

[46] Theodore Mangaphas of Philadelpheia. See above, p. 656.   [47] Sabbas Asidenos.
[48] GA, ch. 7, rev. edn. Wirth, I, p. 12; tr. Macrides, p. 120. See also below, p. 731.
[49] On the various emperors, see above, pp. 662–3.

Grand Komnenos David in Paphlagonia. Despite receiving support from his son-in-law, Kay-Khusraw I, by 1207 Maurozomes had been defeated and imprisoned by Theodore while his lands were absorbed by the sultanate.

Relations between the empire of Nicaea and the Seljuq sultanate should be seen in terms of the family ties between them. While Kay-Khusraw I was married to Maurozomes' daughter, Theodore I Laskaris' wife Anna was the daughter of Alexios III, to whom Kay-Khusraw was indebted. The sultan certainly tried to take advantage of the Byzantine empire's disintegration but, strikingly, his direct assaults were reserved for the lands of other, peripheral rulers. These included Trebizond – capital of the Grand Komnenos Alexios I (1204–22), which Kay-Khusraw attacked in 1205 – and Antalya, which he captured on 5 March 1207.

For the Seljuqs, the situation after 1204 was unique: for the first time their sultanate faced several Greek states in Asia Minor, instead of a single, centralised empire. And yet the sultan, constrained by his family ties, did not exploit the situation to the full. What set Theodore I Laskaris and Kay-Khusraw I against each other was Maurozomes' imprisonment at Theodore's hands, Theodore's coronation as emperor in 1208 and, finally, the appearance of Alexios III Angelos in the sultanate of Rum around 1210.[50] In 1211 the sultan declared open war. In a battle at Antioch-on-the-Maeander some time after 15 June 1211 the Nicaean army was almost defeated, but Theodore managed to kill Kay-Khusraw, and the sultan's eldest son Kay-Kawus I (1211–19) signed an 'inviolable alliance' with him.

Thereafter the Seljuqs did not dare threaten the empire of Nicaea directly. In fact in 1214 the Seljuqs and the Nicaeans simultaneously attacked their common enemy, the empire of Trebizond, whose ruler, the Grand Komnenos Alexios I, was forced to cede western Paphlagonia to Theodore and eastern Paphlagonia, with Sinope as its centre, to Kay-Kawus. The sultanate of Rum became the Nicaean empire's only eastern neighbour. The former rivals pursued different courses: the sultanate, which reached its apogee during the long reign of Kay-Qubad I (1219–37) expanded eastwards; for his part, John III Vatatzes (1221–54) of Nicaea was largely preoccupied with military operations in the Balkans. Yet the Nicaean–Seljuq joint domination of Asia Minor was about to be shattered by the Mongol invasions.

THE COMING OF THE MONGOLS

The Mongol state was founded by Genghis Khan (1206–27) after he succeeded in uniting the Mongol tribes in 1206. He soon began to wage

---

[50] Alexios III was captured by Boniface of Montferrat when the latter was on his way from Corinth to Thessaloniki in November 1204 and Boniface sent the ex-emperor to Montferrat. Around 1209–10 Michael I Angelos Doukas (1205–c. 1215) of Epiros ransomed Alexios III, who by 1211 had left Epiros for Antalya.

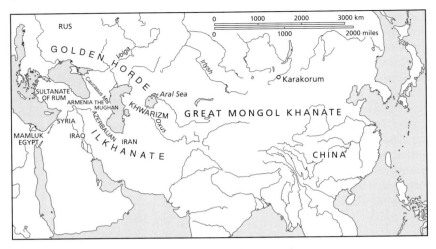

Map 34 The coming of the Mongols

war against his neighbours: the Jurchen emperors in northern China, the Tangut state in north-western China and finally the Khwarizmshahs in central Asia. In 1231 the Mongols destroyed the remnants of the state of the last Khwarizmshah to rule over Iran, Iraq and Azerbaijan, Jalal al-Din Mankburni (1220–31), and this brought them to the borders of the sultanate of Rum. Shortly afterwards, in 1231–2, Sebasteia's hinterland came under attack from Chormaghun, commander-in-chief of the Mongol army in Azerbaijan and Armenia. Kay-Qubad I immediately agreed to pay tribute to the Mongols and a Mongol embassy had arrived in Rum by early September 1236. Before any agreement could be ratified, Kay-Qubad I died on 30 May 1237, but his successor Kay-Khusraw II (1237–46) was swift to send word of his submission to the great khan Ögedei (1229–41): 'I, too, commit myself to the way of agreement and obedience.'[51]

Kay-Khusraw II's deeds did not match his words of compliance, and he failed to establish contact with Chormaghun, nor did he visit the court of the great khan in person. However, the situation changed once again with Ögedei's death in 1241. In the following year, after a lengthy campaign in eastern Europe, Genghis Khan's grandson Batu (1239–55) established a new state, the Golden Horde, and took command of the Mongol forces below the Caucasus range. In 1241–2 a new general, Baiju, was made commander-in-chief of the Mongol troops in Armenia, although Chormaghun nominally preserved his position, despite being struck dumb (or deaf) in battle. Baiju immediately attacked the sultanate. Kay-Khusraw II gathered a large army and called on his allies (including the empires of

51 Ibn Bibi, *Mukhtasar-i Saljuqnamah*, ed. Houtsma, p. 205; German tr. Duda, p. 196.

Trebizond and Nicaea) for help. It was in vain: Baiju completely defeated him in the battle of Köse Dağ on 26 June 1243. While Kay-Khusraw II fled westwards to the Nicaean border, his vizier Muhadhdhab al-Din, moving under his own steam, went first to Baiju and then to Chormaghun. The vizier signed an agreement obliging the sultanate to pay tribute and committing it to becoming a Mongol vassal-state. Batu confirmed these terms during the winter of 1243–4.

The submission of Rum to the Mongols created new problems for John III Vatatzes: the sultanate, together with Cilician Armenia and Trebizond, now became part of the *pax mongolica*. In Asia Minor, the empire of Nicaea was the only state remaining outside Mongol control, and thus it became the next likely target of the Mongol armies. To prevent this, the emperor had to maintain the sultanate of Rum as a buffer zone between the empire and the Mongols.

The enmity between Batu of the Golden Horde and the great khan Güyüg (1246–8) as well as the inner struggles in the Great Mongol khanate before the enthronement of Möngke (1251–9) alleviated the immediate threat to the Nicaean borders. Kay-Khusraw II died in 1246; his elder son, Kay-Kawus II (1246–56, 1257–61), who enjoyed Nicaean support, nominally recognised the supremacy of Batu but refused to go and pay court to the great khan in person. In order to reduce Batu's influence, Güyüg dismissed Baiju and appointed a new general, Eljigidei. He also ordered Kilij Arslan IV to share the throne with his brother Kay-Kawus II.

Although Batu managed to reinstal Baiju in 1251, the position of the Golden Horde in the Caucasus continued to deteriorate. In the same year the great khan Möngke made his brother Hulagu (1258–65), the future Ilkhan, ruler over Iran, Syria, Egypt, Rum, Azerbaijan and Armenia (of these, Egypt and southern Syria had yet to be conquered). Batu, who claimed part of these lands for himself, forbade Hulagu to cross the Oxus. Only after Batu's death in 1255 did Hulagu begin his campaign against the Isma'ili state of the Assassins in northern Iran and the Abbasid caliphate.

Kay-Kawus II, who had imprisoned his brother Kilij Arslan IV by 1256, did not want to exchange nominal submission to the Golden Horde for stricter control at the hands of Hulagu, the future Ilkhan. Besides, Hulagu wanted the plain of Mughan for himself, and ordered Baiju to leave. In August 1256 Baiju arrived unexpectedly at Theodosioupolis (by now called Erzurum). Terrified by the prospect of permanent Mongol settlement in his realm, Kay-Kawus II refused to allow Baiju to remain in the sultanate of Rum and started preparing for war. There was not enough time for Theodore II Laskaris (1254–8) to send him support, but at this very moment Michael Palaiologos – *megas konostaulos* of Nicaea and future emperor – turned up in Konya. He was a refugee who appeared dangerous in Theodore II's eyes because of his noble ancestry, which included links with both the Komnenoi and the Angeloi. It is not entirely clear whether Michael sought refuge in the sultanate simply to avoid possible arrest or whether he really was plotting for the throne of Nicaea. What is certain is that Kay-Kawus II immediately used him against the Mongols; Michael headed the detachment of the Greeks of Rum, fighting under Byzantine banners. However, by 14 October 1256 Baiju had defeated the sultan at Sultanhani and Kay-Kawus fled to the empire of Nicaea; Michael Palaiologos, who escaped to Kastamonu, did the same at the beginning of 1257, when he was pardoned by Theodore II Laskaris.

In this dangerous situation the Mongols were in a strong position to attack the empire of Nicaea; but Nicaean diplomacy rose to the occasion. Between January and March 1257, with Baiju's army still at the borders, a Mongol embassy arrived in Nicaea, sent by the Ilkhan Hulagu. Theodore II gave the envoys a magnificent reception.[52] Hulagu, preoccupied with his struggle against the Abbasids, agreed to restore Kay-Kawus II to the throne, on condition that he would share the sultanate with Kilij Arslan IV. By May 1257 Kay-Kawus II was back in power at Konya.

It was a triumph for Nicaean diplomacy, launching a *rapprochement* between Nicaea and the Ilkhans, while the Nicaean alliance with the Seljuqs remained as strong as ever. Kay-Kawus II, who ruled the western part of the sultanate, even appointed one of the Nicaean military commanders, his friend Michael Palaiologos, as a *beylerbey* (commander-in-chief) at the beginning of 1258.[53] No doubt he did so in order to ensure Nicaean military support. Yet even when united, the Nicaean and Seljuq armies were no match for the Mongols. Imperial *Realpolitik* increasingly required friendly relations with the Mongols of Iran, and it was Michael Palaiologos who first perceived this fact of political life. In 1261 the Mongols finally drove the rebellious Kay-Kawus II out of Rum, but Palaiologos – now Michael VIII (1258–82) – no longer supported his former friend. He detained the sultan in Constantinople; Kay-Kawus II was only liberated three years later, in the autumn or winter of 1264, through the good offices of his brother-in-law Berke (1257–66) of the Golden Horde.

After its restoration in 1261, the Byzantine empire managed to preserve a balance between the Golden Horde and the Ilkhan state. On the one hand, Michael joined the alliance which Mamluk Egypt and the Golden Horde had forged at the end of 1260, united by their mutual animosity towards the Ilkhans. On the other, he successfully negotiated a marriage treaty with the Ilkhan in 1265, marrying his own illegitimate daughter Maria to Hulagu's successor Abaqa (1265–82). The Ilkhans' desire to avoid having to mount a military campaign in Asia Minor helps explain their tolerance of Byzantine

[52] GP, II.25, ed. and French tr. Failler, I, pp. 186–9.
[53] Cahen (2001), p. 189; Korobeinikov, 'Byzantium and the Turks' (DPhil thesis, 2003), pp. 46–72.

neutrality in an otherwise hostile environment. Besides, both states had a common enemy: the nomadic Turks.

THE NEW OLD ENEMY

The Seljuq state in Rum was multi-ethnic: its subjects were Greeks, Syrians, Armenians, Turks, Kurds, Arabs and Persians. Of these, the Turks were for the most part nomads; the Greek and Armenian populations were partly rural and partly urban, as were the Syrians and Arabs in the south-east of Asia Minor. As for the Persian townsfolk, they only moved into Anatolia after the Seljuq conquest. Although the Seljuq aristocracy was predominantly Turkish by origin, the ruling dynasty adopted Iranian names such as Kay-Kawus, Kay-Qubad, and Kay-Khusraw, which were derived from the names of the legendary shahs of the Kayanid dynasty in Iran (see above, pp. 139–40). This was no accident. The vast bureaucratic apparatus, strongly influenced by both Persian language and culture, was the chief instrument with which the sultans ruled their immense Anatolian realm.

When the Mongols finally subdued Rum in 1261, they weakened the sultan's power as much as they could. Between the 1260s and the 1290s semi-dependent Rum lords dominated the region, most powerful of whom was the *parwanah* Mu'in al-Din, the uncrowned head of state from 1260 until 1277.[54] The question of governance was further complicated by Mongol infiltration into the Seljuqs' state apparatus. Deprived of effective control over their finances, army and households, the sultans soon became Mongol puppets.

The Mongol conquests also shifted the ethnic balance in Asia Minor. Under their onslaught, many Turkish nomads had fled from central Asia to Anatolia, but now the Mongol troops also occupied the best pastures of the Anatolian plateau. From the 1260s the number of the Turks who migrated to the Byzantine borders increased sharply. The Turks began to form sizable permanent tribal confederations. The largest of these seems to have been the Turks of Laodicea (Denizli), whose ruler, Mehmed-bey, dared to resist Hulagu in 1262. Although he was killed on the orders of the Ilkhan, his confederation survived until around 1284. Other Turkmen confederations included the Ağaçeri, literally 'men of the forest', who controlled the lands between Melitene and Germanikeia, stretching as far as Cilician Armenia; the confederations of Germiyan and Karaman, based respectively in Kotyaeion (Kütahya) and to the south-east of Konya; the Turks of Kastamonu, close to the southern shores of the Black Sea; and, finally, the Turks of the Pontos, of whom the most prominent was the

---

[54] *Parwanah* was a Persian term, literally meaning butterfly or moth, but used to denote the sultan's personal assistant who delivered his master's orders to ministers of the sultanate.

tribe of *çepni*. Of these confederations at least three – those of Kütahya, Kastamonu and Denizli – occupied lands close to the Byzantine border. Military pressure on the Byzantines increased as the Turks, whose territory the Mongols ravaged, tried to compensate by taking over Byzantine lands for themselves.

The defence of the Nicaean empire, which was an improved variant of the Komnenian military system, relied on three elements: the provincial garrisons or *themata*, situated in the frontier towns and castles; the nomads of Turkish and Cuman origin who were allowed to settle on Nicaean soil; and, finally, the *akritai*, smallholding soldiers installed in the frontier zone (see below, p. 739). Although important during the period of the Nicaean empire, from the 1260s onwards the *akritai* were no match for the Turks, whose powerful confederations were strong enough to resist even the Mongol *tümen*s with some success. The only appropriate response on the part of the Byzantines was to embark on military reform.

Such reform was implemented by Michael VIII Palaiologos. He carried out a cadastral survey of the borderlands in 1264–5 and, as a consequence, converted into a *pronoia* that part of each individual's landed property which was estimated to have an annual revenue of 40 *hyperpera*. This reform changed the status of the *akritai*: those who held state land free of tax, and who had formed irregular military units during the reign of the Laskarids, now became mobile *themata* troops, easily mobilised for a variety of military campaigns.

Michael VIII's second innovation was to maintain closer supervision of the professional Byzantine army along the border, both the *tagmata* and the *themata*. For example, in 1263–4 the Turks of Denizli, who had been defeated by the Mongols in 1262, penetrated as far as Tralles (Aydin). Michael's brother, John the despot, moved his army to Asia Minor from the Balkans, restoring order on the Anatolian frontier in 1264–7 and concluding a peace treaty with the Turks.

The Byzantines managed to maintain their defence system more or less intact up to the 1290s. In the early 1280s Michael VIII succeeded in driving out the Turks who had recently encroached on Byzantine territory, despite being preoccupied at the time with his relations with the west. The Turkish invasion of 1279 had been a direct consequence of their great revolt against the Mongols in 1277–9. The rebels proclaimed as their leader a certain Cimri, maintaining that he was the son of the exiled Kay-Kawus II, Sultan 'Ala' al-Din Siyawush: Kay-Kawus was still remembered for his opposition to the Mongols. The Mongols retaliated mercilessly, devastating not only the epicentre of the revolt, Pamphylia, but also those territories close to the Byzantine border, from Konya to Denizli (Laodicea). The large confederation of the Turks of Denizli was totally dispersed, to be replaced by new confederations, in particular the 'emirate' of the Menteşe. Our Byzantine

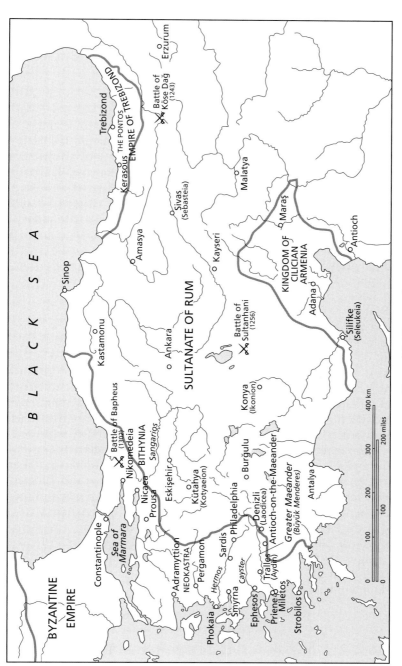

Map 35 Asia Minor c. 1265

BLACK SEA

BYZANTINE EMPIRE

Constantinople

Sea of Marmara

Battle of Bapheus (1302)

Nikomedeia

BITHYNIA

Prousa

Nicaea

Sangarios

Kastamonu

Sinop

Amasya

Sivas (Sebasteia)

Trebizond

Kerasous

THE PONTOS

EMPIRE OF TREBIZOND

Battle of Köse Dağ (1243)

Erzurum

Eskişehir

Kütahya (Kotyaeion)

Ankara

SULTANATE OF RUM

Kayseri

Malatya

Maraş

Antioch

Adramyttion

NEOKASTRA

Pergamon

Sardis

Hermos

Philadelphia

Burğulu

Battle of Sultanhani (1256)

Konya (Ikonion)

KINGDOM OF CILICIAN ARMENIA

Adana

Silifke (Seleukeia)

Phokaia

Smyrna

Ephesos

Priene

Miletos

Strobilos

Cayster

Tralles (Aydın)

Denizli (Laodicea)

Antioch-on-the-Maeander

Greater Maeander (Büyük Menderes)

Antalya

0   100   200   300   400 km

0   100   200 miles

sources record the ensuing invasion that engulfed the lands between the rivers Maeander and Cayster. Michael's response was swift and decisive: he sent his son and co-emperor Andronikos II Palaiologos to the Maeander in 1280, while he himself secured the northern reaches of the Byzantine frontier in a series of military expeditions along the river Sangarios in 1280–2.

Under Michael VIII, Byzantium held onto its Anatolian territories, with the loss of only Strobilos, Stadiotrachia and Antioch-on-the-Maeander. But under Michael's successor, Andronikos II (1282–1328), Byzantine strategy towards the east became non-interventionist (see also below, pp. 806, 808). The Byzantine army – the most vital element in the defence of Asia Minor – does not seem to have been militarily active in the region at all between 1284 and 1295, despite the loss of Tralles in 1284 and a series of turbulent Turkish revolts against the Mongols. The emperor adopted the old Laskarid strategy of rebuilding fortresses and supplying their garrisons with money and soldiers.

Very soon, however, Andronikos ran short of money. He tried to solve his financial problems at the army's expense: in 1284–5 a special 10 per cent tax was imposed on the *pronoia* holders. The emperor went even further than his father in debasing the coinage (see below, p. 809). At the end of the winter of 1292–3 the Turks had crossed the Byzantine border and devastated the theme of Neokastra. The emperor appointed Alexios Philanthropenos as commander-in-chief. Philanthropenos managed to restore the status quo on the border but, unfortunately, he himself rebelled at the end of 1295. Although Andronikos managed to capture and blind Philanthropenos, his army, now in profound crisis, disintegrated. The soldiers, who had suffered greatly as a result of the emperor's financial measures, no longer trusted him. After a severe winter in 1298–9 the Turks crossed the Byzantine borders along the Maeander. Facing ineffective and disorganised Byzantine resistance, by 1302 they had occupied the lowlands between the Maeander and the Hermos rivers and within two years the whole coastline of western Anatolia stretching as far north as Adramyttion was in Turkish hands, save for Phokaia, a Genoese possession. The northern sector of the Byzantine border defences was also breached after the imperial army was defeated at the battle of Bapheus on 27 July 1302 at the hands of Osman, one of the more determined and effective of the Turkish beys in Bithynia. Later attempts by Andronikos to use foreign mercenaries, the Catalans, ended in disaster: the Catalans rebelled and threatened the very existence of the empire in 1305–11 (see below, pp. 811, 835).

CONCLUSION

As we have seen, a strong vein of mutual toleration characterised relations between the Byzantine and the Turkish ruling families in the twelfth and thirteenth centuries. Individual careerists and exiles moved between their respective courts in quest of advancement or asylum, and the Seljuq sultan generally showed little inclination to try and take full advantage of those occasions when the Byzantine administration in western Asia Minor was in disarray. It was, above all, the coming of the Mongols – their erosion of the power of the Rum sultanate to the advantage of individual warlords and their savage measures against local populations in eastern Asia Minor – that prompted the migration of sizable numbers of Turks westwards, swamping the Byzantine defences. Andronikos II's administrative deficiencies and general disregard for Asia Minor further aggravated the situation. But, as so often in Byzantine history, the mainsprings of action lay far beyond the empire's borders or means of control.

The Turkish conquest of 1302–5 was more than a simple nomadic invasion, seeing that sedentary and transhumant elements had long co-existed in the border zone. After the Turks' conquest of what was left of Byzantine Asia Minor, not only did nomads settle in their newly conquered lands, but these lands also soon became the target of Muslim immigration from the depths of central and eastern Asia Minor, leaving the dwindling Greek communities little chance of survival. This rapid change in the ethnic balance meant there was no hope of Byzantium recovering its lost provinces in western Asia Minor. When the Catalans finally departed, they left an empire that was devastated and bankrupt. Byzantium's former possessions in western Anatolia were divided between various Turkish warlords, who managed to establish successful principalities along the coasts of the Aegean and the Sea of Marmara. One such Bithynian *beylik* – that of Osman – would become the cradle of a new formation: the Ottoman Turks.

PART III

THE BYZANTINE LANDS IN THE LATER MIDDLE AGES 1204–1492

AFTER THE FOURTH CRUSADE: THE GREEK RUMP STATES AND THE RECOVERY OF BYZANTIUM

MICHAEL ANGOLD

INTRODUCTION

It was almost unthinkable that the 'queen of cities' should fall. It was in the words of Byzantine contemporaries a 'cosmic cataclysm'. The Byzantine ruling class was disorientated and uprooted. The Constantinopolitan elite sought refuge where they could. Among the common people there was at first a sense of jubilation at their discomfiture: the proud had been humbled. Such was the demoralisation that at all levels of society submission to the conquering crusaders seemed a natural solution. Many leading Byzantines threw in their lot with the Latins. The logothete of the Drome Demetrios Tornikes continued to serve them in this capacity. He was the head of one of the great bureaucratic families which had dominated Constantinople before 1204. In the provinces leading families made deals with the conquerors. Theodore Branas governed the city of Adrianople – the key to Thrace – on behalf of the Venetians. Michael Angelos Doukas – a member of the Byzantine imperial house – took service with Boniface of Montferrat, now ruler of Thessaloniki. The cooperation of the local *archontes* smoothed Geoffrey I of Villehardouin's conquest of the Peloponnese.

The crusaders elected a Latin emperor and created a Latin patriarch of Constantinople. There seemed every possibility that Byzantium would be refashioned in a Latin image. For exactly a year the Latins carried all before them. Then in April 1205 their success came abruptly to an end. They had alienated and underestimated the Bulgarians, who crushed them at the battle of Adrianople. Many of the crusade leaders were killed. The Latin emperor Baldwin of Flanders was led away into captivity, never again to be seen alive.

This defeat revealed how insecure the Latins were in their newly conquered lands. It gave heart to the three Byzantine successor states that were emerging in exile. The most remote was centred on the city of Trebizond, where Alexios and David Komnenos, grandsons of the tyrant Andronikos I Komnenos (1183–5), established themselves early in 1204. David then pushed westwards to secure control of Paphlagonia, which had been held by his grandfather. This brought him into conflict with Theodore Laskaris,

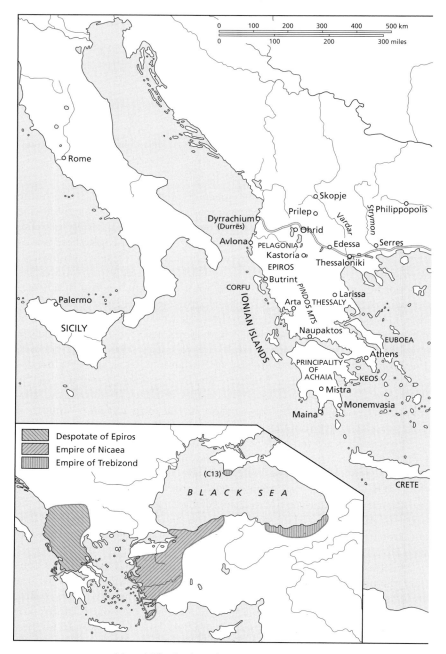

Map 36 The Greek-speaking rump states 1204–1261

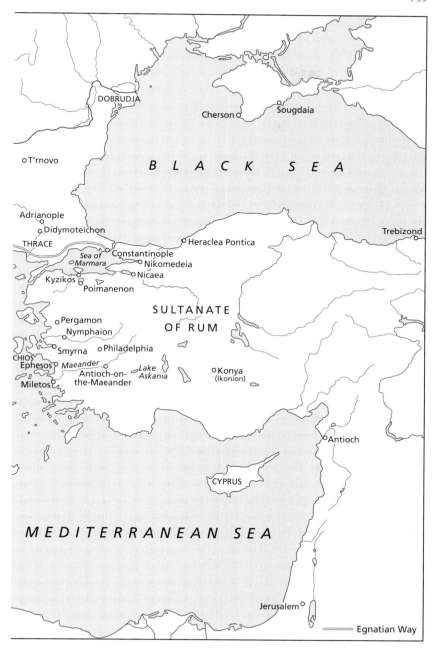

T'rnovo

DOBRUDJA

Cherson ○

Sougdaia

B L A C K   S E A

Adrianople
Didymoteichon
THRACE
Sea of Marmara
Constantinople
Nikomedeia
Kyzikos
Poimanenon
Nicaea

Heraclea Pontica

Trebizond

SULTANATE OF RUM

Pergamon
Nymphaion
Smyrna
Philadelphia
CHIOS
Ephesos
Maeander
Miletos
Antioch-on-the-Maeander
Lake Askania

Konya (Ikonion)

Antioch

CYPRUS

M E D I T E R R A N E A N   S E A

Jerusalem ○

═══ Egnatian Way

who was organising resistance to the Latins from Nicaea. Laskaris was the son-in-law and heir presumptive of Alexios III Angelos (1195–1203). He had escaped from Constantinople in September 1203, soon after his father-in-law had abandoned the capital to the young Alexios Angelos and the soldiers of the Fourth Crusade. Laskaris secured control of the Bithynian cities in his father-in-law's name. By the summer of 1205 it had become clear that Alexios III Angelos was a Latin prisoner. Theodore I Laskaris (1205–21) therefore had himself acclaimed emperor, the better to deal with his various rivals, of whom David Komnenos was the most dangerous. Meanwhile, the foundations of a third Byzantine successor state were being laid in Epiros behind the Pindos mountains by Michael I Angelos Doukas (1204–15) who had quickly abandoned his Latin allegiance.

The Latin defeat at Adrianople allowed the Greeks to ponder the true meaning of the Latin conquest. The horror of the sack of Constantinople began to sink in. Sanctuaries were desecrated, nuns raped and boys of noble family sold into slavery among the Saracens. The atrocity stories that now started to circulate had only a single theme: the crusader sack of Constantinople was a calculated insult to orthodoxy. At the hospital of St Sampson the Latins turned the marble altar screen with its scenes from sacred history into a cover for the common latrine; at the shrine of the Archangel Michael at Anaplous a cardinal smeared the icons of saints with chalk and then threw icons and relics into the sea.[1] But how were the sufferings of Constantinople to be avenged? The orthodox church was effectively without leadership. The patriarch John Kamateros does not cut an impressive figure. He had escaped from Constantinople to the relative security of the Thracian town of Didymoteichon, and had refused an invitation to move to Nicaea, where resistance to the Latins was strongest. When he died in June 1206, it was imperative that a new orthodox patriarch be elected. Otherwise, the patriarchate of Constantinople would pass by default to the Latins. The people and clergy of Constantinople hoped that Pope Innocent III would approve the election of a new orthodox patriarch. They cited the example of the crusader states, where the patriarchal sees of Antioch and Jerusalem had been divided between an orthodox and a Latin incumbent. This initiative appears to have been blocked by the Latin authorities in Constantinople.[2]

The orthodox clergy of Constantinople therefore turned to Theodore Laskaris at Nicaea. He gave his support to the election of a new orthodox patriarch of Constantinople. Michael IV Autoreianos (1208–14) was duly ordained patriarch at Nicaea on 20 March 1208. His first official act was to

---

[1] Cotelerius, *Ecclesiae graecae monumenta*, III, pp. 511–13.
[2] Gill (1973). In general, see now Angold (2003a).

crown and anoint Laskaris emperor on Easter Day. Thus was a Byzantine empire re-created in exile in Nicaea.[3]

AFTERMATH OF THE SACK OF CONSTANTINOPLE

Members of the old elite gravitated to the new capital. The historian Niketas Choniates was one of them. He picked up the threads of old acquaintances. He commiserated with Archbishop Constantine Mesopotamites of Thessaloniki, who had fallen into pirate hands but was now safe in Epiros.[4] He hoped to persuade his brother Michael, the archbishop of Athens, to come to Nicaea. Theodore Laskaris had a ship ready to whisk him away from 'windy Keos' where he had found refuge. The archbishop refused the invitation, preferring to remain within easy reach of his Athenian flock.[5] At Nicaea Niketas Choniates found time to complete his great history, in which he tried to explain why the disaster of 1204 should have overtaken Constantinople. He also looked to the future. He compiled his *Treasury of orthodoxy*, which was designed to counter heresy. The defence of orthodoxy became central to the ideology of exile which he elaborated as court orator for Theodore Laskaris. Exile was punishment for the sins of the past. The parallel with the Israelites was much in Niketas' mind. He compared the waters of Nicaea's Lake Askania to the waters of Babylon. In exile the Byzantines, like the Israelites, would atone for their sins and would recover divine favour. The New Jerusalem would be theirs again. Their immediate task was to preserve the purity of orthodoxy in the face of the Latin threat.[6]

The ideology of exile would at first be virulently anti-Latin in contrast to the more restrained attitudes that prevailed before 1204. The impressions created by the sack of Constantinople were reinforced by the intransigence displayed by the Latin church in subsequent discussions between representatives of the two churches. These discussions only underlined the contempt felt by the Latins for the Greeks. The papal legate Pelagius provided further confirmation of Latin arrogance towards the orthodox church. In 1214 he closed the orthodox churches in Constantinople and persecuted Greek monks who refused to recognise papal primacy. As a counter-blast to his activities, Constantine Stilbes, the metropolitan of Kyzikos, produced his *Against the Latins*. This is one of the key documents of anti-Latin polemic. It marked a decisive shift from reasoned debate to justified prejudice. Stilbes had little to say about theological differences. Instead, he concentrated on

---

[3] Heisenberg, 'Neue Quellen zur Geschichte. II', pp. 5–12. Gounarides (1985) prefers 1207 to the traditional date of 1208. The balance of probabilities still favours 1208 as the date of the election of a new orthodox patriarch at Nicaea and of the coronation of Theodore I Laskaris.

[4] Niketas Choniates, *Orationes*, pp. 204–6.   [5] Michael Choniates, *Epistulae*, pp. 122–7, 129–31.

[6] Niketas Choniates, *Orationes*, pp. 170–200.

two issues: papal primacy and holy war. These were interlinked. They had perverted Latin Christianity and had produced the tragedy of 1204. To take papal primacy first, Stilbes charged that the Latins did not simply regard the pope as the successor of St Peter. It was not even that they identified the two. It was worse than this: they deified the pope and insisted that all Christians submit to his authority. The perversion of papal authority was apparent in the issuing of indulgences. Stilbes was the first Byzantine theologian to draw attention to this Latin practice. What horrified him was not so much that past sins were pardoned, but those that were still to be committed. It was the same with oaths: the pope was capable of releasing Latins not only from those that had already been sworn, but also from those yet to be taken. Papal authority thus undermined the moral order that Christianity was supposed to uphold. It was also used to promote warfare.[7]

The Byzantines had considered, but always rejected, the notion of holy war. They followed Basil of Caesarea's teaching that in all circumstances the taking of human life was wrong. The notion of the crusade disturbed the Byzantines. It was mostly clearly expressed in Anna Komnena's story about the fighting priest. She concluded, 'thus the race is no less devoted to religion than to war'.[8] It was Stilbes who fused this disquiet into an outright condemnation of the Latin church's devotion to war. He accused the Latin church of teaching that men dying in battle went to paradise. This might not have been official doctrine, but beliefs of this kind circulated among crusaders. Latin bishops were supposed to sprinkle naked youths with holy water and in this way to turn them into invincible warriors. Stilbes seems to be garbling the Latin church's role in the making of a knight. Again he was not so far off the mark.

The sack of Constantinople confirmed Stilbes' portrayal of the Latin faith as one perverted by papal primacy and its espousal of war as an instrument of expansion. The crusaders had desecrated the churches of Constantinople and had profaned St Sophia itself. Latin priests and bishops had played an active role in the assault on the City. A bishop had been in the vanguard holding aloft a cross. The Latin clergy had done nothing to prevent the excesses of the crusaders; if anything, they encouraged them. They had desecrated the holy images. Stilbes closed his tract with a demonstration that because of its addiction to war, the Latin church had lapsed into heresy. Stilbes fixed in the Byzantine mind an image of the Latins that would never be erased. Some years later in 1231 when there was talk of a compromise with the Latin authorities on the island of Cyprus, the orthodox clergy and people of Constantinople sent a delegation to Nicaea. They protested

---

[7] Constantine Stilbes, *Against the Latins*, pp. 61–91.
[8] *Al.*, X.8.8, ed. Reinsch and Kambylis, I, p. 307; ed. and French tr. Leib, II, p. 218; tr. Sewter, p. 317. See also Kolbaba (2000), pp. 27–8, 72, 199.

that this was to ignore their sufferings at the hands of the Latins: they had been imprisoned; they had had their beards pulled out. Any deal with the Latins would mean 'a betrayal of the faith handed down from their fathers'. The members of the delegation insisted that an obsession with war had driven the Latins 'raving mad', priests and laity alike. They would take any concession on the part of the Greeks as a sign of weakness and surrender.[9] The events of 1204 brought the Latins into sharper focus. It was part of the way that the Byzantine identity was reconstructed in an anti-Latin sense during the period of exile. The new patriarch Michael Autoreianos even offered spiritual rewards to those Byzantines laying down their lives in the fight against the Latins.[10]

Having laid the foundations of a Byzantine empire in exile Theodore I Laskaris found himself under threat from an unexpected quarter. In 1211 his imperial claims were challenged by his father-in-law Alexios III Angelos, who had the backing of the Seljuq Turks. Laskaris engaged the Seljuq armies at the Pisidian border town of Antioch-on-the-Maeander. The battle started to go against him, so he sought out the Seljuq sultan and killed him in single combat. The Seljuq forces melted away and Alexios III was led off to end his days in a Nicaean monastery. The manner of Laskaris' triumph did wonders for his prestige, but it was a pyrrhic victory. He had lost his best troops – paradoxically, Latin mercenaries. The Latin emperor Henry of Hainault invaded from the north and swept all before him. Laskaris had to cede to the Latins the north-western corner of Asia Minor (see also below, p. 763), placing a wedge between his territories in the north around Nicaea and those in the south around Smyrna, and making communications difficult. The death of David Komnenos in 1212 provided some compensation. It allowed Theodore I Laskaris to annex Paphlagonia, effectively cutting off the empire of Trebizond from the mainstream of Byzantine history. It became instead a 'Greek emirate', and its history involves that of Anatolia and the Black Sea rather than the late Byzantine empire's.

THE RISE OF NICAEA

Theodore I Laskaris died in 1221. His death was followed by civil strife, out of which his son-in-law John III Vatatzes (1221–54) emerged as victor. Later generations remembered Theodore with gratitude, but although he had re-created Byzantium in exile, his success was limited. This contrasted with the fortunes of Theodore Angelos (1215–30, styling himself as Komnenos Doukas) who had taken over the leadership of resistance to the Latins in Epiros. Theodore was a younger cousin of the emperor Alexios III Angelos. In 1217 he was able to waylay a Latin army advancing down

---

[9] *MB*, II, p. 11.   [10] Michael Autoreianos, *Acts*, pp. 117–19.

the Egnatian Way from the Adriatic coast. It was commanded by Peter of Courtenay, the new Latin emperor. The Latins were defeated and Peter of Courtenay disappeared for ever. This Latin defeat bears comparison with that suffered at Adrianople at the hands of the Bulgarians (see above, p. 731 and below, p. 784), and it prepared the way for Theodore Angelos' occupation of Thessaloniki in the autumn of 1224, setting the seal on his military achievements. Angelos had made himself the most powerful ruler in the southern Balkans. He pushed eastwards and by 1228 was within striking distance of Constantinople. To enhance his claims he had himself proclaimed and crowned emperor. Although the existence of rival emperors was nothing new, there were now two Byzantine emperors in exile with claims on Constantinople.

In the background there remained the formidable strength of the Bulgarian tsar Ivan II Asen (1218–41) (see also pp. 788–92). Although he had nominally submitted to papal authority, he too had designs on Latin Constantinople and there were plans afoot for the betrothal of his daughter to the young Latin emperor, Baldwin II; had they been implemented, he would have become regent (see below, pp. 788, 790).

These competing ambitions helped ensure the survival for another thirty years or more of the Latin empire of Constantinople, which was reduced to little more than the City and its immediate hinterland. In the end, it was the so-called Nicaean empire that would emerge as victor. This outcome was far from obvious in 1228, when the forces of Theodore Angelos drove those of the Nicaean emperor John III Vatatzes out of the key Thracian city of Adrianople. It became less unlikely two years later when Angelos invaded Bulgaria. After his defeat and capture by Ivan Asen at the battle of Klokotnitsa (see also p. 790), Angelos was blinded and spent the next seven years in a Bulgarian prison. His Balkan territories as far west as the Adriatic fell into the hands of his captor, with only Thessaloniki, Thessaly and Epiros eluding Bulgarian conquest: these were divided among members of the Angelos dynasty.

Once Ivan Asen had consolidated his new territories, he entered into an alliance with his potential rival, the Nicaean emperor John III Vatatzes, against the Latins of Constantinople. The initiative came from the Nicaean emperor. He was by far the weaker party, but he deployed one tempting bargaining counter: he could offer patriarchal status to the church of Bulgaria. The alliance was sealed by the betrothal of the heir apparent to the Nicaean throne to a daughter of the Bulgarian tsar. There was an ineffective siege of Constantinople in 1235 before the allies broke up acrimoniously. The only positive result was that the Nicaeans gained a permanent foothold in Thrace, providing their emperor John Vatatzes with a base for intervention in the Balkans. After the death of Ivan Asen he took advantage of the ensuing uncertainty to annex much of the southern Balkans. His campaign culminated in December 1246 with his triumphant entry into the city of Thessaloniki. The recovery of Constantinople now seemed a distinct possibility.

Contemporaries conceded that John Vatatzes' great virtue was patience. This, in its turn, was a reflection of the underlying strengths of the Nicaean empire, which Vatatzes knew how to enhance and exploit. He could afford to be patient. He could also afford to keep armies in the field and to maintain an impressive fleet, something that had proved too costly for Byzantine emperors before 1204. This was an indication of the soundness of his fiscal administration. Paradoxically, the loss of Constantinople made for more efficient government. In the years before 1204 it had become bloated and inefficient. In exile, administration had to be simplified. There was no place for the old departments of state (*logothesia*). Central government was reduced to little more than a household administration. The financial side was concentrated in the imperial wardrobe (*vestiarion*). The whole administration was run for much of Vatatzes' reign by one minister, Demetrios Tornikes. On his death in 1247 his duties were split between four secretaries, who in all probability had been his subordinates.

The simplification of central government dramatically reduced its costs, shifting the burden of administration onto the provincial authorities. This was possible because in western Asia Minor the organisation of themes had survived the fall of Constantinople intact and the tax-raising machinery was still in place. However, the main taxes acquired new names. *Synōnē* – land tax – and *kapnikon* – hearth tax – were replaced by *sitarkia* and *agapē*. The meaning of this change of names remains unclear; it may only have been a matter of adopting local terminology, and it does not seem to have entailed any radical reform of the taxation system. Taxpayers continued to be divided according to their means into the same fiscal categories as before: *zeugaratoi, boidatoi, aktēmones* and *aporoi*. The only major fiscal innovation of the period of exile was the expedient known as *epiteleia*, which attached a fiscal value to property. It had three main purposes: it was a way of transferring fiscal obligations from one taxpayer to another; it could be used to safeguard fiscal privileges; and payment of *epiteleia* could be cited as proof of property rights. It acted as a lubricant of the fiscal system at a time when there was a significant growth of privileged property, and its importance is evident from the way it was retained until the demise of the Byzantine empire.[11]

The efficacy of the Byzantine fiscal system depended on maintenance of a cadastral register. John Vatatzes instituted a revision of the cadastral register for his Anatolian provinces early in his reign. This was in keeping with his careful supervision of fiscal administration. He learned on one

[11] Angold (1975a), pp. 202–36.

occasion that two of his receivers were carrying out their duties improperly. He had one beaten so severely that he died. The other had the sense to flee to Trebizond.[12] On another occasion, a local official made a wrong tax assessment. To teach him a lesson the emperor forced him to pay the sum wrongly assessed.

The simplification of government inevitably meant some devolution of authority. The most obvious form this took was the creation of new immunities and *pronoiai*, which entitled the holder to some or all of the state revenues from a particular area. The period of exile saw a decisive growth of privileged property. In these circumstances stringent control over fiscal administration was essential to protect remaining imperial rights and revenues. Some decline of revenue was inevitable, but the emperors of Nicaea were able to compensate for this by building up the imperial demesne.[13] They were able to exploit the confused situation following the fall of Constantinople to appropriate properties without clear title of ownership. They took over, for example, many of the estates in western Anatolia belonging to the monasteries of Constantinople. John Vatatzes insisted on careful management of the imperial demesne, which was undoubtedly a lucrative source of revenue. All the signs are that the period of exile was a time of agrarian prosperity in western Asia Minor. Grain and other foodstuffs could be exported to the Seljuqs of Rum. Later descriptions of the wealth of the Nicaean empire owed something to nostalgia, but seem essentially correct.

John Vatatzes is one of the few medieval rulers credited by contemporaries with an economic policy. He is supposed to have adopted a policy of autarchy. This took the form of a sumptuary law that his subjects should wear clothes made of home-produced cloth.[14] Here was an attempt to stem the tide of imported western and Muslim materials, and this measure seems to have been a response to the sudden appearance of huge quantities of western cloth on the markets of the eastern Mediterranean from the late twelfth century onwards. John Vatatzes' sumptuary law was not likely to make very much difference in the long run, but in the short term he seems to have been able to protect his territories from Italian commercial penetration. Despite the respectable number of Italian, particularly Venetian, commercial documents surviving from the period, there are few indications of Italian trade with the ports of the Nicaean empire. Vatatzes' autarchic policy was intended as an assertion of Byzantine independence. It may have been practical for a time because western Asia Minor was relatively remote from the major trade routes of the Mediterranean. Autarchy had

---

[12] GP, X.9, ed. and French tr. Failler, IV, pp. 324–5.

[13] NG, II.6, ed. Schopen and Bekker, I, pp. 42–3; German tr. van Dieten, I, p. 84.

[14] NG, II.6, ed. Schopen and Bekker, I, pp. 43–4; German tr. van Dieten, I, p. 85; see also Xanalatos (1939).

some political value: it allowed Vatatzes to pose as an emperor who had the well-being of his subjects at heart. This was one of his strengths as emperor.

Another was the presence at Nicaea of the orthodox patriarchate of Constantinople. John Vatatzes was fortunate in the patriarch, Germanos II (1223–40), who supported him loyally in the difficulties he encountered at the beginning of his reign.[15] There was a series of conspiracies against him involving leading court families. The most serious was the work of brothers of the late emperor Theodore I Laskaris. They engineered a Latin invasion of the Nicaean empire, but to no avail. John Vatatzes won a resounding victory over the Latins at Poimanenon in 1224 and followed it up by driving the Latins out of Asia Minor. Vatatzes rewarded the patriarch for his loyalty during this critical period by acceding to his request and issuing a chrysobull protecting episcopal property during a vacancy.[16]

The major achievement of Patriarch Germanos II was to restore the moral standing of the orthodox patriarchate, which had been bruised by its ignominious role in the years leading up to 1204. He connected the depravity of Constantinople before its fall with its ethnically mixed population, describing its population as 'the sordid droppings of prostitutes and adulterous connections, offspring of servant girls bought for cash, sprung willy nilly from the Rhos or the descendants of Hagar and the rest of the racial stew'.[17] Exile provided the opportunity to 'purify the dialect of the tribe' and to create a healthier society. The patriarch reveals something of the motivation behind the growth of a Byzantine proto-nationalism, which otherwise tends to be seen in terms of a nostalgia for a Hellenic past.

This growing nationalism's greatest strength came from its identification with orthodoxy. The defence of orthodoxy was Germanos II's main concern. He renewed the attack on the Bogomil heresy, which had recovered some of its support in the turmoil following the fall of Constantinople (see above, p. 617). But of more immediate importance to the patriarch was the condition of the orthodox communities at Constantinople and in Cyprus which were suffering under Latin rule. Germanos sought to strengthen them in their faith. By ministering to the orthodox beyond the political frontiers of the Nicaean empire he was able to underscore the fact that, although Constantinople might have fallen into Latin hands, orthodoxy still stood, albeit with its centre now at Nicaea. To some this might have seemed an idle boast. The Greeks of the Peloponnese acquiesced in the rule of their Frankish princes, who had the sense to guarantee the rights of orthodox parish priests. Bulgaria still nominally submitted to papal authority. The Serbian grand *župan* Stefan 'the first-crowned' obtained a royal crown

---

[15] For his collected works and an account of his career, see Lagopates, *Germanos*.
[16] Germanos II, 'Bref inédit', ed. Nicole, pp. 74–80.   [17] Lagopates, *Germanos*, p. 282, lines 23–6.

from the papacy in 1217. To avert the possibility that Serbia would drift into the orbit of the Latin church, the patriarch at Nicaea recognised the autocephalous status of the Serbian archbishopric.[18] Germanos II had to face the danger that the orthodox church would fragment along political lines, leaving it an easier prey for the Latin church.

Such considerations bedevilled Germanos II's relations with the orthodox bishops of Epiros, whose primary loyalty was to their ruler Theodore Angelos. The latter's assumption of imperial honours in 1227–8 produced a schism between the orthodox patriarchate at Nicaea and the church in Theodore Angelos' territories. Germanos II refused to accept the validity of Theodore Angelos' imperial coronation. This was performed by Demetrios Chomatenos, the archbishop of Ohrid (1216/17–c. 1236), whose church enjoyed autocephalous status and who increasingly assumed a patriarchal role. Chomatenos' tribunal became a court of appeal for cases throughout Angelos' territories, although this stance became harder to justify after the break-up of Angelos' empire in the wake of his capture by the Bulgarians at the battle of Klokotnitsa in 1230. Two years later this orthodox schism ended when the Epirot bishops recognised the authority of the patriarch at Nicaea. Germanos was vindicated. In 1238 he made a progress around the churches of Epiros which took him as far as Arta.

Germanos' intransigence in his dealings with the Epirot bishops contrasted with the line he took over the Bulgarian church. In 1235 he granted it patriarchal status, but always safeguarding the primacy of honour due to the orthodox patriarch. This concession was made as part of an alliance between the Bulgarian tsar Ivan II Asen and the Nicaean emperor John Vatatzes. It was largely a political move (see below, p. 792). The patriarch was doing the emperor's bidding, though he might have found some consolation in the thought that the alternative was worse: the Bulgarian church would in all likelihood have returned to its Roman allegiance. This would have been a negation of Germanos' endeavours over the preceding three years to bring the Bulgarian church back into the orthodox communion.

NEGOTIATIONS ON CHURCH UNION

Germanos II bowed to one of the facts of Byzantine political life: emperors were always likely to use orthodoxy as a weapon or a bargaining counter in their foreign policy. The emperors of Nicaea continued the practice. In 1207 Theodore I Laskaris turned to Pope Innocent III (1198–1216) for recognition as the leader of the orthodox community. This was done in conjunction with a request that the pope should authorise the election of a new orthodox patriarch of Constantinople. Innocent ignored both

---

[18] Obolensky (1988a), pp. 146–52. See also below, p. 785.

requests. Theodore therefore went ahead with plans for the creation of a new patriarch at Nicaea. Innocent despatched his legate, Cardinal Pelagius, in 1214; his main task was to discipline the Greek church, but he also entered into negotiations with the Nicaean emperor. There was a series of inconclusive debates about a reunion of the churches, first at Constantinople and then at Heraclea Pontica, where Theodore Laskaris was encamped. Laskaris used these as a cover for the completion of a peace treaty with the Latin emperor Henry of Hainault. The lesson was an old one: that there were political advantages to be gained from negotiating over the union of churches. Laskaris tried again in 1219. By this time he had married a Latin princess and had plans to marry one of his daughters to the heir to the Latin empire of Constantinople. The Latin patriarchate was vacant. Laskaris proposed summoning a council that would consider the possibility of the reunion of the churches, as a first step towards the peaceful recovery of Constantinople, but the emperor's complicated manoeuvre was frustrated by opposition from within the orthodox church.

It would have been unrealistic to expect anything concrete to emerge from negotiations over the reunion of the churches, given the hatred engendered by the conquest of Constantinople; this hatred intensified with the subsequent Latin discrimination against the orthodox under their rule. However, a new force was about to make itself felt. By 1220 the Franciscans had established a house at Constantinople and by 1228 the Dominicans too.[19] They introduced a spirit of reasoned dialogue to which the Greeks responded. Patriarch Germanos II first came into contact with the friars in 1232. In that year a party of Franciscans was travelling overland through Asia Minor and was seized by the Seljuq authorities. With the emperor's help, Germanos was able to ransom them and had them brought to Nicaea. He was struck by the Franciscans' poverty and by their humility – so unlike other Latin churchmen – and was also impressed by their desire for peace and reconciliation between Latin and Greek.

It seemed that there was a new spirit abroad in the Latin church which would make possible a reunion of the churches by methods and on terms that were acceptable to the orthodox church. Germanos II induced the Franciscans to act as intermediaries with the papal curia. They were to sound out the possibilities for preliminary discussions that might pave the way for holding a general council of the church, which was the appropriate arena for a reunion of the churches. Some eighteen months later a delegation made up of two Franciscans and two Dominicans set out from Rome for Nicaea, where they were welcomed in January 1234 by emperor and patriarch. The friars' remit went no further than an exchange of views with the patriarch, in which they had much the better of the argument. Their knowledge of

---

[19] Wolff (1944).

Greek patristics made them formidable opponents. One of them read out in Greek the anathema pronounced by Cyril of Alexandria: against those denying that the spirit through which Christ performed his miracles was his own spirit. The friars argued that this supported the Latin position on the procession of the Holy Spirit: that it proceeded from the Father and the Son (*filioque*). Germanos wound up the proceedings on the grounds that nothing more could usefully be done until the orthodox patriarchs of Antioch, Jerusalem and Alexandria arrived to participate in a council. The friars departed; they had not received papal authorisation to take part in a council with representatives of the orthodox church, but they held out the prospect that the reunion of the churches would lead to the restoration of the orthodox patriarchate to Constantinople. They requested to be kept informed of future developments.

Germanos II therefore invited the friars to take part in the council that was assembling at the imperial residence of Nymphaion near Smyrna. They sounded out opinion in Latin Constantinople. To accept the invitation would mean exceeding their instructions, but the situation at Constantinople was so desperate that any contact with the Nicaean court was to be welcomed. The friars therefore journeyed to Nymphaion, but they were simply playing for time. They had no authority to negotiate, but they did make one damaging admission. They insisted that the Latin conquest of Constantinople had never received papal approval. It was the work of 'laymen, sinners and excommunicates presuming on their authority'. The implication was that the pope might one day abandon his support for the Latin empire of Constantinople. But the friars refused to accept that the onus for the sack of Constantinople should fall on the Latins alone. The Greeks had to take their share of the blame for the way they had treated Latins. The friars raised the old accusations that the Greeks washed altars after they had been used by Latins; that they forced Latins to renounce their sacraments as the price of attending orthodox services. The council broke up amidst displays of bad temper. The friars fled for their lives. The Nicaeans resumed the blockade of Constantinople.[20]

Though this episode produced no concrete results and only seemed to confirm the gulf that separated Greek and Latin, it was nevertheless important. Byzantine emperors and patriarchs remained susceptible to the appeal of the friars. Their ideals seemed so different from those of the church militant – the face that the Latin church normally presented to the outside world. Those friars operating out of Constantinople as often as not knew Greek and were well-versed in Greek patristics. They were willing to debate with representatives of the orthodox church on their own

<hr />

[20] Golubovich, 'Disputatio Latinorum', pp. 428–65; Canart, 'Nicéphore Blemmyde'; Roncaglia (1954), pp. 43–84; Gill (1979a), pp. 64–72; Chadwick (2003), pp. 238–45.

terms. Their knowledge of orthodox theology, even their appreciation of Byzantine art, made them seem more sympathetic than perhaps they were. Francis of Assisi was, indeed, to become one of the few western medieval saints to acquire a popular following in the Greek world. Their presence at Constantinople meant that there was always a temptation to enter into negotiations with the Latin church.

The friars were not exclusively in the service of the papacy. Elias of Cortona, the minister general of the Franciscans, was close to Emperor Frederick II (1215–50). He was sent on a mission to Constantinople to broker a peace between the Latin empire and John Vatatzes, who presented him with many gifts and relics. These negotiations laid the foundations for a formal alliance between Frederick and Vatatzes, and this was sealed in 1242/3 by the marriage of the Nicaean emperor to Frederick's bastard daughter, Costanza Lancia.[21] The main advantage Vatatzes derived from this alliance was prestige, and it was under cover of the alliance that he accomplished his major conquests in the southern Balkans, culminating in the occupation of Thessaloniki in 1246. Thereafter the alliance seemed to offer little in the way of concrete reward. The recovery of Constantinople looked as remote as ever, and Vatatzes began to consider other possibilities. His sister-in-law was married to the Hungarian king. She tried to interest him in an understanding with Pope Innocent IV (1243–54), but her efforts only bore fruit when Vatatzes learnt that John of Parma had been made minister general of the Franciscans in July 1247. Why this appointment should have had such an effect on John Vatatzes is not immediately clear. It may have had something to do with Vatatzes' choice of two Franciscans from Constantinople to act as his intermediaries with the papal curia. They may have been able to convince the Nicaean emperor that their new minister general favoured an understanding with the orthodox church.

John of Parma received his commission from Pope Innocent IV on 28 May 1249. His task was to negotiate the return of the Greeks 'in obedience and devotion to the Roman church . . . from which they have for so long withdrawn themselves'. He was given very precise instructions. Orthodox teaching on the procession of the Holy Spirit must conform to that of the Roman church. To this end John of Parma was empowered to convoke in the pope's name a church council for discussions with the orthodox church. He reached the Nicaean court by the autumn of 1249 at the outside. Preliminary discussions must necessarily have focused on one difficult question: under whose auspices was a council to be held? In his instructions to John of

---

[21] Borsari (1951); Merendino (1975). Brezeanu (1974) has redated the marriage of John Vatatzes and Costanza Lancia to 1241/2. The document he relies on is to be dated to 1243 and not, as he supposed, 1242. This means that the marriage can now be safely ascribed to 1242/3 and not 1244, the traditional date for this marriage. See also Martin (2002).

Parma, Innocent IV made the following claim: 'some Greek theologians – as is true – assert that the Roman pontiff, who alone has the authority to convoke a council, is able to effect an agreement between our creed and that of the Greeks – once a council has assembled – on the basis of his authority and that of the council.' Underlying such an assertion there must have been some concession made by the Nicaean emissaries, to the effect that any agreement over the creed reached by a council of the orthodox church must then receive papal approval. The claim that the pope alone has authority to call a council can only have been a papal gloss on the orthodox position. It would not have been acceptable to representatives of the orthodox church.

A council assembled at Nymphaion in the spring of 1250 under the presidency of the Nicaean emperor. The question of the procession of the Holy Spirit was duly debated. John of Parma argued that God the Father operates through the Son and the Son through the Spirit. He then put forward as its corollary the following proposition: just as the Son is from the Father, so the Spirit is from the Son. This left the Greek representatives stunned. They turned for help to their most expert theologian Nikephoros Blemmydes, who was present but had held aloof from the proceedings. Blemmydes protested that there was no scriptural authority for the Son operating through the Spirit. The Son operated in the Spirit, which was quite another matter. Blemmydes' intervention does not seem to have spoiled the irenic atmosphere that prevailed, to judge by the letter sent at the close of the council by the orthodox patriarch Manuel II to Innocent IV. The patriarch claimed that there had been a free and open discussion of the outstanding issues. The official Latin minutes of the council show that the Greeks were apparently willing to make unprecedented concessions over Roman claims to primacy and to accept papal authority over the general council with certain safeguards. In return, the Greeks – somewhat naively – requested the return of Constantinople and the removal of the Latin emperor and patriarch. A Nicaean delegation was despatched to the papal curia with full powers to continue the debate on these issues.

Innocent IV gave his reply early in 1252. He approved the Greek concessions on papal primacy and authority over the council. The addition of the *filioque* to the creed remained a problem. The Greek delegates refused to countenance it unless it could be supported by scriptural authority or some *divinum oraculum*. Innocent IV did not think this reasonable, but in a spirit of reconciliation allowed the orthodox church to omit the *filioque*, pending the final decision of a general council. Innocent IV was unable to offer anything concrete over the return of Constantinople to the Greeks. Negotiations continued, but the pope made his intentions crystal clear by appointing to the Latin patriarchate of Constantinople which had been vacant. There was also vague talk at the papal curia of organising a crusade to aid the Latin empire. The almost simultaneous deaths in 1254 of pope, Nicaean emperor and patriarch put an end to this round of negotiations over the union of churches, but they had been doomed to deadlock ever since the death of Frederick II in December 1250.[22]

John Vatatzes understood that it was in his interests to play off western empire against papacy. To this end he strove to keep alive his alliance with Frederick II, while negotiating with the papacy over the reunion of churches. He continued to supply his father-in-law with troops until the latter's death. Frederick remonstrated with his son-in-law: did he not realise that the pope was trying to drive a wedge between them? Had not this pope excommunicated the Greeks as schismatics, when the true blame for the schism lay with Rome? Frederick was nevertheless, at first, willing to put ships at the disposal of the Nicaean delegation that was making its way to the papal curia. They were playing a complicated diplomatic game. Vatatzes found his continued alliance with Frederick II a useful means of constraining the papacy. Frederick's death in December 1250 meant that the papacy was no longer under such pressure to accommodate the Nicaean emperor.

It has become usual in recent years to emphasise the importance of this episode of Nicaean diplomacy. It is presented as the moment when a reunion of churches on terms acceptable to both sides was most likely to have come about, and that is how it was later seen by Michael VIII Palaiologos (1258–82), who used it as a precedent to justify his unionist policy. Unlike Michael VIII, John Vatatzes seems not to have encountered opposition to rapprochement with the papacy, despite the concessions over papal primacy that he was willing to make. This is all the more surprising in light of the bitter feelings often expressed about the Latins. The loss of Constantinople should have warned against any dealings with the west. The ideal was that in exile the Byzantines would rebuild their strength, but the reality was that the lands of the old Byzantine empire were permeated by western interests, a fact confirmed by the conquest of Constantinople in 1204. While the Nicaean empire was limited to western Asia Minor it was possible to preserve an isolationist stance. However, the moment Vatatzes felt confident enough to aim at the conquest of Constantinople, he had to come to terms with western hegemony. Conditions seemed propitious because of the conflict between western empire and papacy, which Vatatzes sought to exploit. In principle, this was little different from the line of policy pursued by Manuel I Komnenos (1143–80), but Vatatzes was operating, in comparison, from a position of weakness.

This is clearest in his dealings with Frederick II. In the earlier exchanges of letters dating from the 1230s, Frederick fails to accord Vatatzes the

---

[22] Franchi (1981); Gill (1979a), pp. 88–95.

imperial titles. After the marriage of his daughter to Vatatzes he addresses him as emperor of the Greeks, a title that Manuel I Komnenos would have found insulting. It was an unequal alliance, with Vatatzes as the junior partner. Frederick's interest in the Byzantine world is hard to unravel. He inherited his father Henry VI's ambitions, which included hegemony over Byzantium, although this is unlikely to have been one of his major concerns. But any ruler of Sicily had an interest in Corfu and the Ionian islands. George Bardanes, the orthodox bishop of Corfu, had the task of diverting this interest. In a letter written to Frederick in about 1236, he queried the value that such an insignificant possession could have for so great a ruler. He indicated that his lord Manuel Angelos (1230–7), the ruler of Thessaloniki and a younger brother of Theodore Angelos, was willing to recognise Frederick's suzerainty.[23]

It was around this time that a rumour circulated in the west to the effect that Manuel Angelos, John Vatatzes and the Bulgarian tsar Ivan II Asen had offered Frederick homage in return for an alliance against the Latin empire of Constantinople. Homage is unlikely to have been strictly accurate, just a western gloss on an unequal partnership. There were plans at this time for Vatatzes to make a state visit to Frederick's court.[24] By 1238 Vatatzes was sending troops to Italy to help Frederick, and he continued to do so until the latter's death. Frederick's ascendancy extended to the other petty rulers of the Greek east. At the very end of his reign he wrote to the ruler of Epiros insisting that he allow Nicaean troops to pass through his territories on their way to Italy. This episode illustrates the dilemma of the Byzantine states in exile: their interests necessitated recourse to the papacy and the Hohenstaufen, yet the ideology of exile condemned any contact with the Latins. Vatatzes managed to avoid the consequences of this contradiction, but they would come back to haunt Michael VIII.

After Frederick II's death the kingdom of Sicily eventually passed to his bastard son Manfred of Hohenstaufen. He strove to retain Frederick's hegemony over the various Greek rulers, but instead found himself being dragged into the struggle between Nicaea and Epiros. Michael II Angelos Doukas (1230–67), the ruler of Epiros, understood that only with Latin aid would he be able to capitalise on the internal divisions that opened up at the Nicaean court following John Vatatzes' death in November 1254. The new Nicaean emperor was Vatatzes' son Theodore II Laskaris (1254–8), who adopted – perhaps in imitation of Frederick II – a more autocratic stance towards his aristocracy. His chief opponent was Michael Palaiologos, the future emperor, who held the position of grand constable, giving him

[23] Hoeck and Loenertz (1965), pp. 216–18.
[24] Wellas (1983), pp. 130–41; however Longo (1985–6) argues that the John Vatatzes in question was not the emperor, but the governor of Corfu.

command of the Latin mercenaries in Nicaean service. Rather than face a charge of treason, Palaiologos preferred to seek refuge among the Seljuq Turks (see also above, pp. 721–2). He returned to the Nicaean court shortly before Theodore Laskaris' death in August 1258. Thereupon Palaiologos organised a coup with the help of the Latin mercenaries under his command. He respected the constitutional niceties, in the sense that he claimed to rule in the name of Theodore's son John IV Laskaris (1258–61), the legitimate heir to the Nicaean throne. But this was merely a cover for usurpation, which took him inexorably from regent to co-emperor and finally to sole emperor.

This dynastic interlude gave Michael II Angelos Doukas his opportunity. He was able to draw both the Frankish prince of Achaia,[25] William II of Villehardouin (1246–78), and Manfred into an anti-Nicaean coalition. The allied forces met the Nicaean army in the late summer of 1259 at Pelagonia on the Egnatian Way and were completely defeated. The prince together with the flower of the chivalry of the Frankish Peloponnese fell into Nicaean hands. This victory left Michael VIII Palaiologos as the dominant force in the Balkans. It could only be a matter of time before his armies recovered Constantinople. This duly occurred in July 1261 when a small Nicaean force slipped into Constantinople while the Latin garrison was temporarily absent. On 15 August 1261 Michael VIII entered the City in triumph. It was a return to the Promised Land.[26]

THE ACHIEVEMENTS OF A BYZANTINE GOVERNMENT IN EXILE

What, then, was the historical importance of the period of exile?[27] Later generations remembered it as a heroic period. In retrospect it seemed a time of hope, when the body politic was purged of the corruption that characterised Byzantium before 1204, when imperial autocracy was curbed and a more equitable society came into being. The emperor was no longer above society but responsible to it. The historian George Pachymeres illustrated this with a single anecdote. Emperor John Vatatzes caught his son Theodore Laskaris out hunting dressed in cloth of gold. He rebuked the young prince: 'Did he not realise that these vestments of gold and silk were the "blood of the Romans" and should be employed for their

---

[25] The term Morea may be used to describe (a) the physical territory of the Peloponnese in the later middle ages; (b) the Frankish principality in the Peloponnese formed soon after the fall of Constantinople in 1204, which peaked under William II of Villehardouin and which is also known as the principality of Achaia; (c) the area of the Peloponnese that came under imperial Byzantine dominion again in the fourteenth and earlier fifteenth centuries and was, from 1349, a 'despotate', ruled by a member of the imperial family, usually the emperor's son (the 'despot') . For the sake of clarity, we have opted to style the Frankish principality Achaia in this volume and to use Morea to denote the later Byzantine despotate and, occasionally, the physical territory of the Peloponnese.

[26] Geanakoplos (1953).   [27] Ahrweiler (1975b).

benefit, because they were their property?' They were not to be wasted on frivolous pursuits.[28] Public utility was the justification for imperial authority.

Expulsion from Constantinople compelled a reassessment of the limits of imperial authority. Without the validation of the capital emperors needed the moral support of the orthodox church more than ever. This was symbolised by the introduction during the period of exile of the patriarch's anointing with myrrh as a regular feature of the coronation *ordo*. Its meaning was made clear by Patriarch Joseph I (1266–75, 1282–3). In his will he refused to accord Michael VIII Palaiologos the epithet 'holy', much to the latter's indignation. The emperor insisted that it was his by virtue of his unction with myrrh. The patriarch was dismissing him as unworthy of the imperial office. In other words, the rite of unction conferred moral authority on the emperor, but it also left the emperor more vulnerable to ecclesiastical censure[29] – a situation reminiscent of experiences in the west over several centuries.

During the period of exile orthodox patriarchs continued to pay lip service to imperial tutelage. Germanos II's defence of the rights of the patriarchate over the church in Epiros was couched in the traditional terms of 'one church, one empire'. But George Bardanes, the spokesman for the people of Epiros, was far more realistic. He made it clear that the church in Epiros would gladly recognise the authority of the patriarch at Nicaea, but not that of the emperor. He did not understand why imperial authority was necessary to a unit based on common adherence to the orthodox faith. Why was co-existence not possible? 'Let each come to an understanding on these terms and "let each enjoy the Sparta which it has been allotted", not stupidly gazing on the ends of the earth, but being satisfied with one's own territory, fearing God, and honouring in a spirit of brotherly love the appropriate ruler.'[30] It seemed a reasonable plea: the unity of the Byzantine world after 1204 was essentially religious and cultural and no longer dependent upon imperial authority. Political unity was irrelevant or would have to wait until Constantinople was recovered.

It was a point of view that also had its adherents at the Nicaean court. Its leading intellectual and theologian Nikephoros Blemmydes defended the political independence of the Greek ruler of Rhodes; the only unity that mattered was that provided by orthodoxy. He was outraged when in 1256 Theodore II Laskaris compelled the patriarch of the day to place the territories of Michael II of Epiros under interdict.[31] This was blatant exploitation of ecclesiastical power for political purposes. In a quite different

---

[28] GP, I.14, ed. and French tr. Failler, I, pp. 60–3. See now Angelov, D.G. (2007), pp. 204–52, 260–85.
[29] GP, VI.31, ed. and French tr. Failler, II, pp. 638–9; Nicol (1976a).
[30] George Bardanes, *Letter*, ed. Loenertz, p. 117.
[31] Nikephoros Blemmydes, *Autobiography*, ed. Munitiz, pp. 40–2; tr. Munitiz, pp. 89–91.

way Theodore II Laskaris also recognised the divisions of the Byzantine world that exile had fixed. He dedicated his victories in Europe to 'our Holy Mother Anatolia'.[32]

The fall of Constantinople necessitated a reassessment of Byzantine identity. It could hardly be otherwise, since it was so closely bound up with the imperial and universalist pretensions of the capital. In exile the core of the Byzantine identity remained orthodoxy, but it was given a more obviously nationalist twist. In the past, the Byzantines had defined themselves against Hellenes (or pagans) and Jews, and occasionally against Armenians. From the time of the First Crusade the Latins featured more prominently, but it was only after 1204 that they became the 'other' against which the Byzantines measured themselves. This was a negative shift. More positive was the re-evaluation of the meaning of Hellene. It came to be identified with the cultural legacy of classical Greece, stripped of its pagan connotation. This had begun before 1204, but it only received coherent expression after the fall of Constantinople. It is set out most clearly in a letter of Emperor John III Vatatzes to Pope Gregory IX (1227–41). He claimed that his imperial authority had a double validity. On the one hand, it could be traced back to Constantine the Great and, on the other, it was founded in Hellenic wisdom. Orthodoxy and imperial authority fused with a cultural tradition to produce a shift in the Byzantine identity.[33]

This shift inspired the achievements of Byzantine scholars during the period of exile. They were able to recover the intellectual heritage of Byzantium which was threatened by the fall of Constantinople to the Latins. John Vatatzes organised a palace school, which preserved the traditions of higher education.[34] But the most eloquent testimony to Hellenic wisdom's power to inspire comes in the shape of the autobiography of the future patriarch Gregory of Cyprus. He describes how bitterly he resented the Latin conquerors of his native island. They made it virtually impossible for him to get a proper education. Hearing of the fame of Nicaea as a centre of Hellenic education, he ran away from home and made his way to Nicaea. Whatever his disappointments, he treats his search for Hellenic illumination as a form of conversion.[35]

Cultivation of Hellenic wisdom defined the Byzantine elite culturally against the Latins. In 1254 there was a disputation between Nicaean scholars and members of a Hohenstaufen embassy. Theodore II Laskaris presided. He adjudged victory to the Nicaeans and thought it reflected great credit on the Hellenes. Consciousness of a Hellenic past became an integral part of the Byzantine identity, but its expression was the preserve of an intellectual

[32] Theodore II Laskaris, *Epistulae*, ed. Festa, p. 281.   [33] Grumel (1930), pp. 452–4; Angold (1975b).
[34] Constantinides (1982), pp. 5–27; Constantinides (2003), pp. 42–50.
[35] Gregory of Cyprus, *Autobiography*. On the vitality of literary culture at Nicaea and in the early Palaiologan court, see Constantinides (2003); Angelov, D. G. (2003); Gaul (forthcoming).

elite. There was surprisingly little friction between Hellenism and orthodoxy despite their apparent incompatibility. Patriarch Germanos II could
compare John Vatatzes' victories over the Latins to Marathon and Salamis.
This illustrates how Hellenism gave orthodoxy during the period of exile
a more obviously Greek complexion. The orthodox patriarchate did not
hesitate to abandon its rights over the orthodox church in both Serbia and
Bulgaria and came close to doing so in Russia. This was in contrast to the
stubborn and eventually successful defence of its authority over the church
in Epiros. Whatever claims Patriarch Germanos may have continued to
make to universal authority, his stance over the Epirot church indicates a
more obviously nationalist understanding of orthodoxy: it was the faith of
the Greeks.

   Although the recovery of Constantinople from the hated Latins was
always the goal, Constantinople itself became less and less relevant to the
sense of identity that evolved during the period of exile. Political loyalties
became more localised. A sense of common purpose was provided by the
orthodox church and of cultural unity by the Hellenic tradition. At the same
time a rather different structure of government and society was crystallising.
Many of its features can be traced back before 1204, but they were held
in check by the power and tradition of Constantinople. Its fall produced
of necessity a simplification of the machinery of government. Even the
tradition of Roman law weakened, allowing the introduction of the ordeal.[36]
There was a devolution of authority. This took the form of a marked growth
of immunities and *pronoiai*, but it can also be seen in the widespread grant
of urban privileges. Power became increasingly localised.

   Michael VIII ignored these changes at his peril. He was proud to be
hailed as the 'new Constantine', but his autocratic style of government
created many difficulties.[37] His attempt to restore the old ideological and
institutional foundations of the Byzantine empire went counter to the
changes that had occurred during the period of exile. The restored Byzantine empire was not able to escape the legacy of exile. It remained a conglomeration of independent or semi-independent political units. Except
very briefly, Epiros was never persuaded to return under the direct authority of Constantinople, while Asia Minor was never reconciled to Palaiologan
rule. Still more seriously, Michael VIII's efforts to impose union with the
Latin church alienated all sections of orthodox society. This reflected a
shift in attitudes that occurred over the period of exile. An emperor could
no longer use the orthodox faith as a diplomatic bargaining counter with
the Latin west without provoking bitter opposition. The church could
now count on popular support. This had not been the case before 1204.

---

[36] Angold (1980).   [37] Macrides (1980); Macrides (1994b).

Figure 53 Copy *c.* 1480 of an earlier fifteenth-century picture-map showing Constantinople and the Bosporus; this gives a general impression of how the City looked in the later middle ages

Michael VIII's attempt to restore imperial authority to its former eminence only left Byzantine society hopelessly divided. To bewail the recovery of Constantinople, as one Nicaean official did in the summer of 1261, was to show uncanny prescience.[38]

[38] GP, II.28, ed. and French tr. Failler, I, pp. 204–5; Talbot (1993). See also below, p. 804.

THE EMPIRE RESTORED AND THE REIGN OF MICHAEL VIII

These changes would in the long run work against Michael VIII Palaiologos' efforts to restore the Byzantine empire, but failure hardly seemed possible as the emperor took formal possession of Constantinople on 15 August 1261. Early successes suggested that the Byzantine empire would soon be returned to its pre-1204 boundaries. Michael VIII quickly obtained a foothold in the Peloponnese. William II of Villehardouin, prince of Achaia, had fallen into Byzantine hands, along with many of his barons, at the battle of Pelagonia in 1259. He now agreed to come to terms. He ceded to Michael the fortresses of Monemvasia, Mistra and Maina (see below, p. 768). The recovery of the Greek lands beckoned. In 1264 Michael II Angelos Doukas, the ruler of Epiros, accepted the hegemony of the new emperor of Constantinople. Substantial gains had been made in the previous year at the expense of the Bulgarians. Philippopolis, gateway to the Balkans, was recovered together with the ports of the Black Sea coast. Michael VIII then secured control of the Dobrudja, the region at the mouth of the Danube, where he established Turkish colonists. They had come over to Byzantium with the last Seljuq sultan of Rum, Kay-Kawos II, who had fled to Michael in April 1261. Even if it meant accepting baptism, the sultan found this preferable to remaining under the Mongol yoke. Such a spectacular defection gave Michael VIII reason to hope for further gains in Asia Minor. The recovery of Constantinople also put the Venetians on the defensive. They were driven from Constantinople and replaced by the Genoese, who were Byzantine allies. However, the Genoese in their turn were temporarily banned from the capital in 1264, as Michael VIII had no intention of allowing the Italians a dominant position in Constantinople. He built up the Byzantine fleet, which for the last time would be a major force in the waters of the Aegean.[39]

The tragedy of Michael VIII Palaiologos' reign was that he was never able to capitalise on these early successes. He failed to drive the Venetians from their Aegean bases in Crete and Euboea. The Franks of the Peloponnese stubbornly refused to cede any more territory to his armies. The Greek rulers of Epiros and Thessaly threw off their Byzantine allegiance. Opposition to Byzantine rule was stiffened by the appearance of a new figure on the scene, Charles of Anjou, youngest brother of the French king Louis IX (1226–70). Charles' victory at Benevento over Manfred of Hohenstaufen in 1266 established him as papally approved ruler of the kingdom of Sicily and heir to ambitions in the east. In 1267 he entered into separate treaties with William II of Villehardouin, prince of Achaia, and with Baldwin II, the dispossessed Latin emperor of Constantinople. He took the former under his protection, securing succession to the principality of Achaia for his son

[39] Geanakoplos (1959), pp. 119–85.

Philip through a dynastic marriage. He promised the Latin emperor that within seven years he would launch an expedition to recover Constantinople on his behalf. The petty rulers of the Balkans and Greek lands – orthodox and catholic alike – turned to him for support against the pretensions of Michael VIII. The Albanians seized the Byzantine base of Dyrrachium (Durrës), at the head of the Egnatian Way, and in February 1272 recognised Charles of Anjou as their king. Charles thus secured the key positions along the Albanian coast. It was a serious setback for Michael VIII.

The Byzantine emperor sought to counter the Angevin threat in various ways. He strengthened the sea walls of Constantinople. The lesson of the Fourth Crusade was its vulnerability to an attack from the sea. Michael VIII therefore wooed Venice to prevent it from joining the Angevin camp. He finally induced the Venetians to make a treaty with Byzantium rather than with Charles of Anjou in 1268: the Venetians recovered control of their old quarter in Constantinople. However, Byzantium's major diplomatic offensive was directed towards the papacy. Michael employed the age-old ploy of offering a reunion of the churches. The papacy was at first unconvinced of the sincerity or utility of the offer, but this changed in 1271 when Gregory X (1271–6) became pope. He was not interested in supporting Charles of Anjou's designs on Constantinople. His purpose was instead to rescue the crusader states from the Mamluk menace. An alliance with Byzantium might have its uses, but the pope insisted that it must be cemented by reunion on Rome's terms. Essentially, this meant Byzantine recognition of papal supremacy. It was a price that, in the circumstances, Michael VIII thought worth paying. In 1274 he despatched a Byzantine delegation to Lyons where a council of the church was gathering. Without any serious debate of the issues Michael accepted a reunion on papal terms. He cited as a precedent for his actions the negotiations with the papacy initiated by John III Vatatzes.[40] These had produced little, if any, protest, perhaps because they were never brought to a conclusion. But Michael's unionist policies would earn him the hatred of all sections of Byzantine society. Why were people so unwilling to accept his reassurance that almost nothing worthwhile had been conceded? Why did the orthodox church refuse to approach the question of union in a spirit of *oikonomia*?[41]

The answers to these questions reveal that it was not only Charles of Anjou's ambitions that thwarted Michael VIII's plans to restore the Byzantine empire. Michael's unionist policy confirmed the tyrannical nature of his rule. His usurpation of the throne was not easily forgotten. On Christmas Day 1261 he had had the legitimate heir to the imperial throne, John IV Laskaris, blinded and exiled to a fortress on the Sea of Marmara. Patriarch

[40] GP, V.12, ed. and French tr. Failler, II, pp. 478–9.
[41] Nicol (1993), pp. 41–57; Hussey (1986), pp. 220–35; Chadwick (2003), pp. 246–57.

Arsenios protested. He was responsible for protecting the rights of John Laskaris, which the usurper had solemnly sworn before God to uphold. The patriarch therefore excommunicated Michael. It took three years before the emperor could rid himself of Arsenios, but his dismissal only produced a schism within the orthodox church, weakening the authority of subsequent patriarchs. Arsenios gave his support to an uprising around Nicaea in favour of John Laskaris. Michael VIII may have suppressed it with some ease, but thereafter he found the Anatolian provinces increasingly alienated from Constantinopolitan rule. The historian George Pachymeres singled this out as the underlying cause of their subsequent fall to renewed Turkish pressure.[42]

Michael VIII's unionist policy reinforced the growing distrust of his rule. He refused to listen to the reasonable objections of Patriarch Joseph I. As soon as it became clear that the emperor intended to do the pope's bidding, the patriarch retired to a monastery rather than be party to the reunion of the churches. This produced another schism within the orthodox church, when Michael VIII pressed ahead with his designs. Efforts to win support for the union were crude and largely counterproductive. The story goes that when the members of the Byzantine delegation to Lyons returned to Constantinople they were greeted with cries of 'You have become Franks!'[43] It catches a sense of betrayal that spread throughout Byzantine society.

This was confirmed by the harsh way in which Michael VIII and his new patriarch, John Bekkos (1275–82), implemented the union. In 1276 the patriarch convened a council which not only confirmed the union, but placed all who opposed it under ban of excommunication. The next year the emperor and his son publicly swore to recognise the supremacy of the papacy and read out a profession of faith that included the Roman addition of the *filioque*.

Michael's opponents seized on his unionist policy to justify their actions. The Greek rulers of Epiros and Thessaly used it as a pretext for refusing to submit to his authority. John of Thessaly held an anti-unionist council in 1275/6 which attracted many of Michael's opponents within the church. This was blatant exploitation of the unionist issue for political ends. Less easy to explain is the opposition to church union of some of Michael VIII's closest relatives and political associates. Even his favourite sister, the nun Eulogia, turned against him and fled to Bulgaria. Such was the hostility to the union within the imperial family that Michael was compelled to imprison many of his relatives. The papal emissary was taken down to see them languishing in the dungeons of the Great Palace. Michael hoped that their misery would convince the papacy of his sincerity over the union.[44]

---

[42] GP, I.3–6, ed. and French tr. Failler, I, pp. 26–35. See also p. 805.
[43] Geanakoplos (1959), p. 271. See also Geanakoplos (1976), pp. 156–70.
[44] Loenertz (1965).

This opposition from within the imperial family was prompted in the first place by concern for orthodoxy, which was being needlessly compromised by the emperor; but it ran deeper than this. Michael VIII was seen to be using the unionist issue as a way of imposing his arbitrary power over Byzantine church and society. Like all Byzantine emperors, Michael was faced by the conundrum of imperial authority. In theory, he wielded absolute power; in practice, it was limited by obligations to the church and the ruling class, and to society at large. Michael came to power as the leader of an aristocratic faction. He ensured that the chief offices of state went to his close relatives. He also widened his basis of support through a series of shrewd marriages that linked his family to other great houses.[45] At first, his style of government was conciliatory. At the same time as donations to the army and monasteries, he clamped down on the dishonesty and oppression of provincial governors and military commanders. He improved the quality of justice by setting up a court of appeal, the *sekrēton*, and abolished the use of the ordeal by hot iron which had become an instrument of arbitrary government. He showed exaggerated respect for the church and patriarch.[46] This changed once Michael became master of Constantinople. He employed the western notion of the 'law of conquest' to justify a more autocratic approach to government. He claimed that, since he had conquered Constantinople, it belonged to him exclusively, and he used this as a pretext to threaten opponents of the union with confiscation of their property, if they did not comply with his wishes. He was, after all, the 'new Constantine'.[47] He became increasingly remote from his natural basis of support. He made use of western adventurers, such as Benedetto Zaccaria, who received the alum concession at Phokaia near Smyrna.[48] He also relied heavily on trusted bureaucrats, such as the grand logothete George Akropolites, who was a leader of the Byzantine delegation to Lyons.

The humiliating concessions made by Michael VIII to the papacy brought little concrete advantage. This only increased distrust of the emperor. The papacy, for its part, continued to have doubts about Michael's sincerity, so much so that in 1281 Pope Martin IV (1281–5) had him excommunicated. This was at Charles of Anjou's behest, and provided him with the justification he needed for a new assault on Byzantium. This time Charles was able to win over Venice to his cause. Unionist diplomacy had apparently left Byzantium stranded. The Byzantine armies were able to stem the Angevin advance down the Egnatian Way with a victory at Berat in 1281. But salvation came from an unexpected quarter: on 30 March 1282 the inhabitants of Palermo rose up against their hated Angevin rulers. This

[45] Dölger (1950), pp. 275–9.
[46] GP, II.1, ed. and French tr. Failler, I, pp. 130–1; Burgmann and Magdalino (1984).
[47] Macrides (1980); Macrides (1994b).   [48] Geanakoplos (1959), pp. 209–13.

was the famous revolt of the Sicilian Vespers.[49] With Sicily in revolt, Charles had to abandon his plans for an expedition against Constantinople.

Michael VIII saw himself as the saviour of his people. In the autobiographies that he wrote at the end of his life he took sole credit for throwing back the Angevins in Albania and for organising the Sicilian Vespers.[50] He was unable to comprehend his unpopularity; had he not restored the seat of church and empire to Constantinople? This could not be denied, but few would have accepted his other claim: to have ruled according to the best traditions of his family and the imperial office. It seemed much more like a betrayal. It comes as no surprise that, when Michael VIII Palaiologos died on 11 December 1282 in a small Thracian village, the orthodox church refused him a proper burial.[51]

Under Michael VIII Byzantium was for the very last time a major force on the world stage. His diplomatic contacts stretched from Aragon and France in the west to the Ilkhans of Persia in the east; from the Golden Horde on the Caspian to the Mamluks of Egypt.[52] But his efforts left Byzantium exhausted and virtually bankrupt. His legacy was one of schism, poverty and rapid decline. He was a victim of the profound changes which occurred during the period of exile. The defence of orthodoxy against the Latins gave the Byzantine identity an anti-Latin twist. Any compromise with the Latins over dogma was seen as an act of betrayal. Michael VIII was even more vulnerable to accusations of this kind because of the way Laskarid propaganda instilled the notion of the emperor as the servant of his church and people. Political power had become more diffuse. The different regions of the old Byzantine empire developed separate identities and interests. At best, the emperor of Constantinople could expect to exercise a degree of indirect authority. These problems existed before 1204, but Constantinople had – albeit with increasing difficulty – the prestige and resources to hold the empire together. The city that Michael VIII Palaiologos recovered was but a husk. It had been wasted by the years of Latin rule. He made great efforts to restore his new capital, but it was expensive and time-consuming.[53] Constantinople no longer dominated. 1204 had destroyed the myth of Byzantine invulnerability.

[49] Runciman (1958); Geanakoplos (1959), pp. 335–67.
[50] Michael Palaiologos, *Autobiography*, ed. and French tr. Grégoire, pp. 448–68; ed. Dmitrievsky, I, pp. 769–85.
[51] NG, V.7, ed. Schopen and Bekker, I, p. 153; German tr. van Dieten, I, pp. 142–3; see also GP, VI.36, ed. and French tr. Failler, II, pp. 664–7.
[52] Amitai-Preiss (1995), pp. 82–97. See also below, p. 805.
[53] Talbot (1993).

AFTER THE FOURTH CRUSADE: THE LATIN EMPIRE OF CONSTANTINOPLE AND THE FRANKISH STATES

DAVID JACOBY

INTRODUCTION: FRAGMENTED *ROMANIA*

The Latin conquest of Constantinople on 13 April 1204 heralded a new era in the history of the Byzantine lands, known in the Christian west as *Romania*. It dealt a severe blow to the military might, political organisation and prestige of the empire, furthering and hastening its disintegration – begun some twenty-five years earlier – and leading to its dismemberment. In March 1204, about a month before the fall of Constantinople, the leaders of the crusader armies and the commander of the Venetian army and fleet, Doge Enrico Dandolo, reached agreement on five major issues: electing a Latin emperor, the empire's political regime and military organisation, partitioning the lands of *Romania* (the *partitio Romaniae*) and, finally, electing a Latin patriarch of Constantinople and other ecclesiastical matters.

On 9 May 1204 Count Baldwin of Flanders was elected emperor, gaining a quarter of the empire and two imperial palaces in Constantinople. From his domain the new emperor Baldwin I (1204–5) granted many fiefs to crusader knights and mounted sergeants. He also assigned to Venice its share of three-eighths of Constantinople, land outside the City and various revenues. At this stage only Constantinople was in Latin hands. The difficulties encountered by the Latins in the conquest of the Byzantine empire, which was never completed, and the individual expeditions undertaken by various Latin knights and commoners, as well as by the Venetian state, prevented systematic implementation of the partition plan. Instead, the extensive territories occupied by the Latins in the European part of *Romania* and many islands in the Aegean became a mosaic of political entities, many of them small. Most of their rulers were linked to each other within complex webs of vassalage which changed over time (see below, pp. 765–8, 771).

Boniface of Montferrat, who had expected to be elected emperor, gained Thessaloniki from the Venetians, to whom he sold Crete. Although a vassal of Baldwin I, in 1204 Boniface established an independent kingdom extending from Thrace to the area of Corinth in central Greece. After conquering Euboea – called Negroponte by the Latins – in 1205 he granted it first to

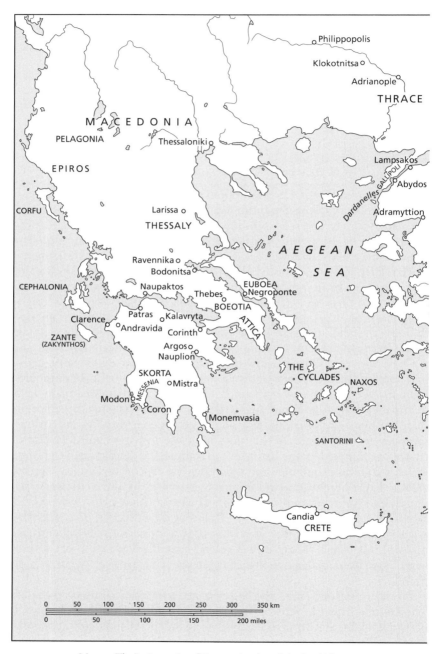

Map 37 The Latin empire of Constantinople and the Frankish states

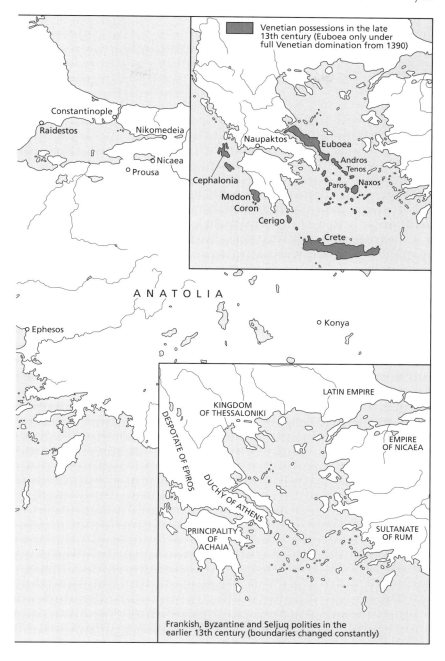

Venetian possessions in the late 13th century (Euboea only under full Venetian domination from 1390)

Constantinople

Raidestos   Nikomedeia

Naupaktos   Euboea

Nicaea   Andros

Prousa   Tenos

Cephalonia   Paros   Naxos

Modon

Coron

Cerigo

Crete

A N A T O L I A

Ephesos   Konya

LATIN EMPIRE

KINGDOM
OF THESSALONIKI

DESPOTATE OF EPIROS

EMPIRE
OF NICAEA

DUCHY OF ATHENS

PRINCIPALITY
OF
ACHAIA

SULTANATE
OF RUM

Frankish, Byzantine and Seljuq polities in the earlier 13th century (boundaries changed constantly)

a French knight and, following the latter's death the same year, to three Veronese noblemen (known as the *terciers*, or *terzieri* in Italian). Thereafter, except for the years 1208–16, the island was divided into three main feudal units until its wholesale occupation by Venice in 1390. On the Greek mainland Boniface awarded several small lordships to French and Italian knights under his suzerainty in Attica and Boeotia. These regions were soon united within the duchy of Athens under Othon of La Roche, who from 1210/11 also held Argos and Nauplion in the Peloponnese from Geoffrey I of Villehardouin, the ruler of the Frankish principality of Achaia.[1] A few years earlier, in 1205, Geoffrey and William of Champlitte had jointly begun the conquest of the Peloponnese and laid the foundations of the principality.

In 1204 or 1205 Marco I Sanudo, nephew of the doge of Venice, established a duchy in the Aegean with its centre at Naxos, which from 1207 he held directly from the Latin emperor. In association with fellow Venetians and foreigners, and with the backing of Venice, Sanudo conquered other islands in the Cyclades in the same year, which he granted out in fief. Small lordships were also created elsewhere in the Aegean. Corfu was occupied by Venice in 1207 and awarded to ten of her citizens, yet lost around 1215 to the Greek ruler of Epiros, Michael I Angelos Doukas (1205–15). Finally, Venice extended its sway in 1207 over the two ports of Modon and Coron in southern Messenia, at the south-western tip of the Peloponnese, and between 1207 and 1211, over the island of Crete (in the face of Genoese opposition). These were the first colonies of an overseas empire, parts of which were to survive up to the time of Napoleon Bonaparte's campaign in Italy in the last years of the eighteenth century. The extreme political and territorial fragmentation of *Romania* in the wake of the Latin conquests was in sharp contrast to the earlier unity of Byzantium. It accounts to a large extent for the diversity of the political and social regimes established in Latin *Romania*, as well as for the nature and orientation of demographic currents and economic activity in the region. While the encounter between the Latins and the overwhelmingly Greek local population generated a break at the political level, it resulted in continuity and some measure of accommodation in other spheres.[2]

---

[1] The term Morea may be used to describe (a) the physical territory of the Peloponnese in the later middle ages; (b) the Frankish principality in the Peloponnese formed soon after the fall of Constantinople in 1204, which peaked under William II of Villehardouin and which is also known as the principality of Achaia; (c) the area of the Peloponnese that came under imperial Byzantine dominion again in the fourteenth and earlier fifteenth centuries and was, from 1349, a 'despotate', ruled by a member of the imperial family, usually the emperor's son (the 'despot') . For the sake of clarity, we have opted to style the Frankish principality Achaia in this volume and to use Morea to denote the later Byzantine despotate and, occasionally, the physical territory of the Peloponnese.

[2] For general background, political history, references to primary sources and studies on the Fourth Crusade and the Latin empire, see: Queller and Madden (1997); Longnon (1949); Wolff (1969); Setton (1976–84), I, pp. 1–105; Carile (1978); Nicol (1988), pp. 124–87; Lock (1995), pp. 36–67, 161–92; Angold

THE COURSE OF EVENTS

The Latin empire led a tumultuous life throughout the fifty-seven years of its existence, up to its collapse in 1261. The imperial and territorial claims of its neighbouring rulers, the Vlacho-Bulgarian kingdom and the two main Byzantine successor states founded after the fall of Constantinople (one in Epiros and the other in western Anatolia, the so-called empire of Nicaea), exposed the Latin empire to almost continuous warfare. War broke out shortly after its establishment. In alliance with Greek leaders in Thrace, the ruler of the Vlacho-Bulgarian kingdom, Kalojan (1197–1207), advanced deep into Latin territory and captured Emperor Baldwin in May 1205 (see also below, p. 784). Henry of Hainault (1206–16), Baldwin's brother and successor, repulsed Kalojan's attacks. After Baldwin's death in 1206, Henry captured extensive territories to the north and succeeded in stabilising the Latin–Bulgarian borders and political relations for a few years. In Anatolia Henry faced Theodore I Laskaris (1205–21), the ruler of the Greek state centred on Nicaea: he managed to surmount his own shifting fortunes by decisively defeating Laskaris in October 1211. This resulted in the renewal of Latin rule in western Anatolia along the entire coastline stretching from Nikomedeia to Adramyttion (see also p. 737). The treaty signed between the two rulers, presumably in the following year, ensured peace between their states until 1224. Henry died in 1216, leaving an empire temporarily strengthened by his military and diplomatic skills, his conciliatory attitude toward his Greek subjects, and his use of Greek troops against his enemies.

The fate of the Latin empire was closely linked to that of the kingdom of Thessaloniki. After the sudden death of Boniface of Montferrat in battle with the Bulgarians in 1207, Henry was forced to intervene against 'Lombard' rebels; they included the *terzieri* of Negroponte, who wished to see William VIII of Montferrat crowned king of Thessaloniki. In 1209 Henry secured the orderly succession of Boniface's son and William's half-brother, the youthful Demetrios. Henry also compelled the lords of Negroponte to submit to himself directly at Thebes, as he did with Geoffrey I of Villehardouin (c. 1209–25/31), lord of Frankish Achaia, at Ravennika. However, the Latin emperor Peter of Courtenay – crowned in Rome by

(2003a), pp. 75–150, 163–92, 210–14, 225–7; Madden (2003). Hendrickx, 'Régestes des empereurs latins' has convenient, but not always reliable, summaries of documents. For a new edition of the treaties between Venice and the Latin emperors, see: *I patti con l'impero latino*, ed. Pozza. On other Frankish states: Longnon (1949); Longnon (1969); Bon (1969); Jacoby (1971), pp. 19–27, 185–95, 253–4, 271–80; Setton (1976–84), I, pp. 1–105; Lock (1995), pp. 68–104; Bredenkamp (1996). Ilieva (1991) should be used with caution. On the Venetian quarter in Constantinople, see below p. 766. On Venice in the Latin empire and the Frankish states: Thiriet (1975), pp. 74–104; Borsari (1966); Jacoby (1971), pp. 185–95, 271–80, 295–300; Jacoby (1993); below pp. 766–7, 771. The territories under exclusive Venetian rule are not treated in this chapter.

Pope Honorius III (1216–27) – was compelled to transfer effective authority in the kingdom of Thessaloniki to William VIII of Montferrat in
1217. Theodore Angelos, who styled himself as Komnenos Doukas, was
the forceful ruler of Epiros (1215–30) and emperor at Thessaloniki (1224–
30). He captured Peter on his way from Rome to Constantinople, taking
advantage of the internal feuds in the Latin kingdom to penetrate into
Macedonia and Thessaly and encircle the city of Thessaloniki, which he
occupied in 1224. Two years later Theodore Angelos reached the walls of
Constantinople, but Ivan II Asen (1218–41), king of the Vlachs and Bulgarians, prevented him from conquering the city which he coveted for
himself. In 1230 Ivan Asen defeated Theodore Angelos and occupied large
tracts of Epirot territories, as far afield as Albania. In the meantime, by
1225, the Nicaean forces of John III Vatatzes (1221–54) had reduced the
Latin hold in western Anatolia to Nikomedeia and a strip of land opposite Constantinople. In 1233 the Latin emperor John of Brienne (1229–37)
launched a short campaign in Anatolia, which failed to produce any lasting
benefits. Two years later he faced a coalition of Vatatzes and Ivan Asen
that endangered the very existence of the Latin empire, by then shrunken
to the city of Constantinople itself. In 1246 Vatatzes wrested Thessaloniki
from the Greek ruler of Epiros. His successor Theodore II Laskaris (1254–
8) was too preoccupied with warfare against neighbours in the Balkans
to move against Constantinople, and gave the City some respite (see also
above, pp. 748–9).

The existence of the Latin empire was thus prolonged by temporary
agreements and shifting alliances with its neighbours, and particularly by
rivalries among the latter. In the long run, however, its ability to survive
was seriously impaired by a chronic absence of adequate financial and military resources and the lack of a firm, permanent and general commitment
from the west to assist it. Papal intervention on the empire's behalf yielded
only limited and temporary results: repeated ecclesiastical negotiations with
its neighbours failed to achieve their submission to the church of Rome
or to reduce their pressure on the empire. Neither papal pleas for help
from western rulers, nor the proclamation of military expeditions to aid
the Latin empire as crusades yielded meaningful, sustained support. The
hard-pressed Baldwin II (1237–61) travelled extensively in the west, first in
1237–9 and again in 1243/4–8, in desperate attempts to enlist help. During
his first absence the barons of the Latin empire mortgaged the Crown of
Thorns, supposedly worn by Christ, as surety for the repayment of 13,134
hyperpyra: this sum had been provided by the Venetian Niccolò Querini
for the consolidation of a number of loans previously advanced to them.
The precious relic was redeemed in 1238 by the king of France, Louis IX
(1226–70), who placed it in the specially built Sainte-Chapelle in Paris.
In 1248 Baldwin II owed 24,000 *hyperpera* to some Venetian merchants in

Constantinople; later, in return for another loan, he mortgaged his only son Philip of Courtenay, who spent several years in Venice in the custody of the creditors. In 1260 Baldwin was compelled to strip lead from the roofs of Constantinople's palaces to raise money for the empire's defence.

The western lay powers each pursued their own interests. Even Venice, despite having an economic stake in the Latin empire's survival, sent naval help only intermittently. In 1260 Venice became aware of the acute danger to Latin rule over Constantinople, yet it was already too late. In the course of its existence the Latin empire was also weakened from within by the growing willingness of its Greek subjects to turn to foreign rulers, particularly those of Epiros and Nicaea who appealed to their Greek identity, and even to assist invading armies. Eventually it was Michael VIII Palaiologos (1258–82) who, after seizing the throne of Nicaea in 1258, reinstated Byzantine rule in the imperial capital three years later and put an end to the Latin empire. Baldwin II escaped to the west, where his efforts to obtain support for the recovery of his state came to nought.[3]

THE LATIN EMPIRE'S MAIN COMPONENTS

The internal structure and development of the Latin empire were rather complex. Various trappings at the coronation of Emperor Baldwin I on 16 May 1204 evoked similar Byzantine ceremonies, and the Byzantine stamp can also be seen in the titles of the emperors, their officers and their dignitaries, as well as in imperial documents. The adoption of these features was partly prompted by the emperors' desire to emphasise the continuity of Byzantine imperial tradition and thereby enhance their own legitimacy. Greek officials serving in the imperial court also acquainted the conquerors with the intricacies of the Byzantine fiscal system and to a large extent ensured its survival.[4] Yet the nature of the political and socio-legal regime of the Latin empire, defined in the treaty of March 1204, and the operation of its government were largely moulded on western feudal patterns and in response to pressing military needs. The conquest and the ensuing distribution of fiefdoms led to the territorialisation and geographical extension of the vassalage network which had existed within the crusader host during the Fourth Crusade. Each fief-holder, however, also swore to render military service to the emperor, the supreme lord.

A novel feature of the Latin empire was the institutional and political position of Venice within its framework, as both subordinate and equal to the emperor. Venice was subordinate in two ways: firstly, as a collective

---

[3] Setton (1976–84), I, pp. 1–153; Barber, M. (1989); Angold (1989). On the Byzantine successor states, see Angold (2003a), pp. 193–217.

[4] Jacoby (1993), p. 143; Lock (1995), pp. 167–71, 189–91.

political entity within the feudal system of government headed by the emperor; and secondly, the individual fief-holders in its portion of the empire undertook to fulfil the same military obligations as their crusader counterparts. In fact, however, Venice played the role of an intermediary between the emperor and its own fief-holders. Its officers apportioned the fiefs among Venetians and foreigners who assumed military and fiscal obligations toward the doge and swore fealty to him; its chief representative in the empire, the *podestà* serving in Constantinople, was responsible for the collective discharge of the military service owed by the fief-holders; and, finally, the Venetians retained a separate military contingent under Venice's own command. On the other hand, Venice maintained exclusive control over other components of its portion of the empire and exercised its authority over those holding property in it. Its decisive contribution to the crusade and the conquest of Constantinople, as well as its separate military contingent, made Venice a political heavyweight with respect to the emperor, establishing virtual parity with the crusader barons in the early years of the Latin empire. In that formative political stage Venetian representatives participated in various governing bodies, whose decisions affected political, territorial, institutional and judicial developments.

The combination of subordination and parity in Venice's position was extended and amplified on a symbolic level by its *podestà*. These Venetian officials used titles and regalian elements borrowed from Byzantium alongside those utilised by the emperors themselves, in order to project a quasi-imperial standing both inside and outside the empire. The great distance from Venice, and political expediency, explain the diplomatic initiative shown by several *podestà* up to the 1230s. It is clear, though, that their policies conformed with the interests of the city of Venice and were closely aligned with it. There are no grounds, therefore, for assuming that the *podestà* adopted an autonomous political course or attempted to bolster their own status at the expense of the Venetian doges. Soon after Baldwin I was proclaimed emperor, Venice obtained the election of a Venetian as patriarch of Constantinople, in accordance with the treaty of March 1204. However, Tommaso Morosini considered himself a representative of Pope Innocent III (1198–16), rather than a Venetian citizen promoting Venice's interests in the Latin empire, which explains his tense relations with the Venetian *podestà*. The patriarchs controlled property yielding substantial revenue in the City.

Venice also took advantage of its major role as a maritime and commercial power. On several occasions Venetian ships helped the emperors in the defence of Constantinople; her subjects played a dominant role in the City's trade; and her quarter there – substantially enlarged in 1204 – was the hub of commercial activity, attracting both Venetian and foreign settlers. Venetian settlers were also established at Raidestos and Gallipoli, ports of call on the Dardanelles belonging to Venice and administered by its representatives until 1235, when they were occupied by John III Vatatzes. In order to reinforce its position in the empire Venice increased the number of its subjects by granting Venetian nationality to Latin foreigners among her fief-holders, Latin city-dwellers, Greeks and descendants of mixed Venetian–Greek parentage known as *gasmouloi*.[5]

The principality of Achaia, the third major Frankish state of Latin *Romania*, survived the Latin empire by some 170 years. It took Geoffrey I of Villehardouin and his sons Geoffrey II of Villehardouin (*c.* 1226/31–46) and William II of Villehardouin (1246–78) until 1248 to conquer the entire Peloponnese, except for the Venetian enclaves of Modon and Coron in southern Messenia. After the fall of the kingdom of Thessaloniki in 1224 the other Frankish lords established in *Romania* rallied around Geoffrey I of Villehardouin. From 1236 the counts of Cephalonia recognised the suzerainty of the princes of Achaia. In return for his promise of help, in 1248 William obtained lifetime suzerainty over all but four of the Aegean islands from Baldwin II, an ascendancy which in fact persisted into the fourteenth century.

Some years later William II of Villehardouin would assert his new position. In 1209 the lord of Euboea, already a vassal of Boniface of Montferrat, had also acknowledged the suzerainty of Venice, yet the agreement was only ratified in 1211. His successors in the three main lordships of Euboea followed suit. This enabled Venice to intervene in the feudal affairs of the island on several occasions, notably from 1256 to 1262, when Venice supported two of these lords who refused to recognise the overlordship of William of Villehardouin. In 1258 William defeated an ally of the rebel lords, the duke of Athens Guy I of La Roche (1225–63), who subsequently acknowledged his vassalic subordination to the prince. Eventually, in 1262, the danger of a Byzantine reconquest prompted all sides to put an end to their conflicts.[6]

The military might of the principality of Achaia was demonstrated on several occasions; in 1236 and again in 1238, Geoffrey II of Villehardouin came to the rescue of Constantinople with his forces, and from May 1249 to May 1250 his brother and successor William joined the French king Louis IX's crusade to Egypt. However, in 1259 the troops of Michael VIII Palaiologos, then still ruling at Nicaea, inflicted a severe defeat upon William, his vassals and allies at Pelagonia in Macedonia. For about two years the

---

[5] Jacoby (1993), pp. 142–64, 194–7; Jacoby (1998); Jacoby (2001b); Jacoby (2006). Venetian naturalisation should not be mistaken for the grant of Venetian citizenship, awarded in that period only to those settled in Venice proper: see Jacoby (1993), pp. 163–4; Jacoby (1981), pp. 217–21.

[6] Jacoby (1971), pp. 21–5, 52, 185–96.

principality was governed by women in lieu of their captive husbands. After the Byzantine recovery of Constantinople in 1261 William agreed, as the price of his release, to cede three important strongholds in the south-eastern Peloponnese to Michael VIII; among them was Monemvasia, which had remained in Frankish hands for only around fourteen years (see also above p. 754).

After regaining a foothold in the peninsula, the following year the Byzantines proceeded to expand. To counter their mounting pressure and in return for promised assistance from the new king of Sicily, Charles I of Anjou (1266–85), William II of Villehardouin agreed in the Treaty of Viterbo (1267) that after his death, the principality of Achaia and its dependencies should be transferred to the king. This move was made with the acquiescence of William's lord, Emperor Baldwin II, who also granted Charles suzerainty over the islands of the Aegean, Corfu and all Latin possessions in Epiros. After the death of William in 1278 Charles took hold of the principality of Achaia and sent his bailiffs to govern it. In 1289 his son Charles II of Anjou (1285–1309) awarded it to William's daughter Isabel of Villehardouin on her second marriage to Florent of Hainault, and the couple took up residence in the principality. Florent established a truce with Byzantium in the same year, yet in 1295 war again broke out.

By now Byzantine rule in the Peloponnese extended from the south-eastern region, recovered by Byzantium in 1262, to Kalavryta in the north, and thus covered a large portion of the peninsula. Florent's most serious problem was the refusal of Helena, mother and regent of the young duke of Athens, Guy II of La Roche (1287–1308), to acknowledge his suzerainty. Yet after coming of age in 1296, the duke did homage to Isabel and Florent. A stronger alliance between the two parties was established in 1299 when Isabel betrothed her little daughter Matilda (Mahaut) of Hainault to Guy.

In 1294 Charles II of Anjou assigned all his eastern dependencies to his son Philip of Taranto, who thus became immediate overlord of Frankish Greece. In 1301 the widowed Isabel of Villehardouin married the count of Piedmont, Philip of Savoy (1301–7), who shortly after arriving in the principality aroused the opposition of various barons and knights with his infringements of Achaian feudal custom. The next year Philip put down a revolt of the indigenous population in the mountainous Skorta region, prompted by new taxes, and in 1303 he campaigned in Epiros in support of Charles, yet later refused to provide further assistance. Since Philip of Savoy delayed doing homage to his immediate overlord, Philip of Taranto, in 1307 Charles declared Isabel to have forfeited her fief. Four years later, Isabel was still claiming her rights and those of her daughter Matilda (Mahaut), but to no effect: Philip of Taranto (1307–13) had definitively become prince of Achaia.

LATIN SETTLEMENT IN *ROMANIA*: LAW,
INSTITUTIONS AND SOCIETY

The establishment of Latin rule over extensive portions of *Romania* opened the way to western immigration and settlement in these territories on a scale much larger than before 1204. With the exception of the Venetians, the new Latin settlers initially came from the ranks of the conquerors, many of whom were knights. The Latin population was gradually reinforced in numbers and became more diversified, the majority of the newcomers hailing from Italian cities. However, our lack of adequate quantitative data makes it impossible to assess the extent of Latin immigration. About 1225 some 450 mounted warriors were dispersed throughout the principality of Achaia, yet it is not clear how many of them lived there with wives and children. In 1210 Othon of La Roche (1204–25), duke of Athens, mentioned localities in which only twelve Latins resided, a reference to feudal lords and their retinues settled in isolated mountain castles or fortified rural mansions. Some of these lords occasionally resided in the houses they owned in cities. Most Latins, however, whether knights or commoners, tended to live permanently in an urban centre, preferably protected by walls, or inside an acropolis, regardless of their previous lifestyle or occupations. Such was the case, for instance, with the crusader knights and Venetian fief-holders in the Gallipoli peninsula. To some extent this marked preference of the Latins for urban settlement in *Romania* derived from economic considerations, in particular those of merchants and craftsmen. Yet it also arose from the psychological urge of a minority group for security, keenly aware of its isolation amidst an overwhelmingly Greek population.

The largest Latin concentration in the conquered territories outside the Venetian colonial empire occurred in Constantinople between 1204 and 1261. The major economic role of the City, as well as Venice's improved position and extended quarter there, attracted primarily Venetian immigrants. In Frankish Achaia the establishment of the princely court at Andravida prompted further settlement in this locality and contributed to its urban development. Italian bankers and merchants took up temporary or permanent residence at Clarence, the port founded near Andravida in the first half of the thirteenth century, and turned it into an economic centre connecting the principality of Achaia with the kingdom of Sicily and Venice. However, Latin migration in *Romania* did not always result in permanent settlement. Some of those established in Latin *Romania* left after a while for other destinations. After the establishment of the Latin empire, knights whose pay was in arrears or who were dissatisfied with their living conditions either returned to the west or left the emperor's service to fight in his neighbours' armies. In addition, some Venetians who had kept up close ties with their kin in Venice, and retained property there, returned home after spending many years in Constantinople or other cities. The Byzantine recovery of the imperial capital in 1261 triggered an exodus of some 3,000 Latins, the majority of whom were undoubtedly Venetian settlers.[7]

As already noted, the conquering knights transplanted their own political organisation and social regime to *Romania*, except in the Venetian portion of the Latin empire. Yet their encounter with the local population required significant accommodations. As in the west, the society of the territories they settled became highly stratified, with a clear distinction between the upper, knightly class and the other strata of society. This distinction was bolstered by the knights' strong class consciousness – expressed in the ceremony of dubbing – and their particular values, lifestyle, mentality and culture. Yet even within this Frankish elite there was pronounced social differentiation. Vassalage and the holding of fiefs entailing military service provided the backbone of the social and political hierarchy, yet only higher- and middle-ranking noblemen exercised judicial and legislative authority and rights of taxation.

The stratified nature of the feudal hierarchy is best known from the principality of Achaia. The barons, one of whom was the Latin archbishop of Patras, enjoyed a strong position, participating in the decisive deliberations of the princely court, and exercising high justice. Among the other tenants-in-chief of the prince, from the second half of the thirteenth century we find some Italian bankers and merchants to whom the princes had granted knighthood and fiefdoms in return for financial assistance. There were several ranks of feudatories below the direct vassals of the prince. The lowest rank included those individuals who were not members of the knightly class: sergeants, owing mounted military service in return for land or a payment, and *archontes*, members of the local elite (see below, pp. 772–3).[8]

Our knowledge of thirteenth-century feudal custom in Frankish Achaia derives mainly from a private legal treatise, known as the *Assizes of Romania*. This compilation was completed between 1333 and 1346 in French, the language of the Frankish knights, yet survives in a Venetian translation presumably prepared in Negroponte in the late fourteenth century.[9] Achaian feudal custom developed from a mixture of imported and local elements. The conquerors and their successors borrowed principles, rules and formulations from their lands of origin, among them Champagne, as well as from the Latin kingdom of Jerusalem, where the Frankish kings

---

[7] Jacoby (1989a), pp. 194–7, 218; Jacoby (1993), pp. 182–9; Jacoby (1997a); Jacoby (2001a); Bon (1969), pp. 318–25, on Andravida and Clarence. Geanakoplos (1959), pp. 112–14, 131–4, argues unconvincingly that there was no mass flight of Latins from Constantinople in 1261, despite mentioning 3,000 fugitives. The Venetians had every reason to fear the Byzantine reconquest of the city.

[8] Jacoby (1971), pp. 271, 291; Jacoby (1973), pp. 901–2; Jacoby (1986); Jacoby (1989a), pp. 189–94.

[9] *Assizes of Romania*, ed. and French tr. Recoura; tr. Topping, with numerous corrections to both in Jacoby (1971), *passim* (index of *Assizes* on pp. 353–6). See now *Assizes of Romania*, ed. Parmeggiani.

and nobility faced many similar problems to their own. Traces of the feudal custom from the kingdom of Sicily also appeared after 1278, when the principality came under Charles I of Anjou's rule. The determining factors in the development of the legal system, though, were legislative acts and judicial precedents established by the princely court of Achaia, registering the dynamics of Frankish problem-solving. Within this framework, the feudal custom of the principality had one novel feature: it incorporated elements of Byzantine law relating to the patrimonial lands held by Greeks and to the status of dependent peasants.

The *Assizes* confirm the strong legal and political position of the prince, reflecting both the tensions which occasionally arose between him and his barons, and the barons' cooperation with the princely court, for which we also have evidence from other sources. The *Assizes* deal extensively with matters of vassalage, fiefdoms, the military service they owed, and with the rights of lords over their peasants, but only marginally with non-feudal holdings, commercial cases and the drafting of wills. The extension of Achaian suzerainty over most islands of the Aegean in 1248 resulted in greater involvement by their Frankish lords, like the dukes of Athens and marquises of Bodonitsa, in the political, military and above all the feudal life of the principality. The collapse of the Latin empire in 1261 increased this involvement – which continued after 1278 under the bailiffs appointed by Charles I of Anjou and the princes ruling the principality directly – spreading Achaian feudal customs throughout the territories subject to the suzerainty of the Frankish princes.[10]

Representatives of Venice served as *baili* in the city of Negroponte (presently Chalkis) from 1211, dealing with judicial cases involving Venetians and their assets on the island. Their jurisdiction increasingly extended to feudal matters, drawing on Achaian custom. In 1262 the island's overlord, William II of Villehardouin, checked their interference in that field (see above, p. 767), and Venice refrained from exercising feudal jurisdiction in Euboea for the next half century or so; however, some Venetian lords in the Aegean continued to submit feudal cases to the Venetian *baili* in Negroponte. This jurisdiction stimulated Venice's interest in the use and preservation of Achaian feudal custom and induced her to sanction a Venetian version of the *Assizes* in 1452; this version acquired legal force throughout Venice's colonial empire, save in Crete. The reliance on Achaian custom contributed decisively to the piecemeal extension of Venetian lordship over Frankish Negroponte and some neighbouring islands, a process completed in 1390.[11] Venice also used other means gradually to undermine the authority of the lords of Euboea in the city of Negroponte.[12]

[10] Jacoby (1971), pp. 24–6, 29–174, 185–7.
[11] Jacoby (1971), pp. 188–202, 210–11, 237–9, 271–81, 295–300.   [12] Jacoby (2002).

As a result of Latin settlement, society in the Latin territories of *Romania*, other than those ruled by Venice, was divided into two distinct groups. While religious affiliation was not of major importance in daily life, it constituted a criterion of basic social stratification and individual identity. The Latins belonging to the Roman church enjoyed the superior status of freemen – *Francus* or Frank being synonymous with both Latin and freeman – while the local society remaining faithful to the Greek church was collectively debased.

Two factors drove this important change in local, formerly Byzantine society. Firstly, the conquering knights projected their own concept of a rigidly stratified society onto it, translating Byzantine social realities into legal terms. Secondly, since the abstract concept of statehood upheld in Byzantium was alien to them, all the prerogatives and functions of the imperial government, which had retained their public nature in the empire, were transferred into the hands of feudal lords. This again was in accordance with the legal system prevailing in western feudal society at that time. The overall privatisation and decentralisation of state authority in judicial and fiscal matters, the twin features of feudalisation in Latin *Romania* (except in Venetian-ruled territories) arrested social trends in Greek society and had a direct bearing on the status of its members.

Before 1204 the basic social and legal distinction within Byzantine society had been between free individuals and slaves. Social as well as economic differentiation among freemen was not expressed in legal terms, and they were all subject to the same imperial laws and courts. The Byzantine elite – the *archontes*, great landlords, high- and middle-ranking imperial officials and imperial dignitaries, mostly living in cities – thus lacked a legal definition. The Frankish knights, however, considered them members of a well-defined socio-legal class, similar to their own yet not equal. The knights' status was hereditary, subject to a legal system different from that governing the bulk of the indigenous population.

With the breakdown of Byzantine imperial government in the years just before and particularly those following the Latin conquest of Constantinople, the *archontes* in many areas of *Romania* assumed control over the local population. By and large, those who negotiated the submission of the cities and territories under their control were allowed to keep all or portions of their patrimonial estates and the dependent peasants living in them. In the duchy of Naxos the small number of Latin settlers prompted the conqueror, Marco I Sanudo, to adopt a conciliatory attitude toward the Greeks, integrating *archontes* among his feudatories. In Frankish Achaia the converging interests of the Frankish knightly class and the *archontes*, more numerous than elsewhere, led to the *archontes* and other Greeks being gradually absorbed into the ranks of the feudatories who owed simple homage, the lowest stratum in the Frankish feudal hierarchy. This legal integration did not affect the status of Greek patrimonial estates, which remained hereditary and were governed by Byzantine law, as before the Latin conquest.

From the mid-thirteenth century, especially after the return of Byzantium to the Peloponnese in 1262, the Frankish leaders' concern to ensure the loyalty, cooperation and military service of the *archontes* led the Franks to grant them fiefdoms under feudal custom, thus furthering their social rise. They even dubbed some *archontes* to knighthood, a status that became hereditary. In most cases, however, this social process did not induce the Greeks to adopt the westerners' creed, nor did it make the Latin knights less reluctant to intermarry with them. The limits of the legal and social assimilation achieved by the *archontes* were also illustrated by the persistence of a cultural gap between the two groups. The *archontes*' social promotion enhanced their status within their own traditional community, yet deprived that community of an elite willing to oppose Latin rule.[13]

As noted above, the entire local population underwent a process of debasement as a result of the conquest. Except for the *archontes*, all Greeks sank into a state of dependency, since in principle they became *paroikoi* or dependent individuals, regardless of their personal status or place of residence before 1204. The *Assizes of Romania* distinguish between only two categories of Greeks, *archontes* and *paroikoi*, the latter also called *villani* by the Latins. In practice, however, the situation was more complex and a distinction apparently existed between local urban and rural populations. Political expediency accounts for Greek autonomy in Adrianople, held since 1206 by the Greek *archōn* Theodore Branas under Venetian lordship. And we may safely assume that the Greek court operating with Latin consent in Thessaloniki in 1213 upheld the rules of Byzantine law regarding the *paroikoi* and their assets, as distinct from those of non-dependent city-dwellers.[14]

However, continuity in the use of the Byzantine term *paroikos* conceals a major change in the legal status and social condition of the Greeks to whom it was applied. Under Byzantine rule, *paroikoi* were peasants considered legally free. As such they had access to imperial courts, although they were attached either to the imperial fisc, to an ecclesiastical institution or to an individual lord, and were subject to important personal restrictions. With the privatisation of governmental authority under Latin rule *paroikoi* were deemed legally unfree, like dependent serfs or villeins in the west; they were therefore members of a legal class from which they could escape only by a formal act of emancipation. The presumption of dependence was so strong that free status had to be duly proven by Greeks who enjoyed it, preferably

---

[13] Jacoby (1973), pp. 889–903; Jacoby (1989a), pp. 180–5, 197–200; Jacoby (1989b), pp. 2–8. The leaders of Slav groups, included among the *archontes* before 1204, benefited from the same social ascent.

[14] Jacoby (1993), pp. 151, 157; Wolff (1969), p. 211.

with the help of documents, if doubts arose. The subjection of the *paroikos* or villein to his lord was far more rigorous than it had been in the Byzantine period. He was considered a mere chattel and tied to the estate of his lord, who wielded almost unlimited authority over him, except for criminal justice which was reserved for competent courts. The legal capacity of the *paroikoi* in their handling of landed property and goods was also far more restricted than in the Byzantine period. Cases of manumission appear to have been rare. Paradoxically, in the absence of Byzantine imperial authority this whole process also adversely affected those dependent peasants who were subject to *archontes* and Greek ecclesiastical institutions. Even lower down the social scale than villeins were the slaves, whose numbers grew as a result of the frequent warfare and piracy in *Romania*. Many slaves were exported to the west or to Muslim countries. In the portion of the Latin empire under its direct rule, Venice adopted the principles and policies of the Frankish knights vis-à-vis the social stratification of Greek society and the privatisation of taxation owed by the peasantry, while maintaining state control over the property and rights it granted out. Moreover, Venice strictly upheld the public nature of Byzantine judicial and fiscal authority as exclusive state prerogatives.[15]

LATIN SETTLEMENT IN *ROMANIA*: ECONOMIC GROWTH

The Latin conquest and the subsequent redistribution of property in the Latins' favour did not alter the nature of *Romania's* economy. Land remained the main source of income, wealth and taxation, the agrarian infrastructure of the countryside was hardly affected, and the basic pattern of agricultural exploitation persisted. This continuity, furthered by the inclusion of Greek officials in the Latins' administration, is illustrated by the survival of Byzantine administrative, fiscal and legal institutions and practices, by the structure of the large estates of Frankish Achaia – documented by fourteenth-century surveys – and by various agricultural contracts. The Latin conquest, however, put an end to the dominance of the Byzantine *archontes* in the financing of economic activities and definitively abolished the Byzantine state's restrictive control over particular branches of manufacture and trade.

Central and western Greece and the Aegean islands, which stayed under Frankish rule longer than the territories recovered by Byzantium in the thirteenth century, saw ever stronger economic interaction between the rural sector, the cities and long-distance maritime trade. The free flow of cash between these sectors of the economy was furthered by various factors: the temporary or permanent presence of Latins, mainly in coastal cities,

[15] Jacoby (1989a), pp. 185–9, 207–16; Jacoby (1989b), pp. 16–18, 20–23; Jacoby (1993), pp. 169–81.

whose population grew; the supply of goods and services to merchants and ships in transit; the expanding western demand for agricultural and industrial commodities; and, finally, the infusion of liquid capital from the west. This last process was promoted from the 1270s at the latest by the activity of mercantile and banking companies from Siena (the Piccolomini and Tolomei), and these were later joined by some from Florence (the Cerchi, Bardi and Peruzzi). The range of their large-scale business stretched from the Latin east to the fairs of Champagne and to England. In Latin Greece, Clarence constituted their main credit centre, but they also operated in Corinth, Thebes and the city of Negroponte.

The Italian merchants and bankers introduced new forms of profit-sharing ventures, credit, business and estate management, as well as ways of marketing, and invested capital in the exploitation of rural land and in manufacturing. Thus in Thebes, Genoese merchants acted as entrepreneurs, financing the production of silk textiles from before 1240. We may safely assume that Venetian merchants acted in a similar capacity, both in Thebes and elsewhere. On the whole, the presence and activity of Italian bankers, merchants and administrators from the second half of the thirteenth century stimulated a growth in agricultural, pastoral and industrial productivity, output and profit, and boosted the economy of the former western provinces of Byzantium occupied by the Latins. Manufacturing, however, took a different course. To be sure, the silk textiles of Thebes and other centres of Latin *Romania* were still shipped to the west in the second half of the thirteenth century. Yet the expanding and diversified manufacture of prized silks in Italy, several of whose types were of Byzantine origin, and the improvements in the quality of glass vessels produced in Venice, partly intended for export to *Romania*, eventually stifled these same industries in western and central Greece and the Aegean islands. These regions increasingly supplied industrial raw materials to the west, while absorbing an ever larger volume of western finished products.

An important aspect of the economic evolution of western and central Greece and the Aegean islands after 1204 was the partial reorientation towards the west of long-distance exports, which had been largely geared towards Constantinople before the Fourth Crusade. The Greek inhabitants of these regions continued to participate in short-range and regional trade and in transportation, by land and by sea, as well as in seasonal fairs. Yet the Latins' overall share in these activities grew at their expense, and from the 1270s the Greeks appear to have relied increasingly on Latin shipping, even in the Aegean. The seaborne commerce of western and central Greece was increasingly subordinated to the requirements, routes and seasonal rhythm of long-distance maritime trade, dominated by Venetian merchants and carriers who took advantage of Venice's naval and diplomatic protection and the infrastructure which its colonies and commercial outposts in the eastern Mediterranean offered. This led to the growing integration of these territories into a triangular trade pattern linking *Romania* with Italy and the Levant. The vigour of the pirates and corsairs preying along the main sea lanes of this network in the second half of the thirteenth century illustrates the overall growth of maritime trade in the eastern Mediterranean in that period.[16]

The economy of Latin Constantinople deserves special attention. It contracted after the Latin conquest of 1204 for want of massive local consumption or investment in high-grade manufacture, but revived shortly afterwards. Its operation became overwhelmingly based on commercial exchanges and the transit and transshipment of goods, functions already performed before the Fourth Crusade. Constantinople's economy was boosted by Venice's treaties with the Seljuq sultans of Rum, the emperors of Nicaea, and various other powers in the eastern Mediterranean along the sea route linking the City to Egypt. The strong position of Venice in Constantinople ensured its merchants – whether itinerant or settled – a dominant share in the City's trade; Pisan, Anconitan, Amalfitan and Provençal merchants also participated in this trade, as did the Genoese from 1232 onwards.

One of the most important economic effects of the Latin conquest of Constantinople was to open up the Black Sea to unrestricted western commerce. At first, however, the Latins appear to have relied upon local traders who had traditionally supplied Constantinople, mainly with wheat, salt, fish, hides and furs. The Latin merchants and carriers gradually extended their ventures in the Black Sea. Yet only after the Mongols consolidated their rule north of the Black Sea from around 1240 did the Latins markedly increase the geographical, commercial and financial range of their operations beyond the coast and penetrate deep inland. Some of them settled in Sougdaia on the southern shore of the Crimea, making it a base for penetration inland to Kiev and beyond, as well as for the export of slaves from Mongol territory to the Mediterranean. Significantly, the Venetians Niccolò and Matteo Polo – father and uncle respectively of the famous Marco – passed through Constantinople and Sougdaia in 1260 before undertaking their journey into inner Asia. Latin Constantinople thus served as an important transit station with a pivotal role in the integration of the Black Sea and Mediterranean trade systems. A sound knowledge and much experience of economic resources, markets and trade routes in the Black Sea and its hinterland were accumulated during the Latin period. They paved the way for the swift and substantial expansion of Genoese and Venetian

---

[16] Jacoby (1997a); Jacoby (2001a). On silk: Jacoby (1994a), pp. 44–8, 51–4; Jacoby (2000b). On piracy and corsairs: Ahrweiler (1966), pp. 322–3, 369–370, 377–8, 381; Geanakoplos (1959), pp. 152–3, 210–15, 302–4, 328, 336–7, 362; Morgan (1976); Balard (1978), I, pp. 39–40.

trade and shipping in that region in the decade following the Byzantine reconquest of Constantinople in 1261.[17]

'GREEK MATTERS'

We have already noted the limited rapprochement between Frankish and Greek social elites. The pursuit of manufacture, trade and shipping by both Latins and Greeks, sometimes jointly, prompted a degree of economic cooperation and social intercourse between them on a daily, practical level in urban centres. These contacts did not, however, affect the deep-seated attitude of the bulk of the Greek population of Latin *Romania* toward the Latins, largely shaped by religious affiliation and ecclesiastical developments. Few Greeks joined the Roman church in the thirteenth century, most remaining within their own religious community. The Latin conquerors of Constantinople first humiliated the Greeks by desecrating their sanctuaries and seizing their relics, many of which were transferred to the west.

The Greek church of Latin *Romania* was soon subjected to papal authority, and its structure was reorganised on the lines of the settlement in southern Italy and Sicily; this provided for the maintenance of the Greek church wherever Greeks constituted the majority of the population. In fact, however, this church gradually lost its bishops and many of its monastic institutions to the advantage of the Latin church. In addition, the conquerors confiscated large portions of its extensive landed property. The growing activity of the Franciscans and the Dominicans from the 1220s put further pressure on the Greek church of Latin *Romania*. Nevertheless, this church displayed considerable vitality, illustrated by its continuous presence and activity among the Greeks, especially in rural areas where the Latin church remained largely absent.

Already in the first years after the conquest the Greek clergy turned to the patriarchal see of Nicaea and the clergy of Epiros for support and inspiration. To the Greeks of Latin *Romania* the clergy conveyed at popular level the staunch theological opposition of the Byzantine church to the papacy, fuelling their opposition to Latin lay rule and Roman ecclesiastical supremacy. As a result, it became the focus and promoter of Greek ethnic awareness and collective identity. Its role in this respect was particularly important in areas such as the principality of Achaia, where the *archontes* refused to oppose the Franks. As noted above, Greek animosity toward the conquerors and their successors contributed to the collapse of the Latin

---

[17] Heyd (1885–6), I, pp. 294–310, II, p. 94; Borsari (1955), pp. 477–88; Balard (1978), I, pp. 38–45, 116; Jacoby (1998); Jacoby (2001b); Jacoby (2005a). Treaties in TT, II, pp. 205–7, 221–5; *Deliberazioni*, ed. Cessi, I, no. 140, pp. 209–10.

empire, yet elsewhere it had limited practical effect.[18] The abiding sense of alienation felt by the Greeks and their affinity for Byzantium were described by the Venetian Marino Sanudo about 1330, more than a century after the Latin conquest:

'Although these places are subjected to the rule of the Franks and obedient to the Roman church, nevertheless almost all the population is Greek and is inclined toward this sect [i.e. the eastern orthodox church], and their hearts are turned toward Greek matters, and when they can show this freely, they do so'.[19]

[18] Wolff (1948); Wolff (1954); Setton (1976–84), I, pp. 1–153, 405–40; Richard (1989); Angold (1989); Angold (2003a), pp. 163–203, 227–47; Jacoby (1989a), pp. 218, 220; Lock (1995), pp. 193–239, 266–310.
[19] *Chroniques*, ed. Hopf, p. 143.

CHAPTER 21

BALKAN POWERS: ALBANIA, SERBIA AND BULGARIA (1200–1300)

ALAIN DUCELLIER

INTRODUCTION

It is widely accepted that the fall of Constantinople in 1204 brought to its knees an empire already on the point of collapse, notably on its Balkan fringes, where three peoples showed new vigour: the Bulgarians, the Serbs and the Albanians. The boundaries between their lands were still very fluid, especially those between Bulgaria and Serbia, and each was at a different stage of evolution towards political and cultural autonomy. Bulgaria under the Asen dynasty, which broke with the Byzantines in 1185–7 and which in 1202 gained Byzantine recognition of its mastery over the lands from Belgrade to Sofia, represented the resurgence of an older state, though with rather different territorial boundaries. Even after two centuries of Byzantine dominance, Bulgaria retained distinctive political and cultural traditions which sustained its self-image as the major power in the Balkans, and, in consequence, implied Bulgarian rights over Constantinople itself.[1]

In Serbia, Stefan Nemanja (c. 1165/8–96) had recently brought together the two old power centres of Raška and Duklja (the latter roughly corresponding to modern Montenegro). Duklja, it is true, retained strong particularist tendencies, and internecine strife within the family of the Nemanjids only made this worse.[2] On the Dalmatian coast, Italian influences spawned short-lived communes, which barely managed to withstand the Serb princes' attempts to absorb them into their realms; the best example is that of Kotor.[3] In any event, Nemanja directed a push southwards from 1183, which enabled him to put pressure on Macedonia beyond Niš. He exerted influence on the Dalmatian coastal region north of Dubrovnik (Ragusa), which oscillated between Byzantine and Norman Sicilian overlordship. Nemanja also drove southwards down the coast as far as the Mati estuary in northern Albania, thus cutting off Duklja from the sea. At the same time the church of Rome attempted to extend its influence

---

[1] Zlatarsky (1970–2), II, pp. 410–11; Dujčev (1956), pp. 327–8. On the impact of the Third and Fourth Crusades on Bulgaria, see Primov (1975a); Asdracha (1976), p. 235. See also above, pp. 688–9, 690.

[2] For syntheses, see Djurović et al. (1970), pp. 5–14, 46–61; above, pp. 683, 686.

[3] Djurović et al. (1970), pp. 83–4.

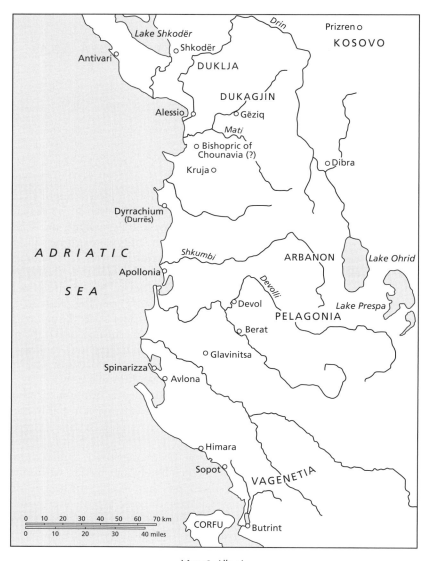

Map 38 Albania

into the region of Albania, spreading outwards from the archiepiscopal seat
at Antivari.[4] Although it seems that Serbia had already gained some self-
awareness as an ethnic identity, it would be premature to see it as amounting to a properly constituted 'state'. Remaining within the Byzantine orbit,

---

[4] Djurović *et al.* (1970), pp. 15–27 and map, p. 16.

Serbia was quite capable of keeping its distance from Constantinople, and at the same time refraining from the Latin church's temptations: in 1200 the young *veliki župan* Stefan (1196–1227) repudiated his wife, Eudocia, daughter of Emperor Alexios III (1195–1203), and she withdrew near-naked to Dyrrachium (Durrës).[5]

As for Albania, its separate identity was real enough, even though it had not made a clean break with Constantinople. The rulers of the region of Arbanon around 1190, Progon and his sons Dhimitër and Gjin, had their base at Kruja. They were virtually self-governing, even though Progon merely had the status of *archōn*; in fact the title of *panhypersebastos*, borne by Dhimitër at the start of the thirteenth century, can only be seen as a sign of his dependence on the Byzantines.[6] Nonetheless, the earliest inscription to mention Progon and Dhimitër, from Gëziq, in the hinterland of Alessio, is written in Latin and calls them *judices*, while noting their dependence on Vladin and George, princes of Duklja. This gives us a snapshot of the political and cultural convergences underway in Arbanon.[7] This Arbanon, the 'Raban' of the *Life of Stefan Nemanja*, had no direct access to the sea, even though the coasts of Epiros were still inhabited mainly by Albanians, for all the Serbs' and Greeks' overlordship. Albanians were also the principal inhabitants of the mountain areas rising above the eastern shore of Lake Shkodër.[8] These lands came under the Roman church during the twelfth century, but the lower reaches were increasingly populated by Albanians. So was the ancient Dardania (modern Kosovo), which lay open to the Albanians via the river system of the Drin, some distance from the Serb power centres of Raška and Duklja. It is hard to see how the Albanians could have spread down from the mountains towards the shores of Lake Shkodër if one does not accept their earlier expansion down from the other side of the mountains, towards Gjakova and Prizren.[9]

There was certainly a religious divide in the region, but it would be wrong to exaggerate its impermeability, particularly as both the Bulgarian and Serbian rulers showed their willingness to be crowned by the pope.[10] It

---

[5] On the religious aspects of Serbian unification, see Kalić (1979); on the Serbian threat and the breach of 1200, see NC, ed. van Dieten, I, pp. 531–2; tr. Magoulias, p. 292; Ostrogorsky (1968), pp. 409–10; Ducellier (1981b), pp. 123 and n. 17, 152. See also above, p. 690.

[6] Soloviev (1934), p. 304; Ducellier (1981b), p. 63.

[7] Shuteriqi (1967), pp. 133–42; Ducellier (1979), p. 28.

[8] *Life of Stefan Nemanja*, ed. Ćorović; tr. Kantor; Ćirković (1988), a notably courageous work.

[9] The question of Illyrian continuity is addressed by Jireček (1916a), pp. 69–70; von Thallóczy and Jireček (1916), pp. 127–8. Drawing heavily on the correspondence of Demetrios Chomatenos, Jireček accepts that, before the Slavs' expansion, the territory occupied by Albanians extended from Scutari (Shkodër) to Avlona and from Prizren to Ohrid. See also Ćirković (1988), p. 347; Mirdita (1981).

[10] See Ćirković (1988), pp. 346–9, who draws a religious borderline along the heights of Dukagjin, and accepts the Albanians' descent towards the lower ground around Lake Shkodër. However, he does not take into account their expansion on the eastern side of the mountain range nor – more surprisingly – the obvious use by them of the Drin valley, which leads straight to Prizren.

was in recognition of continued population growth, rather than by way of punishment, that in 1348 Stefan Dušan (1331–55) required Latin priests from Shkodër to pay their taxes to the orthodox bishop of Prizren, a suffragan of Ohrid.[11] And it is apparent from a charter granted to Dubrovnik by Ivan II Asen (1218–41) in 1230 that the Albanians dominated the central regions of what is now the Albanian republic, in the areas drained by the Devolli river.[12] One is not dealing with Albania in the sense of a tight-knit political or territorial entity; on the other hand the imperial government took account of the ethnic character of the region when the former theme of Dyrrachion became known as *provintia Dirrachii et Arbani*. This was its name, if the *partitio Romaniae* is to be believed (and it probably does reflect pre-1204 realities). Such a name would register the existence of two main centres of Albanian settlement, Arbanon-Raban and Devol.[13]

THE BULGARIAN EMPIRE REVIVED

Each of these three very different entities reacted to the events of 1204 in different ways. For Bulgaria, the *partitio Romaniae* was a direct challenge, since the frontier regions around Philippopolis and Adrianople were doled out to Latins, despite the long-standing Bulgarian claims to them that are enshrined in the treaty of 1202. Renier de Trit held Philippopolis from autumn 1204 to June 1205, when Kalojan retook the town, on his way back from an expedition against Thessaloniki;[14] and in 1206 Venice granted out Adrianople to the 'collaborationist' *archōn* Theodore Branas.[15] This blocked Bulgarian aspirations to dominate the Maritsa valley and gain direct access to the Aegean at last.[16] The Bulgarians were bound to be further disquieted by the fact that the *partitio* of 1204 granted Venice, in addition to the Albanian coastline, the province of Koloneia, between Kastoria and Korça: expansion towards the Adriatic was another long-standing Bulgarian goal.[17]

Tsar Kalojan (1197–1207) managed to contain various separatist tendencies within Bulgaria, and he was able to draw on considerable military resources, especially among the peasantry of the Danube valley. Fully aware of what was happening on the international scene, he hoped to take

---

[11] *Zakonski spomenici*, ed. Novaković, pp. 691–2; Maksimović (1981a), pp. 175–9; Ćirković (1988), p. 348.

[12] *Stare srpske*, ed. Stojanović, II, p. 205; Ćirković (1988), p. 349.

[13] Ducellier (1981b), pp. 97–8. On the *partitio Romaniae*, see above, p. 759.

[14] Asdracha (1976), pp. 236–7; Vlachos (1970), pp. 277–8, with further references.

[15] TT, II, pp. 17–19; Villehard., ch. 423, ed. and French tr. Faral, II, p. 236; tr. Shaw, p. 138; Thiriet (1975), p. 80; Asdracha (1976), p. 239.

[16] Asdracha (1982).

[17] See Andrea Dandolo's 'Liber albus', Archivio di Stato, Venice, fol. 34; Carile (ed.), 'Partitio terrarum', p. 220; Ducellier (1981b), p. 98 and n. 53.

advantage of Byzantium's unexpected collapse and rejected the terms of the *partitio*.[18] His preliminary contacts with the crusaders, which appear to predate the fall of Constantinople, came to nothing. Kalojan saw in Innocent III (1198–1216) – himself unenthusiastic about the course the Fourth Crusade was taking – a guarantor against the crusaders' aggressive ambitions.[19] For the papacy this was an unhoped-for opportunity, a chance to bring Bulgaria within the Roman confession. Neither the Bulgarians nor the inhabitants of Serbia and Bosnia had raised a finger to help Zara, whose enforced submission to Hungary during the crusade ensured that it would remain a catholic city. Indeed, the Bosnians, who were allied with the Hungarians, even took the opportunity to reconcile themselves with Rome in 1203, pledging to deal with Bogomilism:[20] Bosnia was regarded as a main bastion of this dualist heresy.[21] Kalojan obtained recognition of his claim to the imperial title of tsar, and asked Innocent III to nominate a patriarch to head the Bulgarian church. Such demands led negotiations to drag on, and in the end Kalojan had to settle for the relatively modest titles of king for himself and primate for his senior bishop. But the result was that at T'rnovo on 7 November 1204 he received from a cardinal a royal crown, and thus in principle at least came under the pope's wing.[22] In reality, of course, this was a tactical move and Kalojan never gave up his orthodox faith or his imperial ambitions.[23] Up to the end of the second Bulgarian empire, the titles tsar and patriarch remained in use. Thus, for example, at T'rnovo in 1211 the usurper Boril (1207–18) adopted a *synodikon* which, without renouncing Rome, reaffirmed Bulgarian orthodoxy as well as reasserting the traditional struggle of the Bulgarian tsars against Bogomilism.[24] This heresy had never been eradicated from the Bulgarian lands, as events at Philippopolis in 1205 make clear: Villehardouin describes the quarter of the city inhabited by the heretics, which the paltry army of Renier de Trit burnt down.[25]

Kalojan also benefited from offers of service coming from the Greek-speaking *archontes* of Thrace, who were reacting against the intransigence of

[18] It is unfortunately impossible to date Kalojan's embassy to the crusaders precisely: *Gesta Innocentii III papae*, ch. 108, p. cxlvii. But both Robert de Clari and Geoffrey of Villehardouin place it after the first fall of Constantinople on 18 July 1203, and it evidently preceded the Bulgarian–Latin rupture of August 1204: Hendrickx, 'Recherches sur les documents diplomatiques', pp. 135–6; also Wolff (1952).

[19] Innocent III, *Correspondence with the Bulgarians*, ed. Dujčev, pp. 22–3, 30–1, 43–4, 47–8; Italian tr. Dall'Aglio, pp. 52–5, 74–7, 80–5; Asdracha (1976), p. 237.

[20] Ćirković (1964), pp. 48–9.   [21] Dusa (1991), p. 51.

[22] Obolensky (1971), pp. 239–41; Primov (1966), pp. 36–8. See above, p. 690.

[23] Dujčev (1960), p. 43.

[24] Boril, *Synodikon*; Angelov, D. (1961), pp. 253–4. On the orthodox yet 'Roman' character of the T'rnovo council, see Shivarov (1987).

[25] Villehard., ch. 400, ed. and French tr. Faral, II, p. 210; tr. Shaw, p. 132; Asdracha (1976), pp. 60–2 (rich in further references), 237; Primov (1948–9), pp. 145–58; Vlachos (1970), pp. 277–8. The Latins' control of the major Bogomil centres in Macedonia and Thrace may have furthered the spread of their beliefs to the west: Primov (1960), p. 86, preferable to Primov (1975b). See also above, p. 617; Hamilton, B. (2005).

the Latin emperor of Constantinople, Baldwin I (1204–5). These *archontes*, despairing of reaching a *modus vivendi* with the Latins, were even prepared to offer the imperial crown to the Bulgarian tsar at the beginning of 1205. The intrigues of a Bulgaro-Vlach, Šišman, caused uproar in Thessaloniki in May and June, and Boniface of Montferrat, its lord, had to lift his siege of Nauplion in a bid to rescue his wife Maria of Hungary from imprisonment in the acropolis of Thessaloniki.[26]

In the short term at least, Bulgarian policy produced results. On 14 April 1205 the Graeco-Bulgarian coalition, backed up by a formidable squadron of Cuman horsemen,[27] wiped out the Latin army at Adrianople, capturing the Latin emperor himself.[28] This disaster posed such a threat to Constantinople that Theodore I Laskaris (1205–21) was left with a free hand to build up his own power base in Asia Minor, the rump state of Nicaea (see above, pp. 734–5, 737). All too quickly, Kalojan revealed his real ambitions in Thrace; from 1205 to 1207 his armies lived off the land, while local manpower and livestock were carried off to the Danube regions where men and animals were in short supply.[29] Indeed, he was already known as 'killer of Romans' (i.e. of Greeks: *Rōmaioktonos*) because of his earlier treatment of the Greeks, for whom he would always be 'John the Dog' (*Kynoiōannēs*).[30] It is no surprise that the Greeks hated the Bulgarians, all the more so once the new Latin emperor Henry of Hainault (1206–16) abandoned his brother's brutal policy towards the Greek aristocracy. The provincial *archontes* readily came to terms with the Latins, with whom some had already contracted marriage alliances. A case in point is Theodore Branas, whose wife Agnes was the sister of King Philip Augustus of France.

It is a moot point where Kalojan would have gone next if he had not been killed suddenly in October 1207, under the walls of Thessaloniki.[31] In any event, his death brought a reprieve to the Latin empire which, under Henry, managed to hold onto the extreme north-west of Asia Minor. Bulgaria was plunged into turmoil after Boril seized the throne from Kalojan's son, Ivan

---

[26] One should use Krantonelle (1964) with care. See also NC, ed. van Dieten, I, pp. 619–20; tr. Magoulias, pp. 338–40; Villehard., ch. 389, ed. and French tr. Faral, II, p. 198; tr. Shaw, p. 129; Apostolides (1929), p. 336; Hendrickx, 'Recherches sur les documents diplomatiques', pp. 139–40.

[27] Villehardouin speaks only of 14,000 'Turks', but a report on the battle sent to Innocent III has Kalojan attacking the Latins 'cum Turcis et ceteris Crucis Christi inimicis': Theiner (ed.), *Vetera monumenta slavorum meridionalium*, I, p. 41. This has given rise to the notion that the tsar allied with the Bogomils; see for example Derzhavin (1945–8), II, p. 130. Angelov, D. (1961), pp. 251–2 shows that this was an attempt to discredit Kalojan in the pope's eyes; Hansen-Löve (1971).

[28] Gerland (1905), pp. 46–7; Longnon (1949), pp. 77–8. [29] Asdracha (1976), pp. 190–2.

[30] GA, chs. 13–14, rev. edn. Wirth, I, pp. 23–5; tr. Macrides, pp. 139–41, 144–5; Theodore Skoutariotes, *Synopsis chronike*, p. 459; Vlachos (1970), pp. 276, 279–80; Nicol (1957), p. 20; Asdracha (1976), pp. 237–8.

[31] Zlatarsky (1970–2), III, pp. 254–5. Thessaloniki was of particular importance to the Slavs owing to their devotion to St Demetrios, and Kalojan's death was attributed to the saint's intervention: Obolensky (1974), esp. p. 19.

(later Ivan II Asen). Its neighbours fomented this: between the Vardar and Strymon rivers to the west, Alexios Slavos, governor of Melnik, submitted to the Latins, while the Serbian *veliki župan* Stefan recognised Boril's brother, Strez, as lord of the region around Prosek and Strumica.[32]

THE RISE OF THE NEMANJIDS OF SERBIA

With the collapse of the Byzantine empire Serbia's hour had come, although western interference in Dalmatia tended to drive the Serbian empire's centre of gravity further inland. A prime example of this interference was the Venetians' assertion of at least nominal lordship over Dubrovnik in 1205. Under pressure from an aggressive Hungary, and aware of the papacy's aspirations under Honorius III (1216–27), *veliki župan* Stefan revived Kalojan's policies of fifteen years earlier, receiving a royal crown from the papal legate in 1217. Henceforth he would bear the sobriquet *prvovenčani*, 'the first-crowned'. But the Serbs' ambivalent outlook is clear from the fact that in 1219 the king's brother Sava, an Athonite monk, approached the autocephalous archbishop of Nicaea, seeking consecration as autocephalous archbishop of Serbia. This was not simply a question of remaining staunchly orthodox, but of seeing in Nicaea the only authentic remnant of the old empire. Sava and Stefan 'the first-crowned' would have been well aware that normal practice would have been for them to respect the archbishop of Ohrid's authority over Serbia. This would have brought them within the sphere of the despots of Epiros, over-mighty neighbours with an apparently unstoppable programme of expansion. As it was, Stefan had had to provide guarantees to the Epirots, betrothing his son and heir Stefan Radoslav (1227–33) to the daughter of the Epirot ruler Theodore Angelos (1215–30),[33] who himself took control of Thessaloniki in 1224.[34] The Bulgarians for their part were not to forget this alliance with their own worst enemy.

Upon the succession of Stefan Radoslav, the alliance between Serbia and Epiros appeared to be sealed; the Serbian church accepted that it was subordinate to the powerful archbishop of Ohrid, Demetrios Chomatenos, thus abandoning Sava's act of defiance of 1219 (see above, p. 742). However, the Epirot despots' expansionism could only irritate the Serbs, who, like the Bulgarians, were bewitched by dreams of eventually establishing themselves on the shores of the Aegean and the Adriatic. Around the time of his coronation Stefan 'the first-crowned' annexed the area of Peć, even though the Serbs had yet to establish their rule throughout what is now

---

[32] Asdracha (1976), pp. 240–1.

[33] Theodore Angelos styled himself Komnenos Doukas. Nicol (1957), p. 60, and nn. 34–5 on p. 73 distorts matters by talking of 'friendship' between Epiros and Serbia.

[34] Nicol (1957), pp. 62–3, with further references; Longnon (1950), pp. 141–2; Sinogowitz (1952).

Map 39 Theodore Angelos' seizure of Thrace 1225

Kosovo.[35] In 1225 Theodore Angelos managed to expel the Latins from eastern Macedonia, while respecting the small Bulgarian principality of Melnik.
He swept from victory to victory along the coast of Thrace, gaining control
of Kavalla, Xanthi, Gratianopolis, Mosynopolis and Didymoteichon; he
even reached Adrianople, where he drove out the newly installed Nicaeans.[36]
Now that he was a neighbour of the Bulgarian kingdom, Theodore realised
that the Bulgarian threat to his rear could jeopardise his grand plan, which
was for the capture of Constantinople itself. So he devised a tactical alliance
with Ivan II Asen of Bulgaria who had regained power in 1218 and who now
consented to the marriage of his illegitimate daughter, Maria Beloslava,
with Theodore's brother Manuel. This meant that Epiros and Bulgaria were
forging an axis in opposition to Nicaea, but also, indirectly, against Serbia.

THE ALBANIAN HORNETS' NEST

The situation of Albania after the *partitio Romaniae* was quite different.
Venice was assigned, in addition to Dyrrachium and its dependencies, the
chartolarates of Glavinitsa and Vagenetia, regions which the Venetians made
no real effort to hold, and which by 1205 had passed into the hands of the
first of the rulers of Epiros, Michael I Angelos Doukas (1205–15). The rise
of Epiros and the emergence of the new Slav powers of Bulgaria and Serbia
had serious repercussions for Albania. The great trans-Balkan routes across
Albania to the west, the Egnatian Way and the Via de Zenta (which ran
inland from the coast near Lake Shkodër towards Prizren and Priština),
were seriously disrupted by the incessant strife in the area. These routes

---

[35] On the Illyrian-Albanian population there, see Ducellier (1981c); Garašanin (1988b); Pulaha *et al.*
(eds.) (1982), esp. Gashi (1982). See also Prifti *et al.* (eds.) (1990).
[36] Nicol (1957), pp. 104–5; Asdracha (1976), p. 241.

lost their classic role as outlets for eastern goods, starting the irreversible decline of the Epirot and Albanian ports, notably Dyrrachium.[37] In July to August 1205 the Venetian expedition on its way to Constantinople to instal Doge Tommaso Morosini as patriarch seized the opportunity to take over Dyrrachium. A petty duchy was set up there, and Venice sought to draw some economic benefit from it, though this proved small compensation for the resultant tensions with Epiros and Serbia.[38]

Albania thus came under pressure from several sides, not least the Latin archbishopric of Antivari's attempts at catholicising the region.[39] However, given the proximity of an expansionist Serbia and the Epirot principality, little land-locked Arbanon, with its main political centre at Kruja, opted for an orthodox affiliation and subjugation to Epiros, as well as alliance with Serbia.[40] The *archōn* of Arbanon, Progon, had died in 1208, and the attitude of his son, Gjin, is difficult to determine; however, his successor, Dhimitër, clearly saw Venice as the main enemy. This was aggravated by Venice's alliance of 3 July 1208 with George, prince of Duklja and nephew of the Serbian ruler Stefan 'the first-crowned'. A clause in the 1208 treaty even stipulated that Duklja would support Venice if ever the Albanian prince rebelled against the republic.[41] Dhimitër's diplomatic skills are shown in the alliances he struck to counterbalance the effects of this treaty: Dhimitër married Kominia, the daughter of Stefan 'the first-crowned' by his first wife, Eudocia, and he also forged excellent ties with Epiros.[42] Venice, too, was obliged to make an agreement with the Epirots in 1210. This involved Michael Angelos' nominal acceptance that he was a vassal of the republic; in return, Venice recognised his control from the Shkumbi valley as far as Naupaktos.[43]

By 1212 Venice had resolved to give up the Albanian hornets' nest, abandoning its useless and awkwardly situated duchy of Durazzo (Dyrrachium) to Michael Angelos, in circumstances which remain obscure.[44] Even so, Arbanon retained its traditional ties: with Byzantium, Serbia and orthodoxy. When Dhimitër died, probably in 1215, his successor, the Graeco-Albanian

---

[37] Ducellier (1981b), pp. 75–84, 151.

[38] Ducellier (1981b), pp. 126–7; especially important is the still unedited text known as the 'Chronicle of Daniele Barbaro', Cod. Marc. Ital. classe VII, 126=7442, fol. 128, Venice; see also *DBI*, VI, pp. 94–5 (G. Alberigo); Ducellier (1992).

[39] This was despite the fact that traditional orthodoxy was not deemed incompatible with catholicism. After 1187, the bishopric of Kruja seems to have passed into catholic hands: Ducellier (1983), pp. 3–4; Ćirković (1988), pp. 348–9.

[40] Ducellier (1981b), p. 136.

[41] Ducellier (1981b), pp. 138–9; *Acta et diplomata res Albaniae*, ed. von Thallóczy *et al.*, I, no. 134, pp. 42–3.

[42] Kominia was thus a granddaughter of Emperor Alexios III Angelos: Nicol (1957), p. 26; Ducellier (1981b), p. 138.

[43] Nicol (1957), pp. 30–1; Ducellier (1981b), pp. 141–5.   [44] Ducellier (1981b), pp. 149–51.

lord Gregory Kamonas took Kominia as his second wife. He was already married to Gjin's daughter, and now requested canonical dispensation to dissolve his first marriage from Demetrios Chomatenos, the *chartophylax* of Ohrid and already a major figure in Epiros.[45] Relations with Serbia had been damaged by a Slav attack on Shkodër after the collapse of the Venetian duchy of Durazzo and these were now repaired.[46] It was against this 'orthodox bloc' that the new Latin emperor of Constantinople, Peter of Courtenay, launched forth in 1217. He took Dyrrachium by stealth on his way to Constantinople, only to vanish in the Albanian mountain passes,[47] where Theodore Angelos was waiting for him.[48]

IVAN II ASEN OF BULGARIA

This complex network of ties between Greek- and Slavonic-speaking orthodox potentates presupposed an effective Latin threat, and had as its axis the agreement between Epiros and the Bulgarians; however, this alliance could never be more than opportunistic. Bulgaria recovered its strength under Ivan II Asen (1218–41), and Ivan made no secret of his ambition to take Constantinople, which was also the target of the Epirot ruler in his struggle against his Nicaean rival. The Bulgarians also had their eye on the Adriatic, and could not forget that their ambassadors to the pope had been unable to proceed further than Dyrrachium.[49] The death of the Latin emperor Henry in 1216, and the defeat of Peter of Courtenay the following year, revitalised the three powers aiming for Constantinople: Nicaea, Epiros and Bulgaria. The latter realm under Ivan Asen enjoyed its last spell of greatness in the middle ages; from then on, its rulers were primarily concerned with undermining the Greek contenders for the throne in Constantinople, playing off the various factions. The City itself was almost within their sights by 1225, and the Latins were prompted to seek a Bulgarian alliance three years later upon the death of Emperor Robert of Courtenay (1218–28) and with the prospect of a minor, his brother Baldwin, mounting the throne. A marriage was planned between Baldwin II (1237–61) and Ivan's daughter Helena. Ivan was attracted by the prospect of gaining the regency of the Latin empire and in April 1229 he disregarded promises made earlier to

---

[45] Ducellier (1981b), p. 160.

[46] Laskaris (1926), pp. 38–53; Nicol (1957), pp. 49 and n. 6, 71; Ducellier (1981b), p. 160.

[47] GA, ch. 14, rev. edn. Wirth, I, p. 26; tr. Macrides, p. 145; similarly, Theodore Skoutariotes, *Synopsis chronike*, p. 461.

[48] Nicol (1957), p. 50; Ducellier (1981b), pp. 161–3. See above, pp. 737–8.

[49] For 1203, see the Registers of Innocent III, year 6, letter 5: Theiner, *Vetera monumenta slavorum meridionalium*, I, p. 28; Nicol (1957), p. 23 n. 24 (wrongly giving 1204 for 1203). For 1207, see the Registers of Innocent III, year 10, letter 65: *Acta et diplomata res Albaniae*, ed. von Thallóczy et al., I, no. 132, p. 42; Ducellier (1981b), pp. 123, 144–5.

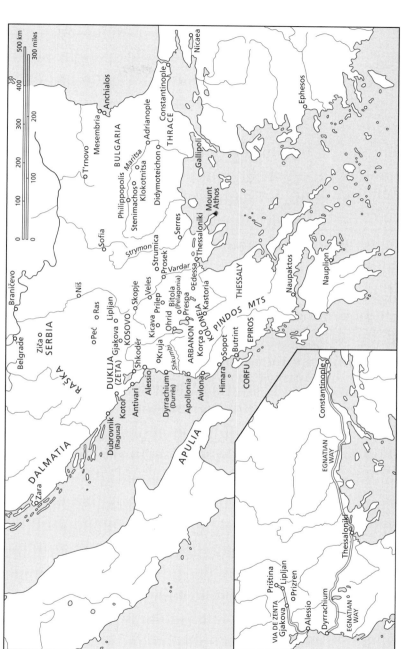

Map 40 Spanning the Egnatian Way

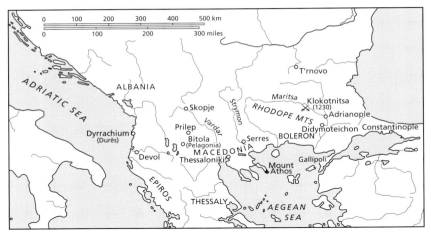

Map 41   Klokotnitsa and Ivan II Asen's counter-offensive 1230

the elderly John of Brienne. However, these plans only resulted in a breach with Theodore Angelos of Epiros.[50]

In spring 1230, taking the view that he could not march on Constantinople without first removing the Bulgarians' threat to his rear,[51] Theodore Angelos decided to attack them. He was crushed in battle at Klokotnitsa in the Maritsa valley,[52] captured and blinded; this defeat sealed the fate of the westernmost of the Greek rump states.[53] In April 1230, Ivan Asen launched a sweeping counter-offensive, gaining Adrianople, Didymoteichon, Boleron, Serres, Pelagonia (Bitola) and Prilep, as well as Thessaly and Albania right up to the gates of Dyrrachium; the town itself apparently escaped his control.[54] It is not clear whether the Bulgarians achieved their ambition of ruling from coast to coast, from the Adriatic to the Aegean. An agreement between Ivan and Dubrovnik of 1230 mentions Skopje, Prilep and

[50] Nicol (1957), p. 108, argues, on uncertain grounds, that the offer came from Ivan II Asen, while Ostrogorsky (1968), pp. 435–6, is likewise unclear. See also GA, chs. 37–8, rev. edn. Wirth, I, p. 60; tr. Macrides, p. 204, 206; Marino Sanudo Torsello, *Liber secretorum fidelium crucis*, pp. 72–3.

[51] Nicol (1957), p. 110, whose explanation is convincing, in contrast to George Akropolites, who explains Theodore's actions solely in terms of unbridled ambition: GA, ch. 25, rev. edn. Wirth, I, p. 41; tr. Macrides, p. 178.

[52] GA, ch. 25, rev. edn. Wirth, I, pp. 41–2; tr. Macrides, pp. 178–9; Zlatarsky (1970–2), III, p. 358. Klokotnitsa is the modern Semica: Nicol (1957), p. 112 n. 14. It was probably after Klokotnitsa that Philippopolis was lost by the Latins, who still held it in 1229: TT, II, pp. 267–8; Asdracha (1976), p. 242 n. 2.

[53] Nicol (1957), pp. 111–12.

[54] Nicol (1957), p. 111; Ducellier (1981b), p. 166; GA, ch. 25, rev. edn. Wirth, I, pp. 42–3; tr. Macrides, p. 179. But for the major evidence, see Uspensky (1901); Zlatarsky (1970–2), III, pp. 587–96.

Devol – acquisitions effectively barring the Serbians from Macedonia – and even Thessaloniki, but no Adriatic port is mentioned there.[55] In any case, the text of this agreement attests a revival of trans-Balkan trade to the advantage of one of the Slav powers, as economic facts caught up with military ones.[56] This also helped to counterbalance the overweening Italian presence in the region's trade.[57] George Akropolites paints quite a favourable picture of Ivan Asen's attitude towards his Greek subjects, although this was probably coloured by Akropolites' desire to cast his *bête noire*, Theodore Angelos, in the worst possible light. However, Ivan avoided Kalojan's mistakes and he does seem to have been regarded favourably by his new subjects; Ivan's recently acquired title 'tsar of the Bulgarians and of the Greeks' offered them a guarantee of sorts.[58] He hoped to give this title further substance by conquering Constantinople from the Latins. Just after his victory at Klokotnitsa in 1230, Ivan visited Mount Athos and showered gifts upon its monasteries: a symbolic expression of his role as supposed successor to the Byzantine emperors.[59] His conquests also enabled him to intervene in the affairs of Serbia, a potent rival whose alliance with Epiros he found hard to forgive. Bulgarian operations led to the downfall of the Serbian ruler Stefan Radoslav,[60] who had withdrawn to Dubrovnik, and then to Dyrrachium.[61]

However, Ivan was a realist and knew he could not take Constantinople on his own. He therefore put together a league of orthodox potentates, including John III Vatatzes, emperor of Nicaea (1221–54), and even Theodore's brother Manuel Angelos (1230–37), emperor at Thessaloniki. Manuel was Ivan's faithless son-in-law and in 1232 he had abandoned plans for church union with Rome and with Frederick II.[62] This league gave Ivan the chance to renounce Kalojan's nominal allegiance to the pope, and he hoped for an immediate dividend, the transformation of the Bulgarian church into a full patriarchate. It is likely that, from 1233, relations with Nicaea were close enough to force the 'unionist' archbishop of T'rnovo to abandon his see and retire to Mount Athos; presumably he had been

---

[55] Ivan II Asen's son-in-law, Manuel, only ruled Epiros by grace of Ivan and also accepted the subordination of his archiepiscopal see to that of T'rnovo: Nicol (1957), pp. 114–15.

[56] An example of the policy of restoring fortifications is Stenimachos, with a commemorative inscription of Ivan II: Zlatarsky (1911 [1912]), pp. 241–2; Asdracha (1976), p. 242.

[57] *Stare srpske*, ed. Stojanović, II, p. 205; *Acta et diplomata res Albaniae*, ed. von Thallóczy *et al.*, I, no. 163, pp. 50–1; Nicol (1957), p. 113 (with citation of the source); Ducellier (1981b), p. 166.

[58] Ivan signs himself thus on the treaty with Dubrovnik: Nicol (1957), p. 111.

[59] Dujčev (1965–96), I, p. 500; Năstase (1983), p. 72.

[60] Documents in *MM*, III, pp. 65–7; Jireček (1911–18), I, pp. 304–5; Marković (1952), pp. 211–19.

[61] Jireček (1911–18), I, p. 304; Krekić (1961), pp. 27–8; Nicol (1957), p. 123.

[62] Ostrogorsky (1968), pp. 436–7; Nicol (1957), pp. 116–17. On John Vatatzes and Frederick (1238), see Norden (1903), pp. 323–5; Borsari (1951), pp. 286–7.

induced to return to orthodoxy by the patriarch of Nicaea.[63] In spring 1235, the Graeco-Bulgarian alliance was further strengthened at Gallipoli by the betrothal of the future Theodore II Laskaris (1254–58) to Ivan II Asen's daughter, who had previously been betrothed to Baldwin II.[64] After lengthy negotiations with the patriarchs of Nicaea and the east,[65] the alliance was reinforced by the formal recognition of the new Bulgarian head church-man, Ioakim, as patriarch; Ioakim went to Nicaea for his consecration.[66] However, for the Bulgarians the problem was that this alliance would clearly involve abandoning any claim to the Byzantine throne; part of the price for the patriarchal title was Ivan's renunciation of his patronage over Mount Athos.[67]

From this point on, the attitude of the Bulgarians becomes rather erratic; Ivan Asen had probably not become Vatatzes' ally simply in order to acquire a patriarchate, and he must have been aware of the dangers Nicaea posed to him. After an abortive joint siege of Latin-held Constantinople in 1235–6, Ivan performed an about-turn and entered into an alliance with the Latins. He broke with Nicaea at the end of 1237, after a terrible pestilence at T'rnovo which carried off his wife and one of his children, as well as Patriarch Ioakim. Ivan believed that he was being punished for breaking his word; Bulgarian writings of this period are full of eschatological references to brilliant triumphs, but also to cautionary punishment for sins.[68] As if to confirm all these prophecies, Ivan himself died in 1241. Soon afterwards the Bulgarian lands were ravaged by a terrible Mongol and Cuman army, putting paid to imperial ambitions for a long time. Nicaea stood to benefit from the settlement of numerous Cumans on the frontiers of Asia and Europe,[69] seeing that the outer fringes of Bulgaria became very vulnerable. The population in Byzantino-Bulgarian borderlands such as the Rhodope range was in fact mostly Bulgarian, ready to assist any action by fellow Bulgarians, as it did after the death of John III Vatatzes in 1254, with long-term consequences.[70]

---

[63] Tarnanidis (1975), pp. 34–5.

[64] GA, ch. 33, rev. edn. Wirth, I, p. 50; tr. Macrides, p. 194; Čankova-Petkova (1969); Asdracha (1976), p. 242.

[65] GA, ch. 33, rev. edn. Wirth, I, pp. 50–1; tr. Macrides, p. 194; Vasilievsky (1885); Ostrogorsky (1968), p. 437; Obolensky (1988), p. 167 and n. 211.

[66] Tarnanidis (1975), pp. 46–9, 52.

[67] *Actes du Protaton*, ed. Papachryssanthou, I, pp. 267–70. On the authenticity of the key document, see also Dujčev (1965–96), I, pp. 502–3; Năstase (1983), p. 78.

[68] GA, ch. 36, rev. edn. Wirth, I, p. 56; tr. Macrides, p. 201; Tapkova-Zaimova and Miltenova (1984), pp. 505–7.

[69] NG, II.5, ed. Schopen and Bekker, I, pp. 36–7; German tr. van Dieten, I, p. 81; Asdracha (1976), pp. 242–3.

[70] GA, ch. 54, rev. edn. Wirth, I, pp. 108–9; tr. Macrides, p. 281; Asdracha (1976), pp. 64, 243. On the ethnic make-up of the local population: Apostolides (1941–42a), p. 79; Apostolides (1941–42b), pp. 93, 97; Asdracha (1976), p. 64.

THE STRUGGLE FOR MASTERY IN EPIROS, ALBANIA AND MACEDONIA

The Bulgarians had drawn Nicaea's rulers and churchmen into Thrace and both Epiros and Arbanon gained some freedom of manoeuvre from this, especially after the death of Ivan Asen. Under the despot Michael II Angelos Doukas (1230–67), who gained control of all Thessaly,[71] Epiros acquired Dyrrachium once more,[72] although in 1250 Michael II had to soothe Nicaea by allowing John Vatatzes' ambassadors free passage to Italy. Dyrrachium had not lost its traditional role as a key transit point between the Balkans and western Europe.[73]

Albania enjoyed an economic upswing during this period. The number of Italian visitors increased, and these included many Venetians, with whom Epiros' rulers were not on good terms. The inhabitants of Dubrovnik were active traders in grain, wood and animal products, making the inhabitants of the Albanian coast less economically dependent on the hinterland, and weakening their traditional ties. A local Slav-dominated merchant class was also developing,[74] assisted by the privileges granted by Michael I Angelos and Dhimitër of Arbanon, and renewed under Michael II in 1237 and 1251.[75] Around 1230, Demetrios Chomatenos noted a degree of acculturation between Italians and Dalmatians, not merely in language and law, but also in the easy co-existence of the Latin and orthodox faithful.[76] In northern Albania, however, relations were less cordial. Around 1250 Giovanni da Pian Carpini, the celebrated archbishop of Antivari, succeeded in profiting from the failure of the Slavs and Epirots to halt the Nicaean conquests; these had resulted in Michael II Angelos ceding Prilep, Veles and even Kruja, the capital of Arbanon, to Vatatzes. With the support of the friars, Carpini sought to secure the loyalty of the people of Arbanon, but this brought him up against the formidable orthodox archbishop of Ohrid. Carpini was therefore unable to gain influence over the border bishoprics of Chounavia and Polatum (Shkodër) and (in admittedly obscure circumstances) these joined the orthodox camp.[77] Even so, the catholic church's activities in the region were proceeding apace, prompting Prince Gulam of Arbanon to abandon Michael II Angelos and join the Nicaean side. Presumably Nicaea looked to him a more effective bulwark against the

---

[71] Nicol (1957), pp. 136–7, 141–2.   [72] Nicol (1957), p. 148; Ducellier (1981b), p. 167.
[73] Festa (ed. and tr.), 'Le lettere greche', pp. 15–16; *MM*, III, pp. 68–9; Ducellier (1981b), pp. 167–8.
[74] Ducellier (1981b), pp. 192–4.   [75] Ducellier (1981b), pp. 186–7.
[76] Ducellier (1981b), pp. 204–5. See Demetrios Chomatenos' *responsa* to Constantine Kabasilas, the Greek metropolitan of Dyrrachium: Demetrios Chomatenos, *Erotapokriseis*; *Acta et diplomata res Albaniae*, ed. von Thallóczy *et al.*, I, no. 164, p. 51.
[77] Šufflay (1916), p. 211; *Acta et diplomata res Albaniae*, ed. von Thallóczy *et al.*, I, no. 164, p. 51; Karpozilos (1973), pp. 46–69; Ducellier (1981b), p. 206; Ducellier (1983), pp. 5–6. After Demetrios Chomatenos' death, the see of Ohrid was occupied by two Bulgarians, but in 1252 it was the Greek Constantine Kabasilas, late of Dyrrachium, who held office there. See also Gelzer (1902), p. 12.

catholic church.[78] At the same time, Nicaea's ruler John Vatatzes renewed the privileges that Kruja had received from Manuel I Komnenos (1143–80), although it is uncertain who controlled the town at this point.[79]

The Nicaean advances threatened the interests of the Bulgarians and Serbs alike. Despite his own weakness, and thanks to the death of John III Vatatzes, the Bulgarian tsar Michael I Asen (1246–56) managed to seize control of western Macedonia all the way to Dibra in 1254, occupying Skopje among other places, although the Nicaeans recovered it two years later. A close *entente* was established between Michael II Angelos and the Serbian ruler Stefan Uroš I (1243–76), who was also interested in dominating Macedonia. It was only in 1256 that Theodore II Laskaris regained control of the route to the Adriatic,[80] recapturing strongholds in Macedonia, including Dyrrachium.[81] Not without reason did Theodore boast of controlling Sofia, Philippopolis, Veles, Skopje and even Serbia, thanks to his latest acquisitions.[82] In the winter of 1256–7, Akropolites reportedly felt free to travel around the region, making his authority felt. He convened the notables (*ekkritoi*) of Arbanon at Dyrrachium, doubtless including Prince Gulam (who subsequently vanishes from sight), and he managed to take control of their polity (such as it was) without protest, installing a thoroughly Byzantine civil, military and fiscal administration.[83] The *ekkritoi* referred to by Akropolites later came to be known as princes, and they would dominate the lands of Albania into modern times. Still loyal to Michael II Angelos of Epiros, these *ekkritoi* proceeded to lead their fellow Albanians in a massive revolt and Michael himself laid siege to Nicaean-occupied Dibra, Ohrid and Prilep,[84] regions which would later become centres of Albanian settlement.[85] However, the revolt did not involve Albania proper or Epiros itself, and Michael's ally, Stefan Uroš, turned the situation to his own advantage: he advanced into central Macedonia, seizing Skopje and pushing south as far as Kicava and Prilep.[86]

---

[78] GA, ch. 49, rev. edn. Wirth, I, p. 91; tr. Macrides, p. 250; Nicol (1957), pp. 151–2; Ducellier (1981b), pp. 168–9.

[79] Andronikos renewed this grant in 1282, as would Stefan Dušan in 1342: Ducellier (1981b), p. 169; von Thallóczy and Jireček (1916), pp. 147–51.

[80] Zlatarsky (1970–72), III, pp. 456–7.

[81] GA, chs. 63, 67, rev. edn. Wirth, I, pp. 133, 140; tr. Macrides, pp. 308, 321; Jireček (1911–18), I, p. 317; Balascev (1911); Nicol (1957), pp. 158–9; Ducellier (1981b), pp. 169–70.

[82] Theodore II Laskaris, *Epistulae*, pp. 280–1; Theodore Skoutariotes, *Synopsis chronike*, p. 526; Nicol (1957), pp. 159–60; Asdracha (1976), p. 172; Ducellier (1981b), p. 170 (with references).

[83] GA, chs. 67–8, rev. edn. Wirth, I, pp. 140–2; tr. Macrides, pp. 321, 323–4; Nicol (1957), pp. 160–2; Ducellier (1981b), p. 171. On Akropolites' approach to writing history, see Macrides (2003b).

[84] GA, ch. 68, rev. edn. Wirth, I, pp. 142–3; tr. Macrides, p. 324; Nicol (1957), pp. 161–2; see also Kravari (1989), p. 47.

[85] Frashëri (1982), pp. 208–9; on modern problems, see Roux (1992), pp. 73–4 and map, p. 77.

[86] GA, ch. 70, rev. edn. Wirth, I, pp. 145–6; tr. Macrides, pp. 328–9; Nicol (1957), p. 163; Kravari (1989), p. 47.

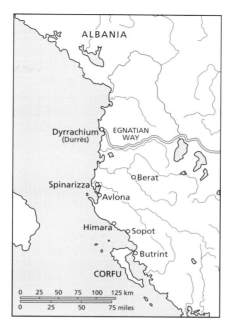

Map 42 Manfred of Hohenstaufen's acquisitions *c.* 1257, and subsequent dowry settlement by
Michael II Angelos of Epiros

Manfred of Hohenstaufen also exploited the troubles in the region, following in the Normans' footsteps. Probably around the end of 1257 he seized
part of central Albania, including Dyrrachium, Berat, Avlona, Spinarizza
and surrounding areas. This was the background to his marriage alliance
with Helena, daughter of Michael II Angelos of Epiros. Staring defeat in
the face, Michael had to recognise Manfred's right to these lands as dowry,
adding for good measure Corfu and the southern Albanian coast, including Himara, Sopot and Butrint.[87] After successful campaigning by John
Palaiologos in the spring of 1259, the Nicaeans regained control of western
Macedonia,[88] and this success was reinforced by Michael VIII Palaiologos'
(1258–82) victory at the battle of Pelagonia that summer.[89] However, Skopje
seems to have remained in Serbian hands until the offensive launched by

[87] We know of this conquest from an act issued at Dyrrachium in February 1258: *MM*, III, pp. 240–2;
Ducellier (1981b), p. 173; Geanakoplos (1953), p. 103 and n. 51; Geanakoplos (1959), p. 49. On Manfred's
dowry, see Nicol (1957), p. 167; Geanakoplos (1959), pp. 50–4, 192; Ducellier (1981b), pp. 173–4. See
now also Hodges *et al.* (2004).
[88] GA, ch. 80, rev. edn. Wirth, I, pp. 165–7; tr. Macrides, pp. 356–7; GP, II.11, ed. and French tr.
Failler, I, p. 151; Nicol (1957), pp. 176–7; Kravari (1989), p. 48.
[89] Geanakoplos (1953), pp. 135–6; Nicol (1956), p. 71; Nicol (1957), p. 182. See above, p. 749.

the Bulgarian tsar Constantine Tich (1257–77). Somehow or other, the city ended up in the Byzantine sphere of influence[90] and in 1303 the Serbian ruler, Stefan Uroš II Milutin (1282–1321), would write of the Serbs' loss of the city, although quite what he meant by this is unclear.[91] In any case, Bulgaria no longer posed a serious threat to its neighbours after 1241. In 1262 Michael VIII succeeded in occupying the coastal towns of Anchialos and Mesembria, promising them as a dowry to his niece Maria, and with the stated intention of never giving them back to the Bulgarians. A Bulgarian counter-attack in 1272 was easily beaten off, showing up the limitations of what was now a divided kingdom.

Bulgaria was riven by political instability for a hundred years, and also menaced externally by the Greeks' formidable allies, the Cuman auxiliaries of the Mongols (see below, p. 805).[92] Yet for all its troubles, Bulgaria was no cultural vacuum. In the mid-fourteenth century, the Bulgarian arch-bishop Iakov was still capable of writing passably good Greek poetry in hexameters, something only Maximos Planoudes could rival.[93] As in Serbia, there were lively manuscript workshops which carried on the Slav–Hellenic tradition; the psalters of Radomir (fig. 55) and Karadimov, the chronicle of Constantine Manasses and the Tomič psalter (fig. 54) are among their products, and they help us understand the fourteenth-century flowering.[94] New forms emerged, such as the 'teratological' (monstrous) letter designs that adorn thirteenth-century manuscripts.[95] However, two dangers still loomed on the fringes of the restored Byzantine empire: the alliance forged between the Angevin kingdom of Naples and Epiros, prompting Charles of Anjou's later intervention, and the Serbs' ambitions of conquest in Macedonia.

Charles of Anjou had taken care to include in the Treaty of Viterbo in 1267 (see above, p. 768) his right to succeed Manfred in Albania.[96] However, it was some time before he staked his claim: partly because of his involvement in the Tunis Crusade of his brother, Louis IX (1226–70),

[90] Kravari (1989), pp. 48 nn. 129 and 130 (with references), 161. Skopje was still in Bulgarian hands in 1268, when Michael VIII's ambassador to Serbia had to bypass the area: GP, V.6, ed. and French tr. Failler, II, pp. 454–5. On the frontier, see Asdracha (1976), pp. 245–7.

[91] *Spomenici za srednevekovnata*, ed. Mošin *et al.*, I, pp. 299, 313; Grujić (1933), p. 273; Kravari (1989), p. 48.

[92] Ostrogorsky (1968), pp. 451, 458. On Michael VIII's grand alliance of Kapchale, Byzantium and Egypt, see Geanakoplos (1959), pp. 81, 290–1; Mansouri (1992a); Mansouri (1992b), pp. 317–24.

[93] Iakov, *Works*, especially the poem on pp. 82–4; Constantinides (1982), pp. 82–3. See below, p. 824.

[94] *Radomirov psaltir*, ed. Makarijoska; Karadimov (Shopov) psalter, Sts Cyril and Methodius National Library, Sofia, MSS. 454 and 1138; see also Khristova *et al.* (1982), pp. 40–1; Boiukliev, 'Shopov psaltir'; Alekseev (1999), p. 187; Constantine Manasses, *Chronicle*, ed. Lampsidis; *Tomič psalter*, I, pp. 46–7. See also Džurova (1997), pp. 190–2.

[95] Džurova (1977), pp. 36–99, and plates III, p. 57, XXI, p. 75, XXIII, p. 77, XXV, p. 79, XXVII, p. 81, XXVIII, p. 82. See fig. 56.

[96] Ducellier (1981b), pp. 230–1.

Figure 54 Illustration from the Tomič Psalter

and partly from uncertainty as to how Michael II Angelos would react to such a bold move. It was only after Michael's death that Charles took over Dyrrachium, which had recently been devastated by a terrible earthquake;[97]

<hr />

[97] Ferjančić (1966), pp. 29–32; Nicol (1972a), p. 171.

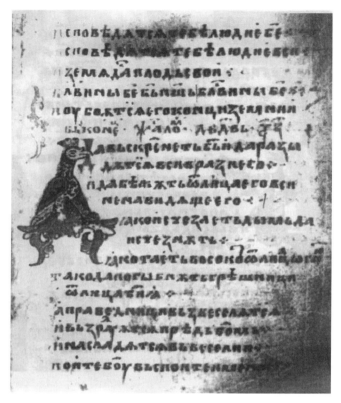

Figure 55   Illustration from the Radomir Psalter

he had himself proclaimed king of Albania there on 21 February 1272.[98]
Charles also gained Avlona, although supporters of the Hohenstaufen were
only expelled from the town in 1274.[99] Michael VIII Palaiologos was well
aware of the danger posed by this Latin coup on his western approaches,
and this made him all the more enthusiastic for union of the two churches
at the council of Lyons (see also pp. 755–6, 803–4). This effectively tied
Charles of Anjou's hands; he would now be attacking a true Christian,
whatever the terms of the Viterbo treaty, and Michael VIII could justify
his own resistance in Albania. This became the theatre for Graeco-Latin
conflict from 1272 to 1284,[100] culminating in the Angevin defeat at Berat in
the spring of 1281; local enthusiasm for the Byzantine initiatives probably

[98] Ducellier (1981b), pp. 176–7, 236–9. Despite Failler's observations in his edition of Pachymeres,
one cannot date this earthquake to 1273: the town was already in ruins before the Angevins took over:
GP, V.8, ed. and French tr. Failler, II, pp. 460–1 and n. 4; Ducellier (1981b), p. 177.
[99] Ducellier (1981b), pp. 234–6.   [100] Ducellier (1981b), pp. 240–62.

Figure 56 Six examples of thirteenth-century 'teratological' letter design

contributed to this.[101] As a result, by 1284 the Angevins had lost virtually all their conquests, Dyrrachium and Avlona among them. They retained only a fraction of the Albanian coastline far to the south, including Butrint and Sopot, which had been ceded to them in 1279 by the despot Nikephoros I Angelos Doukas of Epiros (1267–96).[102] Michael VIII's recovery of the region is symbolised by the fresco found on the outer vestibule of the church of Santa Maria of Apollonia, probably painted around this time. Michael appears with the future emperors Andronikos II (1282–1328) and Michael IX (1294/5–1320).[103] The Angevins continued their vain attempts to regain control of Albania into the mid-fourteenth century, even proposing to exchange it for Aragonese-controlled Sicily: an offer which was, not surprisingly, declined.

[101] Ducellier (1981b), pp. 253–5; Geanakoplos (1959), pp. 333–4.
[102] Ducellier (1981b), p. 249; Nicol (1972a), pp. 184–5; Nicol (1984), pp. 23–5.
[103] Buschhausen and Buschhausen (1976), pp. 143–4 and tables XXI–XXII. See fig. 57.

Figure 57 Wall-painting of Michael VIII and his family, church of Mother of God, Apollonia (Pojan), central Albania

The Angevins' conquest of Albania does, however, show the ability of the local elites to assert themselves. The *archontes* took on Byzantine or Slav titles, either coming to terms with their new master or staying true to the traditional Greek alliance, sometimes at the price of being deported to Apulia.[104] On the coasts, the Angevins' heavy-handed taxation smothered a lively local trade, in which Dubrovnik had shown signs of starting to rival Venice. Albania's major ports underwent serious decline, turning into small staging-posts where the princes only traded in grain, wood, salt, skins and dried fish.[105] Ethnic Albanians became the majority in the area, although important Greek and Slav minorities remained;[106] Pachymeres even describes the repopulation by Albanians after the Dyrrachium earthquake.[107] The divide between coast and hinterland deepened, and trans-Balkan relations would remain disrupted until the coming of the Ottomans' new order.[108] The area became socially and politically unstable. Clan ties unravelled and there was migration inland towards Macedonia and Thessaly, a precursor of the migrations to Italy at the end of the middle ages.[109] Such outflows would long delay Albania's formation as a coherent polity.

[104] Ducellier (1981b), pp. 239, 257–9.
[105] Ducellier (1981b), pp. 276–7, 286–9, especially Spinarizza (Zvërnec).
[106] Ducellier (1981b), pp. 294–5, 298–9.   [107] Ducellier (1981b), pp. 179–80.
[108] Ducellier (1981b), pp. 281–8; Ducellier (1981a), pp. 28–31; Ducellier (1987b).
[109] Ducellier *et al.* (1992), pp. 75–91.

THE CONSOLIDATION OF SERBIAN POWER: STEFAN
UROŠ II MILUTIN

In contrast to the Albanians, the Serbs who now gained ascendancy in Macedonia had a much clearer-cut national identity, for all their internal dynastic difficulties, competition from the Bulgarians and, above all, the Roman revival. The local nobles, the *vlastela*, sought to expand their territories,[110] while the Nemanjid dynasty's most imperial and illustrious ruler, the warrior and statesman Stefan Uroš II Milutin, knew how to keep his nobles happy. He adopted the Byzantine system of *pronoia* (*pronija* in Serbian), enabling him at once to reward and reinforce the nobility while at the same time curbing its excesses.[111] Serbia had come a long way during the thirteenth century, both through cultural osmosis of the many Greek elements remaining in regions under its sway, and by drawing directly on the literary school of Constantinople. This can be seen from Serbian liturgical and hagiographical literature of the period, particularly the 'Panegyric' of Mileševa.[112] There is a world of difference between the rustic conditions which the Greek ambassadors found at the court of Stefan Uroš I in 1266 and the appetite for Byzantine ceremonial and costumes noted by Theodore Metochites while he was negotiating the Graeco-Serbian peace treaty in 1299.[113]

This treaty consolidated Serbia's territorial advances of the previous seventeen years, which had seen the Graeco-Serbian frontier shift twice. The first advance of the Serbs was from a line south of Prizren and Lipljan to the outskirts of Dibra and Veles, almost within sight of Prilep and Ohrid.[114] From 1282 Skopje was definitely in Serb hands; that same year Milutin realised his ambition of reaching the Aegean Sea, when he took Kavalla, perilously close to Thessaloniki.[115] But Milutin did not simply push southwards. Mindful of his ancestors' ambitions in the Adriatic, in 1296 he exploited the death or decrepitude of his former enemies: Nikephoros, despot of Epiros, and *sebastokratōr* John of Thessaly. That same year, Dyrrachium itself came under Serbian rule, and remained so at least until 1304.[116] From this vantage-point, Milutin threatened Dubrovnik and southern Dalmatia, as his predecessors had once done, and as Stefan Dušan would do again in his drive towards the Adriatic.[117] In 1299, the

---

[110] Ostrogorsky (1967), p. 41.

[111] The first examples of *pronija* in Serbia appear after the reconquest of Skopje by the Serbs: Ostrogorsky (1967), p. 42; *Zakonski spomenici*, ed. Novaković, pp. 391–3, 608–21. The very first case of *pronija* dates from 1300: *Zakonski spomenici*, ed. Novaković , p. 614. In general on *pronoia-pronija*, see Ostrogorsky (1954) and below, pp. 810–11.

[112] Capaldo (1989).   [113] *MB*, I, p. 173; Apostolović (1902).

[114] Danilo II *et al.*, *Životi kraljeva*, ed. Daničić, pp. 107, 111; Kravari (1989), p. 49.

[115] Mavromatis (1973), pp. 329–32.   [116] Ducellier (1981b), pp. 327–8; Nicol (1984), pp. 49, 67–8.

[117] Krekić (1973), p. 398. On Dušan's conquests, see Ćirković (2004), pp. 64–6.

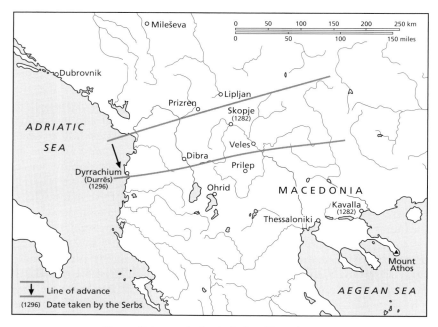

Map 43 Serb expansionism in the late thirteenth century

hard-pressed Andronikos II had no option but to acknowledge the fait accompli. As part of the peace treaty he agreed to his small daughter Simonis' marriage to Milutin, with the Serbian territorial acquisitions serving as her dowry.[118] A chrysobull of Milutin in 1303 for the Athonite monastery of Hilandar and the newly founded house of Pyrgos boasts of his achievement.[119]

Preoccupied by Serbia's apparently unstoppable expansion, the inhabitants of the Balkans would pay all too little heed to the new threat from the Turks in the fourteenth century. And, as so often in the past, Byzantium was caught between foes on two fronts.

---

[118] Simonis was only six years old, and the patriarch was unhappy about the union: GP, IX.30–1, X.3–5, ed. and French tr. Failler, III, pp. 298–303, IV, pp. 312–15; NG, VI.9, ed. Schopen and Bekker, I, pp. 203–4; German tr. van Dieten, I, p. 169; Laskaris (1926), pp. 53–5; Kravari (1989), p. 49, n. 135; Malamut (2000).

[119] *Spomenici za srednovekovnata*, ed. Mošin *et al.*, I, pp. 304–16; Kravari (1989), p. 49. For Hilandar and Zographou, see Dujčev (1966), pp. 31–2.

CHAPTER 22

THE PALAIOLOGOI AND THE WORLD AROUND THEM (1261–1400)

ANGELIKI E. LAIOU

INTRODUCTION

In the course of the fourteenth century, Byzantine society underwent a series of major changes, in some ways similar to those in western Europe, in other ways quite different, and complicated by the presence of external threats that progressively led to the dissolution of the state and the conquest of its territory. While economic, social and cultural developments show considerable vitality, the weakness of the state, radically reducing its ability to provide order and security for its subjects, could not but influence the dynamic of other developments. Innovation, in practice more often than in theory, was not lacking; on the contrary, the responses to new conditions often present interesting if contradictory aspects.

For political history, a new era begins not with the start of the century but rather with the recovery of Constantinople from the Latins by a small expeditionary force of Michael VIII Palaiologos (1258–82), emperor of Nicaea since 1258. This event, which occurred on 25 July 1261, had been long desired by the leaders of the major Greek splinter states, the emperors of Nicaea and the despots of Epiros, and it had certainly been prepared by Michael VIII.[1] The restoration of a Byzantine emperor in the old capital of the empire had certain important consequences. For one thing, it displaced the rulers' focus from Asia to Europe, as they had to deal with western claims. The papacy, Charles of Anjou, the house of Valois and the Venetians all became engaged in various efforts to retake Constantinople, so that there was hostility between Byzantium and at least one western power at almost any time between 1261 and 1314; in 1281, as in 1308, powerful coalitions were aligned against Byzantium. These were deflected, in Michael's day, by masterful diplomacy as well as by a major concession on his part. This was the acceptance, by the Byzantine emperor, of ecclesiastical union with the church of Rome.

The Union of Lyons (1274) (see also above, pp. 755–6) was undertaken to defuse the imminent danger of an attack by Charles of Anjou and his Balkan

---

[1] On the recovery of Constantinople: Geanakoplos (1959), pp. 75–115. See also above, pp. 749, 754.

allies, and indeed the papacy forced Charles to abandon his plans for a time. When, in 1281, Pope Martin IV (1281–5) decided that Michael VIII had not really implemented the union and gave full support to Charles of Anjou, Michael's diplomacy again came into play; he negotiated with the king of Aragon and others, contributing significantly to the attack of Aragon on Sicily, occasioned by the Sicilian Vespers (see above, pp. 757–8). Diplomacy as well as good luck allowed his immediate successors also to survive the western threat. But even as contacts between Byzantines and westerners became closer, through the marriage alliances of the imperial house, through diplomatic negotiations and because of the presence of Italian merchants, the threat of a western offensive kept the emperor occupied in Europe. So also did the effort to create a compact state by recovering the European territories which had been lost at the time of the Fourth Crusade. The results for Asia Minor were disastrous. The most thoughtful historian of the times, George Pachymeres, had this situation in mind when he reported the words of the *prōtasekrētis* Kakos Senachereim who, upon learning of the reconquest of Constantinople, pulled at his beard in dismay and cried, 'Oh, what things I hear! . . . What sins have we committed, that we should live to see such misfortunes? Let no one harbour any hopes, since the Romans hold the City again.'[2]

This, then, is a first contradiction of the Palaiologan state, from the beginning of the dynasty until about 1314. The recovery of Constantinople, considered a divine gift by Michael VIII,[3] forced the empire into political, diplomatic and ideological positions which were often untenable. Anachronistic voices spoke of the universal emperor, and the first three Palaiologoi tried to restore the unity of the geographic space, by restoring at least the European frontiers of the Byzantine empire. But no shadow of universality remained, and geographic integration ran counter to long-term decentralising tendencies, evident in the late twelfth century and exacerbated by the Fourth Crusade. The westerners kept part of their possessions in the principality of Achaia (Morea) and the islands, while the Greek splinter states of the despotate of Epiros and Thessaly retained their independence. The empire of Trebizond was the other Greek splinter state, although its geographic remoteness did not involve it in the power struggles for the recovery of the old Byzantine empire. Non-Greek states, Serbia and Bulgaria, had also become independent, and Serbia in particular was to witness a great expansion in the course of the late thirteenth and the first half of the fourteenth century, aided by financial resources which became available through exploitation of the silver mines at Novo Brdo and elsewhere.

---

[2] GP, II.28, ed. and French tr. Failler, I, pp. 204–5; see also GP, I.1–2, ed. and French tr. Failler, I, pp. 25–7.

[3] Michael Palaiologos, *Autobiography*, ed. and French tr. Grégoire, esp. p. 457; see also GP, I.1, ed. and French tr. Failler, I, pp. 22–5.

Michael VIII tried to make reality conform to ideological imperatives. He fought against the principality of Achaia, rather successfully, and against the Venetians in the Aegean, and tried to reduce the independence of the despotate of Epiros. In Bulgaria, he scored successes with the recovery of some of the Greek-speaking cities of the Black Sea coast, important outlets for the grain which was necessary for the provisioning of Constantinople. At the same time, Michael continued the policy of alliance with the Mongols, first begun by the emperors of Nicaea. The alliance with the Ilkhans of Persia, especially Hulagu Khan (1258–65), was a defence against the Turks, and was continued by Andronikos II (1282–1328), who tried to seal it with a marriage alliance. Michael VIII also made a marriage alliance with the Mongols of the Golden Horde, marrying his illegitimate daughter Euphrosyne Palaiologina to Nogai Khan, as a defence against Bulgaria. This, coupled with an alliance between Michael and Baibars, the sultan of Egypt (1260–77), opened lines of communication between Egypt and the Crimea, from which the Egyptian sultans got their Cuman slave troops. A remote effect, intended or not, was to facilitate the Egyptian conquest of the last crusader outposts in the Holy Land.[4]

The successes of Michael VIII have given him a rather good press, as a consummate diplomat who managed to retain Constantinople against multiple threats, and to enlarge the possessions of his state. At the same time, the cost was heavy and long-term. The policy of union was bitterly contested at home, and was soon repudiated by his successor. Worst of all was the disaffection of Asia Minor. Michael had reached the throne through deposing and blinding young John IV Laskaris (1258–61) (see above, p. 755), offspring of a dynasty which had been based in Asia Minor, and grandson of John III Vatatzes (1221–54), a much-loved emperor, whom the people of Asia Minor considered a saint. The Laskarid dynasty had followers in Asia Minor who were difficult to conciliate; so did the patriarch Arsenios, deposed in 1265 for having excommunicated Michael after the blinding of John Laskaris. The policies of the Laskarids, focused on the defence of Asia Minor, were not continued by Michael VIII; indeed forces were withdrawn from there to fight wars on European soil.[5] The emperor did not even visit the province until the end of his reign. Asia Minor was neglected, heavily taxed and suffered from Turkish attacks. By the end of Michael's reign, the sources speak of depopulation and impoverishment, calling the area beyond the Sangarios river a 'Scythian desert'. The situation was to deteriorate rapidly after 1282.[6]

[4] GP, III.3, III.5, VII.32, ed. and French tr. Failler, I, pp. 234–9, 240–3; III, pp. 98–9. See also above, pp. 758, 796, n. 92.
[5] GP, I.6, ed. and French tr. Failler, I, pp. 34–5.
[6] GP, III.22, VI.29, ed. and French tr. Failler, I, pp. 290–3; II, p. 633.

SUCCESSES AND CONFLICTS (1282–1341)

Political affairs

Despite these problems, the immediate heirs of Michael VIII had some successes. This is a time of significant contradictions: between the ideology of government and actual government, between a progressive impoverishment of the state and the wealth in some segments of society, in the ambivalent relations between Byzantium and the west. Many of these contradictions exploded in the great civil war of 1341–54, which left Byzantium a greatly altered state in a changed world.

Andronikos II and his successor, Andronikos III (1328–41), shifted once again the centre of their interest, from western Europe to Asia Minor and the Balkans. Yet they had to retain close diplomatic relations with western Europe, primarily to ward off an attack and secondarily to seek aid against the Turks. On the whole, there is a shrinkage of the areas of interest and involvement in terms of foreign policy. Here the major successes of Byzantine policy were with regard to the splinter states of Greece: Thessaly, which was acquired piecemeal in 1333, and Epiros, where the city of Ioannina accepted Byzantine overlordship in 1318, and the rest of the despotate in 1340. In the Peloponnese, the process of reconquest proceeded throughout this period; after 1349, the Byzantine possessions, organised as the despotate of the Morea, became one of the most vital parts of the state.

Relations with western Europe were successful as far as the first objective is concerned: there was, in fact, no major expedition against the Byzantine empire. The reduced Byantine diplomatic activities centred around efforts to thwart any coalition of forces that might attack the empire; that is, to make alliances with Ghibelline forces. Matrimonial policy served this purpose, as Andronikos II took as his second wife Yolande-Irene of Montferrat, whose father was allied to Castile, and Andronikos III married Anne of Savoy, daughter of Count Amedeo V. For the rest, Andronikos III had even less close relations with the west than did his grandfather Andronikos II, although the penetration of individual westerners, of western customs and of Venetians and Genoese into the empire continued apace. The second aim, an alliance against the Turks, was not successful, for it hinged upon the union of the churches, discussions on which took place under Andronikos II after 1324, Andronikos III and John VI Kantakouzenos (1347–54), but foundered upon the divergent interests of the papacy and the Byzantine emperors.

The situation in Asia Minor became the nemesis of the Byzantines. The area rapidly fell into the hands of the Turks, especially after the Byzantine defeat at the battle of Bapheus, near Nikomedeia (1302). Andronikos II made a number of efforts to remedy the situation, and for a short time, in 1294, the campaigns of the great general Alexios Philanthropenos raised

Map 44 The empire reconstituted and lost: Byzantium (a) in the late thirteenth century, and (b) in the 1330s

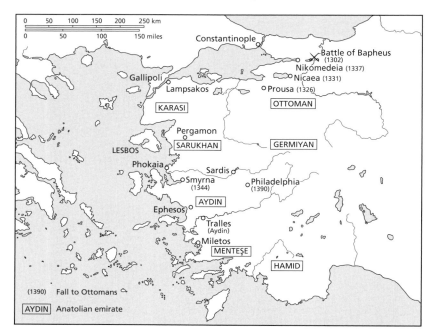

Map 45 The fall of western Asia Minor to the Turks in the first half of the fourteenth century

hopes. But he was opposed by powerful landlords in the area, was pushed into an unsuccessful rebellion, and his successes were short-lived. The countryside was rapidly brought under Turkish control, and one by one the cities were starved into submission. The Ottomans took Prousa in 1326, Nicaea in 1331 and Nikomedeia in 1337. Further south, Ephesos, Smyrna, Miletos, Sardis and Tralles (Aydin) fell to the Seljuq emirates in the first decade of the century. Philadelphia and its immediate region remained as the sole Byzantine possession, until 1390.[7] Andronikos III waged several campaigns in Asia Minor, to no avail. More importantly, after 1329, Andronikos III and, later, John Kantakouzenos had close relations of friendship and alliance with the amir of Sarukhan and with Umur, amir of Aydin. Directed originally against the Genoese lords of Phokaia and Lesbos, this became a more general alliance, in the course of which the Byzantines recognised the Seljuq conquests in Asia Minor.

The realities of government

Despite ideologically driven claims of an all-powerful emperor, in reality government became increasingly weak, and its authority and prerogatives

[7] On Philadelphia see Ahrweiler (1983).

fragmented. In the fourteenth century, the business of government was primarily connected with the collection of taxes, the army and justice. State finances were being eroded by the high cost of pervasive warfare and dwindling resources. For one thing, imperial territories were much more restricted than during the twelfth century, and Asia Minor was lost during this period, so revenues from the land tax were commensurately reduced. War, invasions and inclement weather sometimes made it impossible to collect taxes. Secondly, this was a state and a society administered by privilege. The privileges granted to the aristocracy further eroded the tax base, while treaties with Italian city-states involved commercial privileges for their merchants that considerably reduced the benefits accruing to the state from the very active commercial exchanges in this part of the Mediterranean (see below, pp. 841–4). Some Byzantine merchants, namely those of Ioannina and Monemvasia, were successful in obtaining similar privileges, which worked to their benefit, but had a detrimental effect on the state treasury.[8] The government made some effort to overcome these fiscal difficulties; after 1283, a series of new and extraordinary taxes was introduced, although the hard-pressed peasantry was not always able to pay them. Excise taxes on salt and iron were also levied, in the early fourteenth century, and were much resented. Heavy taxation resulted in annual revenues of 1,000,000 gold coins by 1321: a small sum (Michael VIII had seven times that much), and also a deceptive one, since a civil war, which started in 1321, made the collection of taxes problematic indeed. Other measures were also taken; in order to help pay the high fees of Catalan mercenaries, Andronikos II temporarily stopped the payment of palace officials and soldiers, while in 1343, during the first stages of the great civil war, the empress and regent Anne of Savoy mortgaged the crown jewels to Venice for a loan of 30,000 ducats. The jewels then became a pawn in diplomatic games, as the Venetians tried to negotiate their return against political concessions of some magnitude.[9]

The devaluation of the coinage was in part the result of the same fiscal problems, and also a short-term remedy for the emptiness of imperial coffers. The successive deterioration of the gold coin (from 17 carats in 1230–60 to less than 11 carats by the mid-fourteenth century) has been linked to specific fiscal crises, occasioned in turn by military problems.[10] Sometimes, indeed, the emperors could not meet their military expenses in coin and had to use unminted gold.[11] The issue of gold coins stopped for good at some point between 1354 and 1366, partly, perhaps, because of

[8] On the privileges of Ioannina issued in 1319: MM, V, pp. 77–84; for those of Monemvasia: Schreiner (1978); Schreiner (1981–2), pp. 160–6; Laiou (1980–1), pp. 206–7; Kalligas (1990), pp. 101–34.

[9] On Andronikos II: Laiou (1972), pp. 186–7; on the crown jewels: Bertelè (1962).

[10] For the monetary system of the Palaiologan period, see Morrisson (1991), pp. 308–15.

[11] See, for example, Laiou (1972), p. 189.

a general movement of gold toward western Europe, but undoubtedly also because the state could no longer sustain a gold coinage. Venetian ducats as well as silver coins appear frequently in Byzantine documents of the late Palaiologan period; it is likely that people preferred them to Byzantine issues.

The Palaiologan armed forces, especially native troops, were quite small in number. In 1285 the navy was dismantled, since it was expensive and the death of Charles of Anjou seemed to reduce the threat from the sea. This was a disastrous measure, much deplored by perceptive contemporaries and by people writing in the middle of the fourteenth century.[12] While small fleets were built again in the 1330s and 1340s, the fact remains that for all intents and purposes the Byzantines had abandoned the fleet, and with it the possibility of guaranteeing the security of the seas in the Aegean or even around Constantinople itself; as for the Black Sea, for centuries a closed preserve of the Byzantines, it was dominated by the Italians. Their fleets sailed freely in all these waters (see also below, p. 834). By 1348 the city of Constantinople itself was wide open to attack by the Genoese, and it took a special levy to create a fleet for its defence; not a very successful defence either. Piracy also went unchecked. The piratical expeditions of the Seljuq maritime emirates could not be countered by the Byzantines, nor could the detrimental effects on the islands of the Aegean.[13] When, in the 1330s, the Byzantines discussed with western powers a response to these raids in the guise of a crusade, the Byzantines took a good deal of time to arm twenty ships which, however, never participated in the enterprise, for reasons unknown.[14]

As for the army, native forces were small, while recourse to other expedients was very expensive. The native forces were in part composed of *pronoia*-holders. The *pronoia* is an institution which goes back to the eleventh century, and consists of the grant of land and its revenues in return for service, especially military service since the time of the Komnenoi. Michael VIII, in his efforts to gather support for himself, allowed some *pronoia*-lands to become hereditary, and also gave such lands to members of the senate. By the fourteenth century, one can find military *pronoia*-lands in the hands of two quite distinct groups: the aristocracy, who might have some of their holdings in *pronoia*-land, and soldiers of a lower social and economic level, who, at the lowest strata, might even hold these revenues collectively.[15] The civil wars of the 1320s and the 1340s increased the number of *pronoia*-grants, as rival emperors competed for supporters; the emperors also increasingly

---

[12] GP, VII.26, X.23, XII.26, ed. and French tr. Failler, III, pp. 80–3; IV, pp. 352–5, 578–83; NG, VI.3, VI.11, XVII.7, ed. Schopen and Bekker, I, pp. 174–6, 208–9; II, pp. 866–7; German tr. van Dieten, I, pp. 153, 172; III, p. 219.

[13] Zachariadou (1989b).   [14] Laiou (1970).   [15] Oikonomides (1981), pp. 367–71.

gave these lands, or part of them, in hereditary possession, which undermined the military effectiveness of the restored empire.

Other troops were paid in cash. These can no longer be considered
as constituting a standing army, since they served occasionally, and on
particular campaigns. There may have been an unsuccessful effort to create a
standing army in 1321, to be composed of 1,000 horse in Bithynia and 2,000
in Macedonia and Thrace; the small numbers are noteworthy.[16] For the rest,
the soldiers paid in cash were mostly mercenaries.[17] Occasionally, they were
Greek-speakers, such as the Cretan mercenaries in Asia Minor in the late
thirteenth century. Much more often they were foreign troops, sometimes
already formed into units. The use of foreign mercenaries, known since
the eleventh century, became more frequent in the Palaiologan period.
Italians, Alans, Catalans and others served in the Byzantine army. The
dangers inherent in using such foreign mercenary troops were realised in
Byzantium no less than in fourteenth-century western Europe. What did
not frequently occur was an effort on the part of leaders of mercenaries
to take over the government, as was to happen in Italian cities. Only once
did a comparable situation develop. To deal with the disastrous affairs of
Asia Minor, Andronikos II called in a group of Catalan mercenaries, under
Roger de Flor, to fight against the Turks (see below, p. 835). Soon, the
Catalans developed an interest in acquiring territory, and formed ties with
the kings of Sicily and Aragon, and later with Charles de Valois, husband of
Catherine of Courtenay, the titular Latin empress of Constantinople, and
claimant to its throne. They posed a great threat to the Byzantine state, but
eventually they moved on, conquered Thebes and Athens (in 1311), and set
up a Catalan duchy, which lasted until 1388.

When all else failed, and stakes were high, the emperors had recourse
to a much more dangerous expedient: the use not of mercenaries, but of
the troops of allied foreign rulers. The first half of the fourteenth century
saw two civil wars, which involved a contest for power between two rival
emperors: one from 1321 to 1328 and the other from 1341 to 1354. Both sides
appealed to foreign troops: Serbs and Bulgarians on the first occasion, Serbs
and Turks on the second. The results were catastrophic.

The administration of justice had always been an imperial prerogative
in Byzantium. Unlike medieval western Europe, where judicial authority
had been fragmented and passed, variously, to the church, seigneurial lords
or towns, in Byzantium until the Fourth Crusade, justice was in the hands
of the state, and was administered in imperial courts. The emperor functioned not only as the legislator but also as the ultimate judicial authority,

---

[16] NG, VIII.6, VII.3, ed. Schopen and Bekker, I, pp. 317–18, 223; German tr. van Dieten, II.1, p. 40;
I, p. 179.
[17] For the army, see Bartusis (1992); Oikonomides (1981).

guaranteeing good justice and acting as a judge, both on appeal and sometimes in the first instance. True, Alexios I Komnenos (1081–1118) had given
ecclesiastical courts the right to judge all matters involving marriage.[18]
True, also, the principles of imperial justice were eroded in the late twelfth
century, because of privileges granted to western merchants. Still, the real
changes came after the Fourth Crusade, in the despotate of Epiros, and in
the Palaiologan period. The emperor retained his legislative role, although
occasionally we find synodical or patriarchal decisions being issued as imperial legislation.[19] Justice, however, although ostensibly in imperial hands,
became considerably fragmented and decentralised in the course of the
fourteenth century. The Italian city-states, primarily Venice and Genoa,
sought and received extra-territorial privileges which gave them the right
to be judged by their own courts, even in cases involving Byzantine subjects,
if the defendants were Italian.[20]

In another development, patriarchal courts judged all manner of cases
involving laymen, especially before 1330 and after 1394, when imperial tri-
bunals malfunctioned; by the end of the century, it was quite common
for the patriarchal tribunal to judge even cases involving commercial law.
No wonder that, along with a manual of civil law compiled by a learned
jurist in Thessaloniki in the 1340s (the *Hexabiblos* of Constantine Har-
menopoulos), we also have a compendium of civil and canon law together
(the *Syntagma* of Mathew Blastares, compiled in Thessaloniki in 1335). The
role of clergymen in the judicial system is indicated also by their participation in the highest tribunal of the Palaiologan period, that of the 'general
judges of the Romans'. Established by Andronikos III in 1329, it was an
imperial court, originally consisting of three laymen and a bishop, and was
invested with its authority in a solemn ceremony in the Great Church of
St Sophia. Characteristically, although originally the tribunal sat in Constantinople and its authority extended throughout the empire, soon there
were 'general judges of the Romans' in the provinces; in Thessaloniki as
early as the 1340s, perhaps in Lemnos in 1395, certainly in Serres during the Serbian occupation, in the Morea, as well as in the empire of
Trebizond.[21]

Developments in finances, justice and the army show a dynamic between
the state, in the traditional Byzantine sense of a central government, and
regional forces or particular groups which were agents of decentralisation.
The central government retained its formal right to levy taxes, appoint
army commanders, reform justice and appoint judges. At the same time,
taxes tended to disappear into the hands of regional governors, while army

---

[18] *JG*, ed. Zepos and Zepos, I, p. 312.   [19] *JG*, ed. Zepos and Zepos, I, p. 533–6.
[20] MM, III, pp. 81, 92; *Diplomatarium Veneto-Levantinum*, no. 80, ed. Thomas, I, pp. 164–8.
[21] On the judicial institutions of the Palaiologan period: Lemerle (1948); Lemerle (1949); Lemerle
(1950); Lemerle (1964).

commanders often acted on their own, easily sliding into open rebellion; the *pronoia*-holders, although they held their privileges from the emperor, were not easy to control, and their very privileges resulted from and fostered a particularisation of finances and of military power. As for justice, this too was in some ways decentralised. If one compares the situation to western Europe, it is much closer to the eleventh or twelfth centuries, not to the fourteenth when states were in the process of recovering a control long lost over finances, the army and justice. In important ways, then, the government in the Byzantine empire was undergoing a transformation quite different from that of parts at least of western Europe. It would not necessarily have been negative, had not external circumstances intervened.

Social groups and social relations

Aristocrats and landed estates

Palaiologan society was more structured than at any other time in the history of the Byzantine empire. The aristocracy emerges as a group with considerable power and a high degree of consciousness of its social position; at the same time, and continuing until the end of the formal existence of the state, merchants hold an important economic position and, for a moment, lay claim to political power. These groups prospered economically, certainly until the 1340s.[22]

The development of the Byzantine aristocracy has a long history, in some ways continuous since the tenth century. When the throne was captured by two of the most powerful families (the Komnenoi and the Doukai) in 1081, some important features were consolidated, and continued into the fourteenth century. By then, this was an aristocracy dominated by a few families, linked by intermarriage: their numbers were fewer than in the twelfth century, but most could claim descent from the twelfth-century aristocracy, and those in the highest ranks could name at least one ancestor of imperial stock. Many aristocrats (and the wealthy generally) had fled Constantinople for Nicaea upon its capture in 1204. In Nicaea their power and influence had been somewhat challenged by the policies of John III Vatatzes and Theodore II Laskaris (1254–8). The first had initiated a policy which made some of the army independent of imperial (mostly aristocratic) commanders, and even issued sumptuary laws directed against the aristocracy,[23] while the second had appointed George Mouzalon as regent for his young son. George and his brothers can appropriately be termed the king's men: men from a relatively humble background, who owed their power and

---

[22] On the aristocracy: Laiou (1973); Laiou (1991b); on Palaiologan society, see also Maksimović (1981b), Matschke (1981c); Matschke (1991).

[23] NG, II.6, ed. Schopen and Bekker, I, pp. 42–4; German tr. van Dieten, I, pp. 84–5. See above, pp. 740–1.

loyalty only to the dynasty.[24] The power of the king's men was brought to a bloody end when a conspiracy of aristocrats, led by Michael Palaiologos, murdered them. In the fourteenth century, men who did not initially belong to the highest aristocracy but became powerful through office, civil or military, tended to acquire social prestige by marrying high, and only the most status-conscious person, such as the empress Yolande-Irene of Montferrat, could find fault with their social origins.[25] The most important exception to this statement is Alexios Apokaukos, who progressed from tax-collector to *megas doux* (commander of the fleet). A king's man in some respects, he followed a policy which pitted him against the most vocal representative of the aristocratic class, John Kantakouzenos, and was never considered by that class to be anything but a *parvenu.*[26]

One significant difference between this high aristocracy and that of western Europe was that the Byzantines did not have a nobility. There were no official prerogatives, no official rights and derogations, no privileges legally guaranteed to a specific class and passed from one generation to the next. Undoubtedly, there were attitudes which could eventually have led to the creation of a nobility. High birth counted for a great deal: in the twelfth century, the emperor Manuel I Komnenos (1143–80) had legislated against *mésalliance*;[27] and while in the fourteenth century there was no such state control of marriages, nevertheless matrimonial alliances were very carefully arranged. So much was intermarriage regarded as a feature of the aristocracy that one text dedicated to social reform, the *Dialogue between the rich and the poor* of Alexios Makrembolites, proposed marriages between poor and rich as a remedy for the ills and inequalities of society.[28] This suggestion also indicates a certain opposition to the stratification of society and to the place of the high aristocracy in it.

Aristocratic women played an important role in politics and society. They were the medium through which alliances between aristocratic families were made and since they had property of their own, in the form of both dowry and patrimonial property, they had considerable economic power. Names, lineage, property and family connections were transmitted along the female as well as the male line; and aristocratic women were as acutely conscious and proud of their lineage as their male relatives. As in the twelfth century,

---

[24] Note, however, that George Mouzalon married a Kantakouzene who, after his death, remarried, and is well known as the *prōtovestiarissa* Theodora Palaiologina Kantakouzene Raoulaina: Nicol (1968), pp. 16–19.

[25] Reference is to Nikephoros Choumnos, whose daughter Irene married John Palaiologos, and to Theodore Metochites, whose daughter married a nephew of the reigning emperor, Andronikos II. It was to the marriage of Irene Choumnaina with her son that the empress Yolande-Irene – western-born and not of the highest ancestry herself – objected: GP, X.7, ed. and French tr. Failler, IV, pp. 318–19.

[26] See below, pp. 822–3; JK, I.23, III.14, III.46, ed. Schopen, I, pp. 117–18; II, pp. 89, 278.

[27] Laiou (1992b), p. 44.

[28] On marriage as a remedy: Ševčenko, 'Alexios Makrembolites', pp. 207–8.

the administration of the family property seems to have been in the hands of women; and although literacy may not have reached very low in the social scale, some women of the high aristocracy were learned indeed, and patrons of literary men, scholars, theologians and artists. A number of women, mostly those close to the imperial family, became actively involved in the political and religious controversies of the period, for example Michael VIII's sister and his niece Theodora Raoulaina; the wife and mother of John Kantakouzenos (respectively Irene and Theodora); and Irene Choumnaina Palaiologina.[29]

The aristocracy, both in its highest echelons and at lower levels, was less of a Constantinopolitan group than it had been in the twelfth century. This was partly the result of the rise of regional aristocratic foci of power. Thus the Komnenos Doukas family in Epiros and Thessaly had formed independent states, as did the Grand Komnenoi in Trebizond. There were other important regional magnates, such as the Maliasenoi, the Gabrielopouloi, the Raoul in Epiros and Thessaly, and a number of families in the Morea; many frequently opposed the authority of the central government. Furthermore, with the reconquest of the European provinces, the great families of the reconstituted Byzantine empire acquired lands in Macedonia and Thrace. Typically, members of these families might also be appointed governors of one of the areas where they held their properties, so that regional economic power and political authority were often concomitant. Thus, for example, in the rich agricultural region of Serres, the Tzamplakon family had held estates since the days of the Nicaean empire; in 1326, Alexios Tzamplakon was governor of the city, and in charge of its fiscal administration.[30] The family of John Kantakouzenos, later emperor by rebellion and usurpation, had large estates near Serres; his relative, Andronikos Kantakouzenos, became governor of the city, and Andronikos' successor, Angelos Metochites, likewise belonged to a family with estates in the area.

The aristocracy remained an urban one, preferring residence in the cities to residence on their estates. But, especially in the first half of the century, it was a group whose economic power was based on land. Money was also made from abuse of imperial office and trade in foodstuffs; but land remained both an actual source of wealth and ideologically sanctioned. Despite the fact that the aristocracy was stratified, its members had in common landownership and a degree of privilege, i.e. fiscal privileges granted by the government for all or part of their estates.

The other great landlord in this period was the church. The monasteries, especially those of Mount Athos, acquired very considerable estates, which

---

[29] On female literacy: Laiou (1981), pp. 255–7; on women as patrons of the arts: Buchthal and Belting (1978); Nelson and Lowden (1991); Talbot (1992).

[30] *Archives de Saint-Jean-Prodrome*, nos. 19, 20, ed. Guillou, pp. 74–8. See also Theocharides (1963), esp. pp. 160–4.

were also tax-exempt. Urban monasteries also had property and revenues, although nothing to approach those of the great monasteries of Mount Athos. The political power of the church in this period, as well as its moral authority, went hand in hand with economic power.

The countryside was complex and variegated. Proprietors of medium-sized holdings with production that could be marketed are known to have existed. These might hold imperial privileges, and thus qualify for the label 'gentleman-farmer', like Theodosios Skaranos in the late thirteenth century. They could also be city inhabitants with rural holdings but no visible privileges, such as Theodore Karabas, inhabitant of Thessaloniki, who in all probability was also a merchant, marketing his own products along with those of others.[31] Independent peasants, who paid taxes to the state, and cultivated a plot of land primarily to provide for their families, also appear in our sources, but for the most part when they sell or donate their properties to monasteries; they are under economic stress, at least in Macedonia. In Epiros, the small landowner seems to have been more frequent. Nevertheless, the large estate, held by laymen or clergymen, is the dominant aspect of the countryside. It was cultivated in indirect exploitation, by tenants, including dependent peasants.[32]

The peasantry and country life

The Byzantine dependent peasant, the *paroikos*, is a category which proliferates in the course of the thirteenth and fourteenth centuries. The dependence is from a landlord, lay or ecclesiastical, including a *pronoia*-holder, and takes the form of payment of taxes and dues to the landlord rather than to the state.[33] There is also cultivation of the demesne lands of the landlord but, with some exceptions, labour services seem to have been rather limited, the usual number being twelve days in a year; but twenty-four days and even, once, fifty-two days are attested.[34] On lands which were not his, but which he rented from the landlord, the peasant either paid a fixed rent (*pakton*) or more commonly shared the crop, so that there was a double, or triple, source of revenues for the landlord: the tax (calculated and expected to be paid in coin),[35] the rent (*mortē* or *dekatia*, literally one tenth of the produce, although the normal arrangement would give the landlord one

---

[31] Lefort (1986b); *Actes de Chilandar*, no. 27, ed. Živojinović *et al.*, I, pp. 208–19.

[32] Svoronos (1982), pp. 167–73.

[33] Laiou-Thomadakis (1977); for the peasantry: Lefort (1985); Lefort (1991); Lefort (1993).

[34] Laiou-Thomadakis (1977), pp. 181–2.

[35] But see the case of the peasants of Paphlagonia during Michael VIII's reign: they found payment in coin a great burden, since 'they had the necessary products in more than sufficient quantities, for the land was productive, but they had little coin, because each was only producing what was necessary': GP, III.22, ed. and French tr. Failler, I, pp. 292–3. They were nonetheless forced to pay their taxes in cash, a source of great unhappiness.

third or half of the produce)[36] and some labour services. The dependence, then, was both fiscal and economic. At the same time, it must be stressed that the peasant did own property, particularly the type of property that can be cultivated without much equipment, such as vineyards, olive trees and gardens. This he could leave to his heirs (in a system of partible inheritance, traditional in Byzantium, which leads to considerable instability in the size of the holdings and is not in the best interest of the landlord, but nevertheless survived), or sell, probably without having to obtain the permission of the landlord.[37] The peasant was free in his person, and had freedom of movement.

The legal and economic position of the dependent peasant, and the existence, alongside the large estates, of medium and small holdings, is linked to a type of exploitation which is based primarily on family cultivation of small plots of land, and less on the direct exploitation of domanial reserves.[38] The peasant household in the fourteenth century was both a fiscal unit (upon which the tax was estimated) and an economic unit, a unit of production. It is noteworthy that households and families could be headed by women as well as men, although male heads of household are typical, and that there was no difference in the fiscal obligations of households headed by women. Peasant women like other women in this period could and did own property, much of it in the form of dowry.

Typically, the peasant household consisted of a nuclear family, although it is also typical that most households were extended at some stage, usually while the older generation was alive. Laterally extended households, in which siblings with their own families form one fiscal unit, whether or not they reside together and jointly own or exploit property, are also attested, with varying frequency. Their presence is undoubtedly connected to the system of inheritance and marriage, which divided the economic assets of a household with each generation, and restructured them, through marriage, to which the bride brought a dowry, and the bridegroom also brought property. Joint ownership and exploitation of landed resources, beneficial as it was in economic terms, held only for siblings and first cousins, breaking down after that.[39]

This peasant population, especially in Macedonia where the documents permit a close study, was experiencing an economic decline in the first half of the fourteenth century, visible above all in the reduction of the

---

[36] *MB*, VI, pp. 6, 620–2; see Laiou-Thomadakis (1977), p. 219 and n.121.

[37] An ambiguous text of the late fourteenth century suggests that the landlord may have a right to a tenth of the value of a piece of land that has changed hands; but it is not at all certain that we are dealing with a *paroikos*. For the text, see Fögen (1982), pp. 236–7; but also Laiou-Thomadakis (1977), pp. 44–5.

[38] Svoronos (1956); Svoronos (1982), pp. 153–73.

[39] Laiou (1992b), esp. pp. 167–70; Laiou (1998), pp. 144–60.

property of peasant households, especially the wealthier ones. There are clearly factors at work which act as barriers to the accumulation or even the conservation of peasant holdings, and these cannot include the system of inheritance, since its effects were countered by the reconcentration of property through marriage. The economic decline has been seen by some as a crisis resulting from the overexpansion, into marginal lands, of a population which had been, and was still, expanding.[40] According to this view, there was no demographic crisis in the countryside until the plague of the 1340s. A different interpretation suggests that the population had reached a demographic plateau around 1300, with a subsequent decline. We also find considerable mobility, with the migration both of entire families (among the poorer segment of the rural population) and of individuals (typically, among the wealthier peasants). There is, therefore, in the first half of the century, a crisis in rural society, whether only economic or both economic and demographic. Among its causes one must count the combined effects of wars, civil wars, plunder and pillage by troops both friendly and hostile to the state, all of which brought periodic high points to a crisis that was not yet acute.[41]

Town life and trade

The Byzantine countryside was still a source of considerable wealth, as may be seen in the great fortunes that large proprietors were able to amass. The vitality and wealth of which this society was still capable are more evident in the cities, whose role and population underwent a true transformation. For one thing, although the capital retained its importance, a number of provincial cities emerged as centres of government, primarily in the European provinces, since Asia Minor was, for all intents and purposes, lost within the first three decades. The defence of the cities by their inhabitants at the time of the Catalan attack and later undoubtedly contributed to the growing sense of independence of the urban populations.[42] Some cities acquired imperial privileges which guaranteed a certain degree of self-government in matters both administrative and fiscal.

As for the population of the cities, we lack firm numbers; Constantinople and Thessaloniki may have had 100,000 inhabitants each.[43] It included, as ever, members of the aristocracy, but also groups that are much less visible in the sources: people with landed property, both urban and rural, who might be termed the local gentlefolk, who had some comfortable level of

---

[40] Lefort (1991), pp. 77–8; Lefort (1993), p. 105; for a different view, see Laiou-Thomadakis (1977).

[41] John Kantakouzenos, writing on the first civil war, explained that in 1322 taxes could not be collected, both because of the war and because 'the peasants, from whom the taxes are primarily collected, have left their homes': JK, I.28, ed. Schopen, I, pp. 136–7.

[42] The same is true of Philadelphia in 1304: Ahrweiler (1983), p. 184.

[43] Matschke (1971), pp. 106–7 n. 3.

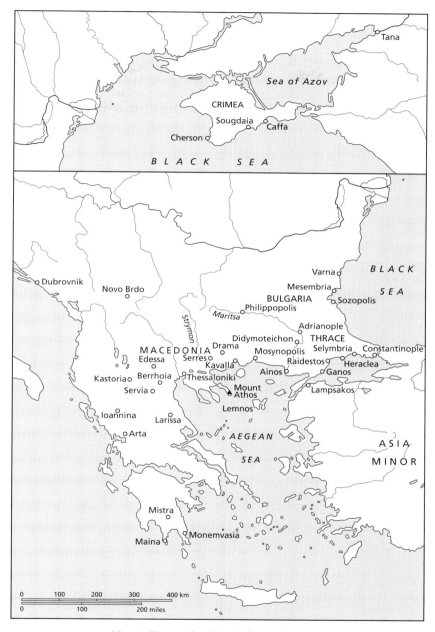

Map 46 Towns and trade in the fourteenth century

affluence and a certain political role, sometimes exercised through offices in the government of the city, including offices in the church.[44] A third group includes merchants and artisans, whose existence is attested in a large number of cities, including Thessaloniki, Adrianople, Ainos, Raidestos, Serres, Ioannina, Arta, Mistra, Monemvasia and Sozopolis. The inhabitants of the coastal cities, in contact with Venetian and Genoese merchants, had commercial activities which were more developed than those of cities of the hinterland. However, the less visible commercial activities of towns and cities of the hinterland must not be neglected.

The role of the cities and urban populations in trade must be seen in conjunction with the larger economic realities of the period. Primary among them is the fact that, until the middle of the century, the cities of Venice and Genoa, as yet untouched by the crisis that affected northern Europe, were predominant in a trading system which they had established, and which included the eastern Mediterranean, Italy and western Europe. For the countries of the eastern Mediterranean and above all for Byzantium which had given substantial commercial privileges to these cities, the result was that their exchange economy functioned within this larger system, and with a specific role: Byzantine exports to the west consisted primarily of foodstuffs and raw materials, and its imports consisted primarily of manufactured products, among which textiles and ceramics were particularly important.

Nevertheless, it should be stressed that this set of economic relations created secondary systems of exchange, in which native merchants participated actively: it was they, for the most part, who carried the merchandise along the land routes; they sailed from port to port in the Aegean, had active economic and financial relations with the Italians, and even, in the case of the Monemvasiots, a booming sea trade of their own. Secondary and dependent this role may have been, but it was significant. Thessaloniki, for example, was the hub of a trade network that included the Balkans west of the Strymon river, as well as Serbia, and reached the sea both in Thessaloniki itself and in Dubrovnik; an important part of the city population consisted of sailors and merchants (see below, p. 846). Other cities, like Adrianople, had merchants who were involved in a second subsystem, including Constantinople, Thrace and Bulgaria, and who had transactions with the Genoese in the towns of the Black Sea.[45] What the Byzantine

---

[44] I use the term 'gentlefolk' to avoid the specifically English and country connotations of the term 'gentry'. This was an urban population but they were also landowners and their wealth came from land and minor office. The *ODB* (see *archontopoulos, ODB*, I, p. 161, M. Bartusis) defines the group as 'nobility of second rank', but since there was no nobility this seems inaccurate. The study of this group remains an important *desideratum*. Among examples are the Mourmouras, Masgidas and Pothos families from Thessaloniki and Serres.

[45] Laiou (1980–1); Laiou (1985); Matschke (1970); Matschke (1971); Oikonomides (1979a), p. 46. On the economy generally, see now *EHB*; Laiou and Morrisson (2007).

merchants could not do was to engage in long-distance trade. The markets of Italy were almost closed to them.[46] As for the Black Sea, Byzantine traders probably had an uninterrupted presence here; that of the Monemvasiots should be particularly noted. The Byzantine presence became fairly massive in the 1340s, when the merchants of Constantinople profited from the conflict between Genoa, Venice and the khans of the Crimea, massive enough to provoke a war with Genoa, and a peace treaty (1352) that included a clause severely limiting the access of Byzantine merchants to Tana and the Sea of Azov. Merchants and bankers were an important group in Constantinople in the first half of the century.

Apart from the participation of the Byzantines in the regional trade which was connected with Italian commerce, there was trade between cities and their hinterland, fuelled partly by the fact that the peasants had to pay their taxes in coin, and partly by the commercialised production of landlords. There was also trade in foodstuffs between different parts of Macedonia.[47] Local production of woollen cloth is attested in Serres and Thessaloniki.[48] But this was small-scale production, for we hear mostly of imports of western cloth.

In those cities where commercial activity was most developed, the merchants (along with other urban inhabitants, including bankers and artisans) were, in this period, identified as a distinct social group. They were usually called the *mesoi*, literally, the 'middle group', being between the landowning aristocracy and the people.[49] They appear to have been conscious enough of their economic interests; they vociferously opposed Emperor John VI Kantakouzenos when, in 1347, he asked for contributions to rebuild the army and the fleet. While presumably a fleet would safeguard their commercial interests, especially in the Black Sea, it may be that their affairs were too deeply intertwined with those of the Italian merchants for them to wish to jeopardise them.[50] This is also the first time in Byzantine history where the literature mentions merchants (or those who become rich through trade) in a way which juxtaposes them to the aristocracy, but certainly includes them among the rich, in the traditional division of rich and poor.[51]

The salient characteristics of the Byzantine city of this period, then, especially of the cities most involved with trade, are the following. They

---

[46] However, notice should be taken of the presence of Byzantine merchants in Alexandria, in the late thirteenth century: *AASS Novembris*, IV, p. 676.

[47] *Texte zur spätbyzantinischen Finanz- und Wirtschaftsgeschichte*, text no. 3, ed. Schreiner, pp. 79–106.

[48] For Thessaloniki, see Matschke (1989). The evidence for production of cloth in significant quantities in this period is limited. For Serres, see *Texte zur spätbyzantinischen Finanz- und Wirtschaftsgeschichte*, text no. 3, entry 53, ed. Schreiner, p. 84.

[49] The most useful discussion is by Oikonomides (1979a), pp. 114–20.

[50] Laiou (1987), p. 103.

[51] Ševčenko, 'Alexios Makrembolites', pp. 206–7. The author himself was of humble social origins: Ševčenko, I. (1974), pp. 74, 86.

are the place of residence of members of the high aristocracy, who also hold political power. A segment of the population, involved in trade, is economically strong but does not participate in the governance of the city. There is in this relatively structured society a growing division between rich and poor, within the close confines of the city. There are, finally, times of insecurity, risk and stress, connected with political troubles. Thus after 1328 Andronikos III had to give relief to creditors impoverished by the civil war, forgiving them the interest on loans. A number of people made a great deal of money, but social tensions were present, and obvious to contemporary observers, from Thomas Magister (Theodoulos Monachos) in the 1320s to Alexios Makrembolites in the early 1340s, who bitterly complained that the rich would have appropriated even the sun if they could, and deprived the poor of its light.[52]

Social tensions, civil wars

Social tensions were to come to the forefront during the civil wars, most clearly during the second civil war, which started in October 1341, and is thus broadly speaking contemporary with other civic rebellions in western Europe. At first, this was a struggle for power at the centre: a dispute for the regency for the nine-year-old heir to the throne, John V Palaiologos (1341–91), between John Kantakouzenos on the one hand, and on the other John V's mother, Anne of Savoy, the patriarch and the *megas doux* Alexios Apokaukos. Before declaring himself emperor, Kantakouzenos had sent letters to the powerful and the military men of the cities, seeking their support; when his letter was read in Adrianople, on 27 October, three men, at least one of whom was almost certainly a merchant, aroused the people of the city, who attacked the aristocrats and burned their houses. Quickly, the civil war spread throughout the cities of Macedonia and Thrace. The most acute aspects of social conflict are visible in Thessaloniki where the opposition to Kantakouzenos was led by a group with radical tendencies, the Zealots (see below, p. 857).

In some cities, like Serres, Kantakouzenos was opposed by members of the aristocracy, and it is certain that social alignments in this civil war were no more perfect than they were in western Europe. But the main lines of division are clear: the aristocracy, of which Kantakouzenos was the richest and most powerful representative, rallied to his side, while in Constantinople, Thessaloniki, Didymoteichon, Adrianople and else-where the merchants, perhaps the bankers, certainly the sailors and, to a varying degree, the *mesoi* generally opposed Kantakouzenos, confis-cated or destroyed his supporters' property, and imprisoned many among them. In his *History*, Kantakouzenos described the civil war in self-serving

---

[52] Ševčenko, 'Alexios Makrembolites', p. 204.

statements. More telling than those is his discussion of the accession to power (in 1339) and the polity of Simone Boccanegra in Genoa. The revolution of 1339 is cast in terms of the Byzantine civil war, and he sees it as an opposition of the people to the nobles 'because they were better than they'. The story of Boccanegra is twisted, undoubtedly consciously, so that all the evils that befell Genoa can be ascribed to him, as the evils resulting from the Byzantine civil war are ascribed to Apokaukos.[53] Although causal connections between the Genoese revolution and the revolution in Thessaloniki have been disproved, the similarities in the social aspects of the conflict are striking.

Since the forces of Kantakouzenos and his allies controlled the countryside, the civil war soon took the form of a struggle for the cities. Cities were difficult to take by assault but, with the countryside looted and in hostile hands, including the Turkish allies of Kantakouzenos, they began to surrender in 1344–5. In 1345, with the assassination of Alexios Apokaukos, the situation changed drastically, and in February 1347 Kantakouzenos entered Constantinople as co-emperor. Thessaloniki resisted until 1350, when, under pressure from the Serbs, it reluctantly accepted both John VI Kantakouzenos and John V Palaiologos. In 1354, John V forced Kantakouzenos to abdicate. This may be considered the end of the civil war.

The civil war was, among other things, an abortive effort to create a state quite different from what had existed in Byzantium, one where the interests of the commercial element would be paramount, while the resources of the landed aristocracy and the church would be used for the needs of defence.[54] At exactly the same time, there was a conflict within the church, between those who adopted a mystical attitude, that posited the possibility of experiencing the Divine Light through a special form of prayer (the hesychasts), and those who believed that God may be experienced in his manifestations but not in his essence. The hesychast controversy divided not only the church but other members of society, those who were interested in theological and religious questions. While political and social attitudes and theological positions did not entirely converge,[55] neither were they parallel. Hesychasm was practised on Mount Athos, and its most vocal proponent was Gregory Palamas; hesychasts were also staunch supporters of Kantakouzenos. The controversy ended with the political victory of Kantakouzenos. He presided over a church council in 1351 which pronounced hesychasm orthodox and its opponents heretical. No wonder that Palamas,

---

[53] JK, IV.26, 32, ed. Schopen, III, pp. 197–8, 234–7.

[54] Most sources of the period refer to the confiscation of the property of the aristocracy. On Apokaukos' plans to create a state that would be primarily maritime and dependent on trade, see JK, III.87, ed. Schopen, II, p. 537.

[55] For example, Nikephoros Gregoras was a supporter of Kantakouzenos in political matters, but a bitter opponent of Palamas and hesychasm.

appointed archbishop of Thessaloniki, was twice prevented by the city government from gaining his see, and was able to enter the city only in 1350, in the wake of Kantakouzenos' triumph.

In the end, Kantakouzenos and the aristocracy won a short-term political victory, but suffered crushing long-term economic defeat. In order to win, Kantakouzenos had appealed to the Serbs in 1342 and the Turks soon afterwards. The regency also made such appeals, unsuccessfully. Kantakouzenos, however, was successful. Stefan Dušan (1331–55) gave him help, but in the process he conquered much of Macedonia, Thessaly, Epiros and part of Greece, sometimes with the agreement of Kantakouzenos, but more often without it. In 1345, he took the large and important city of Serres, and thereafter he called himself emperor of the Serbs and the Romans. The state of Stefan Dušan was large but ephemeral, breaking down after his death in 1355. His successors retained part of it, until the Ottomans conquered it after 1371. As for the Turks, both the amir of Aydin and, more ominously, the Ottomans sent large forces into Europe to help Kantakouzenos; in 1354, they settled in Gallipoli, and from then onwards the Ottoman advance into European territory proceeded rapidly. As a result, the Byzantine state that emerged from the civil war was much smaller and much weaker than before.

Cultural life

The intellectual and artistic production of the fourteenth century is impressive in terms of quantity and in quality. Modern scholars have routinely contrasted these achievements to the weakness of the state; but we have seen that there was both strength and vitality, especially in the first half of the century, not surprisingly the period when intellectual and artistic activity was at its highest. Whether one calls this a renaissance or a revival,[56] the main traits are clear.

There were a considerable number of people whom one may term intellectuals. Many were acquainted with each other, corresponded with each other as the voluminous epistolography of the period shows, were teachers of the next generation (as was the case, for example, for Theodore Metochites and Nikephoros Gregoras). Most, though by no means all, of the intellectuals came from the ranks of the clergy, the aristocracy and officialdom as, more predictably, did their patrons. These were people with a first-rate classical education in Greek; some, like Demetrios Kydones and the monk Maximos Planoudes, also knew and translated Latin. They were polymaths, who wrote on a large number of subjects, including theology, mathematics, astronomy and geography. The latter was of particular importance in the late thirteenth and early fourteenth centuries: Planoudes

---

[56] For the two opposing views, see Runciman (1970); Ševčenko, I. (1984).

is responsible for commissioning the first extant Ptolemaic *Geography* with the full twenty-seven maps.[57] They were also editors and commentators of texts. Finally, the period has considerable literary production, both in high Greek and in the popular language. The great centres of intellectual life were Constantinople (until the 1330s), Thessaloniki and Mistra. But smaller cities could also boast of intellectuals, and artistic production of high quality may be found in the provinces.

The causes of this revival are multiple. The recovery of Constantinople was in itself a stimulus, although there were highly educated people in the empire of Nicaea.[58] Political vicissitudes also influenced attitudes. The profound interest in antiquity, responsible for classicising styles both in writing and in art, may well be connected to new concepts of self-identification which included identification with the ancient Greeks, the Hellenes; this was already clearly evident in the late twelfth century, when intellectuals posited a cultural identification with ancient Greece, to contrast themselves to the westerners.[59] Patronage played an important role. Emperor Andronikos II was deeply interested in intellectual matters, and his most important officials (Nikephoros Choumnos and Theodore Metochites) were among the major scholars of the day. There was, besides, still sufficient money to permit intellectual and artistic production.

Until the end of Andronikos II's reign the imperial court functioned as an important patron. Michael VIII called himself a new Constantine, and he was the first to invest in the rebuilding not only of the walls but of the city which had greatly suffered during the Fourth Crusade and the Latin occupation. The Deesis mosaic in St Sophia is thought to have been made just after the reconquest (fig. 58).[60] Members of the highest aristocracy, relatives of this emperor and his successor, participated in the rebuilding, primarily through the restoration and expansion of monasteries and churches; women were important patrons. The mosaics and frescoes of the period, both in Constantinople and in Thessaloniki, were of the highest quality. Perhaps the best among them are the mosaics and frescoes in the church of the Chora monastery (Kariye Djami), the result of the patronage of Theodore Metochites (fig. 59). It seems that building churches and palaces was considered an important attribute of the aristocracy. The production of manuscripts also flourished, again with some women as patrons.

Aristocratic patronage was also important in other parts of the fourteenth-century Greek world, Thessaly for example. By contrast, it has

[57] This is Codex Urbinas gr. 82, lavishly illustrated, perhaps for Andronikos II. The two other oldest such manuscripts of Ptolemy's *Geography*, Seragliensis gr. 57 and Fabricius gr. 23, are also attributed to Planoudes' activities: Harley and Woodward (1987), I, pp. 191–2, 269–70. See also fig. 67.

[58] For example, George Pachymeres was educated both in Nicaea and in Constantinople, under George Akropolites who was educated in Nicaea. See above, pp. 751–2.

[59] Laiou (1991a), esp. pp. 77–81. See also above, p. 751.

[60] On building activities in the early Palaiologan period, see Talbot (1993); Ousterhout (1991).

Figure 58 The Deesis mosaic in St Sophia, probably made soon after Michael VIII's recovery of Constantinople, which became an imperial capital again; the Mother of God and John the Baptist are shown revering Christ

Figure 59 Grand Logothete Theodore Metochites, mosaic in the church of the Chora monastery, Constantinople

recently been pointed out that in Thessaloniki and Macedonia much of the building was due to ecclesiastical, especially episcopal, patronage.[61] The church of the Holy Apostles in Thessaloniki was built by Patriarch Niphon I (1310–14), while the monasteries of Mount Athos were also important centres of artistic activity. Ecclesiastical patronage reflects the increasing economic and political power of the church.

The period of the civil war and the crises of the mid-fourteenth century brought about changes and a significant reduction of activity, especially in the production of art. Characteristically, when the great eastern arch and part of the dome of St Sophia collapsed (1346), the impoverished John VI sought money for its restoration from the Rus and the inhabitants of the City.[62] In the despotate of the Morea, the patronage of the court of the despot was very active, and the superb frescoes of the Peribleptos date from the second half of the century. Monumental mosaics, a much more expensive medium, were not produced after the 1320s; the mosaics in the great eastern arch, the two eastern pendentives and the dome of St Sophia, completed c. 1354–5, constitute an exception.

The cultural and artistic developments of the fourteenth century also serve as reminders of the fact that Byzantium of this period had an influence far exceeding its political boundaries. Byzantine culture radiated both in the orthodox world (the Slavs, the Georgians, the former Byzantine possessions under Italian occupation) and in the west, carried by artists (among them Theophanes the Greek) who worked in other orthodox states and by intellectuals who began the migration to Italy that would intensify in the fifteenth century.

THE COLLAPSE OF THE STATE AND THE REDISTRIBUTION OF AUTHORITY (1354–1402)

In the second half of the fourteenth century, Byzantium was a tiny and disjointed state in a Mediterranean world that was undergoing its own crisis. Reduced economic circumstances exacerbated the antagonism of Venice and Genoa, which became involved in and fostered the virtually endemic Byzantine dynastic wars, while they also fought for possession of territory, such as the island of Tenedos, which eventually led to the war of Tenedos, otherwise known as the war of Chioggia (1378–81), in which the Byzantines became involved (see below, p. 839). After 1354, the Byzantine 'empire' consisted of Constantinople, Thrace, Thessaloniki (which by now could only be reached by sea) and its immediate hinterland, the islands of the northern Aegean and the despotate of the Morea in the Peloponnese. Even those possessions were insecure, since Thrace was being subjugated

[61] Rautman (1991).   [62] Mango (1962), pp. 66–7.

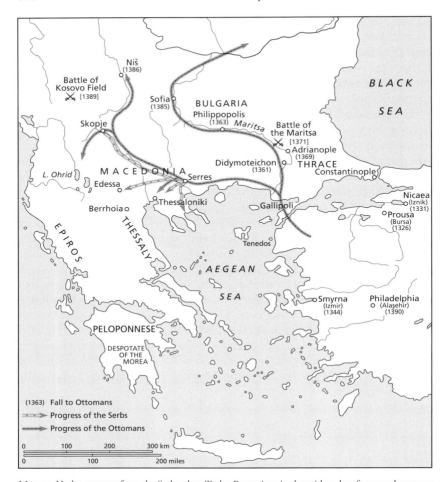

Map 47 Under pressure from the Serbs, then Turks: Byzantium in the mid- to late fourteenth century

by the Ottomans. Raids were soon followed by the conquest of cities,
Didymoteichon falling in 1361, Philippopolis in 1363 and Adrianople in
1369. With the fall of the latter, the road to Macedonia and Bulgaria was
open. In 1371 the Ottoman victory at the battle of the Maritsa destroyed the
Serbian state of Serres; the city passed into Byzantine hands, but only until
1383. At the same time, the Byzantine and Serbian rulers became tributary
to the Ottoman sultan; John V and later his son, Manuel II Palaiologos
(1391–1425), were forced to follow the sultan on campaign.[63]

[63] In 1390–1 Manuel, who fought with the Ottomans in Asia Minor against the other Turkish
emirates and the last Byzantine city, Philadelphia, gave in his letters a moving account of the decline of

After 1371, the Byzantine emperors could rule only with the help or forbearance of the Venetians, the Genoese and the Ottomans. The struggles for the throne among members of the imperial family only exacerbated their dependence, as each sought the help of one or another of these powers. True, there were some efforts to resist these trends. Thus Manuel Palaiologos, later emperor, at a time when he was at odds with his father, went secretly to Thessaloniki, where he established what Demetrios Kydones called a 'new authority'. For a short time he was able to launch expeditions against the Turks; but his successes, though heartening to Byzantines and western Europeans alike,[64] were short-lived, as may be seen by the fall of Serres to the Ottomans in 1383 and of Thessaloniki in 1387. The city, cut off from its hinterland, suffered from lack of food and its population was rent by social tensions and factional disagreements. Even its archbishop abandoned it in 1386–7, along with some of the clergy. Manuel, too, was forced to leave Thessaloniki. He eventually returned to Constantinople, where, in 1391, he succeeded his father on the throne. The first Turkish conquest of Thessaloniki lasted until 1403 (see also below, pp. 857–8).

The other avenue of resistance that some Byzantines could contemplate was cooperation with and help from western Europe. There were sufficient economic and political ties to make such hopes possible, and furthermore by now some of the leaders of western Europe, especially the papacy, were considering the Ottoman advance a threat to Christendom. But Venice and Genoa, weakened by the crises of the mid-century, were pursuing their own interests; France and England were engaged in the Hundred Years War, and the papacy made its help contingent upon a union of the churches, on its own terms. But although there were people in Byzantium who worked actively for the union, the church in general and a large part of the population opposed it. Successive Byzantine emperors (John V, John VII and Manuel II) went to the west in search of aid, but in vain. John V even made a personal conversion to catholicism; an official union was not proclaimed until the Council of Florence (1439) but by then it was much too late. Expeditions such as that of Count Amedeo VI of Savoy were mere palliatives, and the crusade of Nikopolis (1396) was a disaster.

The political crisis was attended by a general economic crisis, as well as a redistribution of dwindling resources and of political power. As in western Europe, there is a general reduction of the population, both in the countryside and in the cities. The picture of the countryside of Thrace and Macedonia is one of devastation and depopulation. The contribution of

the former Byzantine possessions and the population's plight: Manuel II Palaiologos, *Letters*, ed. and tr. Dennis, pp. 42–9, 54–7.

[64] Barker (1969), pp. 47–9; Demetrios Kydones, *Correspondance*, ed. Loenertz, II, p. 175, line 80; German tr. Tinnefeld, III, p. 93.

the Black Death remains an unknown factor. While there is evidence of plague in Constantinople, Macedonia, the Morea, the islands of the Aegean and Mount Athos, there are no particulars that might permit a study of its effects on various segments of the population. In 1384, Patriarch Neilos spoke of the flight of peasants from church lands, attributing it to the invasions.[65]

The aristocracy as a group underwent significant changes in this period. The civil war had impoverished many of them, while the successive conquests of Macedonia by Serbs and Ottomans resulted in a redistribution of property into the hands either of the conquerors, or of those members of the aristocracy who were favourable to them, or of the church. When Byzantine power was temporarily restored in such areas, there were long disputes over the recovery of lands lost by particular families or individuals.[66] Secondly, the aristocracy now became much more involved in trade than it had ever been before, a trend that continued into the fifteenth century.[67] Powerful men who bore aristocratic names invested in commercial and banking activities, closely tied to those of Genoese and Venetian merchants. Emperor John VII seems to have exported grain to Genoa in the 1380s, through his agents. Indeed, despite the great political uncertainty and periodic acute crises in foodstuffs, the grain trade was an active one; some Greeks even brought grain to Caffa in 1386. Moved by hardship, and also by the possibilities trade offered, aristocratic Constantinopolitan ladies invested in commerce with funds from dowry property, despite legal strictures on the use of dowry goods in risky ventures.

A third characteristic of the aristocracy is an increase in the importance of the local aristocracy or gentlefolk, the *archontopouloi* or *archontes* of the Greek sources, the *gentilhomeni picioli* of the Venetian sources.[68] In Serres, they formed part of the ecclesiastical and civil administration of the city under Serbian rule, and some reappear during the first stages of Ottoman rule; so also in Thessaloniki during the first Ottoman occupation. In Ioannina in 1411 they, along with the higher aristocracy, decided on the fate of the city. The emergence of the 'gentlefolk' may be connected with the final stages of decentralisation, which, by cutting the cities off from the capital, placed more decisions in the hands of their inhabitants;[69] it is also

---

[65] MM, II, pp. 61–2.
[66] See Oikonomides (1980); Laiou (1985). John V issued an edict, probably in 1373, which declared that all lands taken illegally from their owners should be restored; but it did not have much effect.
[67] Oikonomides (1979a), pp. 120–2; Laiou (1982), pp. 105–9.
[68] Mertzios (1947), p. 49. The document distinguishes three categories: *gentilhomeni e gentilhomeni picioli e stratioti*. See also Necipoğlu, 'Byzantium between the Ottomans and the Latins' (PhD thesis, 1990); Necipoğlu (forthcoming).
[69] Zachariadou (1989a).

a further sign of the redistribution of power among the upper class. While the enhanced role of the gentlefolk is probably a long-term development (these are families with significant continuity, at least during the fourteenth century), the increased independence of the city populations took place in conditions of crisis, and was typically exercised in decisions to surrender the city to various conquerors.

The most enduring transfer of power of all kinds was to the church collectively, and the monasteries of Mount Athos in particular. Long circumscribed by the existence of a strong central imperial power, the church now expanded its authority and activities and in some ways supplanted the state. The resolution of the hesychast controversy gave the conservative and fiercely orthodox part of the church spiritual and moral power (see also below, p. 857). The weakness in imperial government can be seen in the increase of the church's role in judicial matters and also in what may be termed relief functions, such as caring for the poor, the refugees or the inhabitants of cities in distress. As for economic resources, the monasteries of Athos profited from donations by the Serbian and Wallachian rulers and from privileges granted by the Ottomans; in return, Mount Athos accepted Ottoman overlordship early, perhaps before the conquest of Macedonia.[70] The monasteries also profited from transfers of landed property on the part of aristocratic lay landowners, who could no longer exploit their lands successfully.

The state was well aware of the fact that the church was now the only institution which had resources capable of being tapped. Several times in the course of the century, emperors tried to persuade either the patriarch or other churchmen to give or rent to them church lands, so that soldiers could be compensated from the revenues. But this was usually refused, and Manuel Palaiologos' attempts to confiscate church property in the first phases of the siege of Thessaloniki occasioned a violent outburst on the part of the archbishop. In 1371 Manuel, in desperate straits, took away from the monasteries of Athos and the church of Thessaloniki half their properties, to turn them into *pronoiai* and give them to the soldiers, 'so as to avoid the complete loss of everything'.[71] Part of these lands were restored to the monasteries after 1403. The church, then, wealthy, powerful and with a moral and spiritual sphere of influence that transcended the Byzantine state, encompassing as it did the entire orthodox world, was poised to play a primary role after the Ottoman conquest of Constantinople in 1453.

As the century drew to a close, the only compact Byzantine possessions were in the Peloponnese, where Manuel, the son of John Kantakouzenos,

---

[70] Oikonomides (1976c).   [71] Manuel II Palaiologos, *Prostagma (1408)*, ed. Mošin.

had formed a small but viable state, the despotate of the Morea. Although it, too, suffered Turkish raids, it was relatively prosperous, with a powerful and independent-minded aristocracy, and its capital, Mistra, had considerable intellectual and artistic achievements.[72] It was to survive the fall of Constantinople by seven years. Constantinople, on the other hand, was blockaded by Sultan Bayazid I (1389–1402) for eight long years. Neither the efforts of John le Maingre, Marshal Boucicaut, who had been sent by Charles VI of France with 1,200 soldiers, nor the journey of Manuel II to western Europe to seek aid, would have been sufficient to save the City from the siege and the attendant hunger and suffering. Many inhabitants fled the City, and some were ready to negotiate its surrender.[73] Only the defeat of the Ottoman forces by Timur at the battle of Ankara (1402) granted the Byzantine capital, the despotate of the Morea and the empire of Trebizond another half-century of life (see below, pp. 839, 852).

CONCLUSION

The economy, social structure and political orientation of the Byzantine state were all transformed through the crises of the fourteenth century. The decision to recover Constantinople in 1261 led, on the one hand, to a chimeric dream of reconstituting the old empire, thus negating the reality that, since the late twelfth century, the strongest forces in that area favoured decentralisation, which would have led to smaller, more homogeneous political entities with, perhaps, strong economic and cultural links with each other. The recapture of Constantinople led to another important choice: the orientation toward western Europe which Michael VIII followed almost single-mindedly. This choice, however, could not be retained at the political level. At the economic level, the Byzantine economy of exchange and manufacturing became inextricably connected with the Italian economy. Close cultural contacts with Italy also existed. Internally, there were, in the course of the century, profound changes in the structure of the dominant classes, of the cities, the merchant class. Many of these developments were advantageous to new social groups and new structures just as they harmed old ones; the great civil war resulted from such conflicts, but failed to resolve them. The most serious problem of the Byzantine empire in this period was that its internal development was thwarted and shaped under intense pressure from foreign and hostile powers, the Serbs for a

---

[72] On the despotate of the Morea, see Zakythinos (1975).

[73] *Byzantinischen Kleinchroniken*, ed. Schreiner, I, pp. 184–5; Laonikos Chalkokondyles, *Historiarum demonstrationes*, II, ed. Darkó, I, p. 77; Duc., XIII.7, XIV.1–3, ed. Grecu, pp. 78–9, 80–3; tr. Magoulias, pp. 83, 85–6.

short while, and the Ottomans. As a result, no viable units could coalesce from the process of decentralisation, for surely individual cities, even with their hinterland, were not viable units. The despotate of the Morea was an exception, but its fate followed inexorably that of the rest of the empire and indeed of the Balkans, which eventually were reunited under a new imperial power, the Ottoman state.

CHAPTER 23

LATINS IN THE AEGEAN AND THE BALKANS
(1300–1400)

MICHEL BALARD

By the beginning of the fourteenth century, the Byzantine reconquest of 1261 had made its mark on Latin expansion in the Aegean and the Balkans. With the treaty of Nymphaion on 13 March 1261, Michael VIII Palaiologos (1258–82) granted the Genoese access to the Black Sea. Similar access was granted to the Venetians in the years that followed, and their principal conquests since the Fourth Crusade were recognised. A chain of trading posts and ports of call thus stretched along the main sea routes and was dominated by the Italian maritime republics; Andronikos II Palaiologos (1282–1328) had abandoned the maintenance of a Byzantine fleet as too costly (see above, p. 810). At the heart of this nexus of great trade routes, leading from Italy to Constantinople and the Black Sea, Cyprus and Lesser Armenia, Syria and Alexandria, was the Aegean. Control of its coasts and islands became a vital necessity for the Italian maritime republics and the object of frantic competition; from this sprang the three 'colonial' wars between Genoa and Venice in the course of the fourteenth century. Their only result was a de facto carve-up of the Aegean: Venice had the western and southern coastline, with Messenia, Crete and Negroponte, Genoa the eastern coasts with Chios, Lesbos and the islands of the northern Aegean, while the Catalans would disrupt this Italian maritime and commercial hegemony through their seizure of the duchy of Athens and rapid development of piracy.[1]

As a result, the Aegean and the Balkans found themselves part of a mercantile economy geared to satisfying the needs of the west for foodstuffs and raw materials. They entered a colonial-style exchange system, receiving artisanal products from the west – mainly woollen cloths and linen – in exchange for supplying all that was needed for their manufacture. Local and regional trade was subordinated to the fluctuations and rhythms of long-distance trade dominated by the Italians, to whom Greek traders deferred.[2] These trends were established in two successive phases over the century following the restoration of the Byzantine empire in 1261, and we need to

---

[1] Thiriet (1975); Balard (1978); Pistarino (1990c).
[2] Jacoby (1989b); Balard (1997a); Laiou (1997).

examine these phases before going on to consider the mercantile economy's infrastructure, trade routes and commodities.

THE PHASES OF WESTERN EXPANSION

By the beginning of the fourteenth century, Genoa and Venice were emerging from over four years of conflict, provoked by the Venetians, but which ended with their defeat near the island of Curzola (Korčula) in September 1298. During the war, Andronikos II had sided wholeheartedly with the Genoese, only to be abandoned by them when the Genoese concluded their own peace with the Venetians with the treaty of Milan (25 September 1299). This treaty established their respective spheres of influence. During the war Venice had finally halted Michael VIII's Byzantine reconquest of the Aegean, adding a few islands to its existing possessions. Henceforth, Venetian authority extended firmly over Crete, the partly reconquered Cyclades, Coron and Modon in southern Messenia, and Negroponte (shared with three Latin lords, the *terciers* or *terzieri* in Italian). Venice retained considerable influence in the principality of Achaia (Morea), which Charles II of Anjou (1285–1309) had recently taken from Isabel of Villehardouin and put under the authority of his own son, Philip of Taranto (see above, p. 768). The Venetians enjoyed complete freedom to trade in the Morea and established themselves in its main ports, Clarence and Patras.

The Genoese had gained the rich alum pits of Phokaia on the coast of Asia Minor in the 1260s (see also above, p. 757). In 1304 their admiral Benedetto Zaccaria seized Chios, to protect his trade, and succeeded in securing recognition of the occupation of the island from the *basileus*. At the same time, the Catalan Company, mercenaries rashly summoned by Andronikos II against the Turks and left without pay from the imperial treasury (see above, pp. 809, 811), extended their influence across the Aegean; they ravaged Thrace and then Macedonia, before going on to conquer in 1311 the duchy of Athens, where they remained until 1388. As for the Angevins, they tried to resist the Greek despots of the Morea and began to favour a degree of Italianisation in the principality of Achaia at the expense of the French element which had predominated under the Villehardouins.[3]

The first half of the fourteenth century, at least until 1348, saw all parties consolidate their positions. Venice refused to participate in Charles de Valois' plans for the reconquest of Constantinople and drew closer to Byzantium; a new agreement concluded in 1324 compensated Charles for the losses he had suffered. Five years earlier, a treaty had been signed between Venice and the Catalans, who had been threatening the Venetians' measures to strengthen their authority over the *terciers* in Negroponte. Venice

---

[3] Topping (1975a); Topping (1975b); Jacoby (1997a); Bon (1969); Balard (2002); Laiou (1972).

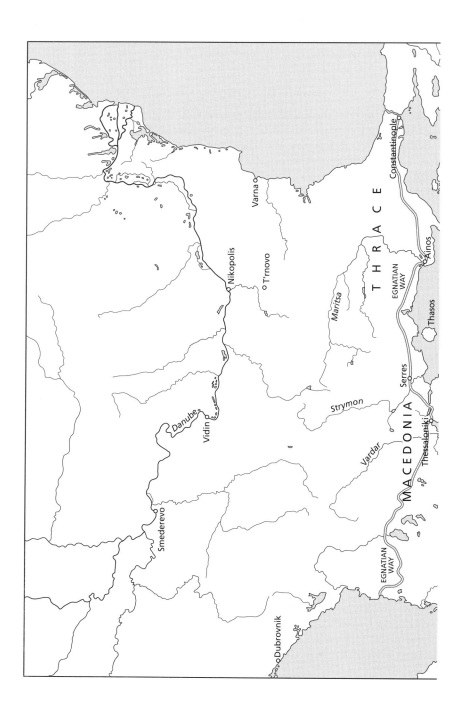

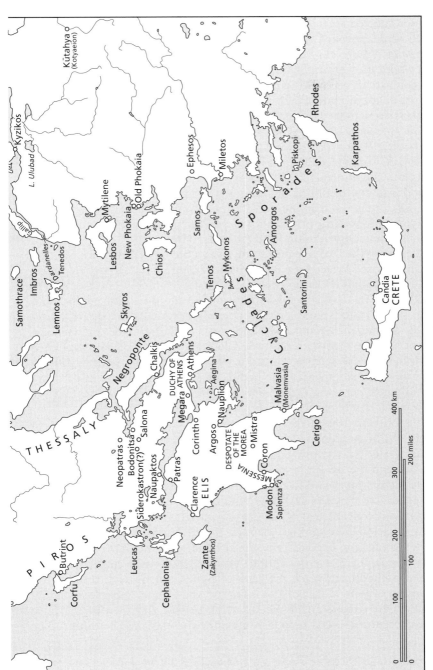

Map 48 Greeks and Latins in the Aegean and Balkans

did not succeed in fully subduing the Cretan revolts of 1332 and 1341, which were provoked by the excessive demands and levies of the local *dominante*. Above all, Venice engaged in the struggle against the Turks, with whom the Catalans had no hesitation in allying: the Venetians played a major part in the Christian union of 1332, the naval league of 1344–5 and the dauphin Humbert II de Viennois' crusade in 1345. In Greece, the Catalans strengthened the duchy of Athens under the control of their vicar-general Alfonso Fadrique (1318–30), seizing Neopatras and Siderokastron, and halting Walter of Brienne's attempt to recover his dukedom. But in 1315–16, the infante Ferrante of Majorca failed in his bid to exploit his rights over the principality of Achaia, which passed from John of Gravina's authority to that of Robert of Taranto. The latter's mother was Catherine de Valois, titular Latin empress of Constantinople, who granted substantial land concessions in the principality to the Florentine banking family of the Acciaiuoli, in compensation for their loans to her.

The fate of the Genoese possessions was more unsettled. Since Martino Zaccaria refused to recognise Byzantine sovereignty over his Aegean possessions, Andronikos III Palaiologos (1328–41) drove him out of Chios in 1329 and Phokaia in 1340, which both returned to the Byzantine empire for a while. But in 1346, exploiting the weak regency of Anne of Savoy and Humbert de Viennois' hesitant leadership of his eastern crusade, the Genoese fleet of Simone Vignoso recaptured Chios and then Phokaia, installing a government of the *mahona* there; this would last for two centuries and was made up of the shipowners who had financed the expedition. In February 1347 an agreement was signed between the Genoese commune and the shipowners, clearly outlining each party's rights on Chios.[4]

This brilliant feat of reconquest, together with Genoese attempts to control traffic to Constantinople and the Black Sea, sparked off the war of the Straits (1351–5) pitching Genoa against a coalition of Venice, the Catalans and the Byzantine empire. The battle of the Bosporus – a hard-fought victory for Genoa in February 1352 – was offset by Venetian success at Alghero (see above, p. 821). The Visconti were instrumental in the peace negotiations concluded at Milan in 1355, whereby the two republics agreed to stop attacking one another; they also agreed that for the next three years neither would send fleets to Tana, the key trading point on the Sea of Azov. The only major effect of this conflict in the Aegean was to enable the Turks to take Gallipoli and reach the gates of Byzantium. In 1355, through the friendship of John V Palaiologos (1341–91), the Genoese Gattilusio family obtained the concession of the island of Lesbos, and then in the early fifteenth century several islands in the northern Aegean. Thereafter, a key

[4] Setton (1975a); Bon (1969); Housley (1992); Argenti (1958), III; Balard (1978); Balard (1997b); Hiestand (1996).

objective for the Venetians was to maintain free passage through the Straits to the Black Sea. Although they gained from the *basileus* the concession of Tenedos at the mouth of the Dardanelles, their occupation of the island in 1376 triggered fresh hostilities with Genoa, the so-called 'war of Chioggia' (see above, p. 827). Essentially an Adriatic conflict, like the previous wars this ended in a stalemate with the treaty of Turin in August 1381.

These rivalries prevented any effective Christian union against the Turks, whose progress in the Aegean was inexorable; they raided the Peloponnesian coast incessantly, and captured Thessaloniki in 1387, taking Neopatras and Salona in 1394. They also blockaded Constantinople, and although pressure on the City was relieved by Boucicaut's expeditionary force, it was only the Turks' crushing defeat at the hands of Timur in 1402 that broke the siege (see above, p. 832 and below, p. 852). To meet these pressing dangers, Venice strove to strengthen Graeco-Latin *Romania* through a policy of annexation. It purchased Nauplion and Argos in 1388 from Marie of Enghien, widow of Pietro Corner and heiress to these lordships, and tightened its control over Negroponte and the Cyclades. The Venetians also enlarged their territory of Coron and Modon in Messenia, took over temporary administration of Patras, and finally offered direct, if ill-fated, aid to the Latin crusaders at Nikopolis in 1396. Crete was their one weak point. The island revolted again from 1363 to 1367, under the leadership of the Venetian fief-holders Gradenigo and Venier, in league with Cretan *archontes* such as John Kalergis. The rebellion was against the weight of taxation imposed by the *Dominante* and its rejection of any debate on the matter with a Cretan deputation. An army of mercenaries sent from Venice suppressed the rebellion with ferocious reprisals. Overall, Venice succeeded in holding her possessions together and protecting them from the Turkish advance, even though it may have aroused the hostility of the Greeks or the petty Latin lords of the Peloponnese.[5]

There were profound changes in mainland Greece in the second half of the fourteenth century. In 1348, when the Greek despotate of the Morea was being established, Stefan Dušan (1331–55) annexed Thessaly and Epiros to his Serb dominions. Great Latin lordships were created: Niccolò Acciaiuoli, grand seneschal of the kingdom of Sicily, was the largest fief-holder of the non-Greek part of the Morea with lands in Messenia, Elis and Corinthia, while his cousin Giovanni was archbishop of Patras from 1360 to 1365. On Niccolò's death, his cousin Nerio inherited part of his Moreot possessions, lost them to the Navarrese Company, but took Megara from the Catalans; most importantly, his acquisition of Athens in 1388 brought eight decades of Catalan occupation to an end. The Tocchi ruled Leucas, Cephalonia and Zante and sought to seize Corinth on the death of Nerio Acciaiuoli in

[5] Thiriet (1975); Gallina (1989); Lock (1995).

1394. Finally, we cannot ignore the remarkable good fortune of the Genoese Zaccaria family, heirs of Martino, the former master of Chios. Centurione I Zaccaria was grand constable and served three times as *bailo* of the Morea. After the death of Peter of San Superan, head of the Catalan Company and self-styled prince of Achaia from 1396 to 1402, Centurione I's grandson Centurione II dispossessed San Superan's heirs and became the last Latin prince of Achaia from 1404 to 1432. Centurione was, in turn, dispossessed by his son-in-law, the Byzantine despot of the Morea, Theodore II Palaiologos (1407–43).[6] Thus through these successive dispossessions the principality passed from Angevin to Navarrese dominion, ending up in the hands of the last scion of an old Genoese family, before reverting to Byzantine control.

At the beginning of the fifteenth century, the Aegean was thus divided between several Latin powers, which were gradually eroded by the advancing Turks and the Byzantine despotate of the Morea. The Venetians organised their possessions into several *regimina*. These included Candia, covering Crete and the island of Cerigo; Negroponte, extending over the island of Euboea, Skyros and the Northern Sporades, and Bodonitsa on the coast of Thessaly; Corfu, comprising the island itself, which had been annexed in 1387, Butrint in Epiros and Naupaktos on the Gulf of Patras; Nauplion and Argos, which encompassed the island of Aegina; and finally Coron and Modon, incorporating the island of Sapienza. Venice also extended her protectorate over the Cyclades, administering Tenos and Mykonos directly, and had several trading posts outside her own territory, such as Thessaloniki in Macedonia, and Ephesos and Miletos on the coast of Asia Minor. Since 1309 Rhodes had been in the hands of the Knights Hospitaller, who for two centuries provided a strong Christian bulwark against the Turks; the island served as a staging-post on the shipping routes to Cyprus and Syria.

The Genoese domain was more limited: Chios, Samos and Old and New Phokaia were held by the *mahona*; there was a Genoese trading post at Ephesos; and Lesbos, Lemnos, Thasos, Imbros, Samothrace and Ainos were held by members of the Gattilusio family, but without strong ties to Genoa. Thessaloniki came under Venetian protection from 1422 to 1430, while the duchy of Athens was in the hands of Antonio Acciaiuoli from 1403 to 1435, and Centurione II Zaccaria held sway over the Morea from 1404 to 1432, although this was gradually reconquered by the Byzantine despotate. Latin commerce developed within this territorial framework, but also in the Byzantine and Turkish domains. The Latins came to dominate the whole of the Aegean and the Balkans, and some of their towers and fortifications mark the landscape to this day.

---

[6] Topping (1975a); Topping (1975b); Bon (1969), I; Zakythinos (1975), I; Setton (1975b); Setton (1975c); Lock (1995).

LONG-DISTANCE TRADE AND ITS INFRASTRUCTURE

Long-distance trade was encouraged by the concession of privileges, which sometimes legalised earlier capture. Venice had obtained complete freedom to trade in Byzantine territories in 1082. Under the agreement made in 1209 with William of Champlitte, Venice secured full ownership of Coron and Modon, possession being confirmed by the treaties concluded in 1268 and 1277 with Michael VIII Palaiologos. In the principality of Achaia, Venice had also enjoyed privileges since the settlement of the Franks in the early thirteenth century. Finally, in 1394 an agreement with Theodore I Palaiologos (1380/1–1407), despot of the Morea, restored the Venetians' customary freedom to trade in the despotate. They were thus able to develop their trading activities throughout the Aegean hindered only by the daily harassment of the tax collectors and agents of the Byzantine fisc. These officials were ready to challenge imperial concessions, especially concerning the export of wheat, which often prompted lengthy negotiations.

From 1261, the Genoese also enjoyed total exemption from the Byzantine *kommerkion*; however, they had to wait for the treaties of 1304 and 1317, concluded with Andronikos II, before they could freely export wheat produced in the empire. John VI Kantakouzenos' (1347–54) attempts to free himself of Genoese economic domination were short-lived: the so-called 'Latin war' (August 1348 – March 1349) was disastrous for the Byzantines. The Pisans also obtained exemption from all customs dues during the reign of Michael VIII. This was not the case with the other Latin nations: although the Catalans managed to reduce their tax paid from three to two per cent in 1320, they never won total exemption. The Narbonnais paid a tax of four per cent throughout the fourteenth century, and the Anconitans two per cent. The Florentines had to wait until 1422 to benefit from reduction of the *kommerkion* by half and the people of Dubrovnik until 1451 to see their duties reduced to two per cent. Despite these variations, the Latins were generally better placed than the Greeks, who had to pay the *kommerkion* at the full rate. This was one of the reasons for Latin supremacy over their Byzantine counterparts.[7]

The second pillar of western trade was the network of colonies and trading posts with permanently settled Latin populations. This emigration naturally extended the vast *inurbamento* movement whereby the Italian mercantile republics drew from their surrounding countryside (*contado*) the human resources necessary for their economic development. We shall leave aside the Cyclades, where the Venetians were no more than a handful of conquering families: on Naxos, the Sanudo and then the Crispo families;

---

[7] Zakythinos (1975), II, p. 258; Laiou (1972); Laiou (1980–1); Balard (1978), II; Antoniadis-Bibicou (1963), pp. 124–33; Giunta (1959), pp. 140–5; for the Komnenian period: Magdalino (1993a), pp. 142–50; Lilie (1984b). See also Chrysostomides (1970); Jacoby (1976); Jacoby (2001a).

on Karpathos, the Corner (Cornaro) family; the Ghisi on Tenos, Mykonos and Amorgos; on Cerigo, the Venier family and on Santorini, the Barozzi. Similarly, in ports of call such as Coron and Modon, the permanent Latin population was insignificant compared with passing merchants and job-seeking sailors. The Latin population must be evaluated quite differently in territories of some substance. For fourteenth-century Negroponte it would be difficult to put the Latins at a figure of more than 2–3,000, out of a total estimated population of 40,000. In Crete the earliest extant census dating from 1576–7 mentions only 407 Venetian families settled in the *cavalerie*, but takes no account of the Latin *bourgeois* in the towns. It seems reasonable to put the number of Venetians on the island at several thousand – 10,000 according to Thiriet, 2,500 according to Jacoby. They divided into fief-holders: *sergenterie* for non-nobles, *cavalerie* for noble Venetians, and *bourgeois* in the towns. Among these fief-holders were the greatest names of the Venetian aristocracy: Dandolo, Gradenigo, Morosini, Venier, Corner and Soranzo. They were subject to heavy levies for the defence and exploitation of their domains, but their common aim was to maximise production from their lands and to secure free trade in cereals from the *Dominante*. The Venetian *bourgeois* of Crete practised crafts or professions in the towns and shared above all in the profits of long-distance trade.[8]

Estimates for the Genoese possessions in the Aegean are just as uncertain. The Gattilusio family admittedly only attracted a handful of fellow citizens at Lesbos, in the northern Aegean, which they occupied at the beginning of the fifteenth century. While dominant at Chios, the Zaccaria had only a few companions and a garrison of 800 soldiers. Under the administration of the *mahona*, a report addressed to the doge of Genoa in 1395 by the *podestà* Niccolò Fatinanti makes it possible to estimate the Latin population at nearly 400 families, i.e. about 2,000 individuals. Among them, the *mahonesi* themselves emerge as the most active participants in long-distance trade; they enjoyed a monopoly on the sale of alum and mastic, the chief products of Phokaia and Chios.[9]

Were the Latins settled in the trading posts and colonies of the Aegean the sole actors in economic life? Or were the Greeks and Jews from the Byzantine empire associated with them in trading activities? Looking at the only official texts – the deliberations of the senate and other Venetian assemblies – one might conclude that the Venetians monopolised trade between the city and its colonies in *Romania*, with their subject populations only minimally involved in local and regional trade, and with profits going exclusively to the citizens of Venice and her fleet. But new evidence is coming to light to

---

[8] Loenertz (1970–8); Koder (1973), pp. 170–3; Thiriet (1975), pp. 270–86; Jacoby (1989a); Jacoby (1997a); Gallina (1989); *Monumenta Peloponnesiaca*, ed. Chrysostomides.
[9] Argenti (1958), I; Balard (1978), I; Pistarino (1990a).

challenge Thiriet's rigid segregation of Venetian colonial society. The study of Cretan notarial acts of the fourteenth century currently underway shows that many associations were formed between Latins, Greeks and Jews for long-distance trading. The fact that Venetian fief-holders and Byzantine *archontes* were the ringleaders of the great Cretan revolt of 1363 suggests some community of interests between the various ethnic elites. On Chios, some Greeks and Jews played an equal role with Latins in long-distance trade: Antonius Argenti, Rabbi Elias and Master Elixeus all invested capital in *societates* with Latins, participating in maritime insurance or the transport of cereals, as well as local trade and the provisioning of small ships between the island and the mainland nearby. In this sense, the increase in maritime and mercantile activities in Latin *Romania* undoubtedly had an impact on the native elite.[10]

However, the Latins controlled the main naval commissioning and navigational organisation. At Venice, the senate strictly regulated the system of *mudae*: the dates of bids and galley sailings, ports of call, merchandise to be loaded and the size of the crews. The system even covered the traffic of unarmed vessels bringing home surplus merchandise. The *mudae* of Cyprus, Syria and Alexandria paid compulsory visits to Modon and Candia, while the *mudae* of *Romania* necessarily put into port in Messenia and Negroponte. The Cyprus *muda* was suppressed in 1373, when the Genoese took Famagusta and wanted to enforce a trading monopoly to benefit the port. On the Genoese side, organisation was laxer: only in 1330 were galleys banned by the *officium Gazarie* from sailing alone for the Levant beyond Sicily. There was no regular convoy, but it was made mandatory for the owners of galleys to sail together (*in conserva*), so as to minimise the risks to precious commodities in transit. There are indications that the Genoese sent two convoys a year to *Romania* before 1350; thereafter it was reduced to one. But Genoa never managed to establish a system of bids comparable to that of the *incanti* at Venice, often leaving it in private hands. The Catalans did not organise regular convoys to the east before the end of the fourteenth century. Besides these regular sailings, unarmed ships would trade along the Aegean coasts; the Venetians put in at Negroponte and Thessaloniki, also at Ephesos and Miletos, while the Genoese shipped great quantities of alum from Phokaia and Chios to Flanders. Private shipments, less well-known than the convoys, should not be underestimated.[11]

As in the west, Latin trade in the Aegean was based on contracts drawn up in the presence of a notary; merchants were bound together for a voyage or longer periods by *colleganze* and *commende, societates* and contracts of exchange, maritime insurances and procurements. The Venetian notarial

---

[10] Jacoby (1973), pp. 889–903; McKee (2000); Balard (1978), I, p. 336; Cosentino (1987); Ilieva (1991).
[11] Stöckly (1995); Balard (1978), II, pp. 576–85; del Treppo (1971); Ashtor (1983); Zachariadou (1983).

deeds from Crete, Coron and Modon, and those of the Genoese notaries of Chios, were no different from those drawn up at Genoa or Venice. The function of these contracts was to raise the necessary capital, insure the ships and cargos and create interdependencies that protected the rights of absent parties. Of particular note are the contracts defining the terms on which the *mahonesi* could exercise their monopoly on the sale of mastic: they divided the production to be sold in the three great geographical zones shared between the Giustiniani families, who made up the *mahona*.[12]

Taken as a whole, these contracts show how diverse were the social origins and class of those involved in the mercantile economy. Although most merchants in the Venetian colonies came from the coasts of the Lagoon, and those of the Genoese trading posts from Liguria, these documents reveal many other traders at work. Catalans, men of Languedoc and Provence, Pisans, Florentines, Lombards and Anconitans, men from southern Italy and Dubrovnik and former refugees from Syria-Palestine were also involved in long-distance trade, either on their own or in association with representatives of the two great Italian maritime republics. The Aegean was truly a 'free trade community' – one where rivalries could develop, but also where individual potential could be fulfilled, given capital, opportunity and a spirit of enterprise.

ROUTES, PRODUCTS AND CONJUNCTURE

There were three distinct areas of Latin trade in the Aegean and the Balkans: the Peloponnese, the Venetian islands and the Genoese possessions. The Peloponnese had long been considered the preserve of Venice, which had gained total freedom of trade upon the creation of a Frankish principality there. Records from the earliest known Venetian assemblies refer to Venetians trading between Clarence and Apulia. This port was in effect the most convenient on the routes between Italy and the principality of Achaia, particularly once the latter passed into the Angevin domain. A Venetian consul saw to it that things ran smoothly, though with some local disruptions. The Venetians brought in metals and cloth, loading their vessels with salt, cereals, cotton, oil, raw silk and raisins from the Morea; the *mudae* were authorised to make a stop at Clarence, and unarmed ships were allowed to collect merchandise left in transit by the galleys. The Genoese also did business at the port, investing almost 4,620 *livres* in sixteen contracts between 1274 and 1345. On a smaller scale, the people of Dubrovnik were also interested in the principality's ports, buying wheat, hides, silk and linen and selling woven cloth, wine and cheeses.

[12] *Pietro Pizolo*, ed. Carbone, I; *Leonardo Marcello*, ed. Chiaudano and Lombardo; *Zaccaria de Fredo*, ed. Lombardo; *Benvenuto de Brixano*, ed. Morozzo della Rocca; Argenti (1958), III; *Notai genovesi*, ed. Balard; Tangheroni (1996).

The second half of the fourteenth century was less favourable from the Latin point of view: Clarence followed the decline of the principality of Achaia and its port suffered stagnation, which Pero Tafur noted on his travels there around 1435. Patras appears to have taken over as the main trading port in the area; the Venetian senate estimated that in 1400 merchandise worth 80,000 ducats had been imported from Patras, with a further 60–70,000 ducats'-worth in 1401. It is understandable that in these circumstances Venice accepted from Patras' archbishop responsibility for protecting the city in 1408, seeking a replacement for the decline of Clarence. The Venetians also played a significant role in the Byzantine despotate until the early fifteenth century, bringing raw materials and manufactured goods and buying wheat, cotton, honey and raw silk. However, Despot Constantine Palaiologos' conquest of Clarence and Patras in 1428 put paid to this cordial relationship. In the absence of conclusive documents, it is hard to evaluate the economic role of the Catalan duchies in this intra-Mediterranean exchange.[13]

To the south of Messenia, the two ports of Coron and Modon were of major interest to Venice. They were, to use an expression of the senate, the 'principal eyes' of the *Dominante*, and of prime strategic importance. They surveilled the movements of enemy fleets and served as a base for the reconquest of rebellious Crete in 1363–4. As staging-posts and warehouses, they received the convoys of merchant galleys which had to call at Modon every year: bills of lading preserved in the Datini archives in Prato list the various commodities – most often of eastern origin such as cotton, sugar and spices – which the galleys would pick up. With their rich agricultural hinterlands, Coron and Modon exported agricultural goods and, most importantly, the products of local stock-raising. Understandably, when faced with Greek and Turkish incursions, Venice tried to protect its two isolated enclaves, and from 1390 to 1430 sought to reunite them territorially through a series of annexations.[14]

It is in the Venetian-dominated islands of the Aegean that we can see the *Dominante*'s mercantile *dirigisme* most clearly; Venice hoped to satisfy its own needs by developing agricultural production there, and aimed to create transit centres for merchandise bound for or coming from the Levant. Crete enjoyed an exceptional position in this respect. It was the point of departure for regional exchanges with the Turkish territories of Asia Minor, which supplied it with slaves, wheat, horses and alum, and to which Crete sent textiles, wine and soap; likewise for exchanges with the Cyclades – which suffered from a chronic shortage of cereals – and with Negroponte,

[13] *Régestes des délibérations*, ed. Thiriet; *Délibérations des assemblées vénitiennes*, ed. Thiriet; Krekić (1961); Bon (1969), I, pp. 320–5; Zakythinos (1975), II, pp. 256–60; Saradi-Mendelovici (1980); Saradi-Mendelovici (1980–1); Schmitt (1995); Balard (2004).

[14] Hodgetts, 'The colonies of Coron and Modon' (PhD thesis, 1974); Thiriet (1976–8).

Coron and Modon. But above all the Cretan ports, first and foremost
Candia, played a vital part in Mediterranean trade. In effect, they saw two
convoys of galleys pass every year: those of Cyprus, then those of Syria and
Alexandria. Before the Genoese capture of Famagusta in 1373, trade with
Cyprus was of prime importance: Crete imported Cypriot salt and sugar
and exported cereals there, and this trade was dominated by the Corner
family, who had possessions in Crete and around Piskopi. The galleys
of Syria and Alexandria brought spices, silk and cotton, with the result
that Crete became the repository for Mediterranean trade's most valuable
products. Finally, the *Dominante* regarded the island as its wheat granary,
since Crete provided more than a third of its supplies; wheat was a state
monopoly and the great landowners could not export it elsewhere without
the senate's authorisation. Other products fostered trade between Crete and
Venice, including wine from Malvasia ('malmsey'), dessert grapes, cotton,
wood, cheeses and hides, and this trade came to dominate the entire Cretan
economy, provoking frequent revolts, even from the ranks of Venetian fief-
holders.[15]

The island of Negroponte, divided between Venice and the *terciers*, was
a compulsory stop for the *muda* to *Romania*, which put in there either
on the outward journey at the end of August, or on its return from Constantinople in November. It was thus pivotal to Venetian trade in lower
Romania, importing and distributing western products such as woollen
and linen cloth, which piled up in the island's warehouses, as well as taking
in products from Greece, such as wood, hides, acorns from kermes oaks
(yielding crimson dye), wax, cotton, cereals and raisins, for transport to the
west. Moreover, Negroponte's principal port of Chalkis was a stop for the
trade in wood, cereals, hides and cloth between Crete and Macedonia. But
there was no longer a question of state-organised trade confined to spring
and autumn passages along the coast of Thessaly; most were left to private
enterprise. Thessaloniki was now the hub of these multi-part voyages. The
Venetians had a consul there and their small merchant colony amassed
wheat from Macedonia and the Bulgarian plains and sold woollen and
linen cloth from the west. Their trade continued, even after the Ottomans
occupied the town. Merchants from Dubrovnik had been active in Thessaloniki since 1234, when its lord, Manuel Angelos (1230–7), granted them a
privilege. The Genoese, too, tried to establish themselves in Thessaloniki;
they had a consul there in 1305 and invested in the town around that time.
However, they did not act in liaison with those making for the Aegean's
east coast, the heart of the Genoese domain from the end of the thirteenth
century on.[16]

---

[15] Thiriet (1975), pp. 328–37; Zachariadou (1983), pp. 159–73; Gallina (1989).
[16] Thiriet (1975), pp. 337–41; Krekić (1961), pp. 67–70; Balard (1978), I, p. 164; Koder (1973).

Figure 60 The shape of the future: illustration of a square-rigged cog

Chios witnessed the development of trade in mastic and alum under the rule of the Zaccaria (1304–29). Alum became very important after 1346, when the *mahonesi* secured control of it. It was indispensable for fixing dye in cloth, and came from the mines of the Old and New Phokaia on the coast of Asia Minor. However, the Giustiniani also tried to control production of alum from other sources in Ottoman territory : Koloneia, Kütahya, Ulubad and Kyzikos. Chios was thus the great repository for alum, which ships and cogs ferried to Flanders for the textile industry. The transport of such a heavy product undoubtedly lay at the root of the medieval 'nautical

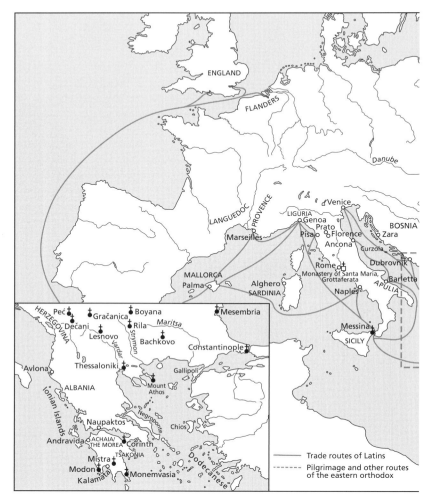

Map 49   Ties material and spiritual: the Roman orthodox and the Romance-speaking worlds

revolution', which saw square-rigged cogs replacing the Latin ships in use in the thirteenth century, putting Genoa ahead of other maritime towns in the race for heavy tonnage (see fig. 60). Until the loss of Phokaia in 1455, Genoese alum occupied a key place in the exchanges between east and west; it stimulated shipbuilding and an increase in the size of ships, and dictated a regular shipping circuit, directly linking Chios with Flanders and England.[17]

[17]   Argenti (1958), III, pp. 488–9; Heers (1971), pp. 274–84; Balard (1978), II, pp. 769–82; Pistarino (1990a); Lane (1974).

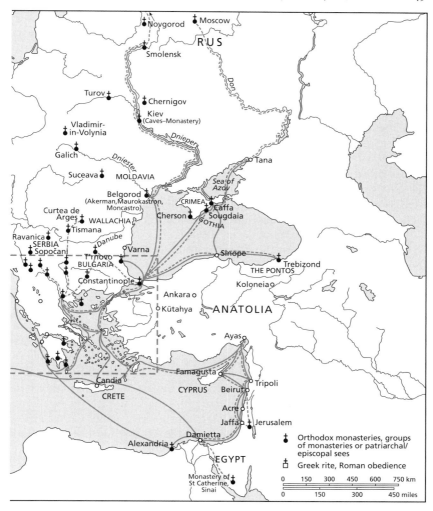

Chios also produced mastic, gum from the *lentiscus* tree, which was highly prized throughout the medieval world. The Giustiniani monopolised both production and distribution through a network of adjudicatory societies, whose members shared in sales of mastic to the west; to *Romania* and Turkey; and to Syria, Egypt and Cyprus. Through this vast commercial complex, the *mahona* made Chios function like a 'plantation economy' in the modern sense of the term: half the island's revenues came from mastic and it formed the basis of the members' wealth. Chios re-exported goods from afar to Asia Minor, via Ephesos and Miletos, while at the same time amassing the products of Anatolia in its warehouses. Finally, the island lay on the axis of two shipping routes, one via the Straits north to Constantinople and the Black Sea, the other leading to Syria and Alexandria by way of Rhodes and Famagusta. It was the hub of Genoese international trade in the east.[18]

From 1355, the Genoese had another base in the same region, the island of Lesbos, which had passed into the hands of the Gattilusio family. Apart from the alum from Kallones on the shore of the island's gulf, the port of Mytilene received Genoese trade on its way from Egypt to Constantinople, via Rhodes and Chios. This trade was primarily in Pontic slaves being exported to Egypt to swell the ranks of the Mamluk army. The seizure of the northern Aegean islands and of the port of Ainos at the mouth of the Maritsa by the Gattilusio at the beginning of the fifteenth century gave the Genoese access to the cornfields of Thrace and the Bulgarian plains.[19]

This picture of western trade in the Aegean would not be complete without some reference to the fluctuations and hindrances characterising fourteenth-century commerce in general. Papal embargoes on trade with the Saracens were heeded to varying degrees until 1345–50, and during the first half of the century this gave great significance to the sea routes to Rhodes, Cyprus and Lesser Armenia, where the harbour of Ayas was the outlet for a famous 'Mongol route' leading to India and China. Crete then had a decisive role as port of call and warehouse for all Venetian shipping, while Negroponte was an essential staging-post for the galleys to Constantinople. In the second half of the century, the issuing of papal licences allowing Latins to traffic in Syria and Egypt led to a proliferation in trading links. Cyprus, partially dominated by the Genoese, was to a large extent abandoned by the Venetian merchant galleys, while Chios added the profits derived from its intermediary role in north–south trade and trafficking with Turkish Anatolia to its large-scale dealings with the west.

Despite everything, western commerce in the Aegean suffered the setbacks which engulfed the fourteenth century as a whole. Both the figures from the *incanti* of Venetian galleys gathered by Thiriet and Stöckly, and those collected from the *Karati Peyre* register by the author, show very high levels of trade with *Romania* in the first half of the fourteenth century, followed by a fall-off in trade from 1350 and a recession lasting until at least 1410–20. Lower production in the west after the Black Death in 1348, an increase in Ottoman incursions in the Aegean, depopulation in Genoese and Venetian territories of which their authorities complained and the development of piracy – which finds an echo in all sources, beginning with the business letters of the Datini archive – all combine to explain this drop. But war never hindered the expansion of business for long; the Venetians and Genoese were able to come to terms with the Turks and the despots of the Morea. As for piracy, it would be a mistake to overestimate its effects; the goods seized by the pirates re-entered the economic system sooner or later, burdened only by an additional tax. After several decades of crisis, western trade resumed its expansion in the Aegean after 1420, more diversified in its agents, its objectives and its results.[20]

[20] Thiriet (1962); Stöckly (1995); Balard (1978), II, pp. 683–4; Edbury (1991); Gertwagen (1998); Jacoby (1997c).

CHAPTER 24

THE ROMAN ORTHODOX WORLD (1393–1492)

ANTHONY BRYER

CHRONOLOGY AND DEFINITION

Byzantines were perhaps more concerned than most medieval people with the insecure business of measuring time and defining authority. There was not much they could do about either, but naming is a taming of the forces of nature and anarchy, and placed the humblest in relation to the stability of God. Byzantines called this order *taxis*. They craved *taxis* all the more in the fifteenth-century *anno domini* (AD), because for orthodox Christians, who counted by the *anno mundi* (AM), it was, quite simply, the end of the secular world. For subjects of either, or both, emperor and patriarch in Constantinople, the world was created on 1 September 5508 BC. Gennadios II Scholarios (1454–6, 1463, 1464–5), Sultan Mehmed II's (1451–81) first patriarch after the fall of Constantinople to the Ottoman Turks on 29 May 1453, put matters in cosmic proportion by foretelling doomsday on 1 September 1492, the end of the seventh millennium AM. In 1393, the first year of the last century of the world, Patriarch Antony IV (1389–90, 1391–7) put matters in *taxis*. Grand Prince Vasilii I of Moscow (1389–1425) had remarked that although there was a church, there did not seem to be a credible emperor in Constantinople. The patriarch replied: 'it is not possible to have a church without an emperor. Yea, even if, by the permission of God, the nations [i.e. the Turks] now encircle the government and residence of the emperor . . . he is still emperor and autocrat of the Romans – that is to say of all Christians.'[1]

The truth was that in 1393 the Ottoman Sultan Bayazid I (1389–1402), who had in 1389 won his throne and the vassalage of Serbia on the battlefield of Kosovo, annexed Bulgaria and was preparing to encircle the government and residence of Manuel II Palaiologos (1391–1425) in Constantinople, a blockade only broken when the sultan was captured by Timur at the battle of Ankara on 28 July 1402.[2] The Mongols, however, soon left Anatolia, but not before reviving the nexus of emirates from which the Ottomans had sprung in what is now Turkey. Thrown into civil war until the emergence of

---

[1] *MM*, II, pp. 190–1; see also Obolensky (1971), pp. 264–6.
[2] Matschke (1981a), pp. 9–39. See also above, pp. 832, 839.

Mehmed I (1413–21), the Ottomans regrouped in their most recent Balkan conquests, giving Byzantium a half-century's respite. By 1453 the City was far from being a bulwark of the west against the hordes of Asia: indeed, the reverse. In secular terms the Ottoman state already ruled far more orthodox Christians than did the Byzantine emperor. It was as a European ruler, based in the Balkans, that Sultan Mehmed II finally took Constantinople as a preliminary to his conquest and reconquest of Anatolia, which occupied the rest of his reign.

The Ottomans were not a people but a dynasty; nor did their Muslim subjects then call themselves Turks. Patriarch Antony used the term 'nation' (Greek *ethnos*, Latin *natio*) pejoratively to describe such barbarians – but he did not call himself Greek either, let alone Hellene, which meant an ancient pagan. He signed himself, in Greek, as 'Our Moderation, Antonios, elect of God, archbishop of Constantinople the New Rome, and ecumenical patriarch'. Today we call his flock Byzantines. But this is as helpful as calling the French Lutetians, after the classical name of their capital in Paris. So far as Antony was concerned, he and his flock were Christian subjects of the first Constantine's New Rome. Hence use is made of their own self-denominator of 'Roman orthodox' to describe them in this chapter.

In the fifteenth century, the Byzantines still called themselves Romans, synonymous with Christians; in Greek their church was termed catholic, or ecumenical. But Emperor John VIII Palaiologos (1425–1448) had to appeal for support to an older Rome and another catholic church against the encircling Turks. John would have been surprised to find himself described in the Latin version of the subsequent decree of the union of the churches as 'emperor of the Greeks', for he had subscribed to it in purple in Florence on 6 July 1439 as 'in Christ God faithful emperor and autocrat of the Romans' – his sprawling signature is in Greek.[3] But the emperor was emphatically 'Roman' and his people soon confirmed their orthodox identity too – by generally rejecting the Council of Florence.

This discussion of time and title may sound antiquarian today, but is vital to an understanding of the identity of the Roman orthodox in the fifteenth century. It coincided roughly with the ninth century of the Muslim era, when the Ottomans first named Byzantines for what they were: subjects of a church that had survived an empire, called 'Rum', or Roman. The definition holds to this day, most vividly when a villager in north-eastern Turkey explains that 'This was Roman country; they spoke Christian here.'

If this chapter were limited to the political history of the Byzantine empire in the fifteenth century, it would be halved by the fall of Constantinople in 1453 which indeed resounded in the west, where historians have made that date one to remember, without quite explaining why. In truth, the change

---

[3] Gill (1959), p. 295; Buckton (ed.) (1994), p. 220. See fig. 62.

Figure 61 The *basileus* under western eyes: portrait medal of John VIII Palaiologos (1425–48) by Pisanello, engraved during the opening stages of the council of union, which met at Ferrara before moving to Florence in 1439 to avoid the plague

of municipal government in Constantinople was important, not so much in the west as to those whom it principally involved: the Roman orthodox. The arrangements made between sultan and patriarch in 1454 may have been shadowy, but they introduced a new order, or *taxis*, which ensured the future of those Roman orthodox incorporated in later conquests of the Morea and the Pontos. Their internal politics still depended on who said what at Florence in 1439, but Roman orthodox bonds which survived the conquest were older and simpler: those of patronage and *patris* – homeland.

This chapter therefore concentrates on the Roman orthodox in the last century of their world: 6901–7000 AM (1393–1492 AD). It concentrates on four homelands, based on Thessaloniki, Mistra, Constantinople and Trebizond. It must exclude other orthodox – whether Greek-speaking or not – who lived under 'Italian' rule along the Adriatic coast and in the Aegean, Dodecanese and Cyprus.[4] It excludes Albania, Bulgaria, Serbia, and Herzegovina and southern Bosnia, as well as the lands north of the Danube which emerged from the fourteenth century as posthumous Byzantine states and were to adopt the very name 'Romania': Wallachia and Moldavia.[5] It

[4] 'Italian' rule encompasses Venice, Genoa, the Knights Hospitallers and local Latin or Frankish lords; it lasted in the Dodecanese until 1523, and in Cyprus until 1571.

[5] In the century from 1397, the Turks gradually subjugated Albania, as they did Serbia between 1389 and 1459. Bulgaria was occupied by the Turks in 1393, with Herzegovina and southern Bosnia falling some 70 years later, in 1463–5. Wallachia (subjugated between 1462 to 1476) and Moldavia (subjugated between 1455 to 1512) also became tribute-payers to the Ottoman empire.

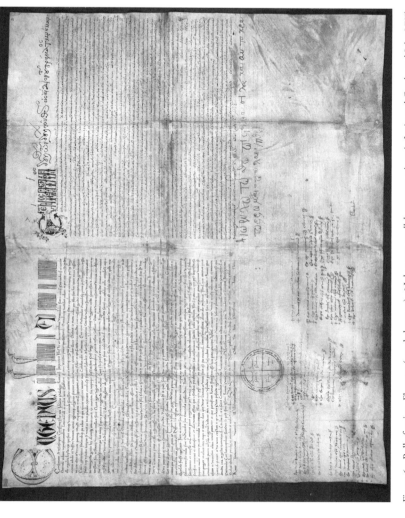

Figure 62 Bull of union, Florence (papal chancery), 6 July 1439; parallel texts are written in Latin and Greek, and John VIII's sprawling signature stands alone beneath the Greek text on the right, in contrast to the array of cardinals, patriarchs and bishops beneath the subscription of Pope Eugenius IV on the left

must even exclude the peoples of the Crimea, whom Mehmed II made tributary in 1475, turning the Black Sea into an Ottoman lake: Khazars, Armenians and Karaite Jews ruled by Crimean Tatar khans, Roman orthodox princes of Gothia and Genoese consuls in Caffa.[6]

By the end of the century only two eastern Christian rulers remained wholly independent of the Ottoman empire. Ethiopia had subscribed to the Union of Florence in 1439, but its Solomonic king, the *negus* Na'od (1478–1508) had an orthodoxy of his own. Moscow had rejected the terms of Florence, so was orthodox enough; Grand Prince Ivan III (1462–1505) had even married the niece of Constantine XI Palaiologos (1449–53), last emperor in Constantinople. But New Rome did not grant Russia its patriarchate until 1589, on the grounds that Old Rome had forfeited the title, and Moscow could enter the bottom of the list as Third Rome.[7]

At the end of the seventh millennium in Constantinople, Patriarch Maximos IV (1491–7) was spared the embarrassment which faces all who foretell a day of judgement which comes and goes without incident, for by 7000 AM most Roman orthodox had adopted the western computation of 1492 AD. Instead, he could say with more conviction than had his predecessor, Antony, a century before, that while since 1453 it was demonstrably possible to have a church without an emperor, it was now possible to have a church with a sultan – indeed for the orthodox a sultan was preferable to a doge or pope. Patriarch Maximos urged the republic of Venice to grant the same rights and freedom of worship to Roman orthodox in the Ionian islands as were available inside the Ottoman empire, while the Roman orthodox church in Cyprus had to wait until 1571 and the Ottoman conquest of the island before regaining its autonomy.[8] Under Sultan Bayazid II in 1492, the identity, survival and even prosperity of the Roman orthodox were more assured than they had seemed to be in 1393, when Bayazid I had threatened an emperor in Constantinople.

THESSALONIKI AND ITS ARCHBISHOPS

The city of Thessaloniki has many names: ancient Thessalonike, Roman Thessalonica, Slav Solun, Venetian Salonicco, Turkish Selanik, Hebrew Slonki and even Salonica to the British. For all these peoples it appeared to be the strategic or commercial key to the Balkans. The city lies near to where the Vardar river crosses the Egnatian Way before debouching into the Aegean Sea. The river, which rises deep in the Balkans, brought Slav traders each 26 October to the fair of St Demetrios, patron of Thessaloniki

[6] Vasiliev (1936a) pp. 160–275; Ducellier (1981b), pp. 323–653; Nicol (1984), pp. 157–216; Imber (1990), pp. 145–254.

[7] Jones and Monroe (1966), p. 57; Runciman (1968), pp. 320–37.   [8] Runciman (1968), p. 212.

and – through the Thessalonican-born evangelists, Sts Cyril and Methodios – of all Slavs. The Egnatian Way runs from the Adriatic coast to Constantinople, so linking Old and New Rome at Thessaloniki.

The Slavs found Thessaloniki was a key which they could not turn. Even the most aggressive of Serbian tsars, Stefan Dušan (1331–55), was unable to take the long-desired city of St Demetrios. By contrast its shallow harbour and October fairs were of limited charm to Italian traders; when offered the key to Thessaloniki in 1423, they accepted without enthusiasm. By then Thessaloniki had developed another reputation. As the second city of the Byzantine and (eventually) Ottoman empire, its relationship with the capital in Constantinople was always uneasy. Even when ruled by a secondary member of the imperial family, Thessaloniki gained a local identity as a sort of city-state of its own, with a recognisable if inchoate local leadership, often headed by the archbishop.

The fourteenth-century urban and peasant uprisings of western Europe were paralleled in Byzantium. In western terms, revolutionary Thessaloniki became a 'commune' from 1342 to 1350. In truth, its urban and artisanal mass was only just critical enough to claim local self-determination behind the great walls of the city, with a still-shadowy political ideology labelled 'Zealot'. But Thessaloniki did not forget those heady days. Its commune was a hardly surprising response to outside pressures: civil war in Byzantium, the Ottoman entry into Europe and the threat of Dušan, all compounded by the Black Death. Yet in Thessaloniki these years are marked by some of the finest surviving late Byzantine decorated churches and by the career of the last great father of the Roman orthodox church: Gregory Palamas. Palamas was archbishop of Thessaloniki from 1347 to 1359. His doctrines were confirmed by the Roman orthodox church in the next century and remain the vital spiritual ideology of the Slav orthodox in particular. The essentially mystical theology of Palamas maintained that the unknowable essence of God could be approached by revelation rather than reason, and hence was in direct opposition to the Aristotelian scholasticism of the western church. On the nearby monastic commune of Mount Athos, Palamism was given expression by hesychasts – best described as 'quietists' – whose spiritual connections with the political Zealots were both obvious and obscure.[9]

The Ottomans first besieged Thessaloniki from 1383 to 1387. Local leadership was divided between its governor, the future emperor Manuel II Palaiologos, and its archbishop, Isidore Glabas (1380–4, 1386–96). Manuel told his subjects to defy the Turkish ultimatum. On St Demetrios' Day 1383 Glabas warned his flock to mend their ways, just as St Paul had twice written to the Thessalonicans on hope, discipline and premature thoughts

---

[9] Meyendorff (1964), pp. 13–115; above, p. 823.

of the end of the world. Thessaloniki duly fell in 1387. In 1393 the archbishop ventured back to his see. He found that the world there had not
ended. Indeed, Ottoman occupation was more tolerable than Manuel had
threatened. Sultan Bayazid I had granted the citizens special favours and
had left the infrastructure of Byzantine local government and its officers
largely in place.[10]

The fact was that the Ottomans could do no other. Vastly outnumbered
by the people they conquered, their problem was manpower: there were
too few Muslims to go round, and of those too few Turks. The solution was
obvious. While the conversion of an orthodox Christian to Islam could be
swift and relatively painless, it takes longer to turn a Roman into a Turk,
which is a theme of this chapter. Yet there were short-cuts. In a sermon
delivered in occupied Thessaloniki in 1395 Archbishop Glabas reported on
an expedient which may date from the first substantial Ottoman establishment in Europe, at Gallipoli in 1354. It is called *devshirme* ('recruitment') in
Turkish and *paidomazoma* ('harvest of children') in Greek. This 'child levy'
took Christians for training in the Ottoman administration and, especially,
in the 'new army' (Turkish *yeni cheri*, root of the English word janissary).
Girls could aspire to the harem. It was such converts who were the most
eager for further conquest. Their advancement, especially after the battle of
Ankara in 1402, led to tension with the old Anatolian Turkish leadership,
which was to come to a head in 1453.

In the aftermath of Timur's victory at Ankara, Thessaloniki reverted to
Byzantium in 1403. Once again its archbishop provided characteristic leadership. Archbishop Symeon of Thessaloniki (1416/17–29), urged his flock
to keep firmly Roman and orthodox. An ardent hesychast, he sought to
restore the identity of the city in the face of Venetian and Ottoman pressure. It was difficult to know who constituted the greater threat: the Turks,
converts from orthodoxy included, who were sent to chastise the Thessalonicans for their sins, or the Venetians who would infect them with the
plague of heresy. From St Sophia in Constantinople Symeon reintroduced
a public liturgy to his own cathedral of St Sophia in Thessaloniki and, as in
Constantinople, regulated a twice-daily street procession of the protecting
icon of the Mother of God called the Hodegetria. But in Constantinople Manuel II Palaiologos was, at the age of seventy-three, more cautious:
in 1423, unable to defend Thessaloniki against the Ottomans, he invited
the republic of Venice to do it for him. Archbishop Symeon tried to rally
his Roman orthodox by chastising them in the name of St Demetrios, on
whose miraculous defence of the city in the past he wrote a great discourse

---

[10] Barker (1969), p. 53; Nicol (1993), p. 287; Vryonis (1956). On late Byzantine Thessaloniki see now
Barker (2003); Bakirtzis (2003); Necipoğlu (2003) and other contributions to the Dumbarton Oaks
Symposium (4–6 May 2001) on 'Late Byzantine Thessalonike' (published in *DOP* 57).

in Venetian-occupied Thessaloniki in 1427–8. Actually, the Venetians were initially welcomed as no great friends of the pope in Rome, but found the place expensive to defend and the locals (like themselves) doing deals with the Turks. The real end came with Archbishop Symeon's death late in 1429. The Ottomans entered a demoralised city on 29 March 1430; the Venetian captains had slipped away, the icon of the Hodegetria was smashed and 7,000 Thessalonicans were taken captive.[11]

What happened next is partly revealed in Ottoman *tahrir defters*, tax and census registers. Short of manpower, the Ottomans targeted cities such as Thessaloniki, first to Islamicise, and then Turkicise. Outside the walls the overwhelmingly peasant population could await assimilation. Sultan Mehmed II had a declared policy of demographic manipulation, today called 'ethnic cleansing', which has good Byzantine precedents. The Ottoman term was *sürgün* (forcible deportation and resettlement), which – along with *devshirme*, noted by Glabas, and natural erosion by conversion – should soon have made Thessaloniki the second Ottoman city of the empire. But this did not happen. The place recovered slowly after 1430, within walls enclosing about 285 hectares, which in medieval Mediterranean terms could encompass a population of 30,000 or more.

In fact Thessaloniki had an adult population of about 10,414 by 1478, which doubled to 20,331 in around 1500 and only tripled to reach 29,220 by 1519. The precision of Ottoman registers is spurious (for it omits tax-evaders and tax-exempt), but the scale is reliable enough. Clearly, resettlement and conversion were belated. In 1478 the city had a Muslim population of 4,320, but its Christian (Roman orthodox) element, with 6,094 souls, was still in an absolute majority with 59 per cent of households. By *c.* 1500 the Christian population had grown to 7,986 but, with 8,575, the Muslim population had doubled to reach, for the first and last time, a simple majority of 42 per cent of the inhabitants of Thessaloniki. But around 1500 a third category was introduced, if incompletely recorded: 3,770 Jews. By 1519, 15,715 Jews were registered: 54 per cent of the population of Thessaloniki, an absolute majority which they maintained until the semi-conversion of many to Islam together with their false Messiah, Sabbatai Zavi (1625–76), after 1666.[12]

The conversion of the major city of the Balkans, from the staunchly Roman orthodox see of Archbishops Palamas, Glabas and Symeon, first into a Muslim stronghold and then into the largest Jewish city in the world, all within four decades, needs explanation. In the past, Byzantine emperors had in turn invited western Christian powers and Ottoman Turks

[11] Dennis (1960); 'Sainte-Sophie de Thessalonique', ed. Darrouzès; Symeon, *Politico-historical works*, ed. Balfour; Vryonis (1986).
[12] Lowry (1986b), pp. 327–32.

to fight their wars for them against orthodox Serbs and Bulgarians, and
regretted the expedient. Now the Ottoman state was faced with a greater,
demographic, war. If Thessaloniki could not be turned Turk, a third urban
element could be introduced. Before 1430 there is evidence for a few Greek-
speaking and Karaite Jews in the city, not even registered in 1478. But after
their conquest of Granada in 1492, the catholic sovereigns, Ferdinand and
Isabel, expelled their Spanish (Sephardic) Jews. Bayazid II welcomed them
via Constantinople, largely to settle in Thessaloniki. It was the greatest
sürgün of all. Ottoman demographic strategy, if such it was, meant that
Thessaloniki did not have a Roman orthodox majority again until after
1912, when it fell to Greece, once more to become a second city.[13]

THE MOREA, THE COUNCIL OF FLORENCE AND PLETHON

The history of the Morea is a late Byzantine success story, which also illustrates the dilemmas faced by Roman orthodox leaders caught between the
west and the Ottomans in the fifteenth century. From 1262 the Peloponnese was steadily recovered from the south by the Byzantines, who shared
it with the shrinking Frankish principality of Achaia, based on Andravida
in the north-west, until the Latins were finally ejected in 1429 (on this
principality, also known as the Frankish principality of Morea, see above
p. 767). From 1349 the Morea was an autonomous despotate, an appanage
of Constantinople usually ruled, like Thessaloniki, by a younger member of
the imperial dynasty. The despots' capital was at Mistra, below a crusader
castle which overlooks ancient Sparta and its plain. Unlike Thessaloniki,
Mistra was new, without strong-minded bishops. As the Frankish *Chronicle
of the Morea* helpfully put it in 1249: '. . . and they named it Myzethras, for
that was how they called it.'[14] The steep streets of Mistra, which cannot
take wheeled traffic, still tumble past monastic enclosures, domed churches
and balconied houses down to the only square and stabling, which is the
courtyard of the despots' palace. Here on 6 January 1449 the despot was
invested, but not crowned, as last Roman orthodox emperor, Constantine
XI Palaiologos. As despot he had been a tributary of the Ottomans since
1447; as emperor he died fighting for Constantinople on 29 May 1453, but
it was not until 29 May 1460 that Mehmed II took Mistra.[15]

The Morean economy was pastoral and transhumant in the highlands,
with lowland agriculture, which included exports to Venice of Kalamata
olives, along with silk and salt. Monemvasia gave its name to exports of
malmsey wine and Corinth to currants. The archives of the despotate are

---

[13] Lowry (1986b), pp. 333–8; Dimitriades (1991).
[14] *Chronicle of the Morea*, ed. Kalonaros, line 2990, p. 125; tr. Lurier, pp. 158–9; Ilieva (1991); Lock
(1995).
[15] Runciman (1980).

Figure 63 Engraving of Mistra in the seventeenth century

largely lost, but it seems to have been run efficiently on late Byzantine fiscal and feudal lines, financing its defence principally through agriculture.[16]

The peoples of the Morea were not as exotic as those of the Crimea, but since the seventh century had included Slav settlers (see above, pp. 257–8). Despite evangelisation as Roman orthodox from the tenth century, Slavs were still evident in Tsakonia, the wild east of the peninsula, while the Maniots in the south had a quite undeserved reputation as the last pagans in Byzantium. Frankish rulers had faced the same problems of manpower as would the Ottomans, who did not settle much either. The Franks left half-castes (*gasmouloi*), great castles, impeccable Cistercian monasteries and, in towns, now forlorn Gothic churches. But they did not take root as deeply as other Latins in the Aegean and Ionian islands. In fact the most substantial demographic introduction in the Morea since the Slavs was Albanian.

However called, Albanians had been moving south before the Ottomans used them to police the Balkans. The Greeks, Bulgarians and Serbs had thrived in the shade of the Byzantine empire. The Albanians seized their turn under Ottoman patronage. They were eager, if sometimes casual, converts to Islam. For example, George, last Roman orthodox mayor (*kephalē*) of Kanina, close to Avlona in southern Albania, turned Turk in 1398, with

[16] Zakythinos (1975), II. On the economy, see also above, pp. 844–5.

the result that his family kept that office until 1943, incidentally supplying the Ottomans with thirty-one successive local *sandjakbey*s, thirteen *beyler-bey*s (of Rumelia, Anatolia and Syria), four field marshals (two Ottoman, one Egyptian, one Greek) and a grand vizier on the way. Muslim members of the Vlora family patronised local Roman orthodox monasteries and died fighting the Latins at Rhodes (1522), Naupaktos (1571) and Candia (1668).[17] The Vlora dynasty, however, was unusual in keeping its identity; Ottoman policy was at best to pension off local ruling families.

Incomplete Ottoman registers show a growth of taxable population in the Morea from about 20,000 to 50,000 non-Muslim households between 1461 and 1512, figures surely too low even if shepherds could not be tracked down over a land mass of 20,000 square kilometres. Yet the indications are clear: the Latin and Muslim population was slight, and of the orthodox over one third was Albanian.[18]

Fifteenth-century Mistra was, however, unmistakably not just Roman orthodox, but Hellene – in the person of Byzantium's last great original thinker: George Gemistos Plethon. A sort of Neoplatonist, Plethon adopted his last name in allusion to Plato and probably inspired Cosimo de' Medici's foundation of a Platonic Academy in Florence. If there was a Byzantine 'Renaissance man', he was Plethon, a maverick who had already dabbled in turn with Zoroastrianism and Judaism (perhaps at the Ottoman court) and whose last autograph fragments of a *Book of laws* exalt Zeus as supreme God. He was an awkward nonconformist to handle in Roman orthodox Constantinople. It was perhaps for his own safety that Manuel II exiled him to Mistra *c.* 1410. But Plethon was soon addressing treatises to Manuel and his son, Despot Theodore II Palaiologos (1407–43) on Platonic Republican lines, urging the division of the citizenry into three classes (of which the most important was its military) and the revival of ancient Hellenic virtues: not those of identity of faith or ethnicity, but of patriotism. He had little time for monks, whose lands threatened to turn Byzantium into a monastic economy of almost Tibetan proportions. Such rhetoric may have been utopian, but Plethon held judicial office at Mistra and was rewarded with estates in the Morea. Perhaps on the principle that patriotism is more important than faith, Plethon was in his old age invited to represent the Roman orthodox church as a lay member of its delegation to the conference with the western church held at Ferrara and Florence in 1438–9.[19]

Like other conferences held under duress, the Council of Florence was soon overtaken by military and political events. The crusade promised by Pope Eugenius IV (1431–47) to save the Constantinople of John VIII Palaiologos from the Ottomans, which the emperor sought in reward for

[17] Vlora (1968–73) II, pp. 271–7.   [18] Beldiceanu and Beldiceanu-Steinherr (1980), pp. 37–46.
[19] Woodhouse (1986). On the resurgence of Byzantine Hellenism, see also pp. 751–2, 825.

union, got as far as the Bulgarian shore of the Black Sea, but came to grief at Varna in 1444. Ostensibly, however, the council considered theological innovations and terms developed in the western church for which the Roman orthodox had no useful equivalent, or sometimes even definition: the addition of *filioque* to the creed; the notion of purgatory; and the question of unleavened bread – matters which hardly bothered most Roman orthodox unless they lived (as in Crete or Cyprus) alongside westerners. But the essential issue was that of authority, and the way that it had developed in Old and New Romes: the primacy of the pope, archbishop of Old Rome and patriarch of the west, over that of the ecumenical patriarch, archbishop of New Rome, to which the orthodox subscribed in 1439; they could at least agree to be 'Roman'. But besides the Ottoman threat, the orthodox delegation was under the additional duress that the agenda and dialectical rules of the great debate were chosen by western scholastics, who ran rings round them. For westerners the union was a matter of discipline: the reincorporation of the wayward orthodox under the authority of a single pope. But for the Roman orthodox it touched their very identity – hence the inclusion of pundits such as Plethon at the Council.[20]

Patriarch Michael III of Anchialos (1170–8) is first credited with identifying the crux of the matter, when he told his emperor: 'Let the Muslim be my material ruler, rather than the Latin my spiritual master. If I am subject to the former, at least he will not force me to share his faith. But if I have to be united in religion with the latter, under his control, I may have to separate myself from God.'[21] His view was to be put more bluntly in words attributed to *megas doux* Luke Notaras on the eve of the fall of Constantinople in 1453: 'Better the turban of the Turk than the tiara of the Latin [pope].'[22] Between 1439 and 1453 lines were drawn which were to dictate Roman orthodox politics thereafter. Spiritual authority in the east had never been focused on a single see, as in the west, but was in effect dispersed among the whole body of the faithful, including the departed. While those alive soon made it clear that they did not accept union, the Byzantine government remained faithful to the expediency of Florence until the bitter end. After 1453 there could be no going back – or forward. What individual delegates did at Florence in 1439 is therefore vital to explaining not just their own fate, but that of the Roman orthodox under the Ottomans.

The Roman orthodox delegation which John VIII and his dying patriarch took to Florence was a final assembly of the Byzantine intelligentsia, a network of patriotic, family and wandering scholarly contacts, in that order, which somehow survived later party politics. We have already met Plethon (who soon got bored), but to take the link of *patris*, a remarkable number of

---

[20] Gill (1959).   [21] Runciman (1955), p. 122; Magdalino (1993a), pp. 292–3.
[22] Duc., XXXVII.10, ed. Grecu, pp. 328–9; tr. Magoulias, p. 210.

the delegates had a connection with Trebizond in the Pontos. For instance the Aristotelian scholar George of Trebizond (1395–c. 1472) was already a convinced unionist and attended the council as a lay member of the papal curia. His reaction to the events of 1453 was to invite Mehmed II to convert to Rome; but he reported so fulsomely on the sultan when they met in Constantinople in 1465, that he found himself in a papal prison. The family of John Eugenikos (1394–c. 1455) also came from Trebizond, on which he wrote patriotic encomia; however, he left Florence before the end of the council, to castigate the union. Otherwise, most Roman orthodox signed the decree of union along with their emperor. Some recanted. Others, convinced by the argument at Florence, entered the western hierarchy itself.

However, Mark Eugenikos, brother of John and bishop of Ephesos (1437–45), refused to sign in 1439. A Palamite, but nevertheless pupil of Plethon, he was in 1456 canonised as a saint by Patriarch Gennadios II, who, as George Scholarios, had attended the council, along with George Amiroutzes from Trebizond and Plethon, as one of a remarkable trio of laymen. Bessarion of Trebizond, bishop of Nicaea (1437–9), had studied with Plethon and Amiroutzes and stayed on in Italy as a cardinal (1439–72). Gregory Mamme attended the council as abbot of the great Constantinopolitan monastery of the Pantokrator. He served as ecumenical patriarch (Gregory III) between 1443 and 1450, before returning west to be made titular Latin patriarch of Constantinople (1451–9). Isidore, from Monemvasia in the Morea, attended as Roman orthodox bishop of Kiev and All Rus (1436–9). Also made a cardinal, he was sent to Moscow as papal legate to Grand Prince Vasilii II (1425–62), who promptly imprisoned him as a unionist. Isidore persisted. He proclaimed the union in Constantinople for Mamme on 12 December 1452, and escaped its fall to become Latin patriarch from 1459 to 1463 – to be succeeded in that office by none other than Bessarion.[23] In the face of so many lures and pressures it was *patris* that held this network together.

Plethon was the first to die, in his nineties, at home in his *patris* of Mistra on 26 June 1452. The last local decree of Constantine Palaiologos as despot was to confirm Plethon's sons on his Laconic lands. But after 1453 Plethon's last work, the *Book of laws*, was forwarded to Patriarch Gennadios, who could do no other than burn it. The book was not just heretical: it was plain pagan. In Mistra another of Plethon's circle had been Cleopa Malatesta, wife of the despot Theodore II Palaiologos, younger brother of John VIII. In 1465 Sigismondo Pandolfo Malatesta (1417–68) penetrated Ottoman Mistra with a Venetian force, and retreated with Plethon's body. He installed the remains in a sarcophagus in the south arcade of his extraordinary Malatesta

²³ Gill (1959); Gill (1964).

Temple in Rimini, part-church, part-pantheon, with an epitaph to 'the greatest philosopher of his time'.[24]

MEHMED II AND GENNADIOS II SCHOLARIOS

There are two common views of the fall of Constantinople. The first is most vividly depicted in a painting presented to Queen Victoria in 1839 by a hero of the War of Independence of modern Greece from the Ottoman Turks, as a history lesson for the young queen (fig. 64). It shows Constantinople on the fateful day: 29 May 1453. Constantine XI had died a martyr; his Latin allies are scuttling away by sea. Christian youths are rounded up in *devshirme*, to become janissaries who wield curved scimitars. The enthroned Sultan Mehmed II supervises the placing of enormous yokes over the Roman orthodox clergy and lay notables of Constantinople. A distinctly pagan-looking lady, personifying Hellas disarmed, weeps under an olive tree. However, escaping to the highlands of the Morea are young braves in white Albanian kilts, ready to fight another day – which dawned in 1821.[25]

A second, revisionist, view of the event is in fact older than the schoolroom one. This maintains that, as heir of the Byzantine emperors, the conquering sultan created for his Roman orthodox subjects a self-governing community, or *millet*, regulated by their patriarch, who now had greater political powers than he had ever enjoyed, especially over the orthodox Slavs, and restored Constantinople as capital of the Roman orthodox world. As late as 1798 Patriarch Anthimos of Jerusalem explained that when the last emperors of Constantinople sold out to papal thraldom in 1439, it was through the particular favour of heaven that the Ottoman empire had been raised to protect the Greeks against heresy, as a safeguard against the politics of the western nations, and as champion of the Roman orthodox church.[26] No wonder the patriarch condemned the heroes of the Morea when they rose against their sultan.

However, what actually happened in 1453 is still obscured by the writing or rewriting of Roman orthodox, Armenian or Jewish tradition two or three generations later. The non-Muslim peoples then claimed that the conqueror had treated them well. This suited the wishful thinking of all parties, Turks included, and allows modern historians to assume that the status quo of a century later had been in place from the start. Would that things were so tidy, and that sleeping myths could lie. Yet, it is worth looking again at what Sultan Mehmed actually did, and ask: who won or lost Constantinople on 29 May 1453? Even that is not a simple question. The Genoese were first off the mark. Three days later they got the sultan to

---

[24] Runciman (1980), p. 117.   [25] *Makriyannis*, ed. and tr. Lidderdale, pl. 1 facing p. 26.
[26] *Movement for Greek independence*, ed. and tr. Clogg, pp. 56–62.

Figure 64 The fall of Constantinople in 1453, by Panayotis Zographos, presented to Queen Victoria, 1839

confirm their privileges in Galata, opposite Constantinople. Dated 1 June 1453, this Turkish charter granted to the Latins is naturally written in Greek – and preserved today in the British Library (fig. 65). But no other community had a ready-made relationship to confirm, or has a document to record a status which had to begin anew through negotiation or accumulated custom.

Among losers, Constantine XI lost his life. He had supported not just union with the Latins, but Mehmed's rival, Orhan – in 1453 there were Turks, too, within Constantinople, if outnumbered by orthodox outside the walls. The sultan's first action after the fall of the City should also give pause for thought. The fate of the emperor would have posed a tricky problem if Mehmed had taken him alive. The sultan knew, however, what to do with his own prime minister, or grand vizier, Halil Djandarlioghlu (1443–53) – put him to death. The Djandarli family was of impeccable Anatolian Turkish descent. It had served the Ottoman dynasty since 1350, supplying its first and four other grand viziers. But Halil, described by both Muslims and Christians as 'friend of the Romans', had cautioned young Mehmed against taking Constantinople. In 1453 the old Anatolian backwoods beys, whom Timur had restored after 1402, and whom Halil represented, were among the losers.[27]

---

[27] Buckton (ed.) (1994), pp. 220–1; Frazee (1983), pp. 5–10; Ménage (1965). Compare with the doubts of some Byzantines as to the advisability of retaking Constantinople in 1261 (above, pp. 753, 804).

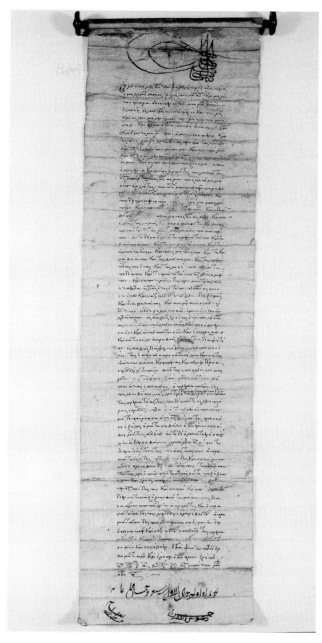

Figure 65 Grant by Mehmed II to the Genoese of Galata (1 June 1453) – only
days after capturing the City – with Mehmed's monogram at the top and the
Arabic signature of an official at the foot

The ruling orthodox dynasties lost, but a handful of secondary families which switched allegiance – such as the Evrenos of Bithynia or the Vlora of Albania – remained influential under new masters. This period lasted only a generation or two, because their usefulness, to the Ottoman state as well as to their old co-religionists, receded by the end of the century. These decades (1453–92) were, however, vital to the new order, because first-generation converts reached the highest ranks of the Ottoman army and government (which came almost to the same thing) before they forgot their origins. Unlike the Djandarli beys, they were eager for conquest – of their native lands in particular. Like all converts, they tried harder and were typically patrons of new mosques and Islamic foundations in the Christian Balkans and the new capital. Their inherited contacts in the Balkans and the Pontos assisted a relatively orderly transfer of power to Mehmed II.[28]

An example is Mahmud Pasha, a convert who served as the sultan's grand vizier from 1455 to 1474 and who successfully dealt with the surrender of the Serbian state in 1459 and of the empire of Trebizond in 1461, both after spirited campaigns. Yet both events were something of family affairs. Mahmud was born an Angelović, so the last prime ministers of Serbia and Trebizond, with whom he negotiated, were respectively his brother and a cousin. The latter was none other than George Amiroutzes – the shadow of Florence fell over such Ottomans too.[29] After executing his own grand vizier in 1453, Mehmed's next action was to look for a credible agent through whom to rule his Roman orthodox subjects. Their emperor was dead. Their patriarch, Gregory III Mamme (1443–50?), had literally gone over to Rome. But *megas doux* Luke Notaras, the last Byzantine prime minister (1449–53), survived. He was outspokenly anti-unionist, and Mehmed seems to have turned to him. What exactly went wrong is obscured by mutual recriminations in later tradition, to do with sexual habits which may be acceptable in one culture, yet scandalous in another. Perhaps the reality is that Notaras would not convert to Islam. It would have lost his credibility not with Venice (where he had a good bank account) but with the Roman orthodox, and therefore his usefulness to the sultan. Like Djandarlioghlu, he and his sons were executed. It was only then, in January 1454, that Mehmed looked to the religious institutions of his overwhelmingly non-Muslim subjects as a way of running them. With hindsight, this expedient seems obvious, even predestined, but it was not so at the time; despite the long experience of Islam in dealing with non-Muslim communities, such institutions had yet to be embedded in the Ottoman state. In effect the Muslim sultan restored the ecumenical patriarchate, so setting a precedent for other community leaders whom the Ottomans brought under their eye in Constantinople: a chief *haham* for Jews (sometime between 1454 and

[28] Inalcik (1973), pp. 23–34; Imber (1990), p. 159.   [29] *PLP*, no. 784.

1492), and a new catholicos for Armenians (sometime between 1461 and 1543), in addition to the privileges granted to western Christians on 1 June 1453, which survived for almost five centuries.[30]

The reconstitution of the see of Constantinople by the sultan is almost as obscure as its traditional foundation by St Andrew. But the evidence of his deed is enough. Mehmed sought out and installed Gennadios II Scholarios as successor of the first-called apostle, and his own first patriarch. It was an inspired choice. Obviously, he could not trust a unionist ally of the papacy, a leading enemy of the Ottomans in the west. The monk Gennadios had rallied the anti-unionists of Constantinople, whose leadership he had inherited from his old teacher, Mark Eugenikos. A veteran of the Council of Florence, Scholarios learned how to deal with the unionists by adapting their own scholastic tools. Now, as patriarch, Gennadios proved adaptable to new facts of life – for example relaxing canon law to allow for the break-up of families and remarriage in the wake of the sack of the City. Even the title he adopted as patriarch was an innovation: 'the servant of the children of God, the humble Gennadios'. In complaining that his bishops were more trouble than the Turks, he recognised that to save the Roman orthodox, the patriarchate must become an Ottoman institution.[31]

Mehmed was quite as remarkable as Gennadios. His stepmother was orthodox. He wrote Greek and hung lamps before his collection of icons. He was a patron of Bellini and curious of all new things. Indeed old Turks complained that 'if you wish to stand in high honour on the sultan's threshold, you must be a Jew or a Persian or a Frank'.[32] Tradition has Mehmed and Scholarios settling the future of the Roman orthodox in *taxis*, a brave new order, and discussing higher theology in a side chapel of the new patriarchal cathedral of the Pammakaristos. But, happily unaware that they were describing what would later be called a *millet*, the fifty-year-old patriarch and twenty-two-year-old sultan appear to have felt their way, apparently making up the rules as they went along. The results are clear. It took a Turk to define a Greek adequately as the son of a Roman orthodox. In so doing, Mehmed ensured the survival of a hitherto endangered people, for the Roman orthodox were thenceforth protected subjects of the sultan's patriarch. The patriarch was responsible to the sultan for regulating the Roman orthodox under canon law – including considerable fiscal franchise over his own flock – in return for privileges and immunities within the Ottoman state.[33]

It was in nobody's interest to question such a rosy tradition later. But it overlooks some harder realities of 1454, one of which was that Mehmed

[30] Braude (1982); Bardakjian (1982); Lewis (1984), pp. 126–36.
[31] GS, ed. Petit et al., IV, p. 206; Turner (1964), pp. 365–72; Turner (1969).
[32] Babinger (1978), p. 508; Raby (1983 [1984]).
[33] Pantazopoulos (1967); Kabrda (1969); Ursinus (1993).

Figure 66 Portrait of Sultan Mehmed II, by Gentile Bellini, 1480

II and his predecessors were primarily sultans of a militant Islamic state, however upstart. They took titles and epithets such as khan, shah, *malik*, 'shadow of God on earth' or, more contentiously, *ghazi* (or holy warrior against the infidel). Mehmed II himself was styled 'ever victorious' and *fatih* (or conqueror). As a pious ruler he founded mosques and charities, which often replaced churches and monasteries; the endowment of St Sophia in Constantinople alone, transferred from cathedral to mosque in 1456/7, numbered over 1,000 properties, including baths, butcheries and beer-shops.[34] The Ottoman state inherited from earlier Islamic practice long-established legal ways of dealing with *dhimmi*s – non-Muslims who, although protected, were unquestionably second-class subjects. Christians

---

[34] Inalcik (1969–70), p. 243.

may have lived under their own canon law, but ultimately it was the sharia, Islamic law, which was supreme.[35]

In turn Patriarch Gennadios may have been adroit in exploiting the position of the underdog, but in truth his encounters with Mehmed in the Pammakaristos can hardly have been meetings of Renaissance minds. Judging by the patriarch's voluminous writings, he was deeply Roman and conventionally orthodox. His exposition of faith, prepared for the sultan, is uncompromising, even polemical. For him, both the prophet and the pope were equivalents of the great beast of the Apocalypse. Gennadios had sharp views on the Armenians, too, and told the Jews that they laboured under an appalling delusion; it was in fact the Roman orthodox who were the chosen people of God.[36]

The fifteenth-century Ottoman empire reunited the Roman orthodox as subjects of their patriarch in Constantinople. Yet it was not the Byzantine empire in disguise. Mehmed was eventually to resettle Constantinople as the centre of the Roman orthodox world and was to be even more effective in making it the governmental capital of an Islamic empire. But these developments were not overnight decisions, let alone plans, and took a decade or more to work through in a sequence whose details remain unclear. In 1453 the City was almost as depopulated as Thessaloniki had been in 1430. The earliest surviving *defter* survey (see above, p. 859), dated 1477, which includes Constantinople and the Frankish trading town of Galata across the Golden Horn, has been variously analysed. A total of 16,326 households were registered, making a population of over 80,000. Of these the absolute majority was already Muslim with 9,517 households. There were 5,162 Christian households, the majority (3,748) Roman orthodox, which had been augmented by resettlement (*sürgün*) from the Morea after 1460, Trebizond after 1461 and the Crimea after 1475 – the last two in quarters of their own. Besides 372 Armenian households and probably under-recorded Latins and gypsies, the final major element was Jewish, already with 1,647 households.[37]

Constantinople, and most of its communities, grew prodigiously in roughly the proportions set in 1477, reaching perhaps 200,000 by 1489 and certainly double that population in 1535. The one exception is the curiously small Roman orthodox element as registered in the *defters*, which by 1489 had hardly grown. While Ottoman statistics can lie, more often they omit. The meetings of patriarch and sultan in the Pammakaristos were off the record, but the *defters* make one wonder if in 1454 Gennadios did not get Mehmed to exempt the refounded patriarchate, its dependants and properties, from the record too. For Gennadios it would only have been a

---

[35] Cahen (1965).   [36] GS, ed. Petit *et al.*, III, p. 468; IV, pp. 211–31.
[37] Inalcik (1974), pp. 238–9; Lowry (1986b), pp. 323–6.

temporary financial precaution. After all, his prediction of the end of the world in 1492 is on record.[38]

ROMAN ORTHODOX BONDS AFTER 1453: THE PONTOS AND AMIROUTZES; MOUNT ATHOS AND MARA

Trebizond in the Pontos, the last Byzantine empire to be conquered by Mehmed II, is a final illustration of the bonds which still held the Roman orthodox world together in the fifteenth century. The strongest tie was patronage; the most enduring, *patris*. The Pontos, in north-eastern Anatolia, was a distinct *patris* to which its patrons, the Grand Komnenoi, emperors of Trebizond (1204–1461), added political identity. As separatist rulers, their legitimacy was all the more Roman orthodox. Like the grand princes of Moscow, their obedience was to the patriarch, not the emperor, in Constantinople. The Grand Komnenos signed himself as 'faithful emperor and autocrat of all Anatolia, of the Iberians and beyond' – initially encompassing the Crimea. This Black Sea coast was perhaps the most densely settled in the Byzantine world. By 1520–3 the population of central Pontos was registered at over 215,000 of whom 92 per cent were still Christian and 86 per cent Roman orthodox, while the rest of Anatolia, about 5.7 million, was already 93 per cent Muslim.[39]

By contrast with the Pontos, the decline of the orthodox church elsewhere in Anatolia had been relatively swift. It succumbed not so much to Islamic missionary zeal as to the loss of its economic base and the withdrawal of the patronage of its imperial officials – for whom all postings from Constantinople were colonial, whether the natives spoke Greek or not.[40] Only just in time to save the identity of such Roman orthodox, Mehmed had halted the structural disintegration of their church by whatever settlement he made with Scholarios in 1454. The result was that ambitious and well-connected Roman orthodox had an alternative to conversion thereafter. They could keep faith and enter patriarchal service. But without political independence the church could only conserve the flock which paid for it, and was perilously dependent upon patrons. Without economic freedom its theological development was frozen at the point when the sultan recognised it: in authority anti-unionist, in spirituality Palamite.

Although the patriarch was an essential officer of the Ottoman system, it was a fundamentally unequal alliance. Sultans supported the church the better to use it – what had emperors done before them? But in the crucial period of conquest the Roman orthodox found a patron who matched, like Mehmed himself, that time of transition alone. She was

[38] GS, ed. Petit *et al.*, IV, pp. 511–12.   [39] Bryer (1991), pp. 316–19.
[40] Vryonis (1971a). See also pp. 328–9.

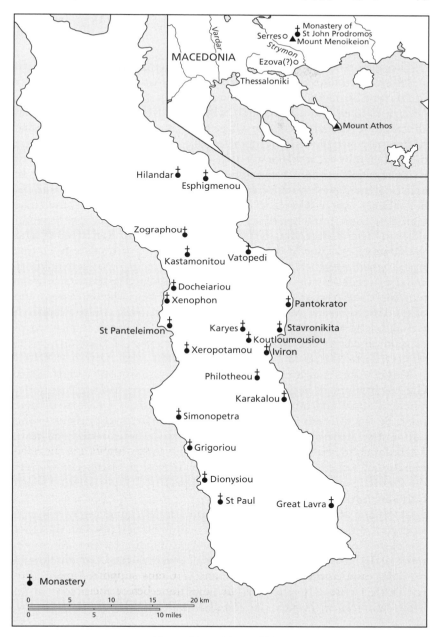

MACEDONIA

Vardar

Serres ○

Strymon

Monastery of
St John Prodromos
Mount Menoikeion

Ezova(?)○

Thessaloniki

Mount Athos

Hilandar
Esphigmenou

Zographou

Kastamonitou   Vatopedi

Docheiariou
Xenophon   Pantokrator

St Panteleimon

Karyes   Stavronikita
              Koutloumousiou
Xeropotamou   Iviron

Philotheou

Karakalou

Simonopetra

Grigoriou

Dionysiou

St Paul   Great Lavra

✝● Monastery

| 0 | 5 | 10 | 15 | 20 km |
| 0 | | 5 | | 10 miles |

Map 50 Mount Athos and Mara

Mara Branković (*c.* 1412–78), daughter of the last despot of Serbia by a sister of the last emperor of Trebizond. In 1435 Mara married Sultan Murad II (1421–51), father of Mehmed II.[41]

The network of marriage alliances in which Mara enmeshed the Ottoman and Roman orthodox dynasties arose from diplomatic expediency – if Serbia could come by dowry rather than conquest, so much the better. But Mara, never a mother, was a formidable widow. Above all she kept her faith, although she resisted a second marriage in 1451 – to her relative, Constantine XI Palaiologos. If she had agreed, the conquest of 1453 would have been even more of a family event than it was. The evidence, not just of tradition but of his acts, reveals how much the sultan revered his Christian stepmother. In 1459 he granted her both the cathedral of St Sophia in Thessaloniki and the fief of Ezova, where she received ambassadors and held a sort of alternative Christian court until her death in 1478.[42] Ezova lies near the Strymon valley in eastern Macedonia between Serres and Mount Athos. Along with the Pontos it was one of the most prosperous areas of the late Byzantine world, where Mehmed allowed some monasteries to keep their holdings and dependent peasants. The Strymon was dominated by the estates of the monasteries of Mount Athos (which Mara and her father endowed) and of the Prodromos on Mount Menoikeion, above Serres (where Patriarch Gennadios II Scholarios retired and is buried). Mehmed II planned to pension off Mara's uncle, the Grand Komnenos David I (1459–61), in the same area after the fall of Trebizond in 1461.[43]

Mount Athos had long been an eremitic and monastic retreat. Since Gregory Palamas, its hesychasts had made it an arbiter of spiritual authority among Roman and other orthodox, countering that of the patriarchate itself. By the fifteenth century its outstations, estates and peasants – who outnumbered the monks by over ten to one – were concentrated from Thessaloniki to Serres, but spread as far as Trebizond; Athos also controlled islands such as Lemnos. It was still to enter its most prosperous days under the Ottomans, when it attracted the patronage of Danubian and Russian orthodox rulers and pilgrims.[44]

In the late fifteenth century, Mara's Ezova in Macedonia was rivalled as a political and economic focus by an even more modest place on the other side of the Roman orthodox world: the village of Doubera, forty kilometres south of Trebizond in the Pontos. The 1515 *defter* registers a solidly Roman orthodox population of only 333 souls (others were probably exempt), but reveals that it was also the *patris* of members of the Amiroutzes family. More significantly, in 1364 the Grand Komnenos Alexios III (1349–90),

---

[41] Duc., XXX.1–3, ed. Grecu, pp. 257–9; tr. Magoulias, pp. 174–6; Nicol (1994), pp. 110–19; Gavrilović (2006), pp. 83–6.

[42] Babinger (1978), pp. 163–4.   [43] *PLP*, no. 12097; Zachariadou (1969); Lowry (1991).

[44] Bryer and Cunningham (eds.) (1996).

who was also founder of an Athonite monastery, had named Doubera as headquarters of the estates of his own nearby pilgrim monastery of Soumela, one of three in the Pontic interior which retained their privileges and tax exemptions after the fall of Trebizond in 1461, just as the Ottomans had favoured some of the monastic economies around Mara's Ezova.[45]

In 1461 Mahmud Pasha sorted out terms of surrender of Trebizond with George Amiroutzes, after a tiresome campaign which left most of the Pontos itself unconquered. Sultan Mehmed deported the Grand Komnenos David and his prime minister, Amiroutzes, as part of a *sürgün* to Constantinople. Thence Amiroutzes wrote to his old compatriot and fellow delegate at Florence, Bessarion, a vivid letter describing the fall of Trebizond – and asking for money to ransom his son and Bessarion's godson, Basil, who was in danger of forcible conversion to Islam. Amiroutzes was an anti-unionist, but evidently not bothered that Bessarion was now a Latin cardinal. He appealed to closer bonds: shared connections of family and *patris*.[46] Had he already solicited Mahmud, who was surely better placed to help?

By 1463 Bessarion had become Isidore of Kiev's successor as Latin patriarch. In the same year someone (the evidence that it was Amiroutzes is only circumstantial) denounced David to Mehmed II. Refusing to apostasise, the imperial family of Trebizond died in gruesome circumstances. Apparently Mara could not, and Amiroutzes would not, intercede. Certainly Amiroutzes had shifted his allegiance to the sultan, for whom he prepared an exposition of Ptolemy's *Geography* with the assistance of his son – called Mehmed. Perhaps this son was the forementioned Basil, who had converted after all? Most Roman orthodox converted to Islam before culturally they turned Turk. But some of their leaders did it the other way round. Contrary to the poor view in which he is held in Greek tradition, George Amiroutzes himself does not seem to have bothered to convert. Apostasy would have denied him playing politics with the patriarchate, while at the sultan's court he could always use his cousin and ally, the grand vizier Mahmud Pasha.[47]

The year 1463 was even more eventful for the Roman orthodox network. Patriarch Joasaph I, one of Gennadios II Scholarios' successors, denounced George Amiroutzes in turn – for his proposed bigamous marriage to the widow of the last Latin duke of Athens. Amiroutzes went ahead all the same. Tradition that he was an exasperating man was confirmed dramatically on Easter Sunday 1463: the affair drove Joasaph to attempt suicide by leaping into the cistern below the Pammakaristos cathedral. Amiroutzes promptly moved in to manage patriarchal finances, using his son, Mehmed, as intermediary with the sultan.[48] Behind a cloud of later tradition may be detected a characteristic trail of patronage and *patris*.

---

[45] Lowry (1986a), p. 128.   [46] *PG*, 116, cols. 723–8.
[47] Nicol (1994), pp. 120–5.   [48] Bryer (1986), pp. 81–6.

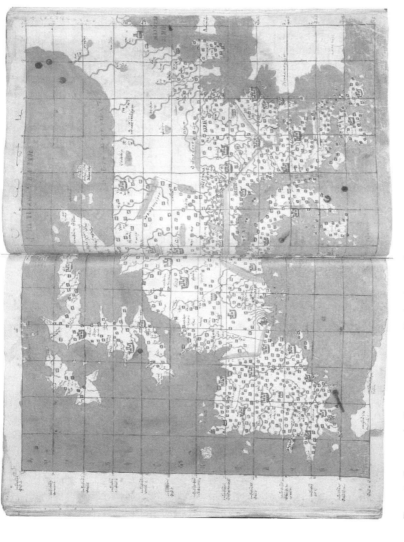

Figure 67 Europe under Ottoman eyes: copy of Ptolemy's map of Europe; Ptolemy's work continued to be closely studied in late Byzantium, as it was in the 'dark age' (see above, pp. 279, 824–5). George Amiroutzes introduced Ptolemy's *Geography* to Mehmed II and translated it into Arabic on the sultan's orders; this copy of the Greek text is believed to be the one donated to St Sophia in 1421, which ended up in Mehmed's library

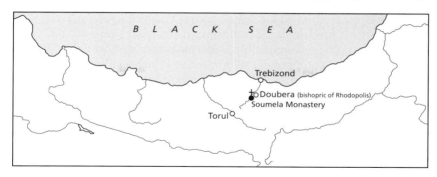

Map 51 The Pontos in the fifteenth century

By 1465 Mehmed had confirmed Amiroutzes' village of Doubera on the estates of Soumela as a monastic immunity. Soumela (and two other nearby mountain monasteries) constituted thereafter the only major economic counterpart to the Macedonian monastic lands protected by Mara, a rival patron.[49] In late 1466 Symeon 'of Trebizond' was presented as candidate for the patriarchate, offering the sultan, for the first time, a bribe of office (called *peshkesh*): 2,000 gold pieces. Monks do not commonly dispose of such sums, and Mehmed had anyway dispossessed the monasteries of the city of Trebizond itself. By elimination, this points to Soumela as Symeon's monastery and brings us back to his sponsor. Putting it bluntly, did Amiroutzes use the resources and connections of Doubera to buy the patriarchate for his candidate?

One consequence is certain. By offering *peshkesh* in 1466, there was no going back. By their own account, the Roman orthodox initiated an auction of their own leadership, which spread to other offices and was to spiral for over three centuries. This was the self-imposed cost of protection of a church by an Islamic state, largely borne by the faithful, whose principal contact with their patriarchate was to raise *peshkesh* and obey canon law. The only beneficiary was the Ottoman treasury. Sultans were not much concerned as to who was patriarch, so long as he was neither unionist nor sponsored by Ottoman commercial or political rivals; in the seventeenth century, French Jesuits and Dutch Calvinists would compete to buy a whole church.[50]

The short-term result was that in 1467 a Serbian party and Mara outbid Symeon with her own candidate. The Pontic party ran Symeon again. During his second term of office in 1472, Symeon swiftly deposed Bishop Pankratios of Trebizond who was implicated in a Turkoman attempt to restore a Grand Komnenos in Trebizond – presumably under pressure

[49] Nicol (1994), pp. 110–19.
[50] *Patriarchat von Konstantinopel*, ed. and German tr. Kresten; Runciman (1968), pp. 193–200, 259–88.

from Amiroutzes who had known all parties involved since 1458, and now knew where his loyalties lay. Seven times the patriarchate went back and forth until in 1482 Symeon finally raised a record *peshkesh* for a third period of office, ousting an opponent of Amiroutzes' marriage of 1463. In 1484 Symeon at last held a synod which repudiated the Union of Florence of 1439.[51]

Patriarch Symeon nevertheless left unfinished business when he died in office in 1486. His death raised the perennial question of whom political funds belong to, for he had neglected to make a will. Who were his heirs? The leaders of the network which had held the Roman orthodox world together had all died: Mahmud Pasha (after 1474), Mara (1478), Mehmed II himself (1481); and of the veterans of Florence, Isidore (1463), Bessarion (1472), Scholarios (*c.* 1472) and Amiroutzes himself (*c.* 1475).

Patriarch Niphon II (1486–8, 1497–8, 1502) was the first successful candidate of new patrons. These were Danubian princes, now Ottoman tributaries, who were to support the monasteries of Athos and the Pontos, too. However, Niphon was unable to claim Symeon's intestate fortune, which was confiscated by Iskender, treasurer of the new sultan, Bayazid II (1481–1512). But the network which reached back to Doubera still held: Iskender was yet another son of George Amiroutzes.[52]

Patris may be even stronger than patronage, and certainly faith, for Doubera village now had even greater aspirations – to empire. In 1479 the future sultan Bayazid II took the last independent corner of the Roman orthodox world, the rocky principality of Torul, south of Trebizond and Soumela; his local consort was Maria 'of Doubera', who as Gulbahar *hatun*, held court in Trebizond until her death in 1505/6. Bayazid's *ulu hatun* ('first lady') was then Ayshe, the daughter of Bozkurt of the Turkoman Dulkadir dynasty and, from 1470, mother of the future sultan Selim I (1512–20). Differing later Ottoman and Roman orthodox accounts can no longer be verified, but can be reconciled. Selim's formative years were in Trebizond, where he was governor from 1489 to 1512 and he wrote in Greek to Venice, styling himself 'emperor of the Pontos and despot of Trebizond'. He confirmed the privileges of Soumela monastery. In turn his son, the future sultan Suleiman, was brought up in Trebizond, presumably by Maria-Gulbahar, from 1494/5.[53]

Maria is a more shadowy figure than Mara of Ezova, but the surest fact about her is vital: her birthplace, or *patris*, was none other than Doubera. The village itself escaped registration until 1515 and Ottoman *defters* are not designed to record any connections she may have had with the families of Amiroutzes, Patriarch Symeon or even Bessarion. But it is a small place.

---

[51] Chrysanthos (1933), pp. 531–41; Laurent (1968).   [52] *PLP*, nos. 787–8.
[53] Chrysanthos (1933), p. 519.

Like Mara of Ezova, Maria of Doubera was probably only the stepmother of a sultan. But in Trebizond Selim gave Gulbahar a marble tomb and in 1514 a mosque fit for an empress.[54]

The fate of the other inhabitants of Trebizond is a final reflection of that of the Roman orthodox. Compared with its hinterland, the city was never populous – in 1436 some 4,000 souls. After its conquest it grew to 6,711 in 1486, 7,017 in 1523, 6,100 in 1553 and reached 10,575 in 1583 – figures about a third of the size of Thessaloniki which also reflect the relative efficiency of Ottoman registrars and omit exempt groups. But the composition is revealing. After 1461 Mehmed instigated a *sürgün*, deporting the Christian leadership and importing Muslims (including recent Albanian converts), so that by around 1486 Trebizond was 19 per cent Muslim and 81 per cent Christian (mostly Roman orthodox). But the Christian population actually grew thereafter, both in numbers and proportion (86 per cent) during the years of Selim's governorship, Suleiman's youth and Gulbahar's widowhood, when the Ottoman state should have been tightening its hold on the place. Trebizond was in danger of becoming totally Christian again and, in contrast to Thessaloniki, Jews were not brought in to break the demographic problem. There was a second *sürgün*. In 1553 the ratio of Christians to Muslims was 53 to 47 per cent, but by 1583 had switched to 46 to 54 per cent. The critical point seems to have been when the Christian element had shrunk to about 55 per cent, when whole parishes (which paid a fixed levy) converted in landslides, leaving faithful individuals unable to afford the balance. Most revealing is that by 1583, 43 per cent of the Muslims of Trebizond are identifiable as first- or second-generation converts. In other words the population of the city, whatever its faith, was then still almost 70 per cent native Pontic: people who kept to their *patris*.[55]

'Conversion' is used here as a convenient term, and indeed has a technical sense in both orthodoxy and Islam, with the difference that under sharia law, conversion or reconversion out of Islam met the penalty of death in the Ottoman empire until 1839. From the fifteenth century on there were a number of attested orthodox martyrs for their faith. Converts to Islam did not find immediate acceptance either. But, following Ottoman registrars, we can only record Roman orthodox by civil status. The spiritual cost of the compromises to which the church and individual faithful were driven in order to survive cannot be recorded, any more than what happened in the countryside. Here, monasteries such as Mara's in Macedonia and Maria's in the Pontos could offer secular as well as spiritual salvation. In the absence of such patrons elsewhere it may not have been too painful to slip in and out of unofficial Islam and orthodoxy within a common peasant culture and local cults of *patris*.

---

[54] Bryer and Winfield (1985), I, pp. 197, 200.   [55] Lowry (1981).

By the reign of Sultan Suleiman I (1520–66) most Roman orthodox who were going to convert to Islam had done so. In the west, Suleiman is called 'the Magnificent', but in the Ottoman empire he is rightly named 'the Law-Giver'. He regularised the local and customary laws inherited through the swift conquests of Constantinople, the Morea, Macedonia and the Pontos, under which most Roman orthodox had continued to live for a century after the fall of Constantinople – beyond even Gennadios Scholarios's prediction of the end of the world in 1492. The politics of the Union of Florence in 1439 could not be forgotten even after 1484. There were to be new patrons in Wallachia, Moldavia and Muscovy, but *patris* may have been the most enduring bond of all. Take, once more, the Soumelan village of Doubera, a steep place hidden in the Pontic undergrowth. After much lobbying the patriarchate created a diocese there in 1863, as influential as it was tiny. The parish church of Doubera became the cathedral of Rhodopolis. Today it is the mosque of Yazlik, a wholly Muslim Turkish village. But its titular bishop wields great influence – especially in Australia, where every second Greek claims to have come from Doubera. Surely this was the home of George Amiroutzes.[56]

---

[56] Bryer and Winfield (1985), I, p. 281; Bryer (1991), pp. 323–5; Balivet (1994).

GLOSSARY (INCLUDING SOME
PROPER NAMES)*

A: Arabic   G: Greek   I: Italian   L: Latin   P: Persian   S: Slavonic
Tc: Turkic   Tsh: Turkish

Abbasids Muslim dynasty which replaced the Umayyads in 750, with their capital in Baghdad

Abkhazians people in western Caucasia on the eastern shore of the Black Sea; subjugated by Justinian, but gained virtual autonomy after Arab invasions of Caucasus; unified with the kingdom of K'art'li in the late tenth century to form Georgia

Achaemenids Persian dynasty which ruled the largest empire of the ancient world (stretching from Central Asia to the Aegean and Egypt) from the sixth to fourth centuries BC

Aghlabids ninth-century dynasty of amirs who ruled northern Africa for the Abbasid caliphs

akritēs **(s.),** *akritai* **(pl.)** smallholding Byzantine soldiers in frontier zone, usually exempt from taxation on condition of military service

aktēmon **(s.),** *aktēmones* **(pl.)** 'without property': fiscal term for a peasant who possessed no draught animals and little or no property, but who might own a small plot and other livestock

Alans warlike nomadic pastoralists speaking a form of Iranian, based in the mountains of the northern Caucasus and on the steppes; by the eleventh century Alans were serving as Byzantine mercenaries

amir [A; P; Tsh] 'commander': originally military, but later applied to local or regional rulers of rank lower than a sultan; ruler over an emirate

Anatolikoi one of the earliest (and most important) themes, named after army of the East (L: Orientales); based in central Anatolia with head-quarters at Amorion

angelology theological doctrine of angels or its study

---

*This is not intended to be a comprehensive guide to the technical terms and foreign words appearing in this book; where possible, these have been explained in context. Only the more problematic proper names receive an entry here. Where not otherwise indicated, italicised foreign words are Greek.

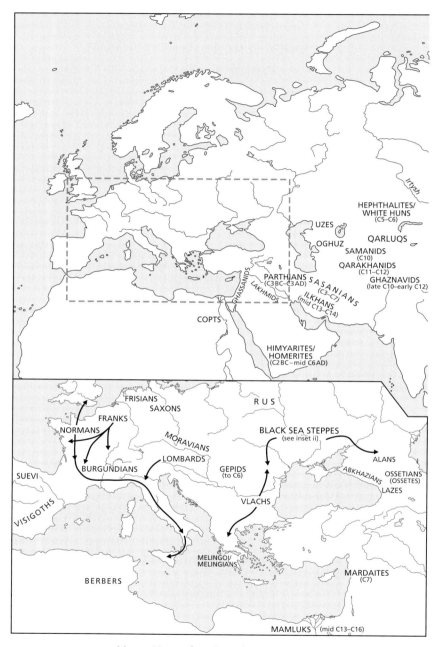

Map 52 Names of peoples, archaic or less familiar

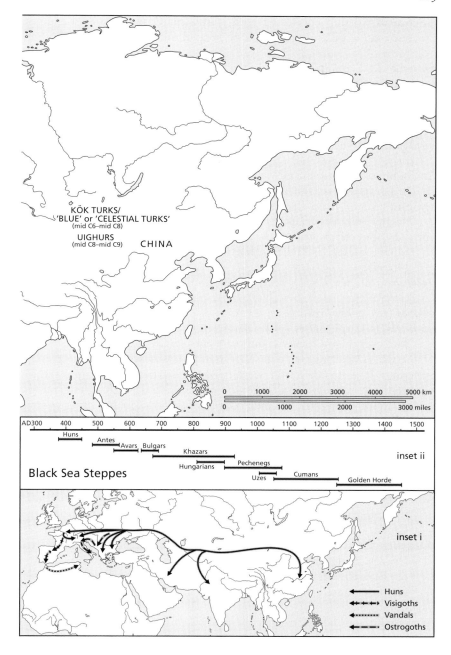

KÖK TURKS/
'BLUE' or 'CELESTIAL TURKS'
(mid C6–mid C8)

UIGHURS
(mid C8–mid C9)   CHINA

| 0 | 1000 | 2000 | 3000 | 4000 | 5000 km |

| 0 | 1000 | 2000 | 3000 miles |

AD300   400   500   600   700   800   900   1000   1100   1200   1300   1400   1500

Huns

Antes

Avars Bulgars

Khazars

Hungarians

Pechenegs

Uzes

Cumans

Golden Horde

inset ii

Black Sea Steppes

inset i

	Huns
	Visigoths
	Vandals
	Ostrogoths

884 G L O S S A R Y

aniconism worship connected with simple material symbols of a deity, such as a pillar or block, not shaped into an image of human form

annona **(s.),** *annonae* **(pl.)** [L] army and civil service rations raised by taxation in kind; state-run shipment of corn from Egypt to supply the population of Constantinople (see also *synōnē*)

Antes Slavic-speaking people, based to the north of the Black Sea by the mid-sixth century, of whom we know little

anthypatos civilian governor of province (L: proconsul); high-ranking dignity

Antiochene of Antioch, a style of theology laying stress on the humanity of Christ and on the literal and historical sense of the Bible

antiphon verses from the Psalter sung alternately by two choirs in the liturgy and the offices

aphthartodocetism an extreme form of monophysitism propounded by Julian, bishop of Halicarnassus (d. *c.* 527); followers also known as Julianists

aplēkton military staging-post; obligation to provide troop accommodation

aporos **(s.),** *aporoi* **(pl.)** fiscal term for those without land or means

apothēkē **(s.),** *apothēkai* **(pl.)** a state depot for grain and other goods; in the seventh and earlier eighth centuries the depot, and the district in which it was situated, was supervised by a *kommerkarios*

appanage (1) term taken from western practice to describe an almost independent territory granted by the emperor to a junior ruling family member, giving him his own court, administration and fiscal system; common in Byzantium from the thirteenth century on; (2) any imperial grant of a large demesne

archōn **(s.),** *archontes* **(pl.)** ruler (other than the *basileus*); holder of imperial title or office; member(s) of the provincial land-holding elite which dominated the towns

Arians followers of a heresy (named after its main proponent, the third-century theologian Arius) which denied the full divinity of Jesus Christ

Arithmos 'number': (1) one of the elite *tagmata*, also known as the Watch (*Vigla*), partly responsible for the policing of Constantinople; (2) middle Byzantine fiscal term referring to the specific number of *paroikos* families granted by the emperor to an individual or ecclesiastical corporation

Armeniakoi one of the earliest themes; based in northern Anatolia with headquarters at Euchaita

Arsacids [P; Armenian; Arshakuni] junior branch of the Parthian royal house which ruled in Armenia until the early fifth century

atabey [Tsh] 'father of the prince': the bey acting as the guardian of an infant ruler; governor of a nation or province who was subordinate to a Muslim monarch

augustus (m.), augusta (f.) senior emperor within a group of co-emperors, or within a single family; honorary title usually bestowed on the wife of the reigning emperor

autocephalous (from *autos* 'self' and *kephalē* 'head'): a completely autonomous ecclesiastical diocese, no longer subordinate to a patriarchate, whose suffragans had the right to elect its 'head'; e.g. Cyprus, Bulgaria, Serbia and Sinai

autokratōr (L: *imperator*) emperor; used from seventh century on to affirm the emperor's self-willed and God-granted rule

automata devices powered by compressed air from bellows or by water, performing in the Magnaura

Avars Turkic-speaking nomadic warriors who appeared in the north Black Sea steppe in the sixth century, installing themselves in Pannonia; destroyed as an independent power by Charlemagne in the 790s

bailo (s.), baili (pl.) [I]'bailiff': general term for administrator; head of the Venetian colony in Constantinople and ambassador to the Byzantine court in the Palaiologan period; there was also a Venetian *bailo* in Euboea

ban [Tc] title of Bosnian and Hungarian rulers

bandon (s.), banda (pl.) (L: *bandum*) originally a battle standard; later a small troop fighting under such a standard in the themes or *tagmata*; the territorial district where such a troop was settled

basileia (L: *imperium*) empire; realm; majesty

basileus (m.), basilissa (f.) main formal designation of the Byzantine emperor from the seventh century on

basilikos (s.), basilikoi (pl.) 'imperial': general term for official specially trusted by the emperor, who carried out diverse missions within the empire or abroad

Berbers name given to several ethnic groups indigenous to north-west Africa; known in Arab sources as the Barbar, and to the Byzantines as Mauri (Moors)

beylerbey [Tsh] 'the bey of the beys': commander-in-chief of the Seljuq army, in charge of organising the sultanate's frontier zone defences

bey [Tsh] ruler or military commander (Turkish equivalent of Arabic amir)

billon alloy containing silver and copper in a Byzantine coin

Bogomilism dualist heresy most probably named after the tenth-century Bulgarian priest Bogomil, which spread from the Balkans to Constantinople and Asia Minor

boidatos (s.), boidatoi (pl.) fiscal term for a peasant possessing a *boidion*, equivalent to owning an ox (*bous*)

Boukellarioi theme formed in the later eighth century in north-west Asia Minor, taking its name from the old Roman regiment, the Bucellarii

boullotēs assistant to the eparch who controlled the quality of products by affixing a seal (*boulla*)

Bulgars Turkic-speaking people from Eurasian steppes; by the late seventh century, groups of Bulgars were based on the middle Volga, the Sea of Azov (the 'Black Bulgars', semi-autonomous within the Khazar khaganate) and close to the Danube delta; the latter gave rise to modern Bulgaria

bull (L: *bulla*; G: *boulla*, 'locket') seal attached to a document (see also chrysobull)

cadaster record of properties and related details, e.g. owners' names and amount of tax payable, used by tax officials

caesar title given to a junior emperor or – from the eleventh century onwards – to imperial relatives or high court officials

Caesaropapism system whereby the monarch exercised unfettered control over the church in his dominions, even in matters of doctrine

caliph (A: *khalifa*) 'successor' of the Prophet Muhammad and so head of the Muslim community (A: *ummah*) or of the Islamic state

caliphate realm of the caliph

castello (s.), *castelli* (pl.) [I] private strongholds, generally castles, but also fortified villages

castrum (s.), *castra* (pl.) [L] see *kastron*

Catalan Company mercenaries from north-eastern Spain, who were employed by Andronikos II but turned against Byzantium and went on to establish themselves in the duchy of Athens, ruling it for much of the fourteenth century

catechumen a person preparing for baptism

catholic (from *katholikos*, 'whole') the undivided church, denoting Chalcedonian Christians in east and west in the early middle ages; later applied exclusively to the western (i.e. Roman catholic) church

catholicos (s.), **catholicoi** (pl.) head of the Armenian church

cenobitic (from *koinos*, 'shared') monastic life in which monks live and pray together in a group, normally in a monastery (opposite of eremitic)

Chalcedonianism from the council of Chalcedon (451): the belief that there are two natures (*physeis*) in the person of Christ, the human and the divine, and that they are joined inseparably; this became the official teaching of the orthodox church, as against monophysitism

Chalke the Bronze Gate: main ceremonial entrance into the Great Palace of Constantinople, through which the emperor passed to go to St Sophia

chartolarate (s.), ***chartolarates*** (pl.) administrative unit in the southwest Balkans

chartophylax head of a church chancery (*chartophylakion*), especially of St Sophia (the patriarchal church)

chartoularios (s.), ***chartoularioi*** (pl.) general term for lower-ranking official with fiscal and archival duties in various bureaus in both central and provincial administration; ecclesiastical office similar to *chartophylax*

chelandion (s.), ***chelandia*** (pl.) Constantinople's sleek warships, perhaps derived from the Greek word for 'eel'

chōrion (s.), ***chōria*** (pl.) a village; technical term for a fiscal unit

Christology theological interpretation of the person and work of Christ

chrysobull 'golden bull', from 'gold' (*chrysos*) and 'seal' (*boulla*): the imperial chancery's most solemn document, usually dated, and bearing the emperor's signature in purple ink and a golden *boulla*

Chrysotriklinos 'golden hall', from 'gold' (*chrysos*) and 'hall' (*triklinos*): large reception hall in the Great Palace, built by Justin II

circus factions associations that staged circus games; fervent supporters' associations of one of the four factions to compete in chariot racing (the Blues, Greens, White and Reds); factional strife disappeared from the seventh century onwards, after chariot-racing and factions were restricted to Constantinople and its surrounds; in the middle empire, factions had a largely ceremonial role, still connected with the Hippodrome

City, the Constantinople; *polis* ('city') came to be used primarily for it

City prefect see eparch

cog large, round, flat-bottomed ship with a single square sail; the workhorse of trading vessels from the fourteenth century on

comes (s.), ***comites*** (pl.) [L] count; in the medieval west, a term for magnates, notionally holding public office with civil and military powers; in reality usually hereditary, belonging to local leading families; for use in Byzantium, see also *komēs*

consul head of government in the Roman republic, a nominal post maintained up to Justinian's reign; thereafter a senior court title (see also *hypatos*)

Copts Egyptian population who spoke the Coptic language; after Egypt's mid-seventh-century conquest by the Arabs, a term for the monophysite Christian population

count of the excubitors (see also L: *comes*) officer of the excubitors (see excubitors)

Cumans (also Scyths, Qipchaqs, Polovtsy) confederation of Turkic-speaking peoples who dominated the Black Sea steppes from the mid-eleventh century, but who were subjugated by the Mongols in the mid-thirteenth century

cura palatii [L] 'care of the palace': see *kouropalatēs*

curia central administration governing the Roman papacy

custom (1) in the west, customary service, or rent, paid in kind or in money, due to a landlord, feudal lord or ruler; (2) western code of conduct, commercial law-code

Cyrilline Chalcedonianism pronouncements on Christ's nature of Patriarch Cyril of Alexandria, endorsed by the council of Chalcedon (451)

Danishmend (T: Danişmendoğulları) Turkoman dynasty that ruled over Cappadocia, Sebasteia and Melitene from late eleventh century, until conquered by the Seljuqs in 1178

Davidic of or pertaining to David, king of Israel, or to his family

demesne western form of land tenure, referring to the lands retained by a lord for his own use (as against lands granted out); initially demesne lands were usually worked by villeins or serfs on the lord's behalf, in fulfilment of their obligations, but this tended to be commuted to monetary payments

despot (*despotēs*) 'lord, master': high imperial title in the Palaiologan period, generally reserved for brothers or sons of the emperor; ruler of a semi-independent imperial territory

diadem originally a head-band, then imperial Roman symbol of majesty from the fourth century on; replaced in the early Byzantine period by a more solid crown (*stemma*), but sometimes used of this crown

dinar [A] (from *dēnarion*; L: *denarius*) standard Islamic gold coin

dioikētēs **(s.),** *dioikētai* **(pl.)** administrator responsible for collecting land tax, usually in a single province

dirham [A] (from *drachma*) standard Islamic silver coin

dishypatos court title often conferred on judges and administrative officials

domestic (*domestikos*; L: *domesticus*) senior official in the church or civil administration; senior military commander, especially of a *tagma*

domestic of the Schools (*domestikos tōn scholōn*) commander of the Schools (crack unit of *tagmata*); commander-in-chief of the armies of the west and the east

Dominante traditional term for Venice

doulos **(s.),** *douloi* **(pl.)** 'slave': emperor's servant, subordinate or subject; external ruler or notable who recognised the emperor's supremacy

doux (see also L: *dux*) head of a *doukaton* (L: *ducatus*), a 'duchy' in one of the western border regions, e.g. Venetia, Naples, Amalfi or Gaeta; from the tenth century on, military commander of a combat unit and/or larger administrative district, e.g. Antioch

droungarios (s.), ***droungarioi*** (pl.) a middle-ranking military officer; commander of the fleet (*tou ploimou*)

droungos (s.), ***droungoi*** (pl.) unit under command of a *droungarios*; subdivision of a theme army

dualist belief in two fundamental principles of good and evil governing the universe

ducat two types of coin from the duchy of Venice: (1) the thirteenth- and early fourteenth-century silver *grosso* [I], first struck in 1201 and imitated a century later at Constantinople under the name of *basilikon*; (2) more commonly, from 1284 onwards, the gold ducat (L: *ducatus aureus*)

dux (s.), ***duces*** (pl.) [L] see also *doux*; in the later Roman and early Byzantine period, commander of a military unit, or of garrison troops

ecumenical councils (from *oikoumenikos*, 'worldwide') conferences of the bishops of the whole church; the first seven 'universal' councils of the orthodox church, given imperial confirmation and the binding force of the law: Nicaea I (325); Constantinople I (381); Ephesus (431); Chalcedon (451); Constantinople II (553); Constantinople III (680–1); Nicaea II (787)

eidikon central treasury

electrum alloy containing silver and gold in a Byzantine coin

emirate(s) see amir

eparch the name of several officials, the most important being the eparch of the City, the civil governor of Constantinople

eparchia (s.), ***eparchiai*** (pl.) ecclesiastical province

epi tou kanikleiou 'keeper of the inkstand': the emperor's senior private secretary, who authenticated documents

ethnos (s.), ***ethnē*** (pl.) 'gentile', 'nation': a people external to Byzantium

ethnikos foreign outsider, member of an *ethnos*

eucharist Christian sacrament in which the body and the blood of Christ are conveyed to believers in the form of consecrated bread and wine; doctrine developed different emphases and ritual varied in different parts of the church

exarch military governor of Byzantine Italy (with his base at Ravenna) or Byzantine Africa (with his base at Carthage); senior official of the patriarchate

exarchate territorial and administrative unit commanded by an exarch; in modern usage, often the exarchate of Ravenna

excubitors (*exkoubitoi*; L: *excubitores*) one of the *tagmata*, elite regiments of the imperial guard, based in the capital

Fatimids Shiite dynasty based in Cairo from the later tenth century; their dominions included north Africa, Palestine and southern Syria

feudatory in the west, and western-occupied *Romania*: (of a person) owing sworn allegiance and services to another; (of a kingdom) under the overlordship of an outside sovereign

filioque [L] 'and from the Son': phrase added by the western church to the text of the Nicene Creed after the declaration that the Holy Spirit proceeds from the Father; major theological point of dispute between the papacy and the Byzantine church

fisc state's treasury and rights to revenue; in the west, royal property paying revenues in kind to support the royal household

fitna [A] literally 'trial': periodic civil wars in the Muslim empire during the first 200 years after Muhammad's death in 632

foideratoi (L: *foederati*) 'federates': originally barbarian tribes settled on Byzantine territory or borderlands on condition that they serve in the army; from the sixth century onwards, elite mounted troops, usually recruited from the barbarians

follis (s.), *folleis* (pl.) principal copper coin worth 288 to the *nomisma*

forum (s.), **fora** (pl.) [L] meeting place in town

Franks a Germanic grouping from the lower Rhine, frequently recruited into the Roman army; united in the early sixth century under Clovis, who extended Frankish rule to most of Roman Gaul and converted to Christianity; in Byzantine usage a broader term to cover all western Christians north of the Alps, including the Normans

Frisians ethnic grouping in north-west Europe, closely related to the Saxons, who inhabited the present-day Netherlands and north-west Germany

gasmouloi from the mid-thirteenth century on, descendants of mixed Greek–Latin (especially Venetian) parentage; recruited in large numbers as mercenaries

gastald Lombard royal official in Italy in charge of a gastaldate, with civil and military powers comparable to counts, and likewise tending to become hereditary

general logothete (*logothetēs tou genikou*) head of the fiscal department which dealt with assessment and collection of taxes

genikon logothesion the general treasury and main fiscal department of government after the seventh century, maintaining the lists of all the taxpayers in the empire; see also general logothete

Gepids eastern Germanic people settled in middle Danube region; dispersed after their defeat by the Avars in 567

Ghassanids monophysite Arab group and the main Arab *foideratoi* of Byzantium

ghazi [A] volunteer warrior fighting for Islam in raids (*ghazawat*) against pagans or Christians, expecting to gain booty or a martyr's death

Ghaznavids Turkic-speaking Muslim state based in present-day Afghanistan from the late tenth to early twelfth century

Gnostic from Gnosticism, the doctrine of salvation through a quasi-intuitive knowledge (*gnōsis*) of the mysteries of God and the origins and destiny of mankind

Golden Horde group of Mongols forming a khanate; dominated the lower Volga and the Black Sea steppes from the later thirteenth to the mid-fifteenth century

Goths Germanic groupings, primarily the Ostrogoths and Visigoths, who raided and settled in large numbers in south-west France, Spain, Italy and the Balkans throughout the fourth and fifth centuries

grand logothete first minister of the Palaiologan empire, in charge of civil administration and foreign affairs

grand *župan* (S: also *veliki* – 'great, grand' – *župan*) paramount ruler of the Serbs

Greek fire devastating and dreaded Byzantine petroleum-based weapon; it was sticky, was ignited at the moment of projection and could not be extinguished by water alone; first known use during the Arab blockade of Constantinople of 674–8; its composition and the technique for projecting it from siphons were state secrets, and the siphons were apparently no longer in use at the time of the Fourth Crusade

Hamdanid Muslim dynasty in Mosul, established in the earlier tenth century; controlled most of upper Mesopotamia, but their power declined in the eleventh century

hatun [Tsh] woman; wife

Helladikoi fleet of the theme of Hellas

Hellenes Greek-speakers, and by extension participants in Greek culture; used pejoratively by Byzantines of their pre-Christian predecessors to mean benighted pagans, but regained positive connotations from around the twelfth century onwards

Hephthalites (White Huns) nomadic people controlling much of the Central Asian steppes in the fifth and sixth centuries

hesychast (-asm) (from *hesychia*, 'peace and quiet') contemplative practice focused on attaining communion with God through inner peace and prayer; term denoting a fourteenth-century movement in Byzantine monasticism

hexagram silver coin introduced by Heraclius in 615 and in use until the early eighth century

hierosynē (L: *sacerdotium*) sacramental priesthood

hijra [A] flight by Muhammad and his followers from Mecca to Medina *c.* 622; the base year of the Muslim calendar

Himyarites (Homerites) predominantly Jewish realm ruling over much of south-west Arabia from the late second century BC until the mid-sixth century AD

holy war belief that waging war on God's behalf was a religious duty

Huns Eurasian nomads who conquered the Alans and expelled the Goths from the Black Sea steppes in the late fourth century; moved westwards, raiding as far as Gaul in the fifth century

hypatos (L: consul) senior court title from the sixth century onwards

hyperpyron **(s.),** *hyperpyra* **(pl.)** (L: *perperum*) 'highly refined': gold coin introduced by Alexios I *c.* 1092; by extension, a unit of account based on this coin; after the gold *hyperpyron* ceased to be struck in the mid-fourteenth century, the term was transferred to the large silver coin that replaced it

hypostasis the individual reality of Christ, as distinguished from His two natures (human and divine)

icon (*eikōn* (s.), *eikones* (pl.)) religious image; picture or portable panel with sacred use and connotations

iconoclast (from *eikōn* 'icon', *klazō* 'smash') 'breaker of images': those after 726 opposed to the veneration of icons, wishing to remove them from public and private view

iconodule (from *eikōn* 'icon', *doulos* 'slave') servant of images (see iconophile)

iconophile (from *eikōn* 'icon', *philos* 'friend') 'image-friendly' i.e. venerator of icons (see iconodule)

Ilkhans leaders of one of the four divisions of the Mongolian empire, centred on Persia, from the mid-thirteenth to fourteenth century; the title of Ilkhan was initially used to signal acknowledgement of primacy of the Great Khan (in Peking)

imam [A] supreme leader of the Muslim community; used by Shiites to denote the Prophet's son-in-law, 'Ali, and his descendants; the officiating priest of a Muslim mosque

imperator [L] 'emperor': used on coins and inscriptions, as part of the imperial nomenclature, throughout the early Byzantine period (G: *autokratōr, basileus*)

imperium [L] kingdom or reign (G: *basileia*)

incanto **(s.),** *incanti* **(pl.)** [I] Venetian system of auctioning the state-owned galleys for commercial use (see also *muda*)

indiction fifteen-year cycle used for dating purposes from the early fourth century onwards, especially in relation to tax-collection

inurbamento [I] the process of moving to live in towns

Ishmaelites Byzantine name for the Arabs, because they were supposedly descended from Ishmael, son of Abraham (see also Saracens)

isosyllabic of a metrical structure in which the syllables are of the same length

Jacobite Syrian monophysites, named after Jacob Baradaeus who helped set up a separate church hierarchy in the sixth century; sometimes applied to monophysites in general

janissary (from Tsh: *yeni cheri*, 'new army') Christian taken under a 'child levy' for training in the Ottoman 'new army' and administration

jihad [A] struggle against one's baser instincts; struggle to make unbelievers submit to the will of God (see also holy war)

judex **(s.),** *judices* **(pl.)** judge; general Latin term for a local magistrate or ruler

Julianists see aphthartodocetism

kapnikon tax on 'hearths' or households

Karabisianoi (from *karabos*, 'ship') a maritime theme in the Aegean, usually based at Samos

Karaites Jewish sect which rejects the Talmud and bases its teaching exclusively on the Scriptures

Karati Peyre taxes raised by Genoese authorities established in Pera (on the north shore of the Golden Horn) from the thirteenth century on

karshuni [A] Arabic written in Syriac letters

kastron **(s.),** *kastra* **(pl.)** (from L: *castrum*) fort, fortress; from the seventh century on could also mean town or city

katepanō from the eighth to twelfth century, a military officer commanding a unit and/or administrative district; from the thirteenth century on, a provincial or regional official

khagan [Tc] title of earlier Turkic supreme rulers (e.g. Avars, Khazars); head of a khaganate

khan [Tc] 'supreme leader': used of pre-Christian Bulgar, and of Turkic and Mongol rulers; head of a khanate

Khazars a Turkic-speaking people who were the major power in the Black Sea steppes, with centres on the lower Volga and Don, from the seventh to later tenth century, when their power was broken by the Rus; major allies of the Byzantines, the majority of Khazars converted to Judaism in the ninth century; their lands were known as Khazaria (in later medieval Italian texts, *Gazaria*)

Khurramites dualist sect in Iran (akin to the Mazdakites) whose movement culminated in Babek's revolt against the Arabs in the mid-ninth century

Kibyrrhaiotai maritime theme in Asia Minor

klasma **(s.),** *klasmata* **(pl.)** 'fragment': land, long abandoned by its tax-paying owner, transferred to public ownership, often for redistribution

kleisoura **(s.),** *kleisourai* **(pl.)** 'pass': administrative district, usually smaller than a theme, in frontier zones especially the Taurus mountains

Knights Hospitaller more fully, 'Knights of the order of the Hospital of St John of Jerusalem': originally a hospice for pilgrims, especially the sick poor; in the twelfth century developed a military wing and acquired extensive properties in western Europe; after 1310 also known as Knights of Rhodes and, from 1530, Knights of Malta

Kök Turks ('Blue or Celestial Turks') Turkic-speaking people who established a Turkic khaganate in the Eurasian steppes from the mid-sixth to the mid-eighth century

komēs **(s.),** *komitai* **(pl.)** count (see also *comes*); military officer of one of several sorts, commanding e.g. the Opsikion, the *tagmata* of the Walls, the *banda* within themes; the count of the stable (*komēs tou staulou*) headed the department that distributed horses and mules to the *tagmata*; term used by medieval Byzantines for western European magnates

kommerkiarios **(s.),** *kommerkiarioi* **(pl.)** tax official, probably the successor of the late Roman *comes commerciorum* [L], the controller of trade on the frontier; from *c.* 650 to *c.* 730 had a key role in raising, storing and issuing to the army revenue mainly in kind; from the mid-eighth century reverted to mainly taxing commerce

kommerkion **(s.),** *kommerkia* **(pl.)** (L: *commercium*) late Roman term for frontier cities where exchanges with foreign merchants were authorised; from the eighth century on, sales tax, normally 10 per cent of the value of the merchandise traded

kontakion **(s.),** *kontakia* **(pl.)** liturgical hymn in honour of a saint or a feast

koubikoularios (L: *cubicularius*) title for dignitaries belonging to the emperor's household

kouratoreia term for imperial estates; areas whose revenues were directly payable to the emperor

kouropalatēs third-highest honorary title after that of emperor (just below *nobelissimos*), initially granted only to members of the imperial family: see *cura palatii*

labarum [L] military standard adopted by Constantine the Great after his vision of the 'cross of light'; this was Christianised by adding to it the '*chrismon*' (the letters Chi (X) and Rho (P) – the first two letters of Christ's name in Greek); by extension, various types of standard or sceptre

Lakhmids Christian (Nestorian) Arab kingdom, clients of Persia in the sixth century

Lazes people living in Lazica, on the eastern coast of the Black Sea

legate, papal personal representative of the pope, entrusted with a mission

legend the lettering or wording on a coin or seal

liturgy all the prescribed services of the church; specifically, the eucharist

livre [F] (L: *libra*) medieval French currency, established by Charlemagne as a unit of account equal to one pound of silver

logothesion **(s.),** ***logothesia*** **(pl.)** central bureaus, instituted in the seventh century

logothete (*logothetēs*, L: *logotheta*) 'accountant': official in charge of one of the *logothesia*; often very high-ranking, logothetes controlled all the principal fiscal bureaus from the seventh century onwards

logothete of the Drome top official in charge of the *logothesion tou dromou*, the bureau which managed the roads, post, intelligence and diplomacy

Lombards a Germanic people living in the northern Balkans and Pannonia, who migrated to Italy in the later sixth century under threat from the Avars

loros long brocade scarf, studded with precious stones, draped around the shoulders and upper body and worn by the emperor and empress; also an attribute of archangels in attendance on Christ

magister militum **(s.),** ***magistri militum*** **(pl.)** [L] 'master of the soldiers': highest-ranking field commander of the late Roman army

magister officiorum [L] 'master of offices': head of the central civil administration and close associate of the emperor in the late Roman empire

magistros **(s.),** ***magistroi*** **(pl.)** holder of the old office of *magister officiorum* [L]; subsequently, a dignity fifth in hierarchical order after the emperor

Magnaura ceremonial hall situated on the periphery of the Great Palace, where the emperor gave audiences to foreign ambassadors and held the most solemn assemblies (*silentia*)

mahona **(n.),** ***mahonesi*** **(adj.)** [I] the Genoese shareholding company that ran Genoa's overseas possessions, comparable to the East India Company

majuscule script – roughly equivalent to capital letters – used almost exclusively for the writing of books from the second to ninth century, until replaced by minuscule (also known as uncial)

malik [A] 'king': title of a ruler ranking lower than the sultan; unlike amir, *malik* was often used of independent rulers, including non-Muslims

Mamluk [A] 'thing possessed', 'slave', particularly one in military service; sultanate of emancipated, mainly Cuman, military slaves which ruled Egypt, Syria and adjoining areas from the mid-thirteenth to early sixteenth century

mancosus **(s.),** ***mancosi*** **(pl.)** an Arabic loan-word which entered the Latin west along with the Arab coins it designated; from the Arabic *manqush* (past participle of the verb *naqash* 'to strike' or 'engrave'); the term has been found on dirhams and has been used in connection with dinars; used in texts from Carolingian Italy to mean either a dinar, or its value in Carolingian currency

manglabitēs member of an elite unit of the imperial bodyguard; title denoting this

Manichaeism dualist doctrine founded by Mani (flayed alive in Persia in 276), whose followers were known as Manichees (see also Mazdakites)

Mardaites a military grouping of uncertain origin installed among the indigenous population in the north of present-day Lebanon and Syria in the seventh century; subsequently served as seafaring borderers on the empire's southern coasts and islands, to counter the Arabs

margrave title of nobility throughout western Europe, originally meaning 'count of a march or border area'; ruler of a margravate

Mariology study of doctrine relating to the Virgin Mary

marzban [P] commander of a Persian frontier province

Mazdakites Persian dualist sect whose radical social doctrines prompted their persecution in the fifth century; doctrine known to the Byzantines as Manichaeism

megas great

megas konostaulos 'grand constable': high-ranking military title; commander of the foreign mercenaries of the Nicaean – and later the restored Byzantine – empire

Melingoi (Melingians) Slav grouping in the Peloponnese which retained its identity and remained Slavic-speaking into the Ottoman period

miaphysite alternative term for monophysite

mikros small

miliarēsion (s.), miliarēsia (pl.) the basic silver coin, introduced by Leo III and worth 12 to the *nomisma*; characteristic of the eighth to eleventh century

mimēsis imitation, particularly with reference to classical literary models

minuscule script with small, rounded letters joined-up for speed of writing (replaced majuscule)

missi (dominici) [L] 'messengers (of the ruler)': emissaries sent by Charlemagne to his various regions

modios (s.), modioi (pl.) measure of weight or of land

Moldavians see Vlachs

monistic (from *monos*) adherent of philosophy that envisages a single reality

monophysite adherent of monophysitism

monophysitism (from *monos* and *physis*) doctrine which emphasised the unity of Christ's person so strongly that it could not easily accept that His two natures (divine and human) were evenly divided in His person;

went against the definition of the faith of the council of Chalcedon (451) (see Chalcedonianism)

monos single

monothelitism (from *monos* and *thelein* 'to will') doctrine recognising the existence of one 'will' in the incarnate Christ beyond the duality of His natures (see monophysitism); a compromise formula put forward during Heraclius' reign and condemned by the sixth ecumenical council held in Constantinople (680–1)

Montanism apocalyptic Christian movement expecting speedy outpouring of the Holy Spirit on the church; the Montanists followed the teachings of Montanus, a second-century Phrygian

Moravians Slavic-speaking inhabitants of the ninth-century polity which arose in central Europe after the dissolution of the Avar khaganate, but was crushed by the Hungarians at the end of the ninth century

muda (s.), mudae (pl.) [L] fourteenth-century trading convoys organised by the Venetian commune to *Romania*, Alexandria, Syria and Flanders; the rights to outfit and man each galley within the *muda* were auctioned (see *incanto*), although the Great Council determined how many galleys should sail to each destination, and the timetable; not all Venetian commerce was carried in these government convoys

Neoplatonism philosophical system loosely based on the ideas of Plato, developed by Plotinus among others; highly influential on Byzantine thought especially through the theological school of Alexandria

Nestorianism doctrine of the Syrian churchman Nestorius (died *c.* 451) which emphasised the duality of Christ's nature (human and divine) so strongly that it could not easily accept the unity of His person

nobelissimos (L: nobelissimus) high-ranking court-title, classed just below caesar, and initially (in the eighth century) reserved for members of the imperial family

nomisma (s.), nomismata (pl.) (L: solidus) gold coin struck at 72 to the pound of gold, valued at 12 *miliarēsia* or 288 *folleis*; from *c.* 1092 onwards Alexios I's new version was generally known as a *hyperpyron*

Normans people from north-west France, originally of Scandinavian origin; in the eleventh century, the duke of Normandy conquered England, other Norman magnates appropriated southern Italy and Sicily and, under the banner of crusading, Antioch

notarios scribe or secretary in government bureau

novella (s.), novellae (pl.) [L] 'new (decree)': issued by an emperor; the Greek equivalent was *neara* (*diataxis* or *nomothesia*)

officium Gazarie [L] the Genoese council of elders responsible for navigation and commerce in the Black Sea (*Gazaria* = Khazaria)

oikonomia the principle of 'economy' or compromise; in ecclesiastical or political contexts, the relaxation of a rule for a greater good

oikos (**s.**) ***oikoi*** (**pl.**) household; stanza of a *kontakion*

oikoumenē the inhabited world

oikoumenikos (L: *universalis*) 'worldwide', ecumenical

Opsikion one of the earliest themes to emerge; based in north-west Asia Minor, closest to Constantinople, with headquarters at Nicaea

Optimatoi theme created in the later eighth century when the Opsikion was split up for political reasons, and when the Optimatoi was demoted from a combat to a rearguard unit

ordo [L] an ordinal, book of rubrics; made to supplement other liturgical books containing texts of prayers, music, lessons, etc.

Origenism attempt to fuse the fundamentals of Greek philosophy with the Christian creed, interpreting the scriptures in a triple sense – literal, moral and allegorical; based on the work of the early third-century philosopher and scholar Origen

orphanotrophos the director of an orphanage, usually a monk; in Constantinople the *orphanotrophoi* became state officials with fiscal responsibilities

orthodoxos (**s.**), ***orthodoxoi*** (**pl.**) (from *orthos* 'correct, true' and *doxa* 'opinion, belief') 'true believers', 'correct thinkers'; later used to distinguish the eastern (orthodox) from the western (Roman Catholic) church

orthodoxy Christianity as defined by correct beliefs, themselves determined at the seven ecumenical councils of the church, and set out in a series of documents and guided by tradition

Ossetians (Ossetes) nomadic pastoralists speaking a form of Iranian, who were related to the Alans; occupied the north-eastern approaches of the Caucasus and also settled in the mountains

Ostrogoths (eastern Goths) groupings of Goths, who adopted Arian Christianity and conquered Italy in the 490s, forming a kingdom based at Ravenna; subjugated in the mid-sixth century by Justinian

Palamism Gregory Palamas' teaching of mystical contemplation, spirituality and ascetic exercises

pallium (**s.**), **pallia** (**pl.**) [L] 'outer garment': vestment; stole-like garment worn by the Roman pope and prelates

panhypersebastos senior court title held by members of the imperial family under the Komnenoi; title bestowed on highly favoured foreigners

parakoimōmenos 'sleeping at the side [of the emperor]': official, usually a eunuch, who was the emperor's chamberlain or personal attendant

paroikos (**s.**), ***paroikoi*** (**pl.**) peasant tenant on private or state land, paying rent as well as tax; from the thirteenth century onwards most peasants seem to have been *paroikoi*

Parthians Persian-based empire led by the Arsacid dynasty, ruling most of Mesopotamia from the later third century BC until its overthrow by the Sasanians in the early third century AD

partitio Romaniae [L] 'dividing-up of the Roman empire': agreement drawn up by Venetians and Crusaders in spring 1204 while besieging Constantinople

patrikios (L: *patricius*) 'patrician': senior court title, often associated with offices such as *stratēgos*

patris fatherland, sense of home and of affinity

patristics study of the church fathers

Paulicians dualist sect forming distinctive communities in the eastern borderlands of Byzantium in the first two-thirds of the ninth century; were then transplanted west to borderlands with Bulgaria

pax mongolica [L] 'Mongol peace': facilitation of communication and commerce resulting from the Mongols' maintenance of order across their vast conquered territories

Pechenegs (also Scyths, Patzinaks) semi-nomadic Turkic-speaking people from the Eurasian steppe; occupied Black Sea steppes from end of the ninth century, and employed by emperors against neighbouring peoples, e.g. Hungarians and Rus; invaded Balkans in 1040s and finally routed in 1091 by the Byzantines and Cumans

philanthrōpia love of mankind, generosity

philos (s.), ***philoi*** (pl.) friend

physis (s.), ***physeis*** (pl.) nature

pinkernēs 'cupbearer' of the emperor; office held by members of the imperial family under the Komnenoi

placitum [L] legal assembly, plea

podestà [I] name given to certain high officials in the Italian city states, notably the chief magistrate; senior Venetian official in Constantinople after 1204

Porphyra chamber in the Great Palace with walls of deep red or purple stone (porphyry), where the empress normally gave birth

porphyrogenitus (s. m.), ***porphyrogenita*** (s. f.), ***porphyrogeniti*** (pl.) [L] 'purple-born': imperial child born 'in the purple' (usually in the Porphyra chamber), i.e. after its father had become emperor

praesentales commanders of early Byzantine core army units, close to the emperor

praetorian prefect official responsible for the largest administrative unit of the empire (prefecture) from Constantine the Great's time

praitōr [L: *praetor*] civilian administrator whose precise function is uncertain, sometimes taking on the role of *doux* or *katepanō*

prince of princes (***archōn tōn archontōn***) title of the foremost of Armenian princes, as recognised by the Byzantine emperor

proedros senior court title; ecclesiastical title used for bishops

prooimion preface, preamble

pronoētēs supervisor; provincial administrative or fiscal official

***pronoia* (s.), *pronoiai* (pl.)** grant of taxes and other revenues from state-owned land or other specified properties, usually in return for military service; introduced from the late eleventh century, it eventually became inheritable

proskynēsis veneration; gesture of respectful greeting or profound reverence, ranging from full prostration to a simple bow

***prostagma* (s.), *prostagmata* (pl.)** imperial ordinance

prōtasekrētis head of imperial chancellery responsible for drafting and keeping imperial records

prōtonotarios top civil official in the thematic administration, first mentioned in ninth century

prōtoproedros high-ranking title with precedence over *proedros*

prōtos first

prōtosebastos high-ranking dignity introduced by Alexios I Komnenos, usually bestowed on the emperor's close relatives

prōtospatharios (L: *protospatharius*) 'first sword bearer': court title initially reserved for a high military commander, later bestowed on lower military officers and other officials

prōtostratōr head groom in charge of the emperor's private stable; commander of the troops and one of the highest Palaiologan dignitaries

***prōtovestiarios* (m.), *prōtovestiarissa* (f.)** 'first keeper of the wardrobe': originally a high-ranking post for a palace eunuch; later a court title conferred on senior civil and military officials

purple, in (the) see *porphyrogenitus*

Qarluqs early Turkic tribal confederation in Transoxania which formed a khanate in the mid-eighth century

quaestor (G: *kouaistōr*) judicial officer, responsible for drafting laws

razzia [I] armed raid, originally by desert-dwellers on settled agricultural land, to conquer, plunder and seize slaves

red-slip type of pottery table- and cooking-ware produced in North Africa and widely distributed around the Mediterranean and across the northwest provinces of the Roman empire from the second to sixth century

***rex* (s.), *reges* (pl.)** [L] 'king'

Rhos Greek form of Rus

***roga* (s.), *rogai* (pl.)** stipend paid to title-holders, senior officials and soldiers annually

***Romaios* (s.), *Romaioi* (pl.)** 'Roman': term used by the Byzantines to describe themselves

Romania 'land of the Romans' (i.e. Byzantines); by the seventh century, a term for the Christian empire of the east; from the thirteenth century, used of the former lands of the Byzantine empire which had been partitioned and were being governed by the Venetians, Franks and other westerners

Rupenids first dynasty to rule Armenian Cilicia, from the late eleventh to early thirteenth century

Rus people of Scandinavian origin who formed a political structure in eastern Europe, between the Gulf of Finland and Middle Dnieper; the land-mass over which they predominated; from the late eleventh century, the term began to denote all inhabitants of this area, from which Russia takes its name

sacrum cubiculum [L] 'sacred chamber': part of the imperial palace

Sallarid tenth- to eleventh-century Muslim dynasty which ruled in the eastern Caucasus and north-western Iran before the Seljuqs; also known as Musafirid or Kangarid

Samaritans followers of a primitive form of Judaism

sandjakbey [Tsh] ruler of a Turkish state administrative unit

Saracens (*Sarakenoi*; L: *Saraceni*) vague term used by westerners and Byzantines of Arabs and, later, of other Muslims, supposed by early Christian churchmen to be the sons of Ishmael by the bond-woman Hagar (see also Ishmaelites)

Sasanians Persian ruling dynasty which overthrew the Parthian Arsacid dynasty in the early third century and ruled modern Iran and parts of Iraq, Pakistan, Afghanistan, Turkmenistan, Uzbekistan and the Gulf Coast of the Arabian peninsula until overthrown by the Arabs in the mid-seventh century

satrap [P] governor of a province in the Persian empire; district administrator

satrapēs see satrap

Saxons Germanic people, conquered and forcibly converted by Charlemagne in the late eighth and early ninth century

Saxony power base of the Ottonian rulers of Germany in the later tenth century

Schools (*scholai*; L: *scholae*) originally any 'office' or body of officials; then more specifically the *scholae palatinae* [L], palace guard created by Diocletian or Constantine the Great; held a mainly ceremonial role by the fifth century; but by the eighth century, a crack unit of the *tagmata*, with an active military role

Scyths classical name for Iranian-speaking nomads of Black Sea steppes; used by Byzantines of several northern peoples, including Bulgars, Pechenegs, Uzes and Cumans

sebastokratōr (s.), *sebastokratores* (pl.) late Byzantine court title normally bestowed on the emperor's sons and other relatives

sebastos (s.), *sebastoi* (pl.) court title introduced by Alexios I Komnenos and conferred on members of the Komnenian elite or foreign rulers;

the root for the higher titles of the *sebastokratōr, panhypersebastos* and *prōtosebastos*

sekrēton (**s.**), *sekrēta* (**pl.**) central administrative and financial bureau

seneschal senior official in important noble western households; royal official in charge of justice and administration in southern France

Septuagint ('**LXX**') the most influential of the Greek versions of the Hebrew Old Testament

shah [P] 'king' (usually of Persia)

silentarios a court attendant whose first duty was to secure order and silence in the palace

silention (**s.**), *silentia* (**pl.**) 'silence': solemn assembly convened by the emperor; the emperor's speeches

simony the purchasing of church office

Sklaviniai regions of Slav settlement and predominance, mainly in Macedonia and Greece

solidus (**s.**), *solidi* (**pl.**) see *nomisma*

sparapet [Armenian] chief Armenian military officer

spatharios (**s.**), *spatharioi* (**pl.**) 'sword-bearer': court title, of decreasing importance from the ninth century

spatharokandidatos court title conferred on lower-rank officials

stemma (**s.**), *stemmata* (**pl.**) imperial metal crown, usually ornamented with pearls and precious stones and surmounted by a cross

stratēgos (**s.**), *stratēgoi* (**pl.**) 'general': from the seventh or eighth century the commander of a theme, who held both civil and military power; during the eleventh century replaced by the terms *doux* or *katepanō*

stratēgos autokratōr commander-in-chief of the Byzantine forces in the west or the east; often used as an equivalent of the domestic of the Schools

strateia (**s.**), *strateiai* (**pl.**) state service of any sort; entitlement to imperial *roga*, carrying with it special military service obligations; from the mid-tenth century, a property whose holder was subject to military service or to supporting a soldier

stratiōtēs (**s.**), *stratiōtai* (**pl.**) 'soldier': holder of a *strateia*; from the mid-tenth century, a holder of 'military land' subject to the obligation to support a soldier

stratiōtikon imperial bureau dealing with military-related taxes and pay

stratōr (**s.**), *stratores* (**pl.**) 'groom': official in the imperial stables

stylites (from *stylē*, 'pillar') from the fifth century onwards, ascetics who fasted and prayed on top of pillars

sultan [A] one of the highest secular titles denoting ruler of a Muslim state; from the mid-eleventh century, title of Seljuq and subsequent Muslim rulers in the Middle East

sürgün [Tsh] forcible deportation and resettlement by Ottoman Turks

suzerain overlord, to whom vassals paid tribute; a dominant state, controlling the foreign relations of a vassal region or people, while allowing them limited self-rule

synkellos 'living in the same cell': high-ranking official in one of the patriarchates; in Constantinople, usually appointed by the emperor to represent his interests

synodikon collection of acts from a synod; liturgical document containing important rulings

synōnē tax or exaction on cultivated land, paid either in kind or in cash (see also *annona*)

tafsīr [A] Koranic commentary

tagma **(s.)**, *tagmata* **(pl.)** 'regiment(s)': elite cavalry and infantry unit(s) stationed in the capital, formed in the eighth century; from the tenth to twelfth centuries, full-time foreign mercenary unit(s)

tarì [A] gold coin (quarter-dinar) struck by the Fatimids and their Norman and Hohenstaufen successors in Sicily

taxis 'good form': battle array; good order in court ceremonial; order and harmony in state, church and society

terciers [French] (I: *terzieri*) three Latin lords, Veronese noblemen, to whom Boniface of Montferrat granted the island of Negroponte in 1205; and their successors until 1390

thema **(s.)**, *themata* **(pl.)** literally 'element', 'topic', 'file'; see theme

theme in the middle Byzantine era, the district where soldiers were quartered, and from which they were recruited; an administrative unit; the army based in such a region

Theotokos 'god-bearing' (from *theos* 'god' and *tokos* 'bringing forth'): description of the Virgin (Mother of God) which emphasised that Mary gave birth to God, and not to a man who became God

Thrakesioi one of the earliest themes, based in western Anatolia with headquarters at Chonai

thughur [A] border region (specifically the Muslim–Byzantine border)

toparch (*toparchēs*) local borderland potentate

tourma **(s.)**, *tourmai* **(pl.)** military unit; subdivision of theme (see also turmarch)

tribunus **(s.)**, *tribuni* **(pl.)** [L] term for indigenous local rulers in southern Italy, which fell out of use in the ninth century

triconch type of church plan in the form of a trefoil

troparion short, sung hymn which forms part of the liturgy

True Cross wooden cross on which Christ was crucified, or fragments – relics – supposedly from it

Turkmen (Turkoman, Turcoman) Turkish nomadic tribesmen from Central Asia who streamed into Anatolia in the eleventh century and subsequently; many were associated with the Seljuqs

tümen [Mongolian] largest Mongol fighting unit, between 3,000 and 10,000 strong

turmarch commander of a *tourma*; senior military commander with fiscal and judicial responsibilities

typikon (s.), *typika* (pl.) monastic foundation charter, setting out the rules and liturgical services to be maintained

Uighurs Turkic confederation which established its own khaganate over the remnants of the Kök Turk empire from *c.* 745 to *c.* 840

Umayyad first Muslim ruling dynasty (661–750)

uncial see majuscule

Uzes a branch of the Oghuz confederation of Turkic-speaking peoples; ousted the Pechenegs from the Black Sea steppes in the mid-eleventh century; invaded Balkans in 1064, but eventually mastered by the Byzantines

Wallachians see Vlachs

veliki župan [S] see grand *župan*

vestarchēs court title conferred on lower-ranking officials

vestēs court title granted to prominent military commanders

vestiarion (L: *vestarium*) 'imperial wardrobe': state treasury for things other than coins

vicegerent deputy (e.g. for God)

Visigoths (western Goths) groupings of Goths who raided into Roman territory in the fourth and fifth centuries, adopting Arian Christianity and establishing kingdoms in present-day south-west France and Spain

vizier [A] high-ranking administrator and adviser appointed by the caliph or sultan; first minister

Vlachs Romance-language-speaking pastoral inhabitants of eastern and south-eastern Europe, descended from Romanised Thracians, other local Balkan populations and Roman colonists; one grouping, the Wallachians, are now found in present-day Romania while another, the Moldavians, are also found in present-day Moldova

Zealots strongly iconophile monks in the late eighth to tenth century; mid-fourteenth century group which briefly established self-government in Thessaloniki, confiscating aristocratic property and redistributing wealth

***zeugaratos* (s.), *zeugaratoi* (pl.)** fiscal term for a peasant who owned a
    pair of oxen

Zoroastrianism [P] early Persian system of religious doctrine established by
    Zarathustra (Zoroaster), venerating fire as a life-force present through-
    out all creation

župan [S] high-ranking title of the south Slavs and (later) the Wallachians
    (see also *grand župan*)

GENEALOGICAL TABLES AND LISTS OF RULERS

Table 1 *Byzantine emperors in Constantinople (c. 500–1204 and 1261–1453)*

Reign	Emperor	Family ties constituting a 'dynasty'*
491–518	Anastasius	
518–527	Justin I	
527–565	Justinian I	
565–578	Justin II	
578–582	Tiberius I	Justinianic
582–602	Maurice	
602–610	Phocas I	
610–641	Heraclius	
641–668	Constans II	
668–685	Constantine IV	
685–695	Justinian II (first reign)	
695–698	Leontius (overthrew Justinian II, exiling him to Cherson)	Heraclian
698–705	Tiberius II Apsimar (overthrew Leontius)	
705–711	Justinian II (second reign)	
711–713	Philippikos	
713–715	Anastasios II	
715–717	Theodosios III	
717–741	Leo III 'the Isaurian'	
741–775	Constantine V	
775–780	Leo IV	Isaurian
780–797	Constantine VI	
797–802	Irene	
802–811	Nikephoros I	
811	Staurakios	
811–813	Michael I	Nikephorian

* 'Dynasty' is here used as a loose yet convenient label for sequences of rulers linked by ties of blood, marriage, adoption or co-emperorship

906

Table 1 *Byzantine emperors (cont.)*

Reign	Emperor	Family ties constituting a 'dynasty'
813–820	Leo V 'the Armenian'	
820–829	Michael II	
829–842	Theophilos	Amorian
842–867	Michael III	
867–886	Basil I	
886–912	Leo VI 'the Wise'	
912–913	Alexander	
913–920	Constantine VII (regency)	
920–944	Romanos I Lekapenos	
945–959	Constantine VII Porphyrogenitus	
959–963	Romanos II	
963–969	Nikephoros II Phokas	
969–976	John I Tzimiskes	Macedonian
976–1025	Basil II	
1025–1028	Constantine VIII	
1028–1034	Romanos III Argyros	
1034–1041	Michael IV 'the Paphlagonian'	
1041–1042	Michael V	
1042	Zoe and Theodora	
1042–1055	Constantine IX Monomachos	
1055–1056	Theodora	
1056–1057	Michael VI Stratiotikos	
1057–1059	Isaac I Komnenos	
1059–1067	Constantine X Doukas	
1068–1071	Romanos IV Diogenes	Doukai
1071–1078	Michael VII Doukas	
1078–1081	Nikephoros III Botaneiates	
1081–1118	Alexios I Komnenos	
1118–1143	John II Komnenos	
1143–1180	Manuel I Komnenos	Komnenoi
1180–1183	Alexios II Komnenos	
1183–1185	Andronikos I Komnenos	
1185–1195	Isaac II Angelos	
1195–1203	Alexios III Angelos	Angeloi
1203–1204	Isaac II and Alexios IV Angelos	
1204	Alexios I Doukas	
[1204–1261]	[Latin Empire – Constantinople recaptured 1261 – see Tables 2 and 6.v]	
1258–1282	Michael VIII Palaiologos (assumed imperial title 1259; emperor at Constantinople 1261)	
1282–1328	Andronikos II Palaiologos	
1294/5–1320	Michael IX Palaiologos	
1328–1341	Andronikos III Palaiologos	
1341–1391	John V Palaiologos	
1347–1354	John VI Kantakouzenos	Palaiologoi
1376–1379	Andronikos IV Palaiologos	
1390	John VII Palaiologos	
1391–1425	Manuel II Palaiologos	
1425–1448	John VIII Palaiologos	
1449–1453	Constantine XI Palaiologos	

Table 2 *Rulers of the Greek 'rump states' (1204–1461)*

Reign	Emperor	Family ties constituting a 'dynasty'
i *Nicaea*		
1205–1221	Theodore I Laskaris	
1221–1254	John III Vatatzes	
1254–1258	Theodore II Laskaris	Laskarid
1258–1261	John IV Laskaris	
1258–1282	Michael VIII Palaiologos (assumed imperial title 1259)	Palaiologoi [see Table 1]
ii *Greek rulers in the western provinces (Epiros and Thessaloniki)*		
1204–1215	Michael I Angelos Doukas of Epiros	
1215–1230	Theodore Angelos emperor at Thessaloniki 1224–1230	
1230–1237	Manuel Angelos emperor and despot at Thessaloniki	
1237–1244	John emperor and despot	Komnenos Doukas (styling themselves Angelos Doukas)
1244–1246	Demetrios Angelos Doukas despot	
1230–1267	Michael II Angelos Doukas despot in Epiros	
1267–1296	Nikephoros I Angelos Doukas despot	
1296–1318	Thomas despot	
iii *Emperors of Trebizond and Grand Komnenoi*		
1204–1222	Alexios I	
[1204–1212	David]~	~ Co-founder of the empire of Trebizond, but nominally subordinate to his brother, Alexios I; sometimes known as David I
1222–1235	Andronikos I Gidos	
1235–1238	John I Axouch	
1238–1263	Manuel I	
1263–1266	Andronikos II	
1266–1280	George	
1280–1297	John II	
1285	Theodora	
1297–1330	Alexios II	
1330–1332	Andronikos III	
1332	Manuel II	
1332–1340	Basil	Grand Komnenoi
1340–1341	Irene Palaiologina	
1341	Anna Anachoutlou (first reign)	
1341	Michael (first reign)	
1341–1342	Anna Anachoutlou (second reign)	
1342–1344	John III	
1344–1349	Michael (second reign)	
1349–1390	Alexios III	
1390–1416/17	Manuel III	
1416/17–1429	Alexios IV	
1429–1458/60	John IV	
1459–1461	David I	

Table 3 *Patriarchs of Constantinople (381–1502)*

Reign	Patriarch
Fourth century	
381–397	Nectarius
398–404	John I Chrysostom
Fifth century	
404–405	Arsacius
406–425	Atticus
426–427	Sisinnius I
428–431	Nestorius
431–434	Maximian
434?–446	Proclus
446–449	Flavian
449–458	Anatolius
458–471	Gennadius I
472–489	Acacius
489–490	Fravitas
490–496	Euphemius
Sixth century	
495–511	Macedonius II
511–518	Timothy I
518–520	John II the Cappadocian
520–535	Epiphanius
535–536	Anthimus I
536–552	Menas
552–565	Eutychius (first patriarchate)
565–577	John III Scholasticus
577–582	Eutychius (second patriarchate)
582–595	John IV Nesteutes 'the faster'
595/6–606	Cyriacus
Seventh century	
607–610	Thomas I
610–638	Sergius I
638–641	Pyrrhus (first patriarchate)
641–653	Paul II
654	Pyrrhus (second patriarchate)
654–666	Peter
667–669	Thomas II
669–675	John V
675–677	Constantine I
677–679	Theodore I (first patriarchate)
679–686	George I
686–687	Theodore I (second patriarchate)
688–694	Paul III
694–706	Callinicus I
Eighth century	
706–712	Kyros
712–715	John VI
715–730	Germanos I
730–754	Anastasios
754–766	Constantine II
766–780	Niketas I
780–784	Paul IV
784–806	Tarasios

(*cont.*)

Table 3 *Patriarchs* (*cont.*)

Reign	Patriarch
Ninth century	
806–815	Nikephoros I
815–821	Theodotos Kassiteras
821–837?	Antony I Kassymatas
837?–843	John VII the Grammarian
843–847	Methodios
847–858	Ignatios (first patriarchate)
858–867	Photios (first patriarchate)
867–877	Ignatios (second patriarchate)
877–886	Photios (second patriarchate)
886–893	Stephen I
893–901	Antony II Kauleas
Tenth century	
901–907	Nicholas I Mystikos (first patriarchate)
907–912	Euthymios I
912–925	Nicholas I Mystikos (second patriarchate)
925–927	Stephen II
927–931	Tryphon
933–956	Theophylact
956–970	Polyeuct
970–974	Basil I Skamandrenos
974–979	Antony III the Stoudite
979–991	Nicholas II Chrysoberges
[991–996]	[vacancy]
996–998	Sisinnios II
Eleventh century	
1001–1019	Sergios II
1019–1025	Eustathios
1025–1043	Alexios the Stoudite
1043–1058	Michael I Keroularios
1059–1063	Constantine III Leichoudes
1064–1075	John VIII Xiphilinos
1075–1081	Kosmas I
1081–1084	Eustratios Garidas
1084–1111	Nicholas III the Grammarian
Twelfth century	
1111–1134	John IX Agapetos
1134–1143	Leo Styppeiotes
1143–1146	Michael II Kourkouas
1146–1147	Kosmas II Attikos
1147–1151	Nicholas IV Mouzalon
1151/2–1153/4	Theodotos II
1153/4 (1 month)	Neophytos I
1154–1157	Constantine IV Chliarenos
1157–1169/70	Luke Chrysoberges
1170–1178	Michael III
1178–1179	Chariton Eugeneiotes
1179–1183	Theodosios Boradiotes
1183–1186	Basil II Kamateros
1186–1189	Niketas II Mountanes

Table 3 *Patriarchs (cont.)*

Reign	Patriarch
1189 (1 month)	Dositheos of Jerusalem (first patriarchate)
1189	Leontios Theotokites
1189–1191	Dositheos of Jerusalem (second patriarchate)
1191–1198	George II Xiphilinos
1198–1206	John X Kamateros
Thirteenth century	
1208–1214	Michael IV Autoreianos
1214–1216	Theodore II Eirenikos
1216	Maximos II
1216/17–1222	Manuel I Sarantenos
1223–1240	Germanos II
1240/1?	Methodios II
1243/4?–1254	Manuel II
1254–1259	Arsenios Autoreianos (first patriarchate)
1260–1261	Nikephoros II
1261–1265	Arsenios Autoreianos (second patriarchate)
1265–1266	Germanos III
1266–1275	Joseph I (first patriarchate)
1275–1282	John XI Bekkos
1282–1283	Joseph I (second patriarchate)
1283–1289	Gregory II (George) of Cyprus
1289–1293	Athanasios I (first patriarchate)
1294–1303	John XII Kosmas
Fourteenth century	
1303–1309	Athanasios I (second patriarchate)
1310–1314	Niphon I
1315–1319	John XIII Glykys
1320–1321	Gerasimos I
1323–1332	Isaias
1334–1347	John XIV Kalekas
1347–1350	Isidore I Boucheiras
1350–1353	Kallistos I (first patriarchate)
1353–1354	Philotheos Kokkinos (first patriarchate)
1355–1363	Kallistos I (second patriarchate)
1364–1376	Philotheos Kokkinos (second patriarchate)
1376/7–1379	Makarios (first patriarchate)
1380–1388	Neilos Kerameus
1389–1390	Antony IV (first patriarchate)
1390–1391	Makarios (second patriarchate)
1391–1397	Antony IV (second patriarchate)
1397	Kallistos II Xanthopoulos
1397–1402, 1403–1410	Matthew I
Fifteenth century	
1410–1416	Euthymios II
1416–1439	Joseph II
1440–1443	Metrophanes II
1443–1450?	Gregory III Mamme
1450	Athanasios II
1454–1456	Gennadios II (George) Scholarios (first patriarchate)

(cont.)

Table 3 *Patriarchs (cont.)*

Reign	Patriarch
1456–1462	Isidore II
1463	Gennadios II (George) Scholarios (second patriarchate)
1463–1464	Sophronios I
1464–1465	Gennadios II (George) Scholarios (third patriarchate)
1465–1466	Joasaph I Kokkas
1466	Mark Xylokaraves
1466–1467	Symeon 'of Trebizond' (first patriarchate)
1466–1471	Dionysios I (first patriarchate)
1471/2–1474	Symeon 'of Trebizond' (second patriarchate)
1475–1476	Raphael
1476–1481/2	Maximos III Manasses
1482–1486	Symeon 'of Trebizond' (third patriarchate)
1486–1488	Niphon II (first patriarchate)
1488–1490	Dionysios I (second patriarchate)
1491–1497	Maximos IV
1497–1498	Niphon II (second patriarchate)
1498–1502	Joachim I
1502	Niphon II (third patriarchate)

Table 4 *Popes of Rome (c. 450–c. 1500)*

Reign	Pope
Fifth century	
440–461	Leo I
461–468	Hilarus
468–483	Simplicius
483–492	Felix III
492–496	Gelasius I
496–498	Anastasius II
Sixth century	
498–514	Symmachus
514–523	Hormisdas
523–526	John I
526–530	Felix IV
530–532	Boniface II
533–535	John II
535–536	Agapetus I
536–537	Silverius
537–555	Vigilius
556–561	Pelagius I
561–574	John III
575–579	Benedict I
579–590	Pelagius II
590–604	Gregory I (the Great)
Seventh century	
604–606	Sabinianus
607	Boniface III

Table 4 *Popes* (*cont.*)

Reign	Pope
608–615	Boniface IV
615–618	Adeodatus I (Deusdedit)
619–625	Boniface V
625–638	Honorius I
640	Severinus
640–642	John IV
642–649	Theodore I
649–655	Martin I
654–657	Eugenius I
657–672	Vitalian
672–676	Adeodatus II
676–678	Donus
678–681	Agatho
682–683	Leo II
684–685	Benedict II
685–686	John V
686–687	Cono
687–701	Sergius I
Eighth century	
701–705	John VI
705–707	John VII
708	Sisinnius
708–715	Constantine
715–731	Gregory II
731–741	Gregory III
741–752	Zacharias
752–757	Stephen II (Stephen III)
757–767	Paul I
768–772	Stephen III (Stephen IV)
772–795	Hadrian I
Ninth century	
795–816	Leo III
816–817	Stephen IV (Stephen V)
817–824	Paschal I
824–827	Eugenius II
827	Valentine
827–844	Gregory IV
844–847	Sergius II
847–855	Leo IV
855–858	Benedict III
858–867	Nicholas I
867–872	Hadrian II
872–882	John VIII
882–884	Marinus I
884–885	Hadrian III
885–891	Stephen V (Stephen VI)
891–896	Formosus, bishop of Porto
896	Boniface VI
896–897	Stephen VI (Stephen VII)
897	Romanus
897	Theodore II
898–900	John IX

(*cont.*)

Table 4 *Popes (cont.)*

Reign	Pope
Tenth century	
900–903	Benedict IV
903	Leo V
904–911	Sergius III
911–913	Anastasius III
913–914	Lando
914–928	John X
928	Leo VI
928–931	Stephen VII (Stephen VIII)
931–935	John XI
936–939	Leo VII
939–942	Stephen VIII (Stephen IX)
942–946	Marinus II
946–955	Agapetus II
955–964	John XII
963–965	Leo VIII
964–966	Benedict V
965–972	John XIII
973–974	Benedict VI
974–983	Benedict VII
983–984	John XIV
985–996	John XV
996–999	Gregory V
Eleventh century	
999–1003	Sylvester II
1003	John XVII
1004–1009	John XVIII
1009–1012	Sergius IV
1012–1024	Benedict VIII
1024–1032	John XIX
1032–1044	Benedict IX (first pontificate)
1045	Sylvester III
1045	Benedict IX (second pontificate)
1045–1046	Gregory VI
1046–1047	Clement II
1047–1048	Benedict IX (third pontificate)
1048	Damasus II
1049–1054	Leo IX
1055–1057	Victor
1057–1058	Stephen IX (Stephen X)
1059–1061	Nicholas II
1061–1073	Alexander II
1073–1085	Gregory VII
1086–1087	Victor III
1088–1099	Urban II
Twelfth century	
1099–1118	Paschal II
1118–1119	Gelasius II
1119–1124	Callixtus II
1124–1130	Honorius II
1130–1143	Innocent II
1143–1144	Celestine II

Table 4 *Popes* (*cont.*)

Reign	Pope
1144–1145	Lucius II
1145–1153	Eugenius III
1153–1154	Anastasius IV
1154–1159	Hadrian IV
1159–1181	Alexander III
1181–1185	Lucius III
1185–1187	Urban III
1187	Gregory VIII
1187–1191	Clement III
1191–1198	Celestine III
Thirteenth century	
1198–1216	Innocent III
1216–1227	Honorius III
1227–1241	Gregory IX
1241	Celestine IV
1243–1254	Innocent IV
1254–1261	Alexander IV
1261–1264	Urban IV
1265–1268	Clement IV
1271–1276	Gregory X
1276	Innocent V
1276	Hadrian V
1276–1277	John XXI
1277–1280	Nicholas III
1281–1285	Martin IV
1285–1287	Honorius IV
1288–1292	Nicholas IV
1294	Celestine V
1294–1303	Boniface VIII
Fourteenth century	
1303–1304	Benedict XI
1305–1314	Clement V
1316–1334	John XXII
1334–1342	Benedict XII
1342–1352	Clement VI
1352–1362	Innocent VI
1362–1370	Urban V
1370–1378	Gregory XI
1378–1389	Urban VI
1389–1404	Boniface IX
Fifteenth century	
1404–1406	Innocent VII
1406–1415	Gregory XII
1417–1431	Martin V
1431–1447	Eugenius IV
1447–1455	Nicholas V
1455–1458	Callixtus III
1458–1464	Pius II
1464–1471	Paul II
1471–1484	Sixtus IV
1484–1492	Innocent VIII
1492–1503	Alexander VI

Table 5.i *Eastern rulers (Sasanian Persia)*

Reign	Shah
224–240	Ardashir I
240–270	Shapur I
270–271	Hormizd I
271–274	Bahram I
274–293	Bahram II
293	Bahram III
293–302	Narseh
302–309	Hormizd II
309–379	Shapur II
379–383	Ardashir II
383–388	Shapur III
388–399	Bahram IV
399–420	Yazdgard I
420–438	Bahram V
438–457	Yazdgard II
457–459	Hormizd III
459–484	Peroz
484–488	Valash
488–496	Kavad I (first reign)
496–498	Zamaspes (Jamasp)
498–531	Kavad I (second reign)
531–579	Khusro I
579–590	Hormizd IV
590	Khusro II (first reign)
590–591	Bahram Chobin
591–628	Khusro II (second reign)
628	Kavad II
628–629	Ardashir III
629	Shahrvaraz
630–631	Boran
633–651	Yazdgard III

Table 5.ii *Eastern rulers (Umayyad caliphate; Abbasid caliphate)*

Reign	Caliph	Dynasty
632–634	Abu Bakr	
634–644	ʿUmar I	Known as the *Rāshidūn*
644–656	ʿUthman	('rightly-guided') caliphs
656–661	ʿAli	
661–680	Muʿawiya I	
680–683	Yazid I	Umayyad (Sufyanid)
683–684	Muʿawiya II	
684–685	Marwan I	
685–705	ʿAbd al-Malik	
705–715	al-Walid I	
715–717	Suleiman	
717–720	ʿUmar II	
720–724	Yazid II	Umayyad (Marwanid)
724–743	Hisham	
743–744	al-Walid II	
744	Yazid III	
744	Ibrahim	
744–750	Marwan II	
749–754	al-Saffah	
754–775	al-Mansur	
775–785	al-Mahdi	
785–786	al-Hadi	
786–809	Harun al-Rashid	
809–813	al-ʾAmin	
813–833	al-Maʾmun	
833–842	al-Muʿtasim	
842–847	al-Wathiq	
847–861	al-Mutawakkil	
861–862	al-Muntasir	
862–866	al-Mustaʿin	
866–869	al-Muʿtazz	Abbasids
869–870	al-Muhtadi	
870–892	al-Muʿtamid	
892–902	al-Muʿtadid	
902–908	al-Muktafi	
908–932	al-Muqtadir	
932–934	al-Qahir	
934–940	al-Radi	
940–944	al-Mutaqqi	
944–946	al-Mustakfi	
946–974	al-Muti	
974–991	al-Taʾi	
991–1031	al-Qadir	
1031–1075	al-Qaʾim	
[1075–1258]	[Abbasid caliphate remained as a nominal commonwealth]	

Table 5.iii *Eastern rulers (Armenian princes: the principal Bagratuni and Artsruni lines)*

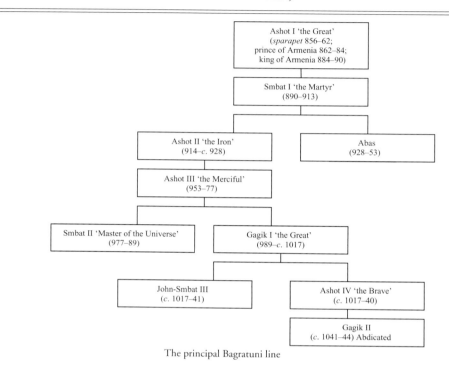

The principal Bagratuni line

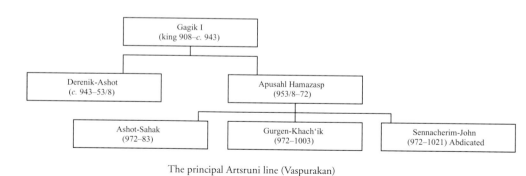

The principal Artsruni line (Vaspurakan)

Table 5.iv *Eastern rulers (Turks: the Seljuq dynasty)*

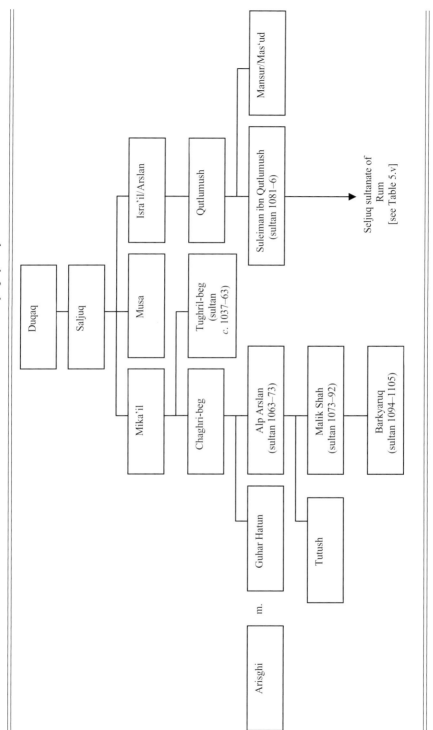

Table 5.v *Eastern rulers (Turks: the Seljuq sultanate of Rum)*

Reign	Sultan
1081–1086	Suleiman ibn Qutlumush
1092–1107	Kilij Arslan I
1107–1116	Malik Shah
1116–1155	Mas'ud
1156–1192	Kilij Arslan II
1192–1196	Kay-Khusraw I (first reign)
1196–1204	Rukn al-Din
1204–1205	Kilij Arslan III
1205–1211	Kay-Khusraw I (second reign)
1211–1219	Kay-Kawus I
1219–1237	Kay-Qubad I
1237–1246	Kay-Khusraw II
1246–1256	Kay-Kawus II (first reign)
1248–1265	Kilij Arslan IV
1257–1261	Kay-Kawus II (second reign)
[1261]	[sultanate of Rum subjugated by the Mongols]

Table 5.vi *Eastern rulers (Turks: the Ottoman beylik and sultanate (c. 1282–1566))*

Reign	Sultan	Dynasty
c. 1282–1326	Osman I	
1326–1362	Orhan	
1362–1389	Murad I	
1389–1402	Bayazid I	
[1402–1413]	[struggle between Mehmed I and his three brothers for the throne]	Osmanli
1413–1421	Mehmed I	
1421–1451	Murad II	
1451–1481	Mehmed II	
1481–1512	Bayazid II	
1512–1520	Selim I	
1520–1566	Suleiman I 'the Magnificent'	

Table 5.vii *Eastern rulers (Mongols: Genghis Khan and his descendants)*

Reign	Ruler	Dynasty (Branch)
1206–1227	Genghis Khan	
1227–1229	[Regency]	
1229–1241	Ögedei Khan	
1241–1246	[Regency]	
1246–1248	Güyüg Khan	Mongol khanate in Central Asia (Great Khans)
1248–1251	[Regency]	
1251–1259	Möngke	
1260–1294	Kublai Khan	
1239–1255	Batu	
c. 1255–c. 1256	Sartaq	
1256/7	Ulaghchi	
1257–1266	Berke	
1267–1281	Möngke-Timur	Golden Horde
1281–1287	Töde-Möngke	
1287–1290	Töle-Buqa	
1290–1312	Toqto'a	
c. 1296–c. 1299	Nogai	Effective ruler after Möngke-Timur; Nogai took the title Khan c. 1296, but was killed during the ensuing civil war
1258–1265	Hulagu	
1265–1282	Abaqa	
1282–1284	Tegüder	
1284–1291	Arghun	Ilkhans of Persia (Ilkhanate)
1291–1295	Gaikhatu	
1295	Baidu	
1295–1304	Ghazan	

Table 6.i *Western rulers (Frankish emperors/senior co-emperors)*

Reign	Ruler	Dynasty
751–768	Pippin III the Short king of the Franks	
800–814	Charlemagne king of the Franks from 768 emperor from 800	
814–840	Louis the Pious	Carolingians
840–855	Lothar I	
855–875	Louis II	
875–877	Charles II the Bald	
877–881	[interregnum]	
881–887	Charles III the Fat	

Table 6.ii *Western rulers (Western emperors of Saxon origin, and their successors)*

Reign	Ruler	Dynasty
919–936	Henry king of the East Franks	Ottonian

962–973	Otto I
	    king of the East Franks from 936
	    crowned emperor by pope in Rome 962	

973–983	Otto II crowned co-emperor by pope in Rome 967	
983–1002	Otto III only crowned emperor by pope in Rome 996	
1002–1024	Henry II crowned emperor by pope in Rome 1014	
1024–1039	Conrad II crowned emperor 1027	Salian
1039–1056	Henry III crowned emperor 1046	
1053–1106	Henry IV crowned emperor by Antipope Clement III 1084	
1099–1125	Henry V crowned emperor 1111	
1125–1137	Lothar III crowned emperor 1133	
1138–1152	Conrad III failed to receive imperial coronation in Rome	Hohenstaufen
1152–1190	Frederick I Barbarossa crowned emperor in Rome in 1155	
1190–1197	Henry VI crowned emperor 1191	
1198–1208	Philip of Swabia claimant, but not crowned emperor in Rome	
1198–1218	Otto IV of Brunswick crowned emperor in Rome 1209	
1215–1250	Frederick II crowned emperor in Rome 1220	

Table 6.iii *Western rulers (Lombard princes of Capua-Benevento and Salerno)*

Reign	Lombard princes of Capua-Benevento
759–787	Arichis II
787–806	Grimoald III
806–817	Grimoald IV
817–833	Sico
833–839	Sicard
839–851	Radelchis I
851–853	Radelgar
853–878	Adelchis
878–881	Gaideris
	(also Guaifer, Waifer, or Waifar)
881–884	Radelchis II (first rule)
884–891	Aiulf II
	(also Aio, Ajo, or Aione)
891–892	Ursus
	(also Orso)
[892–895	Under Byzantine rule]
895–897	Guy IV (Duke of Spoleto)
897–900	Radelchis II (second rule)
900–910	Atenulf I
910–943	Landulf I
	(styled prince from 901)
	Atenulf II
	(styled prince 910–940)
	Atenulf III
	(styled prince 933–943)
943–961	Landulf II
	(styled prince from 939)
961–968/9	Landulf III
	(styled prince from 959; senior co-ruler from 961)
961–981	Pandulf I Ironhead
	(styled prince from 943; senior co-ruler 961–968/9; also Duke of Spoleto from 967 and Prince of Salerno from 978)
981–982	Landulf IV
	(styled prince from 968/9, at Capua 982)
982–1014	Pandulf II
	(also Prince of Capua from 1008)

The Lombard princes of Benevento ruled independently from 774 until 1050, and were also princes of Capua between 900 and 981.

(*cont.*)

Table 6.iii *Lombard princes* (*cont.*)

Reign	Lombard prince of Salerno	Dynasty
880–900	Guaimar I (also Waimar, Gaimar, Guaimaro or Guaimario; deposed)	First dynasty
900–946	Guaimar II (styled prince from 893)	
946–977	Gisulf I (styled prince from 933)	
[978–983	Rule by the princes of Capua and dukes of Amalfi]	

983–999	John II
	    Wido
	    (styled prince 983–988)
		Second dynasty

999–1027	Guaimar III
	(styled prince from 989)
	    John III
	    (styled prince 1015–1018)	

1027–1052	Guaimar IV (styled prince from 1018)	

Regnal years given for the princes of Benevento and of Salerno are those during which they were senior ruler or co-ruler; however, they were often styled prince in association with a father or brother for a longer period of time.

Table 6.iv *Western rulers (Norman rulers of southern Italy)**

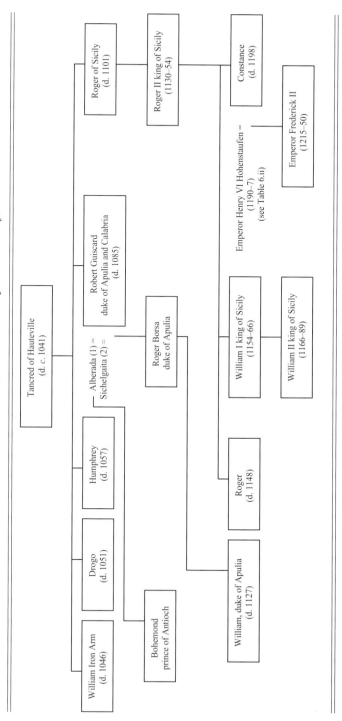

*Simplified, from M. Chibnall, *The Normans*, Oxford (2000)

Table 6.v *Western rulers (Latin emperors in Constantinople)*

Reign	Emperor
1204–1205	Baldwin I of Flanders
1206–1216	Henry of Hainault
1216–1217	Peter of Courtenay
	(defeated and disappears before reaching Constantinople)
1217–1219	Yolanda of Flanders
	(ruling for her husband Peter of Courtenay)
1218–1228	Robert of Courtenay
	(only crowned in 1221 on his return from France)
1229–1237	John of Brienne
	(regent co-emperor for Baldwin II)
1237–1261	Baldwin II
	(emperor from 1228)

Table 6.vi *Western rulers (Rulers of the Frankish principality of Achaia)*

Reign	Ruler	Dynasty
1205–1208	William of Champlitte	
c. 1209–1225/31	Geoffrey I of Villehardouin	
c. 1226/31–1246	Geoffrey II of Villehardouin	Villehardouins
1246–1278	William II of Villehardouin	
1278–1285	bailiffs for Charles I of Anjou	
1285–1289	bailiffs for Charles II of Anjou	Anjevins
1289–1307	Isabel of Villehardouin	
	(married to Florent of Hainault (1289–1297)	
	and to Philip of Savoy (1301–1307))	
1307–1313	Philip of Taranto	
1313–1317	Matilda (Mahaut) of Hainault	
	(daughter of Isabel of Villehardouin and	Period of Anjevin
	Florent of Hainault; married to Louis of	and Aragonese
	Burgundy (1313–1316))	claimants
[1315–1316	failed bid by Ferrante of Majorca]	
1322–1333	John of Gravina	
1333–1364	Robert of Taranto	
1364–1373	Philip II of Taranto	
1373–1381	Joan of Naples and heirs	
	(leased by Joan and her heirs to the Knights	
	Hospitallers from *c.* 1376 on)	
1381–1395	Heirs of Joan of Naples and various	
	other pretenders contested the throne,	
	including the Navarrese Company	
1396–1402	Peter of San Superan	
	(of the Navarrese Company)	
1402–1404	Maria Zaccaria	
1404–1432	Centurione II Zaccaria	

Table 7.i *Balkan rulers (Bulgarian rulers)*

Reign	Khan or tsar	Dynasty
First Bulgarian empire		
c. 680–701	Asparuch	
701–718	Tervel	
[718–725	Unknown]	House of Dulo
725–739	Sevar	
739–756	Kormisos	
756–*c.* 761	Vinech	
c. 760–*c.* 763	Teletz	
c. 763–*c.* 767	Sabin	
c. 767	Umor	Rulers during 'Time of Troubles'
c. 767–*c.* 769	Toktu	
c. 770	Pagan	
c. 770– *c.* 777	Telerig	
c. 777–*c.* 802	Kardam	
c. 803–814	Krum	
c. 815–831	Omurtag	
831–836	Malamir	
836–*c.* 852	Presian	
c. 852–889	Boris	
889–893	Vladimir	House of Krum
893–927	Symeon	
927–969	Peter	
969–971	Boris II (in Byzantine captivity 971–977)	
from 976	Samuel, Aaron, Moses and David (four brothers)	
987/8–1014	Samuel	Kometopouloi
1014–1015	Gabriel-Radomir	
1015–1018	John Vladislav	
[1018–1185	Under Byzantine dominion] Rebels against Byzantine rule:	
1040–1042	Peter Deljan	
c. 1041	Alusjan	
early 1070s	Bodin (acclaimed as 'Tsar Peter')	
Second Bulgarian empire		
1185/6–1196	Asen	
1196–1197	Peter	
1197–1207	Kalojan	
1207–1218	Boril	
1218–1241	Ivan II Asen	
1241–1246	Koloman	
1246–1256	Michael I Asen	
1257–1277	Constantine Tich	
1278–1279	Ivailo	
1279	Ivan III Asen	
1279–1292	George I Terter	
1292–1298	Smilec	
1298–1299	[Regency]	

(*cont.*)

Table 7.i *Bulgarian rulers (cont.)*

Reign	Khan or tsar
1299–1300	Chaka
1300–1322	Theodore Svetoslav
1322	George II Terter
1323–1330	Michael Shishman
1330–1331	Ivan Stefan
1331–1371	Ivan Alexander
1371–1393	Ivan Shishman
[1393–1878	Under Ottoman dominion]

Table 7.ii *Balkan rulers (Serbian rulers: over the core area of Raška)*

Reign	Ruler	Dynasty (Branch)
1083/4–*c.* 1122	Vukan (became independent ruler of Raška with the title *veliki župan* from the early 1090s)	*veliki župan* of Raška
c. 1125–early 1140s	Uroš I	
c. 1145–early 1160s	Uroš II (Desa briefly replaced Uroš II 1153)	
c. 1162	Primislav	
c. 1162	Beloš	
c. 1162–*c.* 1165	Desa	
c. 1165–1168	Tihomir, Stefan Nemanja, Sracimir, Miroslav (joint rule of brothers as *župan*s with Tihomir as *veliki župan*)	
(*c.* 1165/8–1196)	Stefan Nemanja	
1196–1227	*veliki župan* Stefan (*prvovenčani* 'the first-crowned') (crowned king 1217)	Nemanjids (kings of Serbia
1227–1233	Stefan Radoslav	
1233–1243	Stefan Vladislav	
1243–1276	Stefan Uroš I	
1276–1282	Stefan Dragutin	
1282–1321	Stefan Uroš II Milutin	
1321–1331	Stefan Uroš III Dečanski	
1331–1355	Stefan Dušan (king to 1346; crowned tsar 1346)	
1355–1371	Stefan Uroš V (tsar)	
1371–1389	Lazar (pre-eminent prince)	
1389–1427	Stefan Lazarević (prince/lord to 1402; granted by Byzantines title of despot 1402)	
1427–1456	George Branković (prince/lord; despot from 1429)	
1456–1458	Lazar Branković (despot)	
1459	Stefan Tomašević of Bosnia (despot)	

Table 7.iii *Balkan rulers (Hungarian rulers)*

Reign	King	Dynasty
1000–1038	Stephen I	– Árpád
1038–1041	Peter Urseolo (first reign)	
1041–1044	Samuel Aba	} Non-dynastic
1044–1046	Peter Urseolo (second reign)	
1046–1060	Andrew I	
1060–1063	Béla I	
1063–1074	Salomon	
1074–1077	Géza I	
1077–1095	Ladislas I	
1095–1116	Coloman I	
1116–1131	Stephen II	
1131–1141	Béla II	
1141–1162	Géza II	
1162 (January–February)	Stephen III (first reign)	
1162–1163 (July 1162–June 1163)	Ladislas II	} Árpád
1163 (January–June)	Stephen IV	
1163–1172	Stephen III (second reign)	
1172–1196	Béla III (= Béla-Alexios)	
1196–1204	Emeric	
1204–1205	Ladislas III	
1205–1235	Andrew II	
1235–1270	Béla IV	

ALTERNATIVE PLACE NAMES

This list is not intended to be comprehensive, but offers the reader alternative terms for some place names used in *The Cambridge history of the Byzantine empire*. Where equivalents are reasonably close (Cumae or Cuma, Cephalonia or Kefallinía, for example) these have not been given. Similarly, different name forms created through transliteration (Naupaktos or Navpaktos, Lesbos or Lesvos, Boeotia or Viotia) or equivalent name forms in Greek and Latin (Iconion and Iconium, for example) have not normally been included. Two forms are used in the case of certain key towns, where a Turkish or other name had by then effectively superseded the Greek or classical form used in earlier sections (e.g. Ankara in Section III replacing Ankyra in Sections I and II). Where not otherwise specified, places in the table below are to be found in present-day Greece or Turkey and the last-named place is generally the current usage. Further information on alternative place names may be found in entries in the *Oxford dictionary of Byzantium* (*ODB*), or in the comprehensive, if not yet completed, *Tabulae imperii byzantini* (*TIB*) published in Vienna.

Name	Alternatives
Abyssinia	Ethiopia [Africa]
Achaia	Morea
Adramyttion	Adramittium, Edremit
Adrianople	Hadrianoupolis, Edirne
Akhlat	Ahlat, Khilat, Khliat
Akroinon	Afyonkarahisar, Kara Hisar
Albania [Balkans]	see Arbanon
Albania [Caucasus]	Aghuankʻ
Aleppo	Beroea, Berrhoia, Haleb [Syria]
Alessio	Lezhë [Albania]
Amida	Diyarbakir, Diyar Bakr
Amu-Darya (river) [Central Asia]	Oxus
Anazarbos	Ayn Zarba
Anchialos	Acheloos, Pomorie [Bulgaria]
Andravida	Andreville
Ankara	see Ankyra

Name	Alternatives
Ankyra	Ancyra, Ankara
Antalya	see Attaleia
Antioch (on the Orontes)	Antakya
Antioch-on-the-Maeander	Antioch-in-Pisidia, near Yalvaç
Antivari	Tivar, Bar [Montenegro]
Apollonia	Pojan [Albania]
Apollonia	Sozopolis [Pisidia]
Arabissos	near Afşin
Aratsani (river)	eastern or lower branch of Euphrates, Murat
Arbanon	Raban, Albania [Balkans]
Archesh	Arjish, Artzesion, Erçiş
Ardanuji	Adranoutzion, Ardanuch, Ardanuç
Artsn	Artze
Attaleia	Antalya
Avlona	Valona, Vlorë [Albania]
Ayas	L'Aïas, Lajazzo
Aydin	Tralles
Azat (river)	Garni [Armenia]
Belgrade	Singidunum, Beograd [Serbia]
Beroia (Thrace)	Stara Zagora [Bulgaria]
Berrhoia (NE Greece)	Berea, Verria, Veroia
Bitola	Pelagonia, Monastir [Balkans]
Bursa	see Prousa
Butrint [Albania]	Butrinto, Butrot, Buthroton
Caesarea	Kayseri
Caffa	Theodosia, Kefe, Feodosia [Ukraine]
Caput Vada	Ras Kapoudra [Tunisia]
Cayster (river)	Lesser Maeander, Küçük Menderes
Cerigo	Cythere, Kythera
Ceuta [North Africa]	Septem
Chalcedon	Kadiköy
Chalkis (Syria)	Qinnasrin
Chalkis (Greece)	Negroponte, Halkida
Cherson	Sebastopol [Ukraine]
Chorasan	see Khorasan
Clarence	Chiarenza, Glarentza (near Kyllini)
Constantia (Cyprus)	Salamis
Constantinople	Byzantion, Istanbul
Corfu	Kerkyra
Danube (river)	Ister [Balkans]
Dasht-i Kavir [Iran]	Great Kavir
Denizli	Laodicea [Turkey]
Devol [Albania]	Deabolis, Diabolis
Diokleia	see Duklja [Balkans]
Diyar Bakr	see Amida
Dorylaion	Eskişehir
Doubera	Livera, Yazlik
Dristra	Dorostolon, Silistra [Bulgaria]
Dubrovnik [Croatia]	Ragusa
Duklja [Balkans]	Diokleia, Zeta
Dülük	Doliche
Durazzo	see Dyrrachium

(cont.)

Name	Alternatives
Durrës	see Dyrrachium
Dvin [Armenia]	Tibion, Doubios, Dabil
Dyrrachium	Durazzo, Dyrrachion, Durrës [Albania]
Ecbatana	Hamadan [Iran]
Edirne	see Adrianople
Edessa [Greece]	Vodena
Edessa [Mesopotamia]	Urfa
Egnatian Way	Via Egnatia [Balkans]
Emesa	see Homs
Erzurum	see Theodosioupolis
Euboea (island)	Euboia, Evvoia, Negroponte
Euchaita	Avkat, Beyözü
Fergana [Uzbekistan]	Farghana
Galata	Pera
Gangra	Changra, Germanikopolis, Kandari, Çankiri
Gerace [Italy]	Hagia Kyriake
Gerasa	Jerash [Jordan]
Germanikeia	Mar'ash, Maraş, Kahramanmaraş
Ghazna	Ghazni [Afghanistan]
Gjacova	Djakovica [Balkans]
Gurgan	Jurjan, Gorgan [Iran]
Great Kavir	Dasht-i Kavir [Iran]
Hamadan [Iran]	Ecbatana
Hedeby [Denmark]	Haithabu
Heraclea Pontica	Bender Ereğli, Karadeniz Ereğli
Heraclea-Cybistra	Ereğli
Hermos (river)	Gediz
Hierapolis (Phrygia)	Pamukkale
Hierapolis (Syria)	see Membij
Himara	Chimaer, Dhërmi [Albania]
Himyar	Yemen [Arabia]
Homs [Syria]	Emesa, Hims
Iberia	Byzantine name with various meanings, including: (i) general term for Caucasian Georgia, corresponding with K'art'li, the eastern part of the medieval Georgian kingdom; (ii) area of Armenian–Georgian borderland to north-east of Theodosioupolis; (iii) possessions in (ii) of David of Tao inherited by Basil II and turned into 'Iberian theme'
Ikonion	Konya
Istanbul	Constantinople
Izmir	Smyrna
Izmit	Nikomedeia
Iznik	Nicaea
Jaxartes (river)	Syr-Darya [Central Asia]
(al-)Jazira	upper Mesopotamia
Jerash	see Gerasa
Kavalla (Greece)	Christoupolis, Christople
Khliat	see Akhlat
Khorasan	Chorasan, Khurasan [Iran]
Khwarizm	Chwarizm, Khorezm, Khwarazm [Central Asia]
Koloneia	Şebinkarahisar
Konya	Ikonion
Kosovo	Dardania [Balkans]
Kotor	Cattaro [Montenegro]

Name	Alternatives
Kotyaeion	Cotyaeum, Kotaion, Kutaiah, Kütahya
Kütahya	Cotyaeum, Kotaion, Kotyaeion, Kutaiah
Kyzikos	Cyzicus, near Erdek
Laodicea [Syria]	see Latakia
Laodicea [Turkey]	Denizli
Latakia [Syria]	Laodicea
Lepanto	Naupaktos
Lesbos	Mytilene (also island's capital)
Maeander (river)	Greater Maeander, Büyük Menderes
Malatya	Melitene
Malvasia	Monemvasia
Mar'ash	see Germanikeia
Mare nostrum	Mediterranean
Maritsa (river) [Balkans]	Hebros
Marmara (sea of)	Propontis
Martyropolis	see Mayyafariqin
al-Massisa	see Mopsuestia
Mayyafariqin	Martyropolis, Silvan
Medina	Yathrib [Arabia]
Melitene	Malatya
Membij [Syria]	Hierapolis, Mabbug
Merv	Margiana, Marw [Central Asia]
Mesembria	Nesebar [Bulgaria]
Methone	see Modon
Miletos	Palatia, Balat
Modon	Methone, Methoni
Monemvasia	Malvasia
Mopsuestia	al-Massisa, Mamistra, Misis
Morea	Achaia
Naissos	Niš [Serbia]
Nakoleia	Seyitgazi
Naupaktos	Lepanto
Negroponte [town]	see Chalkis
Negroponte [island]	see Euboea
Neocaesarea	Niksar
Nicaea	Nikaia, Iznik
Nikomedeia	Izmit
Niksar	Neocaesarea
Niš [Serbia]	Naissos
Nubia	southern Egypt–northern Sudan [Africa]
Ohrid [Balkans]	Okhrida, Achrida
Outremer	from French for 'overseas' denoting crusading states in Levant, i.e. Syria–Palestine [Middle East]
Oxus (river)	Amu-Darya [Central Asia]
Paradounabon	Paristrion (from Greek 'along Danube')
Pelagonia	region of Macedonia; also town of Bitola
Pera	Galata
Perkri	Berkri
Philadelphia	Alaşehir
Philae	submerged island near Aswan [Egypt]
Philippopolis	Plovdiv [Bulgaria]
Philomelion	Akşehir
Phokaia (Old)	Phocaea, Foça
Phokaia (New)	Foglia, Yenicefoça

(*cont.*)

Name	Alternatives
Piskopi	Episkopi, Telos, Tilos
Polybotos	Bolvadin
Pontos (the)	Black Sea and its shores; more specifically, the south-east shore centred on Trebizond
Propontis	Marmara (sea of)
Prousa	Broussa, Prusa, Brusa, Bursa
Ragusa	Dubrovnik [Croatia]
Raška [Balkans]	core region of emerging Serbian polity centred on Ras (modern Novi Pazar)
Raidestos	Bisanthe, Rhoedestus, Rodosto, Tekirdağ
Rižana [Slovenia]	Risano
Samosata	Shimshat, Shamushat, Samsat (now submerged)
Sangarios (river)	Sakarya
Santorini	Thira
Sebasteia	Sivas
Seleukeia	Silifke
Septem	Ceuta [North Africa]
Serdica	see Sofia [Bulgaria]
Serres	Serrai
Shash	Chash, Tashkent [Central Asia]
Shkodër (lake) [Balkans]	Scutari, Skadarsko
Shkodër (town) [Balkans]	Skadar, Scodra, Scutari
Side	near Manavgat
Singidunum	see Belgrade
Sirmium	Sremska Mitrovica [Balkans]
Sivas	Sebasteia
Smyrna	Izmir
Sofia [Bulgaria]	Serdica, Serdika
Sophon (mount)	Sapanca
Sougdaia	Soldaia, Surozh, Sudak [Ukraine]
Sozopolis [Pisidia]	Apollonia
Sozopolis [Thrace]	Sozopol [Bulgaria]
Spinarizza	Zvërnec [Albania]
Split [Croatia]	Spalato
Strymon (river)	Struma [Balkans]
Surozh	see Sougdaia
Syr-Darya (river)	see Jaxartes
Tana	Tanais, Azak, Azov [Russia]
Tanais (river)	Don [Russia]
Tao	Tayk'
Tayk'	Tao
Tephrike	Divriği
Thamugadi [Tunisia]	Timgad
Theodosioupolis	Karin, Erzurum
Thessalonica	see Thessaloniki
Thessaloniki	Thessalonica, Solun, Salonicco, Selanik, Slonki, Salonica
Thira	Santorini
Tralles	Aydin
Transoxiana	Maverannahr [region south-east of Aral Sea]
Trebizond	Trapezus, Trabzond
T'rnovo	Tărnovo, (Veliko) Turnovo [Bulgaria]
Tyana	Kemerhisar
Tzamandos	Tzamandaw

Name	Alternatives
Ulubad (lake)	Lupajo, Ulubat
Vagharshapat	Echmiadzin, Ejmiatsin, Yejmiadzin [Armenia]
Vardar (river) [Balkans]	Axios
Vaspurakan	Asprakania, region in south-east Armenia forming core of Artsruni realm; annexed by Basil II and turned into theme of Vaspurakan
Velika Morava (river)	Great Morava, Morava [Balkans]
Veroia	see Berrhoia
Yathrib	Medina [Arabia]
Zakynthos	Zante
Zante	Zakynthos
Zara	Zadar [Croatia]
Zeta	see Duklja

BIBLIOGRAPHY

The bibliography is broken down into the following sections:

- Abbreviations
- Primary sources
- Manuscripts
- Secondary works
  - General and frequently cited works
  - Part I (*c.* 500–*c.* 700)
  - Part II (*c.* 700–1204)
  - Part III (1204–1492)
- Unpublished theses

Chronological sectioning for the secondary bibliography is – like the periodisation of history into mutually exclusive compartments – rather arbitrary. **The bibliography of secondary works should therefore be treated as a whole and the reader failing to find a work in one section should try the others**.

Abbreviations

- Often-used primary sources feature in the footnotes in highly abbreviated form. Further details are given in the list of abbreviations, and these provide the key to their place in the Primary sources bibliography.
- Abbreviations of primary sources are marked in the list with an asterisk, to distinguish them from journal titles and series.

Primary sources

- Where forenames of primary text authors are known, they are cited first: 'Michael Psellos', not 'Psellos, Michael'.
- A short-title system has been used for primary sources.

- Wherever possible, details of translations of primary sources into English – and other major western European languages – have been given in the Primary sources bibliography, with corresponding citations when the source features in the footnotes.
- A primary source may have been published in a secondary work. If this secondary work contains substantive material composed by its modern author, it is listed separately as a secondary work, with reference being made to it in the Primary sources listing. For example, *The Chronicle of Monemvasia* is listed as such under Primary sources, but the entry refers the reader to Lemerle (1963), pp. 8–11 (in Secondary works, Part II), where the text forms part of a more general article.

Secondary works

- A list of general and frequently cited works highlights some of the publications underpinning this volume, or offering introductions, syntheses or alternative approaches.
- Many secondary works span more than one chronological part, but in general the reader should find the secondary works cited in a chapter in the corresponding chronological section of the bibliography. Works cited in Part I (chapters 1–4) are normally to be found in the bibliography under Secondary works, Part I, for example. However, if the centre of gravity of the secondary work falls more within another section of the bibliography, it is usually included there; for example, Banaji, J. (2001), *Agrarian change in late antiquity: gold, labour and aristocratic dominance*, Oxford, is cited in the footnotes of chapter 12 (i.e. Part II of *CHBE*), but appears in Secondary works, Part I.
- The secondary bibliography is biased in favour of English-language works, but also gives an idea of some of the more important works available in other European languages.
- A version of the Harvard name and date system has been used for secondary works, except in the case of unpublished theses, which retain a short-title system.
- The use of (ed.) has been retained in the footnotes for edited works. For example, Brubaker, L. (ed.) (1998), *Byzantium in the ninth century: dead or alive?*, Aldershot, is consistently referred to as Brubaker (ed.) (1998), and not Brubaker (1998).
- Where a work has three or more authors or editors, only the first name is given in both the footnotes and in the bibliography (e.g. *Things revealed: studies in early Jewish and Christian literature in honor of Michael E. Stone*, edited by E. G. Chazon, D. Satran and R. A. Clements (Leiden, 2004) appears in both the bibliography and footnotes under Chazon *et al.* (eds.) (2004)).

- A multi-authored volume placed (under its editor's name) in one section of the secondary bibliography may contain pieces listed under an individual author's name in another section. Thus Cheynet (2004) is in Secondary works, Part II, yet Coulon *et al.* (eds.) (2004) – which contains Cheynet (2004) – is in Secondary works, Part III.
- Where an author has published more than one work in a given year, each work has been assigned a separate letter of the alphabet (for example, Mango (2002a), Mango (2002b), etc.). However, these may appear in different sections of the bibliography of secondary works; for example, Mango (2002b) is to be found in Secondary works, Part I, while Mango (2002a) is in Secondary works, Part II.
- Full and regular updates on recent publications can be found in the flagship journal *Byzantinische Zeitschrift*, which now provides an online service to subscribers.

ABBREVIATIONS

*AA**	*Archives de l'Athos*
AAntHung	*Acta antiqua academiae scientiarum hungaricae*
*AASS**	*Acta sanctorum*
ABSA	*Annual of the British school at Athens*
ACIEB 6	*Actes du VIe Congrès international d'études byzantines, Paris 27 juillet–2 août 1948*, 2 vols, Paris (1950–1)
ACIEB 12	*Actes du XIIe Congrès international des études byzantines, Ochride, 10–16 septembre 1961*, 3 vols., Belgrade (1963–4)
ACIEB 13	*Proceedings of the XIIIth International congress of Byzantine studies, Oxford, 5–10 September 1966*, ed. J. Hussey *et al.*, London (1967)
ACIEB 14	*Actes du XIVe Congrès international des études byzantines, Bucarest, 6–12 septembre 1971*, ed. M. Berza and E. Stanescu, 3 vols., Bucharest (1974–6)
ACIEB 15	*Actes du XVe Congrès international d'études byzantines, Athènes, septembre 1976*, 3 vols. in 4 pts., Athens (1979–81)
ACIEB 17	*The 17th International Byzantine congress: major papers (Washington, DC, August 3–8, 1986)*, New York (1986)
ACIEB 18	*XVIII Mezhdunarodnyi kongress vizantinistov (XVIIIth International congress of Byzantine studies), Moscow, August 1991*, 5 vols. (1: *Programme*; 2: *List of participants*; 3 and 4: *Summaries of communications*; 5: *Major papers*), Moscow (1991)

---

* Further bibliographic details in list of Primary Sources.

ACIEB 21	*Proceedings of the 21st International congress of Byzantine studies, London, 2006*, 3 vols, ed. E. Jeffreys, Aldershot (2006)
ACO	*Acta conciliorum oecumenicorum*
AESC	*Annales: économies, sociétés, civilisations*
AFH	*Archivum franciscanum historicum*
Agnel.*	Agnellus of Ravenna, *Liber pontificalis*
AHP	*Archivum historiae pontificiae*
AHR	*American historical review*
AIPHO	*Annuaire de l'Institut de philologie et d'histoire orientales*
AJA	*American journal of archaeology*
*Al.**	Anna Komnena, *Alexiad*
AnBoll	*Analecta bollandiana*
ANL PASC	*Accademia nazionale dei Lincei, problemi attuali di scienza e di cultura, quaderni*
ANRW	*Aufstieg und Niedergang der römischen Welt*, ed. H. Temporini and H. Haase, 87 vols. to date, Berlin and New York (1972–)
AO	*Acta orientalia*
AOH	*Acta orientalia academiae scientiarum hungaricae*
*ARF**	*Annales regni Francorum*
Arist.*	Aristakes of Lastivert, *History*
ASPN	*Archivio storico per le province napoletane*
Attal.*	Michael Attaleiates, *Historia*
Atti 17	*Ravenna da capitale imperiale a capitale esarcale: atti del XVII Congresso internazionale di studio sull'alto medioevo: Ravenna, 6–12 giugno 2004*, 2 vols., Spoleto (2005)
BAR IS	*British archaeological reports international series*
BB	*Byzantinobulgarica*
BBA	*Berliner Byzantinistische Arbeiten*
BBTT	*Belfast Byzantine texts and translations*
BCH	*Bulletin de correspondance hellénique*
BEINE	*The Byzantine and early Islamic Near East*, Princeton, NJ: I: *Problems in the literary source material*, ed. Averil Cameron and L. I. Conrad (1992); II: *Land use and settlement patterns*, ed. G. R. D. King and Averil Cameron (1994); III: *States, resources and armies*, ed. Averil Cameron (1995); IV: *Patterns of communal identity*, ed. Averil Cameron (forthcoming); V: *Trade and exchange*, ed. L. I. Conrad and G. R. D. King (in preparation); VI: *Elites old and new*, ed. J. Haldon and L. I. Conrad (2004)

BF	*Byzantinische Forschungen*
BGA	*Bibliotheca geographorum arabicorum*, ed. M. J. de Goeje, 8 vols., Leiden (1870–94)
BHG	*Bibliotheca hagiographica graeca*, ed. F. Halkin, 3rd edn., 3 vols., Brussels (1957)
BMGS	*Byzantine and modern Greek studies*
BNJ	*Byzantinisch-neugriechische Jahrbücher*
BollGrott	*Bollettino della badia greca di Grottaferrata*
BS	*Byzantine studies/Études byzantines*
BSl	*Byzantinoslavica*
BSo	*Byzantina sorbonensia*
BSOAS	*Bulletin of the School of Oriental and African studies*
BV	*Byzantina vindobonensia*
Byz	*Byzantion*
ByzAust	*Byzantina australiensia*
BZ	*Byzantinische Zeitschrift*
CAH	*The Cambridge ancient history*, 2nd edn., Cambridge: XII: *The crisis of empire*, AD *193–337*, ed. A. K. Bowman *et al.* (2005); XIII: *The late empire*, AD *337–425*, ed. Averil Cameron and P. Garnsey (1998); XIV: *Late antiquity: empire and successors*, AD *425–600*, ed. Averil Cameron *et al.* (2000)
*CC**	*Codex carolinus*
CCCM	*Corpus christianorum, continuatio mediaevalis*
CCSG	*Corpus christianorum, series graeca*
CCSL	*Corpus christianorum, series latina*
*CDC**	*Codex diplomaticus cavensis*
CEFR	*Collection de l'École française de Rome*
CFHB	*Corpus fontium historiae byzantinae*
*CMC**	*Chronica monasterii Casinensis*
CNRS	*Centre national des recherches scientifiques*
CPG	*Clavis patrum graecorum*
CRAI	*Comptes rendus des séances de l'Académie des inscriptions et belles-lettres*
*CS**	*Chronicon Salernitanum*
CSCO	*Corpus scriptorum christianorum orientalium*
CSHB	*Corpus scriptorum historiae byzantinae*
DA	*Deutsches Archiv für Erforschung des Mittelalters*
*DAI**	Constantine VII Porphyrogenitus, *De administrando imperio*, I
*DAI: Comm**	Constantine VII Porphyrogenitus, *De administrando imperio*, II

DBI	*Dizionario biografico degli italiani*, 67 vols. to date, Rome (1960–)
DC*	Constantine VII Porphyrogenitus, *De cerimoniis aulae byzantinae*
DChAE	*Deltion tes Christianikes archaiologikes etaireias*
DGA*	*Discipline générale antique*
DHGE	*Dictionnaire d'histoire et de géographie ecclésiastiques*, ed. A. Baudrillart *et al.*, 28 vols. to date, Paris (1912–)
DOC*	*Catalogue of the Byzantine coins in the Dumbarton Oaks collection*
DOP	*Dumbarton Oaks papers*
DOS*	*Catalogue of Byzantine seals at Dumbarton Oaks*
DOSt	*Dumbarton Oaks studies*
DT*	Constantine VII Porphyrogenitus, *De thematibus*
Duc.*	Ducas, *Istoria Turco-Bizantina*
EB	*Études balkaniques*
EEBS	*Epeteris etaireias Byzantinon spoudon*
EHB	*The economic history of Byzantium: from the seventh through the fifteenth century*, ed. A. E. Laiou *et al.*, *DOSt* 39, 3 vols., Washington, DC (2002)
EHR	*English historical review*
EI	*Encyclopaedia of Islam*, 12 vols., 2nd edn., Leiden (1960–2004)
EO	*Échos d'orient*
Eparch*	Leo VI, *Book of the eparch*
FGHB*	*Fontes graeci historiae bulgaricae*
FM	*Fontes minores*
FSI	*Fonti per la storia d'Italia*
GA*	George Akropolites, *Opera*
Gen.*	Genesios, *Regum libri quattuor*
GMC*	George the Monk (Continued)
GP*	George Pachymeres, *Relations historiques*
GRBS	*Greek, Roman and Byzantine studies*
GS*	Gennadios II Scholarios, *Oeuvres complètes*
HA*	*History of the Albanians*
HAm	*Handes amsorya*
HC	*Histoire du christianisme: des origines à nos jours*, ed. J.-M. Mayeur *et al.*, 14 vols., Paris (1990–2000)
Hell	*Hellenika*
HTR	*Harvard theological review*
HUS	*Harvard Ukrainian studies*
IA	*Iranica antiqua*

IQ	*Islamic quarterly*
IRAIK	*Izvestiia Russkogo arkheologicheskogo instituta v Konstantinopole*
JAOS	*Journal of the American Oriental Society*
JbAC	*Jahrbuch für Antike und Christentum*
JE*	John of Ephesus, *History*
JEH	*Journal of economic history*
JESHO	*Journal of the economic and social history of the orient*
*JG**	*Jus graecoromanum*
JHS	*Journal of Hellenic studies*
JK*	John Kantakouzenos, *Eximperatoris historiarum libri quattor*
JMH	*Journal of medieval history*
JNES	*Journal of Near Eastern studies*
JÖB	*Jahrbuch der österreichischen Byzantinistik*
JRAS	*Journal of the Royal Asiatic society*
JS	*Journal des savants*
JSAI	*Jerusalem studies in Arabic and Islam*
Kek.*	Kekaumenos, *Strategikon*
Kinn.*	John Kinnamos, *History*
LBG	*Lexikon zur byzantinischen Gräzität: besonders des 9.–12. Jahrhunderts*, ed. E. Trapp *et al.*, 2 vols. to date, Vienna (1994–)
*Leg.**	Liudprand of Cremona, *Legatio*
Lew.*	Lewond, *History*
LexMA	*Lexikon des Mittelalters*, ed. R. Auty *et al.*, 9 vols., Munich and Stuttgart (1977–99) (also available online)
LM	*Le Muséon*
*LP**	*Liber pontificalis*
*LPB**	*Les Listes de préséance byzantines*
*LPD**	*Letopis popa Dukljanina*
LThK	*Lexikon für Theologie und Kirche*, ed. W. Kasper *et al.*, 3rd edn., 11 vols., Freiburg im Breisgau (1993–2001)
Mansi*	Mansi (ed.), *Sacrorum conciliorum nova et amplissima collectio*
*MB**	Sathas, *Mesaionike bibliotheke*
MBM	*Miscellanea byzantina monacensia*
ME*	Matthew of Edessa, *Chronicle*
MEFRM	*Mélanges de l'École française de Rome. Moyen âge*
Men.*	Menander the Guardsman, *History*
MGH	*Monumenta Germaniae historica*
MGH AA	*Monumenta Germaniae historica. Auctorum antiquissimorum*, 15 vols., Berlin (1877–1919)

MGH Cap.	*Monumenta Germaniae historica. Capitularia regum Francorum*, 2 vols., Hanover (1883–97)
MGH Ep.	*Monumenta Germaniae historica. Epistolae*, 8 vols., Berlin (1887–1939)
MGH Dip.	*Monumenta Germaniae historica. Diplomata regum et imperatorum Germaniae (Die Urkunden der deutschen Könige und Kaiser)*, 19 vols. to date, Hanover (1879–)
MGH SRG	*Monumenta Germaniae historica. Scriptores rerum Germanicarum in usum scholarum*, 77 vols. to date, Hanover (1871–)
MGH SRG n.s.	*Monumenta Germaniae historica. Scriptores rerum Germanicarum n. s.*, 22 vols. to date, Berlin–Weimar (1922–)
MGH SRL	*Monumenta Germaniae historica. Scriptores rerum Langobardicarum et italicarum saeculorum VI–IX*, Hanover (1878)
MGH SRM	*Monumenta Germaniae historica. Scriptores rerum Merovingicarum*, 7 vols., Hanover (1885–1920)
MGH SS	*Monumenta Germaniae historica. Scriptores*, 38 vols. to date, Hanover (1826–)
MHR	*Mediterranean historical review*
MM*	Miklosich and Müller (eds.), *Acta et diplomata*
MS*	Michael the Syrian, *Chronicle*
MSABK	*Mitteilungen zur spätantiken Archäologie und byzantinischen Kunstgeschichte*
NC*	Niketas Choniates, *History*
NCMH	*The new Cambridge medieval history*, Cambridge: I: *c. 500–c. 700*, ed. P. Fouracre (2005); II: *c. 700–c. 900*, ed. R. McKitterick (1995); III: *c. 900–c. 1024*, ed. T. Reuter (1999); IV: *c. 1024–c. 1198*, ed. D. Luscombe and J. Riley-Smith, 2 vols. (2004); V: *c. 1198–c. 1300*, ed. D. Abulafia (1999); VI: *c. 1300–c. 1415*, ed. M. Jones (2000); VII: *c. 1415–c. 1500*, ed. C. Allmand (1998)
NE*	*Notitiae episcopatuum ecclesiae Constantinopolitanae*
NG*	Nikephoros Gregoras, *Byzantina historia*
*Nicene**	*A select library of Nicene and post-Nicene Fathers of the Christian Church*
Nikeph.*	Nikephoros I, *Breviarium historicum*
NM*	Nicholas I Mystikos, *Letters*
NP*	Niketas the Paphlagonian, *Summorum apostolorum orationes laudatoriae*
OC	*Orientalia christiana*
OCA	*Orientalia christiana analecta*

OCP	*Orientalia christiana periodica*
ODB	*Oxford dictionary of Byzantium*, A. P. Kazhdan *et al.* (eds.), 3 vols., Oxford and New York (1991)
OrChr	*Oriens christianus*
PaP	*Past and present*
PBA	*Proceedings of the British Academy*
PBSR	*Papers of the British school at Rome*
PBW	*Prosopography of the Byzantine world* (http://www.pbw.kcl.ac.uk/)
PG*	Migne (ed.), *Patrologiae cursus completus: series graeca*
Phot.*	Photios, *Epistulae et amphilochia*
PL*	Migne (ed.), *Patrologiae cursus completus: series latina*
PLP	*Prosopographisches Lexikon der Palaiologenzeit*, ed. E. Trapp *et al.*, 15 vols., Vienna (1976–96)
PLRE	*The prosopography of the later Roman empire*, ed. A. H. M. Jones *et al.*, 3 vols. in 4 pts., Cambridge (1971–92)
PMBZ	*Prosopographie der mittelbyzantinischen Zeit*, ed. R.-J. Lilie *et al.*, I: *(641–867), Prolegomena*, 5 vols. and list of abbreviations (1998–2002); II: *(867–1025)* (forthcoming), Berlin and New York
PO	*Patrologia orientalis*, 49 vols. to date, Paris and Turnhout (1904–)
PR *B**	Procopius, *Buildings*
PR *W**	Procopius, *History of the wars*
Psell.*	Michael Psellos, *Chronographia*
PVL*	*Povest' vremennykh let* (see also *RPC*)
QFIAB	*Quellen und Forschungen aus italienischen Archiven und Bibliotheken*
RAC	*Reallexikon für Antike und Christentum*, ed. T. Klauser *et al.*, Stuttgart (1950–)
RbK	*Reallexikon zur byzantinischen Kunst*, ed. K. Wessel and M. Restle, Stuttgart (1963–)
RE	*Paulys Realencyclopädie der classischen Altertumswissenschaft*
REA	*Revue des études arméniennes*
REB	*Revue des études byzantines*
REG	*Revue des études grecques*
RESEE	*Revue des études sud-est européennes*
RH	*Revue historique*
RHC Occ.	*Recueil des historiens des croisades, Historiens occidentaux*, 5 vols. Paris (1841–95)
RHE	*Revue d'histoire ecclésiastique*

RHM	*Römische historische Mitteilungen*
RHR	*Revue de l'histoire des religions*
*RIB**	*Russkaia istoricheskaia biblioteka*
*RKK**	*Die Regesten des Kaiserreichs unter den Karolingern*
RN	*Revue numismatique*
*RPC**	Russian primary chronicle (see also *PVL*)
RSBN	*Rivista di studi bizantini e neoellenici*
SAO	*Studia et acta orientalia*
SBS	*Studies in Byzantine sigillography*, ed. N. Oikonomides et al., 9 vols. to date, Washington, DC and Munich (1987–)
SC	*Sources chrétiennes*
SCH	*Studies in church history*
*SD**	Stephen the Deacon, *Life of Stephen the Younger*
Seb.*	Sebeos, *Armenian history*
SF	*Südost-Forschungen*
SI	*Studia islamica*
Skyl.*	John Skylitzes, *Synopsis historiarum*
Skyl. Con.*	Skylitzes Continuatus, *Chronicle*
SM	*Studi medievali*
Sp	*Speculum*
SSCIS	*Settimane di studio della Fondazione Centro Italiano di studi sull'alto Medioevo*, Spoleto
ST*	Stephen of Taron, *Universal history*
StT	*Studi e testi*
TA*	Thomas Artsruni, *History*
TAPA	*Transactions of the American philological association*
TC*	Theophanes Continuatus, *Chronographia*
Theoph.*	Theophanes, *Chronicle*
Theo. Stud.*	Theodore the Studite, *Letters*
TIB	*Tabula imperii byzantini*, ed. H. Hunger, 10 vols. to date, Vienna (1976–)
TM	*Travaux et mémoires*
TRHS	*Transactions of the Royal Historical Society*
TS*	Theophylact Simocatta, *History*
TT*	*Urkunden zur älteren Handels- und Staatsgeschichte der Republik Venedig*, ed. Tafel and Thomas
TU	*Texte und Untersuchungen*
Vasil.*	Vasiliev, *Byzance et les Arabes*, II.2
Villehard.*	Geoffrey of Villehardouin, *La Conquête de Constantinople*
VV	*Vizantiiskii vremennik*
WBS	*Wiener byzantinistische Studien*

Yov.*   Yovhannes V, *History*
ZDMG   *Zeitschrift der deutschen Morgenländischen Gesellschaft*
ZRVI   *Zbornik Radova Vizantološkog Instituta*

PRIMARY SOURCES

Abu al-Baqa', *al-Manaqib*, ed. S. M. Daradikah and M. 'A. Q. Khuraysat, *Kitab al-manaqib al-mazyadiyah fi akhbar al-muluk al-Asadiyah* [of Abu al-Baqa' Hibat Allah al-Hilli (d. 12th century)], 2 vols., Amman (1984)

Abu 'Ubaydah, *Kitab al-Naqa'id*, ed. A. A. Bevan, *Kitab al-Naqa'id Jarir wa-al-Farazdaq* [of Abu 'Ubaydah Ma'mar ibn al-Muthanna al-Taymi (d. 819)], 3 vols., Leiden (1905–12)

Accessiones ad historiam abbatiae Cassinensis, ed. E. Gattula, Venice (1734)

Acta et diplomata res Albaniae mediae aetatis illustrantia, ed. L. von Thallóczy *et al.*, 2 vols., Vienna (1913–18)

Acta patriarchatus constantinopolitani, see under Miklosich and Müller

Acta sanctae Marinae et sancti Christophori, ed. H. Usener, Bonn (1886)

Acta sanctorum, ed. J. Bolland *et al.*, *Acta sanctorum quotquot toto orbe coluntur*, 71 vols., Antwerp, Brussels and Paris (1643–1940); partial repr. Venice (1734–60); partial repr. Paris (1963–70); repr. first 60 vols., Brussels and Turnhout (1966–71)

Actes de Chilandar, ed. M. Živojinović *et al.*, *Actes de Chilandar: des origines à 1319*, *AA* 20, 1 vol. in 2 pts. to date, Paris (1998–)

Actes de Dionysiou, ed. N. Oikonomides *et al.*, *AA* 4, Paris (1968)

Actes d'Iviron, ed. J. Lefort *et al.*, 4 vols. to date, *AA* 14, 16, 18, 19, Paris (1985–)

Actes de Lavra, ed. P. Lemerle *et al.*, *AA* 5, 8, 10, 11, 4 vols. in 7 pts., Paris, (1970–82)

Actes du Pantocrator, ed. V. Kravari, *AA* 17, 1 vol. to date, Paris (1991–)

Actes du Protaton, ed. D. Papachryssanthou, *AA* 7, 1 vol. in 2 pts., Paris (1975)

Actes de Vatopédi, ed. J. Bompaire *et al.*, *AA* 21–2, 2 vols. to date, Paris (2001–)

Actes de Xénophon, ed. D. Papachryssanthou, *AA* 15, 2 vols., Paris (1986)

Acts of the second council of Nicaea (787), in Mansi, XII, cols. 991–1152; XIII, cols. 1–418

Actus Sylvestri, in Boninus Mombritius, *Sanctuarium seu Vitae sanctorum*, 2 vols., Paris (1910), II, pp. 508–31; ed. P. De Leo, *Il Constitutum Constantini: compilazione agiografica del sec. VIII: note e documenti per una nuova lettura*, Reggio Calabria (1974)

Adalbert of St Maximin, *Reginonis continuatio*, in Regino of Prüm, *Chronicon*, ed. F. Kurze, *Reginonis abbatis Prumiensis chronicon cum continuatione Treverensi*, *MGH SRG* 50, Hanover (1890), pp. 154–79

Adversus Constantinum Caballinum, in *PG* 95, cols. 309–44

Agapetus, *Mirror of princes*, ed. R. Riedinger, *Der Fürstenspiegel für Kaiser Iustinianus von Agapetos Diakonos*, Athens (1995); German tr. W. Blum, *Byzantinische Fürstenspiegel: Agapetos, Theophylakt von Ochrid, Thomas Magister*, Stuttgart (1981), pp. 59–80; partial tr. in *Social and political thought in Byzantium*, ed. Barker, pp. 54–63

Agapius of Membij, *al-'Unwan*, ed. and French tr. A. A. Vasiliev, *Kitab al-'unvan (Histoire universelle écrite par Agapius (Mahboub) de Menbidj)*, PO 5.4 (1910), pp. 557–692; *PO* 7.4 (1911), pp. 457–591; *PO* 8.3 (1912), pp. 399–547; *PO* 11.1 (1915), pp. 9–144, 2 vols. in 4 pts., Paris (1909–15; repr. Paris and Turnhout, 1947–74)

Agathangelos, *History*, ed. G. Ter-Mkrtch'ean and S. Kanayeants', *Patmut'iwn Hayots'*, Tiflis (1909, repr. Delmar, NY, 1980); tr. R. W. Thomson, *Agathangelos: History of the Armenians*, Albany, NY (1976)

Agathias, *Histories*, ed. R. Keydell, *Historiarum libri quinque*, CFHB 2, Berlin (1967); tr. J. D. Frendo, *Agathias, The Histories*, CFHB 2A, Berlin (1975)

Agnellus of Ravenna, *Liber pontificalis*, ed. O. Holder-Egger, *Liber pontificalis ecclesiae Ravennatis*, MGH SRL, Hanover (1878), pp. 265–391; ed. D. Mauskopf Deliyannis, CCCM 199, Turnhout (2006); tr. D. Mauskopf Deliyannis, *The book of pontiffs of the church of Ravenna*, Washington, DC (2004)

Aistulf, *Leges*, ed. and German tr. in F. Beyerle, *Die Gesetze der Langobarden*, Weimar (1947), pp. 358–79

Alcuin, *Letters*, ed. E. Dümmler, MGH Ep. 4, Berlin (1895), pp. 18–493; partial tr. S. Allott, *Alcuin of York, c. AD 732 to 804: his life and letters*, York (1974)

Alexander of Tralles, *Therapeutica*, ed. and German tr. T. Puschmann, *Ein Beitrag zur Geschichte der Medicin*, 2 vols., Vienna (1878–9; repr. with addenda, Amsterdam, 1963)

Alexios I Komnenos, *Ordonnance nouvelle*, in ed. P. Gautier, 'L'Édit d'Alexis Ier Comnène sur la réforme du clergé', REB 31 (1973), pp. 165–201

Amatus of Monte Cassino, *Storia de' Normanni*, ed. V. de Bartholomaeis, FSI 76, Rome (1935); tr. P. N. Dunbar and G. A. Loud, *The history of the Normans*, Woodbridge (2004)

Ammianus Marcellinus, *History*, ed. W. Seyfarth, *Rerum gestarum libri qui supersunt*, 2 vols., Leipzig (1978); partial tr. W. Hamilton, *The later Roman empire AD 354–378*, Harmondsworth (1986)

Analecta sacra et classica spicilegio Solesmensi parata, ed. J. B. Pitra, 7 vols., Paris and Rome (1876–91; repr. Farnborough, 1967)

Analekta hierosolymitikes stachyologias, ed. A. Papadopoulos-Kerameus, 5 vols., St Petersburg (1891–8; repr. Brussels, 1963)

Anania of Shirak, *Geography*, ed. A. Soukry, *Ashkharhats'oyts'Movsesi Khorenats'woy*, Venice (1881; repr. Delmar, NY, 1984); tr. R. H. Hewsen, *The Geography of Ananias of Širak (Ašxarhac'oyc'): the long and short recensions*, Wiesbaden (1992)

Anastasius Bibliothecarius, *Correspondence of Martin I*, PL 129, cols. 585–90

Anastasius of Sinai, *Guidebook*, ed. K. H. Uthemann, *Viae dux*, CCSG 8, Turnhout (1981)

—, *Questions and answers*, ed. M. Richard and J. A. Munitz, *Anastasii Sinaitae Quaestiones et responsiones*, CCSG 59, Turnhout (2006)

—, *Sermons*, ed. K. H. Uthemann, *Sermones duo in constitutionem hominis secundum imaginem Dei necnon Opuscula adversus monotheletas*, CCSG 12, Turnhout (1985)

Andrea, A. J. (tr.), *Contemporary sources for the Fourth Crusade*, Leiden (2000)

Andrea Dandolo, *Chronica*, ed. E. Pastorello, *Andreae Danduli Ducis Venetiarum, Chronica per extensum descripta: aa 46–1280 d.C.*, Bologna (1938–58)

Anna Komnena, *Alexiad*, ed. D. R. Reinsch and A. Kambylis, 2 vols., *CFHB* 40, Berlin and New York (2001); ed. and French tr. B. Leib, 4 vols., Paris (1937–76); tr. E. R. A. Sewter, Harmondsworth (1969)

Annales Bertiniani, ed. F. Grat *et al.*, *Annales de Saint-Bertin*, Paris (1964); tr. J. Nelson, *The Annals of Saint-Bertin*, Manchester (1991)

Annales Mosellani, ed. J. M. Lappenberg, *MGH SS* 16, Hanover (1859), 494–9

Annales regni Francorum, ed. F. Kurze, *MGH SRG* 6, Hanover (1895); tr. B. W. Scholz, *Carolingian chronicles: royal Frankish annals and Nithard's histories*, Ann Arbor, MI (1970)

Anonymi professoris epistulae, ed. A. Markopoulos, *CFHB* 37, Berlin (2000) (contents summarised by Browning (1954), pp. 402–25)

Ansbert, *History of Frederick's expedition*, ed. A. Chroust, *Historia de expeditione Friderici imperatoris*, in *Quellen zur Geschichte des Kreuzzuges Kaiser Friedrichs I., MGH SRG* n.s. 5, Berlin (1928; repr. 1964), pp. 1–115

Anthologia graeca, ed. and tr. W. R. Paton, *The Greek anthology*, 5 vols., London and New York (1916–18)

Archives de l'Athos, ed. P. Lemerle *et al.*, 22 vols. to date, Paris (1937–)

Les Archives de Saint-Jean-Prodrome sur le mont Ménécée, ed. A. Guillou, Paris (1955)

Arethas, archbishop of Caesarea, *Orations*, ed. (with English summaries) R. J. H. Jenkins *et al.*, 'Nine orations of Arethas from Cod. Marc. gr. 524', *BZ* 47 (1954), pp. 1–40

—, *Scripta minora*, ed. L. G. Westerink, 2 vols., Leipzig (1968–72)

Aristakes of Lastivert, *History*, ed. K. N. Yuzbashian, *Patmut'iwn*, Erevan (1973); partial French tr. M. Canard and H. Berbérian, *Récit des malheurs de la nation arménienne*, Brussels (1973); tr. R. Bedrosian, *Aristakes Lastivertc'i's History*, New York (1985)

al-A'sha, *Diwan*, ed. R. Geyer, *Gedichte von 'Abu Basir Maimun ibn Qais al-'A'sa, nebst Sammlungen von Stücken anderer Dichter des gleichen Beinamens und von al-Musayyab ibn 'Alas* [of Abu Bashir Maymun ibn Qays al-A'sha (d. 629)], London (1928)

al-'Askari, *al-'Awa'il*, ed. W. Qassab and M. al-Misri, *Kitab al-'Awa'il* [of Abu Hilal al-Hasan ibn 'Abd Allah ibn Sahl al-'Askari (d. 1004)], 2 vols., 2nd edn., Riyadh (1982)

Asołik, see under Stephen of Taron

Assizes of Romania, ed. and French tr. G. Recoura, *Les Assises de Romanie*, Paris (1930); ed. A. Parmeggiani, *Libro dele uxanze e statuti delo imperio de Romania*, Spoleto (1998); tr. P. Topping, *Feudal institutions as revealed in the Assizes of Romania, the Law Code of Frankish Greece*, Philadelphia (1949; repr. in Topping (1977), no. 1)

Athanasios I, patriarch of Constantinople, *Correspondence*, ed. and tr. A.-M. Talbot, *The correspondence of Athanasius I, patriarch of Constantinople: letters to the emperor Andronicus II, members of the imperial family and officials*, CFHB 7, Washington, DC (1975)

Avitus of Vienne, *Epistulae*, ed. R. Peiper, *MGH AA* 6.2, Berlin (1883), pp. 29–103; tr. D. Shanzer and I. Wood, *Letters and selected prose*, Liverpool (2002)

Ayatkar i zamaspik, ed. and Italian tr. G. Messina, *Libro apocalittico persiano*, Rome (1939)

al-Azdi, *Futuh al-Sham*, ed. W. N. Leeds, '*The Fotooh al-Sham': being an account of the Moslim conquests in Syria* [of Abu Isma'il Muhammad ibn 'Abd Allah al-Basri al-Azdi (d. *c.* 781)], Calcutta (1854)

al-'Azimi, *Ta'rikh Halab*, ed. I. Za'rur, *Ta'rikh Halab* [of Muhammad ibn 'Ali al-'Azimi (d. 1161)], Damascus (1984)

al-Azraqi, *History of Mecca*, ed. R. S. Malhas, *Akhbar Makkah wa-ma ja'a fiha min al-athar* [of Abu al-Walid Muhammad ibn 'Abd Allah ibn Ahmad al-Azraqi (d. *c.* 865)], 2 vols., Beirut (1983)

al-Bakri, *Mu'jam ma sta'jam*, ed. M. al-Saqqa, *Mu'jam ma sta'jam min asma' al-bilad wa-al-mawadi'* [of Abu 'Ubayd 'Abd Allah ibn 'Abd al-'Aziz al-Bakri (d. 1094)], 4 vols., Cairo (1945–51)

—, *al-Mughrib*, ed. W. MacGukin de Slane, *al-Mughrib fi dhikr bilad Ifriqiyah wa-al-Maghrib*, Algiers (1857; repr. Baghdad, 1964)

al-Baladhuri, *Futuh al-buldan*, ed. M. J. de Goeje, *Liber expugnationis regionum/Futuh al-buldan* [of Abu al-Hasan Ahmad ibn Yahya ibn Jabir al-Baladhuri (d. 892)], Leiden (1866); tr. P. K. Hitti and F. C. Murgotten, *The origins of the Islamic state*, 2 vols., New York (1916–24; repr. Piscataway, NJ, 2002)

—, *Ansab al-ashraf*, ed. I. 'Abbas *et al.*, *Ansab al-ashraf*, 5 vols. in 7 pts. to date, Wiesbaden (1978–); ed. M. Hamid Allah, vol. 1 only, Cairo (1959); ed. S. D. Goitein, M. Schloessinger and M. J. Kister, *The Ansab al-ashraf of al-Baladhuri*, 3 vols. in 5 pts., Jerusalem (1936–71)

Bar Hebraeus, *Chronography*, ed. P. Bedjan, *Chronicon syriacum*, Paris (1890); tr. E. A. Wallis Budge, *The chronography of Gregory Abu'l Faraj, the son of Aaron, the Hebrew physician, commonly known as Bar Hebraeus*, 2 vols., London (1932)

Barlaam the Calabrian, *Three treatises*, ed. and tr. T. M. Kolbaba, 'Barlaam the Calabrian: three treatises on papal primacy: introduction, edition, and translation', *REB* 53 (1995), pp. 41–115

Bartolf of Nangis, *Gesta Francorum Iherusalem expugnantium*, *RHC Occ.*, III, pp. 491–543

Basilika, ed. H. J. Scheltema *et al.*, *Basilicorum libri LX*, Series A (Text) 8 vols., Series B (Scholia) 9 vols., Groningen (1953–88)

Bede, *Opera*, ed. C. W. Jones and C. B. Kendall, *Bedae venerabilis opera*, CCSL 123A–C, 3 vols., Turnhout (1975–80)

—, *De temporibus*, in Bede, *Opera* (1975–80), III, pp. 585–611

—, *De temporum ratione*, in Bede, *Opera* (1975–80), II, pp. 263–544; tr. F. Wallis, *The reckoning of time*, Liverpool (1999)

Benvenuto de Brixano, notaio in Candia, 1301–1302, ed. R. Morozzo della Rocca, Venice (1950)

Blockley, R. C. (ed. and tr.), *The fragmentary classicising historians of the later Roman empire: Eunapius, Olympiodorus, Priscus, and Malchus*, 2 vols., Liverpool, (1981–3)

Boiukliev, I., 'Shopov psaltir (tekst i komentar)', *B'lgarski ezik* 13 (1963), pp. 234–54

Book of letters, ed. Y. Izmireants', *Girk' T'ght'ots'*, Tiflis (1901); ed. N. Pogharean, Jerusalem (1994); partial French tr. M. Tallon, *Livre des lettres (Girk T'lt'oc): 1er groupe: documents concernant les relations avec les Grecs*, Beirut (1955) [= *Mélanges de l'Université Saint Joseph* 32, pp. 1–146]; substantially tr. into French in Garsoïan (1999a), pp. 411–583

Boril, *Synodikon*, ed. M. G. Popruženko, *Sinodik tsaria Borila*, Sofia (1928)

Boyce, M. (ed. and tr.), *Textual sources for the study of Zoroastrianism*, Manchester (1984)

Brooks, E. W., 'The Arabs in Asia Minor (641–750) from Arabic Sources', *JHS* 18 (1898), pp. 182–208

Byzantine defenders of images: eight saints' lives in English translation, ed. A.-M. Talbot, Washington, DC (1998)

Byzantine monastic foundation documents: a complete translation of the surviving founders' Typika and testaments, ed. J. C. Thomas and A. C. Hero, *DOSt* 35, 5 vols., Washington, DC (2000)

Die byzantinischen Kleinchroniken, ed. P. Schreiner, *CFHB* 12, 3 vols., Vienna (1975–9)

Byzantium: church, society and civilization seen through contemporary eyes, ed. D. J. Geanakoplos, Chicago (1984)

Campaign organization, ed. and tr. Dennis, *Three Byzantine military treatises*, pp. 246–327

Canart, P., 'Nicéphore Blemmyde et le mémoire adressé aux envoyés de Grégoire IX (Nicée, 1234)', *OCP* 25 (1959), pp. 310–25

Carile, A. (ed.), 'Partitio terrarum Imperii Romanie', *Studi veneziani* 7 (1965), pp. 125–305

Le carte che si conservano nello archivio del capitolo metropolitano della città di Trani (dal IX secolo fino all'anno 1266), ed. A. Prologo, Barletta (1877)

Cassiodorus, *Expositio psalmorum*, ed. M. Adriaen, *CCSL* 98, Turnhout (1958); tr. P. G. Walsh, *Explanation of the psalms*, 3 vols., New York (1990–1)

—, *Variae*, ed. Å.J. Fridh and J. W. Halporn, *Variarum libri XII; De anima*, *CCSL* 96, Turnhout (1973), pp. 1–499; tr. (selection) S. J. B. Barnish, Liverpool (1992)

Cassius Dio, *Roman history*, ed. and tr. E. Cary, 9 vols., London (1914–27)

Catalogue of the Byzantine coins in the Dumbarton Oaks collection and in the Whittemore collection, I: *(491–602)*, ed. A. R. Bellinger (1966); II: *(602–717)*, ed. P. Grierson, 2 vols. (1968); III: *(717–1081)*, ed. P. Grierson, 2 vols. (1973); IV: *(1081–1261)*, ed. M. Hendy, 2 vols. (1999); V: *(1258–1453)*, ed. P. Grierson, 2 vols. (1999), Washington, DC

Catalogue of Byzantine seals at Dumbarton Oaks and in the Fogg Museum of Art, ed. J. Nesbitt *et al.*, 5 vols. to date, Washington, DC (1991–)

Chartae Latinae antiquiores: facsimile edition of the Latin charters: 2nd series, ninth century, ed. G. Cavallo and G. Nicolaj, 25 pts. to date, Olten and Dietikon-Zurich (1997–)

Cheikho, L., *Shu'ara' al-Nasraniyah*, 2 vols., Beirut (1890–1)

Chronica monasterii Casinensis, ed. H. Hoffmann, *Die Chronik von Montecassino*, MGH SS 34, Hanover (1980)

The Chronicle of 811, ed. and French tr. I. Dujčev, 'La Chronique byzantine de l'an 811', *TM* 1 (1965), pp. 205–54; repr. in Dujčev (1965–96), II, pp. 425–89; tr. in Stephenson (2006), pp. 87–90

Chronicle of Brussels, ed. F. Cumont, *Chroniques byzantines du manuscrit 11376*, *Anecdota Bruxellensia* I, Ghent (1894), pp. 13–36

The Chronicle of Monemvasia, ed. in Lemerle (1963), pp. 8–11; ed. and Italian tr. I. Dujčev, *Cronaca di Monemvasia*, Palermo (1976); ed. in Kislinger (2001), pp. 199–206

The Chronicle of the Morea, ed. P. P. Kalonaros, *To chronikon tou Moreos*, Athens (1940); tr. H. E. Lurier, *Crusaders as conquerors: the Chronicle of Morea*, New York (1964)

Chronicle of Tocco, ed. and Italian tr. G. Schirò, *Cronaca dei Tocco di Cefalonia di Anonimo*, CFHB 10, Rome (1975)

Chronicon ad 1234, ed. and Latin and French tr. J.-B. Chabot, *Anonymi auctoris Chronicon ad annum Christi 1234 pertinens*, 4 vols., CSCO 81, 82, 109, 354, Paris (1920–74); partial tr. in *Syrian chronicles*, tr. Palmer *et al.*, pp. 111–221

Chronicon Salernitanum, ed. U. Westerbergh, *Chronicon Salernitanum: a critical edition with studies on literary and historical sources and on languages*, Stockholm (1956)

Chronicon vulturnense del monaco Giovanni, ed. V. Federici, *FSI* 58–60, 3 vols., Rome (1925–38); partial Italian tr. G. de Benedittis, *San Vincenzo al Volturno: dal Chronicon alla storia*, Isernia (1995)

La Chronique de Sainte-Barbe-en-Auge, ed. R.-N. Sauvage, Caen (1907)

Chroniques gréco-romanes inédites et peu connues, ed. C. Hopf, Berlin (1873)

Cinque poeti bizantini: anacreontee dal Barberiniano greco 310, ed. and Italian tr. F. Ciccolella, Alessandria (2000)

Codex bavarus, ed. G. Rabotti, *Breviarium ecclesiae Ravennatis (Codice Bavaro) secoli VII–X*, Rome (1985)

Codex carolinus, ed. W. Gundlach, *MGH Ep.* 3, Berlin (1892), pp. 476–653; partial tr. P. D. King, *Charlemagne: translated sources*, Kendal (1987)

Codex diplomaticus caietanus, 3 vols. in 4 pts., Monte Cassino (1887–1960)

Codex diplomaticus cavensis, ed. M. Morcaldi *et al.*, 10 vols., Milan, Naples and Badia di Cava (1873–1990)

Codex diplomaticus regni Croatiae, Dalmatiae et Slavoniae, ed. T. Smičiklas *et al.*, 19 vols., Zagreb (1904–90)

Commemoratorium de casis Dei vel monasteriis (c. 808), in T. Tobler and M. Molinier (eds.), *Itinera hierosolymitana et descriptiones Terrae Sanctae bellis sacris anteriora et latina lingua exarata sumptibus Societatis illustrandis Orientis latini monumentis*, Geneva (1880), pp. 301–5

Concilium universale Constantinopolitanum tertium, ed. R. Riedinger, *ACO* Series 2 2.1–3, 3 vols. to date, Berlin (1990–)

Confraternity of Thebes, ed. and tr. J. Nesbitt and J. Wiita, 'A confraternity of the Comnenian era', *BZ* 68 (1975), pp. 360–84

Constantine Manasses, *Chronicle*, ed. O. Lampsidis, *Constantini Manassis Breviarium Chronicum*, CFHB 36, 2 vols., Athens (1996)

Constantine VII Porphyrogenitus, *De administrando imperio*, I: ed. G. Moravcsik, tr. R. J. H. Jenkins, 2nd edn., *CFHB* 1, Washington, DC (1967); II: *Commentary*, ed. R. J. H. Jenkins, London (1962)

— *De cerimoniis aulae byzantinae*, ed. J. J. Reiske, 2 vols., *CSHB*, Bonn (1829–30); incomplete ed. and French tr. A. Vogt, *Constantin VII Porphyrogénète: Le Livre des cérémonies*, 2 vols., Paris (1935–9); ed. and French tr. G. Dagron and B. Flusin, *Le Livre des cérémonies* (in preparation); tr. A. Moffatt and M. Tall, *Constantine Porphyrogennetos: the ceremonies*, ByzAust (in preparation); tr. of *DC*, II.15 in Featherstone, *'Di' endeixin'*, pp. 81–112; tr. of *DC*, II.44–5 in Haldon (2000b), pp. 202–35

—, *De thematibus*, ed. A. Pertusi, *StT* 160, Rome (1952)

—, *Excerpta de legationibus*, in *Excerpta historica iussu Imp. Constantini Porphyrogeniti confecta*, I, ed. C. de Boor *et al.*, 4 vols. in 5 pts., Berlin (1903–10)

—, *Military orations*, (i) ed. H. Ahrweiler, 'Un discours inédit de Constantin VII Porphyrogénète', *TM* 2 (1967), pp. 393–404 at pp. 397–9; tr. E. McGeer, 'Two military orations of Constantine VII', in Nesbitt (ed). (2003), pp. 117-20; (ii) ed. R. Vári, 'Zum historischen Exzerptenwerke des Konstantinos Porphyrogennetos' *BZ* 17 (1908), pp. 75–85 at pp. 78–84; tr. McGeer, 'Two military orations', pp. 127–34

—, *Three treatises on imperial military expeditions*, ed. and tr. J. Haldon, *CFHB* 28, Vienna (1990)

Constantine Stilbes, *Against the Latins*, ed. J. Darrouzès, 'Le Mémoire de Constantin Stilbès contre les Latins', *REB* 21 (1963), pp. 50–100

—, *Thesaurus*, ed. J. A. Munitiz, *Theognosti thesaurus*, *CCSG* 5, Louvain (1979)

Constitutio Romana, ed. A. Boretius, *MGH Cap.* 1, Hanover (1883), pp. 322–4

Corippus, *In laudem Iustini Augusti minoris libri IV*, ed. and tr. Averil Cameron, London (1976)

— *Iohannis*, ed. J. Diggle and F. R. D. Goodyear, Cambridge (1970); tr. G. W. Shea, *The Iohannis or De bellis libycis of Flavius Cresconius Corippus*, Lewiston, NY (1998)

Cosmas Indicopleustes, *Christian topography*, ed. and French tr. W. Wolska-Conus, *Topographie chrétienne*, 3 vols., Paris (1968–73); tr. J. W. McCrindle, *The Christian topography of Cosmas, an Egyptian monk*, London (1897)

Cotelerius, J. B., *Ecclesiae graecae monumenta*, 4 vols., Paris (1696)

Council of Hieria (754), *Horos* in Mansi, XIII, cols. 203–364; partial tr. in Gero (1977), pp. 68–94; tr. in *Icon and logos*, ed. Sahas, pp. 44–185; partial German tr. in T. Krannich *et al.* (eds.), *Die ikonoklastische Synode von Hiereia 754: Einleitung, Text, Übersetzung und Kommentar ihres Horos*, Tübingen (2002), pp. 29–69; partial French tr. in Auzépy *et al.* (1996), pp. 46–52

Creeds, councils and controversies: documents illustrating the history of the Church AD 337–461, ed. J. Stevenson, rev. edn. W. H. C. Frend, London (1989)

Cyril of Scythopolis, *Saints' lives*, ed. E. Schwartz, *Kyrillos von Skythopolis*, Leipzig (1939); tr. R. M. Price, *Lives of the monks of Palestine*, Kalamazoo, MI (1991) al-Dabbagh in Ibn Naji, *Ma'alim*, ed. I. Shabbuh *et al.*, *Ma'alim al-iman fi ma'arifat ahl al-Qayrawan* ['Abd al-Rahman ibn Muhammad al-Dabbagh (d. 1299/1300) in Abu al-Qasim ibn Isa ibn Naji (d. 1436)], 3 vols., Cairo (1968)

Danilo II, archbishop *et al.*, *Životi kraljeva i arhiepiskopa srpskih*, ed. D. Daničić (Zagreb, 1866; repr. London, 1972)

De obsidione toleranda, ed. H. van den Berg, tr. D. F. Sullivan, in D. F. Sullivan, 'A Byzantine instruction manual on siege defense: the *De obsidione toleranda*', in Nesbitt (ed.) (2003), pp. 139–266

Délibérations des assemblées vénitiennes concernant la Romanie, ed. F. Thiriet, 2 vols., Paris and The Hague (1966–71)

Deliberazioni del maggior consiglio di Venezia, ed. R. Cessi, 3 vols., Bologna (1931–50)

Demetrios Chomatenos, *Erotapokriseis*, in *Analecta sacra et classica*, ed. Pitra, VI (VII), cols. 618–86

—, *Ponemata diaphora*, ed. G. Prinzing, *CFHB* 38, Berlin and New York (2002)

Demetrios Kydones, *Apologia for unity with Rome*, ed. G. Mercati, *Notizie di Procoro e Demetrio Cidone, Manuele Caleca e Teodoro Meliteniota ed altri appunti per la storia della teologia e della letteratura bizantina del secolo XIV*, *StT* 56, Vatican City, Rome (1931), pp. 359–403; German tr. H.-G. Beck, 'Die "Apologia pro vita sua" des Demetrios Kydones', *Ostkirchliche Studien* 1 (1952), pp. 208–25, 264–82; tr. J. Likoudis, *Ending the Byzantine Greek schism*, New Rochelle, NY (1992), pp. 22–70

—, *Correspondance*, ed. R. J. Loenertz, *StT* 186, 208, 2 vols., Vatican City, Rome (1956–60); German tr. F. Tinnefeld, *Demetrios Kydones, Briefe*, 4 vols. in 5 pts., Stuttgart (1981–2003)

Dendrinos, C. (ed.), 'An unpublished funeral oration on Manuel II Palaeologus († 1425)', in Dendrinos *et al.* (eds.) (2003), pp. 423–56

Denkard VI, tr. S. Shaked, *The wisdom of the Sasanian sages*, Boulder, CO (1979)

Dennis, G. T. (ed. and tr.), *Three Byzantine military treatises*, *CFHB* 25, Washington, DC (1985)

Denys de Thrace et les commentateurs arméniens, ed. N. Adontz, tr. R. Hotterbex, Louvain (1970)

Deusdedit, *Collectio canonum*, ed. V. Wolf von Glanvell, *Die Kanonessammlung des Kardinals Deusdedit*, Paderborn (1905)

Digenis Akritis: the Grottaferrata and Escorial versions, ed. and tr. E. Jeffreys, Cambridge (1998)

al-Dinawari, *al-Akhbar*, ed. V. Guirgass, *Kitab al-akhbar al-tiwal* [of Abu Hanifah Ahmad ibn Dawud al-Dinawari (d. *c.* 895)], 2 vols., Leiden (1888–1912)

Diplomatarium Veneto-Levantinum, I: *1300–1350*, ed. G. M. Thomas, Venice (1880); II: *1351–1454*, ed. G. M. Thomas and R. Predelli, Venice (1899)

Discipline générale antique (IIᵉ–IXᵉ siècles), ed. and French tr. P.-P. Joannou, 2 vols., Rome (1962–3); English tr. ed. by N. P. Tanner, *Decrees of the ecumenical councils*, 2 vols., London and Washington, DC (1990)

Divisio ducatus Beneventani, ed. F. Bluhme in *MGH Leges* (in folio) 4, ed. G. H. Pertz, Hanover (1868), pp. 221–5; ed. in Martin (2005), pp. 201–17

Dmitrievsky, A., *Opisanie liturgicheskikh rukopisei, khraniashchikhsia v bibliotekakh pravoslavnogo vostoka*, 3 vols., Kiev and Petrograd (1895–1917)

Dobschütz, E. von, *Christusbilder: Untersuchungen zur christlichen Legende*, Leipzig (1899)

The Doctrine of Jacob the Newly Baptised, ed. and French tr. G. Dagron and V. Déroche, 'Juifs et Chrétiens dans l'orient du VIIe siècle', *TM* 11 (1991), pp. 17–273

Documenti relativi alla storia di Venezia anteriori al mille, ed. R. Cessi, 2nd edn. by C. F. Polizzi, 2 vols., Venice (1991)

Documenti sulle relazioni delle città toscane coll'oriente cristiano e coi Turchi fino all'anno MDXXXI, ed. G. Müller, Florence (1879)

Documents sur le régime des terres dans la principauté de Morée au XIVe siècle, ed. J. Longnon and P. Topping, Paris (1969)

Dölger, F., *Aus den Schatzkammern des Heiligen Berges: 115 Urkunden und 50 Urkundensiegel aus 10 Jahrhunderten*, Munich (1948)

—, *Beiträge zur Geschichte der byzantinischen Finanzverwaltung: besonders des 10. und 11. Jahrhunderts*, Leipzig (1927); includes edn. of 'The taxation treatise Cod. Marc. gr 173', pp. 113–23; tr. in Brand (1969), pp. 48–57

—, *Regesten der Kaiserurkunden des oströmischen Reiches von 565–1453*, 5 vols., Munich (1924–65); rev. edn. P. Wirth *et al.*, 3 vols. to date (1977–)

—, *Sechs byzantinische Praktika des 14. Jahrhunderts für das Athoskloster Iberon, mit diplomatischen, sprachlichen, verwaltungs- und sozialgeschichtlichen Bemerkungen*, Munich (1949)

Dossier grec de l'Union de Lyon (1273–1277), ed. and French tr. V. Laurent and J. Darrouzès, Paris (1976)

Dubarle, A.-M., 'L'Homélie de Grégoire le Référandaire pour la réception de l'image d'Édesse', *REB* 55 (1997), pp. 5–51

Duca di Candia: ducali e lettere ricevute (1358–1360; 1401–1405), ed. F. Thiriet, Venice (1978)

Duca di Candia: Quaternus consiliorum 1340–1350, ed. P. Ratti Vidulich, Venice (1976)

Ducas, *Istoria Turco-Bizantină, 1341–1462*, ed. V. Grecu, Bucharest (1958); tr. H. J. Magoulias, *Decline and fall of Byzantium to the Ottoman Turks*, Detroit (1975)

Dujčev, I., 'On the treaty of 927 with the Bulgarians', *DOP* 32 (1978), pp. 217–95

Eberwin of Trier, *Ex miraculis sancti Symeonis*, ed. G. Waitz, *MGH SS* 8, Hanover (1848), pp. 209–11

Ecloga, ed. and German tr. L. Burgmann, *Ecloga, das Gesetzbuch Leons III. und Konstantinos V.*, Frankfurt-am-Main (1983); tr. E. H. Freshfield, *A manual of Roman law: the Ecloga*, Cambridge (1926)

Ecloga Basilicorum, ed. L. Burgmann, Frankfurt-am-Main (1988)

Ecloga privata aucta, ed. D. Simon and S. Troianos, 'Eklogadion und Ecloga privata aucta', *FM* 2 (1977), pp. 45–86 (text at pp. 58–74); tr. E. H. Freshfield, *A revised manual of Roman law: founded upon the Ecloga of Leo III and Constantine V, of Isauria, Ecloga privata aucta*, Cambridge (1927)

Eddius Stephanus, *Life of Wilfrid*, ed. W. Levison, *Vita Sancti Wilfridi*, *MGH SRM* 6, Hanover (1913), pp. 193–263; ed. and tr. B. Colgrave, *The life of Bishop Wilfrid, by Eddius Stephanus*, Cambridge (1985)

Einhard, *Life of Charlemagne*, ed. G. Waitz *et al.*, *Vita Karoli magni*, *MGH SRG* 25, Hanover (1911); tr. in P. E. Dutton, *Charlemagne's courtier: the complete Einhard*, Peterborough, Ont. (1998), pp. 15–39

—, *Translatio et miracula sanctorum Marcellini et Petri*, ed. G. Waitz, *MGH SS* 15.1, Hanover (1887), pp. 238–64; tr. in P. E. Dutton, *Charlemagne's courtier: the complete Einhard*, Peterborough, Ont. (1998), pp. 69–130

Elias bar Shinaya, *Chronicle*, ed. E. W. Brooks and J.-B. Chabot, *Opus chronologicum*, *CSCO* 62–3, 2 vols., Paris (1910; repr. Louvain, 1954); French tr. L. J. Delaporte, *La Chronographie d'Élie bar-Šinaya*, Paris (1910)

Elishe, *History*, ed. E. Ter-Minasyan, *Eghishe vasn Vardanay ew Hayots' Paterazmin*, Erevan (1957; repr. Delmar, NY, 1993); tr. R. W. Thomson, *Elishe: History of Vardan and the Armenian war*, Cambridge, MA (1982); French tr. in Langlois, *Historiens de l'Arménie*, II, pp. 183–251

Ennodius, *Panegyricus dictus Theoderico*, in Ennodius, *Opera*, ed. E. Vogel, *MGH AA* 7, Berlin (1885), pp. 203–14; ed. and German tr. C. Rohr, *Der Theoderich-Panegyricus des Ennodius*, Hanover (1995), pp. 195–263

Ephraim, *Historia chronica*, ed. O. Lampsides, *CFHB* 27, Athens (1990)

Epiphanios, *Life of Andrew the Apostle*, *PG* 120, cols. 215–60

Epistolae Langobardicae collectae, ed. W. Gundlach, *MGH Ep.* 3, Berlin (1892), pp. 691–715

Épistoliers byzantins du Xe siècle, ed. J. Darrouzès, Paris (1960)

Epistula ad Theophilum imperatorem, *PG* 95, cols. 345–85; ed. and tr. J. A. Munitiz *et al.*, *The letter of the three patriarchs to Emperor Theophilos and related texts*, Camberley (1997); ed. and German tr. H. Gauer, *Texte zum byzantinischen Bilderstreit: der Synodalbrief der drei Patriarchen des Ostens von 836 und seine Verwandlung in sieben Jahrunderten*, Frankfurt-am-Main (1994), pp. 74–128

Epistulae Austrasicae, ed. W. Gundlach, in *Defensoris Locogiacensis monachi et alia*, ed. M. Rochais *et al.*, *CCSL* 117, Turnhout (1957), pp. 404–70

Eusebius of Caesarea, *Church history*, tr. G. A. Williamson, rev. A. Louth, *The history of the Church from Christ to Constantine*, London (1989)

—, *Life of Constantine*, ed. F. Winkelmann, *Über das Leben des Kaisers Konstantin*, 2nd edn., Berlin (1991); tr. Averil Cameron and S. G. Hall, Oxford (1999)

—, *Werke*, ed. I. A. Heikel *et al.*, 9 vols., Leipzig and Berlin (1902–56)

Eustathios, archbishop of Thessaloniki, *Capture of Thessaloniki*, ed. S. Kyriakidis and Italian tr. V. Rotolo, *La espugnazione di Tessalonica (Historia tes aloseos tes Thessalonikes)*, Palermo (1961); tr. J. R. Melville Jones, *The capture of Thessaloniki, ByzAust* 8, Canberra (1988)

—, *Opera minora*, ed. P. Wirth, *CFHB* 32, Berlin (2000)

Eustathios Boilas, *Testament*, ed. P. Lemerle, 'Le Testament d'Eustathios Boïlas (avril 1059)', ed. in Lemerle (1977), pp. 13–63 (text at pp. 21–9)

Euthymios Tornikes, *Syngraphai*, in *Noctes Petropolitanae*, ed. Papadopoulos-Kerameus, pp. 103–87

Euthymios Zigabenos, *Panoplia dogmatike*, *PG* 128–30; partial tr. in Hamilton and
    Hamilton, *Christian dualist heresies*, pp. 171–4, 180–207
—, *Die Phundagiagiten: ein Beitrag zur Ketzergeschichte des byzantinischen Mittel-
    alters*, ed. G. Ficker, Leipzig (1908), pp. 89–111
Evagrius Scholasticus, *Ecclesiastical history*, ed. J. Bidez and L. Parmentier, London
    (1898); tr. Michael Whitby, Liverpool (2000)
Excavations at Nessana, III: *Non-literary papyri*, ed. C. J. Kraemer, Princeton, NJ
    (1958)
Farmer's law (*Nomos georgikos*), ed. and Russian tr. I. P. Medvedev *et al.*, *Vizan-
    tiiskii zemledel'cheskii zakon'*, Leningrad (1984), pp. 96–128; ed. and tr. W.
    Ashburner, 'The Farmer's Law', *JHS* 30 (1910), pp. 85–108 (edn. at pp. 97–
    108); *JHS* 32 (1912), pp. 68–95 (tr. at pp. 87–95)
al-Fasawi, *al-Ma'rifah*, ed. A. D. 'Umari, *Kitab al-ma'rifah wa-al-ta'rikh* [of Abu
    Yusuf Ya'qub ibn Sufyan al-Fasawi (d. 890/1)], 3 vols., Baghdad (1976)
al-Fasi, *Shifa' al-gharam bi-akhbar al-balad al-haram* [of Taqi al-Din Abu al-Tayyib
    Muhammad ibn Ahmad ibn 'Ali al-Qurashi al-Hashimi al-Hasani al-Fasi (d.
    1429)], 2 vols., Mecca (1956)
Featherstone, J. M., '*Di' endeixin*; display in court ceremonial (*De cerimoniis* II,
    15)', in Cutler and Papaconstantinou (eds.) (2007), pp. 75–112
Festa, N. (ed. and tr.), 'Le lettere greche di Federigo II', *Archivio storico italiano*,
    5th series, vol. 13 (1894), pp. 1–34
Firdausi, *Shahnama*, ed. S. Nafisi, 10 vols., Tehran (1934–6); French tr. J. Mohl, 7
    vols., Paris (1876–8); tr. A. G. and E. Warner, 9 vols., London (1905–25; repr.
    2000)
The First Crusade: the accounts of eye-witnesses and participants, ed. A. C. Krey,
    Princeton (1921; repr. Gloucester, MA, 1958)
Flusin, B., 'Le Panégyrique de Constantin VII Porphyrogénète pour la translation
    des reliques de Grégoire le Théologien (BHG 728)', *REB* 57 (1999), pp. 5–97
Fontes graeci historiae bulgaricae, ed. I. Dujčev *et al.*, 11 vols., Sofia (1954–83)
Fontes historiae Nubiorum, ed. T. Eide *et al.*, 4 vols., Bergen (1994–2000)
Fontes rerum Byzantinarum: rhetorum saeculi XII orationes politicae, ed. V. E. Regel
    and N. I. Novosadskij, St Petersburg (1892; repr. Leipzig, 1982)
Fredegar, *Chronicle*, ed. B. Krusch, *Chronicarum quae dicuntur Fredegarii Scholastici
    libri IV cum continuationibus*, *MGH SRM* 2, Hanover (1889), pp. 1–193; tr.
    J. M. Wallace-Hadrill, *The fourth book of the Chronicle of Fredegar with its
    continuations*, London and New York (1960)
Gallus Anonymus, *Chronicae*, ed. K. Maleczyński, *Chronicae et gesta ducum sive
    principum Polonorum*, Cracow (1952); tr. P. W. Knoll and F. Schaer, *The deeds
    of the princes of the Poles*, Budapest (2003)
Gelzer, H., 'Ungedruckte und wenig bekannte Bistümerverzeichnisse der orien-
    talischen Kirche, I', *BZ* 1 (1892), pp. 245–82
—, 'Ungedruckte und wenig bekannte Bistümerverzeichnisse der orientalischen
    Kirche, II', *BZ* 2 (1893), pp. 22–72
Gemistos Plethon, 'Address to Manuel Palaiologos on affairs in the Peloponnese',
    partial tr. in *Social and political thought in Byzantium*, ed. Barker, pp. 198–206
—, 'Treatise on laws', partial tr. in *Social and political thought in Byzantium*, ed.
    Barker, pp. 212–18

Genesios, *Regum libri quattuor*, ed. A. Lesmüller-Werner and H. Thurn, *CFHB* 14, Berlin (1978); tr. and comm. A. Kaldellis, *On the reigns of the emperors*, *ByzAust* 11, Canberra (1998)

Gennadios II Scholarios, *Oeuvres complètes*, ed. L. Petit *et al.*, 8 vols., Paris (1928–36)

Geoffrey of Villehardouin, *La Conquête de Constantinople*, ed. and French tr. E. Faral, 2 vols., 2nd edn., Paris (1961); tr. M. R. B. Shaw, *Joinville and Villehardouin, Chronicles of the Crusades*, Harmondsworth (1963)

Géométries du fisc byzantin, ed. and French tr. J. Lefort *et al.*, Paris (1991), pp. 38–209

George Akropolites, *Opera*, edn. A. Heisenberg, 2 vols., Leipzig (1903); rev. edn. P. Wirth, Stuttgart (1978); tr. R. Macrides, *George Akropolites: the history*, Oxford (2007)

George Bardanes, *Discussions*, ed. M. P. Roncaglia, *Georges Bardanès, métropolite de Corfou, et Barthélemy de l'ordre franciscain. Les discussions sur le purgatoire (15 oct. – 17 nov. 1231)*, Rome (1953)

—, *Letter*, ed. R.-J. Loenertz, 'Lettre de Georges Bardanès, métropolite de Corcyre, au patriarche oecuménique Germain II 1226–1227 c.', *EEBS* 33 (1964), pp. 87–118

George of Cyprus, *Descriptio orbis Romani*, ed. H. Gelzer, Leipzig (1890)

George the Monk, *Chronicle*, ed. C. de Boor, 2 vols., Leipzig (1904); rev. ed. P. Wirth, Stuttgart (1978)

George the Monk (Continued), see Georgius Monachus Continuatus in TC, pp. 761–924

George Pachymeres, *Relations historiques*, ed. A. Failler and French tr. V. Laurent and A. Failler, *CFHB* 24, 5 vols., Paris (1984–2000)

George of Pisidia, *Poemi*, ed. and Italian tr. A. Pertusi, Ettal (1959)

George Sphrantzes, *Chronicle*, ed. and Romanian tr. V. Grecu, *Memorii, 1401–1477*, Bucharest (1966); ed. and Italian tr. R. Maisano, *Cronaca*, *CFHB* 29, Rome (1990); tr. M. Carroll, *A contemporary Greek source for the siege of Constantinople 1453: the Sphrantzes chronicle*, Amsterdam (1985); tr. M. Philippides, *The fall of the Byzantine empire: a chronicle*, Amhurst, MA (1980)

George Synkellos, *Chronography*, ed. A. A. Mosshammer, *Ecloga chronographica*, Leipzig (1984); tr. W. Adler and P. Tuffin, *The chronography of George Synkellos: a Byzantine chronicle of universal history from the creation*, Oxford (2002)

George Tornikes, *Letters and orations*, ed. and French tr. J. Darrouzès, *Géorges et Démétrios Tornikès. Letters et discours*, Paris (1970)

The Georgian royal annals, ed. S. Qauxc'išvilis, *K'art'lis c'xovreba*, 4 vols., Tbilisi (1955–73) [repr. of Qauxc'išvilis' edition in S. H. Rapp (ed.), *K'art'lis c'xovreba: the Georgian royal annals and their medieval Armenian adaptation*, 2 vols., Delmar, NY (1998)]; ed. and French tr. M. F. Brosset, *Histoire de la Géorgie depuis l'antiquité jusqu'au XIXᵉ siècle*, 2 vols. in 4 pts., St Petersburg (1849–58); tr. R. W. Thomson, *Rewriting Caucasian history: the medieval Armenian adaptation of the Georgian chronicles*, Oxford (1996)

Gerald of Wales, *De principis instructione*, in *Opera*, VIII, ed. G. F. Warner *et al.*, 8 vols., London (1861–91); tr. J. Stevenson, *Concerning the instruction of princes*, London (1858; repr. [with repagination] Felinfach, Dyfed, 1991)

Gerbert of Aurillac, *Letters*, ed. J. Havet, *Lettres de Gerbert, 983–997*, Paris (1889); ed. and French tr. P. Riché and J. P. Callu, *Gerbert d'Aurillac, Correspondance*, 2 vols., Paris (1993)

Germanos I, patriarch of Constantinople, *Historia ecclesiastica et mystica contemplatio*, PG 98, cols. 383–454; ed. and tr. P. Meyendorff, *On the divine liturgy*, Crestwood, NY (1984)

Germanos II, patriarch of Constantinople, 'Bref inédit', ed. J. Nicole, 'Bref inédit de Germain II patriarche de Constantinople (année 1230) avec une recension nouvelle du chrysobulle de l'empereur Jean Ducas Vatacès', *REG* 7 (1894), pp. 68–80

—, *Letter*, ed. and tr. J. Gill, 'An unpublished letter of Germanus, patriarch of Constantinople (1222–1240)', *Byz* 44 (1974), pp. 138–151; repr. in Gill (1979b), no. 3

Gesta Francorum, ed. and tr. R. Hill, *The deeds of the Franks and the other pilgrims to Jerusalem*, London (1962)

Gesta Innocentii III papae, PL 214, pp. xvii–ccxxviii

Golubovich, H., 'Disputatio Latinorum et Graecorum seu relatio apocrisariorum Gregorii IX de gestis Nicaeae in Bithynia et Nymphaeae in Lydia 1234', *AHF* 12 (1919), pp. 418–70

Gottschalk of Orbais, *De praedestinatione*, in ed. C. Lambot, *Oeuvres théologiques et grammaticales de Godescalc d'Orbais*, Louvain (1945), pp. 180–258

Gouillard, J., 'Le Synodikon de l'Orthodoxie: édition et commentaire', *TM* 2 (1967), pp. 1–316

Grčke povelje srpskih vladara, ed. A. Soloviev and V. A. Mošin, Belgrade (1936; repr. London, 1974)

Greek Jewish texts from the Cairo Genizah, ed. and tr. N. de Lange, Tübingen (1996)

Greek papyri in the British Museum, ed. H. I. Bell *et al.*, 6 vols., London (1893–1924)

Greek traditions, ed. A. I. Vinogradov, *Grecheskie predaniia o sv. Apostole Andree*, I: *Zhitiia (S. Andreae apostoli traditio Graeca)*, St Petersburg (2005)

Gregory I (the Great), pope, *Dialogues*, ed. and French tr. A. de Vogüé and P. Antin, SC 251, 260, 265, 3 vols., Paris (1978–80)

—, *Letters*, ed. P. Ewald and L. M. Hartmann, *Registrum epistolarum*, MGH Ep. 1–2, 2 vols., Berlin (1887–99); ed. D. Norberg, *S. Gregorii Magni Registrum epistularum*, CCSL 140, 140A, 2 vols., Turnhout (1982); ed. and French tr. P. Minard, *Registre des lettres*, SC 370, 371, 2 vols., Paris (1991); tr. J. R. C. Martyn, *The letters of Gregory the Great*, 3 vols., Toronto (2004)

—, *Moralia in Job*, ed. M. Adriaen, CCSL 143, 143A, 143B, 3 vols., Turnhout (1979–85); tr. Anon., *Morals on the book of Job*, 3 vols., Oxford (1844–7)

Gregory Akindynos, *Letters*, ed. and tr. A. C. Hero, *Letters of Gregory Akindynos*, CFHB 21, Washington, DC (1983)

Gregory the Cellarer, *Life of Lazaros, AASS Novembris*, III, pp. 508–88; tr. R. P. H. Greenfield, *The life of Lazaros of Mt Galesion: an eleventh-century pillar saint*, Washington, DC (2000)

Gregory of Cyprus, *Autobiography*, in W. Lameere, *La Tradition manuscrite de la correspondance de Grégoire de Chypre, patriarche de Constantinople 1283–1289*,

Brussels and Rome (1937), pp. 176–91; tr. A. Pelendrides, *The Autobiography of George of Cyprus (Ecumenical Patriarch Gregory II)*, London (1993), pp. 21–45

Gregory of Narek, *Book of lamentations*, French tr. A. Mahé and J.-P. Mahé, *Matean oghbergut'ean: le livre de lamentation*, CSCO 584, Louvain (2000)

—, *Discourses*, ed. G. Awetik'ean, *Srboy hawrn meroy Grigori Narekats'woy erkrord matean charits'*, Venice (1827)

Gregory Nazianzen, *Select orations*, tr. in *Nicene*, ed. Wace and Schaff, VII; tr. M. Vinson, *Select orations of St Gregory of Nazianzus*, Washington, DC (2003)

Gregory Palamas, *The one hundred and fifty chapters*, ed. and tr. R. E. Sinkewicz, Toronto (1988)

Gregory of Tours, *Libri historiarum decem*, ed. B. Krusch and W. Levison, *MGH SRM* 1, Hanover (1951); tr. L. Thorpe, *Gregory of Tours: the History of the Franks*, Harmondsworth (1974)

Gr'tski izvori za b'lgarskata istoriia, see *Fontes graeci historiae bulgaricae*

Gunther of Pairis, *Capture of Constantinople*, ed. P. Orth, *Hystoria Constantinopolitana*, Hildesheim (1994); tr. A. J. Andrea, *The capture of Constantinople*, Philadelphia (1997)

Hadrian I, *Letter to Constantine VI and Irene*, in Mansi, XII, cols. 1055–76

Hamilton, J. and Hamilton, B., *Christian dualist heresies in the Byzantine world, c. 650–c. 1450*, Manchester (1998)

Hanawalt, E. A., *An annotated bibliography of Byzantine sources in English translation*, Brookline, MA (1988)

Heisenberg, A., 'Neue Quellen zur Geschichte des lateinischen Kaisertums und der Kirchenunion. I. Der Epitaphios des Nikolaos Mesarites auf seinen Bruder Johannes; II. Die Unionsverhandlungen vom 30. August 1206. Patriarchenwahl und Kaiserkrönung in Nikaia 1208; III. Der Bericht des Nikolaos Mesarites über die politischen und kirchlichen Ereignisse des Jahres 1214', *Sitzungsberichte der Bayerischen Akademie der Wissenschaften, Philosophisch-philologische und historische Klasse*, no. 5 (1922), pp. 3–75; no. 2 (1923), pp. 3–56; no. 3 (1923), pp. 3–96; repr. in Heisenberg (1973), no. 2

Hendrickx, B., 'Recherches sur les documents diplomatiques non conservés, concernant la Quatrième Croisade et l'Empire latin de Constantinople pendant les premières années de son existence, 1200–1206', *Byzantina* 2 (1970), pp. 107–84

—, 'Régestes des empereurs latins de Constantinople, 1204–1261/1272', *Byzantina* 14 (1988), pp. 7–221; repr. Hendrickx, B., *Régestes des empereurs latins de Constantinople, 1204–1261/1272*, Thessalonica (1988)

Herodian, *History*, ed. and tr. C. R. Whittaker, 2 vols., London (1969–70)

'Heron of Byzantium', *Parangelmata poliorcetica – Geodesia*, ed. and tr. in Sullivan, *Siegecraft*, pp. 26–151

Hilduin, *Passion of St Denis (Passio sanctissimi Dionysii)*, PL 106, cols. 23–50

Histoire des Seldjoukides d'Asie Mineure: par un anonyme, ed. F. N. Uzluk, Ankara (1952)

History of the Albanians, ed. V. Arak'elyan, *Patmut'iwn Aghuanits' ashkharhi*, Erevan (1983); tr. C. J. F. Dowsett, *The history of the Caucasian Albanians by Movses Dasxuranci*, London (1961)

Holy women of Byzantium: ten saints' lives in English translation, ed. A.-M. Talbot, Washington, DC (1996)

Hudud al-'alam, tr. V. Minorsky, *The regions of the world: a Persian geography*, 372 AH–982 AD, 2nd edn. C. E. Bosworth, London (1970)

Huyse, P., *Die dreisprächige Inschrift Šaburs I. an der Ka'ba-i Zardušt, Corpus Inscriptionum Iranicarum* III, *Pahlavi inscriptions*, 1: *Royal inscriptions with their Greek and Parthian versions*, 2 vols., London (1999)

Iakov, archbishop of Bulgaria, *Works*, ed. S. G. Mercati, 'Iacobi Bulgariae archiepiscopi opuscula', *Bessarione* 33 (1917), pp. 73–89, 208–27

Ibn 'Abd al-Hakam, *Futuh Misr*, ed. C. C. Torrey, *The history of the conquest of Egypt, North Africa and Spain, known as Futuh Misr of Ibn 'Abd al-Hakam* (d. 870/1), New Haven, CT (1922; repr. New York, 1980)

Ibn 'Abd Rabbih, *Al-'Iqd al-farid* [of Ahmad ibn Muhammad ibn 'Abd Rabbih (d. 940)], ed. A. Amin *et al.*, 7 vols., Cairo (1940–53)

Ibn Abi Dinar, *Al-Mu'nis*, ed. M. Shamman, *Kitab al-Mu'nis fi akhbar Ifriqiyah wa-Tunis* [of Abu 'Abd Allah Muhammad ibn Abi al-Qasim al-Ru'ayni al-Qayrawani al-ma'ruf bi-Ibn Abi Dinar (*fl.* 1698)], Tunis (1967)

Ibn al-'Adim, *Zubdat*, ed. S. Dahhan, *Zubdat al-Halab min ta'rikh Halab* [of Kamal al-Din 'Umar ibn Ahmad Ibn al-'Adim (d. 1262)], 3 vols, Damascus (1951–68)

Ibn 'Asakir, *Ta'rikh madinat Dimashq*, ed. S. al-Munajjid *et al.*, *Ta'rikh madinat Dimashq* [of Abu al-Qasim 'Ali ibn al-Hasan ibn Hibat Allah ibn 'Asakir (d. 1176)], 10 vols. to date, Damascus (1951–); ed. 'U. G. 'Amrawi, 80 vols., Beirut (1995–2000); partial French tr. N. Elisséeff, *La Description de Damas d'Ibn 'Asakir (historien mort à Damas en 571/1176)*, Damascus (1959)

Ibn A'tham al-Kufi, *Kitab al-futuh*, ed. M. 'Abdu'l Mu'id Khan *et al.*, *Kitab al-futuh* [of Abu Muhammad Ahmad ibn A'tham al-Kufi (d. 819)], 8 vols., Hyderabad (1968–75)

Ibn al-Athir, *al-Kamil*, ed. 'A. A. al-Qadi, *Kitab al-kamil fi al-ta'rikh* [of Abu al-Hasan 'Ali 'Izz al-Din Ibn al-Athir (d. 1233)], 11 vols., Beirut (1998); ed. C. J. Tornberg, *Ibn-el-Athiri chronicon, quod perfectissimum inscribitur*, 14 vols., Leiden (1851–76); partial tr. D. S. Richards, *The annals of the Saljuq Turks: selections from al-Kamil fi'l-Ta'rikh of 'Izz al-Din Ibn al-Athir*, London (2002); partial French tr. in Vasil., pp. 129–62

Ibn Bibi, *Mukhtasar-i Saljuqnamah*, ed. M. T. Houtsma, *Histoire des Seldjoucides d'Asie Mineure, d'après l'abrégé du Seldjouknameh d'Ibn-Bibi: texte persan* [of Nasir al-Din Husayn ibn Muhammad Ibn Bibi (*fl.* 18th century)], Leiden (1902); German tr. H. Duda, *Die Seltschukengeschichte des Ibn Bibi*, Copenhagen (1959)

Ibn al-Farra, *Rusul al-muluk*, ed. and tr. M. Vaiou, *Diplomacy in the early Islamic world: a tenth-century treatise on Arab–Byzantine relations* [of Abu 'Ali al-Husayn ibn Muhammad al-ma'ruf bi-Ibn al-Farra (*fl.* 10th century)], London (forthcoming)

Ibn Hajar al-'Asqalani, *Kitab al-isabah fi tamyiz al-sahabah* [of Abu al-Fadl Ahmad ibn 'Ali ibn Hajar al-'Asqalani (d. 1449)], 8 vols. in 4 pts., Cairo (1905–7; repr. 1939)

Ibn Hawqal, *Surat*, ed. J. H. Kramers, *Kitab surat al-'ard: opus geographicum auctore Ibn Haukal* [of Abu al-Qasim Muhammad ibn Hawqal (d. 10th century)], 2 vols., *BGA* 1 (2nd edn.), Leiden (1938–9); partial French tr. in Vasil., pp. 409–21; French tr. J. H. Kramers and G. Wiet, *Configuration de la terre*, 2 vols., Beirut (1964)

Ibn Hisham, *Sirat Rasul Allah*, ed. F. Wüstenfeld, *Kitab sirat Rasul Allah: Das Leben Muhammed's nach Muhammed ibn Ishak* [of Abu Muhammad 'Abd al-Malik ibn Hisham al-Ma'afiri (d. 834)], 2 vols., Göttingen (1858–60); tr. A. Guillaume, *The life of Muhammed*, Oxford (1955; repr. 2004)

Ibn Khaldun, *Al-Muqaddimah*, ed. E. M. Quatremère, *Muqaddimat Ibn Khaldun: Prolégomènes d'Ebn-Khaldoun, texte arabe* [of 'Abd al-Rahman ibn Muhammad ibn Khaldun (d. 1405)], 3 vols, Paris (1858); tr. F. Rosenthal, *The Muqaddimah: an introduction to history*, 3 vols., London (1958)

Ibn Khurradadhbih, *Kitab al-masalik*, ed. and French tr. M. J. de Goeje, *Kitab al-masalik wa-al-mamalik (Liber viarum et regnorum)* [of 'Abu al-Qasim 'Ubayd Allah ibn 'Abd Allah ibn Khurradadhbih (d. 911)], *BGA* 6, Leiden (1889)

Ibn al-Najjar, *Al-Durrah al-thaminah fi ta'rikh al-Madinah* [of Abu 'Abd Allah Muhammad ibn Mahmud ibn al-Najjar (d. 1245)], printed as a supplement to al-Fasi, *Shifa' al-gharam bi-akhbar al-balad al-haram*, II

Ibn Qutaybah, *Kitab al-Ma'arif*, ed. T. 'Ukashah, *Kitab al-ma'arif* [of Abu Muhammad 'Abd Allah ibn Muslim ibn Qutaybah (d. 889)], 2nd edn., Cairo (1969)

Ibn Rustah, *Kitab al-A'laq al-nafisah*, tr. G. Wiet, *Les atours précieux* [of Ahmad ibn 'Umar ibn Rustah (*fl.* 9th /10th century)], Cairo (1955)

Ibn Sa'd, *al-Tabaqat*, ed. E. Sachau, *Biographien Muhammeds, seiner Gefährten und der späteren Träger des Islams, bis zum Jahre 230 der Flucht (Kitab al-tabaqat al-kabir)* [of Muhammad ibn Sa'd (d. 845)], 9 vols. in 15 pts., Leiden (1904–40); *al-Tabaqat al-kubra*, 9 vols., Beirut (1957–68)

Ibn Sallam, *al-Amwal*, ed. M. K. Harras, *Kitab al-amwal* [of Abu 'Ubayd al-Qasim ibn Sallam (d. *c.* 837)], Cairo (1968; repr. Beirut, 1986)

Icon and logos: sources in eighth-century iconoclasm: an annotated translation of the sixth session of the seventh Ecumenical Council (Nicaea, 787), ed. D. J. Sahas, Toronto (1986)

Icon and minaret: sources of Byzantine and Islamic civilization, ed. C. M. Brand, Englewood Cliffs, NJ (1969)

Ignatios the Deacon, *Correspondence*, ed. and tr. C. Mango, *The correspondence of Ignatios the Deacon*, CFHB 39, Washington, DC (1997)

—, *Life of Tarasios, patriarch of Constantinople*, ed. I. A. Heikel, Helsingfors (1981) [= *Acta societatis scientiarum fennicae* 17: 395–423]; ed. and tr. S. Efthymiadis, Aldershot (1998)

Innocent III, pope, *Correspondence with the Bulgarians*, ed. I. Dujčev, 'Prepiskata na papa Innokentiia III s b'lgarite: uvod, tekst i belezhki', *Godishnik na Sofiiskiia universitet: Filosofsko-istoricheski fakultet (Annuaire de l'université Saint Clément d'Ohrida à Sofia: Faculté Historico-Philologique)* 37.3 (1942), pp. 1–116; Italian tr. and comm. F. Dall'Aglio, *Innocenzo III e i Balcani: fede e politica nei Regesta pontifici*, Naples (2003)

Iordanov, I., 'Neizdadeni vizantiiski olovni pechati ot Silistra (III)', *Izvestiia na Narodniia Muzei Varna* 24 [39] (1988), pp. 88–103

—, *Pechatite ot strategiiata v Preslav, 971–1088*, Sofia (1993)

Irene Eulogia Choumnaina Palaiologina, *Correspondence*, ed. and tr. A. C. Hero, *A woman's quest for spiritual guidance: the correspondence of Princess Irene Eulogia Choumnaina Palaiologina*, Brookline, MA (1986)

al-Isfahani, *Al-Aghani*, ed. A. Z. al-'Adawi *et al.*, *Kitab al-Aghani* [of Abu al-Faraj al-Isfahani (d. 967)], 24 vols., Cairo (1927–94)

Islam: from the Prophet Muhammad to the capture of Constantinople, ed. B. Lewis, 2 vols., Oxford (1974; repr. 1987)

Itinerarium Bernardi monachi Franci, in ed. T. Tobler and M. Molinier, *Itinera hierosolymitana et descriptiones Terrae Sanctae bellis sacris anteriora et latina lingua exarata sumptibus Societatis illustrandis Orientis latini monumentis*, Geneva (1880), pp. 309–20

Ivanov, J., *B'lgarski starini iz Makedoniia*, Sofia (1931; repr. 1970)

Jeffery, A., *Materials for the history of the text of the Qur'an*, Leiden (1937)

Jerusalem pilgrims before the Crusades, tr. J. Wilkinson, 2nd edn., Warminster (2002)

Johannes von Gaza und Paulus Silentiarius: Kunstbeschreibungen Justinianischer Zeit, ed. P. Friedländer, Berlin (1912)

John II, metropolitan of Rus, *Canonical responses*, ed. V. N. Beneshevich, 'Otvety mitropolita Ioanna II', *Sbornik pamiatnikov po istorii tserkovnogo prava*, St Petersburg (1915), pp. 108–20

John VIII, pope, *Epistulae*, ed. E. Caspar, *MGH Ep.* 7, Hanover (1928), pp. 1–272

—, *Fragmenta registri*, ed. E. Caspar, *MGH Ep.* 7, Hanover (1928), pp. 273–312

John Apokaukos, *Writings*, ed. N. A. Bees-Seferli, 'Unedierte Schriftstücke aus der Kanzlei des Johannes Apokaukos des Metropoliten von Naupaktos (in Aetolien)', *BNJ* 21 (1971–4), pp. 55–160 (appendix)

John of Biclaro, *Chronicon*, ed. T. Mommsen, *MGH AA* 9, Berlin (1894), pp. 207–20; ed. C. Cardelle de Hartmann and R. Collins, *CCSL* 173A, Turnhout (2001), pp. 59–83; tr. K. Baxter Wolf, *Conquerors and chroniclers of early medieval Spain*, Liverpool (1999), pp. 55–77

John Chrysostom, *Homilies on Genesis*, tr. R. C. Hill, 3 vols., Washington, DC (1986–92)

John Damascene, *Adversus iconoclastas* (*CPG* 8121), *PG* 96, cols. 1347–62

—, *Contra imaginum calumniatores orationes tres*, ed. B. Kotter, *Die Schriften des Johannes von Damaskos*, 5 vols., Berlin (1969–88), III; tr. A. Louth, *Three treatises on the divine images by St John of Damascus*, Crestwood, NY (2003)

John the Deacon, *Cronaca*, ed. G. Monticolo, *Cronache Veneziane antichissime*, *FSI* 9, Rome (1890)

John of Ephesus, *History*, ed. and Latin tr. E. W. Brooks, *Historia ecclesiastica pars tertia*, 2 vols., *CSCO* 105, 106, Paris (1935–6; repr. Louvain 1952)

—, *Lives of the eastern saints*, ed. and tr. E. W. Brooks, *PO* 17 (1923), pp. 1–307; *PO* 18 (1924), pp. 513–698; *PO* 19 (1926), pp. 153–285; repr. Turnhout (1974)

John Kaminiates, *De expugnatione Thessalonicae*, ed. G. Böhlig, *CFHB* 4, Berlin and New York (1973); tr. D. Frendo and A. Photiou, *The capture of Thessaloniki*, *ByzAust* 12, Perth (2000)

John Kantakouzenos, *Eximperatoris historiarum libri quattor*, ed. L. Schopen, 3 vols., *CSHB*, Bonn (1828–32); partial tr. in Miller, 'The history of John Cantacuzenus (book 4)' (PhD thesis, 1975), pp. 147–237

John Kinnamos, *History*, ed. A. Meineke, *Epitome rerum ab Ioanne et Alexio Comnenis gestarum*, *CSHB*, Bonn (1836); tr. C. M. Brand, *Deeds of John and Manuel Comnenus*, New York (1976)

John Klimakos, *Heavenly ladder*, *PG* 88, cols. 631–1210; tr. C. Luibheid and N. Russell, *The ladder of divine ascent*, New York (1982)

John Malalas, *Chronicle*, ed. H. Thurn, *Chronographia*, *CFHB* 35, Berlin and New York (2000); tr. E. Jeffreys *et al.*, *The chronicle of John Malalas*, *ByzAust* 4, Melbourne (1986)

John Mauropous, metropolitan of Euchaita, *Letters*, ed. and tr. A. Karpozilos, *The letters of Ioannes Mauropus, Metropolitan of Euchaita*, *CFHB* 34, Thessalonica (1990)

—, *Quae in Codice Vaticano Graeco 767 supersunt*, ed. P. A. de Lagarde, Göttingen (1882; repr. Amsterdam, 1979)

John Moschus, *Pratum spirituale*, *PG* 87, cols. 2851–3112; tr. J. Wortley, *The spiritual meadow*, Kalamazoo, MI (1992)

John of Nikiu, *Chronicle*, tr. R. H. Charles, *The Chronicle of John, Bishop of Nikiu: translated from Zotenberg's Ethiopic text*, London (1916)

John Skylitzes, *Synopsis historiarum*, ed. H. Thurn, *CFHB* 5, Berlin and New York (1973); tr. J. Wortley, *John Skylitzes, a synopsis of histories*, *BBTT* 10, Belfast (in preparation); French tr. and comm. B. Flusin and J.-C. Cheynet, *Empereurs de Constantinople*, Paris (2003); partial tr. in Tsamakda (2002)

John Tzetzes, *Epistulae*, ed. P. A. M. Leone, Leipzig (1972)

—, *Historiae*, ed. P. A. M. Leone, Naples (1968)

John Zonaras, *Annales* [*Epitomae historiarum*], ed. M. Pinder and T. Büttner-Wobst, 3 vols., *CSHB*, Bonn (1841–97); partial German tr. E. Trapp, *Militärs und Höflinge im Ringen um das Kaisertum: byzantinische Geschichte von 969 bis 1118 nach der Chronik des Johannes Zonaras*, Graz (1986)

Jordanes, *Romana et Getica*, ed. T. Mommsen, *MGH AA* 5.1, Berlin (1882); tr. C. C. Mierow, *The Gothic history of Jordanes*, Princeton (1915; repr. Cambridge, 1966)

Jordanov, I. (ed.), *Corpus of Byzantine seals from Bulgaria*, I: *Byzantine seals with geographical names*, 1 vol. to date, Sofia (2003–)

Joshua the Stylite, *Chronicle*, ed. and tr. W. Wright, *The chronicle of Joshua the Stylite: composed in Syriac AD 507*, Cambridge (1882); tr. F. R. Trombley and J. W. Watt, *The chronicle of Pseudo-Joshua the Stylite*, Liverpool (2000)

Junillus Africanus, *Instituta regularia divinae legis*, ed. and tr. in Maas (2003a), pp. 118–235

Jus graecoromanum, ed. J. Zepos and P. Zepos, 8 vols., Athens (1931; repr. Darmstadt, 1962); partial edn. N. Svoronos with P. Gounaridis, *Les Novelles des empereurs macédoniens concernant la terre et les stratiotes: introduction, édition, commentaires*, Athens (1994); partial tr. E. McGeer, *The land legislation of the Macedonian emperors*, Toronto (2000)

Justinian, *Collectio tripartita*, ed. N. van der Wal and B. H. Stolte, *Collectio tripartita: Justinian on religious and ecclesiastical affairs*, Groningen (1994)

—, *Corpus iuris civilis*, ed. P. Krueger *et al.*, 3 vols, I: *Institutiones, Digesta*; II: *Codex Iustinianus*; III: *Novellae*, Berlin (1895); tr. P. Birks and G. McLeod, *Justinian's Institutes*, Ithaca, NY (1987); tr. A. Watson, *The Digest of Justinian*, 2nd edn., 2 vols., Philadelphia, PA (1998)

Kallistos I, patriarch of Constantinople, *Life of Gregory of Sinai*, ed. I. Pomialovsky, *Bios kai politeia tou en hagiois patros hemon Gregoriou tou Sinaïtou* (= *Zhitie otsa nashego Grigoriia Sinaita*), in *Zapiski istoriko-filologicheskogo fakul'teta imperatorskogo St.-Peterburgskogo Universiteta* 35 (1894)

Karayannopulos, J., 'Fragmente aus dem Vademecum eines byzantinischen Finanzbeamten', in Wirth (ed.) (1966), pp. 318–34; tr. in Brand (1969), pp. 57–60

Karnamak Artakhshir-i Papakan, ed. and tr. E. K. Antia, Bombay (1900); annotated German tr. T. Nöldeke, 'Geschichte des Artachŝîr i Pâpakân, aus dem Pehlewi übersetzt, mit Erläuterungen und einer Einleitung versehen', *Festschrift zur Feier seines fünfzigjährigen Doctorjubiläums am 24. October 1878 Herrn Professor Theodor Benfey gewidmet*, ed. A. Bezzenberger, Göttingen (1878) [= *Beiträge zur Kunde der indogermanischen Sprachen* 4], pp. 22–69

Kekaumenos, *Strategikon*, ed. and Russian tr. G. G. Litavrin, *Sovety i rasskazy Kekavmena*, 2nd edn., St Petersburg (2003); ed. and tr. C. Roueché, *The advice and anecdotes of Kekaumenos: the memoirs of an eleventh-century general* (in preparation)

Khuzistan chronicle, German tr. T. Nöldeke, 'Die von Guidi herausgegebene syrische Chronik', *Sitzungsberichte der philologisch-historischen Classe der Kaiserlichen Akademie der Wissenschaften* 128.9, Vienna (1893), pp. 1–48; first part tr. in *The Roman eastern frontier*, ed. Lieu *et al.*, II, pp. 229–37

Kiril and Methodius, founders of Slavonic writing: a collection of sources and critical studies, ed. I. Dujčev, tr. S. Nikolov, Boulder, CO (1985)

Kniga stepennaia tsarskogo rodosloviia, *Polnoe sobranie russkikh letopisei* 21, 2 vols., St Petersburg (1908–13)

Konstantin Bagrianorodnyi, *Ob upravlenii imperiei*, ed. and Russian tr. G. G. Litavrin *et al.*, Moscow (1989) (Russian edition of Constantine VII Porphyrogenitus, *De administrando imperio*)

Das Konzil von Aachen 809, ed. H. Willjung, *MGH Concilia* 2, Supp. 2, Hanover (1998)

Koran, tr. A. J. Arberry, *The Koran interpreted*, London (1955); tr. M. A. S. Abdel Haleem, *The Qur'an*, Oxford (2005)

Koriwn, *Life of Mashtots'*, ed. M. Abeghean, *Vark' Mashtots'i*, Erevan (1941; repr. with tr. by B. Norehad, Delmar, NY, 1985); German tr. G. Winkler, *Koriwns Biographie des Mesrop Maštoc'*, Rome (1994)

Kresten, O. and Müller, A. E. (eds.), 'Die Auslandsschreiben der byzantinischen Kaiser des 11. und 12. Jahrhunderts: Specimen einer kritischen Ausgabe', *BZ* 86–7 (1993–4), pp. 402–29

Kritobulos of Imbros, *History*, ed. D. R. Reinsch, *Critobuli Imbriotae historiae*, *CFHB* 22, Berlin and New York (1983); German tr. D. R. Reinsch, *Mehmet II. erobert Konstantinopel: die ersten Regierungsjahre des Sultans Mehmet Fatih, des Eroberers von Konstantinopel 1453 : das Geschichtswerk des Kritobulos von Imbros*, Graz (1986); tr. C. T. Riggs, *History of Mehmed the conqueror*, Princeton (1954)

Lagopates, S. N., *Germanos o II, patriarches Konstantinopoleos-Nikaias 1222–1240*, Tripolis (1913)

Langlois, V. (tr.), *Collection des historiens anciens et modernes de l'Arménie*, 2 vols., Paris (1867–9)

Laonikos Chalkokondyles, *Historiarum demonstrationes*, ed. E. Darkó, 2 vols., Budapest (1922–3)

Laurent, V. (ed.), *Le Corpus des sceaux de l'empire byzantin*, 2 vols. in 5 pts., Paris (1963–81)

Lazar of P'arp, *History*, ed. G. Ter-Mkrtch'ean and S. Malkhaseants', *Patmut'iwn Hayots'*, Tiflis (1904; repr. Delmar, NY, 1985); tr. R. W. Thomson, *The History of Lazar P'arpec'i*, Atlanta, GA (1991)

Legenda S. Gerhardi, ed. E. Szentpétery, *Scriptores rerum hungaricarum*, II, Budapest (1938), pp. 463–506

Lemerle, P. (ed.), *Les Plus Anciens Recueils des miracles de saint Démétrius*, 2 vols., Paris (1979–81)

Leo III, pope, *Epistolae X*, ed. K. Hampe, *MGH Ep.* 5, Hanover (1899), pp. 85–104

Leo VI, *Book of the eparch*, ed. and German tr. J. Koder, *Das Eparchenbuch Leons des Weisen*, *CFHB* 33, Vienna (1991); tr. E. H. Freshfield, *Roman law in the later Roman empire: Byzantine guilds, professional and commercial*, Cambridge (1938), pp. 1–50; repr. in *To eparchikon biblion (The book of the eparch)*, intr. I. Dujčev, London (1970), pp. 223–70 [which also contains facsimile of Greek text; edn. by J. Nicole; and Latin and French tr. by J. Nicole]

—, *Funeral oration for Basil I*, ed. and French tr. A. Vogt and I. Hausherr, 'Oraison funèbre de Basil I par son fils Léon le sage', *OC* 26 (1932), pp. 5–79

—, *Naumachica*, ed. and tr. in Pryor and Jeffreys (2006), pp. 483–519

—, *Novels*, ed. P. Noailles and A. Dain, *Les Novelles de Léon le Sage*, Paris (1944)

—, *Tactica*, *PG* 107, cols. 669–1120

Leo Choirosphaktes, *Correspondence*, ed. and French tr. G. Kolias, *Léon Choerosphactès, magistre, proconsul et patrice*, Athens (1939)

—, 'On the bath built by the emperor Leo in the imperial palace', ed. and tr. in Magdalino (1988b), pp. 116–18; ed. and Italian tr. in *Cinque poeti bizantini*, ed. Ciccolella, pp. 91–107

Leo the Deacon, *History*, ed. C. B. Hase, *Historiae libri decem*, *CSHB*, Bonn (1828); tr. A.-M. Talbot and D. F. Sullivan, *The History of Leo the Deacon: Byzantine military expansion in the tenth century*, *DOSt* 41, Washington, DC (2005)

Leo Grammaticus, *Chronographia*, ed. I. Bekker, *CSHB*, Bonn (1842)

Leo of Synada, *Correspondence*, ed. and tr. M. P. Vinson, *The correspondence of Leo, Metropolitan of Synada and Syncellus*, *CFHB* 23, Washington, DC (1985)

Leonardo Marcello, notaio in Candia, 1278–1281, ed. M. Chiaudano and A. Lombardo, Venice (1960)

Leontius of Byzantium, *Opera*, *PG* 86, cols. 1185–1396, 1901–2016

Leontius of Jerusalem, *Adversus Nestorianos, Contra Monophysitas*, *PG* 86, cols. 1399–1902

'Leontius of St Sabas', *Life of Gregory of Agrigento*, *PG* 98, cols. 549–716; ed. A. Berger, *Leontios Presbyteros von Rom: Das Leben des heiligen Gregorios von Agrigent*, *BBA* 60, Berlin (1995)

Letopis popa Dukljanina, ed. F. Šišić, Belgrade and Zagreb (1928)

The letter of Tansar, tr. M. Boyce, Rome (1968)

Lewond, *History*, ed. K. Ezean, *Patmut'iwn Ghewondeay metsi vardapeti Hayots'*, St Petersburg (1887); tr. Z. Arzoumanian, *History of Łewond, the eminent Vardapet of the Armenians*, Wynnewood, PA (1982)

Libellus de cerimoniis aulae imperatoris, ed. in Schramm (1968–71), III, pp. 338–53

Liber pontificalis, ed. L. Duchesne, 2nd edn., 3 vols., Paris (1955–7); tr. R. Davis, 3 vols.: I: *The book of pontiffs: the ancient biographies of the first ninety Roman bishops to AD 715* (2nd edn., 2000); II: *The lives of the eighth-century popes* (1992); III: *The lives of the ninth-century popes* (1995), Liverpool

Libri Carolini see *Opus Caroli regis contra synodum*

Life of Anthony the Younger, ed. A. Papadopoulos-Kerameus, *Pravoslavnii Palestinskii Sbornik* 19.3, St Petersburg (1907), pp. 186–226; ed. F. Halkin, 'Saint Antoine le Jeune et Pétronas le vainqueur des Arabes en 863', *AnBoll* 62 (1944), pp. 210–23; repr. in Halkin (1973), no. 8

Life of Athanasia of Aegina, ed. F. Halkin, *Six inédits d'hagiologie byzantine*, Brussels (1987), pp. 180–95; tr. L. F. Sherry in *Holy women of Byzantium*, ed. Talbot, pp. 137–58

Life of Basil in TC, V, pp. 211–353; ed. and tr. I. Ševčenko, *Chronographiae quae Theophanis Continuati nomine fertur liber V quo Vita Basilii imperatoris amplectitur*, *CFHB* 42, Berlin and New York (forthcoming)

Life of Blasios of Amorion, *AASS Novembris*, IV, pp. 657–69

Life of Clement of Ohrid, see Theophylact of Ohrid

Life of Constantine-Cyril, in B. S. Angelov and K. Kodov (eds.), *Kliment Okhridski, S'brani s'chineniia*, III, Sofia (1973), pp. 89–109; ed. B. N. Floria, *Skazaniia o nachale slavianskoi pis'mennosti*, St Petersburg (2000), pp. 135–78; French tr. in F. Dvornik, *Les Légendes de Constantin et de Méthode vues de Byzance*, Prague (1933), pp. 349–80; tr. in *Medieval Slavic lives*, ed. Kantor, pp. 23–81

Life of Cyril the Phileote, ed. and French tr. E. Sargologos, *La Vie de Saint Cyrille le Philéote, moine byzantin*, Brussels (1964)

Life of David, Symeon and George of Lesbos, ed. J. van den Gheyn, 'Acta graeca ss. Davidis, Symeonis et Georgii Mitylenae in insula Lesbo', *AnBoll* 18 (1899), pp. 209–59; tr. and notes D. Abrahamse and D. Domingo-Forasté in *Byzantine defenders of images*, ed. Talbot, pp. 149–241

Life of Elias the Speleote, *AASS Septembris*, III (11 September), pp. 848–87

Life of Elias the Younger, ed. and Italian tr. G. Rossi Taibbi, *Vita di Sant'Elia il Giovane*, Palermo (1962)

Life of Eustratios of the monastery of Agauroi (Abgar), in *Analekta*, ed. Papadopoulos-Kerameus, IV, pp. 367–400

Life of Euthymios, patriarch of Constantinople, ed. and tr. P. Karlin-Hayter, Brussels (1970)

Life of Euthymios of Sardis, ed. and French tr. J. Gouillard, 'La Vie d'Euthyme de Sardes († 831) une oeuvre du patriarche Méthode', *TM* 10 (1987), pp. 1–101

Life of Euthymios the Younger, ed. L. Petit, 'Vie et office de St Euthyme le jeune', *Bibliothèque hagiographique orientale* 5, Paris (1904), pp. 14–51; ed. F. Dolbeau, 'La Vie latine de saint Euthyme: une traduction inédite de Jean, diacre napolitain', *MEFRM* 93 (1982), pp. 315–35

Life of George of Amastris, ed. and Russian tr. in Vasilievsky (1908–30), III, pp. 1–71

Life of George of Mytilene, ed. I. M. Phountoules, *Oi agioi Georgioi archiepiskopoi Mytilenes*, Athens (1959), pp. 33–43

Life of Germanos, patriarch of Constantinople, ed. and German tr. in L. Lamza, *Patriarch Germanos I. von Konstantinopel (715–730): Versuch einer endgültigen chronologischen Fixierung des Lebens und Wirkens des Patriarchen*, Würzburg (1975), pp. 200–41

Life of Gregentios, ed. and tr. A. Berger and G. Fiacciadori, *Life and works of Saint Gregentios, archbishop of Taphar: introduction, critical edition and translation*, Berlin and New York (2006).

Life of Ignatios, *PG* 105, cols. 487–573

Life of Ioannikios by Peter, ed. J. van den Gheyn, *AASS Novembris* II.1, pp. 384–435; tr. D. F. Sullivan in *Byzantine defenders of images*, ed. Talbot, pp. 243–351

Life of Ioannikios by Sabas, ed. J. van den Gheyn, *AASS Novembris* II.1, pp. 332–383

Life of Irene the empress, ed. F. Halkin, 'Deux impératrices de Byzance, I: La Vie de l'impératrice sainte Irène et le second concile de Nicée II en 787', *AnBoll* 106 (1988), pp. 5–27

Life of Irene of Chrysobalanton, ed. and tr. J. O. Rosenqvist, *The Life of St. Irene, Abbess of Chrysobalanton: a critical edition with introduction, translation, notes and indices*, Uppsala (1986)

Life of John the Almsgiver, ed. H. Delehaye, 'Une vie inédite de saint Jean l'Aumônier', *AnBoll* 45 (1927), pp. 5–74; tr. Dawes and Baynes, *Three Byzantine saints*, pp. 191–270

Life of Leontios of Rostov, ed. A. Titov, *Zhitiia sv. chudotvortsev Leontiia, Isaii, Ignatiia, episkopov rostovskikh*, Moscow (1904)

Life of Luke of Armento, AASS Octobrii, VI (October 13), pp. 337–9

Life of Luke of Steiris, ed. D. Z. Sophianos, *Osios Loukas: o bios tou Osiou Louka tou Steiriote*, Athens (1989); tr. C. L. Connor and W. R. Connor, *The life and miracles of Saint Luke of Steiris*, Brookline, MA (1994)

Life of Mathilda, ed. R. Koepke, *Vita Mahthildis reginae antiquior*, MGH SS 10, Hanover (1852), pp. 573–82; ed. B. Schütte, *Die Lebensbeschreibungen der Königin Mathilde*, MGH SRG 66, Hanover (1994), pp. 109–42; tr. S. Gilsdorf, *Queenship and sanctity: the Lives of Mathilda and the Epitaph of Adelheid*, Washington, DC (2004)

Life of Methodios, in B. S. Angelov and K. Kodov (eds.), *Kliment Okhridski, S'brani s'chineniia*, III, Sofia (1973), pp. 185–92; ed. B. N. Floria, *Skazaniia o nachale slavianskoi pis'mennosti*, St Petersburg (2000), pp. 179–95; French tr. in F. Dvornik, *Les Légendes de Constantin et de Méthode vues de Byzance*, Prague (1933), pp. 381–93; tr. in *Medieval Slavic lives*, ed. Kantor, pp. 97–129

Life of Michael Aragawi, ed. M. A. van den Oudenrijn, *La Vie de Saint Za Mika'el Aragawi*, Fribourg (1939)

Life of Michael Synkellos, ed. and tr. M. B. Cunningham, *The Life of Michael the Synkellos*, BBTT 1, Belfast (1991)

Life of Nicholas, ed. P. Corsi, 'La *Vita* di san Nicola e un codice della versione di Giovanni diacono', *Nicolaus* 7 (1979), pp. 359–80

Life of Niketas of Medikion, *AASS Aprilis*, I, pp. 22–32

Life of Niketas Patrikios, ed. and French tr. D. Papachryssanthou, 'Un confesseur du second iconoclasme: la vie du patrice Nicétas († 836)', *TM* 3 (1968), pp. 309–51

Life of Nikon, ed. and tr. D. F. Sullivan, Brookline, MA (1987)

Life of Nilus the Younger, *PG* 120, cols. 15–166

Life of Peter of Argos, in *Agiou Petrou episkopou Argous Bios kai Logoi*, ed. K. T. Kyriakopoulos, Athens (1976), pp. 232–55

Life of Peter of Atroa, ed. and French tr. V. Laurent, *La Vie merveilleuse de saint Pierre d'Altroa (m. 837)*, Brussels (1956); ed. and French tr. V. Laurent, *La Vita retractata et les miracles posthumes de saint Pierre d'Atroa*, Brussels (1958)

Life of Philaretos the Merciful, ed. and tr. L. Rydén, Uppsala (2002)

Life of Romanos the Neomartyr, ed. and Latin tr. P. Peeters, 'S. Romain le néomartyr († 1 mai 780) d'après un document géorgien', *AnBoll* 30 (1911), pp. 393–427

Life of Stefan Nemanja, ed. V. Ćorović, *Spisi sv. Save, Žitije Stefana Nemanje*, Belgrade and Sremski Karlovci (1928); tr. in *Medieval Slavic lives*, ed. Kantor, pp. 255–95

Life of Stephen Sabaites, *AASS Julii*, III, pp. 531–613

Life of Stephen of Surozh (Sougdaia), ed. and Russian tr. in Vasilievsky (1908–30), III, pp. 72–6 (short *Life*); pp. 77–98 (longer *Life* only in Old Slavonic)

Life of Symeon the New Theologian, ed. and French tr. I. Hausherr, *Un grand mystique byzantin: vie de Syméon le Nouveau Théologien (949–1022) par Nicétas Stéthatos*, Rome (1928)

Life of Symeon Stylites the Younger, ed. P. van den Ven, *La Vie ancienne de S. Syméon Stylite le Jeune, 521–592*, 2 vols., Brussels (1962)

Life of Theodora the empress, ed. A. Markopoulos, 'Bios tes Autokrateiras Theodoras (BHG 1731)', *Symmeikta* 5 (1983), pp. 249–85; tr. M. P. Vinson, in *Byzantine defenders of images*, ed. Talbot, pp. 353–82

Life of Theodora of Thessaloniki, ed. and modern Greek tr. S. A. Paschalides, *O bios tes osiomyroblytidos Theodoras tes en Thessalonike*, Thessalonica (1991), pp. 66–189; tr. A.-M. Talbot in *Holy women of Byzantium*, ed. Talbot, pp. 159–237

Life of Theodore of Sykeon, ed. and French tr. A.-J. Festugière, *Vie de Théodore de Sykéon*, 2 vols., Brussels (1970); tr. Dawes and Baynes in *Three Byzantine saints*, pp. 83–192

Life of Theophanes, in Theoph., ed. de Boor, II, pp. 3–12

Les Listes de préséance byzantines des IXᵉ et Xᵉ siècles, ed. and French tr. N. Oikonomides, Paris (1972)

Liudprand of Cremona, *Antapodosis*, ed. P. Chiesa, *Liudprandi Cremonensis opera omnia*, CCCM 156, Turnhout (1998), pp. 1–150; tr. F. A. Wright, *The works of Liudprand of Cremona*, London (1930), pp. 25–212; French tr. J. Schnapp, *Liutprand de Crémone, Ambassades à Byzance*, Toulouse (2004)

—, *Legatio*, ed. P. Chiesa, *Relatio de legatione Constantinopolitana*, in *Liudprandi Cremonensis opera omnia*, pp. 185–218; tr. B. Scott, London (1993)

—, *Liber de rebus gestis Ottonis magni imperatoris*, ed. P. Chiesa, *Liudprandi Cremonensis opera omnia*, pp. 167–83; tr. Wright, *Works of Liudprand*, pp. 213–32

Livre de la conqueste de la princée de l'Amorée, Chronique de Morée, 1204–1305, ed. J. Longnon, Paris (1911)

Louis I (the Pious), *Pactum Ludovicianum*, in T. Sickel (ed.), *Das Privilegium Otto 1. für die römische Kirche vom Jahre 962*, Innsbruck (1883), pp. 174–7 (text)

Louis II, *Epistula ad Basilium*, ed. W. Henze, *MGH Ep.* 7, Hanover (1928), pp. 386–94

Lughdah al-Isfahani, *Bilad al-'arab*, ed. H. al-Jasir and S. A. al-'Ali, *Bilad al-'arab* [of Abu 'Ali al-Hasan ibn 'Abd Allah Lughdah al-Isfahani (d. 875)], Riyadh (1968)

Lupus of Ferrières, *Letters*, ed. P. K. Marshall, *Servati Lupi epistulae*, Leipzig (1984); tr. G. W. Regenos, *The letters of Lupus of Ferrières*, The Hague (1966)

Lupus Protospatharius, *Annales*, ed. G. H. Pertz, *MGH SS* 5, Hanover (1844), pp. 52–63

McGeer (tr.), *Land legislation of the Macedonian emperors*, see *Jus graecoromanum*

Makriyannis: the memoirs of General Makriyannis, 1797–1864, ed. and tr. H. A. Lidderdale, Oxford (1966)

al-Maliki, *Riyad al-nufus*, ed. H. Mu'nis, *Kitab riad al-nufus: répertoire biographique des savants de Kairouan et de l'Ifrikia de la conquête arabe à l'an 356 de l'hégire (966 de JC)* [of Abi Bakr 'Abd Allah ibn Muhammad al-Maliki (d. c. 1061)], Cairo (1951); ed. B. al-Bakkush, rev. M. al-Matwi, *Kitab Riyad al-nufus fi tabaqat 'ulama' al-Qayrawan wa-Ifriqiyah wa-zuhhadihim wa-nussakihim wa-siyar min akhbarihim wa-fada'ilihim wa-awafihim*, 3 vols., Beirut (1981–4)

Manganeios Prodromos, *Poems*, ed. and tr. E. Jeffreys and M. Jeffreys (in preparation)

Mango, C., *The art of the Byzantine empire, 312–1453: sources and documents*, Toronto (1986)

Manichaean literature: representative texts chiefly from Middle Persian and Parthian writing, tr. J. P. Asmussen, Delmar, NY (1975)

Mansi, J. D. (ed.), *Sacrorum conciliorum nova et amplissima collectio*, 31 vols., Florence (1759–93)

Manuel II Palaiologos, *Letters*, ed. and tr. G. T. Dennis, *The letters of Manuel II Palaeologus*, CFHB 8, Washington, DC (1977)

—, *Oration*, ed. and tr. J. Chrysostomides, *Manuel II Palaeologus: funeral oration on his brother Theodore*, CFHB 26, Thessalonica (1985)

—, *Prostagma (1408)*, in ed. V. Mošin, 'Akti iz Svetogorskih arhiva', *Spomenik* 91 (1939), pp. 164–7

Manuel Holobolos, *Orationes*, ed. M. Treu, in *Programm des königlichen Victoria-Gymnasiums zu Potsdam*, 2 vols., Potsdam (1906–7)

al-Maqrizi, *al-Mawa'iz*, ed. M. Zaynuhum and M. al-Sharqawi, *al-Mawa'iz wa-al-i'tibar bi-dhikr al-khitat wa al-athar al-ma'ruf bi-al-Khitat al-Maqriziyah* [of Abu al-'Abbas Ahmad ibn 'Ali al-Maqrizi (d. 1442)], 3 vols., Cairo (1998);

French tr. P. Casanova, *Description historique et topographique de l'Égypte*, Cairo (1906)

—, *al-Suluk*, ed. M. M. Ziyadah, *Kitab al-suluk li-maʿrifat duwal al-muluk* [of Abu al-ʿAbbas Ahmad ibn ʿAli al-Maqrizi (d. 1442)], 4 vols. in 9 pts., Cairo (1934–72)

Marcellinus, *Chronicle*, ed. T. Mommsen, *MGH AA* 9, Berlin (1894), pp. 37–108; tr. B. Croke, *The chronicle of Marcellinus: a translation and commentary (with a reproduction of Mommsen's edition of the text), ByzAust* 7, Sydney (1995)

Marino Sanudo Torsello, *Liber secretorum fidelium crucis*, in J. B. Bongars (ed.), *Gesta Dei per Francos, Orientalis historia* II, Hanover (1611), pp. 1–316

al-Marzuqi, *al-Azminah, Kitab al-azminah wa-al-amkinah* [of Abu ʿAli Ahmad ibn Muhammad al-Marzuqi (d. 1030)], 2 vols. in 1, Hyderabad (1914)

al-Masʿudi, *Muruj al-dhahab*, ed. C. Pellat, *Muruj al-dhahab wa-maʿadin al-jawhar* [of Abu ʿAli ibn al-Husayn ibn ʿAli al-Masʿudi (d. *c.* 956)], 7 vols., Beirut (1966–79); ed. and French tr. B. de Maynard and P. de Courteille, *Les prairies d'or*, 9 vols., Paris (1861–77); rev. French tr. C. Pellat, 5 vols. to date, Beirut (1962–97)

—, *al-Tanbih*, ed. M. J. de Goeje, *Kitab al-tanbih wa al-ishraf, BGA* 8, Leiden (1894); French tr. B. Carra de Vaux, *Le Livre de l'avertissement et de la revision*, Paris (1896)

Matʿevosyan, A. S. (ed.), *Hayeren dzeragreri hishatakaranner 5–12 dd.*, Erevan (1988)

Matthew of Edessa, *Chronicle*, ed. M. Melikʿ-Adamean and N. Ter-Mikʿayelean, *Patmutʿiwn*, Vagharshapat (1898; repr. with modern Armenian tr. H. Bartʿikyan, Erevan, 1991); tr. A. E. Dostourian, *Armenia and the crusades: tenth to twelfth centuries. The chronicle of Matthew of Edessa*, Lanham, MD (1993)

Maurice, *Strategikon*, ed. G. T. Dennis and German tr. E. Gamillscheg, *CFHB* 17, Vienna (1981); tr. G. T. Dennis, Philadelphia (1984)

Maximos Planoudes, *Epistulae*, ed. M. Treu, Breslau (1890; repr. Amsterdam, 1960); ed. P. A. M. Leone, *Maximi monachi Planudis epistulae*, Amsterdam (1991)

Maximus the Confessor, *Opera*, in *PG* 90–91

—, *Scripta saeculi*, ed. P. Allen and B. Neil, *Scripta saeculi VII vitam Maximi Confessoris illustrantia, CCSG* 39, Turnhout (1999); ed. and tr. P. Allen and B. Neil, *Maximus the Confessor and his companions; documents from exile*, Oxford (2002)

—, *Syriac Life*, ed. S. Brock, 'An early Syriac *Life* of Maximus the Confessor', *AnBoll* 91 (1973), pp. 299–346; repr. Brock (1984), no. 12

Medieval Slavic lives of saints and princes, ed. M. Kantor, Ann Arbor, MI (1983)

Medieval trade in the Mediterranean world: illustrative documents, ed. R. S. Lopez and I. W. Raymond, repr. with foreword by O. R. Constable, New York (2001)

Menander the Guardsman (Protector), *History*, ed. and tr. R. C. Blockley, *The History of Menander the Guardsman*, Liverpool (1985)

Menologion of Basil II, PG 117, cols. 19–614

Methodios, patriarch of Constantinople, *Life of Theophanes*, ed. V. V. Latyshev, *Methodii patriarchae Constantinopolitani vita S. Theophanis Confessoris*, Petrograd (1918)

Michael II and Theophilos, *Letter to Louis I*, in *Concilia aevi Karolini*, ed. A. Werminghoff, *MGH Concilia* 2, 2 vols., Hanover (1906–8), II, pp. 475–80

Michael Attaleiates, *Historia*, ed. I. Bekker, *CSHB*, Bonn (1853); ed. and Spanish tr. I. Pérez Martín, Madrid (2002)

Michael Autoreianos, *Acts*, ed. N. Oikonomides, 'Cinq actes inédits du patriarche Michel Autoreianos', *REB* 25 (1967), pp. 113–45

Michael Choniates, *Epistulae*, ed. F. Kolovou, *CFHB* 41, Berlin and New York (2001)

Michael Gabras, *Letters*, ed. G. Fatouros, *Die Briefe des Michael Gabras (ca. 1290–nach 1350)*, WBS 10, 2 vols., Vienna (1973)

Michael Italikos, *Lettres et discours*, ed. P. Gautier, Paris (1972)

Michael Palaiologos, *Autobiography*, ed. and French tr. H. Grégoire, 'Imperatoris Michaelis Palaeologi de vita sua', *Byz* 29–30 (1959–60), pp. 447–76; ed. A. A. Dmitrievsky, *Opisanie liturgicheskikh rukopisei*, 2 vols. in 3 pts., Kiev (1895, 1901): I, pp. 769–85

Michael Psellos, *Chronographia*, ed. and French tr. E. Renauld, 2 vols., Paris (1926–8); tr. E. A. R. Sewter, *Fourteen Byzantine rulers: the Chronographia of Michael Psellus*, Harmondsworth (1966); ed. and Italian tr. S. Impellizzeri *et al.*, *Imperatori di Bisanzio: cronografia*, 2 vols., Milan (1993)

—, *Letters*, ed. K. N. Sathas, *Istorikoi logoi, epistolai kai alla anekdota*, MB 5, Venice (1876)

—, *Orationes forenses et acta*, ed. G. T. Dennis, Stuttgart (1994)

—, *Orationes panegyricae*, ed. G. T. Dennis, Stuttgart (1994)

—, *Scripta minora*, ed. E. Kurtz and F. Drexl, 2 vols., Milan (1936–41)

Michael the Studite, *Life of Theodore the Studite*, PG 99, cols. 233–328

Michael the Syrian, *Chronicle*, ed. and French tr. J.-B. Chabot, *Chronique de Michel le Syrien, patriarche jacobite d'Antioche (1166–1199)*, 4 vols., Paris (1899–1924)

Migne, J.-P. (ed.), *Patrologia cursus completus: series graeca*, 161 vols., Paris (1857–66)

—(ed.), *Patrologiae cursus completus: series latina*, 221 vols., Paris (1841–64)

Miklosich, F. and Müller, J. (eds.), *Acta et diplomata graeca medii aevi sacra et profana collecta*, 6 vols., Vienna (1860–90)

Miracles of Anastasius the Persian, in *Acta M. Anastasii Persae*, ed. H. Usener, Bonn (1894), pp. 14–20

Miracles of Demetrius (Miracula Sancti Demetrii), AASS Octobris, IV, pp. 104–97

Miracles of Genesius (Miracula Sancti Genesii), ed. G. Waitz, in *MGH SS* 15.1, Hanover (1837), pp. 169–72

Monumenta Bulgarica: a bilingual anthology of Bulgarian texts from the 9th to the 19th centuries, ed. T. Butler, Ann Arbor, MI (1996)

Monumenta Peloponnesiaca: documents for the history of the Peloponnese in the 14th and 15th centuries, ed. J. Chrysostomides, Camberley (1995)

Monumenti ravennati de' secoli di mezzo, ed. M. Fantuzzi, 6 vols., Venice (1801–4)

Morrisson, C., *Catalogue des monnaies byzantines de la Bibliothèque Nationale*, 2 vols., Paris (1970)

Moses of Khoren, *History*, ed. M. Abeghean and S. Yarut'iwnean, *Patmut'iwn Hayots'*, Tiflis (1913; repr. Delmar, NY, 1981); tr. R. W. Thomson, *Moses Khorenats'i: History of the Armenians*, Cambridge, MA (1978; rev. edn. Ann Arbor, MI, 2006)

The movement for Greek independence, 1770–1821: a collection of documents, ed. and tr. R. Clogg, London (1976)

Muhammad ibn Habib, *al-Muhabbar*, ed. I. Lichtenstädter, *Kitab al-muhabbar* [of Abu Ja'far Muhammad ibn Habib (d. 860)], Hyderabad (1942)

La Narratio de rebus Armeniae, ed. G. Garitte, *CSCO* 132, Louvain (1952); French tr. J.-P. Mahé, 'La Narratio de rebus Armeniae', *REA* n. s. 25 (1994–5), pp. 429–38

Nestor-Iskander, *Tale of Constantinople*, tr. W. K. Hanak and M. Philippides, *The tale of Constantinople: of its origin and capture by the Turks in the year 1453*, New Rochelle, NY (1994)

Nicholas I, pope, *Epistulae*, ed. E. Perels, *MGH Ep.* 6, Berlin (1925), pp. 267–690

—, *Responsa ad consulta Bulgarorum*, in Nicholas I, *Epistulae*, pp. 568–600; German tr. L. Heiser, *Die Responsa ad consulta Bulgarorum des Papstes Nikolaus I. (858–867): ein Zeugnis päpstlicher Hirtensorge und ein Dokument unterschiedlicher Entwicklungen in den Kirchen von Rom und Konstantinopel*, Trier (1979), pp. 400–88

Nicholas I Mystikos, patriarch of Constantinople, *Letters*, ed. and tr. R. J. H. Jenkins and L. G. Westerink, *CFHB* 6, Washington, DC (1973)

—, *Miscellaneous writings*, ed. and tr. L. G. Westerink, *CFHB* 20, Washington, DC (1981)

Nicholas Mesarites, 'Discourse', ed. P. G. Nikopoulos, 'Anekdotos logos eis Arsenion Autoreianon patriarchen Konstantinoupoleos (Discours inédit à Arsène Autoreianos, patriarche de Constantinople)', *EEBS* 45 (1981–2), pp. 406–61

Die nichtliterarischen lateinischen Papyri Italiens aus der Zeit 445–700, ed. J.-O. Tjäder, 3 vols., Lund (1954–82)

Nihayat al-arab, ed. M. B. Danish-Pazhuh, *Nihayat al-arab fi-akhbar al-Furs wa-al-'Arab*, Tehran (1995)

Nikephoros I, patriarch of Constantinople, *Against the iconoclast*, ed. A. Papadopoulos-Kerameus, 'Episemon engraphon kata ton eikonomachon kai Manichaion', in *Analekta*, I, pp. 454–60

—, *Antirrhetici*, *PG* 100, cols. 205–533; French tr. M.-J. Mondzain-Baudinet, *Discours contre les iconoclastes*, Paris (1989)

—, *Breviarium historicum*, ed. C. de Boor, Leipzig (1880); ed. and tr. C. Mango, *Short history*, *CFHB* 13, Washington, DC (1990)

—, *De Magnete*, ed. J. B. Pitra, *Spicilegium solesmense complectens sanctorum patrum scriptorumque ecclesiasticorum anecdota hactenus opera*, 4 vols., Paris (1852–8), I, pp. 302–35, 552–3; ed. and tr. J. M. Featherstone, 'Opening scenes of the second iconoclasm: Nicephorus's *Critique* of the citations from Macarius Magnes', *REB* 60 (2002), pp. 65–111

—, *Refutatio*, ed. J. M. Featherstone, *CCSG* 33, Louvain (1997)

Nikephoros II Phokas, *Praecepta militaria*, ed. and tr. in McGeer (1995), pp. 3–78

Nikephoros, metropolitan of Rus, *Sermon*, 'Pouchenie mitropolita Nikifora v nedeliu Syropustnuiu', in Makarii, *Istoriia russkoi tserkvi*, II, ed. A. V. Nazarenko, Moscow (repr. 1995), pp. 569–71

—, *Works*, ed. S. M. Polianskii, *Tvoreniia mitropolita Nikifora*, Moscow (2006)

Nikephoros Basilakes, *Orationes et epistulae*, ed. A. Garzya, Leipzig (1984)

Nikephoros Basilakes, *Progimnasmi e monodie*, ed. and Italian tr. A. Pignani, Naples (1983)

Nikephoros Blemmydes, *Autobiography*, ed. A. Heisenberg, *Curriculum vitae et carmina*, Leipzig (1896); ed. J. A. Munitiz, *Autobiographia: sive curriculum vitae; necnon epistula universalior*, CCSG 13, Turnhout (1984); tr. J. A. Munitiz, *Nikephoros Blemmydes: a partial account*, Louvain (1988)

Nikephoros Bryennios, *Histoire*, ed. and French tr. P. Gautier, *CFHB* 9, Brussels (1975)

Nikephoros Gregoras, *Byzantina historia*, ed. L. Schopen and I. Bekker, 3 vols., *CSHB*, Bonn (1829–55); German tr. J.-L. van Dieten, *Rhomäische Geschichte*, 5 vols., Stuttgart (1973–94)

—, *Letters*, ed. P. A. M. Leone, *Nicephori Gregorae Epistulae*, 2 vols., Matino (1982–3)

Nikephoros Ouranos, *Taktika*, chs. 56–65, ed. and tr. in McGeer (1995), pp. 88–163

Niketas Byzantinos, *Confutatio falsi libri quem scripsit Mohamedes Arabs*, *PG* 105, cols. 669–842

Niketas Choniates, *History*, ed. J.-L. van Dieten, *CFHB* 11, 2 vols., Berlin and New York (1975); tr. H. J. Magoulias, *O City of Byzantium: annals of Niketas Choniates*, Detroit (1984)

—, *Orationes et epistulae*, ed. J.-L. van Dieten, *CFHB* 3, Berlin and New York (1972); comm. J.-L. van Dieten, *Niketas Choniates: Erläuterung zu den Reden und Briefen nebst einer Biographie*, Berlin and New York (1971)

—, *Treasury of orthodoxy (Thesaurus orthodoxae fidei)*, in *PG* 139–40; prologue ed. in J.-L. van Dieten, *Zur Überlieferung und Veröffentlichung der Panoplia dogmatike des Niketas Choniates*, Amsterdam (1970), pp. 50–9

Niketas the Paphlagonian, *Summorum apostolorum orationes laudatoriae*, *PG* 105, cols. 16–373

Niketas Stethatos, *Life of Symeon the New Theologian*, ed. and French tr. I. Hausherr and G. Horn, *Un grand mystique byzantin: vie de Syméon le Nouveau Théologien (949–1022)*, *OC* 12, no. 45, Rome (1928)

Nikolaos Mesarites, *Ekphrasis*, ed. and tr. G. Downey, 'Nikolaos Mesarites: description of the church of the Holy Apostles at Constantinople', *Transactions of the American Philosophical Society* 47 (1957), pp. 855–924

The Nikon chronicle, Nikonovskaia Letopis', Polnoe sobranie russkikh letopisei 9–13, St Petersburg (1862; repr. Moscow, 1965); tr. S. A. Zenkovsky and B. J. Zenkovsky, *The Nikonian Chronicle*, 5 vols., Princeton (1984–9)

Noctes Petropolitanae, ed. A. Papadopoulos-Kerameus, St Petersburg (1913; repr. Leipzig, 1976)

Nomos georgikos see *Farmer's law*

The Normans in Europe, ed. E. M. C. van Houts, Manchester (2000)

Notai genovesi in Oltremare. Atti rogati a Chio da Donato di Chiavari, 17 febbraio–12 novembre 1394, ed. M. Balard, Genoa (1988)

Notai genovesi in Oltremare. Atti rogati a Chio da Giuliano de Canella, 2 novembre 1380–31 marzo 1381, ed. E. Basso, Athens (1993)

Notai genovesi in Oltremare. Atti rogati a Chio da Gregorio Panissaro (1403–1405), ed. P. Piana Toniolo, Genoa (1995)

Notitiae episcopatuum ecclesiae Constantinopolitanae, ed. J. Darrouzès, Paris (1981)

Notker Balbulus [the Stammerer], *Gesta Karoli magni imperatoris*, ed. H. F. Haefele, *Taten Kaiser Karls des Grossen, MGH SRG* n.s. 12, Berlin (1959); tr. L. Thorpe, *Two Lives of Charlemagne*, Harmondsworth (1969)

Nuova serie di documenti sulle relazioni di Genova coll'impero bizantino, ed. A. Sanguineti and G. Bertolotto, *Atti della Società ligure di storia patria* 28 (1896–8), pp. 343–499

Odo of Deuil, *Expedition*, ed. and tr. V. G. Berry, *De profectione Ludovici VII in orientem*, New York (1948)

Odorico, P., 'Il calamo d'argento: un carme inedito in onore di Romano II', *JÖB* 37 (1987), pp. 65–93

'Office inédit en l'honneur de Nicéphore Phocas', ed. L. Petit, *BZ* 13 (1904), pp. 398–420

Opus Caroli, ed. A. Freeman and P. Meyvaert, *Opus Caroli regis contra synodum (Libri Carolini), MGH Concilia* 2, Supp. 1, Hanover (1998)

Otto I, *Diplomata*, ed. T. Sickel, *Die Urkunden Konrad I., Heinrich I. und Otto I., MGH Dip.* 1, Hanover (1879–84; repr. Munich, 1980)

Otto II, *Diplomata*, ed. T. Sickel, *Die Urkunden Otto des II., MGH Dip. 2.1,* Hanover (1888; repr. Munich, 1980)

Otto III, *Diplomata*, ed. T. Sickel, *Die Urkunden Otto des III., MGH Dip.* 2.2, Hanover (1893; repr. Berlin, 1957)

Pactum Lotharii I, ed. A. Krause, in A. Boretius and A. Krause (eds.), *MGH Cap.* 2, Hanover (1890), pp. 130–5

Pagans and Christians in late antiquity: a sourcebook, ed. A. D. Lee, London (2000)

Papsturkunden 896–1046, ed. H. Zimmermann, 3 vols., Vienna (1984–9)

Parastaseis syntomoi chronikai, in ed. T. Preger, *Scriptores originum Constantinopolitanarum*, 2 vols., Leipzig (1901–7), I, pp. 19–73; tr. Averil Cameron and J. Herrin, *Constantinople in the early eighth century: the Parastaseis syntomoi chronikai*, Leiden (1984)

Paschal chronicle, ed. L. Dindorf, *Chronicon paschale, CSHB*, 2 vols., Bonn (1832); tr. Michael Whitby and Mary Whitby, Liverpool (1989)

Passion of St Anastasia, ed. F. Halkin, *Légendes grecques de 'martyres romaines'*, Subsidia Hagiographica 55, Brussels (1973), pp. 86–131

Das Patriarchat von Konstantinopel im ausgehenden 16. Jahrhundert: der Bericht des Leontios Eustratios im Cod. Tyb. MB 10, ed. and German tr. O. Kresten, Vienna (1970)

I patti con l'impero latino di Costantinopoli: 1205–1231, ed. M. Pozza, *Pacta Veneta* 10, Venice (2004)

Paul the Deacon, *Historia Langobardorum*, ed. L. Bethmann and G. Waitz, *MGH SRL*, Hanover (1878), pp. 45–187; tr. W. D. Foulke, Philadelphia (1907; repr. 2003)

Paul the Silentiary, *Description of the church of St Sophia (Ekphrasis tou naou tes Hagias Sophias)*, in *Johannes von Gaza*, ed. Friedländer, pp. 227–56; partial tr.

in Trypanis (ed.), *Greek verse*, pp. 417–18; partial tr. in Lethaby and Swainson (1894), pp. 35–60

P'awstos Buzand, *Epic history*, ed. K'. Patkanean, *Buzandaran Patmut'iwnk'*, St Petersburg (1883; repr. Delmar, NY, 1984); tr. N. G. Garsoïan, *The epic histories attributed to P'awstos Buzand: Buzandaran Patmut'iwnk'*, Cambridge, MA (1989)

Peira, ed. C. E. Zacharia von Lingenthal, *Peira Eustathiou tou Romaiou*, in *Jus graecoromanum*, IV, pp. 9–260

Le pergamene di Conversano, ed. G. Coniglio, Bari (1975)

Periplus Maris Erythraei, ed. and tr. L. Casson, Princeton (1989)

Petit, L., 'Le Monastère de Notre Dame de Pitié en Macédoine', *IRAIK* 6 (1900), pp. 1–153

Philippidis-Braat, A., 'La Captivité de Palamas chez les Turcs: dossier et commentaire', *TM* 7 (1979), pp. 109–221

Philotheos, *Kletorologion*, ed. and French tr. Oikonomides, in *Les Listes de préséance*, pp. 65–235

Photios, patriarch of Constantinople, *Bibliotheca*, ed. and French tr. R. Henry, 9 vols., Paris (1959–91); partial tr. N. G. Wilson, London (1994)

—, *Epistulae et amphilochia*, ed. B. Laourdas and L. G. Westerink, 6 vols., Leipzig (1983–8)

—, *Homilies*, ed. B. Laourdas, *Omiliai*, Thessalonica (1959); tr. C. Mango, *The homilies of Photius, Patriarch of Constantinople*, *DOSt* 3, Cambridge, MA (1958)

—, *Letter to Khan Boris of Bulgaria*, in Photios, *Epistulae et amphilochia*, ed. Laourdas and Westerink, I, pp. 1–39; tr. D. S. White and J. R. Berrigan, *The patriarch and the prince: the letter of Patriarch Photios of Constantinople to Khan Boris of Bulgaria*, Brookline, MA (1982)

Pietro Pizolo, notaio in Candia, I: *1300*; II: *1304–1305*, ed. S. Carbone, 2 vols., Venice (1978–85)

Placiti cassinesi, ed. M. Inguanez, I: *I placiti cassinesi del secolo X con periodi in volgare*, II: *Documenti cassinesi dei secoli XI–XIII con volgare*, 4th edn., Monte Cassino (1942)

I placiti del 'Regnum Italiae', ed. C. Manaresi, 3 vols. in 5 pts., *FSI* 92, 96, 97, Rome (1955–60)

Plea of Rižana, in *I placiti del 'Regnum Italiae'*, ed. Manaresi, I, no. 17, pp. 48–56; ed. and Italian tr. in A. Petranović and A. Margetić, 'Il placito del Risano', *Atti del Centro di ricerche storiche, Rovigno* 14, Trieste–Rovigno (1983–4), pp. 55–75 (text and Italian tr. at pp. 56–69)

Poetae latini medii aevi, ed. E. Dümmler *et al.*, *MGH*, 6 vols., Hanover (1881–1979)

Poupardin, R., *Recueil des actes des rois de Provence (855–928)*, Paris (1920)

Povest' vremennykh let, ed. V. P. Adrianova-Peretts and D. S. Likhachev, 2nd edn. rev. M. B. Sverdlov, St Petersburg (1996); tr. S. H. Cross and O. P. Sherbowitz-Wetzor, *Russian primary chronicle*, Cambridge, MA (1953)

Preger, T. (ed.) *Scriptores originum Constantinopolitanorum*, 2 vols., Leipzig (1901–7)

Priscian, *De laude Anastasii imperatoris*, ed. and tr. P. Coyne, Lewiston, NY (1991)

—, *Grammatici latini*, ed. H. Keil, 8 vols., Leipzig (1855–80)

Priscus, in Blockley, *Historians*, I, pp. 48–70, 113–23; II, pp. 222–400

Procopius, *Buildings*, ed. and tr. H. B. Dewing and G. Downey, Cambridge, MA and London (1940)

—, *History of the wars*, ed. and tr. H. B. Dewing, 5 vols., Cambridge, MA and London (1914–28); German tr. (bks. V–VIII) D. Coste, *Prokop, Gothenkrieg*, Leipzig (1885; repr. Munich, 1966)

—, *Secret history*, ed. and tr. H. B. Dewing, *The anecdota or secret history*, Cambridge, MA and London (1935); tr. G. A. Williamson, London (1966)

Pseudo-Dionysios of Tell-Mahre, *Chronicle*, ed. and partial Latin tr. J.-B. Chabot; French tr. (vol. II) R. Hespel, *Incerti auctoris chronicon Pseudo-Dionysianum vulgo dictum*, CSCO 91, 104, 121, 507, 4 vols., Paris and Louvain (1927–89); partial tr. W. Witakowski, *Pseudo-Dionysius of Tel-Mahre, Chronicle (known also as the Chronicle of Zuqnin). Part III*, Liverpool (1996)

Pseudo-Gregory II, *Letters to Leo III*, ed. and French tr. in Gouillard (1968), pp. 276–305

Pseudo-al-Jahiz, *al-Taj*, ed. A. Zaki, *Kitab al-Taj fi akhlaq al-muluk*, Cairo (1914); French tr. C. Pellat, *Le Livre de la couronne, Kitab at-Tag (fi Ahlaq al-Muluk); ouvrage attribué à Gahiz*, Paris (1954)

Pseudo-Kodinos, *Treatise on the dignities and offices*, ed. and French tr. J. Verpeaux, *Traité des offices*, Paris (1966)

Pseudo-Methodius, *Apocalypse*, ed. W. J. Aerts and G. A. A. Kortekaas, *Die Apokalypse des Pseudo-Methodius: die ältesten griechischen und lateinischen Übersetzungen*, CSCO 569–70, 2 vols., Louvain (1998); German tr. G. J. Reinink, *Die syrische Apokalypse des Pseudo-Methodius*, CSCO 540–1, 2 vols., Louvain (1993)

Pseudo-Shapuh, tr. R. W. Thomson, 'The anonymous story-teller (also known as "Pseudo-Šapuh")', *REA* 21 (1988–9), pp. 171–232

Pseudo-Symeon, *Chronicle*, in Theophanes Continuatus, *Chronographia*, pp. 603–760

Radomirov psaltir (Le psautier de Radomir), ed. L. Makarijoska, Skopje (1997)

Ralles, G. A. and Potles, M., *Syntagma ton theion kai ieron kanonon*, 6 vols., Athens (1852–9; repr. Athens, 1966)

Ramón Muntaner, *Chronicle*, tr. R. Hughes, *The Catalan expedition to the east: from the Chronicle of Ramón Muntaner*, Woodbridge (2006)

Raqiq al-Qayrawani, *Ta'rikh Ifriqiyah*, ed. al-Munji al-Ka'bi, *Ta'rikh Ifriqiyah wa-al-maghrib* [of Ibrahim ibn al-Qasim Raqiq al-Qayrawani (*fl.* 11th century)], Tunis (1968)

Readings in late antiquity: a sourcebook, ed. M. Maas, London (2000)

Regesta pontificum romanorum: ab condita ecclesia ad annum post Christum natum MCXCVIII, ed. P. Jaffé *et al.*, 2 vols., Leipzig (1885–8)

Die Regesten des Kaiserreichs unter den Karolingern, 751–918, ed. J. F. Böhmer, rev. E. Mühlbacher, *Regesta imperii* 1, Innsbruck (1908; repr. Hildesheim, 1966)

Les Régestes des actes du patriarcat de Constantinople, ed. V. Grumel *et al.*, 7 vols., Paris (1932–91)

Régestes des délibérations du Sénat de Venise concernant la Romanie, ed. F. Thiriet, 3 vols., Paris and The Hague (1958–71)

Das Register des Patriarchats von Konstantinopel, ed. and German tr. H. Hunger *et al.*, *CFHB* 19, 3 vols. to date, Vienna (1981–)

Religions of late antiquity in practice, ed. R. Valantasis, Princeton, NJ (2000)

Rhodian sea-law (Nomos Rodion Nautikos), ed. W. Ashburner, Oxford (1909; repr. Aalen, 1976); tr. in E. H. Freshfield, *A manual of later Roman law*, Cambridge (1927); German tr. in Letsios (1996), pp. 253–66

Rippin, A. and Knappert, J. (eds. and trs.), *Textual sources for the study of Islam*, Manchester (1986)

Robert de Clari, *Conquest of Constantinople*, ed. P. Lauer, *La Conquête de Constantinople*, Paris (1924); tr. E. H. McNeal, *The conquest of Constantinople*, New York (1936; repr. 1966)

The Roman eastern frontier and the Persian wars, ed. S. N. Lieu *et al.*, 2 vols., London (1991–2002)

Romanus the Melodist, *Sancti Romani melodi cantica: cantica genuina*, ed. P. Maas and C. A. Trypanis, Oxford (1963); English tr. M. Carpenter, *Kontakia of Romanos, Byzantine melodist*, 2 vols., Columbia, MO (1970–3); English tr. (selection) E. Lash, *St Romanos the Melodist, Kontakia, On the life of Christ*, San Francisco (1996)

Rus primary chronicle see *Povest' vremennykh let*

Russian travelers to Constantinople in the fourteenth and fifteenth centuries, ed. and tr. G. Majeska, *DOSt* 19, Washington, DC (1984)

Russkaia istoricheskaia biblioteka, 39 vols., St Petersburg (1872–1927)

'Sainte-Sophie de Thessalonique d'après un rituel', ed. J. Darrouzès, *REB* 34 (1976), pp. 45–78

Šandrovskaja, V. S. and Seibt, W., *Byzantinische Bleisiegel der Staatlichen Eremitage mit Familiennamen*, 1 vol. to date, Vienna (2005–)

Sathas, K. N., *Mesaionike bibliotheke*, 7 vols., Venice and Paris (1872–94)

Schlumberger, G. L., *Sigillographie de l'empire byzantin*, Paris (1884)

Scriptor incertus, *De Leone Armenio*, in Leo Grammaticus, *Chronographia*, ed. Bekker, pp. 335–62; ed. and Italian tr. F. Iadevaia, *Scriptor incertus*, Messina (1987)

Sebeos, *Armenian history*, ed. G. Abgaryan, *Patmut'iwn Sebeosi*, Erevan (1979); tr. and comm. R. W. Thomson and J. D. Howard-Johnston, *The Armenian History attributed to Sebeos*, 2 vols., Liverpool (1999)

Seibt, W. and A.-K. Wassiliou, *Die byzantinischen Bleisiegel in Österreich*, I: *Kaiserhof*; II: *Zentral- und Provinzialverwaltung*, 2 vols., Vienna (1978–2004)

A select library of Nicene and post-Nicene Fathers of the Christian Church: second series, ed. H. Wace and P. Schaff, 14 vols., Oxford (1890–1900); repr. Grand Rapids, MI, 1951–)

Ševčenko, I., 'Alexios Makrembolites and his "Dialogue between the rich and the poor"', *ZRVI* 6 (1960), pp. 187–228

—, 'Nicolas Cabasilas' "anti-Zealot" discourse: a reinterpretation', *DOP* 11 (1957), pp. 79–171

—(ed.), 'Poems on the deaths of Leo VI and Constantine VII in the Madrid manuscript of Skylitzes', *DOP* 23–4 (1969–70), pp. 185–228

Severus, patriarch of Antioch, *Letters*, ed. and tr. E. W. Brooks, *The sixth book of the select letters of Severus, patriarch of Antioch, in the Syriac version of Athanasius of Nisibis*, 2 vols., London (1902–4)

Seyrig, ed. J.-C. Cheynet *et al.*, *Les Sceaux byzantins de la collection Henri Seyrig*, Paris (1991)

Shahid, I. (ed. and tr.), *The martyrs of Najran: new documents*, Brussels (1971)

Sibt ibn al-Jawzi, *Mir'at al-zaman fi ta'rikh al-a'yan*, ed. A. Sevim, Ankara (1968)

Il sinodo lateranense dell'ottobre 649: rassegna critica di fonti dei secolo VII–XII, ed. R. Riedinger, comm. P. Conte, Vatican City, Rome (1989)

Skirmishing, ed. and tr. Dennis, *Three Byzantine military treatises*, pp. 143–239; ed. and French tr. G. Dagron and H. Mihăescu, *Le Traité sur la guérilla (De velitatione) de l'empereur Nicéphore Phocas (963–969)*, Paris (1986)

Skylitzes Continuatus, *Chronicle*, ed. E. T. Tsolakes, *E synecheia tes chronographias tou Ioannou Skylitse*, Thessalonica (1968)

Social and political thought in Byzantium from Justinian I to the last Palaeologus: passages from Byzantine writers and documents, ed. E. Barker, Oxford (1957)

Socrates Scholasticus, *Ecclesiastical history*, tr. R. W. Thomson, *The Armenian adaptation of the Ecclesiastical History of Socrates Scholasticus*, Louvain (2001)

Sozomen, *Church history (Ekklesiastike historia)*, ed. J. Bidez and G. C. Hansen, *Kirchengeschichte*, 2nd edn., Berlin (1995)

Spomenici za srednovekovnata i ponovata istorija na Makedonija, ed. V. Mošin *et al.*, 5 vols., Skopje (1975–88)

Stare srpske povelje i pisma, ed. L. Stojanović, *Zbornik za istoriju, jezik i kniževnost srpskog naroda* 19, 24, 2 vols., Belgrade (1929–34)

Stephen the Deacon, *Life of Stephen the Younger*, ed. and French tr. M.-F. Auzépy, *La Vie d'Étienne le Jeune par Étienne le Diacre*, Aldershot (1997)

Stephen of Siwnikʻ, *Meknutʻiwn kʻerakanin*, in *Denys de Thrace*, ed. Adontz, pp. 181–219

Stephen of Taron (Stephanos Asołik, Stepʻanos Taronetsʻi Asoghik), *Universal history*, ed. S. Malkhaseantsʻ, *Patmutʻiwn tiezerakan*, St Petersburg (1885); tr. T. W. Greenwood, *The universal history of Stephen of Taron*, Oxford (in preparation); *Histoire universelle*, I, French tr. E. Dulaurier, Paris (1883); II, French tr. F. Macler, Paris (1917)

Sternbach, L., 'Christophorea', *Eos* 5 (1899), pp. 7–21

Storia della badia di Monte-Cassino, ed. L. Tosti, 3 vols., Naples (1842–3)

Suidae lexicon, ed. A. Adler, 5 vols., Leipzig (1928–38; repr. Stuttgart, 1967–71; repr. Munich, 2001–4); see also www.stoa.org/sol

Sullivan, D. F. (ed. and tr.), *Siegecraft: two tenth-century instructional manuals*, *DOSt* 36, Washington, DC (2000)

Svod drevneishikh pis'mennykh izvestii o slavianakh (Corpus testimoniorum vetustissimorum ad historiam slavicam pertinentium), ed. L. A. Gindin *et al.*, 2 vols., Moscow (1991–5)

Symeon, archbishop of Thessalonica, *Politico-historical works (1416/17 to 1429)*, *WBS* 13, ed. D. Balfour, Vienna (1979)

Symeon [Magister] the Logothete, *Chronicle*, ed. S. Wahlgren, *Symeonis magistri et logothetae Chronicon*, CFHB 44.1, Berlin (2006)

Symeon Metaphrastes, *Life of Thomas the Apostle*, ed. in Volk (1996), pp. 148–67

Symeon the New Theologian, *Hymnen*, ed. A. Kambylis, Berlin and New York (1976)

—, *Traités théologiques et éthiques*, ed. and French tr. J. Darrouzès, SC 122, 129, 2 vols., Paris (1966–7)

Synaxarion of Constantinople, ed. H. Delehaye, *Synaxarium ecclesiae Constantinopolitanae: Propylaeum ad Acta Sanctorum Novembris*, Brussels (1902)

The synaxarion of the monastery of the Theotokos Evergetis, ed. and tr. R. Jordan, I: *September–February*; II: *the movable cycle (March to August)*, 2 vols. to date, BBTT 6.5, 6.6, Belfast (2000–5)

Synodicon orientale, ed. and French tr. J.-B. Chabot, Paris (1902)

Synodicon of orthodoxy, ed. and French tr. J. Gouillard, 'Le synodikon de l'Orthodoxie: édition et commentaire', TM 2 (1967), pp. 1–316 at pp. 44–118

Synodicon vetus, ed. and tr. J. Duffy and J. Parker, *The Synodicon vetus*, CFHB 15, Washington, DC (1979)

Syrian chronicles, tr. A. Palmer *et al.*, *The seventh century in the West-Syrian chronicles*, Liverpool (1993)

al-Tabari, *Tafsir*, ed. M. Z. 'al-Ghumrawi *et al.*, *Tafsir al-Qu'ran* [of Abu Ja'far Muhammad ibn Jarir al-Tabari (d. 922/3)], 30 vols., Cairo (1903)

—, *Ta'rikh*, ed. M. J. de Goeje *et al.*, *Annales quos scripsit Abu Djafar Mohammed ibn Djarir at-Tabari, Ta'rikh al-rusul wa-al-muluk*, 15 vols., Leiden (1879–1901); general ed. of translation E. Yarshater, *The history of al-Tabari*, 39 vols., Albany, NY (1985–99), tr. C. E. Bosworth (V, XXXIII), Y. Friedmann (XII), H. Kennedy (XXIX), M. G. Morony (XVIII), S. D. Powers (XXIV); partial German tr. T. Nöldeke, *Geschichte der Perser und Araber zur Zeit der Sasaniden*, Leiden (1879)

Tacitus, *The Annals*, ed. and tr. J. Jackson, 4 vols., Cambridge MA (1931–7)

Tafel and Thomas, see *Urkunden zur älteren Handels- und Staatsgeschichte der Republik Venedig*

Taktikon Uspensky, ed. and French tr. Oikonomides, *Les Listes de préséance*, pp. 46–63

Tarihî takvimler, ed. O. Turan, *Istanbul'un fethinden önce yazilmis tarihî takvimler*, Ankara (1954)

Texte zur spätbyzantinischen Finanz- und Wirtschaftsgeschichte in Handschriften der Biblioteca Vaticana, ed. P. Schreiner, StT 344, Vatican City, Rome (1991)

Thawdhurus Abu Qurrah, bishop of Harran, *Treatise*, tr. S. H. Griffith, *A treatise on the veneration of the holy icons written in Arabic by Theodore Abu Qurrah, Bishop of Harran (c. 755–c. 830 AD)*, Louvain (1997)

Thegan, *Deeds of Louis the Pious*, in *Thegan, Die Taten Kaiser Ludwigs, Astronomus, Das Leben Kaiser Ludwigs*, ed. and German tr. E. Tremp, MGH SRG 64, Hanover (1995), pp. 168–259

Theiner, A. (ed.), *Vetera monumenta slavorum meridionalium historiam illustrantia*, 2 vols., Rome (1863–75)

Theodore II Laskaris, *Christian theology*, ed. C. T. Krikones, *Theodorou II Laskareos, Peri christianikes theologias logoi*, Thessalonica (1988)

—, *Encomium*, ed. and Italian tr. L. Tartaglia, *Encomio dell'imperatore Giovanni Duca*, Naples (1990)

—, *Epistulae*, ed. N. Festa, *Theodori Ducae Lascaris Epistulae CCXVII*, Florence (1898)

—, 'In praise of the great city of Nicaea', ed. L. Bachmann, *Theodori Ducae Lascaris imperatoris in laudem Nicaea urbis oratio*, Rostock (1847); ed. in Georgiopoulou, 'Theodore II Dukas Laskaris' (PhD thesis, 1990), pp. 140–72; tr. in Foss (1996a), pp. 133–53

—, *Opuscula rhetorica*, ed. A. Tartaglia, Munich (2000)

Theodore of Alania, *Alanikos*, *PG* 140, cols. 387–414

—, *Encomium*, ed. A. D. Karpozilos, 'An unpublished encomium by Theodore bishop of Alania', *Byzantina* 6 (1974), pp. 226–49

Theodore Daphnopates, *Correspondance*, ed. and French tr. J. Darrouzès and L. G. Westerink, Paris (1978)

—, *Life of Theodore the Studite*, *PG* 99, cols. 113–232

Theodore Metochites, 'Nicene oration', ed. K. N. Sathas, *MB* 1, Venice (1872), pp. 139–53; tr. in Foss (1996a), pp. 165–95

—, *Poems*, ed. and tr. J. M. Featherstone, *Theodore Metochites's poems 'to himself'*, *BV* 23, Vienna (2000)

Theodore Prodromos, *Katomyomachia*, ed. and German tr. H. Hunger, *Der byzantinische Katz-Mäuse-Krieg*, *BV* 3, Vienna (1968)

—, *Poems*, ed. W. Hörandner, *Historische Gedichte*, *WBS* 11, Vienna (1974)

The Theodore psalter, ed. and tr. C. Barber, Champaign, IL (2000)

Theodore Skoutariotes, *Synopsis chronike*, ed. K. N. Sathas, *MB* 7, Paris (1894), pp. 1–556

Theodore Spandounes, *On the origin of the Ottoman emperors*, ed. K. N. Sathas, *De la origine deli Imperatori Ottomani, Documents inédits relatifs à l'histoire de la Grèce au moyen âge*, Paris (1890), pp. iii–l (preface), pp. 133–261 (text); ed. and tr. D. M. Nicol, Cambridge (1997)

Theodore the Studite, *Antirrhetici*, *PG* 99, cols. 328–436

—, *Epigrams*, *PG* 99, cols. 1780–1812; ed. and German tr. P. Speck, *Jamben auf verschiedene Gegenstände*, Berlin (1968); French tr. F. de Montleau, *Les Grandes Catéchèses*, I: *Les Épigrammes I–XXIX*, Bégrolles-en-Mauges (2002), pp. 571–599

—, *Letters*, *PG* 99, cols. 903–1679; ed. G. Fatouros, *Theodori Studitae Epistulae*, 2 vols., *CFHB* 31.1–2, Berlin (1991–2)

—, *Panegyric to Theophanes the Confessor*, ed. and French tr. S. Efthymiadis, 'Le Panégyrique de s. Théophane le Confesseur pour s. Théodore Stoudite', *AnBoll* 111 (1993), pp. 259–90

Theodosios the Deacon, *De Creta capta*, ed. H. Criscuolo, Leipzig (1979)

Theodosios the Monk, *Letter*, ed. C. O. Zuretti, 'La espugnazione di Siracusa nell' 880', in *Centenario della nascità di Michele Amari*, ed. E. Besta *et al.*, Palermo (1910), I, pp. 165–73

Theodosius, *Codex Theodosianus*, ed. T. Mommsen and P. Meyer, *Theodosiani libri XVI cum constitutionibus Sirmondianis*, 2 vols., Berlin (1905; repr. 1971); tr. C. Pharr *et al.*, *The Theodosian code and novels and the Sirmondian constitutions*, Princeton, NJ (1952)

Theognostos of Sarai, *Questions*, 'Otvety konstantinopol'skogo patriarshogo sobora na voprosy saraiskogo episkopa (Feognosta)', *RIB* VI, St Petersburg (1880), cols. 129–40 (Slavonic version), appendix 1, cols. 5–12 (Greek text)

Theophanes, *Chronicle*, ed. C. de Boor, 2 vols., Leipzig (1883–5); tr. C. Mango and R. Scott, *The Chronicle of Theophanes Confessor*, Oxford (1997)

Theophanes Continuatus, *Chronographia*, ed. I. Bekker, *CSHB*, Bonn (1838)

Theophylact of Ohrid, *Discourses*, ed. and French tr. P. Gautier, *Discours, traités, poésies, Théophylacte d' Achrida*, *CFHB* 16.1, Thessalonica (1980)

—, *Letters*, ed. and French tr. P. Gautier, *Lettres, Théophylacte d'Achrida*, *CFHB* 16.2, Thessalonica (1986)

—, *Life of Clement of Ohrid*, ed. A. Milev, *Gr'tskite zhitiia na Kliment Okhridski*, Sofia (1966); ed. I. G. Iliev, 'The long *Life* of Clement of Ohrid: a critical edition', *BB* 9 (1995), pp. 62–120

—, *Martyrium ss. quindecim illustrium martyrum*, *PG* 126, cols. 151–222

Theophylact Simocatta, *History*, ed. C. de Boor and P. Wirth, *Theophylacti Simocattae Historiae*, Stuttgart (1972); tr. Michael Whitby and Mary Whitby, *The history of Theophylact Simocatta*, Oxford (1986)

Theotokos Evergetis, ed. and French tr. P. Gautier, 'Le *Typikon* de la Théotokos Évergétis', *REB* 40 (1982), pp. 5–101; tr. R. Jordan in *Byzantine monastic foundation documents*, ed. Thomas and Hero, II, pp. 454–506

Thietmar of Merseburg, *Chronicon*, ed. R. Holtzmann, *Die Chronik des Bischofs Thietmar von Merseburg und ihre Korveier überarbeitung*, *MGH SRG* n.s. 9, Berlin (1935); tr. D. A. Warner, *Ottonian Germany: the Chronicon of Thietmar of Merseburg*, Manchester (2001)

Thomas Artsruni, *History*, ed. K. Patkanean, *Patmut'iwn tann Artsruneats'*, St Petersburg (1887; repr. Tiflis, 1917; repr. Delmar, NY, 1991); tr. R. W. Thomson, *The history of the house of the Artsrunik'*, Detroit (1985)

Three Byzantine saints: contemporary biographies of St Daniel the Stylite, St Theodore of Sykeon and St John the Almsgiver, tr. E. Dawes and N. H. Baynes, Crestwood, NY (1996)

Timarion, ed. R. Romano, *Pseudo-Luciano, Timarione*, Naples (1974); tr. B. Baldwin, Detroit (1984)

Tomič psalter, ed. A. Džurova, *Tomichov psaltir*, 2 vols., Sofia (1990)

I trattati con Bisanzio 992–1198, ed. M. Pozza and G. Ravegnani, *Pacta Veneta* 10, Venice (1993)

Trypanis, C. A. (ed.), *Penguin book of Greek verse*, Harmondsworth (1971)

'Le Typikon du Christ Pantocrator', ed. and French tr. P. Gautier, *REB* 32 (1974), pp. 1–145

Ukhtanes, *History of Armenia*, tr. Z. Arzoumanian, *Bishop Ukhtanes of Sebastia, History of Armenia, Part II: History of the severance of the Georgians from the Armenians*, Fort Lauderdale, FL (1985)

Urkunden zur älteren Handels- und Staatsgeschichte der Republik Venedig, ed. G. L. F. Tafel and G. M. Thomas, 3 vols., Vienna (1856–7)

Die Urkunden Pippins, Karlmanns und Karls des Grossen (Pippini, Carlomanni, Caroli Magni diplomata), ed. E. Mühlbacher *et al.*, *MGH Die Urkunden der Karolinger (Diplomata Karolinorum)* 1, Hanover (1906)

al-ʿUsfuri, *al-Tabaqat*, ed. A. D. al-ʿUmari, *Kitab al-tabaqat* [of Khalifah ibn Khayyat al ʿUsfuri (d. 854/5)], 2 vols., Baghdad (1967)

Vasiliev, A. A., *Byzance et les Arabes*, II.2: *Extraits des sources Arabes*, tr. M. Canard, Brussels (1950)

Das Verbrüderungsbuch der Abtei Reichenau, ed. J. Autenrieth *et al.*, *MGH Libri memoriales et necrologia* n.s. 1, Hanover (1979)

Victor of Tunnuna, *Chronicle*, ed. T. Mommsen, *MGH AA* 9, Berlin (1894), pp. 178–206; ed. C. Cardelle de Hartmann, *CCSL* 173A, Turnhout (2001), pp. 1–55; ed. and Italian tr. A. Placanica, *Vittore da Tunnuna, Chronica: chiesa e impero nell'età di Giustiniano*, Florence (1997)

Villehardouin, see Geoffrey of Villehardouin

Walter Map, *De nugis curialium*, ed. and tr. M. R. James, rev. C. N. L. Brooke and R. A. B. Mynors, *Courtier's trifles*, Oxford (1983)

al-Waqidi, *Kitab al-maghazi*, ed. M. Jones, *The Kitab al-maghazi of al-Waqidi* [of Abu ʿAbd Allah Muhammad ibn ʿUmar ibn Waqid al-Waqidi (d. 822)], 3 vols., London (1966)

Wellesz, E., *The Akathistos hymn*, Copenhagen (1957)

Widukind of Corvey, *Res gestae Saxonicae*, ed. P. Hirsch and H.-E. Lohmann, *Die Sachsengeschichte des Widukind von Korvei*, *MGH SRG* 60, Hanover (1935); ed. and German tr. A. Bauer and R. Rau, *Quellen zur Geschichte der sächsischen Kaiserzeit*, 2nd edn., Darmstadt (1977)

William of Apulia, *Gesta Roberti Wiscardi*, ed. and French tr. M. Mathieu, *La Geste de Robert Guiscard par Guillaume de Pouille*, Palermo (1961)

William of Tyre, *Chronicon*, ed. R. B. C. Huygens, *CCCM* 63, 63A, 2 vols., Turnout (1986); tr. E. A. Babcock and A. C. Krey, *A history of deeds done beyond the sea, by William, Archbishop of Tyre*, 2 vols., New York (1943)

Wilson, N. and Darrouzès, J., 'Restes du cartulaire de Hiéra-Xérochoraphion', *REB* 26 (1968), pp. 5–47

Yahya of Antioch, *History*, ed. and French tr. I. Kratchkovsky, A. Vasiliev *et al.*, *Histoire de Yahya-ibn-Saʿid d'Antioche*, 3 vols., *PO* 18, 23, 47, Paris and Turnhout (1924–97); Italian tr. B. Pirone, *Cronache dell' Egitto fatimide e dell' impero bizantino (937–1033)*, Milan (1998)

al-Yaʿqubi, *Kitab al-buldan* [of Ahmad ibn Abi Yaʿqub al-Yaʿqubi (d. *c.* 897)], ed. M. J. de Goeje, *BGA* 7, pp. 231–373

—, *Taʾrikh*, ed. M. T. Houtsma, *Ibn-Wadhih qui dicitur al-Jaʿqubi Historiae*, 2 vols., Leiden (1883)

Yaqut, *Muʿjam al-buldan*, ed. F. Wüstenfeld, *Jacut's Geographisches Wörterbuch* [of Yaqut ibn ʿAbd Allah al-Hamawi (d. 1229)], 6 vols., Leipzig (1866–73)

Yovhannes V, catholicos, *History*, ed. M. Emin, *Hovhannes Draskhanakertts'i, Patmut'iwn Hayots'*, Moscow (1853; repr. Tiflis, 1912; repr. Delmar, NY, 1980); tr. K. Maksoudian, *Yovhannes Drasxanakertc'i, History of Armenia*, Atlanta, GA

(1987); French tr. P. Boisson-Chenorhokian, *Histoire d'Arménie*, CSCO 605, Louvain (2004)

Zaccaria de Fredo, notaio in Candia, 1352–1357, ed. A. Lombardo, Venice (1968)

Zacharias, pope, *Versio graeca Gregorii Dialogorum, PL* 77, cols. 147–430

Zacharias of Mytilene, *Ammonius (De mundi opificio contra philosophos disputatio)*, ed. and Italian tr. M. M. Colonna, *Ammonio*, Naples (1973)

—, *Chronicle*, ed. and Latin tr. E. W. Brooks, *Historia ecclesiastica*, CSCO 83–4, 87–8, 4 vols., Paris (1919–24); tr. F. J. Hamilton and E. W. Brooks, *The Syriac chronicle known as that of Zachariah of Mitylene*, London (1899; repr. New York, 1979)

—, *Life of Severus*, in ed. and French tr. M.-A. Kugener, *Sévère, Patriarche d'Antioche, 512–518: textes syriaques, PO* 2.1 (1907), pp. 7–115

—, *Lives of Isaiah and Peter the Iberian (fragment)*, in ed. E. W. Brooks, *Vitae virorum apud monophysitas celeberrimorum*, CSCO 7–8, 2 vols., Paris (1907), I, pp. 1–12 (tr.); II, pp. 1–18 (text)

Zacos, ed. J.-C. Cheynet, *Sceaux de la collection Zacos (Bibliothèque Nationale de France) se rapportant aux provinces orientales de l'empire byzantin*, Paris (2001)

Zacos, G. *et al.*, *Byzantine lead seals*, 2 vols., Basle (1972–85)

Zahir al-Din Nishapuri (d. 1184/5 or 1187), *Saljuq'namah*, ed. I. Afshar, Tehran (1953); tr. K. A. Luther, *The history of the Seljuq Turks from The Jami' al-tawarikh: an Ilkhanid adaptation of the Saljuq-nama of Zahir al-Din Nishapuri*, ed. C. E. Bosworth, Richmond (2001); ed. A. H. Morton, *The Saljuqnama of Zahir al-Din Nishapuri: a critical text making use of the unique manuscript in the library of the Royal Asiatic Society*, Warminster (2004)

Zakonski spomenici srpskih država srednjeg veka, ed. S. Novaković, Belgrade (1912)

Zuhayr ibn Abi Sulma (d. *c.* 609), *Sharh Diwan*, Cairo (1944)

MANUSCRIPTS

Andrea Dandolo, 'Liber albus', Archivio di Stato, Venice

'Chronicle of Daniele Barbaro', Biblioteca Nazionale Marciana, Cod. Marc. Ital. classe VII, 126=7442, Venice

Gregory I, pope, 'Dialogues', Vat. gr. 1666, Vatican

Karadimov (Shopov) psalter, Sts Cyril and Methodius National Library, MSS. 454 and 1138, Sofia

Mahomet II, 'Grant of privileges to inhabitants of Galata 1453', British Library, MS. Gr. Eg. 2817, London

'Psalter of Basil II', Biblioteca Nazionale Marciana, Cod. gr. 17, Venice

Pseudo-Dionysius the Areopagite, Bibliothèque Nationale de France, MS. gr. 437, Paris

Ptolemy, 'Geography', Biblioteca Apostolica Vaticana, Codex Urbinas gr. 82, Vatican City; Seragliensis gr. 57, Topkapi Palace, Istanbul; Fabricius gr. 23, Königlichen Bibliothek, Copenhagen.

Ptolemy, 'Handy Tables', Biblioteca Apostolica Vaticana, MS. gr. 1291, Vatican City

'Tale of St Christomeus', Cod. Bresc. A III 3, fols. 142–5, Brescia
'Tale of St Christomeus', Cod. Hier. Sab. 373, fols. 117–29, Jerusalem
'Theodore Psalter of 1066', British Library, Additional MS. 19352, London
'Uspensky Gospels', Rossiiskaia Natsionalnaia Biblioteka, RNB gr. 219, St Peters-
 burg
al-Washsha', 'Kitab al-fadil', British Library, MS. Or. 6499, London

SECONDARY WORKS

GENERAL AND FREQUENTLY CITED WORKS

Ahrweiler, H. (1966), *Byzance et la mer: la marine de guerre, la politique et les institutions maritimes de Byzance aux VIIe–XVe siècles*, Paris
—(1971), *Études sur les structures administratives et sociales de Byzance*, London
Ahrweiler, H. and Laiou, A. E. (eds.) (1998), *Studies on the internal diaspora of the Byzantine empire*, Washington, DC
Angold, M. (1995), *Church and society in Byzantium under the Comneni, 1081–1261*, Cambridge
—(1997), *The Byzantine empire, 1025–1204: a political history*, 2nd edn., London
Balard, M. *et al.* (eds.) (2005), *Byzance et le monde extérieur: contacts, relations, échanges (Actes de trois séances du XXe Congrès international des études byzantines, Paris, 19–25 août 2001)*, BSo 21, Paris
Barker, J. W. (1969), *Manuel II Palaeologus, 1391–1425: a study in late Byzantine statesmanship*, New Brunswick, NJ
Baun, J. (2007), *Tales from another Byzantium: celestial journey and local community in the medieval Greek Apocrypha*, Cambridge
Beck, H.-G. (1959), *Kirche und theologische Literatur im Byzantinischen Reich*, Munich
—(1971), *Geschichte der byzantinischen Volksliteratur*, Munich
—(1978), *Das byzantinische Jahrtausend*, Munich
Beckwith, J. (1979), *Early Christian and Byzantine art*, 2nd edn., Harmondsworth
Brand, C. M. (1968), *Byzantium confronts the west, 1180–1204*, Cambridge, MA (repr. Aldershot, 1992)
Brandes, W. (2002a), *Finanzverwaltung in Krisenzeiten: Untersuchungen zur byzantinischen Administration im 6.–9. Jahrhundert*, Frankfurt-am-Main
Brown, P. (1971), *The world of late antiquity: AD 150–750*, London
—(1982), *Society and the holy in late antiquity*, London
Brown, T. S. (1984), *Gentlemen and officers: imperial administration and aristocratic power in Byzantine Italy, 554–800*, London
Browning, R. (1983), *Medieval and modern Greek*, 2nd edn., Cambridge
—(1992), *The Byzantine empire*, 2nd edn., Washington, DC
Brubaker, L. (1999a), *Vision and meaning in ninth-century Byzantium: image as exegesis in the homilies of Gregory of Nazianzus*, Cambridge
—(ed.) (1998), *Byzantium in the ninth century: dead or alive?*, Aldershot
Brubaker, L. and Haldon, J. (2001), *Byzantium in the iconoclast era (c. 680–850): the sources. An annotated survey*, Aldershot
Cameron, Averil (1985), *Procopius and the sixth century*, London

—(2006b), *The Byzantines*, Oxford

Cavallo, G. (ed.) (1997), *The Byzantines*, tr. T. Dunlap *et al.*, Chicago

Cavallo, G. *et al.* (eds.) (1991), *Scritture, libri e testi nelle aree provinciali di Bisanzio: atti del seminario di Erice, 18–25 settembre 1988*, 2 vols., Spoleto

Charanis, P. (1961), 'The Armenians in the Byzantine empire', *BSl* 22, pp. 196–240; rev. edn. repr. Lisbon (1963); repr. in Charanis (1972a), no. 5

Cheynet, J.-C. (1990), *Pouvoir et contestations à Byzance (963–1210)*, BSo 9, Paris

—(2006), *The Byzantine aristocracy and its military function*, Aldershot

Connor, C. L. (2004), *Women of Byzantium*, New Haven and London

Constantelos, D. (1991), *Byzantine philanthropy and social welfare*, 2nd edn., New Rochelle, NY

Cormack, R. (1985), *Writing in gold: Byzantine society and its icons*, London

—(2000), *Byzantine art*, Oxford

Cross, F. L. and Livingstone, E. A. (eds.) (2005), *The Oxford dictionary of the Christian church*, 3rd edn., Oxford

Curta, F. (2006), *Southeastern Europe in the middle ages 500–1250*, Cambridge

Dagron, G. (1976), 'Minorités ethniques et religieuses dans l'orient byzantin à la fin du Xe et au XIe siècle: l'immigration syrienne', *TM* 6, pp. 177–216; repr. in Dagron (1984a), no. 10

—(1984a), *La Romanité chrétienne en orient*, London

—(2003), *Emperor and priest*, tr. J. Birrell, Cambridge; rev. and tr. of G. Dagron, *Empereur et prêtre: étude sur le césaropapisme byzantin*, Paris, 1996

Dagron, G. *et al.* (eds.) (1993), *Évêques, moines et empereurs (610–1054)*, HC 4, Paris

Dölger, F. (1953), *Byzanz und die europäische Staatenwelt*, Ettal (repr. Darmstadt, 1976)

Ducellier, A. (1981b), *La Façade maritime de l'Albanie au moyen âge: Durazzo et Valona du XIe au XVe siècle*, Thessalonica

Dujčev, I. (1965–96), *Medioevo bizantino-slavo*, 4 vols. in 5 pts., Rome (I–III), Sofia (IV)

Easterling, P. and Handley, C. (eds.) (2001), *Greek scripts: an illustrated introduction*, London

Esler, P. F. (ed.) (2000), *The early Christian world*, 2 vols., London

Falkenhausen, V. von (1967), *Untersuchungen über die byzantinische Herrschaft in Süditalien vom 9. bis ins 11. Jahrhundert*, Wiesbaden

—(1978), *La dominazione bizantina nell'Italia meridionale dal IX all'XI secolo*, Bari (Italian tr. of von Falkenhausen (1967))

Farmakides, A. (1983), *A manual of modern Greek*, I: *For university students elementary to intermediate*, New Haven and London

Fine, J. V. A. (1983), *The early medieval Balkans: a critical survey from the sixth to the late twelfth century*, Ann Arbor, MI

—(1987), *The late medieval Balkans*, Ann Arbor, MI

Foss, C. (1975), 'The Persians in Asia Minor and the end of antiquity', *EHR* 90, pp. 721–47; repr. in Foss (1990a), no. 1; repr. in Bonner (ed.) (2004), no. 1, pp. 3–29

—(1976), *Byzantine and Turkish Sardis*, Cambridge, MA

—(1977a), 'Archaeology and the "twenty cities" of Byzantine Asia', *AJA* 81, pp. 469–86; repr. in Foss (1990a), no. 2

—(1977b), 'Late antique and Byzantine Ankara', *DOP* 31, pp. 29–87; repr. in Foss (1990a), no. 6

—(1979a), *Ephesus after antiquity: a late antique, Byzantine and Turkish city*, Cambridge

Garland, L. (ed.) (2006), *Byzantine women: varieties of experience, 800–1200*, Aldershot

Gay, J. (1904), *L'Italie méridionale et l'empire byzantin depuis l'avènement de Basile Ier jusqu'à la prise de Bari par les Normands (867–1071)*, Paris

Geanakoplos, D. J. (1959), *Emperor Michael Palaeologus and the west, 1258–1282: a study in Byzantine–Latin relations*, Cambridge, MA

Gregory, T. E. (2005), *A history of Byzantium*, Malden, MA

Hackel, S. (ed.) (1981), *The Byzantine saint: papers given at the fourteenth spring symposium of Byzantine studies, Birmingham, 1980*, London

Haldon, J. (1993), 'Military service, military lands and the status of soldiers: current problems and interpretations', *DOP* 47, pp. 1–67; repr. in Haldon (1995a), no. 7

—(1997a), *Byzantium in the seventh century: the transformation of a culture*, 2nd edn., Cambridge

—(1999a), *Warfare, state and society in the Byzantine world, 565–1204*, London

—(2005b), *Byzantium: a history*, Stroud

—(2005c), *The Palgrave atlas of Byzantine history*, Basingstoke

Harris, J. (ed.) (2005), *Palgrave advances in Byzantine history*, Basingstoke

Harvey, A. (1989), *Economic expansion in the Byzantine empire, 900–1200*, Cambridge

Hendy, M. F. (1985), *Studies in the Byzantine monetary economy, c. 300–1450*, Cambridge

Herrin, J. (1987), *The formation of Christendom*, Oxford

—(2001), *Women in purple: rulers of medieval Byzantium*, London

—(2007), *Byzantium: the surprising life of a medieval empire*, London

Hewsen, R. H. (2001), *Armenia: a historical atlas*, Chicago

Holmes, C. (2005), *Basil II and the governance of empire (976–1025)*, Oxford

Holton, D. *et al.* (2004), *Greek: an essential grammar of the modern language*, London

Horden, P. and Purcell, N. (2000), *The corrupting sea: a study of Mediterranean history*, Oxford

Hornblower, S. and Spawforth, A. (eds.) (2003), *The Oxford classical dictionary*, 3rd edn., Oxford

Horrocks, G. (1997), *Greek: a history of the language and its speakers*, London

Howard-Johnston, J. D. (ed.) (1988), *Byzantium and the west, c. 850–c. 1200: proceedings of the eighteenth spring symposium of Byzantine studies, Oxford, 30 March–1 April 1984* [= *BF* 13], Amsterdam

Hunger, H. (1978), *Die hochsprachliche profane Literatur der Byzantiner*, 2 vols., Munich

Hussey, J. M. (1986), *The orthodox church in the Byzantine empire*, Oxford

—(ed.) (1966–7), *The Cambridge medieval history*, IV: *The Byzantine empire*, 2 vols., Cambridge

Jacoby, D. (1997b), *Trade, commodities and shipping in the medieval Mediterranean*, Aldershot

James, L. (ed.) (forthcoming), *Blackwell companion to the Byzantine world*, Oxford

Jeffreys, E. (ed.) (2003), *Rhetoric in Byzantium: papers from the thirty-fifth spring symposium of Byzantine studies, Exeter College, University of Oxford, March 2001*, Aldershot

—(ed.) (2006), *Byzantine style, religion and civilization: in honour of Sir Steven Runciman*, Cambridge

Jeffreys, E. *et al.* (eds.) (2008, forthcoming), *The Oxford handbook of Byzantine studies*, Oxford

Kaegi, W. E. (1992), *Byzantium and the early Islamic conquests*, Cambridge

—(2003a), *Heraclius, emperor of Byzantium*, Cambridge

Kaplan, M. (1992), *Les Hommes et la terre à Byzance du VIe au XIe siècle: propriété et exploitation du sol, BSo* 10, Paris

Kazhdan, A. P. and Ronchey, S. (1999), *L'aristocrazia bizantina: dal principio dell'XI alla fine del XII secolo*, 2nd edn., Palermo

Kazhdan, A. P. *et al.* (eds.) (1991), *Oxford dictionary of Byzantium*, 3 vols., Oxford

Kennedy, H. (ed.) (2002), *An historical atlas of Islam*, 2nd edn., Leiden

Krautheimer, R. and Ćurčič, S. (1986), *Early Christian and Byzantine architecture*, 4th edn., Harmondsworth

Kravari, V. *et al.* (eds.) (1989–91), *Hommes et richesses dans l'empire byzantin*, 2 vols., I: *IVe–VIIe siècle*, II: *VIIIe–XVe siècle*, Paris

Kreutz, B. M. (1991), *Before the Normans: southern Italy in the ninth and tenth centuries*, Philadelphia

Krueger, D. (ed.) (2006), *A people's history of Christianity*, III: *Byzantine Christianity*, Minneapolis

Krumbacher, K. (1897), *Geschichte der byzantinischen Literatur von Justinian bis zum Ende des oströmischen Reiches (527–1453)*, 2nd edn., Munich

Kühn, H.-J. (1991), *Die byzantinische Armee im 10. und 11. Jahrhundert: Studien zur Organisation der Tagmata*, Vienna

Laiou, A. E. *et al.* (eds.) (2002), *The economic history of Byzantium: from the seventh through the fifteenth century*, 3 vols., Washington, DC

Laiou, A. E. and Morrisson, C. (2007), *The Byzantine economy*, Cambridge

Laiou, A. E. and Simon, D. (eds.) (1994), *Law and society in Byzantium: ninth-twelfth centuries*, Washington, DC

Lemerle, P. (1986), *Byzantine humanism: the first phase*, tr. H. Lindsay and A. Moffatt, *ByzAust* 3, Canberra; tr. of Lemerle, P. (1971), *Le Premier Humanisme byzantin*, Paris

—(1979), *The agrarian history of Byzantium from the origins to the twelfth century: the sources and problems*, tr. G. Mac Niocaill, Galway

Lightfoot, C. S. (1998), 'The survival of cities in Byzantine Anatolia: the case of Amorium', *Byz* 68, pp. 56–71

Lilie, R.-J. (1976), *Die byzantinische Reaktion auf die Ausbreitung der Araber: Studien zur Strukturwandlung des byzantinischen Staates im 7. und 8. Jahrhundert*, *MBM* 22, Munich

—(1984b), *Handel und Politik zwischen dem byzantinischen Reich und den italienischen Kommunen Venedig, Pisa und Genua in der Epoche der Komnenen und der Angeloi, 1081–1204*, Amsterdam

—(1993a), *Byzantium and the Crusader States, 1096–1204*, tr. J. C. Morris and J. E. Ridings, Oxford

Lilie, R.-J. *et al.* (eds.) (1998–2002), *Prosopographie der mittelbyzantinischen Zeit, Prolegomena* and 6 vols., Berlin and New York

Lock, P. (1995), *The Franks in the Aegean, 1204–1500*, London

Lowden, J. (1997), *Early Christian and Byzantine art*, London

McCormick, M. (1990), *Eternal victory: triumphal rulership in late antiquity, Byzantium, and the early medieval west*, 2nd edn., Cambridge

—(2001), *Origins of the European economy: communications and commerce AD 300–900*, Cambridge

McGeer, E. (1995), *Sowing the dragon's teeth: Byzantine warfare in the tenth century*, DOSt 33, Washington, DC

Magdalino, P. (1993a), *The empire of Manuel I Komnenos 1143–1180*, Cambridge

—(1996a), *Constantinople médiévale: études sur l'évolution des structures urbaines*, Paris; English tr. 'Medieval Constantinople', in Magdalino (2007b), no. 1

—(ed.) (1994), *New Constantines: the rhythm of imperial renewal in Byzantium, 4th–13th centuries. Papers from the twenty-sixth spring symposium of Byzantine studies, March 1992*, Aldershot

—(ed.) (2003), *Byzantium in the year 1000*, Leiden

Maguire, E. and Maguire, H. (2007), *Other icons: art and power in Byzantine secular culture*, Princeton

Maguire, H. (1981), *Art and eloquence in Byzantium*, Princeton

—(ed.) (1997), *Byzantine court culture from 829 to 1204*, Washington, DC

Malamut, E. (1988), *Les Îles de l'empire byzantin VIIIe–XIIe siècles*, BSo 8, 2 vols., Paris

Mango, C. (1979), *Byzantine architecture*, London

—(1980), *Byzantium: the empire of New Rome*, London

—(1990), *Le Développement urbain de Constantinople (IVe–VIIe siècles)*, 2nd edn., Paris

—(1991), 'Greek culture in Palestine after the Arab conquest', in Cavallo *et al.* (eds.) (1991), I, pp. 149–60

—(ed.) (2002), *The Oxford history of Byzantium*, Oxford

Martin, J.-M. (1993), *La Pouille du VIe au XIIe siècle*, Rome

Mathews, T. F. (1998), *The art of Byzantium: between antiquity and the Renaissance*, London

Miller, T. S. (2003), *The orphans of Byzantium: child welfare in the Christian empire*, Washington, DC

Morris, R. (1995), *Monks and laymen in Byzantium, 843–1118*, Cambridge

—(ed.) (1990), *Church and people in Byzantium: twentieth spring symposium of Byzantine studies, Manchester, 1986*, Birmingham

Morrisson, C. *et al.* (eds.) (2004), *Le Monde byzantin*, I: *L'Empire romain d'orient (330–641)*, Paris

Mullett, M. (1997), *Theophylact of Ohrid: reading the letters of a Byzantine archbishop*, Aldershot

Nicol, D. M. (1979), *Church and society in the last centuries of Byzantium*, Cambridge

—(1988), *Byzantium and Venice: a study in diplomatic and cultural relations*, Cambridge

—(1993), *The last centuries of Byzantium 1261–1479*, 2nd edn., Cambridge

Obolensky, D. (1971), *The Byzantine commonwealth: Eastern Europe 500–1453*, London

—(1988a), *Six Byzantine portraits*, Oxford

Oikonomides, N. (1976b), *Documents et études sur les institutions de Byzance, 7ᵉ–15ᵉ s.*, London

—(1992a), *Byzantium from the ninth century to the Fourth Crusade*, Aldershot

—(1997a), 'Title and income at the Byzantine court', in Maguire (ed.) (1997), pp. 199–215; repr. in Oikonomides (2004), no. 17

—(2002), 'The role of the Byzantine state in the economy', in *EHB*, III, pp. 973–1058

Ostrogorsky, G. (1968), *A history of the Byzantine state*, tr. J. Hussey, 2nd edn., Oxford

Ousterhout, R. (1998), 'Reconstructing ninth-century Constantinople', in Brubaker (ed.) (1998), pp. 115–30

—(1999), *Master builders of Byzantium*, Princeton

Pratsch, T. (2005a), *Der hagiographische Topos: griechische Heiligenviten in mittelbyzantinischer Zeit*, Berlin and New York

Rapp, S. H. and Awde, N. (eds.) (forthcoming), *Historical atlas of Georgia*, London; tr. of Muskhelishvili, D. *et al.* (eds.) (2003), *Sakartvelos istoriis atlasi (Historical atlas of Georgia)*, Tbilisi

Riley-Smith, J. (ed.) (1991), *The atlas of the Crusades*, London

Ringrose, K. M. (2003), *The perfect servant: eunuchs and the social construction of gender in Byzantium*, Chicago

Rodley, L. (1994), *Byzantine art and architecture: an introduction*, Cambridge

Rosenqvist, J. O. (2007), *Die byzantinische Literatur. Vom 6. Jahrhundert bis zum Fall Konstantinopels 1453*, Berlin and New York

Runciman, S. (1965), *The fall of Constantinople: 1453*, Cambridge

—(1977), *The Byzantine theocracy*, Cambridge

Ševčenko, I. (1988–9), 'Religious missions seen from Byzantium', *HUS* 12–13, pp. 7–27

—(1992a), 'Re-reading Constantine Porphyrogenitus' in Shepard and Franklin (eds.) (1992), pp. 167–95

Shepard, J. and Franklin, S. (eds.) (1992), *Byzantine diplomacy*, Aldershot

Stephenson, P. (2000), *Byzantium's Balkan frontier: a political study of the northern Balkans, 900–1204*, Cambridge

Talbert, R. J. A. *et al.* (eds.) (2000), *The Barrington atlas of the Greek and Roman world*, Princeton

Talbot, A.-M. (2001), *Women and religious life in Byzantium*, Aldershot

Talbot Rice, D. (1968), *Byzantine art*, 2nd edn., Harmondsworth

Treadgold, W. (1988), *The Byzantine revival, 780–842*, Stanford

—(1997), *A history of the Byzantine state and society*, Stanford

—(2001), *A concise history of Byzantium*, Basingstoke

Treitinger, O. (1956), *Die oströmische Kaiser- und Reichsidee nach ihrer Gestaltung im höfischen Zeremoniell: vom oströmischen Staats- und Reichsgedanken*, Darmstadt

Tsiknakis, K. G. (ed.) (1997), *To empolemo Byzantio, 9os–12os ai. (Byzantium at War, 9th–12th centuries)*, Athens

Vasiliev, A. A. (1935–68), *Byzance et les Arabes*, 2 vols., I: *La Dynastie d'Amorium (820–867)*, II.1: *La Dynastie macédonienne (867– 959)*, ed. and French tr. H. Grégoire and M. Canard, Brussels

Venning, T. (ed.) (2005), *A chronology of the Byzantine empire*, Basingstoke

Whitby, Michael (1988), *The emperor Maurice and his historian: Theophylact Simocatta on Persian and Balkan warfare*, Oxford

Whittow, M. (1996a), *The making of orthodox Byzantium, 600–1025*, London

Wickham, C. (2005), *Framing the early middle ages: Europe and the Mediterranean 400–800*, Oxford

Wilson, N. G. (1996), *Scholars of Byzantium*, 2nd edn., London

SECONDARY WORKS, PART I (c. 500–c. 700)

Abadie-Reynal, C. (ed.) (2003), *Les Céramiques en Anatolie aux époques hellénistique et romaine: actes de la table ronde d'Istanbul, 23–24 mai 1996*, Paris

'Abd al-Ghani, 'A. (1993), *Ta'rikh al-Hirah fi al-Jahiliya wa-al-Islam*, Damascus

Abdalla, A. M. *et al.* (eds.) (1979–84), *Studies in the history of Arabia*, 2 vols., Riyadh

Abel, F.-M. (1938), 'L'Île de Jotabe', *Revue Biblique* 47: 510–38

Abu Wandi, R. *et al.* (1996), *'Isa wa-Maryam fi l'Qur'an wa-al-tafasir*, Amman

Adams, J. N. *et al.* (eds.) (2002), *Bilingualism in ancient society: language contact and the written text*, Oxford

Adontz, N. (1934), 'Les Légendes de Maurice et de Constantin V, empereurs de Byzance', *Mélanges Bidez (Annuaire de l'Institut de Philologie et d'Histoire Orientales et Slaves* 2), pp. 1–12

—(1970), *Armenia in the period of Justinian: the political conditions based on the Naxarar system*, tr. and rev. N. G. Garsoïan, Lisbon

al-Afghani, S. (1960), *Aswaq al-'Arab fi al-Jahiliyah wa-al-Islam*, Damascus

Ahlwardt, W. (1872), *Bemerkungen über die Ächteit der alten arabischen Gedichte*, Greifswald

Ahrens, K. (1930), 'Christliches im Qoran', *ZDMG* 84, pp. 15–68, 148–90

Albert, M. *et al.* (eds.) (1993), *Christianismes orientaux*, Paris

Alexander, P. J. (1985), *The Byzantine apocalyptic tradition*, Berkeley

Allen, P. (1979), 'The "Justinianic" plague', *Byz* 49, pp. 5–20

—(2000), 'The definition and enforcement of orthodoxy', in *CAH*, XIV, pp. 811–34

Allen, P. and Jeffreys, E. (eds.) (1996), *The sixth century: end or beginning?*, *ByzAust* 10, Brisbane

Alston, R. (2001), 'The population of late Roman Egypt and the end of the ancient world', in Scheidel (ed.) (2001), pp. 161–204

—(2002), 'Managing the frontiers: supplying the frontier troops in the sixth and seventh centuries', in Erdkamp (ed.) (2002), pp. 398–419

Altheim, F. and Stiehl, R. (1954), *Ein asiatischer Staat: Feudalismus unter den Sasaniden und ihren Nachbarn*, Wiesbaden

Altheim, F. and Stiehl, R. (1957), *Finanzgeschichte der Spätantike*, Frankfurt-am-Main

Altheim, F. and Stiehl, R. (1971–3), *Christentum am Roten Meer*, 2 vols., Berlin and New York

Amory, P. (1997), *People and identity in Ostrogothic Italy, 489–554*, Cambridge

Andreescu-Treadgold, I. and Treadgold, W. (1997), 'Procopius and the imperial panels of S. Vitale', *The Art Bulletin* 79, pp. 708–23

Angold, M. (2001), *Byzantium: the bridge from antiquity to the middle ages*, London

Arafat, W. (1958), 'Early critics of the authenticity of the poetry of the *Sira*'', *BSOAS* 21, pp. 453–63

—(1965), 'An aspect of the forger's art in early Islamic poetry', *BSOAS* 28, pp. 477–82

—(1968), 'Fact and fiction in the history of pre-Islamic idol-worship', *IQ* 12, pp. 9–21

Arjava, A. (1996), *Women and law in late antiquity*, Oxford

al-Askar, A. (2002), *Al-Yamama in the early Islamic era*, Reading

Azpeitia, J. (2005), 'Deir Sim'ân, monastère nord-ouest: présentation de l'église (avec un appendice épigraphique par Alain Desreumaux)', *TM* 15, pp. 37–65

Back, M. (1978), *Die sassanidischen Staatsinschriften*, Leiden

Badawi, 'A. R. (ed.) (1962), *Mélanges Taha Husain*, Cairo

Baddeley, O. and Brunner, E. (1996), *The Monastery of Saint Catherine*, London

Bagnall, R. (1993), *Egypt in late antiquity*, Princeton

—(ed.) (2007), *Egypt in the Byzantine world, 300–700*, Cambridge

Baillie, M. (1999), *Exodus to Arthur: catastrophic encounters with comets*, London

Baird, D. (2000), 'Konya Plain survey', *Anatolian archaeology* 6, p. 15

—(2004), 'Settlement expansion on the Konya Plain, Anatolia: 5th–7th centuries AD', in Bowden *et al.* (eds.) (2004), pp. 217–46

Baker, D. (ed.) (1976), *The orthodox churches and the west, SCH* 13, Oxford

Bakhit, M. A. (ed.) (1987), *Proceedings of the second symposium on the history of Bilad al-Sham during the early Islamic period up to 40 AH/640 AD*, 3 vols., Amman

Baldwin, B. (1978), 'Menander Protector', *DOP* 32, pp. 99–125

Bálint, C. (2000), 'Byzantinisches zur Herkunftsfrage des vielteiligen Gürtels', in Bálint (ed.) (2000), pp. 99–162

—(ed.) (2000), *Kontakte zwischen Iran, Byzanz und der Steppe im 6.–7. Jahrhundert*, Budapest and Naples

Balty, J. (1989), 'Mosaïques antiques de Syrie et de Jordanie', in Piccirillo (ed.) (1989), pp. 149–60

Banaji, J. (2001), *Agrarian change in late antiquity: gold, labour and aristocratic dominance*, Oxford

Barbero, A. and Loring, M. I. (2005), 'The formation of the Sueve and Visigothic kingdoms in Spain', in *NCMH*, I, pp. 162–92

Bardill, J. (2004), *Brickstamps of Constantinople*, 2 vols., Oxford

Barford, P. M. (2001), *The early Slavs: culture and society in early medieval eastern Europe*, London

Barnwell, P. S. (1992), *Emperor, prefects and kings: the Roman west, 395–565*, London

Bashear, S. (1984), *Muqaddima fi l-ta'rikh al-akhar*, Jerusalem

—(1997), *Arabs and others in early Islam*, Princeton

Baynes, N. H. (1910), 'Rome and Armenia in the fourth century', *EHR* 25, pp. 625–43; repr. in Baynes (1955), pp. 186–208

—(1949), 'The supernatural defenders of Constantinople', *AB* 67, pp. 165–77; repr. in Baynes (1955), pp. 248–60

—(1955), *Byzantine studies and other essays*, London

Beaucamp, J. *et al.* (2004), *Recherches sur la Chronique de Jean Malalas*, Paris

Bekkum, W. J. van (2002), 'Jewish messianic expectations in the age of Heraclius', in Reinink and Stolte (eds.) (2002), pp. 95–112

Bellamy, J. A. (1985), 'A new reading of the Namarah inscription', *JAOS* 105, pp. 31–51

Berbérian, H. (1964), 'Autobiographie d'Anania Sirakec'i', *REA* n.s. 1, pp. 189–94

Birkeland, H. (1956), *The Lord guideth: studies on primitive Islam*, Oslo

Blachère, R. (1952–66), *Histoire de la littérature arabe des origines à la fin du XVe siècle de J-C*, 3 vols., Paris

—(1956), 'Regards sur l'"acculturation" des arabo-musulmans jusque vers 40/661', *Arabica* 3, pp. 247–65

Blockley, R. C. (1992), *East Roman foreign policy*, Leeds

Böhlig, A. (1980), *Die Gnosis,* III: *Der Manichäismus*, Zurich and Munich

Bonifay, M. *et al.* (eds.) (1998), *Fouilles à Marseille: les mobiliers (Ier–VIIe siècles ap. J. C.)*, Paris

Bonner, M. (ed.) (2004), *Arab–Byzantine relations in early Islamic times*, Aldershot

Bosworth, C. E. (1983), 'Iran and the Arabs before Islam', in Yarshater (ed.) (1983), I, pp. 593–612

Boudignon, C. (2004), 'Maxime le Confesseur était-il Constantinopolitain?', in Janssens *et al.* (eds.) (2004), pp. 11–44

Bousquet, G. H. (1954), 'Une explication marxiste de l'Islam par un ecclésiastique épiscopalien', *Hespéris* 41, pp. 231–47

Bowden, W. *et al.* (eds.) (2004), *Recent research on the late antique countryside*, Leiden

Bowersock, G. W. (1983), *Roman Arabia*, Cambridge, MA

—(2004), 'Riflessioni sulla periodizzazione dopo "esplosione di tardoantico" di Andrea Giardina', *Studi storici* 45, pp. 7–13

Bowersock, G. W. *et al.* (eds.) (1999), *Late antiquity: a guide to the postclassical world*, Cambridge, MA

Bowman, J. (1967), 'The debt of Islam to monophysite Syrian Christianity', in MacLaurin (ed.) (1967), pp. 201–40

Boyce, M. (1957), 'Some reflections about Zurvanism', *BSOAS* 19.2, pp. 304–16

—(1979), *Zoroastrians, their religious beliefs and practices*, London

—(1983) 'Parthian writings and literature', in Yarshater (ed.) (1983), II, pp. 1151–65

—(1990), 'Some further reflections on Zurvanism', *Iranica varia: papers in honor of Professor Ehsan Yarshater*, Leiden, pp. 20–9

Boyd, S. and Mundell Mango, M. (eds.) (1992), *Ecclesiastical silver plate in sixth-century Byzantium: papers of the symposium held May 16–18, 1986, at the Walters Art Gallery, Baltimore, and Dumbarton Oaks, Washington, DC*, Washington, DC

Braund, D. (1994), *Georgia in antiquity: a history of Colchis and Transcaucasian Iberia, 550 BC – AD 562*, Oxford

Brock, S. (1980), 'The Orthodox–Oriental Orthodox conversations of 532', *Apostolos Varnavas* 41, pp. 219–27; repr. in Brock (1984), no. 11

—(1982), 'Christians in the Sasanid empire: a case of divided loyalties', in Mews (ed.) (1982), pp. 1–19

—(1984), *Syriac perspectives on late antiquity*, London

—(1994), 'The church of the east in the Sasanian empire up to the sixth century and its absence from the councils in the Roman empire', in *Syriac dialogue: non-official consultation on dialogue within the Syriac tradition* 1, Vienna (1994), pp. 69–86

—(1999), *From Ephrem to Romanos: interactions between Syriac and Greek in late antiquity*, Aldershot

—(ed.) (2001), *The hidden pearl: the Syrian Orthodox Church and its ancient Aramaic heritage*, 4 vols., Rome

Brown, P. (1976), 'Eastern and western Christendom in late antiquity: a parting of the ways', in Baker (ed.) (1976), pp. 1–24; repr. in Brown (1982), pp. 166–95

—(1988), *The body and society: men, women and sexual renunciation in early Christianity*, New York

—(1992), *Power and persuasion in late antiquity: towards a Christian empire*, Madison, WI

—(1998), 'Christianisation and religious conflict', in *CAH*, XIII, pp. 632–64

—(2000), 'Holy men', in *CAH*, XIV, pp. 781–810

—(2003), *The rise of western Christendom: triumph and diversity, AD 200–1000*, 2nd edn., Oxford

Browne, E. G. (1900), 'Some account of the Arabic work entitled *Nihayatu'l-irab fi akhbari'l-Furs wa'l-'Arab*, particularly of that part which treats of the Persian kings', *JRAS* n.s. 32, pp. 195–259

Browning, R. (1987), *Justinian and Theodora*, 2nd edn., London

Brubaker, L. (1997b), 'Memories of Helena: patterns in imperial female matronage in the fourth and fifth centuries', in James (ed.) (1997), pp. 52–75

—(2004c), 'Sex, lies and textuality: the *Secret history* of Procopius and the rhetoric of gender in sixth-century Byzantium', in Brubaker and Smith (eds.) (2004), pp. 83–101

—(2005), 'The age of Justinian: gender and society', in Maas (ed.) (2005), pp. 427–47

Brubaker, L. and Smith, J. M. H. (eds.) (2004), *Gender in the early medieval world: east and west, 300–900*, Cambridge

Brunschvig, R. (1976a), 'Coup d'oeil sur l'histoire des foires à travers l'Islam', in Brunschvig (1976b), I, pp. 113–44

—(1976b), *Études d'islamologie*, 2 vols., Paris

Burns, T. S. and Eadie, J. W. (eds.) (2001), *Urban centers and rural contexts in late antiquity*, East Lansing, MI

Bury, J. B. (1923), *History of the later Roman empire from the death of Theodosius I to the death of Justinian, AD 395 to AD 565*, 2 vols., London

Butzer, K. W. (1957), 'Der Umweltfaktor in der grossen arabischen Expansion', *Saeculum* 8, pp. 359–71

Cameron, Alan (1969), 'The last days of the Academy at Athens', *Proceedings of the Cambridge Philological Society*, 195, n.s. 15, pp. 7–30; repr. in Cameron, Alan (1985), no. 13

—(1976), *Circus factions: Blues and Greens at Rome and Byzantium*, Oxford

—(1985), *Literature and society in the early Byzantine world*, London

Cameron, Averil (1969–70), 'Agathias on the Sassanians', *DOP* 23–24, pp. 67–183

—(1975), 'The empress Sophia', *Byz* 45, pp. 5–21; repr. in Cameron, Averil (1981), no. 11

—(1976), 'The early religious policies of Justin II', in Baker (ed.) (1976), pp. 51–67; repr. in Cameron, Averil (1981), no. 10

—(1978), 'The Theotokos in sixth-century Constantinople', *Journal of theological studies* 29, pp. 79–108; repr. in Cameron, Averil (1981), no. 16

—(1979a), 'Images of authority: elites and icons in late sixth-century Byzantium', *PaP* 84, pp. 3–35; repr. in Cameron, Averil (1981), no. 18

—(1979b), 'The Virgin's robe: an episode in the history of early seventh-century Constantinople', *Byz* 49, pp. 42–56; repr. in Cameron, Averil (1981), no. 17

—(1981), *Continuity and change in sixth century Byzantium*, London

—(1991a), 'The eastern provinces in the seventh century AD: Hellenism and the emergence of Islam', in Said (ed.) (1991), pp. 287–313; repr. in Cameron, Averil (1996b), no. 4

—(1991b), *Christianity and the rhetoric of empire: the development of Christian discourse*, Berkeley

—(1992a), 'Byzantium and the past in the seventh century: the search for redefinition', in Fontaine and Hillgarth (eds.) (1992), pp. 250–76; repr. in Cameron, Averil (1996b), no. 5

—(1992b), 'New themes and styles in Greek literature: seventh–eighth centuries', in *BEINE*, I, pp. 81–105

—(1992c), 'The language of images: the rise of icons and Christian representation', in Wood (ed.) (1992b), pp. 1–42

—(1993), *The Mediterranean world in late antiquity AD 395–600*, London

—(1996a), 'Byzantines and Jews: some recent work on early Byzantium', *BMGS* 20, pp. 249–74

—(1996b), *Changing cultures in early Byzantium*, Aldershot

—(2000), 'The early cult of the Virgin', in Vassilaki (ed.) (2000), pp. 3–15

—(2002a), 'Blaming the Jews: the seventh-century invasions of Palestine in context', *TM* 14, pp. 57–78

—(2002b), 'The "long" late antiquity: a late twentieth-century model', in Wiseman (ed.) (2002), pp. 165–91

— (2005), 'Introduction', in Vassilaki (ed.) (2005), pp. xvii–xxxii

—(2006a), 'Constantine and the "peace of the church"', in Mitchell and Young (eds.) (2006), pp. 538–51

—(ed.) (2003), *Fifty years of prosopography: the later Roman empire, Byzantium and beyond*, PBA 118, Oxford

Cameron, Averil and Kuhrt, A. (eds.) (1983), *Images of women in antiquity*, London

Caseau, B. *et al.* (eds.) (2006), *Pèlerinages et lieux saints dans l'antiquité et le moyen âge*, Paris

Casiday, A. and Norris, F. W. (eds.) (2007), *The Cambridge history of Christianity*, II: *Constantine to c. 600*, Cambridge

Caskel, W. (1927–30), 'Die einheimischen Quellen zur Geschichte Nord-Arabiens vor dem Islam', *Islamica* 3, pp. 331–41

—(1930), 'Aijam al-'Arab. Studien zur altarabischen Epik', *Islamica* 3.5 *Supplement*, pp. 1–99

—(1953), *Die Bedeutung der Beduinen in der Geschichte der Araber*, Cologne

—(1962), 'Der arabische Stamm vor dem Islam und seine gesellschaftliche und juridische Organisation', *Dalla tribù allo stato: atti del convegno internazionale (Roma,13–16 aprile 1961)*, ANL PASC 54, Rome, pp. 139–49

—(1966), *Gamharat an-nasab: das genealogische Werk des Hišam ibn Muhammad al-Kalbi*, 2 vols., Leiden

Caton, S. C. (1990), 'Anthropological theories of tribe and state formation in the Middle East: ideology and the semiotics of power', in Khoury and Kostiner (eds.) (1990), pp. 74–108

Chadwick, H. (2001), *The church in ancient society: from Galilee to Gregory the Great*, Oxford

—(2006), *Studies on ancient Christianity*, Aldershot

Charles, H. (1936), *Le Christianisme des arabes nomades sur le limes et dans le désert syro-mésopotamien aux alentours de l'hégire*, Paris

Chaumont, M.-L. (1958), 'Le Culte d'Anahita à Staxr et les premiers Sassanides', *Revue de l'histoire des religions* 153, pp. 154–75

—(1960), 'Recherches sur le clergé zoroastrien: le herbad', *RHR* 158, pp. 54–80, 161–79

—(1976), 'L'Arménie entre Rome et l'Iran, I: de l'avènement d'Auguste à l'avènement de Dioclétien', *ANRW* II, 9.1, pp. 71–194

—(1988), *La Christianisation de l'empire iranien: des origines aux grandes persécutions du IVᵉ siècle*, CSCO 499, Louvain

Chavarría, A. and Lewit, T. (2004), 'Archaeological research on the late antique countryside: a bibliographic essay', in Bowden *et al.* (2004), pp. 3–51

Chazon, E. G. *et al.* (eds.) (2004), *Things revealed: studies in early Jewish and Christian literature in honor of Michael E. Stone*, Leiden

Chelhod, J. (1971), *Le Droit dans la société bedouine*, Paris

Christensen, A. (1925), *Le Règne du roi Kawadh I et le communisme Mazdakite*, Copenhagen

—(1944), *L'Iran sous les sassanides*, 2nd edn., Copenhagen

Christides, V. (1972), 'The names *Arabes, Sarakenoi,* etc and their false Byzantine etymologies', *BZ* 65, pp. 329–33

Chrysos, E. (1992), 'Byzantine diplomacy, AD 300–800: means and ends', in Shepard and Franklin (eds.) (1992), pp. 25–39

——(2003), 'Romans and foreigners', in Cameron, Averil (ed.) (2003), pp. 119–36

Chrysos, E. and Schwarcz, A. (eds.) (1989), *Das Reich und die Barbaren,* Vienna

Chrysostomides, J. (ed.) (1988), *Kathegetria: essays presented to Joan Hussey for her 80th birthday,* Camberley

Clover, F. M. (1993), *The late Roman west and the Vandals,* Aldershot

Clover, F. M. and Humphreys, R. S. (eds.) (1989), *Tradition and innovation in late antiquity,* Madison, WI

Conrad, L. I. (1981), 'The *Qusur* of medieval Islam: some implications for the social history of the Near East', *Al-Abhath* 29, pp. 7–23

——(1987a), 'Abraha and Muhammad: some observations apropos of chronology and literary topoi in the early Arabic historical tradition', *BSOAS* 50, pp. 225–40

——(1987b), 'Al-Azdi's History of the Arab conquests in Bilad al-Sham: some historiographical observations', in Bakhit (ed.) (1987), I, pp. 28–62

——(1992), 'The conquest of Arwad: a source-critical study in the historiography of the early medieval Near East', in *BEINE,* I, pp. 317–401

——(1994), 'Epidemic disease in central Syria in the late sixth century: some new insights from the verse of Hassan ibn Thabit', *BMGS* 18, pp. 12–58

——(1996a), 'The Arabs and the Colossus', *JRAS* 6, pp. 165–87

——(1996b), 'Die Pest und ihr soziales Umfeld im Nahen Osten des frühen Mittelalters', *Der Islam* 73, pp. 81–112

——(1998), 'Futuh', in Meisami and Starkey (eds.) (1998), I, pp. 237–40

——(2002), 'Heraclius in early Islamic *kerygma*', in Reinink and Stolte (eds.) (2002), pp. 113–56

——(forthcoming), *Muhammadanea Edessensis: the rise of Islam in eastern Christian historiography under the early 'Abbasids,* Princeton

——(in preparation), 'The early Arab urban foundations in Iraq and Egypt: implications for trade and exchange', in *BEINE,* V

Cook, M. (1983), *Muhammad,* Oxford

Cook, M. and Crone, P. (1977), *Hagarism: the making of the Islamic world,* Cambridge

Corsi, P. (1983), *La spedizione italiana di Costante II,* Bologna

Cosentino, S. (1996–2000), *Prosopografia dell'Italia bizantina (493–804),* I: *A-F*; II: *G-O,* 2 vols. to date, Bologna

Courtois, C. (1955), *Les Vandales et l'Afrique,* Paris

Croke, B. (1992), *Christian chronicles and Byzantine history, 5th–6th centuries,* Aldershot

Crone, P. (1980), *Slaves on horses: the evolution of the Islamic polity,* Cambridge

——(1986), 'The tribe and the state', in Hall (ed.) (1986), pp. 48–77

——(1987), *Meccan trade and the rise of Islam,* Princeton

——(1991), 'Kavad's heresy and Mazdak's revolt', *Iran* 29, pp. 21–42; repr. in Crone (2005), no. 1, pp. 1–50

——(1992), 'Serjeant and Meccan trade', *Arabica* 39, pp. 216–40

—(1993), 'Tribes and states in the Middle East', *JRAS* 3, pp. 353–75

—(1994), 'The first-century concept of *Higra*', *Arabica* 41, pp. 352–87

—(2005), *From Kavad to al-Ghazali: religion, law and political thought in the Near East, c. 600–c. 1100*, Aldershot

Crow, J. *et al.* (2001), 'The water supply of Constantinople: archaeology and hydrogeology of an early medieval city', *Environmental Geology* 40, pp. 1325–33

Crow, J. and Bayliss R. (2005), 'Water for the Queen of Cities: a review of recent research in the Byzantine and early Ottoman water supply of Constantinople', *Basilissa* 1, pp. 28–49

Cunningham, M. B. and Allen, P. (eds.) (1998), *Preacher and audience: studies in early Christian and Byzantine homiletics*, Leiden

Curta, F. (2001a), *The making of the Slavs: history and archaeology of the lower Danube region, c. 500–700*, Cambridge

—(2001b), 'Peasants as "makeshift soldiers for the occasion": sixth-century settlement patterns in the Balkans', in Burns and Eadie (eds.) (2001), pp. 119–217

—(2001c), 'The "Prague type": a critical approach to pottery classification', in Kountoura-Galake (ed.) (2001), pp. 171–88

—(2004), 'Barbarians in dark-age Greece: Slavs or Avars?', in Stepanov and Vachkova (eds.) (2004), pp. 513–50

—(2005a), 'Antes, people', in *International encyclopaedia for the middle ages-online: a supplement to LexMA-Online*, (http://www.brepolis.net/bme), Turnhout

—(2005b), 'Female dress and "Slavic" bow fibulae in Greece', *Hesperia* 74, pp. 101–46

—(2005c), 'Before Cyril and Methodius: Christianity and barbarians beyond the sixth- and seventh-century Danube frontier', in Curta (ed.) (2005), pp. 180–219

Curtis, J. (ed.) (2000), *Mesopotamia and Iran in the Parthian and Sasanian periods: rejection and revival c. 238 BC – AD 642*, London

Cutler, A. (2005), 'Silver across the Euphrates: forms of exchange between Sasanian Persia and the late Roman empire', *MSABK* 4, pp. 9–37

Dabrowa, E. (ed.) (1994), *The Roman and Byzantine army in the east*, Cracow

Dagron, G. (1974), *Naissance d'une capitale: Constantinople et ses institutions de 330 à 451*, Paris

—(1977), 'Le Christianisme dans la ville byzantine', *DOP* 31, pp. 1–25

Dark, K. and Özgümüs, F. (1998–2005), *Istanbul rescue archaeology survey*, 5 vols., London

Daryaee, T. (2003), 'The Persian Gulf trade in late antiquity', *Journal of World History* 14, pp. 1–16

Deichmann, F. W. (1969–89), *Ravenna: Hauptstadt des spätantiken Abendlandes*, 2 vols. in 5 pts. + indices, Wiesbaden

Delierneux, N. (2001), 'Pratiques et vénération orientales et occidentales des images chrétiennes dans l'antiquité tardive: à propos de quelques ambiguïtés', *Revue Belge de philologie et d'histoire* 79.2, pp. 373–420

Déroche, V. (1991), 'La Polémique anti-judaïque au VIᵉ et VIIᵉ siècle. Un mémento inédit, les *Képhalaia*', *TM* 11, pp. 275–312

Devreese, R. (1937), 'La Fin inédite d'une lettre de saint Maxime: un baptême forcé de Juifs et de Samaritains à Carthage en 632', *Revue des sciences religieuses* 17, pp. 25–35

Dignas, B. and Winter, E. (2007), *Rome and Persia in late antiquity: neighbours and rivals*, Cambridge

Djaït, H. (1986), *Al-Kufa: naissance de la ville islamique*, Paris

Donner, F. M. (1977), 'Mecca's food supplies and Muhammad's boycott', *JESHO* 20, pp. 249–66

—(1981), *The early Islamic conquests*, Princeton

—(1989), 'The role of nomads in the Near East in late antiquity (400–800 CE)', in Clover and Humphreys (eds.) (1989), pp. 73–88; repr. in Peters (ed.) (1999), pp. 21–33

—(1998), *Narratives of Islamic origins: the beginnings of Islamic historical writing*, Princeton

Dostal, W. (1979), *Der Markt von San'a'*, Vienna

—(1984), 'Towards a model of cultural evolution in Arabia', in Abdalla *et al.* (eds.) (1984), II, pp. 185–91

Draguet, R. (1924), *Julien d'Halicarnasse et sa controverse avec Sévère d'Antioche sur l'incorruptibilité du corps du Christ*, Louvain

Drake, H. A. *et al.* (eds.) (2006), *Violence in late antiquity: perceptions and practices*, Aldershot

Drijvers, J. W. (2002), 'Heraclius and the *restitutio crucis*. Notes on symbolism and ideology', in Reinink and Stolte (eds.) (2002), pp. 175–90

Duchesne-Guillemin, J. (1983), 'Zoroastrian religion', in Yarshater (ed.) (1983), II, pp. 866–908

Dunlop, D. M. (1957), 'Sources of gold and silver in Islam according to al-Hamdani (10th century AD)', *SI* 8, pp. 29–49

Durliat, J. (1982), 'Les Attributions civiles des évêques byzantins: l'exemple du diocèse d'Afrique (553–709)', *JÖB* 32, pp. 73–84

Dussaud, R. (1955), *La Pénétration des Arabes en Syrie avant l'Islam*, Paris

Dvornik, F. (1966), *Early Christian and Byzantine political philosophy: origins and background, DOSt* 9, 2 vols., Washington, DC

Edwards, M. (2006), 'The first council of Nicaea', in Mitchell and Young (eds.) (2006), pp. 552–68

Efthymiades, S. (2004), 'A day and ten months in the life of a lonely bachelor: the other Byzantium in *Miracula S. Artemii* 18 and 22', *DOP* 58, pp. 1–26

Engelhardt, I. (1974), *Mission und Politik in Byzanz: ein Beitrag zur Strukturanalyse byzantinischer Mission zur Zeit Justins und Justinians, MBM* 19, Munich

Engemann, J. (2005), 'Diplomatische "Geschenke" – Objekte aus der Spätantike', *MSABK* 4, pp. 39–64

Eph'al, I. (1982), *The ancient Arabs: nomads on the borders of the fertile crescent, 9th–5th centuries BC*, Leiden

Erdkamp, P. (ed.) (2002), *The Roman army and the economy*, Amsterdam

Evans, J. A. S. (1996), *The age of Justinian: the circumstances of imperial power*, London

—(2002), *The Empress Theodora: partner of Justinian*, Austin, TX

Fahd, T. (ed.) (1989), *L'Arabie préislamique et son environnement historique et culturel: actes du Colloque de Strasbourg, 24–27 juin 1987*, Leiden

Farès, B. (1932), *L'Honneur chez les Arabes avant l'Islam*, Paris

Farquharson, P. (1996), 'Byzantium, planet earth and the solar system', in Allen and Jeffreys (eds.) (1996), pp. 263–9

Feissel, D. and Gascou, J. (eds.) (2004), *La Pétition à Byzance*, Paris

Feissel, D. and Philippidis-Braat, A. (1985), 'Inventaires en vue d'un recueil des inscriptions historiques de Byzance, III: Inscriptions du Péloponnèse (à l'exception de Mistra)', *TM* 9, pp. 267–395

Fenster, E. (1968), *Laudes constantinopolitanae, MBM* 9, Munich

Ferluga, J. (1991), 'L'Esarcato', in Berardi *et al.* (eds.) (1990–6), II.1, pp. 351–77

Février, P.-A. (1983), 'Approches récentes de l'Afrique byzantine', *Revue de l'Occident musulman et de la Méditerranée* 35, pp. 25–53

Fisher, W. B. (ed.) (1968), *The Cambridge history of Iran*, I: *The land of Iran*, Cambridge

Flusin, B. (1992), *Saint Anastase le Perse et l'histoire de la Palestine au début du VIIe siècle*, 2 vols., Paris

—(2004), 'Le Monachisme', in Morrisson *et al.* (eds.) (2004), pp. 236–54

Fontaine, J. and Hillgarth, J. N. (eds.) (1992), *The seventh century: change and continuity: proceedings of a joint French and British colloquium at the Warburg Institute, 8–9 July 1988*, London

Foss, C. (1990a), *History and archaeology of Byzantine Asia Minor*, London

—(1995), 'The Near Eastern countryside in late antiquity: a review article', in Humphrey (ed.) (1995–2002), I, pp. 213–34

—(1997), 'Syria in transition, AD 550–750: an archaeological approach', *DOP* 51, pp. 189–269

—(2002a), 'The empress Theodora', *Byz* 72, pp. 141–76

Foss, C. and Winfield, D. (1986), *Byzantine fortifications: an introduction*, Pretoria

Fowden, E. K. (1999), *The barbarian plain: Saint Sergius between Rome and Iran*, Berkeley

Fowden, G. (1993), *Empire to commonwealth: consequences of monotheism in late antiquity*, Princeton

—(2002), 'Elefantiasi del tardoantico?', *Journal of Roman archaeology* 15, pp. 681–6

Freeman, P. and Kennedy, D. (eds.) (1986), *The defence of the Roman and Byzantine east*, 2 vols., Oxford

Frend, W. H. C. (1972), *The rise of the monophysite movement: chapters in the history of the church in the fifth and sixth centuries*, Cambridge

Frye, R. N. (1959), 'Zurvanism again', *HTR* 52, pp. 63–73

—(1983a), 'The political history of Iran under the Sasanians', in Yarshater (ed.) (1983), I, pp. 116–80

—(1983b), 'Bahrain under the Sasanians', in Potts (ed.) (1983), pp. 167–70

—(1984), *The history of ancient Iran*, Munich

Fück, J. (1950), *'Arabiya. Untersuchungen zur arabischen Sprach- und Stilgeschichte*, Berlin

—(1981), *Arabische Kultur und Islam im Mittelalter: Ausgewählte Schriften*, Weimar

Gabra, G. (2002), *Coptic monasteries: Egypt's monastic art and architecture*, Cairo

Gabrieli, F. (1959), 'La letteratura beduina preislamica', in Gabrieli (ed.) (1959), pp. 95–114

—(ed.) (1959), *L'antica società beduina*, Rome

Garsoïan, N. G. (1976), 'Prolegomena to a study on the Iranian elements in Arsacid Armenia', *HAm* 90, pp. 177–234; repr. in Garsoïan (1985), no. 10

—(1983), 'Secular jurisdiction over the Armenian church (fourth–seventh centuries)', *HUS* 7, pp. 220–50; repr. in Garsoïan (1985), no. 9

—(1984–5), 'The early-mediaeval Armenian city: an alien element?', *Journal of the Ancient Near Eastern Society* 16–17, pp. 67–83; repr. in Garsoïan (1999c), no. 7

—(1985), *Armenia between Byzantium and the Sasanians*, London

—(1988), 'Some preliminary precisions on the separation of the Armenian and imperial churches: 1. The presence of "Armenian" bishops at the first five oecumenical councils', in Chrysostomides (ed.) (1988), pp. 249–85; repr. in Garsoïan (1999c), no. 3

—(1996), 'Quelques précisions préliminaires sur le schisme entre les églises byzantine et arménienne au sujet du concile de Chalcédoine: 2. La date et les circonstances de la rupture', in Garsoïan *et al.* (eds.) (1996), pp. 99–112; repr. in Garsoïan (1999c), no. 4

—(1999a), *L'Église arménienne et le grand schisme d'Orient*, *CSCO* 574, Louvain

—(1999b), 'La Menace perse', in Garsoïan (1999a), pp. 135–239

—(1999c), *Church and culture in early medieval Armenia*, Aldershot

Garsoïan, N. G. *et al.* (eds.) (1982), *East of Byzantium: Syria and Armenia in the formative period*, Washington, DC

Garsoïan, N. G. and Mahé, J.-P. (1997), *Des Parthes au califat: quatre leçons sur la formation de l'identité arménienne*, Paris

Gaube, H. (1984), 'Arabs in sixth-century Syria: some archaeological observations', *Proceedings of the First International Conference on Bilad al-Sham, 20–25 April 1974*, Amman

Geiger, A. (1833), *Was hat Mohammed aus dem Judenthume aufgenommen?*, Bonn

Gellner, E. (1973a), *Cause and meaning in the social sciences*, ed. I. C. Jarvie and J. Agassi, London

—(1973b), 'The concept of kinship', in Gellner (1973a), pp. 163–82

Gershevitch, I. (ed.) (1985), *The Cambridge history of Iran,* II: *The Median and Achaemenian periods*, Cambridge

Ghirshman, R. (1962), *Iran: Parthians and Sassanians*, tr. S. Gilbert and J. Emmons, London

Giardina, A. (1999), 'Esplosione di tardoantico', *Studi storici* 40, pp. 157–80

—(2000), 'The family in the late Roman world', in *CAH*, XIV, pp. 392–415

—(2004), 'Tardoantico: appunti sul dibattito attuale', *Studi storici* 45, pp. 41–6

Gibb, H. A. R. (1962), 'Pre-Islamic monotheism in Arabia', *HTR* 55, pp. 269–80; repr. in Peters (ed.) (1999), pp. 295–306

Gibbon, E. (1776–88), *The history of the decline and fall of the Roman empire*, 6 vols., London

Göbl, R. (1954), 'Aufbau der Münzprägung (des Sasanidenstaates)', in Altheim and Stiehl (1954), pp. 51–128

—(1971), *Sasanian numismatics*, tr. P. Severin, Braunschweig

—(1983), 'Sasanian coins', in Yarshater (ed.) (1983), I, pp. 322–38

Goetz, H.-W. *et al.* (eds.) (2003), *Regna and gentes: the relationship between late antique and early medieval peoples and kingdoms in the transformation of the Roman world*, Leiden

Goffart, W. (1957), 'Byzantine policy in the west under Tiberius II and Maurice: the pretenders Hermengild and Gundovald', *Traditio* 13, pp. 73–118

—(1971), 'Zosimus, the first historian of Rome's fall', *AHR* 76, pp. 412–41

—(1981), 'Rome, Constantinople and the barbarians', *AHR* 86, pp. 275–306

Goitein, S. D. (1966), *Studies in Islamic history and institutions*, Leiden

Goldziher, I. (1967–71), *Muslim studies*, ed. and tr. S. M. Stern and C. R. Barber, 2 vols., London

Goodblatt, D. M. (1979), 'The poll tax in Sassanian Babylonia: the Talmudic evidence', *JESHO* 22, pp. 233–95

Goubert, P. (1951–65), *Byzance avant l'Islam*, 2 vols. in 3 pts., Paris

Graf, D. F. and O'Connor, M. (1977), 'The origin of the term Saracen and the Rawwafa inscriptions', *BS* 4, pp. 52–66

Gray, P. T. R. (1979), *The defense of Chalcedon in the east (451–553)*, Leiden

—(2005), 'The legacy of Chalcedon: christological problems and their significance', in Maas (ed.) (2005), pp. 215–38

Greatrex, G. (1997), 'The Nika riot: a reassessment', *JHS* 117, pp. 60–86

—(1998), *Rome and Persia at war, 502–532*, Leeds

—(2005), 'Byzantium and the east in the sixth century', in Maas (ed.) (2005), pp. 477–509

Gregory, T. E. (1992 [1993]), '*Kastro* and *diateichisma* as responses to early Byzantine frontier collapse', *Byz* 62, pp. 235–53

—(1993), *The Hexamilion and the fortress, Isthmia* 5, Princeton

Griffith, S. H. (1985), 'The Gospel in Arabic: an inquiry into its appearance in the first Abbasid century', *OrChr* 69, pp. 126–67

Grignaschi, M. (1971), 'La riforma tributaria di Hosro I e il feudalismo sassanide', in *La Persia nel medioevo: atti del convegno internazionale (Roma, 31 marzo–5 aprile 1970), ANL PASC* 160, Rome, pp. 87–147

Grillmeier, A. (1975–96) *Christ in Christian tradition*, I: 2nd edn., tr. J. Bowden, *From the apostolic age to Chalcedon (451)*; II: *From the council of Chalcedon (451) to Gregory the Great (590–604)*, pt. 1, tr. P. Allen and J. Cawte, *Reception and contradiction: the development of discussion about Chalcedon from 451 to the beginning of the reign of Justinian*; pt. 2, with T. Hainthaler, tr. J. Cawte and P. Allen, *The church of Constantinople in the sixth century*; pt. 4, with T. Hainthaler, tr. O. C. Dean, *The church of Alexandria with Nubia and Ethiopia after 451*, London

Groom, N. (1981), *Frankincense and myrrh: a study of the Arabian incense trade*, London

Grunebaum, G. E. von (1963), 'The nature of Arab unity before Islam', *Arabica* 10, pp. 4–23; repr. in Peters (ed.) (1999), pp. 1–19

Guidi, M. [Morony, M.] (1991), 'Mazdak', *EI*, VI, pp. 949–52

Guillaumont, A. (1962), *Les 'képhalaia gnostica' d'Évagre le Pontique et l'histoire de l'Origénisme chez les grecs et chez les syriens*, Paris

Guillou, A. (1969), *Régionalisme et indépendance dans l'empire byzantin au VIIe siècle: l'exemple de l'exarchat et de la pentapole d'Italie*, Rome

Gunn, J. D. (ed.) (2000), *The years without summer: tracing AD 536 and its aftermath, BAR IS* 872, Oxford

Haarer, F. (2006), *Anastasius I: politics and empire in the late Roman world*, Liverpool

Haas, C. (1997), *Alexandria in late antiquity: topography and social conflict*, Baltimore

Hahn, I. (1959), 'Sassanidische und spätrömische Besteuerung', *AAntHung* 7, pp. 149–60

Haldon, J. (1979), *Recruitment and conscription in the Byzantine army c. 550–950: a study on the origins of the stratiotika ktemata*, Vienna

—(1986a), 'Ideology and social change in the seventh century: military discontent as a barometer', *Klio* 68, pp. 139–90

—(1992a), 'The works of Anastasius of Sinai: a key source for the history of seventh-century east Mediterranean society and belief', in *BEINE*, I, pp. 107–47

—(1995c), 'Seventh-century continuities: the *Ajnād* and the "thematic myth"', in *BEINE*, III, pp. 379–423

—(2004), 'The fate of the late Roman senatorial elite: extinction or transformation?', in *BEINE*, VI, pp. 179–234

—(2005a), 'Economy and administration: how did the empire work?', in Maas (ed.) (2005), pp. 28–59

—(2006a), '"Greek Fire" revisited: recent and current research', in Jeffreys, E. (ed.) (2006), pp. 290–325

Haldon, J. and Byrne, M. (1977), 'A possible solution to the problem of Greek fire', *BZ* 70, pp. 91–9

Hall, J. A. (ed.) (1986), *States in history*, Oxford

Hallaq, W. B. and Little, D. P. (eds.) (1991), *Islamic studies presented to Charles J. Adams*, Leiden

Hammur, 'I. M. (1979), *Aswaq al-'arab*, Beirut

Hannestad, K. (1961), 'Les Forces militaires d'après la guerre gothique de Procope', *Classica et Mediaevalia* 21, pp. 136–83

Hardy, E. R. (1968), 'The Egyptian policy of Justinian', *DOP* 22, pp. 21–41

Harries, J. (1999), *Law and empire in late antiquity*, Cambridge

Harries, J. and Wood, I. (eds.) (1993), *The Theodosian code: studies in the imperial law of late antiquity*, London

Harris, A. (2003), *Byzantium, Britain and the west: the archaeology of cultural identity AD 400–650*, Stroud

—(2004), 'Shops, retailing and the local economy in the early Byzantine world: the example of Sardis', in Dark (ed.) (2004), pp. 82–122

Harrison, R. M. (1989), *A temple for Byzantium: the discovery and excavation of Anicia Juliana's palace-church in Istanbul*, London

—(2001), *Mountain and plain: from the Lycian coast to the Phrygian plateau in the late Roman and early Byzantine period*, ed. W. Young, Ann Arbor, MI

Hatcher, J. (1994), 'England in the aftermath of the Black Death', *PaP* 144, pp. 3–35

Hatlie, P. (2007), *The monks and monasteries of Constantinople, ca. 350–850*, Cambridge

Hattersley-Smith, K. (1996), *Byzantine public architecture between the fourth and early eleventh centuries AD, with special reference to the towns of Byzantine Macedonia*, Thessalonica

Hawting, G. R. (1982), 'The origins of the Islamic sanctuary at Mecca', in Juynboll (ed.) (1982), pp. 25–47

—(1999), *The idea of idolatry and the emergence of Islam: from polemic to history*, Cambridge

Hayes, J. W. (1972), *Late Roman pottery*, London

Heather, P. (1991), *Goths and Romans 332–489*, Oxford

—(1996), *The Goths*, Oxford

—(2005), *The fall of the Roman empire: a new history of Rome and the barbarians*, London

Heck, G. W. (1999), 'Gold mining in Arabia and the rise of the Islamic state', *JESHO* 42, pp. 364–95

—(2003), '"Arabia without spices": an alternate hypothesis', *JAOS* 123, pp. 547–76

Heinzer, F. and Schönborn, C. (eds.) (1982), *Maximus Confessor: actes du symposium sur Maxime le Confesseur (Fribourg, 2–5 septembre 1980)*, Fribourg

Hendy, M. F. (2002), 'East and west: the transformation of late Roman financial structures', *Roma fra oriente e occidente = SSCIS* 49, II, pp. 1307–70

Henninger, J. (1966), 'Altarabische Genealogie (zu einem neuerschienenen Werk)', *Anthropos* 61, pp. 852–70

Herrin, J. (1983a), 'In search of Byzantine women: three avenues of approach', in Cameron and Kuhrt (eds.) (1983), pp. 167–89

Herrmann, G. (1977), *The Iranian revival*, Oxford

Hill, S. (1996), *The early Byzantine churches of Cilicia and Isauria*, Aldershot

Hinds, M. (1996), *Studies in early Islamic history*, ed. J. Bacharach *et al.*, Princeton

Honoré, A. M. (1971), *Justinian's Digest: work in progress*, Oxford

—(1978), *Tribonian*, London

Horden, P. (2005), 'Mediterranean plague in the age of Justinian', in Maas (ed.) (2005), pp. 134–60

Horovitz, J. (2002), *The earliest biographies of the Prophet and their authors*, ed. L. I. Conrad, Princeton

Howard-Johnston, J. D. (1994), 'The official history of Heraclius' Persian campaigns', in Dabrowa (ed.) (1994), pp. 57–87

—(1995a), 'The two great powers in late antiquity: a comparison', in *BEINE*, III, pp. 157–226; repr. in Howard-Johnston (2006a), no. 1

—(1999), 'Heraclius' Persian campaigns and the revival of the east Roman empire, 622–630', *War in history* 6, pp. 1–44; repr. in Howard-Johnston (2006a), no. 8

—(2002), 'Armenian historians of Heraclius: an examination of the aims, sources and working-methods of Sebeos and Movses Daskhurantsi'', in Reinink and Stolte (eds.) (2002), pp. 41–62; repr. in Howard-Johnston (2006a), no. 5

—(2006a), *East Rome, Sasanian Persia and the end of antiquity: historiographical and historical studies*, Aldershot

Hoyland, R. G. (1997), *Seeing Islam as others saw it: a survey and evaluation of Christian, Jewish and Zoroastrian writings on early Islam*, Princeton

—(2001), *Arabia and the Arabs: from the bronze age to the coming of Islam*, London

Humbach, H. and Skjærvø, P. O. (1978–83), *The Sassanian inscription of Paikuli*, 3 vols. in 4 pts., Wiesbaden

Humfress, C. (2005), 'Law and legal practice in the age of Justinian', in Maas (ed.) (2005), pp. 161–84

Humphrey, J. H. (ed.) (1995–2002), *The Roman and Byzantine Near East: some recent archaeological research*, 3 vols., Ann Arbor, MI and Portsmouth, RI

Humphries, R. S. (1991), *Islamic history: a framework for inquiry*, 2nd edn., Princeton

Hundsbichler, H. (ed.) (1994), *Kommunikation zwischen Orient und Okzident: Alltag und Sachkultur. Internationaler Kongress, Krems an der Donau, 6. bis 9. Oktober 1992*, Vienna

Husayn, T. (1927), *Fi al-adab al-Jahili*, Cairo

Izutsu, T. (2002), *Ethico-religious concepts in the Qur'an*, Montreal

Jabbur, J. S. (1959), 'Abu-al-Duhur': the Ruwalah *'Utfah'*, in Kritzeck and Bayly Winder (eds.) (1959), pp. 195–8

—(1995), *The Bedouins and the desert: aspects of nomadic life in the Arab east*, tr. L. I. Conrad, ed. S. J. Jabbur and L. I. Conrad, Albany, NY

Jacob, G. (1897), *Altarabisches Beduinenleben*, Berlin

James, L. (2001), *Empresses and power in early Byzantium*, London

Janssens, B. *et al.* (eds.) (2004), *Philomathestatos: studies in Greek and Byzantine texts presented to Jacques Noret for his sixty-fifth birthday*, Louvain

Jézégou, M.-P. (1998), 'Le Mobilier de l'épave Saint-Gervais 2 (VIIᵉ s.) à Fos-sur-Mer (B.-du Rh.)', in Bonifay *et al.* (eds.) (1998), pp. 343–51

Jones, A. H. M. (1955), 'The economic life of the towns of the Roman empire', *La Ville,* II: *Institutions économiques et sociales (Recueils de la Société Jean Bodin 7)*, pp. 161–94

—(1964), *The later Roman empire, 284–602: a social, economic and administrative survey*, 3 vols. + maps, Oxford

Juynboll, G. H. A. (ed.) (1982), *Studies on the first century of Islamic society*, Carbondale, IL

Kaegi, W. E. (1968) *Byzantium and the decline of Rome*, Princeton

—(1977), 'The first Arab expedition against Amorium', *BMGS* 3, pp. 19–22; repr. in Kaegi (1982), no. 14

—(1982), *Army, society and religion in Byzantium*, London

—(2001), 'Byzantine Sardinia and Africa face the Muslims: a rereading of some seventh-century evidence', *Bizantinistica* 3, pp. 1–24

—(2002), 'Society and institutions in Byzantine Africa', in Corrias and Cosentino (eds.) (2002), pp. 15–28

—(2003b), 'The earliest Muslim penetrations of Anatolia', in Avramea *et al.* (eds.) (2003), pp. 269–82

—(forthcoming), 'Byzantine Sardinia threatened: its changing situation in the seventh century', *Convegno sui Bizantini in Sardegna: 'Forme e caratteri della presenza bizantina nel Mediterraneo occidentale: la Sardegna (secoli VI–XI),' 22 marzo 2003*, to be published in the proceedings of that congress

—(in preparation), 'The terminal wave of shocks for Constans II', in Kaegi, W. E. (in preparation), *Byzantium and Islam in North Africa*

Kaldellis, A. (2004), *Procopius of Caesarea: tyranny, history, and philosophy at the end of antiquity*, Philadelphia

Kaplony, A. (1996), *Konstantinopel und Damaskus: Gesandtschaften und Verträge zwischen Kaisern und Kalifen 639–750*, Berlin

Kazemi, F. and McChesney, R. D. (eds.) (1988), *A way prepared: essays on Islamic culture in honor of Richard Bayly Winder*, New York

Kazhdan, A. P. (1975), *Armiane v sostave gospodstvuiushchego klassa Vizantiiskoi imperii v XI–XII vv.*, Erevan

Keenan, J. G. (2000), 'Egypt', in *CAH*, XIV, pp. 612–37

Kelly, C. (2004), *Ruling the later Roman empire*, Cambridge, MA

Kennedy, H. (1985), 'From *Polis* to *Madina*: urban change in late antique and early Islamic Syria', *PaP* 106, pp. 3–27

—(2000), 'Syria, Palestine and Mesopotamia', in *CAH*, XIV (2000), pp. 588–611

Khoury, P. S. and Kostiner, J. (eds.) (1990), *Tribes and state formation in the Middle East*, Berkeley

Kister, M. J. (1965), 'The market of the Prophet', *JESHO* 8, pp. 272–6; repr. in Kister (1980), no. 9

—(1968), 'Al-Hira: some notes on its relations with Arabia', *Arabica* 15, pp. 143–69; repr. in Kister (1980), no. 3; repr. in Peters (ed.) (1999), pp. 81–107

—(1979), 'Some reports concerning al-Ta'if', *JSAI* 1, pp. 1–18; repr. in Kister (1980), no. 11

—(1980), *Studies in Jahiliyya and early Islam*, London

—(1990), *Society and religion from Jahiliyya to Islam*, Aldershot

—(1997), *Concepts and ideas at the dawn of Islam*, Aldershot

—(2002), 'The struggle against Musaylima and the conquest of Yamama', *JSAI* 27, pp. 1–56

Kitzinger, E. (1954), 'The cult of images in the age before iconoclasm', *DOP* 8, pp. 83–150

—(1977), *Byzantine art in the making: main lines of stylistic development in Mediterranean art, 3rd–7th century*, London

Klíma, O. (1957), *Mazdak: Geschichte einer sozialen Bewegung im Sassanidischen Persien*, Prague

—(1977), *Beiträge zur Geschichte des Mazdakismus*, Prague

Kobylinski, Z. (2005), 'The Slavs', in *NCMH*, I, pp. 524–44

Koder, J. (1978), 'Zur Frage der slavischen Siedlungsgebiete im mittelalterlichen Griechenland', *BZ* 71, pp. 315–31

—(1996), 'Climatic change in the fifth and sixth centuries?', in Allen and Jeffreys (eds.) (1996), pp. 270–85

Köpstein, H. and Winkelmann, F. (eds.) (1976), *Studien zum 7. Jahrhundert in Byzanz: Probleme der Herausbildung des Feudalismus, BBA* 47, Berlin

Kozelj, T. and Wurch-Kozelj, M. (2005), 'Les Carrières de marbre à Thasos à l'époque proto-byzantine: extraction et production', *TM* 15, pp. 465–86

Krauss, S. (1916), 'Talmudische Nachrichten über Arabien', *ZDMG* 70, pp. 321–53

Krieger, R. (1992), *Untersuchungen und Hypothesen zur Ansiedlung der Westgoten, Burgunden und Ostgoten*, Bern

Kritzeck, J. and Bayly Winder, R. (1959), *The world of Islam: studies in honor of Philip K. Hitti*, London

Krueger, D. (2003), 'Writing and redemption in the hymns of Romanos the Melodist', *BMGS* 27, pp. 2–44

—(2005), 'Christian piety and practice in the sixth century', in Maas (ed.) (2005), pp. 291–315

Kubiak, W. B. (1987), *Al-Fustat: its foundation and early urban development*, Cairo

Labourt, J. (1904), *Le Christianisme dans l'empire Perse sous la dynastie Sassanide (224–632)*, Paris

Lammens, H. (1928), *L'Arabie occidentale avant l'Hégire*, Beirut

Lancaster, W. (1997), *The Rwala Bedouin today*, 2nd edn., Prospect Heights, IL

Lange, N. de (1992), 'Jews and Christians in the Byzantine empire: problems and prospects', in Wood (ed.) (1992), pp. 15–32

—(2005a), 'Jews in the age of Justinian', in Maas (ed.) (2005), pp. 401–26

Lavan, L. (2001), 'The late-antique city: a bibliographic essay', in Lavan (ed.) (2001), pp. 9–26

—(ed.) (2001), *Recent research in late-antique urbanism*, Portsmouth, RI

Lavan, L. and Bowden, W. (eds.) (2003), *Theory and practice in late antique archaeology*, Leiden

Lecker, M. (1986), 'On the markets of Medina (Yathrib) in pre-Islamic and early Islamic times', *JSAI* 8, pp. 133–47; repr. in Lecker (1998), no. 9

—(1993), 'Idol worship in pre-Islamic Medina (Yathrib)', *LM* 106, pp. 331–46; repr. in Lecker (1998), no. 1; repr. in Peters (ed.) (1999), pp. 129–44

—(1994), 'Kinda on the eve of Islam and during the *ridda*', *JRAS* 4, pp. 333–56; repr. in Lecker (1998), no. 15

—(1998), *Jews and Arabs in pre- and early Islamic Arabia*, Aldershot

Leder, S. (1992), 'The literary use of the *Khabar*: a basic form of historical writing', in *BEINE*, I, pp. 277–315

Lee, A. D. (1993), *Information and frontiers: Roman foreign relations in late antiquity*, Cambridge

—(2005), 'The empire at war', in Maas (ed.) (2005), pp. 113–33

—(2007a), *War in late antiquity*, Oxford

—(2007b), 'Warfare and the state', in Sabin *et al.* (eds.) (2007), II, pp. 379–423

Lenski, N. (ed.) (2006), *The Cambridge companion to the age of Constantine*, Cambridge

Lethaby, W. R. and Swainson, H. (1894), *The church of Sancta Sophia Constantinople: a study of Byzantine building*, London

Letsios, D. G. (1996), *Nomos Rhodion Nautikos: das Seegesetz der Rhodier: Untersuchungen zu Seerecht und Handelsschiffahrt in Byzanz*, Rhodes

Liebeschuetz, J. H. W. G. (1992), 'The end of the ancient city', in Rich (ed.) (1992), pp. 1–49

—(2001), *Decline and fall of the Roman city*, Oxford

Lieu, S. N. C. (1994), *Manichaeism in Mesopotamia and the Roman East*, Leiden

Little, L. K. (ed.) (2007), *Plague and the end of antiquity: the pandemic of 541–750*, New York

Loginov, S. D. and Nikitin, A. B. (1993a), 'Sasanian coins of the third century from Merv', *Mesopotamia* 28, pp. 225–46

—(1993b), 'Coins of Shapur II from Merv', *Mesopotamia* 28, pp. 247–69

—(1993c), 'Sasanian coins of the late fourth to seventh centuries from Merv', *Mesopotamia* 28, pp. 271–312

Loseby, S. (2005), 'The Mediterranean economy', in *NCMH*, I, pp. 605–38

Lounghis, T. C. (1994), 'Die byzantinischen Gesandten als Vermittler materieller Kultur vom 5. bis ins 11. Jahrhundert', in Hundsbichler (ed.) (1994), pp. 49–67

—(2005), 'The adaptability of Byzantine political ideology to western realities as a diplomatic message (476–1096)', *Comunicare e significare nell'alto medioevo* = *SSCIS* 52, pp. 335–61

Louth, A. (1996a), *Maximus the Confessor*, London

—(1996b), 'A Christian theologian at the court of the caliph: some cross-cultural reflections', *Dialogos: Hellenic studies review* 3, pp. 4–19

—(2000), 'Palestine under the Arabs 650–750: the crucible of Byzantine orthodoxy', in Swanson (ed.) (2000), pp. 67–77

—(2001), *Denys the Areopagite*, London

—(2002), *St John Damascene: tradition and originality in Byzantine theology*, Oxford

—(2004), 'Conciliar records and canons', in Young *et al.* (eds.) (2004), pp. 391–5

Lozachmeur, H. (ed.) (1995), *Présence arabe dans le croissant fertile avant l'Hégire*, Paris

Lukonin, V. G. (1961), *Iran v epokhu pervykh Sasanidov*, Leningrad

Maas, M. (1986), 'Roman history and Christian ideology in Justinianic reform legislation', *DOP* 40, pp. 17–31

—(1992), *John Lydus and the Roman past: antiquarianism and politics in the age of Justinian*, London

—(1995), 'Fugitives and ethnography in Priscus of Panium', *BMGS* 19, pp. 146–61

—(2003a), *Exegesis and empire in the early Byzantine Mediterranean*, Tübingen

—(2003b), '"Delivered from their ancient customs": Christianity and the question of cultural change in early Byzantine ethnography', in Mills and Grafton (eds.) (2003), pp. 152–88

—(ed.) (2005), *The Cambridge companion to the age of Justinian*, Cambridge

MacAdam, H. I. (1983), 'Epigraphy and village life in southern Syria during the Roman and early Byzantine periods', *Berytus* 31, pp. 103–27; repr. in MacAdam (2002), no. 12

—(1989), 'Strabo, Pliny the Elder and Ptolemy of Alexandria: three views of ancient Arabia and its peoples', in Fahd (ed.) (1989), pp. 289–320; repr. in MacAdam (2002), no. 5

—(2002), *Geography, urbanisation and settlement patterns in the Roman Near East*, Aldershot

MacCormack, S. (1981), *Art and ceremony in late antiquity*, Berkeley

McCormick, M. (2000), 'Emperor and court', in *CAH*, XIV, pp. 135–63

Macdonald, M. C. A. (1993), 'Nomads and the Hawran in the late Hellenistic and Roman periods: a reassessment of the epigraphic evidence', *Syria* 70, pp. 303–413

—(1995a), 'North Arabia in the first millennium BCE', in Sasson (ed.) (1995), II, pp. 1355–69

—(1995b), 'Quelques réflexions sur les Saracènes, l'inscription de Rawwafa et l'armée romaine', in Lozachmeur (ed.) (1995), pp. 93–101

MacLaurin, E. C. B. (ed.) (1967), *Essays in honour of G. W. Thatcher*, Sydney

Macrides, R. and Magdalino, P. (1988), 'The architecture of *ekphrasis*: construction and context of Paul the Silentiary's poem on Hagia Sophia', *BMGS* 12, pp. 47–82

Madgearu, A. (2001a), 'The end of town-life in Scythia Minor', *Oxford journal of archaeology* 20, pp. 207–17

Magness, J. (1993), *Jerusalem ceramic chronology, circa 200–800 CE*, Sheffield

—(2003), *The archaeology of the early Islamic settlement in Palestine*, Winona Lake, IN

Mahé, J.-P. (1997), 'Confession religieuse et identité nationale dans l'église arménienne du VIIe au XIe siècle', in Garsoïan and Mahé (1997), pp. 79–105

Malmberg, S. (2005), 'Visualising hierarchy at imperial banquets', in Mayer and Trzcionka (eds.) (2005), pp. 11–24

Manandian, H. (1965), *The trade and cities of Armenia in relation to ancient world trade*, tr. from 2nd edn. by N. G. Garsoïan, Lisbon

Mango, C. (1975b), *Byzantine literature as a distorting mirror: an inaugural lecture delivered before the University of Oxford on 21 May 1974*, Oxford; repr. in Mango (1984), no. 2

—(1993), *Studies on Constantinople*, Aldershot

—(2000), 'The Triumphal Way of Constantinople and the Golden Gate', *DOP* 54, pp. 173–88

—(2002b), 'Introduction', in Mango (ed.) (2002), pp. 1–16

Marcone, A. (2004), 'La tarda antichità o della difficoltà della periodizzazione', *Studi storici* 45, pp. 25–36

Markey, T. (1989), 'Germanic in the Mediterranean: Lombards, Vandals and Visigoths', in Clover and Humphreys (eds.) (1989), pp. 51–71

Martindale, J. R. (2001), *Prosopography of the Byzantine empire, I: 641–867* (CD-Rom), Aldershot

Mathews, T. F. (1971), *The early churches of Constantinople: architecture and liturgy*, University Park, PA

Mayerson, P. (1963), 'The desert of southern Palestine according to Byzantine sources', *Proceedings of the American Philosophical Society* 107, pp. 160–72

Meeker, M. E. (1979), *Literature and violence in north Arabia*, Cambridge

Meer, F. van der and Mohrmann, C. (1966), *Atlas of the early Christian world*, ed. and tr. M. F. Hedlund and H. H. Rowley, 3rd edn., London

Megaw, A. H. S. (2006), 'The Campanopetra reconsidered: the pilgrimage church of the Apostle Barnabas?', in Jeffreys, E. (ed.) (2006), pp. 394–404

Meier, M. (2003), *Das andere Zeitalter Justinians: Kontingenzerfahrung und Kontingenzbewältigung im 6. Jahrhundert n. Chr.*, Göttingen

Meisami, J. S. and Starkey, P. (eds.) (1998), *Encyclopedia of Arabic literature*, 2 vols., London

Merrills, A. H. (2005), *History and geography in late antiquity*, Cambridge

Mews, S. (ed.) (1982), *Religion and national identity*, Oxford

Meyendorff, J. (1989), *Imperial unity and Christian divisions: the church 450–680 AD*, Crestwood, NY

Michaud, H. (1960), *Jésus selon le Coran*, Neuchâtel

Millar, F. (1993a), 'Hagar, Ishmael, Josephus and the origins of Islam', *Journal of Jewish Studies* 44, pp. 23–45

—(1993b), *The Roman Near East, 31 BC–AD 337*, Cambridge, MA

—(2000), 'Pagan and Christian voices from late antiquity' [review of *CAH*, XIII], *Journal of Roman archaeology* 13, pp. 752–63

Mills, K. and Grafton, A. (eds.) (2003), *Conversion in late antiquity and the early middle ages: seeing and believing*, Rochester, NY

Mitchell, M. M. and Young, F. M. (eds.) (2006), *The Cambridge history of Christianity*, I: *Origins to Constantine*, Cambridge

Momigliano, A. (1955), 'Cassiodorus and Italian culture of his time', *PBA* 41, pp. 207–45

Moorhead, J. (1981), 'The monophysite response to the Arab invasions', *Byz* 51, pp. 579–91

—(1982), 'The last years of Theoderic', *Historia* 32, pp. 106–20

—(1983), 'Italian loyalties during Justinian's Gothic war', *Byz* 53, pp. 575–96

—(1994), *Justinian*, London

—(2001), *The Roman empire divided, 400–700*, London

—(2005), 'Ostrogothic Italy and the Lombard invasions', in *NCMH*, I, pp. 140–61

Morony, M. G. (1984), *Iraq after the Muslim conquest*, Princeton

Morrisson, C. (1989), 'Monnaie et prix à Byzance du Vᵉ au VIIᵉ siècle', in Kravari *et al.* (eds.) (1989–91), I, pp. 239–60

Morrisson, C. and Sodini, J.-P. (2002), 'The sixth-century economy', in *EHB*, I, pp. 171–220

Müller, W. W. (1978), *Weihrauch: ein arabisches Produkt und seine Bedeutung in der Antike*, *RE* Supplement-Band XV, Munich

Mullett, M. and Scott, R. (eds.) (1981), *Byzantium and the classical tradition: University of Birmingham, thirteenth spring symposium of Byzantine studies, 1979*, Birmingham

Mundell Mango, M. (1986), *Silver from early Byzantium: the Kaper Koraon and related treasures*, Baltimore

—(2000), 'Byzantine, Sasanian and central Asian silver', in Bálint (ed.) (2000), pp. 267–84

—(2005), 'A new stylite at Androna in Syria', *TM* 15, pp. 329–42

Musil, A. (1928), *The manners and customs of the Rwala Bedouins*, New York

Nagel, T. (1967), *Die Qisas al-Anbiya': ein Beitrag zur arabischen Literaturgeschichte*, Bonn

Nau, F. (1933), *Les Arabes chrétiens de Mésopotamie et de Syrie du VIIe au VIIIe siècle*, Paris

Nedungatt, G. and Featherstone, J. M. (eds.) (1995), *The Council in Trullo revisited*, Rome

Nelson, C. (ed.) (1973), *The desert and the sown: nomads in the wider society*, Berkeley

Newby, G. D. (1988), *A history of the Jews of Arabia: from ancient times to their eclipse under Islam*, Columbia, SC

Nicholson, R. A. (1907), *A literary history of the Arabs*, London (repr. London, 1998)

Nimmo-Smith, J. (2006), 'Magic at the crossroads in the sixth century', in Jeffreys, E. (ed.) (2006), pp. 224–37

Nöldeke, T. (1887a), *Die Ghassänischen Fürsten aus dem Hause Gafna's*, Berlin

—(1887b), *Aufsätze zur persischen Geschichte*, Leipzig

—(1920), *Das Iranische Nationalepos*, 2nd edn., Leipzig

Noth, A. (1994), *The early Arabic historical tradition: a source-critical study*, 2nd edn., with L. I. Conrad, tr. M. Bonner, Princeton

O'Connor, M. P. (1986), 'The etymology of "Saracen" in Aramaic and pre-Islamic Arabic contexts', in Freeman and Kennedy (eds.) (1986), II, pp. 603–32

O'Donnell, J. (2004), 'Late antiquity: before and after', *TAPA* 134, pp. 203–13

Olinder, G. (1927), *The kings of Kinda and the family of Akil al-Murar*, Lund

Ostrogorsky, G. (1962), 'La Commune rurale byzantine', *Byz* 32, pp. 139–66; repr. in Ostrogorsky (1973a), pp. 44–71

—(1973a), *Zur byzantinischen Geschichte: ausgewählte kleine Schriften*, Darmstadt

—(1973b), 'Die Entstehung der Themenverfassung. Korreferat zu A. Pertusi, La formation des thèmes byzantins', repr. in Ostrogorsky (1973a), pp. 72–9

Panella, C. (1989), 'Gli scambi nel mediterraneo occidentale dal IV al VII secolo dal punto di vista di alcune "merci"', in Kravari *et al.* (eds.) (1989–91), I, pp. 129–41

Papathomopoulos, M. (1984), 'Greek sources for the history of the Arabs in the pre-Islamic period', *Graeco-Arabica* 3, pp. 203–5

Parrinder, G. (1965), *Jesus in the Qur'an*, London

Patlagean, E. (1977), *Pauvreté économique et pauvreté sociale à Byzance, 4e–7e siècles*, Paris

—(1981), *Structure sociale, famille, chrétienté à Byzance: IVe–XIe siècle*, London

Pazdernik, C. (2005), 'Justinianic ideology and the power of the past', in Maas (ed.) (2005), pp. 185–212

Peeters, P. (1935), 'Sainte Sousanik, martyre en Arméno-Géorgie', *AnBoll* 53, pp. 5–48

Pellat, C. (1953), *Le Milieu basrien et la formation de Gahiz*, Paris

—(1962–3), 'Concept of *hilm* in Islamic ethics', *Bulletin of the Institute of Islamic Studies* 6–7, pp. 1–12; repr. in Pellat (1976), no. 9

—(1973), *Risalah fi al-hilm 'inda al-'Arab*, Beirut

—(1976), *Études sur l'histoire socio-culturelle de l'Islam, VIIe–XVe s.*, London

Peltomaa, L. M. (2001), *The image of the Virgin Mary in the Akathistos hymn*, Leiden

Pentcheva, B. V. (2002), 'The supernatural protector of Constantinople: the Virgin and her icons in the tradition of the Avar siege', *BMGS* 26, pp. 2–41

Peters, F. E. (1984), 'The Arabs on the frontiers of Syria before Islam', *Proceedings of the First International Conference on Bilad al-Sham, 20–25 April 1974*, Amman, pp. 141–73

——(1988), 'The commercial life of Mecca before Islam', in Kazemi and McChesney (eds.) (1988), pp. 3–26

——(ed.) (1999), *The Arabs and Arabia on the eve of Islam*, Aldershot

Piccirillo, M. (ed.) (1989), *Mosaïques byzantines de Jordanie*, Lyons

Piéri, D. (2005), 'Nouvelles productions d'amphores de Syrie du Nord aux époques protobyzantine et omeyyade', *TM* 15, pp. 583–95

Pigulevskaia [=Pigulevskaja], N. V. (1937), 'K voprosu o podatnoi reforme Khosroia Anushervana', *Vestnik drevnei istorii* 1, pp. 143–54

——(1946), *Vizantiia i Iran na rubezhe VI i VII vekov*, Moscow and Leningrad

——(1963), *Les Villes de l'état Iranien aux époques Parthe et Sassanide*, Paris

Pohl, W. (2003), 'A non-Roman empire in central Europe: the Avars', in Goetz *et al.* (eds.) (2003), pp. 571–95

——(ed.) (1997), *Kingdoms of the empire: the integration of barbarians in late antiquity*, Leiden

Pohl, W. and Reimitz, H. (eds.) (1998), *Strategies of distinction: the construction of the ethnic communities, 300–800*, Leiden

Potter, D. S. (1990), *Prophecy and history in the crisis of the Roman empire: a historical commentary on the Thirteenth Sibylline Oracle*, Oxford

Potts, D. T. (ed.) (1983), *Dilmun: new studies in the archaeology and early history of Bahrain*, Berlin

Poulter, A. G. (1983), 'Town and country in Moesia Inferior', in Poulter (ed.) (1983a), II, pp. 74–118

——(2000), 'The Roman to Byzantine transition in the Balkans: preliminary results on Nicopolis and its hinterland', *Journal of Roman Archaeology* 13, pp. 346–58

——(ed.) (1983), *Ancient Bulgaria: papers presented to the International Symposium on the Ancient History and Archaeology of Bulgaria, University of Nottingham, 1981*, 2 vols., Nottingham

Pringle, D. (2001), *The defence of Byzantine Africa from Justinian to the Arab conquest: an account of the military history and archaeology of the African provinces in the sixth and seventh centuries*, 2nd edn., *BAR IS* 99, Oxford

Rapp, C. (2005), 'Literary culture under Justinian', in Maas (ed.) (2005), pp. 376–97

Reinink, G. J. (2002), 'Heraclius, the new Alexander: apocalyptic prophecies during the reign of Heraclius', in Reinink and Stolte (eds.) (2002), pp. 81–94

Reinink, G. J. and Stolte, B. (eds.) (2002), *The reign of Heraclius (610–641): crisis and confrontation*, Louvain

Renoux, C. (1993), 'Langue et littérature arméniennes', in Albert *et al.* (eds.) (1993), pp. 107–66

Retsö, J. (2003), *The Arabs in antiquity: their history from the Assyrians to the Umayyads*, London

Rich, J. (ed.) (1992), *The city in late antiquity*, London

Richards, J. (1980), *Consul of God: the life and times of Gregory the Great*, London

Riedinger, R. (1982), 'Die Lateransynode von 649 und Maximos der Bekenner', in Heinzer and Schönborn (eds.) (1982), pp. 111–21

Rippin, A. (1991), 'RHMNN and the hanifs', in Hallaq and Little (eds.) (1991), pp. 153–68

—(2005), *Muslims: their religious beliefs and practices*, 3rd edn., London

Robin, C. (1991) (ed.), *L'Arabie antique de Karib'il à Mahomet: nouvelles données sur l'histoire des Arabes grâce aux inscriptions*, Aix-en-Provence

Robinson, N. (1991), *Christ in Islam and Christianity: the representation of Jesus in the Qur'an and the classical Muslim commentaries*, Basingstoke

Roisl, H. N. (1981), 'Totila und die Schlacht bei den Busta Gallorum, Ende Juni/Anfang Juli 552', *JÖB* 30, pp. 25–50

Rompay, L. van (2005), 'Society and community in the Christian east', in Maas (ed.) (2005), pp. 239–66

Rösch, G. (1978), *Onoma basileias: Studien zum offiziellen Gebrauch der Kaisertitel in spätantiker und frühbyzantinischer Zeit*, BV 10, Vienna

Rosenthal, E. I. J. (1961), *Judaism and Islam*, London and New York

Rothstein, G. (1899), *Die Dynastie der Lahmiden in al-Hira*, Berlin

Rotter, G. (1993), 'Der *veneris dies* im vorislamischen Mekka, eine neue Deutung des Namens "Europa" und eine Erklärung für *kobar* = Venus', *Der Islam* 70, pp. 112–32

RouECHÉ, C. (2004), *Aphrodisias in late antiquity: the late Roman and Byzantine inscriptions*, rev. 2nd edn., <http://insaph.kcl.ac.uk/ala2004>

Rouché, C. *et al.* (eds.) (2002), *De aedificiis: le texte de Procope et les réalités*, Turnhout

Rousseau, P. (1996), 'Inheriting the fifth century: who bequeathed what?', in Allen and Jeffreys (eds.) (1996), pp. 1–19

Rubin, U. (1984), 'Al-Samad and the high god: an interpretation of Sura CXII', *Der Islam* 61, pp. 197–214

—(1986), 'The Ka'ba: aspects of its ritual functions and position in pre-Islamic and early Islamic times', *JSAI* 8, pp. 97–131; repr. in Peters (ed.) (1999), pp. 313–47

—(1990), '*Hanifiyya* and Ka'ba: an inquiry into the Arabian pre-Islamic background of *Din Ibrahim*', *JSAI* 13, pp. 85–112; repr. in Peters (ed.) (1999), pp. 267–94

—(1995), *The eye of the beholder: the life of Muhammad as viewed by the early Muslims – a textual analysis*, Princeton

Rubin, Z. (1986), 'Diplomacy and war in the relations between Byzantium and the Sassanids in the fifth century AD', in Freeman and Kennedy (eds.) (1986), II, pp. 677–95

—(1995), 'The reforms of Khusro Anushirwan', in *BEINE*, III, pp. 227–97

—(2002), '*Res gestae divi saporis*: Greek and Middle Iranian in a document of Sasanian anti-Roman propaganda', in Adams *et al.* (eds.) (2002), pp. 267–97

—(2004), 'Nobility, monarchy and legitimation under the later Sasanians', in *BEINE*, VI, pp. 235–73

Ruprechtsberger, E. M. (1989), 'Byzantinische Befestigungen in Algerien und Tunesien', *Antike Welt* 20.1, pp. 3–21

Russell, J. R. (1987), *Zoroastrianism in Armenia*, Cambridge, MA

Sabin, P. *et al.* (eds.) (2007), *The Cambridge history of Greek and Roman warfare*, 2 vols., Cambridge

Said, S. (ed.) (1991), *Hellenismos: quelques jalons pour une histoire de l'identité grecque (Actes du colloque de Strasbourg, 25–27 octobre 1989)*, Leiden

Sarkissian, K. (1965), *The council of Chalcedon and the Armenian church*, New York

Sarris, P. (2002), 'The Justinianic plague: origins and effects', *Continuity and Change* 17, pp. 169–82

—(2004), 'The origins of the manorial economy: new insights from late antiquity', *EHR* 119, pp. 279–311

—(2006), 'Aristocrats and aliens in early Byzantine Constantinople', in Jeffreys, E. (ed.) (2006), pp. 413–27

Sartre, M. (1982), 'Tribus et clans dans le *Hawran* antique', *Syria* 59, pp. 77–91

Sasson, J. M. (ed.) (1995), *Civilizations of the ancient Near East*, 4 vols., New York

Schäfer, P. (1997), *Judeophobia: attitudes towards the Jews in the ancient world*, Cambridge, MA

Scharf, R. (2001), *Foederati: von der völkerrechtlichen Kategorie zur byzantinischen Truppengattung*, Vienna

Scheidel, W. (ed.) (2001), *Debating Roman demography*, Leiden

Schick, R. (1995), *The Christian communities of Palestine from Byzantine to Islamic rule: a historical and archaeological study*, Princeton

Schippmann, K. (1990), *Grundzüge der Geschichte des sasanidischen Reiches*, Darmstadt

Schneider, D. M. (1984), *A critique of the study of kinship*, Ann Arbor, MI

Schreiner, P. (1985), 'Eine merowingische Gesandschaft in Konstantinopel (590?)', *Frühmittelalterliche Studien* 19, pp. 195–200

—(1998), 'Der *Liber Pontificalis* und Byzanz: Mentalitätsgeschichte im Spiegel einer Quelle, mit einem Exkurs: Byzanz und der Liber Pontificalis (Vat. gr. 1455)', in Borchardt and Bünz (eds.), (1998), I, pp. 33–48

Schulze, W. *et al.* (2006), 'Heraclian countermarks on Byzantine copper coins in seventh-century Syria', *BMGS* 30, pp. 1–27

Scott, R. (1981), 'The classical tradition in Byzantine historiography', in Mullett and Scott (eds.) (1981), pp. 61–74

—(1996), 'Writing the reign of Justinian: Malalas *versus* Theophanes', in Allen and Jeffreys (eds.) (1996), pp. 20–34

Segal, J. B. (1984), 'Arabs in Syriac literature before the rise of Islam', *JSAI* 4, pp. 89–123

Seibt, W. (ed.) (2002), *Die Christianisierung des Kaukasus: Referate des Internationalen Symposions (Wien 9. bis 12. Dezember 1999)*, Vienna

Serjeant, R. B. (1962), '*Haram* and *Hawtah*: the sacred enclave in Arabia', in Badawi (ed.) (1962), pp. 41–58; repr. in Peters (ed.) (1999), pp. 167–84

—(1990), '*Meccan trade and the rise of Islam*: misconceptions and flawed polemics', *JAOS* 110, pp. 472–86

Ševčenko, I. (1980), 'A shadow outline of virtue: the classical heritage of Greek Christian literature (second to seventh century)', in Weitzmann (ed.) (1980), pp. 53–73; repr. in Ševčenko, I. (1982a), no. 2

Seyrig, H. (1941), 'Antiquités syriennes: postes romains sur la route de Médine',
    Syria 22, pp. 218–23
Shahid, I. (1958), 'The last days of Salih', *Arabica* 5, pp. 145–58
—(1984), *Rome and the Arabs: a prolegomenon to the study of Byzantium and the
    Arabs*, Washington, DC
—(1989), *Byzantium and the Arabs in the fifth century*, Washington, DC
—(1995–2002), *Byzantium and the Arabs in the sixth century*, 2 vols. in 3 pts.,
    Washington, DC
—(2000), 'Byzantium and the Arabs in the sixth century: à propos of a recent
    review', *BF* 26, pp. 125–60
—(2002), 'The thematization of Oriens: final observations', *Byz* 72, pp. 192–249
Shaked, S. (forthcoming), 'Zoroastrians and others in Sasanian Iran', in *BEINE*,
    IV
Shaki, M. (1981), 'The *Denkard* account of the history of the Zoroastrian scriptures',
    Archív Orientalní 49, pp. 114–25
Sharf, A. (1971), *Byzantine Jewry: from Justinian to the Fourth Crusade*, London
Shaw, B. D. (1982–3), '"Eaters of flesh, drinkers of milk": the ancient Mediterranean
    ideology of the pastoral nomad', *Ancient Society* 13–14, pp. 5–31; repr. in Shaw
    (1995), no. 6
—(1995), *Rulers, nomads and Christians in Roman North Africa*, Aldershot
Simon, R. (1967), 'L'Inscription Ry 506 et la préhistoire de la Mecque', *AOH* 20,
    pp. 325–37
—(1989), *Meccan trade and Islam: problems of origin and structure*, tr. F. Sós,
    Budapest; tr. of R. Simon, *A mekkai kereskedelem kialakulása és jellege*,
    Budapest, 1975
Smith, S. (1954), 'Events in Arabia in the sixth century AD', *BSOAS* 16,
    pp. 425–68
Solodukho, I. A. (1948), 'Podati i povinnosti v Irake v III-V vv. nashei ery', *Sovetskoe
    vostokovedenie* 5, pp. 55–72
Spanu, P. G. (1998), *La Sardegna bizantina tra VI e VII secolo*, Oristano
Speck, P. (2003c), 'The Virgin's help for Constantinople', *BMGS* 27, pp. 266–71
Spieser, J.-M. (2001), *Urban and religious spaces in late antiquity and early Byzan-
    tium*, Aldershot
Stathakopoulos, D. C. (2004), *Famine and pestilence in the late Roman empire and
    early Byzantine empire: a systematic survey of subsistence crises and epidemics*,
    Aldershot
Stein, E. (1920), 'Des Tiberius Constantinus Novelle "peri epiboles" und der Edic-
    tus domni Chilperici regis', *Klio* 16, pp. 72–4
—(1949–59), *Histoire du bas-empire*, I: *De l'état romain à l'état byzantin, 284–476*;
    II: *De la disparition de l'empire d'Occident à la mort de Justinien, 476–565*, Paris;
    repr. Amsterdam, 1968
Stepanov, T. and Vachkova, V. (eds.) (2004), *Civitas divino-humana: in honorem
    annorum LX Georgii Bakalov*, Sofia
Stewart, F. (1994), *Honor*, Chicago
Stolte, B. (1999), 'Desires denied: marriage, adultery and divorce in early Byzantine
    law', in James (ed.) (1999), pp. 77–86

—(2003–4[2005]), 'Is Byzantine law Roman law?', *Acta Byzantina Fennica* n.s. 2, pp. 111–26

Stratos, A. N. (1968–80), *Byzantium in the seventh century*, tr. M. Ogilvie-Grant and H. T. Hionides, 5 vols., Amsterdam

Swanson, R. N. (ed.) (2000), *The Holy Land, holy lands and Christian history*, SCH 36, Oxford

Sweet, L. E. (1965), 'Camel raiding of north Arabian Bedouin: a mechanism of ecological adaptation', *American anthropologist* 67, pp. 1132–50

Taft, R. F. (1978), *The great entrance: a history of the transfer of gifts and other pre-anaphoral rites of the liturgy of St John Chrysostom*, OCA 200, 2nd edn., Rome

—(2001), *Divine liturgies: human problems in Byzantium, Armenia, Syria and Palestine*, Aldershot

Tapper, R. (1990), 'Anthropologists, historians and tribespeople on tribe and state formation in the Middle East', in Khoury and Kostiner (eds.) (1990), pp. 48–73

Tchalenko, G. (1953–58), *Villages antiques de la Syrie du Nord*, 3 vols., Paris

Teall, J. (1965), 'The barbarians in Justinian's armies', *Sp* 40, pp. 294–322

Teixidor, J. (1977), *The pagan god: popular religion in the Greco-Roman Near East*, Princeton

Ter-Minassiantz, E. (1904), *Die armenische Kirche in ihren Beziehungen zu den syrischen Kirchen bis zum Ende des 13. Jahrhunderts*, Leipzig

Themelis, P. (2005), 'Eleutherna: the protobyzantine city', *TM* 15, pp. 343–56

Thomson, R. W. (1982), 'The formation of the Armenian literary tradition', in Garsoïan *et al.* (eds.) (1982), pp. 135–50; repr. Thomson (1994), no. 4

—(1988–9), 'Mission, conversion and Christianization: the Armenian example', *HUS* 12–13, pp. 28–45; repr. Thomson (1994), no. 3

—(1994), *Studies in Armenian literature and Christianity*, Aldershot

—(1995), *A bibliography of classical Armenian literature to 1500 AD*, Turnhout

—(1998), 'The defence of Armenian orthodoxy in Sebeos', in Ševčenko and Hutter (eds.) (1998), pp. 329–41

—(2007), 'Supplement to *A bibliography of classical Armenian literature to 1500 AD*: publications 1993–2005', *LM* 120, pp. 163–223

Tougher, S. (2004), 'Social transformation, gender transformation? The court eunuch, 300–900', in Brubaker and Smith (eds.) (2004), pp. 70–82

Toumanoff, C. (1963), *Studies in Christian Caucasian history*, Washington, DC

Treadgold, W. (1990), 'The break in Byzantium and the gap in Byzantine studies', *BF* 15, pp. 289–316

—(2007), *Early Byzantine historians*, Basingstoke

Trimingham, J. S. (1979), *Christianity among the Arabs in pre-Islamic times*, London

Trombley, F. (1997), 'War and society in rural Syria *c.* 502–613 AD: observations on the epigraphy', *BMGS* 21, pp. 154–209

Tsafrir, Y. and Foerster, G. (1994), 'From Scythopolis to Baysan: changing concepts of urbanism', in *BEINE*, II, pp. 95–115

Van Dam, R. (2005), 'Merovingian Gaul and the Frankish conquests', in *NCMH*, I, pp. 193–231

Van Der Horst, P. W. (2004), '*Twenty-five questions to corner the Jews*: a Byzantine anti-Jewish document from the seventh century', in Chazon *et al.* (eds.) (2004), pp. 289–301

Vanhaverbeke, H. *et al.* (2004), 'Late antiquity in the territory of Sagalassos', in Bowden *et al.* (eds.) (2004), pp. 247–79

Vermoere, M. *et al.* (2003), 'Pollen sequences from the city of Sagalassos (Pisidia, south-west Turkey)', *Anatolian studies* 53, pp. 161–73

Villiers, A. (1940), *Sons of Sinbad*, London

Walmsley, A. (1996), 'Byzantine Palestine and Arabia: urban prosperity in late antiquity', in Christie and Loseby (eds.) (1996), pp. 126–58

—(2007), *Early Islamic Syria: an archaeological assessment*, London

Ward-Perkins, B. (1998), 'The cities', in *CAH*, XIII, pp. 371–410

—(2000a), 'Land, labour and settlement', in *CAH*, XIV, pp. 315–45

—(2000b), 'Specialized production and exchange', in *CAH*, XIV, pp. 346–91

—(2005), *The fall of Rome and the end of civilization*, Oxford

Watrous, L. V. *et al.* (2004), *The plain of Phaistos: cycles of social complexity in the Mesara region of Crete*, Los Angeles

Watson, P. (1992), 'Change in foreign and regional economic links with Pella in the seventh century AD: the ceramic evidence', in Canivet and Rey-Coquais (eds.) (1992), pp. 233–48

Watt, W. M. (1953), *Muhammad at Mecca*, Oxford

—(1979), 'The Qur'an and belief in a high god', *Der Islam* 56, pp. 205–11

Watts, E. (2004), 'Justinian, Malalas and the end of Athenian philosophical teaching in AD 529', *Journal of Roman Studies* 94, pp. 168–82

Webb, R. (1999), 'The aesthetics of sacred space: narrative, metaphor, and motion in *ekphraseis* of church buildings', *DOP* 53, pp. 59–74

Weitzmann, K. (ed.) (1980), *Age of spirituality: a symposium*, Princeton

Welch, A. T. (1979), 'Allah and other supernatural beings: the emergence of the Qur'anic doctrine of *tawhid*'', *Journal of the American Academy of Religion* 47, *Dec. suppl.*, pp. 733–58

Wellesz, E. (1956), 'The "Akathistos": a study in Byzantine hymnography', *DOP* 9/10, pp. 141–74

Wellhausen, J. (1897), *Reste arabischen Heidentums*, 2nd edn., Berlin

Whitby, Mary (1998), 'Defender of the cross: George of Pisidia on the emperor Heraclius and his deputies', in Whitby, Mary (ed.) (1998), pp. 247–73

—(2002), 'George of Pisidia's presentation of the emperor Heraclius and his campaigns: variety and development', in Reinink and Stolte (eds.) (2002), pp. 157–73

—(ed.) (1998), *The propaganda of power: the role of panegyric in late antiquity*, Leiden

Whitby, Michael (1992), 'Greek historical writing after Procopius: variety and vitality', in *BEINE*, I, pp. 25–80

—(1994), 'The Persian king at war', in Dabrowa (ed.) (1994), p. 227–63

Whitehouse, D. and Williamson, A. (1973), 'Sasanian maritime trade', *Iran* 11, pp. 29–48

Whittow, M. (1990), 'Ruling the late Roman and early Byzantine city: a continuous history', *PaP* 129, pp. 3–29

—(1999), 'Rome and the Jafnids: writing the history of a sixth-century tribal dynasty', in Humphrey (ed.) (1995–2002), II, pp. 207–24

—(2001), 'Recent research on the late-antique city in Asia Minor: the second half of the sixth century revisited', in Lavan (ed.) (2001), pp. 137–53

Widengren, G. (1956), 'Recherches sur le féodalisme iranien', *Orientalia Suecana* 5, pp. 79–182

—(1961), 'The status of the Jews in the Sassanian empire', *IA* 1, pp. 117–62

—(1965), *Die Religionen Irans*, Stuttgart

—(1967), *Der Feudalismus im alten Iran*, Cologne

—(1976), 'Iran, der grosse Gegner Roms: Königsgewalt, Feudalismus, Militärwesen', *ANRW* II, 9.1, pp. 219–306

Wiesehöfer, J. (1996), *Ancient Persia: from 550 BC to 650 AD*, tr. A. Azodi, London

Wikander, S. (1946), *Feuerpriester in Kleinasien und Iran*, Lund

Winkelmann, F. (1993), *Studien zu Konstantin dem Grossen und zur byzantinischen Kirchengeschichte: ausgewählte Aufsätze*, ed. W. Brandes and J. Haldon, Birmingham

Winkler, G. (1982), *Das armenische Initiationsrituale*, OCA 217, Rome

—(2000), *Über die Entwicklungsgeschichte des armenischen Symbolums*, OCA 262, Rome

Wiseman, T. P. (ed.) (2002), *Classics in progress: essays on ancient Greece and Rome*, Oxford

Wolfram, H. (1988), *History of the Goths*, tr. T. J. Dunlap, Berkeley

Wolski, J. (1976), 'Iran und Rom: Versuch einer historischen Wertung der gegenseitigen Beziehungen' *ANRW* II, 9.1, pp. 195–214

Wood, D. (ed.) (1992a), *Christianity and Judaism, SCH* 29, Oxford

—(1992b), *The church and the arts, SCH* 28, Oxford

Yarshater, E. (1971), 'Were the Sasanians heirs to the Achaemenids?', in *La Persia nel medioevo: atti del convegno internazionale (Roma, 31 marzo–5 aprile 1970)*, ANL PASC 160, Rome, pp. 517–33

—(ed.) (1983), *The Cambridge history of Iran*, III: *The Seleucid, Parthian and Sasanian periods*, 2 vols., Cambridge

Young, F. *et al.* (eds.) (2004), *The Cambridge history of early Christian literature*, Cambridge

Zaehner, R. C. (1955), *Zurvan: a Zoroastrian dilemma*, Oxford

—(1975), *The dawn and twilight of Zoroastrianism*, London

Zeyadeh, A. (1994), 'Settlement patterns, an archaeological perspective: case studies from northern Palestine and Jordan', in *BEINE*, II, pp. 117–31

Zuckerman, C. (2004), *Du village à l'empire: autour du registre fiscal d'Aphroditô, 525–526*, Paris

SECONDARY WORKS, PART II (*c*. 700–1204)

Abashidze, M. and Rapp, S. H. (2004), 'The Life and Passion of Kostanti-Kaxay', *LM* 117, pp. 137–74

Abulafia, D. (1984), 'Ancona, Byzantium and the Adriatic 1155–1173', *PBSR* 52,
    pp. 195–216; repr. in Abulafia (1987), no. 9
—(2004), 'The Italian other: Greeks, Muslims, and Jews', in Abulafia (ed.) (2004),
    pp. 215–36, 267–9
—(ed.) (2004), *Italy in the central middle ages, 1000–1300*, Oxford
Abulafia, D. and Berend, N. (eds.) (2002), *Medieval frontiers: concepts and practices*,
    Aldershot
Adontz, N. (1933), 'La Portée historique de l'oraison funèbre de Basile I par son
    fils Léon VI le sage', *Byz* 8, pp. 501–13
—(1933–4), 'L'Âge et l'origine de l'empereur Basile I (867–886)', *Byz* 8, pp. 475–500
    and *Byz* 9, pp. 223–60
Aerts, W. J. (1972), 'The Monza Vocabulary', in Bakker *et al.* (eds.) (1972), pp. 36–73
Afinogenov, D. E. (1994), '*Kōnstantinoupolis episkopon echei*: the rise of the patriar-
    chal power in Byzantium from Nicaenum II to Epanagoga, I: from Nicaenum
    II to the second outbreak of iconoclasm', *Erytheia* 15, pp. 45–65
—(1996), '*Kōnstantinoupolis episkopon echei*, II: from the second outbreak of icon-
    oclasm to the death of Methodios', *Erytheia* 17, pp. 43–71
—(1997), *Konstantinopol'skii patriarkhat i ikonoborcheskii krizis v Vizantii (784–
    847)*, Moscow
—(1999), 'The date of Georgios Monachos reconsidered', *BZ* 92, pp. 437–47
—(2001), 'The conspiracy of Michael Traulos and the assassination of Leo V:
    history and fiction', *DOP* 55, pp. 329–38
—(2004), 'Le Manuscrit grec Coislin 305: la version primitive de la *Chronique* de
    Georges le Moine', *REB* 62, pp. 239–46
Agapitos, P. A. (1989), 'E eikona tou autokratora Basileiou I ste philomakedonike
    grammateia, 867–959', *Hell* 40, pp. 285–322
—(1991), *Narrative structure in the Byzantine vernacular romances: a textual and
    literary study of Kallimachos, Belthandros and Libistros, MBM* 34, Munich
—(2003), 'Ancient models and novel mixtures: the concept of genre in Byzan-
    tine funerary literature from Photios to Eustathios of Thessalonike', in Nagy
    et al. (eds.) (2003), pp. 5–23
Ahrweiler, see also Glykatzi and Glykatzi-Ahrweiler
Ahrweiler, H. (1960), *Recherches sur l'administration de l'empire byzantin aux
    IXe–XIe siècles*, Paris [= *BCH* 84, pp. 1–109]; repr. in Ahrweiler (1971),
    no. 8
—(1962a), 'L'Asie Mineure et les invasions arabes', *RH* 227, pp. 1–32
—(1962b), 'Une inscription méconnue sur les Mélingues du Taygète', *BCH* 86,
    pp. 1–10; repr. in Ahrweiler (1971), no. 15
—(1975a), *L'Idéologie politique de l'empire byzantin*, Paris
—(ed.) (1988), *Géographie historique du monde méditerranéen, BSo* 7, Paris
Akinean, A. and Ter-Pawghosean, P. (1968a), 'Vahanay Nikiay episkoposi bank'',
    HAm 82, pp. 257–80
—(1968b), 'Patchen t'ght'oyn metsi hayrapatin Kostandinupolsi P'otay ar Ashot
    ishkhanats' ishkhan', *HAm* 82, pp. 439–50
Alekseenko, N. (2003), 'Les Relations entre Cherson et l'empire, d'après le
    témoignage des sceaux des archives de Cherson', *SBS* 8, pp. 75–83

Alexander, P. J. (1953), 'The iconoclastic council of St Sophia (815) and its definition (*horos*)', *DOP* 7, pp. 35–66; repr. in Alexander (1978), no. 8

—(1958a), *The patriarch Nicephorus of Constantinople: ecclesiastical policy and image worship in the Byzantine empire*, Oxford

—(1958b), 'Church councils and patristic authority: the iconoclastic councils of Hiereia (754) and St Sophia (815)', *Harvard Studies in Classical Philology* 63, pp. 493–505; repr. in Alexander (1978), no. 9

—(1962), 'The strength of empire and capital as seen through Byzantine eyes', *Sp* 37, pp. 339–357; repr. in Alexander (1978), no. 3

—(1973), 'Les Débuts des conquêtes arabes en Sicile et la tradition apocalyptique byzantino-slave', *Bollettino del Centro di studi filologici e linguistici siciliani* 12, pp. 7–35; repr. in Alexander (1978), no. 14

—(1977), 'Religious persecution and resistance in the Byzantine empire of the eighth and ninth centuries: methods and justifications', *Sp* 52, pp. 238–64; repr. in Alexander (1978), no. 10

—(1978), *Religious and political history and thought in the Byzantine empire*, London

Alexiou, M. (1982–3), 'Literary subversion and the aristocracy in twelfth-century Byzantium: a stylistic analysis of the *Timarion* (ch. 6–10), *BMGS* 8, pp. 29–45

—(1986), 'The poverty of *écriture* and the craft of writing: towards a reappraisal of the Prodromic poems', *BMGS* 10, pp. 1–40

Alishan, G. (1881), *Shirak: teghagrut'iwn patkerats'oyts'*, Venice

Althoff, G. (1991), 'Vormundschaft, Erzieher, Lehrer – Einflüsse auf Otto III', in von Euw and Schreiner (eds.) (1991), II, pp. 277–89

—(2003), *Otto III*, tr. P. G. Jestice, University Park, PA

Althoff, G. *et al.* (eds.) (1988), *Person und Gemeinschaft im Mittelalter: Karl Schmid zum fünfundsechzigsten Geburtstag*, Sigmaringen

Alvermann, D. (1995), 'La battaglia di Ottone II contro i Saraceni nel 982', *Archivio storico per la Calabria e la Lucania* 62, pp. 115–30

Amari, M. (1933–9), *Storia dei musulmani di Sicilia*, ed. C. A. Nallino, 2nd edn., 3 vols. in 5 pts., Catania

Amsellem, E. (1999), 'Les Stigand: des Normands à Constantinople', *REB* 57, pp. 283–8

Anastasi, R. (1969), *Studi sulla Chronographia di Michele Psello*, Catania

Anastos, M. V. (1957), 'The transfer of Illyricum, Calabria and Sicily to the jurisdiction of the patriarchate of Constantinople in 732–733', *RSBN* 9, pp. 14–31; repr. in Anastos (1979), no. 9

—(1968), 'Leo III's edict against the images in the year 726–727 and Italo-Byzantine relations between 726 and 730', *BF* 3, pp. 5–41; repr. in Anastos (1979), no. 8

—(1979), *Studies in Byzantine intellectual history*, London

—(1993), 'The coronation of Emperor Michael IV in 1034 by Empress Zoe and its significance', in Langdon *et al.* (eds.) (1993), I, pp. 23–43; repr. in Anastos (2001b), no. 7

—(2001a), 'Constantinople and Rome: a survey of the relations between the Byzantine and the Roman churches', in Anastos (2001b), no. 8, pp. i–vi, 1–119

—(2001b), *Aspects of the mind of Byzantium: political theory, theology and ecclesiastical relations with the See of Rome*, ed. S. Vryonis and N. Goodhue, Aldershot

Anca, A. S. (2005), 'Ehrerweisung durch Geschenke in der Komnenenzeit: Gewohnheiten und Regeln des herrscherlichen Schenkens', *MSABK* 4, pp. 185–94

Andel, T. H. van *et al.* (1986), 'Five thousand years of land use and abuse in the southern Argolid', *Hesperia* 55, pp. 103–28

Angelidi, C. (1994), 'Un texte patriographique et édifiant: le "discours narratif" sur les Hodégoi', *REB* 52, pp. 113–49

Angelidi, C. and Papamastorakis, T. (2000), 'The veneration of the Virgin Hodegetria and the Hodegon monastery', in Vassilaki (ed.) (2000), pp. 272–87

Angelov, D. *et al.* (eds.) (1984), *Sbornik v pamet na Prof. Stancho Vaklinov*, Sofia

Angold, M. (1985), 'The shaping of the medieval Byzantine city', *BF* 10, pp. 1–38

—(1991), 'The Byzantine state on the eve of the battle of Manzikert', in Bryer and Ursinus (eds.) (1991), pp. 9–34

—(1999), 'The road to 1204: the Byzantine background to the Fourth Crusade', *JMH* 25, pp. 257–78

—(ed.) (1984), *The Byzantine aristocracy, IX to XIII centuries*, BAR IS 221, Oxford

Ankori, Z. (1959), *Karaites in Byzantium: the formative years, 970–1110*, New York

Antoniadis-Bibicou, see Bibicou

Antonopoulou, T. (1997), *The homilies of the emperor Leo VI*, Leiden

Archer, L. J. *et al.* (eds.) (1994), *Women in ancient societies: an illusion of the night*, Basingstoke

Argant, J. (2003), 'Données palynologiques', in Geyer and Lefort (eds.) (2003), pp. 175–200

Arnaldi, G. (1987), 'Le origini del patrimonio di S. Pietro', in Arnaldi *et al.* (1987), pp. 3–151

Arnaldi, G. *et al.* (1987), *Comuni e signorie nell'Italia nordorientale e centrale: Lazio, Umbria e Marche, Lucca, Storia d'Italia* 7.2, Turin

Arnaldi, G. and Cavallo G. (eds.) (1997), *Europa medievale e mondo bizantino: contatti effettivi e possibilità di studi comparati*, Rome

Arslan, E. A. and Morrisson, C. (2002), 'Monete e moneta a Roma nell'alto medioevo', *Roma fra oriente e occidente* = *SSCIS* 49, II, pp. 1255–1305

Arthur, P. (1997), 'Un gruppo di ceramiche alto medievale da Hierapolis (Pamukkale, Denizli), Turchia occidentale', *Archeologia medievale* 24, pp. 531–40

—(2002), *Naples, from Roman town to city-state: an archaeological perspective*, London

Arutiunova-Fidanian, V. A. (1980), *Armiane-khalkidoniti na vostochnikh granitsakh vizantiiskoi imperii (XIv.)*, Erevan

—(1988–9), 'The ethno-confessional self-awareness of Armenian Chalcedonians', *REA* n.s. 21, pp. 345–63

Arutjunova-Fidanjan, see Arutiunova-Fidanian

Astruc, C. *et al.* (1970), 'Les Sources grecques pour l'histoire des Pauliciens d'Asie Mineure: texte critique et traduction', *TM* 4, pp. 1–227

Atherden, M. A. and Hall, J. A. (1994), 'Holocene pollen diagrams from Greece', *Historical biology* 9, pp. 117–30

—(1999), 'Human impact on vegetation in the White Mountains of Crete since AD 500', *The Holocene* 9, pp. 183–93

Augenti, A. (1996), *Il Palatino nel medioevo: archeologia e topografia (secoli VI–XIII)*, Rome

Auzépy, M.-F. (1988), 'La Place des moines à Nicée II (787)', *Byz* 58, pp. 5–21

—(1990), 'La Destruction de l'icône du Christ de la Chalcé par Léon III: propagande ou réalité?', *Byz* 60, pp. 445–92

—(1992), 'L'Analyse littéraire et l'historien: l'exemple des vies de saints iconoclastes', *BSl* 53, pp. 57–67

—(1994a), 'Constantin V, l'empereur isaurien et les Carolingiens', in Redon and Rosenberger (eds.) (1994), pp. 49–64

—(1994b), 'De la Palestine à Constantinople (VIIIᵉ–IXᵉ siècles): Étienne le Sabaïte et Jean Damascène', *TM* 12, pp. 183–218

—(1995a), 'L'*Adversus Constantinum Caballinum* et Jean de Jérusalem', *BSl* 56, pp. 323–38

—(1995b), 'La Carrière d'André de Crète', *BZ* 88, pp. 1–12

—(1997), 'Francfort et Nicée II', in Berndt (ed.) (1997), I, pp. 279–300

—(1999), *L'Hagiographie et l'iconoclasme byzantin: le cas de la Vie d'Étienne le Jeune*, Aldershot

—(2000), 'La Gothie aux VIIIᵉ–IXᵉ siècles d'après les sources ecclésiastiques et hagiographiques', in *Materialy po arkheologii, istorii i etnografii Tavrii* 7, pp. 324–31 [= *Materials in archaeology, history and ethnography of Tauria*, VII, ed. A. Aïbabin, Simferopol, 2000]

—(2001), 'Les Isauriens et l'espace sacré: l'église et les reliques', in Kaplan (ed.) (2001), pp. 13–24

—(2002), 'Constantin, Théodore et le dragon', in Nikolaou (ed.) (2002), pp. 87–96

—(2003), 'Les Monastères', in Geyer and Lefort (eds.) (2003) pp. 431–58

—(2004), 'Les Enjeux de l'iconoclasme', *Cristianità d'occidente e cristianità d'oriente (secoli VI–XI)* = *SSCIS* 51, pp. 127–69

Auzépy, M.-F. *et al.* (1996), *La Chrétienté orientale du début du VIIᵉ siècle au milieu du XIᵉ siècle: textes et documents*, Paris

Avramea, A. (1997), *Le Péloponnèse du IVᵉ au VIIIᵉ siècle: changements et persistances*, *BSo* 15, Paris

—(2001), 'Les Slaves dans le Péloponnèse', in Kountoura-Galake (ed.) (2001), pp. 293–302

Avramea, A. *et al.* (eds.) (2003), *Byzantio, kratos kai koinonia: mneme Nikou Oikonomide (Byzantium, state and society: in memory of Nikos Oikonomides)*, Athens

Azzara, C. (1994), *Venetiae: determinazione di un'area regionale fra antichità e alto medioevo*, Treviso

Baker, D. (ed.) (1973), *Sanctity and secularity: the church and the world*, *SCH* 10, Oxford

Bakker, W. F., *et al.* (eds.) (1972), *Studia byzantina et neohellenica neerlandica*, Leiden

Balard, M. (1976), 'Amalfi et Byzance (Xᵉ–XIIᵉ siècles)', *TM* 6, pp. 85–95

Balard, M. *et al.* (eds.) (1998), *Eupsychia: mélanges offerts à Hélène Ahrweiler*, 2 vols., *BSo* 16, Paris

Ball, J. L. (2005), *Byzantine dress: representations of secular dress in eighth- to twelfth-century painting*, Basingstoke

Bănescu, N. (1946), *Les Duchés byzantins de Paristrion (Paradounavon) et de Bulgarie*, Bucharest

Barber, C. (1997), 'Homo byzantinus?', in James (ed.) (1997), pp. 185–99

—(2002), *Figure and likeness: on the limits of representation in Byzantine iconoclasm*, Princeton

Barbu, D. (1989), 'Monde byzantin ou monde orthodoxe', *RESEE* 27, pp. 259–71

Bardill, J. (2006), 'Visualizing the Great Palace of the Byzantine emperors at Constantinople: archaeology, text and topography', in Bauer (ed.) (2006), pp. 5–46

Barišić, F. (ed.) (1963–4), *Mélanges Georges Ostrogorsky = ZRVI* 8, 2 vols., Belgrade

Barnard, L. W. (1974), *The Graeco-Roman and oriental background of the iconoclastic controversy*, Leiden

Barnea, I. (1983), 'Sigilii bizantine inedite din Dobrogea, I', *Pontica* 16, pp. 263–72

—(1987), 'Sceaux byzantins de Dobroudja', *SBS* 1, pp. 77–88

Barnes, H. and Whittow, M. (1993), 'The Oxford University/British Institute of Archaeology at Ankara survey of medieval castles of Anatolia (1992). Mastaura Kalesi: a preliminary report', *Anatolian studies* 43, pp. 117–35

Barzos, K. (1984), *E genealogia ton Komnenon*, 2 vols., Thessalonica

Bass, G. F. *et al.* (eds.) (2004), *Serçe Limani: an eleventh-century shipwreck*, I: *The ship and its anchorage, crew and passengers*, College Station, TX

Bauer, F. A. (2006), 'Potentieller Besitz: Geschenke im Rahmen des byzantinischen Kaiserzeremoniells', in Bauer (ed.) (2006), pp. 135–70

—(ed.) (2006), *Visualisierungen von Herrschaft: frühmittelalterliche Residenzen – Gestalt und Zeremoniell*, Istanbul

Baun, J. (2000), 'Middle Byzantine "tours of hell": outsider theodicy?', in Smythe (ed.) (2000), pp. 47–60

—(2008), 'Last things', in Noble and Smith (eds.) (2008), pp. 606–24

Bavant, B. (1979), 'Le Duché byzantin de Rome: origine, durée et extension géographique', *MEFRM* 91, pp. 41–88

Bazzana, A. (ed.) (1999), *Archéologie des espaces agraires méditerranéens au moyen âge: actes du colloque de Murcie (Espagne) tenu du 8 au 12 mai 1992*, Castrum 5, Madrid

Beaton, R. and Ricks, D. (eds.) (1993), *Digenes Akrites: new approaches to Byzantine heroic poetry*, Aldershot

Beaton, R. and Roueché, C. (eds.) (1993), *The making of Byzantine history: studies dedicated to Donald M. Nicol*, Aldershot

Beaucamp, J. (1977), 'La Situation juridique de la femme à Byzance', *Cahiers de civilisation médiévale, Xe–XIIe siècles* 20, pp. 145–76

—(2004), 'La Christianisation du droit à Byzance: l'exemple du statut des femmes', *Cristianità d'occidente e cristianità d'oriente (secoli VI–XI) = SSCIS* 51, pp. 917–55

Beaucamp, J. and Dagron, G. (eds.) (1998), *La Transmission du patrimoine: Byzance et l'aire méditerranéenne*, Paris

Becher, M. (2002), 'Die Kaiserkrönung im Jahr 800: eine Streitfrage zwischen Karl dem Grossen und Papst Leo III.', *Rheinische Vierteljahrsblätter* 66, pp. 1–38

Beck, H.-G. (1965), 'Konstantinopel: zur Sozialgeschichte einer frühmittelalterlichen Haupstadt', *BZ* 58, pp. 11–45; repr. in Beck (1972), no. 10

—(1966), 'Senat und Volk von Konstantinopel: Probleme der byzantinischen Verfassungsgeschichte', *Bayerische Akademie der Wissenschaften. Philosophisch-Historische Klasse. Sitzungsberichte 1966*, pp. 1–75; repr. in Beck (1972), no. 12

—(1967), 'Christliche Mission und politische Propaganda im byzantinischen Reich', *La conversione al Cristianesimo nell'Europa dell'alto medioevo* = *SSCIS* 14, pp. 649–74; repr. in Beck (1972), no. 4

—(1969), 'The Byzantine church in the age of Photius', in Kempf *et al.* (1969), pp. 174–93

—(1972), *Ideen und Realitäten in Byzanz*, London

Beihammer, A. D. (2000), *Nachrichten zum byzantinischen Urkundenwesen in arabischen Quellen (565–811)*, Bonn

—(2004), 'Die Kraft der Zeichen: Symbolische Kommunikation in der byzantinisch-arabischen Diplomatie des 10. und 11. Jahrhunderts', *JÖB* 54, pp. 159–89

Beletsky, D. V. and Vinogradov, A. I. (2005), 'Freski Sentinskogo khrama i problemy istorii alanskogo khristianstva v X v.', *Rossiiskaia arkheologiia* no. 1, pp. 130–42

Belke, K. *et al.* (eds.) (2000), *Byzanz als Raum: zu Methoden und Inhalten der historischen Geographie des östlichen Mittelmeerraumes*, Vienna

Belletzkie, R. J. (1980), 'Pope Nicholas I and John of Ravenna: the struggle for ecclesiastical rights in the ninth century', *Church history* 49, pp. 262–72

Bellier, P. *et al.* (1986), *Paysages de Macédoine: leurs caractères, leur évolution à travers les documents et les récits des voyageurs*, Paris

Belting, H. (1962), 'Studien zum beneventanischen Hof im 8. Jahrhundert', *DOP* 16, pp. 141–93

—(1994), *Likeness and presence: a history of the image before the era of art*, tr. E. Jephcott, Chicago; tr. of Belting, H. (1990), *Bild und Kult. Eine Geschichte des Bildes vor dem Zeitalter der Kunst*, Munich

Bendall, S. and Nesbitt, J. (1990), 'A "poor" token from the reign of Constantine V', *Byz* 60, pp. 432–5

Berardi, D. *et al.* (eds.) (1990–6), *Storia di Ravenna*, 5 vols. in 6 pts., Venice

Berger, A. (1988), *Untersuchungen zu den Patria Konstantinupoleos*, Bonn

—(2001), 'Das Dossier des heiligen Gregentios, ein Werk der Makedonenzeit', *Byzantina* 22, pp. 53–65

Berndt, R. (ed.) (1997), *Das Frankfurter Konzil von 794: Kristallisationspunkt karolingischer Kultur*, 2 vols., Mainz

Berschin, W. (1988), *Greek letters and the Latin middle ages: from Jerome to Nicholas of Cusa*, tr. J. C. Frakes, Washington, DC

Bertolini, O. (1941), *Roma di fronte a Bisanzio e ai Longobardi*, Bologna

—(1950), 'Sergio, arcivescovo di Ravenna (744–769) e i papi del suo tempo', *Studi romagnoli* 1, pp. 43–88; repr. in Bertolini, O. (1968), II, pp. 551–91

—(1967), 'Quale fu il vero obbiettivo assegnato in Italia da Leone III "Isaurico" all'armata di Manes, stratego dei Cibyrreoti?', *BF* 2, pp. 15–49

—(1968), *Scritti scelti di storia medioevale*, ed. O. Banti, 2 vols., Livorno

—(1972), *Roma e i Longobardi*, Rome

Bertolini, P. (1970), 'La serie episcopale napoletana nei sec. VIII e IX: ricerche sulle fonti per la storia dell'Italia meridionale nell'alto medioevo', *Rivista di storia della chiesa in Italia* 24, pp. 349–440

—(1974), 'La chiesa di Napoli durante la crisi iconoclasta: appunti sul codice Vaticano Latino 5007', in *Studi sul medioevo cristiano offerti a Rafaello Morghen per il 90. anniversario dell'Istituto Storico Italiano (1883–1973)*, 2 vols., Rome (1974), I, pp. 101–27

Beshevliev, V. (1963), *Die protobulgarischen Inschriften, BBA* 23, Berlin; rev. Bulgarian edn. *P'rvo-B'lgarski nadpisi*, Sofia (1979); 2nd edn. Sofia (1992)

—(1978), *Bulgarisch-byzantinische Aufsätze*, London

—(1981), *Die protobulgarische Periode der bulgarischen Geschichte*, Amsterdam

Bibicou, H. (1959–60), 'Une page d'histoire diplomatique de Byzance au XIe siècle: Michel VII Doukas, Robert Guiscard et la pension des dignitaires', *Byz* 29–30, pp. 43–75

Bintliff, J. (1996), 'The Frankish countryside in central Greece: the evidence from archaeological field survey', in Lock and Sanders (eds.) (1996), pp. 1–18

—(2000), 'Reconstructing the Byzantine countryside: new approaches from landscape archaeology', in Belke *et al.* (eds.) (2000), pp. 37–63

Biraben, J.-N. and Le Goff, J. (1969), 'La Peste dans le haut moyen âge', *Annales. Économies, Sociétés, Civilisations* 24, pp. 1484–1510

Birkenmeier, J. W. (2002), *The development of the Komnenian army, 1081–1180*, Leiden

Bischoff, B. (1951), 'Das griechische Element in der abendländischen Bildung des Mittelalters', *BZ* 44, pp. 27–55; repr. in Bischoff (1966–81), II, pp. 246–75

—(1966–81), *Mittelalterliche Studien: ausgewählte Aufsätze zur Schriftkunde und Literaturgeschichte*, 3 vols., Stuttgart

—(1977), 'Irische Schreiber im Karolingerreich', in *Jean Scot Érigène et l'histoire de la philosophie: Laon, 7–12 juillet 1975, Colloques internationaux du CNRS* 561, Paris, pp. 47–58

—(1984), *Anecdota novissima: Texte des vierten bis sechzehnten Jahrhunderts*, Stuttgart

Bischoff, B. and Lapidge, M. (1994), *Biblical commentaries from the Canterbury school of Theodore and Hadrian*, Cambridge

Blankinship, K. Y. (1994), *The end of the jihad state: the reign of Hisham ibn 'Abd al-Malik and the collapse of the Umayyads*, Albany, NY

Bloch, H. (1984), 'Der Autor der *Graphia aureae urbis Romae*', *DA* 40, pp. 55–175

—(1988), 'Peter the Deacon's vision of Byzantium and a rediscovered treatise in his *Acta S. Placidi*', *Bisanzio, Roma e l'Italia nell'alto medioevo = SSCIS* 34, pp. 797–847

Blöndal, S. (1978), *The Varangians of Byzantium: an aspect of Byzantine military history*, rev. and trans. B. S. Benedikz, Cambridge

Boase, T. S. R. (1978), 'The history of the kingdom', in Boase (ed.) (1978), pp. 1–33

—(ed.) (1978), *The Cilician kingdom of Armenia*, Edinburgh

Böhlendorf-Arslan, B. (2004), *Glasierte byzantinische Keramik aus der Türkei*, 3 vols., Istanbul

Bojović, B. and Georgiev, B. (1997), 'La Littérature autochtone (hagiographique et historiographique) en Bulgarie médiévale', *Cahiers balkaniques* 4, pp. 21–44

Bonarek, J. (2003), *Romajowie i obcy w kronice Jana Skylitzesa: identyfikacja etniczna Bizantyńczyków i ich stosunek do obcych w świetle kroniki Jana Skylitzesa*, Torun

Bonner, M. (1996), *Aristocratic violence and holy war: studies in the jihad and the Arab-Byzantine frontier*, New Haven and London

Borchardt, K. and Bünz, E. (eds.) (1998), *Forschungen zur Reichs-, Papst- und Landesgeschichte: Peter Herde zum 65. Geburtstag*, 2 vols., Stuttgart

Borgolte, M. (1976), *Der Gesandtenaustausch der Karolinger mit den Abbasiden and mit den Patriarchen von Jerusalem*, Munich

Borsari, S. (1950–1), 'Monasteri bizantini nell'Italia meridionale longobarda (sec. X e XI)', *ASPN* n.s. 32, pp. 1–16

—(1959), 'Istituzioni feudali e parafeudali nella Puglia bizantina', *ASPN* n.s. 37, pp. 123–35

—(1963), *Il monachesimo bizantino nella Sicilia e nell'Italia meridionale prenormanne*, Naples

—(1966–7), 'Aspetti del dominio bizantino in Capitanata', *Atti della Accademia Pontaniana* n.s. 16, pp. 55–66

Bortoli, A. and Kazanski, M. (2002), 'Kherson and its region', in *EHB*, II, pp. 659–65

Boscolo, A. (1978), *La Sardegna bizantina e alto-giudicale*, Sassari

Bosworth, C. E. (1968), 'The political and dynastic history of the Iranian world (AD 1000–1217)', in Boyle (ed.) (1968), pp. 1–202

—(1992), 'The city of Tarsus and the Arab–Byzantine frontiers in early and middle 'Abbasid times', *Oriens* 33, pp. 268–86; repr. in Bosworth (1996), no. 14

—(1996), *The Arabs, Byzantium and Iran: studies in early Islamic history and culture*, Aldershot

Bouhot, J.-P. (1976), *Ratramne de Corbie: histoire littéraire et controverses doctrinales*, Paris

Bouras, C. (1982), *Nea Moni on Chios: history and architecture*, tr. D. A. Hardy, Athens

—(2002), 'Aspects of the Byzantine city, eighth-fifteenth centuries', in *EHB*, II, pp. 497–528

—(2005), 'Originality in Byzantine architecture', *TM* 15, pp. 99–108

Bourin, M. *et al.* (eds.) (1996), *L'Anthroponymie: document de l'histoire sociale des mondes méditerranéens médiévaux*, CEFR 226, Rome

Boyle, J. A. (ed.) (1968), *The Cambridge history of Iran*, V: *The Saljuq and Mongol periods*, Cambridge

Bozhilov, I. (1983), *Tsar Simeon Veliki (893–927): Zlatniiat vek na srednovekovna B'lgariia*, Sofia

—(1986a), 'L'Idéologie politique du tsar Syméon: Pax Symeonica', *BB* 8, pp. 73–88

—(1986b), 'Preslav et Constantinople: dépendance et indépendance culturelles', in *ACIEB* 17, pp. 429–54

Božilov, see Bozhilov

Brand, C. M. (1969), 'Two Byzantine treatises on taxation', *Traditio* 25, pp. 35–60

—(1984), 'The Fourth Crusade: some recent interpretations', *Medievalia et humanistica* n.s. 12, pp. 33–45

—(1989), 'The Turkish element in Byzantium, eleventh-twelfth centuries', *DOP* 43, pp. 1–25

Brandes, W. (1989), *Die Städte Kleinasiens im 7. und 8. Jahrhundert*, Berlin

—(1998), '"Juristische" Krisenbewältigung im 7. Jahrhundert? Die Prozesse gegen Martin I. und Maximos Homologetes', *FM* 10, pp. 141–212

—(1999), 'Byzantine cities in the seventh and eighth centuries – different sources, different histories?', in Brogiolo and Ward-Perkins (eds.) (1999), pp. 29–57

—(2002b), review of W. Treadgold's *A history of the Byzantine state and society*, *BZ* 95, pp. 716–25

Brandes, W. and Haldon, J. (2000), 'Towns, tax and transformation: state, cities and their hinterlands in the east Roman world *c.* 500–800', in Brogiolo *et al.* (eds.) (2000), pp. 141–72

Brenot, C. *et al.* (1978), *Etudes de numismatique danubienne: trésors, lingots, imitations, monnaies de fouilles IVe–XIIe siècle = Sirmium* 8, Rome

Brett, G. (1954), 'The automata in the Byzantine "Throne of Solomon"', *Sp* 29, pp. 477–87

Brogiolo, G. P. *et al.* (eds.) (2000), *Towns and their territories between late antiquity and the early middle ages*, Leiden

Brogiolo, G. P. and Ward-Perkins, B. (eds.) (1999), *The idea and ideal of the town between late antiquity and the early middle ages*, Leiden

Brokkar, W. G. (1972), 'Basil Lacapenos', *Studia byzantina et neohellenica neerlandica* 3, pp. 199–234

Brooks, E. W. (1899), 'The campaign of 716–718 from Arabic sources', *JHS* 19, pp. 19–33

—(1900), 'Byzantines and Arabs in the time of the early Abbasids, I', *EHR* 15, pp. 728–747

—(1901), 'Byzantines and Arabs in the time of the early Abbasids, II', *EHR* 16, pp. 84–91

—(1911), 'The age of Basil I', *BZ* 20, pp. 486–91

Brousselle, I. (1996), 'L'Intégration des Arméniens dans l'aristocratie byzantine au IXe siècle', in Garsoïan *et al.* (eds.) (1996), pp. 43–54

Brown, P. (1973), 'A dark age crisis: aspects of the iconoclastic controversy', *EHR* 88, pp. 1–34; repr. in Brown (1982), pp. 251–301

Brown, T. S. (1979), 'The church of Ravenna and the imperial administration in the seventh century', *EHR* 94, pp. 1–28

—(1986), '*Romanitas* and *campanilismo*: Agnellus of Ravenna's view of the past', in Holdsworth and Wiseman (eds.) (1986), pp. 107–14

—(1988a), 'The background of Byzantine relations with Italy in the ninth century: legacies, attachments and antagonisms', in Howard-Johnston (ed.) (1988), pp. 27–45

—(1988b), 'The interplay between Roman and Byzantine traditions and local sentiment in the exarchate of Ravenna', *Bisanzio, Roma e l'Italia nell'alto medioevo = SSCIS* 34, pp. 127–60

—(1990), 'Louis the Pious and the papacy: a Ravenna perspective', in Godman and Collins (eds.) (1990), pp. 297–307

—(1992), 'Otranto in medieval history', in Michaelides *et al.* (eds.) (1992), I, pp. 27–39

—(1993), 'Ethnic independence and cultural deference: the attitude of the Lombard principalities to Byzantium *c.* 876–1077', *Bsl* 54, pp. 5–12

—(1995), 'Justinian II and Ravenna', *BSl* 56, pp. 29–36

Brown, T. S. and Christie, N. (1989), 'Was there a Byzantine model of settlement in Italy?', *MEFRM* 101, pp. 377–99

Browning, R. (1954), 'The correspondence of a tenth-century Byzantine scholar', *Byz* 24, pp. 397–452; repr. in Browning (1977), no. 9

—(1962), 'An unpublished funeral oration on Anna Comnena', *Proceedings of the Cambridge Philological Society* 188, pp. 1–12; repr. in Browning (1977), no. 7

—(1965), 'Notes on the *Scriptor incertus de Leone Armenio*', *Byz* 35, pp. 389–411

—(1975a), 'Enlightenment and repression in Byzantium in the eleventh and twelfth centuries', *PaP* 69, pp. 3–22

—(1975b), *Byzantium and Bulgaria: a comparative study across the early medieval frontier*, London

—(1975c), 'Homer in Byzantium', *Viator* 6, pp. 15–33; repr. in Browning (1977), no. 17

—(1977), *Studies on Byzantine history, literature and education*, London

—(1978), 'Literacy in the Byzantine world', *BMGS* 4, pp. 39–54

Brubaker, L. (1985), 'Politics, patronage and art in ninth-century Byzantium: the "Homilies" of Gregory of Nazianzus in Paris (B. N. gr. 510)', *DOP* 39, pp. 1–13

—(1997a), 'Material culture and the myth of Byzantium', in Arnaldi and Cavallo (eds.) (1997), pp. 33–41

—(1998), 'Icons before iconoclasm?', *Morfologie sociali e culturali in Europa fra tarda antichità e alto medioevo = SSCIS* 45, pp. 1215–54

—(1999b), 'The Chalke gate, the construction of the past, and the Trier ivory', *BMGS* 23, pp. 258–85

—(2004a), 'The elephant and the ark: cultural and material interchange across the Mediterranean in the eighth and ninth centuries', *DOP* 58, pp. 175–95

—(2004b), 'Aniconic decoration in the Christian world (6th–11th century): east and west', *Cristianità d'occidente e cristianità d'oriente (secoli VI–XI) = SSCIS* 51, pp. 573–90

—(2006), 'The *Christian Topography* (Vat. gr. 699) revisited: image, text, and conflict in ninth-century Byzantium', in Jeffreys, E. (ed.) (2006), pp. 3–24

Brubaker, L. and Linardou, K. (eds.) (2007), *Eat, drink, and be merry (Luke 12:19) – Food and wine in Byzantium: papers of the 37th annual spring symposium of Byzantine studies, in honour of Professor A. A. M. Bryer*, Aldershot

Brühl, C. (1968), *Fodrum, gistum, servitium regis: Studien zu den wirtschaftlichen Grundlagen des Königtums im Frankenreich und in den fränkischen*

Nachfolgestaaten Deutschland, Frankreich und Italien vom 6. bis zur Mitte des 14. Jahrhunderts, 2 vols., Cologne

—(1977), 'Purpururkunden', in Jäschke and Wenskus (eds.) (1977), pp. 3–21

—(1989), 'Die Kaiserpfalz bei St Peter und die Pfalz Ottos III. auf dem Palatin (Neufassung 1983)', in Brühl (1989–97), I, pp. 3–31

—(1989–97), *Aus Mittelalter und Diplomatik: gesammelte Aufsätze*, 3 vols., Hildesheim

Bryer, A. and Herrin, J. (eds.) (1977), *Iconoclasm*, Birmingham

Buckler, G. (1929), *Anna Comnena: a study*, Oxford

Buckton, D. (1988), 'Byzantine enamel and the west', in Howard-Johnston (ed.) (1988), pp. 235–44

—(2006), 'Byzantine enamels in the twentieth century', in Jeffreys, E. (ed.) (2006), pp. 25–37

Bulgakova, V. (2004), *Byzantinische Bleisiegel in Osteuropa: die Funde auf dem Territorium Altrusslands*, Wiesbaden

Bullough, D. A. (1955), 'The counties of the *Regnum Italiae* in the Carolingian period, 774–888: a topographical study', *PBSR* 23, pp. 148–68

Burgarella, F. (1983), 'Bisanzio in Sicilia e nell'Italia meridionale: i riflessi politici', in Guillou *et al.* (1983), pp. 129–248

Burgmann, L. (1981), 'Die Novellen der Kaiserin Eirene', *FM* 4, pp. 1–36

—(2005), 'Zur diplomatischen Terminologie in der Peira', in Hoffmann and Monchizadeh (eds.) (2005), pp. 457–67

Burgmann, L. *et al.* (eds.) (1985), *Cupido legum*, Frankfurt-am-Main

Burke, J. and Scott, R. (eds.) (2000), *Byzantine Macedonia: identity, image and history, ByzAust* 13, Melbourne

Bury, J. B. (1912), *A history of the eastern Roman empire from the fall of Irene to the accession of Basil I (AD 802–867)*, London

Büttner, E. (2007), *Erzbischof Leon von Ohrid (1037–1056): Leben und Werk (mit den Texten seiner bisher unedierten asketischen Schrift und seiner drei Briefe an den Papst)*, Bamberg

Cahen, C. (1968), *Pre-Ottoman Turkey: a general survey of the material and spiritual culture and history c. 1071–1330*, tr. J. Jones-Williams, London

—(2001), *The formation of Turkey: the Seljukid sultanate of Rūm: eleventh to fourteenth century*, ed. and tr. P. M. Holt, Harlow

Cameron, Alan (1970), 'Michael Psellus and the date of the Palatine Anthology', *GRBS* 11, pp. 339–50

Cameron, Averil (1987), 'The construction of court ritual: the Byzantine *Book of ceremonies*', in Cannadine and Price (eds.) (1987), pp. 106–36

Canard, M. (1953), *Histoire de la dynastie des H'amdanides de Jazira et de Syrie*, Paris

—(1965), 'La Campagne arménienne du sultan seldjuqide Alp Arslan et la prise d'Ani en 1064', *REA* n.s. 2, pp. 239–59

Canivet, P. and Rey-Coquais, J.-P. (eds.) (1992), *La Syrie de Byzance à l'Islam, VIIe–VIIIe siècles: actes du colloque international Lyon – Maison de l'Orient méditerranéen, Paris – Institut du monde arabe, 11–15 Septembre 1990*, Damascus

Cannadine, D. and Price, S. (eds.) (1987), *Rituals of royalty: power and ceremonial in traditional societies*, Cambridge

Carile, A. (1996), 'L'Istria tra Bisanzio e Venezia', in *Istria e Dalmazia: un viaggio nella memoria (Atti del Convegno di studi, Bologna, 10 marzo 1995)*, Bologna, pp. 37–52

—(1998), 'Produzione e usi della porpora nell'impero bizantino', in Longo (ed.) (1998), pp. 243–75

Carile, A. and Fedalto, G. (1978), *Le origini di Venezia*, Bologna

Cassandro, G. (1969), 'Il ducato bizantino', in *Storia di Napoli* (1967–78), II.1, pp. 3–408

Cavallo, G. (1988), 'Le tipologie della cultura nel riflesso delle testimonianze scritte', *Bisanzio, Roma e l'Italia nell'alto medioevo* = *SSCIS* 34, pp. 467–516

—(1997), 'Una storia comune della cultura: realtà o illusione?' in Arnaldi and Cavallo (eds.) (1997), pp. 19–32

Cavallo, G. and Mango, C. (eds.) (1995), *Epigrafia medievale greca e latina: ideologia e funzione. Atti del seminario di Erice, 12–18 settembre 1991*, Spoleto

Cavanagh, W. *et al.* (1996–2002), *Continuity and change in a Greek rural landscape: the Laconia survey*, 2 vols., London

Cessi, R. (1951), *Le origini del ducato veneziano*, Naples

Chalandon, F. (1900–12), *Les Comnène; études sur l'empire byzantin au XIe et au XIIe siècles*, I: *Essai sur le règne d'Alexis Ier Comnène (1081–1118)*, II: *Jean II Comnène (1118–1143) et Manuel I Comnène (1143–1180)*, 2 vols., Paris

Charanis, P. (1953), 'The term "Helladikoi" in Byzantine texts of the sixth, seventh and eighth centuries', *EEBS* 23, pp. 615–20; repr. in Charanis (1972), no. 17

—(1972), *Studies on the demography of the Byzantine empire*, London

—(1973), *Social, economic and political life in the Byzantine empire*, London

—(1975), 'Cultural diversity and the breakdown of Byzantine power in Asia Minor', *DOP* 29, pp. 1–20

Cheïra, M. A. (1947), *La Lutte entre arabes et byzantins*, Alexandria

Cheynet, J.-C. (1980), 'Mantzikert: un désastre militaire?', *Byz* 50, pp. 410–38; repr. in Cheynet (2006), no. 13

—(1983), 'Dévaluation des dignités et dévaluation monétaire dans la seconde moitié du XIe siècle', *Byz* 53, pp. 453–77; repr. in Cheynet (2006), no. 6

—(1985), 'Du stratège de thème au duc: chronologie de l'évolution au cours du XIe siècle', *TM* 9, pp. 181–94; repr. in Cheynet (2006), no. 11

—(1995), 'Les Effectifs de l'armée byzantine (X^e–XIIe s.)', *Cahiers de civilisation médiévale*, 38, pp. 319–35; repr. in Cheynet (2006), no. 12

—(1996), 'L'Anthroponymie aristocratique à Byzance', in Bourin *et al.* (eds.) (1996), pp. 267–94; English tr. 'Aristocratic anthroponimy in Byzantium', in Cheynet (2006), no. 3

—(1998a), 'Théophile, Théophobe et les Perses', in Lampakes (ed.) (1998), pp. 39–50

—(1998b), 'La Résistance aux Turcs en Asie Mineure entre Mantzikert et la Première Croisade', in Balard *et al.* (eds.) (1998), I, pp. 131–47; repr. in Cheynet (2006), no. 14

—(2000), 'L'Aristocratie byzantine (VIIIe–XIIIe siècle)', *JS*, pp. 281–322; English tr. 'The Byzantine aristocracy, 8th–13th centuries', in Cheynet (2006), no. 1

—(2003), 'L'Apport de la sigillographie aux études byzantines', *VV* 62 (87), pp. 47–58

—(2004), 'Byzance et l'orient latin: le legs de Manuel Comnène', in Coulon *et al.* (eds.) (2004), pp. 115–25

—(2005), 'L'Iconographie des sceaux des Comnènes', in Ludwig (ed.) (2005), pp. 53–67

Cheynet, J.-C. *et al.* (2004), 'Une inscription d'Akroïnos datant de Constantin Porphyrogénète', *REB* 62, pp. 215–28

Cheynet, J.-C. *et al.* (eds.) (2007), *Le Monde byzantin*, II: *L'Empire Byzantin (641–1204)*, Paris

Cheynet, J.-C. and Vannier, J.-F. (1990), *Études prosopographiques, BSo* 5, Paris

Chiesa, P. (1989), 'Traduzioni e traduttori dal greco nel IX secolo: sviluppi di una tecnica', in Leonardi and Menestò (eds.) (1989), pp. 172–200

—(1992), 'Le biografie greche e latine di papa Martino I', in *Martino I papa (649–653) e il suo tempo: atti del XXVIII convegno storico internazionale, Todi 13–16 ottobre 1991*, Spoleto, pp. 211–41

—(2002), 'Traduzioni e traduttori a Roma nell'alto medioevo', *Roma fra oriente e occidente = SSCIS* 49, pp. 455–87

Cholij, R. (2002), *Theodore the Stoudite: the ordering of holiness*, Oxford

Christides, V. (1984), *The conquest of Crete by the Arabs (ca. 824): a turning point in the struggle between Byzantium and Islam*, Athens

Christie, Neil (ed.) (1991), *Three south Etrurian churches: Santa Cornelia, Santa Rufina and San Liberato*, London

Christie, Neil and Loseby, S. T. (eds.) (1996), *Towns in transition: urban evolution in late antiquity and the early middle ages*, Aldershot

Christie, Niall and Yazigi, M. (eds.) (2006), *Noble ideals and bloody realities: warfare in the middle ages*, Leiden

Christophilopoulou, A. (1951), 'Silention', *BZ* 44, pp. 79–85

Chrysos, E. (1975), 'Die "Krönung" Symeons in Hebdomon', *Cyrillomethodianum* 3, pp. 169–73

—(2004a), *L'Empire byzantin: 565–1025*, Aix-en-Provence

—(2004b), '1054: schism?', in *Cristianità d'occidente e cristianità d'oriente (secoli VI–XI) = SSCIS* 51, Spoleto, pp. 547–71

Chrysos, E. *et al.* (eds.) (1999), *Griechenland und das Meer: Beiträge eines Symposions in Frankfurt im Dezember 1996*, Mannheim und Möhnesee

Chrysostomides, J. (1982), 'A Byzantine historian: Anna Comnena', in Morgan (ed.) (1982), pp. 30–46

Ciccolella, F. (1998), 'Three anacreontic poems assigned to Photius', *OCP* 64, pp. 305–28

Ciggaar, K. N. (1996), *Western travellers to Constantinople: the west and Byzantium, 962–1204*, Leiden

—(2002), 'Bilingual word lists and phrase lists: for teaching or for travelling?', in Macrides (ed.) (2002), pp. 165–78

Cilento, N. (1966), *Le origini della signoria capuana nella Longobardia minore*, Rome

—(1971), *Italia meridionale longobarda*, 2nd edn., Naples

Citarella, A. O. (1967), 'The relations of Amalfi with the Arab world before the crusades', *Sp* 42, pp. 299–312

—(1968), 'Patterns in medieval trade: the commerce of Amalfi before the crusades', *JEH* 28, pp. 531–55

Classen, P. (1952), '*Romanum gubernans imperium*: zur Vorgeschichte der Kaisertitulatur Karls des Grossen', *DA* 9, pp. 103–21; repr. with revisions in Classen (1983), pp. 187–204

—(1981), 'Italien zwischen Byzanz und dem Frankenreich', *Nascità dell'Europa ed Europa carolingia, un'equazione da verificare* = *SSCIS* 27, pp. 919–67

—(1983), *Ausgewählte Aufsätze*, ed. J. Fleckenstein *et al.*, Sigmaringen

—(1985), *Karl der Grosse, das Papsttum and Byzanz: die Begründung des karolingischen Kaisertums*, ed. H. Fuhrmann and K. Märtl, 3rd edn., Sigmaringen

Claude, D. (1985), *Der Handel im westlichen Mittelmeer während des Frühmittelalters: Bericht über ein Kolloquium der Kommission für die Altertumskunde Mittel- und Nordeuropas im Jahre 1980*, Göttingen

Clucas, L. (1981), *The trial of John Italos and the crisis of intellectual values in Byzantium in the eleventh century*, *MBM* 26, Munich

Coates-Stephens, R. (1997), 'Dark age architecture in Rome', *PBSR* 65, pp. 177–232

Cobb, P. M. (2001), *White banners: contention in 'Abbasid Syria, 750–880*, Albany, NY

—(forthcoming), 'Islamic empire in Syria, 705–763', in Robinson, C. F. (ed.) (forthcoming), *The new Cambridge history of Islam*, I: *The formation of the Islamic world, sixth to eleventh century*, Cambridge

Connor, C. L. (1991), *Art and miracles in medieval Byzantium: the crypt at Hosios Loukas and its frescoes*, Princeton

Cormack, R. (1992), 'But is it art?', in Shepard and Franklin (eds.) (1992), pp. 219–36

—(1997a), *Painting the soul: icons, death masks, and shrouds*, London

—(1997b), 'Women and icons, and women in icons', in James (ed.) (1997), pp. 24–51

Corrias, P. and Cosentino, S. (eds.) (2002), *Ai confini dell'impero: archeologia, arte e storia della Sardegna bizantina*, Cagliari

Corrigan, K. A. (1992), *Visual polemics in the ninth-century Byzantine psalters*, Cambridge

Cosentino, S. (2004), 'La Flotte byzantine face à l'expansion musulmane: aspects d'histoire institutionnelle et sociale (VIIᵉ–Xᵉ siècle)', *BF* 28, pp. 3–20

—(2005), 'Re-analysing some Byzantine bullae from Sardinia', in Ludwig (ed.) (2005), pp. 69–81

Costambeys, M. (2007), *Power and patronage in early medieval Italy: local society, Italian politics and the Abbey of Farfa, c. 700–900*, Cambridge

Cowdrey, H. E. J. (1982), 'Pope Gregory VII's "crusading" plans of 1074', in Kedar *et al.* (eds.) (1982), pp. 27–40

—(1998), *Pope Gregory VII, 1073–1085*, Oxford

Cowe, S. P. (1992), 'An Armenian Job fragment from Sinai and its implications', *OrChr* 76, pp. 123–57

Cresci, L. R. (1991), 'Cadenze narrative e interpretazione critica nell'opera storica di Michele Attaliate', *REB* 49, pp. 197–218

Crisci, E. (2000), 'La produzione libraria nelle aree orientali di Bisanzio tra i secoli VII e VIII: i manoscritti superstiti', in Prato (ed.) (2000), I, pp. 3–28

Criscuolo, U. (1982 [1983]), '*Politikos anēr*: contributo al pensiero politico di Michele Psello', *Rendiconti dell'Accademia di archeologia, lettere e belle arti, Napoli* 57, pp. 129–63

Crostini, B. (2003), 'Christianity and Judaism in eleventh-century Constantino-ple', in Ruggieri and Pieralli (eds.) (2003), pp. 169–87

Cubitt, C. (ed.) (2003), *Court culture in the early middle ages: the proceedings of the First Alcuin Conference*, Turnhout

Cunningham, M. (2003), 'Dramatic device or didactic tool? The function of dia-logue in Byzantine preaching', in Jeffreys, E. (ed.) (2003), pp. 101–13

Curradi, C. (1977), 'I conti Guidi nel secolo X', *Studi romagnoli* 28, pp. 17–64

Curta, F. (ed.) (2005), *East central and eastern Europe in the early middle ages*, Ann Arbor, MI

Custurea, G. (2000), *Circulatia monedei bizantine în Dobrogea: secolele IX–XI*, Constanta

Cutler, A. (1984), *The aristocratic psalters in Byzantium*, Paris

—(2001), 'Gifts and gift exchange as aspects of the Byzantine, Arab and related economies', *DOP* 55, pp. 247–78

—(2003), 'Imagination and documentation: eagle silks in Byzantium, the Latin west and 'Abbasid Baghdad', *BZ* 96, pp. 67–72

Cutler, A. and Papaconstantinou, A. (eds.) (2007), *The material and the ideal: essays in medieval art and archaeology in honour of Jean-Michel Spieser*, Lieden

Cutler, A. and Spieser, J.-M. (1996), *Byzance médiévale, 700–1204*, Paris

Dagron, G. (1983), 'Byzance et le modèle islamique au Xe siècle: à propos des *Constitutions tactiques* de l'empereur Léon VI', *CRAI*, pp. 219–42

—(1984b), *Constantinople imaginaire: études sur le recueil des Patria*, Paris

—(1987), '"Ceux d'en face": les peuples étrangers dans les traités militaires byzantins', *TM* 10, pp. 207–32

—(1991), '"Ainsi rien n'échappera à la réglementation": état, église, corporations, confréries: à propos des inhumations à Constantinople (IVe–Xe siècle)', in Kravari *et al.* (eds.) (1989–91), II, pp. 155–82

—(1993), 'Le Christianisme byzantin du VIIe au milieu du XIe siècle' in Dagron *et al.* (1993), pp. 1–348

—(1994), 'Nés dans la pourpre', *TM* 12, pp. 105–42

—(1997), 'Apprivoiser la guerre: Byzantins et Arabes ennemis intimes', in Tsiknakis (ed.) (1997), pp. 37–49

—(2000), 'L'Organisation et le déroulement des courses d'après le *Livre des cérémonies*', *TM* 13, pp. 3–200

—(2002), 'The urban economy, seventh-twelfth centuries', in *EHB*, II, pp. 393–461

—(2005), 'Architecture d'intérieur: le *Pentapyrgion*', *TM* 15, pp. 109–17

Dalarun, J. (ed.) (1991), *La Calabre de la fin de l'antiquité au moyen âge: actes de la table ronde, Rome 1–2 décembre 1989*, MEFRM 103.2, Rome

Dark, K. (2001), *Byzantine pottery*, Stroud

—(2004), 'Houses, streets and shops in Byzantine Constantinople from the fifth to the twelfth centuries', *JMH* 30, pp. 83–107

—(2005), 'Archaeology', in Harris (ed.) (2005), pp. 166–84

—(ed.) (2004), *Secular buildings and the archaeology of everyday life in the Byzantine empire*, Oxford

Darrouzès, J. (1970), *Recherches sur les 'offikia' de l'église byzantine*, Paris

—(1975), 'Listes épiscopales du concile de Nicée II (787)', *REB* 33, pp. 5–76

—(1987), 'Le Patriarche Méthode contre les iconoclastes et les Stoudites', *REB* 45, pp. 15–57

Davids, A. (ed.) (1995), *The empress Theophano: Byzantium and the west at the turn of the first millennium*, Cambridge

Davies, W. and Fouracre, P. (eds.) (1986), *The settlement of disputes in early medieval Europe*, Cambridge

Day, G. W. (1988), *Genoa's response to Byzantium, 1155–1204: commercial expansion and factionalism in a medieval city*, Urbana, IL

Dédéyan, G. (1975), 'L'Immigration arménienne en Cappadoce au XIᵉ siècle', *Byz* 45, pp. 41–117

—(2003), *Les Arméniens entre Grecs, Musulmans et Croisés: étude sur les pouvoirs arméniens dans le Proche-Orient méditerranéen (1068–1150)*, 2 vols., Lisbon

Deér, J. (1957), 'Die Vorrechte des Kaisers in Rom (772–800)', *Schweizer Beiträge zur allgemeinen Geschichte* 15, pp. 5–63; repr. in Wolf (ed.) (1972), pp. 30–115

—(1961), 'Der Globus des spätrömischen und des byzantinischen Kaisers. Symbol oder Insignie?', *BZ* 54, pp. 53–85, 291–318

De Gregorio, G. and Kresten, O. (eds.) (1998), *Documenti medievali greci e latini: studi comparativi. Atti del Seminario di Erice, 23–29 ottobre 1995*, Spoleto

Delehaye, H. (1909), *Les Légendes grecques des saints militaires*, Paris

Delogu, P. (1977), *Mito di una città meridionale (Salerno, secoli VIII–XI)*, Naples

Delogu, P. *et al.* (1980), *Longobardi e bizantini, Storia d'Italia* 1, Turin

Del Treppo, M. (1956), 'La vita economica e sociale in una grande abbazia del Mezzogiorno: San Vicenzo al Volturno nell'alto medioevo', *ASPN* n.s. 35, pp. 31–110

Demus, O. (1970), *Byzantine art and the west*, London

—(1984), *The mosaics of San Marco in Venice*, 2 vols. in 4 pts., Chicago

Denkova, L. (1993), 'Bogomilism and literacy (an attempt of a general analysis of a tradition)', *EB* 29.1, pp. 90–6

Dennis, G. T. (1997), 'Imperial panegyric: rhetoric and reality', in Maguire (ed.) (1997), pp. 131–40

—(2001a), 'Death in Byzantium', *DOP* 55, pp. 1–7

—(2001b), 'Defenders of the Christian people: holy war and Byzantium', in Laiou and Mottahedeh (eds.) (2001), pp. 31–9

Déroche, V. (1993), 'L'Autorité des moines à Byzance du VIIIᵉ au Xᵉ siècle', *Revue bénédictine* 103, pp. 241–54

—(2002), 'Représentations de l'Eucharistie dans la haute époque byzantine', *TM* 14, pp. 167–80

Der Nersessian, S. (1969), 'The kingdom of Cilician Armenia', in Setton (ed.) (1969–89), II, pp. 630–59

Detorakes, T. E. (1987), 'Byzantio kai Europe: agiologikes scheseis (527–1453)', in *Byzantio kai Europe: 1 diethnes Byzantinologike synantese, Delphoi, 20–24 Iouliou 1985*, Athens, pp. 85–99

Devisse, J. (1975–6), *Hincmar, archevêque de Reims, 845–882*, 3 vols., Geneva

Devreesse, R. (1935), 'Le Texte grec de l'Hypomnesticum de Théodore Spoudée: le supplice, l'exil et la mort des victimes illustres du monothélisme', *AnBoll* 53, pp. 49–80

Devroey, J.-P. (2003), *Économie rurale et société dans l'Europe franque, VIe–IXe siècles*, I: *Fondements matériels, échanges et lien social*, Paris

Diaconu, P. (1970), *Les Petchénègues au Bas-Danube*, Bucharest

——(1978), *Les Coumans au Bas-Danube aux XIe et XIIe siècles*, Bucharest

Diaconu, P. *et al.* (1972–7), *Păcuiul lui Soare*, 2 vols., Bucharest

Diehl, C. (1905), *Études byzantines*, Paris

Dimitroukas, I. (1997), *Reisen und Verkehr im byzantinischen Reich: vom Anfang des 6. Jhr. bis zur Mitte des 11. Jhr*, 2 vols., Athens

Dionisotti, A. C. (1988), 'Greek grammars and dictionaries in Carolingian Europe', in Herren and Brown (eds.) (1988), pp. 1–56

Ditten, H. (1993), *Ethnische Verschiebungen zwischen der Balkanhalbinsel und Kleinasien vom Ende des 6. bis zur zweiten Hälfte des 9. Jahrhunderts*, BBA 59, Berlin

Dölger, F. (1938–9), 'Die Kaiserurkunde der Byzantiner als Ausdruck ihrer politischen Anschauungen', *Historische Zeitschrift* 159, pp. 229–50; repr. in Dölger (1953), pp. 9–33

——(1940), 'Der Bulgarenherrscher als geistlicher Sohn des byzantinischen Kaisers', in Georgiev *et al.* (eds.) (1940), pp. 219–32; repr. in Dölger (1953), pp. 183–96

Dölger, F. and Karayannopulos, J. (1968), *Byzantinische Urkundenlehre*, I: *Die Kaiserurkunden*, Munich

Doorninck, F. van (2002), 'The Byzantine ship at Serçe Limani: an example of small-scale maritime commerce with Fatimid Syria in the early eleventh century', in Macrides (ed.) (2002), pp. 137–48

Dorfmann-Lazarev, I. (2004), *Arméniens et Byzantins à l'époque de Photius: deux débats théologiques après le triomphe de l'orthodoxie*, CSCO 609, Louvain

Duby, G. (1971), *La Société aux XIe et XIIe siècles dans la région mâconnaise*, 2nd edn., Paris

Ducellier, A. *et al.* (1986), *Byzance et le monde orthodoxe*, Paris

Duffy, J. and Peradotto, J. (eds.) (1988), *Gonimos: Neoplatonic and Byzantine studies presented to Leendert G. Westerink at 75*, Buffalo, NY

Dümmler, E. (1887–8), *Geschichte des Ostfränkischen Reiches*, 2nd edn., 3 vols., Leipzig

Dunn, A. (1992), 'The exploitation and control of woodland and scrubland in the Byzantine world', *BMGS* 16, pp. 235–98

——(1994), 'The transition from *polis* to *kastron* in the Balkans (3rd–8th/9th century): general and regional perspectives', *BMGS* 18, pp. 60–80

——(1999), 'From *polis* to *kastron* in southern Macedonia: Amphipolis, Khrysoupolis and the Strymon delta', in Bazzana (ed.) (1999), pp. 399–413

——(2006), 'The rise and fall of towns, loci of maritime traffic, and silk production: the problem of Thisvi-Kastorion', in Jeffreys, E. (ed.) (2006), pp. 38–71

Durand, A. (1998), *Les Paysages médiévaux du Languedoc: X^e–XIIe siècles*, Toulouse

Durand, J. and Flusin, B. (eds.) (2004), *Byzance et les reliques du Christ*, Paris

Dvornik, F. (1948), *The Photian schism: history and legend*, Cambridge

——(1958), *The idea of apostolicity in Byzantium and the legend of the apostle Andrew*, DOSt 4, Cambridge, MA

——(1970), *Byzantine missions among the Slavs: SS Constantine-Cyril and Methodius*, New Brunswick, NJ

—(1974), *Photian and Byzantine ecclesiastical studies*, London

Eastmond, A. (ed.) (2001), *Eastern approaches to Byzantium*, Aldershot

Eastmond, A. and James, L. (eds.) (2003), *Icon and word: the power of images in Byzantium*, Aldershot

Edwards, R. W. (1987), *The fortifications of Armenian Cilicia, DOSt* 23, Washington, DC

Eickhoff, E. (1966), *Seekrieg und Seepolitik zwischen Islam and Abendland: das Mittelmeer, 650–1040*, Berlin

El-Cheikh, N. M. (2004a), *Byzantium viewed by the Arabs*, Cambridge, MA

—(2004b), 'Byzantine leaders in Arabic-Muslim texts', in *BEINE*, VI, pp. 109–31

Eleuteri, P. and Rigo, A. (1993), *Eretici, dissidenti, musulmani ed ebrei a Bisanzio: una raccolta eresiologica del XII secolo*, Venice

Engberg, S. G. (2004), 'Romanos Lekapenos and the mandilion of Edessa', in Durand and Flusin (eds.) (2004), pp. 123–42

Epstein, A. W. (1980), 'The political content of the painting of Saint Sophia at Ohrid', *JÖB* 29, pp. 315–29

—(1986), *Tokale Kilise: tenth-century metropolitan art in Byzantine Cappadocia, DOSt* 22, Washington, DC

Erkens, F.-R. (2000), 'Graecisca sublimitas: Byzanz' Attraktivität und der abendländische Westen', in Wieczorek and Hinz (eds.) (2000), II, pp. 749–53

Esbroeck, M. van (1971a), 'Un nouveau témoin du livre d'Agathange', *REA* n.s. 8, pp. 13–167

—(1971b), 'Témoignages littéraires sur les sépultures de saint Grégoire l'Illuminateur', *AnBoll* 89, pp. 387–418

—(2003), 'Der armenische Ikonoklasmus', *OrChr* 87, pp. 144–53

Euw, A. von (1991), 'Ikonologie der Heiratsurkunde der Kaiserin Theophanu', in von Euw and Schreiner (eds.) (1991), II, pp. 175–91

Euw, A. von and Schreiner, P. (eds.) (1991), *Kaiserin Theophanu: Begegnung des Ostens und Westens um die Wende des ersten Jahrtausends*, 2 vols., Cologne

Evans, H. C. and Wixom, W. D. (eds.) (1997), *The glory of Byzantium: art and culture of the middle Byzantine era, AD 843–1261*, New York

Falkenhausen, V. von (1968), 'Taranto in epoca bizantina', *SM* 9, pp. 133–66

—(1968–9), 'A medieval Neapolitan document', *Princeton University Library Chronicle* 30, pp. 171–82

—(1970), 'Eine byzantinische Beamtenurkunde aus Dubrovnik', *BZ* 63, pp. 10–23

—(1973), 'Zur byzantinischen Verwaltung Luceras am Ende des 10. Jahrhunderts', *QFIAB* 53, pp. 395–406

—(1978–9 [1985]), 'Chiesa greca e chiesa latina in Sicilia prima della conquista araba', *Archivio storico siracusano* n.s. 5, pp. 137–55

—(1983), 'I Longobardi meridionali', in Guillou *et al.* (1983), pp. 251–364

—(1988), 'San Pietro nella religiosità bizantina', *Bisanzio, Roma e l'Italia nell'alto medioevo = SSCIS* 34, pp. 627–58

—(1989a), 'La vita di S. Nilo come fonte storica per la Calabria bizantina', *Atti del congresso internazionale su S. Nilo di Rossano 28 Settembre–1 Ottobre 1986*, Rossano-Grottaferrata, pp. 271–305

—(1989b), 'Die Städte im byzantinischen Italien', *MEFRM* 101, pp. 401–64

—(1997), 'Bishops', in Cavallo (ed.) (1997), pp. 172–96

—(2003), 'Between two empires: southern Italy in the reign of Basil II', in Magdalino (ed.) (2003), pp. 135–59

—(2005), 'Griechische Beamte in der *duana de secretis* von Palermo: eine prosopographische Untersuchung', in Hoffmann and Monchizadeh (eds.) (2005), pp. 381–411

Farag, W. (1977), *The truce of Safar* AH *359: December–January 969–970*, Birmingham

Fasoli, G. (1979), 'Il dominio territoriale degli arcivescovi di Ravenna fra l'VIII e l'XI secolo', in Mor and Schmidinger (eds.) (1979), pp. 87–140

Featherstone, J. M. (2003), 'Olga's visit to Constantinople in *De cerimoniis*', *REB* 61, pp. 241–51

—(2006), 'The Great Palace as reflected in the *De cerimoniis*', in Bauer (ed.) (2006), pp. 47–62

Feissel, D. (1987), 'Bulletin épigraphique: inscriptions chrétiennes et byzantines', *REG* 100, pp. 347–87

Felix, W. (1981), *Byzanz und die islamische Welt im früheren 11. Jahrhundert: Geschichte der politischen Beziehungen von 1001 bis 1055*, BV 14, Vienna

Ferluga, J. (1976), *Byzantium on the Balkans: studies on the Byzantine administration and the Southern Slavs from the VIIth to the XIIth centuries*, Amsterdam

—(1978), *L'amministrazione bizantina in Dalmazia*, 2nd edn., Venice

—(1988), 'L'Italia bizantina dalla caduta dell'Esarcato di Ravenna alla metà del secolo IX', *Bisanzio, Roma e l'Italia nell'alto medioevo* = SSCIS 34, pp. 169–93

Fiori, F. (2001), *Costantino hypatos e doux di Sardegna*, Bologna

Fisher, E. A. (1993), 'Michael Psellos on the rhetoric of hagiography and the *Life of St Auxentius*', *BMGS* 17, pp. 43–55

—(1994), 'Image and ekphrasis in Michael Psellos' sermon on the crucifixion', *BSl* 55, pp. 44–55

Floria, B. N. (ed.) (2002), *Khristianstvo v stranakh vostochnoi, iugo-vostochnoi i tsentral'noi Evropy na poroge vtorogo tysiacheletiia*, Moscow

Floria, B. N. *et al.* (2000), *Sud'by kirillo-mefodievskoi traditsii posle Kirilla i Mefodiia*, St Petersburg

Flusin, B. (2001), 'L'Empereur hagiographe: remarques sur le rôle des premiers empereurs macédoniens dans le culte des saints', in Guran and Flusin (eds.) (2001), pp. 29–54

Fögen, M.-T. (1994), 'Legislation in Byzantium: a political and a bureaucratic technique', in Laiou and Simon (eds.) (1994), pp. 53–70

—(1998), 'Reanimation of Roman law in the ninth century: remarks on reasons and results', in Brubaker (ed.) (1998), pp. 11–22

Fonkič, B. L. (2000), 'Aux origines de la minuscule stoudite (les fragments moscovite et parisien de l'œuvre de Paul d'Égine)', in Prato (ed.) (2000), I, pp. 169–86

Foss, C. (1985–96), *Survey of medieval castles of Anatolia*, I: *Kütahya*, II: *Nicomedia*, 2 vols., Oxford and Ankara

—(1990b), 'Byzantine Malagina and the lower Sangarius', *Anatolian Studies* 40, pp. 161–83; repr. in Foss (1996c), no. 7

—(1994), 'The Lycian coast in the Byzantine age', *DOP* 48, pp. 1–52

—(1996a), *Nicaea: a Byzantine capital and its praises: with the speeches of Theodore Laskaris, In praise of the great city of Nicaea, and Theodore Metochites, Nicene oration*, Brookline, MA

—(1996b), 'The cities of Pamphylia in the Byzantine age', in Foss (1996c), no. 4

—(1996c), *Cities, fortresses and villages of Byzantine Asia Minor*, Aldershot

—(1997), 'Syria in transition, AD 550–750: an archaeological approach', *DOP* 51, pp. 189–269

—(2002b), 'Pilgrimage in medieval Asia Minor', *DOP* 56, pp. 129–51

Foss, C. and Scott, J. A. (2002), 'Sardis' in *EHB*, II, pp. 615–22

Fossier, R. (1999), 'Rural economy and country life', in *NCMH*, III, pp. 27–63

France, J. (1984), 'Anna Comnena, the *Alexiad* and the First Crusade', *Reading Medieval Studies* 10, pp. 20–38

François, V. (2005), 'La Vaisselle de table à Byzance: un artisanat et un marché peu perméables aux influences extérieures', in Balard *et al.* (eds.) (2005), pp. 211–23

François, V. and Spieser, J.-M. (2002), 'Pottery and glass in Byzantium', in *EHB*, II, pp. 593–609

Franklin, S. (1983), 'The empire of the *Rhomaioi* as viewed from Kievan Russia: aspects of Byzantino-Russian cultural relations', *Byz* 53, pp. 507–37; repr. in Franklin (2002a), no. 2

—(2002a), *Byzantium-Rus-Russia*, Aldershot

—(2002b), *Writing, society and culture in early Rus, c. 950–1300*, Cambridge

—(2006), 'Kievan Rus' (1015–1125)', in Perrie (ed.) (2006), pp. 73–97

Franklin, S. and Mavroudi, M. (eds.) (2007), 'Byzantino-Slavica and Byzantino-Arabica. Studies in the translation and transmission of text', *BSl* 65, pp. 7–67

Franklin, S. and Shepard, J. (1996), *The emergence of Rus, 750–1200*, London

Frankopan, P. (1996), 'A victory of Gregory Pakourianos against the Pechenegs', *BSl* 57, pp. 278–81

—(2002), 'The imperial governors of Dyrrakhion in the reign of Alexios I Komnenos', *BMGS* 26, pp. 65–103

—(2004a), 'Byzantine trade privileges to Venice in the eleventh century: the chrysobull of 1092', *JMH* 30, pp. 135–60

—(2004b), 'Co-operation between Constantinople and Rome before the First Crusade: a study of the convergence of interests in Croatia in the late eleventh century', *Crusades* 3, pp. 1–13

Franses, R. (2003), 'When all that is gold does not glitter: on the strange history of looking at Byzantine art', in Eastmond and James (eds.) (2003), pp. 13–24

Freely, J. and Çakmak, A. S. (2004), *Byzantine monuments of Istanbul*, Cambridge

Freeman, A. (1985), 'Carolingian orthodoxy and the fate of the *Libri Carolini*', *Viator* 16, pp. 65–108

Frohnes, H. *et al.* (eds.) (1974–8), *Kirchengeschichte als Missionsgeschichte*, 2 vols., Munich

Frolow, A. (1961), *La Relique de la vraie croix: recherches sur le développement d'un culte*, Paris

—(1965), *Les Reliquaires de la vraie croix*, Paris

Frye, R. N. (ed.) (1975), *The Cambridge history of Iran*, IV: *The period from the Arab invasion to the Saljuqs*, Cambridge

Gadolin, A. R. (1970), *A theory of history and society with special reference to the Chronographia of Michael Psellus*, Stockholm

Galasso, G. (1959–60), 'Le città campane nell'alto medioevo', *Archivio storico per le province napoletane* 77 (n.s. 38), pp. 9–42 and 78 (n.s. 39), pp. 9–53

Galatariotou, C. (1987), 'Byzantine *ktētorika typika*: a comparative study', *REB* 45, pp. 77–138

—(1988), 'Byzantine women's monastic communities: the evidence of the *typika*', *JÖB* 38, pp. 263–90

—(1991), *The making of a saint: the life, times and sanctification of Neophytos the recluse*, Cambridge

Garitte, G. (1960), 'Un opuscule grec traduit de l'arménien sur l'addition de l'eau au vin eucharistique', *LM* 73, pp. 297–310

Garland, L. (1999), *Byzantine empresses: women and power in Byzantium, AD 527–1204*, London

—(2005), 'The rhetoric of gluttony and hunger in twelfth-century Byzantium', in Mayer and Trzcionka (eds.) (2005), pp. 43–55

—(2006), 'Street life in Constantinople: women and the carnivalesque', in Garland (ed.) (2006), pp. 162–76

—(ed.) (1997), *Conformity and non-conformity in Byzantium: papers given at the eighth conference of the Australian association for Byzantine studies, University of New England, Australia, July 1993*, BF 24, Amsterdam

Garsoïan, N. G. (1998), 'The problem of Armenian integration into the Byzantine empire', in Ahrweiler and Laiou (eds.) (1998), pp. 53–124; repr. in Garsoïan (1999c), no. 8

Garsoïan, N. G. *et al.* (eds.) (1996), *L'Arménie et Byzance: histoire et culture*, BSo 12, Paris

Gautier, P. (1969), 'L'Obituaire du typikon du Pantocrator', *REB* 27, pp. 235–62

—(1971), 'Le Synode des Blachernes (fin 1094): étude prosopographique', *REB* 29, pp. 213–84

Gay, G. [= J.] (1917), *L'Italia meridionale e l'impero bizantino dall'avvento di Basilio I alla resa di Bari ai Normanni (867–1071)*, Florence; repr. Bologna, 2001 (Italian tr. of Gay (1904))

Georgiev, S. *et al.* (eds.) (1940), *Sbornik v pamet na Prof. Pet'r Nikov*, Sofia

Gero, S. (1973), *Byzantine iconoclasm during the reign of Leo III, with particular attention to the oriental sources*, CSCO 346, Louvain

—(1975), 'The eucharistic doctrine of the Byzantine iconoclasts and its sources', *BZ* 68, pp. 4–22

—(1977), *Byzantine iconoclasm during the reign of Constantine V, with particular attention to the oriental sources*, CSCO 384, Louvain

Geyer, B. (2002), 'Physical factors in the evolution of the landscape and land use', in *EHB*, I, pp. 31–45

Geyer, B. and Lefort, J. (eds.) (2003), *La Bithynie au moyen âge*, Paris

Gill, M. A. V. (2002), *Amorium reports, finds I: the glass (1987–1997)*, BAR IS 1070, Oxford

Given, M. and Knapp, A. B. (2003), *The Sydney Cyprus survey project: social approaches to regional archaeological survey*, Los Angeles

Gjuzelev, V. and Pillinger, R. (eds.) (1987), *Das Christentum in Bulgarien und auf der übrigen Balkanhalbinsel in der Spätantike und im frühen Mittelalter: II. Internationales Symposium Haskovo (Bulgarien), 10.–13. Juni 1986*, Vienna

Glykatzi and Glykatzi-Ahrweiler, see Ahrweiler

Godman, P. and Collins, R. (eds.) (1990), *Charlemagne's heir: new perspectives on the reign of Louis the Pious (814–840)*, Oxford

Goitein, S. D. (1967–93), *A Mediterranean society: the Jewish communities of the Arab world as portrayed by the documents of the Cairo Geniza*, 6 vols., Berkeley

Goldberg, E. J. (2006), *Struggle for empire: kingship and conflict under Louis the German, 817–876*, Ithaca, NY

Gordon, M. (2001), *The breaking of a thousand swords: a history of the Turkish military of Samarra, AH 200–275/815–889 CE*, Albany, NY

Górecki, D. M. (1986), 'The Slavic theory in Russian pre-revolutionary historiography of the Byzantine farmer community', *Byz* 56, pp. 77–107

—(1989), 'The *strateia* of Constantine VII: the legal status, administration and historical background', *BZ* 82, pp. 157–76

—(1997), 'Prescription in the Macedonian Novels on preemption: a linguistic, legal and political inquiry', *BSl* 58, pp. 113–30

—(1998), 'Fiscal control of unproductive land in tenth-century Byzantium: policies and politics', *FM* 10, pp. 239–60

—(2004), 'The rural community of the *Nomos georgikos* : governing body (art. 81)' and fiscal liability (art. 18)', *BSl* 62, pp. 79–94

Görich, K. (1993), *Otto III. Romanus Saxonicus et Italicus: kaiserliche Rompolitik und sächsische Historiographie*, Sigmaringen

Gouillard, J. (1961), 'Deux figures mal connues du second iconoclasme', *Byz* 31, pp. 371–401; repr. in Gouillard (1981), no. 6

—(1965), 'L'Hérésie dans l'empire byzantin des origines au XIIᵉ siècle', *TM* 1, pp. 299–324; repr. in Gouillard (1981), no. 1

—(1968), 'Aux origines de l'iconoclasme: le témoignage de Grégoire II?', *TM* 3, pp. 243–307; repr. in Gouillard (1981), no. 4

—(1969), 'Un "quartier" d'émigrés palestiniens à Constantinople au IXᵉ siècle?', *RESEE* 7, pp. 73–6

—(1981), *La vie religieuse à Byzance*, London

Gouma-Peterson, T. (ed.) (2000), *Anna Komnene and her times*, New York

Grabar, A. (1936), *L'empereur dans l'art byzantin: recherches sur l'art officiel de l'empire d'Orient*, Paris; repr. London, 1971

Greenwood, T. W. (2002), 'Sasanian echoes and apocalyptic expectations: a re-evaluation of the *Armenian History* attributed to Sebeos', *LM* 115, pp. 323–97

—(2004), 'A corpus of early medieval Armenian inscriptions', *DOP* 58, pp. 27–91

—(2006a), 'Failure of a mission? Photius and the Armenian church', *LM* 119, pp. 115–59

—(2006b), 'The discovery of the relics of St Grigor and the development of Armenian tradition in ninth-century Byzantium', in Jeffreys, E. (ed.) (2006), pp. 177–91

—(2008), '"New light from the east": chronography and ecclesiastical history through a late seventh-century Armenian source', *Journal of early Christian studies* 16, pp. 197–254

Grégoire, H. (1908), 'Note sur une inscription gréco-araméenne trouvée à Faraša (Ariaramneia-Rhodandos)', *CRAI*, pp. 434–47

—(1937), 'Du nouveau sur l'histoire bulgaro-byzantine: Nicétas Pégonitès, vainqueur du roi bulgare, Jean Vladislav', *Byz* 12, pp. 283–91

—(1953), 'La Carrière du premier Nicéphore Phocas', *Hell* 4, pp. 232–54

—(1966), 'The Amorians and Macedonians 842–1025' in Hussey (ed.) (1966–7), I, pp. 105–92

Gregory, T. E. (1974), 'The gold coinage of the emperor Constantine VII', *The American Numismatic Society Museum Notes* 19, pp. 87–118

—(1980), 'The political program of Constantine Porphyrogenitus', *ACIEB* 15, IV, pp. 122–30

Gress-Wright, D. (1977), 'Bogomilism in Constantinople', *Byz* 47, pp. 163–85

Grierson, P. (1962), 'The tombs and obits of the Byzantine emperors (337–1042)', *DOP* 16, pp. 1–63

—(1981), 'The Carolingian empire in the eyes of Byzantium', in *Nascita dell'Europa ed Europa carolingia, un'equazione da verificare* = *SSCIS* 27, pp. 885–916

—(1982), *Byzantine coins*, London

Griffith, S. H. (1982), 'Eutychius of Alexandria on the emperor Theophilus and iconoclasm in Byzantium: a tenth century moment in Christian apologetics in Arabic', *Byz* 52, pp. 154–90; repr. in Griffith (1992), no. 4

—(1992), *Arabic Christianity in the monasteries of ninth-century Palestine*, Aldershot

—(1996), 'The Muslim philosopher al-Kindi and his Christian readers: three Arab Christian texts on "The Dissipation of Sorrows"', *Bulletin of the John Rylands University Library of Manchester* 78, pp. 111–27; repr. in Griffith (2002), no. 9

—(2002), *The beginnings of Christian theology in Arabic: Muslim–Christian encounters in the early Islamic period*, Aldershot

Groenman-van Waateringe, W. and van Wijngaarden-Bakker, L. H. (eds.) (1987), *Farm life in a Carolingian village: a model based on botanical and zoological data from an excavated site*, Assen-Maastricht

Grosdidier de Matons, J. (1976), 'Psellos et le monde de l'irrationnel', *TM* 6, pp. 325–49

Grousset, R. (1947), *Histoire de l'Arménie des origines à 1071*, Paris

Grumel, V. (1951–2), 'L'Annexion de l'Illyricum oriental, de la Sicile et de la Calabre au patriarcat de Constantinople', *Recherches de science religieuse* 40, pp. 191–200

Grünbart, M. (1998), 'Die Familie Apokapes im Lichte neuer Quellen', *SBS* 5, pp. 29–41

—(ed.) (2007), *Theatron: Rhetorische Kultur in Spätantike und Mittelalter (Rhetorical culture in late antiquity and the middle ages)*, Berlin and New York

Grünbart, M. *et al.* (eds.) (2007), *Material culture and well-being in Byzantium, 400–1453*, Vienna

Guilland, R. (1967), *Recherches sur les institutions byzantines*, 2 vols., Berlin

—(1969), *Études de topographie de Constantinople byzantine*, 2 vols., Berlin

Guillou, A. (1963), 'Inchiesta sulla popolazione greca della Sicilia e della Calabria nel medio evo', *Rivista Storica Italiana* 75, pp. 53–68; repr. in Guillou (1970), no. 9

—(1965), 'La Lucanie byzantine: étude de géographie historique', *Byz* 35, pp. 119–49; repr. in Guillou (1970), no. 10

—(1970), *Studies on Byzantine Italy*, London

—(1974), 'Production and profits in the Byzantine province of Italy (tenth to eleventh centuries): an expanding society', *DOP* 28, pp. 89–109

—(1975–6 [1979]), 'La Sicilia bizantina: un bilancio delle ricerche attuali', *Archivio storico siracusano* n.s. 4, pp. 45–89

—(1976), 'La Soie du Katépanat d'Italie', *TM* 6, pp. 69–84

—(1977), 'La Sicile byzantine. Etat de recherches', *BF* 5, pp. 95–145

—(1978), *Culture et société en Italie byzantine (VIᵉ–XIᵉ s.)*, London

—(1983), 'L'Italia bizantina dalla caduta di Ravenna all'arrivo dei Normanni', in Guillou *et al.* (1983), pp. 3–126

Guillou, A. *et al.* (1983), *Il mezzogiorno dai bizantini a Federico II, Storia d'Italia* 3, Turin

Gunn, J. D. (ed.) (2000), *The years without summer: tracing AD 536 and its aftermath*, BAR IS 872, Oxford

Günsenin, N. (1990), *Les Amphores byzantines (Xᵉ–XIIIᵉ siècles): typologie, production, circulation d'après les collections turques*, Lille

—(1998), 'Le Vin de *Ganos*: les amphores *et la mer*', in Balard *et al.* (eds.) (1998), I, pp. 281–7

—(2002), 'Medieval trade in the Sea of Marmara: the evidence of shipwrecks', in Macrides (ed.) (2002), pp. 125–35

Gutas, D. (1998), *Greek thought, Arabic culture: the Graeco-Arabic translation movement in Baghdad and early 'Abbasid society (2nd–4th/8th–10th centuries)*, New York

Györffy, G. (1976), 'Rôle de Byzance dans la conversion des Hongrois', in Kuczyński *et al.* (eds.) (1976), pp. 169–80

—(1994), *King Saint Stephen of Hungary*, Boulder, CO

Haendler, G. (1958), *Epochen karolingischer Theologie: eine Untersuchung über die karolingischen Gutachten zum byzantinischen Bilderstreit*, Berlin

Haldon, J. (1984), *Byzantine praetorians: an administrative, institutional and social survey of the Opsikion and the Tagmata, c. 580–900*, Bonn

—(1992b), 'The army and the economy: the allocation and redistribution of surplus wealth in the Byzantine state', *MHR* 7, pp. 133–53

—(1994), 'Synōnē: re-considering a problematic term of middle Byzantine fiscal administration', *BMGS* 18, pp. 116–53; repr. in Haldon (1995a), no. 8

—(1995a), *State, army and society in Byzantium*, Aldershot

—(1995b), 'Strategies of defence, problems of security: the garrisons of Constantinople in the middle Byzantine period', in Mango and Dagron (eds.) (1995), pp. 143–55

—(1997b), 'The organisation and support of an expeditionary force: manpower and logistics in the middle Byzantine period', in Tsiknakis (ed.) (1997), pp. 111–51; repr. in Haldon (ed.) (2007), pp. 409–49

—(1999b), 'The idea of the town in the Byzantine empire', in Brogiolo and Ward-Perkins (eds.) (1999), pp. 1–23

—(2000a), 'Production, distribution and demand in the Byzantine world, *c.* 660–840', in Hansen and Wickham (eds.) (2000), pp. 225–64

—(2000b), 'Theory and practice in tenth-century military administration: chapters 11, 44 and 45 of the *Book of Ceremonies*', *TM* 13, pp. 201–352

—(2001a), *The Byzantine wars: battles and campaigns of the Byzantine era*, Stroud

—(2001b), 'Byzantium in the dark centuries: some concluding remarks', in Kountoura-Galake (ed.) (2001), pp. 455–62

—(2003a), review of W. Brandes' *Finanzverwaltung in Krisenzeiten*, *BZ* 96, pp. 717–28

—(2003b), 'Approaches to an alternative military history of the period ca. 1025–1071', in Vlysidou (ed.) (2003), pp. 45–74

—(2006b), 'Roads and communications in the Byzantine empire: wagons, horses and supplies', in Pryor (ed.) (2006), pp. 131–58

—(ed.) (2007), *Byzantine warfare*, Aldershot

Haldon, J. and Brubaker, L. (forthcoming), *Byzantium in the iconoclast era (680–850): a history*, Cambridge

Haldon, J. and Kennedy, H. (1980), 'The Arab-Byzantine frontier in the eighth and ninth centuries: military organisation and society in the borderlands', *ZRVI* 19, pp. 79–116; repr. in Bonner (ed.) (2004), no. 6, pp. 141–78

Haldon, J. and Ward-Perkins, B. (1999), 'Evidence from Rome for the image of Christ on the Chalke gate in Constantinople', *BMGS* 23, pp. 286–96

Halkin, F. (1973), *Études d'épigraphie grecque et d'hagiographie byzantine*, Aldershot

Hamarneh, B. (2003), *Topografia cristiana ed insediamenti rurali nel territorio dell'odierna Giordania nelle epoche bizantina ed islamica: V–IX sec.*, Vatican City, Rome

Hamilton, B. (1979), *Monastic reform, Catharism and the crusades, 900–1300*, London

Hamilton, S. (2001), '"Most illustrious king of kings": evidence for Ottonian kingship in the Otto III prayerbook (Munich, Bayerische Staatsbibliothek, Clm 30111)', *JMH* 27, pp. 257–88

Hannick, C. (1978), 'Die byzantinischen Missionen', in Frohnes *et al.* (eds.) (1974–8), II, pp. 279–359

—(1988), 'Das musikalische Leben in der Frühzeit Bulgariens', *BSl* 49, pp. 23–37

—(1993), 'Les Nouvelles Chrétientés du monde byzantin: Russes, Bulgares et Serbes', in Dagron *et al.* (eds.) (1993), pp. 909–39

Hansen, I. L. and Wickham, C. (eds.) (2000), *The long eighth century: production, distribution and demand*, Leiden

Harris, J. (2003a), *Byzantium and the crusades*, London

Harrison, R. M. and Hayes, J. W. (1986–92), *Excavations at Saraçhane in Istanbul*, I: *The excavations, structures, architectural decoration, small finds, coins, bones and molluscs*; II: *The pottery*, 2 vols., Princeton

Hartmann, W. (1989), *Die Synoden der Karolingerzeit im Frankenreich und in Italien*, Paderborn

Harvey, A. (1995), 'The middle Byzantine economy: growth or stagnation?', *BMGS* 19, pp. 243–61

—(1996), 'Financial crisis and the rural economy', in Mullett and Smythe (eds.) (1996), pp. 167–84

—(2003), 'Competition for economic resources: the state, landowners and fiscal privileges', in Vlysidou (ed.) (2003), pp. 169–77

Hatlie, P. (1996), 'Redeeming Byzantine epistolography', *BMGS* 20, pp. 213–48

Hattendorf, J. B. and Unger, R. W. (eds.) (2003), *War at sea in the middle ages and the Renaissance*, Woodbridge

Hayes, J. W. and Martini, I. P. (eds.) (1994), *Archaeological survey in the lower Liri valley, central Italy, under the direction of Edith Mary Wightman*, BAR IS 595, Oxford

Hehl, E.-D. *et al.* (eds.) (2002), *Das Papsttum in der Welt des 12. Jahrhunderts*, Stuttgart

Helms, M. W. (1993), *Craft and the kingly ideal: art, trade, and power*, Austin, TX

Hendy, M. F. (1969), *Coinage and money in the Byzantine empire 1081–1261*, DOSt 12, Washington, DC

—(1970), 'Byzantium, 1081–1204: an economic reappraisal', *TRHS* 5th series, 20, pp. 31–52

—(1986), 'The coins', in Harrison and Hayes (1986–92), I, pp. 278–373

—(1989a), 'Byzantium, 1081–1204: the economy revisited, twenty years on', in Hendy (1989b), no. 3, pp. 1–48

—(1989b), *The economy, fiscal administration and coinage of Byzantium*, Northampton

Henning, J. (2005), 'Ways of life in eastern and western Europe during the early middle ages: which way was "normal"?', in Curta (ed.) (2005), pp. 41–59

Hergenröther, J. (1867–89), *Photius, Patriarch von Constantinopel: sein Leben, seine Schriften and das griechische Schisma*, 3 vols., Regensburg

Herren, M. W. and Brown, S. A. (eds.) (1988), *The sacred nectar of the Greeks: the study of Greek in the west in the early middle ages*, London

Herrin, J. (1973), 'Aspects of the process of Hellenization in the early middle ages', *ABSA* 68, pp. 113–26

—(1975), 'Realities of Byzantine provincial government: Hellas and Peloponnesos, 1180–1205', *DOP* 29, pp. 253–86

—(1982), 'Women and the faith in icons in early Christianity', in Samuel and Stedman Jones (eds.) (1982), pp. 56–83

—(1983b), 'In search of Byzantine women: three avenues of approach', in Cameron and Kuhrt (eds.) (1983), pp. 167–89

—(1992), 'Constantinople, Rome and the Franks in the seventh and eighth centuries', in Shepard and Franklin (eds.) (1992), pp. 91–107

—(1994), 'Public and private forms of religious commitment among Byzantine women', in Archer *et al.* (eds.) (1994), pp. 181–203

—(2000a), 'The imperial feminine in Byzantium', *PaP* 169, pp. 3–35

—(2000b), 'Blinding in Byzantium', in Scholz and Makris (eds.) (2000), pp. 56–68

—(2004), 'The pentarchy: theory and reality in the ninth century', *Cristianità d'occidente e cristianità d'oriente (secoli VI–XI)* = SSCIS 51, pp. 591–628

—(2006), 'Changing functions of monasteries for women during Byzantine icon-oclasm', in Garland (ed.) (2006), pp. 1–15

Hetherington, P. (2006), 'The image of Edessa: some notes on its later fortunes', in Jeffreys, E. (ed.) (2006), pp. 192–205

Hiestand, R. (1964), *Byzanz und das Regnum Italicum im 10. Jahrhundert*, Zurich

Hild, F. and Hellenkemper, H. (1990), *Kilikien und Isaurien, TIB* 5, 2 vols., Vienna

Hild, F. and Restle, M. (1981), *Kappadokien: Kappadokia, Charsianon, Sebasteia und Lykandos, TIB* 2, Vienna

Hill, B. (1997), 'Imperial women and the ideology of womanhood in the eleventh and twelfth centuries', in James (ed.) (1997), pp. 76–99

Hodges, R. and Mitchell, J. (eds.) (1985), *San Vicenzo al Volturno: the archaeology, art and territory of an early medieval monastery, BAR IS* 252, Oxford

Hodges, R. and Whitehouse, D. (1983), *Mohammed, Charlemagne, and the origins of Europe: archaeology and the Pirenne thesis*, London

Hoffmann, H. (1969), 'Die Anfänge der Normannen in Süditalien', *QFIAB* 49, pp. 95–144

Hoffmann, J. (1974), *Rudimente von Territorialstaaten im byzantinischen Reich (1071–1210): Untersuchungen über Unabhängigkeitsbestrebungen und ihr Verhältnis zu Kaiser und Reich, MBM* 17, Munich

Hoffmann, L. M. and Monchizadeh, A. (eds.) (2005), *Zwischen Polis, Provinz und Peripherie: Beiträge zur byzantinischen Geschichte und Kultur*, Wiesbaden

Hohlweg, A. (1965), *Beiträge zur Verwaltungsgeschichte des Oströmischen Reiches unter den Komnenen, MBM* 1, Munich

Holdsworth, C. and Wiseman, T. P. (eds.) (1986), *The inheritance of historiography 350–900*, Exeter

Holmes, C. (2001), '"How the east was won" in the reign of Basil II', in Eastmond (ed.) (2001), pp. 41–56

—(2002a), 'Byzantium's eastern frontier in the tenth and the eleventh century', in Abulafia and Berend (eds.) (2002), pp. 83–104

—(2002b), 'Written culture in Byzantium and beyond: contexts, contents and interpretations', in Holmes and Waring (eds.) (2002), pp. 1–31

—(2006), 'Constantinople in the reign of Basil II', in Jeffreys, E. (ed.) (2006), pp. 326–39

Holmes, C. and Waring, J. (eds.) (2002), *Literacy, education and manuscript transmission in Byzantium and beyond*, Leiden

Holo, J. (2000), 'A Genizah Letter from Rhodes evidently concerning the Byzantine reconquest of Crete', *JNES* 59, pp. 1–12

—(forthcoming), *Byzantine Jewry in the Mediterranean economy*, Cambridge

Holtzmann, W. and Guillou, A. (1961), 'Zwei Katepansurkunden aus Tricarico', *QFIAB* 41, pp. 1–28; repr. in Guillou (1970), no. 7

Honigmann, E. (1935), *Die Ostgrenze des byzantinischen Reiches von 363 bis 1071 nach griechischen, arabischen, syrischen und armenischen Quellen*, Brussels

Hörandner, W. (2003), 'Court poetry: questions of motifs, structure and function', in Jeffreys, E. (ed.) (2003), pp. 75–87

Hörandner, W. and Grünbart, M. (eds.) (2003), *L'Épistolographie et la poésie épigrammatique: projets actuels et questions de méthodologie (Actes de la 16ᵉ table ronde, XXᵉ Congrès international d'études byzantines, Paris 2001)*, Paris

Horbury, W. (ed.) (1999), *Hebrew study from Ezra to Ben-Yehuda*, Edinburgh

Horden, P. (1986), 'The confraternities of Byzantium', *SCH* 23, pp. 25–45

Horníčková, K. (1999), 'The Byzantine reliquary pectoral crosses in central Europe', *Bsl* 60, pp. 213–50

Houts, E. M. C. van (1985), 'Normandy and Byzantium in the eleventh century', *Byz* 55, pp. 544–59; repr. in Van Houts (1999), no. 1

—(1999), *History and family traditions in England and the continent, 1000–1200*, Aldershot

Hovsep'yan, G. (1951), *Yishatakarankʻ dzeragratsʻ*, Antilias

Howard-Johnston, J. D. (1983a), 'Byzantine Anzitene', in Mitchell (ed.) (1983), pp. 239–90

—(1983b), 'Urban continuity in the Balkans in the early middle ages', in Poulter (ed.) (1983), II, pp. 242–54

—(1995b), 'Crown lands and the defence of imperial authority in the tenth and eleventh centuries', *BF* 21, pp. 75–100

—(2006b), 'A short piece of narrative history: war and diplomacy in the Balkans, winter 921/2–spring 924', in Jeffreys, E. (ed.) (2006), pp. 340–60

Hunger, H. (1964), *Prooimion: Elemente der byzantinischen Kaiseridee in den Arengen der Urkunden*, Vienna

—(1965), *Reich der neuen Mitte: der christliche Geist der byzantinischen Kultur*, Graz

—(1968), 'Zehn unedierte byzantinischen Beamten-Siegel', *JÖB* 17, pp. 179–95

—(1969–70), 'On the imitation (*mimēsis*) of antiquity in Byzantine literature', *DOP* 23/24, pp. 15–38; repr. in Hunger (1973), no. 15

—(1973), *Byzantinische Grundlagenforschung: gesammelte Aufsätze*, London

—(1994), 'Heimsuchung und Schirmherrschaft über Welt und Menschheit: *Mēter Theou hē Episkepsis*', *SBS* 4, pp. 33–43

Hurbanič, M. (2005), 'The Byzantine missionary concept and its revitalisation in the ninth century: some remarks on the content of Photius' encyclical letter *Ad archiepiscopales thronos per orientem obtinentes*', *BSl* 63, pp. 103–16

Hussey, J. M. (1960), *Ascetics and humanists in eleventh-century Byzantium*, London

Huxley, G. (1975), 'The emperor Michael III and the battle of Bishop's Meadow (AD 863)', *GRBS* 16, pp. 443–50

Iliev, I. G. (1992), 'The manuscript tradition and the authorship of the long *Life* of St Clement of Ohrid', *BSl* 53, pp. 68–73

Iordanov, I. (1984), 'Molybdobulles de Boris-Mihail (865–889) et de Siméon (893–913)', *EB* 20.4, pp. 89–93

—(2003), 'The katepanate of Paradounavon according to the sphragistic data', *SBS* 8, pp. 63–74

Irigoin, J. (1969), 'L'Italie méridionale et la tradition des textes antiques', *JÖB* 18, pp. 37–55

Ivaniševič, V. (1988), 'Vizantijski novac (491–1092) iz zbirke Narodnog Muzeja u Požarevcu', *Numizmatičar* 11, pp. 87–104

—(1993), 'Opticaj Vizantijskih folisa XI veka na prostoru centralnog Balkana', *Numizmatičar* 16, pp. 79–92

Ivanišević, V. and Radić, V. (1997), 'Četiri ostave vizantijskog novca iz zbirke Narodnog Muzeja u Beogradu', *Numizmatičar* 20, pp. 131–46

Ivanov, S. A. (2002), 'Casting pearls before Circe's swine: the Byzantine view of mission', *TM* 14, pp. 295–301

—(2003), *Vizantiiskoe missionerstvo. Mozhno li sdelat' iz 'varvara' khristianina?*, Moscow

—(2006), *Holy fools in Byzantium and beyond*, tr. S. Franklin, Oxford

—(2007), 'Mission impossible: ups and downs in Byzantine missionary activity from the eleventh to the fifteenth century', in Shepard (ed.) (2007), pp. 251–65

Ivison, E. A. (2000), 'Urban renewal and imperial revival in Byzantium (730–1025)', *BF* 26, pp. 1–46

Jacob, A. (1972), 'Une lettre de Charles le Chauve au clergé de Ravenne?', *RHE* 67, pp. 409–22

Jacoby, D. (1994b), 'Italian privileges and trade in Byzantium before the Fourth Crusade: a reconsideration', *Anuario de estudios medievales* 24, pp. 349–69; repr. in Jacoby (1997b), no. 2

—(1995), 'The Jews of Constantinople and their demographic hinterland', in Mango and Dagron (eds.) (1995), pp. 221–32

—(2000a), 'Byzantine trade with Egypt from the mid-tenth century to the Fourth Crusade', *Thesaurismata* 30, pp. 25–77

James, L. (1996), *Light and colour in Byzantine art*, Oxford

—(ed.) (1997), *Women, men and eunuchs: gender in Byzantium*, London

—(ed.) (1999), *Desire and denial in Byzantium*, Aldershot

—(ed.) (2007), *Art and text in Byzantine culture*, Cambridge

James, L. and Lambert, S. (eds.) (forthcoming), *Languages of love and hate: art and rhetoric in medieval discussions of the crusades*, Turnhout

Janin, R. (1975), *Les Églises et les monastères des grands centres byzantins: Bithynie, Hellespont, Latros, Galésios, Trébizonde, Athènes, Thessalonique*, Paris

Janković, M. (1981), *Srednjovekovno naselje na Velikom Gradcu u X–XI veku*, Belgrade

Jäschke, K.-U. and Wenskus, R. (eds.) (1977), *Festschrift für Helmut Beumann zum 65. Geburtstag*, Sigmaringen

Jeffreys, E. (1982), 'The sevastokratorissa Eirene as literary patroness: the monk Iakovos', *JÖB* 32, pp. 63–71

—(1998), 'The novels of mid-twelfth century Constantinople: the literary and social context', in Ševčenko and Hutter (eds.) (1998), pp. 191–9

—(2004), 'Notes towards a discussion of the depiction of the Umayyads in Byzantine literature', in *BEINE*, VI, pp. 133–47

—(2007), 'Rhetoric in Byzantium', in Worthington (ed.) (2007), pp. 166–84

Jeffreys, E. and Jeffreys, M. J. (1994), 'Who was Eirene the sevastokratorissa?', *Byz* 64, pp. 40–68

Jeffreys, M. J. (2003), '"Rhetorical" texts', in Jeffreys, E. (ed.) (2003), pp. 87–100

Jehel, G. (ed.) (2000), *Orient et Occident du IXe au XVe siècle: actes du colloque d'Amiens, 8–10 octobre 1998*, Paris

Jenkins, R. J. H. (1948), 'Constantine VII's portrait of Michael III', *Bulletin de la classe des lettres et des sciences morales et politiques, Académie Royale de Belgique*, 5th series, 34, pp. 71–7; repr. in Jenkins (1970), no. 1

—(1954), 'The classical background of the *Scriptores post Theophanem*', *DOP* 8, pp. 13–30; repr. in Jenkins (1970), no. 4

—(1965), 'The chronological accuracy of the "Logothete" for the years AD 867–913', *DOP* 19, pp. 91–112; repr. in Jenkins (1970), no. 3

—(1966), *Byzantium: the imperial centuries AD 610–1071*, London

—(1970), *Studies on Byzantine history of the 9th and 10th centuries*, London

Jenkins, R. J. H. and Mango, C. (1956), 'The date and significance of the tenth homily of Photius', *DOP* 9–10, pp. 125–40; repr. in Jenkins (1970), no. 2

Johns, J. (1995), 'The Greek church and the conversion of Muslims in Norman Sicily?', *BF* 21, pp. 133–57

—(2002), *Arabic administration in Norman Sicily: the royal diwan*, Cambridge

Jolivet-Lévy, C. (1987), 'L'Image du pouvoir dans l'art byzantin à l'époque de la dynastie macédonienne (867–1056)', *Byz* 57, pp. 441–70

—(2001), *La Cappadoce médiévale: images et spiritualité*, Paris

Jones, L. (2001–2), 'The visual expression of Bagratuni rulership: ceremonial and portraiture', *REA* n.s. 28, pp. 341–98

Jones, L. and Maguire, H. (2002), 'A description of the jousts of Manuel I Komnenos', *BMGS* 26, pp. 104–48

Jordan, R. (2000), 'John of Phoberou: a voice crying in the wilderness', in Smythe (ed.) (2000), pp. 61–73

Jordanov, I., see Iordanov, I.

Jotischky, A. (2004), *Crusading and the crusader states*, Harlow

Jurukova, J. (1984), 'La Titulature des souverains du premier royaume bulgare d'après les monuments de la sphragistique', in Angelov *et al.* (eds.) (1984), pp. 224–30

Jurukova, J. and Penchev, V. (eds.) (1990), *B'lgarski srednovekovni pechati i moneti*, Sofia

Kaczynski, B. M. (1988), *Greek in the Carolingian age: the St Gall manuscripts*, Cambridge, MA

Kaegi, W. E. (1964), 'The contribution of archery to the Turkish conquest of Anatolia', *Sp* 39, pp. 96–108; repr. in Haldon (ed.) (2007), pp. 237–49

—(1967), 'Some reconsiderations on the themes (seventh-ninth centuries)', *JÖB* 16, pp. 39–53

—(1978), review of R.-J. Lilie's *Die byzantinische Reaktion auf die Ausbreitung der Araber*, *Sp* 53, pp. 399–404

—(1981), *Byzantine military unrest 471–843: an interpretation*, Amsterdam

—(1999), review of W. Treadgold's *Byzantium and its army 284–1081*, *Sp* 74, pp. 521–4

Kahane, H. and Kahane, R. (1968–76), 'Abendland and Byzanz: Sprache', *Reallexikon der Byzantinistik*, I, cols. 345–639, Amsterdam

Kalavrezou, I. (1997), 'Helping hands for the empire: imperial ceremonies and the cult of relics at the Byzantine court', in Maguire (ed.) (1997), pp. 53–79

—(ed.) (2003), *Byzantine women and their world*, Cambridge, MA

Kaldellis, A. (1999), *The argument of Psellos' Chronographia*, Leiden

Kalić, J. (1988), 'La Région de Ras à l'époque byzantine' in Ahrweiler (ed.) (1988), pp. 127–40

—(2000), 'Raška istraživanja', *Istorijski Časopis* 47, pp. 11–24

Kamp, N. and Wollasch, J. (eds.) (1982), *Tradition als historische Kraft: interdisziplinäre Forschungen zur Geschichte des früheren Mittelalters*, Berlin

Kaplan, M. (1991a), 'Maisons impériales et fondations pieuses: réorganisation de la fortune impériale et assistance publique de la fin du VIIIᵉ à la fin du Xᵉ siècle', *Byz* 61, pp. 340–64

—(1991b), 'La Place des soldats dans la société villageoise byzantine (VIIᵉ–Xᵉ siècles)', in *Le Combattant au moyen âge: actes du XVIIIᵉ congrès de la société des historiens médiévistes de l'enseignement supérieur public, Montpellier 1987*, Rouen, 1991; 2nd edn. Paris, 1995, pp. 45–55

—(1993), 'La Place du schisme de 1054 dans les relations entre Byzance, Rome et l'Italie', *BSl* 54, pp. 29–37

—(1997), *La Chrétienté byzantine du début du VIIᵉ siècle au milieu du XIᵉ siècle: images et reliques, moines et moniales, Constantinople et Rome*, Paris

—(2001), 'Quelques remarques sur la vie rurale à Byzance au IXᵉ siècle d'après la correspondance d'Ignace le Diacre', in Kountoura-Galake (ed.) (2001), pp. 365–76

—(ed.) (2001), *Le Sacré et son inscription dans l'espace à Byzance et en Occident: études comparées, BSo 18*, Paris

Kaplan, M. and Morrisson, C. (2004), 'L'Économie byzantine: perspectives historiographiques' [review article of *EHB* and *DOC* IV and V], *RH* 306, pp. 391–411

Karlin-Hayter, P. (1971), 'Etudes sur les deux histoires du règne du Michel III', *Byz* 41, pp. 452–96; repr. in Karlin-Hayter (1981), no. 4

—(1981), *Studies in Byzantine political history: sources and controversies*, London

—(1989), 'Michael III and money', *BSl* 50, pp. 1–8

—(1991a), 'Le *De Michaele* du Logothète: construction et intentions', *Byz* 61, pp. 365–95

—(1991b), 'L'Enjeu d'une rumeur: opinion et imaginaire à Byzance au IXᵉ s.', *JÖB* 41, pp. 85–111

Karpozilos, A. (1982), *Symbole ste melete tou biou kai tou ergou tou Ioanne Mauropodos*, Ioannina

Kazanski, M. *et al.* (eds.) (2000), *Les Centres proto-urbains russes entre Scandinavie, Byzance et orient*, Paris

Kazhdan, A. P. (1977), 'Once more about the "alleged" Russo-Byzantine treaty (ca. 1047) and the Pecheneg crossing of the Danube', *JÖB* 26, pp. 65–77

—(1983), 'Certain traits of imperial propaganda in the Byzantine empire from the eighth to the fifteenth centuries', in Makdisi *et al.* (eds.) (1983), pp. 13–28

—(1988–9), 'Rus'–Byzantine princely marriages in the eleventh and twelfth centuries', *HUS* 12–13, pp. 414–29

—(1992), 'Ignatios the Deacon's letters on the Byzantine economy', *BSl* 53, pp. 197–201

—(1997), 'The formation of Byzantine family names in the ninth and tenth centuries', *BSl* 58, pp. 90–109

—(1999), *A history of Byzantine literature, 650–850*, Athens

Kazhdan, A. P. and Epstein, A. W. (1985), *Change in Byzantine culture in the eleventh and twelfth centuries*, Berkeley

Kazhdan, A. P. and Franklin, S. (1984), *Studies on Byzantine literature of the eleventh and twelfth centuries*, Cambridge

Kazhdan, A. P. and McCormick, M. (1997), 'The social world of the Byzantine court', in Maguire, H. (ed.) (1997), pp. 167–97

Kazhdan, A. P. and Maguire, H. (1991), 'Byzantine hagiographical texts as sources on art', *DOP* 45, pp. 1–22

Kazhdan, A. P. and Talbot, A.-M. (1991–2), 'Women and iconoclasm', *BZ* 84–85, pp. 391–408; repr. in Talbot (2001), no. 3

Kedar, H.-E. *et al.* (eds.) (1982), *Outremer: studies in the history of the crusading kingdom of Jerusalem presented to Joshua Prawer*, Jerusalem

Keller, H. (1997), 'Ottonische Herrschersiegel. Beobachtungen und Fragen zu Gestalt und Aussage und zur Funktion im historischen Kontext', in Krimm and John (eds.) (1997), pp. 3–51; repr. in Keller (2002), pp. 131–66, 275–97

—(2002), *Ottonische Königsherrschaft: Organisation und Legitimation königlicher Macht*, Darmstadt

Kempf, F. *et al.* (1969), *History of the church*, III: *The church in the age of feudalism*, tr. A. Biggs, London

Kennedy, H. (1981), *The early Abbasid caliphate: a political history*, London

—(1992), 'Byzantine-Arab diplomacy in the Near East from the Islamic conquests to the mid-eleventh century', in Shepard and Franklin (eds.) (1992), pp. 133–43; repr. in Bonner (ed.) (2004), no. 4, pp. 81–91

—(2001), *The armies of the caliphs: military and society in the early Islamic state*, London

—(2004a), *The court of the caliphs: the rise and fall of Islam's greatest dynasty*, London

—(2004b), *The prophet and the age of the caliphates: the Islamic Near East from the sixth to the eleventh century*, 2nd edn., Harlow

Kermeli, E. and Özel, O. (eds.) (2006), *The Ottoman empire: myths, realities and 'black holes': contributions in honour of Colin Imber*, Istanbul

Kessler, H. L. and Wolf, G. (eds.) (1998), *The holy face and paradox of representation: papers from a colloquium held at the Bibliotheca Hertziana, Rome and the Villa Spelman, Florence, 1996*, Bologna

Keys, D. (1999), *Catastrophe: an investigation into the origins of the modern world*, London

Kindlimann, S. (1969), *Die Eroberung von Konstantinopel als politische Forderung des westens im Hochmittelalter: Studien zur Entwicklung der Idee eines lateinischen Kaiserreichs in Byzanz*, Zurich

Kirsten, E. (1958), 'Die byzantinische Stadt', *Berichte zum XI. Internationalen Byzantinisten-Kongress, München, 1958*, Munich, 1958, pp. 1–48

Kislinger, E. (1981), 'Der junge Basileios I. und die Bulgaren', *JÖB* 30, pp. 137–50

—(1983), 'Eudokia Ingerina, Basileios I. und Michael III.', *JÖB* 33, pp. 119–36

—(1987), 'Michael III. Image und Realität', *Eos* 75, pp. 387–400

—(2000), 'Elpidios (781/782) – ein Usurpator zur Unzeit', in *Byzantino-sicula* III: *Miscellanea di scritti in memoria di Bruno Lavagnini*, Palermo (2000), pp. 193–202

—(2001), *Regionalgeschichte als Quellenproblem: die Chronik von Monembasia und das sizilianische Demenna, eine historisch-topographische Studie*, Vienna

Kitzinger, E. (1954), 'The cult of images in the age before iconoclasm', *DOP* 8, pp. 83–150

Klaić, N. (1971), *Povijest Hrvata u ranom srednjem vijeku*, Zagreb

Klein, H. (2004), 'Eastern objects and western desires: relics and reliquaries between Byzantium and the west', *DOP* 58, pp. 283–314

—(2006), 'Sacred relics and imperial ceremonies at the Great Palace of Constantinople', in Bauer (ed.) (2006), pp. 79–100

Koch, G. (ed.) (2000), *Byzantinische Malerei: Bildprogramme, Ikonographie, Stil: Symposion in Marburg vom 25.–29.6.1997*, Wiesbaden

Koder, J. (1984), *Der Lebensraum der Byzantiner: historisch-geographischer Abriss ihres mittelalterlichen Staates im östlichen Mittelmeerraum*, Graz

—(2000), 'Macedonians and Macedonia in Byzantine spatial thinking', in Burke and Scott (eds.) (2000), pp. 12–28

—(2002), 'Maritime trade and the food supply for Constantinople in the middle ages', in Macrides (ed.) (2002), pp. 109–24

Koder, J. and Hild, F. (1976), *Hellas und Thessalia, TIB* 1, Vienna

Kolbaba, T. M. (1998), 'Fighting for Christianity: holy war in the Byzantine empire', *Byz* 68, pp. 194–221; repr. in Haldon (ed.) (2007), pp. 43–70

—(2001), 'Byzantine perceptions of Latin religious "errors": themes and changes from 850 to 1350', in Laiou and Mottahedeh (eds.) (2001), pp. 117–43

—(2003), 'The legacy of Humbert and Cerularius: the tradition of the "schism of 1054" in Byzantine texts and manuscripts of the twelfth and thirteenth centuries', in Dendrinos *et al.* (eds.) (2003), pp. 47–61

—(2005), 'On the closing of the churches and the rebaptism of Latins: Greek perfidy or Latin slander?', *BMGS* 29, pp. 39–51

—(2006), 'The orthodoxy of the Latins in the twelfth century', in Louth and Casiday (eds.) (2006), pp. 199–214

—(2008), 'Latin and Greek Christians', in Noble and Smith (eds.) (2008), pp. 213–29

Kolditz, S. (2002), 'Leon von Synada und Liudprand von Cremona. Untersuchungen zu den Ost-West-Kontakten des 10. Jahrhunderts', *BZ* 95, pp. 509–83

Konstantinou, E. (ed.) (2005), *Methodios und Kyrillos in ihrer europäischen Dimension*, Frankfurt-am-Main

Korobeinikov, D. (2004a), 'The revolt in Kastamonu, *c.* 1291–1293', *BF* 27, pp. 87–118

—(2007), 'A sultan in Constantinople: the feasts of Ghiyath al-Din Kay-Khusraw I', in Brubaker and Linardou (eds.) (2007), pp. 93–108

Kostaneants', K. (1913), *Vimakan Taregir Ts'uts'ak zhoghovatsoy ardzanagrut 'eants 'hayots' (Letopis' na kamniakh: sobranie-ukazatel' armianskikh nadpisei)*, St Petersburg

Kountoura-Galake, E. (1983), 'E epanastase tou Bardane Tourkou', *Symmeikta* 5, pp. 203–15

—(1996b), *O Byzantinos kleros kai e koinonia ton 'skoteinon aionon'*, Athens

—(1997), 'New fortresses and bishoprics in eighth-century Thrace', *REB* 55, pp. 279–89

—(1998), 'The Armeniac theme and the fate of its leaders', in Lampakes (ed.) (1998), pp. 27–38

—(2004), 'Iconoclast officials and the formation of surnames during the reign of Constantine V', *REB* 62, pp. 247–53

—(ed.) (2001), *Oi skoteinoi aiones tou Byzantiou, 7os–9os ai. (The dark centuries of Byzantium, 7th–9th centuries)*, Athens

Koutrakou, N.-C. (1994), *La Propagande impériale byzantine: persuasion et réaction (VIIIᵉ–Xᵉ siècles)*, Athens

—(1995), 'La Rumeur dans la vie politique byzantine: continuité et mutations (VIIIᵉ–Xᵉ siècles)', *BSl* 56, pp. 63–81

—(2000), '"Spies of towns": some remarks on espionage in the context of Arab-Byzantine relations (VIIth–Xth centuries)', *Graeco-Arabica* 7–8, pp. 243–66

Kovalev, R. K. (2005), 'Creating Khazar identity through coins: the special issue dirhams of 837/8', in Curta (ed.) (2005), pp. 220–53

Kresten, O. (1975), '*Pallida Mors Sarracenorum*: zur Wanderung eines literarischen Topos von Liudprand von Cremona bis Otto von Freising und zu seiner byzantinischen Vorlage', *RHM* 17, pp. 23–75

—(1977), 'Zur Echtheit des *sigillion* des Kaisers Nikephoros I. für Patras', *RHM* 19, pp. 15–78

—(1992–3), 'Der "Anredestreit" zwischen Manuel I. Komnenos und Friedrich I. Barbarossa nach der Schlacht von Myriokephalon', *RHM* 34–35, pp. 65–110

—(1998), 'Zur Chrysographie in den Auslandsschreiben der byzantinischen Kaiser', *RHM* 40, pp. 139–86

—(2000a), 'Zur angeblichen Heirat Annas, der Tochter Kaiser Leons VI., mit Ludwig III. "dem Blinden"', *RHM* 42, pp. 171–211

—(2000c), '"Staatsempfänge" im Kaiserpalast von Konstantinopel um die Mitte des 10. Jahrhunderts: Beobachtungen zu Kapitel II 15 des sogenannten "Zeremonienbuches"', *Sitzungsberichte der philosophisch-historischen Klasse, Österreichische Akademie der Wissenschaften* 670, pp. 1–61

Kriaras, E. (1968), 'Psellos', *RE* Suppl. 11, pp. 1124–82

—(1972), 'O Michael Psellos', *Byzantina* 4, pp. 53–128

Krimm, K. and John, H. (eds.) (1997), *Bild und Geschichte: Studien zur politischen Ikonographie: Festschrift für Hansmartin Schwarzmaier zum fünfundsechzigsten Geburtstag*, Sigmaringen

Kuczyński, S. K. *et al.* (eds.) (1976), *Cultus et cognitio: studia z dziejów średniowiecznej kultury (Festschrift für Alexander Gieysztor)*, Warsaw

Kunze, K. (1969), *Studien zur Legende der heiligen Maria Aegyptiaca im deutschen Sprachgebiet*, Berlin

Laiou, A. E. (2002a), 'Exchange and trade, seventh-twelfth centuries', in *EHB*, II, pp. 697–770

—(2002b), 'The human resources', in *EHB*, I, pp. 47–55

—(2002c), 'Economic and non-economic exchange', in *EHB*, II, pp. 681–96

—(2002d), 'The Byzantine economy: an overview', in *EHB*, III, pp. 1145–64

Lamberz, E. (1997), 'Studien zur Überlieferung der Akten des VII. Ökumenischen Konzils: Der Brief Hadrians I. an Konstantin VI. und Irene (JE 2448)', *DA* 53, pp. 1–43

—(2001), '"Falsata Graecorum more?" Die griechische Version der Briefe Papst Hadrians I. in den Akten des VII. Ökumenischen Konzils', in Sode and Takács (eds.), pp. 213–29

—(2004), *Die Bischofslisten des VII. Ökumenischen Konzils (Nicaenum II)*, Munich

Lampakes, S. (ed.) (1998), *E Byzantine Mikra Asia, 6os–12os ai. (Byzantine Asia Minor, 6th–12th centuries)*, Athens

Lampropoulou, A. *et al.* (2001), 'Symbole sten ermeneia ton archaiologikon tekmerion tes Peloponnesou kata tous "skoteinous aiones"', in Kountoura-Galake (ed.) (2001), pp. 198–229

Langdon, J. S. *et al.* (eds.) (1993), *To Hellenikon: studies in honor of Speros Vryonis, Jr*, 2 vols., New Rochelle, NY

Lange, N. de (1999), 'A thousand years of Hebrew in Byzantium', in Horbury (ed.) (1999), pp. 147–61

—(2000), 'Hebrews, Greeks or Romans? Jewish culture and identity in Byzantium', in Smythe (ed.) (2000), pp. 105–18

—(2005b), 'A corpus of Hebrew inscriptions from the territories of the Byzantine empire: report on a project', *Bulletin of Judaeo-Greek Studies* 35, pp. 35–9

—(2006), 'Can we speak of Jewish orthodoxy in Byzantium?', in Louth and Casiday (eds.) (2006), pp. 167–78

Laurent, J. (1980), *L'Arménie entre Byzance et l'Islam depuis la conquête arabe jusqu'en 886*, rev. edn. M. Canard, Lisbon

Lauxtermann, M. (2003–), *Byzantine poetry from Pisides to Geometres: texts and contexts*, 1 vol. to date, *WBS* 24, Vienna

Lavermicocca, N. (2003), *Bari bizantina: capitale mediterranea*, Bari

Lee, A. D. and Shepard, J. (1991) 'A double life: placing the *Peri Presbeon*', *BSl* 52, pp. 15–39

Lefort, J. (1976), 'Rhétorique et politique: trois discours de Jean Mauropous en 1047', *TM* 6, pp. 265–303

—(2002), 'The rural economy, seventh–twelfth centuries', in *EHB*, I, pp. 231–310

—(2005), 'Les Villages de Macédoine orientale au moyen âge (X^e–XIVe siècle)', in Lefort *et al.* (eds.) (2005), pp. 288–99

Lefort, J. *et al.* (eds.) (2005), *Les Villages dans l'empire byzantin: IVe–XVe siècle*, Paris

Leib, B. (1958), 'Les Silences d'Anne Comnène, ou ce que n'a pas dit l'Alexiade', *BSl* 19, pp. 1–11

—(1977), 'Aperçus sur l'époque des premiers Comnènes', *Collectanea Byzantina* [= *OCA* 204], Rome, pp. 1–64

Lemerle, P. (1960), *Prolégomènes à une édition critique et commentée des 'Conseils et récits' de Kékauménos*, Brussels

—(1963), 'La Chronique improprement dite de Monemvasie: le contexte historique et légendaire', *REB* 21, pp. 5–49; repr. in Lemerle (1980), no. 2

—(1965), 'Thomas le Slave', *TM* 1, pp. 255–97; repr. in Lemerle (1980), no. 3

—(1967), '"Roga" et rente d'état aux Xᵉ–XIᵉ siècles', *REB* 25, pp. 77–100; repr. in Lemerle (1978), no. 16

—(1973), 'L'Histoire des Pauliciens d'Asie Mineure d'après les sources grecques', *TM* 5, pp. 1–144; repr. in Lemerle (1980), no. 4

—(1977), *Cinq études sur le XIᵉ siècle byzantin*, Paris

—(1980), *Essais sur le monde byzantin*, London

Leonardi, C. and Menestò, E. (eds.) (1989), *Giovanni Scoto nel suo tempo: l'organizzazione del sapere in età carolingia. Atti del XXIV convegno internazionale, Todi, 11–14 ottobre 1987*, Spoleto

Letsios, D. (2004), 'Jewish communities in the Aegean during the middle ages', in Chrysostomides *et al.* (eds.) (2004), pp. 109–30

Lewis, B. (1977), 'Sources for the economic history of the Middle East', in Lewis *et al.* (1977), pp. 1–17

Lewis, B. *et al.* (1977), *Wirtschaftsgeschichte des Vorderen Orients in islamischer Zeit*, Leiden

Leyser, K. J. (1973), 'The tenth century in Byzantine–western relationships', in Baker (ed.) (1973), pp. 29–63; repr. in Leyser (1982), pp. 103–37

—(1982), *Medieval Germany and its neighbours, 900–1250*, London

—(1988), 'Ends and means in Liudprand of Cremona', in Howard-Johnston (ed.) (1988), pp. 119–43; repr. in Leyser (1994), pp. 125–42

—(1994), *Communications and power in medieval Europe: the Carolingian and Ottonian centuries*, ed. T. Reuter, London

—(1995), '*Theophanu divina gratia imperatrix augusta*: western and eastern emperorship in the later tenth century', in Davids (ed.) (1995), pp. 1–27

Lidov, A. (2006), 'Spatial icons: the miraculous performance with the Hodegetria of Constantinople', in Lidov (ed.) (2006), pp. 349–57 (a résumé of 'Prostranstvennye ikony: chudotvornoe deistvo s Odigitriei Konstantinopol'skoi', in Lidov (ed.) (2006), pp. 325–48)

—(ed.) (2006), *Hierotopy: creation of sacred spaces in Byzantium and medieval Russia*, Moscow

Lightfoot, C. S. (2002), 'Byzantine Anatolia: reassessing the numismatic evidence', *RN* 158, pp. 229–39

—(ed.) (2003), *Amorium reports 2: research papers and technical reports, BAR IS 1170*, Oxford

Lightfoot, C. S. *et al.* (1998), 'The Amorium project: the 1996 excavation season', *DOP* 52, pp. 323–36

—(2001), 'The Amorium project: the 1998 excavation season', *DOP* 55, pp. 371–99

—(2004), 'The Amorium project: excavation and research in 2001', *DOP* 58, pp. 355–70

Lilie, R.-J. (1984a), 'Die zweihundertjährige Reform: zu den Anfängen der Themen-organisation im 7. and 8. Jahrhundert', *BSl* 45, pp. 27–39, 190–201

—(1987a), 'Der erste Kreuzzug in der Darstellung Anna Komnenes', *Poikila Byzantina* 6, pp. 49–148

—(1987b), 'Die byzantinischen Staatsfinanzen im 8. und 9. Jahrhundert und die stratiotika ktemata', *BSl* 48, pp. 49–55

—(1989), 'Die lateinische Kirche in der Romania vor dem vierten Kreuzzug. Versuch einer Bestandaufnahme', *BZ* 82, pp. 202–20

—(1991), 'Twelfth-century Byzantine and Turkish states', in Bryer and Ursinus (eds.) (1991), pp. 35–51

—(1993b), 'Anna Komnene und die Lateiner', *BSl* 54, pp. 169–82

—(1996), *Byzanz unter Eirene und Konstantin VI. (780–802)*, Frankfurt-am-Main

—(1999), *Die Patriarchen der ikonoklastischen Zeit: Germanos I.–Methodios I. (715–847)*, Frankfurt-am-Main

—(2004), *Byzanz und die Kreuzzüge*, Stuttgart

Litavrin, G. G. (1977), *Vizantiiskoe obshchestvo i gosudarstvo v X–XI vv.*, Moscow

—(1999a), 'K voprosu ob obstoiatel'stvakh, meste i vremeni kreshcheniia kniagini Ol'gi', in Litavrin (1999b), pp. 429–37

—(1999b), *Vizantiia i slaviane: sbornik statei*, St Petersburg

—(2000), *Vizantiia, Bolgariia, drevniia Rus' (IX–nachalo XII v.)*, St Petersburg

— (ed.)(2006), *Vizantiiskie ocherki: trudy rossiiskikh uchenykh k XXI mezhdunarodnomu kongressu vizantinistov*, St Petersburg

Littlewood, A. R. (1999), 'The Byzantine letter of consolation in the Macedonian and Komnenian periods', *DOP* 53, pp. 19–41

—(ed.) (1995), *Originality in Byzantine literature, art and music: a collection of essays*, Oxford

Littlewood, A. R. *et al.* (eds.) (2002), *Byzantine garden culture*, Washington, DC

Liubarsky, I. N. (1978), *Mikhail Psell, lichnost' i tvorchestvo: k istorii vizantiiskogo predgumanizma*, Moscow

—(1987), 'Der Kaiser als Mime: zum Problem der Gestalt des byzantinischen Kaisers Michael III.', *JÖB* 37, pp. 39–50

—(1993), 'New trends in the study of Byzantine historiography', *DOP* 47, pp. 131–8

—(1994), 'George the Monk as a short-story writer', *JÖB* 44, pp. 255–64

—(1996), 'Why is the *Alexiad* a masterpiece of Byzantine literature?', in Rosenqvist (ed.) (1996), pp. 127–42; repr. in Gouma-Peterson (ed.) (2000), pp. 169–85

Ljubarskij, J., see Liubarsky, I. N.

Llewellyn, P. A. B. (1971), *Rome in the dark ages*, London

—(1981), 'The names of the Roman clergy, 401–1046', *Rivista di storia della chiesa in Italia* 35, pp. 355–70

—(1986), 'The popes and the constitution in the eighth century', *EHR* 101, pp. 42–67

Lock, P. and Sanders, G. D. R. (eds.) (1996), *The archaeology of medieval Greece*, Oxford

Loenertz, R.-J. (1950), 'Le Panégyrique de S. Denys l'Aréopagite par S. Michel le Syncelle', *AnBoll* 68, pp. 94–107; repr. in Loenertz (1970), pp. 149–62

—(1951), 'La Légende parisienne de S. Denys l'Aréopagite: sa genèse et son premier témoin', *AnBoll* 69, pp. 217–37; repr. in Loenertz (1970), pp. 163–83

—(1970), *Byzantina et Franco-Graeca: articles parus de 1935 à 1966*, ed. P. Schreiner, Rome

—(1974), '"*Constitutum Constantini*": destination, destinataires, auteur, date', *Aevum* 48, pp. 199–245

Longo, O. (ed.) (1998), *La porpora, realtà e immaginario di un colore simbolico: atti del convegno di studio, Venice, 24–25 ottobre 1996*, Venice

Lopez, R. S. (1945), 'The silk industry in the Byzantine empire', *Sp* 20, pp. 1–42; repr. in Lopez (1978), no. 3

—(1976), 'Beati monoculi: the Byzantine economy in the early middle ages', in Kuczyński *et al.* (eds.) (1976), pp. 341–52; repr. in Lopez (1978), no. 1

—(1978), *Byzantium and the world around it: economic and institutional relations*, London

Loud, G. A. (1988), 'Byzantine Italy and the Normans', in Howard-Johnston (ed.) (1988), pp. 215–33; repr. in Loud (1999), no. 3

—(1991), 'Anna Komnena and her sources for the Normans of southern Italy', in Wood and Loud (eds.) (1991), pp. 41–57; repr. in Loud (1999), no. 13

—(1994a), 'Montecassino and Byzantium in the tenth and eleventh centuries', in Mullett and Kirby (eds.) (1994), pp. 30–55; repr. in Loud (2000b), no. 2

—(1994b), 'The Liri valley in the middle ages', in Hayes and Martini (eds.) (1994), pp. 53–68; repr. in Loud (2000b), no. 1

—(1999), *Conquerors and churchmen in Norman Italy*, Aldershot

—(2000a), *The age of Robert Guiscard: southern Italy and the Norman conquest*, Harlow

—(2000b), *Montecassino and Benevento in the middle ages: essays in south Italian church history*, Aldershot

Lounghis, T. C. (1980), *Les Ambassades byzantines en Occident: depuis la fondation des états barbares jusqu'aux Croisades (407–1096)*, Athens

—(2002), 'The Byzantine historians on politics and people from 1042 to 1081', *Byz* 72, pp. 381–403

Louth, A. (2006), 'Photios as a theologian', in Jeffreys, E. (ed.) (2006), pp. 206–23

Louth, A. and Casiday, A. (eds.) (2006), *Byzantine orthodoxies: papers from the thirty-sixth spring symposium of Byzantine studies, University of Durham, 23–25 March 2002*, Aldershot

Louvi-Kitzi, A. (2002), 'Thebes', in *EHB*, II, pp. 631–8

Lowden, J. (1992), 'The luxury book as diplomatic gift', in Shepard and Franklin (eds.) (1992), pp. 249–60

Luchterhandt, M. (2006), 'Stolz und Vorurteil: der Westen und die byzantinische Hofkultur im Frühmittelalter', in Bauer (ed.) (2006), pp. 171–212

Ludwig, C. (1998), 'The Paulicians and ninth-century Byzantine thought', in Brubaker (ed.) (1998), pp. 23–35

—(ed.) (2005), *Siegel und Siegler: Akten des 8. Internationalen Symposions für Byzantinische Sigillographie*, Frankfurt-am-Main

Luzzati Laganà, F. (1983), 'Il ducato di Napoli', in Guillou *et al.* (1983), pp. 327–39

—(1982 [1983]), 'Le firme greche nei documenti del Ducato di Napoli', *SM* 23, pp. 729–52

Maas, M. (1990), 'Photius' treatment of Josephus and the high priesthood', *Byz* 60, pp. 183–94

McCabe, A. (2007), *A Byzantine encyclopaedia of horse medicine: the sources, compilation and transmission of the Hippiatrica*, Oxford

McCormick, M. (1985), 'Analyzing imperial ceremonies', *JÖB* 35, pp. 1–20

—(1987), 'Byzantium's role in the formation of early medieval civilization: approaches and problems', *Illinois classical studies* 12, pp. 207–20

—(1994a), 'Textes, images et iconoclasme dans le cadre des relations entre Byzance et l'Occident carolingien', *Testo e immagine nell'alto medioevo* = SSCIS 41, pp. 95–162

—(1994b), 'Diplomacy and the Carolingian encounter with Byzantium down to the accession of Charles the Bald', in McGinn and Otten (eds.) (1994), pp. 15–48

—(1997), 'Byzantium and the early medieval west: problems and opportunities', in Arnaldi and Cavallo (eds.) (1997), pp. 1–17

—(1998a), 'Bateaux de vie, bateaux de mort: maladie, commerce, transports annonaires et le passage économique du bas-empire au moyen âge', in *Morfologie sociali e culturali in Europa fra tarda antichità e alto medioevo* = SSCIS 45, pp. 35–122

—(1998b), 'The imperial edge: Italo-Byzantine identity, movement and integration, AD 650–950', in Ahrweiler and Laiou (eds.) (1998), pp. 17–52

—(2002), 'Byzantium on the move: imagining a communications history', in Macrides (ed.) (2002), pp. 3–29

—(2005), 'La Lettre diplomatique byzantine du premier millénaire vue de l'Occident et l'énigme du papyrus de Paris', in Balard *et al.* (eds.) (2005), pp. 135–49

McGeer, E. (1988), 'Infantry versus cavalry: the Byzantine response', *REB* 46, pp. 135–45; repr. in Haldon (ed.) (2007), pp. 335–45

—(1991), 'Tradition and reality in the *Taktika* of Nikephoros Ouranos', *DOP* 45, pp. 129–40

McGinn, B. and Otten, W. (eds.) (1994), *Eriugena: east and west. Papers of the eighth international colloquium of the society for the promotion of Eriugenian studies, Chicago and Notre Dame, 18–20 October 1991*, Notre Dame, IL

McKitterick, R. (1993), 'Ottonian intellectual culture in the tenth century and the role of Theophano', *Early Medieval Europe* 2, pp. 53–74; also published in Davids (ed.) (1995), pp. 169–93

—(2004), *History and memory in the Carolingian world*, Cambridge

—(ed.) (1990), *The uses of literacy in early mediaeval Europe*, Cambridge

McKitterick, R. and Quinault R. (eds.) (1997), *Edward Gibbon and empire*, Cambridge

McQueen, W. B. (1986), 'Relations between the Normans and Byzantium, 1071–1112', *Byz* 56, pp. 427–76

Macrides, R. (1988), 'Killing, asylum and the law in Byzantium', *Sp* 63, pp. 509–38; repr. in Macrides (1999), no. 10

—(1990), 'Nomos and kanon on paper and in court', in Morris (ed.) (1990), pp. 61–86; repr. in Macrides (1999), no. 6

—(1991), 'Perception of the past in the twelfth-century canonists', in Oikonomides (ed.) (1991), pp. 589–600; repr. in Macrides (1999), no. 7

—(1992a), 'Dynastic marriages and political kinship', in Shepard and Franklin (eds.) (1992), pp. 263–80

—(1994a), 'The competent court', in Laiou and Simon (eds.) (1994), pp. 117–30; repr. in Macrides (1999), no. 8

—(1996), 'The historian in the history', in Constantinides *et al.* (eds.) (1996), pp. 205–24

—(2000), 'The pen and the sword: who wrote the *Alexiad*?', in Gouma-Peterson (ed.) (2000), pp. 63–81

—(2002), 'Constantinople: the crusaders' gaze', in Macrides (ed.) (2002), pp. 193–212

—(ed.) (2002), *Travel in the Byzantine world: papers from the thirty-fourth spring symposium of Byzantine studies, Birmingham, April 2000*, Aldershot

Madgearu, A. (1999), 'The military organization of Paradunavon', *BSl* 60, pp. 421–46

—(2001b), 'Rethinking the Byzantine Balkans: a recent book on the 10th–12th centuries', *RESEE* 39, pp. 203–12

Magdalino, P. (1981), 'The Byzantine holy man in the twelfth century', in Hackel (ed.) (1981), pp. 51–66; repr. in Magdalino (1991), no. 7

—(1987), 'Observations on the Nea Ekklesia of Basil I', *JÖB* 37, pp. 51–64; repr. in Magdalino (2007b), no. 5

—(1988a), 'Basil I, Leo VI and the feast of the prophet Elijah', *JÖB* 38, pp. 193–6; repr. in Magdalino (2007b), no. 6

—(1988b), 'The bath of Leo the Wise and the "Macedonian Renaissance" revisited: topography, iconography, ceremonial, ideology', *DOP* 42, pp. 97–118

—(1989), 'Honour among Romaioi: the framework of social values in the world of *Digenes Akrites* and Kekaumenos', *BMGS* 13, pp. 183–218; repr. in Magdalino (1991), no. 3

—(1991), *Tradition and transformation in medieval Byzantium*, Aldershot

—(1993b), 'The history of the future and its uses: prophecy, policy and propaganda', in Beaton and Roueché (eds.) (1993), pp. 3–34

—(1994), 'Justice and finance in the Byzantine state, ninth to twelfth centuries', in Laiou and Simon (eds.) (1994), pp. 93–115

—(1996b), 'Eustathios and Thessalonica', in Constantinides *et al.* (eds.) (1996), pp. 225–38

—(1997), 'The non-juridical legislation of the emperor Leo VI', in Troianos (ed.) (1997), pp. 169–82

—(1998), 'The road to Baghdad in the thought world of ninth century Byzantium', in Brubaker (ed.) (1998), pp. 195–213

—(2000a), 'The maritime neighborhoods of Constantinople: commercial and residential functions, sixth to twelfth centuries', *DOP* 54, pp. 209–26; repr. in Magdalino (2007b), no. 3

—(2000b), 'Constantinople and the outside world', in Smythe (ed.) (2000), pp. 149–62; repr. in Magdalino (2007b), no. 11

—(2002), 'The Byzantine reception of classical astrology', in Holmes and Waring (eds.) (2002), pp. 33–57

—(2003), 'Prosopography and Byzantine identity', in Cameron, Averil (ed.) (2003), pp. 41–56

—(2004), 'L'Église du Phare et les reliques de la Passion à Constantinople (VIIe/VIIIe–XIIIe siècles)', in Durand and Flusin (eds.) (2004), pp. 15–30

—(2005), 'Prophecies on the fall of Constantinople', in Laiou (ed.) (2005), pp. 41–53

—(2006), *L'Orthodoxie des astrologues: la science entre le dogme et la divination à Byzance, VIIe–XIVe siècle*, Paris

—(2007a), 'Isaac II, Saladin and Venice', in Shepard (ed.) (2007), pp. 93–106; tr. of 'Isaac II Ange, Saladin et Venise', in Kaplan, M. (ed.) (forthcoming), *Byzance et ses confins*, Paris

—(2007b), *Studies on the history and topography of Byzantine Constantinople*, Aldershot

Magdalino, P. and Nelson, R. (1982), 'The emperor in Byzantine art of the twelfth century', *BF* 8, pp. 123–83; repr. in Magdalino (1991), no. 6

Maguire, H. (1996), *The icons of their bodies: saints and their images in Byzantium*, Princeton

—(1997), 'Images of the court', in Evans and Wixom (eds.) (1997), pp. 182–91

Mahé, J.-P. (1991), 'Basile II et Byzance vus par Grigor Narekac'i', *TM* 11, pp. 555–73

—(1993), 'L'Église arménienne de 611 à 1066' in Dagron *et al.* (eds.) (1993), pp. 457–547

Maisano, R. (ed.) (1993), *Storia e tradizione culturale a Bisanzio fra XI e XII secolo: atti della prima Giornata di studi bizantini sotto il patrocinio della Associazione Italiana di Studi Bizantini (Napoli, 14–15 febbraio 1992)*, Naples

Makdisi, G. *et al.* (eds.) (1983), *Prédication et propagande au moyen âge: Islam, Byzance, Occident* (Penn–Paris–Dumbarton Oaks Colloquia 3), Paris

Makk, F. (1989), *The Árpáds and the Comneni: political relations between Hungary and Byzantium in the 12th century*, tr. G. Novák *et al.*, Budapest

Maksimović, L. (1997), 'Organizacija Vizantijske vlasti u novoosvojenim oblastima posle 1018 godine', *ZRVI* 36, pp. 31–43

Maksimović, L. and Popović, M. (1993), 'Les Sceaux byzantins de la région danubienne en Serbie, II – La collection du Musée National de Belgrade', *SBS* 3, pp. 113–42

Maksoudian, K. (1988–9), 'The Chalcedonian issue and the early Bagratids. The Council of Širakawan', *REA* n.s. 21, pp. 333–44

Malamut, E. (1993), *Sur la route des saints byzantins*, Paris

—(1995), 'L'Image byzantine des Petchénègues', *BZ* 88, pp. 105–47

—(2004a), 'Les Itinéraires sacrés de Grégoire le Décapolite', *Cristianità d'occidente e cristianità d'oriente (secoli VI–XI) = SSCIS* 51, pp. 1191–1220

—(2005), 'Thessalonique 830–904', in Hoffmann and Monchizadeh (eds.) (2005), pp. 159–90

Maliaras, N. (1991), *Die Orgel im byzantinischen Hofzeremoniell des 9. und des 10. Jahrhunderts: eine Quellenuntersuchung, MBM* 33, Munich

Maltese, E. V. (1993), 'I *Theologica* di Psello e la cultura filosofica bizantina', in Maisano (ed.) (1993), pp. 51–69

Maltezou, C. A. (1995), 'Venetian *habitatores, burgenses* and merchants in Constantinople and its hinterland (twelfth-thirteenth centuries)', in Mango and Dagron (eds.) (1995), pp. 233–41

Manacorda, D. (2001), *Crypta Balbi: archeologia e storia di un paesaggio urbano*, Milan

Mandić, L. and Mihajlovski, R. (2000), 'A XIth century Byzantine seal from Heraclea near Bitola', *REB* 58, pp. 273–7

Mango, C. (1959), *The brazen house: a study of the vestibule of the imperial palace of Constantinople*, Copenhagen

—(1963a), 'The conciliar edict of 1166', *DOP* 17, pp. 315–30; repr. in Mango (1993), no. 18

—(1963b), 'Antique statuary and the Byzantine beholder', *DOP* 17, pp. 53–75; repr. in Mango (1984), no. 5

—(1967), 'When was Michael III born?', *DOP* 21, pp. 253–58; repr. in Mango (1984), no. 14

—(1973a), 'Eudocia Ingerina, the Normans, and the Macedonian dynasty', *ZRVI* 14–15, pp. 17–27; repr. in Mango (1984), no. 15

—(1973b), 'La Culture grecque et l'Occident au VIIIe siècle', in *I problemi dell'occidente nel secolo VIII = SSCIS* 20, pp. 683–721; repr. in Mango (1984), no. 6

—(1975a), 'The availability of books in the Byzantine empire, AD 750–850', in *Byzantine books and bookmen: a Dumbarton Oaks colloquium*, Washington, DC, pp. 29–45; repr. in Mango (1984), no. 7

—(1976), 'Les Monuments de l'architecture du XIe siècle et leur signification historique et sociale', *TM* 6, pp. 351–65

—(1977), 'The liquidation of iconoclasm and the patriarch Photios', in Bryer and Herrin (eds.) (1977), pp. 133–40; repr. in Mango (1984), no. 8

—(1981a), 'Daily life in Byzantium', *JÖB* 31, pp. 338–53

—(1981b), 'Discontinuity with the classical past in Byzantium', in Mullett and Scott (eds.) (1981), pp. 48–57

—(1983), 'The two lives of St Ioannikios and the Bulgarians', *HUS* 7, pp. 393–404

—(1984), *Byzantium and its image: history and culture of the Byzantine empire and its heritage*, London

—(2002a), 'A journey round the coast of the Black Sea in the ninth century', *Palaeoslavica* 10, pp. 255–64

—(2005), 'The meeting-place of the first ecumenical council and the Church of the Holy Fathers at Nicaea', *DChAE* 26, pp. 27–34

Mango, C. and Ševčenko, I. (1972), 'Three inscriptions of the reigns of Anastasius I and Constantine V', *BZ* 65, pp. 379–93

Mango, M. see Mundell Mango, M.

Maniatis, G. C. (2004), 'The wheat market in Byzantium, 900–1200: organization, marketing and pricing strategies', *BSl* 62, pp. 103–24

Mansouri, T. (2000), 'Présence byzantine en terre d'islam (VIIe–XIe siècle): sources d'informations et moyens de propagande', in Jehel (ed.) (2000), pp. 235–53

Manzano Moreno, E. (1998), 'Byzantium and al-Andalus in the ninth century', in Brubaker (ed.) (1998), pp. 215–27

Marazzi, F. (1991), 'Il conflitto fra Leone III Isaurico e il papato fra il 725 e il 733, e il "definitivo" inizio del medioevo a Roma: un'ipotesi in discussione', *PBSR* 59, pp. 231–57

Margetić, L. (1988), 'Quelques aspects du plaid de Rižana', *REB* 46, pp. 125–34

Markopoulos, A. (1992), 'An anonymous laudatory poem in honor of Basil I', *DOP* 46, pp. 225–32, repr. in Markopoulos (2004), no. 14

—(1994), 'Constantine the Great in Macedonian historiography: models and approaches', in Magdalino (ed.) (1994), pp. 159–70, repr. Markopoulos (2004), no. 15

—(2003), 'Byzantine history writing at the end of the first millennium', in Magdalino (ed.) (2003), pp. 183–97

—(2004), *History and literature of Byzantium in the 9th–10th centuries*, Aldershot

—(ed.) (1989), *Konstantinos VII o Porphyrogennetos kai e epoche tou: 2 Diethnes Byzantinologike Synantese, Delphoi, 22–26 Iouliou 1987 (Constantine VII and his age: Second international Byzantine congress, Delphi, 22–26 July 1987)*, Athens

Martin, J.-M. (1980), 'Eléments préféodaux dans les principautés de Bénévent et de Capoue (fin du VIIIe siècle–début du XIe siècle): modalités de privatisation du pouvoir', *Structures féodales et féodalisme dans l'Occident méditerranéen (Xe–XIIIe siècles): colloque international organisé par le Centre National de la Recherche Scientifique et l'École Française de Rome, Rome, 10–13 octobre 1978, CEFR* 44, Rome, pp. 553–86

—(2005), *Guerre, accords et frontières en Italie méridionale pendant le haut moyen âge: Pacta de Liburia, Divisio principatus Beneventani et autres actes*, Rome

Martin, J.-M. and Noyé, G. (1991), 'Les Villes de l'Italie byzantine (IXe–XIe siècle)', in Kravari *et al* (eds.) (1989–91), II, pp. 27–62

Martin, M. E. (1978), 'The chrysobull of Alexius I Comnenus to the Venetians and the early Venetian Quarter in Constantinople', *BSl* 39, pp. 19–23

Martin-Hisard, B. (1996), 'L'Empire byzantin dans l'oeuvre de Lewond', in Garsoïan *et al.* (eds.) (1996), pp. 135–44

—(2000), 'Constantinople et les *archontes* caucasiens dans le *Livre des cérémonies* II, 48', *TM* 13, pp. 359–530

—(2001), 'Moines et monastères géorgiens du 9e siècle: la *Vie* de saint Grigol de Xancta', *REB* 59, pp. 5–94

—(2002), 'Moines et monastères géorgiens du 9e siècle: la *Vie* de saint Grigol de Xancta. Deuxième partie: une mise en perspective historique', *REB* 60, pp. 5–64

Mayer, W. and Trzcionka, S. (eds.) (2005), *Feast, fast or famine: food and drink in Byzantium, ByzAust* 15, Brisbane

Mayr-Harting, H. (2001), 'Liudprand of Cremona's account of his legation to Constantinople (968) and Ottonian imperial strategy', *EHR* 116, pp. 539–56

Mazzarino, S. (1940), 'Su un'iscrizione trionfale di Turris Libisonis', *Epigraphica* 2, pp. 292–313

Meersseman, G. G. (1963), *Kritische glossen op de Griekse Theophilus-legende (7e eeuw) en haar Latijnse vertaling (9e eeuw)*, Brussels

Megaw, A. H. S. (1966), 'The Skripou screen', *ABSA* 61, pp. 1–32

Ménager, L. R. (1958–9), 'La "Byzantinisation" religieuse de l'Italie méridionale (IXe–XIIe siècles) et la politique monastique des Normands d'Italie', I: *RHE* 53, pp. 747–74; II: *RHE* 54, pp. 5–40

Mercati, S. G. (1970a), *Collectanea byzantina*, 2 vols., Bari

—(1970b), 'Sull' epitafio di Basilio II Bulgaroctonos', repr. in Mercati (1970a), II, pp. 226–31

Merores, M. (1911), *Gaeta im frühen Mittelalter (8. bis 12. Jahrhundert): Beiträge zur Geschichte der Stadt*, Gotha

Meyer-Plath, B. and Schneider, A. M. (1938–43), *Die Landmauer von Konstantinopel*, 2 vols., Berlin

Michaelides, D. *et al.* (eds.) (1992), *Excavations at Otranto*, 2 vols., Lecce

Miller, T. S. (1997), *The birth of the hospital in the Byzantine empire*, 2nd edn, Baltimore

Miller, T. S. and Nesbitt, J. (eds.) (1995), *Peace and war in Byzantium: essays in honor of George T. Dennis SJ*, Washington, DC

Millingen, A. van (1899), *Byzantine Constantinople, the walls of the city and adjoining historical sites*, London

Minorsky, V. (1953), 'Caucasica IV', *BSOAS* 15, pp. 504–29

Mirti, P. *et al.* (2001), 'Glass fragments from the Crypta Balbi in Rome: the composition of eighth-century fragments', *Archaeometry* 43, pp. 491–502

Mitchell, S. (ed.) (1983), *Armies and frontiers in Roman and Byzantine Anatolia: proceedings of a colloquium held at University College, Swansea, in April 1981, BAR IS* 156, Oxford

Moffatt, A. (1995), 'The master of ceremonies' bottom drawer: the unfinished state of the *De ceremoniis* of Constantine Porphyrogennetos', *BSl* 56, pp. 377–88

Mor, C. G. (1951), 'La lotta fra la chiesa greca e la chiesa latina in Puglia nel secolo X', *Archivio storico pugliese* 4, pp. 58–64

—(1952–3), *L'età feudale*, 2 vols., Milan

Mor, C. G. and Schmidinger, H. (eds.) (1979), *I poteri temporali dei vescovi in Italia e in Germania nel medioevo*, Bologna

Moravcsik, G. (1961), 'Sagen und Legenden über Kaiser Basileios I.', *DOP* 15, pp. 59–126

Mordek, H. (1988), 'Rom, Byzanz and die Franken im 8. Jahrhundert: zur Überlieferung und kirchenpolitischen Bedeutung der Synodus Romana Papst Gregors III. vom Jahre 732 (mit Edition)', in Althoff *et al.* (eds.) (1988), pp. 123–56

Morgan, D. O. (ed.) (1982), *Medieval historical writing in the Christian and Islamic worlds*, London

Morris, R. (1976), 'The powerful and the poor in tenth-century Byzantium: law and reality', *PaP* 73, pp. 3–27

—(1981), 'The political saint of the eleventh century', in Hackel (ed.) (1981), pp. 43–50

—(1985), 'Monasteries and their patrons in the tenth and eleventh centuries', *BF* 10, pp. 185–231

—(1986), 'Dispute settlement in the Byzantine provinces in the tenth century', in Davies and Fouracre (eds.) (1986), pp. 125–47

—(1988), 'The two faces of Nikephoros Phokas', *BMGS* 12, pp. 83–115

—(2003), 'Beyond the *De ceremoniis*', in Cubitt (ed.) (2003), pp. 235–54

—(2006a), review of L. Neville's *Authority in Byzantine provincial society, 950–1100*, *EHR* 121, pp. 507–9

—(2006b), 'The *epoptēs* Thomas at work', in Kermeli and Özel (eds.) (2006), pp. 23–37

—(2008), 'The problem of property', in Noble and Smith (eds.) (2008), pp. 327–44

Morrisson, C. (1976), 'La Dévaluation de la monnaie byzantine au XIᵉ siècle: essai d'interprétation', *TM* 6, pp. 3–48

—(1998), 'La Sicile byzantine: une lueur dans les siècles obscurs', *Numismatica e antichità classiche quaderni Ticinesi* 27, pp. 307–34

—(2001), 'Survivance de l'économie monétaire à Byzance (VIIᵉ–IXᵉ s.)', in Kountoura-Galake (ed.) (2001), pp. 377–97

—(2002), 'Byzantine money: its production and circulation', in *EHB*, III, pp. 909–66

Morrisson, C. and Cheynet, J.-C. (2002), 'Prices and wages in the Byzantine world', in *EHB*, II, pp. 815–78

Moss, C. and Kiefer, K. (eds.) (1995), *Byzantine east, Latin west: art-historical studies in honor of Kurt Weitzmann*, Princeton

Mouriki, D. (1985), *The mosaics of Nea Moni on Chios*, tr. R. Burgi, 2 vols., Athens

Mousheghian, K. *et. al.* (2000a), *History and coin finds in Armenia: coins from Duin*, Wetteren

—(2000b), *History and coin finds in Armenia: coins from Ani*, Wetteren

Müller-Wiener, W. (1961), 'Mittelalterliche Befestigungen im südlichen Ionien', *Istanbuler Mitteilungen* 11, pp. 5–122

—(1977), *Bildlexikon zur Topographie Istanbuls*, Tübingen

Mullett, M. (1984), 'The "disgrace" of the ex-Basilissa Maria', *BSl* 45, pp. 202–11

—(1988), 'Byzantium: a friendly society?', *PaP* 118, pp. 3–24

—(1990a), 'Patronage in action: the problems of an eleventh-century bishop', in Morris (ed.) (1990), pp. 125–47

—(1990b), 'Writing in early mediaeval Byzantium', in McKitterick (ed.) (1990), pp. 156–85

—(2003), 'The detection of relationship in middle Byzantine literary texts: the case of letters and letter-networks', in Hörander and Grünbart (eds.) (2003), pp. 63–74

Mullett, M. and Kirby, A. (eds.) (1994), *The Theotokos Evergetis and eleventh-century monasticism: papers of the third Belfast Byzantine international colloquium, 1–4 May 1992, BBTT 6.1*, Belfast

Mullett, M. and Kirby, A. (eds.) (1997), *Work and worship at the Theotokos Evergetis, 1050–1200: papers of the fourth Belfast Byzantine international colloquium, 14–17 September 1995, BBTT 6.2*, Belfast

Mullett, M. and Smythe, D. (eds.) (1996), *Alexios I Komnenos: papers of the second Belfast Byzantine international colloquium, 14–16 April 1989, BBTT 4.1*, Belfast

Mütherich, F. (1987), 'Das Verzeichnis eines griechischen Bilderzyklus in dem St Galler Codex 48', *DOP* 41, pp. 415–23; repr. in Mütherich (2004), pp. 524–39

—(2004), *Studies in Carolingian manuscript illumination*, London

Muthesius, A. (1995), *Studies in Byzantine and Islamic silk weaving*, London

—(1997), *Byzantine silk weaving: AD 400 to AD 1200*, ed. E. Kislinger and J. Koder, Vienna

Nagy, G. *et al.* (eds.) (2003), *Modern Greek literature: critical essays*, London

Nazarenko, A. V. (2001), *Drevniaia Rus' na mezhdunarodnykh putiakh*, Moscow

Necipoğlu, N. (ed.) (2001), *Byzantine Constantinople: monuments, topography and everyday life*, Leiden

Nerlich, D. (1999), *Diplomatische Gesandtschaften zwischen Ost- und Westkaisern 756–1002*, Bern

Nesbitt, J.W. (ed.) (2003), *Byzantine authors: literary activities and preoccupations*, Leiden

Neville, L. (2004), *Authority in Byzantine provincial society, 950–1100*, Cambridge

—(2006), 'Taxing Sophronia's son-in-law: representations of women in provincial documents', in Garland (ed.) (2006), pp. 77–89

Nichanian, M. and Prigent, V. (2003), 'Les Stratèges de Sicile: de la naissance du thème au règne de Léon V', *REB* 61, pp. 97–141

Nickles, H. G. (1937), 'The *Continuatio Theophanis*', *TAPA* 68, pp. 221–7

Nicol, D. M. (1962), 'Byzantium and the papacy in the eleventh century', *Journal of ecclesiastical history* 13, pp. 1–20; repr. in Nicol (1972b), no. 2

Nikolaou, K. (ed.) (2002), *Anoche kai katastole stous Mesous Chronous: mneme Lenou Maurommate (Toleration and repression in the Middle Ages: in memory of Lenos Mavrommatis)*, Athens

Nikolov, A. (2003), '"A useful tale about the Latins": an Old Bulgarian translation of a lost Byzantine anti-Latin text of the end of 11th–early 12th century', *Scripta & e-scripta* 1, pp. 99–119

Nixon, L. *et al.* (2000), *Sphakia survey: the internet edition* (www.sphakia.classics.ox.ac.uk)

Noble, T. F. X. (1984), *The republic of St Peter: the birth of the papal state, 680–825*, Philadelphia

Noble, T. F. X. and Smith, J. M. H. (eds.) (2008), *The Cambridge history of Christianity*, III: *Early medieval Christianities, c. 600–c. 1100*, Cambridge

Noonan, T. S. (2000), 'The fur road and the silk road: the relations between central Asia and northern Russia in the early middle ages', in Bálint (ed.) (2000), pp. 285–301

Nordhagen, P. J. (1988), 'Italo-Byzantine wall painting of the early middle ages: an eighty-year-old enigma in scholarship', *Bisanzio, Roma e l'Italia nell'alto medioevo = SSCIS* 34, pp. 593–626

Northedge, A. (2001), 'The palaces of the Abbasids at Samarra', in Robinson (ed.) (2001), pp. 29–67

Noyé, G. (1988), 'Quelques observations sur l'évolution de l'habitat en Calabre du Ve au XIe siècle', *RSBN* n.s. 25, pp. 57–138

—(1998), 'Byzance et Italie méridionale', in Brubaker (ed.) (1998), pp. 229–43

—(2000), 'Economie et société dans la Calabre byzantine (IVe–XIe siècle)', *JS*, pp. 209–80

Obolensky, D. (1948), *The Bogomils: a study in Balkan neo-manichaeism*, Cambridge

—(1963), 'The principles and methods of Byzantine diplomacy', in *ACIEB* 12, I, pp. 45–61; repr. in Obolensky (1994), pp. 1–22

—(1986), 'Theophylaktos of Ohrid and the authorship of the *Vita Clementis*', *Byzantion: aphieroma ston Andrea N. Strato; Byzance: hommage à André N. Stratos; Byzantium: tribute to Andreas N. Stratos*, II, Athens (1986), pp. 601–18

—(1988b), 'The Balkans in the ninth century: barrier or bridge?', in Howard-Johnston (ed.) (1988), pp. 47–66; repr. in Haldon (ed.) (2007), pp. 295–314

—(1993), 'Byzantium, Kiev and Cherson in the tenth century', *BSl* 54, pp. 108–13

Odorico, P. (ed.) (forthcoming), *L'Éducation au gouvernement et à la vie: la tradition des 'règles de vie' de l'antiquité au moyen-âge: Actes du congrès international, Pise, mars 2005*, Paris

Odorico, P. and Agapitos, P. A. (eds.) (2002), *Pour une 'nouvelle' histoire de la littérature byzantine: problèmes, méthodes, approches, propositions: Actes du Colloque international philologique Nicosie – Chypre 25–28 mai 2000*, Paris

Odorico, P. and Agapitos, P. A. (eds.) (2004), *Les Vies des saints à Byzance: genre littéraire ou biographie historique? Actes du IIe Colloque international philologique 'EPMHNEIA', Paris, 6–8 juin 2002*, Paris

Ohnsorge, W. (1958), *Abendland und Byzanz: gesammelte Aufsätze zur Geschichte der byzantinisch–abendländischen Beziehungen und des Kaisertums*, Darmstadt

—(1983), *Ost-Rom und der Westen: gesammelte Aufsätze zur Geschichte der byzantinisch-abendländischen Beziehungen und des Kaisertums*, Darmstadt

Oikonomides, N. (1963), 'Le Serment de l'impératrice Eudocie (1067): un épisode de l'histoire dynastique de Byzance', *REB* 21, pp. 101–28; repr. in Oikonomides (1976b), no. 3

—(1964), 'Une liste arabe des stratèges byzantins du VIIe siècle et les origines du thème de Sicile', *RSBN* n.s. 1, pp. 121–30; repr. in Oikonomides (1976b), no. 7

—(1966), 'The donations of castles in the last quarter of the 11th century (Dölger, *Regesten* no. 1012)', in Wirth (ed.) (1966), pp. 413–17; repr. in Oikonomides (1976b), no. 14

—(1971), 'À propos des relations ecclésiastiques entre Byzance et la Hongrie au XIe siècle: le métropolite de Turquie', *RESEE* 9, pp. 527–33; repr. in Oikonomides (1976b), no. 20

—(1972), 'Quelques boutiques de Constantinople au Xe siècle: prix, loyers, imposition (*Cod. Patmiacus 171*)', *DOP* 26, pp. 345–56; repr. in Oikonomides (1992a), no. 8

—(1974), 'L'Organisation de la frontière orientale de Byzance aux Xe–XIe siècles et le taktikon de l'Escorial', *ACIEB* 14, I, pp. 285–302; repr. in Oikonomides (1976b), no. 24

—(1976a), 'L'Évolution de l'organisation administrative de l'empire byzantin au XIe siècle (1025–1118)', *TM* 6, pp. 125–52; repr. in Oikonomides (1992a), no. 10

—(1979b), 'L'*Épopée* de Digénis et la frontière orientale de Byzance aux Xe et XIe siècles', *TM* 7, pp. 375–97; repr. in Oikonomides (1992a), no. 17

—(1981, 1984, 1985), 'Mesembria in the ninth century: epigraphical evidence', *BS* 8, 11 and 12, pp. 269–73; repr. in Oikonomides (1992a), no. 2

—(1983), 'Les Danishmendides entre Byzance, Bagdad et le sultanat d'Iconium', *RN* 25, pp. 189–207; repr. in Oikonomides (1992a), no. 19

—(1986a), 'Silk trade and production in Byzantium from the sixth to the ninth century: the seals of *kommerkiarioi*', *DOP* 40, 33–53; repr. in Oikonomides (2004), no. 8

—(1986b), 'The "Peira" of Eustathios Romaios: an abortive attempt to innovate in Byzantine law', *FM* 7, pp. 169–192; repr. in Oikonomides (1992a), no. 12

—(1988a), 'Middle-Byzantine provincial recruits: salary and armament', in Duffy and Peradotto (eds.) (1988), pp. 121–36; repr. in Oikonomides (2004), no. 10; repr. in Haldon (ed.) (2007), pp. 151–66

—(1989), 'Commerce et production de la soie à Byzance', in Kravari *et al.* (eds.) (1989–91), I, pp. 187–92

—(1991), 'Le Kommerkion d'Abydos, Thessalonique et le commerce bulgare au IXe siècle', in Kravari *et al.* (eds.) (1989–91), II, pp. 241–8

—(1993), 'Le Marchand byzantin des provinces (IXe–XIe s.)', *Mercati e mercanti nell'alto medioevo: l'area euroasiatica e l'area mediterranea* = *SSCIS* 40, pp. 633–60; repr. in Oikonomides (2004), no. 12

—(1995), 'The concept of "holy war" and two tenth-century Byzantine ivories', in Miller and Nesbitt (eds.) (1995), pp. 62–86

—(1996a), *Fiscalité et exemption fiscale à Byzance (IXe–XIe s.)*, Athens

—(1996b), 'St Andrew, Joseph the Hymnographer and the Slavs of Patras', in Rosenqvist (ed.) (1996), pp. 71–8; repr. in Oikonomides (2004), no. 24

—(1997b), 'The economic region of Constantinople: from directed economy to free economy and the role of the Italians', in Arnaldi and Cavallo (eds.) (1997), pp. 221–38; repr. in Oikonomides (2004), no. 13

—(1999–2000), 'A note on the campaign of Staurakios in the Peloponnese (783/4)', *ZRVI* 38, pp. 61–5; repr. in Oikonomides (2004), no. 26

—(2004), *Social and economic life in Byzantium*, ed. E. Zachariadou, Aldershot

—(ed.) (1991), *To Byzantio kata ton 12 aiona: kanoniko dikaio, kratos kai koinonia (Byzantium in the 12th century: canon law, state and society)*, Athens

Oikonomides, N. *et al.* (1998), 'Seals published 1931–1986', *SBS* 5, pp. 43–201

Osborne, J. (2003), 'Papal court culture during the pontificate of Zacharias (AD 741–52)', in Cubitt (ed.) (2003), pp. 223–34

Osborne, J. *et al.* (eds.) (2004), *Santa Maria Antiqua al Foro Romano cento anni dopo: atti del colloquio internazionale, Roma, 5–6 maggio 2000*, Rome

Ostrogorsky, G. (1929), *Studien zur Geschichte des byzantinischen Bilderstreites*, Breslau; repr. Amsterdam, 1964

—(1930), 'Les Débuts de la querelle des images', *Mélanges Charles Diehl*, 2 vols., Paris, I, pp. 235–56

—(1959), 'Byzantine cities in the early middle ages', *DOP* 13, pp. 45–66

—(1966), 'Agrarian conditions in the Byzantine empire in the middle ages', in Postan (ed.) (1966), pp. 205–34

O'Sullivan, S. (2004), 'Sebeos' account of an Arab attack on Constantinople in 654', *BMGS* 28, pp. 67–88

Ousterhout, R. (2001), 'Architecture, art and Komnenian ideology at the Pantokrator monastery', in Necipoğlu (ed.) (2001), pp. 133–50

—(2006), *A Byzantine settlement in Cappadocia, DOSt* 42, Washington, DC

Pahlitzsch, J. (2001), *Graeci und Suriani im Palästina der Kreuzfahrerzeit: Beiträge und Quellen zur Geschichte des griechisch-orthodoxen Patriarchats von Jerusalem*, Berlin

Pals, J. P. (1987), 'Observations on the economy of the settlement', in Groenman-van Waateringe and van Wijngaarden-Bakker (eds.) (1987), pp. 118–29

Panella, C. and Saguì, L. (2001), 'Consumo e produzione a Roma tra tardoantico e altomedioevo: le merci, i contesti', in *Roma nell'alto medioevo = SSCIS* 48, pp. 757–820

Papaioannou, E. N. (2001), 'The "usual miracle" and an unusual image: Psellos and the icons of Blachernai', *JÖB* 51, pp. 177–88

Papathanassiou, A. N. (1996), '"Homeritarum leges": an interpretation', *Proche-Orient Chrétien* 46, pp. 27–71

Parani, M. G. (2003), *Reconstructing the reality of images: Byzantine material culture and religious iconography (11th to 15th centuries)*, Leiden

Paroli, L. (1992a), 'La ceramica invetriata tardo-antica e medievale nell'Italia centro-meridionale', in Paroli (ed.) (1992), pp. 33–61

—(1992b), 'Ceramiche invetriate da un contesto dell'VIII secolo della Crypta Balbi – Roma', in Paroli (ed.) (1992), pp. 351–77

—(2004), 'Roma dal V al IX secolo: uno sguardo attraverso le stratigrafie archeologiche', in Paroli and Venditelli (eds.) (2004), pp. 11–40

—(ed.) (1992), *La ceramica invetriata tardoantica e altomedievale in Italia: atti del seminario, Certosa di Pontignano, Siena, 23–24 febbraio 1990*, Florence

Paroli, L. and Venditelli, L. (eds.) (2004), *Roma dall'antichità al medioevo,* II: *Contesti tardoantichi e altomedievali*, Milan

Patlagean, E. (1984a), 'Sainteté et pouvoir', in Hackel (ed.) (1981), pp. 88–105

—(1984b), 'Les Débuts d'une aristocratie byzantine et le témoignage de l'historiographie: système des noms et liens de parenté aux IXe–Xe siècles', in Angold (ed.) (1984), pp. 23–43

—(1986), 'Aveux et désaveux d'hérétiques à Byzance (XIe–XIIe siècles)', in *L'Aveu: antiquité et moyen-âge: actes de la table ronde organisée par l'École Française de Rome avec le concours du CNRS et de l'Université de Trieste, Rome, 28–30 mars 1984*, Rome (1986), pp. 243–60

—(1993), 'Byzance et les marchés du grand commerce, vers 839–vers 1030: entre Pirenne et Polanyi', *Mercati e mercanti nell'alto medioevo: l'area euroasiatica e l'area mediterranea = SSCIS* 40, pp. 587–632

—(1994), 'La Double Terre Sainte de Byzance: autour du XIIe siècle', *Annales – histoire, sciences sociales* 49, pp. 459–69

—(1997), 'The poor', in Cavallo (ed.) (1997), pp. 15–42

—(2001), *Figures du pouvoir à Byzance (IXe–XIIe siècle)*, Spoleto

—(2004), 'Ecrire l'histoire économique de Byzance: à propos d'un ouvrage récent' [Review of *EHB*], *Le Moyen Age: revue d'histoire et de philologie* 110, pp. 659–69

Patoura, S. (1994), *Oi aichmalotai os paragontes epikoinonias kai plerophoreses (4os–10os ai.)*, Athens

Pattenden, P. (1983), 'The Byzantine early warning system', *Byz* 53, pp. 258–99

Peacock, A. C. S. (2005), 'Nomadic society and the Seljuq campaigns in Caucasia', *Iran and the Caucasus* 9.2, pp. 205–30

Pellat, C. (1954), 'Gahiziana, I: le *Kitab al-Tabassur bi-l-Tigara* attribué à Gahiz', *Arabica* 1, pp. 153–65

Peri, V. (1971), 'Leone III e il "filioque": echi del caso nell'agiografia greca', *Rivista di storia della chiesa in Italia* 25, pp. 3–58

Perrie, M. (ed.) (2006), *The Cambridge history of Russia,* I: *From early Rus' to 1689*, Cambridge

Pertusi, A. (1965), 'Venezia e Bisanzio nel secolo XI', in *La Venezia del Mille, Storia della civiltà veneziana* 10, Florence, pp. 117–60

—(1979), 'Venezia e Bisanzio, 1000–1204', *DOP* 33, pp. 1–22

Pevny, O. Z. (ed.) (2000), *Perceptions of Byzantium and its neighbors (843–1261)*, New York

Philippart, G. (1974), 'Jean évêque d'Arezzo (IXe s.), auteur du *De assumptione* de Reichenau', *AnBoll* 92, pp. 345–6

Phillips, J. (1996), *Defenders of the Holy Land: relations between the Latin east and the west, 1119–1187*, Oxford

—(2004), *The Fourth Crusade and the sack of Constantinople*, London

Piccirillo, M. (1993), *The mosaics of Jordan*, ed. P. M. Bikai and T. A. Dailey, Amman

Pirivatrić, S. (1997 [1998]), *Samuilova država: obim i karakter*, Belgrade

Pitarakis, B. (1998), 'Mines anatoliennes exploitées par les Byzantins: recherches récentes', *RN* 153, pp. 141–85

Poblome, J. and Waelkens, M. (2003), 'Sagalassos and Alexandria: exchange in the eastern Mediterranean', in Abadie-Reynal (ed.) (2003), pp. 179–91

Podskalsky, G. (1982), *Christentum und theologische Literatur in der Kiever Rus' (988–1237)*, Wiesbaden

Polat, M. (1999), *Die Umwandlungsprozess von Kalifat zur Dynastie: Regierungspolitik und Religion beim ersten Umayyadenherrscher Muʿawiya ibn Abi Sufyan*, Frankfurt-am-Main

Polemis, D. I. (1968), *The Doukai: a contribution to Byzantine prosopography*, London

Politis, L. (1973), *A history of modern Greek literature*, Oxford

Popović, M. (1982), *Beogradska tvrđava*, Belgrade

—(1991), 'Les Forteresses du système défensif byzantin en Serbie au XIe–XIIe siècle', *Starinar* 42, pp. 169–85

—(1999), *Tvrđava Ras (The fortress of Ras)*, Belgrade

Popović, M. and Ivanišević, V. (1988), 'Grad Braničevo u srednjem veku', *Starinar* 39, pp. 125–79

Popović, V. (1978), 'Catalogue des monnaies byzantines du musée de Srem' in Brenot *et al.* (1978), pp. 179–93

—(1980), 'Continuité culturelle et tradition littéraire dans l'église médiévale de Sirmium', in *Les Nécropoles romaines et médiévales de Mačvanska Mitrovica (= Sirmium: recherches archéologiques en Syrmie* 12), ed. V. Popović, Belgrade, pp. i–iv

Poppe, A. (1981), 'The building of the church of St Sophia in Kiev', *JMH* 7, pp. 15–66; repr. in Poppe (1982), no. 4

—(1982), *The rise of Christian Russia*, Aldershot

Postan, M. M. (ed.) (1966), *The Cambridge economic history of Europe*, I: *The agrarian life of the middle ages*, 2nd edn. Cambridge

Poupardin, R. (1907), *Les Institutions politiques et administratives des principautés lombardes de l'Italie méridionale (IXᵉ–XIᵉ siècles)*, Paris

Prato, G. (ed.) (2000), *I manoscritti greci tra riflessione e dibattito: atti del V colloquio internazionale di paleografia greca, Cremona, 4–10 ottobre 1998*, 3 vols., Florence

Pratsch, T. (1998), *Theodoros Studites (759–826) – zwischen Dogma und Pragma: der Abt des Studiosklosters in Konstantinopel im Spannungsfeld von Patriarch, Kaiser und eigenem Anspruch*, Frankfurt-am-Main

—(2005b), 'Leon (* um 939; † vor 6. April 945): der Sohn Konstantin VII. Porphyrogennetos', *BZ* 98, pp. 484–95

Prigent, V. (2002), 'Les Evêchés byzantins de la Calabre septentrionale au VIIIᵉ siècle', *MEFRM* 114, pp. 931–53

—(2004), 'Les Empereurs isauriens et la confiscation des patrimoines pontificaux d'Italie du Sud', *MEFRM* 116, pp. 557–94

Prinz, O. (1985), 'Eine frühe abendländische Aktualisierung der lateinischen Übersetzung des Pseudo-Methodios', *DA* 41, pp. 1–23

Prinzing, G. (1993a), 'Das Bamberger Gunthertuch in neuer Sicht', *BSl* 54, pp. 218–31

—(1995), 'Zu Odessos/Varna (im 6. Jh.), Belgrad (1096) und Braničevo (um 1163). Klärung dreier Fragen aus Epigraphik, Prosopographie und Sphragistik', *BSl* 56, pp. 219–25

—(2002), 'Das Papsttum und der orthodox geprägte Südosten Europas 1180–1216', in Hehl *et al.* (eds.) (2002), pp. 137–84

—(2005), 'Zum Austausch diplomatischer Geschenke zwischen Byzanz und seinen Nachbarn in Ostmittel- und Südosteuropa', *MSABK* 4, pp. 139–71

Prinzing, G. *et al.* (eds.) (2001), *Byzantium and east central Europe*, Cracow

Prinzing, G. and Salamon, M. (eds.) (1999), *Byzanz und Ostmitteleuropa, 950–1453: Beiträge zu einer table-ronde des XIX International Congress of Byzantine Studies, Copenhagen 1996*, Wiesbaden

Pryor, J. H. (1988), *Geography, technology and war: studies in the maritime history of the Mediterranean, 649–1571*, Cambridge

—(2002), 'Types of ships and their performance capabilities', in Macrides (ed.) (2002), pp. 33–58

—(2003), 'Byzantium and the sea: Byzantine fleets and the history of the empire in the age of the Macedonian emperors, *c.* 900–1025 CE', in Hattendorf and Unger (eds.) (2003), pp. 83–104

—(2004), 'The *stadiodromikon* of the *De cerimoniis* of Constantine VII, Byzantine warships and the Cretan expedition of 949', in Chrysostomides *et al.* (eds.) (2004), pp. 77–108

—(ed.) (2006), *Logistics of warfare in the age of the crusades*, Aldershot

Pryor, J. H. and Jeffreys, E. (2006), *The age of the Dromon: the Byzantine navy, ca. 500–1204*, Leiden

Queller, D. E. and Madden, T. F. (1997), *The Fourth Crusade: the conquest of Constantinople*, 2nd edn., Philadelphia

Rapp, S. H. (2003), *Studies in medieval Georgian historiography: early texts and Eurasian contexts, CSCO* 601, Louvain

Ravegnani, G. (2004), *I bizantini in Italia*, Bologna

Redgate, A. E. (1998), *The Armenians*, Oxford

Redon, O. and Rosenberger, B. (eds.) (1994), *Les Assises du pouvoir: temps médiévaux, territoires africains. Pour Jean Devisse*, Saint-Denis

Reinach, T. (1924), 'Un contrat de mariage du temps de Basile le Bulgaroctone', in *Mélanges offerts à M. Gustave Schlumberger, membre de l'Institut, à l'occasion du quatre-vingtième anniversaire de sa naissance (17 octobre 1924)*, 2 vols., Paris, 1924, I, pp. 118–32

Reinert, S. W. (1998), 'The Muslim presence in Constantinople 9th–15th centuries: some preliminary observations', in Ahrweiler and Laiou (eds.) (1998), pp. 125–50

Reinsch, D. R. (1986), 'Eustathios Rhomaios' Opusculum über das Hypobolon', *FM* 7, pp. 239–52

—(1989), 'Ausländer und Byzantiner im Werk der Anna Komnene', *Rechthistorisches Journal* 8, pp. 257–74

—(1996a), 'Zur literarischen Leistung der Anna Komnene', in Rosenqvist, (ed.) (1996), pp. 113–25

—(2000a), 'Women's literature in Byzantium? The case of Anna Komnene', in Gouma-Peterson (ed.) (2000), pp. 83–105

—(2000b), 'Literarische Bildung in Konstantinopel im 7. und 8. Jahrhundert. Das Zeugnis der Homiletik', in Prato (ed.) (2000), I, pp. 29–46

—(2005), 'Die Kultur des Schenkens in den Texten der Historiker der Komnenenzeit', *MSABK* 4, pp. 173–83

Reinsch, D. R. and Agapitos, P. A. (eds.) (2000), *Der Roman im Byzanz der Komnenenzeit: Referate des Internationalen Symposiums an der Freien Universität Berlin, 3. bis 6. April 1998*, Frankfurt-am-Main

Rentschler, M. (1981), *Liudprand von Cremona: eine Studie zum ost–westlichen Kulturgefälle im Mittelalter*, Frankfurt-am-Main

Rheidt, K. (2002), 'The urban economy of Pergamon', in *EHB*, II, pp. 623–9

Ricci, A. (1998), 'The road from Baghdad to Byzantium and the case of the Bryas palace in Istanbul', in Brubaker (ed.) (1998), pp. 131–49

Riley-Smith, J. (2002), *What were the crusades?*, 3rd edn., Basingstoke

Ringrose, K. M. (1999), 'Passing the test of sanctity: denial of sexuality and involuntary castration', in James (ed.) (1999), pp. 123–37

Robinson, C. F. (ed.) (2001), *A medieval Islamic city reconsidered: an interdisciplinary approach to Samarra*, Oxford

Rochow, I. (1991), *Byzanz im 8. Jahrhundert in der Sicht des Theophanes: quellenkritisch-historischer Kommentar zu den Jahren 715–813*, Berlin

—(1994), *Kaiser Konstantin V. (741–775): Materialen zu seinem Leben und Nachleben*, Frankfurt-am-Main

—(2001), 'Zu den diplomatischen Beziehungen zwischen Byzanz und dem Kalifat in der Zeit der syrischen Dynastie (717–802)', in Sode and Takács (eds.) (2001), pp. 305–25

Rodley, L. (1985), *Cave monasteries of Byzantine Cappadocia*, Cambridge

—(2003), 'The Byzantine court and Byzantine art', in Cubitt (ed.) (2003), pp. 255–73

Romančuk, A. I. (2005), 'Das byzantinische Cherson (Chersonesos): Meer und Barbaren – einige historische Aspekte', in Hoffmann and Monchizadeh (eds.) (2005), pp. 75–91

Romeo, R. (ed.) (1979–81), *Storia della Sicilia*, 10 vols., Naples

Rosenqvist, J. O. (ed.) (1996), *Leimōn: studies presented to Lennart Rydén on his sixty-fifth birthday*, Uppsala

Rotman, Y. (2004), *Les Esclaves et l'esclavage de la Méditerranée antique à la Méditerranée médiévale, VIᵉ–XIᵉ siècles*, Paris

Rotter, G. (1982), *Die Umayyaden und der zweite Bürgerkrieg (680–692)*, Wiesbaden

Rouan, M.-F. (1981), 'Une lecture "iconoclaste" de la Vie d'Étienne le Jeune', *TM* 8, pp. 415–36

Roueché, C. (2002), 'The literary background of Kekaumenos', in Holmes and Waring (eds.) (2002), pp. 111–38

—(2003), 'The rhetoric of Kekaumenos', in Jeffreys, E. (ed.) (2003), pp. 23–37

—(forthcoming), 'The place of Kekaumenos in the admonitory tradition', in Odorico (ed.) (forthcoming)

Ruggieri, V. and Pieralli, L. (eds.) (2003), *Eukosmia: studi miscellanei per il 75° di Vincenzo Poggi S.J.*, Soveria Mannelli (Catanzaro)

Ruggini, L. C. (1980), 'La Sicilia fra Roma e Bisanzio', in Romeo (ed.) (1979–81), III, pp. 1–96

Runciman, S. (1929), *The emperor Romanus Lecapenus and his reign; a study of tenth-century Byzantium*, Cambridge

—(1930), *A history of the first Bulgarian empire*, London

—(1955), *The eastern schism*, Oxford

Russell, J. (2002), 'Anemurion', in *EHB*, I, pp. 221–8

Rydén, L. (1984), 'The portrait of the Arab Samonas in Byzantine literature', *Graeco-Arabica* 3, pp. 101–8

Samuel, R. and Stedman Jones, G. (eds.) (1982), *Culture, ideology and politics: essays for Eric Hobsbawm*, London

Sanders, G. D. R. (2003), 'Recent developments in the chronology of Byzantine Corinth', in Williams and Bookidis (eds.) (2003), pp. 385–99

Sansterre, J.-M. (1983), *Les Moines grecs et orientaux à Rome aux époques byzantine et carolingienne: milieu du VIᵉ s.–fin du IXᵉ s.*, 2 vols., Brussels

—(1984), 'Où le diptyque consulaire de Clementinus fut-il remployé à une fin liturgique?', *Byz* 54, pp. 641–7

—(1988), 'Le Monachisme byzantin à Rome', *Bisanzio, Roma e l'Italia nell'alto medioevo = SSCIS* 34, pp. 701–46

—(1989), 'Otton III et les saints ascètes de son temps', *Rivista di storia della chiesa in Italia* 43, pp. 377–412

—(1990), 'Le Monastère des Saints Boniface et Alexis sur l'Aventin et l'expansion du christianisme dans le cadre de la "Renovatio Imperii Romanorum" d'Otton III: une révision', *Revue Benedictine*, 100, pp. 493–506

—(1992), 'Monaci e monasteri greci a Ravenna', in Berardi *et al.* (eds.) (1990–6), II.1, pp. 323–9

—(1996), 'Les Informations parvenues en Occident sur l'avènement de l'empereur Léon V et le siège de Constantinople par les Bulgares en 813', *Byz* 66, pp. 373–80

—(2002), 'Entre deux mondes? La vénération des images à Rome et en Italie d'après les textes des VIe–XIe siècles', *Roma fra oriente e occidente = SSCIS* 49, pp. 993–1052

—(2004), 'Les Moines d'Occident et le monachisme d'Orient du VIe au XIe siècle: entre textes anciens et réalités contemporaines', *Cristianità d'occidente e cristianità d'oriente (secoli VI–XI) = SSCIS* 51, pp. 289–332

Saurma-Jeltsch, L. E. (2004), 'Das Gebetbuch Ottos III: dem Herrscher zur Ermahnung und Verheissung bis in alle Ewigkeit', *Frühmittelalterliche Studien* 38, pp. 55–88

Savvides, A. G. K. (1990), 'O Byzantino-Armenikos oikos Kourkoua (90s–120s ai. m. Ch.)', *Deltion eraldikes kai genealogikes etairias ellados* 8, pp. 5–31

—(2004a), *Georgios Maniakes: kataktesis kai yponomeuse sto Byzantio tou endekatou aiona (1030–1043 m. Ch.)*, Athens

Savvides, A. G. K. and Hendrickx, B. (eds.) (2006–), *Encyclopaedic prosopographical lexicon of Byzantine history and civilization*, 1 vol. to date, Turnhout

Saxer, V. (2001), 'La chiesa di Roma dal V al X secolo: amministrazione centrale ed organizzazione territoriale', in *Roma nell'alto medioevo = SSCIS* 48, pp. 493–637

Schenk, K. (1880), *Kaiser Leon III.: ein Beitrag zur Geschichte des Bilderstreits. Erster Theil*, Halle

Schieffer, T. (1935), *Die päpstlichen Legaten in Frankreich vom Vertrage von Meersen (870) bis zum Schisma von 1130*, Berlin

Schminck, A. (1986), *Studien zu mittelbyzantinischen Rechtsbüchern*, Frankfurt-am-Main

—(2000), 'The beginnings and origins of the "Macedonian" dynasty', in Burke and Scott (eds.) (2000), pp. 61–8

Schneider, A. M. and Karnapp, W. (1938), *Die Stadtmauer von Iznik (Nicaea)*, Berlin

Schneidmüller, B. and Weinfurter, S. (eds.) (2000), *Otto III. – Heinrich II. Eine Wende?*, 2nd edn., Stuttgart

Scholz, C. (2005), 'Probleme bei der Erforschung der Integration Bulgariens in das byzantinische Reich, 1018–1186', in Hoffmann and Monchizadeh (eds.) (2005), pp. 337–47

Scholz, C. and Makris, G. (eds.) (2000), *Polypleuros nous: Miscellanea für Peter Schreiner zu seinem 60. Geburtstag*, Munich

Schramm, G. (1981), *Eroberer und Eingesessene: geographische Lehnnamen als Zeugen der Geschichte Südosteuropas im ersten Jahrtausend n. Chr.*, Stuttgart

Schramm, P. E. (1957), *Kaiser, Rom und Renovatio: Studien zur Geschichte des römischen Erneuerungsgedankens vom Ende des karolingischen Reiches bis zum Investiturstreit*, 2nd edn., Darmstadt

—(1968–71), *Kaiser, Könige und Päpste: gesammelte Aufsätze zur Geschichte des Mittelalters*, 4 vols. in 5 pts., Stuttgart

Schramm, P. E. and Mütherich, F. (1962), *Denkmale der deutschen Könige und Kaiser: ein Beitrag zur Herrschergeschichte von Karl dem Grossen bis Friedrich II. 768–1250*, Munich

Schreiner, P. (1984), 'Das Herrscherbild in der byzantinischen Literatur des 9. bis 11. Jahrhunderts', *Saeculum* 35, pp. 132–51

—(1987), 'Das Christentum in Bulgarien vor 864', in Gjuzelev and Pillinger (eds.) (1987), pp. 51–61

—(1988), 'Der byzantinische Bilderstreit: kritische Analyse der zeitgenössischen Meinungen und das Urteil der Nachwelt bis heute', *Bisanzio, Roma e l'Italia nell'alto medioevo* = SSCIS 34, pp. 319–407

—(1991), 'Réflexions sur la famille impériale à Byzance (VIIIᵉ–Xᵉ siècles)', *Byz* 61, pp. 181–93

—(1997), 'Soldiers', in Cavallo (ed.) (1997), pp. 74–94

—(2003), 'Zur griechischen Schrift im hochmittelalterlichen Westen: Der Kreis um Liudprand von Cremona', *RHM* 45, pp. 305–17

—(2004), 'Diplomatische Geschenke zwischen Byzanz und dem Westen ca. 800–1200: Eine Analyse der Texte mit Quellenanhang', *DOP* 58, pp. 251–82

—(2006), 'Zu Gast in den Kaiserpalästen Konstantinopels: Architektur und Topographie in der Sicht fremdländischer Betrachter', in Bauer (ed.) (2006), pp. 101–34

Schwarz, U. (1978), *Amalfi im frühen Mittelalter (9.–11. Jahrhundert): Untersuchungen zur Amalfitaner Überlieferung*, Tübingen

Segal, J. B. (1970), *Edessa: 'the blessed city'*, Oxford

Seibert, H. (2000), 'Herrscher und Mönchtum im spätottonischen Reich. Vorstellung – Funktion – Interaktion', in Schneidmüller and Weinfurter (eds.) (2000), pp. 205–66

Seibt, W. (1976), *Die Skleroi: eine prosopographisch-sigillographische Studie*, BV 9, Vienna

—(1978), 'Die Eingliederung von Vaspurakan in das byzantinische Reich (etwa Anfang 1019 bzw. Anfang 1022)', *HAm* 92, pp. 49–66

—(1993), '*Armenika themata* als terminus technicus der byzantinischen Verwaltungsgeschichte des 11. Jahrhunderts', *BSl* 54, pp. 134–41

—(1999), 'Siegel als Quelle für Slawenarchonten in Griechenland', *SBS* 6, pp. 27–36

—(2003a), 'Weitere Beobachtungen zu Siegeln früher Slawenarchonten in Griechenland', in Avramea *et al.* (eds.) (2003), pp. 459–66

—(2003b), 'Seals and the prosopography of the Byzantine empire', in Cameron, Averil (ed.) (2003), pp. 95–102

Ševčenko, I. (1979–80), 'Constantinople viewed from the eastern provinces in the middle Byzantine period', *HUS* 3–4, pp. 712–47; repr. in Ševčenko, I. (1982a), no. 6

—(1992b), 'The search for the past in Byzantium around the year 800', *DOP* 46, pp. 279–93

Ševčenko, I. and Hutter, I. (eds.) (1998), *Aetos: studies in honour of Cyril Mango*, Stuttgart and Leipzig

Ševčenko, N. P. (1991), 'Icons in the liturgy', *DOP* 45, pp. 45–57

—(1995), '"Servants of the Holy Icon"', in Moss and Kiefer (eds.) (1995), pp. 547–56

Shahid, I. (2002), 'The thematization of Oriens: final observations', *Byz* 72, pp. 192–249

Sharf, A. (1971), *Byzantine Jewry: from Justinian to the Fourth Crusade*, London

Shepard, J. (1973), 'The English and Byzantium: a study of their role in the Byzantine army in the later eleventh century', *Traditio* 29, pp. 53–92

—(1975), 'John Mauropous, Leo Tornicius and an alleged Russian army: the chronology of the Pecheneg crisis of 1048–1049', *JÖB* 24, pp. 61–89

—(1975–6), 'Scylitzes on Armenia in the 1040s and the role of Catacalon Cecaumenus', *REA* n.s. 11, pp. 269–311

—(1978–9), 'Why did the Russians attack Byzantium in 1043?', *BNJ* 22, pp. 147–212

—(1988a), 'When Greek meets Greek: Alexius Comnenus and Bohemond in 1097–1098', *BMGS* 12, pp. 185–277

—(1988b), 'Aspects of Byzantine attitudes and policy towards the west in the tenth and eleventh centuries', in Howard-Johnston (ed.) (1988), pp. 67–118

—(1991), 'Symeon of Bulgaria – Peacemaker', *Annuaire de l'Université de Sofia "St. Kliment Ohridski", Centre de Recherches Slavo-Byzantines "Ivan Dujčev"* 83, pp. 9–48

—(1992), 'A suspected source of Scylitzes' *Synopsis Historion*: the great Catacalon Cecaumenus', *BMGS* 16, pp. 171–81

—(1995a), 'Slavs and Bulgars', in *NCMH*, II, pp. 228–48

—(1995b), 'A marriage too far? Maria Lekapena and Peter of Bulgaria', in Davids (ed.) (1995), pp. 121–49

—(1995c), 'Imperial information and ignorance: a discrepancy', *BSl* 56, pp. 107–16

—(1997), 'Byzantine soldiers, missionaries and diplomacy under Gibbon's eyes', in McKitterick and Quinault (eds.) (1997), pp. 78–100

—(1998), 'The Khazars' formal adoption of Judaism and Byzantium's northern policy', *Oxford Slavonic Papers* 31, pp. 11–34

—(1999), 'Bulgaria: the other Balkan "empire"', in *NCMH*, III, pp. 567–85

—(2001), 'Constantine VII, Caucasian openings and the road to Aleppo', in Eastmond (ed.) (2001), pp. 19–40

—(2002a), 'Spreading the word: Byzantine missions', in Mango (ed.) (2002), pp. 230–47

—(2002b), 'Emperors and expansionism: from Rome to middle Byzantium' in Abulafia and Berend (eds.) (2002), pp. 55–82

—(2005), '"How St James the Persian's head was brought to Cormery": a relic collector around the time of the First Crusade' in Hoffmann and Monchizadeh (eds.) (2005), pp. 287–335

—(2006a), 'Byzantium's overlapping circles', *ACIEB* 21, I, pp. 15–55

—(2006b), 'The origins of Rus' (*c.* 900–1015)', in Perrie (ed.) (2006), pp. 47–72

—(2007), 'Invisible Byzantiums', in Grünbart *et al.* (eds.) (2007), pp. 225–34

—(ed.) (2007), *The expansion of orthodox Europe: Byzantium, the Balkans and Russia*, Aldershot

Shivarov, N. *et al.* (eds.) (1989), *Mezhdunaroden simpozium 1100 godini ot blazhenata konchina na sv. Metodii*, 2 vols., Sofia

Sidéris, G. (2002), '"Eunuchs of light": power, imperial ceremonial and positive representations of eunuchs in Byzantium (4th–12th centuries AD)', in Tougher (ed.) (2002), pp. 161–75

Silvas, A. (2006), 'Kassia the nun *c.* 810–*c.* 865: an appreciation', in Garland (ed.) (2006), pp. 17–39

Simeonova, L. (1993), 'Power in Nicholas Mysticus' letters to Symeon of Bulgaria: notes on the political vocabulary of a tenth-century Byzantine statesman', *BSl* 54, pp. 89–94

—(1998a), *Diplomacy of the letter and the cross: Photios, Bulgaria and the papacy, 860s–880s*, Amsterdam

—(1998b), 'In the depths of tenth-century Byzantine ceremonial: the treatment of Arab prisoners of war at imperial banquets', *BMGS* 22, pp. 75–104; repr. in Haldon (ed.) (2007), pp. 549–79

—(2000), 'Foreigners in tenth-century Byzantium: a contribution to the history of cultural encounter', in Smythe (ed.) (2000), pp. 229–44

Simon, D. (1973), *Rechtsfindung am byzantinischen Reichsgericht*, Frankfurt-am-Main

—(1986), 'Das Ehegüterrecht der Peira: Ein systematischer Versuch', *FM* 7, pp. 193–238

—(1994), 'Legislation as both a world order and a legal order', in Laiou and Simon (eds.) (1994), pp. 1–25

Simpson, A. J. (2006), 'Before and after 1204: the versions of Niketas Choniates' *Historia*', *DOP* 60, pp. 189–221

Şimşek, C. (1995), 'İkinci sezon Hierapolis Roma hamami (Müze Binasi) Kazi Çalişmalari', *Müze Kurtarma Kazilari Semineri* 5, pp. 243–63

Sironis, N. (1998), 'Historicity and poetry in ninth-century homiletics: the homilies of Patriarch Photios and George of Nicomedia', in Cunningham and Allen (eds.) (1998), pp. 295–316

Šišić, F. (1917), *Geschichte der Kroaten,* I, Zagreb

Skinner, P. (1992), 'Noble families in the duchy of Gaeta in the tenth century', *PBSR* 60, pp. 353–77

—(1995), *Family power in southern Italy: the duchy of Gaeta and its neighbours, 850–1139*, Cambridge

Skoulatos, B. (1980), *Les Personnages byzantins de l'Alexiade: analyse proso-pographique et synthèse*, Louvain

Smith, J. M. H. (ed.) (2000), *Early medieval Rome and the Christian west: essays in honour of Donald A. Bullough*, Leiden

Smith, M. H. (1978), *'And taking bread . . .': Cerularius and the azyme controversy of 1054*, Paris

Smythe, D. (1999), 'In denial: same-sex desire in Byzantium', in James (ed.) (1999), pp. 139–48

—(2005), 'Gender', in Harris (ed.) (2005), pp. 157–65

—(ed.) (2000), *Strangers to themselves: the Byzantine outsider: papers from the thirty-second spring symposium of Byzantine studies, University of Sussex, Brighton, March 1998*, Aldershot

Sode, C. (2005), 'Der Brief der Kaiser Michael II. und Theophilos an Kaiser Ludwig den Frommen', in Hoffmann and Monchizadeh (eds.) (2005), pp. 141–58

Sode, C. and Takács, S. (eds.) (2001), *Novum millennium: studies on Byzantine history and culture dedicated to Paul Speck*, Aldershot

Sodini, J.-P. and Villeneuve, E. (1991), 'Le Passage de la céramique byzantine à la céramique omeyyade en Syrie du nord, en Palestine et en Transjordanie', in Canivet and Rey-Coquais (eds.) (1992), pp. 195–218

Solier, Y. *et al.* (1981), 'Les Épaves de Gruissan', *Archaeonautica* 3, pp. 7–264

Sophocleus, S. (1994), *Icons of Cyprus: 7th–20th century*, Nicosia

—(2000), 'Le Peintre Theodoros Apsevdis et son entourage, Chypre 1183 et 1192', in Koch (ed.) (2000), pp. 307–20

Sot, M. *et al.* (eds.) (1990), *Haut moyen-âge: culture, éducation et société. Études offertes à Pierre Riché*, La Garenne-Colombes

Soustal, P. (1991), *Thrakien: Thrake, Rodope und Haimimontos, TIB 6*, Vienna

Spatharakis, I. (1976), *The portrait in Byzantine illuminated manuscripts*, Leiden

—(1981), *Corpus of dated illuminated Greek manuscripts: to the year 1453*, 2 vols., Leiden

Speck, P. (1974), *Die Kaiserliche Universität von Konstantinopel: Präzisierungen zur Frage des höheren Schulwesens in Byzanz im 9. und 10. Jahrhundert*, Munich

—(1978), *Kaiser Konstantin VI.: die Legitimation einer Fremden und der Versuch einer eigenen Herrschaft*, 2 vols., Munich

—(1981), *Artabasdos, der rechtgläubige Vorkämpfer der göttlichen Lehren: Untersuchungen zur Revolte des Artabasdos und ihrer Darstellung in der byzantinischen Historiographie*, Bonn

—(1990), *Ich bin's nicht, Kaiser Konstantin ist es gewesen: die Legenden vom Einfluss des Teufels, des Juden und des Moslem auf den Ikonoklasmus*, Bonn

—(1998), 'Byzantium: cultural suicide?', in Brubaker (ed.) (1998), pp. 73–84

—(2000), 'Die griechischen Quellen zur Bekehrung der Bulgaren und die zwei ersten Briefe des Photios', in Scholz and Makris (eds.) (2000), pp. 342–59

—(2003a), *Understanding Byzantium: studies in Byzantine historical sources*, ed. S. Takács, Aldershot

—(2003b), 'Ein weiterer interpolierter Text in den Akten des Konzils von 787. Der Brief des Patriarchen Germanos an Thomas von Klaudiupolis', in Avramea *et al.* (eds.) (2003), pp. 481–90

Spieser, J.-M. (1991), 'La Céramique byzantine médievale', in Kravari *et al.* (eds.) (1989–91), II, pp. 249–60

Spinei, V. (2003), *The great migrations in the east and south east of Europe from the ninth to the thirteenth century*, tr. D. Badulescu, Cluj-Napoca

Stănescu, E. (1966), 'Les Réformes d'Isaac Comnène', *RESEE* 4, pp. 35–69

Starr, J. (1939), *The Jews in the Byzantine empire, 631–1204*, Athens; repr. Farnborough, 1969

Stefan, G. *et al.* (1967), *Dinogetia*, Bucharest

Steindorff, L. (1984), *Die dalmatinischen Städte im 12. Jahrhundert: Studien zu ihrer politischen Stellung und gesellschaftlichen Entwicklung*, Cologne

Stein-Wilkeshuis, M. (1991), 'A Viking-age treaty between Constantinople and northern merchants, with its provisions on theft and robbery', *Scando-Slavica* 37, pp. 35–47

Stepanov, T. (2001), 'The Bulgar title KANASUBIGI: reconstructing the notions of divine kingship in Bulgaria, AD 822–836', *Early Medieval Europe* 10, pp. 1–19

—(2005), 'Ruler and political ideology in *pax nomadica*: early medieval Bulgaria and the Uighur Qaganate', in Curta (ed.) (2005), pp. 152–61

Stephenson, P. (1994), 'Manuel I Comnenus and Geza II: a revised context and chronology for Hungaro-Byzantine relations, 1148–1155', *BSl* 55, pp. 251–78

—(1996), 'John Cinnamus, John II Comnenus and the Hungarian campaign of 1127–1129', *Byz* 66, pp. 177–87

—(1999a), 'Byzantine policy towards Paristrion in the mid-eleventh century: another interpretation', *BMGS* 23, pp. 43–66

—(1999b), 'Political authority in Dalmatia during the reign of Manuel I Comnenus (1143–1180)', in Prinzing and Salamon (eds.) (1999), pp. 127–50

—(2003a), *The legend of Basil the Bulgar-Slayer*, Cambridge

—(2003b), 'The Balkan frontier in the year 1000', in Magdalino (ed.) (2003), pp. 109–33

—(2003c), 'Anna Comnena's *Alexiad* as a source for the Second Crusade?', *JMH* 29, pp. 41–54

—(2005), 'The tomb of Basil II', in Hoffmann and Monchizadeh (eds.) (2005), pp. 227–38

—(2006), '"About the emperor Nikephoros and how he leaves his bones in Bulgaria": a context for the controversial *Chronicle of 811*', *DOP* 60, pp. 87–109

— (2007), 'Imperial Christianity and sacred warfare in Byzantium', in Wellman (ed.) (2007) pp. 81–93

— (ed.) (in preparation), *The Byzantine world*, London

Stiegemann, C. and Wemhoff, M. (eds.) (1999), *799: Kunst und Kultur der Karolingerzeit. Karl der Grosse und Papst Leo III. in Paderborn. Katalog der Ausstellung*, 2 vols., Mainz

Stiernon, D. (1967), *Constantinople IV, Histoire des conciles oecuméniques* 5, Paris

Stoclet, A. J. (1990), 'Les Établissements francs à Rome au VIIIᵉ siècle: "hospitale intus basilicam beati Petri, domus Nazarii, scola Francorum", et palais de Charlemagne', in Sot *et al.* (eds.) (1990), pp. 231–47

Stolte, B. (1998), 'Not new but novel: notes on the historiography of Byzantine law', *BMGS* 22, pp. 264–79

Stommel, H. and Stommel, E. (1983), *Volcano weather: the story of 1816, the year without a summer*, Newport, RI

Stone, A. F. (2001), 'Eustathian panegyric as a historical source', *JÖB* 51, pp. 225–58

—(2003a), 'Dorylaion revisited: Manuel I Komnenos and the refortification of Dorylaion and Soublaion in 1175', *REB* 61, pp. 183–99

—(2003b), 'The oration of Eustathios of Thessaloniki for Agnes of France: a snapshot of political tension between Byzantium and the west', *Byz* 73, pp. 112–26

—(2004), 'Stemming the Turkish tide: Eustathios of Thessaloniki on the Seljuk Turks', *BSl* 62, pp. 125–42

—(2005), 'Eustathios and the wedding banquet for Alexios Porphyrogennetos', in Mayer and Trzcionka (eds.) (2005), pp. 33–42

Striker, C. L. (1981), *The Myrelaion (Bodrum Camii) in Istanbul*, Princeton

Striker, C. L. and Kuban, Y. D. (eds.) (1997), *Kalenderhane in Istanbul: the buildings, their history, architecture and decoration. Final reports on the archaeological exploration and restoration at Kalenderhane Camii 1966–1978*, Mainz

Strunk, O. (1964), 'The Latin antiphons for the octave of the epiphany', in Barišić (ed.) (1963–4), II, pp. 417–26; repr. in Strunk (1977), pp. 208–19

—(1977), *Essays on music in the Byzantine world*, New York

Sullivan, D. F. (2003), 'Byzantium besieged: prescription and practice', in Avramea *et al.* (eds.) (2003), pp. 509–21

Sutherland, J. (1975), 'The mission to Constantinople in 968 and Liudprand of Cremona', *Traditio* 31, pp. 55–83

Svoronos, N. (1951), 'Le Serment de fidélité à l'empereur byzantin et sa signification constitutionnelle', *REB* 9, pp. 106–42; repr. in Svoronos (1973), no. 6

—(1959), 'Recherches sur le cadastre byzantin et la fiscalité aux XIᵉ et XIIᵉ siècles: le cadastre de Thèbes', *BCH* 83, pp. 1–166; repr. in Svoronos (1973), no. 3

—(1967), 'Société et organisation intérieure dans l'empire byzantin au XIᵉ siècle: les principaux problèmes', *ACIEB* 13, pp. 373–89; repr. in Svoronos (1973), no. 9

—(1973), *Études sur l'organisation intérieure, la société et l'économie de l'empire byzantin*, London

Swiencickyj, I. (1940), 'Byzantinische Bleisiegel in den Sammlungen von Lwow' in Georgiev *et al.* (eds.) (1940), pp. 434–41

Tachiaos, A.-E. N. (2001), *Cyril and Methodius of Thessalonica: the acculturation of the Slavs*, Crestwood, NY

Taft, R. F. (1984), *Beyond east and west: problems in liturgical understanding*, Washington, DC; 2nd edn., Rome, 1997

—(1992), *The Byzantine rite: a short history*, Collegeville, MN

Taha, A. D. (1989), *The Muslim conquest and settlement of North Africa and Spain*, London

Talbot, A.-M. (1997), 'Women', in Cavallo (ed.) (1997), pp. 117–43; repr. in Talbot (2001), no. 1

Tăpkova-Zaimova, V. (1979), *Byzance et les Balkans à partir du VIᵉ siècle: les mouvements ethniques et les états*, London

—(1986), 'Les Problèmes du pouvoir dans les relations bulgaro-byzantines (jusqu'au XIIᵉ s.)', *BB* 8, pp. 124–30

—(1993), 'L'Administration byzantine au Bas Danube (fin du Xᵉ–XIᵉ s.)', *BSl* 54, pp. 95–101

Taviani, see Taviani-Carozzi

Taviani-Carozzi, H. (1980), 'Pouvoir et solidarités dans le principauté de Salerne à la fin du Xᵉ siècle', *Structures féodales et féodalisme dans l'Occident méditerranéen (Xᵉ–XIIIᵉ siècles): colloque international organisé par le Centre National de la*

Recherche Scientifique et l'École Française de Rome, Rome, 10–13 octobre 1978,
CEFR 44, Rome, pp. 587–606

—(1991a), 'Caractères originaux des institutions politiques et administratives dans
les principautés lombardes d'Italie méridionale au Xe siècle', *Il secolo di ferro:*
mito e realtà del secolo X = *SSCIS* 38, pp. 273–326

—(1991b), *La Principauté lombarde de Salerne (IXe–XIe siècle): pouvoir et sociéte en*
Italie lombarde méridionale, Rome

Tellenbach, G. (1934), *Römischer und christlicher Reichsgedanke in der Liturgie des*
frühen Mittelalters, Heidelberg (1934) (= *Sitzungsberichte der Heidelberger*
Akademie der Wissenschaften, Philosophisch-historische Klasse, Jahrgang 1934/5,
1. Abhandlung)

—(1982), 'Kaiser, Rom und Renovatio: ein Beitrag zu einem grossen Thema', in
Kamp and Wollasch (eds.) (1982), pp. 231–53

Ter-Ghewondyan, A. (1976), *The Arab emirates in Bagratid Armenia*, tr. N.
Garsoïan, Lisbon

Thierry, N. (1977), *Peintures d'Asie Mineure et de Transcaucasie aux Xe et XIe s.*,
London

—(1983–94), *Haut moyen-âge en Cappadoce: les églises de la région de Çavusin*, 2
vols., Paris

—(1985), 'Un portrait de Jean Tzimiskès en Cappadoce', *TM* 9, pp. 477–84

—(2002), *La Cappadoce de l'antiquité au moyen âge*, Turnout

Thomas, R. D. (1991), 'Anna Comnena's account of the First Crusade: history and
politics in the reigns of the emperors Alexius I and Manuel I Comnenus',
BMGS 15, pp. 269–312

Thomson, F. J. (1982), 'Chrysostomica Palaeoslavica. A preliminary study of the
sources of the Chrysorrhoas (Zlatostruy) collection', *Cyrillomethodianum* 6,
pp. 1–65

—(1989), 'Continuity in the development of Bulgarian culture during the period
of Byzantine hegemony and the Slavonic translations of works by three Cappadocian fathers', in Shivarov *et al.* (eds.) (1989), II, pp. 140–53

—(1993), 'The Symeonic florilegium – problems of its origin, content, textol-
ogy and edition, together with an English translation of the eulogy of Tsar
Symeon', *Palaeobulgarica* 17, pp. 37–53

—(1999), *The reception of Byzantine culture in mediaeval Russia*, Aldershot

Thümmel, H. G. (1991), *Bilderlehre und Bilderstreit: Arbeiten zur Auseinanderset-*
zung über die Ikone und ihre Begründung vornehmlich im 8. und 9. Jahrhundert,
Würzburg

Tinnefeld, F. (1971), *Kategorien der Kaiserkritik in der byzantinischen Historiographie,*
von Prokop bis Niketas Choniates, Munich

—(1973), '"Freundschaft" in den Briefen des Michael Psellos: Theorie und Wirklichkeit', *JÖB* 22, pp. 151–68

—(1989), 'Michael I. Kerullarios, Patriarch von Konstantinopel (1043–1058): kritische Überlegungen zu einer Biographie', *JÖB* 39, pp. 95–127

—(1991), 'Die Braut aus Byzanz – Fragen zu Theophanos Umfeld und
gesellschaftlicher Stellung vor ihrer abendländischen Heirat', in Wolf (ed.)
(1991), pp. 247–61

—(1995), 'Byzanz und die Herrscher des Hauses Hohenstaufen (1138–1259)', *Archiv für Diplomatik* 41, pp. 105–27

—(2003), 'Intellectuals in late Byzantine Thessalonike', *DOP* 57, pp. 153–72

—(2005a), '*Mira varietas*: Exquisite Geschenke byzantinischer Gesandtschaften in ihrem politischen Kontext (8.–12. Jh.)', *MSABK* 41, pp. 121–37

—(2005b), 'Zum Stand der Olga-Diskussion', in Hoffmann and Monchizadeh (eds.) (2005), pp. 531–67

Todt, K.-P. (2000), 'Die Frau als Selbstherrscher: Kaiserin Theodora, die letzte Angehörige der Makedonischen Dynastie', *JÖB* 50, pp. 139–71

—(2001), 'Region und griechisch-orthodoxes Patriarchat von Antiocheia in mittelbyzantinischer Zeit (969–1084)', *BZ* 94, pp. 239–67

— (2002), 'Die letzte Papstreise nach Byzanz: Der Besuch Papst Konstantins I. in Konstantinopel im Jahre 711: zugleich ein Beitrag zur Geschichte der Papstreisen', *Zeitschrift für Kirchengeschichte* 113, pp. 24–50

Totev, T. (1987), 'Les Monastères de Pliska et de Preslav aux IXᵉ–Xᵉ siècles (aperçu archéologique)', *BSl* 48, pp. 185–200

Toubert, P. (1973), *Les Structures du Latium médiéval: le Latium méridional et la Sabine du IXᵉ siècle à la fin du XIIᵉ siècle*, 2 vols., Rome

—(1976), 'Pour une histoire de l'environnement économique et social du Mont Cassin (IXᵉ–XIIᵉ siècles)', *CRAI*, pp. 689–702

Tougher, S. (1997a), 'Byzantine eunuchs: an overview, with special reference to their creation and origin', in James (ed.) (1997), pp. 168–84

—(1997b), *The reign of Leo VI (886–912): politics and people*, Leiden

—(1999), 'Michael III and Basil the Macedonian: just good friends?', in James (ed.) (1999), pp. 149–58

—(2002), 'In or out? Origins of court eunuchs', in Tougher (ed.) (2002), pp. 143–59

—(2006), '"The Angelic Life": monasteries for eunuchs', in Jeffreys, E. (ed.) (2006), pp. 238–52

—(ed.) (2002), *Eunuchs in antiquity and beyond*, London

Toynbee, A. J. (1973), *Constantine Porphyrogenitus and his world*, Oxford

Treadgold, W. (1979), 'The chronological accuracy of the "Chronicle" of Symeon the Logothete for the years 813–845', *DOP* 33, pp. 157–97

—(1983a), 'The military lands and the imperial estates in the middle Byzantine empire', *HUS* 7, pp. 619–31

—(1983b), 'Remarks on the work of Al-Jarmi on Byzantium', *BSl* 44, pp. 205–12

—(1984), 'The Bulgars' treaty with the Byzantines in 816', *Rivista di studi bizantini e slavi* 4, pp. 213–20

—(1992) 'The army in the works of Constantine Porphyrogenitus', *RSBN* n.s. 29, pp. 77–162

—(1995), *Byzantium and its army, 284–1081*, Stanford

—(2002), 'The struggle for survival (641–780)', in Mango (ed.) (2002), pp. 129–52

—(2003), review of P. Stephenson's *Byzantium's Balkan Frontier*, *Sp* 78, pp. 1001–3

—(2004a), 'The historicity of imperial bride-shows', *JÖB* 54, pp. 39–52

—(2004b), 'The prophecies of the patriarch Methodius', *REB* 62, pp. 229–37

—(2006), 'Byzantium, the reluctant warrior', in Christie and Yazigi (eds.) (2006), pp. 209–33

Trilling, J. (1997), 'Daedalus and the nightingale: art and technology in the myth of the Byzantine court', in Maguire (ed.) (1997), pp. 217–30

Tritle, L. (1977), 'Tatzates' flight and the Byzantine-Arab peace treaty of 782' *Byz* 47, pp. 279–300

Troianos, S. (ed.) (1997), *Analecta Athenensia ad ius byzantinum spectantia*, I, Athens

Tsamakda, V. (2002), *The illustrated Chronicle of Ioannes Skylitzes in Madrid*, Leiden

Tsougarakis, D. (1988), *Byzantine Crete: from the fifth century to the Venetian conquest*, Athens

Turan, O. (1953), 'Les Souverains seldjoukides et leurs sujets non-musulmans', *Studia Islamica* 1, pp. 65–100

Turlej, S. (2001), *The Chronicle of Monemvasia: the migration of the Slavs and church conflicts in the Byzantine source from the beginning of the ninth century*, tr. M. Dąbrowska, Cracow

Tyerman, C. (2004), *Fighting for Christendom: holy war and the crusades*, Oxford

Vaissière, E. de la (2004), *Histoire des marchands sogdiens*, 2nd edn., Paris

Vanhaverbeke, H. and Waelkens, M. (2003), *The Chora of Sagalassos: the evolution of the settlement pattern from prehistoric until recent times*, Turnhout

Vásáry, I. (2005), *Cumans and Tatars: oriental military in the pre-Ottoman Balkans, 1185–1365*, Cambridge

Vasiliev, A. A. (1929–30), 'Manuel Comnenus and Henry Plantagenet', *BZ* 29, pp. 233–44

—(1946), *The Russian attack on Constantinople in 860*, Cambridge, MA

—(1952), *History of the Byzantine empire, 324–1453*, 2nd edn., 2 vols., Madison, WI

Vasilievsky, V. G. (1908–30), *Trudy*, 4 vols., St Petersburg

Vassilaki, M. (2005), 'Praying for the salvation of the empire?', in Vassilaki (ed.) (2005), pp. 263–74

—(ed.) (2000), *Mother of God: representations of the Virgin in Byzantine art*, Milan

—(ed.) (2005), *Images of the Mother of God: perceptions of the Theotokos in Byzantium*, Aldershot

Vauchez, A. *et al.* (eds.) (1993), *Apogée de la papauté et expansion de la chrétienté (1054–1274)*, HC 5, Paris

Vavřínek, V. (1978), 'The introduction of the Slavonic liturgy and the Byzantine missionary policy', in Vavřínek (ed.) (1978), pp. 255–81

—(ed.) (1978), *Beiträge zur byzantinischen Geschichte im 9.–11. Jahrhundert: Akten des Colloquiums Byzanz auf dem Höhepunkt seiner Macht, Liblice, 20.–23. September 1977*, Prague

—(ed.) (1993), *Byzantium and its neighbours from the mid-9th till the 12th centuries: papers read at the Byzantinological symposium, Bechyne, 1990*, Prague [= *BSl* 54]

Vavřínek, V. and Zástěrová, B. (1982), 'Byzantium's role in the formation of Great Moravian culture', *BSl* 43, pp. 161–88

Vehse, O. (1927), 'Das Bündnis gegen die Sarazenen vom Jahre 915', *QFIAB* 19, pp. 181–204

Ven, P. van den (1955–7), 'La Patristique et l'hagiographie au concile de Nicée de 787', *Byz* 25–7, pp. 325–62

Venedikov, I. (1962), 'La Population byzantine en Bulgarie au début du IXe siècle', *BB* 1, pp. 261–77

Vinson, M. (2004), 'Romance and reality in the Byzantine bride shows', in Brubaker and Smith (eds.) (2004), pp. 102–20

Vlasto, A. P. (1970), *The entry of the Slavs into Christendom*, Cambridge

Vlysidou, V. N. (1991), *Exoterike politike kai esoterikes antidraseis ten epoche tou Basileiou 1*, Athens

—(ed.) (2003), *E autokratoria se krise? To Byzantio ton 11 aiona, 1025–1081 (The empire in crisis? Byzantium in the eleventh century, 1025–1081)*, Athens

Vlysidou, V. N. *et al.* (eds.) (1998), *E Mikra Asia ton thematon (Asia Minor and its themes)*, Athens

Vogt, A. (1908), *Basile Ier, empereur de Byzance (867–886) et la civilisation byzantine à la fin du IXe siècle*, Paris; repr. Hildesheim, 1973

Volk, R. (1996), 'Symeon Metaphrastes: ein Benutzer des *Barlaam-Romans*', *RSBN* 33, pp. 67–180

Vroom, J. (2003), *After antiquity: ceramics and society in the Aegean from the 7th to the 20th century AC: a case study from Boeotia, central Greece*, Leiden

—(2005a), *Byzantine to modern pottery in the Aegean, 7th to 20th century: an introduction and field guide*, Utrecht

—(2005b), 'Middle Byzantine ceramic finds from Limyra in Lycia', *TM* 15, pp. 617–24

Vryonis, S. (1963), 'Byzantine *demokratia* and the guilds in the eleventh century', *DOP* 17, pp. 287–314; repr. in Vryonis (1971b), no. 3

—(1971a), *The decline of medieval Hellenism in Asia Minor and the process of Islamization from the eleventh through the fifteenth century*, Berkeley

—(1971b), *Byzantium: its internal history and relations with the Muslim world*, London

—(2001), '*The decline of medieval Hellenism in Asia Minor and the process of Islamization from the eleventh through the fifteenth century*: the book in the light of subsequent scholarship, 1971–1998', in Eastmond (ed.) (2001), pp. 1–15

Wahlgren, S. (2001), 'Symeon the Logothete: some philological remarks', *Byz* 71, pp. 251–62

Walker, P. E. (1977), 'The "crusade" of John Tzimisces in the light of new Arabic evidence', *Byz* 47, pp. 301–27

Walmsley, A. (2000), 'Production, exchange and regional trade in the Islamic east Mediterranean: old structures, new systems?', in Hansen and Wickham (eds.) (2000), pp. 265–343

—(2005), 'The village ascendant in Byzantine and early Islamic Jordan: socio-economic forces and cultural responses', in Lefort *et al.* (eds.) (2005), pp. 511–22

Walter, C. (1982), *Art and ritual of the Byzantine church*, Aldershot

Waring, J. (2002), 'Literacies of lists: reading Byzantine monastic inventories', in Holmes and Waring (eds.) (2002), pp. 165–86

Wasilewski, T. (1964), 'Le Thème byzantin de Sirmium-Serbie au XIe et XIIe siècle', *ZRVI* 8, pp. 465–82

Weiss, G. (1973), *Oströmische Beamte im Spiegel der Schriften des Michael Psellos*, Munich

—(1977), 'Die juristische Bibliothek des Michael Psellos', *JÖB* 26, pp. 79–102

Weitzmann, K. (1971a), 'The Mandylion and Constantine Porphyrogennetos', in Weitzmann (1971b), pp. 224–46

—(1971b), *Studies in classical and Byzantine manuscript illumination*, Chicago

—(1972), *Ivories and steatites*, Washington, DC

Wellhausen, J. (2004), 'Arab wars with the Byzantines in the Umayyad period', tr. M. Bonner, in Bonner (ed.) (2004), no. 2, pp. 31–64; tr. of Wellhausen, J. (1901), 'Die Kämpfe der Araber mit den Römäern in der Zeit der Umaijiden', *Nachrichten von der Königlichen Gesellschaft der Wissenschaften zu Göttingen, philologisch-historische Klasse*, Heft 4, pp. 414–47

Wellman, J. K. (ed.) (2007), *Belief and bloodshed: religion and violence across time and tradition*, Lanham, MD

Wendling, W. (1985), 'Die Erhebung Ludwigs d. Fr. zum Mitkaiser im Jahre 813 und ihre Bedeutung für die Verfassungsgeschichte des Frankenreiches', *Frühmittelalterliche Studien* 19, pp. 201–38

Wentzel, H. (1971), 'Das byzantinische Erbe der ottonischen Kaiser: Hypothesen über den Brautschatz der Theophano', *Aachener Kunstblätter* 40, pp. 15–39

Wessel, S. (2003), 'The Nouthesia and the Law of Moses', *Byz* 73, pp. 520–42

Westermann-Angerhausen, H. (1995), 'Did Theophano leave her mark on the Ottonian sumptuary arts ?', in Davids (ed.) (1995), pp. 244–64

Weyl Carr, A. (2000), 'The Mother of God in public', in Vassilaki (ed.) (2000), pp. 325–37

—(2002), 'Icons and the object of pilgrimage in middle Byzantine Constantinople', *DOP* 56, pp. 75–92

Wharton, A. J. (1988), *Art of empire: painting and architecture of the Byzantine periphery: a comparative study of four provinces*, University Park, PA

Whitby, Mary (ed.) (2007), *Byzantines and crusaders in non-Greek sources, 1025–1204*, Oxford

White, M. M. (2006), 'Byzantine visual propaganda and the inverted heart motif', *Byz* 76, pp. 330–63

Whittow, M. (1995), 'Rural fortifications in western Europe and Byzantium, tenth to twelfth century', *BF* 21, pp. 57–74

—(1996b), 'How the east was lost: the background to the Komnenian *reconquista*', in Mullett and Smythe (eds.) (1996), pp. 55–67

—(2003), 'Decline and fall? Studying long-term change in the east', in Lavan and Bowden (eds.) (2003), pp. 404–23

—(ed.) (forthcoming), *Byzantium: the economic turn*, Oxford

Wickham, C. (1981), *Early medieval Italy: central power and local society, 400–1000*, London

—(1985), 'The *Terra* of San Vicenzo al Volturno in the 8th to 12th centuries: the historical framework', in Hodges and Mitchell (eds.) (1985), pp. 227–58

—(1998), 'Ninth-century Byzantium through western eyes', in Brubaker (ed.) (1998), pp. 245–56

—(2000a), 'Overview: production, distribution and demand, II', in Hansen and Wickham (eds.) (2000), pp. 345–77

—(2000b), '"The Romans according to their malign custom": Rome in Italy in the late ninth and tenth centuries', in Smith (ed.) (2000), pp. 151–67

—(2004), 'The Mediterranean around 800: on the brink of the second trade cycle', *DOP* 58, pp. 161–74

Wieczorek, A. and Hinz, H.-M. (eds.) (2000), *Europas Mitte um 1000*, 3 vols., Stuttgart

Williams, C. K. and Bookidis, N. (eds.) (2003), *Corinth, the centenary, 1896–1996*, Athens

Winkelmann, F. (1985), *Byzantinische Rang- und Ämterstruktur im 8. und 9. Jahrhundert: Faktoren und Tendenzen ihrer Entwicklung*, Berlin

—(1987), *Quellenstudien zur herrschenden Klasse von Byzanz im 8. und 9. Jahrhundert*, BBA 54, Berlin

Winnifrith, T. (1987), *The Vlachs: the history of a Balkan people*, London

Wirth, P. (ed.) (1966), *Polychronion: Festschrift Franz Dölger zum 75. Geburtstag*, Heidelberg

Wolf, G. (ed.) (1972), *Zum Kaisertum Karls des Grossen: Beiträge und Aufsätze*, Darmstadt

—(ed.) (1991), *Kaiserin Theophanu: Prinzessin aus der Fremde – des Westreichs Grosse Kaiserin*, Cologne

Wolska-Conus, W. (1976), 'Les Écoles de Psellos et de Xiphilin sous Constantin IX Monomaque', *TM* 6, pp. 223–43

—(1979), 'L'École de droit et l'enseignement du droit à Byzance au XIᵉ siècle: Xiphilin et Psellos', *TM* 7, pp. 1–107

Wood, I. and Loud, G. A. (eds.) (1991), *Church and chronicle in the middle ages*, London

Worthington, I. (ed.) (2007), *A companion to Greek rhetoric*, Oxford

Wright, D. H. (1985), 'The date of the Vatican illuminated "Handy Tables" of Ptolemy and its early additions', *BZ* 78, pp. 355–62

Yannopoulos, P. A. (1993), 'Métropoles du Péloponnèse mésobyzantin: un souvenir des invasions avaro-slaves', *Byz* 63, pp. 388–400

—(2000), 'Les Vicissitudes historiques de la *Chronique* de Théophane', *Byz* 70, pp. 527–53

Yarnley, C. J. (1972), 'Philaretos: Armenian bandit or Byzantine general?', *REA* n.s. 9, pp. 331–53

Yun, B. (1994), 'Economic cycles and structural changes', in Brady *et al.* (eds.) (1994–5), I, pp. 113–45

Yuzbashian, K. N. (1973–4), 'L'Administration byzantine en Arménie aux Xᵉ–XIᵉ siècles', *REA* n.s. 10, pp. 139–83

Zangger, E. *et al.* (1997), 'The Pylos Regional Archaeological Project, part II: landscape evolution and site preservations', *Hesperia* 66, pp. 549–641

Zanini, E. (1998), *Le Italie bizantine: territorio, insediamenti ed economia nella provincia bizantina d'Italia (VI–VIII secolo)*, Bari

Zarov, I. (2003), *Vizantiskata estetika i srednovekovniot živopis vo Makedonija od XI i XII vek*, Skopje

Zettler, A. (1983), 'Cyrill und Method im Reichenauer Verbrüderungsbuch', *Frühmittelalterliche Studien* 17, pp. 280–98

Živković, T. (1999), 'The date of creation of the theme of Peloponnesus', *Symmeikta* 13, pp. 141–55

Zuckerman, C. (1988), 'The reign of Constantine V in the miracles of St Theodore the recruit', *REB* 46, pp. 191–210

—(1994), 'Chapitres peu connus de l'*Apparatus Bellicus*', *TM* 12, pp. 359–89

—(2000a), 'Deux étapes de la formation de l'ancien état russe', in Kazanski *et al.* (eds.) (2000), pp. 95–120

—(2000b), 'Le Voyage d'Olga et la première ambassade espagnole à Constantinople en 946', *TM* 13, pp. 647–72

—(2000c), 'À propos du *Livre des cérémonies*, II, 48. I: Les Destinataires des lettres impériales en Caucasie de l'est. II: Le Problème d'Azia/Asia, le pays des Ases. III: L'Albanie caucasienne au Xᵉ siècle', *TM* 13, pp. 531–94

—(2005), 'Learning from the enemy and more: studies in "dark centuries" Byzantium', *Millennium* 2, pp. 79–135

SECONDARY WORKS, PART III (1204–1492)

Aalst, V. D. van and Ciggaar, K. N. (eds.) (1990), *The Latin empire: some contributions*, Hernen

Abulafia, D. (1987), *Italy, Sicily and the Mediterranean, 1100–1400*, London

Ahrweiler, H (1958), 'La Politique agraire des empereurs de Nicée', *Byz* 28, pp. 51–66, 135–6

—(1965), 'L'Histoire et la géographie de la région de Smyrne entre les deux occupations turques (1081–1317)', *TM* 1, pp. 1–204

—(1975b), 'L'Expérience nicéenne', *DOP* 29, pp. 21–40

—(1983), 'La Région de Philadelphie au XIVᵉ siècle (1290–1390), dernier bastion de l'hellénisme en Asie Mineure', *CRAI*, pp. 175–97

Akbaygil, I. *et al.* (eds.) (2003), *Iznik throughout history*, tr. R. Urgan, Istanbul

Alekseev, A. (1999), *Tekstologiia slavianskoi Biblii*, St Petersburg

Amitai-Preiss, M. J. (1995), *Mongols and Mamluks: the Mamluk-Ilkhanid war 1260–81*, Cambridge

Angelov, D. (1956), 'Certains aspects de la conquête des peuples balkaniques par les Turcs', *BSl* 17, pp. 220–75; repr. in Angelov, D. (1978), no. 12

—(1961), *Bogomilstvoto v B'lgariia*, Sofia; French tr. *Le Bogomilisme en Bulgarie*, Toulouse, 1972

—(1978), *Les Balkans au moyen âge: la Bulgarie des Bogomils aux Turcs*, London

Angelov, D. G. (2003), 'Byzantine imperial panegyric as advice literature (1204–c. 1350)', in Jeffreys, E. (ed.) (2003), pp. 55–72

—(2004), 'Plato, Aristotle and "Byzantine political philosophy"', *Mélanges de l'Université Saint-Joseph* 57, pp. 499–523

—(2005), 'Byzantine ideological reactions to the Latin conquest of Constantinople', in Laiou (ed.) (2005), pp. 293–310

—(2007), *Imperial ideology and political thought in Byzantium, 1204–1330*, Cambridge

Angold, M. (1975a), *A Byzantine government in exile: government and society under the Laskarids of Nicaea 1204–1261*, Oxford

—(1975b), 'Byzantine "nationalism" and the Nicaean empire', *BMGS* 1, pp. 49–70

—(1980), 'The interaction of Latins and Byzantines during the period of the Latin empire, 1204–1261: the case of the ordeal', in *ACIEB* 15, IV, pp. 1–10

—(1984), 'Archons and dynasts: local aristocracies in the cities of the later Byzantine empire', in Angold (ed.) (1984), pp. 236–53

—(1989), 'Greeks and Latins after 1204: the perspective of exile', *MHR* 4, pp. 63–86, repr. in Arbel *et al.* (eds.) (1989), pp. 63–86

—(1993), 'Administration of the empire of Nicaea', *BF* 19, pp. 127–38

—(2003a), *The Fourth Crusade: event and context*, Harlow

—(2003b), 'The city Nicaea ca. 1000–ca. 1400', in Akbaygil *et al.* (eds.) (2003), pp. 27–51

—(2006), 'Byzantium and the west, 1204–1453', in Angold (ed.) (2006), pp. 53–78

—(ed.) (2006), *The Cambridge history of Christianity*, V: *Eastern Christianity*, Cambridge

Antoniadis-Bibicou, H. (1963), *Recherches sur les douanes à Byzance*, Paris

Apostolides, K. M. (1929), 'Dyo engrapha ek Philippoupoleos apo ton archon tou 19ou aionos', *Thrakika* 2, pp. 325–68

—(1941–42a), 'Romania-Zagora kai ta tes Thrakes oria epi tes byzantiakes autokratorias', *Archeion tou Thrakikou Laographikou kai Glossikou Thesaurou* 8, pp. 65–82

— (1941–42b), 'E dia ton aionon ethnike physiognomia tes Thrakes', *Archeion tou Thrakikou Laographikou kai Glossikou Thesaurou* 8, pp. 83–122

Apostolović, M. (1902), 'Todora Metohita poslanica o diplomatskom putu u Srbiju', *Letopis matice srpske* 216, pp. 25–58

Arbel, B. (ed.) (1996), *Intercultural contacts in the medieval Mediterranean*, London

Arbel, B. *et al.* (eds.) (1989), *Latins and Greeks in the eastern Mediterranean after 1204*, London

Argenti, P. P. (1958), *The occupation of Chios by the Genoese and their administration of the island (1346–1566)*, 3 vols., Cambridge

Arnaldi, G., *et al.* (eds.) (1997), *Storia di Venezia*, III: *La formazione dello stato patrizio*, Rome

Asdracha, C. (1976), *La Région des Rhodopes aux XIIIᵉ et XIVᵉ siècles; étude de géographie historique*, Athens

—(1982), 'Modes d'affirmation des pouvoirs locaux bulgares pendant le moyen âge tardif', *P'rvi mezhdunaroden kongres po b'lgaristika, Sofia, 23 mai–3 iuni 1981. Dokladi*, Part I: *B'lgarskata d'rzhava prez vekovete.* 1: *Srednovekovnata b'lgarska d'rzhava prez vekovete; B'lgarskata d'rzhava prez epokhata na kapitalizma*, Sofia, pp. 76–87

Ashtor, E. (1983), *Levant trade in the later middle ages*, Princeton

Atiya, A. S. (1934), *The crusade of Nicopolis*, London; repr. New York, 1978

—(1938), *The crusade in the later middle ages*, London; repr. New York, 1965

Babinger, F. (1978), *Mehmed the Conqueror and his time*, tr. R. Manheim, Princeton

Bakalopulos, see Vakalopoulos

Baker, D. (ed.) (1973), *Relations between east and west in the middle ages*, Edinburgh

Bakirtzis, C. (2003), 'The urban continuity and size of late Byzantine Thessalonike', *DOP* 57, pp. 35–64

Balard, M. (1966), 'Les Génois en Romanie entre 1204 et 1261: recherches dans les minutiers notariaux génois', *Mélanges d'archéologie et d'histoire. École française de Rome* 78, pp. 467–502

—(1978), *La Romanie génoise, XIIᵉ–début du XVᵉ siècle*, 2 vols., Genoa and Rome

—(1995), 'The Greeks of Crimea under Genoese rule in the XIVth and XVth centuries', *DOP* 49, pp. 23–32

—(1997a), 'Les Hommes d'affaires occidentaux ont-ils asphyxié l'économie byzantine?', in Arnaldi and Cavallo (eds.) (1997), pp. 255–65

—(1997b), 'La lotta contro Genova', in Arnaldi *et al.* (eds.) (1997), pp. 87–126

—(2002), 'Chio, centre économique en mer Egée (XIVᵉ–XVᵉ siècles)', *TM* 24, pp. 13–19

—(2004), 'Clarence, escale génoise aux XIIIᵉ–XIVᵉ siècles', in Doumerc and Picard (eds.) (2004), pp. 185–203

Balard, M. *et al.* (eds.) (1987), *Les Italiens à Byzance*, Paris

Balard, M. and Ducellier, A. (eds.) (1995), *Coloniser au moyen âge*, Paris

Balard, M. and Ducellier, A. (eds.) (1999), *Le Partage du monde: échanges et colonisation dans la Méditerranée médiévale*, Paris

Balard, M. and Ducellier, A. (eds.) (2002), *Migrations et diasporas méditerranéennes (Xᵉ–XVIᵉ siècles): actes du colloque de Conques, octobre 1999, BSo* 19, Paris

Balascev, G. (1911), 'Pismo ot imperatora Teodora II Laskar po skljucvaneto mira s car Michaila Asena (1256 g.)', *Minalo* II, 5–6

Balfour, D. (1982–3), 'Saint Gregory of Sinai's life story and spiritual profile – the works of Gregory the Sinaïte', *Theologia* 53, pp. 30–62, 417–29, 697–709, 1102–18; *Theologia* 54, pp. 153–83

—(1984), 'Was St Gregory Palamas St Gregory the Sinaite's pupil?', *St Vladimir's Theological Quarterly* 28, pp. 115–30

Balivet, M. (1994), *Romanie byzantine et pays de Rum turc: histoire d'un espace d'imbrication gréco-turque*, Istanbul

Balletto, L. (ed.) (1997), *Oriente e occidente tra medioevo ed età moderna. Studi in onore di G. Pistarino*, 2 vols., Acqui Terme

Barber, M. (1989), 'Western attitudes to Frankish Greece in the thirteenth century', *MHR* 4, pp. 111–28; repr. in Arbel *et al.* (eds.) (1989), pp. 111–28; repr. in Barber (1995), no. 10

—(1995), *Crusaders and heretics, 12th–14th centuries*, Aldershot

Bardakjian, K. B. (1982), 'The rise of the Armenian patriarchate of Constantinople', in Braude and Lewis (eds.) (1982), I, pp. 89–100

Barker, J. W. (2003), 'Late Byzantine Thessalonike: a second city's challenges and responses', *DOP* 57, pp. 5–54

Baronas, D. (2004), 'The three martyrs of Vilnius: a fourteenth-century martyrdom and its documentary sources', *AnBoll* 122, pp. 83–134

—(2007), 'Byzantium and Lithuania: north and south look at each other', in Kaimakamova *et al.* (eds.) (2007), pp. 303–17

Bartusis, M. (1982), 'On the status of *stratiotai* during the late Byzantine period', *ZRVI* 21, pp. 53–9

—(1988), 'The *kavallarioi* of Byzantium', *Sp* 63, pp. 343–50

—(1991), 'The cost of late Byzantine warfare and defense', in Bryer and Ursinus (eds.) (1991), pp. 75–89

—(1992), *The late Byzantine army: arms and society 1204–1453*, Philadelphia

Beaton, R. (1996), *The medieval Greek romance*, 2nd edn., London

Beldiceanu, N. and Beldiceanu-Steinherr, I. (1980), 'Recherches sur la Morée (1461–1512)', *SF* 39, pp. 17–74

Belting, H. *et al.* (1978), *The mosaics and frescoes of St Mary Pammakaristos (Fethiye Camii) at Istanbul, DOSt* 15, Washington, DC

Bernicolas-Hatzopoulos, D. (1983), 'The first siege of Constantinople by the Ottomans (1394–1402) and its repercussions on the civilian population of the city', *BS* 10, pp. 39–51

Bertelè, T. (1962), 'I gioelli della corona bizantina dati in pegno alla repubblica veneta nel sec. XIV e Mastino II della Scala', *Studi in onore di Amintore Fanfani*, II, Milan, pp. 87–188

—(1978), *Numismatique byzantine: suivie de deux études inédites sur les monnaies des Paléologues*, French edn. C. Morrisson, Wetteren

Bianconi, D. (2005), *Tessalonica nell'età dei paleologi: le pratiche intellettuali nel riflesso della cultura scritta*, Paris

Biliarsky, I. (1993), 'Le rite du couronnement des tsars dans les pays slaves et la promotion d'autres *axiai*', *OCP* 59, pp. 91–139

—(2001), 'Some observations on the administrative terminology of the second Bulgarian empire (13th–14th centuries)', *BMGS* 25, pp. 69–89

Bisaha, N. (2004), *Creating east and west: Renaissance humanists and the Ottoman Turks*, Philadelphia

Bojovic, B. I. (1995), *L'Idéologie monarchique dans les hagio-biographies dynastiques du moyen âge serbe, OCA* 248, Rome

—(2001), 'Une monarchie hagiographique: la théologie du pouvoir dans la Serbie médiévale (XIIᵉ–XVᵉ siècles)', in Guran and Flusin (eds.) (2001), pp. 61–72

Bon, A. (1969), *La Morée franque: recherches historiques, topographiques et archéologiques sur la principauté d'Achaïe 1205–1430*, 2 vols., Paris

Borsari, S. (1951), 'Federico II e l'oriente bizantino', *Rivista storica italiana* 63, pp. 279–91

—(1955), 'I rapporti tra Pisa e gli stati di Romania nel duecento', *Rivista storica italiana* 67, pp. 477–92

—(1966), *Studi sulle colonie veneziane in Romania nel XIII secolo*, Naples

—(2007), *L'Eubea veneziana*, Venice

Bosch, U. V. (1965), *Kaiser Andronikos III. Palaiologos: Versuch einer Darstellung der byzantinischen Geschichte in den Jahren 1321–1341*, Amsterdam

Bouras, C. (2001), 'The impact of Frankish architecture on thirteenth-century Byzantine architecture', in Laiou and Mottahedeh (eds.)(2001), pp. 247–62

Bowman, S. B. (1985), *The Jews of Byzantium (1204–1453)*, Tuscaloosa, AL

Brady, T. A. *et al.* (eds.) (1994–5), *Handbook of European history, 1400–1600: late middle ages, renaissance and reformation*, 2 vols., Leiden

Brătianu, G. I. (1929), *Recherches sur le commerce génois dans la mer Noire au XIIIᵉ siècle*, Paris

—(1936), *Privilèges et franchises municipales dans l'empire byzantin*, Paris

Braude, B. (1982), 'Foundation myths of the *millet* system', in Braude and Lewis (eds.) (1982), I, pp. 69–88

Braude, B. and Lewis, B. (eds.) (1982), *Christians and Jews in the Ottoman Empire*, 2 vols., New York and London

Bredenkamp, F. (1996), *The Byzantine empire of Thessaloniki, 1224–1242*, Thessalonica

Brezeanu, S. (1974), 'Notice sur les rapports de Frédéric II de Hohenstaufen avec Jean III Vatatzès', *RESEE* 12, pp. 583–5

Bryer, A. A. M. (1980), *The empire of Trebizond and the Pontos*, London

—(1986), 'Rural society in Matzouka', in Bryer and Lowry (eds.) (1986), pp. 51–96

—(1988), *Peoples and settlement in Anatolia and the Caucasus, 800–1900*, London

—(1991), 'The Pontic Greeks before the diaspora', *Journal of Refugee Studies* 4, pp. 315–34

Bryer, A. A. M. *et al.* (2002), *The post-Byzantine monuments of the Pontos: a source book*, Aldershot

Bryer, A. A. M. and Cunningham, M. (eds.) (1996), *Mount Athos and Byzantine monasticism: papers from the twenty-eighth spring symposium of Byzantine studies, Birmingham, March 1994*, London

Bryer, A. A. M. and Lowry, H. W. (eds.) (1986), *Continuity and change in late Byzantine and early Ottoman society: papers given at a symposium at Dumbarton Oaks in May 1982*, Birmingham and Washington, DC

Bryer, A. A. M. and Ursinus, M. O. H. (eds.) (1991), *Manzikert to Lepanto: the Byzantine world and the Turks, 1071–1571: papers given at the nineteenth spring symposium of Byzantine studies, Birmingham, March 1985, BF* 16, Amsterdam

Bryer, A. A. M. and Winfield, D. (1985), *The Byzantine monuments and topography of the Pontos, DOSt* 20, 2 vols., Washington, DC

Buchthal, H. and Belting, H. (1978), *Patronage in thirteenth-century Constantinople: an atelier of late Byzantine book illumination and calligraphy, DOSt* 16, Washington, DC

Buckton, D. (ed.) (1994), *Byzantium: treasures of Byzantine art and culture from British collections*, London

Burgmann, L. *et al.* (eds.) (1985), *Cupido legum*, Frankfurt-am-Main

Burgmann, L. and Magdalino, P. (1984), 'Michael VIII on maladministration: an unpublished novel of the early Palaiologan period', *FM* 6, pp. 377–90

Buschhausen, Heide and Buschhausen, Helmut (1976), *Die Marienkirche von Apollonia in Albanien: Byzantiner, Normannen und Serben im Kampf um die Via Egnatia, BV* 8, Vienna

Cahen, C. (1965), 'Dhimma', in *EI*, II, pp. 227–31

Čankova-Petkova, G. (1969), 'Griechisch-bulgarische Bündnisse in den Jahren 1235 und 1246', *BB* 3, pp. 49–79

Capaldo, M. (1989), 'Contributi allo studio delle collezioni agiografico-omiletiche in area slava: struttura e preistoria del "Panegirico di Mileševa"', *Europa orientalis* 8, pp. 209–51

Capaldo, M. *et al.* (eds.) (2003–6), *Lo spazio letterario del medioevo*, III: *Le culture circostanti*, Rome

Carile, A. (1978), *Per una storia dell'impero latino di Costantinopoli, 1204–1261*, 2nd edn., Bologna

Chadwick, H. (2003), *East and west, the making of a rift in the church: from apostolic times until the council of Florence*, Oxford

Charanis, P. (1948), 'The monastic properties and the state in the Byzantine empire', *DOP* 4, pp. 51–118; repr. in Charanis (1973), no. 1

—(1951), 'On the social structure and economic organization of the Byzantine empire in the thirteenth century and later', *BSl* 12, pp. 94–153; repr. in Charanis (1973), no. 4

Chrysanthos [Philippides, metropolitan of Trebizond] (1933), 'E ekklesia Trapezountos', *Archeion Pontou* 4–5, pp. 1–904

Chrysos, E. (ed.) (1992), *To despotato tes Epeirou [The despotate of Epirus]: praktika diethnous symposiou gia to despotato tes Epeirou: Arta, 27–31 Maiou 1990*, Arta

Chrysostomides, J. (1970), 'Venetian commercial privileges under the Palaeologi', *Studi veneziani* 12, pp. 267–356

Chrysostomides, J. *et al.* (eds.) (2004), *The Greek islands and the sea: proceedings of the first international colloquium held at the Hellenic Institute, Royal Holloway, University of London, 21–22 September 2001*, Camberley

Chrysostomides, J. and Dendrinos, C. (eds.), (2006), *'Sweet land of Cyprus': lectures on the history and culture of Cyprus*, Camberley

Ćirković, S. (1964), *Istorija srednjovekovne Bosanske države*, Belgrade

—(1988), 'Les Albanais à la lumière des sources historiques des Slaves du sud', in Garašanin (ed.) (1988a), pp. 341–59

—(2004), *The Serbs*, tr. V. Tošić, Oxford

Clucas, L. (ed.) (1988), *The Byzantine legacy in eastern Europe*, Boulder, CO

Constantelos, D. J. (1972), 'Emperor John Vatatzes' social concern: basis for canonization', *Kleronomia* 4, pp. 92–104

—(1998), *Christian Hellenism: essays and studies in continuity and change*, New Rochelle, NY

Constantinides, C. N. (1982), *Higher education in Byzantium in the thirteenth and early fourteenth centuries 1204–ca. 1310*, Nicosia

—(2003), 'Teachers and students of rhetoric in the late Byzantine period', in Jeffreys, E. (ed.) (2003), pp. 39–52

Constantinides, C. N. *et al.* (eds.) (1996), *Philellēn: studies in honour of Robert Browning*, Venice

Cosentino, S. (1987), *Aspetti e problemi del feudo Veneto-Cretese, secoli XIII–XIV*, Bologna

Coulon, D. *et al.* (eds.) (2004), *Chemins d'outre-mer: études sur la Méditerranée médiévale offertes à Michel Balard, BSo 20*, 2 vols., Paris

Cowan, A. (ed.) (2000), *Mediterranean urban culture, 1400–1700*, Exeter

Cowe, S. P. (2006), 'The Armenians in the era of the crusades (1050–1350)', in Angold (ed.) (2006), pp. 404–29

Crummey, R. O. (1987), *The formation of Muscovy, 1304–1613*, London

Ćurčić, S. (1979), *Gračanica: King Milutin's church and its place in late Byzantine architecture*, University Park, PA

Ćurčić, S. and Hadjitryphonos, E. (1997), *Secular medieval architecture in the Balkans 1300–1500 and its preservation*, Thessalonica

Ćurčić, S. and Mouriki, D. (eds.) (1991), *The twilight of Byzantium: aspects of cultural and religious history in the late Byzantine empire*, Princeton

Dąbrowska, M. (2005), '"Vasilissa, ergo gaude . . .": Cleopa Malatesta's Byzantine CV', *BSl* 63, pp. 217–24

Dade, E. (1938), *Versuche zur Wiedererrichtung der lateinischen Herrschaft in Konstantinopel im Rahmen der abendländischen Politik 1261 bis etwa 1310*, Jena

Dall'Aglio, F. (2002), 'The Bulgarian siege of Thessaloniki in 1207: between history and hagiography', *Eurasian Studies* 1, pp. 263–82

Dendrinos, C. *et al.* (eds.) (2003), *Porphyrogenita: essays on the history and literature of Byzantium and the Latin East in honour of Julian Chrysostomides*, Aldershot

Dennis, G. T. (1960), *The reign of Manuel II Palaeologus in Thessalonica, 1382–1387*, OCA 159, Rome

—(1982), *Byzantium and the Franks 1350–1420*, London

Derzhavin, N. S. (1945–8), *Istoriia Bolgarii*, 4 vols., Moscow

Dimitriades, V. (1991), 'Byzantine and Ottoman Thessaloniki', in Bryer and Ursinus (eds.) (1991), pp. 265–9

Dimnik, M. (2004), 'Kievan Rus', the Bulgars and the southern Slavs, *c.* 1020–*c.* 1200', in *NCMH*, IV.2, pp. 254–76

Djourova see Džurova

Djurović, M. *et al.* (1970), *Istorija Crne Gore*, II.1: *Od kraja XII do kraja XV vijeka: Crne Gora u doba Nemanjića*, Titograd

Dölger, F. (1949), 'Einiges über Theodora die Griechin, Zarin der Bulgaren (1308–1330)', *AIPHO* 9, pp. 211–21; repr. in Dölger (1961), pp. 222–30

—(1950), 'Zwei byzantinische Reiterheroen erobern die Festung Melnik', *Ephemerides Instituti Archaeologici Bulgarici* 16, pp. 275–9; repr. in Dölger (1961), pp. 299–305

—(1961), *Paraspora: 30 Aufsätze zur Geschichte, Kultur und Sprache des byzantinischen Reiches*, Ettal

Dotson, J. E. (2006), 'Ship types and fleet composition at Genoa and Venice in the early thirteenth century', in Pryor (ed.) (2006), pp. 63–75

Doumerc, B. and Picard, C. (eds.) (2004), *Byzance et ses périphéries (Mondes grec, balkanique et musulman): hommage à Alain Ducellier*, Toulouse

Ducellier, A. (1979), 'Les Albanais du XIe au XIIIe siècle, nomades ou sédentaires?', *BF* 7, pp. 23–36; repr. in Ducellier (1987a), no. 6

—(1981a), 'L'Économie albanaise au moyen âge: une traite coloniale', *Albanie* 11, pp. 28–31; repr. in Ducellier (1987a), no. 16

—(1981c), 'Les Albanais ont-ils envahi le Kosovo?', *Albanie* 13, pp. 10–14; repr. in Ducellier (1987a), no. 10

—(1983), 'Aux frontières de la romanité et de l'orthodoxie au moyen âge: le cas de l'Albanie', *L'Histoire à Nice: actes du Colloque international 'Entre l'Occident et l'Orient' (Antibes–Juan les Pins, 21–31 octobre 1981)*, Nice, pp. 129–50; repr. in Ducellier (1987a), no. 11

—(1987a), *L'Albanie entre Byzance et Venise X^e–XVe siècles*, London

—(1987b), 'La Côte albanaise au moyen âge: exutoires locaux ou ports de transit?', repr. in Ducellier (1987a), no. 19

—(1992), 'La Penisola Balcanica vista dall'osservatorio veneziano nei sec. XIV e XV', in Gensini (ed.) (1992), pp. 297–314

Ducellier, A. *et al.* (1992), *Les Chemins de l'exil: bouleversements de l'est européen et migrations vers l'ouest à la fin du moyen âge*, Paris

Dujčev, I. (1956), 'V'stanieto v 1185 g. i negovata khronologiia', *Izvestiia na Instituta za istoriia* 6, pp. 327–58

—(1960), 'Les Slaves et Byzance', *Etudes historiques à l'occasion du XIe congrès international des sciences historiques, Stockholm, août 1960*, Sofia, pp. 31–77; repr. in Dujčev (1965–96), IV.1, no. 9

—(1964), 'Le Mont Athos et les Slaves au moyen âge', in Rousseau (ed.) (1963–4), II, pp. 121–44; repr. in Dujčev (1965–96), I, pp. 487–510

—(1966), 'Chilandar et Zographou au moyen âge', *Hilandarski Zbornik* 1, pp. 21–32; repr. in Dujčev (1965–96), III, pp. 489–506

—(1973), 'Contribution à l'histoire de la conquête turque en Thrace aux dernières décades du XIVe siècle', *EB* 9.2, pp. 80–92

Dunbabin, J. (1998), *Charles I of Anjou: power, kingship and state-making in thirteenth-century Europe*, London

Durand, J. and Lafitte, M.-P. (eds.) (2001), *La Trésor de la Sainte-Chapelle*, Paris

Đurić, V. (ed.) (1979), *Međunarodni naučni skup Sava Nemanjić-Sveti Sava: istorija i predanje, Decembar 1976 (Colloque scientifique international Sava Nemanjić– Saint Sava: histoire et tradition: décembre, 1976)*, Belgrade

Dusa, J. (1991), *The medieval Dalmatian episcopal cities: development and transformation*, New York

Džurova, A. (1977), 'Le Manuscript pendant le deuxième royaume bulgare (1185–1396)', *Cyrillomethodianum* 4, pp. 36–99

—(1997), *V'vedenie v slavianskata kodikologiia: vizantiiskiat kodeks i retseptsiiata mu sred slavianite*, Sofia

Eastmond, A. (2003a), '"Local" saints, art and regional identity in the orthodox world after the Fourth Crusade', *Sp* 78, pp. 707–49

—(2003b), 'Byzantine identity and relics of the True Cross in the thirteenth century', in Lidov (ed.) (2003), pp. 205–15

—(2004), *Art and identity in thirteenth-century Byzantium: Hagia Sophia and the empire of Trebizond*, Aldershot

Edbury, P. (1991), *The kingdom of Cyprus and the crusades, 1191–1371*, Cambridge

—(2002), 'Latins and Greeks on crusader Cyprus', in Abulafia and Berend (eds.) (2002), pp. 133–42

Evans, H. C. (ed.) (2004), *Byzantium: faith and power (1261–1557)*, New York

Fennell, J. L. I. (1995), *A history of the Russian church to 1448*, London

Ferjančić, B. (1966), 'Kada je umro Despot Mihailo II Angeo?', *ZRVI* 9, pp. 29–32

—(1974), *Tesalija u XIII i XIV veku*, Belgrade

Fisher, E. A. (2002–3), 'Planoudes, Holobolos and the motivation for translation', *GRBS* 43, pp. 77–104

Fleet, K. (ed.) (forthcoming), *The Cambridge history of Turkey*, I: *Byzantium– Turkey, 1071–1453*, Cambridge

Fögen, M.-T. (1982), 'Zeugnisse byzantinischer Rechtspraxis im 14. Jahrhundert', *FM* 5, pp. 215–80

—(1985), 'Horror iuris: byzantinische Rechtsgelehrte disziplinieren ihren Metropoliten', in Burgmann *et al.* (eds.) (1985), pp. 47–71

—(ed.) (1991), *Fremde der Gesellschaft*, Frankfurt-am-Main

—(ed.) (1995), *Ordnung und Aufruhr im Mittelalter: historische und juristische Studien zur Rebellion*, Frankfurt-am-Main

Foss, C. (1979b), 'Late Byzantine fortifications in Lydia', *JÖB* 28, pp. 297–320

Francès, E. (1962), 'La Féodalité byzantine et la conquête turque', *SAO* 4, pp. 69–90

Franchi, A. (1981), *La svolta politico-ecclesiastica tra Roma e Bizanzio, 1249–1254: la legazione di Giovanni da Parma, il ruolo di Federico II: studio critico sulle fonti*, Rome

—(1984), *I vespri siciliani e le relazioni tra Roma e Bisanzio: studio critico sulle fonti*, Palermo

François, V. (1995), *La Céramique byzantine à Thasos*, Athens and Paris

—(2003), 'Elaborate incised ware: une preuve du rayonnement de la culture byzantine à l'époque paléologue', *BSl* 61, pp. 151–68

—(2004), 'Réalités des échanges en Méditerranée orientale du XIIe au XVIIIe siècles: l'apport de la céramique', *DOP* 58, pp. 241–9

Frashëri, K. (1982), 'Trojet e shqiptarëve në shek. XV', in Pulaha *et al.* (eds.) (1982), pp. 199–210

Frazee, C. A. (1983), *Catholics and sultans: the church and the Ottoman empire, 1453–1923*, Cambridge

Fryde, E. (2000), *The early Palaeologan renaissance (1261–c. 1360)*, Leiden

Gallina, M. (1989), *Una società coloniale nel trecento: Creta fra Venezia e Bisanzio*, Venice

Garašanin, M. V. (ed.) (1988a), *Iliri i Albanci (Les Illyriens et les Albanais)*, Belgrade

—(1988b), 'Zaključna razmatranja' in Garašanin (ed.) (1988a), pp. 361–75

Gashi, S. (1982), 'Prania e etnosit shqiptar në Kosovë gjatë shekujve XIII-XIV në dritën e burimeve kishtare serbe', in Pulaha *et. al.* (eds.) (1982), pp. 239–64

Gasparis, C. (2005), 'The period of Venetian rule on Crete: breaks and continuities during the thirteenth century', in Laiou (ed.) (2005), pp. 233–46

Gaul, N. (2002), 'Eunuchs in the later Byzantine empire, *c.* 1250–1400', in Tougher (ed.) (2002), pp. 199–218

—(forthcoming), *Thomas Magistros und die spätbyzantinische Sophistik: Studien zum Humanismus urbaner Eliten der frühen Palaiologenzeit*, Wiesbaden

Gavrilović, S. *et al.* (eds.) (1981–3), *Istorija srpskog naroda*, 6 vols., Belgrade

Gavrilović, Z. (1991), 'The portrait of King Marko at Markov Manastir (1376–1381)', in Bryer and Ursinus (eds.) (1991), pp. 415–28

—(2001), *Studies in Byzantine and Serbian medieval art*, London

—(2006), 'Women in Serbian politics, diplomacy and art at the beginning of Ottoman rule', in Jeffreys, E. (ed.) (2006), pp. 72–90

Geanakoplos, D. J. (1953), 'Greco-Latin relations on the eve of the Byzantine restoration: the battle of Pelagonia – 1259', *DOP* 7, pp. 99–141

—(1976), *Interaction of the 'sibling' Byzantine and western cultures in the middle ages and Italian renaissance 330–1600*, New Haven and London

—(1989), *Constantinople and the west: essays on the late Byzantine (Palaeologan) and Italian renaissances and the Byzantine and Roman churches*, Madison, WI

Gelzer, H. (1902), *Der Patriarchat von Achrida, Geschichte und Urkunden*, Leipzig

Gensini, S. (ed.) (1992), *Europa e Mediterraneo tra medioevo e prima età moderna: l'osservatorio italiano*, Pisa

Gerland, E. (1905), *Geschichte des lateinischen Kaiserreiches von Konstantinopel*, I: *Geschichte der Kaiser Balduin I. und Heinrich 1204–1216*, Bad Homburg v. d. Höhe

Gerstel, S. E. J. (2001), 'Art and identity in the medieval Morea', in Laiou and Mottahedeh (eds.) (2001), pp. 263–85

Gerstel, S. E. J. and Talbot, A.-M. (2006), 'The culture of lay piety in medieval Byzantium, 1054–1453', in Angold (ed.) (2006), pp. 79–100

Gertwagen, R. (1998), 'L'isola di Creta e i suoi porti (dalla fine del XII alla fine del XV secolo)', in Ortalli (ed.) (1998), pp. 337–74

—(2006), 'Harbours and facilities along the eastern Mediterranean sea lanes to *Outremer*', in Pryor (ed.) (2006), pp. 95–118

Giannelli, C. (1946), 'Un progetto di Barlaam Calabro per l'unione delle chiese', in *Miscellanea Giovanni Mercati*, III: *Letteratura e storia bizantina* [= StT 123], pp. 157–208

Gill, J. (1959), *The Council of Florence*, Cambridge

—(1964), *Personalities of the Council of Florence, and other essays*, Oxford

—(1973), 'Innocent III and the Greeks: apostle or aggressor?', in Baker (ed.) (1973), pp. 95–108

—(1974), 'The church union of the council of Lyons (1274) portrayed in the Greek documents', *OCP* 40, pp. 5–45; repr. in Gill (1979b), no. 5

—(1975), 'John Beccus, patriarch of Constantinople 1275–1282', *Byzantina* 7, pp. 253–266; repr. in Gill (1979b), no. 6

—(1977), 'The tribulations of the Greek church in Cyprus, 1196–c. 1280', *BF* 5, pp. 73–93; repr. in Gill (1979b), no. 4

—(1979a), *Byzantium and the papacy, 1198–1400*, New Brunswick, NJ

—(1979b), *Church union: Rome and Byzantium, 1204–1453*, London

Giunta, F. (1959), *Aragonesi e Catalani nel Mediterraneo*, II: *La presenza catalana nel Levante dalle origini a Giacomo II*, Palermo

Giuzelev [Gyuzelev], V. and Miltenova, A. (eds.) (2002), *Srednovekovna khristianska Evropa, iztok i zapad: tsennosti, traditsii, obshtuvane (Medieval Christian Europe, east and west: traditions, values, communications)*, Sofia

Glycofrydi-Leontsini, A. (2003), 'Demetrius Cydones as a translator of Latin texts', in Dendrinos *et al.* (eds.) (2003), pp. 175–85

Glykatzi and Glykatzi-Ahrweiler, see Ahrweiler

Godfrey, J. (1980), *1204: the unholy crusade*, Oxford

Gothóni, R. (2004), 'Mount Athos during the last centuries of Byzantium', in Rosenqvist (ed.) (2004), pp. 57–69

Gounarides, P. (1985), 'E chronologia tes anagoreuses kai tes stepses tou Theodorou I tou Laskareos', *Symmeikta* 6, pp. 59–71

Grujić, R. (1933), 'Kada je Nemanjin unuk po kćeri, Bugarski car Konstantin Tih, mogao vladati u Skopskoj oblasti?', *Glasnik Skopskog naučnog društva* 12, pp. 272–3

Grumel, V. (1930), 'L'Authenticité de la lettre de Jean Vatatzès, empereur de Niceé, au Pape Grégoire IX', *EO* 29, pp. 450–8

Guilland, R. (1922), 'Le Palais de Théodore Métochite', *REG* 35, pp. 82–95

—(1926), *Essai sur Nicéphore Grégoras: l'homme et l'oeuvre*, Paris

Guillou, A. (ed.) (1982), *La civiltà bizantina dal XII al XV secolo: aspetti e problemi, Corsi di studi* 3, Rome

Gundlach, R. and Weber, H. (eds.) (1992), *Legitimation und Funktion des Herrschers: vom ägyptischen Pharao zum neuzeitlichen Diktator,* Stuttgart

Guran, P. (2001), 'Jean VI Cantacuzène, l'hésychasme et l'empire. Les miniatures du codex Parisinus graecus 1242', in Guran and Flusin (eds.) (2001), pp. 73–121

Guran, P. and Flusin, B. (eds.) (2001), *L'Empereur hagiographe: culte des saints et monarchie byzantine et post-byzantine*, Bucharest

Haldon, J. (1986b), 'Limnos, monastic holdings in the Byzantine state: ca. 1261–1453', in Bryer and Lowry (eds.) (1986), pp. 161–215

Halecki, O. (1930), *Un empereur de Byzance à Rome: vingt ans de travail pour l'union des églises et pour la défense de l'empire d'orient 1355–1375*, Warsaw; repr. London, 1972

Hamilton, B. (1980), *The Latin church in the Crusader states: the secular church*, London

—(2005), 'The Albigensian Crusade and the Latin empire of Constantinople', in Laiou (ed.) (2005), pp. 335–43

Hanak, W. K. (2004), 'One source, two renditions: *The tale of Constantinople* and its fall in 1453', *BSl* 62, pp. 239–50

Hansen-Löve, A. A. (1971), 'Die Darstellung der Schlacht bei Adrianopel (1205) in der "Chronik von Morea"', *EB* 7.3, pp. 102–12

Harley, J. B. and Woodward, D. (eds.) (1987–), *The history of cartography*, 2 vols. in 4 pts. to date, Chicago and London

Harris, J. (1995a), *Greek émigrés in the west, 1400–1520*, Camberley

—(1995b), 'A worthless prince? Andreas Palaeologus in Rome, 1465–1502', *OCP* 61, pp. 537–54

—(2003b), 'Laonikos Chalkokondyles and the rise of the Ottoman Turks', *BMGS* 27, pp. 153–70

—(2004), 'The last crusades: the Ottoman threat', in Madden (ed.) (2004), pp. 172–99

Harvey, A. (2000), 'Economic conditions in Thessaloniki between the two Ottoman occupations', in Cowan (ed.) (2000), pp. 115–124, 245–248

Hausherr, I. (1956), 'L'Hésychasme, étude de spiritualité', *OCP* 22, pp. 5–40, 247–85

Heers, J. (1971), *Gênes au XVe siècle: activité économique et problèmes sociaux,* Paris

Heisenberg, A. (1973), *Quellen und Studien zur spätbyzantinischen Geschichte*, London

Hetherington, P. (2003), 'The jewels from the crown: symbol and substance in the later Byzantine imperial regalia', *BZ* 96, pp. 157–68

Heyd, W. (1885–6), *Histoire du commerce du levant au moyen âge*, 2 vols., Leipzig

Hiestand, R. (1996), 'Nova Francia – nova Graecia: Morea zwischen Franken, Venezianern und Griechen', in Lauer and Schreiner (eds.) (1996), pp. 55–72

Hinterberger, M. (1999), *Autobiographische Traditionen in Byzanz*, WBS 22, Vienna

Hjort, Ø. (2004), '"Oddities" and "refinements": aspects of architecture, space and narrative in the mosaics of Kariye Camii', in Rosenqvist (ed.) (2004), pp. 27–43

Hodges, R. *et al.* (2004), *Byzantine Butrint: excavations and surveys 1994–9*, Oxford

Hoeck, J. M. and Loenertz, R.-J. (1965), *Nikolaos-Nektarios von Otranto, Abt von Casole: Beiträge zur Geschichte der ost-westlichen Beziehungen unter Innozenz III. und Friedrich II.*, Ettal

Hopwood, K. (1991), 'Nomads or bandits? The pastoralist/sedentarist interface in Anatolia', in Bryer and Ursinus (eds.) (1991), pp. 179–94

Housley, N. (1992), *The later crusades, 1274–1580: from Lyons to Alcazar*, Oxford

Hrochová, V. (1967), 'Le Commerce vénitien et les changements dans l'importance des centres de commerce en Grèce du 13ᵉ au 15ᵉ siècles', *Studi veneziani* 9, pp. 3–34

—(1989), *Aspects des Balkans médiévaux*, Prague

Hult, K. (2004), 'Theodore Metochites as a literary critic', in Rosenqvist (ed.) (2004), pp. 44–56

Hunger, H. (1959), 'Von Wissenschaft und Kunst der frühen Palaiologenzeit', *JÖB* 8, pp. 123–55

Ilieva, A. (1991), *Frankish Morea, 1205–1262: socio-cultural interaction between the Franks and the local population*, Athens

—(1995), 'Images of towns in Frankish Morea; the evidence of the *Chronicles* of the Morea and of the Tocco', *BMGS* 19, pp. 94–119

Imber, C. (1990), *The Ottoman empire, 1300–1481*, Istanbul

Inalcik, H. (1969–70), 'The policy of Mehmed II toward the Greek population of Istanbul and the Byzantine buildings of the city', *DOP* 23–4, pp. 229–49; repr. in Inalcik (1978), no. 6

—(1973), *The Ottoman empire: the classical age, 1300–1600*, London

—(1974), 'Istanbul', in *EI*, IV, pp. 224–48

—(1978), *The Ottoman empire: conquest, organization and economy*, London

—(1985), 'The rise of the Turcoman maritime principalities in Anatolia, Byzantium, and crusades', *BF* 9, pp. 179–217

Iorga, N. (2000), *Byzantium after Byzantium*, tr. L. Treptow, Oxford

Irmscher, J. (1972), 'Nikäa als "Mittelpunkt des griechischen Patriotismus"', *BF* 4, pp. 114–37

Jackson, P. (2005), *The Mongols and the west, 1221–1410*, Harlow

Jackson, P. and Lockhart, L. (eds.) (1986), *The Cambridge history of Iran*, VI: *The Timurid and Safavid periods*, Cambridge

Jacoby, D. (1967), 'Les *Archontes* grecs et la féodalité en Morée franque', *TM* 2, pp. 421–81

—(1971), *La Féodalité en Grèce médiévale: les 'assises de Romanie': sources, application et diffusion*, Paris

—(1973), 'The encounter of two societies: western conquerors and Byzantines in the Peloponnesus after the Fourth Crusade', *AHR* 78, pp. 873–906; repr. in Jacoby (1979), no. 2

—(1974), 'Catalans, Turcs et Vénitiens en Romanie (1305–1332): un nouveau témoignage de Marino Sanudo Torsello', *Studi medievali* 3rd series 15, pp. 217–61

—(1976), 'Les États latins en Romanie: phénomènes sociaux et économiques (1204–1350 environ)', *XVe Congrès international d'études byzantines: rapports et co-rapports*, Athens (1976); repr. in Jacoby (1979), no. 1

—(1979), *Recherches sur la Méditerranée orientale du XIIe au XVe siècle: peuples, sociétés, économies*, London

—(1981), 'Les Vénitiens naturalisés dans l'empire byzantin: un aspect de l'expansion de Venise en Romanie du XIIIe au milieu du XVe siècle', *TM* 8, pp. 217–35; repr. in Jacoby (1989c), no. 9

—(1986), 'Knightly values and class consciouness in the crusader states of the eastern Mediterranean', *MHR* 1, pp. 158–86; repr. in Jacoby (1989c), no. 1

—(1989a), 'Social evolution in Latin Greece', in Setton (ed.) (1969–89), VI, pp. 175–221

—(1989b), 'From Byzantium to Latin Romania: continuity and change', *MHR* 4, pp. 1–44; repr. in Arbel *et al.* (eds.) (1989), pp. 1–44; repr. in Jacoby (2001c), no. 8

—(1989c), *Studies on the crusader states and on Venetian expansion*, Northampton

—(1993), 'The Venetian presence in the Latin empire of Constantinople 1204–1261: the challenge of feudalism and the Byzantine inheritance', *JÖB* 43, pp. 141–201; repr. in Jacoby (2001c), no. 6

—(1994a), 'Silk production in the Frankish Peloponnese: the evidence of fourteenth-century surveys and reports', in Kalligas (ed.) (1994), pp. 41–61; repr. in Jacoby (1997b), no. 8

—(1997a), 'Italian migration and settlement in Latin Greece: the impact on the economy', in Mayer (ed.) (1997), pp. 97–127; repr. in Jacoby (2001c), no. 9

—(1997c), 'Byzantine Crete in the navigation and trade networks of Venice and Genoa', in Balletto (ed.) (1997), I, pp. 517–40

—(1998), 'Venetian settlers in Latin Constantinople (1204–1261): rich or poor?', in Maltezou (ed.) (1998), pp. 181–204; repr. in Jacoby (2001c), no. 7

—(2000b), 'The production of silk textiles in Latin Greece', in *Technognosia ste latinokratoumene Ellada: emerida, Athena, 8 Fevrouariou 1997, Gennadeios Bibliotheke*, Athens, pp. 22–35; repr. in Jacoby (2005b), no. 12

—(2001a), 'Changing economic patterns in Latin Romania: the impact of the west', in Laiou and Mottahedeh (eds.) (2001), pp. 197–233; repr. in Jacoby (2005b), no. 9

—(2001b), 'The Venetian quarter of Constantinople from 1082 to 1261: topographical considerations', in Sode and Takács (eds.) (2001), pp. 153–70; repr. in Jacoby (2005b), no. 3

—(2001c), *Byzantium, Latin Romania and the Mediterranean*, Aldershot

—(2002), 'La Consolidation de la domination de Venise dans la ville de Négrepont (1205–1390): un aspect de sa politique coloniale', in Maltezou and Schreiner (eds.) (2002), pp. 151–87

—(2004a), 'Silk economics and cross-cultural artistic interaction: Byzantium, the Muslim world and the Christian west', *DOP* 58, pp. 197–240

—(2004b), 'The demographic evolution of Euboea under Latin rule, 1205–1470', in Chrysostomides *et al.* (eds.) (2004), pp. 131–79

—(2005a), 'The economy of Latin Constantinople, 1204–1261', in Laiou (ed.) (2005), pp. 195–214

—(2005b), *Commercial exchange across the Mediterranean: Byzantium, the Crusader Levant, Egypt and Italy*, Aldershot

—(2005c), 'Les Latins dans les villes de Romanie jusqu'en 1261: le versant méditerranéen des Balkans', in Balard *et al.* (eds.) (2005), pp. 13–26

—(2006), 'The Venetian government and administration in Latin Constantinople, 1204–1261: a state within a state', in Ortalli *et al.* (eds.) (2006), I, pp. 21–82

Jeffreys, E. and Jeffreys, M. J. (1983), *Popular literature in late Byzantium*, London

Jeffreys, E. and Jeffreys, M. J. (1986), 'The oral background of Byzantine popular poetry', *Oral Tradition* 1, pp. 504–47

Jeffreys, M. J. (1975), 'The *Chronicle of the Morea*: priority of the Greek version', *BZ* 68, pp. 304–50

Jerusalimskaja, A. A. (2003), 'Les Soieries byzantines à la lumière des influences orientales: les thèmes importés et leurs interpretations dans le monde occidental', *Bulletin du CIETA* 80, pp. 16–25

Jireček, K. (1911–18), *Geschichte der Serben*, 2 vols., Gotha

—(1916a), 'Albanien in der Vergangenheit', in von Thallóczy (ed.) (1916), I, pp. 63–93

—(1916b), 'Skutari und sein Gebiet im Mittelalter', in von Thallóczy (ed.) (1916), I, pp. 94–124

Jones, A. H. M. and Monroe, E. (1966), *A history of Ethiopia*, Oxford

Jugie, M. (1928), 'Démetrius Cydonès et la théologie latine à Byzance du XIVe et XVe siècles', *EO* 27, pp. 385–402

Kabrda, J. (1969), *Le Système fiscal de l'église orthodoxe dans l'empire ottoman d'après les documents turcs*, Brno

Kaimakamova, M. *et al.* (eds.) (2007), *Byzantium, new peoples and powers: the Byzantino-Slav contact-zone, from the ninth to the fifteenth century*, Cracow

Kalić, J. (1979), 'Crkvene prilike u srpskim zemljama do stvaranja arhiepiskopije 1219. godine', in Đurić (ed.) (1979), pp. 27–53

Kalligas, H. A. (1990), *Byzantine Monemvasia: the sources*, Monemvasia

—(ed.) (1994), *Travellers and officials in the Peloponnese. Descriptions – reports – statistics, in honour of Sir Steven Runciman*, Monemvasia

Karlin-Hayter, P. (1990), 'Indissolubility and the "greater evil": three thirteenth-century divorce cases', in Morris (ed.) (1990), pp. 87–105

Karpov, S. P. (1986), *L'impero di Trebisonda, Venezia, Genova e Roma, 1204–1461: rapporti politici, diplomatici e commerciali*, tr. E. Zambelli, Rome; tr. of Karpov, S. P. (1981), *Trapezundskaia imperiia i zapadnoevropeiskie gosudarstva v XIII–XV vv.*, Moscow

—(1993), 'The grain trade in the southern Black Sea region: the thirteenth to the fifteenth century', *MHR* 8, pp. 55–73

—(1995a), 'New documents on the relations between the Latins and the local populations in the Black Sea area (1392–1462)', *DOP* 49, pp. 33–41

—(1995b), 'On the origin of medieval Tana', *BSl* 56, pp. 227–35

—(2000), *La navigazione veneziana nel Mar Nero: XIII–XV sec.*, tr. G. Fanti and M. Bakhmatova, Ravenna; tr. of Karpov, S. P. (1994), *Putiami srednevekovykh morekhodov: chernomorskaia navigatsiia Venetsianskoi respubliki v XIII-XV vv.*, Moscow

—(2004), 'Les Empereurs de Trébizonde, débiteurs des Génois', in Coulon *et al.* (eds.) (2004), pp. 489–94

—(2005), 'The Black Sea region, before and after the Fourth Crusade', in Laiou (ed.) (2005), pp. 283–92

Karpov, S. P. and Mogarichev, I. M. (eds.) (1995), *Vizantiia i srednevekovyi Krym*, Simferopol

Karpozilos, A. D. (1973), *The ecclesiastical controversy between the kingdom of Nicaea and the principality of Epiros 1217–1233*, Thessalonica

Kazhdan, A. P. (1980), 'L'*Histoire* de Cantacuzène en tant qu'oeuvre littéraire', *Byz* 50, pp. 279–335; repr. in Kazhdan (1993a), no. 16

—(1982), 'The fate of the intellectual in Byzantium', *The Greek Orthodox Theological Review* 27, pp. 83–97; repr. in Kazhdan (1993a), no. 15

—(1993a), *Authors and texts in Byzantium*, Aldershot

—(1993b), 'State, feudal and private economy in Byzantium', *DOP* 47, pp. 83–100

—(1995), 'The Italian and late Byzantine City', *DOP* 49, pp. 1–22

Khristova, D. *et al.* (1982), *B'lgarski r'kopisi ot XI do XVIII vek, zapazeni v B'lgariia. Svoden katalog*, Sofia

Kianka, F. (1995), 'Demetrios Kydones and Italy', *DOP* 49, pp. 99–110

Kiilerich, B. (2004), 'Aesthetic aspects of Palaiologan art in Constantinople: some problems', in Rosenqvist (ed.) (2004), pp. 11–26

Koder, J. (1973), *Negroponte: Untersuchungen zur Topographie und Siedlungsgeschichte der Insel Euboia während der Zeit der Venezianerherrschaft*, TIB 1, Vienna

Kolbaba, T. M. (1995), 'Conversion from Greek orthodoxy to Roman catholicism in the fourteenth century', *BMGS* 19, pp. 120–34

—(1997), 'Meletios Homologetes *On the customs of the Italians*', *REB* 55, pp. 137–68

—(2000), *The Byzantine lists: errors of the Latins*, Urbana, IL

Kordoses, M. S. (1987), *Southern Greece under the Franks (1204–1262): a study of the Greek population and the orthodox church under the Frankish dominion*, Ioannina

Korobeinikov, D. (2003), 'Orthodox communities in eastern Anatolia in the thirteenth and fourteenth centuries, I: the two patriarchates: Constantinople and Antioch', *Al-Masaq* 15, pp. 197–214

—(2004b), 'Diplomatic correspondence between Byzantium and the Mamluk sultanate in the fourteenth century', *Al-Masaq* 16, pp. 53–74

—(2005), 'Orthodox communities in eastern Anatolia in the thirteenth and fourteenth centuries, II: the time of troubles', *Al-Masaq* 17, pp. 1–29

Kovačević-Kolić, D. (2004), 'Les Métaux précieux de Serbie et le marché Européen (XIVe–XVe siècles)', *ZRVI* 41, pp. 191–203

Krantonelle, A. (1964), *E kata ton Latinon, Helleno-Boulgarike sympraxis en Thrake 1204–1206*, Athens

Kraus, C. R. (2007), *Kleriker im späten Byzanz: Anagnosten, Hypodiakone, Diakone, Priester 1261–1453*, Wiesbaden

Krausmüller, D. (2006), 'The rise of hesychasm', in Angold (ed.) (2006), pp. 101–26

Kravari, V. (1989), *Villes et villages de Macédoine occidentale*, Paris

Krekić, B. (1961), *Dubrovnik (Raguse) et le levant au moyen âge*, Paris and The Hague

—(1973), 'Le relazioni fra Venezia, Ragusa e le popolazioni serbo-croate', in Pertusi (ed.) (1973–4), I. 1, pp. 389–401

Kremmydas, V. *et al.* (eds.) (1986), *Aphieroma ston Niko Svorono*, 2 vols., Rethymnon

Kresten, O. (2000b), *Die Beziehungen zwischen den Patriarchaten von Konstantinopel und Antiocheia unter Kallistos I. und Philotheos Kokkinos im Spiegel des Patriarchatsregisters von Konstantinopel*, Mainz

Kypraiou, E. (ed.) (1991–2), *Euphrosynon: aphieroma ston Manole Chatzedake*, 2 vols., Athens

Laiou, A. E. (1970), 'Marino Sanudo Torsello, Byzantium and the Turks; the background to the Anti-Turkish League of 1332–1334', *Sp* 45, pp. 374–92

—(1972), *Constantinople and the Latins: the foreign policy of Andronicus II, 1282–1328*, Cambridge, MA

—(1973), 'The Byzantine aristocracy in the Palaeologan period: a story of arrested development', *Viator* 4, pp. 131–51; repr. in Laiou (1992c), no. 6

—(1977) [Laiou-Thomadakis], *Peasant society in the late Byzantine empire: a social and demographic study*, Princeton

—(1980–1), 'The Byzantine economy in the Mediterranean trade system: thirteenth–fifteenth centuries', *DOP* 34–5, pp. 177–222; repr. in Laiou (1992c), no. 7

—(1981), 'The role of women in Byzantine society', *JÖB* 31, pp. 233–60; repr. in Laiou (1992c), no. 1

—(1982), 'The Greek merchant of the Palaeologan period: a collective portrait', *The Proceedings of the Academy of Athens*, pp. 96–132; repr. in Laiou (1992c), no. 8

—(1984), 'Observations on the results of the Fourth Crusade: Greeks and Latins in port and market', *Medievalia et humanistica* n.s. 12, pp. 47–60

—(1985), 'In the medieval Balkans: economic pressures and conflicts in the fourteenth century', in Vryonis (ed.) (1985), pp. 137–62; repr. in Laiou (1992c), no. 9

—(1987), 'Un notaire vénitien à Constantinople: Antonio Bresciano et le commerce international en 1350', in Balard *et al.* (eds.) (1987), pp. 79–151

—(1991a), 'The foreigner and the stranger in twelfth-century Byzantium: means of propitiation and acculturation', in Fögen (ed.) (1991), pp. 71–98

—(1991b), 'Sto Byzantio ton Palaiologon: oikonomika kai politistika phainomena', in Kypraiou (ed.) (1991–2), I, pp. 283–96

—(1992a), 'Venetians and Byzantines: investigation of forms of contact in the fourteenth century', *Thesaurismata* 22, pp. 29–43

—(1992b), *Mariage, amour et parenté à Byzance aux XIe–XIIIe siècles*, Paris

—(1992c), *Gender, society and economic life in Byzantium*, Aldershot

—(1993), 'On political geography: the Black Sea of Pachymeres', in Beaton and Roueché (eds.) (1993), pp. 94–121

—(1995a), 'Italy and the Italians in the political geography of the Byzantines (14th century)', *DOP* 49, pp. 73–98

—(1995b), 'Peasant rebellion: notes on its vocabulary and typology', in Fögen (ed.) (1995), pp. 99–117

—(1995c), 'E Thessalonike, e endochora tes kai o oikonomikos tes choros sten epoche ton Palaiologon', in *Byzantine Makedonia, 324–1430 m. Ch., Thessalonike, 29–31 Oktobriou 1992: diethnes symposio*, Thessalonica, pp. 183–94

—(1997), 'Byzantium and the commercial revolution', in Arnaldi and Cavallo (eds.) (1997), pp. 239–53

—(1998), 'Marriage prohibitions, marriage strategies and the dowry in thirteenth-century Byzantium', in Beaucamp and Dagron (eds.) (1998), pp. 129–60

—(2000), 'The economy of Byzantine Macedonia in the Palaiologan period', in Burke and Scott (eds.) (2000), pp. 199–211

—(2002e), 'The agrarian economy, thirteenth–fifteenth centuries', in *EHB*, III, pp. 311–75

—(ed.) (1980) [Laiou-Thomadakis], *Charanis studies: essays in honor of Peter Charanis*, New Brunswick, NJ

—(ed.) (2005), *Urbs capta: the Fourth Crusade and its consequences*, Paris

—(ed.) (in preparation), *Le Monde byzantin*, III: *1204–1453*, Paris

Laiou, A. E. and Mottahedeh, R. P. (eds.) (2001), *The crusades from the perspective of Byzantium and the Muslim world*, Washington, DC

Laiou, A. E. and Simon, D. (1992), 'Eine Geschichte von Mühlen und Mönchen: der Fall der Mühlen von Chantax', *Bullettino dell'Istituto di diritto romano 'Vittorio Scialoja'*, 3rd series 30, pp. 619–76

Laiou-Thomadakis, see under Laiou

Lampropoulos, K. (1988), *Ioannes Apokaukos: symbole sten ereuna tou biou kai tou syngraphikou ergou tou*, Athens

Lane, F. C. (1974), 'Progrès technologiques et productivité dans les transports maritimes de la fin du moyen âge au début des temps modernes', *RH* 510, pp. 277–302

Langdon, J. S. (1992), *Byzantium's last imperial offensive in Asia Minor: the documentary evidence for and hagiographical lore about John III Ducas Vatatzes' crusade against the Turks, 1222 or 1225 to 1231*, New Rochelle, NY

Langdon, J. S. et al. (eds.) (1993), *To Hellenikon: studies in honor of Speros Vryonis, Jr.*, 2 vols., New Rochelle, NY

Laskaris, M. (1926), *Vizantijske princeze u srednjovekovnoj Srbiji*, Belgrade; repr. 1990

Lauer, R. and Schreiner, P. (eds.) (1996), *Die Kultur Griechenlands in Mittelalter und Neuzeit: Bericht über das Kolloquium der Südosteuropa-Kommission 28.–31. Oktober 1992*, Göttingen

Laurent, V. (1938), 'Grégoire X (1271–1276) et le projet d'une ligue antiturque', *EO* 37, pp. 257–73

—(1968), 'Les Premiers Patriarches de Constantinople sous domination Turque (1454–1476)', *REB* 26, pp. 229–63

—(ed.) (1948), *Mémorial Louis Petit*, Bucharest

Lefort, J. (1982), *Villages de Macédoine: notices historiques et topographiques sur la Macédoine orientale au moyen âge*, I: *La Chalcidique occidentale*, Paris

—(1985), 'Radolibus: populations et paysage', *TM* 9, pp. 195–234; repr. in Lefort (2006), no. 6, pp. 161–200

—(1986a), 'Population and landscape in eastern Macedonia during the middle ages: the example of Radolibos', in Bryer and Lowry (eds.) (1986), pp. 11–21

—(1986b), 'Une exploitation de taille moyenne au XIIIe siècle en Chalcidique', in Kremmydas *et al.* (eds.) (1986), I, pp. 362–72; repr. in Lefort (2006), no. 7, pp. 201–9

—(1991), 'Population et peuplement en Macédoine orientale, IXe–XVe siècle', in Kravari *et al.* (eds.) (1991), II, pp. 63–82; repr. in Lefort (2006), no. 9, pp. 229–47

—(1993), 'Rural economy and social relations in the countryside', *DOP* 47, pp. 101–13; repr. in Lefort (2006), no. 12, pp. 279–92

—(2006), *Société rurale et histoire du paysage à Byzance*, Paris

—(ed.) (1986), *Paysages de Macédoine, leurs caractères, leur évolution à travers les documents et les récits des voyageurs*, Paris

Lemerle, P. (1945), *Philippes et la Macédoine orientale à l'époque chrétienne et byzantine: recherches d'histoire et d'archéologie*, 2 vols., Paris

—(1948), 'Le Juge général des Grecs et la réforme judiciaire d'Andronic III', in Laurent (ed.) (1948), pp. 292–316; repr. in Lemerle (1978), no. 10

—(1949), 'Recherches sur les institutions judiciaires à l'époque des Paléologues, I: le tribunal impérial', *AIPHO* 9, pp. 369–84; repr. in Lemerle (1978), no. 11

—(1950), 'Recherches sur les institutions judiciaires à l'époque des Paléologues, II: le tribunal du patriarcat ou tribunal synodal', *AnBoll* 68, pp. 318–33; repr. in Lemerle (1978), no. 12

—(1957), *L'Émirat d'Aydin, Byzance et l'Occident: recherches sur 'La Geste d'Umur pacha'*, Paris

—(1964), 'Documents et problèmes nouveaux concernant les juges généraux', *DChAE* 4, pp. 29–44; repr. in Lemerle (1978), no. 14

—(1978), *Le monde de Byzance: histoire et institutions*, London

Lewis, B. (1984), *The Jews of Islam*, London

Lidov, A. (ed.) (2003), *Eastern Christian relics*, Moscow

Lingas, A. (2006), 'Medieval Byzantine chant and the sound of orthodoxy', in Louth and Casiday (eds.) (2006), pp. 131–50

Lock, P. (2006), 'Freestanding towers in the countryside of Rhodes', in Jeffreys, E. (ed.) (2006), pp. 374–93

Loenertz, R.-J. (1965), 'Mémoire d'Ogier, protonotaire, pour Marco et Marchetto nonces de Michel VIII Paléologue auprès du pape Nicholas III, 1278 printemps-été', *OCP* 31, pp. 374–408

—(1970–8), *Byzantina et Franco-Graeca*, ed. P. Schreiner *et al.*, 2 vols., Rome

Loenertz, R.-J. and Schreiner, P. (1975), *Les Ghisi: dynastes vénitiens dans l'Archipel, 1207–1390*, Florence

Longnon, J. (1949), *L'Empire latin de Constantinople et la principauté de Morée*, Paris

—(1950), 'La Reprise de Salonique par les Grecs en 1224', *ACIEB* 6, pp. 141–6

—(1969), 'The Frankish states in Greece 1204–1311', in Setton (ed.) (1969–89), II, pp. 235–74

Longo, A. A. (1985–6), 'Per la storia di Corfù nel XIII secolo', *RSBN* n.s. 22–3, pp. 209–43

Lounghis, T. C. (2003), 'Byzantines logies apopseis peri chrematos kai agoras to 14 aiona', in *Chrema kai agora sten epoche ton Palaiologon*, ed. N. G. Moschonas, Athens, 2003, pp. 349–63

Lowry, H. W. (1981), *Trabzon şehrinin islâmaşma ve Türkleşmesi, 1461–1583*, Istanbul

—(1986a), 'Privilege and property in Ottoman Maçuka during the opening decades of the *Tourkokratia*, 1461–1553', in Bryer and Lowry (eds.) (1986), pp. 97–128

—(1986b), '"From lesser wars to the mightiest war": the Ottoman conquest and the transformation of Byzantine urban centers in the fifteenth century', in Bryer and Lowry (eds.) (1986), pp. 321–38

—(1991), 'The fate of Byzantine monastic properties under the Ottomans: examples from Mount Athos, Limnos and Trabzon', in Bryer and Ursinus (eds.) (1991), pp. 275–311

Luttrell, A. T. (1982), *Latin Greece, the Hospitallers, and the Crusades, 1291–1440*, Aldershot

—(1992), *The Hospitallers of Rhodes and their Mediterranean world*, Aldershot

McKee, S. (2000), *Uncommon dominion: Venetian Crete and the myth of ethnic purity*, Philadelphia

Macrides, R. (1980), 'The new Constantine and the new Constantinople – 1261?', *BMGS* 6, pp. 13–41

—(1981), 'Saints and sainthood in the early Palaiologan period', in Hackel (ed.) (1981), pp. 67–87

—(1992b), 'Bad historian or good lawyer? Demetrios Chomatenos and novel 131', *DOP* 46, pp. 187–96; repr. in Macrides (1999), no. 12

—(1994b), 'From the Komnenoi to the Palaiologoi: imperial models in decline and exile', in Magdalino (ed.) (1994), pp. 269–82

—(1999), *Kinship and justice in Byzantium, 11th–15th centuries*, Aldershot

—(2003a), 'The thirteenth century in Byzantine historical writing', in Dendrinos *et al.* (eds.) (2003), pp. 63–76

—(2003b), 'George Akropolites' rhetoric', in Jeffreys, E. (ed.) (2003), pp. 201–11

—(2004), 'The ritual of petition', in Yatromanolakis and Roilos (eds.) (2004), pp. 356–70

—(2005), '1204: the Greek sources', in Laiou (ed.) (2005), pp. 141–50

Madden, T. F. (2003), *Enrico Dandolo and the rise of Venice*, Baltimore

—(ed.) (2004), *Crusades: the illustrated history*, London

Magdalino, P. (1977), 'A neglected authority for the history of the Peloponnese in the early thirteenth century: Demetrios Chomatianos, archbishop of Bulgaria', *BZ* 70, pp. 316–23

Majeska, G. P. (1991), 'Russo-Byzantine relations 1240–1453: a traffic report', *ACIEB* 18, V, pp. 27–51

—(2003), 'Russian pilgrims and the relics of Constantinople', in Lidov (ed.) (2003), pp. 387–96

Maksimović, L. (1973), 'Geneza i karakter apanaža u Vizantiji', *ZRVI* 14–15, pp. 103–54

—(1981a), 'Trijumf Vizantije početkom XI veka', in Gavrilović *et al.* (eds.) (1981–3), I, pp. 170–9

—(1981b), 'Charakter der sozial-wirtschaftlichen Struktur der spätbyzantinischen Stadt', *JÖB* 31, pp. 149–88

—(1988), *The Byzantine provincial administration under the Palaiologoi*, tr. M. Heppell, Amsterdam

—(2000), 'Byzantinische Herrscherideologie und Regierungsmethoden im Falle Serbien: ein Beitrag zum Verständnis des byzantinischen Commonwealth', in Scholz and Makris (eds.) (2000), pp. 174–92

—(2002), 'L'Empire de Stefan Dušan: genèse et caractère', *TM* 14, pp. 414–28

—(2004), 'Verija u politici Stefana Dušana', *ZRVI* 41, pp. 341–52

—(2005), 'La Serbie et les contrées voisines avant et après la IVᵉ croisade', in Laiou (ed.) (2005), pp. 269–82

Malamut, E. (1997), 'Echanges d'ambassades dans les Balkans (1204–1260): signes d'une idéologie politique', in Mornet and Morenzoni (eds.) (1997), pp 621–34

—(2000), 'Les Reines de Milutin', *BZ* 93, pp. 490–507

—(2002a), 'Les Ambassades du dernier empereur de Byzance', *TM* 14, pp. 429–48

—(2002b), 'La Circulation des Ms grecs en Europe, milieu XIVᵉ–milieu XVᵉ siècle', in Giuzelev and Miltenova (eds.) (2002), pp. 85–113

—(2003), 'Cinquante ans à Thessalonique: de 1280 à 1330', *ZRVI* 40, pp. 263–96

—(2004b), 'Travellers in the Aegean Islands from the twelfth to the sixteenth century', in Chrysostomides *et al.* (eds.) (2004), pp. 181–97

Maltezou, C. A. (1978 [1979]), 'Il quartiere veneziano di Costantinopoli (scali marittimi)', *Thesaurismata* 15, pp. 30–61

—(2003), 'Ellenes kai Italoi emporoi sten Anaia tes Mikras Asias (arches 14ou ai.)', in Dendrinos *et al.* (eds.) (2003), pp. 253–63

—(ed.) (1998), *Plousioi kai phtochoi sten koinonia tes Ellenolatinikes Anatoles (Ricchi e poveri nella società dell'oriente grecolatino)*, Venice

Maltezou, C. A. and Schreiner, P. (eds.) (2002), *Bisanzio, Venezia e il mondo franco-greco (XIII–XV secolo)*, Venice

Mango, C. (1962), *Materials for the study of the mosaics of St Sophia at Istanbul*, *DOSt* 8, Washington, DC

—(1988–9), 'The tradition of Byzantine chronography', *HUS* 12–13, pp. 360–72

Mango, C. and Dagron, G. (eds.) (1995), *Constantinople and its hinterland: papers from the twenty-seventh spring symposium of Byzantine studies, Oxford, April 1993*, Aldershot

Maniatis, G. C. (2001), 'The domain of private guilds in the Byzantine economy, tenth to fifteenth centuries', *DOP* 55, pp. 339–69

Mansouri, M. T. (1992a), *Recherches sur les relations entre Byzance et l'Egypte, 1259–1453: d'après les sources arabes*, Tunis

—(1992b), 'Byzantins, Mamluks et Mongols aux alentours de 1265: la politique étrangère de Michel VIII Paléologue au début de son règne', *Byzantiaka* 12, pp. 315–24

Marjanović-Dušanić, S. (2004), 'Molitve svetih Simeona i Save u vladarskom programu kralja Milutina', *ZRVI* 41, pp. 235–50

Marković, M. (1952), 'Vizantijske povelje Dubrovačkog arhiva', *ZRVI* 1, pp. 205–62

Martin, J. (1995), *Medieval Russia, 980–1584*, Cambridge

Martin, J.-M. (2002), '*O felix Asia!* Frédéric II, l'Empire de Nicée et le "césaropapisme"', *TM* 14, pp. 473–83

Mathew, G. (1963), *Byzantine aesthetics*, London

Matschke, K.-P. (1969), 'Rolle und Aufgaben des Gouverneurs von Konstantinopel in der Palaiologenzeit', *BB* 3, pp. 81–101

—(1970), 'Zum Charakter des byzantinischen Schwarzmeerhandels im 13. bis 15. Jahrhundert', *Wissenschaftliche Zeitschrift der Karl-Marx-Universität Leipzig* 19, pp. 447–58

—(1971), *Fortschritt und Reaktion in Byzanz im 14. Jahrhundert. Konstantinopel in der Bürgerkriegsperiode von 1341 bis 1354*, Berlin

—(1979), 'Geldgeschäfte, Handel und Gewerbe in spätbyzantinischen Rechenbüchern und in der spätbyzantinischen Wirklichkeit: ein Beitrag zu den Produktions- und Austauschverhältnissen im byzantinischen Feudalismus', *Jahrbuch für Geschichte des Feudalismus* 3, pp. 181–204

—(1981a), *Die Schlacht bei Ankara und das Schicksal von Byzanz*, Weimar

—(1981b) 'Bemerkungen zu den sozialen Trägern des spätbyzantinischen Seehandels', *BB* 7, pp. 253–61

—(1981c), 'Sozialschichten und Geisteshaltungen', *JÖB* 31, pp. 189–212

—(1989), 'Tuchproduktion und Tuchproduzenten in Thessalonike und in anderen Städten und Regionen des späten Byzanz', *Byzantiaka* 9, pp. 47–87

—(1991), 'Bemerkungen zu den Mikro- und Makrostrukturen der spätbyzantinischen Gesellschaft', *ACIEB* 18, V, pp. 152–95

—(1984a), 'Byzantinische Politiker und byzantinische Kaufleute im Ringen um die Beteiligung am Schwarzmeerhandel in der Mitte des 14. Jh.', *Mitteilungen des Bulgarischen Forschungsinstituts in Österreich* 6, pp. 75–90

—(1984b), 'Grund- und Hauseigentum in und um Konstantinopel in spätbyzantinischer Zeit', *Jahrbuch für Wirtschaftsgeschichte* 4, pp. 103–28

—(1993), 'Die spätbyzantinische Öffentlichkeit', in Tanz (ed.) (1993), pp. 155–223

—(1995), 'The Notaras family and its Italian connections', *DOP* 49, pp. 59–72

—(1997), 'Some merchant families in Constantinople before, during and after the fall of the city 1453', *Balkan studies* 38, pp. 219–38

—(2002a), 'The late Byzantine urban economy, thirteenth-fifteenth centuries', in *EHB*, II, pp. 463–95

—(2002b), 'Commerce, trade, markets and money: thirteenth-fifteenth centuries', in *EHB*, II, pp. 771–806

—(2005), 'Bemerkungen zur Stadtgeschichte Thessalonikes in spätbyzantinischer Zeit', in Hoffmann and Monchizadeh (eds.) (2005), pp. 433–44

Mavromatis, L. (1973), 'La Prise de Skopje par les Serbes: date et signification', *TM* 5, pp. 329–34

—(1978), *La Fondation de l'empire serbe: le kralj Milutin*, Thessalonica

Mayer, H. E. (ed.) (1997), *Die Kreuzfahrerstaaten als multikulturelle Gesellschaft: Einwanderer und Minderheiten im 12. und 13. Jahrhundert*, Munich

Mazarakis, A. (ed.) (1996), *Praktika synedriou 'Oi Gatelouzoi tes Lesbou', 9–11 septembriou 1994, Mytilini*, Athens

Ménage, V. (1965), 'Djandar', in *EI*, II, pp. 444–5

Merendino, E. (1975), 'Federico II e Giovanni III Vatatzes', in *Byzantino-sicula*, II: *Miscellanea di scritti in memoria di Giuseppe Rossi Taibbi*, Palermo, pp. 371–83

Mergiali, S. (1996), *L'Enseignement et les lettrés pendant l'époque des paléologues (1261–1453)*, Athens

Mergiali-Sahas, S. (2001a), 'A Byzantine ambassador to the west and his office during the fourteenth and fifteenth centuries: a profile', *BZ* 94, pp. 588–604

—(2001b), 'Byzantine emperors and holy relics: use, and misuse, of sanctity and authority', *JÖB* 51, pp. 41–60

Mertzios, K. (1947), *Mnemeia Makedonikes istorias*, Thessalonica

Metcalf, D. M. (1979), *Coinage in south-eastern Europe, 820–1396*, 2nd edn., London

Meyendorff, J. (1964), *A study of Gregory Palamas*, tr. G. Lawrence, London

—(1971), 'Spiritual trends in Byzantium in the late thirteenth and early fourteenth centuries', in *Art et Société à Byzance sous les Paléologues: actes du colloque organisé par l'Association internationale des études byzantines à Venise en Septembre 1968*, Venice, 1971, pp. 53–71; repr. in Underwood (ed.) (1966–75), IV, pp. 93–106

—(1974a), *Byzantine hesychasm: historical, theological and social problems: collected studies*, London

—(1974b), 'Society and culture in the fourteenth century: religious problems', *ACIEB* 14, I, pp. 111–24; repr. in Meyendorff (1974a), no. 8

—(1974c), *St Gregory Palamas and orthodox spirituality*, tr. A. Fiske, Crestwood, NY

—(1979), *Byzantine theology: historical trends and doctrinal themes*, 2nd edn., New York

—(1981), *Byzantium and the rise of Russia: a study of Byzantino-Russian relations in the fourteenth century*, Cambridge

—(1988), 'Mount Athos in the fourteenth century: spiritual and intellectual legacy', *DOP* 42, pp. 157–65

Micheau, F. (2006), 'Eastern Christianities (eleventh to fourteenth century): Copts, Melkites, Nestorians and Jacobites', in Angold (ed.) (2006), pp. 373–403

Miller, W. (1908), *The Latins in the Levant: a history of Frankish Greece, 1204–1566*, London; repr. New York, 1979

—(1921), *Essays on the Latin Orient*, Cambridge; repr. New York, 1983

Mirdita, Z. (1981), *Antroponimia e Dardanisë në kohën romake (L'anthroponymie de la Dardanie à l'époque romaine)*, Pristina

Molin, K. (2001), *Unknown crusader castles*, London and New York

Mollat du Jourdin, M. *et al.* (eds.) (1990), *Un temps d'épreuves (1274–1449), HC* 6, Paris

Monfasani, J. (1995), *Byzantine scholars in Renaissance Italy: Cardinal Bessarion and other emigrés: selected essays*, Aldershot

—(2004), *Greeks and Latins in Renaissance Italy: studies on humanism and philosophy in the 15th century*, Aldershot

Morgan, G. (1976), 'The Venetian claims commission of 1278', *BZ* 69, pp. 411–38

Mornet, E. and Morenzoni, F. (eds.) (1997), *Milieux naturels, espaces sociaux: études offertes à Robert Delort*, Paris

Morrisson, C. (1991), 'Monnaie et finances dans l'empire byzantin, X^e–XVe siècle', in Kravari *et al.* (eds.) (1989–91), II, pp. 291–315

—(2005), 'L'Ouverture des marchés après 1204: un aspect positif de la IVe croisade?', in Laiou (ed.) (2005), pp. 215–32

Mouriki, D. (1991), 'The wall paintings of the Pantanassa at Mistra: models of a painter's workshop in the fifteenth century', in Čurčič and Mouriki (eds.) (1991), pp. 217–50

Müller, A. E. (2005), 'Zur Datierung des Chrysobulls Michaels VIII. für Ochrid: nicht August 1272, sondern Juli 1273', in Hoffmann and Monchizadeh (eds.) (2005), pp. 427–32

Munitiz, J. A. (1981), 'Self-canonisation: the 'Partial Account' of Nikephoros Blemmydes', in Hackel (ed.) (1981), pp. 164–8

—(1990), 'A reappraisal of Blemmydes' first discussion with the Latins', *BSl* 51, pp. 20–6

—(1992), 'Hagiographical autobiography in the thirteenth century', *BSl* 53, pp. 243–9

—(2003), 'Blemmydes revisited: the letters of Nicephorus Blemmydes to Patriarch Manuel II', in Dendrinos *et al.* (eds.) (2003), pp. 369–87

Năstase, D. (1983), 'Le Patronage du Mont Athos au XIIIe siècle', *Cyrillomethodianum* 7, pp. 71–87

—(1985), 'Le Mont Athos pendant l'occupation latine de Constantinople: quelques considérations', *BNJ* 22, pp. 126–30

Năsturel, P. Ş. (1986), *Le Mont Athos et les Roumains: recherches sur leurs relations du milieu du XIVe siècle à 1654*, OCA 227, Rome

Necipoğlu, N. (1992), 'Ottoman merchants in Constantinople during the first half of the fifteenth century', *BMGS* 16, pp. 158–69

—(2000), 'Constantinopolitan merchants and the question of their attitudes towards Italians and Ottomans in the late Palaiologan period', in Scholz and Makris (eds.) (2000), pp. 251–63

—(2003), 'The aristocracy in late Byzantine Thessalonike: a case study of the city's *archontes* (late 14th and early 15th centuries)', *DOP* 57, pp. 133–52

—(forthcoming), *Politics and society in the later Byzantine empire: Byzantium between the Ottomans and the Latins*, Cambridge

—(ed.) (2001), *Byzantine Constantinople: monuments, topography and everyday life*, Leiden

Nelson, R. S. (1991), *Theodore Hagiopetrites, a late Byzantine scribe and illuminator*, 2 vols., Vienna

Nelson, R. S. and Lowden, J. (1991), 'The Palaeologina group: additional manuscripts and new questions', *DOP* 45, pp. 59–68

Nicol, D. M. (1956), 'The date of the battle of Pelagonia', *BZ* 49, pp. 68–71

—(1957), *The despotate of Epiros*, Oxford

—(1968), *The Byzantine family of Kantakouzenos (Cantacuzenus) ca. 1100–1460: a genealogical and prosopographical study*, DOSt 11, Washington, DC

—(1971), 'The Byzantine reaction to the second council of Lyons, 1274', *SCH* 7, pp. 113–46; repr. in Nicol (1972b), no. 6

—(1972a), 'The relations of Charles of Anjou with Nikephoros of Epiros', *BF* 4, pp. 170–94; repr. in Nicol (1986), no. 5

—(1972b), *Byzantium: its ecclesiastical history and relations with the western world: collected studies*, London

—(1974), 'Byzantium and England', *Balkan Studies* 15, pp. 179–203; repr. in Nicol (1986), no. 17

—(1976a), '*Kaisersalbung*: the unction of emperors in late Byzantine coronation ritual', *BMGS* 2, pp. 37–52; repr. in Nicol (1986), no. 1

—(1976b), 'Refugees, mixed population and local patriotism in Epiros and western Macedonia after the Fourth Crusade', *XVᵉ Congrès international d'études byzantines: rapports et co-rapports: Histoire*, Athens, 1976; repr. in Nicol (1986), no. 4

—(1982), 'Thessalonica as a cultural centre in the fourteenth century', *E Thessalonike metaxy Anatoles kai Dyseos: praktika symposiou tessarakontaeteridos tes Etaireias Makedonikon Spoudon, 30 Oktobriou–1 Noembriou 1980*, Thessalonica, pp. 121–31; repr. in Nicol (1986), no. 10

—(1984), *The despotate of Epiros, 1267–1479: a contribution to the history of Greece in the middle ages*, Cambridge

—(1986), *Studies in late Byzantine history and prosopography*, London

—(1989), 'Popular religious roots of the Byzantine reaction to the second council of Lyons', in Ryan (ed.) (1989), pp. 321–39

—(1994), *The Byzantine lady: ten portraits, 1250–1500*, Cambridge

—(1996), *The reluctant emperor: a biography of John Cantacuzene, Byzantine emperor and monk, c. 1295–1383*, Cambridge

Norden, W. (1903), *Das Papsttum und Byzanz*, Berlin

Nörr, D. and Simon, D. (eds.) (1984), *Gedächtnisschrift für Wolfgang Kunkel*, Frankfurt-am-Main

Nystazopoulou, M. (1964), 'O "Alanikos" tou episkopou Alanias Theodorou kai e eis ton patriarchikon thronon anarrhesis Germanou tou 2 (chronologike diakribosis)', *EEBS* 33, pp. 270–8

Nystazopoulou-Pélékidis, M. (1973), 'Venise et la Mer Noire du XIᵉ au XVᵉ siècle', in Pertusi (ed.) (1973–4), I, pp. 541–82

—(1983), 'Sur la diplomatique byzantine à l'époque de l'empire de Nicée', *Byzantiaka* 3, pp. 161–73

Obolensky, D. (1974), 'The cult of St Demetrius of Thessaloniki in the history of Byzantine-Slav relations', *Balkan studies* 15, pp. 3–20; repr. in Obolensky (1982), no. 4; repr. in Obolensky (1994), pp. 281–300

—(1982), *The Byzantine inheritance of eastern Europe*, London

—(1994), *Byzantium and the Slavs*, Crestwood, NY

Oikonomides, N. (1969), 'Le Haradj dans l'empire byzantin du XVᵉ siècle', *Actes du Iᵉʳ Congrès international des études balkaniques et sud-est européennes*, III, Sofia, pp. 681–8; repr. in Oikonomides (1976b), no. 19

—(1976c), 'Monastères et moines lors de la conquête ottomane', *SF* 35, pp. 1–10

—(1976d), 'La Décomposition de l'empire byzantin à la veille de 1204 et les origines de l'empire de Nicée: à propos de la "Partitio Romaniae"', *XVe Congrès international d'études byzantines: rapports et co-rapports*, Athens, 1976; repr. in Oikonomides (1992a), no. 20

—(1979a), *Hommes d'affaires grecs et latins à Constantinople (XIIIe–XVe siècles)*, Paris and Montreal

—(1980), 'The properties of the Deblitzenoi in the fourteenth and fifteenth centuries', in Laiou-Thomadakis (ed.) (1980), pp. 176–98

—(1981), 'À propos des armées des premiers Paléologues et des compagnies de soldats', *TM* 8, pp. 353–71; repr. in Oikonomides (2005), no. 16

—(1985), 'La Chancellerie impériale de Byzance du 13e au 15e siècle', *REB* 42, pp. 167–95

—(1986c), 'Ottoman influence on late Byzantine fiscal practice', *SF* 45, pp. 1–24

—(1988b), 'Byzantium and the western powers in the thirteenth to fifteenth centuries', in Howard-Johnston (ed.) (1988), pp. 319–32; repr. in Oikonomides (2005), no. 17

—(1992b), 'Byzantine diplomacy, AD 1204–1453: means and ends', in Shepard and Franklin (eds.) (1992), pp. 73–88; repr. in Oikonomides (2005), no. 23

—(2005), *Society, culture, and politics in Byzantium*, ed. E. A. Zachariadou, Aldershot

Ortalli, G. (ed.) (1998), *Venezia e Creta: atti del convegno internazionale di studi, Iraklion-Chanià, 30 settembre–5 ottobre 1997*, Venice

Ortalli, G. *et al.* (eds.) (2006), *Quarta crociata. Venezia – Bisanzio – Impero Latino*, 2 vols., Venice

Ostrogorsky, G. (1954), *Pour l'histoire de la féodalité byzantine*, tr. H. Grégoire, Brussels

—(1956), *Quelques problèmes d'histoire de la paysannerie byzantine*, Brussels

—(1958), 'Byzance, état tributaire de l'empire turc', *ZRVI* 5, pp. 49–58

—(1965), *Serska oblast posle Dušanove smrti*, Belgrade

—(1967), 'Problèmes des relations byzantino-serbes au XIVe siècle', *ACIEB* 13, pp. 41–55

Ousterhout, R. (1987), *The architecture of the Kariye Camii in Istanbul*, DOSt 25, Washington, DC

—(1991), 'Constantinople, Bithynia and regional developments in later Palaeologan architecture', in Ćurčić and Mouriki (eds.) (1991), pp. 75–110

—(2000), 'Contextualizing the later churches of Constantinople: suggested methodologies and a few examples', *DOP* 54, pp. 241–50

—(2002), *The art of the Kariye Camii*, London

Pantazopoulos, N. J. (1967), *Church and law in the Balkan peninsula during the Ottoman rule*, Thessalonica

Papadopoulou, E. and Dialete, D. (eds.) (1996), *Byzantium and Serbia in the 14th century*, Athens

Pertusi, A. (ed.) (1973–4), *Venezia e il Levante fino al secolo XV: atti del I convegno internazionale di storia della civiltà Veneziana (Venezia, 1–5 giugno 1968)*, 2 vols., Florence

Peschlow, U. (2001), 'Die befestigte Residenz von Mermerkule: Beobachtungen an einem spätbyzantinischen Bau im Verteidigungssystem von Konstantinopel', *JÖB* 51, pp. 385–403

Pistarino, G. (1990a), 'Duecentocinquant'anni dei Genovesi a Chio', in Pistarino (1990c), pp. 243–80

—(1990b), 'I Gattilusio di Lesbo e d'Enos signori nell'Egeo', in Pistarino (1990c), pp. 383–420

—(1990c), *Genovesi d'oriente*, Genoa

—(1995), *Chio dei Genovesi nel tempo di Cristoforo Colombo*, Rome

Podskalsky, G. (1977), *Theologie und Philosophie in Byzanz: der Streit um die theologische Methodik in der spätbyzantinischen Geistesgeschichte (14.–15. Jahrhundert), seine systematischen Grundlagen und seine historische Entwicklung*, Munich

—(2000), *Theologische Literatur des Mittelalters in Bulgarien und Serbien, 865–1459*, Munich

Polyviannyi, D. I. (2000), *Kul'turnoe svoeobrazie srednevekovoi Bolgarii v kontektse vizantiisko-slavianskoi obshchnosti IX–XV vekov*, Ivanovo

Popović, D. (2003), 'Relics and politics in the middle ages: the Serbian approach', in Lidov (ed.) (2003), pp. 161–80

Prifti, K. *et al.* (eds.) (1990), *E vërteta mbi Kosovën dhe shqiptarët në Jugosllavii*, Tirana

Primov, B. (1948), 'B'lgari, G'rtsi i Latintsi v Plovdiv prez 1204–1205 g.. Roliata na Bogomilite', *Izvestiia na B'lgarskoto istorichesko druzhestvo (Bulletin de la société historique bulgare)* 22–24, pp. 145–58

—(1960), 'Medieval Bulgaria and the dualist heresies in western Europe', *Études historiques à l'occasion du XIe congrès international des sciences historiques, Stockholm, août 1960*, Sofia, pp. 79–106

—(1966), 'Mezhdunarodno znachenie na Vtorata B'lgarska D'rzhava v perioda na neinoto s'zdavane i utv'rzhdavane', *Istoricheski Pregled* 22.1, pp. 22–46

—(1975a), *Les Bougres: histoire du pope Bogomile et de ses adeptes*, Paris

—(1975b), 'The Third and Fourth Crusades and Bulgaria', *Études historiques à l'occasion du XIVe congrès international des sciences historiques, San Francisco, 1975* (= *Études historiques* 7), pp. 43–69

—(1980), 'Spread and influence of Bogomilism in Europe', *BB* 6, pp. 317–37

Prinzing, G. (1972), *Die Bedeutung Bulgariens und Serbiens in den Jahren 1204–1219: im Zusammenhang mit der Entstehung und Entwicklung der byzantinischen Teilstaaten nach der Einnahme Konstantinopels infolge des 4. Kreuzzuges*, MBM 12, Munich

—(1992), 'Das byzantinische Kaisertum im Umbruch: zwischen regionaler Aufspaltung und erneuter Zentrierung in den Jahren 1204–1282', in Gundlach and Weber (eds.) (1992), pp. 129–83

—(1993b), 'Das Verwaltungssystem im epirotischen Staat der Jahre 1210–ca. 1246', *BF* 19, pp. 113–26

—(2004), 'A quasi-patriarch in the state of Epiros: the autocephalous archbishop of "Boulgaria" (Ohrid) Demetrios Chomatenos', *ZRVI* 41, pp. 165–82

Pulaha, S. *et al.* (eds.) (1982), *Shqiptarët dhe trojet e tyre*, Tirana

Raby, J. (1983 [1984]), 'Mehmed the Conqueror's Greek scriptorium', *DOP* 37, pp. 15–34

Radošević, N. (1987), 'Nikejski carevi u savremenoj im retorici', *ZRVI* 26, pp. 69–85

Rautman, M. (1991), 'Aspects of monastic patronage in Palaeologan Macedonia', in Ćurčić and Mouriki (eds.) (1991), pp. 53–74

Reinert, S. W. (1993), 'The Palaiologoi, Yildirim Bayezid and Constantinople: June 1389–March 1391', in Langdon *et al.* (eds.) (1993), I, pp. 289–365

—(2002), 'Fragmentation (1204–1453)', in Mango (ed.) (2002), pp. 248–83

Reinsch, D. R. (1996b), 'Lieber der Turban oder was? Bemerkungen zum Dictum des Lukas Notaras', in Constantinides *et al.* (eds.) (1996), pp. 377–89

—(2003), 'Kritobulos of Imbros – learned historian, Ottoman *raya* and Byzantine patriot', *ZRVI* 40, pp. 297–311

Richard, J. (1989), 'The establishment of the Latin church in the empire of Constantinople (1204–27)', *MHR* 4, pp. 45–62; repr. in Arbel *et al.* (eds.) (1989), pp. 45–62

Richter, G. (1990), 'Johannes Bekkos und sein Verhältnis zur römischen Kirche', *BF* 15, pp. 167–217

Riebe, A. (2005), *Rom in Gemeinschaft mit Konstantinopel: Patriarch Johannes XI. Bekkos als Verteidiger der Kirchenunion von Lyon (1274)*, Wiesbaden

Robbert, L. B. (1985), 'Venice and the crusades', in Setton (ed.) (1969–89), V, pp. 379–451

Roberg, B. (1990), *Das Zweite Konzil von Lyon (1274)*, Paderborn

Rock, S. (2006), 'Russian piety and orthodox culture, 1380–1589', in Angold (ed.) (2006), pp. 253–75

Roncaglia, M. (1954), *Les Frères mineurs et l'église grecque orthodoxe au XIIIᵉ siècle 1231–1274*, Cairo

Ronchey, S. (2006), 'Orthodoxy on sale: the last Byzantine, and the lost Crusade', *ACIEB* 21, I, pp. 313–42

Rosenqvist, J. O. (ed.) (2004), *Interaction and isolation in late Byzantine culture: papers read at a colloquium held at the Swedish Research Institute in Istanbul, 1–5 December 1999*, Istanbul

Rousseau, O. (ed.) (1963–4), *Le Millénaire du mont Athos, 963–1963: études et mélanges*, 2 vols., Venice and Chevetogne

Roux, M. (1992), *Les Albanais en Yougoslavie, minorité nationale, territoire et développement*, Paris

Rowell, S. C. (1994), *Lithuania ascending: a pagan empire within east-central Europe, 1295–1345*, Cambridge

Rubin, M. and Simons, W. (eds.) (forthcoming), *The Cambridge history of Christianity*, IV: *Christianity in western Europe, c. 1100–c. 1500*, Cambridge

Runciman, S. (1958), *The Sicilian Vespers: a history of the Mediterranean world in the late thirteenth century*, Cambridge

—(1968), *The great church in captivity: a study of the patriarchate of Constantinople from the eve of the Turkish conquest to the Greek war of independence*, Cambridge

—(1970), *The last Byzantine renaissance*, Cambridge

—(1980), *Mistra: Byzantine capital of the Peloponnese*, London

Russell, N. (2003), 'Palamism and the circle of Demetrius Cydones', in Dendrinos *et al.* (eds.) (2003), pp. 153–74

—(2006), 'Prochoros Cydones and the fourteenth-century understanding of orthodoxy', in Louth and Casiday (eds.) (2006), pp. 75–91

Ryan, C. (ed.) (1989), *The religious roles of the papacy: ideals and realities 1150–1300*, Toronto

Sakellariou, E. (2003), 'Latin Morea in the late middle ages: observations on its demography and economy', in Dendrinos *et al.* (eds) (2003), pp. 301–16

Saradi-Mendelovici, E. (1980), 'A propos de la ville de Patras aux 13ᵉ–15ᵉ siècles', *REB* 38, pp. 219–32

—(1980–1), 'E mesaionike Glarentza', *Diptycha* 2, pp. 61–71

Saradi[-Mendelovici], H. (1992), *Le Notariat byzantin du IXᵉ au XVᵉ siècles*, Athens

Savvides, A. G. K. (1981), *Byzantium in the Near East: its relations with the Seljuk sultanate of Rum in Asia Minor, the Armenians of Cilicia and the Mongols, AD c. 1192–1237*, Thessalonica

—(1987), *Byzantina stasiastika kai autonomistika kinemata sta Dodekanesa kai ste Mikra Asia, 1189–1240 m. Ch.*, Athens

—(1992–3), 'Tamerlane, Byzantium and Spain (with notes on Clavijo's visit to Trebizond in AD 1404)', *Archeion Pontou* 44, pp. 46–58

—(2003), *Oi Alanoi tou Kaukasou kai oi metanasteuseis tous sten ystere archaioteta kai sto mesaiona*, Athens

—(2004b), *E idryse Monkolikes Autokratorias: o Tzennkis Chan, oi epigonoi tou kai o kosmos tes Anatoles, 1206–1294 m. Ch.*, Athens

—(2005), *Oi megaloi Komnenoi tes Trapezountas kai tou Pontou. Istorike episkopese tes Byzantines autokratorias tou Mikrasiatikou Ellenismou, 1204–1461*, Athens

—(2006), *Istoria tou Byzantiou me apospasmata apo tis peges*, III: *E ystere Byzantine autokratoria kai o mesaionikos Ellenismos (1025–1461)*, 2nd edn., Athens

Schlumberger, G. L. (1902), *Expédition des 'Almugavares' ou routiers catalans en Orient de l'an 1302 à l'an 1311*, Paris

Schmitt, O. J. (1995), 'Zur Geschichte der Stadt Glarentza im 15. Jahrhundert', *Byz* 65, pp. 98–135

Schreiner, P. (1978), 'Ein Prostagma Andronikos' III. für die Monembasioten im Pegai (1328) und das gefälschte Chrysobull Andronikos' II. für die Monembasioten im byzantinischen Reich', *JÖB* 27, pp. 203–28

—(1981–2), 'Paratereseis dia ta pronomia tes Monembasias', *Praktika tou 2. diethnous synedriou Peloponnesiakon spoudon*, I, Athens, pp. 160–6

—(1994), 'Das byzantinische Rechnungswesen im Rahmen der Mittelmeerwelt mit besonderer Berücksichtigung spätbyzantinischer Kontobücher des 13. bis 15. Jahrhunderts', in *Kommunikation zwischen Orient und Okzident: Alltag und Sachkultur: internationaler Kongress Krems an der Donau 6. bis 9. Oktober 1992*, Vienna, pp. 117–41

—(1995), 'L'Importance culturelle des colonies occidentales en territoire byzantin', in Balard and Ducellier (eds.) (1995), pp. 288–93, 295–7

—(2005), 'Statistische Beobachtungen zu echten und gefälschten byzantinischen Kaiserschreiben an westliche Herrscher und Institutionen (565–1453)', in Balard *et al.* (eds.) (2005), pp. 165–9

Seibt, W. (ed.) (1996), *Geschichte und Kultur der Palaiologenzeit: Referate des internationalen Symposions zu Ehren von Herbert Hunger (Wien, 30. November bis 3. Dezember 1994)*, Vienna

Setton, K. M. (1975a), *Catalan domination of Athens*, 2nd edn., London

—(1975b), 'The Catalans in Greece, 1311–1380', in Setton (ed.) (1969–89), III, pp. 167–224

—(1975c), 'The Catalans and Florentines in Greece, 1380–1462', in Setton (ed.) (1969–89), III, pp. 225–77

—(1976–84), *The papacy and the Levant (1204–1571)*, 4 vols., Philadelphia

—(ed.) (1969–89), *A history of the crusades*, 6 vols., 2nd edn., Madison, WI

Ševčenko, I. (1961), 'The decline of Byzantium seen through the eyes of its intellectuals', *DOP* 15, pp. 167–86; repr. in Ševčenko, I. (1981), no. 2

—(1962), *Études sur la polémique entre Théodore Métochite et Nicéphore Choumnos: la vie intellectuelle et politique à Byzance sous les premiers Paléologues*, Brussels

—(1967), 'Russo-Byzantine relations after the eleventh century', *ACIEB* 13, pp. 93–104; repr. in Ševčenko, I. (1991), no. 20, pp. 267–84

—(1974), 'Society and intellectual life in the fourteenth century', in *ACIEB* 14, I, pp. 69–92; repr. in Sĕvčenko, I. (1981), no. 1

—(1975), 'Theodore Metochites, the Chora and the intellectual trends of his time', in Underwood (ed.) (1966–75), IV, pp. 17–91; English version with appendices and footnotes of Ševčenko, I. (1971), 'Théodore Métochites, Chora et les courants intellectuels de l'époque', in *Art et Société à Byzance sous les Paléologues: actes du colloque organisé par l'Association internationale des études byzantines à Venise en Septembre 1968*, Venice, pp. 13–39

—(1978), 'Agapetus east and west: the fate of a Byzantine "Mirror of Princes"', *RESEE* 16, pp. 3–44; repr. in Ševčenko, I. (1982a), no. 3

—(1981), *Society and intellectual life in late Byzantium*, London

—(1982a), *Ideology, letters and culture in the Byzantine world*, London

—(1982b), 'Nicéphore Blemmydès, *Autobiographies* (1264 et 1265)', in Guillou (ed.) (1982), pp. 111–37

—(1984), 'The Palaeologan renaissance', in Treadgold (ed.) (1984b), pp. 144–71

—(1991), *Byzantium and the Slavs in letters and culture*, Cambridge, MA and Naples

—(2002), 'Palaiologan learning', in Mango (ed.) (2002), pp. 284–93

Ševčenko, N. P. (2006), 'Art and liturgy in the later Byzantine empire', in Angold (ed.) (2006), pp. 127–53

Shawcross, C. T. M. (2005), 'Oral residue and narrative structure in the *Chronicle of Morea*', *Byz* 75, pp. 210–33

—(2008), '"Do thou nothing without counsel": political assemblies and the ideal of good government in the thought of Theodore Palaeologus and Theodore Metochites', *Al-Masaq* 20, pp. 90–117

—(2008, forthcoming), 'In the name of the true emperor: politics of resistance after the Palaiologan usurpation', *BSl* 66

—(forthcoming a), *The Chronicle of Morea: historiography in Crusader Greece*, Oxford

—(forthcoming b), 'Greeks and Franks after the Fourth Crusade: identity in the *Chronicle of Morea*', in James and Lambert (eds.) (forthcoming)

Shepard, J. (2006c), 'The Byzantine commonwealth, 1000–1550', in Angold (ed.) (2006), pp. 3–52

—(2006d), 'Manners maketh Romans? Young barbarians at the emperor's court', in Jeffreys, E. (ed.) (2006), pp. 135–58

Shivarov, N. (1987), 'Otnosno niakoi s'obrazheniia i motivi za svikvaneto na T'rnovskiia s'bor prez 1211 g. i za negoviia obrazets', *Annuaire de l'université de Sofia 'St Kliment Ohridski'. Centre des recherches slavo-byzantines 'Ivan Dujčev'* 1, pp. 89–99

Shuteriqi, D. (1967), 'Një mbishkrim i Arbërit (1190–1216) dhe mbishkrime të tjera gjetur në Mirditë', *Studime historike* 21(4). 3, pp. 131–58

Simon, D. (1984), '*Princeps legibus solutus*: die Stellung des byzantinischen Kaisers zum Gesetz', in Nörr and Simon (eds.) (1984), pp. 449–92

—(1986), 'Byzantinische Provinzialjustiz', *BZ* 79, pp. 310–43

Sinogowitz, B. (1952), 'Zur Eroberung Thessalonikes im Herbst 1224', *BZ* 45, p. 28

Skrzhinskaia, E. C. (1947), 'Genueztsy v Konstantinople v XIV v.', *VV* 1(26), pp. 213–34

Soloviev, A. V. (1934), 'Eine Urkunde des Panhypersebastos Demetrios, Megas Archon von Albanien', *BZ* 34, pp. 304–10

Soulis, G. C. (1984), *The Serbs and Byzantium during the reign of Tsar Stephen Dušan (1331–1355) and his successors*, Washington, DC

Stanescu, E. (1974), 'Byzance et les pays roumains 11ᵉ–15ᵉ siècles', *ACIEB* 14, I, pp. 393–431

Stauridou-Zaphraka, A. (1990), *Nikaia kai Epeiros ton 13 aiona: ideologike antiparathese sten prospatheia tous na anaktesoun ten autokratoria*, Thessalonica

—(2005), 'The political ideology of the state of Epiros', in Laiou (ed.) (2005), pp. 311–23

Stiernon, D. (1977), 'Le Problème de l'union gréco-latine vu de Byzance: de Germain II à Joseph Iᵉʳ (1232–1273)', in *1274, année charnière, mutations et continuités: Lyon–Paris, 30 septembre–5 octobre 1974, Colloques internationaux du CNRS* 558, Paris, pp. 139–66

Stöckly, D. (1995), *Le système de l'incanto des galées du marché à Venise (fin XIIIᵉ-milieu XVᵉ siècle)*, Leiden

Šufflay, M. von (1916), 'Die Kirchenzustände im vortürkischen Albanien: die orthodoxe Durchbruchszone im katholischen Damme', in von Thallóczy (ed.) (1916), I, pp. 188–281

Svoronos, N. (1956), 'Sur quelques formes de la vie rurale à Byzance: petite et grande exploitation', *AESC* 11, pp. 325–35

—(1982), 'Le Domaine de Lavra sous les Paléologues', in *Actes de Lavra*, IV, pp. 65–173

Tachiaos, A.-E. N. (1984–5), 'The testament of Photius Monembasiotes, metropolitan of Russia (1408–31): Byzantine ideology in XVth-century Muscovy', *Cyrillomethodianum* 8–9, pp. 77–109

Tafrali, O. (1913), *Thessalonique au quatorzième siècle*, Paris; repr. Thessalonica, 1933

Talbot, A.-M. (1985), 'Late Byzantine nuns: by choice or necessity?', *BF* 9, pp. 103–17; repr. in Talbot (2001), no. 17

—(1992), 'Empress Theodora Palaiologina, wife of Michael VIII', *DOP* 46, pp. 295–303; repr. in Talbot (2001), no. 5

—(1993), 'The restoration of Constantinople under Michael VIII', *DOP* 47, pp. 243–61

Talbot Rice, D. (1968a), *Byzantine painting: the last phase*, London

—(1968b), *The church of Haghia Sophia at Trebizond*, Edinburgh

Tangheroni, M. (1996), *Commercio e navigazione nel medioevo*, Rome and Bari

Tanz, S. (ed.) (1993), *Mentalität und Gesellschaft im Mittelalter: Gedenkschrift für Ernst Werner*, Frankfurt-am-Main

Tăpkova-Zaimova, V. and Miltenova, V. (1984), 'The problem of prophecies in Byzantine and Bulgarian literature', *Balkan Studies* 25, pp. 499–510

Tarnanidis, I. (1975), 'Byzantine–Bulgarian ecclesiastical relations during the reigns of Ioannis Vatatzis and Ivan Ašen II, up to the year 1235', *Cyrillomethodianum* 3, pp. 28–52

Thallóczy, L. von (ed.) (1916), *Illyrisch–Albanische Forschungen*, 2 vols., Munich

Thallóczy, L. von and Jireček, K. (1916), 'Zwei Urkunden aus Nordalbanien', in von Thallóczy (ed.) (1916), I, pp. 125–51

Theocharides, G. I. (1963) 'Oi Tzamplakones: Symbole eis ten Byzantinen Makedoniken prosopographian tou ID' aionos', *Makedonika* 5, pp. 125–83

Thiriet, F. (1962), 'Quelques observations sur le trafic des galées vénitiennes d'après les chiffres des *incanti* (XIVe–XVe siècles)', in *Studi in onore di Amintore Fanfani*, III, Milan, pp. 495–522; repr. in Thiriet (1977), no. 8

—(1975), *La Romanie vénitienne au moyen âge: le développement et l'exploitation du domaine colonial vénitien (XIIe–XVe siècles)*, 2nd edn., Paris

—(1976–8), 'La Messénie méridionale dans le système colonial des Vénitiens en Romanie', *Praktika tou 1. Diethnous synedriou Peloponnesiakon spoudon*, Athens, pp. 86–98

—(1977), *Études sur la Romanie gréco-vénitienne (X^e–XVe siècles)*, London

Thomson, F. J. (1998), 'Gregory Tsamblak: the man and the myths' *Slavica Gandensia* 25, pp. 5–149

—(2005), 'Mediaeval Bulgarian and Serbian theological literature: an essential vademecum' [review of G. Podskalsky, *Theologische Literatur des Mittelalters in Bulgarien und Serbien, 865–1459*], *BZ* 98, pp. 503–49

—(2006), 'Il testo biblico dai libri liturgici alla Bibbia di Ostrog (1581)', in Capaldo *et al.* (eds.) (2003–6), pp. 245–87

Tiepolo, M.-F. and Tonetti, E. (eds.) (2002), *I greci a Venezia: atti del Convegno internazionale di studio, Venezia, 5–7 novembre 1998*, Venice

Todt, K.-P. (1991), *Kaiser Johannes VI. Kantakuzenos und der Islam: politische Realität und theologische Polemik im palaiologenzeitlichen Byzanz*, Würzburg

Topping, P. (1975a), 'The Morea, 1311–1364', in Setton (ed.) (1969–89), III, pp. 104–40

—(1975b), 'The Morea, 1364–1460', in Setton (ed.) (1969–89), III, pp 141–66

—(1977), *Studies on Latin Greece AD 1205–1715*, London

Toth, I. (2007), 'Rhetorical *theatron* in late Byzantium: the example of Palaiologan imperial orations', in Grünbart (ed.) (2007), pp. 429–48

Treadgold, W. (ed.) (1984), *Renaissances before the Renaissance: cultural revivals of late antiquity and the middle ages*, Stanford

Treppo, M. del (1971), *I mercanti catalani e l'espansione della corona d'Aragona nel Mediterraneo*, Naples

Troianos, S. N. (2005), 'Das Gottesurteil im Prozessrecht der byzantinischen Kirche', in Hoffmann and Monchizadeh (eds.) (2005), pp. 469–90

Turner, C. J. G. (1964), 'Pages from the late Byzantine philosophy of history', *BZ* 57, pp. 345–73

—(1969), 'The career of George-Gennadius Scholarius', *Byz* 39, pp. 420–55

Tyerman, C. J. (1982), 'Marino Sanudo Torsello and the lost crusade: lobbying in the fourteenth century', *TRHS* 5th series, 32, pp. 57–73

Underwood, P. (ed.) (1966–75), *The Kariye Djami*, 4 vols., Princeton

Ursinus, M. O. H. (1993), 'Millet', in *EI*, VI, pp. 61–4

Uspensky, F. I. (1901), 'O drevnostiakh goroda Tyrnova', *IRAIK* 7, pp. 1–24

Vakalopoulos, A. E. (1962), 'Les Limites de l'empire byzantin depuis la fin du XIVe siècle jusqu'à sa chute (1453)', *BZ* 55, pp. 56–65

Vasiliev, A. A. (1936a), *The Goths in the Crimea*, Cambridge, MA

—(1936b), 'The foundation of the empire of Trebizond (1204–1222)', *Sp* 11, pp. 3–37

Vasilievsky, V. G. (1885), 'Obnovlenie Bolgarskogo Patriarshestva pri tsare Ioanne Asene II v 1235 godu', *Zhurnal Ministerstva Narodnogo Prosveshcheniia* 238, pp. 1–56 and 206–38

Verpeaux, J. (1959), *Nicéphore Choumnos, homme d'état et humaniste byzantin (ca. 1250/1255–1327)*, Paris

Vlachos, T. (1970), 'Kalojan plündert Thrakien und Makedonien', *Byzantina* 2, pp. 269–83

Vlora, E. B. (1968–73), *Lebenserinnerungen*, 2 vols., Munich

Vodoff, V. (1989), *Princes et principautés russes X–XVII siècles*, Northampton

Vryonis, S. (1956), 'Isidore Glabas and the Turkish "Devshirme"', *Sp* 31, pp. 433–43; repr. in Vryonis (1971b), no. 13

—(1986), 'The Ottoman conquest of Thessaloniki in 1430', in Bryer and Lowry (eds.) (1986), pp. 281–321

—(ed.) (1985), *Byzantine studies in honor of Milton V. Anastos*, Malibu, CA

Walter, C. (1978), 'The iconographical sources for the coronation of Milutin and Simonida at Gračanica', in *L'Art byzantin au début du XIVe siècle: Symposium de Gračanica 1973*, Belgrade, pp. 183–200; repr. in Walter (1993), no. 4

—(1993), *Prayer and power in Byzantine and papal imagery*, Aldershot

Weiss, G. (1969), *Joannes Kantakuzenos, Aristokrat, Staatsmann, Kaiser und Mönch, in der Gesellschaftsentwicklung von Byzanz im 14. Jahrhundert*, Wiesbaden

Weissbrod, U. (2003), *'Hier liegt der Knecht Gottes . . .': Gräber in byzantinischen Kirchen und ihr Dekor (11. bis 15. Jahrhundert): unter besonderer Berücksichtigung der Höhlenkirchen Kappadokiens*, Wiesbaden

Wellas, M. B. (1983), *Griechisches aus dem Umkreis Kaiser Friedrichs II.*, Munich

Werner, E. (1974), 'Gesellschaft und Kultur im XIV. Jahrhundert: sozial-ökonomische Fragen', *ACIEB* 14, I, pp. 93–110

Wilson, N. G. (1992), *From Byzantium to Italy: Greek studies in the Italian renaissance*, London

Wolf, G. *et al.* (eds.) (2004), *Mandylion: intorno al 'Sacro Volto' da Bisanzio a Genova*, Milan

Wolff, R. L. (1944), 'The Latin empire of Constantinople and the Franciscans', *Traditio* 2, pp. 213–37; repr. in Wolff (1976), no. 7

—(1948), 'The organization of the Latin Patriarchate of Constantinople, 1204–1261: social and administrative consequences of the Latin conquest', *Traditio* 6, pp. 33–60; repr. in Wolff (1976), no. 8

—(1952), 'Baldwin of Flanders and Hainaut, first Latin emperor of Constantinople: his life, death and resurrection, 1172–1225', *Sp* 27, pp. 281–322; repr. in Wolff (1976), no. 4

—(1954), 'Politics in the Latin patriarchate of Constantinople, 1204–1261', *DOP* 8, pp. 227–303; repr. in Wolff (1976), no. 9

—(1969), 'The Latin empire of Constantinople, 1204–1261', in Setton (1969–89), II, pp. 187–233; repr. in Wolff (1976), no. 1

—(1976), *Studies in the Latin empire of Constantinople*, London

Woodhouse, C. M. (1986), *George Gemistos Plethon: the last of the Hellenes*, Oxford

Xanalatos, D. (1939), 'Wirtschaftliche Aufbau- und Autarkiemassnahmen im XIII. Jahrhundert', *Leipziger Vierteljahrschrift für Südosteuropa* 3, pp. 129–39

Xhufi, P. (1987), 'Shqiptarët përballë anzhuinëve (1276–1285)', *Studime Historike* 41(24).2, pp. 199–222

Yatromanolakis, D. and Roilos, P. (eds.) (2004), *Greek ritual poetics*, Washington, DC

Zachariadou, E. A. (1969), 'Early Ottoman documents of the Prodromos monastery (Serres)', *SF* 28, pp. 1–12; repr. in Zachariadou (1985), no. 15

—(1970 [1971]), 'The conquest of Adrianople by the Turks', *Studi veneziani* 12, pp. 211–17; repr. in Zachariadou (1985), no. 12

—(1980), 'The Catalans of Athens and the beginning of the Turkish expansion in the Aegean area', *Studi medievali* 3rd series 21, pp. 821–38; repr. in Zachariadou (1985), no. 5

—(1983), *Trade and crusade: Venetian Crete and the emirates of Menteshe and Aydin 1300–1415*, Venice

—(1985), *Romania and the Turks (c. 1300–c. 1500)*, London

—(1987), 'Notes sur la population de L'Asie Mineure turque au XIVe siècle', *BF* 12, pp. 223–31

—(1989a), 'Ephemeres apopeires gia autodioikese stis Ellenikes poleis kata ton 14 kai 15 aiona', *Ariadne* 5, pp. 345–51

—(1989b), 'Holy war in the Aegean during the fourteenth century', *MHR* 4, pp. 212–25

—(2004b), 'Changing masters in the Aegean', in Chrysostomides *et al.* (eds.) (2004), pp. 199–212

—(2006a), 'Mount Athos and the Ottomans 1350–1550', in Angold (ed.) (2006), pp. 154–68

—(2006b), 'The great church in captivity, 1453–1568', in Angold (ed.) (2006), pp. 169–85

Zakythinos, D. A. (1948), *Crise monétaire et crise économique à Byzance du XIIIᵉ au XVᵉ siècle*, Athens

—(1975), *Le Despotat grec de Morée*, I: *Histoire politique*; II: *Vie et institutions*, rev. edn. C. Maltézou, 2 vols., London

Živojinović, M. (1991), 'The trade of Mount Athos monasteries', *ZRVI* 29–30, pp. 101–16

Zlatarsky, V. N. (1911 [1912]), 'Asenoviiat nadpis pri Stanimaka', *Izvestiia na B'lgarskoto arkheologichesko druzhestvo* 2, pp. 231–47

—(1970–2), *Istoriia na b'lgarskata d'rzhava prez srednite vekove*, 3 vols. in 4 pts., Sofia

UNPUBLISHED THESES

Carroll, A. (2005), 'The role of the Varangian guard in Byzantine rebellions', PhD thesis, Queen's University Belfast

Conrad, L. I. (1981), 'The plague in the early medieval Near East', PhD thesis, Princeton University

Cook, D. B. (2002), 'The beginnings of Islam in Syria during the Umayyad period', PhD thesis, University of Chicago

Delouis, O. (2005), 'Saint Jean-Baptiste de Stoudios à Constantinople. La Contribution d'un monastère à l'histoire de l'empire byzantin (v. 454–1204)', PhD thesis, University of Paris-I

Forsyth, J. (1977), 'The Byzantine–Arab Chronicle (938–1034) of Yahya b. Sa'id al-Antaki', PhD thesis, University of Michigan

Frankopan, P. (1998), 'The foreign policy of the emperor Alexios I Komnenos (1081–c. 1100)', DPhil thesis, University of Oxford

Georgiopoulou, S. (1990), 'Theodore II Dukas Laskaris (1222–1258) as an author and an intellectual of the thirteenth century', PhD thesis, Harvard University

Gilliland, J. (2005), 'The career and writings of Demetrius Kydones: a study of Byzantine politics and society, c. 1347–c. 1373', DPhil thesis, University of Oxford

Hodgetts, A. C. (1974), 'The colonies of Coron and Modon under Venetian administration, 1204–1400', PhD thesis, University of London

Keshk, K. M. (2002), 'The depiction of Mu'awiya in the early Islamic sources', PhD thesis, University of Chicago

Korobeinikov, D. A. (2003), 'Byzantium and the Turks in the thirteenth century', DPhil thesis, University of Oxford

Miller, T. S. (1975), 'The history of John Cantacuzenus (book 4): text, translation and commentary', PhD thesis, The Catholic University of America, Washington, DC

Necipoğlu, N. (1990), 'Byzantium between the Ottomans and the Latins: a study of political attitudes in the late Palaeologan period 1370–1460', PhD thesis, Harvard University

Nichanian, M. (2004), 'Aristocratie et pouvoir impérial à Byzance VIIe–IXe siècle', PhD thesis, University of Paris-IV

Pazdernik, C. F. (1997), 'A dangerous liberty and a servitude free from care: political *eleutheria* and *douleia* in Procopius of Caesarea and Thucydides of Athens', PhD thesis, Princeton University

Prigent, V. (2006), 'La Sicile byzantine VIe–Xe siècle', PhD thesis, University of Paris-IV

Sarantis, A. C. (2005), 'The Balkans during the reign of Justinian: barbarian invasions and imperial responses', DPhil thesis, University of Oxford

Shawcross, C. T. M. (2005), 'The Chronicle of Morea: historiography in crusader Greece', DPhil thesis, University of Oxford

Sidéris, G. (2001), 'Eunuques et pouvoir à Byzance du Ve au Xe siècle', PhD thesis, University of Paris-I

Sophoulis, P. (2005), 'A study of Byzantine–Bulgar relations, 775–816', DPhil thesis, University of Oxford

Thompson, S. (2001), 'The kingdom of Provence and its rulers, *c.* 870–*c.* 950', PhD thesis, University of Cambridge

Vaiou, M. (2002), 'Diplomatic relations between the 'Abbasid caliphate and the Byzantine empire: methods and procedures', DPhil thesis, University of Oxford

Vinogradov, A. I. (2001), 'Grecheskie zhitiia apostola Andreiia', PhD thesis, University of Moscow

Waring, J. S. (1999), 'Byzantine monastic libraries in the eleventh and twelfth centuries', PhD thesis, Queen's University Belfast

White, M. M. (2004), 'Military saints in Byzantium and Rus, 900–1200', PhD thesis, University of Cambridge

PICTURE ACKNOWLEDGEMENTS

Every effort has been made to secure necessary permissions to reproduce copyright material in this work, though in some cases it has proved impossible to trace copyright holders. If any omissions are brought to our notice, we will be happy to include appropriate acknowledgements on reprinting.

The following abbreviations have been used:

BN   Bibliothèque Nationale de France, Paris
BNE   Biblioteca Nacional de España Madrid
Bod.   Bodleian Library, University of Oxford
UL   Syndics of Cambridge University Library
Vat.   Biblioteca Apostolica Vaticana, Vatican City

1   Photo: Jonathan Shepard
2a   Photo: Peter and Vanessa Winchester
2b   Photo: Jonathan Shepard
3   Image courtesy of Bildarchiv Foto Marburg
4   Photo: Peter and Vanessa Winchester
5   From Ghirshman (1962), fig. 235. Photo: Claude Deffarge-Rapho. Image courtesy of UL
6   From *Album of Armenian palaeography*, ed. M. Stone *et al.* (Aarhus, 2002), no. 3, p. 114, courtesy of Aarhus University Press. Image courtesy of Bod.
7a   From Pringle (2001), pp. 546–7. Used by kind permission of Denys Pringle
7b   From Pringle (2001), plate XXXIV(a). Used by kind permission of Denys Pringle
8a   © 1990, Photo Scala, Florence
8b   © Fratelli Alinari, BGA-F-003918-0000
9a   From Tsamkda (2002), plate 70. Illustration from BNE cod. Vitr. 26-2, fol. 34 v. Image courtesy of BNE
9b   Photo: John Haldon
10   © The Trustees of the British Museum, 099755

11a From *DOC*, III.1, plate XIII (Constantine VI, 1.4). Image courtesy of UL

11b From *DOC*, III.1, plate XV (Irene, 1a.5). Image courtesy of UL

12 From Cutler and Spieser (1996), p. 49. Illustration from Vat. MS gr. 1291, fol. 9 r. Image courtesy of Bod.

13 From Mango (ed.) (2002), p. 219. Illustration from St Petersburg, National Library of Russia, cod. gr. 219, fols. 158 v. and 159 r. Image courtesy of UL

14 © The British Library Board. All rights reserved. Theodore Psalter of 1066, British Library Additional MS 19352, fol. 27 v. (detail)

15 From Tsamakda (2002), plate 189. Illustration from BNE cod. Vitr. 26-2, fol. 77 v. Image courtesy of BNE

16 From Brubaker (1999a), fig. 5, between pp. xxiii and 1. Illustration from BN cod. gr. 510, fol. C v. Image courtesy of UL

17 From A. Wharton Epstein, *Tokalı Kilise: tenth-century metropolitan art in Byzantine Cappadocia* (Washington, DC, 1986), plate 97. Photo: David Page. Image courtesy of UL

18a From Horníčková (1999), p. 220. Illustration from Budapest, Magyar Nemzeti Múzeum, inv. no. 1939.96

18b From Horníčková (1999), p. 238. Illustration from Budapest, Magyar Nemzeti Múzeum, inv. no. 1893.75.1348

19 © Biblioteca Apostolica Vaticana (Vatican City), Codex Vatican. Slav. 3

20 From Mango (ed.) (2002), p. 238. Image supplied by Oxford University Press

21 Photo: Theo van Lint

22 Photo: Tim Greenwood

23 Photo: Nancy Alderson

24 Photo: Theo van Lint

25a From Kaegi (1992), cover illustration. Illustration from the American Numismatic Society, New York, 170.63.1

25b From *The Cambridge illustrated history of the Islamic world*, ed. F. Robinson (Cambridge, 1996), p. 13. Illustration from the American Numismatic Society, New York

26 From *Cambridge illustrated history of the Islamic world*, ed. Robinson, p. 15. Illustration from Robert Harding Picture Library, London

27 From Mouriki (1985), II, plate 230. Photo: M. Vernados. Image courtesy of UL

28 From DOC, III.1, plate XVII (Michael I, 3.6). Image courtesy of UL

29 From *Codices graeci Bibliothecae Vaticanae selecti*, ed. E. Follieri, fasc. IV, tab. 11. Illustration from Vat. MS gr. 1666, fol. 154 v. Image courtesy of Bod.

48   Photo: Peter and Vanessa Winchester

49   From Magdalino (1993a), cover. Illustration from Vat. MS gr. 1176, fol. 11 r.

50   From DOS, I, no. 16.1, pp. 48–9

51   From Tsamakda (2002), plate 509. Illustration from BNE cod. Vitr. 26-2, fol. 215 r. Image courtesy of BNE

52a   From L. A. Durnovo, *Haykakan manrankarch'ut'yun. Miniatures arméniennes* (Yerevan, 1967), plate 13. Illustration from 'Gospel Book of 1066, Sebasteia', Yerevan, Matenadaran, MS 311

52b   From Durnovo, *Haykakan manrankarch'ut'yun*, plate 12. Illustration from 'Gospel Book of 1066, Sebasteia', Yerevan, Matenadaran, MS 311

53   *Liber insularum Archipelagi* of Cristoforo Buondelmonti, *c.* 1485 © The British Library Board. All rights reserved. MS Arundel 93, fol. 155 r.

54   From A. Džurova, *Tomichov psaltir v dva toma*, II (Sofia, 1990) (facsimile). Illustration from Moscow, State Historical Museum, cod. no. 2752, fol. 137 r.

55   From *Radomirov psaltir (Le Psautier de Radomir)*, ed. L. Makarijoska (Skopje, 1997), p. 325. Illustration from Mount Athos, Zographou Monastery, no. 1 d. 13 (formerly no. H47) (also known as the 'Zograf Psalter')

56   From Džurova (1977), plate XXVIII, p. 82. Illustration from Zagreb, Bibliothèque de l'Académie Yougoslave, cod. Iva 109 and cod. Iva III 9

57   From Buschhausen and Buschhausen (1976), table XXI, p. 101. Image courtesy of Dr H. Buschhausen

58   Photo: Peter and Vanessa Winchester

59   From S. Runciman, *Byzantine style and civilisation* (Harmondsworth, 1975), p. 174. Photo: Byzantine Institute Inc. Courtesy of Dumbarton Oaks, Byzantine Photograph and Fieldwork Archives, Washington, DC

60   Photo: Michel Balard

61   From Buckton (ed.) (1994), plate 232, p. 219. Illustration from London, British Museum, CM 1907, 2-4, 2

62   © The British Library Board. All rights reserved. Cotton MS Cleopatra E.iii, fols. 80 v. and 81

63   From Runciman (1980), fig. 2, p. 41. Illustration from Bernard Randolph, *The present state of the Morea, called anciently Peloponnesus*, 3rd edn. (London: Will. Notts *et al.*, 1689), between pp. 8 and 9

64   From *Makriyannis: the memoirs of General Makriyannis, 1797–1864*, ed. and tr. H. A. Lidderdale (London, 1966), plate 1, p. 26

65   © The British Library Board. All rights reserved. Egerton MS
     2817
66   Courtesy of the National Gallery, London
67   From *Turks: a journey of a thousand years*, ed. D. Roxburgh
     (London, 2005), no. 241, pp. 284–5. Illustration from Istanbul,
     Topkapı Sarayı Müzesi, GI 27

INDEX

NOTE: Page references in italics refer to maps or illustrations. Material within entries is arranged predominantly alphabetically, although some of the longer entries begin with a chronologically-ordered section, to help orient the reader.

Footnotes are only referred to where the subject is not mentioned in the corresponding page of the text. Personal names of Byzantines and other individuals in the early and middle periods are generally listed by first name followed by family name (for example, John Skylitzes rather than Skylitzes, John). For the later period, some (mainly western) individuals are listed by surname (for example, Dandolo, Enrico). Entries for commonly occurring first names are sequenced thus: Byzantine emperors, patriarchs of Constantinople, popes, and then all others in alphabetical order.

visual media 54–8, 78–9; church and 56, (canons) 247, 248; east-west influence 426, 429–30, 448, 464; 11th-century creativity 33; emperors' authority projected through 54–5; idealisation 78–9; and imperial ideology 55, 56, 78; keeping up appearances 55–6; lack of comprehension of classical 278; Muslim use of Byzantine 398; private secular art 56–8; study resources 58n20, 78, 79, 94; see also architecture; building; coinage; iconography; icons; manuscripts (illuminations); mosaics; patronage; portraits; seals; wall-paintings

Vitalian, revolt of 105, 199–200

Viterbo 446; treaty of 768, 796; map 434

Viviers 218; map 197

viziers 904; grand see Halil Djandarlioghlu; Mahmud Pasha

Vlachs 71, 653, 664, 689, 904; 'Bulgarian imitative' coins 689; Vlach-Bulgarian revolt 41, 650, 655–6, 661, 687–9, 691; map 882

Vladimir Sviatoslavich, prince of Rus 48, 299, 325–7, 525, 548–9

Vladimir-in-Volynia; map 848

Vladin, prince of Duklja 781

Vlora family of Albania 861–2, 868

Vojislav family see Michael and Stefan Vojislav

volcanic eruptions 280–1, 478–9

Volga Bulgars 326–7

Vonitsa 678; map 667

Vramshapur, king of eastern Armenia 160, 161

Vrt'anes (Armenian monophysite leader) 338

al-Walid, caliph 384

Wallachia 50, 674, 831, 854; maps 91, 666, 848; see also Vlachs

wall-paintings 55, 58, 79, 316, 672

walls, city 468; Ephesos 470, 485; Melitene 701; Niš 685; Sirmium 668; unwalled cities in Asia Minor 699–701; see also under Constantinople

Walls, Long, in Thrace 127, 471

Walter of Brienne, duke of Athens 838

wardrobe, imperial, see vestiarion

warehouses (apothēkai) 271–2

warfare: Basil II's control of peasantry vital 586; church's blessing 202, (see also holy war); civil 822–3; and economy 14, 188, 370, 405, 511, 809, 818; iconoclast period 254, 255–60; icons as banners 226, 227, 242; on multiple fronts 11, 32, 60–1, 531, 536, (west left exposed) 219, 372, 412; Muslim-Byzantine, styles 367–8, 387, 498–9, (Muslim innovation) 372–3; rulers' personal leadership in battle 394, (caliphs) 38, 365, 370, 388, 389, 390, 394, (emperors) 32, 38, 273, 297, 374, 394, 399; tax collection

prevented by 809; 10th-century revival 60; see also armies; army, imperial; generals; holy war; jihad; legitimation of rule (military); military manuals and treatises; military technology; navies; navy, imperial; siege warfare

warlords: Arab frontier 387, 388, 389; Roman 9th-century local 448; Turkish 727

water supplies: Arabian oases 183; Constantinople 5, 114, 255, 404, 471, 485; Persian qanats 132; Rome 206

wealth: growing disparities in late empire 806, 821, 822; of Komnenian empire 647–8; land as basis of 774, 815, 818; under Palaiologoi 806; see also under Constantinople; Nicaea, empire of; officials, imperial; Rome

weights and measures, regulation of 498

Wessex, kingdom of 542

west 3, 9–10, 196–220; 5th-century demise of western empire 25–6, 99, 196, 198, 203–5; 6th century 128, 197, 196–220, (relations with east) 128, 196–212, 210–12, 218–20; 8th-9th-century 395–430, 431–87; A D 900–1025 40, 537–59; Komnenian relations with 36, 41, 627–8, 633–4, 640–1, 648–53; Palaiologan relations with 36, 757, 803–4, 806, 827, 832, (aid sought against Turks) 3, 10, 806, 829, 832, 858

balance of power and influence with Byzantium 10; Black Death 850; Byzantine attitude to 6th-century kingdoms 199, 201, 212; Christianisation brings turbulence 25; coinage 484; growth of influence in east 51, 72–4; imperial ideology and relations with 408–9, 417, 430, (and Franks) 5, 409, 417, 418, 419, 432; Italy as pivotal to relations 396–7, 431; law of conquest 757; separation from east by Slav settlement 128; maps 197, 396, 848; see also individual states, peoples and rulers, church and Christianity (EAST-WEST RELATIONS); culture (east-west contacts); feudalism; Jerusalem (east-west encounter); Latin empire; Latins; papacy; translation; and under diplomacy; economy; missions

Wido, duke of Spoleto 422

widows 66, 67, 68, 261, 269

William I, king of Sicily 638

William II, king of Sicily 36, 639–40, 651, 658, 660

William II of Villehardouin, prince of Achaia 767–8, 771; and Charles of Anjou 754–5, 768; Michael VIII defeats 749, 754, 767–8, 795

William VIII, marquess of Montferrat 763–4

William of Champlitte 762, 841

William of Tyre 85n47, 636